HANDBOOK OF LOGIC
IN ARTIFICIAL INTELLIGENCE
AND LOGIC PROGRAMMING

Editors

Dov M. Gabbay, C. J. Hogger, and J. A. Robinson

HANDBOOKS OF LOGIC IN COMPUTER SCIENCE

and

ARTIFICIAL INTELLIGENCE AND LOGIC PROGRAMMING

Executive Editor
Dov M. Gabbay

Administrator
Jane Spurr

Handbook of Logic in Computer Science

Handbook of Logic in Artificial Intelligence and
Logic Programming

HANDBOOK OF LOGIC IN ARTIFICIAL INTELLIGENCE AND LOGIC PROGRAMMING

Volume 5
Logic Programming

Edited by
DOV M. GABBAY

and

C. J. HOGGER
Imperial College of Science, Technology and Medicine
London

and

J. A. ROBINSON
Syracuse University, New York

CLARENDON PRESS · OXFORD
1998

Oxford University Press, Great Clarendon Street, Oxford OX2 6DP

Oxford New York

Athens Auckland Bangkok Bogota Bombay
Buenos Aires Calcutta Cape Town Dar es Salaam
Delhi Florence Hong Kong Istanbul Karachi
Kuala Lumpur Madras Madrid Melbourne
Mexico City Nairobi Paris Singapore
Taipei Tokyo Toronto Warsaw
and associated companies in
Berlin Ibadan

Oxford is a trade mark of Oxford University Press

Published in the United States by
Oxford University Press Inc., New York

© The contributors listed on pp. xiv–xv, 1998

'Constraint logic programming: a survey' by J. Jaffar and M. J. Maher was
previously published in the Journal of Logic
Programming 19/20, 503–82. It is reproduced with
permission from Elsevier

A catalogue record for this book is available from the British Library

Library of Congress Cataloging in Publication Data
(Data available)

ISBN 0 19 853792 1

Typeset by the authors using LaTeX

Printed in Great Britain by
Bookcraft (Bath) Ltd
Midsomer Norton, Avon

Preface

I am very happy to present to the community the fifth and last volume of our Handbook series, covering the area of Logic and Logic Programming.

The ideas and methods of logic programming gave a substantial push to the development of logic itself. Ideas like negation as failure, goal directed presentation of a logic, metalevel features in the object level are applicable to any logical system and not only to the classical Horn clause fragment.

The central role and success of these ideas in logic programming provided an example to follow for research into similar developments for general logics.

Logic programming is also a central tool in the new and wide area of non-monotonic logic and artificial intelligence. The methods of abduction, the use of constraints and higher order features have all interacted and supported the new systems of logic designed to cope with practical common sense reasoning.

The Handbooks

The *Handbook of Logic in Artificial Intelligence and Logic Programming* and its companion, the *Handbook of Logic in Computer Science*, have been created in response to a growing need for an in-depth survey of the application of logic in AI and computer science.

We see the creation of the Handbook as a combination of authoritative exposition, comprehensive survey, and fundamental reasearch exploring the underlying unifying themes in the various areas. The intended audience is graduate students and researchers in the areas of computing and logic, as well as other people interested in the subject. We assume as background some mathematical sophistication. Much of the material will also be of interest to logicians and mathematicians.

The tables of contents of the volumes were finalized after extensive discussions between Handbook authors and second readers. The first two volumes present the background logic and mathematics extensively used in artificial intelligence and logic programming. The point of view is application oriented. The other volumes present major areas in which the methods are used. These include: Volume 1—Logical foundations; Volume 2—Deduction methodologies; Volume 3—Nonmonotonic reasoning and uncertain reasoning; Volume 4—Epistemic and temporal reasoning.

The chapters, which in many cases are of monographic length and scope, are written with emphasis on possible unifying themes. The chapters have an overview, introduction, and main body. A final part is dedicated to more specialized topics.

Chapters are written by internationally renowned researchers in their respective areas. The chapters are co-ordinated and their contents were discussed in joint meetings. Each chapter has been written using the following procedures:

1. A very detailed table of contents was discussed and co-ordinated at several meetings between authors and editors of related chapters. The discussion was in the form of a series of lectures by the authors. Once an agreement was reached on the detailed table of contents, the authors wrote a draft and sent it to the editors and to other related authors. For each chapter there is a second reader (the first reader is the author) whose job it has been to scrutinize the chapter together with the editors. The second reader's role is very important and has required effort and serious involvement with the authors.

   Second readers for this volume include (in alphabetical order) K. Apt, M. Bruynooghe, G. Dowek, K. Fine, J. P. Gallagher, F. van Harmelen, K. Inoue, B. Jayaraman, P. Kanellakis. R. Kowalski, J-L. Lassez, J. Lloyd, M. Leuschel, D. W. Loveland, M. Maher, J. Meseguer, D. Miller, G. Nadathur, T. Przymusinski, K. Satoh, D. J. Sherman, and E. Wimmers.

2. Once this process was completed (i.e. drafts seen and read by a large enough group of authors), there were other meetings on several chapters in which authors lectured on their chapters and faced the criticism of the editors and audience. The final drafts were prepared after these meetings.

3. We attached great importance to group effort and co-ordination in the writing of chapters. The first two parts of each chapter, namely the introduction-overview and main body are not completely under the discretion of the author, as he/she had to face the general criticism of all the other authors. Only the third part of the chapter is entirely for the authors' own personal contribution.

The Handbook meetings were generously financed by OUP, by SERC contract SO/809/86, by the Department of Computing at Imperial College, and by several anonymous private donations. We would like to thank our colleagues, authors, second readers, and students for their effort and professionalism in producing the manuscripts for the Handbook. We would particularly like to thank the staff of OUP for their continued and enthusiastic support, Mrs L. Rivlin for help with design, and Mrs Jane Spurr, our OUP Adminstrator for her dedication and efficiency.

London   D. M. Gabbay
July 1997

Contents

Proof Procedures for Logic Programming
Donald W. Loveland and Gopalan Nadathur

The Role of Abduction in Logic Programming
A. C. Kakas, R. A. Kowalski and F. Toni

Semantics for Disjunctive and Normal Disjunctive Logic Programs

Jorge Lobo, Jack Minker and Arcot Rajasekar

Negation as Failure, Completion and Stratification

J. C. Shepherdson

Meta-Programming in Logic Programming

P. M. Hill and J. Gallagher

Higher-Order Logic Programming
Gopalan Nadathur and Dale Miller

Transformation of Logic Programs

Index

Contributors

J. Gallagher Department of Computer Science, University of Bristol, University Walk, Bristol BS8 3PN.

P. M. Hill School of Computer Studies, The University of Leeds, Leeds LS2 9JT.

J. Jaffar Department of Information Systems and Computer Science, National University of Singapore, Kent Ridge, Singapore 0511.

A. C. Kakas Department of Computer Science, University of Cyprus, PO Box 537, CY-1678 Nicosia, Cyprus.

R. A. Kowalski Department of Computing, Imperial College of Science, Technology and Medicine, 180 Queen's Gate, London SW7 2BZ.

J. Lobo Department of Computer Science, University of Illionois at Chicago Circle, Chicago, Illinois, USA.

D. W. Loveland Computer Science Department, Box 91029, Duke University, Durham, NC 27708–0129, USA.

M. J. Maher IBM Thomas J. Watson Research Center, PO Box 704, Yorktown Heights, NY 10598, USA.

D. Miller Computer and Information Science, University of Pennsylvania, Philadelphia, PA 19104–6389, USA.

J. Minker Department of Computer Science and Institute for Advanced Computer Studies, University of Maryland, College Park, Maryland 20742, USA.

G. Nadathur Department of Computer Science, University of Chicago, 1100 East 58th Street, Chicago, Illinois 60637, USA.

M. J. O'Donnell Department of Computer Science, University of Chicago, 1100 East 58th Street, Chicago, Illinois 60637, USA.

A. Pettorossi Electronics Department, University of Rome II, Via della Ricerca Scientifica, I-00133 Roma, Italy.

M. Proietti Viale Manzoni 30, I-00185 Roma, Italy.

A. Rajasekar San Diego Supercomputer Center, La Jolla, California 92093, USA.

J. Shepherdson Department of Mathematics, University of Bristol, University Walk, Bristol BS8 3PN.

F. Toni   Department of Computing, Imperial College of Science, Technology and Medicine, 180 Queen's Gate, London SW7 2BZ.

Introduction: Logic and Logic Programming Languages

Michael J. O'Donnell

Contents

1 Introduction

1.1 Motivation

Logic, according to Webster's dictionary [Webster, 1987], is *'a science that deals with the principles and criteria of validity of inference and demonstration: the science of the formal principles of reasoning.'* Such *'principles and criteria'* are always described in terms of a *language* in which inference, demonstration, and reasoning may be expressed. One of the most useful accomplishments of logic for mathematics is the design of a particular formal language, the *First Order Predicate Calculus* (FOPC). FOPC is so successful at expressing the assertions arising in mathematical discourse that mathematicians and computer scientists often identify logic with classical logic expressed in FOPC. In order to explore a range of possible uses of logic in the design of programming languages, we discard the conventional identification of logic with FOPC, and formalize a general schema for a variety of logical systems, based on the dictionary meaning of the word. Then, we show how logic programming languages may be designed systematically for any sufficiently effective logic, and explain how to view Prolog, Datalog, λProlog, Equational Logic Programming, and similar programming languages, as instances of the general schema of logic programming. Other generalizations of logic programming have been proposed independently by Meseguer [Meseguer, 1989], Miller, Nadathur, Pfenning and Scedrov [Miller *et al.*, 1991], Goguen and Burstall [Goguen and Burstall, 1992].

The purpose of this chapter is to introduce a set of basic concepts for understanding logic programming, not in terms of its historical development, but in a systematic way based on retrospective insights. In order to achieve a systematic treatment, we need to review a number of elementary definitions from logic and theoretical computer science and adapt them to the needs of logic programming. The result is a slightly modified logical notation, which should be recognizable to those who know the traditional notation. Conventional logical notation is also extended to new and analogous concepts, designed to make the similarities and differences between logical relations and computational relations as transparent as possible. Computational notation is revised radically to make it look similar to logical notation. The chapter is self-contained, but it includes references to the logic and theoretical computer science literature for those who wish to explore connections.

There are a number of possible motivations for developing, studying, and using logic programming languages. Many people are attracted to Prolog, the best known logic programming language, simply for the special programming tools based on unification and backtracking search that it provides. This chapter is not concerned with the utility of particular logic programming languages as programming tools, but with the value of concepts from logic, particularly semantic concepts, in the design, implementation, and use of programming languages. In particular, while denotational and algebraic semantics provide excellent tools to *describe* important aspects of programming systems, and often to prove correctness of implementations, we will see that logical semantics can exploit the strong traditional consensus about the meanings of certain logical notations to *prescribe* the behavior of programming systems. Logical semantics also provides a natural approach, through proof systems, to verifiably correct implementations, that is sometimes simpler than the denotational and algebraic approaches. A comparison of the three styles of semantics will show that denotational and algebraic semantics provide *descriptive* tools, logical semantics provides *prescriptive* tools, and the methods of algebraic semantics may be used to translate logical semantics into denotational/algebraic semantics.

In this chapter, a relation is called *computable* if and only if its characteristic function is total recursive, and a relation is *semicomputable* if and only if the set of ordered pairs in the relation is recursively enumerable. Recursion theorists and theoretical computer scientists often refer to computable sets as *decidable* sets, but logicians sometimes call a theory *decidable* when every formula is either provable or refutable in the theory. The two meanings of 'decidable' are closely connected, but not identical, and we avoid confusion by choosing a different word. When some component of a relation is a finite set, the set is assumed to be represented by a list of its members for the purpose of discussing computability and semicomputability.

1.2   A notational apology

In order to understand logic programming rigorously in terms of formal concepts from mathematical logic, and at the same time intuitively, we need to look closely at the details of several formal relations from logic and from theory of computation. We must come to understand the formal similarities and differences between these relations, and how those formal properties arise from the intuitive similarities and differences in our intended applications of these relations. Unfortunately, the conventional notations for logic and computation look radically different, and take advantage of different simplifying assumptions, which obscures those connections that are essential to intuitive applications of the corresponding concepts. So, we will make visually small variations on conventional logical notation, extending it to deal with questions and their answers as well as the traditional assertions and their semantic interpretations. Then, we will radically redesign conventional recursion-theoretic notation in order to display visually the connections between computational relations and logical relations. In order to be prepared for the strange look of the notations, we need to review them all briefly in advance, although the precise definitions for the concepts that they denote will be introduced gradually through Sections 2–3.

The important domains of conventional logical objects for our study are the sets of

- logical assertions, or formulae $\mathbf{F}$
- sets of formulae, or theories $\mathbf{T} \in 2^{\mathbf{F}}$
- semantic interpretations, or models $\mathbf{M}$
- sets of models, representing knowledge $\mathbf{K} \in 2^{\mathbf{M}}$
- proofs, or derivations $\mathbf{D}$

We add the unconventional domain of

- questions $\mathbf{Q}$

Answers to questions are particular formulae, so no additional domain is required for them. The domains of conventional computational objects are the sets of

- programs **P**
- inputs **I**
- computations **C**
- outputs **O**

In recursion-theoretic treatments of computation, programs, inputs, and outputs are all integers, but our analysis is more convenient when they are allowed to be different domains. We will find strong intuitive analogies and formal connections between

- programs and sets of formulae
- inputs and questions
- computations and proofs
- outputs and formulae (intended as answers to questions)

In order to understand the analogies and formal connections thoroughly, we must investigate a number of relations between domains with varying arities from two to four. In all cases, we will use *multiple infix* notation. That is, each n-ary relation will be denoted by $n - 1$ symbols separating its arguments. With some care in the geometrical design of the separator symbols, we get a reasonably mnemonic notation.

There are two quaternary relational notations from which all the other notations may be derived. Let Q be a question, **T** a set of formulae, D a proof, and F a formula. The notation

$$Q \mathbin{?\!\vdash} \mathbf{T} \mid D - F$$

means that in response to the question Q, given the postulates in **T**, we may discover the proof D of the answer F. Similarly, let I be an input, P a program, C a computation, and O an output. The notation

$$I \triangleright P \mathbin{\|} C \to O$$

means that in response to the input I, the program P may perform the computation C, yielding output O. The correspondence between the arguments Q and I, **T** and P, D and C, F and O displays the crucial correspondence between logic and computation that is at the heart of logic programming.

There are two closely related trinary notations.

$$Q \mathbin{?\!\vdash} \mathbf{T} \vdash F$$

means that there exists a proof D such that $Q \mathbin{?\!\vdash} \mathbf{T} \mid D - F$, and

$$I \triangleright P \longmapsto O$$

means that there exists a computation C such that $I \triangleright P \parallel C \rightarrow O$. The symbol $\vdash$ in $Q \mathbin{?\!\!-} \mathbf{F} \vdash F$ is the conventional symbol for proof in mathematical logic; we take the liberty of decomposing it into the two symbols $\mid$ and $-$ for the quaternary notation. The conventional recursion-theoretic notation for our $I \triangleright P \longmapsto O$ is $\phi_P(I) = O$. The computational symbol $\longmapsto$ and its components $\parallel$ and $\rightarrow$ are designed to have similar shapes to $\vdash$, $\mid$, and $-$.

Other relations from logic do *not* correspond directly to computational relations, but can be understood by their connections to the quaternary form, in which the logic/computation correspondence is direct and transparent. In Section 3.2 I define $Q \mathbin{?\!\!-} \mathbf{T} \mid D - F$ to hold exactly when both

$$Q \mathbin{?\!\!-} F \qquad \text{and} \qquad \mathbf{T} \mid D - F$$

where $Q \mathbin{?\!\!-} F$ means that F is an answer (not necessarily a correct one) to the question Q, and $\mathbf{T} \mid D - F$ means that D is a proof of F, using postulates in the set $\mathbf{T}$. $\mathbf{T} \mid D - F$ is a conventional concept from mathematical logic (often written $\mathbf{T}, D \vdash F$ or $\mathbf{T} \vdash_D F$). The question–answer relation $\mathbin{?\!\!-}$ is not conventional. Notice that each separating symbol in the quaternary notation $Q \mathbin{?\!\!-} \mathbf{T} \mid D - F$ is used exactly once in the binary and trinary forms from which it is defined, so the notational conjunction of symbols suggests the logical conjunction of the denoted relations. Unfortunately, while the symbol $\mathbin{?\!\!-}$ appears between the question Q and the answer formula F in the binary notation $Q \mathbin{?\!\!-} F$, it is not adjacent to F in the quaternary notation $Q \mathbin{?\!\!-} \mathbf{T} \mid D - F$. The dash component $-$ of the symbol $\mathbin{?\!\!-}$ mimics the $-$ symbol at the end of the quaternary notation, and the similar component of the $\vdash$ symbol from the trinary notation above, as a reminder that the $\mathbin{?\!\!-}$ symbol is expressing a relation to the final answer formula F, rather than to the set $\mathbf{T}$ of postulated formulae.

The quaternary computational relation is also defined as the conjunction of a binary and a trinary relation, but the arguments involved in these relations do *not* correspond to the arguments of the binary and trinary relations from logic. In Section 3.3 I define $I \triangleright P \parallel C \rightarrow O$ to hold exactly when both

$$I \triangleright P \parallel C \qquad \text{and} \qquad C \rightarrow O$$

where $I \triangleright P \parallel C$ means that the program P on input I may perform the computation C, and $C \rightarrow O$ means that the computation C yields output O. In this case, the mnemonic suggestion of the conjunction of the trinary and binary relations in the quaternary notation works out perfectly, as all argument positions are adjacent to the appropriate separator symbols.

A few other derived notations are useful for denoting relations from logic. These all agree with conventional notation in mathematical logic.

$$\mathbf{T} \vdash F$$

means that there exists a proof D such that $\mathbf{T} \mid D - F$—that is, F is formally derivable from $\mathbf{T}$. Corresponding to the relation $\vdash$ of *formal derivability* is the relation $\models$ of *semantic entailment*.

$$\mathbf{T} \models F$$

means that F is semantically entailed by $\mathbf{T}$. Similarly,

$$Q \mathbin{?\!\!-} \mathbf{T} \models F$$

means that F is an answer to Q semantically entailed by $\mathbf{T}$ ($Q \mathbin{?\!\!-} F$ and $\mathbf{T} \models F$) in analogy to $Q \mathbin{?\!\!-} \mathbf{T} \vdash F$. The mathematical definition of semantic entailment involves one more semantic relation. Let M be a model, and F a formula.

$$M \models F$$

means that F is true in M.

Table 1 displays all of the special notations for semantic, proof-theoretic, and computational relations. The precise meanings and applications of these notations are developed at length in subsequent sections. The notation described above is subscripted when necessary to distinguish the logical and computational relations of different systems.

Logic		Computation
Semantics	**Proof**	
	$Q \mathbin{?\!\!-} \mathbf{T} \mid D - F$	$I \triangleright\ P \mathbin{\|} C \to O$
$Q \mathbin{?\!\!-} \mathbf{T} \models F$	$Q \mathbin{?\!\!-} \mathbf{T} \vdash F$	$I \triangleright\ P \mapsto O$
		$I \triangleright\ P \mathbin{\|} C$
$Q \mathbin{?\!\!-} F$		
		$C \to O$
	$\mathbf{T} \mid D - F$	
$\mathbf{T} \models F$	$\mathbf{T} \vdash F$	
$M \models F$		

Table 1. Special notations for logical and computational relations

2 Specifying logic programming languages

Logic typically develops its *'principles and criteria of validity of inference'* by studying the relations between *notations* for assertions, the *meanings* of those assertions, and *derivations* of notations expressing true assertions. Mathematical logic formalizes these concepts using *logical formulae* as notations, sets of *models* to analyze meanings and characterize truth, and *demonstrations* or *proofs* as derivations of true formulae and inferences. The structure of formulae alone is *syntax*, their relation to models is *semantics*, and their relation to proofs is *proof theory*. Syntax is not relevant to the present discussion. We must examine formal systems of semantics, and augment them with formal concepts of questions and their answers, in order to understand the specification of a logic programming language. In Section 3 we see how formal systems of proof provide a natural approach to the implementation of computations for logic programming.

2.1 Semantic systems and semantic consequences

A *semantic system* relates a set $\mathbf{F}$ of logical formulae to a set $\mathbf{M}$ of formal models, each representing a conceivable state of the world in enough detail to determine when a given formula represents a true assertion in that state of the world.

Definition 2.1.1. A *semantic system* is a system $\mathcal{S} = \langle \mathbf{F}, \mathbf{M}, \models \rangle$, where

1. $\mathbf{F}$ is a set of *logical formulae*
2. $\mathbf{M}$ is a set of *models*
3. $\models$ is a relation on $\mathbf{M} \times \mathbf{F}$

Let $\mathbf{K} \subseteq \mathbf{M}$. **Theory**$(\mathbf{K}) = \{F \in \mathbf{F} : M \models F \text{ for all } M \in \mathbf{K}\}$.
Let $\mathbf{T} \subseteq \mathbf{F}$. **Models**$(\mathbf{T}) = \{M \in \mathbf{M} : M \models F \text{ for all } F \in \mathbf{T}\}$.

Intuitively, $M \models F$ is intended to mean that formula F *holds in*, or *is valid in*, or *is satisfied by*, model M. **Theory**$(\mathbf{K})$ is the fullest possible description of $\mathbf{K}$ using a set of formulae in the language of the system. **Models**$(\mathbf{T})$ represents the state of knowledge given implicitly by the formulae in $\mathbf{T}$—knowing $\mathbf{T}$ we know that reality corresponds to one of the models in **Models**$(\mathbf{T})$, but we do not know which one. Notice the antimonotone relation between $\mathbf{F}$ and $\mathbf{M}$:

$$\mathbf{T}_1 \subseteq \mathbf{T}_2 \text{ if and only if } \mathbf{Models}(\mathbf{T}_1) \supseteq \mathbf{Models}(\mathbf{T}_2)$$
$$\mathbf{K}_1 \subseteq \mathbf{K}_2 \text{ if and only if } \mathbf{Theory}(\mathbf{K}_1) \supseteq \mathbf{Theory}(\mathbf{K}_2)$$
$$\mathbf{Models}(\mathbf{T}_1 \cup \mathbf{T}_2) = \mathbf{Models}(\mathbf{T}_1) \cap \mathbf{Models}(\mathbf{T}_2)$$
$$\mathbf{Models}(\mathbf{T}_1 \cap \mathbf{T}_2) = \mathbf{Models}(\mathbf{T}_1) \cup \mathbf{Models}(\mathbf{T}_2)$$
$$\mathbf{Theory}(\mathbf{K}_1 \cup \mathbf{K}_2) = \mathbf{Theory}(\mathbf{K}_1) \cap \mathbf{Theory}(\mathbf{K}_2)$$
$$\mathbf{Theory}(\mathbf{K}_1 \cap \mathbf{K}_2) = \mathbf{Theory}(\mathbf{K}_1) \cup \mathbf{Theory}(\mathbf{K}_2)$$

In order to provide satisfactory intuitive insight, a semantic system must relate the syntactic structure of formulae to the determination of

8 *Michael J. O'Donnell*

truth. For example, well-known sets of formulae often come with a syntactic operator to construct, from two formulae A and B, their *logical conjunction* $A \wedge B$. The semantics for conjunctions is defined structurally, by the rule $\mathbf{M} \models A \wedge B$ *if and only if* $\mathbf{M} \models A$ *and* $\mathbf{M} \models B$. The formal analysis of this chapter deals only with the abstract relation of a model to a formula that holds in the state of the world represented by that model, not the internal structure of that relation, because we are interested here in the *use* of semantics for understanding logic programming, rather than the deeper structure of semantics itself. Goguen's and Burstall's *institutions* [Goguen and Burstall, 1992] are similar to semantic systems, but they capture in addition the structural connection between syntax and semantics through category theory, and show that the functions **Models** and **Theory** form a *Galois connection*.

Notice that the sets $\mathbf{F}$ of formulae and $\mathbf{M}$ of models are not required to be given effectively. In well-known semantic systems, the set of formulae is normally computable, since formulae are normally finite syntactic objects, and it is easy to determine mechanically whether a given object is a formula or not. Infinite formulae, however, have important uses, and they can be given practical computational interpretations, so we do *not* add any formal requirement of computability. The set of models, on the other hand, is typically quite complex, because models represent conceivable states of an external world, rather than finite constructions of our own minds. In fact, for many semantic systems there are technical set-theoretic problems even in regarding the collection of models in the system as a set, but those problems do not affect any of the results of this chapter.

In this chapter, basic concepts are illustrated through a running example based on the *shallow implicational calculus* (SIC), designed to be almost trivial, but just complex enough to make an interesting example. More realistic examples are treated toward the end of the chapter.

Example 2.1.2. Let **At** be a set of *atomic propositional formulae*. The set $\mathbf{F}_{\text{Sh}}$ of formulae in the *shallow implicational calculus* is the smallest set such that:

1. $\mathbf{At} \subseteq \mathbf{F}_{\text{Sh}}$
2. If $a, b \in \mathbf{At}$, then $(a \Rightarrow b) \in \mathbf{F}_{\text{Sh}}$

The set $\mathbf{M}_{\text{Sh}}$ of models in SIC is defined by

$$\mathbf{M}_{\text{Sh}} = 2^{\mathbf{At}}$$

The semantic relation $\models_{\text{Sh}} \subseteq \mathbf{M}_{\text{Sh}} \times \mathbf{F}_{\text{Sh}}$ is defined by:

1. For $a \in \mathbf{At}$, $M \models_{\text{Sh}} a$ if and only if $a \in M$
2. $M \models_{\text{Sh}} (a \Rightarrow b)$ if and only if either $b \in M$ or $a \notin M$

Now $\langle \mathbf{F}_{Sh}, \mathbf{M}_{Sh}, \models_{Sh} \rangle$ is a semantic system, representing the classical concept of meaning for the implicational formulae of SIC.

SIC is just the restriction of the classical propositional calculus [Andrews, 1986; Kleene, 1952; Gallier, 1986] to atomic propositional formulae, and implications between atomic propositional formulae. It is called 'shallow' because no nesting of implications is allowed. Since the truth of formulae in SIC (as in the propositional calculus) is determined entirely by the truth of atomic formulae, a model merely specifies the set of atomic formulae that are true in a given conceivable state of the world. Following the tradition of material implication in classical logic, an implication is true precisely when its conclusion is true, or its hypothesis is false.

For the formal definition of a logic programming language, the important thing about a semantic system is the *semantic-consequence* relation that it defines, determining when the truth of a set of formulae justifies inferring the truth of an additional formula.

Definition 2.1.3 ([Andrews, 1986; Gallier, 1986]). Let $\mathcal{S} = \langle \mathbf{F}, \mathbf{M}, \models \rangle$ be a semantic system. The *semantic-consequence* relation defined by $\mathcal{S}$ is $\models \subseteq 2^{\mathbf{F}} \times \mathbf{F}$, where $\mathbf{T} \models F$ if and only if $M \models F$ for all $M \in \mathbf{Models}(\mathbf{T})$.

The semantic-consequence relation $\models$ is *compact* if and only if, for all $\mathbf{T} \subseteq \mathbf{F}$ and $F \in \mathbf{F}$, whenever $\mathbf{T} \models F$ there exists a finite subset $\mathbf{T}^{\mathbf{f}} \subseteq \mathbf{T}$ such that $\mathbf{T}^{\mathbf{f}} \models F$.

Intuitively, $\mathbf{T} \models F$ means that F is a *semantic consequence* of $\mathbf{T}$, since F must be true whenever all formulae in $\mathbf{T}$ are true. Semantic consequences are often called *logical consequences*; our terminology is chosen to highlight the contrast between semantic consequences and the *provable consequences* of Definition 3.1.4. Notice that $\mathbf{Theory}(\mathbf{Models}(\mathbf{T}))$ is the set of semantic consequences of $\mathbf{T}$. It is easy to show that an arbitrary relation $\models$ on $2^{\mathbf{F}} \times \mathbf{F}$ is the semantic-consequence relation of some semantic system if and only if it is

1. *reflexive*: $F \in \mathbf{T}$ implies that $\mathbf{T} \models F$
2. *monotone*: $\mathbf{T} \models F$ and $\mathbf{T} \subseteq \mathbf{U}$ imply that $\mathbf{U} \models F$
3. *transitive*: $\mathbf{T} \models F$ and $\mathbf{T} \cup \{F\} \models G$ imply that $\mathbf{T} \models G$

In order for a semantic-consequence relation to be useful for logic programming, or for rigorous formal reasoning, it must be sufficiently effective. Well-known semantic systems normally define semantic-consequence relations that are compact—their behavior on arbitrary sets is determined by their behavior on finite sets. Normal semantic-consequence relations are semicomputable, but not necessarily computable, when restricted to finite sets of formulae in the first component. Fortunately, semicomputability is enough for logic programming.

Example 2.1.4. The semantic-consequence relation $\models_{Sh}$ of the shallow implicational calculus of Example 2.1.2 is compact, and has a particularly simple behavior:

1. for atomic formulae $a \in \mathbf{At}$, $\mathbf{T} \models_{\mathrm{Sh}} a$ if and only if there is a finite sequence $\langle a_0, \ldots, a_m \rangle$ of atomic formulae such that $a_0 \in \mathbf{T}$, and $(a_i \Rightarrow a_{i+1}) \in \mathbf{T}$ for all $i < m$, and $a_m = a$

2. $\mathbf{T} \models_{\mathrm{Sh}} (a \Rightarrow b)$ if and only if there is a finite sequence $\langle a_0, \ldots, a_m \rangle$ of atomic formulae such that $a_0 \in \mathbf{T} \cup \{a\}$, and $(a_i \Rightarrow a_{i+1}) \in \mathbf{T}$ for all $i < m$, and $a_m = b$

We may think of the implications in $\mathbf{T}$ as directed edges in a graph whose vertices are atomic formulae. Atomic formulae in $\mathbf{T}$ are marked *true*. An atomic formula a is a semantic consequence of $\mathbf{T}$ precisely if there is a directed path from some atomic formula in $\mathbf{T}$ to a. Similarly, an implication $a \Rightarrow b$ is a semantic consequence of $\mathbf{T}$ precisely if there is a directed path from a, or from an atomic formula in $\mathbf{T}$, to b. Notice that SIC satisfies the *deduction property*: [Andrews, 1986; Kleene, 1952; Gallier, 1986]

$$\mathbf{T} \models_{\mathrm{Sh}} (a \Rightarrow b) \text{ if and only if } \mathbf{T} \cup \{a\} \models_{\mathrm{Sh}} b$$

A semantic system provides a conceptual tool for analyzing a primitive sort of communication in a monologue. A state of implicit knowledge is naturally represented by the set of models corresponding to conceivable states of the world that are consistent with that knowledge. Notice that larger sets of models represent smaller amounts of knowledge. For a general discussion of knowledge as sets of models, the shortcomings of such representations, and problems and paradoxes that arise when subtle sorts of knowledge are considered, see [Fagin *et al.*, 1984]. The knowledge involved in formal analysis of the examples of logic programming in this chapter is simple enough to be represented by sets of models without presenting the problems that arise in a more general setting. Explicit knowledge is naturally represented by a set of formulae. **Models(T)** is the implicit knowledge given explicitly by $\mathbf{T}$. Similarly, **Theory(K)** is the strongest explicit representation of the implicit knowledge $\mathbf{K}$ that is expressible in a given language, but there is no guarantee that an agent with implicit knowledge $\mathbf{K}$ can effectively produce all of the explicit knowledge **Theory(K)**.

Consider a *speaker*, whose state of knowledge is represented by $\mathbf{K_s}$, and an *auditor* with initial knowledge $\mathbf{K_a^0}$. The speaker wishes to communicate some of her knowledge to the auditor, so she utters a set of formulae $\mathbf{T} \subseteq \mathbf{Theory}(\mathbf{K_s})$. The impact of the speaker's utterance on the auditor's state of knowledge is to remove from the auditor's set of models those that do not satisfy $\mathbf{T}$. That is, $\mathbf{K_a^0}$ is replaced by $\mathbf{K_a^1} = \mathbf{K_a^0} \cap \mathbf{Models}(\mathbf{T})$. Notice that, if the auditor's initial knowledge is minimal, that is if $\mathbf{K_a^0}$ is the set of all models in the semantic system, then $\mathbf{K_a^1} = \mathbf{Models}(\mathbf{T})$, so the formulae implied by the new knowledge, $\mathbf{Theory}(\mathbf{K_a^1})$, are exactly the semantic consequences of $\mathbf{T}$. In logic programming systems, the programmer plays the part of the speaker above, the processor plays the part of the auditor, the program is the utterance, and the logical meaning of the program is the resulting state of knowledge produced in the auditor/processor. Inputs to, computations of, and outputs from logic programs are treated later.

Notice that this style of semantic analysis of communication does not give either speaker or auditor direct access to inspect or modify the models constituting the other's state of implicit knowledge. Rather, all such access is mediated by the utterance of explicit logical formulae. Also, notice that there is no attempt to construct a *unique* model to represent a state of knowledge, or the information communicated by an utterance. Rather, an increase in implicit knowledge is represented by a reduction in the variability of members of a set of models, any one of which might represent the real state of the world. Unless the semantic-consequence relation of a semantic system is very easy to compute—which it seldom is—the difference between implicit knowledge and effectively utterable explicit knowledge can be quite significant. The *proof systems* of Section 3.1 help describe a way in which implicit knowledge is made explicit, and yield a rough description of the computations of logic programs.

The preceding scheme for representing communication of knowledge deals naturally with a sequence of utterances, by iterating the process of shrinking the auditor's set of models. There is no provision, however, for analyzing any sort of interactive *dialogue*, other than as a pair of formally unrelated monologues. The *query systems* of the next section introduce a primitive sort of interactive question-answering dialogue.

2.2 Query Systems, questions and answers

Semantic systems and semantic-consequence relations are conventional subjects for logical investigation. They suffice for discussions of the truth of a formula and the validity of the inference of a new formula from a given set of formulae. In order to analyze the relation between input to a logic program and the corresponding output, we need a formal basis for discussing questions and their answers. Mathematical logicians have given very little attention to this branch of logic—one exception is the formal treatment by Belnap and Steel [Belnap Jr. and Steel, 1976]. *Query systems* are an abstraction of the common formal schema from a number of instances of question–answer domains defined by Belnap and Steel.

Definition 2.2.1. A *query system* is a system $\mathcal{Q} = \langle \mathbf{F}, \mathbf{Q}, ?\!\vdash \rangle$, where

1. $\mathbf{F}$ is a set of *logical formulae*

2. $\mathbf{Q}$ is a set of *questions*

3. $?\!\vdash$ is a relation on $\mathbf{Q} \times \mathbf{F}$

Questions, like formulae, are normally finite syntactic objects, and the set of all questions is normally computable, but we allow exceptions to the normal case.

$Q \mathrel{?\!\!-} F$ is intended to mean that F is an *answer* to Q. $\mathrel{?\!\!-}$ is intended only to determine the acceptable form for an answer to a question, *not* to carry any information about *correctness* of an answer. For example, it is reasonable to say that '$2 + 2 = 5$' is an incorrect answer to 'what is $2 + 2$?', while '$2 + 2 = 2^2$' is correct, but not an answer. The correctness or incorrectness of an answer is evaluated semantically with respect to explicit knowledge.

Definition 2.2.2. Let $\mathcal{Q} = \langle \mathbf{F_Q}, \mathbf{Q}, \mathrel{?\!\!-} \rangle$ be a query system, and let $\mathcal{S} = \langle \mathbf{F_S}, \mathbf{M}, \models \rangle$ be a semantic system with $\mathbf{F_Q} \subseteq \mathbf{F_S}$.

$Q \mathrel{?\!\!-} \mathbf{T} \models F$ means that $F \in \mathbf{F_Q}$ is a *semantically correct* answer to $Q \in \mathbf{Q}$ for explicit knowledge $\mathbf{T} \subseteq \mathbf{F_S}$, defined by

$$Q \mathrel{?\!\!-} \mathbf{T} \models F \text{ if and only if } Q \mathrel{?\!\!-} F \text{ and } \mathbf{T} \models F$$

A question $Q \in \mathbf{Q}$ is *semantically answerable* for explicit knowledge $\mathbf{T} \subseteq \mathbf{F_S}$ if and only if there exists a formula $F \in \mathbf{F_Q}$ such that F is a semantically correct answer to Q in $\mathbf{T}$.

Meseguer [Meseguer, 1989; Meseguer, 1992] proposes a different notion of question answering, in which a question is a formula, and an answer is a proof (in an abstract notation omitting many details) of the formula. (This is an interesting twist on the *formulae as types* concept [Howard, 1980; Tait, 1967], which is more usually applied by letting a program specification be a formula, and a program be a proof of the formula [Constable *et al.*, 1986].)

Several interesting query systems may be defined for the shallow implicational calculus.

Example 2.2.3. Let **imp** be a new formal symbol, and let $\mathbf{F_{Sh}}$ be the set of formulae in SIC defined in Example 2.1.2. Let

$$\mathbf{Q_{S1}} = \{\mathbf{imp}(F) : F \in \mathbf{At}\}$$

Define the relation $\mathrel{?\!\!-}_{S1} \subseteq \mathbf{Q_{S1}} \times \mathbf{F_{Sh}}$ by

$$\mathbf{imp}(c) \mathrel{?\!\!-}_{S1} (a \Rightarrow b) \text{ if and only if } a = c$$

Now $\langle \mathbf{F_{Sh}}, \mathbf{Q_{S1}}, \mathrel{?\!\!-}_{S1} \rangle$ is a query system representing the conceivable answers to questions of the form 'what atomic formula does a imply?'

The query system of Example 2.2.3 above is susceptible to two sorts of answers that may be intuitively unsatisfying. First, in a state of knowledge in which an atomic formula b is known to be true, $(a \Rightarrow b)$ is a correct answer to questions $\mathbf{imp}(a)$ for all atomic formulae a. This problem may be avoided by considering states of knowledge in which only implications are known, or it may be addressed by changing the underlying semantic system to one with a *relevant* interpretation of implication [Anderson and Belnap Jr., 1975]. Second, $(a \Rightarrow a)$ is a correct answer to the question $\mathbf{imp}(a)$. $(a \Rightarrow a)$ is a *tautology*, that is, it holds in all models, so it cannot give any information about a state of knowledge. We could define a new query system, in which only nontautologies are considered to be answers. Since, for most useful logics, the detection of tautologies ranges from intractable to impossible, such a technique is generally unsatisfying. A better approach is to let a question present a set of atomic formulae that must not be used in an answer, since the questioner considers them to be insufficiently informative. We may find later that certain nontautological formulae are uninformative for various reasons, and this technique reserves the flexibility to handle those cases.

Example 2.2.4. Let **rest-imp** be a new formal symbol, and let

$$\mathbf{Q}_{S2} = \{\mathbf{rest\text{-}imp}(a, \mathbf{A}) : a \in \mathbf{At} \text{ and } \mathbf{A} \subseteq \mathbf{At}\}$$

Define the relation $?\!\!-_{S2} \subseteq \mathbf{Q}_{S2} \times \mathbf{F}_{Sh}$ by

$$\mathbf{rest\text{-}imp}(c, \mathbf{C}) \ ?\!\!-_{S1} \ (a \Rightarrow b) \text{ if and only if } a = c \text{ and } b \notin \mathbf{C}$$

Now $\langle \mathbf{F}_{Sh}, \mathbf{Q}_{S1}, ?\!\!-_{S1} \rangle$ is a query system representing the conceivable answers to questions of the form 'what atomic formula not in $\mathbf{A}$ does a imply?'

The new query system of Example 2.2.4 may be used very flexibly to guide answers toward the most informative implications of an atomic formula a. If the explicit knowledge available to the auditor to answer questions is finite, then there are only a finite number of atomic formulae that can appear in an answer, so the sets of prohibited formulae may simply be listed. In more sophisticated languages than SIC, we need some sort of finite notation for describing large and even infinite sets of prohibited answers.

Query systems allow a further enrichment of the analysis of communication. Once a speaker has communicated some implicit knowledge $\mathbf{K}$ to an auditor by uttering formulae, a *questioner* (sometimes, but not always, identical with the speaker) may ask a question Q, which the auditor tries to answer by discovering a formula F such that $Q \ ?\!\!- F$ (F is an answer to the question Q), and $F \in \mathbf{Theory}(\mathbf{K})$ (Q is correct according to the implicit knowledge $\mathbf{K}$).

So, given a set $\mathbf{T}$ of formulae expressing the knowledge $\mathbf{Models}(\mathbf{T})$, a question Q provides an additional constraint on the search for a formula F such that $\mathbf{T} \models F$, to ensure that $Q \ ?\!\!- F$ as well. In many cases, there is more than one correct answer F such that $Q \ ?\!\!- \mathbf{T} \models F$. Depending on the context, the questioner may want a single answer chosen nondeterministically from the set of correct answers, or a best answer under some criterion. The case where the questioner wants a list of all answers may be modelled by representing that list by a single formula giving the conjunction of all the list elements. A particularly useful criterion for best answer uses the logical consequence relation.

Definition 2.2.5. Let $\mathcal{Q} = \langle \mathbf{F_Q}, \mathbf{Q}, ?{-} \rangle$ be a query system, and let $\mathcal{S} = \langle \mathbf{F_S}, \mathbf{W}, \models \rangle$ be a semantic system with $\mathbf{F_Q} \subseteq \mathbf{F_S}$. F is a *consequentially strongest* correct answer to the question Q for explicit knowledge $\mathbf{T}$ if and only if

1. $Q ?{-} \mathbf{T} \models F$

2. for all $G \in \mathbf{F_Q}$, whenever $Q ?{-} \mathbf{T} \models G$, then $\{F\} \models G$

Consequentially strongest answers are not necessarily unique, but all consequentially strongest answers are semantically equivalent. Notice that the comparison of strength for two answers F and G is done without taking into account the knowledge $\mathbf{T}$. That is, we require $\{F\} \models G$, rather than $\mathbf{T} \cup \{F\} \models G$. This makes sense because $\mathbf{T}$ is known to the auditor, but not necessarily to the questioner. Even if the questioner knows $\mathbf{T}$, he may not be able to derive its consequences. The whole purpose of the communication between questioner and auditor is to give the questioner the benefit of the auditor's knowledge and inferential power. So, the value of an answer to the questioner must be determined independently of the knowledge used by the auditor in its construction (the alternative form $\mathbf{T} \cup \{F\} \models G$ holds trivially by monotonicity, so it carries no information anyway).

In order to illustrate the use of consequentially strongest answers, we extend SIC to deal with conjunctions of implications.

Example 2.2.6. Expand the formulae of SIC to the set

$$\mathbf{F_{Sc}} = \mathbf{F_{Sh}} \cup \{F_1 \wedge \cdots \wedge F_m : F, G \in \mathbf{F_{Sh}}\}$$

of formulae in the *shallow implicational-conjunctive calculus* (SICC). The semantic systems and proof systems of Examples 2.1.2, 3.1.3, 3.1.2 extend in the natural way to deal with conjunctive formulae. Let **conj-imp** be a new formal symbol, and let

$$\mathbf{Q_{Sc}} = \{\mathbf{conj\text{-}imp}(a) : a \in \mathbf{At}\}$$

Define the relation $?{-}_{\mathrm{Sc}} \subseteq \mathbf{Q_{Sc}} \times \mathbf{F_{Sc}}$ by

$$\mathbf{conj\text{-}imp}(c) \; ?{-}_{\mathrm{Sc}} \; (a_1 \Rightarrow b_1) \wedge \cdots \wedge (a_m \Rightarrow b_m) \qquad \text{if and only if} \\ a_i = c \text{ for all } i \leq m$$

Now $\langle \mathbf{F}_{\text{Sc}}, \mathbf{Q}_{\text{Sc}}, \overset{?}{\vdash}_{\text{Sc}} \rangle$ is a query system representing the conceivable answers to questions of the form 'what are some atomic formulae implied by a?' A consequentially strongest answer to **conj-imp**(a) is a conjunction of *all* of the implications with hypothesis a that hold in a given state of knowledge.

The concept of consequentially strongest answers is particularly helpful in systems where a potentially infinite answer is produced incrementally. The entire infinite answer may often be read as an infinite conjunction of finite formulae, and the requirement of consequentially strongest answers guarantees that the incremental production of the answer does not stop prematurely, before all available information is expressed.

In logic programming systems, the *user* of a program plays the part of the questioner. The input is the question, and the output is the answer, if any, discovered and proved by the processor/auditor. This scenario allows the knowledge resources of a programmer/speaker to be combined with the deductive powers of a processor/auditor, in order to answer questions from the user/questioner.

2.3 Examples of logic programming languages

Now we can design a wide variety of logic programming languages, by defining appropriate semantic systems and query systems.

2.3.1 Programming in first-order predicate calculus

Several logic programming systems, particularly Prolog and Relational Databases, are essentially sublanguages of a general language for logic programming in FOPC.

Definition 2.3.1 ([Andrews, 1986; Kleene, 1952; Gallier, 1986]).
Let **V** be a countably infinite set. Members of **V** are called *variables,* and are written u, v, w, x, y, z, sometimes with subscripts.

Let $\mathbf{Fun}_i$ be a countably infinite set for each $i \geq 0$, with $\mathbf{Fun}_i$ and $\mathbf{Fun}_j$ disjoint when $i \neq j$. Members of $\mathbf{Fun}_i$ are called *function symbols of arity i,* and are written f, g, h, sometimes with subscripts. A function symbol of arity 0 in $\mathbf{Fun}_0$ is called a *constant,* and may be written a, b, c, d, e.

Let $\mathbf{Pred}_i$ be a countably infinite set for each $i \geq 0$, with $\mathbf{Pred}_i$ and $\mathbf{Pred}_j$ disjoint when $i \neq j$, $\mathbf{Pred}_i$ and $\mathbf{Fun}_j$ disjoint for all i and j. Members of $\mathbf{Pred}_i$ are called *predicate* or *relation symbols of arity i,* and are written P, Q, R, sometimes with subscripts. A predicate symbol of arity 0 in $\mathbf{Pred}_0$ is called a *propositional symbol,* and is closely analogous to an atomic propositional formula in **At** as used in Example 2.1.2.

The set $\mathbf{T}_P$ of *terms* in FOPC is defined inductively as the least set such that:

1. if $x \in \mathbf{V}$ then $x \in \mathbf{T}_P$
2. if $a \in \mathbf{Fun}_0$ then $a \in \mathbf{T}_P$

3. if $f \in \mathbf{Fun}_i$ for some $i > 0$ and $t_1, \ldots, t_i \in \mathbf{T}_P$, then $f(t_1, \ldots, t_i) \in \mathbf{T}_P$

Terms are intended to represent objects in some universe of discourse. $f(t_1, \ldots, t_i)$ is intended to represent the result of applying the function denoted by f to the objects represented by $t_1, \ldots, t_i$. We often take the liberty of writing binary function application in infix notation. For example, if $+ \in \mathbf{Fun}_2$ we may write $(t_1 + t_2)$ for $+(t_1, t_2)$. A *ground term* is a term containing no variables.

The set $\mathbf{F}_P$ of *formulae* in FOPC is defined inductively as the least set such that:

1. True, False $\in \mathbf{F}_P$
2. if $P \in \mathbf{Pred}_0$, then $P \in \mathbf{F}_P$
3. if $P \in \mathbf{Pred}_i$ for some $i > 0$ and $t_1, \ldots, t_i \in \mathbf{T}_P$, then $P(t_1, \ldots, t_i) \in \mathbf{F}_P$
4. if $A, B \in \mathbf{F}_P$, then $(A \wedge B), (A \vee B), (A \Rightarrow B), (\neg A) \in \mathbf{F}_P$
5. if $A \in \mathbf{F}_P$ and $x \in \mathbf{V}$, then $(\exists x : A), (\forall x : A) \in \mathbf{F}_P$

Formulae in FOPC are intended to represent assertions about the objects represented by their component terms. True and False are the trivially true and false assertions, respectively. $P(t_1, \ldots, t_i)$ represents the assertion that the relation denoted by P holds between $t_1, \ldots, t_i$. $(A \wedge B)$, $(A \vee B)$, $(A \Rightarrow B)$, $(\neg A)$ represent the usual conjunction, disjunction, implication, and negation. $(\exists x : A)$ represents 'there exists x such that A,' and $(\forall x : A)$ represents 'for all x A.' Parentheses may dropped when they can be inferred from normal precedence rules.

In a more general setting, it is best to understand $\mathbf{Fun}_i$ and $\mathbf{Pred}_i$ as parameters giving a *signature* for first-order logic, and let them vary to produce an infinite class of predicate calculi. For this chapter, we may take $\mathbf{Fun}_i$ and $\mathbf{Pred}_i$ to be arbitrary but fixed. In many texts on mathematical logic, the language of FOPC includes a special binary predicate symbol '$\doteq$' for equality. We follow the Prolog tradition in using the *pure first-order predicate calculus*, without equality, and referring to it simply as FOPC.

The intended meanings of FOPC formulae sketched above are formalized by the traditional semantic system defined below. First, we need a set of models for FOPC.

Definition 2.3.2 ([Andrews, 1986; Kleene, 1952; Gallier, 1986]).
Let $\mathbf{U}$ be an infinite set, called the *universe*. Let $U \subseteq \mathbf{U}$.
A *variable assignment* over U is a function $\nu : \mathbf{V} \to U$.
A *predicate assignment* over U is a function
$$\rho : \bigcup \{\mathbf{Pred}_i : i \geq 0\} \to \bigcup \{2^{(U^i)} : i \geq 0\}$$
such that $P \in \mathbf{Pred}_i$ implies $\rho(P) \subseteq U^i$ for all $i \geq 0$.
A *function assignment* over U is a function
$$\tau : \bigcup \{\mathbf{Fun}_i : i \geq 0\} \to \bigcup \{U^{(U^i)} : i \geq 0\}$$
such that $f \in \mathbf{Fun}_i$ implies $\tau(f) : U^i \to U$ for all $i \geq 0$.
If $U \subseteq \mathbf{U}$, τ is a function assignment over U, and ρ is a predicate

assignment over U, then $\langle U, \tau, \rho \rangle$ is a *model of FOPC*. $\mathbf{M}_P$ is the set of all models of FOPC.

Notice that FOPC models assign values to function and predicate symbols, but not to variables. The exclusion of variable assignments from models is the only technically significant distinction between variables and constant symbols. A function assignment and a variable assignment together determine a valuation of terms. With a predicate assignment, they also define a valuation of formulae.

Definition 2.3.3 ([Andrews, 1986; Kleene, 1952; Gallier, 1986]).
Let τ be a function assignment over U, ν a variable assignment over U. The *term valuation* $\tau_\nu : \mathbf{T}_P \to U$ is defined inductively by

1. if $x \in \mathbf{V}$, then $\tau_\nu(x) = \nu(x)$
2. if $f \in \mathbf{Fun}_i$, and $t_1, \ldots, t_i \in \mathbf{T}_P$, then
   $\tau_\nu(f(t_1, \ldots, t_i)) = \tau(f)(\tau_\nu(t_1), \ldots, \tau_\nu(t_i))$

In addition, let ρ be a predicate assignment over U. The *formula valuation* $\rho_{\tau,\nu} : \mathbf{F}_P \to \{0, 1\}$ is defined inductively by

1. $\rho_{\tau,\nu}(\text{False}) = 0$
2. $\rho_{\tau,\nu}(\text{True}) = 1$
3. if $P \in \mathbf{Pred}_i$, and $t_1, \ldots, t_i \in \mathbf{T}_P$, then $\rho_{\tau,\nu}(P(t_1, \ldots, t_i)) = 1$ if and only if $\langle \tau_{\tau,\nu}(t_1), \ldots, \tau_{\tau,\nu}(t_i) \rangle \in \rho(P)$
4. $\rho_{\tau,\nu}(A \wedge B) = 1$ if and only if $\rho_{\tau,\nu}(A) = 1$ and $\rho_{\tau,\nu}(B) = 1$
5. $\rho_{\tau,\nu}(A \vee B) = 1$ if and only if $\rho_{\tau,\nu}(A) = 1$ or $\rho_{\tau,\nu}(B) = 1$
6. $\rho_{\tau,\nu}(A \Rightarrow B) = 1$ if and only if $\rho_{\tau,\nu}(A) = 0$ or $\rho_{\tau,\nu}(B) = 1$
7. $\rho_{\tau,\nu}(\neg A) = 1$ if and only if $\rho_{\tau,\nu}(A) = 0$
8. $\rho_{\tau,\nu}(\exists x : A) = 1$ if and only if $\rho_{\tau,\nu'}(A) = 1$ for some ν' such that $y \neq x$ implies $\nu(y) = \nu'(y)$
9. $\rho_{\tau,\nu}(\forall x : A) = 1$ if and only if $\rho_{\tau,\nu'}(A) = 1$ for all ν' such that $y \neq x$ implies $\nu(y) = \nu'(y)$

Now, we may define an appropriate semantic system for FOPC.

Definition 2.3.4. The classical semantic system for FOPC is $\langle \mathbf{F}_P, \mathbf{M}_P, \models_P \rangle$, where $\langle U, \tau, \rho \rangle \models_P F$ if and only if $\rho_{\tau,\nu}(F) = 1$ for all variable assignments ν over U.

FOPC is particularly well suited to defining relations, letting variables stand for the parameters in the relations. For such purposes, it is important to distinguish between uses of variables that are *bound* by the quantifiers $\exists$ and $\forall$, and those that are *free* to be used as relational parameters.

Definition 2.3.5 ([Andrews, 1986; Kleene, 1952; Gallier, 1986]).
An occurrence of a variable x in a formula is *bound* if and only if it is located within a subformula of the form $(\exists x : F)$ or the form $(\forall x : F)$. An occurrence of a variable x in a formula is *free* if and only if it is not bound.

A *sentence* is a formula with no free occurrences of variables. If $F \in \mathbf{F}_P$ is a formula, and all free occurrences of variables in F are among $x_1, \ldots, x_i$, then the sentence $(\forall x_1 : \cdots \forall x_i : F)$ is a *closure* of F. It is easy to see that F is semantically equivalent to each of its closures.

Let $x_1, \ldots, x_i$ be a list of variables with no repetitions, and let $t_1, \ldots, t_i \in \mathbf{T}_P$. $F[t_1, \ldots, t_i/x_1, \ldots, x_i]$ is the formula that results from substituting the term t_j for every free occurrence of the variable x_j in the formula F, for each j, $1 \leq j \leq i$, renaming bound variables of F when necessary so that the variables of $t_1, \ldots, t_i$ are free in the result [Andrews, 1986; Kleene, 1952; Gallier, 1986] . When $G = F[t_1, \ldots, t_i/x_1, \ldots, x_i]$, we say that G is an *instance* of F, and that F is *more general* than G. These relations apply naturally to terms as well as formulae.

G is a *variable renaming* of F if and only if $G = F[y_1, \ldots, y_i/x_1, \ldots, x_i]$, for some list of variables $y_1, \ldots, y_i$ with no repetitions (equivalently, G is an instance of F and F is an instance of G, since we get $F = G[x_1, \ldots, x_i/y_1, \ldots, y_i]$).

It is very natural to think of a query system in which we may ask what substitutions for the free variables of a formula make it true.

Definition 2.3.6 ([Belnap Jr. and Steel, 1976]). Let **what** be a new formal symbol. Let

$$\mathbf{Q}_P = \{(\mathbf{what}\ x_1, \ldots, x_i : F) : F \in \mathbf{F}_P\}$$

Define the relation $\overset{?}{\vdash}_P \subseteq \mathbf{Q}_P \times \mathbf{F}_P$ by

$$(\mathbf{what}\ x_1, \ldots, x_i : F) \overset{?}{\vdash}_P G$$

if and only if

$$G = F[t_1, \ldots, t_i/x_1, \ldots, x_i] \text{ for some } t_1, \ldots, t_i \in \mathbf{T}_P$$

Now $\langle \mathbf{F}_P, \mathbf{Q}_P, \overset{?}{\vdash}_P \rangle$ is a query system representing the conceivable single answers to questions of the form 'for what terms $t_1, \ldots, t_i$ does $F[t_1, \ldots, t_i/x_1, \ldots, x_i]$ hold?'

The query system above has a crucial role in the profound theoretical connections between logic and computation. For each finite (or even semi-computable) set $\mathbf{T} \subseteq \mathbf{F}_P$ of formulae, and each question $Q = (\mathbf{what}\ x_1, \ldots, x_i : F)$, the set

$$\{\langle t_1, \ldots, t_i \rangle : Q \overset{?}{\vdash}_P \mathbf{T} \models_P F[t_1, \ldots, t_i/x_1, \ldots, x_i]\}$$

is semicomputable. If we use some constant symbol $c \in \mathbf{Fun}_0$ to represent the number 0, some unary function symbol $f \in \mathbf{Fun}_1$ to represent the successor function, and some binary predicate symbol E to represent the equality relation, then we may define all semicomputable sets of integers by formulae in a simple and natural way. We let $\mathbf{R} \subseteq \mathbf{F}_P$ be a finite set of postulates for *Robinson's arithmetic* (system Q of [Mostowski *et al.*, 1953])—a primitive theory sufficient for deriving answers to all addition and multiplication problems. Then *every* semicomputable set is of the form

$$\{j : (\textbf{what } x : F) \overset{?}{\vdash}_P \mathbf{R} \models_P F[f^j(c)/x]\}$$

for some formula $F \in \mathbf{F}_P$. Similarly, every partial computable function ϕ may be defined by choosing an appropriate formula $F \in \mathbf{F}_P$, and letting $\phi(i)$ be the unique number j such that

$$(\textbf{what } y : F[f^i(c)/x]) \overset{?}{\vdash}_P \mathbf{R} \models_P F[f^i(c), f^j(c)/x, y]$$

Notice that the FOPC questions $(\textbf{what } x_1, \ldots, x_i : F)$ do not allow trivial tautological answers, such as the correct answer $(a \Rightarrow a)$ to the question $\textbf{imp}(a)$ ('what atomic formula does a imply?', Example 2.2.3, Section 2.2). In fact, $(\textbf{what } x_1, \ldots, x_i : F)$ has a tautological answer if and only if F is a tautology. FOPC questions avoid this problem through the distinction between predicate symbols and function symbols. When we try to find an answer $F[t_1, \ldots, t_i/x_1, \ldots, x_i]$ to the question $(\textbf{what } x_1, \ldots, x_i : F)$, the information in the question $(\textbf{what } x_1, \ldots, x_i : F)$ is carried largely through predicate symbols, while the information in the answer $F[t_1, \ldots, t_i/x_1, \ldots, x_i]$ is carried entirely by the function symbols in $t_1, \ldots, t_i$, since the predicate symbols in the formula F are already fixed by the question. It is the syntactic incompatibility between the formula given in the question and the terms substituted in by the answer that prevents tautological answers. Suppose that FOPC were extended with a symbol **choose**, where $(\textbf{choose } x : F)$ is a term such that $(\exists x : F)$ implies $F[(\textbf{choose } x : F)/x]$. Then $F[(\textbf{choose } x : F)/x]$ would be a trivially (but not quite tautologically) correct answer to $(\textbf{what } x : F)$ except when no correct answer exists.

The absence of trivial tautological answers does *not* mean that all answers to FOPC questions are equally useful. In some cases a question has a most general semantically correct answer. This provides a nice syntactic way to recognize certain consequentially strongest answers, and a useful characterization of all answers even when there is no consequentially strongest answer.

Proposition 2.3.7. *If G' is an instance of G, then G' is a semantic consequence of G ($G \models_P G'$). It follows immediately that if G is a semantically correct answer to $Q \in \mathbf{Q}_P$ ($Q \overset{?}{\vdash}_P \mathbf{T} \models_P G$), then G' is also a semantically correct answer ($Q \overset{?}{\vdash}_P \mathbf{T} \models_P G'$).*

If G' is a variable renaming of G, then they are semantically equivalent.

Definition 2.3.8. Let $\mathbf{T} \subseteq \mathbf{F}_P$ be a set of formulae, and let $Q = (\mathbf{what}\ x_1,$ $\ldots, x_i : F) \in \mathbf{Q}_P$ be a question. G is a *most general* answer to Q for explicit knowledge $\mathbf{T}$ if and only if

1. $Q \ ?\!\!\vdash_P \mathbf{T} \models_P G$
2. for all $G_0 \in \mathbf{F}_P$, if G is an instance of G_0 and $Q \ ?\!\!\vdash_P \mathbf{T} \models_P G_0$, then G_0 is a variable renaming of G.

A set $\mathbf{A} \subseteq \mathbf{F}_P$ of formulae is a *most general set* of correct answers to Q for $\mathbf{T}$ if and only if

1. each formula $F \in \mathbf{A}$ is a most general answer to Q for $\mathbf{T}$
2. for all formulae $G \in \mathbf{F}_P$, if $Q \ ?\!\!\vdash_P \mathbf{T} \models_P G$, then G is an instance of some $F \in \mathbf{A}$
3. for all formulae $F_1, F_2 \in \mathbf{A}$, if F_2 is an instance of F_1, then $F_2 = F_1$

It is easy to see that for each question $Q \in \mathbf{Q}_P$ and set of formulae $\mathbf{T} \subseteq \mathbf{F}_P$ there is a most general set of correct answers (possibly empty or infinite). Furthermore, the most general set of correct answers is unique up to variable renaming of its members.

Notice that it is very easy to generate all correct answers to a question in $\mathbf{Q}_P$ from the most general set—they are precisely the instances of its members. If Q has a consequentially strongest answer, then it has a consequentially strongest answer that is also most general. If the most general set of correct answers is the singleton set $\{F\}$, then F is a consequentially strongest answer.

Example 2.3.9. Let $G \in \mathbf{Pred}_2$ be a binary predicate symbol, where $G(t_1, t_2)$ is intended to assert that t_1 is strictly larger than t_2. Suppose that objects in the universe have left and right portions, and that $l, r \in \mathbf{Fun}_1$ denote the operations that produce those portions. A minimal natural state of knowledge about such a situation is

$$\mathbf{T}_0 = \{\forall x : G(x, l(x)) \wedge G(x, r(x))\}$$

A natural question is $Q = (\mathbf{what}\ x, y : G(x, y))$. The most general set of answers is

$$\mathbf{A}_0 = \{G(x, l(x)),\ G(x, r(x))\}$$

Other answers include $G(l(x), r(l(x)))$, $G(r(x), l(r(x)))$, etc.

$\mathbf{T}_0$ has only the specific knowledge that a whole is larger than its portions, but not the general knowledge that the relation G is a strict ordering relation. Let

$$\mathbf{T}_1 = \quad \mathbf{T}_0 \cup \{\forall x, y, z : (G(x, y) \wedge G(y, z)) \Rightarrow$$
$$G(x, z),\ \forall x, y : \neg(G(x, y) \wedge G(y, x))\}$$

For this extended knowledge, the most general set of answers to Q is the infinite set

$\mathbf{A}_1 = \mathbf{A}_0 \cup \{G(x, l(l(x))), G(x, l(r(x))), G(x, r(r(x))), G(x, l(l(l(x)))), \ldots\}$

The first formula added to $\mathbf{T}_1$ above, which expresses the transitivity of ordering, leads to the additional answers.

In some cases, it is convenient to allow conjunctions of answers to questions in $\mathbf{Q}_P$ to be conjoined into a single answer.

Definition 2.3.10. Let **conj-what** be a new formal symbol. Let

$$\mathbf{Q}_{P\wedge} = \{(\mathbf{conj\text{-}what}\ x_1, \ldots, x_i : F) : F \in \mathbf{F}_P\}$$

Define the relation $?{-}_{P\wedge} \subseteq \mathbf{Q}_{P\wedge} \times \mathbf{F}_P$ by

$$(\mathbf{conj\text{-}what}\ x_1, \ldots, x_i : F)\ ?{-}_{P\wedge}\ G$$

if and only if

$$G = F[t_1^1, \ldots, t_i^1 / x_1, \ldots, x_i] \wedge \cdots \wedge F[t_1^n, \ldots, t_i^n / x_1, \ldots, x_i] \text{ for some } t_1^1, \ldots, t_i^n \in \mathbf{T}_P$$

Now $\langle \mathbf{F}_{P\wedge}, \mathbf{Q}_{P\wedge}, ?{-}_{P\wedge} \rangle$ is a query system representing the conceivable conjunctive answers to questions of the form 'for what terms $t_1, \ldots, t_i$ does $F[t_1, \ldots, t_i / x_1, \ldots, x_i]$ hold?'

Answers to $(\mathbf{conj\text{-}what}\ x_1, \ldots, x_i : F)$ are precisely conjunctions of answers to $(\mathbf{what}\ x_1, \ldots, x_i : F)$. $(\mathbf{conj\text{-}what}\ x_1, \ldots, x_i : F)$ may have a consequentially strongest answer even though $(\mathbf{what}\ x_1, \ldots, x_i : F)$ does not. In particular, whenever the most general set of answers to $(\mathbf{what}\ x_1, \ldots, x_i : F)$ is finite, the conjunction of those answers is a consequentially strongest answer to $(\mathbf{conj\text{-}what}\ x_1, \ldots, x_i : F)$.

2.3.2 Prolog

The most famous programming language associated with logic programming, and the one that instigated scientists to study logic programming as a specialty within computer science, is Prolog [Kowalski, 1974; van Emden and Kowalski, 1976], the creation of Kowalski and Colmerauer. The name 'Prolog' is usually associated with a group of very similar programming languages based on logic programming in Horn clauses—a particular sublanguage of the first-order predicate calculus. Prolog as it is actually used deviates from pure logic programming in several ways: it fails to produce some logically entailed answers; in rare cases it produces logically incorrect answers; and it contains constructs that are not definable naturally in FOPC, and which are normally understood in conventional imperative ways. Furthermore, the criteria by which Prolog chooses one of several possible answers cannot be explained naturally in terms of the semantics of FOPC. The discrepancy between Prolog and Horn-clause logic programming is closely comparable to the discrepancy between Lisp and the purely functional language based on the lambda calculus that is sometimes called 'pure lazy Lisp'. In spite of the discrepancies, the best way to understand Prolog is to conceive of it as an approximation to, and extension of, a Horn-clause logic programming language.

The essential idea behind Prolog is to find correct answers to predicate calculus questions in $\mathbf{Q}_P$ of Section 2.3.1 above. In principle, all such answers are computable. Currently known implementation techniques require fairly stringent conditions on the sets of formulae that may be used as explicit knowledge for question answering, and on the questions that may be asked, in order to search for and generate proofs in a relatively simple and disciplined way. Prolog is based on the restriction of programs to sets of *Horn clauses,* and questions to simple conjunctions of positive atomic formulae.

Definition 2.3.11. A formula $F \in \mathbf{F}_P$ is a *Horn clause* if and only if it is in one of the forms

1. $F = (R_1(t_{1,1}, \ldots, t_{1,i_1}) \wedge \cdots \wedge R_m(t_{m,1}, \ldots, t_{m,i_m}) \Rightarrow P(u_1, \ldots, u_j))$
2. $F = (R_1(t_{1,1}, \ldots, t_{1,i_1}) \wedge \cdots \wedge R_m(t_{m,1}, \ldots, t_{m,i_m}) \Rightarrow \text{False})$
3. $F = (\text{True} \Rightarrow P(u_1, \ldots, u_j))$
4. $F = (\text{True} \Rightarrow \text{False})$

where $R_1, \ldots, R_m, P$ are predicate symbols, and $t_{1,1}, \ldots, t_{m,i_m}, u_1, \ldots, u_j$ are terms.

A *pure Prolog program* is a finite set of Horn clauses.

A *pure Prolog input* is a question of the form

$$(\textbf{what } x_1, \ldots, x_i : P_1(t_{1,1}, \ldots, t_{1,i_1}) \wedge \cdots \wedge P_m(t_{m,1}, \ldots, t_{m,i_m}))$$

where $x_1, \ldots, x_i$ are precisely the free variables of $P_1(t_{1,1}, \ldots, t_{1,i_1}) \wedge \cdots \wedge P_m(t_{m,1}, \ldots, t_{m,i_m})$.

In order to promote readability of programs, within the limitations of older keyboards and printers, typical Prolog implementations replace the conventional logical symbol '$\wedge$' by ';', they write the arguments to implications in the reverse of the usual order and replace the symbol '$\Leftarrow$' by ':−'. Also, they denote the symbol 'False' in the conclusion of an implication, and 'True' in the hypothesis, by the empty string. Predicate symbols are written in lower case, and variables are written in upper case. So, the four forms of Horn clause in actual Prolog programs look like

1. $p(u_1, \ldots, u_j) :\!- r_1(t_{1,1}, \ldots, t_{1,i_1}); \cdots; r_m(t_{m,1}, \ldots, t_{m,i_m})$
2. $:\!- r_1(t_{1,1}, \ldots, t_{1,i_1}); \cdots; r_m(t_{m,1}, \ldots, t_{m,i_m})$
3. $p(u_1, \ldots, u_j) :\!- (\text{or } p(u_1, \ldots, u_j))$
4. $:\!-$ (or the empty string)

Since a question always requests substitutions for all free variables, the header 'what $x_1, \ldots, x_i$' is omitted and the question is abbreviated in the form

$$r_1(t_{1,1}, \ldots, t_{1,i_1}); \cdots; r_m(t_{m,1}, \ldots, t_{m,i_m})$$

Since the substitution in an answer of the form

$$(R_1(t_{1,1}, \ldots, t_{1,i_1}) \wedge \cdots \wedge R_m(t_{m,1}, \ldots, t_{m,i_m}))[s_1, \ldots, s_i/x_1, \ldots, x_i]$$

completely determines the answer, actual Prolog output presents only the substitution, in the form

$$x_1 = s_1; \cdots; x_i = s_i$$

These notational variations and abbreviations have a substantial impact on the way Prolog programs, inputs, and outputs *look,* but they are completely transparent to the logical meaning.

When a pure Prolog input is presented to a pure Prolog program, all possible answers may be derived systematically by treating each clause of form 1 as a recursive part of a definition of the procedure P in terms of calls to the procedures $R_1, \ldots, R_m$. Because the same predicate symbol P may appear in the conclusion of more than one clause, each clause normally provides only a part of the definition of P. Clauses of form 3 are nonrecursive parts of the definition of a procedure P. Clauses of form 2 are somewhat peculiar: they act like extra hardcoded parts of the input. Clauses of form 4 are useless in programs, but allowed by the formal definition. Different implementations may or may not prohibit the degenerate forms. Prolog tries to choose more general answers instead of their instances, but it does not guarantee that all answers produced are most general. An understanding of the precise correspondence of Prolog to the answering of pure Prolog input questions using pure Prolog programs requires a lot of detail that must wait until the chapter 'Horn clause logic programming'.

A notable variation on Prolog is λProlog [Nadathur and Miller, 1990; Nadathur and Miller, 1988]. This language extends predicate calculus logic programming into the *omega-order predicate calculus,* also called *type theory* [Andrews, 1986]. Higher-order predicate calculi add variables ranging over predicates, quantification over such variables, and predicates that apply to other predicates. λProlog generalizes the Horn clauses of FOPC to the hereditary Harrop formulae of the omega-order predicate calculus [Miller *et al.*, 1991].

2.3.3 Relational databases and Datalog

Relational databases [Date, 1986; Codd, 1970] were invented by Codd, completely independently of the development of Prolog and logic programming in the programming language community. Nonetheless, relational databases and their queries may be understood very naturally in terms of logic programming concepts. This point has been noted by the Prolog community, leading to the definition of Datalog [Maier and Warren, 1988], a variant of relational databases in the style of Prolog. Gallaire, Minker, and Nicolas have developed the concept of *deductive databases* [Gallaire *et al.*, 1984] to capture the logical content of relational databases and their variants. Reiter [Reiter, 1984] has shown how a logical view of databases has advantages of robustness under several useful generalizations of database functionality. My proposed approach to logic programming applies logic to programming languages in essentially the same way that Reiter applies logic to databases.

Like Prolog, relational database systems find correct answers to predicate calculus questions in $\mathbf{Q}_P$ of Section 2.3.1. The different natural assumptions and performance requirements of the database world lead to far more stringent restrictions on the sets of formulae that may be used for question answering. The questions, which correspond to database queries, are essentially unrestricted. Because of the stringent restrictions on knowledge formulae, which limit answers to a predetermined finite set of possibilities, actual relational database implementations do not deviate from pure logic programming, except by offering constructs that go beyond the logical definitions. On purely relational queries, they produce precisely all of the semantically correct answers.

Definition 2.3.12. A *pure relational database* is a finite set of formulae of the form $P(c_1, \ldots, c_i)$, where $P \in \mathbf{Pred}_i$ is a predicate symbol and $c_1, \ldots, c_i \in \mathbf{Fun}_0$ are constant symbols.

A pure relational database as defined above is the natural logical view of the contents of a relational database system at any given time. The constant symbols are the objects that may appear in fields of relations in the database. Each predicate symbol represents one of the relations in the database. Each formula $P(c_1, \ldots, c_i)$ represents the presence of the tuple $\langle c_1, \ldots, c_i \rangle$ in the relation P.

Pure relational database query languages are equivalent to $\mathbf{Q}_P$—all queries of the form $(\mathbf{what}\ x_1, \ldots, x_i : F)$ are allowed. Because of the simplicity of the formulae in the database, restrictions on the queries are not required for tractable implementation. Notice the complementarity of Prolog and relational database query languages. Prolog allows relatively powerful Horn clauses as knowledge formulae, but restricts queries to conjunctions of atomic formulae. Relational database query languages restrict knowledge formulae to the very simple form of predicate symbols applied to constant symbols, but allow unrestricted FOPC **what** queries.

The simplicity of the formulae in a pure relational database guarantees that the set of answers to $(\mathbf{what}\ x_1, \ldots, x_i : F)$ is finite, and relational database query systems actually produce *all* the semantically correct answers. Equivalently, we may think of a relational database query system as producing the consequentially strongest answer (unique up to the order of the conjuncts) to (**conj-what** $x_1, \ldots, x_i : F$). The consequentially strongest answer to the **conj-what** form of the question is simply the conjunction of all the answers to the **what** form.

Datalog restricts queries to the Prolog form, but allows Horn clauses with no function symbols (no 'functors' in Prolog jargon) to be added to the formulae of the database to provide additional knowledge for the purpose of answering a given query. The Horn clauses are thought of as defining new relations to be used in the query, rather than as adding information to the database.

A variety of notations have been used for the expression of FOPC queries in relational database systems. These variant notations may look very different from FOPC at first glance, but in fact they are equivalent in querying power. The complete translations between notations are clumsy to define formally, so we consider the general principles behind the notation, and illustrate the translation with examples. I use Codd's language DSL ALPHA [Date, 1986; Codd, 1971], often called *relational calculus*, for the database notation.

Instead of referring directly to objects in the universe **U**, relational database languages generally refer to tuples in relations, because they correspond to records in a conventional file. Instead of the positional notation $P(t_1, \ldots, t_i)$, they give *domain names* $D_1, \ldots, D_i$ to the parameter positions. The name of a relation (predicate symbol) is treated as a variable ranging over the set of tuples in that relation. The value of the domain D in an arbitrary tuple of the relation P is denoted by the record notation $P.D$. $P.D = c$ means that the value in the domain D of an unknown tuple in the relation P is c, and $P.D = Q.E$ means that the value in the domain D of some tuple in P is the same as that in domain E of some tuple in Q. Because of the absence of function symbols with arity greater than 0, this use of equality does not introduce the general capabilities of FOPC with equality, it merely captures the limited sort of equality information that is represented in pure FOPC by multiple occurrences of constants and variables, and by binding variables to constants. In principle, the equation $x \doteq c$ can be understood as $P_c(x)$, where P is a special predicate postulated to hold on c, and to not hold on all other constant symbols. For example, if P and Q are binary predicates and D, E, F, G are appropriate domain names, then the DSL ALPHA expression

$$P.D = c \wedge P.E = Q.F \wedge Q.G = d$$

is equivalent to the FOPC formula

$$P(c, x) \wedge Q(x, d)$$

Additional variables may be declared in DSL ALPHA to range over the tuples of a relation in the database, and these variables may be quantified with ∀ and ∃. So, in the presence of the declarations

RANGE X P

RANGE Y Q

which declare the variable X to range over tuples of the relation P and Y to range over tuples of Q, the expression

$$\forall X(X.D = c \lor \exists Y(X.E = Y.F \land Y.G = d))$$

is equivalent to the FOPC formula

$$\forall x_1 : \forall x_2 : (P(x_1, x_2) \Rightarrow (x_1 \doteq c \lor Q(x_2, d))).$$

Notice that the existential quantifier in the DSL ALPHA expression is left out of the FOPC formula, because one of its components is bound to the constant d, and the other to the E component of the variable X, whose quantification occurs before that of Y. In general, a FOPC quantifier is required for each domain position of a quantified tuple in a DSL ALPHA expression that is not bound by equality either to a constant or to a component of a variable that has already been quantified. With the same RANGE declarations above, the DSL ALPHA expression

$$\forall X \exists Y(X.D = Y.G)$$

is equivalent to the FOPC formula

$$\forall x_1 : \forall x_2 : P(x_1, x_2) \Rightarrow \exists y : Q(y, x_1)$$

So, there are some syntactic subtleties in translating quantification from DSL ALPHA into FOPC, but they are all solvable with sufficient care.

There is one semantic problem that prevents DSL ALPHA from expressing everything that can be expressed by FOPC formulae with only 0-ary function symbols. That is the limitation of the range of quantified variables in DSL ALPHA to the set of tuples actually occurring in a relation in the database, while FOPC may quantify over an abstract universe **U**. There is no expression in DSL ALPHA semantically equivalent to $\forall x : P(x)$, since DSL ALPHA can only express the fact that every object in a tuple of the database satisfies the predicate P. Because these objects are exactly those mentioned by the knowledge formulae, however, the restricted quantification of DSL ALPHA yields the same answers to queries as the unrestricted quantification of FOPC, so in terms of the behavior of query-answering systems the notations are equivalent. Another way of viewing this semantic difference is to suppose that each database implicitly contains a *closed world assumption* [Reiter, 1978] expressing the fact that only the objects mentioned in the database exist. In FOPC with equality, the closed world assumption may be expressed by the formula $\forall x : x \doteq c_0 \vee \cdots \vee x \doteq c_n$, where $c_0, \ldots, c_n$ are all of the constant symbols appearing in the database. Without equality, we can only express the fact that every object acts just like one of $c_0, \ldots, c_n$ (i.e., it satisfies exactly the same formulae), and even that requires an infinite number of formulae.

Given the translation of DSL ALPHA expressions to FOPC formulae suggested above, we may translate DSL ALPHA queries into FOPC questions. DSL ALPHA queries have the general form

$$\underline{\text{GET }} Q(P_1.D_1, \ldots, P_i.D_i) : E$$

where $P_1, \ldots, P_i$ are relations in the database, Q is a new relational symbol not occurring in the database, $D_1, \ldots, D_i$ are domain names, and E is an expression. Appropriate declarations of the ranges of variables in E must be given before the query. Let F be a FOPC formula equivalent to E, using the variables $x_1, \ldots, x_i$ for the values $P_1.D_1, \ldots, P_i.D_i$. Then, the effect of the DSL ALPHA query above is to assign to Q the relation (set of tuples) answering the question

$$\textbf{what } x_1, \ldots, x_i : F$$

That is,

$$Q = \{\langle c_1, \ldots, c_i \rangle : (\textbf{what } x_1, \ldots, x_i : F) \; ?\!\vdash_P \textbf{D} \models_P$$
$$F[c_1, \ldots, c_i/x_1, \ldots, x_i]\}$$

where $\textbf{D}$ is the set of formulae in the database. Equivalently, the value of Q may be thought of as an abbreviation for the consequentially strongest answer to $\textbf{conj-what } x_1, \ldots, x_i : F$ for $\textbf{D}$, which is just the conjunction of all the answers to $\textbf{what } x_1, \ldots, x_i : F$.

Another type of notation for relational database queries avoids explicit quantification entirely, and uses the relational operations of *projection, join*, etc. to define new relations from those in the database. Notation in the style of DSL ALPHA above is called *relational calculus*, because of the similarity to predicate calculus in the use of explicit quantification. The alternate approach through operations on relations is called *relational algebra*, because the equations that express the properties of the relational operations resemble well-known definitions of algebras. In fact, each notation has its own algebra and its own calculus, and the difference is just the way in which relations are denoted. Most recent work on relational databases refers to the relational algebra notation, which looks even more distant from FOPC than the relational calculus notation, but is still easily translatable into FOPC. See [Date, 1986; Codd, 1972] for a description of relational algebra notation for database queries, and a translation to the relational calculus notation.

2.3.4 Programming in equational logic

Another natural logical system in which to program is equational logic. A large number of programming languages may be viewed essentially as different restrictions of programming in equational logic.

Definition 2.3.13. Let the set $\mathbf{V}$ of variables, the sets $\mathbf{Fun}_0, \mathbf{Fun}_1, \ldots$ of constant and function symbols, and the set $\mathbf{T}_P$ of terms be the same as in FOPC (see Definition 2.3.1). Let $\doteq$ be a new formal symbol (we add the dot to distinguish between the formal symbol for equality in our language and the meaningful equality symbol $=$ used in discussing the language). The set $\mathbf{F}_{\doteq}$ of *equational formulae* (or simply *equations*) is

$$\mathbf{F}_{\doteq} = \{t_1 \doteq t_2 : t_1, t_2 \in \mathbf{T}_P\}$$

Models for equational logic are the same as models for FOPC, omitting the predicate assignments. Although $\doteq$ behaves like a special binary predicate symbol, it is given a fixed meaning (as are $\wedge$, $\vee$, $\neg$, $\Rightarrow$, $\exists$, $\forall$), so it need not be specified in each model. An equational formula $t_1 \doteq t_2$ holds in a model precisely when t_1 denotes the same object as t_2 for every variable assignment.

Definition 2.3.14.   Let the infinite universe $\mathbf{U}$ and the set of function assignments be the same as in FOPC (Definition 2.3.4). If $U \subseteq \mathbf{U}$ and τ is a function assignment over U, then $\langle U, \tau \rangle$ is a *model of equational logic*. $\mathbf{M}_{\doteq}$ is the set of all models of equational logic.
    Let the set of variable assignments be the same as in FOPC (Definition 2.3.2), as well as the definition of a term valuation τ_ν from a function assignment τ and variable assignment ν (Definition 2.3.3). The classical semantic system for equational logic is $\langle \mathbf{F}_{\doteq}, \mathbf{M}_{\doteq}, \models_{\doteq} \rangle$, where $\langle U, \tau \rangle \models_{\doteq} t_1 \doteq t_2$ if and only if $\tau_\nu(t_1) = \tau_\nu(t_2)$ for all variable assignments ν over U.

Models of equational logic are essentially *algebras* [Cohn, 1965; Grätzer, 1968; Mac Lane and Birkhoff, 1967] . The only difference is that algebras are restricted to *signatures*—subsets, usually finite, of the set of constant and function symbols. Such restriction does not affect any of the properties discussed in this chapter. If $\mathbf{T}$ is a finite subset of $\mathbf{T}_{\doteq}$, then the set of algebras **Models(T)** (restricted, of course, to an appropriate signature) is called a *variety*. For example, the *monoids* are the models of $\{m(x, m(y, z)) \doteq m(m(x, y), z),\ m(x, e) \doteq x,\ m(e, x) \doteq e\}$ restricted to the signature with one constant symbol e and one binary function symbol m.

Perhaps the simplest sort of question that is naturally answered by an equation is 'what is t_0?' for a term t_0. For each term t_1, the equation $t_0 \doteq t_1$ is an answer to this question. The trouble with such a primitive question is that it admits too many answers. For example, the tautology $t_0 \doteq t_0$ is always a correct answer to 'what is t_0?'. This problem is closely analogous to the problem of the tautological answer $(a \Rightarrow a)$ to the question $\mathbf{imp}(a)$ ('what atomic formula does a imply?', Example 2.2.3, Section 2.2). For the shallow implicational calculus, we avoided undesired answers simply by listing a set $\mathbf{A}$ of them, in the form $\mathbf{rest\text{-}imp}(a, \mathbf{A})$ ('what atomic formula not in $\mathbf{A}$ does a imply?', Example 2.2.4). Since the number of terms t_1 making $t_0 \doteq t_1$ true is generally infinite, we need a finite notation for describing the prohibited answers. A particularly useful way is to give a finite set of terms with variables, and prohibit all instances of those terms from appearing as subterms in an answer term.

Definition 2.3.15. Let $x_1, \ldots, x_i$ be a list of variables with no repetitions, and let $t, t_1, \ldots, t_i \in \mathbf{T}_P$. $t[t_1, \ldots, t_i/x_1, \ldots, x_i]$ is the formula that results from substituting the term t_j for every occurrence of the variable x_j in the term t, for each j, $1 \leq j \leq i$. When $s = t[t_1, \ldots, t_i/x_1, \ldots, x_i]$, we say that s is an *instance* of t, and that t is *more general* than s.

The concepts of substitution, instance, and generality for terms are analogous to the corresponding concepts defined for formulae in Definition 2.3.5, simplified because all occurrences of variables in terms are free.

Definition 2.3.16. Let $t_1, \ldots, t_i \in \mathbf{T}_P$ be terms. A term s is a *normal form* for $\{t_1, \ldots, t_i\}$ if and only if no subterm of s is an instance of a term in $\{t_1, \ldots, t_i\}$.

Let **norm** be a new formal symbol. Let

$$\mathbf{Q}_{\doteq} = \{(\mathbf{norm}\, t_1, \ldots, t_i : t) : t, t_1, \ldots, t_i \in \mathbf{T}_P\}$$

Define the relation $?\!\!\vdash_{\doteq} \,\subseteq \mathbf{Q}_{\doteq} \times \mathbf{F}_{\doteq}$ by

$$(\mathbf{norm}\, t_1, \ldots, t_i : t) \; ?\!\!\vdash_{\doteq} \; (s_1 \doteq s_2)$$

if and only if $s_1 = t$ and s_2 is a normal form for $\{t_1, \ldots, t_i\}$.

Now $\langle \mathbf{F}_{\doteq}, \mathbf{Q}_{\doteq}, ?\!\!\vdash_{\doteq} \rangle$ is a query system representing the answers to questions of the form 'what normal form for $t_1, \ldots, t_i$ is equal to t?'

For every semicomputable set $\mathbf{T} \subseteq \mathbf{F}_{\doteq}$, the set of equations $(t \doteq s)$ such that $(\mathbf{norm}\, t_1, \ldots, t_i : t) \; ?\!\!\vdash_{\doteq} \mathbf{T} \models_{\doteq} (t \doteq s)$ is semicomputable. It is easy to define a query system with conjunctive equational answers, similar to the conjunctive FOPC answers of Definition 2.3.10. Such a step is most useful when *infinite* conjunctions are allowed, so it is reserved for Section 7.1 of the chapter 'Equational Logic Programming.'

Example 2.3.17. Let $a \in \mathbf{Fun}_0$ be a constant symbol representing *zero*, let $s \in \mathbf{Fun}_1$ be a unary function symbol representing the *successor* function, and let $p \in \mathbf{Fun}_2$ be a binary function symbol representing *addition*. A natural state of knowledge about these symbols is

$$\mathbf{T} = \{p(a, x) \doteq x, \; p(s(x), y) \doteq s(p(x, y))\}$$

A natural question is $(\mathbf{norm}\, p(x, y) : p(s(s(a)), s(s(s(a)))))$. The unique correct answer is $(p(s(s(a)), s(s(s(a)))) \doteq s(s(s(s(s(a))))))$. That is, the answer to the question 'what is a term for 2 plus 3, not using the plus operator?' is '2 plus 3 equals 5.'

Another question, peculiar but formally legitimate, is $(\mathbf{norm}\, s(s(x)), s(p(x, y)) : s(s(a)))$. Correct answers include $(s(s(a)) \doteq p(s(a), s(a)))$, $(s(s(a)) \doteq p(s(a), p(s(a), a)))$, $(s(s(a)) \doteq p(p(s(a), a), s(a)))$, etc. The answers to this question express 2 as sums of 1 and 0. The simplest form is 1 plus 1; all other forms simply add extraneous 0s.

Every partial computable function ϕ may be defined similarly by letting $\phi(i)$ be the unique j such that

$$(\mathbf{norm}\, t_1, \ldots, t_i : f(s^i(a))) \; ?\!\!-_{\doteq} \; \mathbf{T} \models_{\doteq} (f(s^i(a)) \doteq s^j(a))$$

for appropriately chosen $t_1, \ldots, t_i$ and finite set $\mathbf{T}$ of equations defining f. In principle, we might ask for most general or consequentially strongest answers to questions in $\mathbf{Q}_{\doteq}$. In practice, multiple answers to such questions are usually incomparable.

A more powerful form of equational question answering involves the solution of equations.

Definition 2.3.18. Let **solve** be a new formal symbol. Let

$$\mathbf{Q}_{s\doteq} = \{(\mathbf{solve}\, x_1, \ldots, x_i : t_1 \doteq t_2) : t_1, t_2 \in \mathbf{T}_P\}$$

Define the relation $?\!\!-_{s\doteq}$ by

$$(\mathbf{solve}\, x_1, \ldots, x_i : t_1 \doteq t_2) \; ?\!\!-_{s\doteq} \; (s_1 \doteq s_2)$$

if and only if there are terms $u_1, \ldots, u_i \in \mathbf{T}_P$ such that $s_1 = t_1[u_1, \ldots, u_i/ x_1, \ldots, x_i]$ and $s_2 = t_2[u_1, \ldots, u_i/x_1, \ldots, x_i]$.

Now $\langle \mathbf{Q}_{s\doteq}, \mathbf{F}_{\doteq}, ?\!\!-_{s\doteq} \rangle$ is a query system representing the answer to questions of the form 'what values of $x_1, \ldots, x_i$ solve the equation $t_1 \doteq t_2$?'

Notice the close analogy between the question $(\mathbf{solve}\, x_1, \ldots, x_i : t_1 \doteq t_2)$ above, and the FOPC question $(\mathbf{what}\, x_1, \ldots, x_i : F)$ of Definition 2.3.6, Section 2.3.1. Syntactically, the equational question is merely the special case of the FOPC question where the formula F is restricted to be an equation. The semantics of equational logic lead, however, to very different typical uses for, and implementations of, equation solving.

2.3.5 Functional and equational programming languages

A wide variety of nonprocedural programming languages have been inspired by Backus' proposal of *functional programming languages* [Backus, 1974; Backus, 1978] defined by equations. The previous development of Lisp by McCarthy [McCarthy, 1960], although not originally conceived in terms of functional programming, fits in retrospect into the functional approach, and its success has boosted the interest in functional languages substantially. Languages for the algebraic description of abstract data types [Guttag and Horning, 1978; Wand, 1976; Futatsugi *et al.*, 1985] use equations in individual programs, rather than in the language design, and one experimental language is defined explicitly in terms of equational logic programming [Hoffmann and O'Donnell, 1982; Hoffmann *et al.*, 1985; O'Donnell, 1985]. The essential idea behind functional, algebraic, and equational, programming languages is to find correct answers to normalization questions in $\mathbf{Q}_{\dot{=}}$ of Section 2.3.4 above. A number of different styles are used to specify these languages, often obscuring the logic programming content. In this section, 'functional programming languages' include all programming languages that *can be* described naturally as answering normalization questions, and we view them as a form of equational logic programming, whether or not they are conventionally thought of in that way. Actual functional languages differ widely on a number of dimensions:

- the notation in which terms are written;
- the way in which the knowledge formulae are determined by the language design and the program;
- the way in which questions are determined by the language design, the program, and the input;
- deviations from pure equational logic programming.

Because of the complexity of these variations, the discussion in this section is organized around the various decisions involved in designing a functional programming language, rather than around a survey of the most important languages.

The style in which many functional programming languages are specified creates an impression that there are fundamental logical differences between functional programming and equational logic programming. This impression is false—functional programming and equational logic programming are two different ways of describing the same behaviors. The different styles of description may encourage different choices in language design, but they do *not* introduce any fundamental logical deviations. In particular, 'higher order' functional programming languages are *not* higher order in any fundamental logical sense, and may be described very naturally by first-order equational logic [Goguen, 1990]. The chapter 'Equational Logic Programming,' Section 1.2, provides more discussion of the connection between functional and equational programming ideologies.

Determining equational knowledge from language design and program. The equational formulae used as explicit knowledge for answering normalization questions in functional programming languages are derived from the language design itself and from the program that is being executed. In principle, they could also be given in the input, but this possibility has not been exploited explicitly. Many functional languages are processed by interactive interpreters, which blur the distinction between program and input, and many functional languages have mechanisms, such as *lambda abstraction* [McCarthy, 1960] or the *let* construct, that simulate the introduction of certain equations within an input term. Interactive interpretive processing, and the simulation of additional equations within terms, provide implicitly a lot of the power of explicit equations in the input.

Most functional languages are designed around substantial sets of primitive operations, defined by equations. For example, the primitives *cons* (construct ordered pair), *car* (first component of pair), and *cdr* (second component of pair) in Lisp are defined by the two equations $(car(cons(x, y)) \doteq x)$ and $(cdr(cons(x, y)) \doteq y)$ [McCarthy, 1960]. Primitive operators that manipulate term structure, or provide program control structures, are usually defined by explicitly given small finite sets of equations. Primitive operators for basic mathematical operations are defined by large or infinite sets of equations that must be described rather than listed. For example, the conventional arithmetic operation of addition is defined by the equations $add(0, 0) \doteq 0$, $add(0, 1) \doteq 1,\dots$, $add(1, 0) \doteq 1$, $add(1, 1) \doteq 2,\dots$, $add(2, 0) \doteq 2$, $add(2, 1) \doteq 3$, $add(2, 2) \doteq 4,\dots$.

Most functional programming languages have rich enough primitive sets of operators defined by equations in the language design that it is not necessary to introduce new equations in a program—the goals of the program may be accomplished by appropriate combinations of primitive operations. In particular, many functional languages have operators that simulate the introduction of additional local equations within a term. Even in languages with powerful primitives, it is often convenient to introduce explicit equations defining new operators in a given program. A few functional languages have weak primitives, and depend upon equations in programs for their expressive power.

Most functional languages impose restrictions on the equations that may be introduced by programs, in order to allow simple and efficient proof searches in the implementation. Typical restrictions are surveyed in the chapter 'Equational Logic Programming,' Section 2.3.2. In most languages, the restrictions on equations in programs allow each equation $f(t_1, \dots, t_i) \doteq t$ in a program to be treated as a part of the definition of a procedure to compute f. Note the similarity to the treatment of clauses in Prolog programs (Section 2.3.2).

Determining a question from language design, program, and input. Recall that the form of a normalization question is $(\text{norm } t_1, \ldots, t_i : t)$. An answer to such a question gives a term equal to t that does not contain a subterm of any of the forms $t_1, \ldots, t_i$. The determination of a question divides naturally into the determination of the prohibited forms $t_1, \ldots, t_i$ and the term t to normalize.

In most functional programming languages, the prohibited forms $t_1, \ldots, t_i$ are determined by partitioning the set of symbols into *constructors, primitive functions*, and *defined functions*. Constructors are intended to be computationally inert—they are treated as elements of a data structure. The use of constructors in equations is highly restricted to ensure this inertness. The binary symbol *cons* in Lisp is the archetypal constructor. In languages that distinguish constructors, the prohibited forms in normalization questions are precisely the terms $f(x_1, \ldots, x_i)$, where f is a primitive function or a defined function of arity i. That is, the normal forms for questions in constructor systems are precisely the *constructor expressions*—terms composed entirely of variables and constructors. The set of constructors may be fixed by the language design, or a program may be allowed to introduce new constructors, in explicit declarations of the symbols or in recursive type definitions.

In a functional language without constructors, the prohibited forms may be implicit in the equations of a program. Most functional languages infer from the presentation of the equation $t_1 \doteq t_2$ that the left-hand side t_1 is to be transformed into the right-hand side t_2. Such an inference is not justified directly by the semantics of equational logic, but it is often justified by restrictions on the form of equations imposed by the language. So, the prohibited forms in questions are often taken to be precisely the terms on the left-hand sides of equations in the program.

The term to be normalized is typically in the form

$$(t^{\text{la}}[t_1^{\text{pr}}, \ldots, t_{i_{\text{pr}}}^{\text{pr}} / x_1, \ldots, x_{i_{\text{pr}}}])[t_1^{\text{in}}, \ldots t_{i_{\text{in}}}^{\text{in}} / y_1, \ldots, y_{i_{\text{in}}}]$$

where t^{la} is fixed by the language design, $t_1^{\text{pr}}, \ldots, t_{i_{\text{pr}}}^{\text{pr}}$ are determined by the program, and $t_1^{\text{in}}, \ldots, t_{i_{\text{in}}}^{\text{in}}$ are determined by the input. In principle, other forms are possible, but it seems most natural to view the language design as providing an operation to be applied to the program, producing an operation to be applied to the input. For example, in a pure Lisp *eval* interpreter, $t^{\text{la}} = eval(x_1, nil)$. The program to be evaluated is t_1^{pr} (the second argument *nil* to the *eval* function indicates an empty list of definitions under which to evaluate the program). Pure Lisp has no input—conceptual input may be encoded into the program, or extralogical features may be used to accomplish input. A natural extension of pure Lisp to allow definitions of symbols in a program yields $t^{\text{la}} = eval(x_1, x_2)$, t_1^{pr} is the expression given by the program to be interpreted, and t_2^{pr} is a list of bindings representing the definitions given in the program. In a language, unlike Lisp, where a program designates a particular defined function f as the *main* procedure to be executed on the input, we can have $t^{\text{la}} = x_1$ (the language design does not contribute to the term to be normalized), $t_1^{\text{pr}} = f(y_1)$ where f is the designated main function, and t_1^{in} is the input. In yet other languages, the term to be normalized is given entirely by the input.

Notational variations and abbreviations. Functional programming languages vary widely in the notations used for terms, using all sorts of prefix, infix, postfix, and mixfix forms. A survey of the possibilities is pointless. All current functional languages determine the prohibited forms in questions implicitly, either from the language design or from the left-hand sides of equations in a program. Questions are presented by specifying some or all of the term to be normalized—other parts of the term may be implicit as described above. Outputs always present only the normal form s rather than the equation $t \doteq s$, since the question term t is already given explicitly or implicitly.

Deviations from pure equational logic programming. Implementations of functional programming languages have generally come closer to the ideal of pure equational logic programming than Prolog systems have to pure Horn-clause logic programming, largely because of a simpler correspondence between logical and procedural concepts in functional languages than in Prolog. Many functional languages extend pure logic programming with side-effect-producing operations, similar to those in Prolog. These extensions are usually used to deal with input and output. Some functional languages avoid such extensions by modelling the entire input and output as an expression, called a *stream,* that lists the atomic elements of the input and output [Karlsson, 1981; Thompson, 1990; Hudak and Sundaresh, 1988; Hudak, 1992; Gordon, 1992; Dwelly, 1988]; others use a functional representation of input and output based on *continuations* [Perry, 1991; Hudak and Sundaresh, 1988; Hudak, 1992]. Also see [Williams and Wimmers, 1988] for an implicit approach to functional I/O. A protocol that decouples the temporal order of input and output from its representation in a functional program has been proposed as well [Rebelsky, 1993; Rebelsky, 1992] .

The purely functional subsets of functional programming languages usually avoid giving incorrect answers. Implementations of Lisp before the 1980s are arguably incorrect in that their use of *dynamic scope* [Stark, 1990; Moses, 1970] for parameter bindings gives answers that are incorrect according to the conventional logical equations for substitution of terms for parameters, taken from the lambda calculus [Church, 1941; Stenlund, 1972; Barendregt, 1984] . Since the equations for manipulating bindings were never formalized precisely in the early days of Lisp, implementors may argue that their work is correct with respect to an unconventional definition of substitution. Early Lispers seem to have been unaware of the logical literature on variable substitution, and referred to the dynamic binding problem as the 'funarg' problem.

Essentially all functional programming languages before the 1980s fail to find certain semantically correct answers, due to infinite evaluation of irrelevant portions of a term. In conventional Lisp implementations, for example, the defining equation $car(cons(x, y)) \doteq x$ is not applied to a term $car(cons(t_1, t_2))$ until both t_1 and t_2 have been converted to normal forms. If the attempt to normalize t_2 fails due to infinite computation, then the computation as a whole fails, even though a semantically correct answer might have been derived using only t_1. Systems that fail to find a normal form for $car(cons(t_1, t_2))$ unless *both* of t_1 and t_2 have normal forms are said to have *strict cons* functions. The discovery of *lazy evaluation* [Friedman and Wise, 1976; Henderson and Morris, 1976; O'Donnell, 1977] showed how to avoid imposing unnecessary strictness on *cons* and other functions, and many recent implementations of functional programming languages are guaranteed to find all semantically correct answers. Of course, it is always possible to modify defining equations so that the strict interpretation of a function is semantically complete.

Example 2.3.19. Consider Lisp, with the standard equations

$$car(cons(x, y)) \doteq x \text{ and } cdr(cons(x, y)) \doteq y$$

To enforce strict evaluation of lists, even in a lazily evaluated implementation of equational logic programming, add new function symbols *test*, *strict*, *and*, and a new constant *true*, with the equations

$$test(true, x) \doteq x, \qquad and(true, true) \doteq true,$$
$$strict(cons(x, y)) \doteq and(strict(x), strict(y)), \qquad strict(a) \doteq true$$

for each atomic symbol a. Then, redefine *car* and *cdr* by

$$car(cons(x, y)) \doteq test(strict(y), x) \text{ and } cdr(cons(x, y)) \doteq test(strict(x), y)$$

Lazy evaluation with the new set of equations has the same effect as strict evaluation with the old set.

Some definitions of functional programming language specify strictness explicitly. One might argue that the strict version of *cons* was intended in the original definition of Lisp [McCarthy, 1960], but strictness was never stated explicitly there.

2.3.6 Equation solving and predicate calculus with equality

Given successful applications of logic programming in the pure first-order predicate calculus without equality, and in pure equational logic, it is very tempting to develop languages for logic programming in the first-order predicate calculus with equality (FOPC$_{\doteq}$). Unfortunately, there is a mismatch between the style of questions used in the two sorts of logic programming. FOPC logic programming uses questions of the form (**what** $x_1, \ldots, x_i : F$) (Definition 2.3.6), whose answers supply substitutions for the variables $x_1, \ldots, x_i$ satisfying F. Equational logic programming uses questions of the form (**norm** $t_1, \ldots, t_i : t$) (Definition 2.3.16), whose answers supply normal forms equal to t, not containing the forms $t_1, \ldots, t_i$. The implementation techniques for answering these two sorts of questions do not appear to combine well.

The most natural idea for achieving logic programming in FOPC$_{\doteq}$ is to use the FOPC style of question, and extend it to deal with equations. In principle that is feasible, because the formal equality symbol $\doteq$ may be treated as another binary predicate symbol in **Pred**$_2$, and Horn clauses expressing its crucial properties are easy to find. Unfortunately, the natural Horn clauses for the equality predicate, when treated by current implementation techniques for FOPC logic programming, yield unacceptably inefficient results. In practice, a satisfactory realization of logic programming in FOPC$_{\doteq}$ will require new techniques for solving equations—that is, for answering questions of the form (**solve** $x_1, \ldots, x_i : t_1 \doteq t_2$) (Definition 2.3.18). An interesting experimental language incorporating significant steps toward logic programming in FOPC$_{\doteq}$ is EqL [Jayaraman, 1985], but this language only finds solutions consisting of constructor expressions. The problem of finding nonconstructor solutions is much more difficult.

It is also possible to define FOPC logic programming in terms of a normalization-style query. Consider a question 'what acceptable formula implies F_0', which presents a goal formula F_0, and some description of which answer formulae are acceptable and which are prohibited (the problem of describing such prohibited formulae is more complex in FOPC than in equational logic because of the structural properties of the logical connectives $\wedge, \vee, \ldots$). An answer to such a question is an implication of the form $F_1 \Rightarrow F_0$, where F_1 is an acceptable formula. The conventional FOPC questions (**what** $x_1, \ldots, x_i : F_0$) may be understood as a variant of the 'what implies F_0' questions, where the acceptable formulae are precisely those of the form $x_1 \doteq t_1 \wedge \cdots \wedge x_i \doteq t_i$. The proposed new style of FOPC question may be seen as presenting a set of constraints expressed by F_0, and requesting a normalized expression of constraints F_1 such that every solution to the constraints expressed by F_1 is also a solution to the constraints of F_0. *Constraint Logic Programming* [Jaffar and Lassez, 1987; Lassez, 1991] has taken some steps in this direction, although Constraint

Logic Programming generally views the normalized constraints expressed by F_1 not as a final result to be output as an answer, but as something to be solved by techniques outside of FOPC, such as numerical techniques for solving linear systems of equations.

3 Implementing logic programming languages

Semantic systems and query systems are convenient tools for specifying logic programming languages: we require a language to provide semantically correct answers to questions. In order to implement logic programming languages, we first develop sound (correct) and complete (powerful) *proof systems* to provide effective certificates of the semantic correctness of inferences. Then, we convert proof systems to *programming systems* that process inputs and programs efficiently to produce outputs, by introducing *strategies* for choosing incrementally which proofs to construct. In this chapter we consider only the abstract forms of implementations, far above the level of actual code for real machines. Truly practical implementations do, however, follow these abstract forms quite closely.

3.1 Proof systems and provable consequences

A semantic-consequence relation determines in principle whether it is correct to infer one logical formula from others. In order to give a formal justification for an inference, we need a notation for *proofs*. We reserve the initial P for programs, so D is used to stand for proofs, which might also be called *demonstrations* or *derivations*.

Definition 3.1.1. A *proof system* is a system $\mathcal{D} = \langle \mathbf{F}, \mathbf{D}, | - \rangle$, where

1. $\mathbf{F}$ is a set of *formulae*
2. $\mathbf{D}$ is a set of *proofs*
3. $| -$ is a relation on $2^{\mathbf{F}} \times \mathbf{D} \times \mathbf{F}$ (when $\langle \mathbf{T}, D, F \rangle$ are in the relation $| -$, we write $\mathbf{T} | D - F$)
4. $| -$ is monotone (if $\mathbf{T} | D - F$ and $\mathbf{T} \subseteq \mathbf{U}$, then $\mathbf{U} | D - F$)

The proof system $\mathcal{D}$ is *compact* if and only if, for all $\mathbf{T} \subseteq \mathbf{F}$, $P \in \mathbf{D}$, and $F \in \mathbf{F}$, whenever $\mathbf{T} | D - F$ there exists a finite subset $\mathbf{T}^{\mathrm{f}} \subseteq \mathbf{T}$ such that $\mathbf{T}^{\mathrm{f}} | D - F$.

$\mathbf{T} | D - F$ is intended to mean that D is a *proof* of F which is allowed to use hypotheses in $\mathbf{T}$. The fact that D is not *required* to use all hypotheses leads to monotonicity (4). There are a number of proposals for systems of 'nonmonotonic logic,' but they may be regarded as studies of different relations between proofs and formulae than the notion of derivability represented by $| -$ above, rather than as arguments about the properties of $| -$. The controversy about nonmonotonic logic is not relevant to the discussion in this chapter, and fans of nonmonotonic relations between proofs and formulae may translate into their own notation if they like.

In well-known proof systems, proofs as well as formulae are finite syntactic objects, and the set **D** of all proofs is computable. There are important uses, however, for infinite proofs of infinite formulae, so we do not add a formal requirement of computability. Typically, a proof D determines uniquely the conclusion formula F and minimum hypothesis set **T** such that $\mathbf{T} \mid D - F$, but there is no need to require such a property. Meseguer [Meseguer, 1989] proposed a similar general notion of *proof calculus*.

It is straightforward to design a proof system for SIC. The following proof system follows the conventional style of textbooks in logic. Proofs are sequences of formulae, each one either a hypothesis, a postulate, or a consequence of earlier formulae in the proof.

Example 3.1.2. Let $\mathbf{F}_{\mathrm{Sh}}$ be the set of formulae in SIC. The set of *linear proofs* in SIC is $\mathbf{P}_{\mathrm{Sl}} = \mathbf{F}_{\mathrm{Sh}}^{+}$, the set of nonempty finite sequences of formulae. The proof relation $\mid -_{\mathrm{Sl}}$ is defined by

$$\mathbf{T} \mid \langle F_0, \ldots, F_m \rangle -_{\mathrm{Sl}} F \text{ if and only if } F_m = F \text{ and,}$$
$$\text{for all } i \leq m, \text{ one of the following cases holds:}$$

1. $F_i \in \mathbf{T}$
2. $F_i = (a \Rightarrow a)$ for some atomic formula $a \in \mathbf{At}$
3. $F_i = b$, and there exist $j, k < i$ such that $F_j = a$ and $F_k = (a \Rightarrow b)$ for some atomic formulae $a, b \in \mathbf{At}$
4. $F_i = (a \Rightarrow c)$, and there exist $j, k < i$ such that $F_j = (a \Rightarrow b)$ and $F_k = (b \Rightarrow c)$ for some atomic formulae $a, b, c \in \mathbf{At}$

Now $\langle \mathbf{F}_{\mathrm{Sh}}, \mathbf{P}_{\mathrm{Sl}}, \mid -_{\mathrm{Sl}} \rangle$ is a compact proof system, representing the *Hilbert*, or *linear*, style of proof for implications.

Intuitively, a linear or Hilbert-style proof is a finite sequence of formulae, each one being either a *hypothesis* (case 1 above), a *postulate* (case 2 above, expressing the postulate scheme of *reflexivity* of implication), or the consequence of previous formulae by a *rule of inference* (case 3 above, expressing the rule of *modus ponens*, and case 4, expressing the rule of *transitivity* of implication). The conclusion of a linear proof is the last formula in the list.

An alternative proof system for SIC, less conventional but more convenient for some purposes, follows the *natural deduction* style of proof [Prawitz, 1965]. Natural deduction proofs are trees, rather than sequences, to display the actual logical dependencies of formulae. They also allow the introduction and discharging of temporary assumptions in proofs, to mimic the informal style in which we prove $a \Rightarrow b$ by assuming a and proving b.

Example 3.1.3. Let $\mathbf{F}_{\mathrm{Sh}}$ be the set of formulae in the shallow implicational calculus defined in Example 2.1.2. Let **assume**, **modus-ponens**, and **deduction-rule** be new formal symbols.

The set $\mathbf{P}_{\text{Sn}}$ of *natural deduction proofs* in SIC and the proof relation $\vdash_{\text{Sn}} \subseteq 2^{\mathbf{F}_{\text{Sh}}} \times \mathbf{P}_{\text{Sn}} \times \mathbf{F}_{\text{Sh}}$ are defined by simultaneous inductive definition to be the least set and relation such that:

1. for each atomic formula $a \in \mathbf{At}$, and each set of formulae $\mathbf{T} \subseteq \mathbf{F}_{\text{Sh}}$,

$$\mathbf{assume}(a) \in \mathbf{P}_{\text{Sn}}$$

and

$$\mathbf{T} \cup \{a\} \mid \mathbf{assume}(a) \vdash_{\text{Sn}} a$$

2. if $\alpha, \beta \in \mathbf{P}_{\text{Sn}}$, and $\mathbf{T} \mid \alpha \vdash_{\text{Sn}} a$ for some atomic formula $a \in \mathbf{At}$, and $\mathbf{U} \mid \beta \vdash_{\text{Sn}} (a \Rightarrow b)$, then

$$\mathbf{modus\text{-}ponens}(\alpha, \beta) \in \mathbf{P}_{\text{Sn}} \text{ and } \mathbf{T} \cup \mathbf{U} \mid \mathbf{modus\text{-}ponens}(\alpha, \beta) \vdash_{\text{Sn}} b$$

3. if $\beta \in \mathbf{P}_{\text{Sn}}$ and $\mathbf{T} \cup \{a\} \mid \beta \vdash_{\text{Sn}} b$ for some atomic formula $a \in \mathbf{At}$, then

$$\mathbf{deduction\text{-}rule}(a, \beta) \in \mathbf{P}_{\text{Sn}} \text{ and } \mathbf{T} \mid \mathbf{deduction\text{-}rule}(a, \beta) \vdash_{\text{Sn}} (a \Rightarrow b)$$

Now $\langle \mathbf{F}_{\text{Sh}}, \mathbf{P}_{\text{Sn}}, \vdash_{\text{Sn}} \rangle$ is a compact proof system, representing the *natural deduction* style of proof for implications.

Intuitively, $\mathbf{assume}(a)$ is a trivial proof of a from hypothesis a. $\mathbf{modus\text{-}ponens}$ (α, β) is the result of using a proof α of some atomic formula a, a proof β of an implication $(a \Rightarrow b)$, and combining the results along with the rule of *modus ponens* to conclude b. The set of hypotheses for the resulting proof includes all hypotheses of α and all hypotheses of β. $\mathbf{deduction\text{-}rule}(a, \beta)$ is the result of taking a proof β of b from hypotheses including a, and discharging some (possibly 0) of the assumptions of a from the proof, to get a proof of $(a \Rightarrow b)$ by the *deduction rule*. In clause 3 of the inductive definition above, notice that the hypothesis set $\mathbf{T}$ may contain a, in which case $\mathbf{T} \cup \{a\} = \mathbf{T}$. It is this case that allows for the possibility that one or more assumptions of a remain undischarged in an application of the deduction rule.

The style of proof formalized in Example 3.1.3 is called *natural deduction*, since it mimics one popular informal style of proof in which an implication is proved by assuming its hypothesis and deriving its conclusion. Natural deduction style [Prawitz, 1965], and the similar style of sequent derivation [Gentzen, 1935; Kleene, 1952], both due to Gentzen, are the styles of proof most commonly treated by research in *proof theory* [Stenlund, 1972; Prawitz, 1965; Takeuti, 1975; Schutte, 1977; Girard *et al.*, 1989]. In proof theory, natural deduction rules are expressed very naturally as terms in a typed lambda calculus, where the type of a lambda term is the formula that it proves [Howard, 1980; Tait, 1967].

In many cases, we are interested only in the provability of an inference, and not the proof itself. So, we let each proof system define a *provable-consequence* relation, analogous to the semantic-consequence relation associated with a semantic system.

Definition 3.1.4. Let $\mathcal{D} = \langle \mathbf{F}, \mathbf{D}, \vdash \rangle$ be a proof system. The *provable-consequence* relation defined by $\mathcal{D}$ is $\vdash \subseteq 2^{\mathbf{F}} \times \mathbf{F}$, where

$\mathbf{T} \vdash F$ if and only if there exists a proof $D \in \mathbf{D}$ such that $\mathbf{T} \mid D - F$.

The provable-consequence relation $\vdash$ is *compact* if and only if, for all $\mathbf{T} \subseteq \mathbf{F}$, and $F \in \mathbf{F}$, whenever $\mathbf{T} \vdash F$ then there exists a finite subset $\mathbf{T}^{\mathrm{f}} \subseteq \mathbf{T}$ such that $\mathbf{T}^{\mathrm{f}} \vdash F$.

Intuitively, $\mathbf{T} \vdash F$ means that F is *provable* from hypotheses in $\mathbf{T}$. It is easy to show that an arbitrary relation $\vdash$ on $2^{\mathbf{F}} \times \mathbf{F}$ is the provable-consequence relation of some proof system if and only if it is *monotone* ($\mathbf{T} \vdash F$ and $\mathbf{T} \subseteq \mathbf{U}$ imply that $\mathbf{U} \vdash F$). See [Meseguer, 1989] for another abstract definition of provable consequence relations, with more stringent requirements.

Most well-known semantic/provable-consequence relations are compact, and semicomputable on the finite sets of formulae. The trinary proof relations of proof systems (restricted to finite sets of hypotheses) are normally computable. That is, in a reasonable proof system we can determine definitely and mechanically whether or not a supposed proof is in fact a proof of a given conclusion from a given finite set of hypotheses. It is easy to see that a proof system with semicomputable set $\mathbf{D}$ of proofs and semicomputable trinary proof relation $\mid -$ also has a semicomputable provable-consequence relation, and that compactness of the proof system implies compactness of the provable-consequence relation. In fact, every semicomputable provable-consequence relation is defined by some proof system with computable $\mathbf{D}$ and trinary proof relation $\mid -$. In this respect the trinary proof relation acts as a *Gödel T-predicate* [Kleene, 1952] to the binary provable consequence relation.

3.2   Soundness and completeness of proof systems

The behavior of a proof system may be evaluated in a natural way with respect to a semantic system with the same or larger set of formulae. We say that the proof system is *sound* for the semantic system when every provable consequence is a semantic consequence, and that the proof system is *complete* when every semantic consequence is provable. Roughly, soundness means correctness, and completeness means maximal power within the constraints imposed by the set of formulae available in the proof system.

Definition 3.2.1. Let $\mathcal{D} = \langle \mathbf{F_D}, \mathbf{D}, \mid - \rangle$ be a proof system, and let $\mathcal{S} =$

$\langle \mathbf{F}_S, \mathbf{M}, \models \rangle$ be a semantic system, with $\mathbf{F}_D \subseteq \mathbf{F}_S$.

$\mathcal{D}$ is *sound* for S if and only if, for all $\mathbf{T} \subseteq \mathbf{F}$ and $F \in \mathbf{F}_D$,

$$\mathbf{T} \vdash F \text{ implies } \mathbf{T} \models F$$

$\mathcal{D}$ is *complete* for S if and only if, for all $\mathbf{T} \subseteq \mathbf{F}$ and $F \in \mathbf{F}_D$,

$$\mathbf{T} \models F \text{ implies } \mathbf{T} \vdash F$$

Each of the proposed proof systems for SIC is sound and complete for the semantic system of SIC. The following proofs of completeness for SIC are similar in form to completeness proofs in general, but unusually simple. Given a set of hypotheses $\mathbf{T}$, and a formula F that is not provable from $\mathbf{T}$, we construct a model M satisfying exactly the set of provable consequences of $\mathbf{T}$ within some sublanguage $\mathbf{F}_F$ containing F (**Theory**$(M) \cap \mathbf{F}_F \supseteq$ **Theory**(**Models**($\mathbf{T}$)) $\cap \mathbf{F}_F$). In our example below, $\mathbf{F}_F$ is just the set of all shallow implicational formulae ($\mathbf{F}_{Sh}$), and the model construction is particularly simple.

Example 3.2.2. Each of the proof systems $\langle \mathbf{F}_{Sh}, \mathbf{P}_{Sn}, \vdash_{Sn} \rangle$ of Example 3.1.3 and $\langle \mathbf{F}_{Sh}, \mathbf{P}_{Sl}, \vdash_{Sl} \rangle$ of Example 3.1.2 is sound and complete for the semantic system $\langle \mathbf{F}_{Sh}, \mathbf{M}_{Sh}, \models_{Sh} \rangle$ of Example 2.1.2.

The proofs of soundness involve elementary inductions on the size of proofs. For the natural deduction system, the semantic correctness of a proof follows from the correctness of its components; for the linear system correctness of a proof $\langle F_0, \ldots, F_{m+1} \rangle$ follows from the correctness of the prefix $\langle F_0, \ldots, F_m \rangle$.

The proofs of completeness require construction, for each set $\mathbf{T}$ of formulae, of a model $M = \{a \in \mathbf{At} : \mathbf{T} \vdash_{Sn} a\}$ (or $\mathbf{T} \vdash_{Sl} a$). So $M \models_{Sh} a$ for all atomic formulae $a \in \mathbf{T} \cap \mathbf{At}$ trivially. It is easy to show that $M \models_{Sh} (a \Rightarrow b)$ for all implications $(a \Rightarrow b) \in \mathbf{T}$ as well, since either $a \notin M$, or b follows by modus ponens from a and $a \Rightarrow b$, so $b \in M$. Finally, it is easy to show that $M \models_{Sh} F$ if and only if $\mathbf{T} \vdash_{Sn} F$ (or $\mathbf{T} \vdash_{Sl} F$).

In richer languages than SIC, containing for example disjunctions or negations, things may be more complicated. For example, if the disjunction $(A \lor B)$ is in the set of hypotheses $\mathbf{T}$, each model satisfying $\mathbf{T}$ must satisfy one of A or B, yet neither may be a logical consequence of $\mathbf{T}$, so one of them must be omitted from $\mathbf{F}_F$. Similarly, in a language allowing negation, we often require that every model satisfy either A or $\neg A$. Such considerations complicate the construction of a model substantially.

Notice that the formal definitions above do *not* restrict the nature of semantic systems and proof systems significantly. All sorts of nonsensical formal systems fit the definitions. Rather, the relationships of soundness and completeness provide us with conceptual tools for evaluating the behavior of a proof system, with respect to a semantic system that we have already accepted as appropriate. Logic is distinguished from other technical sciences, not by the formal definition of the systems that it studies, but rather by the use of logical concepts to evaluate these systems. The distinction between logic programming and other forms of programming is similarly based on the approach to evaluating the systems, rather than the formal qualities of the systems.

While formal studies may reveal pleasing or disturbing properties of semantic systems, there is also an unavoidable intuitive component in the evaluation of a semantic system. A semantic system is reasonable only if it accurately captures enough of the structure of the mental meaning that we want to associate with a formula to allow a sensible determination of the correctness or incorrectness of steps of reasoning. Since different people have different intuitive notions about the proper meanings of formulae, and the same person may find different intuitions useful for different purposes, we should be open minded about considering a broad variety of semantic systems. But, the mere satisfaction of a given form of definition, whether the form in Definition 2.1.1 above, or one of the popular 'denotational' forms using lattices or chain-complete partial orderings and fixpoints, does not make a 'semantics' meaningful. A number of additional mathematical and philosophical dissertations are needed to give practical aid in the evaluation and selection of semantic proposals. The best one-sentence advice that I can offer is to always ask of a proposed semantic system, 'for a given formula F, what does the semantic system tell about the information regarding the world that is asserted by F.' For this chapter, I use only systems of semantics based on first-order classical forms of logic that have been shaken down very thoroughly over the years. In these systems, the individual models clearly present enough alleged facts about a possible state of the world to determine the truth or falsehood of each formula. So, the information asserted by a formula is that the world under discussion is one of the ones satisfying the formula in the sense of $\models$. There are many reasons to prefer nonclassical logics for programming and for other purposes. But, we must never rest satisfied with 'semantic' treatments of these logics until they have been connected convincingly to an intuitive notion of *meaning*.

A semantic system and a sound proof system may be used to analyze the process by which implicit knowledge is made explicit—we are particularly interested in the derivation of explicit knowledge in order to answer a question. Consider an agent with *implicit* knowledge given by the set **K** of models consistent with that knowledge, and represent the agent's *explicit* knowledge by a set **T** of formulae that he can utter effectively. The correctness of the explicit knowledge requires that $\mathbf{T} \subseteq \mathbf{Theory(K)}$. Suppose that the agent knows that the proof system is sound, and suppose that he can recognize at least some cases when the relation $\mathbf{T} \mid D - F$ holds—often this capability results from computing the appropriate decision procedure for a computable proof system (or enumeration procedure for a semicomputable proof system), with an appropriate finite subset of **T**. Then, whenever he finds a formula F and a proof D such that $\mathbf{T} \mid D - F$, the agent may add the formula F to his explicit knowledge. The soundness of the proof system guarantees that $F \in \mathbf{Theory(K)}$. Notice that sound proofs can never extend explicit knowledge beyond the bound determined by implicit knowledge, which is **Theory(K)**.

Definition 3.2.3. Let $\mathcal{Q} = \langle \mathbf{F_Q}, \mathbf{Q}, ?- \rangle$ be a query system, and let $\mathcal{D} = \langle \mathbf{F_D}, \mathbf{D}, \mid - \rangle$ be a proof system with $\mathbf{F_Q} \subseteq \mathbf{F_D}$.

$Q ?- \mathbf{T} \vdash F$ means that $F \in \mathbf{F_Q}$ is a *provably correct* answer to $Q \in \mathbf{Q}$ for explicit knowledge $\mathbf{T} \subseteq \mathbf{F_S}$, defined by

$$Q ?- \mathbf{T} \vdash F \text{ if and only if } Q ?- F \text{ and } \mathbf{T} \vdash F$$

Similarly,

$$Q ?- \mathbf{T} \mid D - F \text{ if and only if } Q ?- F \text{ and } \mathbf{T} \mid D - F$$

If $\mathcal{P}$ is sound, then provable correctness implies semantic correctness (Definition 2.2.2). If $\mathcal{P}$ is complete, then semantic correctness implies provable correctness.

Going back to the communication analysis of previous sections, let $\mathbf{K_s}$ be the speaker's implicit knowledge, let $\mathbf{K_a^0}$ be the auditor's initial implicit knowledge, and let $\mathbf{T_a^0}$ be the auditor's initial explicit knowledge. When the speaker utters a set of formulae $\mathbf{T_u}$, consistent with her implicit knowledge, the auditor's implicit knowledge improves as before to $\mathbf{K_a^1} = \mathbf{K_a^0} \cap \mathbf{Models(T_u)}$, and the auditor's explicit knowledge improves to $\mathbf{T_a^1} = \mathbf{T_a^0} \cup \mathbf{T_u}$. Let a questioner ask a question Q of the auditor. Without further communication from the speaker, the auditor may improve his explicit knowledge by proving new formulae from hypotheses in $\mathbf{T_a^1}$ in order to answer the question Q. If the auditor's initial explicit knowledge is empty, then $\mathbf{T_a^1} = \mathbf{T_u}$, so the formulae derivable in this way are exactly the provable consequences of $\mathbf{T_u}$, and the answers that may be found are exactly the provably correct answers to Q for $\mathbf{T_u}$. If the proof system used by the auditor is sound, then all such answers are semantically correct; if the proof system is complete then all semantically correct answers are provable. Now let the speaker be a programmer who utters a set of formulae constituting a logic program, let the auditor be a processor, and let the questioner be a user whose question is given as input to the program. Then, computations performed by the processor take the form of search for and construction of proofs deriving the explicit knowledge needed to produce an output answer, from the explicit knowledge given in the program.

3.3 Programming systems

A *programming system* represents the computational behavior of a processor. In order to understand logic programming, we consider an arbitrary, possibly ineffective and nondeterministic, programming system, and then show how to evaluate its behavior logically with respect to a given semantic system and query system. We choose an unconventional formal notation for programming systems in order to expose the close analogy of sets of formulae to programs, questions to inputs, proofs to computations, answers to outputs.

Definition 3.3.1. A *programming system* is a system $\mathcal{P} = \langle \mathbf{P}, \mathbf{I}, \mathbf{C}, \mathbf{O}, \triangleright [\!], \rightarrow \rangle$, where

1. $\mathbf{P}$ is a set of *programs*
2. $\mathbf{I}$ is a set of *inputs*
3. $\mathbf{C}$ is a set of *computations*
4. $\mathbf{O}$ is a set of *outputs*
5. $\triangleright [\!]$ is a relation on $\mathbf{I} \times \mathbf{P} \times \mathbf{C}$ (when $\langle I, P, C \rangle$ are in the relation $\triangleright [\!]$, we write $I \triangleright P [\!] C$)
6. For each $I \in \mathbf{I}$ and $P \in \mathbf{P}$, there is at least one $C \in \mathbf{C}$ with $I \triangleright P [\!] C$
7. $\rightarrow$ is a relation on $\mathbf{C} \times \mathbf{O}$
8. For each $C \in \mathbf{C}$, there is at most one $O \in \mathbf{O}$ with $C \rightarrow O$ (that is, $\rightarrow$ is a partial function from $\mathbf{C}$ to $\mathbf{O}$)

We define the relation $\triangleright [\!] \rightarrow \subseteq \mathbf{I} \times \mathbf{P} \times \mathbf{C} \times \mathbf{O}$ by

$$I \triangleright P [\!] C \rightarrow O \text{ if and only if } I \triangleright P [\!] C \text{ and } C \rightarrow O$$

$I \triangleright P [\!] C$ is intended to mean that, when input I is presented to program P, one possible resulting computation is C. $C \rightarrow O$ is intended to mean that the computation C produces output O. Multiple computations for a given P and I are allowed, indicating nondeterminism, but each computation produces at most one output. The intended meaning of a nondeterministic computation relation is that we do not know which of the several possible computations will occur for a given input and output [Dijkstra, 1976]. The choice may be determined by unknown and time-dependent factors, or it may be random. In order to guarantee some property of the result of computation, we must ensure that it holds for all possible nondeterministic choices.

In well-known programming systems from theory textbooks, programs, inputs, and outputs (like formulae, proofs, and questions) are finite syntactic objects, and the sets $\mathbf{P}$, $\mathbf{I}$, and $\mathbf{O}$ are computable. Infinite computations, in the form of infinite sequences of finite memory-state descriptions, are allowed, but in theory textbooks the infinite computations normally have no output. On the other hand, the straightforward abstractions of well-known programming systems from real life (abstracted only by ignoring all bounds on time and space resources in the computation) allow infinite computations to consume infinite inputs and produce infinite outputs.

In many cases, we are interested only in the input–output behavior of a program, and not in the computations themselves. So, we let each programming system define a trinary relation determining the possible outputs for a given program and input.

Definition 3.3.2. Let $\mathcal{P} = \langle \mathbf{P}, \mathbf{I}, \mathbf{C}, \mathbf{O}, \rhd\ (\!|, \rightarrow \rangle$ be a programming system. The *computed-output* relation defined by $\mathcal{P}$ is $\rhd\ (\!\!\rightarrow\, \subseteq\, \mathbf{P} \times \mathbf{I} \times \mathbf{O}$, where

$$I \rhd\ P\ (\!\!\rightarrow O \text{ if and only if there exists a computation } C \in \mathbf{C}$$
$$\text{such that } I \rhd\ P\ (\!|\ C \rightarrow O.$$

For a programming system to be useful, the computed-output relation $\rhd\ (\!\!\rightarrow$ must be sufficiently effective to allow a mechanical implementation. Computed-output relations in theory textbooks, like provable-consequence relations, are normally semicomputable; computation and output relations $\rhd\ (\!|$ and $\rightarrow$, like trinary proof relations $\mid -$, are normally computable (and even primitive recursive). If $C, \rhd\ (\!|$, and $\rightarrow$ are all semicomputable, then so is $\rhd\ (\!\!\rightarrow$. In fact, every semicomputable computed-output relation $\rhd\ (\!\!\rightarrow$ may be defined from computable $C, \rhd\ (\!|$, and $\rightarrow$. Systems with infinite inputs and/or infinite outputs require more liberal, and less conventional, notions of effectiveness.

The programming systems of Definition 3.3.1 are not required to be deterministic, or effective. They are a simple generalization of the programming systems, also called *indexings* and *Gödel numberings*, of recursion theory [Machtey and Young, 1978; Kleene, 1952]. Our $I \rhd\ P\ (\!\!\rightarrow O$ corresponds to the recursion-theoretic notation $\phi_P(I) = O$. Recursion theory normally considers only *determinate* programming systems.

Definition 3.3.3. A programming system $\mathcal{P} = \langle \mathbf{P}, \mathbf{I}, \mathbf{C}, \mathbf{O}, \rhd\ (\!|, \rightarrow \rangle$ is *determinate* if and only if, for each program P and input I, there is at most one output O such that $I \rhd\ P\ (\!\!\rightarrow O$. That is, $\rhd\ (\!\!\rightarrow$ is a partial function from $\mathbf{P} \times \mathbf{I}$ to $\mathbf{O}$.

A programming system $\mathcal{P} = \langle \mathbf{P}, \mathbf{I}, \mathbf{C}, \mathbf{O}, \rhd\ (\!|, \rightarrow \rangle$ is *deterministic* if and only if, for each program P and input I, there is a unique computation C such that $I \rhd\ P\ (\!|\ C$. That is, $\rhd\ (\!|$ is a partial function from $\mathbf{P} \times \mathbf{I}$ to $\mathbf{C}$.

Determinism implies determinacy, but not the converse—a nondeterministic programming system may provide many computations that yield the same determinate output.

A number of different programming systems may be defined to answer questions in the shallow implicational calculus, depending on the type of question and the stringency of requirements for the answer.

Example 3.3.4. Let $\mathbf{F}_\Rightarrow = \{(a \Rightarrow b) : a, b \in \mathbf{At}\}$ be the set of implicational SIC formulae ($\mathbf{F}_{\mathrm{Sh}} - \mathbf{At}$, with $\mathbf{F}_{\mathrm{Sh}}$ and $\mathbf{At}$ defined in Example 2.1.2). The set of *implicational logic programs* ($\mathbf{P}_\Rightarrow$) is the set of finite subsets of $\mathbf{F}_\Rightarrow$.

Let the set of inputs to implicational logic programs be $\mathbf{Q}_{\mathrm{S1}}$—the set of questions of the form $\mathbf{imp}(a)$ ('what atomic formula does a imply?') defined in Example 2.2.3.

The set of *naive implicational computations* ($\mathbf{C}_{\mathrm{S1}}$) is the set of nonempty finite and infinite sequences of atomic formulae.

The computation relation $\triangleright\; [\![_{\mathrm{S1}}$ is defined by $\mathbf{imp}(a) \triangleright \mathbf{T}\; [\![_{\mathrm{S1}}\; \langle c_0, c_1, \ldots \rangle$ if and only if

1. $c_0 = a$
2. $(c_{i-1} \Rightarrow c_i) \in \mathbf{T}$ for all $i > 0$ in the (finite or infinite) range of the sequence $\langle c_0, \ldots \rangle$

The output relation $\rightarrow_{\mathrm{S1}}$ is defined by

$$\langle c_0, \ldots, c_m \rangle \rightarrow_{\mathrm{S1}} (c_0 \Rightarrow c_m)$$

Infinite computations have no output.

Now $\langle \mathbf{P}_\Rightarrow, \mathbf{Q}_{\mathrm{S1}}, \mathbf{C}_{\mathrm{S1}}, \mathbf{F}_\Rightarrow, \triangleright\; [\![_{\mathrm{S1}}, \rightarrow_{\mathrm{S1}} \rangle$ is a programming system, computing answers to questions of the form 'what atomic formula does a imply?'

The programming system above behaves nondeterministically and indeterminately in proving some implication of a. Its computations may halt at any point and output the latest atomic conclusion found. Loops in the graph of implications lead to infinite computations with no output. Notice that each finite computation $\langle c_0, \ldots c_i, \ldots, c_m \rangle$, with output $(c_0 \Rightarrow c_m)$, translates very easily into the linear proof

$$\langle (c_0 \Rightarrow c_0), \ldots, (c_{i-1} \Rightarrow c_i), (c_0 \Rightarrow c_i), \ldots, (c_{m-1} \Rightarrow c_m), (c_0 \Rightarrow c_m) \rangle$$

of $(c_0 \Rightarrow c_m)$ in the proof system of Example 3.1.2. The first line is an instance of the reflexive rule, and subsequent lines alternate between implications in $\mathbf{T}$, and applications of transitivity.

In order to avoid uninformative outputs, such as $(a \Rightarrow a)$, we need a programming system with a slightly more sophisticated notion of when to stop a computation.

Example 3.3.5. Let **fail** be a new formal symbol, and let the set of *naive implicational computations with failure* be

$$\mathbf{C}_{\mathrm{S2}} = \mathbf{C}_{\mathrm{S1}} \cup \{\langle c_0, \ldots, c_m, \mathbf{fail} \rangle : c_0, \ldots, c_m \in \mathbf{At}\}$$

(the set of finite and infinite sequences of atomic formulae, possibly ending in the special object **fail**).

Let the set of inputs to implicational logic programs be $\mathbf{Q}_{S2}$—the set of questions of the form **rest-imp**$(a, \mathbf{A})$ ('what atomic formula not in $\mathbf{A}$ does a imply?').

The computation relation $\triangleright \, \mathbb{I}_{S2}$ is defined by **rest-imp**$(a, \mathbf{A}) \triangleright \mathbf{T} \, \mathbb{I}_{S2} \langle c_0, \ldots \rangle$ if and only if

1. $c_0 = a$
2. if $c_i \in \mathbf{A}$, and there is a $d \in \mathbf{At}$ such that $(c_i \Rightarrow d) \in \mathbf{T}$, then the sequence has an $i + 1$st element c_{i+1}, and $(c_i \Rightarrow c_{i+1}) \in \mathbf{T}$
3. if $c_i \in \mathbf{A}$, and there is no $d \in \mathbf{At}$ such that $(c_i \Rightarrow d) \in \mathbf{T}$, then the sequence has an $i + 1$st element, and $c_{i+1} = \mathbf{fail}$
4. if $c_i \in \mathbf{At} - \mathbf{A}$, then either there is no $i+1$st element, or $(c_i \Rightarrow c_{i+1}) \in \mathbf{T}$
5. if $c_i = \mathbf{fail}$, then there is no $i + 1$st element

So, $\triangleright \, \mathbb{I}_{S2}$ allows computations to terminate only when an atomic formula outside of $\mathbf{A}$ has been found, or a dead end in the implication graph has been reached.

The output relation $\rightarrow_{S2}$ is defined by

$$\langle c_0, \ldots, c_m \rangle \rightarrow_{S2} (c_0 \Rightarrow c_m) \text{ for } c_m \in \mathbf{At}$$

Infinite computations and finite computations ending in **fail** have no output.

Now $\langle \mathbf{P}_\Rightarrow, \mathbf{Q}_{S2}, \mathbf{C}_{S2}, \mathbf{F}_\Rightarrow, \triangleright \, \mathbb{I}_{S2}, \rightarrow_{S2} \rangle$ is a programming system, computing answers to questions of the form 'what atomic formula not in $\mathbf{A}$ does a imply?'

The programming system of Example 3.3.5 is nondeterministic and indeterminate. It avoids useless answers, but it still may fall into infinite or finite failing computations, even when a legitimate answer exists. It also may find an answer, but fail to output it and proceed instead into a failure or an infinite computation. Successful computations translate into proofs as in Example 3.3.4.

We may further strengthen the behavior of a programming system by letting it back up and try new proofs after finite failures, and by insisting that answers be output as soon as they are found.

Example 3.3.6. Let the set of inputs to implicational logic programs again be $\mathbf{Q}_{S2}$—the set of questions of the form **rest-imp**$(a, \mathbf{A})$ ('what atomic formula not in $\mathbf{A}$ does a imply?').

Let **print** be a new formal symbol. The set of *backtracking implicational computations* ($\mathbf{C}_{S3}$) is the set of nonempty finite and infinite sequences of finite sets of atomic formulae, possibly ending in the special form **print**(a) where a is an atomic formula (**fail** of Example 3.3.5 is represented now by the empty set).

The computation relation $\triangleright \, \mathbb{I}_{S3}$ is defined by **rest-imp**$(a, \mathbf{A}) \triangleright \mathbf{T} \, \mathbb{I}_{S3} \langle C_0, \ldots \rangle$ if and only if

1. $\mathbf{C}_0 = \{a\}$
2. if $\mathbf{C}_i \subseteq \mathbf{A}$ and $\mathbf{C}_i \neq \emptyset$, then there is an $i + $1st element, and

$$\mathbf{C}_{i+1} = \mathbf{C}_i - \{c\} \cup \{d : (c \Rightarrow d) \in \mathbf{T}\}$$

   for some atomic formula $c \in \mathbf{C}_i$
3. if $\mathbf{C}_i \subseteq \mathbf{At}$, and $\mathbf{C}_i - \mathbf{A} \neq \emptyset$, then there is an $i + $1st element, and $\mathbf{C}_{i+1} = \mathbf{print}(c)$ for some $c \in \mathbf{C}_i - \mathbf{A}$
4. if $\mathbf{C}_i = \emptyset$, or $\mathbf{C}_i = \mathbf{print}(c)$, then there is no $i + $1st element

So, $\triangleright \llbracket_{S3}$ allows a computation to replace any atomic formula that has already been proved with the set of atomic formulae that it implies directly in $\mathbf{T}$. A computation halts precisely when it chooses a unique atomic formula not in $\mathbf{A}$ to output, or when it fails by producing the empty set. The output relation $\rightarrow_{S3}$ is defined by

$$\langle\{a\}, \ldots, \mathbf{print}(b)\rangle \rightarrow_{S3} (a \Rightarrow b)$$

Infinite computations, and finite computations ending in $\emptyset$, have no output. Now $\langle \mathbf{P}_\Rightarrow, \mathbf{Q}_{S2}, \mathbf{C}_{S3}, \mathbf{F}_\Rightarrow, \triangleright \llbracket_{S3}, \rightarrow_{S3} \rangle$ is another programming system, computing answers to questions of the form 'what atomic formula not in $\mathbf{A}$ does a imply?'

The programming system of Example 3.3.6 is nondeterministic and indeterminate. It is less susceptible to missing answers than that of Example 3.3.5. The new system does not get stuck with a failure when a single path in the implication graph leads to a dead end: a computation ends in $\emptyset$ only when *all* paths have been followed to a dead end. When there is a finite path to an answer, and also a cycle, the nondeterministic choice of which formula to replace at each step determines which path is followed in the computation, and so determines success or infinite computation. The translation of a computation in the latest system to a proof is not quite as transparent as in Examples 3.3.4 and 3.3.5, but it is still simple. Each successful computation $\langle\{c_0\}, \mathbf{C}_1, \ldots, \mathbf{C}_{m-1}, \mathbf{print}(c_m)\rangle$ must contain a sequence of atomic formulae $\langle c_0, c_1, \ldots, c_{m-1}, c_m \rangle$, where for $i < m\ c_i \in \mathbf{C}_i$, and for adjacent pairs c_i, c_{i+1}, either $c_i = c_{i+1}$, or $(c_i \Rightarrow c_{i+1}) \in \mathbf{T}$. This sequence of atomic formulae transforms to a linear proof as before.

A final example of a programming system illustrates the use of incremental output from possibly infinite computations to produce consequentially strong answers.

Example 3.3.7. Let the set of inputs to implicational logic programs be $\mathbf{Q}_{Sc}$—the set of questions of the form $\mathbf{conj\text{-}imp}(a)$ ('what are some atomic formulae that a implies?') from Example 2.2.6.
The set of *conjunctive implicational computations* $(\mathbf{C}_{S4})$ is the set of nonempty finite or infinite sequences of finite sets of atomic formulae (the same

as $\mathbf{C}_{S3}$, without the final elements $\mathbf{print}(a)$.

The computation relation$\triangleright$ $[\![]\!]_{S4}$ is defined by $\mathbf{conj\text{-}imp}(a)\triangleright \mathbf{T} [\![]\!]_{S4} \langle \mathbf{C}_0,\ldots\rangle$ if and only if

1. $\mathbf{C}_0 = \{a\}$
2. if $\mathbf{C}_i \neq \emptyset$, then there is an $i + 1$st element, and

$$\mathbf{C}_{i+1} = (\mathbf{C}_i - \{c\}) \cup \{d : (c \Rightarrow d) \in \mathbf{T}\}$$

   for some atomic formula $c \in \mathbf{C}_i$
3. if $\mathbf{C}_i = \emptyset$, then there is no $i + 1$st element

The computations above are the same as those of Example 3.3.6, except that we never choose a single atomic formula to output. $\emptyset$ is no longer regarded as a failure.

The output relation $\rightarrow_{S4}$ is defined by $\langle \mathbf{C}_0,\ldots\rangle \rightarrow_{S4} (a \Rightarrow b_1) \wedge \cdots \wedge (a \Rightarrow b_m)$ if and only if

1. $\mathbf{C}_0 = \{a\}$
2. $\{b_1,\ldots b_m\} = \mathbf{C}_0 \cup \mathbf{C}_1 \cup \cdots$, and $b_1,\ldots b_m$ are given in the order of first appearance in the sequence $\mathbf{C}_0,\ldots$, with ties broken by some arbitrary ordering of atomic formulae

Notice that even infinite computations have output.

Now $\langle \mathbf{P}_\Rightarrow, \mathbf{Q}_{Sc}, \mathbf{C}_{S4}, \mathbf{F}_\Rightarrow, \triangleright [\![]\!]_{S4}, \rightarrow_{S4}\rangle$ is a programming system, computing answers to questions of the form 'what are some atomic formulae that a implies?'

The programming system above should be thought of as producing its output incrementally at each computation step. It is nondeterministic and indeterminate. Even though the computation may be infinite, it never fails to produce an answer, although the output may be the trivial formula $a \Rightarrow a$. The strength of the answer produced depends on the nondeterministic choices of the atomic formula replaced in each computation step.

3.4 Soundness and completeness of programming systems

A query system determining what constitutes an answer, and the semantic-consequence relation of a semantic system determining the correctness of an answer, yield criteria for evaluating the behavior of a programming system, similar to the criteria for evaluating a proof system in Section 3.1. We define *soundness* and *completeness* of programming systems, in analogy to the soundness and completeness of proof systems. Logic programming is distinguished from other sorts of programming by the use of such logical concepts to evaluate programming systems.

There is only one sensible concept of soundness for a programming system: every output is a correct answer to the input program. When a given question has more than one correct answer, completeness criteria vary depending on the way in which we expect an output answer to be chosen.

Definition 3.4.1. Let $\mathcal{P} = \langle \mathbf{P}, \mathbf{I}, \mathbf{C}, \mathbf{O}, \triangleright \,\rrbracket, \rightarrow \rangle$ be a programming system, let $\mathcal{S} = \langle \mathbf{F_S}, \mathbf{M}, \models \rangle$ be a semantic system, and let $\mathcal{Q} = \langle \mathbf{F_Q}, \mathbf{Q}, ?\!\!\vdash \rangle$ be a query system, with $\mathbf{P} \subseteq 2^{\mathbf{F_S}}$, $\mathbf{I} \subseteq \mathbf{Q}$, and $\mathbf{O} \subseteq \mathbf{F_S} \cap \mathbf{F_Q}$.

$\mathcal{P}$ is *sound* for $\mathcal{S}$ and $\mathcal{Q}$ if and only if, for all $P \in \mathbf{P}$ and $I \in \mathbf{I}$,

$$I \triangleright P \rrbracket \mapsto O \text{ implies } I ?\!\!\vdash P \models O$$

$\mathcal{P}$ is *weakly complete* for $\mathcal{S}$ and $\mathcal{Q}$ if and only if, for all $P \in \mathbf{P}$ and $I \in \mathbf{I}$ such that I is semantically answerable for P (Definition 2.2.2), and for all computations $C \in \mathbf{C}$ such that $I \triangleright P \rrbracket C$, there exists $O \in \mathbf{O}$ such that

$$C \rightarrow O \text{ and } I ?\!\!\vdash P \models O$$

(O is unique because $\rightarrow$ is a partial function).

$\mathcal{P}$ is *consequentially complete* for $\mathcal{S}$ and $\mathcal{Q}$ if and only if $\mathcal{P}$ is weakly complete and, in addition, O above is a consequentially strongest correct answer ($\{O\} \models N$ for all $N \in \mathbf{F_Q}$ such that $I ?\!\!\vdash P \models N$).

So, a programming system is sound if all of its outputs are correct answers to input questions, based on the knowledge represented explicitly by programs. A system is weakly complete if, whenever a correct answer exists, every computation outputs some correct answer. A system is consequentially complete if, whenever a correct answer exists, every computation outputs a consequentially strongest correct answer. Notice that, for consequential completeness, the strength of the output answer is judged against all possible answers in the query system, not just those that are possible outputs in the programming system, so we cannot achieve consequential completeness by the trickery of disallowing the truly strongest answers.

A programming system provides another approach to analyzing a simple form of communication. While semantic systems, proof systems, and query systems yield insight into the meaning of communication and criteria for evaluating the behavior of communicating agents, programming systems merely describe that behavior. A programmer provides a program P to a processor. A user (sometimes, but not always, identical with the programmer) provides an input I, and the processor performs a computation C such that $I \triangleright P \rrbracket C$ from which the output O, if any, such that $C \rightarrow O$, may be extracted. We allow the mapping from computation to output to depend on purely conventional rules that are adopted by the three agents. What aspects of a computation are taken to be significant to the output is really a matter of convention, not necessity. Often, only the string of symbols displayed on some printing device is taken to be the output, but in various contexts the temporal order in which they are displayed (which may be

different from the printed order if the device can backspace), the temporal
or spatial interleaving of input and output, the speed with which output
occurs, the color in which the symbols are displayed, which of several devices is used for display, all may be taken as significant. Also, convention
determines the treatment of infinite computation as having no output, null
output, or some nontrivial and possibly infinite output produced incrementally. The presentation of input to a computation is similarly a matter of
accepted convention, rather than formal computation.

In logic programming, where the programmer acts as speaker, the processor as auditor, and the user as questioner, soundness of the programming system guarantees that all outputs constitute correct answers. Various forms of completeness guarantee that answers will always be produced
when they exist. In this sense, soundness and completeness mean that a
programming system provides a correct and powerful implementation of
the auditor in the speaker-auditor-questioner scenario of Section 2.2.

There is a close formal correspondence between programming systems
and pairs of proof and query systems: inputs correspond to questions,
programs correspond to sets of hypotheses, computations to proofs, and
outputs to theorems (for a different correspondence, in which programs
in the form of lambda terms correspond to natural deduction proofs, see
[Howard, 1980; Tait, 1967; Constable *et al.*, 1986]—compare this to the interpretation of formulae as queries and proofs as answers [Meseguer, 1989]).
Notice that both quaternary relations $Q \,?\!\!- \mathbf{T} \mid D - F$ and $I \rhd P \, [\!]\, C \to O$
are typically computable, while both of the trinary relations $Q \,?\!\!- \mathbf{T} \vdash F$
and $I \rhd P \, [\!\!\to\!] \, O$ are typically semicomputable. Furthermore, the definitions of the trinary relations from the corresponding quaternary relations
are analogous. In both cases we quantify existentially over the third argument, which is variously a proof or a computation.

There is an important difference, however, between the forms of definition of the provable-answer relation $Q \,?\!\!- \mathbf{T} \mid D - F$, and of the computational relation $I \rhd P \, [\!]\, C \to O$, reflecting the difference in intended uses
of these relations. This difference has only a minor impact on the relations definable in each form, but a substantial impact on the efficiency of
straightforward implementations based on the definitions. In the query-
proof domain, we relate formulae giving explicit knowledge (program) to
the proofs (computations) that can be constructed from that knowledge,
yielding formulae (outputs) that are provable consequences of the given
knowledge in the relation $\mathbf{T} \mid D - F$. We independently relate questions
(inputs) to the answers (outputs) in the relation $Q \,?\!\!- F$, and then take
the conjunction of the two. There is no formal provision for the question
(input) to interact with the knowledge formulae (program) to guide the
construction of the proof (computation)—the question (input) is only used
to select a completed proof. In the computational domain, we relate inputs
(questions) directly to programs (knowledge formulae) to determine com-

putations (proofs) that they can produce in the relation $I \rhd P \Box C$. Then, we extract outputs (answer formulae) from computations (proofs) in the relation $C \to O$. The relation $I \rhd P \Box C$ provides a formal concept that may be used to represent the interaction of input (question) with program (knowledge) to guide the construction of the computation (proof).

Given a proof system and a query system, we can construct a programming system with essentially the same behavior. This translation is intended as an exercise in understanding the formal correspondence between proofs and computations. Since our requirements for proof systems and programming systems are quite different, this construction does *not* normally lead to useful implementations.

Proposition 3.4.2. *Let* $\mathcal{D} = \langle \mathbf{F}, \mathbf{D}, \vert - \rangle$ *be a proof system, and let* $\mathcal{Q} = \langle \mathbf{F}, \mathbf{Q}, ?\!- \rangle$ *be a query system. Define the programming system*

$$\mathcal{P} = \langle 2^{\mathbf{F}}, \mathbf{Q}, (\mathbf{D} \times \mathbf{F}) \cup \{\mathbf{fail}\}, \mathbf{F}, \rhd \Box, \to \rangle$$

where

1. $Q \rhd \mathbf{T} \Box \langle P, F \rangle$ *if and only if* $Q ?\!- \mathbf{T} \mid P - F$
2. $Q \rhd \mathbf{T} \Box \mathbf{fail}$ *if and only if there are no* P *and* F *such that* $Q ?\!- \mathbf{T} \mid P - F$
3. $\langle P, F \rangle \to G$ *if and only if* $F = G$
4. $\mathbf{fail} \to F$ *is false for all* $F \in \mathbf{F}$

Then,

$$Q ?\!- \mathbf{T} \mid P - F \text{ if and only if } Q \rhd \mathbf{T} \Box \langle P, F \rangle \to F$$

Therefore,

$$Q ?\!- \mathbf{T} \vdash F \text{ if and only if } Q \rhd \mathbf{T} \mapsto F$$

If $\mathcal{D}$ above is sound for some semantic system $\mathcal{S}$, then $\mathcal{P}$ is sound for $\mathcal{S}$ and $\mathcal{Q}$, but the converse fails because some formulae may never occur as answers to questions. Proposition 3.4.2 shows that a proof may be interpreted as a nondeterministically chosen computation that outputs a theorem.

Because hypotheses to proofs are sets of formulae, rather than single formulae, and the proof relation must be monotone with respect to the subset relation, there are computational relations $\rhd \mapsto$ defined by programming systems that are not the same as the relation $?\!- \vdash$ of any proof and query systems. Intuitively, in order to mimic an arbitrary programming system with a proof system and a query system, we must augment the output O resulting from input I into a formula asserting that *input* I *produces output* O. This augmentation is almost trivial, in the sense that echoed input may just as well be regarded as an implicit part of the output. Informal question answering uses such implicit augmentation: in response to the question 'what is the capital city of Idaho?' the abbreviated answer 'Boise' is generally accepted as equivalent to the full answer 'the capital city of Idaho is Boise.'

Proposition 3.4.3. *Let* $\mathcal{P} = \langle \mathbf{P}, \mathbf{I}, \mathbf{C}, \mathbf{O} \rangle$ *be a programming system. Define the proof system* $\mathcal{D} = \langle \mathbf{P} \cup (\mathbf{I} \times \mathbf{O}), \mathbf{C}, | - \rangle$*, where*

1. $\mathbf{T} \mid C - \langle I, O \rangle$ *if and only if* $I \triangleright P \, [\![\, C \to O$ *for some* $P \in \mathbf{T}$
2. $\mathbf{T} \mid C - P$ *is false for all* $P \in \mathbf{P}$

Also define the query system $\mathcal{Q} = \langle \mathbf{I} \times \mathbf{O}, \mathbf{I}, ?\!\!- \rangle$*, where*

1. $I \,?\!\!- \langle J, O \rangle$ *if and only if* $I = J$.

Then,

$$I \triangleright P \, [\![\, C \to O \text{ if and only if } I \,?\!\!- \{P\} \mid C - \langle I, O \rangle$$

Therefore,

$$I \triangleright P \longmapsto O \text{ if and only if } I \,?\!\!- \{P\} \vdash \langle I, O \rangle$$

As in the construction of Proposition 3.4.2, soundness of $\mathcal{D}$ implies soundness of $\mathcal{P}$, but the converse fails, and completeness does not transfer either way. Proposition 3.4.3 shows that a computation may be interpreted as a proof that a given program and input produce a certain output.

Example 3.4.4. The programming systems of Examples 3.3.4, 3.3.5, 3.3.6, and 3.3.7 are all sound for their appropriate semantic and query systems. The proof of soundness is easy—every computation can be transformed easily into a proof in a sound proof system.

The programming system of naive implicational computations in Example 3.3.4 is not weakly complete. Consider the program

$$\{a \Rightarrow b, \ b \Rightarrow a, \ a \Rightarrow c\}$$

Given the input question **imp**(a) ('what logical formula does a imply?'), a possible computation is the infinite sequence

$$\langle a, b, a, b, \ldots \rangle$$

which has no output. There are three correct answers,

$$a \Rightarrow a, \, a \Rightarrow b, \text{ and } a \Rightarrow c$$

each of which is found by a short computation.

The programming system of naive implicational computations with failure in Example 3.3.5 is not weakly complete. Consider the program

$$\{a \Rightarrow b, \ a \Rightarrow c, \ c \Rightarrow a, \ a \Rightarrow d\}$$

Given the input question **rest-imp**$(a, \{a, b, c\})$ ('what logical formula not in $\{a, b, c\}$ does a imply?'), two possible computations with no output are

$$\langle a, b, \textbf{fail} \rangle \text{ and } \langle a, c, a, c, \ldots \rangle$$

There is a correct answer, $a \Rightarrow d$, which is found by the computation $\langle a, d \rangle$.

The programming system of backtracking implicational computations in Example 3.3.6 avoids the finite failure of the naive computations with failure, but is still not weakly complete because of infinite computations. It succeeds on the program and question above, with the unique computation

$$\langle \{a\}, \{b, c, d\}, \{d\} \rangle$$

but fails on a slightly trickier case. Consider the program

$$\{a \Rightarrow b, \ a \Rightarrow c, \ c \Rightarrow a, \ a \Rightarrow d, \ d \Rightarrow e\}$$

and the question **rest-imp**$(a, \{a, b, c, d\})$. There is no finite failing computation, and the correct answer $a \Rightarrow e$ is output by the computation

$$\langle \{a\}, \{b, c, d\}, \{b, d\}, \{a, d\}, \{a, e\}, \textbf{print}(e) \rangle$$

But there is still an infinite computation that misses the output:

$$\langle \{a\}, \{b, c, d\}, \{b, a, d\}, \{b, c, d\}, \ldots \rangle$$

The programming system of conjunctive implicational computations in Example 3.3.7 is weakly complete, simply because every computation outputs some correct answer of the form $(a \Rightarrow a) \wedge \ldots$, where in the worst case only the first conjunct is given. This system was clearly aimed, however, toward producing consequentially strong answers. It is not consequentially complete. Consider again the program

$$\{a \Rightarrow b, \ a \Rightarrow c, \ c \Rightarrow a, \ a \Rightarrow d, \ d \Rightarrow e\}$$

and the new question **conj-imp**(a). The computation

$$\langle \{a\}, \{b, c, d\}, \{b, c, e\}, \{b, a, e\}, \{b, c, d, e\}, \{b, a, d, e\}, \{b, c, d, e\}, \ldots \rangle$$

outputs the consequentially strongest answer

$$(a \Rightarrow a) \wedge (a \Rightarrow b) \wedge (a \Rightarrow c) \wedge (a \Rightarrow d) \wedge (a \Rightarrow e)$$

But the computation

$$\langle \{a\}, \{b, c, d\}, \{b, a, d\}, \{b, c, d\}, \ldots \rangle$$

outputs only the weaker answer

$$(a \Rightarrow a) \wedge (a \Rightarrow b) \wedge (a \Rightarrow c) \wedge (a \Rightarrow d)$$

missing the conjunct $a \Rightarrow e$.

In each case above, the failure of completeness results from the possibility of unfortunate choices for the next computational step.

Most practical implementations of logic programming languages are not complete, and many are not even sound. Nonetheless, soundness and completeness are useful standards against which to judge implementations. Most implementations are sound and complete for well-characterized subsets of their possible programs and inputs. The cases where soundness and/or completeness fail are typically considered at least peculiar, and sometimes pathological, and they are the topics of much discussion and debate. The history of programming languages gives some hope for a trend toward stricter adherence at least to soundness criteria. For example, early Lisp processors employed dynamic scoping, which is essentially an unsound implementation of logical substitution. Modern Lisp processors are usually statically scoped, and provide sound implementations of substitution [Muchnick and Pleban, 1980; Brooks *et al.*, 1982; Rees Clinger, 1986]. As compiler technology matured, the logically correct static scoping was found to be more efficient than dynamic scoping, although early work assumed the contrary.

In spite of the close formal correspondence outlined above between proof and computation, our natural requirements for proof systems and programming systems differ significantly. The requirements for correctness, formalized as soundness, are essentially the same—everything that is proved/computed must be a logical consequence of given information. But, the requirements for power, formalized as completeness, vary substantially.

Proofs are thought of as things to search for, using any available tools whether formal, intuitive, or inspirational, and we only demand formal or mechanical verification of the correctness of a proof, not mechanical discovery of the proof. So, proofs are quantified existentially in the definition of completeness of a proof system, and we are satisfied with the mere existence of a proof of a given true formula. Computations, on the other hand, are thought of as being generated on demand by a computing agent in order to satisfy the requirement of a user. So, we require that a complete programming system be guaranteed to produce a sufficiently strong correct answer whenever a correct answer exists. Since we do not know which of several possible computations will be generated nondeterministically by the computing agent, we quantify universally over computations.

Because of the requirement that *all* computations in a complete programming system yield correct answers, merely mimicking the relational behavior of a proof system, as in Proposition 3.4.2, is not sufficient for useful implementation. Practical implementations must use complete *strategies* for choosing proofs in order to provide programming systems with the desired guaranteed results.

3.5   Proof-theoretic foundations for logic programming

Given a suitable proof system, a practical implementation of a logic programming language still must solve the difficult problem of searching the set of proofs for one that provides an answer to a given input question. Methods for choosing and generating proofs are called *proof strategies*. While logical semantics provides the conceptual tools for specifying logic programming languages, *proof theory* [Stenlund, 1972; Prawitz, 1965; Takeuti, 1975; Schutte, 1977; Girard *et al.*, 1989]. provides the tools for developing proof strategies. Once a proof strategy has been defined, the remaining problems in implementation are the invention of appropriate algorithms and data structures for the strategy, and the details of code generation or interpreting. The organization of logic programming into the application of semantics to specification, and the application of proof theory to implementation, does *not* mean, however, that the former precedes the latter in the design of a logic programming language. Design normally requires the simultaneous consideration of specification and implementation, and the designer must search the two spaces of semantic specifications and proof-theoretic strategies in parallel for a compatible pair of ideas. In different circumstances either topic can be the primary driver of design decisions. In writing this chapter, I have not been able to develop the proof theoretic side of logic programming design as thoroughly as the semantic side, merely because I ran out of time, pages, and energy. In this section, I will only outline the issues involved in applying proof theory to logic programming.

The choice of a proof strategy affects both the power and the complexity of an implementation, but not the soundness. Given a sound proof system, a proof strategy can only choose (or fail to find) a correct proof, it cannot expand the class of proofs. But, a given proof strategy may be incapable of discovering certain provably correct answers, so it may yield an incomplete computing system, even when starting with a complete proof system. So, there is great value in proof theoretic theorems demonstrating that, whenever a formula F is provable, there is a proof in some usefully restricted form. Even when these do not lead to complete implementations, they can improve the power/complexity tradeoff dramatically. Fortunately, proof theorists have concentrated a lot of attention on such results, particularly in the form of *proof normalization* theorems, which show that all proofs may be reduced to a normal form with special structure. Many normalization results are expressed as *cut elimination* theorems, showing that a particular version of *modus ponens* called the *cut* rule may be removed from proofs. Cut elimination theorems are usually associated with the predicate calculus and its fragments, variants, and extensions. The impact of cut elimination on proof strategies has been studied very thoroughly, leading to an excellent characterization of the sequent-style proof systems that are susceptible to generalizations of the simple goal-directed proof strategy used in Prolog [Miller *et al.*, 1991]. These proof-theoretic methods have been applied successfully in some novel logics where the model-theoretic semantics are not yet properly understood.

In the term rewriting literature, there are similar results on the normalization of equational proofs. Many of these come from *confluence* (also called *Church–Rosser*) results. A system of equations

$$\{l_1 \doteq r_1, \ldots, l_m \doteq r_m\}$$

presented with each equation oriented in a particular left–right order, is *confluent* precisely if every proof of an equation $s \doteq t$ may be transformed into a rewriting of each of s and t to a common form u. *Rewriting* means here that an equational hypothesis $l_i \doteq r_i$ may only be used from left to right, to replace instances of l_i by corresponding instances of r_i but not the reverse. The restriction of equational proofs to rewritings allows complete strategies that are much simpler and more efficient than those that search through all equational proofs. See Sections 2.2 and 2.3 of the chapter 'Equational Logic Programming' in this volume, as well as [Klop, 1991], for more on the application of term rewriting to equational proofs.

4 The uses of semantics

The development of logic programming systems from logics, given above, provides a particular flavor of semantics, called *logical semantics,* for logic programming languages. Logical semantics, rather than competing directly with other flavors of programming language semantics, provides different insights, and is useful for different purposes. The careful comparison of different styles of semantics is a wide-open area for further research. In this section, I sketch the sort of relations that I believe should be explored between logical semantics, denotational semantics, and algebraic semantics. Meseguer proposes two sorts of logic programming—'weak' logic programming uses essentially the same notion of logical semantics as mine, while 'strong' logic programming uses the theory of a single model, such as a model derived by algebraic semantics [Meseguer, 1989].

4.1 Logical semantics vs. denotational semantics

Roughly, denotational semantics [Scott, 1970; Scott and Strachey, 1971; Stoy, 1977] takes the meaning of a program to be an abstract description of its input/output behavior, where inputs and outputs are uninterpreted tokens. Denotational semantics assigns to each program a unique value carrying that meaning. One problem of denotational semantics is how to deal with observable computational behavior, such as nontermination, that does not produce output tokens in the concrete sense. This problem was solved by expanding the domains of input and output, as well as the domains of program meanings, to partially ordered sets (usually chain-complete partial orderings [Markowsky, 1976] or lattices [Scott, 1976]) containing objects representing abstract computational behaviors, not all of which produce tokens as output [Reynolds, 1973; Scott, 1982]. In practice, the definition of appropriate domains is often the most challenging task in creating a denotational semantic description of a programming language, and *domain theory* has become a definite specialty in theoretical computer science [Schmidt, 1986; Stoy, 1977; Zhang, 1991; Gunter, 1992; Winksel, 1993].

The denotational approach provides a useful tool for characterizing what a particular type of implementation actually does, but it does not give any intuitive basis for discussing what an implementation *ought* to do. Logical semantics, on the other hand, begins with an interpretation of input and output. It does not directly address techniques for analyzing the behavior of programs—that is left to a metalanguage. But it *does* provide an intuitive basis for distinguishing logically reasonable behaviors from other behaviors.

For example, denotational semantics for functional languages was initially defined using eager evaluation [Backus, 1978] The domains that were used to define eager evaluation are not rich enough to represent lazy evaluation. In fact the definition of domains for lazy evaluation [Winksel, 1993] posed difficult technical problems, causing resistance to the use of lazy evaluation. Denotational semantics for lazy evaluation matured long after the idea had been implemented, and informal evidence for its utility had been presented. [Friedman and Wise, 1976; Henderson and Morris, 1976] Logical semantics for equational programming, on the other hand, *requires* lazy evaluation for completeness, and the demand for lazy evaluation from this point of view precedes its invention as a programming tool—at latest it goes back to [O'Donnell, 1977] and the essential roots are already there in work on combinatory logic and the lambda calculus [Curry and Feys, 1958]. Once lazy evaluation was explained denotationally, that explanation became a very useful tool for analysis and for deriving implementations. In general logical semantics predicts and prescribes useful techniques, while denotational semantics explains and analyzes them.

4.2 Logical semantics vs. initial/final-algebra and Herbrand semantics

Semantics that use initial or final algebras or Herbrand models [Guttag and Horning, 1978; Goguen *et al.*, 1978; Meseguer and Goguen, 1985] to represent the meanings of programs provide systematic techniques for deriving denotational-like semantics from logical semantics. Logical semantics determines a large class of models consistent with a given program. Algebraic semantic techniques construct a single model, depending on the language in which output is expressed as well as the given program, whose output theory is the same as that of the class of models given by logical semantics. This single model can be used for the same sorts of analysis as denotational semantics (although it is not always based on a lattice or chain-complete partial ordering). Such single-model semantics must be reconsidered whenever the output language expands, since in the larger language the theory of the single model may *not* be the same as the theory of the class of models consistent with the program.

For example, consider a language (based on ideas from Lucid [Ashcroft and Wadge, 1977]) with symbols *cons*, *first*, *more*, *a*, *b*, satisfying the equations

$$
\begin{aligned}
first(cons(x,y)) &\doteq first(x) \\
first(a) &\doteq a \\
\cdot first(b) &\doteq b \\
more(cons(x,y)) &\doteq y \\
more(a) &\doteq a \\
more(b) &\doteq b
\end{aligned}
$$

Assume that only the symbols a and b are allowed as output—that is, we are only interested in deriving equations of the forms $s \doteq a$ and $t \doteq b$, where s and t are arbitrary input terms. Algebraic semantic techniques typically interpret this system over a universe of infinite flat (i.e., not nested) lists with elements from the set $\{a, b\}$, where after some finite prefix, all elements of the list are the same. $cons(s,t)$ is interpreted as the list beginning with the first element of s, followed by all the elements of t. In this algebraic interpretation, $cons(cons(a,b),b) \doteq cons(a,b)$ and $cons(b, cons(a,a)) \doteq cons(b,a)$ hold, although neither is a semantic consequence of the given equations. If, however, we add the conventional symbols *car* and *cdr*, and define them by the equations

$$
\begin{aligned}
car(cons(x,y)) &\doteq x \\
cdr(cons(x,y)) &\doteq y
\end{aligned}
$$

then we must expand the universe of the algebraic interpretation to the universe of binary trees with leaves marked a and b. There is no way to define the functions *car* and *cdr* in the flat list model so that they satisfy the new equations. If we take the full equational theory of the flat list model, and add the defining equations for *car* and *cdr*, then the resulting theory trivializes. Every two terms s and t are equal by the derivation

$$
s \doteq cdr(car(cons(cons(a,s),b)))
$$

$$\doteq \quad cdr(car(cons(a,b)))$$
$$\doteq \quad cdr(car(cons(cons(a,t),b)))$$
$$\doteq \quad t$$

Of course, nobody would apply algebraic semantics in this way—taking the model for a smaller language and trying to interpret new function symbols in the same universe. But, what the example shows is that an algebraic model of a given system of equations may not preserve all of the relevant information about the behavior of those equations in extended languages. The set of models associated with a system of equations by logical semantics is much more robust, and carries enough information to perform extensions such as the example above.

In general, algebraic semantic techniques, based on initial models, final models, and Herbrand universes, provide useful tools for determining, in a given program, the minimum amount of information that a data structure must carry in order to support the computational needs of that program. They do *not,* and are not intended to, represent the inherent information given by the formulae in the program, independently of a particular definition of the computational inputs and outputs that the program may operate on.

Acknowledgements

I am very grateful for the detailed comments that I received from the readers, Bharay Jayaraman, José Meseguer, Dale Miller, Gopalan Nadathur and Ed Wimmers. All of the readers made substantial contributions to the correctness and readability of the chapter.

References

[Anderson and Belnap Jr., 1975] Alan Ross Anderson and Nuel D. Belnap Jr. *Entailment—the Logic of Relevance and Necessity*, volume 1. Princeton University Press, Princeton, NJ, 1975.

[Andrews, 1986] Peter B. Andrews. *An Introduction to Mathematical Logic and Type Theory: To Truth Through Proof.* Computer Science and Applied Mathematics. Academic Press, New York, NY, 1986.

[Ashcroft and Wadge, 1977] E. Ashcroft and W. Wadge. Lucid: A non-procedural language with iteration. *Communications of the ACM,* 20(7):519–526, 1977.

[Backus, 1974] John Backus. Programming language semantics and closed applicative languages. In *Proceedings of the 1st ACM Symposium on Principles of Programming Languages*, pages 71–86. ACM, 1974.

[Backus, 1978] John Backus. Can programming be liberated from the von Neumann style? a functional style and its algebra of programs. *Communications of the ACM*, 21(8):613–641, 1978.

[Barendregt, 1984] Hendrik Peter Barendregt. *The Lambda Calculus: Its Syntax and Semantics*. North-Holland, Amsterdam, 1984.

[Belnap Jr. and Steel, 1976] Nuel D. Belnap Jr. and T. B. Steel. *The Logic of Questions and Answers*. Yale University Press, New Haven, CT, 1976.

[Brooks *et al.*, 1982] R. A. Brooks, R. P. Gabriel, and Guy L. Steele. An optimizing compiler for lexically scoped Lisp. In *Proceedings of the 1982 ACM Compiler Construction Conference*, June 1982.

[Church, 1941] A. Church. *The Calculi of Lambda-Conversion*. Princeton University Press, Princeton, New Jersey, 1941.

[Codd, 1970] E. F. Codd. A relational model of data for large shared data banks. *Communications of the ACM*, 13(6), June 1970.

[Codd, 1971] E. F. Codd. A data base sublanguage founded on the relational calculus. In *Proceedings of the 1971 ACM SIGFIDET Workshop on Data Description, Access and Control*, 1971.

[Codd, 1972] E. F. Codd. Relational completeness of data base sublanguages. In *Data Base Systems*, volume 6 of *Courant Computer Science Symposia*. Prentice-Hall, Englewood Cliffs, NJ, 1972.

[Cohn, 1965] P. M. Cohn. *Universal Algebra*. Harper and Row, New York, NY, 1965.

[Constable *et al.*, 1986] Robert L. Constable, S. F. Allen, H. M. Bromley, W. R. Cleaveland, J. F. Cremer, R. W. Harper, D. J. Howe, Todd B. Knoblock, N. P. Mendler, Prakesh Panangaden, J. T. Sasaki, and Scott F. Smith. *Implementing Mathematics with the Nuprl Proof Development System*. Prentice-Hall, Englewood Cliffs, NJ, 1986.

[Curry and Feys, 1958] H. B. Curry and R. Feys. *Combinatory Logic*, volume 1. North-Holland, Amsterdam, 1958.

[Date, 1986] C. J. Date. *An Introduction to Database Systems*. Systems Programming. Addison-Wesley, Reading, MA, 4 edition, 1986.

[Dijkstra, 1976] Edsger W. Dijkstra. *A Discipline of Programming*. Prentice-Hall, Englewood Cliffs, NJ, 1976.

[Dwelly, 1988] Andrew Dwelly. Synchronizing the I/O behavior of functional programs with feedback. *Information Processing Letters*, 28, 1988.

[Fagin *et al.*, 1984] Ronald Fagin, Joseph Y. Halpern, and Moshe Y. Vardi. A model-theoretic analysis of knowledge. In *Proceedings of the 25th Annual IEEE Symposium on Foundations of Computer Science*, pages 268–278, 1984.

[Friedman and Wise, 1976] Daniel Friedman and David S. Wise. Cons should not evaluate its arguments. In *3rd International Colloquium on*

Automata, Languages and Programming, pages 257–284. Edinburgh University Press, 1976.

[Futatsugi *et al.*, 1985] K. Futatsugi, Joseph A. Goguen, J.-P. Jouannaud, and José Meseguer. Principles of OBJ2. In *12th Annual Symposium on Principles of Programming Languages*, pages 52–66. ACM, 1985.

[Gallaire *et al.*, 1984] Hervé Gallaire, Jack Minker, and J. M. Nicolas. Databases: A deductive approach. *ACM Computing Surveys*, 16(2), June 1984.

[Gallier, 1986] Jean H. Gallier. *Logic for Computer Science—Foundations of Automatic Theorem Proving*. Harper & Row, New York, NY, 1986.

[Gentzen, 1935] Gerhard Gentzen. Untersuchungen über das logische schließen. *Mathematische Zeitschrift*, 39:176–210, 405–431, 1935. English translation in [Gentzen, 1969].

[Gentzen, 1969] Gerhard Gentzen. Investigations into logical deductions, 1935. In M. E. Szabo, editor, *The Collected Works of Gerhard Gentzen*, pages 68–131. North-Holland, Amsterdam, 1969.

[Girard *et al.*, 1989] Jean-Yves Girard, Yves Lafont, and Paul Taylor. *Proofs and Types*. Cambridge Tracts in Theoretical Computer Science. Cambridge University Press, Cambridge, UK, 1989.

[Goguen and Burstall, 1992] Joseph A. Goguen and Rod M. Burstall. Institutions: Abstract model theory for specification and programming. *Journal of the ACM*, 39(1):95–146, January 1992.

[Goguen *et al.*, 1978] Joseph A. Goguen, James Thatcher, and Eric Wagner. An initial algebra approach to the specification, correctness and implementation of abstract data types. In Raymond Yeh, editor, *Current Trends in Programming Methodology*, pages 80–149. Prentice-Hall, 1978.

[Goguen, 1990] Joseph A. Goguen. Higher order functions considered unnecessary for higher order programming. In David A. Turner, editor, *Research Topics in Functional Programming*, pages 309–351. Addison-Wesley, 1990.

[Gordon, 1992] Andrew D. Gordon. *Functional Programming and Input/Output*. PhD thesis, University of Cambridge, 1992.

[Grätzer, 1968] G. Grätzer. *Universal Algebra*. Van Nostrand, Princeton, NJ, 1968.

[Gunter, 1992] Carl A. Gunter. *Semantics of Programming Languages: Structures and Techniques*. Foundations of Computing. MIT Press, Cambridge, MA, 1992.

[Guttag and Horning, 1978] John V. Guttag and J. J. Horning. The algebraic specification of abstract data types. *Acta Informatica*, 10(1):1–26, 1978.

[Henderson and Morris, 1976] P. Henderson and J. H. Morris. A lazy evaluator. In *3rd Annual ACM Symposium on Principles of Programming Languages*, pages 95–103. SIGPLAN and SIGACT, 1976.

[Hoffmann and O'Donnell, 1982] C. M. Hoffmann and M. J. O'Donnell. Programming with equations. *ACM Transactions on Programming Languages and Systems*, 4(1):83–112, 1982.

[Hoffmann et al., 1985] C. M. Hoffmann, M. J. O'Donnell, and R. I. Strandh. Implementation of an interpreter for abstract equations. *Software — Practice and Experience*, 15(12):1185–1203, 1985.

[Howard, 1980] William Howard. The formulas-as-types notion of construction. In John P. Seldin and J. R. Hindley, editors, *To H. B. Curry: Essays on Combinatory Logic, Lambda-Calculus, and Formalism*, pages 479–490. Academic Press, New York, NY, 1980.

[Hudak and Sundaresh, 1988] Paul Hudak and Raman S. Sundaresh. On the expressiveness of purely functional I/O systems. Technical Report YALEU/DCS/RR665, Yale University, New Haven, CT, December 1988.

[Hudak, 1992] Report on the programming language Haskell, a non-strict, purely functional language, version 1.2. *ACM SIGPLAN Notices*, 27(5), May 1992.

[Jaffar and Lassez, 1987] Joxan Jaffar and Jean-Louis Lassez. Constraint logic programming. In *Fourteenth Annual ACM Symposium on Principles of Programming Languages*, pages 111–119, 1987.

[Jayaraman, 1985] Bharat Jayaraman. Equational programming: A unifying approach to functional and logic programming. Technical Report 85-030, The University of North Carolina, 1985.

[Karlsson, 1981] K. Karlsson. Nebula, a functional operating system. Technical report, Chalmers University, 1981.

[Kleene, 1952] Steven Cole Kleene. *Introduction to Metamathematics*, volume 1 of *Biblioteca Mathematica*. North-Holland, Amsterdam, 1952.

[Klop, 1991] Jan Willem Klop. Term rewriting systems. In S. Abramsky, Dov M. Gabbay, and T. S. E. Maibaum, editors, *Handbook of Logic in Computer Science*, volume 1, chapter 6. Oxford University Press, Oxford, 1991.

[Kowalski, 1974] R. Kowalski. Predicate logic as a programming language. In *Information Processing 74*, pages 569–574. North-Holland, 1974.

[Lassez, 1991] Jean-Louis Lassez. From LP to CLP: Programming with constraints. In T. Ito and A. R. Meyer, editors, *Theoretical Aspects of Computer Software: International Conference*, volume 526 of *Lecture Notes in Computer Science*. Springer-Verlag, 1991.

[Mac Lane and Birkhoff, 1967] Saunders Mac Lane and G. Birkhoff. *Algebra*. Macmillan, New York, NY, 1967.

[Machtey and Young, 1978] Michael Machtey and Paul Young. *An Introduction to the General Theory of Algorithms.* Theory of Computation. North-Holland, New York, NY, 1978.

[Maier and Warren, 1988] David Maier and David S. Warren. *Computing with Logic—Logic Programming with Prolog.* Benjamin Cummings, Menlo Park, CA, 1988.

[Markowsky, 1976] G. Markowsky. Chain-complete posets and directed sets with applications. *Algebra Universalis*, 6:53–68, 1976.

[McCarthy, 1960] John McCarthy. Recursive functions of symbolic expressions and their computation by machine, part I. *Communications of the ACM*, 3(4):184–195, 1960.

[Meseguer and Goguen, 1985] José Meseguer and Joseph A. Goguen. Initiality, induction, and computability. In Maurice Nivat and John Reynolds, editors, *Algebraic Methods in Semantics*, pages 459–541. Cambridge University Press, 1985.

[Meseguer, 1989] José Meseguer. General logics. In H.-D. Ebbinghaus et. al., editor, *Logic Colloquium '87: Proceedings of the Colloquium held in Granada, Spain July 20–25, 1987*, Amsterdam, 1989. Elsevier North-Holland.

[Meseguer, 1992] José Meseguer. Multiparadigm logic programming. In H. Kirchner and G. Levi, editors, *Proceedings of the 3rd International Conference on Algebraic and Logic Programming, Volterra, Italy, September 1992*, Lecture Notes in Computer Science. Springer-Verlag, 1992.

[Miller et al., 1991] Dale Miller, Gopalan Nadathur, Frank Pfenning, and Andre Scedrov. Uniform proofs as a foundation for logic programming. *Annals of Pure and Applied Logic*, 51:125–157, 1991.

[Moses, 1970] Joel Moses. The function of FUNCTION in LISP, or why the FUNARG problem should be called the environment problem. *ACM SIGSAM Bulletin*, 15, 1970.

[Mostowski et al., 1953] Andrzej Mostowski, Raphael M. Robinson, and Alfred Tarski. *Undecidability and Essential Undecidability in Arithmetic*, chapter II, pages 37–74. Studies in Logic and the Foundations of Mathematics. North-Holland, Amsterdam, 1953. Book author: Alfred Tarski in collaboration with Andrzej Mostowski and Raphael M. Robinson. Series editors: L. E. J. Brouwer, E. W. Beth, A. Heyting.

[Muchnick and Pleban, 1980] Steven S. Muchnick and Uwe F. Pleban. A semantic comparison of Lisp and Scheme. In *Proceedings of the 1980 Lisp Conference*, pages 56–64, 1980. Stanford University.

[Nadathur and Miller, 1988] Gopalan Nadathur and Dale Miller. An overview of λProlog. In *Proceedings of the 5th International Conference on Logic Programming*, pages 810–827, Cambridge, MA, 1988. MIT Press.

[Nadathur and Miller, 1990] Gopalan Nadathur and Dale Miller. Higher-order Horn clauses. *Journal of the ACM*, 37(4):777–814, October 1990.

[O'Donnell, 1977] Michael James O'Donnell. *Computing in Systems Described by Equations*, volume 58 of *Lecture Notes in Computer Science*. Springer-Verlag, 1977.

[O'Donnell, 1985] Michael James O'Donnell. *Equational Logic as a Programming Language*. Foundations of Computing. MIT Press, Cambridge, MA, 1985.

[Perry, 1991] Nigel Perry. *The Implementation of Practical Functional Programming Languages*. PhD thesis, Imperial College of Science, Technology and Medicine, University of London, 1991.

[Prawitz, 1965] Dag Prawitz. *Natural Deduction—a Proof-Theoretic Study*. Alqvist and Wiksell, Stockholm, 1965.

[Rebelsky, 1992] Samuel A. Rebelsky. I/O trees and interactive lazy functional programming. In Maurice Bruynooghe and Martin Wirsing, editors, *Proceedings of the Fourth International Symposium on Programming Language Implementation and Logic Programming*, volume 631 of *Lecture Notes in Computer Science*, pages 458–472. Springer-Verlag, August 1992.

[Rebelsky, 1993] Samuel A. Rebelsky. *Tours, a System for Lazy Term-Based Communication*. PhD thesis, The University of Chicago, June 1993.

[Rees Clinger, 1986] The Revised[3] report on the algorithmic language Scheme. *ACM SIGPLAN Notices*, 21(12):37–79, 1986.

[Reiter, 1978] Raymond Reiter. On closed world databases. In Hervé Gallaire and Jack Minker, editors, *Logic and Databases*, pages 149–178. Plenum Press, 1978. also appeared as [Reiter, 1981].

[Reiter, 1981] Raymond Reiter. On closed world databases. In Bonnie Lynn Webber and Nils J. Nilsson, editors, *Readings in Artificial Intelligence*, pages 119–140. Tioga, Palo Alto, CA, 1981.

[Reiter, 1984] Raymond Reiter. Towards a logical reconstruction of relational database theory. In Michael L. Brodie, John Mylopoulos, and Joachim W. Schmidt, editors, *On Conceptual Modelling—Perspectives from Artificial Intelligence, Databases, and Programming Languages*, Topics in Information Systems, pages 191–233. Springer-Verlag, 1984.

[Reynolds, 1973] John C. Reynolds. On the interpretation of Scott's domains. In *Proceedings of Convegno d'Informatica Teorica*, Rome, Italy, February 1973. Instituto Nazionale di Alta Matematica (Citta Universitaria).

[Schmidt, 1986] David A. Schmidt. *Denotational Semantics: A Methodology for Language Development*. Allyn and Bacon, 1986.

[Schutte, 1977] Kurt Schutte. *Proof Theory.* Springer-Verlag, New York, NY, 1977.

[Scott and Strachey, 1971] Dana Scott and Christopher Strachey. Toward a mathematical semantics for computer languages. In *Proceedings of the Symposium on Computers and Automata*, pages 19–46, Polytechnic Institute of Brooklyn, 1971.

[Scott, 1970] Dana Scott. *Outline of a Mathematical Theory of Computation*, volume PRG-2 of *Oxford Monographs*. Oxford University Press, Oxford, UK, 1970.

[Scott, 1976] Dana Scott. Data types as lattices. *SIAM Journal on Computing*, 5(3), 1976.

[Scott, 1982] Dana Scott. Domains for denotational semantics. In M. Nielsen and E. M. Schmidt, editors, *Automata, Languages and Programming—Ninth Colloquium*, volume 140 of *Lecture Notes in Computer Science*, pages 577–613. Springer-Verlag, Berlin, 1982.

[Stark, 1990] W. Richard Stark. *LISP, Lore, and Logic—An Algebraic View of LISP Programming, Foundations, and Applications*. Springer-Verlag, New York, NY, 1990.

[Stenlund, 1972] Sören Stenlund. *Combinators, λ-Terms, and Proof Theory*. D. Reidel, Dordrecht, Netherlands, 1972.

[Stoy, 1977] Joseph E. Stoy. *Denotational Semantics: The Scott-Strachey Approach to Programming Language Theory*. MIT Press, Cambridge, MA, 1977.

[Tait, 1967] William W. Tait. Intensional interpretation of functionals of finite type. *Journal of Symbolic Logic*, 32(2):187–199, 1967.

[Takeuti, 1975] Gaisi Takeuti. *Proof Theory.* North-Holland, Amsterdam, 1975.

[Thompson, 1990] Simon Thompson. Interactive functional programs, a method and a formal formal semantics. In David A. Turner, editor, *Research Topics in Functional Programming*. Addison-Wesley, 1990.

[van Emden and Kowalski, 1976] M. H. van Emden and R. A. Kowalski. The semantics of predicate logic as a programming language. *Journal of the ACM*, 23(4):733–742, 1976.

[Wand, 1976] Mitchell Wand. First order identities as a defining language. *Acta Informatica*, 14:336–357, 1976.

[Webster, 1987] *Webster's Ninth New Collegiate Dictionary*. Merriam-Webster Inc., Springfield, MA, 1987.

[Williams and Wimmers, 1988] John H. Williams and Edward L. Wimmers. Sacrificing simplicity for convenience: Where do you draw the line? In *Proceedings of the Fifteenth Annual ACM Symposium on Principles of Programming Languages*, pages 169–179. ACM, 1988.

[Winksel, 1993] Glynn Winksel. *The Formal Semantics of Programming Languages—An Introduction*. Foundations of Computing. MIT Press, Cambridge, MA, 1993.

[Zhang, 1991] Guo-Qiang Zhang. *Logic of Domains*. Progress in Theoretical Computer Science. Birkhauser, Boston, MA, 1991.

Equational Logic Programming
Michael J. O'Donnell

Contents

1 Introduction to equational logic programming

1.1 Survey of prerequisites

Sections 2.3.4 and 2.3.5 of the chapter 'Introduction: Logic and Logic Programming Languages' are crucial prerequisites to this chapter. I summarize their relevance below, but do not repeat their content.

Logic programming languages in general are those that compute by deriving semantic consequences of given formulae in order to answer questions. In equational logic programming languages, the formulae are all equations expressing postulated properties of certain functions, and the questions ask for equivalent normal forms for given terms. Section 2.3.4 of the 'Introduction ...' chapter gives definitions of the models of equational logic, the semantic consequence relation

$$\mathbf{T} \models_{\doteq} (t_1 \doteq t_2)$$

($t_1 \doteq t_2$ is a semantic consequence of the set $\mathbf{T}$ of equations, see Definition 2.3.14), and the question answering relation

$$(\mathbf{norm}\ t_1, \ldots, t_i : t)\ {?\!\!-}_{\doteq} (t \doteq s)$$

($t \doteq s$ asserts the equality of t to the normal form s, which contains no instances of $t_1, \ldots, t_i$, see Definition 2.3.16). Since this chapter is entirely about Equational Logic, we drop the subscripts and write $\models$ for $\models_{\doteq}$ and ${?\!\!-}$ for ${?\!\!-}_{\doteq}$. The composed relation

$$(\mathbf{norm}\ t_1, \ldots, t_i : t)\ {?\!\!-}\ \mathbf{T} \models (t \doteq s)$$

($t \doteq s$ is a semantically correct answer to the question $(\mathbf{norm}\ t_1, \ldots, t_i : t)$ for knowledge $\mathbf{T}$, see Definition 2.2.2) means that s is a normal form—a term containing no instances of $t_1, \ldots, t_i$—whose equality to t is a semantic consequence of the equations in $\mathbf{T}$. Equational logic programming languages in use today all take sets $\mathbf{T}$ of equations, prohibited forms $t_1, \ldots, t_i$, and terms t to normalize, and they compute normal forms s satisfying the relation above.

Section 2.3.5 of the 'Introduction ...' chapter explains how different equational languages variously determine $\mathbf{T}$, $t_1, \ldots, t_i$, and t from the language design, the program being executed, and the input. An alternate style of equational logic programming, using questions of the form $(\mathbf{solve}\ x_1, \ldots, x_i : t_1 \doteq t_2)$ that ask for substitutions for $x_1, \ldots, x_i$ solving the equation $(t_1 \doteq t_2)$, is very attractive for its expressive power, but much harder to implement efficiently (see Section 7.2).

There is a lot of terminological confusion about equational logic programming. First, many in the Prolog community use 'logic' to mean the first-order predicate calculus (FOPC), while I stick closer to the dictionary meaning of logic, in which FOPC is one of an infinity of possible logical systems. Those who identify logic with FOPC often use the phrase 'equational logic programming' to mean some sort of extension of Prolog using equations, such as logic programming in FOPC with equality. In this chapter, 'equational logic programming' means the logic programming of pure equational logic, as described in the chapter 'Introduction: Logic and Logic Programming Languages.'

A second source of confusion is that many equational logic programming languages have been invented under different labels. Lisp [McCarthy, 1960], APL [Iverson, 1962], Red languages [Backus, 1974], functional programming languages [Backus, 1978; Hudak, 1992], many dataflow languages [Ashcroft and Wadge, 1985; Pingali and Arvind, 1985; Pingali and Arvind, 1986], and languages for algebraic specification of abstract datatypes [Futatsugi *et al.*, 1985; Guttag and Horning, 1978; Wand, 1976] are all forms of equational logic programming languages, although they are seldom referred to as such. This chapter focuses on a generic notion of equational logic programming, rather than surveying particular languages.

1.2 Motivation for programming with equations

From a programmer's point of view, an equational logic programming language is the same thing as a functional programming language[Backus, 1978]. The advantages of functional programming languages are discussed in [Hudak, 1989; Bird and Wadler, 1988; Field and Harrison, 1988]— equational logic programming languages offer essentially the same advantages to the programmer. Functional programming and equational logic programming are different views of programming, which provide different ways of designing and describing a language, but they yield essentially the same class of possible languages. The different styles of design and description, while they allow the same range of possibilities, influence the sense of naturalness of different languages, and therefore the relative importance of certain features to the designer and implementer. The most important impact of the equational logic programming view on language design is the strong motivation that it gives to implement *lazy,* or *demand-driven,* computation.

In the conventional view of functional programming, computation is the *evaluation* of an input term in a *unique* model associated with the programming language. This view makes it very natural to evaluate a term of the form $f(s_1, \ldots, s_n)$ by first evaluating all of the arguments s_i, and then applying the function denoted by f to the values of the arguments. If the attempt to evaluate one of the arguments leads to infinite computation, then the value of that argument in the model is said to be an object called 'undefined' (the word is used here as a *noun,* although the dictionary recognizes it only as an adjective), and typically denoted by the symbol $\bot$. But, since the value $\bot$ is indicated by the behavior of infinite computation, there is no chance to actually apply the function denoted by f to it, so that every function is forced to map $\bot$ to $\bot$. Such functions are called *strict* functions.

Early functional programming languages required all primitive functions to be strict, except for the conditional function *cond*. The normal

Michael J. O'Donnell

way to evaluate a term of the form $cond(s, t, u)$ is to evaluate s, then use
its value to determine which of t or u to evaluate, omitting the other. The
function denoted by $cond$ is thus not strict, since for example the value
of $cond(true, 0, \bot)$ is 0 rather than $\bot$. Only Backus seems to have been
annoyed by the inconsistency between the nonstrictness of the conditional
function and the strictness of all other primitives. He proposed a strict
conditional, recovering the selective behavior of the nonstrict conditional
through a higher-order coding trick [Backus, 1978]. In effect, he took advantage of the nearly universal unconscious acceptance of a nonstrict interpretation of function *application,* even when the function to be applied
is strict.

In the equational logic programming view, computation is the derivation of an equivalent normal form for an input term using the information
given by a set of equations describing the symbols of the programming
language. The equivalence of input to output holds in *all* of the infinitely
many models of those equations. This view makes it very natural to apply equations involving f to derive an equivalent form for $f(s_1, \ldots, s_n)$ at
any time, possibly before all possible derivation has been performed on the
arguments s_i. The natural desire for *completeness* of an implementation requires that infinite computation be avoided whenever possible. Notice that
the equational logic programming view does not *assign* a value $\bot$ denoting
'undefined' (the noun) to a term with infinite computational behavior. In
fact, in each individual model all functions are total. Rather, we might observe that a term is *undefined* (the word is now an adjective, as approved by
the dictionary) if there is no equivalent term suitable for output, although
each model of the given equations assigns it some value. So, equational
logic programming leads naturally to computational behavior that is not
strict—in fact, a logically complete implementation of equational logic programming must make functions as unstrict as possible. The preference for
nonstrictness comes from regarding undefinedness as our inability to discover the value of a function, rather than the inherent lack of a semantic
value.

The contrast between strict and nonstrict treatments of functions is
best understood by comparing the conventional implementation of *cond,*
true and *false* to that of *cons, car* and *cdr* in Lisp.

Example 1.2.1. The following equations define the relationship between
cond, true, and *false*:

$$\mathbf{T}_{cond} = \{(cond(true, x, y) \doteq x),\ (cond(false, x, y) \doteq y)\}$$

Similarly the following equations define the relationship between *cons, car,*
and *cdr*:

$$\mathbf{T}_{cons} = \{(car(cons(x, y)) \doteq x),\ (cdr(cons(x, y)) \doteq y)\}$$

These equations were given, without explicit restriction, in the earliest published definition of Lisp [McCarthy, 1960].

Notice the formal similarity between $\mathbf{T}_{cond}$ and $\mathbf{T}_{cons}$ in Example 1.2.1 above. In both cases, two equations provide a way to select one of the two subterms denoted by the variables x and y. In $\mathbf{T}_{cond}$, the selection is determined by the first argument to *cond*, in $\mathbf{T}_{cons}$ it is determined by the function symbol applied to the term headed by *cons*. Yet in all early Lisp implementations *cons* is evaluated strictly, while *cond* is not. The equation $(car(cons(0, s)) \doteq 0)$ is a logical consequence of $\mathbf{T}_{cons}$, even when s leads to infinite computation, so a complete implementation of equational logic programming must *not* treat *cons* strictly.

In the Lisp and functional programming communities, nonstrict evaluation of functions other than the conditional is called *lazy evaluation*. The power of lazy evaluation as a programming tool is discussed in [Friedman and Wise, 1976; Henderson and Morris, 1976; Henderson, 1980; Hudak, 1989; Bird and Wadler, 1988; Field and Harrison, 1988; O'Donnell, 1985]. Lazy evaluation is *demand-driven*—computation is performed only as required to satisfy demands for output. So, the programmer may define large, and even infinite, data structures as intermediate values, and depend on the language implementation to compute only the relevant parts of those structures. In particular, lazily computed lists behave as *streams* [Karlsson, 1981; Hudak and Sundaresh, 1988], allowing a straightforward encoding of pipelined coroutines in a functional style.

Many modern implementations of functional programming languages offer some degree of lazy evaluation, and a few are now uniformly lazy. But, in the functional programming view, lazy evaluation is an optional added feature to make programming languages more powerful. The basic denotational semantic approach to functional programming makes strictness very natural to describe, while denotational semantics for lazy evaluation seems to require rather sophisticated use of domain theory to construct models with special values representing all of the relevant nonterminating and partially terminating behaviors of terms [Winksel, 1993]. In the equational logic programming view, lazy evaluation is required for logical completeness, and strict evaluation is an arbitrary restriction on derivations that prevents certain answers from being found.

The functional and equational views also diverge in their treatments of certain terms that are viewed as pathological. From the functional programming view, pathological terms seem to require specialized logical techniques treating errors as values, and even new types of models called *error algebras* [Goguen, 1977]. For example, in a language with stacks, the term *pop(empty)* is generally given a value which is a token denoting the erroneous attempt to pop an empty stack. Given a set of equations, equational logic programming provides a conceptual framework, based on well-understood traditional concepts from mathematical logic, for prescribing completely the computational behavior of terms. The judgement that a particular term is pathological is left to the consumer of that answer, which might be a human reader or another program. For example, the term *pop(empty)* need not be evaluated to an error token: it may be output as a normal form, and easily recognized as a pathological case by the consumer. Or, an explicit equation $pop(empty) \doteq e$ may be added to the program, where *e* gives as much or as little detailed information about the particular error as desired.

So, for the programmer there is nothing to choose between lazy functional programming and equational logic programming—these are two styles for describing the same programming languages, rather than two different classes of programming languages. To the language designer or implementor, the functional programming view provides a connection to a large body of previous work, and offers some sophisticated tools for the thorough description of the processing of erroneous programs and the use of varying degrees of strictness or laziness. The equational logic programming view offers a deeper explanation of the logical content of computations, a way of defining correctness of the computation of answers independently of the classification of programs as correct or erroneous, and a strong motivation for uniformly lazy evaluation. It also connects equational/functional programming to other sorts of logic programming in a coherent way, which may prove useful to future designs that integrate equational/functional programming with other styles.

1.3   Outline of the chapter

The next part of this chapter is primarily concerned with problems in the implementation of equational logic programming and some interesting variants of it. Those problems arise at four very different levels of abstraction—logic, strategy, algorithm, and code. At the level of pure logic, Section 2 discusses two different formal systems of proof for equational logic—inferential proof and term rewriting proof—and argues that the latter is logically weaker in general, but more likely to provide efficient computation for typical equational programs. The *confluence property* of sets of equations is introduced, and shown to be a useful way of guaranteeing that term rewriting proof can succeed. Next, Section 3 treats high-level strategic questions in the efficient search for a term rewriting proof to answer a given question. The crucial problem is to choose the next rewriting step out of a number of possibilities, so as to guarantee that all correct answers are found, and to avoid unnecessary steps. Then, Section 4 discusses the design of efficient algorithms and data structures for finding and choosing rewriting steps, and for representing the results of rewriting. Section 5 contains a brief description of the conventional machine code that a compiler can generate based on these algorithms and data structures. Section 6 discusses briefly some of the problems involved in parallel implementation of equational logic programming. Finally, Section 7 treats several possible extensions to the functionality of equational logic programming and the problems that arise in their semantics and implementation.

2 Proof systems for equational logic

The basic idea in implementations of equational logic programming is to search for a proof that provides a correct answer to a given question. The basic idea behind proofs in equational logic is that the equation $t_1 \doteq t_2$ allows t_1 and t_2 to be used interchangeably in other formulae. As in Definition 3.1.1, of the chapter 'Introduction: Logic and Logic Programming Languages,' $\mathbf{T} \mid D - F$ means that D is a correct proof of the formula F from hypotheses in $\mathbf{T}$. $\mathbf{T} \vdash F$ means that there exists a proof of F from hypotheses in $\mathbf{T}$. In this chapter, subscripts on the generic symbols $\mid -$ and $\vdash$ are omitted whenever the particular proof system is clear from the context.

In Sections 2.1 and 2.2, we consider two different styles of equational proof. Inferential proofs derive equations step by step from other equations. Term rewriting proofs use equations to transform a given term into a provably equivalent term by substituting equals for equals.

2.1 Inferential proofs

In order to explore a variety of approaches to proving equations, we first define generic concepts of rules of inference and proofs using rules, and then consider the power of various sets of rules.

Definition 2.1.1. Let the set $\mathbf{V}$ of variables, the sets $\mathbf{Fun}_i$ of i-ary function symbols, and the set $\mathbf{T}_P$ of terms, be the same as in Definition 2.3.1 of the 'Introduction ...' chapter Section 2.3, and let the set of *equational formulae*, or simply *equations*, be $\mathbf{F}_{\doteq} = \{t_1 \doteq t_2 : t_1, t_2 \in \mathbf{T}_P\}$, as in Definition 2.3.13 in Section 2.3.4 of the chapter 'Introduction: Logic and Logic Programming Languages.'

An *equational rule of inference* is a binary relation

$$\mathcal{R} \subseteq 2^{\mathbf{F}_{\doteq}} \times \mathbf{F}_{\doteq}$$

When $\mathbf{T} \, \mathcal{R} \, F$, we say that F *follows from* $\mathbf{T}$ by rule $\mathcal{R}$. Members of $\mathbf{T}$ are called *hypotheses* to the application of the rule, and F is the *conclusion*. When $\emptyset \, \mathcal{R} \, F$, we call F a *postulate*. (It is popular now to call a postulated formula F an *axiom*, although the dictionary says that an axiom must be self-evident, not just postulated.) Rules of inference are usually presented in the form

$$\frac{H_1,\ldots,H_m}{C}$$

Where $H_1 \ldots, H_m$ are schematic descriptions of the hypotheses, and C is a schematic description of the conclusion of an arbitrary application of the rule. Notice that the union of rules of inference is itself a rule.

The set of *inferential equational proofs* is $\mathbf{P}_{\doteq} = \mathbf{F}_{\doteq}^+$, the set of nonempty finite sequences of equations. Given a rule of inference $\mathcal{R}$, the proof relation

$$\vdash_{\mathcal{R}} \subseteq 2^{\mathbf{F}_{\doteq}} \times \mathbf{P}_{\doteq} \times \mathbf{F}_{\doteq}$$

is defined by

$$\mathbf{T} \mid \langle F_0,\ldots,F_m \rangle \vdash_{\mathcal{R}} F \text{ if and only if } F_m = F \text{ and,}$$
for all $i \le m$, one of the following cases holds:

1. $F_i \in \mathbf{T}$
2. There exist $j_1,\ldots,j_n < i$ such that $\{F_{j_1},\ldots,F_{j_n}\} \, \mathcal{R} \, F_i$

So, a proof of F from hypotheses in $\mathbf{T}$ using rule $\mathcal{R}$ is a sequence of equations, each one of which is either a hypothesis, or it follows from previous equations by the rule $\mathcal{R}$. The following are popular rules of inference for proofs in equational logic.

Definition 2.1.2.

$$\text{Reflexive} \quad \frac{}{s \doteq s}$$

$$\text{Symmetric} \quad \frac{s \doteq t}{t \doteq s}$$

$$\text{Transitive} \quad \frac{r \doteq s, \ s \doteq t}{r \doteq t}$$

$$\text{Instantiation} \quad \frac{s \doteq t}{s[r/x] \doteq t[r/x]}$$

$$\text{Substitution} \quad \frac{s \doteq t}{r[s/x] \doteq r[t/x]}$$

$$\text{Congruence} \quad \frac{s_1 \doteq t_1,\ldots,s_m \doteq t_m}{f(s_1,\ldots,s_m) \doteq f(t_1,\ldots,t_m)}$$

Now, when $\mathcal{R}$ is the union of any of the rules presented above, $\langle \mathbf{F}_{\doteq}, \mathbf{P}_{\doteq},$ $| -_{\mathcal{R}} \rangle$ is a compact proof system (Definition 2.1.3, Section 2.1).

The rules above are somewhat redundant. Every proof system using a subset of these rules is sound, and those using the Reflexive, Symmetric, Transitive and Instantiation rules, and at least one of Substitution and Congruence, are also complete.

Proposition 2.1.3. *Let $\mathcal{R}$ be the union of any of the rules in Definition 2.1.2. Then $\langle \mathbf{F}_{\doteq}, \mathbf{P}_{\doteq}, | -_{\mathcal{R}} \rangle$ is a sound proof system for the standard semantic system of Definition 2.3.14, Section 2.3.4 of the chapter 'Introduction: Logic and Logic Programming Languages.' That is, $\mathbf{T} \vdash_{\mathcal{R}} (t_1 \doteq t_2)$ implies $\mathbf{T} \models (t_1 \doteq t_2)$.*

The proof of soundness is an elementary induction on the number of steps in a formal equational proof, using the fact that each of the rules of inference proposed above preserves truth.

Proposition 2.1.4. *Let $\mathcal{R}$ be the union of the Reflexive, Symmetric, Transitive, and Instantiation rules, and at least one of the Substitution and Congruence rules. Then $\langle \mathbf{F}_{\doteq}, \mathbf{P}_{\doteq}, | -_{\mathcal{R}} \rangle$ is a complete proof system. That is, $\mathbf{T} \models (t_1 \doteq t_2)$ implies $\mathbf{T} \vdash_{\mathcal{R}} (t_1 \doteq t_2)$.*

To prove completeness, we construct for each set $\mathbf{T}$ of equations, a term model $M_{\mathbf{T}}$ such that $\mathbf{Theory}(\{M_{\mathbf{T}}\})$ contains exactly the semantic consequences of $\mathbf{T}$. For each term $t \in \mathbf{T}_P$,

$$|t|_{\mathbf{T}} = \{s : \mathbf{T} \vdash_{\mathcal{R}} (s \doteq t)\}$$

Because $\mathcal{R}$ includes the Reflexive, Symmetric, and Transitive rules, provable equality is an equivalence relation on terms, and $|t|_{\mathbf{T}}$ is the equivalence class containing t. Now, construct the model

$$M_{\mathbf{T}} = \langle U_{\mathbf{T}}, \tau_{\mathbf{T}} \rangle$$

whose universe is

$$U_{\mathbf{T}} = \{|t|_{\mathbf{T}} : t \in \mathbf{T}_P\}$$

and whose function assignment is defined by

$$\tau_{\mathbf{T}}(f)(|t_1|_{\mathbf{T}}, \ldots, |t_i|_{\mathbf{T}}) = |f(t_1, \ldots, t_i)|_{\mathbf{T}}$$

Either of the rules Substitution and Congruence is sufficient to guarantee that $\tau_{\mathbf{T}}$ is well defined. Finally, the Instantiation rule guarantees that $\mathbf{T} \vdash (s \doteq t)$ if and only if $\tau_{\mathbf{T}\nu}(s) = \tau_{\mathbf{T}\nu}(t)$ for all variable assignments ν, which by Definition 2.3.14 is equivalent to $\mathbf{T} \models (s \doteq t)$.

Notice that each inference by the Congruence rule is derivable by k applications of the Substitution rule, combined by the Transitive rule. In effect, Congruence is just a special form of multiple simultaneous substitution. Similarly, each inference by the Substitution rule is derivable by repeated applications of the Congruence rule and additional instances of the Reflexive rule (this can be proved easily by induction on the structure of the term r on which substitution is performed in the Substitution rule).

In the rest of this chapter, the symbols $\vdash_{\inf}$ and $\vdash_{\inf}$ refer to a sound and complete system of inferential equational proof, when the precise rules of inference are not important.

2.2   Term rewriting proofs

The most commonly used methods for answering normal form questions (**norm** $t_1, \ldots, t_i : t$) all involve replacing subterms by equal subterms, using the Substitution rule, to transform the term t into an equivalent normal form. Substitution of subterms according to given rules is called *term rewriting,* and is an interesting topic even when the rewriting rules are not given by equations (see the chapter 'Equational Reasoning and Term Rewriting Systems' in Volume 1). In this chapter, we are concerned only with the use of term rewriting to generate equational proofs—this technique is also called *demodulation* [Loveland, 1978] in the automated deduction literature.

Definition 2.2.1. Let $\mathbf{T} = \{l_1 \doteq r_1, \ldots, l_n \doteq r_n\}$ be a set of equations. Recall that an *instance* of a formula or term is the result of substituting terms for variables (Definition 2.3.5 in Section 2.3.1 of the chapter 'Introduction: Logic and Logic Programming Languages').

A term s_1 *rewrites to* s_2 *by* $\mathbf{T}$ (written $s_1 \xrightarrow{\mathbf{T}} s_2$) if and only if there is a term t, a variable x with exactly one occurrence in t, and an instance $l_i' \doteq r_i'$ of an equation $l_i \doteq r_i$ in $\mathbf{T}$, such that $s_1 = t[l_i'/x]$ and $s_2 = t[r_i'/x]$. That is, s_2 results from finding exactly one instance of a left-hand side of an equation in $\mathbf{T}$ occurring as a subterm of s_1, and replacing it with the corresponding right-hand side instance.

A *term rewriting sequence* for $\mathbf{T}$ is a nonempty finite or infinite sequence $\langle u_0, u_1, \ldots \rangle$ such that, for each i, $u_i \xrightarrow{\mathbf{T}} u_{i+1}$.

Term rewriting sequences formalize the natural intuitive process of replacing equals by equals to transform a term. A term rewriting sequence may be viewed as a somewhat terse proof.

Definition 2.2.2. Let $\mathbf{T}_P^+$ be the set of nonempty finite sequences of terms in $\mathbf{T}_P$. The proof relation $\vdash_{tr}$ is defined by $\mathbf{T} \vdash \langle u_0, \ldots, u_m \rangle \vdash_{tr} (s \doteq t)$ if and only if $u_0 = s$, $u_m = t$, and for each $i < m$, $u_i \xrightarrow{\mathbf{T}} u_{i+1}$.

Then $\langle \mathbf{F}_{\doteq}, \mathbf{T}_P^+, \vdash_{tr} \rangle$, is a compact proof system, representing the *term rewriting* style of equational proof.

A term rewriting proof for **T** represents an inferential proof from hypotheses in **T** in a natural way.

Proposition 2.2.3. *If* $\mathbf{T} \vdash_{\mathrm{tr}} (s \doteq t)$, *then* $\mathbf{T} \vdash_{\mathrm{inf}} (s \doteq t)$.

Let $\langle u_0, \ldots, u_n \rangle$ *be the term rewriting sequence such that*

$$\mathbf{T} \mid \langle u_0, \ldots, u_n \rangle \dashv_{\mathrm{tr}} (s \doteq t)$$

In particular, $u_0 = s$ and $u_n = t$. The proof of the proposition is an elementary induction on n.

BASIS: *For $n = 0$, $s = u_0 = u_n = t$, so $\mathbf{T} \mid \langle u_0 \doteq u_0 \rangle \dashv_{\mathrm{inf}} (s \doteq t)$, by the Reflexive rule.*

INDUCTION: *For $n > 0$, since a nonempty prefix of a term rewriting proof is also a term rewriting proof, we have $\mathbf{T} \mid \langle u_0, \ldots, u_{n-1} \rangle \dashv_{\mathrm{tr}} (s \doteq u_{n-1})$. By the induction hypothesis, there is a D such that $\mathbf{T} \mid D \dashv_{\mathrm{inf}} (s \doteq u_{n-1})$. It is easy to extend D to D' so that $\mathbf{T} \mid D' \dashv (s \doteq t)$, by adding the following steps:*

- *the appropriate equation from **T**;*

- *a sequence of applications of the Instantiation rule to produce the appropriate instance of the equation above;*

- *one application of the Substitution rule to produce $u_{n-1} \doteq t$;*

- *one application of the Transitive rule to produce $s \doteq t$.*

Since inferential proof is sound, it follows that term rewriting proof is also sound.

Example 2.2.4. Let $\mathbf{T} = \{ f(a, f(x, y)) \doteq f(y, x), \; g(x) \doteq x \}$.

$$\langle f(g(a), f(g(b), c)), \; f(a, f(g(b), c)), \; f(c, g(b)), \; f(c, b) \rangle$$

is a term rewriting proof of

$$f(g(a), f(g(b), c)) \doteq f(c, b)$$

from **T**. The corresponding inferential proof from the induction in Proposition 2.2.3 is given below. Line numbers are added on the left, and rules cited on the right, for clarity: formally the proof is just the sequence of equations. The key occurrences of the terms in the term rewriting sequence above are boxed to show the correspondence.

$\langle$

1	$f(g(a), f(g(b), c))$	$\doteq$	$\boxed{f(g(a), f(g(b), c))}$	,	*Reflexive*
2	$g(x)$	$\doteq$	x	,	*Hypothesis*
3	$g(a)$	$\doteq$	a	,	*Instantiation,2*
4	$f(g(a), f(g(b), c))$	$\doteq$	$f(a, f(g(b), c))$	,	*Substitution,3*
5	$f(g(a), f(g(b), c))$	$\doteq$	$\boxed{f(a, f(g(b), c))}$	,	*Transitive,1, 3*
7	$f(a, f(x, y))$	$\doteq$	$f(y, x)$	,	*Hypothesis*
8	$f(a, f(g(b), y))$	$\doteq$	$f(y, g(b))$	,	*Instantiation,7*
9	$f(a, f(g(b), c))$	$\doteq$	$f(c, g(b))$	,	*Instantiation,8*
10	$f(a, f(g(b), c))$	$\doteq$	$f(c, g(b))$	,	*Substitution,9*
11	$f(g(a), f(g(b), c))$	$\doteq$	$\boxed{f(c, g(b))}$	,	*Transitive,1, 10*
12	$g(x)$	$\doteq$	x	,	*Hypothesis*
13	$g(b)$	$\doteq$	b	,	*Instantiation,12*
14	$f(c, g(b))$	$\doteq$	$f(c, b)$	,	*Substitution,13*
15	$f(g(a), f(g(b), c))$	$\doteq$	$\boxed{f(c, b)}$		*Transitive,1, 14*

$\rangle$

Steps 5, 10, and 12 above are redundant (they reproduce the results already obtained in steps 4, 9, 2), but the systematic procedure in the induction of Proposition 2.2.3 includes them for uniformity.

So, a term rewriting proof is a convenient and natural shorthand for an inferential proof.

Not every inferential proof corresponds to a term rewriting proof. First, the proofs corresponding to term rewriting sequences do not use the Symmetric rule. This represents a serious incompleteness in term rewriting proof. Section 2.3 shows how restrictions on equational hypotheses can avoid the need for the Symmetric rule, and render term rewriting complete for answering certain normal form questions.

Example 2.2.5. Let $\mathbf{T} = \{a \doteq b, \ c \doteq b, \ c \doteq d\}$. $\mathbf{T} \models (a \doteq d)$, and $\mathbf{T} \vdash_{\inf} (a \doteq d)$, by one application of the Symmetric rule and two applications of the Transitive rule. But, there is no term rewriting sequence from a to d, nor from d to a, nor from a and d to a common form equal to both.

Second, term rewriting proofs limit the order in which the Instantiation, Substitution, and Transitive rules are applied. This second limitation does not affect the deductive power of the proof system.

Proposition 2.2.6. Let $\mathbf{T} = \{l_1 \doteq r_1, \ldots, l_n \doteq r_n\}$ be a set of equations. Let $\mathbf{T}^R = \{r_1 \doteq l_1, \ldots, r_n \doteq l_n\}$. $\mathbf{T}^R$ is the same as $\mathbf{T}$ except that the left and right sides of equations are interchanged—equivalently, $\mathbf{T}^R$ contains *the results of applying the Symmetric rule to the equations in* **T**.

For all equations $(s \doteq t)$, if **T** $\vdash_{\inf} (s \doteq t)$ (equivalently, if **T** $\models (s \doteq t)$) then **T** $\cup$ **T**^{R} $\vdash_{\mathrm{tr}} (s \doteq t)$.

The proof of the proposition, given in more detail in [O'Donnell, 1977], works by permuting the steps in an arbitrary inferential proof of $s \doteq t$ into the form:

1. hypotheses;
2. applications of the Symmetric rule;
3. applications of the Instantiation rule;
4. applications of the Substitution rule;
5. applications of the Transitive rule.

The reflexive rule is only needed in the degenerate case when $s = t$ (s and t are the same term). In this form, it is easy to represent each of the applications of the Transitive rule as concatenating two term rewriting sequences. The crucial quality of the permuted form of the proof is that all uses of the Instantiation rule come before any use of the Transitive and Substitution rules.

The implementor of a logic programming system often faces a trade-off between the cost of an individual proof, and the cost of the search for that proof. The discipline of term rewriting can be very advantageous in reducing the number of possible steps to consider in the search for a proof to answer a question, but it increases the lengths of proofs in some cases. Section 4.3.3 shows how clever uses of Instantiation sometimes reduce the length of a proof substantially compared to term rewriting proofs. Efficient implementations of programming languages have not yet succeeded in controlling the costs of search for a proof with the more sophisticated approaches to Instantiation, so term rewriting is the basis for almost all implementations.

2.3 The confluence property and the completeness of term rewriting

Term rewriting is often much more efficient than an undisciplined search for an equational proof. But, for general sets **T** of equational hypotheses, term rewriting is not complete, due to its failure to apply the Symmetric rule. It is tempting, then, to use each equation in both directions, and take advantage of the completeness result of Proposition 2.2.6. Unfortunately, known techniques for efficient term rewriting typically fail or become inefficient when presented with the reversed forms of equations. So, we find special restrictions on equations that imply the completeness of term rewriting for the answering of particular normal form questions. The *confluence property*, also called the *Church–Rosser property*, provides the key to such restrictions.

Definition 2.3.1. Let $\rightarrow$ be a binary relation, and $\rightarrow^*$ be its reflexive–transitive closure. $\rightarrow$ is *confluent* if and only if, for all s, t_1, t_2 in its domain such that $s \rightarrow^* t_1$ and $s \rightarrow^* t_2$, there exists a u such that $t_1 \rightarrow^* u$ and $t_2 \rightarrow^* u$ (see Figure 1 B)

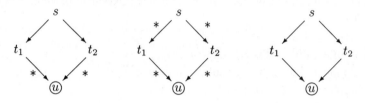

A. Local confluence   B. Confluence   C. One-step confluence

The circle around u indicates that it is existentially quantified, the uncircled s, t_1, t_2 are universally quantified.

Fig. 1. Confluence and related properties.

Two similar properties that are very important in the literature are *local confluence,* which is weaker than confluence, and *one-step confluence,* which is stronger than confluence.

Definition 2.3.2 ([Newman, 1942]). Let $\rightarrow$ be a binary relation, and $\rightarrow^*$ be its reflexive–transitive closure. $\rightarrow$ is *locally confluent* if and only if, for all s, t_1, t_2 in its domain such that $s \rightarrow t_1$ and $s \rightarrow t_2$, there exists a u such that $t_1 \rightarrow^* u$ and $t_2 \rightarrow^* u$ (see Figure 1 A).

While confluence guarantees that divergent term rewriting sequences may always be rewritten further to a common form, local confluence guarantees this only for single step term rewriting sequences.

Definition 2.3.3 ([Newman, 1942]). Let $\rightarrow$ be a binary relation. $\rightarrow$ is *locally confluent* if and only if, for all s, t_1, t_2 in its domain such that $s \rightarrow t_1$ and $s \rightarrow t_2$, there exists a u such that $t_1 \rightarrow u$ and $t_2 \rightarrow u$ (see Figure 1 C).

While confluence guarantees that divergent term rewriting sequences may always be rewritten further to a common form, one-step confluence guarantees that for single step divergences, there is a single-step convergence.

Proposition 2.3.4. *One-step confluence implies confluence implies local confluence.*

The first implication is a straightforward induction on the number of steps in the diverging rewrite sequences. The second is trivial.

2.3.1 Consequences of confluence

When the term rewriting relation $\overset{\text{T}}{\to}$ for a set **T** of equations has the confluence property, term rewriting is sufficient for deriving all logical consequences of **T**, in the sense that $\mathbf{T} \models (s \doteq t)$ implies that s and t rewrite to some common form u.

Proposition 2.3.5 ([Curry and Feys, 1958]). *Let* **T** *be a set of equations, and let* $\overset{\text{T}}{\to}$ *be the term rewriting relation for* **T** *(Definition 2.2.1). If* $\overset{\text{T}}{\to}$ *is confluent, then for all terms* s *and* t *such that* $\mathbf{T} \models (s \doteq t)$, *there is a term* u *such that* $\mathbf{T} \vdash_{\text{tr}} (s \doteq u)$ *and* $\mathbf{T} \vdash_{\text{tr}} (t \doteq u)$.

The proof of the proposition is an elementary induction on the length of an inferential proof D *such that* $\mathbf{T} \mid D \dashv_{\text{inf}} (s \doteq t)$.

So, confluent term rewriting is nearly complete, in the sense that every logical consequence $s \doteq t$ of a set of equations **T** may be derived by choosing an appropriate term u, and finding two term rewriting proofs and a trivial inferential proof as follows:

1. $\mathbf{T} \vdash_{\text{tr}} (s \doteq u)$
2. $\mathbf{T} \vdash_{\text{tr}} (t \doteq u)$
3. $\{s \doteq u,\ t \doteq u\} \vdash_{\text{inf}} (s \doteq t)$ trivially, by one application of Symmetry and one application of Transitivity.

The near-completeness of confluent term rewriting leads to its use in theorem proving [Knuth and Bendix, 1970; Loveland, 1978]. For equational logic programming, term rewriting can answer all normal form queries in a confluent system, when the prohibited terms in normal forms are all the left-hand sides of equations.

Proposition 2.3.6. *Let* $\mathbf{T} = \{l_1 \doteq r_1, \ldots, l_m \doteq r_m\}$ *be a set of equations, with confluent term rewriting relation* $\overset{\text{T}}{\to}$, *and let* t *be any term. If*

$$(\textbf{norm}\ l_1, \ldots, l_m : t)\ \text{?-} \ \mathbf{T} \models (t \doteq s)$$

then

$$(\textbf{norm}\ l_1, \ldots, l_m : t)\ \text{?-} \ \mathbf{T} \vdash_{\text{tr}} (t \doteq s)$$

The proof is elementary. By confluence, t *and* s *rewrite to a common form* u. *Since* s *is a normal form, it is not rewritable, and must be the same as* u.

So, for equations **T** with confluent rewriting relation, term rewriting based on **T** is sufficient for answering all queries requesting normal forms that prohibit left-hand sides of equations in **T**. From now on, a *normal form* will mean a normal form for the left-hand sides of whatever set of equations we are discussing (see Definition 2.3.16 in the chapter 'Introduction: Logic and Logic Programming Languages' for the general concept of *normal form*).

The most famous consequence of the confluence property is uniqueness of normal forms.

Proposition 2.3.7.   *Let* $\mathbf{T} = \{l_1 \doteq r_1, \ldots, l_m \doteq r_m\}$ *be a set of equations, with confluent term rewriting relation* $\overset{\mathbf{T}}{\to}$. *If*

$$(\mathbf{norm}\, l_1, \ldots, l_m : t) \,?\!\!-\, \mathbf{T} \models (t \doteq s_1)$$

and

$$(\mathbf{norm}\, l_1, \ldots, l_m : t) \,?\!\!-\, \mathbf{T} \models (t \doteq s_2)$$

then $s_1 = s_2$ (s_1 *and* s_2 *are the same term).*

The proof is elementary. By confluence, s_1 and s_2 rewrite to a common form u. Since s_1 and s_2 are normal forms, they are not rewritable, and must be the same as u.

So, equational logic programs using confluent systems of equations have uniquely defined outputs. This is an interesting property to note, but it is not essential to the logic programming enterprise—logic programs in FOPC are allowed to have indeterminate answers (Section 2.3.1 of the 'Introduction' chapter), and this freedom is often seen as an advantage. In efficient equational logic programming, confluence is required for the completeness of term rewriting, and uniqueness of answers is an accidental side-effect that may be considered beneficial or annoying in different applications. Confluence, in effect, guarantees that the order of applying rewrite steps cannot affect the normal form. In Section 3 we see that the order of application of rewrite rules *can* affect the efficiency with which a normal form is found, and in some cases whether or not the unique normal form is found at all.

2.3.2   Testing for confluence

Proposition 2.3.8. *Confluence is an undecidable property of finite sets of equations.*

The proof is straightforward. Given an arbitrary Turing Machine $\mathcal{M}$, *modify* $\mathcal{M}$ *so that, if it halts, it does so in the special configuration* I_f. *Encode configurations (instantaneous descriptions) of* $\mathcal{M}$ *as terms (just let the tape and state symbols be unary function symbols), and provide rewriting rules to simulate the computation of* $\mathcal{M}$. *So far, we have a system of equations in which an arbitrary encoding of an initial configuration* I_0 *rewrites to* I_f *if and only if* $\mathcal{M}$ *halts on* I_0. *Choose a new symbol a not used in encoded configurations, and add two more equations:* $I_0 \doteq a$ *and* $I_f \doteq a$. *The extended system is confluent if and only if* $\mathcal{M}$ *halts on* I_0.

For practical purposes in programming language implementations, we need a *sufficient* condition for confluence that is efficient to test.

Orthogonality. A particularly useful sort of condition for guaranteeing confluence is *orthogonality*, also called *regularity* (but not connected in any sensible way to the regular languages). Orthogonality is a set of restrictions on rewrite rules insuring that they do not interfere with one another in certain pathological ways. We consider three versions of orthogonality. *Rewrite-orthogonality* insures that the rewrites performed by the rules do not interfere, while the stronger condition of *rule-orthogonality* prohibits even the appearance of interference based on an inspection of the left-hand sides of the rules, and ignoring the right-hand sides. *Constructor-orthogonality* is an even stronger and simpler syntactic condition that guarantees rule-orthogonality. In other literature on term rewriting, 'orthogonality' and 'regularity' refer to the stronger form, rule-orthogonality.

Definition 2.3.9. Let $\mathbf{T} = \{l_1 \doteq r_1, \ldots, l_n \doteq r_n\}$ be a set of equations. $\mathbf{T}$ is *rewrite-orthogonal* if and only if the following conditions hold:

1. (Nontrivial) No left-hand side l_i of an equation $l_i \doteq r_i$ in $\mathbf{T}$ consists entirely of a variable.
2. (Rule-like) Every variable in the right-hand side r_i of an equation $l_i \doteq r_i$ in $\mathbf{T}$ occurs in the left-hand side l_i as well.
3. (Left-linear) No variable occurs more than once in the left-hand side l_i of an equation $l_i \doteq r_i$ in $\mathbf{T}$.
4. (Rewrite-Nonambiguous) Let l_i and l_j be left-hand sides of equations in $\mathbf{T}$, and let s be a term with a single occurrence of a new variable y (not occurring in any equation of $\mathbf{T}$). If

$$s[l_i[t_1, \ldots, t_m/x_1, \ldots, x_m]/y] = l_j[t'_1, \ldots, t'_n/x'_1, \ldots, x'_n]$$

then either s is an instance of l_j, or

$$s[r_i[t_1, \ldots, t_m/x_1, \ldots, x_m]/y] = r_j[t'_1, \ldots, t'_n/x'_1, \ldots, x'_n]$$

In clause 4 the nested substitution may be hard to read.

$$s[r_i[t_1, \ldots, t_m/x_1, \ldots, x_m]/y]$$

is the result of substituting $t_1, \ldots, t_m$ for $x_1, \ldots, x_m$ in r_i, to produce $r'_i = r_i[t_1, \ldots, t_m/x_1, \ldots, x_m]$, then substituting r'_i for y in s. Clause 4 is best understood by considering an example where it fails. The set of equations $\{f(g(v, w), x) \doteq a,\ g(h(y), z) \doteq b\}$ is rewrite-ambiguous because, in the term $f(g(h(c), d), e)$, there is an instance of $f(g(w, x))$ and an instance of $g(h(y), z)$, and the two instances share the symbol g. Furthermore, $f(g(h(c), d), e)$ rewrites to a using the first equation, and to a different result, $f(b, e)$, using the second equation.

Nontriviality and the Rule-like property are required in order for the interpretation of the equations as term rewriting rules to make much sense.

Left-linearity is of practical importance because the application of a rule with repeated variables on the left-hand side requires a test for equality. Non-left-linear systems also fail to be confluent in rather subtle ways, as shown in Example 2.3.16 below. Rewrite-nonambiguity says that if two rewriting steps may be applied to the same term, then they are either completely independent (they apply to disjoint sets of symbols), or they are equivalent (they produce the same result). Example 2.3.16 below shows more cases of rewrite-ambiguity and its consequences.

One simple way to insure rewrite-nonambiguity is to prohibit all interference between left-hand sides of rules.

Definition 2.3.10 (Klop [1991; 1980]).   Let $\mathbf{T} = \{l_1 \doteq r_1, \ldots, l_n \doteq r_n\}$ be a set of equations. $\mathbf{T}$ is *rule-orthogonal* if and only if $\mathbf{T}$ satisfies conditions 1–3 of Definition 2.3.9 above, and also

    4′ (Rule-Nonambiguous) Let l_i and l_j be left-hand sides of equations in $\mathbf{T}$, and let s be a term with a single occurrence of a new variable y (not occurring in any equation of $\mathbf{T}$). If

$$s[l_i[t_1, \ldots, t_m/x_1, \ldots, x_m]/y] = l_j[t'_1, \ldots, t'_n/x'_1, \ldots, x'_n]$$

    then either s is an instance of l_j, or $s = y$ and $i = j$.

Rule-nonambiguity says that if two rewriting steps may be applied to the same term, then they are either completely independent, or they are identical (the same rule applied at the same place). Notice that rule nonambiguity depends only on the left-hand sides of equations, not the right-hand sides. In fact, only the Rule-like condition of rule-orthogonality depends on right-hand sides.

Definition 2.3.11.   Two systems of equations are *left-similar* if the multisets of left-hand sides of equations are the same, except for renaming of variables.

Proposition 2.3.12.   *A set $\mathbf{T}$ of equations is rule-orthogonal if and only if*

- $\mathbf{T}$ *satisfies the rule-like restriction, and*
- *every rule-like set of equations left-similar to $\mathbf{T}$ is rewrite-orthogonal.*

That is, rule-orthogonality holds precisely when rewrite-orthogonality can be guaranteed by the forms of the left-hand sides alone, independently of the right-hand sides.

An even simpler way to insure rule-nonambiguity is to use a *constructor* system, in which symbols appearing leftmost in rules are not allowed to appear at other locations in left-hand sides.

Definition 2.3.13.   Let $\mathbf{T} = \{l_1 \doteq r_1, \ldots, l_n \doteq r_n\}$ be a set of equations. $\mathbf{T}$ is *constructor-orthogonal* if and only if $\mathbf{T}$ satisfies conditions 1–3 of

Definition 2.3.9 above, and the symbols of the system partition into two disjoint sets—the set $\mathbf{C}$ of *constructor symbols*, and the set $\mathbf{D}$ of *defined symbols*, satisfying

4″ (Symbol-Nonambiguous)

- Every left-hand side of an equation in $\mathbf{T}$ has the form $f(t_1, \ldots, t_m)$, where $f \in \mathbf{D}$ is a defined symbol, and $t_1, \ldots, t_m$ contain only variables and constructor symbols in $\mathbf{C}$.
- Let l_i and l_j be left-hand sides of equations in $\mathbf{T}$. If there exists a common instance s of l_i and l_j, then $i = j$.

In most of the term-rewriting literature, 'orthogonal' and 'regular' both mean *rule-orthogonal*. It is easy to see that constructor orthogonality implies rule-orthogonality, which implies rewrite-orthogonality. Most functional programming languages have restrictions equivalent or very similar to constructor-orthogonality.

Orthogonal systems of all varieties are confluent.

Proposition 2.3.14. *Let* $\mathbf{T}$ *be a constructor-, rule- or rewrite-orthogonal set of equations. Then the term rewriting relation* $\xrightarrow{\mathbf{T}}$ *is confluent.*

Let $\rightarrow$ *be the rewrite relation that is to be proved confluent. The essential idea of these, and many other, proofs of confluence is to choose another relation* $\rightarrow'$ *with the one-step confluence property (Definition 2.3.3, whose transitive closure is the same as the transitive closure of* $\rightarrow$. *Since confluence is defined entirely in terms of the transitive closure,* $\rightarrow$ *is confluent if and only if* $\rightarrow'$ *is confluent.* $\rightarrow'$ *is confluent because one-step confluence implies confluence. To prove confluence of orthogonal systems of equations, the appropriate* $\rightarrow'$ *allows simultaneous rewriting of any number of disjoint subterms.*

Theorem 10.1.3 of the chapter 'Equational Reasoning and Term-Rewriting Systems' in Section 10.1 of Volume 1 of this handbook is the rewrite-orthogonal portion of this proposition, which is also proved in [Huet and Lévy, 1991; Klop, 1991]. The proof for rewrite-orthogonal systems has never been published, but it is a straightforward generalization. [O'Donnell, 1977] proves a version intermediate between rule-orthogonality and rewrite-orthogonality.

In fact, for nontrivial, rule-like, left-linear systems, rule-nonambiguity captures precisely the cases of confluence that depend only on the left-hand sides of equations.

Proposition 2.3.15. *A nontrivial, rule-like, left-linear set* $\mathbf{T}$ *of equations is rule-nonambiguous if and only if, for every set of equations* $\mathbf{T}'$ *left-similar to* $\mathbf{T}$, $\xrightarrow{\mathbf{T}'}$ *is confluent.*

($\Rightarrow$) is a direct consequence of Propositions 2.3.14 and 2.3.12. ($\Leftarrow$) is straightforward. In a rule-ambiguous system, simply fill in each right-hand

side with a different constant symbol, not appearing on any left-hand side, to get a nonconfluent system.

In the rest of this chapter, we use the term 'orthogonal' in assertions that hold for both rewrite- and rule-orthogonality. To get a general understanding of orthogonality, and its connection to confluence, it is best to consider examples of nonorthogonal systems and investigate why they are not confluent, as well as a few examples of systems that are not rule orthogonal, but are rewrite orthogonal, and therefore confluent.

Example 2.3.16. The first example, due to Klop [Klop, 1980], shows the subtle way in which non-left-linear systems may fail to be confluent. Let

$$\mathbf{T}_1 = \{eq(x,x) \doteq \mathit{true},\ f(x) \doteq eq(x,f(x)),\ a \doteq f(a)\}$$

eq represents an equality test, a very useful operation to define with a non-left-linear equation. Now

$$f(a) \overset{\mathbf{T}_1}{\to} eq(a,f(a)) \overset{\mathbf{T}_1}{\to} eq(f(a),f(a)) \overset{\mathbf{T}_1}{\to} \mathit{true}$$

and also

$$f(a) \overset{\mathbf{T}_1}{\to} f(f(a)) \overset{\mathbf{T}_1}{\to} f(eq(a,f(a))) \overset{\mathbf{T}_1}{\to} f(eq(f(a),f(a))) \overset{\mathbf{T}_1}{\to} f(\mathit{true})$$

true is in normal form, and $f(\mathit{true})$ rewrites infinitely as

$$f(\mathit{true}) \overset{\mathbf{T}_1}{\to} eq(\mathit{true},f(\mathit{true})) \overset{\mathbf{T}_1}{\to} eq(\mathit{true},eq(\mathit{true},f(\mathit{true}))) \overset{\mathbf{T}_1}{\to} \cdots$$

The system is not confluent, because the attempt to rewrite $f(\mathit{true})$ to *true* yields an infinite regress with $f(\mathit{true}) \overset{\mathbf{T}_1}{\to} eq(\mathit{true},f(\mathit{true}))$. Notice that $\overset{\mathbf{T}_1}{\to}$ has unique normal forms. The failure of confluence involves a term with a normal form, and an infinite term rewriting sequence from which that normal form cannot be reached. Non-left-linear systems that satisfy the other requirements of rule-orthogonality always have unique normal forms, even when they fail to be confluent [Chew, 1981]. I conjecture that this holds for rewrite-orthogonality as well.

A typical rewrite-ambiguous set of equations is

$$\mathbf{T}_2 = \{c(a,y) \doteq a,\ c(x,b) \doteq b\}$$

c represents a primitive sort of *nondeterministic choice* operator. $\mathbf{T}_2$ violates condition (4′) because

$$w[c(a,y)[b/y]/w] = c(a,b) = c(x,b)[a/x]$$

but

$$w[a[b/y]/w] = a \neq b = b[a/x]$$

$\overset{\mathbf{T_2}}{\to}$ is not confluent, as $c(a,b) \overset{\mathbf{T_2}}{\to} a$ by the first equation, and $c(a,b) \overset{\mathbf{T_2}}{\to} b$ by the second equation, but a and b are in normal form.

By contrast, consider the set

$$\mathbf{T}_{or+} = \{or(true, y) \doteq true, \ or(x, true) \doteq true\}$$

of equations defining the *positive parallel or* operator. Although $\mathbf{T}_{or+}$ is rule-ambiguous, it is *rewrite*-nonambiguous:

$$w[or(true, y)[true/y]/w] = or(true, true) = or(x, true)[true/x]$$

and w is not an instance of $or(x, true)$, but the corresponding right-hand sides are both *true*:

$$w[true[true/y]/w] = true = true[true/x]$$

$\mathbf{T}_{or+}$ is rewrite-orthogonal, so $\overset{\mathbf{T}_{or+}}{\to}$ is confluent.

A more subtle example of a rewrite-orthogonal set of equations that is rule-ambiguous is the *negative parallel or:*

$$\mathbf{T}_{or-} = \{or(false, y) \doteq y, \ or(x, false) \doteq x\}$$

Although

$$w[or(false, y)[false/y]/w] = or(false, false) = or(x, false)[false/x]$$

and w is not an instance of $or(x, false)$, the substitution above unifies the corresponding right-hand sides as well:

$$y[false/y] = false = x[false/x]$$

$\mathbf{T}_{or-}$ is rewrite-orthogonal, so $\overset{\mathbf{T}_{or-}}{\to}$ is confluent.

Another type of rewrite-ambiguous set of equations is

$$\mathbf{T}_3 = \{f(g(x, y)) \doteq g(f(x), f(y)), \ g(i, z) \doteq z\}$$

These equations express the fact that f is a *homomorphism* for g (i.e., f *distributes* over g), and that i is a *left identity* for g. The left-hand sides of the two equations overlap in $f(g(i, z))$, with the symbol g participating in instances of the left-hand sides of both equations. Condition (4) is violated, because

$$f(w)[g(i, z)[y/z]/w] = f(g(i, y)) = f(g(x, y))[i/x]$$

but $f(w)$ is not an instance of $f(g(x,y))$. $\overset{\mathbf{T_3}}{\rightarrow}$ is not confluent, as $f(g(i,i)) \overset{\mathbf{T_3}}{\rightarrow}$ $g(f(i), f(i))$ by the first equation, and $f(g(i,i)) \overset{\mathbf{T_3}}{\rightarrow} f(i)$ by the second equation, but both $g(f(i), f(i))$ and $f(i)$ are in normal form. While the previous examples of ambiguity involved two rules applying to precisely the same term, the ambiguity in $\mathbf{T_3}$ comes from two overlapping applications of rules to a term and one of its subterms. Some definitions of orthogonality/regularity treat these two forms of ambiguity separately.

By contrast, consider the set

$$\mathbf{T_4} = \{f(g(x,y)) \doteq f(y),\ g(i,z) \doteq z\}$$

Although $\mathbf{T_4}$ is rule-ambiguous, it is *rewrite*-nonambiguous:

$$f(w)[g(i,z)[y/z]/w] = f(g(i,y)) = f(g(x,y))[i/x]$$

and $f(w)$ is not an instance of $f(g(x,y))$, but the corresponding right-hand sides yield

$$f(w)[z[z/z]/w] = f(z) = f(y)[i, z/x, y]$$

$\mathbf{T_4}$ is rewrite-orthogonal, so $\overset{\mathbf{T_4}}{\rightarrow}$ is confluent.

Condition (4) may also be violated by a single self-overlapping equation, such as

$$\mathbf{T_5} = \{f(f(x)) \doteq g(x)\}$$

The left-hand side $f(f(x))$ overlaps itself in $f(f(f(x)))$, with the second instance of the symbol f participating in two different instances of $f(f(x))$. Condition (4) is violated, because

$$f(y)[f(f(x))/y] = f(f(f(x))) = f(f(x))[f(x)/x]$$

but $f(y)$ is not an instance of $f(f(x))$. $\overset{\mathbf{T_5}}{\rightarrow}$ is not confluent, as $f(f(f(a))) \overset{\mathbf{T_5}}{\rightarrow}$ $g(f(a))$ and $f(f(f(a))) \overset{\mathbf{T_5}}{\rightarrow} f(g(a))$, but both $g(f(a))$ and $f(g(a))$ are in normal form.

A final example of overlapping left-hand sides is

$$\mathbf{T_6} = \{f(g(a,x),y) \doteq a,\ g(z,b) \doteq b\}$$

The left-hand sides of the two equations overlap in $f(g(a,b),y)$, with the symbol g participating in instances of the left-hand sides of both equations. Condition (4) is violated, because

$$f(w,y)[g(z,b)[a/z]/w] = f(g(a,b),y) = f(g(a,x),y)[b/x]$$

but $f(w,y)$ is not an instance of $f(g(a,x),y)$. $\overset{\mathbf{T_6}}{\rightarrow}$ is not confluent, as $f(g(a,b),c) \overset{\mathbf{T_6}}{\rightarrow} a$ by the first equation, and $f(g(a,b),c) \overset{\mathbf{T_6}}{\rightarrow} f(b,c)$ by the second equation, but both a and $f(b,c)$ are in normal form.

The equations for combinatory logic

$$\mathbf{T}_{SK} = \{@(@(@(S,x),y),z) \doteq @(@(x,z),@(y,z)), \ @(@(K,x),y) \doteq x\}$$

are rule-orthogonal, but not constructor-orthogonal, since the symbol @ (standing for application of a function to an argument) appears leftmost and also in the interior of left-hand sides. In more familiar notation, $@(\alpha, \beta)$ is written $(\alpha\beta)$, and leftward parentheses are omitted, so the equations look like

$$Sxyz \doteq xz(yz), \ Kxy \doteq x$$

Many functional programming languages vary the definition of constructor-orthogonality to allow pure applicative systems (the only symbol of arity greater than zero is the apply symbol @) in which the *zeroary* symbols (S and K in the example above) are partitioned into defined symbols and constructors.

The equations for addition of Horner-rule form polynomials in the symbolic variable V (V is a variable in the polynomials, but is treated formally as a constant symbol in the equations) are

$$\mathbf{T}_{poly} = \{ \quad +(+(w,*(V,x)),+(y,*(V,z))) \doteq +(+(w,y),*(V,+(x,z))),$$
$$+(w,+(y,*(V,z))) \doteq +(+(w,y),*(V,z)),$$
$$+(+(w,*(V,x)),y) \doteq +(+(w,y),*(V,x)) \quad \}$$

This system is rule-orthogonal, but not constructor-orthogonal, because the symbols $+$ and $*$ appear leftmost and also in the interior of left-hand sides. In the more familiar infix form for $+$ and $*$, the equations look like

$$(w + V * x) + (y + V * z) \doteq (w + y) + V * (x + z),$$
$$w + (y + V * z) \doteq (w + y) + V * z,$$
$$(w + V * x) + y \doteq (w + y) + V * x$$

No natural variation on the definition of constructor-orthogonality seems to allow these equations. The only obvious way to simulate their behavior with a constructor-orthogonal system is to use two different symbols for addition, and two different symbols for multiplication, depending on whether the operation is active in adding two polynomials, or is merely part of the representation of a polynomial in Horner-rule form.

Although the polynomial example above shows that some natural sets of equations are rule-orthogonal but not constructor-orthogonal, Thatte has an automatic translation from rule-orthogonal to constructor-orthogonal systems [Thatte, 1985] showing that in some sense the programming power of the two classes of systems is the same. I still prefer to focus attention on the more general forms of orthogonality, because they deal more directly with the intuitive forms of equations, and because I believe that improved equational logic programming languages of the future will deal with even more general sets of equations, so I prefer to discourage dependence on the special properties of constructor systems.

Knuth–Bendix Methods. Although overlapping left-hand sides of equations *may* destroy the confluence property, there are many useful equational programs that are confluent in spite of overlaps. In particular, the equation expressing the associative property has a self-overlap, and equations expressing distributive or homomorphic properties often overlap with those expressing identity, idempotence, cancellation, or other properties that collapse a term. These overlaps are usually benign, and many useful equational programs containing similar overlaps are in fact confluent.

Example 2.3.17. Consider the singleton set

$$\mathbf{T}_7 = \{g(x, g(y, z)) \doteq g(g(x, y), z)\}$$

expressing the *associative* law for the operator g. This equation has a self-overlap, violating condition (4) of rewrite-orthogonality (Definition 2.3.9) because

$$g(w, u)[g(x, g(y, z))/u] = g(w, g(x, g(y, z)))$$
$$= g(x, g(y, z))[w, x, g(y, z)/x, y, z]$$

but the corresponding right-hand sides disagree:

$$g(w, u)[g(g(x, y), z)/u] = g(w, g(g(x, y), z))$$
$$\neq$$
$$g(g(w, x), g(y, z)) = g(g(x, y), z)[w, x, g(y, z)/x, y, z]$$

Nonetheless, $\overset{\mathbf{T}_7}{\rightarrow}$ is confluent. For example, while

$$g(a, g(b, g(c, d))) \overset{\mathbf{T}_7}{\rightarrow} g(a, g(g(b, c), d))$$

and

$$g(a, g(b, g(c, d))) \overset{\mathbf{T}_7}{\rightarrow} g(g(a, b), g(c, d))$$

by different applications of the equation, the two results rewrite to a common normal form by

$$g(a, g(g(b, c), d)) \overset{\mathbf{T}_7}{\rightarrow} g(g(a, g(b, c)), d) \overset{\mathbf{T}_7}{\rightarrow} g(g(g(a, b), c), d)$$

and

$$g(g(a, g(b, c)), d) \overset{\mathbf{T}_7}{\rightarrow} g(g(g(a, b), c), d)$$

Consider also the set

$$\mathbf{T_8} = \{f(g(x,y)) \doteq g(f(x), f(y)), \ g(i, z) \doteq z, \ f(i) \doteq i\}$$

expressing the distribution of f over g, and the fact that i is a left identity for g and a fixed point for f. The first and second equations overlap, violating condition (4) of rewrite-orthogonality, because

$$f(w)[g(i, z)/w] = f(g(i, z)) = f(g(x, y))[i, z/x, y]$$

but the corresponding right-hand sides disagree:

$$f(w)[z/w] = f(z) \neq g(f(i), f(z)) = g(f(x), f(y))[i, z/x, y]$$

Nonetheless, $\overset{\mathbf{T_8}}{\rightarrow}$ is confluent. For example, while

$$f(g(i, a)) \overset{\mathbf{T_8}}{\rightarrow} g(f(i), f(a))$$

by the first equation and

$$f(g(i, a)) \overset{\mathbf{T_8}}{\rightarrow} f(a)$$

by the second equation, the first result rewrites to the second, which is in normal form, by

$$g(f(i), f(a)) \overset{\mathbf{T_8}}{\rightarrow} g(i, f(a)) \overset{\mathbf{T_8}}{\rightarrow} f(a)$$

Notice that $\mathbf{T_8} = \mathbf{T_3} \cup \{f(i) \doteq i\}$, and that confluence failed for $\mathbf{T_3}$ (Example 2.3.16).

Experience with equational logic programming suggests that most naively written programs contain a small number of benign overlaps, which are almost always similar to the examples above. An efficient test for confluence in the presence of such overlaps would be extremely valuable.

The only known approach to proving confluence in spite of overlaps is based on the Knuth–Bendix procedure [Knuth and Bendix, 1970]. This procedure relies on the fact that local confluence (Definition 2.3.2) is often easier to verify than confluence, and that local confluence plus termination imply confluence.

Proposition 2.3.18 ([Newman, 1942]). *If $\rightarrow$ is locally confluent, and there is no infinite sequence $s_0 \rightarrow s_1 \rightarrow \cdots$, then $\rightarrow$ is confluent.*

The proof is a simple induction on the number of steps to normal form.

Unfortunately, a system with nonterminating rewriting sequences may be locally confluent, but not confluent.

Example 2.3.19. $\mathbf{T_1}$ of Example 2.3.16 is locally confluent, but not confluent.

94   *Michael J. O'Donnell*

Consider also the set of equations

$$\mathbf{T}_9 = \{a \doteq b,\ b \doteq a,\ a \doteq c,\ b \doteq d\}$$

$\overset{\mathbf{T}_9}{\to}$ is locally confluent, but not confluent. Notice how confluence fails due to the two-step rewritings $a \overset{\mathbf{T}_9}{\to} b \overset{\mathbf{T}_9}{\to} d$ and $b \overset{\mathbf{T}_9}{\to} a \overset{\mathbf{T}_9}{\to} c$ (see Figure 2).

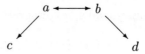

Fig. 2. $\mathbf{T}_9$ is locally confluent, but not confluent.

Another example, without a rewriting loop, is the set of equations

$$\mathbf{T}_{10} = \{f(x) \doteq g(h(x)),\ g(x) \doteq g(h(x)),\ f(x) \doteq c,\ g(x) \doteq d\}$$

$\overset{\mathbf{T}_{10}}{\to}$ is locally confluent, but not confluent. Again, confluence fails due to the two-step rewritings $f(x) \overset{\mathbf{T}_{10}}{\to} g(h(x)) \overset{\mathbf{T}_{10}}{\to} d$ and $g(x) \overset{\mathbf{T}_{10}}{\to} f(h(x)) \overset{\mathbf{T}_{10}}{\to} c$ (see Figure 3).

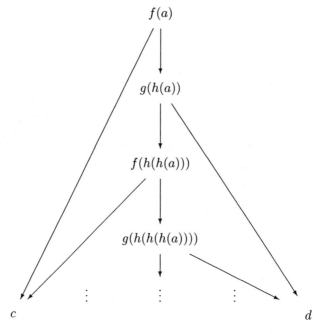

Fig. 3. $\mathbf{T}_{10}$ is locally confluent, but not confluent.

The Knuth–Bendix procedure examines overlaps one at a time to see whether they destroy the local confluence property. Given a pair of equations $l_1 \doteq r_1$ and $l_2 \doteq r_2$ be such that their left-hand sides overlap—i.e., there is a term $s \neq y$ with one occurrence of y such that

$$s[l_1[t_1, \ldots, t_m/x_1, \ldots, x_m]/y] = l_2[t_1', \ldots, t_n'/x_1', \ldots, x_n']$$

but s is not an instance of l_2. For each s, l_1 and l_2, use the smallest $t_1, \ldots, t_m$ and $t_1', \ldots, t_n'$ that satisfy this equation. The results of rewriting the instance of s above in two different ways, according to the overlapping instances of equations, are $c_1 = s[r_1[t_1, \ldots, t_m/x_1, \ldots, x_m]/y]$ and $c_2 = r_2[t_1', \ldots, t_n'/x_1', \ldots, x_n']$. The pair $\langle c_1, c_2 \rangle$ is called a *critical pair*. A finite set of equations generates a finite set of critical pairs, since only a finite number of ss can be compatible with some l_2, but not an instance of l_2. The procedure checks all critical pairs to see if they rewrite to a common normal form. If so, the system is locally confluent.

Proposition 2.3.20 ([Huet, 1980]). *Let* **T** *be a set of equations. If for every critical pair* $\langle c_1, c_2 \rangle$ *of* **T** *there is a term d such that $c_1 \overset{T}{\to}{}^* d$ and $c_2 \overset{T}{\to}{}^* d$, then $\overset{T}{\to}$ is locally confluent.*

This proposition, and the Knuth–Bendix method, apply even to non-left-linear sets of equations. For example, the local confluence of $\mathbf{T}_1$ in Example 2.3.16 may be proved by inspecting all critical pairs.

When some critical pair cannot be rewritten to a common form, the Knuth–Bendix procedure tries to add an equation to repair that failure of local confluence. For equational logic programming, we would like to use just the part of the procedure that checks local confluence, and leave it to the programmer to decide how to repair a failure. Although, in principle, the search for a common form for a critical pair might go on forever, in practice a very shallow search suffices. I have never observed a natural case in which more than two rewriting steps were involved. Unfortunately, many useful equational programs have nonterminating term rewriting sequences, so local confluence is not enough. The design of a variant of the Knuth–Bendix procedure that is practically useful for equational logic programming is an open topic of research—some exploratory steps are described in [Chen and O'Donnell, 1991]. A number of methods for proving termination are known [Dershowitz, 1987; Guttag *et al.*, 1983], which might be applied to portions of an equational program even if the whole program is not terminating, but we have no experience with the practical applicability of these methods. If the rewriting of the terms c_1 and c_2 in a critical pair to a common form d (see Proposition 2.3.20) takes no more than one rewriting step (this is *one-step confluence*, Definition 2.3.3), then we get confluence and not just local confluence. Rewrite-orthogonal systems are those whose critical pairs are all trivial—the members of the pair are equal, and so the reduction to a common form takes zero steps. Unfortunately, all of the important examples so far of confluent but not rewrite-orthogonal equational programs have the basic structure of associativity or distributivity (see Example 2.3.17) and require two rewriting steps to resolve their critical pairs.

The sets of equations in Example 2.3.17 pass the Knuth–Bendix test for local confluence, and a number of well-known techniques can be used to prove that there is no infinite term rewriting sequence in these systems. But, we need to recognize many variations on these example systems, when they are embedded in much larger sets of equations which generate some infinite term rewriting sequences, and no completely automated method has yet shown practical success at that problem (although there are special treatments of commutativity and associativity [Baird *et al.*, 1989; Dershowitz *et al.*, 1983]). On the other hand, in practice naturally constructed systems of equations that are locally confluent are almost always confluent. Surely someone will find a useful and efficient formal criterion to distinguish the natural constructions from the pathological ones of Example 2.3.19.

3   Term rewriting proof strategies

Given an orthogonal set of equations $\mathbf{T} = \{l_1 \doteq r_1, \ldots, l_m \doteq r_m\}$, or any set with confluent term rewriting relation $\overset{\mathbf{T}}{\to}$, we may now answer all questions of the form (**norm** $l_1, \ldots, l_m : t$) by exploring term rewriting sequences starting with t. Confluence guarantees that if there is an answer, some term rewriting sequence will find it (Proposition 2.3.6). Furthermore, confluence guarantees that no finite number of term rewriting steps can be catastrophic, in the sense that if $s \overset{\mathbf{T}}{\to}^* t$ and if s rewrites to a normal form, then t rewrites to the same normal form. Confluence, however, does not guarantee that no infinite term rewriting sequence can be catastrophic.

Example 3.0.1.   Consider the set of equations

$$\mathbf{T}_{11} = \{car(cons(x,y)) \doteq x,\ a \doteq f(a)\}$$

The first equation is the usual definition of the *car* (left projection) function of Lisp, the second is a silly example of an equation leading to infinite term rewriting. $\mathbf{T}_{11}$ is orthogonal, so $\overset{\mathbf{T}_{11}}{\to}$ is confluent. But $car(cons(b,a))$ rewrites to the normal form b, and also in the infinite rewriting sequence $car(cons(b,a)) \overset{\mathbf{T}_{11}}{\to} car(cons(b,f(a))) \overset{\mathbf{T}_{11}}{\to} \cdots$.

Notice that, due to confluence, no matter how far we go down the infinite term rewriting sequence $car(cons(b,a)) \overset{\mathbf{T}_{11}}{\to} car(cons(b,f(a))) \overset{\mathbf{T}_{11}}{\to} \cdots$, one application of the first equation leads to the normal form b. Nonetheless, a naive strategy might fail to find that normal form by making an infinite number of unfortunate rewrites. In fact, the usual recursive evaluation techniques used in Lisp and other term-evaluating languages correspond to term rewriting strategies that choose infinite sequences whenever possible. A breadth-first search of all possible rewriting sequences is guaranteed to find all normal forms, but at the cost of a lot of unnecessary work.

For efficient implementation of equational logic programming, we need strategies for choosing term rewriting steps so that

- a small number of term rewriting sequences is explored, preferably only one;
- if there is a normal form, it is found, preferably by the shortest or cheapest sequence possible.

Some theoretical work on sequencing in the lambda calculus has already been explored under the title of *one-step strategies* [Barendregt, 1984].

3.1 Complete and outermost complete rewriting sequences

In orthogonal systems of equations, there are two useful results on strategies that are guaranteed to find normal forms. The formal notation for stating these results precisely is somewhat involved (see the chapter 'Equational Reasoning and Term Rewriting Systems' in Volume 1), so I only give rough definitions here. The concepts in this section can be extended to nonorthogonal systems, but in some cases there are very subtle problems in the extensions, and they have never been treated in the literature.

Definition 3.1.1 ([Huet and Lévy, 1991]). A *redex* is an occurrence of an instance of a left-hand side of an equation in a term. An *outermost* redex is one that is not nested inside any other redex. When α is a redex in s, and $s \xrightarrow{\text{T}}^* t$, the *residuals* of α in t are the redexes in t that correspond in the obvious way to α in s—they are essentially explicit copies of α, except that some rewriting step may have rewritten a subterm of α, so that some copies may be modified. All residuals of α are occurrences of instances of the same left-hand side as α.

Example 3.1.2. Consider the rule-orthogonal set of equations

$$\mathbf{T}_{12} = \{f(x) \doteq g(x,x),\ g(h(x),y) \doteq h(x),\ a \doteq b\}$$

The term $g(f(f(h(a))), f(h(a)))$ has five redexes: two occurrences each of the terms a and $f(h(a))$, and one occurrence of $f(f(h(a)))$. The latter two are both instances of the left-hand side $f(x)$ of the first equation. The leftmost occurrence of $f(h(a))$ is nested inside $f(f(h(a)))$, so it is not outermost. Each occurrence of a is nested inside an occurrence of $f(h(a))$, so neither is outermost. The rightmost occurrence of $f(h(a))$, and the sole occurrence of $f(f(h(a)))$, are both outermost redexes. In the rewriting sequence below, the leftmost occurrence of $f(h(a))$, and its residuals in each succeeding term, are boxed.

$$g(f(\boxed{f(h(a))}), f(h(a))) \xrightarrow{\mathbf{T}_{12}} g(g(\boxed{f(h(a))}, \boxed{f(h(a))}), f(h(a)))$$

$$\xrightarrow{\mathbf{T}_{12}} g(g(\boxed{f(h(b))}, \boxed{f(h(a))}), f(h(a)))$$

$$\xrightarrow{\mathbf{T}_{12}} g(g(g(h(b), h(b)), \boxed{f(h(a))}), f(h(a)))$$

$$\xrightarrow{\mathbf{T}_{12}} g(g(h(b), \boxed{f(h(a))}), f(h(a)))$$

$$\xrightarrow{\mathbf{T}_{12}} g(h(b), f(h(a)))$$

$$\xrightarrow{\mathbf{T}_{12}} h(b)$$

Notice how the leftmost occurrence of $f(h(a))$ in the first term of the sequence is copied into two occurrences in the second, due to the rewriting of a redex in which it is nested. The first of these is changed to $f(h(b))$ in the third term of the sequence, but it is still a residual of the original leftmost $f(h(a))$. In the fourth term of the sequence, $f(h(b))$ is rewritten, eliminating one of the residuals. In the sixth term, the remaining residual, still in the form $f(h(a))$, is eliminated due to rewriting of a redex in which it is nested. Another occurrence of $f(h(a))$ remains, but it is a residual of the rightmost occurrence of that term in the first term of the sequence.

In general, a residual α of a redex is eliminated when α is rewritten (or, in rewrite-orthogonal systems, when a redex overlapping α is rewritten). α is copied zero, one, or more times (zero times eliminates the residual) when another redex in which α is nested is rewritten. α remains the same when another redex disjoint from α is rewritten. Finally, α is modified in form, but remains an instance of the same left-hand side, when another redex nested inside α is rewritten.

In orthogonal systems, the nontrivial, rule-like, and nonambiguous qualities of equations (restrictions 1, 2, 4 or 4' of Definition 2.3.9 or 2.3.10) guarantee that a given redex may be rewritten in precisely one way. So, a term rewriting strategy need only choose a redex to rewrite at each step. The most obvious way to insure that all normal forms are found is to rewrite every redex fairly.

Definition 3.1.3 ([O'Donnell, 1977]). A finite or infinite term rewriting sequence $t_0 \to t_1 \to \cdots$ is *complete* (also called *fair*) if and only if, for every i and every redex α in t_i, there exists a $j > i$ such that t_j contains no residual of α.

A complete term rewriting sequence is fair to all redexes, in the sense that every redex α (or its residuals, which are essentially the later versions of the redex) eventually gets eliminated, either by rewriting α (with rewrite-orthogonality, a redex overlapping α), or by making zero copies of α while rewriting another redex in which α is nested. Complete term rewriting sequences are maximal, in the sense that they produce terms that are rewritten further than every other sequence. Since nothing is rewritten further than a normal form, complete sequences produce a normal form whenever there is one.

Proposition 3.1.4 ([O'Donnell, 1977]). *Let* $\mathbf{T}$ *be an orthogonal set of equations, let* $t_0 \xrightarrow{\mathbf{T}} t_1 \xrightarrow{\mathbf{T}} \cdots$ *be a complete rewriting sequence, and let* s *be any term such that* $t_0 \xrightarrow{\mathbf{T}}^* s$. *There exists an* i *such that* $s \xrightarrow{\mathbf{T}}^* t_i$. *In particular, if* s *is in normal form, then* $t_i = s$.

Computing a single complete term rewriting sequence is generally cheaper than searching breadth-first among a number of sequences, but fair rewriting strategies (such as the strategy of adding new redexes to a queue, and rewriting all residuals of the head redex in the queue) typically perform a substantial number of superfluous rewriting steps, and can easily waste an exponentially growing amount of work in some cases. Since a residual α of a redex may only be eliminated by rewriting α, or some redex inside which α is nested, we need only be fair to the outermost redexes in order to be sure of finding normal forms.

Definition 3.1.5 ([O'Donnell, 1977]). A finite or infinite term rewriting sequence $t_0 \to t_1 \to \cdots$ is *outermost complete* or *outermost fair* (called *eventually outermost* in [O'Donnell, 1977]) if and only if, for every i and every outermost redex α in t_i, there exists a $j > i$ such that the unique residual of α in t_{j-1} is either eliminated by rewriting in t_j, or is no longer outermost in t_j (equivalently, no residual of α is outermost in t_j).

Since, for the least j satisfying the definition above, α remains outermost from t_i through t_{j-1} and cannot be copied, there is no loss of generality in requiring the residual of α in t_{j-1} to be unique.

Proposition 3.1.6 ([O'Donnell, 1977]). *Let* $\mathbf{T}$ *be a rule-orthogonal set of equations, let* $t_0 \xrightarrow{\mathbf{T}} t_1 \xrightarrow{\mathbf{T}} \cdots$ *be an outermost complete rewriting sequence, and let* s *be a (unique) normal form for* t_0. *There exists an* i *such that* $t_i = s$.

[O'Donnell, 1977] proves this proposition for a form of orthogonality intermediate between rule- and rewrite-orthogonality. I conjecture that the proof generalizes to rewrite-orthogonality.

The requirement that $\mathbf{T}$ be orthogonal, and not just confluent, is essential to Proposition 3.1.6.

Example 3.1.7. Consider the set of equations

$$\mathbf{T}_{13} = \{f(g(x,b)) \doteq b, \ g(x,y) \doteq g(f(x),y), \ a \doteq b\}$$

These equations are confluent, but not rewrite-orthogonal, since the left-hand sides of the first and second equations overlap in $f(g(x, b))$, but the corresponding right-hand sides yield $b \neq f(g(f(x), b))$. The natural outermost complete rewriting sequence starting with $f(g(b, a))$ is the infinite one

$$f(g(b, a)) \stackrel{\mathbf{T}_{13}}{\rightarrow} f(g(f(b), a)) \stackrel{\mathbf{T}_{13}}{\rightarrow} f(g(f(f(b)), a)) \stackrel{\mathbf{T}_{13}}{\rightarrow} \cdots$$

But $f(g(b, a))$ rewrites to normal form by

$$f(g(b, a)) \stackrel{\mathbf{T}_{13}}{\rightarrow} f(g(b, b)) \stackrel{\mathbf{T}_{13}}{\rightarrow} b$$

The problem is that rewriting the nonoutermost redex a to b creates a new outermost redex for the first equation *above* the previously outermost one for the second equation. This leapfrogging effect allows an inner redex to kill an outer one indirectly, by creating another redex even closer to the root. There should be some interesting conditions, weaker than rewrite-orthogonality, that prohibit this leapfrogging effect and guarantee outermost termination for confluent systems.

The obvious way to generate outermost-complete rewriting sequences is to alternate between finding all outermost redexes, and rewriting them all. The order in which the outermost redexes are rewritten is irrelevant since they are all disjoint and cannot cause copying or modification of one another. Unfortunately, this strategy often generates a lot of wasted work. For example, consider a system containing the equations $\mathbf{T}_{cond}$ for the conditional function from Example 1.2.1

$$\mathbf{T}_{cond} = \{cond(true, x, y) \doteq x, \ cond(false, x, y) \doteq y\}$$

In a term of the form $cond(r, s, t)$, there will usually be outermost redexes in all three of r s and t. But, once r rewrites to either *true* or *false*, one of s and t will be thrown away, and any rewriting in the discarded subterm will be wasted. The *ad hoc* optimization of noticing when rewriting of one outermost redex immediately causes another to be nonoutermost sounds tempting, but it probably introduces more overhead in detecting such cases than it saves in avoiding unnecessary steps. Notice that it will help the *cond* example only when r rewrites to *true* or *false* in one step. So, we need some further analysis to choose which among several outermost redexes to rewrite.

3.2 Sequentiality analysis and optimal rewriting

For rewrite-orthogonal systems of equations in general, it is impossible to choose reliably a redex that *must* be rewritten in order to reach normal form, so that there is no risk of wasted work.

Example 3.2.1. Let $\mathbf{T}_c$ be equations defining some general-purpose programming system, such as Lisp. The forms of the particular equations in $\mathbf{T}_c$ are not important to this example, merely the fact that they are powerful enough for general-purpose programming. Assume that in the system $\mathbf{T}_c$ there is an effective way to choose a redex that must be rewritten to reach normal form (this is the case for typical definitions of Lisp). Now, add the *positive parallel-or* equations

$$\mathbf{T}_{or+} = \{\, or(true, x) \doteq true,\ or(x, true) \doteq true \,\}$$

and consider the system $\mathbf{T}_c \cup \mathbf{T}_{or+}$.

For an arbitrary given term $or(s, t)$, we would like to choose either s or t to rewrite first. If s rewrites to *true*, but t does not, then it is crucial to choose s, else work (possibly infinitely much work) will be wasted. Similarly, if t rewrites to *true*, but s does not, it is crucial to choose t. If *neither* s nor t rewrites to *true*, then both must be rewritten to normal form in order to normalize the whole term, so we may choose either. If *both* s and t rewrite to *true* then, ideally, we would like to choose the one that is cheapest to rewrite, but suppose that we are satisfied with either choice in this case also.

Suppose that we have an effective way to choose s or t above. Then, we have a *recursive separation* of the terms $or(s, t)$ in which s rewrites to *true* and t has no normal form from those in which t rewrites to *true* and s has no normal form. Such a separation is known to be impossible. (It would lead easily to a computable solution of the halting problem. See [Machtey and Young, 1978] for a discussion of *recursive inseparability*.) So, we cannot decide effectively whether to rewrite redexes in s or in t without risking wasted work.

The case where *both* s and t rewrite to *true* poses special conceptual problems for sequentiality theory. Although it is necessary to rewrite *one* of s or t in order to reach the normal form *true*, it is neither necessary to rewrite s, nor necessary to rewrite t. The criterion of choosing a redex that *must* be rewritten fails to even *define* a next rewriting step mathematically, and the question of computability does not even arise. Notice that this latter case is problematic for $\mathbf{T}_{or+}$ alone, without the addition of $\mathbf{T}_c$.

The difficulty in Example 3.2.1 above appears to depend on the unifiability of the left-hand sides of the two equations in $\mathbf{T}_{or+}$, which is allowed in rewrite-orthogonal systems, but not rule-orthogonal systems. A more subtle example, due to Huet and Lévy, shows that rule-orthogonality is still not sufficient for effective sequencing.

Example 3.2.2 ([Huet and Lévy, 1991]). Replace the parallel-or equations of Example 3.2.1 by the following:

$$\mathbf{T}_{14} = \{\, f(x, a, b) \doteq c,\ f(b, x, a) \doteq c,\ f(a, b, x) \doteq c \,\}$$

and consider the system $\mathbf{T}_c \cup \mathbf{T}_{14}$. Given a term of the form $f(r, s, t)$, we cannot decide whether to rewrite redexes in r, in s, or in t without risking wasted work, because we cannot separate computably the three cases

- $r \to^* a$ and $s \to^* b$
- $r \to^* b$ and $t \to^* a$
- $s \to^* a$ and $t \to^* b$

Unlike the parallel-or example, it is impossible for more than one of these three cases to hold. There is always a mathematically well-defined redex that *must* be rewritten in order to reach a normal form, and the problem is entirely one of choosing such a redex effectively. In fact, for sets $\mathbf{T}$ of equations such that $\mathbf{T} \cup \mathbf{T}_{14}$ is *terminating* (every term has a normal form), the choice of whether to rewrite r, s, or t in $f(r, s, t)$ is effective, but usually unacceptably inefficient.

So, some further analysis of the form of equations beyond checking for orthogonality is required in order to choose a good redex to rewrite next in a term rewriting sequence. Analysis of equations in order to determine a good choice of redex is called *sequentiality analysis*.

3.2.1 Needed redexes and weak sequentiality

The essential ideas for sequentiality analysis in term rewriting are due to Huet and Lévy [Huet and Lévy, 1991], based on a notion of sequential predicate by Kahn [Kahn and Plotkin, 1978]. A redex that may be rewritten without risk of wasted work is called a *needed redex*.

Definition 3.2.3 ([Huet and Lévy, 1991]). Given an orthogonal set $\mathbf{T}$ of equations and a term t_0, a redex α in t_0 is a *needed redex* if and only if, for every term rewriting sequence $t_0 \xrightarrow{\mathbf{T}} t_1 \xrightarrow{\mathbf{T}} \cdots \xrightarrow{\mathbf{T}} t_m$, either

- there exists an i, $1 \le i \le m$ such that a residual of α is rewritten in the step $t_{i-1} \xrightarrow{\mathbf{T}} t_i$, or
- α has at least one residual in t_m.

A needed redex is a redex whose residuals can never be completely eliminated by rewriting other redexes. So, the rewriting of a needed redex is not wasted work, since at least one of its residuals has to be rewritten in order to reach normal form. Huet and Lévy defined needed redexes only for terms with normal forms, but the generalization above is trivial. A system is *weakly sequential* if there is always a needed redex to rewrite.

Definition 3.2.4. A rewrite-orthogonal set of equations is *weakly sequential* if and only if every term that is not in normal form contains at least one needed redex. A set of equations is *effectively weakly sequential* if and only if there is an effective procedure that finds a needed redex in each term not in normal form.

The word 'sequential' above is conventional, but may be misleading to those interested in parallel computation. A weakly sequential system is not *required* to be computed sequentially—typically there is great opportunity for parallel evaluation. Rather, a weakly sequential system *allows* sequential computation without risk of wasted rewriting work. In this respect 'sequentializable' would be a more enlightening word than 'sequential.'

The parallel-or system $\mathbf{T}_{or+}$ of Example 3.2.1 is rewrite-orthogonal, but not weakly sequential, because the term

$$or(or(true, a), or(true, a))$$

has two redexes, neither of which is needed, since either can be eliminated by rewriting the other, then rewriting the whole term to *true*. Rule-orthogonality guarantees weak sequentiality.

Proposition 3.2.5 ([Huet and Lévy, 1991]). *A nontrivial, rule-like, and left-linear set of equations (Definition 2.3.9) is weakly sequential if and only if it is rule-orthogonal.*

The proof of (⇐) is in [Huet and Lévy, 1991]. It involves a search through all rewriting sequences (including infinite ones), and does not yield an effective procedure. (⇒) is straightforward, since when two redexes overlap neither is needed.

Proposition 3.2.5 above shows that no analysis based on weak sequentiality can completely sequentialize systems whose confluence derives from rewrite-orthogonality, or from a Knuth–Bendix analysis. Section 3.2.4 discusses possible extensions of sequentiality beyond rule-orthogonal systems.

The system $\mathbf{T}_c \cup \mathbf{T}_{14}$ of Example 3.2.2 is rule-orthogonal, and therefore weakly sequential. For example, in a term of the form $f(r, s, t)$, where $r \to^* a$ and $s \to^* b$, both r and s contain needed redexes. The subsystem $\mathbf{T}_{14}$, without the general-purpose programming system $\mathbf{T}_c$, is *effectively* weakly sequential, but only because it is terminating. I conjecture that effective weak sequentiality is undecidable for rule-orthogonal systems.

3.2.2 Strongly needed redexes and strong sequentiality

The uncomputability of needed redexes and the weak sequential property are addressed analogously to the uncomputability of confluence: by finding efficiently computable sufficient conditions for a redex to be needed, and for a system to be effectively weakly sequential. A natural approach is to ignore right-hand sides of equations, and detect those cases of needed redexes and effectively weakly sequential systems that are guaranteed by the structure of the left-hand sides. To this end we define ω-rewriting, in which a redex is replaced by an arbitrary term.

Definition 3.2.6 ([Huet and Lévy, 1991]). Let $\mathbf{T} = \{l_1 \doteq r_1, \ldots, l_n \doteq r_n\}$ be a rule-orthogonal set of equations.

A term s_1 ω-*rewrites to* s_2 *by* **T** (written $s_1 \xrightarrow{\mathrm{T}}_{\omega} s_2$) if and only if there is a term t, a variable x with exactly one occurrence in t, an instance l'_i of a left-hand side l_i in **T**, and a term r such that $s_1 = t[l'_i/x]$ and $s_2 = t[r/x]$. That is, s_2 results from finding exactly one instance of a left-hand side of an equation in **T** occurring as a subterm of s_1, and replacing it with an arbitrary term. The definition of residual (Definition 3.1.1) generalizes naturally to ω-rewriting.

Now, a *strongly needed redex* is defined analogously to a needed redex, using ω-rewriting instead of rewriting.

Definition 3.2.7 ([Huet and Lévy, 1991]). Given a rule-orthogonal set **T** of equations and a term t_0, a redex α in t_0 is *strongly needed* if and only if, for every ω-rewriting sequence $t_0 \xrightarrow{\mathrm{T}}_{\omega} t_1 \xrightarrow{\mathrm{T}}_{\omega} \cdots \xrightarrow{\mathrm{T}}_{\omega} t_m$, either

- there exists an i, $1 \leq i \leq m$ such that a residual of α is rewritten in the step $t_{i-1} \xrightarrow{\mathrm{T}}_{\omega} t_i$, or

- α has at least one residual in t_m.

Because of rule-orthogonality, the property of being strongly needed depends only on the location of a redex occurrence, and not on its internal structure. So, we call an arbitrary occurrence in a term *strongly needed* if and only if a redex substituted in at that location is strongly needed. [Huet and Lévy, 1991] defines *strong indexes,* and shows that they determine exactly the strongly needed redexes. It is easy to see that every strongly needed redex is needed, and outermost. And, it is easy to detect whether a given redex is strongly needed (see Section 4 and [Huet and Lévy, 1991]). A system of equations is strongly sequential if there is always a strongly needed redex to be rewritten, except in a normal form term.

Definition 3.2.8 ([Huet and Lévy, 1991]). A rule-orthogonal set of equations is *strongly sequential* if and only if every term that is not in normal form contains at least one strongly needed redex.

It is obvious that every strongly sequential system is effectively weakly sequential, but the converse does not hold.

Example 3.2.9. The system $\mathbf{T}_{14}$ of Example 3.2.2, although it is effectively weakly sequential, is *not* strongly sequential. $f(f(a, b, c), f(a, b, c), f(a, b, c))$ ω-rewrites to $f(f(a, b, c), a, b)$, which is a redex, so the first redex $f(a, b, c)$ is not strongly needed. Similarly, $f(f(a, b, c), f(a, b, c), f(a, b, c))$ ω-rewrites to the redexes $f(b, f(a, b, c), a)$ and $f(a, b, f(a, b, c))$, so the second and third redexes are not strongly needed. All three redexes are weakly needed.

By contrast, consider the strongly sequential system

$$\mathbf{T}_{15} = \{f(g(b, b), h(x, b)) \doteq b, \ f(g(c, x), h(c, c)) \doteq c, \ h(x, d) \doteq d, \ a \doteq b\}$$

In the term $f(g(a, a), h(a, a))$, the first and last occurrences of a are strongly needed, but the second and third are not.

Notice that ω-rewriting allows different redexes that are occurrences of instances of the same left-hand side to be rewritten inconsistently in different ω-rewriting steps. Such inconsistency is critical to the example above, where in one case $f(a, b, c)$ ω-rewrites to a, and in another case it ω-rewrites to b.

Strong sequentiality is independent of the right-hand sides of equations.

Proposition 3.2.10. *If* $\mathbf{T}_1$ *and* $\mathbf{T}_2$ *are left-similar (see Definition 2.3.11), and* $\mathbf{T}_1$ *is strongly sequential, then so is* $\mathbf{T}_2$.

The proof is straightforward, since $\mathbf{T}_1$ *and* $\mathbf{T}_2$ *clearly have the same* ω-*rewriting relations (Definition 3.2.6).*

It is *not* true, however, that a system is strongly sequential whenever all left-similar systems are weakly sequential. The system of Example 3.2.2 and all left-similar systems are weakly sequential, but not strongly sequential. But in that case, no given redex is needed in all of the left-similar systems. An interesting open question is whether a redex that is needed in all left-similar systems must be strongly needed.

For finite rule-orthogonal sets of equations, strong sequentiality is decidable.

Proposition 3.2.11 ([Huet and Lévy, 1991; Klop and Middeldorp, 1991]). *Given a finite rule-orthogonal set* $\mathbf{T}$ *of equations, it is decidable whether* $\mathbf{T}$ *is strongly sequential.*

The details of the proof are quite tricky, but the essential idea is that only a finite set of terms, with sizes limited by a function of the sizes of left-hand sides of equations, need to be checked for strongly needed redexes.

In developing the concept of *strongly needed* redexes and connecting it to the concept of *weakly needed* redexes, Huet and Lévy define the intermediately powerful concept of an *index*. Roughly, an index is a needed redex that can be distinguished from other redexes just by their relative positions in a term, without knowing the forms of the redexes themselves [Huet and Lévy, 1991]. Every index is a weakly needed redex, but not vice versa. *Strong* indexes are equivalent to strongly needed redexes. A system in which every term not in normal form has at least one index is called *sequential*. The precise relation between sequentiality in all left-similar systems, and strong sequentiality, is an interesting open problem.

All of the sequentiality theory discussed in this section deals with sequentializing the process of rewriting a term to normal form. Example 7.1.6 in Section 7.1 shows that even strongly sequential systems may require a parallel evaluation strategy for other purposes, such as a complete procedure for rewriting to head-normal form.

3.2.3   Optimal rewriting

From a naive point of view, the natural strategy of rewriting a strongly
needed redex at each step does not lead to minimal-length rewriting sequences ending in normal form. The problem is that the rewriting of a
strongly needed redex may cause another needed (but not strongly needed)
redex to be copied arbitrarily many times. Since strongly needed redexes
are always outermost, they are particularly likely to cause such copying.

Example 3.2.12.   In the strongly sequential system of equations

$$\mathbf{T}_{16} = \{f(x) \doteq g(x, x)\}$$

given the initial term $f(f(a))$, both redexes, $f(f(a))$ and $f(a)$, are needed,
but only the outermost one is strongly needed. By rewriting a strongly
needed redex at each step, we get the 3-step sequence

$$f(f(a)) \overset{\mathbf{T}_{16}}{\to} g(f(a), f(a)) \overset{\mathbf{T}_{16}}{\to} g(g(a,a), f(a)) \overset{\mathbf{T}_{16}}{\to} g(g(a,a), g(a,a))$$

But, there is a 2-step sequence

$$f(f(a)) \overset{\mathbf{T}_{16}}{\to} f(g(a,a)) \overset{\mathbf{T}_{16}}{\to} g(g(a,a), g(a,a))$$

which does not rewrite the unique strongly needed redex in the first step.

It is easy to construct further examples in which the number of steps
wasted by rewriting strongly needed redexes is arbitrarily large.

Proposition 3.2.13. *Given an arbitrary strongly sequential system of
equations, and a term, there is no effective procedure to choose a redex at
each step so as to minimize the length of the rewriting sequence to normal
form.*

I am not aware of a treatment of this point in the literature. The basic
idea is to use the equations

$$\mathbf{T}_{17} = \{f(x, y) \doteq g(x, x, h(y)), \; a \doteq b, \; g(x, x, 0) \doteq 0\}$$

similar to $\mathbf{T}_{16}$ of Example 3.2.12, and add additional equations to define h
as the evaluator for Lisp or some other general-purpose computing system.
Now, start with a term of the form $f(a, p)$, where p is an arbitrary program.
If evaluation of p halts with value 0 (that is, if $h(p)$ rewrites to 0), then
an optimal rewriting sequence rewrites $f(a, p)$ to $g(a, a, h(p))$ in the first
step, and never rewrites the occurrences of a. If evaluation of p halts with
any value other than 0, then an optimal sequence rewrites a to b in the
first step (else it must be rewritten twice later). An effective method for
choosing the first step would yield a recursive separation of the programs
that halt with output 0 from those that halt with output 1, which is known
to be impossible [Machtey and Young, 1978].

Notice that, when there is a normal form, breadth-first search over all rewriting sequences yields a very expensive computation of a minimal sequence. But, no effective procedure can choose some redex in all cases (even in the absence of a normal form), and minimize the number of rewriting steps when there is a normal form.

The uncomputability of minimal-length rewriting strategies in Proposition 3.2.13 sounds discouraging. The number of rewriting steps is *not*, however, a good practical measure of the efficiency of a sequencing strategy. Given equations, such as $f(x) \doteq g(x, x)$ in Example 3.2.12, with more than one occurrence of the same variable x on the right-hand side, normal sensible implementations do *not* make multiple copies of the subterm substituted for that variable. Rather, they use multiple pointers to a single copy. Then, only one actual computing step is required to rewrite all of the apparent multiple copies of a redex within that substituted subterm. So, in Example 3.2.12, the strategy of choosing a strongly needed redex actually leads to only two steps, from $f(f(a))$ to $g(f(a), f(a))$, and then directly to $g(g(a, a), g(a, a))$. The normal form is represented in practice with only one copy of the subterm $g(a, a)$, and two pointers to it for the two arguments of the outermost g. If we charge only one step for rewriting a whole set of shared redexes, then rewriting strongly needed redexes is optimal.

Proposition 3.2.14. *Consider multiple-rewriting sequences, in which in one step all of the shared copies of a redex are rewritten simultaneously. Given a strongly sequential set of equations and a term, the strategy of rewriting at each step a strongly needed redex and all of its shared copies leads to normal form in a minimal number of steps.*

This proposition has never been completely proved in print. I claimed a proof [O'Donnell, 1977] but had a fatal error [Berry and Lévy, 1979; O'Donnell, 1979]. The hard part of the proposition—that the rewriting of a strongly needed redex is never a wasted step—was proved by Huet and Lévy [Huet and Lévy, 1991]. The remaining point—that rewriting a strongly needed redex never causes additional rewriting work later in the sequence—seems obvious, but has never been treated formally in general. Lévy [Lévy, 1978] treated a similar situation in the lambda calculus, but in that case there is no known efficient implementation technique for the sequences used in the optimality proof. Although the formal literature on optimal rewriting is still incomplete, and extensions of optimality theory to systems (such as the lambda calculus) with bound variables are extremely subtle, for most practical purposes Huet's and Lévy's work justifies the strategy of rewriting all shared copies of a strongly needed redex at each step. Optimality aside, rewriting strategies that always choose a strongly needed redex are examples of *one-step normalizing strategies,* which provide interesting theoretical problems in combinatory logic and the lambda calculus [Barendregt, 1984].

3.2.4   Extensions to sequentiality analysis

Proposition 3.2.5 seems to invalidate rewrite-orthogonal systems for efficient or optimal sequential rewriting. A closer look shows that the definition of weakly needed redexes and weak sequentiality is inappropriate for rewrite-orthogonal systems. When two redexes from a rewrite-orthogonal system overlap, we get the same result by rewriting either one. So, there is no need for a sequential strategy to choose between them, and we might as well allow an arbitrary selection. This observation suggests a more liberal concept of needed redex.

Definition 3.2.15. Given a rewrite-orthogonal set $\mathbf{T}$ of equations and a term t_0, a redex α in t_0 is a *rewrite-needed redex* if and only if, for every term rewriting sequence $t_0 \xrightarrow{\mathbf{T}} t_1 \xrightarrow{\mathbf{T}} \cdots \xrightarrow{\mathbf{T}} t_m$, either

- there exists an i, $1 \le i \le m$ such that a residual of α is rewritten in the step $t_{i-1} \xrightarrow{\mathbf{T}} t_i$, or
- there exists an i, $1 \le i \le m$ such that a redex overlapping a residual of α is rewritten in the step $t_{i-1} \xrightarrow{\mathbf{T}} t_i$, or
- α has at least one residual in t_m.

This is the same as Definition 3.2.3 of needed redex, except that when one redex is reduced, we give credit to all redexes that overlap it. We generalize Definition 3.2.4 with the new version of needed redexes.

Definition 3.2.16. An orthogonal set of equations is *weakly rewrite-sequential* if and only if every term that is not in normal form contains at least one rewrite-needed redex. A set of equations is *effectively weakly rewrite-sequential* if and only if there is an effective procedure that finds a rewrite-needed redex in each term not in normal form.

Three sorts of overlaps between left-hand sides of equations have different impacts on weak rewrite-sequentiality. Recall (Definition 2.3.9) that the problematic overlaps occur when there is a term s, and left-hand sides l_i and l_j, such that

$$s[l_i[t_1, \ldots, t_m/x_1, \ldots, x_m]/y] = l_j[t'_1, \ldots, t'_n/x'_1, \ldots, x'_n]$$

Rewrite-nonambiguity requires that either s is an instance of l_j, or the corresponding right-hand sides r_i and r_j satisfy

$$s[r_i[t_1, \ldots, t_m/x_1, \ldots, x_m]/y] = r_j[t'_1, \ldots, t'_n/x'_1, \ldots, x'_n]$$

1. Sometimes the structure of the inner term l_i is entirely subsumed by the structure of the outer term l_j—that is, the substituted terms $t'_1, \ldots, t'_n$ are trivial, and

$$s[l_i[t_1, \ldots, t_m/x_1, \ldots, x_m]/y] = l_j$$

In this case, the equation $l_j \doteq r_j$ is redundant, since every possible application of it can be accomplished by applying $l_i \doteq r_i$ instead.

2. Sometimes the structure of the inner term l_i extends below the structure of the outer term l_j—that is, the substituted terms $t_1, \ldots, t_m$ are trivial, and

$$s[l_i/y] = l_j[t'_1, \ldots, t'_n/x'_1, \ldots, x'_n]$$

Overlaps of this sort appear not to destroy weak rewrite-sequentiality.

3. Otherwise, neither set of substituted terms $t_1, \ldots, t_m$ nor $t'_1, \ldots, t'_n$ is trivial. This is the interesting case. Weak rewrite-sequentiality may hold or not, depending on the extent to which redexes in substituted subterms are copied or eliminated by the right-hand sides.

Figure 4 illustrates the three types of overlap with suggestive pictures.

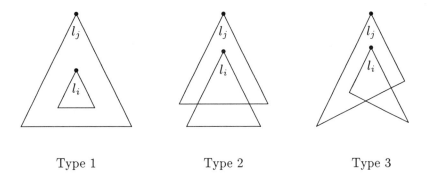

Type 1 Type 2 Type 3

Fig. 4. The three types of left-hand-side overlap.

Example 3.2.17. Consider the set

$$\mathbf{T}_{18} = \{f(g(h(x))) \doteq f(h(x)), \ g(x) \doteq x\}$$

The overlap here is of type 1, since

$$f(y)[g(x)[h(x)/x]/y] = f(g(h(x)))$$

The first equation is redundant since it is essentially a special case of the second.

Next, consider

$$\mathbf{T}_{19} = \{f(g(x), a) \doteq f(x, a), \ g(h(x)) \doteq h(x)\}$$

The overlap here is of type 2, since

$$f(y,a)[g(h(x))/y] = f(g(h(x)),a) = f(g(x),a)[h(x)/x]$$

$\mathbf{T}_{19}$ is weakly rewrite-sequential. In a term of the form $f(s,t)$, in which $s \overset{\mathbf{T}_{19}}{\twoheadrightarrow} g(h(s'))$ and also $t \overset{\mathbf{T}_{19}}{\twoheadrightarrow} a$, it is always safe to rewrite t first, since by rewriting s to $g(h(s'))$ and then rewriting this to $h(s')$, we cannot eliminate the redexes in t.

Now, consider

$$\mathbf{T}_{20} = \{f(g(a,x)) \doteq f(a),\ g(x,a) \doteq a\}$$

The overlap here is of type 3, since

$$f(y)[g(x,a)[a/x]/y] = f(g(a,a)) = f(g(a,x))[a/x]$$

is the smallest substitution showing the overlap, and neither substitution is trivial. $\mathbf{T}_{20}$ is not weakly rewrite-sequential, since the term $f(g(g(a,a), g(a,a)))$ has the two rewrite sequences

$$f(g(g(a,a),g(a,a))) \overset{\mathbf{T}_{20}}{\twoheadrightarrow} f(g(a,g(a,a))) \overset{\mathbf{T}_{20}}{\twoheadrightarrow} f(a)$$

which shows that the rightmost occurrence of $g(a,a)$ is not needed and

$$f(g(g(a,a),g(a,a))) \overset{\mathbf{T}_{20}}{\twoheadrightarrow} f(g(g(a,a),a)) \overset{\mathbf{T}_{20}}{\twoheadrightarrow} f(a)$$

which shows that the leftmost occurrence of $g(a,a)$ is not needed.

Modify the previous example slightly, by changing the right-hand sides:

$$\mathbf{T}_{21} = \{f(g(a,x)) \doteq f(x),\ g(x,a) \doteq x\}$$

The result is still a type 3 overlap, but the system is weakly rewrite-sequential, since the redexes that are not needed immediately in the creation of an outer redex are preserved for later rewriting.

The positive parallel-or equations in $\mathbf{T}_{or+}$ of Examples 2.3.16 and 3.2.1 give another example of a type 3 overlap where weak rewrite-sequentiality fails. On the other hand, the negative parallel-or equations of $\mathbf{T}_{or-}$ in Example 2.3.16 have type 2 overlap, but they are sequential. In a term of the form $or(s,t)$ where $s \overset{\mathbf{T}_{or-}}{\twoheadrightarrow} false$ and $t \overset{\mathbf{T}_{or-}}{\twoheadrightarrow} false$, it is safe to rewrite either s or t first, since the redexes in the other, unrewritten, subterm are preserved for later rewriting.

Theories extending sequentiality analysis, through concepts such as weak rewrite-sequentiality, are open topics for research. I conjecture that weak rewrite-sequentiality is an undecidable property of rewrite-orthogonal systems, and that the natural concept of strong rewrite-sequentiality has essentially the same properties as strong sequentiality, except for allowing type 2 overlaps. Optimality is very subtle in these extensions, since the amount of sharing may vary depending on which of two overlapping redexes is reduced. More interesting and powerful extensions of sequentiality will require analysis of right-hand sides to deal with type 3 overlaps. Such analysis should be related in interesting ways to *strictness analysis* in functional programming languages [Mycroft, 1980; Hughes, 1985b] , which detects partial strictness properties of defined functions. *Abstract interpretation* [Abramsky and Hankin, 1987; Cousot and Cousot, 1977] provides a promising approach to sequentiality analysis based on right-hand sides.

Extensions of useful sequentiality analysis to systems whose confluence is established by variations on the Knuth–Bendix procedure will require the concept of residual to be generalized so that the residual of a redex α may be an arbitrarily long rewriting *sequence* used in resolving a critical pair involving α. Variations on sequentiality analysis for incremental and parallel implementations of equational logic programming are discussed in Sections 6 and 7, respectively.

4 Algorithms and data structures to implement equational languages

The basic idea of implementing equational logic programming for strongly sequential systems is straightforward. Represent terms as linked structures with sharing, in the time-honored style of Lisp [McCarthy *et al.*, 1965; McCarthy, 1960]. At every step, find a strongly needed redex and rewrite it, halting if and when the sequence ends with a normal form. A lot of work is required to reduce these basic ideas to efficient practice. At the abstract level of algorithm and data-structure design, the problem breaks naturally into three components: a data structure to represent terms, a pattern-matching and sequencing algorithm to find strongly needed redexes, and a driving procedure to invoke the pattern-matcher/sequencer, perform the chosen rewrites, and incorporate the results into the term data structure.

4.1 Data structures to represent terms

The natural data structure for terms is a linked structure in a heap, with sharing allowed. Each occurrence of a symbol f in a term is represented by a node of storage containing f and pointers to its arguments. Sharing is accomplished by allowing several different argument pointers to point to the same node. There are a number of optimizations that coalesce small nodes, or break large nodes into linked sequences, that have been explored in the literature on Lisp compilers [Bobrow and Clark, 1979]. In this section, we consider data structures at an abstract level with precisely one symbol per

heap node, and assume that such optimizations are applied at a lower level
of implementation.

4.1.1 A conceptual model for term data structures

Some useful techniques for implementing equational logic programming
require more than the linked heap structures representing terms. For example, it is sometimes better to represent the rewriting of s to t by a link
from the head node of the representation of s pointing to the head node
of t, rather than by an actual replacement of s by t. This representation
still uses a heap, but the heap now represents a portion of the infinite
rewriting graph for a starting term, rather than just a single term at some
intermediate stage in rewriting to normal form. Other techniques involve
the memoing of intermediate steps to avoid recomputation—these require
more efficient table lookup than may be achieved with a linked heap. Fortunately, there is a single abstract data structure that subsumes all of the
major proposals as special cases, and which allows a nice logical interpretation [Sherman, 1990]. This data structure is best understood in terms of
three tables representing three special sorts of functions.

Definition 4.1.1. For each $i \geq 0$ let $\mathbf{Fun}_i$ be a countably infinite set of
function symbols of arity i. The 0-ary function symbols in $\mathbf{Fun}_0$ are called
constant symbols. $\mathbf{T}_P^0$ is the set of ground terms (terms without variables)
constructed from the given function symbols (see Definition 2.3.1 of the
chapter 'Introduction: Logic and Logic Programming Languages'). Let $\mathbf{P}$
be a countably infinite set. Members of $\mathbf{P}$ are called *parameters,* and are
written $\alpha, \beta, \ldots$, sometimes with subscripts. Formally, parameters behave
just like the *variables* of Definition 2.3.1, but their close association with
heap addresses later on makes us think of them somewhat differently.

An *i-ary signature* is a member of $\mathbf{Fun}_i \times \mathbf{P}^i$. The signature $\langle f, \langle \alpha_1, \ldots,$
$\alpha_i \rangle \rangle$, is normally denoted by $f(\alpha_1, \ldots, \alpha_i)$. $\mathbf{Sig}$ denotes the set of signatures
of all arities.

Let $\mathbf{nil}$ be a symbol distinct from all function symbols, parameters, and
signatures.

A *parameter valuation* is a function $\mathbf{val} : \mathbf{P} \to \mathbf{Sig} \cup \{\mathbf{nil}\}$.

A *parameter replacement* is a function $\mathbf{repl} : \mathbf{P} \to \mathbf{P} \cup \{\mathbf{nil}\}$.

A *signature index* is a function $\mathbf{ind} : \mathbf{Sig} \to \mathbf{P} \cup \{\mathbf{nil}\}$.

A parameter valuation, parameter replacement, or signature index is
finitely based if and only if its value is $\mathbf{nil}$ for all but a finite number of
arguments.

The conventional representation of a term by a linked structure in a
heap may be understood naturally as a table representing a finitely based
parameter valuation. The parameters are the heap addresses, and the
signatures are the possible values for data nodes. $\mathbf{val}(\alpha)$ is the signature
stored at address α. But, we may also think of parameters as additional

Table 1. Parameter valuation representing $f(g(a, f(a, a)), f(a, a))$.

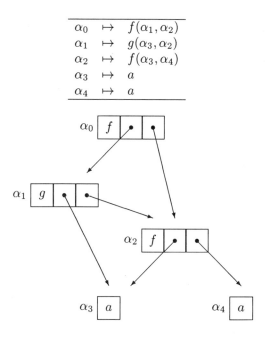

α_0	$\mapsto$	$f(\alpha_1, \alpha_2)$
α_1	$\mapsto$	$g(\alpha_3, \alpha_2)$
α_2	$\mapsto$	$f(\alpha_3, \alpha_4)$
α_3	$\mapsto$	a
α_4	$\mapsto$	a

Fig. 5. Linked structure representing $f(g(a, f(a, a)), f(a, a))$.

0-ary symbols, of signatures as terms of height 1 built from parameters, and of the function **val** as a set of formulae asserting equalities between parameters and signatures. Each value $\mathbf{val}(\alpha) = f(\beta_1, \ldots, \beta_i) \neq \mathbf{nil}$ of the valuation function represents the formula $\alpha \doteq f(\beta_1, \ldots, \beta_i)$. When **val** represents the contents of a heap with the head symbol of a term t stored at address α, then $\alpha \doteq t$ is a logical consequence of the equations represented by **val**.

Example 4.1.2. Consider the finitely based parameter valuation **val** given by Table 1. All values of **val** not shown in the tables are **nil**. The linked heap structure associated with **val** is shown in Figure 5. The set of equations represented by **val** is

$$\{\alpha_0 \doteq f(\alpha_1, \alpha_2), \ \alpha_1 \doteq g(\alpha_3, \alpha_2), \ \alpha_2 \doteq f(\alpha_3, \alpha_4), \ \alpha_3 \doteq a, \ \alpha_4 \doteq a\}$$

Logical consequences of these equations include $\alpha_2 \doteq f(a, a)$, $\alpha_1 \doteq g(a, f(a, a))$, and $\alpha_0 \doteq f(g(a, f(a, a)), f(a, a))$.

It is useful to have a notation for the term represented explicitly by a parameter valuation at a particular parameter.

Definition 4.1.3. Let **val** be a parameter valuation. The partial function **val*** : $\mathbf{P} \to \mathbf{T}_P^0$ is defined inductively by

$$\mathbf{val}^*(\alpha) = f(\mathbf{val}^*(\beta_1), \ldots, \mathbf{val}^*(\beta_i))$$

when $\mathbf{val}(\alpha) = f(\beta_1, \ldots, \beta_i)$. Notice that the case where f is a constant symbol, and therefore $i = 0$, provides a basis for the inductive definition. If a value of **nil** is encountered anywhere in the induction, or if the induction fails to terminate because of a loop, **val*** is undefined.

When $\mathbf{val}^*(\alpha)$ is well-defined, the equation $\alpha \doteq \mathbf{val}^*(\alpha)$ is always a logical consequence of the equations represented by **val**.

Optimized implementations of equational logic programming languages sometimes find it more efficient to link together nodes representing left- and right-hand sides of equations, rather than to actually perform rewriting steps. Such linking can be implemented by an additional pointer in each node of a heap structure. The information in these links is naturally represented by a parameter replacement function. Given a set **T** of equations, it first appears that we should think of the function **repl** as a set of formulae asserting that one term rewrites to another—that is, $\mathbf{repl}(\alpha) = \beta \neq \mathbf{nil}$ represents the formula $\mathbf{val}^*(\alpha) \overset{\mathbf{T}}{\to}^* \mathbf{val}^*(\beta)$. But further rewriting steps on subterms of the term represented by α may invalidate such a relation. There are also implementations that make efficient use of data structures for which **val*** is ill defined. So, the proper logical interpretation of $\mathbf{repl}(\alpha) = \beta$ as a formula is merely $\alpha \doteq \beta$. An efficient implementation manipulates **val** and **repl** so that β is in some way a better starting point for further rewriting than α. The precise sense in which it is better varies among different implementations. **val** and **repl** together yield a set of terms for each parameter, all of which are known to be equal. The set $\mathbf{val}^*_{\mathbf{repl}}(\alpha)$ defined below is the set of terms that may be read by starting at α and following links in **val** and **repl**.

Definition 4.1.4. Let **val** be a parameter valuation and let **repl** be a parameter replacement. The function $\mathbf{val}^*_{\mathbf{repl}} : \mathbf{P} \to 2^{\mathbf{T}_P^0}$ is defined so that $\mathbf{val}^*_{\mathbf{repl}}(\alpha)$ is the least set satisfying

1. If $\mathbf{val}(\alpha) = f(\beta_1, \ldots, \beta_i)$, then

$$\mathbf{val}^*_{\mathbf{repl}}(\alpha) \supseteq \{f(t_1, \ldots, t_i) : t_1 \in \mathbf{val}^*_{\mathbf{repl}}(\beta_1) \wedge \cdots \wedge t_i \in \mathbf{val}^*_{\mathbf{repl}}(\beta_i)\}$$

2. If $\mathbf{repl}(\alpha) \neq nil$, then $\mathbf{val}^*_{\mathbf{repl}}(\alpha) \supseteq \mathbf{val}^*_{\mathbf{repl}}(\mathbf{repl}(\alpha))$

In the presence of loops, $\mathbf{val}^*_{\mathbf{repl}}(\alpha)$ may be infinite. Even without loops, its size may be exponential in the size of the data structure representing **val** and **repl**. The power of such data structures derives from this ability to represent large sets of equivalent terms compactly. When $\mathbf{val}^*(\alpha)$ is well defined, $\mathbf{val}^*(\alpha) \in \mathbf{val}^*_{\mathbf{repl}}(\alpha)$. Another special member of $\mathbf{val}^*_{\mathbf{repl}}(\alpha)$

Table 2. Parameter valuation and replacement.

val			repl		
α_0	$\mapsto$	$f(\alpha_1, \alpha_3)$	α_0	$\mapsto$	α_4
α_1	$\mapsto$	$f(\alpha_2, \alpha_3)$	α_1	$\mapsto$	nil
α_2	$\mapsto$	a	α_2	$\mapsto$	nil
α_3	$\mapsto$	b	α_3	$\mapsto$	α_5
α_4	$\mapsto$	$g(\alpha_2, \alpha_3)$	α_4	$\mapsto$	nil
α_5	$\mapsto$	c	α_5	$\mapsto$	nil

is particularly interesting—the one reached by following **repl** links as much as possible.

Definition 4.1.5. Let **val** be a parameter valuation and let **repl** be a parameter replacement. The partial function $\mathbf{val}^{max}_{\mathbf{repl}} : \mathbf{P} \to \mathbf{T}^0_P$ is defined inductively by

$$\mathbf{val}^{max}_{\mathbf{repl}}(\alpha) = \mathbf{val}^{max}_{\mathbf{repl}}(\mathbf{repl}(\alpha))$$

when $\mathbf{repl}(\alpha) \neq \mathbf{nil}$.

$$\mathbf{val}^{max}_{\mathbf{repl}}(\alpha) = f(\mathbf{val}^{max}_{\mathbf{repl}}(\beta_1), \ldots, \mathbf{val}^{max}_{\mathbf{repl}}(\beta_i))$$

when $\mathbf{repl}(\alpha) = \mathbf{nil}$ and $\mathbf{val}(\alpha) = f(\beta_1, \ldots, \beta_i)$. As with $\mathbf{val}^*$, $\mathbf{val}^{max}_{\mathbf{repl}}$ is undefined if **nil** is encountered as a value of **val**, or if the induction fails to terminate because of a loop.

Example 4.1.6. Consider the finitely based parameter valuation **val** and parameter replacement **repl** given by Table 2. All values of **val** and **repl** not shown in the tables are **nil**. These tables represent some of the consequences of the equations

$$\mathbf{T}_{22} = \{f(f(x,y),z) \doteq g(x,z), \ b \doteq c\}$$

when used to rewrite the term $f(f(a,b),b)$ The linked heap structure associated with **val** and **repl** is shown in Figure 6. The rightmost link in each node α points to $\mathbf{repl}(\alpha)$. By following links from α_0 in the table we can construct the six ground terms in $\mathbf{val}^*_{\mathbf{repl}}(\alpha_0)$: $\mathbf{val}^*(\alpha_0) = f(f(a,b),b)$, $f(f(a,b),c)$, $f(f(a,c),b)$, $f(f(a,c),c)$, $g(a,b)$, and $\mathbf{val}^{max}_{\mathbf{repl}}(\alpha_0) = g(a,c)$. Every equality between these terms is a logical consequence of $\mathbf{T}_{22}$, and all of these equalities may be read immediately from the data structure by following links from α_0.

A prime weakness of data structures based on parameter valuations and replacements is that both functions require a parameter as argument. Given a newly constructed signature, there is no direct way, other than

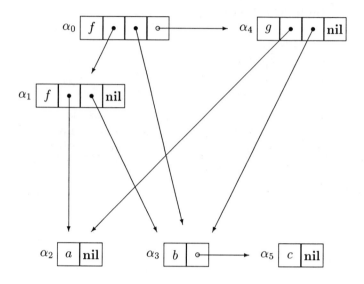

Fig. 6. Linked structure showing **val** and **repl** links.

searching through the parameter valuation, to discover whether information on that signature is already available. Signature indexes are intended
precisely to allow a newly constructed signature to be translated to an
equivalent parameter. While finitely based parameter valuations and replacements are normally implemented by direct memory access, using parameters as addresses, the number of possible signatures is generally too
great to allow such an implementation of a finitely based signature index.
General-purpose table-look-up methods are used instead, usually hash tables [Knuth, 1973]. A typical application of a hash-table representation of
a signature index is the *hashed cons* optimization in Lisp [Spitzen *et al.*,
1978], where every newly constructed node is looked up in a hash table to
see whether it already exists in the heap—if it does the existing node may be
shared instead of creating another copy in the heap. The most obvious use
of a signature index **ind**, such as the hashed cons application, requires that
whenever $\mathbf{ind}(f(\beta_1, \ldots, \beta_i)) = \alpha \neq \mathbf{nil}$, then $\mathbf{val}(\alpha) = f(\beta_1, \ldots, \beta_i)$; that
is, **val** is a partial inverse to **ind**. It may be advantageous in some cases to
let $\mathbf{ind}(f(\beta_1, \ldots, \beta_i))$ be a parameter known to be equal to $f(\beta_1, \ldots, \beta_i)$.
The proper logical interpretation of $\mathbf{ind}(f(\beta_1, \ldots, \beta_i)) = \alpha \neq \mathbf{nil}$ is merely
the formula $f(\beta_1, \ldots, \beta_i) \doteq \alpha$. So, **ind** provides the same type of logical information as **val**, but allows access to that information through a signature
argument, instead of a parameter argument.

4.1.2   Logical interpretation of term data structures

Each point in the graph of a parameter valuation **val**, a parameter replacement **repl**, and a signature index **ind** represents an equation. An entire data structure consisting of finitely based functions **val**, **repl**, and **ind** represents a suitably quantified conjunction of these equations. For definiteness, suppose that inputs and outputs are rooted at the parameter α_0. Then the logical meaning of **val**, **repl**, and **ind** is the conjunction of all their equations, with all parameters *except* α_0 existentially quantified.

Definition 4.1.7. Let **val**, **repl**, **ind** be a parameter valuation, a parameter replacement, and a signature index, respectively, all three finitely based. Let $\alpha_1, \ldots, \alpha_n$ be all of the parameters β occurring in the finite basis of the domain of **val** or of **repl** ($\textbf{val}(\beta) \neq nil$ or $\textbf{repl}(\beta) \neq nil$), or in the range of **repl**, or as a component of a signature in the finite basis of the domain of **ind** or in the range of **val**, except for the input/output parameter α_0. The *logical interpretation* of **val**, **repl**, **ind** is the formula $F_{\textbf{val},\textbf{repl},\textbf{ind}}$ defined by

$$F_{\textbf{val},\textbf{repl},\textbf{ind}} = (\exists \alpha_1, \ldots \alpha_n : G)$$

where G is the conjunction of all the equations

1. $\beta \doteq f(\gamma_1, \ldots, \gamma_i)$ where $\textbf{val}(\beta) = f(\gamma_1, \ldots, \gamma_i)$
2. $\beta \doteq \gamma$ where $\textbf{repl}(\beta) = \gamma$
3. $f(\beta_1, \ldots, \beta_i) \doteq \gamma$ where $\textbf{ind}(f(\beta_1, \ldots, \beta_i)) = \gamma$

Example 4.1.8. Consider the finitely based parameter valuation **val** and parameter replacement **repl** discussed in Example 4.1.6, and shown in Table 2 and Figure 6. If α_0 is the parameter used for the root of the input and output, then the logical interpretation of **val** and **repl** is

$$\exists \alpha_1, \ldots, \alpha_5 : \quad \alpha_0 \doteq f(\alpha_1, \alpha_3) \wedge \alpha_1 \doteq f(\alpha_2, \alpha_3) \wedge \alpha_2 \doteq a \wedge \alpha_3 \doteq b \wedge$$
$$\alpha_4 \doteq g(\alpha_2, \alpha_3) \wedge \alpha_5 \doteq c \wedge \alpha_0 \doteq \alpha_4 \wedge \alpha_3 \doteq \alpha_5$$

The interpretation of parameter valuations, parameter replacements, and signature indexes as encodings of existentially quantified conjunctions of equations makes it much easier to insure correctness of proposed algorithms for manipulating data structures based on these functions. The essential idea is that a transformation of a data structure from a state representing $\textbf{val}_0$, $\textbf{repl}_0$, $\textbf{ind}_0$ to one representing $\textbf{val}_1$, $\textbf{repl}_1$, $\textbf{ind}_1$ in the computation of an equational program $\textbf{T}$ is logically permissible if and only if the formula represented by $\textbf{val}_1$, $\textbf{repl}_1$, $\textbf{ind}_1$ is a logical consequence of $\textbf{T}$ plus the formula represented by $\textbf{val}_0$, $\textbf{repl}_0$, $\textbf{ind}_0$. So, an evaluation algorithm may take input s, start in a state where $\textbf{val}^{max}(\alpha_0) = s$, and apply permissible transformations to reach a state where $t \in \textbf{val}^{max}_{\textbf{repl}}(\alpha_0)$, for some normal form t. The permissibility of the transformations guarantees that t is a correct answer.

The interpretation of the term data structures as sets of formulae applies the concepts of logic programming to the implementation of a logic programming language. A similar use of logical concepts within the implementation of a logic programming language occurs in recent presentations of *unification* algorithms (used in the implementation of Prolog) as processes that derive solutions to equations, where every intermediate step represents a new and simpler set of equations to be solved [Kapur *et al.*, 1982; Martelli and Montanari, 1976]. The view of unification as transformation of equations to be solved clarifies the correctness of a number of clever and efficient algorithmic techniques.

Similarly, the logical view of term data structures shows immediately that a wide range of transformations of such data structures are correct, leaving an implementer free to choose the ones that appear to be most efficient. In order to represent new terms during a computation, we must be careful not to introduce spurious information about the input/output parameter α_0, nor to postulate the solvability of nontrivial equations. The concept of *reachability,* defined below, may be used to enforce both of these conditions.

Definition 4.1.9.   The set of parameters *reachable* from a given parameter α is defined inductively by

1. α is reachable from α

2. If β is reachable from α, and one of the following holds as well

    (a) $\mathbf{val}(\gamma) = f(\ldots, \beta, \ldots)$
    (b) $\mathbf{val}(\beta) = f(\ldots, \gamma, \ldots)$
    (c) $\mathbf{repl}(\gamma) = \beta$
    (d) $\mathbf{repl}(\beta) = \gamma$
    (e) $\mathbf{ind}(f(\ldots, \gamma, \ldots)) = \beta$
    (f) $\mathbf{ind}(f(\ldots, \beta, \ldots)) = \gamma$

    then γ is reachable from α

Permissible transformations include

1. Building new terms: when α is not reachable from any of $\alpha_0, \beta_1, \ldots, \beta_i$, reassign $\mathbf{val}(\alpha) := f(\beta_1, \ldots, \beta_i)$. (This allows both bottom-up and top-down construction of directed-acyclic representations of terms, using names completely unconnected to α_0. More liberal conditions than the unreachability of α from $\alpha_0, \beta_1, \ldots, \beta_i$ are possible, but they are somewhat complex to define.)

2. Representing rewriting in **repl**: when some $s \in \mathbf{val}^*_{\mathbf{repl}}(\alpha)$ rewrites to some $t \in \mathbf{val}^*_{\mathbf{repl}}(\beta)$, reassign $\mathbf{repl}(\alpha) := \beta$.

3. Rewriting in **val**: when $\mathbf{repl}(\alpha) \neq nil$, reassign $\mathbf{val}(\alpha) := \mathbf{val}(\mathbf{repl}(\alpha))$.

4. Compressing paths in **repl**: when **repl**(**repl**(α)) $\neq$ *nil*,
   reassign **repl**(α) := **repl**(**repl**(α)).
5. Rewriting arguments in **val**: when **val**(α) = $f(\beta_1, \ldots, \beta_i)$ and
   repl(β_j) $\neq$ *nil*, reassign **val**(α) := $f(\beta_1, \ldots, \textbf{repl}(\beta_j), \ldots, \beta_i)$.
6. Opportunistic sharing: when **ind**(**val**(α)) $\neq$ *nil*, α,
   reassign **repl**(α) := **ind**(**val**(α))
7. Indexing: when **val**(α) = $f(\beta_1, \ldots, \beta_i)$,
   reassign **ind**($f(\beta_1, \ldots, \beta_i)$) := α.
8. Garbage collecting: reassign **val**(α) := *nil*, and/or **repl**(α) := *nil*,
   and/or **ind**($f(\ldots)$) := *nil*. (This is always *permissible*, because it
   only erases assertions. It is *desirable* only when the information removed is not useful for the remainder of the computation.)

A straightforward evaluator scans $\textbf{val}_{\textbf{repl}}^{max}(\alpha_0)$ to find an instance of a left-
hand side s of an equation rooted at some node β, uses transformation 1
repeatedly to build a copy of the corresponding right-hand side t in free
nodes rooted at γ, then links β to γ by transformation 2. Transformations
3–5 allow the same term $\textbf{val}_{\textbf{repl}}^{max}(\alpha_0)$ to be scanned more efficiently, by
reducing the number of **repl** links that must be followed. Transformations
6 and 7 are used for optimizations such as *hashed cons, congruence closure*,
and *memo functions* to avoid re-evaluating the same subterm when it is
constructed repeatedly in a computation. Section 4.3 discusses several
optimizations using transformations 3–7.

The existential quantification of all parameters other than α_0 is required for the logical correctness of transformation 1 (term building), which
changes the meaning of some existentially quantified parameter, without
affecting any assertion about α_0. 2–8 are permissible independent of the
quantification. Notice that only transformation 2 depends on the given
equational program, and only 2 adds information to the data structure. 1
is needed to build new terms required by 2, but by itself 1 does not change
the logical assertions about α_0. 3–8 can only *reduce* the information given
by **val** and **repl**, but they may improve the efficiency of access to information that is retained. 3–7 never change $\textbf{val}_{\textbf{repl}}^{max}(\alpha_0)$. Transformation 8
is normally applied only to nodes that are inaccessible from α_0, in which
case 8 also preserves $\textbf{val}_{\textbf{repl}}^{max}(\alpha_0)$.

The logical interpretation introduced in Definition 4.1.7 seems to be
the most natural one for explaining currently known techniques for implementing equational logic programming, but others are possible, and might
lead to useful extensions of, or variations on, the current sort of equational logic programming. Let $\alpha_1, \ldots, \alpha_n$ be all of the parameters used in
val, **repl**, **ind**, other than the input/output parameter α_0, and let G be
the conjunction of all the equations represented by points in the graphs
of **val**, **repl**, **ind**, just as in Definition 4.1.7. Two other interesting logical
interpretations worthy of study are

1. $(\exists \alpha_0, \alpha_1, \ldots, \alpha_n : G) \Rightarrow (\exists \alpha_1, \ldots, \alpha_n : G)$
2. $\forall \alpha_0, \alpha_1, \ldots, \alpha_n : (G \Rightarrow (input \doteq \alpha_0))$, where *input* is a new zeroary symbol

The first proposal above allows introduction of arbitrary structures not connected to the input/output variable α_0. The second one allows for solution of equations, where every solution to the output is guaranteed to be a solution to the input problem as well.

4.2   Pattern-matching and sequencing methods

Given a representation of a term, the implementation of an equational logic program must perform *pattern-matching* to discover instances of left-hand sides of equations that may be rewritten, and must apply *sequencing* techniques to determine which of several such redexes to rewrite. These two conceptual tasks appear to be inextricably connected, so it is best to provide a single procedure to do both—that is, to find the next appropriate redex to rewrite in a given term. In order to find and choose a redex in a term, a procedure traverses the term until it has gathered enough information about the symbols in the term to make its choice. The full details of pattern-matching and sequencing methods are too long for this chapter. So, I describe two basic approaches to the problem and illustrate them by examples. The reader who needs more detail should consult [Huet and Lévy, 1991; Hoffmann and O'Donnell, 1979; Hoffmann *et al.*, 1985; O'Donnell, 1985; Klop, 1991; Klop and Middeldorp, 1991].

4.2.1   Representing sequencing information by Ω-terms

A natural way to represent partial information about a term is to present the known structure as a term, with a special symbol (Ω) representing unknown portions.

Definition 4.2.1.   The set $\mathbf{T}_P^\Omega$ of Ω-*terms* is defined in the same way as the set $\mathbf{T}_P$ of terms (Definition 2.3.1 of the chapter 'Introduction: Logic and Logic Programming Languages'), except the new constant Ω is added to the set $\mathbf{Fun}_0$ of symbols of arity 0.

An Ω-term s is *less defined than* an Ω-term t, written $s \sqsubseteq t$, if and only if s is the result of replacing zero or more subterms of t by Ω.

$s \sqcap t$ denotes the greatest lower bound of s and t.

When Ω-terms s and t have a common upper bound (that is, when there is a u such that $s \sqsubseteq u$ and $t \sqsubseteq u$), we write $s \uparrow t$.

The Ω in an Ω-term behaves formally much like a variable, except that each occurrence of the same symbol Ω is treated as a *unique* variable, occurring only at that location.

There is an elegant and simple procedure, called *melting*, for computing all of the possible effects of ω-rewriting on an Ω-term.

Definition 4.2.2.   The function $\mathbf{patt} : \mathbf{T}_P \to \mathbf{T}_P^\Omega$ is defined by

$$\mathbf{patt}(t) = t[\Omega, \ldots, \Omega/x_1, \ldots, x_m]$$

where $x_1, \ldots, x_m$ are all of the variables occurring in t.

Extend **patt** to sets of equations $\mathbf{T} = \{l_1 \doteq r_1, \ldots, l_n \doteq r_n\}$ by

$$\mathbf{patt}(\mathbf{T}) = \{\mathbf{patt}(l_1), \ldots, \mathbf{patt}(l_n)\}$$

Given a set $\mathbf{T}$ of equations, and an Ω-term $s \in \mathbf{T}_P^\Omega$, s is transformed into $\mathbf{melt}_\omega^{\mathbf{T}}(s)$ by the following extremely simple polynomial-time procedure:

1. If $s = t[u/x]$, where $u \neq \Omega$ and $u \uparrow p$ for some $p \in \mathbf{patt}(\mathbf{T})$, then replace s by $t[\Omega/x]$.
2. Repeat (1) above until it is not applicable.

If s is an Ω-term representing current information about a term t that we are rewriting to normal form, then $\mathbf{melt}_\omega^{\mathbf{T}}(s)$ represents precisely the information in s that is guaranteed to hold for all t' such that $t \xrightarrow{\mathbf{T}}_\omega^* t'$. By marking an occurrence with a new inert symbol, and melting, we can determine whether ω-rewriting may eliminate that occurrence without rewriting it—that is, we determine whether the occurrence is strongly needed.

Proposition 4.2.3. *Let s be an Ω-term, and let α be an occurrence in s. Let s' be the result of replacing α in s with a new constant symbol, $\bullet$. α is strongly needed if and only if $\mathbf{melt}_\omega^{\mathbf{T}}(s)$ contains an occurrence of $\bullet$.*

Huet and Lévy [Huet and Lévy, 1991] propose a pattern-matching and sequencing technique that accumulates an Ω-term s_α (initially just Ω), representing information about the subterm at a particular node α in a term t. At each step, they choose a strongly needed occurrence of Ω in s_α, and extend s_α by reading the symbol at the corresponding subterm occurrence in t. The information in s_α may be used to control pattern-matching and sequencing as follows:

1. If there is a pattern $p \in \mathbf{patt}(\mathbf{T})$ such that $p \sqsubseteq s_\alpha$, then α is a redex occurrence (in strongly sequential systems we always get $s_\alpha = p$, but it is better to think of the more general case).
2. If there is no pattern $p \in \mathbf{patt}(\mathbf{T})$ such that $s_\alpha \uparrow p$, then α is not currently a redex occurrence.
3. If $\mathbf{melt}_\omega^{\mathbf{T}}(s_\alpha) \neq \Omega$, then α will never be a redex occurrence.
4. It is safe to query the symbol in t corresponding to a strongly needed occurrence of Ω in s_α, and to rewrite any redex occurring there, since it must be strongly needed.

In cases 2 and 3, Huet and Lévy move to a proper descendant α' of α corresponding to the largest subterm s' of s_α, containing the newly read symbol, such that $s' \uparrow p$ for some $p \in \mathbf{patt}(\mathbf{T})$ (because of strong sequentiality, in fact $s' \sqsubseteq p$). Then they let $s_{\alpha'} = s'$ and proceed at α'. In case 1, the fact that we have reached α by safe moves implies that the redex is strongly

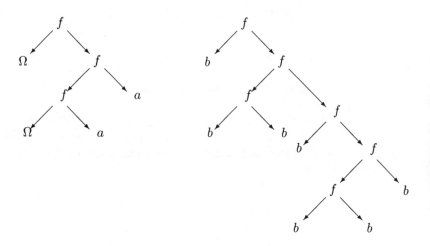

Fig. 7. Pictures of terms for sequencing example

needed. So, they rewrite, and continue processing at an appropriate ancestor of α, rereading whatever symbols have been changed by rewriting at α.

Example 4.2.4. Consider the strongly sequential system

$$\mathbf{T}_{23} = \{f(x, f(f(y, a), a)) \doteq a, \ b \doteq a\}$$

$$\mathbf{patt}(\mathbf{T}_{23}) = \{f(\Omega, f(f(\Omega, a), a)), \ b\}$$

and search for a strongly needed redex in the term

$$t = f(b, f(f(b, b), f(b, f(f(b, b), b))))$$

with occurrences Λ (the root), 1 (leftmost b), 2 ($f(f(b, b), f(b, f(f(b, b), b)))$),
2.1 (leftmost $f(b, b)$), 2.1.1, 2.1.2 (second and third bs), 2.2 ($f(b, f(f(b, b), b)))$
2.2.1 (fourth b), 2.2.2 ($f(f(b, b), b)$), 2.2.2.1 (rightmost $f(b, b)$), 2.2.2.1.1,
2.2.2.1.2, 2.2.2.2 (fifth, sixth and seventh bs). The pattern $f(\Omega, f(f(\Omega, a), a))$,
and the term t, are shown pictorially in Figure 7. The occurrence of Ω chosen for expansion at each step is underlined, and the subterm replacing it is shown in a box.

- Start at the root of t, with $s_\Lambda = \underline{\Omega}$.
  - ∗ There is only one choice, so read the f at the root, and expand to $s_\Lambda = \boxed{f(\Omega, \underline{\Omega})}$.
  - ∗ Only the rightmost Ω is strongly needed, so read the corresponding symbol, and expand to $s_\Lambda = f(\Omega, \boxed{f(\Omega, \underline{\Omega})})$.

* Only the rightmost Ω is strongly needed, so expand to
  $s_\Lambda = f(\Omega, f(\Omega, \boxed{f(\Omega, \Omega)}))$.

* The new Ω-term is incompatible with left-hand side patterns (the f conflicts with an a in the pattern), so we find the largest subterm containing the box that is compatible with a pattern. That subterm is the second principal subterm at 2,
  $s' = f(\Omega, \boxed{f(\Omega, \Omega)})$, so initialize s_2 to s' and continue at 2.

- Now process the second principal subterm of t,
  $t_2 = f(f(b, b), f(b, f(f(b, b), b)))$, with $s_2 = f(\Omega, f(\Omega, \underline{\Omega}))$.

  * Only the rightmost Ω is strongly needed, so expand to
    $s_2 = f(\Omega, f(\Omega, \boxed{f(\Omega, \Omega)}))$.

  * The new Ω-term is incompatible with the patterns (the f conflicts with an a in the pattern), so we find $s' = f(\Omega, f(\Omega, \Omega))$, initialize $s_{2.2}$ to s', and continue at 2.2.

- Now process the subterm $t_{2.2} = f(b, f(f(b, b), b))$ at 2.2, with $s_{2.2} = f(\Omega, f(\Omega, \underline{\Omega}))$.

  * Only the rightmost Ω is strongly needed, so expand to
    $s_{2.2} = f(\Omega, \boxed{f(\Omega, \Omega)})$.

  * Only the rightmost Ω is strongly needed, so expand to
    $s_{2.2} = f(\Omega, f(\Omega, \boxed{b}))$.

  * The new Ω-term is incompatible with the patterns (the b conflicts with an a in the pattern), so we find $s' = b$, initialize $s_{2.2.2.2}$ to s', and continue at 2.2.2.2.

- Now process the subterm $t_{2.2.2.2} = b$ at 2.2.2.2, with $s_{2.2.2.2} = b$. $b \sqsubseteq s_{2.2.2.2}$, and $b \in \mathbf{patt}(\mathbf{T}_{23})$, so this subterm is a strongly needed redex. Rewrite it to a, yielding

$$t = f(b, f(f(b, b), f(b, f(f(b, b), a))))$$

and continue at 2.2, using the last value for $s_{2.2}$ before reading 2.2.2.2:
$s_{2.2} = f(\Omega, f(\Omega, \underline{\Omega}))$.

  * Expand the fourth Ω again, but this time we read an a instead of a b, yielding $s_{2.2} = f(\Omega, f(\Omega, \boxed{a}))$.

  * Only the rightmost Ω is strongly needed, so expand to
    $s_{2.2} = f(\Omega, f(\boxed{f(\Omega, \Omega)}, a))$.

  * Only the rightmost Ω is strongly needed, so expand to
    $s_{2.2} = f(\Omega, f(f(\Omega, \boxed{b}), a))$.

  * Again the new Ω-term is incompatible with the patterns, and further processing at 2.2.2.1.2 rewrites the b to a, yielding

$$t = f(b, f(f(b, b), f(b, f(f(b, a), a))))$$

We continue at 2.2, with the last version of $s_{2.2}$ before reading 2.2.2.1.2. Extend $s_{2.2} = f(\Omega, f(f(\Omega, \underline{\Omega}), a))$ again, this time to $s_{2.2} = f(\Omega, f(f(\Omega, \boxed{a}), a))$.

* Now $f(\Omega, f(f(\Omega, a), a)) \sqsubseteq s_{2.2}$, and $f(\Omega, f(f(\Omega, a), a)) \in \mathbf{patt}(\mathbf{T}_{23})$, so we have a strongly needed redex, which we rewrite to a, yielding
$$t = f(b, f(f(b, b), a))$$

- Continue at 2 with the last Ω-term before reading 2.2: $s_2 = f(\Omega, \Omega)$.
    * Expand the rightmost Ω again, but this time we read an a instead of an f, yielding $s_2 = f(\Omega, \boxed{a})$.
    * The new Ω-term is incompatible with the patterns, and there is no compatible subterm, so we move back toward the root.
- Continue at Λ with the last Ω term before reading 2.2:
$s_\Lambda = f(\Omega, f(\Omega, \underline{\Omega}))$.
    * This time we read an a instead of an f, yielding:
    $s_\Lambda = f(\Omega, f(\Omega, \boxed{a}))$.
    * Only the rightmost Ω is strongly needed, so expand to
    $s_\Lambda = f(\Omega, f(\boxed{f(\Omega, \underline{\Omega})}, a))$.
    * Only the rightmost Ω is strongly needed, so expand to
    $s_\Lambda = f(\Omega, f(f(\Omega, \boxed{b}), a))$.
    * As before, the Ω-term is incompatible with the patterns; further processing at 2.1.2 discovers that b is a redex, and rewrites it to a, yielding
    $$t = f(b, f(b, a), a)$$
    Then we continue at Λ with $s_\Lambda = f(\Omega, f(f(\Omega, \underline{\Omega}), a))$ again, this time reading an a and extending to $s_\Lambda = f(\Omega, f(f(\Omega, \boxed{a}), a))$.
    * Now we have a redex pattern $f(\Omega, f(f(\Omega, a), a))$ at the root. We rewrite to a and start over at the root.
- In general, there might be more computation at the root, but in this example we immediately get $s_\Lambda = a$, which is incompatible with the patterns. Since there is nowhere left to go, we have a normal form.

Huet and Lévy use Ω-terms in a pattern-matching and sequentializing method that succeeds for every strongly sequential system of equations. Several similar but less general methods have been proposed in order to simplify the method in special cases [O'Donnell, 1985; Strandh, 1988; Strandh, 1989; Durand and Salinier, 1993; Durand, 1994; Ramakrishnan and Sekar, 1990].

4.2.2 Representing Sequencing Information by Sets of Subpatterns

Another natural approach to pattern-matching and sequencing is to focus on the left-hand sides of equations, and represent information about a term according to the ways that it does and does not match portions of those left-hand sides.

Definition 4.2.5. Let $\mathbf{T}$ be a set of equations. $\mathbf{U_T}$ is the set of all subterms of members of $\mathbf{patt(T)}$.

A *subpattern set* for $\mathbf{T}$ is a subset $B \subseteq \mathbf{U_T}$.

Subpattern sets may be used to present information about pattern-matching and sequencing in several ways:

1. A *match set* is a subpattern set containing all of the subpatterns known to match at a particular node in a term.
2. A *possibility set* is a subpattern set containing all of the subpatterns that might match at a particular node in a term, as the result of ω-rewriting the proper subterms of that node.
3. A *search set* is a subpattern set containing subpatterns to search for at a particular node, in order to contribute to a redex.

Notice that match sets and possibility sets always contain Ω (except in the unusual case when $\mathbf{T}$ has no occurrence of a variable), because everything matches Ω. Search sets never contain Ω, since it is pointless to search for something that is everywhere; they always contain $\mathbf{patt(T)}$, since finding an entire redex occurrence is always useful.

In order to control pattern-matching and sequencing with subpattern sets, associate a match set M_α and a possibility set P_α with each node in a term t. Initially, $M_\alpha = \{\Omega\}$ and $P_\alpha = \mathbf{U_T}$ for all α. At all times the subterm at α will match every subpattern in M_α, but no subpattern that is not in P_α. That is, $[M, P]$ is an interval in the lattice of subpattern sets in which the true current description of the subterm at α always resides. At every visit to a node α, update M_α and P_α based on the symbol f at α and the information at the children $\alpha_1, \ldots, \alpha_n$ of α as follows:

$$
\begin{aligned}
M_\alpha \;:=\; & M_\alpha \cup \\
& \{f(m_1, \ldots, m_n) \in \mathbf{U_T} : m_1 \sqsubseteq m'_1, \ldots, m_n \sqsubseteq m'_n \text{ for some} \\
& \qquad\qquad\qquad\qquad m'_1 \in M_{\alpha_1}, \ldots, m'_n \in M_{\alpha_n}\}
\end{aligned}
$$

$$
\begin{aligned}
P'_\alpha \;:=\; & P_\alpha \cap \\
& (\{f(p_1, \ldots, p_n) \in \mathbf{U_T} : p_1 \sqsubseteq p'_1, \ldots, p_n \sqsubseteq p'_n \text{ for some} \\
& \qquad\qquad\qquad p'_1 \in P_{\alpha_1}, \ldots, p'_n \in P_{\alpha_n}\} \cup \{\Omega\})
\end{aligned}
$$

$$
P_\alpha \;:=\; \begin{cases} P'_\alpha & \text{if } P'_\alpha \cap \mathbf{patt(T)} = \emptyset \\ \mathbf{U_T} & \text{otherwise} \end{cases}
$$

P'_α represents the set of all subpatterns that may match at node α, as the result of ω-rewriting at *proper* descendants of α. Notice the similarity between the calculation of P_α and the process of melting—$\mathbf{U_T}$ above plays the role of Ω in melting.

Similarly, keep a search set S_α at each node that is visited in the traversal, entering at the root with $S_\Lambda = \mathbf{patt}(\mathbf{T})$. When moving from a node α to the ith child $\alpha.i$ of α, update the search set at $\alpha.i$ by

$$S_{\alpha.i} := \mathbf{patt}(\mathbf{T}) \cup$$
$$\{s : s \text{ is the } i\text{th principal subterm of a member of } S_\alpha \cap P'_\alpha\}$$

The information in M_α, P_α, S_α, and the corresponding information at the children $\alpha_1, \ldots \alpha_n$ of α, may be used to control pattern-matching and sequencing as follows:

1. If $M_\alpha \cap \mathbf{patt}(\mathbf{T}) \neq \emptyset$, then α is a redex occurrence.
2. If $P_\alpha \cap \mathbf{patt}(\mathbf{T}) = \emptyset$, then α will never be a redex occurrence.
3. If $M_\alpha \cap S_\alpha \neq \emptyset$, then α contributes to a possible redex at one of its ancestors.
4. If $P_\alpha \cap S_\alpha = \emptyset$, then the symbol at α will never contribute to a redex occurrence.
5. If there is no Ω-term $s \in S_\alpha$ whose ith principal subterm is in $M_{\alpha.i}$, then it is safe to move to $\alpha.i$ and process it further—in particular, any redex occurrence reached by safe moves is strongly needed.

Hoffmann and I proposed a pattern-matching and sequencing method based on match/possibility/search sets. The method appears heuristically to succeed on most naturally defined orthogonal systems, but Jiefei Hong noticed that there are some strongly sequential systems for which it fails.

Example 4.2.6. Consider the strongly sequential system

$$\mathbf{T}_{24} = \{f(g(a,x),a) \doteq d, \ f(g(x,a),b) \doteq e, \ c \doteq a\}$$

and search for a strongly needed redex in the term $f(g(c,c),c)$ with occurrences Λ (the root), 1 (the subterm $g(c,c)$), 1.1, 1.2, and 2 (the three occurrences of c, from left to right).

- Initially, we search at Λ, with

$$S_\Lambda = \mathbf{patt}(\mathbf{T}_{24}) = \{f(g(a,\Omega),a), \ f(g(\Omega,a),b), \ c\} \qquad M_\Lambda = \{\Omega\}$$

$$P_\Lambda = \mathbf{U}_{\mathbf{T}_{24}} = \{f(g(a,\Omega),a), f(g(\Omega,a),b), c, g(a,\Omega), g(\Omega,a), a, b, \Omega\}$$

Update M_Λ and P_Λ based on $M_1 = M_2 = \{\Omega\}$, $P_1 = P_2 = \mathbf{U}_{\mathbf{T}_{24}}$, and the symbol f at the root—in this case M_Λ and P_Λ do not change, and

$$P'_\Lambda = \{f(g(a,\Omega),a), \ f(g(\Omega,a),b), \ \Omega\}$$

From condition (5) above, it is safe to move to either of 1 or 2.

Suppose that we choose arbitrarily to move to 1.

- Now, we search at 1, with

$$S_1 = \{f(g(a, \Omega), a), \; f(g(\Omega, a), b), \; c, \; g(a, \Omega), \; g(\Omega, a)\}$$

$$M_1 = \{\Omega\} \qquad\qquad P_1 = \mathbf{U_{T_{24}}}$$

Update M_1 and P_1 to

$$M_1 = \{\Omega\} \quad P_1 = P_1' = \{g(a, \Omega), \; g(\Omega, a), \; \Omega\}$$

The possibility set decreases in this case, because there is no left-hand side with g at the root. Now by condition (5), it is *not* safe to move to the first child of 1, 1.1, because $g(\Omega, a) \in S_1$ has Ω as its first principal subterm, and $\Omega \in M_{1.1}$. Similarly, it is not safe to move to 1.2, because of $g(a, \Omega) \in S_1$. The method suggested in [Hoffmann and O'Donnell, 1979] is not capable of backing up to parents and siblings of 1 in order to decide which of the children of 1 to visit first.

On the other hand, suppose we choose arbitrarily to move from Λ to 2 instead of 1.

- Now, we search at 2, with

$$S_2 = \{f(g(a, \Omega), a), \; f(g(\Omega, a), b), \; c, \; a, \; b\}$$

$$M_2 = \{\Omega\} \qquad\qquad P_2 = \mathbf{U_T}$$

Update M_2 and P_2 to

$$M_2 = \{c, \; \Omega\} \quad P_2' = \{c, \Omega\} \quad P_2 = \mathbf{U_T}$$

Since $c \in M_2 \cap \mathbf{patt(T)}$, there is a redex, which is strongly needed since we found it by safe moves, and we rewrite c to a, yielding $f(g(c, c), a)$. Recalculate M_2 and P_2 to

$$M_2 = \{a, \; \Omega\} \quad P_2 = P_2' = \{a, \; \Omega\}$$

$a \in M_2 \cap S_2$, so continue back at Λ trying to complete a redex using the a at 2.

- Search again at Λ; update M_Λ, P_Λ' and P_Λ again. M_Λ and P_Λ do not change, but now

$$P_\Lambda' = \{f(g(a, \Omega), a), \; \Omega\}$$

It is still safe to move to 1.

- Search at 1 with

$$S_1 = \{f(g(a,\Omega),a),\ f(g(\Omega,a),b),\ c,\ g(a,\Omega)\}$$

$$M_1 = \{\Omega\} \qquad\qquad P_1 = \mathbf{U_T}$$

Notice that information from 2 has led to a smaller search set, not containing $g(\Omega, a)$. Update M_1 and P_1 to

$$M_1 = \{\Omega\} \quad P_1 = P_1' = \{g(a,\Omega),\ g(\Omega,a),\ \Omega\}$$

This time it is safe to move to 1.1, but not to 1.2, so we choose the former.

• Search at 1.1 with

$$S_{1.1} = \{f(g(a,\Omega),a),\ f(g(\Omega,a),b),\ c,\ a\}$$

$$M_{1.1} = \{\Omega\} \qquad\qquad P_{1.1} = \mathbf{U_T}$$

The results are the same as in the search at 2 above—c rewrites to a and we continue back at 1.

• Search again at 1, update M_1, P_1 again to

$$M_1 = \{g(a,\Omega),\ \Omega\} \quad P_1 = P_1' = \{g(a,\Omega),\ \Omega\}$$

$g(a,\Omega) \in M_1 \cap S_1$, so continue back at Λ

• Search one more time at Λ, recalculating M_Λ, P_Λ to

$$M_\Lambda = \{f(g(a,\Omega),a),\ \Omega\} \quad P_\Lambda' = \{f(g(a,\Omega),a),\ \Omega\} \quad P_\Lambda = \mathbf{U_T}$$

$f(g(a,\Omega),a) \in M_\Lambda \cap \mathbf{patt(T)}$, so there is a redex at Λ. Rewrite it, yielding d. Update M_Λ, P_Λ to

$$M_\Lambda = \{\Omega\} \quad P_\Lambda = P_\Lambda' = \{\Omega\}$$

$P_\Lambda \cap \mathbf{patt(T)} = \emptyset$, so the d at Λ will never change. Since Λ now has no children, we are done, and d is a normal form.

$\mathbf{T}_{24}$ shows that for some strongly sequential systems, the success of the subpattern set analysis depends on the choice of traversal order. In the strongly sequential system

$$\mathbf{T}_{25} = \{f(g(a,x),g(a,x)) \doteq b,\ f(g(x,a),h(a,x)) \doteq c,$$
$$f(h(a,x),g(x,a)) \doteq d,\ f(h(x,a),h(x,a)) \doteq e\}$$

no order of traversal allows the subpattern set analysis to succeed. The only way to sequence with $\mathbf{T}_{25}$ is to visit *both* of the children of an f before descending to grandchildren. The Huet–Lévy method allows this breadth-first behavior, but the Hoffmann–O'Donnell method does not.

4.2.3 Applying the sequencing techniques

Neither Ω-terms nor subpattern sets should be computed explicitly at run time. Rather, at compile time we compute the finite set of values that can possibly occur while executing a given system of equations **T**, along with tables of the operations required to update them at run time. It is natural to think of Ω-terms and subpattern sets as components of the state of a finite automaton, and the tables of operations as a representation of the transition graph. A key problem is that the number of states may grow exponentially in the size of **T**. [Hoffmann and O'Donnell, 1982] analyzes the number of match sets associated with a set of patterns. There is no published analysis of the number of Ω-terms, nor of possibility and search sets, but it appears that all three may grow at an exponential rate also. Most implementations of equational logic programming appear to use methods that are equivalent to highly restricted forms of the Ω-term method.

The Huet–Lévy Ω-term method is the only published method that succeeds for all strongly sequential systems. The only published method using subpatterns fails in cases, such as $\mathbf{T}_{25}$, where it is necessary to back up before reaching the leaves of a pattern, in order to carry information about sequencing to a sibling. I conjecture that a simple variation in the algorithm of [Hoffmann and O'Donnell, 1979] will succeed on all strongly sequential systems. Besides the superior generality of the Huet–Lévy algorithm, Ω-term methods have the advantage of a simple notation, making it relatively easy to discover restrictions that control the number of possible values. On the other hand, subpattern sets express the significance of information for pattern matching purposes in a particularly transparent way. The subpattern set method also has the advantage of separating clearly the information that is passed up the tree (match and possibility sets) from the information that is passed down the tree (search sets). Match and possibility sets may be associated with nodes in a heap representation of a tree, taking advantage of sharing in the heap. Search sets and Ω-terms depend on the path by which a node was reached, so they must be stored on a traversal stack, or otherwise marked so that they are not shared inappropriately.

4.3 Driving procedures for term rewriting

4.3.1 A recursive schema for lazy evaluation

It is natural to drive the conventional strict evaluation of a term by a recursive procedure, *eval*, shown in Figure 8. For each function symbol f that appears in a term, there is a predefined procedure $\bar{f}$ to compute the value of that function on given arguments. The simplicity of recursive evaluation is appealing, and it has a direct and transparent correspondence to the semantic definition of the value of a term (Definition 2.3.3 of the chapter 'Introduction: Logic and Logic Programming Languages). It is straightforward to let the value of a term be its normal form, and use the recursive *eval*

Procedure *eval*(t)
> Let $t = f(t_1, \ldots, t_n)$;   (1)
> **For** $i := 1, \ldots, n$ **do**   (2)
> > $v_i := eval(t_i)$ (3)
>
> **end for**;
> **Return** $\bar{f}(v_1, \ldots, v_n)$ (4)

end procedure *eval*

Fig. 8. Recursive schema for strict evaluation.

above to find the normal form of its input. But, the structure of the procedure is heavily biased toward strict evaluation. Even the conditional function *cond* requires a special test between lines (1) and (2) to avoid evaluating both branches. Lazy functional languages have been implemented with conventional recursive evaluation, by adding new values, called *suspensions, thunks,* or *closures* to encode unevaluated subterms [Peyton Jones, 1987; Bloss *et al.*, 147–164]. The overhead of naive implementations of suspensions led to early skepticism about the performance of lazy evaluation. Clever optimizations of suspensions have improved this overhead substantially, but it is still arguably better to start with an evaluation schema that deals with lazy evaluation directly.

For orthogonal systems of equations, a function symbol that contributes to a redex occurrence at a proper ancestor cannot itself be at the root of a redex. So, a term may be normalized by a recursive procedure that rewrites its argument only until the root symbol can never be rewritten.

Definition 4.3.1.   Let **T** be a set of equations, and t be a term. t is a *(weak) head-normal form* for **T** if and only if there is no redex u such that $t \xrightarrow{\text{T}}^{*} u$.

t is a *strong head-normal form* for **T** if and only if there is no redex u such that $t \xrightarrow[\omega]{\text{T}}^{*} u$.

Head normality is undecidable, but strong head normality is easy to detect by melting.

Proposition 4.3.2.   *Let t be a term. t is a strong head-normal form for* **T** *if and only if* $\text{melt}_\omega^{\text{T}}(t) \neq \Omega$.

Let t be an Ω-term. The following are equivalent:

- u *is a strong head-normal form for* **T**, *for all* $u \sqsupseteq t$
- $\text{melt}_\omega^{\text{T}}(t) \neq \Omega$.

The procedure *head-eval* in Figure 9 below rewrites its argument only to strong head-normal form, instead of all the way to normal form. The tests whether t is in strong head-normal form (1), whether t is a redex (2), and the choice of a safe child i (5), may be accomplished by any

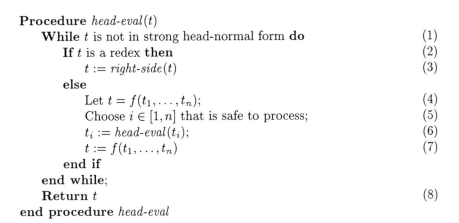

Procedure *head-eval*(t)
 While t is not in strong head-normal form **do** (1)
  If t is a redex **then** (2)
   $t := \textit{right-side}(t)$ (3)
  else
   Let $t = f(t_1, \ldots, t_n)$; (4)
   Choose $i \in [1, n]$ that is safe to process; (5)
   $t_i := \textit{head-eval}(t_i)$; (6)
   $t := f(t_1, \ldots, t_n)$ (7)
  end if
 end while;
 Return t (8)
end procedure *head-eval*

Fig. 9. Recursive schema to find head-normal form.

pattern-matching and sequencing method that succeeds on the given system of equations. The procedure *right-side* called by *head-eval* above builds and returns the right-hand side instance corresponding to a given redex. *right-side* contains the information about function symbols analogous to that contained in the collection of $\bar{f}$s used by the strict evaluator *eval*. In a detailed implementation, pattern-matching and sequencing require some additional data structures, and possibly some additional values returned by *head-eval*.

In order to produce a normal form for t, *head-eval* must be called recursively on the subterms of t, as shown by the procedure *norm* in Figure 10 below. Section 7 shows how other schemes for calling *head-eval*, more so-

Procedure *norm*(t)
 $t := \textit{head-eval}(t)$; (1)
 Let $t = f(t_1, \ldots, t_n)$; (2)
 For $i := 1, \ldots, n$ **do** (3)
  $t_i := \textit{norm}(t_i)$ (4)
 end for;
 $t := f(t_1, \ldots, t_n)$; (5)
 Return t (6)
end procedure *norm*

Fig. 10. Recursive schema to normalize a term lazily.

phisticated than *norm*, may be used to generalize the behavior of input and output in equational logic programming.

4.3.2   Using the term data structure in rewriting

The basic recursive schema of *head-eval* may manipulate the tables **val**, **repl** and **ind** in a variety of different ways, with various advantages and disadvantages in performance. In most cases, particularly in implementations of orthogonal systems of equations, the pattern-matching and sequencing method operates on $\mathbf{val}_{\mathbf{repl}}^{max}(\alpha_0)$, where α_0 is a heap address that initially represents the root of the input term. $\mathbf{val}_{\mathbf{repl}}^{max}(\alpha_0)$ is typically the closest thing to a normal form for the original input that can be read easily from **val**, **repl** and **ind**, so we achieve the best progress by rewriting it further. It is also clearly correct to run the pattern-matcher/sequencer on another term in $\mathbf{val}_{\mathbf{repl}}^{*}(\alpha_0)$. I am not aware of any current implementation that does this, but it is likely to be necessary in complete implementations of nonconfluent systems, and equation solving systems (Section 7.2), which will presumably need to explore several rewriting sequences in parallel. The details of access to **val** and **repl** for pattern-matching/sequencing fit into the implementation of the conditions tested in lines (1) and (2) of *head-eval*, and in the choice of i in line (5). If the calculation of $\mathbf{val}_{\mathbf{repl}}^{max}(\alpha_0)$ follows **repl** links, it is usually desirable to compress the paths using transformations (4) and (5) from Section 4.1.2, which speeds up future calculations of $\mathbf{val}_{\mathbf{repl}}^{max}(\alpha_0)$. The benefits of transformations (4) and (5) are essentially the same as the benefits of path compression in the UNION/FIND algorithm [Aho *et al.*, 1974] (think of **repl** as representing a partition of terms into equivalence classes of terms that have been proved equal).

The implementation of *right-side*, called in line (3) of *head-eval*, is the only place where updating of **val**, **repl** and **ind** is required. Suppose that we are applying the equation $l \doteq r$ to rewrite the term t, represented in the heap with root node α. The most obvious implementation of *right-side* builds all of the nonvariable structure of r in newly allocated heap nodes in **val**, using pointers to pre-existing structure for the variable substitutions (this is essentially what a conventional Lisp implementation does). Let β be the root node of the constructed representation of the appropriate instance of r. Once the instance of r is built, β may be copied into α. Unfortunately, when r consists of a single variable, as in $car(cons(x,y)) \doteq x$, β may have already been shared extensively, and this copying loses an obvious opportunity for further sharing [O'Donnell, 1977]. The natural alternative to copying β is to assign $\mathbf{repl}(\alpha) := \beta$ (represent the rewriting step by a link, instead of rewriting in place). This avoids any loss of sharing, and if path compression is applied in calculating $\mathbf{val}_{\mathbf{repl}}^{max}(\alpha_0)$, it appears to have an acceptable cost in overhead for access to the heap. In many programs, a more sophisticated implementation of *right-side* can save an exponentially growing amount of wasted work by sharing identical subterms of r. Many natural programs have such identical subterms of right-hand sides, and in practice this makes the difference between efficiency and infeasibility often enough to be well worth the effort. The cost of detecting identical subterms of right-hand sides using the tree isomorphism algorithm [Aho *et al.*, 1974] is quite modest, and can be borne entirely at compile time.

4.3.3 Dynamic exploitation of sharing and memoing of ground terms

There are several ways that the signature index **ind** may be used to improve sharing dynamically and opportunistically at run time (these are examples of transformations (6) and (7) of Section 4.1.2). A further sophistication of *right-side* builds the structure of the instance of r from the leaves and variable instances up, and for each constructed signature $f(\alpha_1, \ldots, \alpha_n)$ it checks $\mathbf{ind}(f(\alpha_1, \ldots, \alpha_n))$. If the result is *nil*, *right-side* builds a new heap node β containing signature $f(\alpha_1, \ldots, \alpha_n)$, and updates **ind** by $\mathbf{ind}(f(\alpha_1, \ldots, \alpha_n)) := \beta$. If the result is $\gamma \neq nil$ it shares the pre-existing representation rooted at γ. This technique is essentially the same as the *hashed cons* optimization in Lisp implementations [Spitzen *et al.*, 1978]. There are more places where it may be valuable to check the signature index for opportunistic sharing. Immediately after line (6) of *head-eval*, the signature at the root α of the heap representation of t may have changed, due to rewriting of t_i and path-compression. A sophisticated implementation may check $\mathbf{ind}(\mathbf{val}(\alpha))$, and if the result is $\beta \neq nil, \alpha$, reassign $\mathbf{repl}(\alpha) := \beta$, so that further path compression will replace links pointing to α by links to β, thus increasing sharing. If $\mathbf{ind}(\mathbf{val}(\alpha)) = nil$, then reassign $\mathbf{ind}(\mathbf{val}(\alpha)) := \alpha$. Finally, when *head-eval* is called recursively on a subterm rooted at the heap address α, the signature at α may be modified as the result of rewriting of a shared descendant of α that was visited previously by a path not passing through α. So, the same checking of **ind** and updating of **repl** or **ind** may be performed in step (1) of *head-eval*, after any implicit path compression, but before actually testing for strong head-normal form.

The opportunistic sharing techniques described above have a nontrivial cost in overhead added to each computation step, but in some cases they reduce the number of computation steps by an exponentially growing amount. See [Sherman, 1990] for more details on opportunistic sharing, and discussion of the tradeoff between ovehead on each step and number of steps. The method that checks new opportunities for sharing at every node visit as described above is called *lazy directed congruence closure*. An even more aggressive strategy, called *directed congruence closure* [Chew, 1980], makes extra node visits wherever there is a chance that a change in signature has created new sharing opportunities, even though the pattern-matcher/sequencer has not generated a need to visit all such nodes (i.e., when the signature at a shared node changes, directed congruence closure visits all parents of the node, many of which might never be visited again by *head-eval*). Directed congruence closure may reduce the number of steps in lazy directed congruence closure by an exponential amount, but the added overhead appears heuristically large, and changes the structure of the implementation significantly from the recursive schema of *head-eval*.

Opportunistic sharing strategies are generalizations of the idea of *memo functions* [Keller and Sleep, 1986; Mitchie, 1968; Field and Harrison, 1988]. Most memoing techniques limit themselves to remembering equalities of the form $f(t_1, \ldots, t_n) \doteq u$, where the t_is and u are all in normal form. Lazy directed congruence closure and its variants can remember partial evaluations as well, as can the *lazy memo functions* of Hughes [Hughes, 1985a]. There is a nice theoretical characterization of the memoing power of directed congruence closure.

Proposition 4.3.3 ([Chew, 1980]). *At any step in the process of rewriting a term, there is a set* **G** *of ground instances of equations that have been applied in rewriting. Using directed congruence closure, we never apply a ground instance that is a semantic consequence of* **G**.

Not only does directed congruence closure avoid ever doing the same rewriting step twice in different contexts, it only performs a new rewriting step when new substitution of terms for variables in the given equations is absolutely necessary to derive that step.

4.3.4 Sharing and memoing nonground terms—paramodulation

The next natural step beyond directed congruence closure is sharing/ memoing nonground terms. Abstractly in theorem-proving language, this amounts to applying *paramodulation* [Robinson and Wos, 1969; Loveland, 1978; Gallier, 1986] to derive new equations with variables, instead of using demodulation to merely rewrite a given term. Paramodulation takes two equations $p \doteq q[r/x]$ and $s \doteq t$ and substitutions σ_r, σ_s of terms for variables such that $r\sigma_r = s\sigma_s$, and derives the new equation $p\sigma_r \doteq q\sigma_r[t\sigma_s/x]$, which follows from the first two by instantiation, substitution, and transitivity. Paramodulation sometimes improves the lengths of proofs by exponentially growing amounts compared to pure term rewriting [Loveland, 1978].

Example 4.3.4. Consider the set $\mathbf{T}_{rev}$ of equations defining list reversal (*rev*) and appending an element to the end of a list (*app*).

$$\mathbf{T}_{rev} = \{ \quad rev(nil) \doteq nil,$$
$$rev(cons(x, y)) \doteq app(x, rev(y)),$$
$$app(x, nil) \doteq x,$$
$$app(x, cons(y, z)) \doteq cons(y, app(x, z)) \quad \}$$

The number of rewriting steps required to append an element to a list of i elements is $i + 1$. But, consider applying paramodulation instead. One step of paramodulating the last equation in $\mathbf{T}_{rev}$ with itself yields

$app(w, cons(x, cons(y, z))) \doteq cons(x, cons(y, app(w, z)))$, which moves the appended element w past the first two elements in the list. The new equation paramodulates again with $app(x, cons(y, z)) \doteq cons(y, app(x, z))$ to move the appended element past three list elements, but paramodulating the new equation with itself does even better, moving the appended element past four list elements. It is straightforward to produce a sequence of equations, each by paramodulating the previous one with itself, so that the ith equation in the sequence moves an appended element past 2^i list elements. So, paramodulation reduces the number of steps involved in normalizing $app(\alpha, \beta)$, where β is a list of i elements, from $i + 1$ to $\mathcal{O}(\log i)$.

The improvement in normalizing $rev(\alpha)$ is less dramatic, but perhaps more useful in practice. If α has i elements, then rewriting requires $\Omega(i^2)$ steps to normalize $rev(\alpha)$, because it involves appending to the end of a sequence of lists of lengths $0, 1, \ldots, i$. But, we may produce a sequence of equations, each by paramodulating the previous one with

$$app(x, cons(y, z)) \doteq cons(y, app(x, z))$$

so that the ith equation in the sequence appends an arbitrary element to a list of length i. The whole sequence requires only i steps of paramodulation, so a list of i elements may be reversed by $\mathcal{O}(i)$ paramodulation steps.

There are several problems in reducing the ideas on paramodulation suggested in Example 4.3.4 to useful practice. First, we need a way to control paramodulation—that is, to choose useful steps of paramodulation to perform (equivalently, useful derived nonground equations to save and use along with the originally given program equations for further evaluation steps). Sequential strategies for lazy evaluation appear to solve this problem in principle. Whenever a sequential rewriting process discovers that a ground term s rewrites in one step to a ground term t, and existing links in the **repl** table rewrite t further to u, ground sharing techniques such as lazy directed congruence closure in effect save the derived ground equation $s \doteq u$ for later use as a single step (this is accomplished by setting **repl**$(\alpha) := \gamma$ where $t = \mathbf{val}^*_{\mathbf{repl}}(\alpha)$ and $u = \mathbf{val}^*_{\mathbf{repl}}(\gamma)$). A method for nonground sharing should save instead the nonground equation $s' \doteq u'$, where s' is the generalization of s containing all of the symbol instances in s that were scanned by the sequential rewriting process in order to rewrite s to u, with unique variables replacing the unscanned portions of s. The appropriate generalization u' of u is easy to derive from the same information that determines s'. The equation $s' \doteq u'$ may be derived by paramodulation, using the same equations that were used to rewrite s to u. This strategy for driving paramodulation by the same sequentializing process that drives rewriting accomplishes the improvement of list reversal from quadratic to a linear number of inference steps in Example 4.3.4 above.

A second problem is to deal efficiently with the more general sets of equations that we get by adding the results of paramodulation to the original program equations. Notice that, even when the original program is orthogonal, there are overlaps between the original equations and the results of paramodulation. When several different equations apply to the same subterm, we probably should choose the most specific one, but that may not always be uniquely determined (see Figure 4 in Section 3.2.4 for the different sorts of overlap). At least in Example 4.3.4 above, choosing the most specific applicable equation accomplishes the improvement of list appending from linear to logarithmic.

Finally, we need an efficient data structure for representing sets of non-ground equations, with a good way to add the new equations that result from paramodulation. Suffix trees [Aho *et al.*, 1974] appear to provide a good basis for representing dynamically increasing sets of patterns and/or equations [Strandh, 1984], but it is not at all clear how to generalize these ideas efficiently to terms instead of strings (a good dissertation project: implement string rewriting with as much sharing as possible at both ends of a substring—this is essentially nonground sharing with only unary functions). A more detailed examination of Example 4.3.4 above reveals that, although the number of abstract steps required to reverse a list of length i using paramodulation is only $\mathcal{O}(i)$, each abstract step involves an equation with a larger left-hand side than the one before. So, while the number of steps decreases, the cost of pattern-matching in each step increases, and the total cost for reversal remains $\Omega(i^2)$. The exponential improvement in appending to the end of a list still yields a net win, but it is not clear how often such exponential improvements will arise in practice. In order to decrease the total cost of reversal to $\mathcal{O}(i)$, we need a way to make the pattern matching process incremental, so that the work done to match a smaller pattern may be reused in matching a larger pattern derived from it. I cannot find a reason why such efficient incremental pattern matching is impossible, but no known technique accomplishes it today.

Another starting point for research on nonground sharing is the work on sharing in the lambda calculus [Staples, 1982; Lamping, 1990; Kathail, 1984; Gonthier *et al.*, 1992]. Some surprisingly powerful data structures have been discovered already, but the overhead of using them is still not understood well enough to determine their practical impact.

4.3.5   Storage allocation

Essentially all of the known ideas for automatic storage allocation and deallocation are applicable to the **val/repl/ind** heap [Cohen, 1981; Appel, 1991]. Unfortunately, one of the most attractive methods in current practice—generational garbage collection [Lieberman and Hewitt, 1983]—has been analyzed on the assumption that it is rare for old nodes in the heap to point to much more recently allocated ones. The **repl** links in lazy implementations of equational logic programming appear to violate that assumption. I know of no experimental or theoretical study of the efficiency of generational garbage collection with lazy evaluation. The aggressive sharing techniques also call into question the normal definition of 'garbage' nodes as those that *cannot* be reached starting from some set of directly accessible root nodes. In the discussion above, the directly accessible nodes are α_0 and all of the nodes entered in the **ind** table. With the more aggressive approaches to sharing, every node in the heap is usually accessible from nodes in **ind**, so there is no garbage according to the strict definition. On the other hand, nodes that are inaccessible from α_0 (the root of the term being rewritten to normal form) contain information that may be recalculated from the α_0-accessible nodes and the equational program, so, while they are not useless garbage, they are not *essential* to the calculation of a final result. I am not aware of any published literature on deallocation of useful but inessential nodes in a heap, which might be called 'rummage sale' instead of 'garbage collection.' Phillip Wadler proposed that a garbage-collection/rummage-sale procedure might also perform rewriting steps that reduce the size of the given term. Such a technique appears to provide the space-saving benefits of strictness analysis [Mycroft, 1980; Hughes, 1985b], avoiding both the compile-time cost and the nonuniformity in the run-time control. Research is needed on the practical impact of various heuristic strategies for looking ahead in a rewriting sequence in search of a smaller version of the current term.

5 Compiling efficient code from equations

Conventional approaches to compiling functional programs, following early Lisp compilers, associate a block of machine code with each function symbol f, and use the recursive schema for *eval* in Figure 8, with some representation of *suspensions* to encode partially evaluated terms as a new sort of value [Peyton Jones, 1987]. A natural and less explored alternative is to associate a block of machine code with each state in a finite automaton whose states are derived from an analysis of the program using Ω-terms or subpattern sets [Bondorf, 1989; Durand *et al.*, 1991]. The state-based approach has no explicit representation of suspensions, although in effect terms that it must build in the heap are implicit suspensions. And, a naive implementation of the state-based approach leads to more and smaller recursive procedures than the symbol-based approach. Of course, sophisticated symbol-based compilers may optimize by compiling multiple specialized versions of a single function for different sorts of arguments, and sophisticated state-based compilers may optimize by inlining some of the recursive calls. The *supercombinator* method [Hughes, 1982] introduces new symbols internal to the implementation, reducing the dependence of symbol-based compiling on the actual symbols in the source program. After such optimizations, it is not clear whether symbol-based compiling and state-based compiling will actually generate different code. The function symbols appear to be conceptually tied to the programmer's view of her program, while the automaton states appear to be conceptually tied to the computational requirements of the program. I conjecture that in the long run the state-based approach will prove more convenient for achieving the best run-time performance, while the symbol-based approach will maintain a more intuitive connection between program structure and performance.

Both the function-based and state-based methods compile the information in the set of equations constituting a program, but they both treat the input term and all of the intermediate terms produced in rewriting to normal form as static data structures, which must be interpreted by the compiled equational code. The Tigre system [Koopman and Lee, 1989; Koopman, 1990] by contrast compiles each function symbol *in the term being evaluated* into a block of code—the entire term becomes a self modifying program that reduces itself to normal form. Tigre compiles only a particular extension of the combinator calculus; an interesting generalization would be a Tigre-like compiler for an arbitrary orthogonal system.

Several abstract machine languages have been proposed as intermediate languages for equational compilers, or as real machine languages for specialized term-rewriting machines. Landin's SECD machine [Landin, 1965] is designed to support evaluation of lambda terms. The G Machine [Johnsson, 1984; Augustsson, 1984; Burn *et al.*, 1988] is intended as a specialized machine language or intermediate language for term rewriting in general. Equational Machine (EM) code [Durand *et al.*, 1991; Strandh, 1988] is designed to support state-based compiling of equational programs, and the optimizations that seem most important in that approach. Several other abstract machine proposals are in [Cardelli, 1983; Cardelli, 1984; Cousineau *et al.*, 1985]. Turner proposes to compile equational systems into the combinator calculus, using the well-known capability of the combinator calculus to encode substitution in the lambda calculus [Turner, 1979]. Then, an implementation of the combinator calculus, fine tuned for performance, can support essentially all equational logic programming languages. The impact of such translations of one rewriting system to another is ill understood—in particular the effects on sharing and parallelism (see Section 6) are quite subtle. The Warren Abstract Machine (WAM) [Warren, 1983], intended as an intermediate language for Prolog compilers, has also been used in theorem provers as a representation for terms—*t* is represented by WAM code to unify an arbitrary input with *t*. I am not aware of any published study of the applicability of such a WAM encoding of terms to functional or equational logic programming.

6 Parallel implementation

One of the primary early motivations for studying functional programming languages was the apparent opportunities for parallel evaluation [Backus, 1978]. So, it is ironic that most of the effort in functional and equational logic programming to date involves sequential implementation. A variety of proposals for parallel implementation may be found in [Peyton Jones, 1987].

Both strictness analysis and sequentiality analysis are used primarily to choose a sequential order of computation that avoids wasted steps. An important open topic for research is the extension of sequentiality analysis to support parallel computation. Huet and Lévy's sequentiality analysis is already capable of identifying more than one strongly needed redex in a term. A parallel implementation might allocate processors first to the strongly needed redexes, and then to other more speculative efforts. It appears that sequentiality analysis can be generalized rather easily (although this has not been done in print) to identify strongly needed *sets* of redexes, where no individual redex is certain to be needed, but at least one member of the set is needed. For example, with the positive parallel-or equations in $\mathbf{T}_{or+}$ of Examples 2.3.16 and 3.2.1, it is intuitively clear that if α is needed in t, and β is needed in u, then at least one of α and β must be rewritten in $or(t, u)$ (although neither is *needed* according to the formal Definition 3.2.3). Further research is required on the practical impact of heuristic strategies for allocating parallel processors to the members of strongly needed sets. It is natural to give priority to the singleton sets (that is, to the strongly needed redexes), but it is not clear whether a set of size 2 should be preferred to one of size 3—perhaps other factors than the size of the set should be considered. Strongly needed redex sets are essentially *disjunctive* assertions about the need for redexes—more general sorts of boolean relations may be useful (e.g., either *all* of $\alpha_1, \ldots, \alpha_m$ or *all* of $\beta_1, \ldots, \beta_n$ are needed).

Unfortunately, since strongly needed redexes are all outermost, sequentiality analysis as known today can only help with parallelism between different arguments to a function. But, one of the most useful qualities of lazy programming is that it simulates a parallel producer–consumer relationship between a function and its arguments. It seems likely that much of the useful parallelism to be exploited in equational logic programming involves parallel rewriting of nested redexes. An analysis of nonoutermost needed redexes appears to require the sort of abstract interpretation that is used in strictness analysis [Mycroft, 1980; Hughes, 1985b]—it certainly will depend on right-hand sides as well as left-hand sides of equations. Unfortunately, most of the proposed intermediate languages for compiling equational programs are inherently sequential, and a lot of work is required to convert current sequential compiling ideas to a parallel environment. The idea of compiling everything into combinators may not be useful for parallel implementation. The known translations of lambda terms into combinators eliminate some apparent parallelism between application of a function and rewriting of the definition of the function (although no direct implementation is known to support all of this apparent parallelism either). Only very preliminary information is available on the inherent *parallel* power of rewriting systems: even the correct definition of such power is problematic [O'Donnell, 1985].

At a more concrete level, there are a lot of problems involved in parallelizing the heap-based execution of evaluation/rewriting sequences. A data structure, possibly distributed amongst several processors, is needed to keep track of the multiple locations at which work is proceeding. If any speculative work is done on redexes that are not known to be needed, there must be a way to kill off processes that are no longer useful, and reallocate their processing to to useful processes (although aggressive sharing through the signature index confuses the question of usefulness of processes in the same way that it confuses the usefulness of heap nodes).

Sharing presents another challenge. Several different processors may reach a shared node by different paths. It is important for data integrity that they do not make simultaneous incompatible updates, and important for efficiency that they do not repeat work. But, it is incorrect for the first process to lock all others completely out of its work area. Suppose we are applying a system of equations including $car(cons(x,y)) \doteq x$. There may be a node α in the heap containing the signature $cons(\beta_1, \beta_2)$ shared between two parents, one of them containing $cons(\alpha, \delta)$ and the other containing $car(\alpha)$. A process might enter first through the *cons* parent, and perform an infinite loop rewriting inside β_2. If a second process enters through the *car* node, it is crucial to allow it to see the *cons* at α, to link to β_1, and depending on the context above possibly to continue rewriting at β_1 and below.

Abstractly, we want to lock node/state pairs, and allow multiple processes to inspect the same node, as long as they do so in different states, but when a process reaches a node that is already being processed *in the same state* it should wait, and allow its processor to be reassigned, since any work that it tries to do will merely repeat that of its predecessor. It is not at all clear how to implement such a notion of locking with acceptable overhead. Perhaps a radically different approach for assigning work to processors is called for, that does not follow the structure of current sequential implementations so closely. For example, instead of the shared-memory approach to the heap in the preceding discussion, perhaps different sections of the heap should be assigned to particular processors for a relatively long period, and demands for evaluation should be passed as messages between processors when they cross the boundaries of heap allocation.

7 Extensions to equational logic programming

7.1 Incremental infinite input and output

The logic programming approach to answering normal form queries leads naturally to the use of lazy evaluation to guarantee completeness. But, once we commit to lazy evaluation, the basic scheme of normal form queries seems too limited. Inside an equational computation, it is natural to conceive of procedures consuming and producing potentially infinite terms incrementally, in the manner of communicating coroutines. It is perfectly sensible to define objects that correspond intuitively to infinite terms, as long as only finite portions of these infinite terms are required to produce output. It is annoying that the full flexibility of incremental demand-driven computation in the internal computation is not available at the input/output interface. Aside from the loss of input/output programming power *per se*, such a discrepancy between internal and external communication tends to encourage large, unwieldy, monolithic programs, and discourage the collections of small, separate, modular programs that are more desirable in many ways.

The desired abstract behavior of a demand-driven incremental I/O interface is essentially clear. The consumer of output demands the symbol at the root of the output. The equational program computes until it has produced a head-normal form equivalent to the input, then it outputs the root symbol of that head-normal form, and recursively makes the principal subterms available to the consumer of output, who can demand symbols down different paths of the output tree in any order. During the computation of a head-normal form, the equational program generates demands for symbols in the input. The producer of input is responsible only for providing those input symbols that are demanded. In this way, both input and output terms are treated incrementally as needed, and each may be infinite.

A direct generalization of equational logic programming by extending the set of terms to include infinite ones is semantically problematic.

Example 7.1.1. Consider the system of equations

$$\mathbf{T}_{27} = \{a \doteq f(c, a), \; b \doteq f(c, f(c, b))\}$$

The natural infinite output to expect from input a is $f(c, f(c, \ldots))$. b produces the same infinite output. So, if in our semantic system $f(c, f(c, \ldots))$ is a generalized term, with a definite value (no matter what that value is), then $\mathbf{T}_{27} \models (a \doteq b)$. But, according to the semantics of Definition 2.3.14 in Section 2.3.4 of the chapter 'Introduction: Logic and Logic Programming Languages', $\mathbf{T}_{27} \not\models_{\doteq} (a \doteq b)$, because there are certainly models in which the equation $x \doteq f(c, x)$ has more than one solution. For example, interpret f as integer addition, and c as the identity element zero. Every integer n satisfies $n = 0 + n$.

Even if we replace the second equation with the exact substitution of b for a in the first, that is $b \doteq f(c,b)$, it does not follow by standard equational semantics that $a \doteq b$. With some difficulty we may define a new semantic system, with a restricted set of models in which all functions have sufficient continuity properties to guarantee unique values for infinite terms. But it is easy to see that the logical consequence relation for such a semantic system is not semicomputable (recursively enumerable). It is always suspect to say that we understand a system of logic according to a definition of meaning that we cannot apply effectively.

Instead, I propose to interpret outputs involving infinite terms as abbreviations for infinite conjunctions of formulae in the first-order predicate calculus (FOPC) (such infinite conjunctions, and infinite disjunctions as well, are studied in the formal system called $L_{\omega_1,\omega}$ [Karp, 1964]).

Definition 7.1.2. The *first-order predicate calculus with equality* (FOPC$_{\doteq}$) is the result of including the equality symbol $\doteq$ in the set **Pred**$_2$ of binary predicate symbols, and combining the semantic rules for FOPC (Definitions 2.3.1–2.3.4, Section 2.3.1 of the chapter 'Introduction: Logic and Logic Programming Languages') and Equational Logic (Definitions 2.3.13–2.3.14, Section 2.3.4 of the 'Introduction ...' chapter) in the natural way (a model for FOPC$_{\doteq}$ satisfies the restrictions of a model for FOPC and the restrictions of a model for equational logic).

$L_{\omega_1,\omega,\doteq}$ is the extension of FOPC$_{\doteq}$ to allow countably infinite conjunctions and disjunctions in formulae. Let $\mathbf{F}_{P,\omega_1,\omega,\doteq}$ be the set of formulae in $L_{\omega_1,\omega,\doteq}$. Extend the semantic system for FOPC$_{\doteq}$ to a semantic system for $L_{\omega_1,\omega,\doteq}$ by the following additional rules for infinite conjunctions and disjunctions:

1. $\rho_{\tau,\nu}(\bigwedge\{A_1, A_2, \ldots\}) = 1$ if and only if $\rho_{\tau,\nu}(A_i) = 1$ for all $i \geq 1$
2. $\rho_{\tau,\nu}(\bigvee\{A_1, A_2, \ldots\}) = 1$ if and only if $\rho_{\tau,\nu}(A_i) = 1$ for some $i \geq 1$

That is, an infinite conjunction is true precisely when all of its conjuncts are true; and an infinite disjunction is true precisely when at least one of its disjuncts is true.

A set T of terms is a *directed set* if and only if, for every two terms $t_1, t_2 \in T$, there is a term $t_3 \in T$ such that t_3 is an instance of t_1 and also an instance of t_2.

Let U be a countable directed set of linear terms. For each $u \in U$, let $\vec{y}_u$ be a list of the variables occurring in u. Let t be a finite ground term. The *conjunctive equation* of t and U is the infinite conjunction

$$\bigwedge\{(\exists \vec{y}_u : (t \doteq u)) : u \in U\}$$

$\mathbf{T}_P^\omega$ is the set of finite and infinite terms.

The *term limit* of a directed set U (written $\lim(U)$) is the possibly infinite term resulting from overlaying all of the terms $u \in U$, and substituting the new symbol $\bot$ for any variables that are not overlaid by nonvariable symbols. Since members of U are pairwise consistent, every location in the limit gets a unique symbol, or by default comes out as $\bot$. To see more rigorously that the term limit of U is well defined, construct a (possibly transfinite) *chain*, $\langle t_0 \sqsubseteq t_1 \sqsubseteq \cdots \rangle$. First, $t_0 = \bot$. Given t_α, choose (axiom of choice) an $s \in U$ such that $s \not\sqsubseteq t_\alpha$, and let $t_{\alpha+1}$ be the overlay of s with t_α. At limit ordinals λ, let t_λ be the limit of the chain of terms preceding λ. With a lot of transfinite induction, we get to a t_β such that, for all $s \in U$, $s \sqsubseteq t_\beta$, at which point the chain is finished. $\lim(U)$ is the limit of that chain.

The *canonical set* of an infinite term t (written **approx**(t)) is the set of all finite linear terms t' (using some arbitrary canonical scheme for naming the variables) such that t is an instance of t'. **approx**(t) is a directed set, and $\lim(\textbf{approx}(t)) = t$.

A careful formal definition of infinite terms and limits is in [Kenneway *et al.*, 1991; Dershowitz *et al.*, 1991], but an intuitive appreciation suffices for this section.

When the finite input t produces the infinite output $\lim(U)$, instead of interpreting the output as the equation $t \doteq \lim(U)$, interpret it as the conjunctive equation of t and U. Notice that a *chain* (a sequence $u_1, u_2, \ldots$ such that u_{i+1} is an instance of u_i) is a special case of a directed set. The infinite outputs for finite inputs may be expressed by chains, but the generality of directed sets is needed with infinite outputs for infinite inputs below.

Infinite inputs require a more complex construction, since they introduce universal quantification that must be nested appropriately with the existential quantification associated with infinite output. Also, different orders in which a consumer explores the output may yield different sequences of demands for input, and this flexibility needs to be supported by the semantics.

Definition 7.1.3. Let T and U be directed sets of linear terms such that no variable occurs in both $t \in T$ and $u \in U$. For each term $t \in T$ and $u \in U$, let $\vec{x}_t$ and $\vec{y}_u$ be lists of the variables occurring in t and u, respectively. Let $f : T \to 2^U$ be a function from terms in T to directed subsets of U, such that when t_2 is an instance of t_1, every member of $f(t_2)$ is an instance of every member of $f(t_1)$. The *conjunctive equation* of T and U by f is the infinite conjunction

$$\bigwedge \{(\forall \vec{x}_t : \exists \vec{y}_u : (t \doteq u)) : t \in T \text{ and } u \in f(t)\}$$

Definition 7.1.4. Let $s_1, \ldots, s_i \in \mathbf{T}_P$ be terms. A term u is an *incre-*

mental normal form for $\{s_1, \ldots, s_i\}$ if and only if no nonvariable subterm of u unifies with a term in $\{s_1, \ldots, s_i\}$. Equivalently, u is an incremental normal form if and only if u is a normal form and every substitution of normal forms for variables leaves u in normal form. Equivalently, u is an incremental normal form if and only if melting preserves u_Ω, where u_Ω results from substituting Ω for each variable in u.

Let $\mathbf{norm}^\omega$ be a new formal symbol. Let

$$\mathbf{Q}_{\doteq}^\omega = \{(\mathbf{norm}^\omega\, s_1, \ldots, s_i : t_\omega) : t_\omega \in \mathbf{T}_P^\omega, s_1, \ldots, s_i \in \mathbf{T}_P\}$$

Define the relation $\overset{?}{\vdash}{}_{\doteq}^\omega \subseteq \mathbf{Q}_{\doteq}^\omega \times \mathbf{F}_{P,\omega_1,\omega,\doteq}$ by

$$(\mathbf{norm}^\omega\, s_1, \ldots, s_i : t_\omega) \overset{?}{\vdash}{}_{\doteq}^\omega A$$

if and only if there exists a directed set U and a monotonic (in the instance ordering $\sqsubseteq$) function $f : \mathbf{approx}(t_\omega) \to 2^U$ such that

1. A is the conjunctive equation of $\mathbf{approx}(t_\omega)$ and U by f;
2. u is in incremental normal form, for all $u \in U$.

Now $\langle \mathbf{F}_{P,\omega_1,\omega,\doteq}, \mathbf{Q}_{\doteq}^\omega, \overset{?}{\vdash}{}_{\doteq}^\omega \rangle$ is a query system representing the answers to questions of the form 'what set of incremental normal forms for $s_1, \ldots, s_i$ is conjunctively equal to t?' In an implementation of equational logic programming based on $\mathbf{norm}^\omega$, the consumer of output generates demands causing the computation of some $u \in U$. Some of the symbols in u are demanded directly by the consumer, others may be demanded by the system itself in order to get an incremental normal form. The implementation demands enough input to construct $t \in \mathbf{approx}(t_\omega)$ such that $u \in f(t)$. By modelling the input and output as directed sets, rather than sequences, we allow enough flexibility to model all possible orders in which the consumer might demand output. The function f is used to model the partial synchronization of input with output required by the semantics of equational logic. Unfortunately, the trivial output $y, y, \ldots$, with term limit $\bot$, always satisfies 1–2 above. The most useful implementation would provide *consequentially strongest* answers (Definition 2.2.5, Section 2.2 of the chapter 'Introduction: Logic and Logic Programming Languages')—that is, they would demand the minimum amount of input semantically required to produce the demanded output. If consequentially strongest answers appear too difficult to implement, a more modest requirement would be that $\lim(U)$ is maximal among all correct answers—that is, all semantically correct output is produced, but not necessarily from the minimal input. The techniques outlined above do not represent sharing information, either within the input, within the output, or between input and output. Further research is needed into semantic interpretations of sharing information.

Example 7.1.5. Consider the system

$$\mathbf{T}_{28} = \{f(g(x,y)) \doteq h(h(g(x,y)))\}$$

and the infinite input term

$$t_\omega = f(g(t_\omega, t_\omega))$$

and the query

$$\mathbf{norm}^\omega\ f(g(x,y)) : t_\omega$$

The natural desired answer A to this query is the conjunction of

$\forall x_1:$	$\exists y_1:$	x_1	$\doteq$	y_1
$\forall x_1:$	$\exists y_1:$	$f(x_1)$	$\doteq$	y_1
$\forall x_1, x_2:$	$\exists y_1, y_2:$	$f(g(x_1,x_2))$	$\doteq$	$h(h(g(y_1,y_2)))$
$\forall x_1, x_2:$	$\exists y_1, y_2:$	$f(g(f(x_1),x_2))$	$\doteq$	$h(h(g(y_1,y_2)))$

$$\forall x_1, x_2, x_3: \quad \exists y_1, y_2, y_3: \quad f(g(f(g(x_1,x_2)),x_3))) \doteq h(h(g(h(h(g(y_1,y_2)))),y_3)))$$

$$\forall x_1, x_2: \quad \exists y_1, y_2: \quad f(g(x_1,f(x_2))) \doteq h(h(g(y_1,y_2)))$$

$$\forall x_1, x_2, x_3: \quad \exists y_1, y_2, y_3: \quad f(g(x_1,f(g(x_2,x_3)))) \doteq h(h(g(y_1,h(h(g(y_2,y_3)))))))$$

$$\vdots$$

A represents the infinite output $t'_\omega = h(h(g(t'_\omega, t'_\omega)))$. U does not contain all approximations to t'_ω, but only the ones that have gs as the rootmost non-$\bot$ symbols. The monotone function mapping partial inputs to the portions of output that they determine is:

$$\bot \mapsto \bot$$
$$f(\bot) \mapsto \bot$$
$$f(g(\bot,\bot)) \mapsto h(h(g(\bot,\bot)))$$
$$f(g(f(\bot),\bot)) \mapsto h(h(g(\bot,\bot)))$$
$$f(g(f(g(\bot,\bot)),\bot)) \mapsto h(h(g(h(h(g(\bot,\bot))),\bot)))$$
$$f(g(\bot,f(\bot))) \mapsto h(h(g(\bot,\bot)))$$
$$f(g(\bot,f(g(\bot,\bot)))) \mapsto h(h(\bot,g(h(h(g(\bot,\bot))))))$$
$$\vdots$$

A natural approach to representing sharing information would be to use $\forall x_1, x_2 \ : \ f(g(x_1, x_2)) \ \doteq \ h(h(g(x_1, x_2)))$ instead of $\forall x_1, x_2 \ : \ \exists y_1, y_2 \ : \ f(g(x_1, x_2)) \doteq h(h(g(y_1, y_2)))$, etc., but this idea has yet to be explored.

It is simple in principle to modify an implementation of equational logic programming to deal incrementally with infinite input queries and output answers in the query system $\mathbf{Q}_{\doteq}^{\omega}$. The practical details of such an implementation are interesting and challenging. The *tours* protocol [Rebelsky, 1992; Rebelsky, 1993] provides one design for incremental input and output of infinite terms. Implementations based on the recursive scheme for *head-eval* in Figure 9 may be adapted relatively simply to incremental input and output, simply by replacing the scheme for *norm* in Figure 10 by a scheme that issues calls to *head-eval* only as symbols are demanded by the consumer of output. Unfortunately, such adaptations are not normally complete, because of sequentializing problems. The trouble is that conjunctive behavior (which is easy to sequentialize) in the application of a rule corresponds to disjunctive behavior (which is impossible to sequentialize) in the production of strong head-normal forms, and vice versa.

Example 7.1.6. Consider the following equation defining the *negative sequential-or:*

$$\mathbf{T}_{or-s} = \{\, or(\textit{false}, \textit{false}) \doteq \textit{false}\,\}$$

This equation causes no problem in sequentializing the rewriting of a term to a finite normal form, since it requires *both* arguments to *or*. But, $or(s, t)$ is a strong head-normal form if and only if *either* of s or t is a strong head-normal form $\neq \textit{false}$. So, it is not safe to rewrite s, because of the possibility that s has no strong head-normal form, while t rewrites to strong head-normal form $u \neq \textit{false}$. For symmetric reasons, it is not safe to rewrite t. Only a parallel rewriting of both s and t is complete, and such parallel rewriting is very likely to waste steps.

By contrast, the positive parallel-or equations $\mathbf{T}_{or+}$ of Examples 2.3.16 and 3.2.1 prevent sequential computation of a finite normal form, but pose no problem to sequential head-normalization of $or(s, t)$ by rewriting s and t—*both* arguments must rewrite to strong head-normal forms $\neq \textit{true}$ in order to head-normalize $or(s, t)$.

So, to achieve complete implementations of equational logic programming with incremental input and output, we must solve the sticky problems of efficient implementation of parallel rewriting, even if the parallelism is simulated by multitasking on a sequential processor. In the meantime, sequential and incomplete implementations are likely to be practically useful for many problems—the incompleteness appears to be no more serious than the incompleteness of Prolog, which is widely accepted.

Beyond the incremental evaluation of an input that increases over time, there is an even more challenging problem to evaluate a *changing* input. In principle, changing input may be reduced to increasing input by representing the entire edit history of a term as another term [Rebelsky, 1993]. In practice, there is a lot of research required to achieve practical efficiency. A highly efficient general scheme for re-evaluation after a change in input will be extremely valuable. There are several techniques known for re-evaluation in special structures, such as attributed parse trees [Demers *et al.*, 1981; Pugh and Teitelbaum, 1989], but none approaches the generality or fine-grainedness of equational re-evaluation. A late result for the λ-calculus that I have not had a chance to review is in [Field and Teitelbaum, 1990]. Powerful memo techniques seem to be crucial to efficient re-evaluation of a changed input term. In some sense efficient re-evaluation is precisely the intelligent reuse of partial results from the previous evaluation. I conjecture that nonground memoing will be especially valuable for this problem.

Finally, we should study implementations of equational logic programming in which the set of equations is changing. Changing sets of equations arise in rapid recompiling during program development, in applications that use equations as inputs rather than as programs, and in methods based on nonground memoing or paramodulation (Section 4.3.4). Very little is known about this problem—all that I am aware of is a technique for incremental maintenance of a finite automaton for pattern matching [Strandh, 1984].

7.2 Solving equations

Queries of the form (**solve** $x_1, \ldots, x_n : s \doteq t$) (Definition 2.3.18, Section 2.3.4 of the chapter 'Introduction: Logic and Logic Programming Languages') require the solution of the equation $s \doteq t$ for the values of $x_1, \ldots, x_n$. This appears to be much more difficult than finding normal forms, and to offer more programming power. In particular, it appears that solving equations is the essential problem in the most natural approach to combining the useful qualities of Prolog and lazy functional programming. Notice that **solve** queries are quite similar to the **what** queries processed by Prolog (Section 2.3.1 of the 'Introduction ...' chapter). A combination of the methods for solving equations with the techniques of Prolog should provide a way of answering **what** queries in the first-order predicate calculus with equality.

Much of the theory of term rewriting falls short of dealing with the problems posed by equation solving. Confluence appears to help—if the given set $\mathbf{T}$ of equations is confluent, then we may seek an instance s' of s and t' of t, and a term u, such that $s' \xrightarrow{\mathbf{T}}^* u$ and $t' \xrightarrow{\mathbf{T}}^* u$, ignoring the symmetric rule and applying equations only from left to right. But, for a complete implementation, it is not sufficient to rewrite needed redexes. That is, it may be that there is a u such that $s' \xrightarrow{\mathbf{T}}^* u$ and $t' \xrightarrow{\mathbf{T}}^* u$, but no such u may be reached by rewriting only needed redexes (Definition 3.2.3, Section 3.2.3). Outermost complete rewriting (Definition 3.1.5, Section 3.1) is similarly insufficient. Complete rewriting sequences (Definition 3.1.3) come a bit closer. If s' and t' have a common form, then a complete rewriting sequence starting with s' is guaranteed eventually to produce a term u such that $t' \xrightarrow{T}^* u$. But, another complete rewriting sequence starting with t' is not guaranteed to produce the same u. Finally, even if we generate rewriting sequences from s' and t' that both contain u, it is not clear how to synchronize the sequences so that u appears in both of them at the same time.

No thoroughly satisfactory method is known for a complete implementation of equation solving in an arbitrary strongly sequential system. But, enough is known to make two observations that are likely to be useful in such an implementation.

1. Suppose we are solving $f(s_1,\ldots,s_m) \doteq g(t_1,\ldots,t_n)$, where $f \neq g$. It suffices to rewrite only needed redexes until the head symbols agree. Unfortunately, it is hard to know whether to rewrite $f(s_1,\ldots,s_m)$ or $g(t_1,\ldots,t_n)$ or both, but within each we can use the same sort of sequentializer that rewrites a single term to normal form.

2. There are only two cases in which it is helpful to instantiate a variable:

   (a) when the instantiation creates a redex at a proper ancestor of the variable, which we immediately rewrite (so, in the situation of (1) above, the redex must be needed);

   (b) when the instantiation unifies corresponding subterms of s and t.

   In each case, we should substitute the most general (smallest) term that achieves the redex or the unification.

Jayaraman noticed (1) [Jayaraman, 1985], and used it to implement a system called EqL for solving equations $s \doteq t$ only in the case where instances s' of s and t' of t reduce to a common form consisting entirely of constructor symbols in a constructor-orthogonal system (Definition 2.3.13, Section 2.3.2). For this purpose, it suffices to rewrite s' and t' to head-normal forms. If the head symbols agree, recursively solve equations between the corresponding arguments, otherwise there is no solution. It should be straightforward to generalize EqL to find solutions in normal form in strongly sequential rewrite- and rule-orthogonal systems. If we want all solutions, even those that are not in normal form, we must somehow explore in parallel the attempt to rewrite the head symbol of s' and the attempt to solve the equation without head rewriting one or both of them (and a similar parallelism for t'). This introduces all of the problems of parallelism discussed in Section 6, and it probably limits or eliminates the ability to do path compression on **repl** links (Section 4.3), since it is not sufficient to work only on the most rewritten form of a term ($\mathbf{val}_{\mathbf{repl}}^{max}(\alpha_0)$, where α_0 is the root of the heap representation of the term being rewritten).

Heuristically, it appears that the majority of the individual steps in solving an equation are unlikely to create such parallelism. But, EqL's uniform requirement of finding a solution in normal form is likely to introduce the same huge inefficiencies in some cases as strict evaluation (notice that the individual evaluations of s', t' to normal form are lazy, but the equation solution is not lazy, as it may take steps that are required to reach normal form, but not to solve the equation). If these heuristic observations are accurate, even an implementation with rather high overhead for parallelism may be very valuable, as long as the cost of parallelism is introduced only in proportion to the actual degree of parallelism, rather than as a uniform overhead on sequential evaluation as well.

Among the theoretical literature on term rewriting, the most useful material for equation solving will probably be that on *narrowing* [Fay, 1979] (see the chapter 'Equational Reasoning and Term Rewriting Systems in Volume 1), which is a careful formalization of observation (2) above. Information on sequencing narrowing steps seems crucial to a truly efficient implementation: some new results are in [Antoy *et al.*, 1994].

7.3   Indeterminate evaluation in subset logic

Until now, I have considered only quantified conjunctions of equations as formulae, else I cannot claim to be using equational logic. The discipline of equational logic constrains the use of term rewriting systems, and leads us to insist on confluent systems with lazy evaluation. Lazy evaluation appears to be mostly a benefit, but the restriction to confluent systems is annoying in many ways, and it particularly weakens the modularity of equational logic programming languages, since orthogonality depends on the full textual structure of left-hand sides of equations, and not just on an abstract notion of their meanings. As well as improving the techniques for guaranteeing confluence, we should investigate nonconfluent term rewriting. Since, without confluence, term rewriting cannot be semantically complete for equational logic, we need to consider other logical interpretations of term rewriting rules.

A natural alternative to equational logic is *subset logic* [O'Donnell, 1987]. Subset logic has the same terms as equational logic, the formulae are the same except that they use the backward subset relation symbol $\supseteq$ instead of $\doteq$ (Definition 2.3.13, Section 2.3.4 of the chapter 'Introduction: Logic and Logic Programming Languages'). Subset logic semantics are the same as equational (Definition 2.3.14, Section 2.3.4 of the 'Introduction ...' chapter), except that every term represents a *subset* of the universe of values instead of a single value, function symbols represent functions from subsets to subsets that are extended pointwise from functions of individual values (i.e., $f(S) = \bigcup \{f(\{x\}) : x \in S\}$). Subset logic is complete with the *reflexive, transitive,* and *substitution* rules of equality, omitting the *sym-*

metric rule (Definition 2.1.2, Section 2.1). So, term rewriting from left to right is complete for subset logic, with no restrictions on the rules. Technically, it doesn't matter whether the left side of a rule is a subset of the right, or *vice versa,* as long as the direction is always the same. Intuitively, it seems more natural to think of rewriting as producing a subset of the input term, since then a term may be thought of as denoting a set of possible answers. Thus, a single line of a subset logic program looks like $l \supseteq r$. Note that normal forms do not necessarily denote singleton sets, although it is always possible to construct models in which they do.

Subset logic programming naturally supports programs with indeterminate answers. When a given input s rewrites to two different normal forms t and u, subset logic merely requires that $s \supseteq t$ and $s \supseteq u$ are true, from which it does not follow that $t \doteq u$ is true, nor $t \supseteq u$, nor $u \supseteq t$. While equational logic programming extends naturally to infinite inputs and outputs, without changing its application to finite terms, such extension of subset logic programming is more subtle. If only finite terms are allowed, then infinite computations may be regarded as a sort of failure, and a finite normal form must be found whenever one exists. If incremental output of possibly infinite normal forms is desired, then there is no effective way to give precedence to the finite forms when they exist. The most natural idea seems to be to follow all possible rewriting paths, until one of them produces a stable head symbol (that is, the head symbol of a strong head-normal form) for output. Whenever such a symbol is output, all rewriting paths producing different symbols at the same location are dropped. Only a reduction path that has already agreed with all of the symbols that have been output is allowed to generate further output. The details work out essentially the same as with infinite outputs for equational programs, merely substituting $\supseteq$ for $\doteq$. It is not at all clear whether this logically natural notion of commitment to a symbol, rather than a computation path, is useful. I cannot find a natural semantic scheme to support the more conventional sort of commitment to a computation path instead of an intermediate term, although a user may program in such a way that multiple consistent computation paths never occur and the two sorts of commitment are equivalent.

Efficient implementation of nonconfluent rewriting presents a very interesting challenge. It is obviously unacceptable to explore naively the exponentially growing set of rewriting sequences. A satisfying implementation should take advantage of partial confluent behavior to prune the search space down to a much smaller set of rewriting sequences that is still capable of producing all of the possible outputs. The correct definition of the right sort of partial confluence property is not even known. It is *not* merely confluence for a subset of rules, since two rules that do not interfere with one another may interfere differently with a third, so that the order in which the two noninterfering rules are applied may still make a difference to the outcome. Pattern-matching and sequencing techniques must be generalized as well, and a good data structure designed to represent simultaneously the many different rewritings under consideration as compactly as possible. A good complete implementation of nonconfluent rewriting will probably allow the prohibited terms in normal forms (Definition 2.3.16, Section 2.3.4 of the chapter 'Introduction: Logic and Logic Programming Languages') to be different from the left-hand sides of rules. Sharing of equivalent subterms becomes problematic since it may be necessary to reduce two different occurrences of the same subterm in two different ways. The difficulties in discovering a complete implementation of subset logic programming would be well rewarded, since this style of programming can capture the useful indeterminate behavior of Prolog, while avoiding the repeated generation of the same solution by slightly different paths that slows some Prolog programs down substantially.

Even an incomplete implementation of nonconfluent rewriting might be very valuable. In the spirit of logic programming, such an implementation should depend on inherent structural properties of the rules in a program to determine which of a set of possible rewriting steps is chosen when the redex patterns overlap. From the point of view of implementation, the most natural approach appears to be to select an outermost connected component of overlapping redex patterns, but to rewrite within the component from innermost out. It is not clear how to resolve the ambiguous case where two redex patterns have the same root, nor has anyone proposed a sensible semantic explanation based on logic programming for any principle for choosing between conflicting rules.

Jayaraman has a different concept of subset logic programming [Jayaraman, 1992]. Meseguer's *rewriting logic* has the same rules as my subset logic, with a different semantic justification. [Meseguer, 1992]

7.4 Relational rewriting

Equation solving can lead to a combination of Prolog and functional programming through logic programming in the first-order predicate calculus with equality. Subset logic programming, implemented with nonconfluent term rewriting, can lead to an implementation of predicate calculus programming in a sort of indeterminate functional programming. Another intriguing way to reconcile some of the good qualities of Prolog and functional programming is relational logic programming. Relational logic programming can be approached as a generalization of terms to systems of relational constraints, or as a purification of Prolog by removing the function symbols (called 'functors' in Prolog).

A relational formula is a FOPC formula with no function symbols (this prohibition includes zeroary functions, or constants). The natural analogue to a term in relational logic is a conjunction of atomic formulae, which may be represented as a hypergraph (like a graph, but edges may touch more than two nodes) with nodes standing for variables and hyperedges (edges touching any number of nodes, not necessarily two) representing predicate symbols. Two fundamental problems stand in the way of a useful implementation of relational logic programming through hypergraph rewriting.

1. We need an efficient implementation of hypergraph rewriting. The pattern-matching problem alone is highly challenging, and no practical solution is yet known.

2. We need a semantic system that makes intuitive sense, and also supports computationally desirable methods of hypergraph rewriting.

A first cut at (2) might use the semantic system for FOPC, and express rewrite rules as formulae of the form

$$\forall \vec{x} : \exists \vec{y} : (A_1 \wedge \cdots \wedge A_m) \Leftarrow (B_1 \wedge \cdots \wedge B_n)$$

These clauses differ from the Horn clauses of Prolog in two ways. The quantification above is $\forall \vec{x} : \exists \vec{y} :$, where clauses are universally quantified. And, the consequence of the implication above is a conjunction, where Horn clauses allow at most one atomic formula in the consequence, and even general clauses allow a disjunction, rather than a conjunction. Notice that, with Prolog-style all-universal quantification, the implication distributes over conjunctions in the consequence ($(A_1 \wedge A_2) \Leftarrow B$ is equivalent to $(A_1 \Leftarrow B) \wedge (A_2 \Leftarrow B)$). But, if existentially quantified variables from $\vec{y}$ appear in $A_1, \ldots, A_m$, the distribution property does not hold.

Since the consequence and hypothesis of our formula are both conjunctions of atomic formulae, they may be represented by hypergraphs, and it is natural to read the formula as a hypergraph rewrite rule. A natural sort of hypergraph rewriting will be sound for deriving universally quantified implications from $\forall \exists$ implications, as long as the existentially quantified variables $\vec{y}$ correspond to nodes in the graph that participate *only* in the hyperedges representing $A_1, \ldots, A_m$. The universally quantified variables in $\vec{x}$ correspond to nodes that may connect in other ways as well as by hyperedges representing $A_1, \ldots, A_m$, so they are the interface nodes to the unrewritten part of the hypergraph. Interestingly, the final result of a computation on input I is an implication $\forall \vec{w} : I \Leftarrow O$. This implication does not give a solution to the goal I, as in Prolog. Rather, it rewrites the goal I into a (presumably simpler or more transparent) goal O, such that every solution to O is also a solution to I. This is formally similar to functional and equational logic programming, in that the class of legitimate outputs is a subclass of the legitimate inputs—in Prolog inputs are formulae and outputs are substitutions. Constraint logic programming [Jaffar and Lassez, 1987; Lassez, 1991] is perhaps heading in this direction.

The semantic treatment suggested above is not very satisfactory, as it rules out lazy evaluation, and even storage reclamation (an intermediate part of a hypergraph that becomes disconnected from the input and output cannot be thrown away, even though it cannot affect the nature of a solution, since if any part of the hypergraph is unsolvable, the whole conjunction is unsolvable). Also, the logically sound notion of unification of the left-hand side of a rule with a portion of a hypergraph in order to rewrite it seems far too liberal with this semantic system—without the single-valued quality of functions, additional relations can be postulated to hold anywhere. I conjecture that the first problem can be solved by a semantic system in which every unquantified formula is solvable, so that a disconnected portion of the hypergraph may be discarded as semantically irrelevant. One way to achieve this would be to use some sort of measured universe [Cohn, 1980], and require every atomic predicate to hold for all but a subset of measure 0—then every finite intersection of atomic predicates (equivalently, the value of every finite conjunction of atomic formulae) has a solution. Such a semantic system is not as weird as it first seems, if we understand the universe as a space of *concepts,* rather than real objects, and think of each predicate symbol as giving a tiny bit of information about a concept. We can conceive of every combination of information (such as a green unicorn with a prime number of feet that is a large power of 2), even though most such combinations never enter our notion of reality. Although the question of solvability becomes trivial in this semantic system, implications between solutions still have interesting content. The problem of limiting unifications in a useful way appears more difficult. I suggest that nonclassical 'relevant' interpretations of implication [Anderson and Belnap Jr., 1975] are likely to be helpful.

Acknowledgements

I am very grateful for the detailed comments that I received from the readers, Bharat Jayaraman, Donald W. Loveland, Gopalan Nadathur and David J. Sherman.

References

[Abramsky and Hankin, 1987] S. Abramsky and C. Hankin. *Abstract Interpretation of Declarative Languages.* Ellis Horwood, Chichester, UK, 1987.

[Aho et al., 1974] A. V. Aho, John E. Hopcroft, and J. D. Ullman. *The Design and Analysis of Computer Algorithms.* Addison-Wesley, 1974.

[Anderson and Belnap Jr., 1975] Alan Ross Anderson and Nuel D. Belnap Jr. *Entailment—the Logic of Relevance and Necessity,* volume 1. Princeton University Press, Princeton, NJ, 1975.

[Antoy et al., 1994] Sergio Antoy, Rachid Echahed, and Michael Hanus. A needed narrowing strategy. In *Proceedings of the 21st ACM Symposium* on *Principles of Programming Languages*, pages 268–279. ACM, January 1994.

[Appel, 1991] Andrew Appel. Garbage collection. In Peter Lee, editor, *Topics in Advanced Language Implementation Techniques*. MIT Press, 1991.

[Ashcroft and Wadge, 1985] E. A. Ashcroft and W. W. Wadge. *Lucid, the Dataflow Programming Language*. Academic Press, London, UK, 1985.

[Augustsson, 1984] Lennart Augustsson. A compiler for lazy ML. In *ACM Symposium on Lisp and Functional Programming*, August 1984.

[Backus, 1974] John Backus. Programming language semantics and closed applicative languages. In *Proceedings of the 1st ACM Symposium on Principles of Programming Languages*, pages 71–86. ACM, 1974.

[Backus, 1978] John Backus. Can programming be liberated from the von Neumann style? a functional style and its algebra of programs. *Communications of the ACM*, 21(8):613–641, 1978.

[Baird et al., 1989] T. Baird, G. Peterson, and R. Wilkerson. Complete sets of reductions modulo associativity, commutativity, and identity. In *Proceedings of the 3rd International Conference on Rewriting Techniques and Applications*, volume 355 of *Lecture Notes in Computer Science*, pages 29–44, 1989.

[Barendregt, 1984] Hendrik Peter Barendregt. *The Lambda Calculus: Its Syntax and Semantics*. North-Holland, Amsterdam, 1984.

[Berry and Lévy, 1979] Gérard Berry and Jean-Jacques Lévy. Letter to the editor, *SIGACT News*, **11**, 3–4, 1979.

[Bird and Wadler, 1988] R. Bird and P. Wadler. *Introduction to Functional Programming*. Prentice-Hall, New York, NY, 1988.

[Bloss et al., 147–164] A. Bloss, Paul Hudak, and J. Young. Code optimizations for lazy evaluation. *Lisp and Symbolic Computation: an International Journal*, 1, 147–164.

[Bobrow and Clark, 1979] D. Bobrow and D. Clark. Compact encodings of list structure. *ACM Transactions on Programming Languages and Systems*, 1(2):266–286, 1979.

[Bondorf, 1989] Anders Bondorf. A self-applicable partial evaluator for term-rewriting systems. In *International Joint Conference on the Theory and Practice of Software Development*, volume 352 of *Lecture Notes in Computer Science*. Springer-Verlag, 1989.

[Burn et al., 1988] G. L. Burn, Simon L. Peyton Jones, and J. D. Robson. The spineless g-machine. In *Proceedings of the 1988 ACM Conference on Lisp and Functional Programming*, pages 244–258, 1988.

[Cardelli, 1983] Luca Cardelli. The functional abstract machine. *Polymorphism*, 1(1), 1983.

[Cardelli, 1984] Luca Cardelli. Compiling a functional language. In *Proceedings of the ACM Symposium on Lisp and Functional Programming*, August 1984.

[Chen and O'Donnell, 1991] Yiyun Chen and Michael James O'Donnell. Testing confluence of nonterminating overlapping systems of rewrite rules. In *Conditional and Typed Rewriting Systems 2nd International CTRS Workshop, Montreal, June 1990*, volume 516 of *Lecture Notes in Computer Science*, pages 127–136. Springer-Verlag, 1991.

[Chew, 1980] Leslie Paul Chew. An improved algorithm for computing with equations. In *21st Annual Symposium on Foundations of Computer Science*, pages 108–117. IEEE, 1980.

[Chew, 1981] Leslie Paul Chew. Unique normal forms in term rewriting systems with repeated variables. In *13th Annual ACM Symposium on Theory of Computing*, pages 7–18, 1981.

[Cohen, 1981] J. Cohen. Garbage collection of linked data structures. *Computing Surveys*, 13(3), September 1981.

[Cohn, 1980] Donald L. Cohn. *Measure Theory*. Birkhauser, Boston, MA, 1980.

[Cousineau et al., 1985] G. Cousineau, P.-L. Curien, and M. Mauny. The categorical abstract machine. In *Symposium on Functional Programming Languages and Computer Architecture*, volume 201 of *Lecture Notes in Computer Science*. Springer-Verlag, 1985.

[Cousot and Cousot, 1977] P. Cousot and R. Cousot. Abstract interpretation: A unified framework for static analysis of programs by construction or approximation of fixpoints. In *Fourth Annual ACM Symposium on Principles of Programming Languages*. ACM, 1977.

[Curry and Feys, 1958] H. B. Curry and R. Feys. *Combinatory Logic*, volume 1. North-Holland, Amsterdam, 1958.

[Demers et al., 1981] Alan Demers, Thomas Reps, and Tim Teitelbaum. Incremental evaluation of attribute grammars with application to syntax-directed editors. In *Conference Record of the 13th Annual ACM Symposium on Principles of Programming Languages*, pages 105–116. ACM, 1981.

[Dershowitz, 1987] Nachum Dershowitz. Termination of rewriting. *Journal of Symbolic Computation*, 3:69–116, 1987.

[Dershowitz et al., 1983] Nachum Dershowitz, Jieh Hsiang, N. Josephson, and David A. Plaisted. Associative–commutative rewriting. In *Proceedings of the 8th International Joint Conference on Artificial Intelligence*, pages 940–944, August 1983.

[Dershowitz et al., 1991] Nachum Dershowitz, Simon Kaplan, and David A. Plaisted. Rewrite, rewrite, rewrite, rewrite, rewrite. *Theoretical Computer Science*, 83:71–96, 1991.

[Durand, 1994] Irène Durand. Bounded, strongly sequential, and forward-branching term-rewriting systems. *Journal of Symbolic Computation*, **18**, 319–352, 1994.

[Durand and Salinier, 1993] Irène Durand and Bruno Salinier. Constructor equivalent term rewriting systems. *Information Processing Letters*, 47, 1993.

[Durand et al., 1991] Irène Durand, David J. Sherman, and Robert I. Strandh. Optimization of equational programs using partial evaluation. In *Proceedings of the ACM/IFIP Symposium on Partial Evaluation and Semantics-Based Program Manipulation, New Haven, CT*, 1991.

[Fay, 1979] M. Fay. First order unification in equational theories. In *Proceedings of the 4th Workshop on Automated Deduction*, volume 87 of *Lecture Notes in Computer Science*, pages 161–167. Springer-Verlag, 1979.

[Field and Harrison, 1988] A. J. Field and P. G. Harrison. *Functional Programming*. Addison-Wesley, 1988.

[Field and Teitelbaum, 1990] John Field and Tim Teitelbaum. Incremental reduction in the lambda calculus. In *Proceedings of the 1990 ACM Conference on Lisp and Functional Programming*, pages 307–322. ACM Press, 1990.

[Friedman and Wise, 1976] Daniel Friedman and David S. Wise. Cons should not evaluate its arguments. In *3rd International Colloquium on Automata, Languages and Programming*, pages 257–284. Edinburgh University Press, 1976.

[Futatsugi et al., 1985] K. Futatsugi, Joseph A. Goguen, J.-P. Jouannaud, and José Meseguer. Principles of OBJ2. In *12th Annual Symposium on Principles of Programming Languages*, pages 52–66. ACM, 1985.

[Gallier, 1986] Jean H. Gallier. *Logic for Computer Science—Foundations of Automatic Theorem Proving*. Harper & Row, New York, NY, 1986.

[Goguen, 1977] Joseph A. Goguen. Abstract errors for abstract data types. In E. J. Neuhold, editor, *Proceedings of IFIP Working Conference on Formal Description of Program Concepts*. North-Holland, 1977.

[Gonthier et al., 1992] Georges Gonthier, Martín Abadi, and Jean-Jacques Lévy. The geometry of optimal lambda reduction. In *Conference Record of the 19th Annual ACM Symposium on Principles of Programming Languages*, pages 15–26. ACM, 1992.

[Guttag and Horning, 1978] John V. Guttag and J. J. Horning. The algebraic specification of abstract data types. *Acta Informatica*, 10(1):1–26, 1978.

[Guttag et al., 1983] John V. Guttag, Deepak Kapur, and David Musser. On proving uniform termination and restricted termination of rewriting systems. *SIAM Journal on Computing*, 12:189–214, 1983.

[Henderson, 1980] P. Henderson. *Functional Programming—Application and Implementation.* Prentice-Hall, 1980.

[Henderson and Morris, 1976] P. Henderson and J. H. Morris. A lazy evaluator. In *3rd Annual ACM Symposium on Principles of Programming Languages*, pages 95–103. SIGPLAN and SIGACT, 1976.

[Hoffmann and O'Donnell, 1979] C. M. Hoffmann and M. J. O'Donnell. Interpreter generation using tree pattern matching. In *6th Annual Symposium on Principles of Programming Languages*, pages 169–179. SIGPLAN and SIGACT, 1979.

[Hoffmann and O'Donnell, 1982] C. M. Hoffmann and M. J. O'Donnell. Pattern matching in trees. *Journal of the ACM*, 29(1):169–179, 1982.

[Hoffmann et al., 1985] C. M. Hoffmann, M. J. O'Donnell, and R. I. Strandh. Implementation of an interpreter for abstract equations. *Software — Practice and Experience*, 15(12):1185–1203, 1985.

[Hudak, 1989] Paul Hudak. Conception, evolution, and application of functional programming languages. *ACM Computing Surveys*, 21(3):359–411, 1989.

[Hudak, 1992] Report on the programming language Haskell, a non-strict, purely functional language, version 1.2. *ACM SIGPLAN Notices*, 27(5), May 1992.

[Hudak and Sundaresh, 1988] Paul Hudak and Raman S. Sundaresh. On the expressiveness of purely functional I/O systems. Technical Report YALEU/DCS/RR665, Yale University, New Haven, CT, December 1988.

[Huet, 1980] G. Huet. Confluent reductions: Abstract properties and applications to term rewriting. *Journal of the ACM*, 27(4):797–821, October 1980.

[Huet and Lévy, 1991] Gérard Huet and Jean-Jacques Lévy. Computations in orthogonal rewriting systems. In Jean-Louis Lassez and Gordon Plotkin, editors, *Computational Logic—Essays in Honor of Alan Robinson*, pages 395–443. MIT Press, Cambridge, MA, 1991.

[Hughes, 1982] R. J. M. Hughes. Super-combinators: A new implementation method for applicative languages. In *ACM Symposium on Lisp and Functional Programming*, August 1982.

[Hughes, 1985a] J. Hughes. Lazy memo-functions. In *Functional Programming Languages and Computer Architecture*, volume 201 of *Lecture Notes in Computer Science*, pages 129–146. Springer-Verlag, 1985.

[Hughes, 1985b] R. J. M. Hughes. Strictness detection in non-flat domains. In Neil Jones and Harald Ganzinger, editors, *Workshop on Programs as Data Objects*, volume 217 of *Lecture Notes in Computer Science*. Springer-Verlag, 1985.

[Iverson, 1962] K. E. Iverson. *A Programming Language.* John Wiley and Sons, New York, NY, 1962.

[Jaffar and Lassez, 1987] Joxan Jaffar and Jean-Louis Lassez. Constraint logic programming. In *14th Annual ACM Symposium on Principles of Programming Languages*, pages 111–119, 1987.

[Jayaraman, 1985] Bharat Jayaraman. Equational programming: A unifying approach to functional and logic programming. Technical Report 85-030, The University of North Carolina, 1985.

[Jayaraman, 1992] Bharat Jayaraman. Implementation of subset-equational programming. *The Journal of Logic Programming*, 12(4), April 1992.

[Johnsson, 1984] Thomas Johnsson. Efficient compilation of lazy evaluation. In *Proceedings of the ACM SIGPLAN'84 Symposium on Compiler Construction*, 1984. SIGPLAN Notices 19(6) June, 1984.

[Kahn and Plotkin, 1978] Gilles Kahn and Gordon Plotkin. Domaines concrets. Technical report, IRIA Laboria, LeChesnay, France, 1978.

[Kapur et al., 1982] Deepak Kapur, M. S. Krishnamoorthy, and P. Narendran. A new linear algorithm for unification. Technical Report 82CRD-100, General Electric, 1982.

[Karlsson, 1981] K. Karlsson. Nebula, a functional operating system. Technical report, Chalmers University, 1981.

[Karp, 1964] Carol R. Karp. *Languages with Expressions of Infinite Length*. North-Holland, Amsterdam, 1964.

[Kathail, 1984] Arvind and Vinod Kumar Kathail. Sharing of computation in functional langauge implementations. In *Proceedings of the International Workshop on High-Level Computer Architecture*, 1984.

[Keller and Sleep, 1986] R. M. Keller and M. R. Sleep. Applicative caching. *ACM Transactions on Programming Languages and Systems*, 8(1):88–108, 1986.

[Kenneway et al., 1991] J. R. Kenneway, Jan Willem Klop, M. R. Sleep, and F. J. de Vries. Transfinite reductions in orthogonal term rewriting systems. In *Proceedings of the 4th International Conference on Rewriting Techniques and Applications*, volume 488 of *Lecture Notes in Computer Science*. Springer-Verlag, 1991.

[Klop, 1980] Jan Willem Klop. *Combinatory Reduction Systems*. PhD thesis, Mathematisch Centrum, Amsterdam, 1980.

[Klop, 1991] Jan Willem Klop. Term rewriting systems. In S. Abramsky, Dov M. Gabbay, and T. S. E. Maibaum, editors, *Handbook of Logic in Computer Science*, volume 1, chapter 6. Oxford University Press, Oxford, 1991.

[Klop and Middeldorp, 1991] Jan Willem Klop and A. Middeldorp. Sequentiality in orthogonal term rewriting systems. *Journal of Symbolic Computation*, 12:161–195, 1991.

[Knuth, 1973] Donald E. Knuth. *The Art of Computer Programming— Sorting and Searching*, volume 3. Addison-Wesley, Reading, MA, 1973.

[Knuth and Bendix, 1970] Donald E. Knuth and P. Bendix. Simple word problems in universal algebras. In J. Leech, editor, *Computational Problems in Abstract Algebra*, pages 127–146. Pergamon Press, Oxford, 1970.

[Koopman, 1990] Philip J. Koopman. *An Architecture for Combinator Graph Reduction*. Academic Press, Boston, MA, 1990.

[Koopman and Lee, 1989] Philip J. Koopman and Peter Lee. A fresh look at combinator graph reduction. In *Proceedings of the SIGPLAN'89 Conference on Programming Language Design and Implementation*, October 1989.

[Lamping, 1990] John Lamping. An algorithm for optimal lambda calculus reduction. In *Conference Record of the 17th Annual ACM Symposium on Principles of Programming Languages*, pages 16–30. ACM, 1990.

[Landin, 1965] P. J. Landin. A correspondence between ALGOL 60 and Church's lambda-notation: Part I. *Communications of the ACM*, 8(2):89–101, 1965.

[Lassez, 1991] Jean-Louis Lassez. From LP to CLP: Programming with constraints. In T. Ito and A. R. Meyer, editors, *Theoretical Aspects of Computer Software: International Conference*, volume 526 of *Lecture Notes in Computer Science*. Springer-Verlag, 1991.

[Lévy, 1978] Jean-Jacques Lévy. *Reductions Correctes et Optimales dans le Lambda-Calcul*. PhD thesis, Université Paris, January 1978.

[Lieberman and Hewitt, 1983] Henry Lieberman and Carl Hewitt. A realtime garbage collector based on the lifetimes of objects. *Communications of the ACM*, 26(6):419–429, June 1983.

[Loveland, 1978] Donald W. Loveland. *Automated Theorem Proving: A Logical Basis*. Elsevier North-Holland, New York, NY, 1978.

[Machtey and Young, 1978] Michael Machtey and Paul Young. *An Introduction to the General Theory of Algorithms*. Theory of Computation. North-Holland, New York, NY, 1978.

[Martelli and Montanari, 1976] A. Martelli and U. Montanari. Unification in linear time and space: A structured presentation. Technical Report B76-16, Institut di Elaborazione delle Informazione, Consiglio Nazionale delle Ricerche, Pisa, Italy, 1976.

[McCarthy, 1960] John McCarthy. Recursive functions of symbolic expressions and their computation by machine, part I. *Communications of the ACM*, 3(4):184–195, 1960.

[McCarthy et al., 1965] John McCarthy, Paul W. Abrahams, Daniel J. Edwards, Timothy P. Hart, and Michael I. Levin. *LISP 1.5 Programmer's Manual*. MIT Press, Cambridge, MA, 1965.

[Meseguer, 1992] José Meseguer. Multiparadigm logic programming. In

H. Kirchner and G. Levi, editors, *Proceedings of the 3rd International Conference on Algebraic and Logic Programming, Volterra, Italy, September 1992*, Lecture Notes in Computer Science. Springer-Verlag, 1992.

[Mitchie, 1968] D. Mitchie. 'Memo' functions and machine learning. *Nature*, 1968.

[Mycroft, 1980] Alan Mycroft. The theory and practice of transforming call-by-need into call-by-value. In *International Symposium on Programming*, volume 83 of *Lecture Notes in Computer Science*. Springer-Verlag, 1980.

[Newman, 1942] M. H. A. Newman. On theories with a combinatorial definition of 'equivalence'. *Annals of Mathematics*, 43(2):223–243, 1942.

[O'Donnell, 1977] Michael James O'Donnell. *Computing in Systems Described by Equations*, volume 58 of *Lecture Notes in Computer Science*. Springer-Verlag, 1977.

[O'Donnell, 1979] Michael James O'Donnell. Letter to the editor, *SIGACT News*, **11**, 2, 1979.

[O'Donnell, 1985] Michael James O'Donnell. *Equational Logic as a Programming Language*. Foundations of Computing. MIT Press, Cambridge, MA, 1985.

[O'Donnell, 1987] Michael James O'Donnell. Tree-rewriting implementation of equational logic programming. In Pierre Lescanne, editor, *Rewriting Techniques and Applications — Bordeaux, France, May 1987 — Proceedings*, volume 256 of *Lecture Notes in Computer Science*. Springer-Verlag, 1987.

[Peyton Jones, 1987] Simon L. Peyton Jones. *The Implementation of Functional Programming Languages*. Prentice-Hall, Englewood Cliffs, NJ, 1987.

[Pingali and Arvind, 1985] Keshav Pingali and Arvind. Efficient demand-driven evaluation, part 1. *ACM Transactions on Programming Languages and Systems*, 7(2):311–333, April 1985.

[Pingali and Arvind, 1986] Keshav Pingali and Arvind. Efficient demand-driven evaluation, part 2. *ACM Transactions on Programming Languages and Systems*, 8(1):109–139, January 1986.

[Pugh and Teitelbaum, 1989] William Pugh and Tim Teitelbaum. Incremental computation via function caching. In *Conference Record of the Sixteenth Annual ACM Symposium on Principles of Programming Languages*, pages 315–328. ACM, 1989.

[Ramakrishnan and Sekar, 1990] I. V. Ramakrishnan and R. C. Sekar. Programming in equational logic: Beyond strong sequentiality. In *Proceedings of the IEEE Conference on Logic in Computer Science*, 1990.

[Rebelsky, 1992] Samuel A. Rebelsky. I/O trees and interactive lazy functional programming. In Maurice Bruynooghe and Martin Wirsing, editors, *Proceedings of the 4th International Symposium on Programming Language Implementation and Logic Programming*, volume 631 of *Lecture Notes in Computer Science*, pages 458–472. Springer-Verlag, August 1992.

[Rebelsky, 1993] Samuel A. Rebelsky. *Tours, a System for Lazy Term-based Communication*. PhD thesis, The University of Chicago, June 1993.

[Robinson and Wos, 1969] G. A. Robinson and L. Wos. Paramodulation and theorem-proving in first-order logic with equality. *Machine Intelligence*, 4:135–150, 1969.

[Sherman, 1990] David J. Sherman. Lazy directed congruence closure. Technical Report 90-028, The University of Chicago, 1990.

[Spitzen *et al.*, 1978] Jay M. Spitzen, Karl N. Levitt, and Lawrence Robinson. An example of hierarchical design and proof. *Communications of the ACM*, 21(12):1064–1075, December 1978.

[Staples, 1982] John Staples. Two-level expression representation for faster evaluation. In Hartmut Ehrig, Manfred Nagl, and Grzegorz Rozenberg, editors, *Graph Grammars and their Application to Computer Science: 2nd International Workshop*, volume 153 of *Lecture Notes in Computer Science*. Springer-Verlag, 1982.

[Strandh, 1984] R. I. Strandh. Incremental suffix trees with multiple subject strings. Technical Report JHU/EECS-84/18, The Johns-Hopkins University, 1984.

[Strandh, 1988] Robert I. Strandh. *Compiling Equational Programs into Efficient Machine Code*. PhD thesis, The Johns Hopkins University, Baltimore, MD, 1988.

[Strandh, 1989] Robert I. Strandh. Classes of equational programs that compile into efficient machine code. In *Proceedings of the 3rd International Conference on Rewrite Techniques and Applications*, 1989.

[Thatte, 1985] Satish Thatte. On the correspondence between two classes of reduction systems. *Information Processing Letters*, 1985.

[Turner, 1979] D. A. Turner. A new implementation technique for applicative languages. *Software—Practice and Experience*, 9:31–49, 1979.

[Wand, 1976] Mitchell Wand. First order identities as a defining language. *Acta Informatica*, 14:336–357, 1976.

[Warren, 1983] David H. D. Warren. An abstract Prolog instruction set. Technical Report 309, Artificial Intelligence Center, SRI International, Menlo Park, CA, October 1983.

[Winksel, 1993] Glynn Winksel. *The Formal Semantics of Programming Languages—An Introduction*. Foundations of Computing. MIT Press, Cambridge, MA, 1993.

Proof Procedures for Logic Programming

Donald W. Loveland and Gopalan Nadathur

Contents

1 Building the framework: the resolution procedure

A proof procedure is an algorithm (technically, a semi-decision procedure) which identifies a formula as valid (or unsatisfiable) when appropriate, and may not terminate when the formula is invalid (satisfiable). Since a proof procedure concerns a logic the procedure takes a special form, superimposing a search strategy on an inference calculus. We will consider a certain collection of proof procedures in the light of an inference calculus format that abstracts the concept of logic programming. This formulation allows us to look beyond SLD-resolution, the proof procedure that underlies Prolog, to generalizations and extensions that retain an essence of logic programming structure.

The inference structure used in the formulation of the logic programming concept and first realization, Prolog, evolved from the work done in the subdiscipline called automated theorem proving. While many proof procedures have been developed within this subdiscipline, some of which appear in Volume 1 of this handbook, we will present a narrow selection,

namely the proof procedures which are clearly ancestors of the first proof
procedure associated with logic programming, SLD-resolution. Extensive
treatment of proof procedures for automated theorem proving appear in
Bibel [Bibel, 1982], Chang and Lee [Chang and Lee, 1973] and Loveland
[Loveland, 1978].

1.1   The resolution procedure

Although the consideration of proof procedures for automated theorem
proving began about 1958 we begin our overview with the introduction of
the resolution proof procedure by Robinson in 1965. We then review the
linear resolution procedures, model elimination and SL-resolution procedures. Our exclusion of other proof procedures from consideration here
is due to our focus, not because other procedures are less important historically or for general use within automated or semi-automated theorem
process.

   After a review of the general resolution proof procedure, we consider
the linear refinement for resolution and then further restrict the procedure format to linear input resolution. Here we are no longer capable of
treating full first-order logic, but have forced ourselves to address a smaller
domain, in essence the renameable Horn clause formulas. By leaving the
resolution format, indeed leaving traditional formula representation, we see
there exists a linear input procedure for all of first-order logic. This is the
model elimination(ME) procedure, of which a modification known as the
SL-resolution procedure was the direct inspiration for the SLD-resolution
procedure which provided the inference engine for the logic programming
language Prolog. The ME–SL-resolution linear input format can be translated into a very strict resolution restriction, linear but not an input restriction, as we will observe.

   The resolution procedure invented by Alan Robinson and published in
1965 (see [Robinson, 1965]) is studied in depth in the chapter on resolution-
based deduction in Volume 1 of this handbook, and so quickly reviewed
here. The resolution procedure is a refutation procedure, which means
we establish unsatisfiability rather than validity. Of course, no loss of
generality occurs because a formula is valid if and only if (iff) its negation
is unsatisfiable. The formula to be tested for unsatisfiability is "converted
to conjunctive normal form with no existential quantifiers present". By this
we mean that with a given formula F to be tested for unsatisfiability, we
associate a logically equivalent formula F' which is in conjunctive normal
form (a conjunction of clauses, each clause a disjunction of atomic formulas
or negated atomic formulas, called *literals*) with no existential quantifiers.
F' may be written without any quantifiers, since we regard F, and therefore
F', as a closed formula, so the universal quantifiers are implicitly assumed
to be present preceding each clause. (Thus we are free to rename variables
of each clause so that no variable occurs in more than one clause.) The

formula F' is derivable from F by standard logical equivalences plus the use of Skolem functions to replace quantifiers. We shall say that F' is in *Skolem conjunctive form* and that F' is the *Skolem conjunctive form of F*. Precise algorithms for conversion are given in many textbooks, including Chang and Lee [Chang and Lee, 1973] and Loveland [Loveland, 1978].

The formula

$$\neg P(x, f(x)) \vee Q(x, g(x), z)$$

is the Skolem conjunctive form of

$$\forall x[P(x, f(x)) \supset \exists y \forall z Q(x, y, z)],$$

where $g(x)$ is a Skolem function introduced for the y that occurs in the intermediate formula

$$\forall x[\neg P(x, f(x)) \vee \exists y \forall z Q(x, y, z)].$$

(Recall that an existentially quantified variable is replaced by a new function letter followed by arguments consisting of all universally quantified variables where the universal quantifier contains the existential quantifier within its scope.) The formula

$$\forall z \exists x \forall y (A(y, y) \vee [B(y, z) \wedge C(x, y)])$$

has

$$(A(y, y) \vee B(y, z)) \wedge (A(w, w) \vee C(a, w))$$

as its Skolem conjunctive form formula, where a is a Skolem function having 0 arguments. Note that in this example immediate Skolemization, before applying the distributive law and then importing the quantifiers, would have introduced a Skolem function $f(z)$ instead of the Skolem constant a used above. For pragmatic reasons regarding the cost of search in automated proof procedures it is best to seek Skolem functions with the fewest number of arguments. We have adopted the traditional logic notation of capital letters for predicate letters, and non-capitals for variables, function and constant letters. Variables are represented by end of the alphabet letters.

For those accustomed to logic programming notation, based on clauses as implications, it is a natural question to ask: why use conjunctive normal form? The resolution procedure (and hence its restrictions) does not distinguish between positive literals (atomic formula, or atoms) and negative literals (negated atoms). Also, the general resolution procedure (and many variants) requires symmetric calling access to all literals of a clause. Thus the symmetry of OR as the connective in the clause is very suitable. Of course, we could present the entire set of procedures using implicative form but there is no insight gained and the presentation would differ from the traditional presentations for no essential reason. Therefore, we will invoke a notation change in the middle of the paper, but this reflects common sense and historical precedent, so we forsake uniform notation.

Resolution procedures are based on the resolution inference rule

$$\frac{C_1 \lor a \quad \neg a \lor C_2}{C_1 \lor C_2}$$

where $C_1 \lor a$ and $\neg a \lor C_2$ are two known clauses, with C_1 and C_2 representing arbitrary disjuncts of literals. The literals a and $\neg a$ are called the *resolving literals*. The derived clause is called the *resolvent*. The similarity of the inference rule to Gentzen's cut rule is immediately clear and the rule can be seen as a generalization of *modus ponens*. The resolvent is true in any model for the two given clauses, so the inference rule preserves validity.

The resolution inference rule just given is the propositional rule, also called the *ground* resolution rule for a reason given later. We postpone discussion of the very similar first-order inference rule to delay some complications.

Because the Skolem conjunctive format is so uniform in style, it is convenient to simplify notation when using it. We drop the OR symbol in clauses and instead simply concatenate literals. Clauses themselves are either written one per line or separated by commas. When the non-logical symbols are all single letters it is also convenient to drop the parentheses associated with predicate letters and the commas between arguments. Thus the Skolem conjunctive form formula $(P(a) \lor P(b)) \land (\neg P(a)) \land (\neg P(b))$ is shortened to $PaPb, \neg Pa, \neg Pb$ by use of the simplifying notation.

Using the just-introduced shorthand notation for a formula in this form, often called a *clause set*, we present a refutation of a clause set. We use the terms *input clause* to designate a clause from the *input* clause set given by the user to distinguish such clauses from derived clauses of any type.

1.	$PaPb$	input clause
2.	$Pa\neg Pb$	input clause
3.	$\neg PaPb$	input clause
4.	$\neg Pa\neg Pb$	input clause
5.	Pa	resolvent of clauses 1, 2
6.	$\neg Pa$	resolvent of clauses 3, 4
7.	contradiction	Pa and $\neg Pa$ cannot both hold

Note that in line 5 the two identical literals are merged.

Since each resolvent is true in any model satisfying the two parent clauses, a satisfiable clause set could not yield two contradictory unit clauses. Thus $Pa, \neg Pa$ signals an unsatisfiable input clause set. The resolution inference rule applied to Pa and $\neg Pa$ yields the empty clause, denoted □. This is customarily entered instead of the word "contradiction", as we do hereafter.

We have noted that the ground resolution inference system is *sound*, i.e. will not deduce □ if the original clause set is satisfiable. We now note that this inference system is complete, i.e. for every propositional unsatisfiable clause set there is a resolution refutation. A proof appears in Chang and Lee [Chang and Lee, 1973] or Loveland [Loveland, 1978]. A proof by induction on the number of "excess" literal occurrences in the clause set (the number of literal occurrences minus the number of clauses in the set) is not difficult and the reader may enjoy trying the proof himself.

Above, we have given a proof of unsatisfiability, or a refutation. There is no indication there as to how such a proof might be found. Descriptions of search algorithms that employ the resolution inference rule comprise proof procedures for resolution. Perhaps the most natural proof procedure for resolution is the level saturation procedure, where all resolvents at a certain level are determined before beginning the next level. Because we enumerate all resolvents eventually, we have a complete proof procedure. We define all the given, or input, clauses to be at level 0. A resolvent is at level $k + 1$ if the parent clauses are at level k and j, for $j \leq k$. For the preceding example we list the clauses by level:

Level 0: $PaPb, Pa\neg Pb, \neg PaPb, \neg Pa\neg Pb$
Level 1: $Pa, Pb, \neg Pa, \neg Pb, \neg PaPa, \neg PbPb$
Level 2: □ , and all Level 0 and Level 1 clauses.

Level 2 resolvents include all previously obtained clauses because the tautologies $\neg PaPa$ and $\neg PbPb$ as one parent clause will always produce the other parent clause as the resolvent. Thus we can remove tautologies without affecting completeness. This is true for almost all resolution restrictions also. (An exception can occur when clauses are ordered, such as in the locking, or indexing, strategy. For example, see Loveland [1978].)

Other deletion rules can be advantageous, given that only clause □ is sought. Once Pa is produced, resolving thereafter with $PaPb$ or $Pa\neg Pb$ is counterproductive because the resolvents again contain Pa. It is almost immediate that, when trying to derive the (length 0) clause □, there is no need to retain a clause that contains another existing clause as a subclause. Eliminating a clause $C_1 \vee C_2$ when C_2 also exists, for clauses C_1 and C_2, is known as subsumption elimination. This generalizes at the first-order level (noted later) and can get reasonably technical, with various options. This is studied in detail in Loveland [1978]. Also see Wos et al. [1991].

A variant of the level saturation proof procedure that has proved useful in practice employs a unit preference search strategy. (See Wos et al. [Wos et al., 1964].) Here resolvents at higher levels than the current level being "saturated" are computed whenever one of the parents is a unit clause (one-literal clause). The intuition here is that the resolvent is always at least one literal less in cardinality ("shorter") than the longer parent clause, which is progress since the goal clause is the empty clause, having length 0.

Except for merging, these unit clause resolutions must be the resolutions that occur near the end of refutations, so it makes sense to "look ahead" in this limited way.

Having treated the level-saturation resolution proof procedure, which is a breadth-first search ordering, it is natural to ask about depth-first search procedures. This is of particular interest to logic programmers who know that this is the search order for Prolog. We want to do this in a manner that preserves completeness. (Why it is desirable to preserve completeness is a non-trivial question, particularly at the first-order level where searches need not terminate and the combinatorial explosion of resolvent production is the dominant problem. Two points speak strongly for considering completeness: 1) these inference systems have such a fine-grained inference step that incompleteness in the inference proof procedures leads to some very simple problems being beyond reach and 2) it is best to understand what one has to do to maintain completeness to know what price must be paid if completeness is sacrificed. We will make some further specific comments on this issue later.)

Before presenting a depth-first proof procedure let us observe that at the propositional, or ground, level there are only a finite number of resolvents possible beginning with any given (finite) clause set. This follows directly from two facts: 1) no new atoms are created by the resolution inference rule, and 2) a literal appears at most once in a clause, so there is an upper bound on the number of literals in any resolvent.

A straightforward depth-first proof procedure proceeds as follows. If there are n input clauses then we temporarily designate clause n as the *focus* clause. In general the focus clause is the last resolvent still a candidate for inclusion in a resolution refutation (except for the first clause assignment, to clause n). We begin by resolving focus clause n against clause 1, then clause 2, etc. until a new non-subsumed non-tautological clause is created as a resolvent. This resolvent is labeled clause $n+1$ and becomes the new focus clause. It is resolved against clause 1, clause 2, etc. until a new clause is created that is retained. This becomes the new focus clause and the pattern continues. If $\square$ is obtained the refutation is successful. Otherwise, some focus clause m creates no new surviving clause and *backtracking* is begun. The clause $m-1$ is relabeled the focus clause (but clause m is retained) and clause $m-1$ is resolved against those clauses not previously tried, beginning with clause $j+1$ where clause j is the clause that paired with clause $m-1$ to produce clause m. The first retained resolvent is labeled clause $m+1$. Clause $m+1$ now becomes the focus clause and the process continues as before. This backtracking is close to the backtracking employed by Prolog.

The above depth-first procedure does differ from that used in Prolog, however. The primary difference is that after one backtracks from a clause that yields no new resolvent, the clause is not removed. If we are interested in a complete procedure then we might need to consider using this "abandoned" clause C with clauses of higher index not yet defined, and hence not yet tried with C. Suppose hypothetically that a four clause given set has only the following resolution refutation (excluding renumbering): clause 3 and clause 4 create a resolvent (clause 5), clause 1 and clause 2 create a resolvent (clause 6), and $\Box$ is the resolvent of clause 5 and clause 6. The depth-first search starts its search by creating clause 5 as before, failing to create any new resolvent using clause 5, and backtracks by restarting with clause 4. Clause 4 first pairs with itself, but automatically skips this since no nontautologous clause resolves with itself, and fails when paired with clause 5. We have exhausted our first chosen focus clause; when this happens the backtracking continues backwards through all clauses. Thus, clause 3 is the new focus clause, does create a resolvent when paired with clause 4, but that is subsumed by (is identical to) clause 5. Clause 3 subsequently fails as the focus clause and clause 2 becomes the focus clause, and produces a resolvent when paired with clause 1. This new clause 6 immediately becomes the focus clause, is eventually paired with clause 5 and $\Box$ is produced. The point of all this is that clause 5 had to be retained to be used when clause 6 was finally created.

The reader may object to the supposition that clause 5 fails to produce any resolvent, but the contention that it would always pair with a lower indexed clause if it is ever used in a refutation would require a theorem about behavior of resolution refutations. The depth-first search utilized here is simply designed to sweep the same proof space as swept by the breadth-first search, but in a different order.

It does happen that clauses that exhaust their pairings and force a backtrack do not need to be retained. (That is, clause 5 above would either yield a resolvent under some pairing or could be removed upon backtracking.) This is a consequent of the existence of linear resolution refinements. The linear refinement asserts that if a clause set is unsatisfiable then there is a resolution refutation such that each resolvent has the preceding clause as one of the parent clauses and the other parent clause must appear earlier in the deduction or be an input clause. The preceding parent clause is called the *near parent* clause. The other clause, the *far parent* clause, can be defined more precisely as follows: The far parent clause must be either an input clause or an *ancestor* clause, where the set of ancestor clauses of a clause C is the smallest set of clauses containing the near parent clause of C and the ancestors of the near parent clause of C. Again note that this is a condition on proof form, not on search. There exists a linear refutation with any input clause as first near-parent clause if that clause is in a minimally unsatisfiable subset of the input clauses. We call the first near-parent clause the *top* clause of the linear deduction. We give a linear refutation of the clause set given earlier. It is common to list the top clause as the last input clause.

A linear refutation:

1.	$PaPb$	input clause
2.	$Pa\neg Pb$	input clause
3.	$\neg PaPb$	input clause
4.	$\neg Pa\neg Pb$	input clause
5.	$\neg Pb$	resolvent of 2, 4
6.	Pa	resolvent of 1,5
7.	Pb	resolvent of 3,6
8.	$\square$	resolvent of 5,7

The last step in the above refutation involved two resolvents. This is true of every refutation of this clause set, since no input clause is a one-literal clause and $\square$ must have two one-literal parents. This provides an example that not every clause set has a linear refutation where the far parent is always a input clause. Clauses 4, 5 and 6 are the ancestors of clause 7 in the above example. This definition of ancestor omits clauses 1, 2 and 3 as ancestors of clause 7 but our intent is to capture the derived clauses used in the derivation of clause 7.

The linear restriction was independently discovered by Loveland (see [Loveland, 1970], where the name *linear* was introduced and a stronger restriction *s-linear* resolution also was introduced) and by Luckham (where the name *ancestor filter* was used; see [Luckham, 1970].) A proof of completeness of this restriction also is given in Chang and Lee [Chang and Lee, 1973] and Loveland [Loveland, 1978].

With this result we can organize our depth-first search to discard any clause when we backtrack due to failure of that clause to lead to a proof. It follows that we need only try a given resolvent with clauses of lower index than the resolvent itself and that all retained resolvents are elements of the same (linear) proof attempt. Use of this restriction permits a great saving in space since only the current proof attempt clauses are retained. However, a large cost in search effectiveness may be paid because of much duplication of resolvent computation. In a proof search the same clause (or close variant) is often derived many times through different proof histories. In a breadth-first style search the redundant occurrences can be eliminated by subsumption check. This is a check not available when resolved clauses are eliminated upon backtracking as usually done in the depth-first linear resolution procedures. Each recreation of a clause occurrence usually means a search to try to eliminate the occurrence. This produces the high search price associated with depth-first search procedures.

The redundant search problem suffered by depth-first linear resolution procedures may make this approach unwise for proving deep mathematical theorems, where much computation is needed and few heuristic rules exist to guide the search. Depth-first linear resolution is often just the right procedure when there is a fairly strong guidance mechanism suggesting which clauses are most likely to be useful at certain points in the search. This principle is at work in the success of Prolog, which implements a depth-first linear strategy. When using Prolog, the user generally uses many predicate names, which means that relatively few literals are possible matches. This trims the branching rate. Secondly, the user orders the clauses with knowledge of how he expects the computation to proceed. Clearly, when some information exists to lead one down essentially correct paths, then there is a big win over developing and retaining all possible deductions to a certain depth. Besides logic programming applications, the depth-first approach is justified within artificial intelligence (AI) reasoning system applications where the search may be fairly restricted with strong heuristic guidance. When such conditions hold, depth-first search can have an additional advantage in that very sophisticated implementation architectures exist (based on the Warren Abstract Machine; see [Aït-Kaci, 1990]) allowing much higher inference rates (essentially, the number of resolution operations attempted) than is realized by other procedure designs. This speed is realized for a restricted linear form called linear input procedures, which we discuss later, which is usually implemented using depth-first search mode.

It is important to realize that the linear resolution restriction need not be implemented in a depth-first manner. For example, one might begin with several input clauses "simultaneously" (either with truly parallel computation on a parallel computer or by interleaving sequential time segments on a sequential machine) and compute all depth $n + 1$ resolvents using all depth n parents before proceeding to depth $n + 2$ resolvents. This way subsumption can be used on the retained clauses (without endangering completeness) yet many resolution rule applications are avoided, such as between two input clauses not designated as start clauses for a linear refutation search.

The mode of search described above is very close to the set-of-support resolution restriction introduced by Wos et al. [1964; 1965]. A refutation of a clause set S with set-of-support $T \subseteq S$ is a resolution refutation where every resolvent has at least one parent a resolvent or a member of T. Thus two members of $S - T$ cannot be resolved together. To insure completeness it suffices to determine that $S - T$ is a satisfiable set. The primary difference between this restriction and the quasi-breadth-first search for linear resolution described in the preceding paragraph is that for the linear refutation search of the previous paragraph one could choose to segregate clauses by the deduction responsible for its creation (labeled by initial parents), and not resolve clauses from different deductions. This reduces the branching factor in the search tree. If this is done, then any subsuming clause must acquire the deduction label of the clause it subsumes. The resulting refutation will not be linear if a subsuming clause is utilized, but usually the refutation existence, and not the style of refutation, is what matters. One could call such refutations *locally linear* refutations. Loveland [Loveland,

1978] discusses linear restrictions with subsumption.

Before concluding this discussion of search strategies, we consider oriented clause sets. So far, we have treated the clause set as non-oriented, in that no clause or subset of clauses received special notice *a priori*. Such is the situation when an arbitrary logical formula is tested for unsatisfiability. However, often the clause set derives from a theorem of form $A \supset B$, where A is a set of axioms of some theory and B is the theorem statement believed to hold in the theory. Analogously, A may be viewed as a logic programming program and B is the query. It is well-known that testing the validity of $A \supset B$ answers the question: Is B a logical consequence of A?

We test $A \supset B$ for validity by testing $A \wedge \neg B$ for unsatisfiability. The conversion to Skolem conjunctive form of $A \wedge \neg B$ permits A and $\neg B$ to be converted separately and the two clause sets conjoined. The clause set S_A from A is called the theory base, database or axiom set, and the clause set S_B from $\neg B$ is called the goal set, query set or theorem statement (set). In practice, the cardinality of set S_A is usually much larger than the cardinality of S_B. Also, there is often no assurance that all the clauses of S_A are needed in the proof, whereas usually all clauses of S_B are needed. Moreover, S_A is usually a consistent clause set. Thus, the support set T is usually a subset of S_B, and linear refutations are started with one parent from S_B.

In this oriented clause set setting there are natural notions of direction of search. A linear refutation with one parent from S_B is called a *backchaining, goal-oriented*, or *top-down* refutation and the associated search is a *backchaining* or *goal-oriented* search. If the linear refutation begins with both parents from S_A then it is a *forward chaining, forward-directed*, or *bottom-up* refutation, with the same labels applied to the associated search. The same labels apply to the set-of-support refinement with support set $T \subset S_B$ or $T \subset S_A$. If top-down and bottom-up refutations are sought simultaneously, then the search is said to be *bidirectional*. The idea of bidirectionality is to share resolvents between the bottom-up and top-down searches, in effect having search trees growing bottom-up and top-down which meet and provide a complete proof path from data to goal. If this occurs, the search trees involved are roughly half the depth of a search tree strictly top-down or a tree strictly bottom-up. Since the number of tree nodes (resolvents) of any level generally grows exponentially with the depth of the level a tremendous potential savings exists in search size. Automated theorem provers use bidirectional search sometimes, but use is by no means universal. One problem is what clauses from S_A are appropriate. In back-chaining systems, often definitions are expanded forward several steps, a case of forward chaining.

A study of bidirectional search in a more general setting that resolution inference was done by Pohl [Pohl, 1971]. A related study on search strategies, explicitly considering resolution, is given in Kowalski [Kowalski, 1970].

Before proceeding to further restrictions of resolution we need to present the first-order version of the resolution procedure. The more common presentation of first-order resolution uses two inference rules, binary resolution and binary factoring. Binary resolution is the first-order counterpart of the propositional resolution rule given earlier and factoring is the generalization of the merging of literals that removes duplication in the propositional case. ("Binary" refers to action limited to two literals; if factoring is incorporated within the resolution rule then several literals in one or both parent clauses might be "removed" from the resolvent.)

To present the binary resolution and factoring rules of inference, unification must be introduced. Substitution θ is a unifier of expressions l_1 and l_2 iff $l_1\theta \equiv l_2\theta$. For our use it suffices to consider l_1 and l_2 as (first-order) atoms of first-order terms. Substitution σ is a most general unifier (mgu) of l_1 and l_2 iff $l_1\sigma \equiv l_2\sigma$ and for any substitution γ such that $l_1\gamma = l_2\gamma$, there is a λ such that $\gamma = \sigma\lambda$. We defer to the chapter on unification in Volume 1 of this handbook for further discussion of this topic. Also see the chapter on resolution-based deduction in the same volume.

Two clauses are variable disjoint if they share no common variables.

We now present the inference rules for first-order resolution.

Binary resolution. Given variable disjoint clauses $C_1 \lor a_1$ and $C_2 \lor \neg a_2$, where a_1 and a_2 are atoms and C_1 and C_2 are disjunctions of literals, we deduce resolvent $(C_1 \lor C_2)\sigma$ from $C_1 \lor a_1$ and $C_2 \lor \neg a_2$, where σ is the mgu of a_1 and a_2; in summary:

$$\frac{C_1 \lor a_1 \quad C_2 \lor \neg a_2}{(C_1 \lor C_2)\sigma}$$

Binary factoring. Given clause $C \lor l_1 \lor l_2$, where l_1 and l_2 are literals and C is a disjunction of literals, we deduce factor $(C \lor l)\sigma$ where σ is the mgu of l_1 and l_2, i.e. $l_1\sigma = l = l_2\sigma$; in summary:

$$\frac{C \lor l_1 \lor l_2}{(C \lor l)\sigma}$$

We illustrate the use of these rules by giving a refutation of the clause set

$$\{PxQx, Px\neg Qy, \neg PxQf(x), \neg Px\neg Qx\}$$

Because the resolution rule requires the two parent clauses to be variable disjoint, clauses may have their variables renamed prior to the application of the resolution rule. This is done without explicit reference; we say that clause Px and clause $\neg PxRf(x)$ has resolvent $Rf(x)$ when the actual resolution rule application would first rename Px as (say) Py and then use

$$\frac{Py \quad \neg PxRf(x)}{Rf(x)}$$

We give a linear refutation:

1. $PxQx$ — input clause
2. $Px\neg Qy$ — input clause
3. $\neg PxQf(x)$ — input clause
4. $\neg Px\neg Qx$ — input clause
5. $\neg Qx\neg Qy$ — resolvent of 2, 4
6. $\neg Qx$ — factor of 5
7. Px — resolvent of 1, 6
8. $Qf(x)$ — resolvent of 3,7
9. $\Box$ — resolvent of 6,8

The soundness of resolution procedures at the first-order level, that $\Box$ is derived only when the input clause set is unsatisfiable, is an immediate consequence of the fact that resolution and factoring preserve validity. The completeness of resolution procedures, that $\Box$ is derivable whenever the input clause set is unsatisfiable, utilizes the Skolem–Herbrand–Gödel theorem (a model-theoretic version of a very difficult proof-theoretic theorem of Herbrand). The Skolem–Herbrand–Gödel theorem asserts that a first-order formula (resp., clause set) is unsatisfiable iff a finite conjunction of ground formula (resp. clause set) instances is unsatisfiable. By a ground formula instance we mean a copy of the formula with the variables replaced by variable-free terms composed of symbols from the (non-variable) term alphabet of the formula. The set of such terms is called the *Herbrand universe*. (If no constant individual appears in the formula, one is included by decree.) The standard completeness proof for a first-order resolution proof procedure has two parts: 1) a proof of the ground version of the procedure and 2) a "lifting" argument that relates the first-order search to a ground-level search by establishing that for any ground deduction of that class of deductions defined by the proof procedure there is a first-order deduction in that clause with that ground deduction as a ground instance. In particular, use of most general unifiers assures us that if clauses C_1 and C_2 have ground instances $C_1\theta$ and $C_2\theta$ in the ground deduction then the resolvent C_3 of C_1 and C_2 has $C_3\theta$ as a resolvent of $C_1\theta$ and $C_2\theta$. One can find more on the general nature of such arguments in Volume 1 of this handbook. Proofs of completeness of various restrictions of resolution must be argued separately; many such proofs appear in Chang and Lee [Chang and Lee, 1973] and Loveland [Loveland, 1978].

The search component of first-order proof procedures is as discussed for the propositional (or ground) procedures, with one notable exception.

Since a set of resolvents generated from a finite set of clauses can be infinite, pure depth-first search may not terminate on some search paths. Rather, it always utilizes the last resolvent successfully and never backtracks. (This is well-known to Prolog users.) To insure that a refutation can be found when one exists, a variation of pure depth-first called iterative deepening is sometimes used. Iterative deepening calls for repeated depth-first search to bounds $d + nr$, for $d > 0$, $r > 0$ and $n = 0, 1, 2, ...$, where the user sets the parameters d and r prior to the computation. Frequently, $r = 1$ is used. The advantage of small storage use, and speed for input linear search, is retained and yet some similarity to breadth-first search is introduced. The cost is recomputation of earlier levels. However, if one recalls that for complete binary trees (no one-child nodes and all leaves at the same level) there are as many leaves as interior nodes, and the proportion of leaves grows as the branching factor grows, one sees that recomputation is not as frightening as it first appears. Perhaps the more important downside to iterative deepening is that if you are structured so as to find the solution while sweeping a small portion of the entire search space with sufficient depth bound then a depth bound just too low makes the procedure sweep the entire search space before failing and incrementing. This is a primary reason why Prolog employs pure depth-first search. (Also, of course, because very frequently Prolog does not have infinite search branches, at least under the clause ordering chosen by the user.)

Seeking linear refutations at the first-order level introduces a technical issue regarding factoring. The complication arises because we wish to enforce the notion of linearity strongly. In particular, if a factor of a far parent is needed that was not produced when that clause was a near parent, then the factor would have to be entered as a line in the deduction, violating the condition that the near parent always participates in creation of the next entry (by resolution or factoring). To avoid this violation we will agree that for linear resolution, unless otherwise noted, a resolution operation can include use of a factor of the far parent ancestor or input clause. Actually, for most versions of linear resolution, including the general form introduced already, this caveat is not needed provided that the given set has all its factors explicitly given also. (That is, the given set is closed under the factoring inference rule.) A fuller treatment of this issue, and much of what follows regarding linear resolution refinements and variants, is found in Loveland [Loveland, 1978].

1.2 Linear resolution refinements

There are several restrictions of linear resolution, and several combinations that multiply the possibilities for variations of linear resolutions. We will settle for one variant, among the most restricted of possibilities. Our interest in the particular form is that it is a resolution equivalent to the model elimination (SL-resolution) procedure that we study next.

We need to be more precise about the notion of clause subsumption before considering the next refinement. The idea of subsumption is to recognize when one formula makes a second formula redundant. This concept of subsumption can be expressed as follows: formula C subsumes formula D iff $\forall \bar{x} C$ implies $\forall \bar{y} D$, where $\bar{x}$ (resp. $\bar{y}$) denotes the free variables of C (resp. D). For example, $\forall x(P(x) \vee \neg P(f(x)))$ implies $\forall y(P(y) \vee \neg P(f(f(y))))$; here, two instances of clause $Px \neg Pf(x)$ are needed to infer $\forall y(Py \neg Pf(f(y)))$, namely, $Px \neg Pf(x)$ and $Pf(x) \neg Pf(f(x))$. Since we need an expedient test for subsumption, a form of subsumption used most often in resolution provers is a more limited form we call θ-subsumption: clause C θ-subsumes clause D if there exists a substitution θ such that the literals of $C\theta$ are also in D (we write this as $C\theta \subseteq D$, accepting the view of a clause as a set of literals), and that the number of literals of C does not exceed the number of literals of D. Without the literal count requirement every factor would be subsumed by its parent, and discarding clauses based on subsumption would generally not be possible. For many resolution strategies including breadth-first, linear and set-of support resolution, θ-subsumed clauses can be removed from further consideration.

We do not claim that the check for θ-subsumption always carries an acceptable cost; its use especially when C is a multiliteral clause has been controversial. However, strong use of θ-subsumption has been well defended (see [Wos *et al.*, 1991]). Certainly the test is much faster than the general definition because only one instance of C is involved.

We now introduce a small modification of the resolution inference rule that utilizes the θ-subsumption criterion. We say that C is an *s-resolvent* (for subsumption resolvent) of near parent clause C_1 and far parent clause C_2 if C is (a factor of) a resolvent C_3 where C θ-subsumes a substitution instance of near parent $C_1 - l$, l the resolving literal. We amplify our reference to "substitution instance" below. Sometimes a factor of the standard resolvent is needed to satisfy the θ-subsumption restriction, and at other times no s-resolvent exists. We will see that this highly constrains the resolvent; moreover, we can limit any resolution where the far parent is a non-input ancestor clause to s-resolution in the s-linear restriction we define shortly. We give examples of s-resolution:

Example 1.2.1.

Near parent clause:	$PxQaRx$
Far parent clause:	$Qy\neg Rf(x)$
S-resolvent:	$Pf(x)Qa$
Standard resolvent:	$Pf(x)QaQy$

Example 1.2.2.

> Near parent clause: $PxQaRx$
>
> Far parent clause: $Qb\neg Rf(x)$
>
> No s-resolvent exists

The first example illustrates the reason we must allow s-resolvent C to θ-subsume only an instance of near parent clause C_1. In this example, the standard resolvent contains $Pf(x)$, created by the resolution operation from parent literal Px. Clearly, there is no instance of the resolvent that will θ-subsume near parent clause $PxQaRx$, but instance $Pf(x)QaRf(x)$ is θ-subsumed by $Pf(x)Qa$, here a factor of the standard resolvent.

The s-resolution operation can be quite costly to perform. The direct approach involves computing the resolvent and checking the θ-subsumption condition. The latter would most often cause rejection, so *a priori* tests on the parents would be desirable. We do not pursue this further because we finesse this issue later.

In pursuit of the strongly restricted form of linear resolution, we introduce the notion of ordered clause, with the intention of restricting the choice of resolving literal. By decreasing the choice we decrease the branching factor of the search tree. We set the convention that the rightmost literal of a clause is to be the resolving literal; however, we merge leftward, so that in the resolution operation the substitution instance demanded by the unifier of the resolution operation may create a merge left situation where the intended resolving literal disappears from the rightmost position! Then we say that such a resolution operation application fails.

The class of orderings for the restricted linear resolution we define permits any ordering the user chooses for input clauses except that each literal of each input clause must be rightmost in some ordered clause. Thus a 3-literal input clause must have at least three ordered clauses derived from it. A resolvent-ordered clause has leftmost the surviving descendents of the literals of the near parent ordered clause, in the order determined by the near parent ordered clause, while the surviving descendents of the far parent can be ordered in any manner the user wishes, i.e. is determined by the particular ordering the user has chosen.

The ordering applied to the input clauses is superfluous, except to the input clause chosen as first near parent clause (called the *top* clause), because all other uses of input clauses are as far parent clauses in a resolution operation. By definition of resolvent ordered clause, the literals descendent from the far parent can be ordered as desired when determining the resolvent. Of course, it is important that any ordering of input clauses provide that every literal of every input clause be rightmost, and thus accessible as a resolving literal. The notion of "top clause" is often used with arbitrary linear deductions, but is needed for ordered clause linear deductions because the first resolution step is not symmetrical in the parent clauses;

one clause provides the leftmost literals of the ordered resolvent.

An *ordered s-linear deduction* of clause A from a set S of clauses is an ordered clause linear deduction of A from the fully factored set S_f of S where any resolvent without a input clause as a parent clause is an s-resolvent. If the fully factored input set is used then factors of ancestor clauses need not be derived in the deduction. This is true because it can be shown that factors of s-resolvents need not be computed.

Given a resolution refutation $B_1, \ldots, B_n$, it seems intuitive that if B_i θ-subsumes B_j, $i < j$, we have made no progress towards $\square$ in the interval $[i, j]$. We call a deduction *weakly tight* if for no $i < j$ is $B_i \subseteq B_j$. Full tightness, that for no $i < j$ does B_i θ-subsume B_j, is the ideal condition to enforce, but it is not clear that it is enforceable. A careful definition excludes clauses from θ-subsuming their factors but this hints at the care needed. Also, since s-resolution results in a shorter clause than the near parent (resolving literal of the near parent is removed at least) its use is a win when available. A deduction satisfies the *weak subsumption rule* if an s-resolvent is used whenever both parent clauses are derived clauses and the near parent clause is variable-free. In particular this rule says that for the propositional case no consideration to resolution with input clauses is needed when an s-resolvent exists. The rule is called "weak" because the unconstrained demand that s-resolution be used when available yields an incomplete procedure. The reason is intuitive; s-resolution always works when the right terms are at hand, but s-resolution where free variables occur can lead to forcing a wrong instantiation.

An ordered s-linear deduction is a TOSS deduction (weakly tight ordered s-linear resolution with the weak subsumption rule) if the deduction is weakly tight and satisfies the weak subsumption rule.

S-linear deductions exist that are neither weakly tight nor satisfy the weak subsumption rule.

We give two examples of ordered s-linear (actually, TOSS) deductions. The first example is one of the simplest examples where factoring is required in almost all resolution formats. Any order of input clauses is permitted.

1.	$PxPy$	input
2.	$\neg Px \neg Py$	input, top clause
3.	$\neg PxPy$	resolvent of 1,2
4.	$\neg Px$	S-resolvent of 2,3
5.	Px	resolvent of 1,4
6.	$\square$	S-resolvent of 4,5

This refutation uses an s-resolution with a input clause as one parent. Here the far parent is the top clause. The top clause can be treated like a derived clause, so that if derived clause 3 above had been ground, s-resolution could be forced. Actually, in this case no alternative need be considered anyway, because if the resolvent has every literal simply a variant of its parent literal no instantiation has been eliminated by this action. That is, the weak subsumption rule can be extended to force s-resolution if the s-resolvent does not instantiate the literals inherited from the near parent clause.

The second example has a more dramatic instance of s-resolution and illustrates how regular factoring of resolvents can then be dropped. However, it is seen from this example that there is a possible price to pay for banning factoring in that a longer proof is required. It is controversial whether factoring is better included or excluded in linear deductions. It is a trade-off of a reduced branching factor versus shorter proofs and hence shorter proof trees. (Recall that Prolog avoids factoring; factoring within linear resolution is optional in the Horn clause domain.)

The clause order is determined by $P < Q < R$ in the following example.

Example 1.2.3.

1.	Qx	input
2.	$PxRx$	input
3.	$\neg PxRf(y)$	input
4.	$\neg Px \neg Rx$	input
5.	$Px\neg Qy\neg Rz$	input, top clause
6.	$Px\neg QyPz$	resolvent of 2,5
7.	$Px\neg QyRf(z)$	resolvent of 3,6
8.	$Px\neg Qy\neg Pf(z)$	resolvent of 4,7
9.	$Px\neg Qy$	s-resolvent of 6,8
10.	Px	resolvent of 1,9
11.	$Rf(x)$	resolvent of 3,10
12.	$\neg Pf(x)$	resolvent of 4,11
13.	$\square$	s-resolvent of 10,12

By factoring at step 6, steps 7 and 8 would have been omitted. In essence, step 7 through step 9 are repeated at step 11 through step 13, each sequence "removing" Px. These redundant proof segments are common when factoring is not used.

The TOSS restriction is not the strongest restriction possible; one can superimpose a restriction on the choice of far parent of s-resolutions. The added restriction is based on a restriction introduced by Andrews [Andrews, 1976], called *resolution with merging*. A resolvent may often contain a literal with parenthood in both parent clauses, such as literal Pa in resolvent $PaPx$ with parent clauses $PaQx$ and $PaPx\neg Qx$. This occurs because identical literals are merged. At the general level, unifiable literals may remain separate in the resolvent, but factoring then permits their "merging". Thus, $PxQy$ and $Px\neg Qy$ yields resolvent $PxPz$ with factor Px. When such a factor contains a literal with parenthood in both parent clauses, mimicking the ground case, we call this a *merge factor* and the pertinent literal(s) *merge literal(s)*.

An MTOSS deduction (a TOSS deduction with merging) is a TOSS deduction where s-resolution occurs only when the rightmost literal of the far parent is a descendent of a merge literal.

Although the MTOSS restriction is as constraining a principle as is known regarding limiting resolution inferences when both parent clauses are derived, the merge condition has not received much attention in implementation. Actually, the TOSS and even the s-resolution restriction have not received much attention regarding implementations explicitly. As suggested earlier, a strongly related format has received much attention.

The focus of the preceding consideration of linear restrictions is to reduce the need to resolve two derived clauses together. Why is this interesting? For several (related) reasons. One of the problems in proof search is the branching factor, how many alternative inferences could be pursued at a given point in a partial deduction. Since all input clauses are deemed always eligible (at least for linear resolution) the branching factor is reduced by tightening conditions for resolving two derived clauses. A second reason is that the input clauses can be viewed as given operators. In a linear deduction the far parent clause can be seen as modifying the near parent clause, transforming the near parent clause to a new but related clause. S-resolution is pleasing in this regard because it says that one needs to deviate from applying the given "operators" only when the near parent is modified by removal of the literal receiving current attention, the resolving literal. (The ordering previously specified for linear deductions is useful in this viewpoint because it creates a focus on a given literal and its descendents before considering another literal of the clause.) An implementation consideration for limiting derived-clause resolution is that one can precondition the input clauses to optimize the resolution operation when a input clause is used in the resolution. Indeed, this is what Prolog does; compilers exist based on this principle.

To the extent that the above points have validity then the ideal linear resolution is the *linear input* format, where every resolvent has a input clause as far parent clause. (The word "linear" in "linear input" is redundant as use of a input clause as one parent forces a deduction to be linear, but the term is common and makes explicit that input resolution is a linear resolution restriction.)

Linear input resolution has been shown earlier not to be complete for first-order logic, but it is complete over a very important subset. A formula is a *Horn formula* if it is in prenex normal form with its quantifier-free part (matrix) in conjunctive normal form, where each clause has at most one positive literal. A *Horn (clause) set* is a clause set where each clause has at most one positive literal. That every unsatisfiable Horn set has a linear input refutation is immediate from the completeness of linear resolution and the observation that if one takes a clause of all-negative literals (a *negative clause*) as top clause then every derived clause is a negative clause and resolution between derived clauses is impossible. A negative clause must exist in each unsatisfiable set, for otherwise a model consisting of positive literals exists. The completeness proof for linear resolution shows that a refutation exists using as top clause any clause that is in a minimally unsatisfiable subset of the input clause set.

How much wider a class than Horn sets can linear input resolution handle? Essentially, no wider class. It can be shown (see Loveland [Loveland, 1978]) that if ground clause set S has a linear input refutation then there is a possible renaming of literals such that S_1, a renaming of S, is a Horn set. A ground set S_1 is a renaming of S if S and S_1 differ only in that for some atoms the positive and negated occurrences of that atom have been interchanged. This is equivalent to renaming each atom of a selected set of atoms by a new negated atom at every occurrences and replacing $\neg\neg A$ by A. Thus the ground set

$$\{\neg PaPbPc\neg Pd, \neg Pb\neg Pd, Pd\neg Pe, \neg Pc\neg Pe, Pe, Pa\}$$

is not Horn, because the first clause has two positive literals, but does have a linear input refutation, as the reader can easily check. However, the set is convertible to a Horn set by interchanging Pa, Pb, Pc with their negations.

This theorem that ground clause sets with linear input refutations are renamable Horn sets need not hold at the general level. This is because a literal within a clause C has several ground instances, some instances requiring renaming and others not, and without finding the refutation (or at least the instances needed) it is not possible to decide whether or not to rename the literal occurrence within C.

Horn sets are considered further when we focus on logic programming. We move on with our review of related theorem-proving procedures.

Apparently the linear input format is desirable, and sophisticated and effective architectures for Prolog implementations have indeed affirmed its desirability, but we seem condemned by the theorem just considered to clause sets whose ground image is a renamable Horn set. Actually, the manner of overcoming this problem was discovered before linear resolution was understood as such. The means of having linear input format complete for all of first-order logic is to alter the underlying resolution structure.

The *model elimination* (*ME*) procedure (see [Loveland, 1968; Loveland, 1969; Loveland, 1978]), introduced almost simultaneously with the resolution procedure, uses the notion of *chain*, analogous to an ordered clause but with two classes of literals, *A-literals* and *B-literals*. The set of *B*-literals in a chain can be regarded as a derived clause as resolution would obtain. SL-resolution [Kowalski and Kuehner, 1971], also a linear input procedure, uses the ME device of two classes of literals to achieve completeness for first-order logic. In this respect it is not strictly a resolution procedure in spite of its name (it differs from ME primarily in introducing a factoring operation) so does not conflict with the relationship between Horn clause sets and linear input resolution as its label might suggest.

As is well-known to logic programming experts, the procedure supporting Prolog is a linear input procedure applied to Horn clauses, but adapted pragmatically after experimentation with SL-resolution. ME owes its current success to a series of implementations by Mark Stickel [Stickel, 1984; Stickel, 1988]; the implementations are collected under the name Prolog Technology Theorem Prover. Recently, parallel implementations of ME have appeared [Bose *et al.*, 1991; Schumann and Letz, 1990; Astrachan and Loveland, 1991]. (Some impressive sequential implementations accompany the parallel versions; e.g., see [Astrachan and Stickel, 1992; Letz *et al.*, 1991].) These implementations have used the Warren Abstract Machine (WAM) architecture [Warren, 1983; Aït-Kaci, 1990] so successful in implementing Prolog.

We present a summary of the model elimination and SL-resolution procedures. We present the ME procedure and then note the distinctions introduced by SL-resolution.

There is great similarity between TOSS deductions and ME deductions; for a proper variant of the TOSS procedure there is an isomorphism with ME. (The variant allows no merging or factoring.) For that reason we will present an example, first with a ground TOSS refutation and then with a corresponding ME refutation. This will be helpful in following the description of ME. Following the informal, simplified introduction to ME and the examples we give a formal, precise definition of (one version of) ME.

The model elimination procedure has two inference operations, extension and reduction. Extension corresponds closely to the resolution operation and reduction is related to factoring. Whereas the resolution operation deletes both resolving literals, the corresponding *extension* operation retains the "resolving" literal of the "near parent" chain, the preceding chain, but promotes the descendent of the literal from a B-literal to an A-literal. A-literals capture and retain all the ancestor information that is really needed, it turns out. (We will drop the reference to descendent and identify the successor literal with the parent, even when instantiation occurs. This will cause no confusion as it is natural to think dynamically of literals passing to newly derived chains in a procedural way.) The counterpart of s-resolution is the *reduction* operation (not related to "reduction" in logic programming parlance) where the rightmost B-literal is removed because it is complementary (using unification in the general case) to an A-literal to its left. Factoring is not needed in ME, as mentioned; reduction can be seen to incorporate factoring and even merging, so merging of ground literals is not done either. (Factoring is explicitly done in

SL-resolution although not needed for completeness.) Chains are ordered, like ordered clauses, and the rightmost B-literal is always the literal acted upon. Any A-literal that becomes rightmost is dropped. The ME procedure we describe is called *weak ME* in [Loveland, 1978], and was the first ME procedure introduced [Loveland, 1968].

We now give our two related examples. We take our examples from [Loveland, 1978], p. 170.

Example 1.2.4. We choose the clause ordering for resolvents that is the reverse order of their presentation in the prefix. Recall that the ordering only affects literals from the far parent; literals from the near parent have the order of the near parent.

A TOSS refutation:

1.	$\neg Pa$	input
2.	$\neg Pc$	input
3.	$\neg PbPd$	input
4.	$\neg PbPc\neg Pd$	input
5.	$PaPbPc$	input, top clause
6.	$PaPb$	resolvent of 2,5
7.	$PaPd$	resolvent of 3,6
8.	$PaPc\neg Pb$	resolvent of 4,7
9.	$PaPc$	s-resolvent of 6,8
10.	Pa	resolvent of 2,9
11.	$\square$	resolvent of 1,10

Now we give the ME counterpart.

Example 1.2.5. The chain-ordering for derived chains is as for the preceding example, namely to extend with literals in reverse order to their appearance in the prefix, the input clause set.

An ME refutation:

1.	$\neg Pa$	input clause
2.	$\neg Pc$	input clause
3.	$\neg PbPd$	input clause
4.	$\neg PbPc\neg Pd$	input clause
5.	$PaPbPc$	input, top clause
6a.	$PaPb[Pc]$	extend with 2
	(A-literal is then deleted as it is rightmost)	
6b.	$PaPb$	
7.	$Pa[Pb]Pd$	extend with 3
8.	$Pa[Pb][Pd]Pc\neg Pb$	extend with 4
9.	$Pa[Pb][Pd]Pc$	reduce
	(A-literal Pb allows the reduction)	
10.	Pa	extend with 2

11. □   extend with 1

We now present the specifications for the (weak) model elimination procedure.

A chain is a sequence of literals, where each literal is in one of two classes, A-literal or B-literal. The input clauses define elementary chains, consisting of all B-literals. Each input clause must define at least one chain for each literal of the input clause, with that literal rightmost. (This provides that each literal of each input clause is accessible as a resolving literal.)

Not every literal sequence is a useful chain. We will use only admissible chains. A chain is *admissible* iff:

(1) complementary B-literals are separated by an A-literal;
(2) no B-literal is to the right of an identical A-literal;
(3) no two A-literals have the same atom; and
(4) the rightmost literal is a B-literal.

The reason for condition (1) is that complementary B-literals not separated by an A-literal originate in the same clause, and the offending non-admissible chain would incorporate a tautologous clause. This can arise even if the associated input clause that contributed those literals is not tautologous because the derived chain undergoes instantiation. Reason (2) comes from the procedure design, from one basic view of ME as using the A-literals to attempt to define a model of the clause and where each attempt at a model is eliminated in turn in the process of obtaining a refutation. No redundant entries in a model specification is needed and the B-literal could only become an A-literal later. Reason (3), that no identical or complementary A-literals need occur combines the just mentioned relationship to models and recognition that the reduction operation should have been used when the right A-literal was a B-literal in an earlier chain. Reason (4) reflects automatic removal of rightmost A-literals.

A (weak) model elimination refutation is a sequence of chains, beginning with a top chain selected from the input elementary chains, ending with □, where each successor chain is derived by extension or reduction defined below.

Each inference rule takes a single chain as the parent chain. The extension operation also uses an *auxiliary* chain, for our purposes always a input elementary chain.

Given an admissible parent chain K and a variable-disjoint auxiliary elementary chain K_1, chain K_2 is formed by the *extension* rule if the rightmost literals of K and K_1 can be made complementary literals by unifier σ. The derived chain K_2 is then formed by deleting the rightmost literal of $K_1\sigma$, promoting the rightmost literal of K to A-literal, and appending the B-literals of $K_1\sigma$ to the right of $K\sigma$ in any order chosen by a user-given ordering rule. If no literals of $K_1\sigma$ exist, all rightmost A-literals of $K\sigma$ are dropped.

Given an admissible parent chain K, chain K_2 is formed by the *reduction* rule if there exists an A-literal which can be made complementary to the rightmost literal by unifier σ. The derived chain K_1 is then formed by deleting the rightmost literal of $K\sigma$ and any A-literals that would then become rightmost.

The ordering rule that dictates the order of appended B-literals from the auxiliary chain in extension is arbitrary. In SL-resolution this freedom to process in user-desired order is described by a selection function that selects from the B-literals to the right of the rightmost A-literal the literal to next use for extension. In ME this is captured by assuming an oracle ordering rule that places the literals in order that the user chooses for his/her selection sequence. Although B-literals between A-literals carry their order forward under both inference rules, clearly this is a descriptive and processing convenience only. The order can be changed at any time by rationalizing that the ordering rule could have made this new selection initially. No inference depends on nonrightmost B-literals to place any constraints on reordering. The selection function mechanism of SL-resolution makes this ordering freedom clear.

The ME procedure also possesses a lemma mechanism that allows certain derived elementary chains to be added to the set of input chains. This must be done with great selectivity because the auxiliary set can explode in size very quickly. Also, the ability to use the derived chain in the manner of the compiled input clauses seems to be lost. It seems that only unit clause lemmas are worth retaining, and only a selected subset of those. The lemma device has recently proved itself in the METEOR implementation (see [Astrachan and Stickel, 1992]).

To prove substantial mathematical theorems using a linear input proof procedure will take some substantial added devices. In spite of the very high inference rate achievable due to the effective implementation techniques that takes advantage of the fixed set providing the far parent clauses (chains), the tremendous number of redundant calculations overwhelm the search. Some manner of recording computed search subtrees when successful (lemmas) and when failed, is needed. Such a methodology, called caching, is being studied and has had some success (see [Astrachan and Stickel, 1992]). Success with devices like caching are needed if linear input provers are to be useful in proving substantial mathematical theorems. Not only do procedures that employ a breadth-first search style keep clauses for subsumption use, but forward-chaining systems tend to create more ground literals because of a frequent property of axioms. Axioms are often Horn clauses and the positive literal often contains only variables shared with another literal. By resolving the positive literal last it is often a ground literal when resolved.

Although possibly not the optimal procedural format for proving mathematical theorems, the linear input format is excellent for situations where strong search guidance exists, as previously noted. One of the situations where such guidance is often possible is in the logic programming domain. We now explore this domain.

2   The logic programming paradigm

Logic programming as a phrase has come to have two meanings. Many people familiar only with Prolog regard logic programming in a very narrow sense; the use of Horn clause logic in a manner implemented by Prolog. In its broadest sense logic programming is a philosophy regarding computation, asserting that deduction and computation are two sides of the same concept. This viewpoint is built on the following general observation: an answer that can be computed using a problem-specific algorithm can also be determined by a proof procedure presented with the axioms of the appropriate theory and the problem as a theorem to be proven. In its fullest sense, then, logic programming is concerned with the development and use of logics whose proof procedures best fit our well-understood notion of good computation procedures. The advantage of good computation models for the proof search is that the user then understands the computational implications of the problem formulation as (s)he develops the problem specification.

In this section we will look at the notion of logic programming in its fullest sense, by a systematic presentation of the logical structures that preserve good computation properties. This is done by preserving the important procedural qualities possessed by Horn clause logic that makes Prolog so successful. Thus it is appropriate to begin by a review of logic programming in the narrow sense mentioned above, which will reflect the historical development of logic programming as a field of study. This will bring us back to the subject matter of the preceding section, for the inference engine that underlies Prolog is a restricted form of linear resolution using a revised notation.

2.1   Horn clause logic programming

We first need to define *Horn clause logic*. If we recall that a clause is a disjunction of literals, then a *Horn clause* is a clause with at most one positive literal, or *atom*. Clauses with one atom are called *definite* clauses. One formulation of Horn clause logic is as a refutation logic of the type we have already studied with the clause set restricted to Horn clauses. Simple restrictions of refutation systems already considered give us complete refutation procedures for this logic. One restriction is to linear resolution; simply impose an input restriction on a standard linear resolution system. That is, the far parent clause must be from the input clause set. A simple observation extends the completeness of linear resolution for first-order logic to a completeness argument for linear input resolution over Horn logic. That is done as follows: Start with a negative clause (all literals are negative; there always is such a clause if the clause set is unsatisfiable) and then note that *any* linear deduction must also be an input deduction because every derived clause is a negative clause. (Since no two negative clauses can resolve with each other no two derived clauses can resolve together.) One can show that if a refutation exists then one exists starting with a negative clause. Thus, since in general an unsatisfiable clause set always has a linear refutation, there must be a refutation among the linear input deductions for each unsatisfiable Horn clause set. Finally, clauses can be ordered arbitrarily and resolution done on only the rightmost, or only the leftmost, literal of the current clause. This is clear because the subdeduction that "removes" that literal can only use input clauses, so is totally independent of the other literals of the clause.

A second approach to structure a linear procedure for Horn clause logic is to restrict the model elimination (SL-resolution) procedure by removing the reduction rule. This leaves only extension as an inference rule which makes no use of A-literals so the need for two types of literals has gone. If the A-literals are removed then extension is simply the binary resolution inference rule. Thus ME also collapses to a linear input resolution refutation procedure within the Horn clause domain. Again we note that if we begin with a chain from a negative clause then reduction is never called so that the above restriction is equivalent to the full ME procedure on the class of Horn clause sets. Thus this restriction is complete for Horn clause logic. This restriction clearly does not use factoring so we see that linear input resolution without factoring is complete for the Horn clause domain. In ME (SL-resolution) we can only order (select from) the most recently added literals. However, with only the extension rule of inference, we can reorder (select from) the entire clause at each step. Extension makes no reference to any literal within the current chain other than the literal extended on, so any literal may be chosen first. This restriction of ME (SL-resolution) to Horn clauses, with the changes noted, is called *SLD-resolution* for SL-resolution for definite clauses. SLD-resolution was so-named by Apt and van Emden for the reason outlined here (and, probably more importantly, because the development of Prolog's underlying logic, SLD-resolution, followed historically from SL-resolution). However, independent of the activity directly leading to Prolog, Robert Hill [Hill, 1974] defined and proved complete for Horn clause logic this ordered linear input procedure, which he called LUSH resolution, for linear, unrestricted selection resolution for Horn clauses.

Horn clause logic provides the mechanism that defines "pure Prolog", the first-order logic part of Prolog. (We assume that the reader is familiar with the search control aspects of Prolog and with negation-as-failure, and knows that these are not practically definable within first-order Horn clause logic. Someone wishing further amplification of these qualities of Prolog should consult some of the other chapters of this volume.) To better capture the direct notion of proof and computation important to the presentation of Prolog we need to adopt another view of Horn clause logic. The new viewpoint says that we are not interested simply in whether or not a set of clauses is unsatisfiable. We now are interested in answers to a query made in the context of a database, to use one vocabulary common in logic programming. In a more compatible terminology, we seek a constructive proof of an existentially quantified theorem where the existential variables are instantiated so as to make the theorem true. (It happens that only one instantiation of these existential variables is needed for any Horn clause problem; this is a consequence of the need for only one negative clause in any (minimal) unsatisfiable Horn clause set, ground sets in particular.) Along with a notion of answer we will also emphasize a direct proof system, meaning that conceptually we will consider proofs from axioms with the theorem as the last line of the deduction. This is important even though our customary proof search will be a backward chaining system that begins with the proposed theorem (query).

The alternate viewpoint begins with a different representation for a Horn clause. The definite clauses have the generic form $A_1 \vee \neg A_2 \vee \neg A_3 \vee \ldots \vee \neg A_n$ which we now choose to represent in the (classically) logically equivalent form $A_1 \leftarrow A_2, A_3 \ldots, A_n$ where the latter expression is the implication $A_2 \wedge A_3 \wedge \ldots \wedge A_n \supset A_1$ written with the consequent on the left to facilitate the clause presentation when backchaining in the proof search mode, and with the comma replacing AND. Negative clause $\neg A_1 \vee \neg A_2 \vee \neg A_3 \vee \ldots \vee \neg A_n$ is written $\leftarrow A_1, A_2, A_3, \ldots, A_n$ which as an implication is read $A_1 \wedge A_2 \wedge A_3 \wedge \ldots \wedge A_n \supset FALSE$ (i.e., that the positive conjunction is contradictory). In particular, we note that the negative literals appear as atoms on the right of $\leftarrow$ (conjoined together) and the positive literal appears on the left.

We now consider the problem presentation. Theorem proving problems are often of the form $A \supset B$, where A is a set of axioms and B is the proposed theorem. The validation of $A \supset B$ is equivalent to the refutability of its negation, $A \wedge \neg B$. To assure that $A \wedge \neg B$ is a Horn clause set we can start with Horn clauses as axioms and let B have form $\exists \overline{x}(B_1 \wedge B_2 \wedge \ldots \wedge B_r)$, where $\exists \overline{x}$ means the existential closure of all variables in the expression it quantifies. This form works for B because $\neg \exists \overline{x}(B_1 \wedge B_2 \wedge \ldots \wedge B_r)$ is logically equivalent to a negative Horn clause. In Horn clause logic programming (i.e. for Prolog) the problem format is explicitly of the form $P \supset Q$, where P, the *program*, is a set of definite Horn clauses and Q, the *query*, is of form $\exists \overline{x}(B_1 \wedge B_2 \wedge \ldots \wedge B_r)$. The notation $\leftarrow B_1, \ldots, B_r$ that we use for this formula is suggestive of a query if the $\leftarrow$ is read here as a query mark. Indeed, ?- is the prefix of a query for most Prolog implementations. (The existential quantifier is not notated.)

We have just seen that the Prolog query is an existentially quantified conjunction of atoms. As already noted, it is central to logic programming that the proof search yield a substitution instance for each existentially quantified query variable and not just confirmation that the query instance follows from the program clause set. We call this *answer extraction*. Answer extraction is not original to logic programming; it goes back to work in question-answering systems of Green and Raphael [Green and Raphael, 1968; Green, 1969] for natural language systems and robotics in particular. Again, we note that for Horn clause sets only one query instance is needed; every Horn clause program implies (at most) a single query instance, a *definite* answer.

We emphasize that we have shifted from resolution theorem proving, which focuses on refutability and with a very symmetric input set (no distinguished literal or clauses) to a focus on logical consequence and input asymmetry. Asymmetry occurs at the clause level with a designated consequent atom and at the problem level with a designated query.

We now focus more closely on answer extraction. Given program P and query Q a *correct answer substitution* θ for P, Q is a substitution over Q such that $Q\theta$ is a logical consequence of P. For program P and query Q the *computed answer substitution* θ is the substitution applied to all variables of Q as determined at the successful termination of the SLD-resolution procedure. The key statements of soundness and completeness for Horn clause logic programming is that for SLD-resolution every computed answer is correct and if a correct answer exists then there exists a finite SLD-resolution deduction yielding a computed answer. Of course, this is a direct translation of results known to the resolution theory community. (We hasten to note that many important results in logic programming are not direct derivatives of work in the automated theorem proving field.)

Finally, we remark that the backchaining, problem reduction proof search mode inherited from linear resolution is an artifact of practicality only. The goal-oriented search has proved very advantageous, especially since user search control (e.g. ordering of clauses in the program) means that a small fraction of the search space is expanded in depth-first goal-oriented search. Conceptually, it is also useful to consider proofs in a forward direction, from facts through implied facts to the query instance.

We present a small example in the two formats of SLD-resolution to illustrate the isomorphism between the logic programming notation and the resolution notation for linear input deductions. We give the problem in the logic programming style first. Note that s, t, u, v, w, x, y, z are variables and a, b, c are constant terms. The substitutions that participate in the computed answer are indicated. The format is x/t where x is a variable and t is the replacement term.

Program:
    1. $p(a, a, b)$
    2. $p(c, c, b)$
    3. $p(x, f(u, w), z) \leftarrow p(x, u, y), p(y, w, z)$
    4. $p(x, g(s), y) \leftarrow p(y, s, x)$
Query:
    5. $\leftarrow p(a, t, c)$
Derivation:

6.	$\leftarrow p(a, u, y), p(y, w, c)$	using clause 3
	Substitution: $t/f(u, w)$	
7.	$\leftarrow p(b, w, c)$	using clause 1
	Substitution: u/a	
8.	$\leftarrow p(c, s, b)$	using clause 4
	Substitution: $w/g(s)$	
9.	success	using clause 2
	Substitution: s/c	

Answer:
    $p(a, f(a, g(c)), c)$

That the deduction form is that of ordered clause input linear resolution is clear by comparing the above to the resolution deduction that follows.

Given clauses:
    1. $p(a, a, b)$
    2. $p(c, c, b)$
    3. $p(x, f(u, w), z), \neg p(x, u, y), \neg p(y, w, z)$
    4. $p(x, g(s), y) \neg p(y, s, x)$
    5. $\neg p(a, t, c)$
Derivation:

6.	$\neg p(a, u, y), \neg p(y, w, c)$	resolvent of 3,5
	Substitution: $t/f(u, w)$	
7.	$\neg p(b, w, c)$	resolvent of 1,6
	Substitution: u/a	
8.	$\neg p(c, s, b)$	resolvent of 4,7
	Substitution: $w/g(s)$	
9.	□	resolvent of 2,8
	Substitution: s/c	

2.2   A framework for logic programming

We have now completed our review of SLD-resolution and its role in Horn clause logic programming. Horn clause logic programming provides the core concepts underlying Prolog, the so-called pure Prolog. But is the quite restricted form given by Horn clause logic the only meaningful logic for logic programming? Do more powerful (and useful) logics exist? The idea of using arbitrary clauses as opposed to Horn clauses has been championed by [Kowalski, 1979]. In a similar fashion, the use of full first-order logic — as opposed to logic in clausal form — has been advocated and explored [Bowen, 1982]. In a more conservative direction, extending the structure of Horn clauses by limited uses of connectives and quantifiers has been suggested. The best known extension of pure Horn clause logic within the logic programming paradigm permits negation in goals, using the notion of negation-as-failure. However, the idea of using implications and universal quantifiers and, in fact, arbitrary logical connectives in goals has also been advocated [Gabbay and Reyle, 1984a; Lloyd and Topor, 1984; McCarty, 1988a; McCarty, 1988b; Miller, 1989b; Miller *et al.*, 1991].

There is a wide spectrum of logical languages between those given by Horn clause logic and full quantificational logic, especially if the derivability relation to be used is also open to choice. An obvious question that arises in this situation is whether some of these languages provide more natural bases for logic programming than do others. We argue for an affirmative answer to this question in this subsection. In particular, we describe a criterion for determining whether or not a given predicate logic provides an adequate basis for logic programming. The principle underlying this criterion is that a logic program in a suitable logical language must satisfy dual needs: it should function as a specification of a problem while serving at the same time to describe a programming task. It is primarily due to the specification requirement that an emphasis is placed on the use of symbolic logic for providing the syntax and the metatheory of logic programming. The programming task description requirement, although less well recognized, appears on reflection to be of equal importance. The viewpoint we adopt here is that the programming character of logic programming arises from thinking of a program as a description of a search whose structure is determined by interpreting the logical connectives and quantifiers as *fixed* search instructions. From this perspective, the connectives and quantifiers appearing in programs must exhibit a duality between a search-related interpretation and a logical meaning. Such a duality in meaning cannot be attributed to these symbols in every logical language. The criterion that we describe below is, in essence, one for identifying those languages in which this can be done.

To provide some concreteness to the abstract discussion above, let us reconsider briefly the notions of programs and queries in the context of Horn clause logic. As has previously been noted, one view of a query in this setting is as a formula of the form $\exists \overline{x}\,(p_1(\overline{x}) \wedge \ldots \wedge p_n(\overline{x}))$; $\overline{x}$ is used here to denote a sequence of variables and $p_i(\overline{x})$ represents an atomic formula in which some of these variables appear free. The SLD-resolution procedure described in the previous subsection tries to find a proof for such a query by looking for specific substitutions for the variables in $\overline{x}$ that make each of the formulas $p_i(\overline{x})$ follow from the program. This procedure can, thus, be thought to be the result of assigning particular search interpretations to existential quantifiers and conjunctions, the former being interpreted as specifications of (infinite) OR branches with the branches being parameterized by substitutions and the latter being interpreted as specifications of AND branches. This view of the logical symbols is of obvious importance from the perspective of programming in Horn clause logic. Now, it is a nontrivial property of Horn clause logic that a query has a constructive proof of the kind described above if it has any proof at all from a given program. It is this property that permits the search-related interpretation of the logical symbols appearing in queries to co-exist with their logical or declarative semantics and that eventually underlies the programming utility of Horn clauses.

Our desire is to turn the observations made in the context of Horn clause logic into a broad criterion for recognizing logical languages that can be used in a similar fashion in programming. However, the restricted syntax of logic in clausal form is an impediment to this enterprise and we therefore enrich our logical vocabulary before proceeding further. In particular, we shall allow the logical symbols $\wedge$, $\vee$, $\supset$, $\forall$, $\exists$, $\top$ and $\bot$ to appear in the formulas that we consider. The first five of these symbols do not need an explanation. The symbols $\top$ and $\bot$ are intended to correspond to truth and falsity, respectively. We shall also use the following syntactic variables with the corresponding general connotations:

$\mathcal{D}$ A set of formulas, finite subsets of which serve as possible programs of some logic programming language.

$\mathcal{G}$ A set of formulas, each member of which serves as a possible query or goal for this programming language.

A An atomic formula excluding $\top$ and $\bot$.

D A member of $\mathcal{D}$, referred to as a program clause.

G A member of $\mathcal{G}$, referred to as a goal or query.

$\mathcal{P}$ A finite set of formulas from $\mathcal{D}$, referred to as a (logic) program.

Using the current vocabulary, computation in logic programming can be viewed as the process of constructing a derivation for a query G from a program $\mathcal{P}$. The question that needs to be addressed, then, is that of the restrictions that must be placed on $\mathcal{D}$ and $\mathcal{G}$ and the notion of derivation to make this a useful viewpoint.

Towards answering this question, we shall describe a proof-theoretic criterion that captures the idea of computation-as-search. The first step in this direction is to define the search-related semantics that is to be attributed to the logical symbols. This may be done by outlining the structure of a simple nondeterministic interpreter for programs and goals. This interpreter either succeeds or does not succeed, depending on the program $\mathcal{P}$ and the goal G that it is given in its initial state. We shall write $\mathcal{P} \vdash_O G$ to indicate that the interpreter succeeds on G given $\mathcal{P}$; the subscript in $\vdash_O$ signifies that this relation is to be thought of as the "operational" semantics of an (idealized) interpreter. The behavior of this interpreter is characterized by the following search instructions corresponding to the various logical symbols; the notation $[x/t]G$ is used here to denote the result of substituting t for all free occurrences of x in G:

SUCCESS $\mathcal{P} \vdash_O \top$.

AND $\mathcal{P} \vdash_O G_1 \wedge G_2$ only if $\mathcal{P} \vdash_O G_1$ and $\mathcal{P} \vdash_O G_2$.

OR $\mathcal{P} \vdash_O G_1 \vee G_2$ only if $\mathcal{P} \vdash_O G_1$ or $\mathcal{P} \vdash_O G_2$.

INSTANCE $\mathcal{P} \vdash_O \exists x\, G$ only if there is some term t such that $\mathcal{P} \vdash_O [x/t]G$.

AUGMENT $\mathcal{P} \vdash_O D \supset G$ only if $\mathcal{P} \cup \{D\} \vdash_O G$.

GENERIC $\mathcal{P} \vdash_O \forall x\, G$ only if $\mathcal{P} \vdash_O [x/c]G$, where c is a constant that does not appear in $\mathcal{P}$ or in G.

These instructions may be understood as follows: The logical constant $\top$ signifies a successfully completed search. The connectives $\wedge$ and $\vee$ provide, respectively, for the specification of an AND and a nondeterministic OR node in the search space to be explored by the interpreter. The quantifier $\exists$ specifies an infinite nondeterministic OR node whose branches are parameterized by the set of all terms. Implication instructs the interpreter to augment its program prior to searching for a solution to the consequent of the implication. Finally, universal quantification is an instruction to introduce a new constant and to try to solve the goal that results from the given one by a (generic) instantiation with this constant.

    Certain comments about the search instructions are in order before we proceed further. First of all, it is necessary to counter a possible impression that their structure is arbitrary. If $\vdash_O$ were interpreted as derivability in almost any reasonable logical system, then the conditions pertaining to it that are contained in the instructions AND, OR, INSTANCE, AUGMENT and GENERIC would be true in the reverse direction. Thus, in order to maintain a duality between a logical and a search-related reading of the logical symbols, the operational interpretation of these symbols is forced to satisfy the listed conditions in this direction. The instructions provided above represent, in this sense, a strengthening of the logical character of the relevant connectives and quantifiers in a way that permits a search-related meaning to be extracted for each of them. Further, the search interpretations that are so obtained are, quite evidently, of a natural kind. The interpretations for $\exists$ and $\wedge$ are, as we have observed, the ones accorded to them within the framework of Horn clauses, the notions of success and disjunctive search are meaningful ones, and some of the programming utility of the AUGMENT and GENERIC search operations will be discussed later in this section.

The second point to note is that we have addressed only the issue of the success/failure semantics for the various logical symbols through the presentation of the idealized interpreter. In particular, we have not described the notion of the *result* of a computation. There is, of course, a simple way in which this notion can be elaborated: existentially quantified goals are to be solved by finding instantiations for the quantifiers that yield solvable goals, and the instantiations of this kind that are found for the top-level existential quantifiers in the original goal can be provided as the outcome of the computation. However, in the interest of developing as broad a framework as possible, we have not built either this or any other notion of a result into our operational semantics. We note also that our interpreter has been specified in a manner completely independent of any notion of unification. Free variables that appear in goals are not placeholders in the sense that substitutions can be made for them and substitutions are made only in the course of instantiating quantifiers. Of course, a practical interpreter for a particular language whose operational semantics satisfies the conditions presented here might utilize a relevant form of unification as well as a notion of variables that can be instantiated. We indicate how such an interpreter might be designed in the next section by considering this issue in the context of specific languages described there.

In a sense related to that of the above discussion, we observe that our search instructions only partially specify the behavior to be exhibited by an interpreter in the course of solving a goal. In particular, they do not describe the action to be taken when an atomic goal needs to be solved. A natural choice from this perspective turns out to be the operation of backchaining that was used in the context of Horn clause logic. Thus, an instruction of the following sort may often be included for dealing with atomic goals:

ATOMIC $\mathcal{P} \vdash_O A$ only if A is an instance of a clause in $\mathcal{P}$ or $\mathcal{P} \vdash_O G$ for an instance $G \supset A$ of a clause in $\mathcal{P}$.

There are two reasons for not including an instruction of this kind in the prescribed operational semantics. First, we are interested at this juncture only in describing the manner in which the connectives and quantifiers in a goal should affect a search for a solution and the particular use that is to be made of program clauses is, from this perspective, of secondary importance. Second, such an instruction requires program clauses to conform to a fairly rigid structure and as such runs counter to the desire for generality in the view of logic programming that we are developing.

A notable omission from the logical connectives that we are considering is that of $\neg$. The interpretation of negation in most logical systems corresponds to an inconsistency between a proposition and a set of assumptions. In contrast, the natural search-related meaning for this symbol seems to be that of failure in finding a solution to a given goal. There is, thus, a considerable variance between the two desired views of the symbol. Further, the search-related view assumes that the abilities of the system of derivation can be circumscribed in some fashion. It appears difficult to represent this kind of an ability within a proof system and so we do not make an attempt to do this here. It is easy to provide for an alternative view of negation that is close to its logical interpretation as is done in [Miller, 1989b]. There is, however, no need to add an explicit negation symbol for this purpose since it can be treated as defined in terms of $\supset$ and $\perp$. As for the symbol $\perp$ itself, there is a natural tendency to read it as failure. Once again, this does not correspond to the usual interpretation of $\perp$ within logical systems where it is considered to be a proposition that is "true" when there is a contradiction in the assumptions. In including an interpretation of $\perp$ that is close to its logical meaning, a choice has to be made between two competing views of the consequences of discovering a contradiction. The search instructions described above are compatible with either view. The view that is ultimately adopted is dependent on the logical system that is chosen to provide the declarative semantics; in particular, on which of the notions of provability that are described below is used.

The declarative semantics to be associated with the various connectives and quantifiers can be formalized by means of sequent-style proof systems. We digress briefly to summarize the central notions pertaining to such systems. The basic unit of assertion within these systems is that of a *sequent*. This is a pair of finite (possibly empty) sets of formulas $\langle \Gamma, \Theta \rangle$ that is written as $\Gamma \longrightarrow \Theta$. The first element of this pair is commonly referred to as the antecedent of the sequent and the second is called its succedent. A sequent corresponds intuitively to the assertion that at least one of the formulas in its succedent holds given as assumptions all those in its antecedent. (Although we shall not be concerned with the situation where Θ is empty, this usually corresponds to a contradiction in the assumptions.) A *proof* for a sequent is a finite tree constructed using a given set of *inference figures* and such that the root is labeled with the sequent in question and the leaves are labeled with designated *initial sequents*. Particular sequent systems are characterized by their choice of inference figures and initial sequents.

Figure 1 contains the inference figure schemata of interest in this paper. Actual inference figures are obtained from these by instantiating Γ, Θ and Δ by sets of formulas, B, C, and P by formulas, t by a term and c by a constant. There is, in addition, a proviso on the choice of constant for c: it should not appear in any formula contained in the lower sequent in the same figure. The notation B, Γ (Θ, B) that is used in the schemata is to be read as an abbreviation for $\{B\} \cup \Gamma$ $(\{B\} \cup \Theta)$ and a set of formulas can be viewed as being of this form even if $B \in \Gamma$ ($B \in \Theta$). The initial sequents in the proof systems that we consider are of the form $\Gamma \longrightarrow \Theta$ where $\top \in \Theta$ or $\Gamma \cap \Theta$ contains either $\bot$ or an atomic formula.

Sequent-style proof systems of the kind we have described generally have three *structural* inference figure schemata, which we have not listed. Two of these schemata, usually called *interchange* and *contraction*, ensure that the order and multiplicity of formulas in sequents are unimportant in a situation where the antecedents and succedents are taken to be lists instead of sets. Our use of sets, and the interpretation of the notation B, Γ (Θ, B) that is explained above, obviates these schemata. The third kind of structural inference figure schema, commonly referred to as *thinning* or *weakening*, permits the addition of a formula to the antecedent or succedent of a sequent whose proof has already been constructed. Such inference figures are required when the antecedent and the succedent of an initial sequent are permitted to have at most one formula. Our choice of initial sequents, once again, obviates these inference figures.

We shall call an arbitrary proof that is obtained using the schemata in Figure 1 a **C**-proof. Placing additional restrictions on the use of the schemata in Figure 1 results in alternative notions of derivations. One such notion that is of interest to us in this paper is that of an **I**-proof. A proof of this kind is a **C**-proof in which each sequent occurrence has a singleton set as its succedent. As a further refinement, if we disallow the use of the inference figure schema $\bot$-R in an **I**-proof, we obtain the notion of an **M**-proof. We shall need these three notions of derivability later in this chapter and so we introduce special notation for them. We write $\Gamma \vdash_C B$, $\Gamma \vdash_I B$, and $\Gamma \vdash_M B$, if the sequent $\Gamma \longrightarrow B$ has, respectively, a **C**-proof, an **I**-proof, and an **M**-proof; if the set Γ is empty, it may be omitted from the left side of these three relations. The three relations that are thus defined correspond to provability in, respectively, classical, intuitionistic and minimal logic. More detailed discussions of these kinds of sequent proof systems and their relationship to other presentations of the corresponding logics can be found in [Fitting, 1969; Gentzen, 1969; Prawitz, 1965; Troelstra, 1973]. It is relevant to note that in our presentation of these three provability relations we have excluded a structural inference figure schema called *cut*. As a result of this omission, the correspondence between our presentation and the customary definitions of the respective derivability relations depends on a fundamental theorem for the logics in question that is referred to as the cut-elimination theorem.

The framework of sequent systems provides a convenient means for formalizing the desired duality in interpretation for the logical connectives and quantifiers. The first step in this direction is to formalize the behavior of the idealized interpreter within such systems. We do this by identifying the notion of a *uniform proof*. This is an **I**-proof in which any sequent whose succedent contains a non-atomic formula occurs only as the lower sequent

$$\frac{B, C, \Gamma \longrightarrow \Theta}{B \wedge C, \Gamma \longrightarrow \Theta} \wedge\text{-L} \qquad \frac{\Gamma \longrightarrow \Theta, B \qquad \Gamma \longrightarrow \Theta, C}{\Gamma \longrightarrow \Theta, B \wedge C} \wedge\text{-R}$$

$$\frac{B, \Gamma \longrightarrow \Theta \qquad C, \Gamma \longrightarrow \Theta}{B \vee C, \Gamma \longrightarrow \Theta} \vee\text{-L}$$

$$\frac{\Gamma \longrightarrow \Theta, B}{\Gamma \longrightarrow \Theta, B \vee C} \vee\text{-R} \qquad \frac{\Gamma \longrightarrow \Theta, C}{\Gamma \longrightarrow \Theta, B \vee C} \vee\text{-R}$$

$$\frac{\Gamma \longrightarrow \Theta, B \qquad C, \Gamma \longrightarrow \Delta}{B \supset C, \Gamma \longrightarrow \Theta \cup \Delta} \supset\text{-L} \qquad \frac{B, \Gamma \longrightarrow \Theta, C}{\Gamma \longrightarrow \Theta, B \supset C} \supset\text{-R}$$

$$\frac{[x/t]P, \Gamma \longrightarrow \Theta}{\forall x\, P, \Gamma \longrightarrow \Theta} \forall\text{-L} \qquad \frac{\Gamma \longrightarrow \Theta, [x/t]P}{\Gamma \longrightarrow \Theta, \exists x\, P} \exists\text{-R}$$

$$\frac{[x/c]P, \Gamma \longrightarrow \Theta}{\exists x\, P, \Gamma \longrightarrow \Theta} \exists\text{-L} \qquad \frac{\Gamma \longrightarrow \Theta, [x/c]P}{\Gamma \longrightarrow \Theta, \forall x\, P} \forall\text{-R}$$

$$\frac{\Gamma \longrightarrow \Theta, \bot}{\Gamma \longrightarrow \Theta, B} \bot\text{-R}$$

Fig. 1. Inference figure schemata

of an inference figure that introduces the top-level logical symbol of that formula. Suppose now that the sequent $\Gamma \longrightarrow G$ appears in a uniform proof. Then the following conditions must be satisfied with respect to this sequent:

o If G is $\top$, the sequent is initial.
o If G is $B \wedge C$ then the sequent is inferred by $\wedge$-R from $\Gamma \longrightarrow B$ and $\Gamma \longrightarrow C$.
o If G is $B \vee C$ then the sequent is inferred by $\vee$-R from either $\Gamma \longrightarrow B$ or $\Gamma \longrightarrow C$.
o If G is $\exists x\, P$ then the sequent is inferred by $\exists$-R from $\Gamma \longrightarrow [x/t]P$ for some term t.
o If G is $B \supset C$ then the sequent is inferred by $\supset$-R from $B, \Gamma \longrightarrow C$.
o If G is $\forall x\, P$ then the sequent is inferred by $\forall$-R from $\Gamma \longrightarrow [x/c]P$, where c is a constant that does not occur in the given sequent.

The structure of a uniform proof thus reflects the search instructions associated with the logical symbols. We can, in fact, define $\vdash_O$ by saying that $\mathcal{P} \vdash_O G$, *i.e.*, the interpreter succeeds on the goal G given the program $\mathcal{P}$, if and only if there is a uniform proof of the sequent $\mathcal{P} \longrightarrow G$. We observe now that the logical symbols exhibit the desired duality between a logical and a search-related meaning in exactly those situations where the existence of a proof within a given logical system ensures the existence of a uniform proof. We use this observation to define our criterion for establishing the suitability of a logical language as the basis for logic programming: letting $\vdash$ denote a chosen proof relation, we say that a triple $\langle \mathcal{D}, \mathcal{G}, \vdash \rangle$ is an *abstract logic programming language* just in case, for all finite subsets $\mathcal{P}$ of $\mathcal{D}$ and all formulas G of $\mathcal{G}$, $\mathcal{P} \vdash G$ if and only if $\mathcal{P} \longrightarrow G$ has a uniform proof.

2.3 Abstract logic programming languages

Abstract logic programming languages as described in the previous subsection are parameterized by three components: a class of formulas each member of which can serve as a program clause, another class of formulas that corresponds to possible queries and a derivability relation between formulas. Within the framework envisaged, the purpose of the derivability relation is to provide a declarative semantics for the various logical symbols used. This purpose is realized if a well understood proof relation, such as the relation $\vdash_C$, $\vdash_I$, or $\vdash_M$, is used. Once a particular declarative semantics is chosen, it must be verified that this accords well with the desired operational or search semantics for the logical symbols. In general, this will be the case only when the permitted programs and queries are restricted in some fashion. In determining if the desired duality is realized in any given situation, it is necessary to confirm that the existence of a proof for a goal from a program entails also the existence of a uniform proof. If this is the case, then our logical language has a proof procedure that is goal-directed and whose search behavior is substantially determined by the logical symbols that appear in the goal being considered. Viewed differently, the defining criterion for an abstract logic programming language is one that ensures that a procedure of this kind may be used for finding proofs without an inherent loss of completeness.

Even though our criterion for identifying logical languages that can serve as the bases for logic programming seems to have content at an intuitive level, it is necessary to demonstrate that it actually serves a useful purpose. An important requirement in this regard is that it have a definite discriminatory effect. Towards showing that it does have such an effect, we first consider some recently proposed extensions to Horn clause logic and show that they fail to qualify as abstract logic programming languages. These extensions utilize the negation symbol that may be introduced into our setting by defining $\neg P$ to be $(P \supset \bot)$. With this understanding, the first non-example is one where $\mathcal{D}$ consists of the universal closures of atoms or formulas of the form $(B_1 \wedge \ldots \wedge B_n) \supset A$ where A is an atom and B_i is a literal, $\mathcal{G}$ consists of the existential closure of conjunctions of atoms and $\vdash$ corresponds to classical provability (see, for example, [Fitting, 1985]). Within the language defined by this triple, the set $\{p \supset q(a), \neg p \supset q(b)\}$ constitutes a program and the formula $\exists x \, q(x)$ corresponds to a query. This query is provable from the program in question within classical logic and the following is a **C**-proof for the relevant sequent:

$$
\cfrac{\cfrac{\cfrac{p \longrightarrow \bot, p}{\longrightarrow \neg p, p} \supset\text{-R}}{p \supset q(a) \longrightarrow \neg p, \exists x \, q(x)} \qquad \cfrac{\cfrac{q(a) \longrightarrow q(a)}{q(a) \longrightarrow \exists x \, q(x)} \exists\text{-R}}{q(a) \longrightarrow \exists x \, q(x)} \supset\text{-L}}{p \supset q(a), \neg p \supset q(b) \longrightarrow \exists x \, q(x)} \qquad \cfrac{\cfrac{q(b) \longrightarrow q(b)}{q(b) \longrightarrow \exists x \, q(x)} \exists\text{-R}}{} \supset\text{-L.}
$$

There is, however, no uniform proof for $\exists x \, q(x)$ from the program being considered; such a proof would require $q(t)$ to be derivable from $\{p \supset q(a), \neg p \supset q(b)\}$ for some particular t, and this clearly does not hold. Thus, the language under consideration fails to satisfy the defining criterion for abstract logic programming languages. Another non-example along these lines is obtained by taking $\mathcal{D}$ to be the collection of (the universal closures of) positive and negative Horn clauses, $\mathcal{G}$ to consist of the existential closure of a conjunction of literals containing at most one negative literal and $\vdash$ to be classical provability [Gallier and Raatz, 1987]. This triple fails to be an abstract logic programming language since

$$\neg p(a) \vee \neg p(b) \vdash_C \exists x \, \neg p(x)$$

although no particular instance of the existentially quantified goal can be proved. For a final non-example, let $\mathcal{D}$ and $\mathcal{G}$ consist of arbitrary formulas and let $\vdash$ be provability in classical, intuitionistic or minimal logic. This triple, once again, does not constitute an abstract logic programming language, since, for instance,

$$p(a) \vee p(b) \vdash \exists x \, p(x)$$

regardless of whether $\vdash$ is interpreted as $\vdash_C$, $\vdash_I$ or $\vdash_M$ whereas there is no term t such that $p(t)$ is derivable even in classical logic from $p(a) \vee p(b)$.

To conclude that our criterion really makes distinctions, it is necessary to also exhibit positive examples of abstract logic programming languages. We provide examples of this kind now and the syntactic richness of these examples will simultaneously demonstrate a genuine utility for our criterion.

The first example that we consider is of a logical language that is slightly richer than Horn clause logic. This language is given by the triple $\langle \mathcal{D}_1, \mathcal{G}_1, \vdash_C \rangle$ where $\mathcal{G}_1$ is the collection of first-order formulas defined by the syntax rule

$$G ::= \top \mid A \mid G \wedge G \mid G \vee G \mid \exists x \, G$$

and $\mathcal{D}_1$ is similarly defined by the rule

$$D ::= A \mid G \supset A \mid D \wedge D \mid \forall x\, D.$$

As observed in Subsection 2.1, a positive Horn clause is equivalent in classical logic to a formula of the form $\forall \bar{x}\,(B \supset A)$ where B is a conjunction of atoms. This form is subsumed by the D formulas defined above. The queries within the Horn clause logic programming framework are of the form $\exists \bar{x}\, B$ where B is a conjunction of atoms. Formulas of this sort are, once again, contained in the set denoted by $\mathcal{G}_1$. It is thus evident that the paradigm of programming provided for by Horn clause logic is subsumed by the triple $\langle \mathcal{D}_1, \mathcal{G}_1, \vdash_C \rangle$ if indeed this turns out to be an adequate basis for logic programming. That this is the case is the content of the following proposition:

Proposition 2.3.1. *The triple $\langle \mathcal{D}_1, \mathcal{G}_1, \vdash_C \rangle$ constitutes an abstract logic programming language.*

The reader interested in a proof of this proposition is referred, amongst other places, to [Miller *et al.*, 1991]. Although we do not present a proof here, it is instructive to consider the structure of such a proof. As noted already, the nontrivial part consists of showing that the existence of a classical proof guarantees also the existence of a uniform proof. There are two observations that lead to this conclusion in the case of interest. First, if $\mathcal{P}$ is a finite subset of $\mathcal{D}_1$ and G is a member of $\mathcal{G}_1$, then an inductive argument on the heights of derivations shows that the sequent $\mathcal{P} \longrightarrow G$ has a **C**-proof only if it has one in which (a) the inference figure $\perp$-R does not appear and (b) there is only one formula in the succedent of each sequent appearing in the proof. Second, in a derivation of the sort engendered by the first observation, the inference figures $\wedge$-L, $\supset$-L and $\forall$-L can be moved above $\wedge$-R, $\vee$-R and $\exists$-R if these immediately precede them. Thus, the derivation of the restricted form determined by the first observation can in fact be transformed into a uniform proof for the same sequent.

The outline of the proof for Proposition 2.3.1 brings out certain additional aspects that should be noted. To begin with, a derivation of the kind described in the first observation is obviously an **I**-proof and an **M**-proof. The content of this observation may thus be rephrased in the following fashion: the notions of provability in classical, intuitionistic and minimal logic are indistinguishable from the perspective of sequents of the form $\mathcal{P} \longrightarrow G$, assuming that $\mathcal{P}$ is a finite subset of $\mathcal{D}_1$ and G is an element of $\mathcal{G}_1$. The second point to note is that we are assured of the existence of a uniform proof regardless of whether the sequent in question has a proof in classical, intuitionistic or minimal logic. Thus, the triples $\langle \mathcal{D}_1, \mathcal{G}_1, \vdash_C \rangle$, $\langle \mathcal{D}_1, \mathcal{G}_1, \vdash_I \rangle$ and $\langle \mathcal{D}_1, \mathcal{G}_1, \vdash_M \rangle$ all determine the *same* abstract logic programming language.

We have already observed that the programming paradigm based on Horn clauses is subsumed by the abstract logic programming language $\langle \mathcal{D}_1, \mathcal{G}_1, \vdash_C \rangle$. There is a correspondence in the converse direction as well. Using the equivalence of $G \supset A$ and $\neg G \vee A$, the operations of prenexing and anti-prenexing, de Morgan's laws and the distributivity of $\vee$ over $\wedge$, it can be seen that each formula in $\mathcal{D}_1$ is equivalent in classical logic to a conjunction of positive Horn clauses. Each formula in $\mathcal{G}_1$ can, in a similar fashion, be seen to be classically equivalent to the negation of a conjunction of negative Horn clauses. Now, it is easily observed that the union of a set S_1 of positive Horn clauses and a set S_2 of negative Horn clauses has a refutation only if S_1 augmented with some particular element of S_2 also has a refutation. Thus, the idea of solving a goal from a program in the abstract logic programming language $\langle \mathcal{D}_1, \mathcal{G}_1, \vdash_C \rangle$ can be reduced, by a process of translation, to logic programming using Horn clause logic. However, there are several advantages to not carrying out such a reduction and to utilizing the syntax for programs and goals embodied in the triple $\langle \mathcal{D}_1, \mathcal{G}_1, \vdash_C \rangle$ instead. First of all, preserving the richer syntax can lead to a more compact notation, given that the size of the conjunctive normal form of a formula can be exponentially larger than that of the formula itself. Second, this syntax allows for the explicit use of the symbols $\vee$ and $\exists$ in programs and goals with their associated search interpretations. These symbols provide useful programming primitives and also engender a syntax that is closer to the one used in practice; for instance, Prolog programmers often use disjunctions in the bodies of clauses with the intention of signifying a disjunctive search. Finally, the reduction described above depends significantly on the use of classical logic. The translation to clausal form is questionable if the abstract logic programming language under consideration is thought to be defined by the triple $\langle \mathcal{D}_1, \mathcal{G}_1, \vdash_I \rangle$ or the triple $\langle \mathcal{D}_1, \mathcal{G}_1, \vdash_M \rangle$ instead. This point is of particular relevance since the enrichment to this abstract logic programming language that we consider below is based on abandoning classical logic in favor of intuitionistic or minimal logic.

The language $\langle \mathcal{D}_1, \mathcal{G}_1, \vdash_C \rangle$ does not utilize the framework developed in the previous subsection fully. In particular, the symbols corresponding to the search operations AUGMENT and GENERIC are excluded from the syntax of goal formulas in this language. When we consider adding $\supset$ to the logical symbols already permitted in goals, we see that the use of classical logic to provide the declarative semantics does not accord well with the intended search interpretation for the various symbols. Consider, for example, the goal formula $p \vee (p \supset q)$. Given the desired search semantics for $\vee$ and $\supset$, we would expect an interpreter that attempts to solve this goal in the context of an empty program to fail; the interpreter should succeed only if either p is solvable from the empty program or q is solvable from a program containing just p, and clearly neither is the case. This expectation is manifest in the fact that the sequent $\longrightarrow p \vee (p \supset q)$ does not have a uniform proof. There is, however, a **C**-proof for this sequent as witnessed by the following derivation:

$$\frac{\dfrac{\dfrac{p \longrightarrow p, q}{\longrightarrow p, p \supset q} \supset\text{-R}}{\longrightarrow p \vee (p \supset q), p \supset q} \vee\text{-R}}{\longrightarrow p \vee (p \supset q)} \vee\text{-R}.$$

(The last inference figure in this derivation introduces a formula already in the succedent which need not be written, given our treatment of antecedents and succedents as sets.) The problem in this case arises from the fact that the formulas $p \vee (p \supset q)$ and $(p \supset p) \vee (p \supset q)$ are equivalent in classical logic. However, the search semantics of these two formulas are incompatible: the former permits the clause p to be used only in finding a solution for q, whereas the latter makes it available even in solving p. A problem of a similar nature arises when we consider interactions between $\exists$ and $\supset$. The "query" $\exists x\, (p(x) \supset q)$, for instance, has a classical proof from a program consisting of the clause $((p(a) \wedge p(b)) \supset q)$ although it has no derivation consistent with the search interpretation of $\exists$. In general, a derivability relation that is weaker than that of classical logic is needed for determining the declarative semantics of a logic programming language incorporating the AUGMENT search operation, and intuitionistic or minimal provability appear to be possible choices. It may appear somewhat paradoxical that a weaker derivability relation should provide the basis for a richer logic programming language. However, this apparent paradox disappears when we consider the equivalence of $\langle \mathcal{D}_1, \mathcal{G}_1, \vdash_C \rangle$, $\langle \mathcal{D}_1, \mathcal{G}_1, \vdash_I \rangle$ and $\langle \mathcal{D}_1, \mathcal{G}_1, \vdash_M \rangle$; intuitionistic and minimal derivability provide, in a certain sense, a tighter analysis of the declarative semantics of the same language.

We describe replacements for $\mathcal{D}_1$ and $\mathcal{G}_1$ that realize the richer syntax for programs and goals considered above. In particular, let G- and D-formulas be given now by the following mutually recursive syntax rules:

$$G ::= \top \mid A \mid G \wedge G \mid G \vee G \mid \forall x\, G \mid \exists x\, G \mid D \supset G,$$
$$D ::= A \mid G \supset A \mid \forall x\, D \mid D \wedge D.$$

We shall use $\mathcal{G}_2$ and $\mathcal{D}_2$ to refer to the classes of G- and D-formulas so defined. There is a correspondence between these D-formulas and those described by the logician Harrop [Harrop, 1960; Troelstra, 1973]. Assuming that the symbol B represents arbitrary formulas, the so-called *Harrop formulas* are equivalent in intuitionistic and minimal logic to the H-formulas defined by the rule

$$H ::= A \mid B \supset A \mid \forall x\, H \mid H \wedge H.$$

An interesting property of Harrop formulas, proved in [Harrop, 1960], is the following: if $\mathcal{P}$ is a finite set of Harrop formulas and C is a non-atomic formula, then $\mathcal{P} \vdash_I C$ only if there is an **I**-proof of $\mathcal{P} \longrightarrow C$ in which

the last inference rule introduces the logical connective of C. Thus, an
I-proof of a sequent whose antecedent is a set of Harrop formulas can be
made uniform "at the root." This observation does not in itself imply the
existence of a uniform proof for $\mathcal{P} \longrightarrow C$ whenever it has an I-proof: there
may be sequents in such a derivation whose antecedents contain formulas
that are not Harrop formulas and whose proofs can therefore not be made
uniform at the root. For example, consider the situation when $\mathcal{P}$ is empty
and C is $(p \vee q) \supset (q \vee p)$. Following Harrop's observation, we see that a
proof of the resulting sequent can be obtained from one for $p \vee q \longrightarrow q \vee p$.
However, the antecedent of this sequent does not contain an H-formula
and it is easily seen that a derivation for the sequent in intuitionistic logic
cannot have the introduction of the disjunction in the succedent as its
last step. Now, by further restricting the syntax of the H-formulas and
of the formulas that we attempt to show follow from them, it is possible
to ensure the applicability of Harrop's observation at each sequent in a
derivation. This idea is, in fact, reflected in the definitions of the formulas
in $\mathcal{G}_2$ and $\mathcal{D}_2$ above. Viewed differently, every subformula of a formula
in $\mathcal{D}_2$ that appears in a positive context has the top-level structure of a
Harrop formula. The members of $\mathcal{D}_2$ are, for this reason, referred to as
hereditary Harrop formulas.

We shall show presently that the triple $\langle \mathcal{D}_2, \mathcal{G}_2, \vdash_I \rangle$ defines an abstract
logic programming language. Before we do this, we illustrate the nature of
programming in this language.

Example 2.3.2. The problem that we consider here is commonly referred
to as the sterile jar problem. Assume that the following facts are given to
us: a jar is sterile if every germ in it is dead, a germ in a heated jar is
dead and a particular jar has been heated. The task is to represent this
information so that the conclusion that there is some jar that is sterile can
be drawn.

There is an obvious division of labor for the representation task at hand:
the information that is provided is best represented by a program and the
conclusion that is to be drawn can be thought of as a goal. Let *sterile* be
a unary predicate corresponding to the sterility of jars, let $germ(X)$ and
$dead(X)$ represent the assertions that X is a germ and that (the germ) X
is dead, let $heated(Y)$ represent the fact that (the jar) Y has been heated
and let $in(X, Y)$ correspond to the assertion that (the germ) X is in (the
jar) Y. Letting j be a constant that denotes the given jar, the assumptions
of the problem can be represented by the following formulas:

$\forall y ((\forall x (germ(x) \supset (in(x, y) \supset dead(x)))) \supset sterile(y)),$
$\forall y \forall x ((heated(y) \wedge (in(x, y) \wedge germ(x))) \supset dead(x)),$ and
$heated(j).$

It is easily seen that each of these formulas is a member of $\mathcal{D}_2$ and so they
collectively constitute a program in the language under consideration. We

shall denote this program by $\mathcal{P}$. An interesting aspect of these formulas is the translation into logical notation of the defining characteristic of sterility for jars. In determining that a given jar is sterile, it is necessary to verify that any germ that is in the jar is dead. Two forms of hypothetical reasoning arise in this context. First, we are interested exclusively in the germs that are in the jar and we only need to ascertain that these are dead. However, this property must hold of every germ hypothesized to be in the jar, not just those whose existence is known of explicitly at some point. These two requirements are reflected in the embedded universal quantifier and implications that appear in the first program clause above. Further, as the reader may observe from the discussion that follows, the programming interpretation for these two logical symbols and the use of the instruction ATOMIC described in the previous subsection yields exactly the desired "procedure" for determining the sterility of a jar.

The conclusion that we wish to draw can be represented by the formula

$$\exists x \, sterile(x).$$

This formula is obviously a member of $\mathcal{G}_2$ and, hence, a goal in our extended language. We may think of reaching the desired conclusion by constructing a uniform proof for this goal from the program $\mathcal{P}$. Using the search interpretation of the existential quantifier, such a proof may be obtained by, first of all, constructing a proof for $sterile(j)$ from the same program. Note that we have exhibited clairvoyance in the choice of the instantiating term. Such foresight can, of course, not be expected of an actual procedure that looks for uniform proofs and we will discuss ways of dealing with this issue in an actual implementation. Now, the search instructions do not dictate the next step in finding a proof for $sterile(j)$. However, we may think of using the instruction ATOMIC for this purpose; as we shall see presently, ATOMIC turns out to be a derived rule in the context of constructing uniform proofs. Using this instruction with respect to the first program clause in the list above produces the (sub)goal

$$\forall x \, (germ(x) \supset (in(x,j) \supset dead(x)))$$

with the program still being $\mathcal{P}$. At this stage the instructions GENERIC and (two instances of) AUGMENT will be used, giving rise to the goal $dead(c)$ and the program $\mathcal{P} \cup \{germ(c), in(c,j)\}$, where c is assumed to be a new constant. The situation that has been produced reflects an attempt to show that jar j is sterile by showing that any (generic) germ that is assumed to be in it is dead. To proceed further, we may use ATOMIC with respect to the second clause in the list above, yielding the goal

$$(heated(j) \wedge (in(c,j) \wedge germ(c)));$$

once again, some foresight is needed in the choice of instance for the formula from the program. Invoking the instruction AND twice now results in the atomic goals $heated(j)$, $in(c,j)$, and $germ(c)$ that are to be solved from the program $\mathcal{P} \cup \{germ(c), in(c, j)\}$. Each of these goals can be immediately solved by using the ATOMIC instruction.

We could think of extracting a result from the uniform proof that has been constructed. This result can be the instantiation for the existentially quantified variable in the original goal that yields the uniform proof. Intuitively, this corresponds to exhibiting j as an example of a sterile jar.

The following proposition shows that the classes $\mathcal{D}_2$ and $\mathcal{G}_2$ constitute satisfactory replacements for $\mathcal{D}_1$ and $\mathcal{G}_1$ respectively. We present a proof of this proposition here to illustrate the kind of analysis involved in establishing such a property.

Proposition 2.3.3. *The triple* $\langle \mathcal{D}_2, \mathcal{G}_2, \vdash_I \rangle$ *constitutes an abstract logic programming language.*

Proof. Let $\mathcal{P}$ be a finite set of $\mathcal{D}_2$ formulas and G be a $\mathcal{G}_2$ formula. Since a uniform proof is also an **I**-proof, $\mathcal{P} \vdash_O G$ only if $\mathcal{P} \vdash_I G$. Thus we only need to show that the converse holds.

Let Γ be a finite subset of $\mathcal{D}_2$. We claim, then, that there cannot be an **I**-proof for $\Gamma \longrightarrow \perp$. This claim is established by an induction on the sizes of proofs, where the size of a proof is the number of sequents appearing in it. So suppose the claim is not true and let Γ be such that the derivation of $\Gamma \longrightarrow \perp$ is of least size. Now, the size of this derivation cannot be 1 since $\perp$ cannot be a member of Γ. If the size is greater than 1, then the possible structures for the formulas in $\mathcal{D}_2$ dictates that the last rule in the derivation must be one of $\supset$-L, $\forall$-L, or $\wedge$-L. In each of these cases, there must be a derivation of smaller size for a sequent $\Gamma' \longrightarrow \perp$ where Γ' is a set of $\mathcal{D}_2$ formulas. This contradicts our assumption about Γ.

Now let Δ be a finite subset of $\mathcal{D}_2$ and G' be a member of $\mathcal{G}_2$ and assume that $\Delta \longrightarrow G'$ has an **I**-proof of size l. We claim then that

(1) if $G' = G_1 \wedge G_2$ then $\Delta \longrightarrow G_1$ and $\Delta \longrightarrow G_2$ have **I**-proofs of size less than l,

(2) if $G' = G_1 \vee G_2$ then either $\Delta \longrightarrow G_1$ or $\Delta \longrightarrow G_2$ has an **I**-proof of size less than l,

(3) if $G' = \exists x \, G_1$ then there is a term t such that $\Delta \longrightarrow [t/x]G_1$ has an **I**-proof of size less than l,

(4) if $G' = D \supset G_1$ then $\Delta \cup \{D\} \longrightarrow G_1$ has an **I**-proof of size less than l, and

(5) if $G' = \forall x \, G_1$ then there is a constant c that does not appear in any of the formulas in $\Delta \cup \{\forall x \, G_1\}$ for which $\Delta \longrightarrow [c/x]G_1$ has an **I**-proof of size less than l.

This claim is proved, once again, by induction on the size of the derivation for $\Delta \longrightarrow G'$. If this size is 1, G' must be atomic and so the claim is vacuously true. For the case when the size is $s + 1$, we consider the possibilities for the last inference figure. The argument is trivial when this is one of ∧-R, ∨-R, ∃-R, ⊃-R, and ∀-R. From the previous claim, this figure cannot be ⊥-R. Given the structure of the formulas in Δ, the only remaining cases are ∀-L, ∧-L and ⊃-L. Consider the case for ∀-L, *i.e.*, when the last figure is of the form

$$\frac{[t/x]P, \Theta \longrightarrow G'}{\forall x\, P, \Theta \longrightarrow G'}$$

The argument in this case depends on the structure of G'. For instance, let $G' = \forall x\, G_1$. The upper sequent of the above figure is of a kind to which the inductive hypothesis is applicable. Hence, there is a constant c that does not appear in any of the formulas in $\Theta \cup \{[t/x]P, \forall x\, G_1\}$ for which $[t/x]P, \Theta \longrightarrow [c/x]G_1$ has an **I**-proof of size less than s. Adding below this derivation a ∀-L inference figure, we obtain an **I**-proof of size less than $s + 1$ for $\forall x\, P, \Theta \longrightarrow [c/x]G_1$. Observing now that c cannot appear in $\forall x\, P$ if it is does not appear in $[t/x]P$, the claim is verified in this case. The analysis for the cases when G' has a different structure follows an analogous pattern. Further, similar arguments can be provided when the last inference figure is an ∧-L or an ⊃-L.

Now let $\mathcal{P} \longrightarrow G$ have an **I**-proof. It follows from the second claim that it must then have a uniform proof. The proof of the claim in fact outlines a mechanism for moving the inference figure that introduces the top-level logical connective in G to the end of the **I**-proof. A repeated use of this observation yields a method for transforming an **I**-proof of $\Gamma \longrightarrow G$ into a uniform proof for the same sequent.   ∎

The proof of Proposition 2.3.3 reveals a relationship between derivability in intuitionistic and minimal logic in the context of interest. In particular, let $\mathcal{P}$ be a finite subset of $\mathcal{D}_2$ and let G be a formula in $\mathcal{G}_2$. We have observed, then, that an **I**-proof of the sequent $\mathcal{P} \longrightarrow G$ cannot contain uses of the inference figure ⊥-R in it. Thus any **I**-proof of such a sequent must also be an **M**-proof. In other words, these two notions of provability are indistinguishable from the perspective of existence of derivations for sequents of the form $\mathcal{P} \longrightarrow G$. It follows from this that $\langle \mathcal{D}_2, \mathcal{G}_2, \vdash_I \rangle$ and $\langle \mathcal{D}_2, \mathcal{G}_2, \vdash_M \rangle$ constitute the same abstract logic programming languages. We note that the introduction of implication together with its desired search interpretation leads to a distinction between classical provability on the one hand and intuitionistic and minimal provability on the other. It may be asked whether a similar sort of distinction needs to be made between intuitionistic and minimal provability. It turns out that a treatment of negation and an interpretation of the idea of a contradiction requires these two notions to be differentiated. We do not discuss this issue any further here, but the interested reader may refer to [Miller, 1989b] for some thoughts in this direction.

We have raised the issue previously of what the behavior of the (idealized) interpreter should be when an atomic goal is encountered. We have also suggested that, in the case of the language $\langle \mathcal{D}_2, \mathcal{G}_2, \vdash_M \rangle$, the instruction ATOMIC might be used at such a point. Following this course is sound with respect to the defined operational semantics as the following proposition shows.

Proposition 2.3.4. *Let $\mathcal{P}$ be a finite subset of $\mathcal{D}_2$ and let A be an atomic formula. If A is an instance of a clause in $\mathcal{P}$ or if there is an instance $(G \supset A)$ of a clause in $\mathcal{P}$ such that $\mathcal{P} \longrightarrow G$ has a uniform proof, then $\mathcal{P} \longrightarrow A$ has an uniform proof.*

Proof. If A is an instance of a formula in $\mathcal{P}$, we can obtain a uniform proof of $\mathcal{P} \longrightarrow A$ by appending below an initial sequent some number of $\forall$-L inference figures. Suppose $(G \supset A)$ is an instance of a clause in $\mathcal{P}$ and that $\mathcal{P} \longrightarrow G$ has a uniform proof. We can then obtain one for $\mathcal{P} \longrightarrow A$ by using an $\supset$-L inference figure followed by some number of $\forall$-L below the given derivation and the initial sequent $A, \mathcal{P} \longrightarrow A$. ∎

Using ATOMIC as a means for solving atomic goals in conjunction with the instructions for solving the other kinds of goals also yields a complete strategy as we now observe.

Proposition 2.3.5. *Let $\mathcal{P}$ be a finite subset of $\mathcal{D}_2$ and let A be an atomic formula. If the sequent $\mathcal{P} \longrightarrow A$ has a uniform proof containing l sequents, then either A is an instance of a clause in $\mathcal{P}$ or there is an instance $(G \supset A)$ of a clause in $\mathcal{P}$ such that $\mathcal{P} \longrightarrow G$ has an uniform proof containing fewer than l sequents.*

Proof. The following may be added as a sixth item to the second claim in the proof of Proposition 2.3.3 and established by the same induction: the sequent $\mathcal{P} \longrightarrow A$ has an **I**-proof containing l sequents only if either A is an instance of a clause in $\mathcal{P}$ or there is an instance $(G \supset A)$ of a clause in $\mathcal{P}$ such that $\mathcal{P} \longrightarrow G$ has an **I**-proof containing fewer than l sequents. The claim when embellished in this way easily yields the proposition. ∎

The abstract logic programming language $\langle \mathcal{D}_2, \mathcal{G}_2, \vdash_I \rangle$ incorporates each of the search primitives discussed in the previous subsection into the syntax of its goals. It provides the basis for an actual language that contains two new search operations, AUGMENT and GENERIC, in addition to those already present in Prolog. At least one use for these operations in a practical setting is that of realizing scoping mechanisms with regard to program clauses and data objects. Prolog provides a means for augmenting a program through the nonlogical predicate called *assert* and for deleting clauses through a similar predicate called *retract*. One problem with these predicates is that their effects are rather global: an *assert* makes a new clause available in the search for a proof for every goal and a *retract* removes it from consideration in every derivation. The AUGMENT operation provides a more controlled means for augmenting programs: this operation makes program clauses available only during the search for solutions to *particular* goals. Consider, for instance, a goal whose structure is given schematically by

$$(D_1 \supset (G_1 \wedge (D_2 \supset G_2))) \wedge G_3,$$

where D_1 and D_2 represent formulas from $\mathcal{D}_2$ and G_1, G_2 and G_3 represent formulas from $\mathcal{G}_2$. Assume further that we are attempting to solve this goal from a program given by $\mathcal{P}$. The search interpretation for $\supset$ requires such a solution to be obtained by solving G_1 from the program $\mathcal{P} \cup \{D_1\}$, G_2 from the program $\mathcal{P} \cup \{D_1, D_2\}$ and G_3 from $\mathcal{P}$. The AUGMENT operation thus provides a means for making additions to a program in a well structured fashion. This idea can be exploited to realize block structuring in logic programming as well as to provide a (logically justified) notion of *modules* in this programming paradigm. The reader is referred to [Miller, 1989b] and [Miller, 1989a] for illustrative examples and for a general exploration of these abilities.

Just as the AUGMENT operation is useful in giving program clauses a scope, the GENERIC operation is useful in controlling the availability of objects. To understand this possibility, consider a goal that is given schematically by $\exists x \, ((\forall y \, G_1(x,y)) \wedge G_2(x))$. Solving this goal involves finding a term t such that for some "new" constant c the goals $G_1(t,c)$ and $G_2(t)$ are solvable. Note that the constant c is available only in the context of solving the goal $G_1(t,c)$. In particular, it cannot appear within t and thus cannot be transmitted into the context of solving $G_2(t)$ or "outwards" as an answer substitution. Further, while it can appear in terms created in the course of solving $G_1(t,c)$ and is, in this sense, available as an object in this context, it cannot be directly manipulated by the clauses that are utilized in solving this goal. The latter is a consequence of the fact that the quantifier $\forall y$ determines the *lexical* scope of c and thus controls the context in which it can be referred to directly. Viewed differently, the GENERIC operation provides a means for introducing a new constant whose lexical scope is determined by the symbol representing the operation and whose dynamic scope is the goal that is spawned as a result of the operation.

The GENERIC and AUGMENT operations can be used in tandem to realize the notion of abstract data types in logic programming. The essential idea that needs to be captured in this context is that of limiting direct access to particular objects to only those program clauses that are supposed to implement operations on them, while allowing these objects and the operations defined on them to be used in a larger context. To see how this requirement might be realized in our context, consider a goal of the form $\exists x \forall y \, (D(x,y) \supset G(x))$, where y does not appear in $G(x)$. From one perspective, the variable y is a constant whose name is visible only in the program clauses contained in $D(x,y)$. Once this constant is "created," it can be used in the course of solving $G(x)$. However, the only way it can be referred to by name, and hence directly manipulated, in this context is by using one of the clauses in $D(x, y)$.

Although the above discussion provides the intuition guiding a realization of information hiding and of abstract data types in logic programming, a complete realization of these notions requires an ability to quantify over function symbols as well. This kind of a "higher-order" ability can be incorporated into the language we have presented without much difficulty. However, we do not do this here and refer the interested reader to [Miller *et al.*, 1991] and [Nadathur and Miller, 1988] instead. We also note that a more detailed discussion of the scoping mechanism provided by the GENERIC operation appears in [Miller, 1989a] and the language described there also incorporates a higher-order ability.

We consider now the issue of designing an actual interpreter or proof procedure for the abstract logic programming languages discussed in this subsection. Let us examine first the language $\langle \mathcal{D}_1, \mathcal{G}_1, \vdash_C \rangle$. The notion of a uniform proof determines, to a large extent, the structure of an interpreter for this language. However, some elaboration is required of the method for choosing terms in the context of the INSTANCE instruction and of the action to be taken when atomic goals are encountered. Propositions 2.3.4 and 2.3.5 and the discussion of SLD-resolution suggest a course that might be taken in each of these cases. Thus, if a goal of the form $\exists x\, G(x)$ is encountered at a certain point in a search, a possible strategy is to delay the choice of instantiation for the quantifier till such time that this choice can be made in an educated fashion. Such a delaying strategy can be realized by instantiating the existential quantifier with a "placeholder" whose value may be determined at a later stage through the use of unification. Placeholders of this kind are what are referred to as logic variables in logic programming parlance. Thus, using the convention of representing placeholders by capital letters, the goal $\exists x\, G(x)$ may be transformed into one of the form $G(X)$ where X is a new logic variable. The use of such variables is to be "cashed out" when employing ATOMIC in solving atomic goals. In particular, given a goal A that possibly contains logic variables, the strategy will be to look for a program clause of the form $\forall \overline{y}\, A'$ or $\forall \overline{y}\, (G \supset A')$ such that A unifies with the atom that results from A' by replacing all the universally quantified variables in it with logic variables. Finding such a clause results, in the first case, in an immediate success or, in the second case, in an attempt to solve the resulting instance of G. The interpreter that is obtained by incorporating these mechanisms into a search for a uniform proof is still nondeterministic: a choice has to be made of a disjunct in the context of the OR instruction and of the program clause to use with respect to the ATOMIC instruction. This nondeterminism is, however, of a more tolerable kind than that encountered in the context of the IN-STANCE instruction. Moreover, a deterministic but incomplete procedure can be obtained by making these choices in a fixed manner as is done in the case of Prolog.

In devising an actual interpreter for $\langle \mathcal{D}_2, \mathcal{G}_2, \vdash_I \rangle$, we need also to think of a treatment of the search primitives embodied in $\supset$ and $\forall$. From inspecting the instructions corresponding to these symbols, it appears that relatively straightforward mechanisms can be used for this purpose. Thus, consider the situation when a goal of the form $D \supset G$ is encountered. We might proceed in this case by enhancing the program with the clause D and then attempting to solve G. Similarly, assume that we desire to solve the goal $\forall x\, G(x)$. We might think now of generating a new constant c and of attempting to solve the goal $G(c)$ that results from instantiating the universal quantifier with this constant.

The mechanisms outlined above can, in principle, be used to implement the new search primitives. However, some care must be taken to ensure that they mesh properly with the devices that are used in implementing the language $\langle \mathcal{D}_1, \mathcal{G}_1, \vdash_C \rangle$. One possible source of unwanted interaction is that between the use of logic variables to deal with INSTANCE and of new constants to realize GENERIC: since instantiations for existential quantifiers may be determined only after the introduction of new constants for dealing with universal quantifiers that appear within their scope, some method is needed for precluding the appearance of such constants in the instantiating terms. As a concrete example, consider solving the goal $\exists x\, \forall y\, p(x, y)$ from the program $\{\forall x\, p(x, x)\}$; we assume that p is a predicate symbol here. Following the strategy outlined up to this point in a naive fashion results in a success: the initial goal would be reduced to one of the form $p(X, c)$, and this can be unified with the (only) program clause by instantiating X to c. Notice, however, that this is an erroneous solution since the instantiation determined for X leads to a violation of the condition of newness on c at the time that it is generated.

To prevent incorrect solutions of the kind described above, it is necessary to limit possible instantiations for logic variables in some relevant manner. Some devices such as raising [Miller, 1992], lifting [Paulson, 1987] and dynamic Skolemization [Fitting, 1990] have been proposed for this purpose. (Static Skolemization, the device generally used in the setting of classical logic, does not work in the current context.) These devices preserve the usual unification process but build the constraints that have to be satisfied into the "logic variable" that is used in connection with INSTANCE or the new "constant" that is introduced in connection with GENERIC. An alternative approach that is described in [Nadathur, 1993] is to modify the naive treatment of INSTANCE and GENERIC only to the extent of including a numeric label with logic variables and constants and to constrain unification to respect the information contained in these labels. This approach requires much less bookkeeping than the earlier mentioned ones and is, in fact, simple enough to be incorporated into an abstract machine for the language described in this subsection [Nadathur *et al.*, 1993].

An adequate implementation of AUGMENT must consider two additional aspects. One of these arises from the fact that different programs might have to be considered at distinct points in a search. An efficient means is therefore needed for realizing changing program contexts. The additions to and the depletions from the program generally follow a stack discipline and can, in principle, be implemented using such a device. A complicating factor, however, is the imposition of determinism on the interpreter that we have outlined and the consequent need for backtracking when a failure is encountered along a solution path that is being explored. To understand why this might be a problem, let us consider a goal of the form $\exists x\,((D \supset G_1(x)) \wedge G_2(x))$ in the context of a program $\mathcal{P}$. Under the scheme being considered, the program would first be augmented with D and an attempt would be made to solve the goal $G_1(X)$, where X is a logic variable. Suppose that this attempt succeeds with a certain binding for X and also leaves behind an alternative (partially explored) solution path for $G_1(X)$. An attempt would now be made to solve the appropriate instance of $G_2(X)$ after removing D from the program. Assume, however, that the attempt to solve this instance of $G_2(X)$ fails. It is necessary, at this point, to continue the exploration of the alternative solution path for $G_1(X)$. However, this exploration must be carried out in the context of the appropriate program. In particular, all the clauses that were added in the course of trying to solve $G_2(X)$ must be removed and the clause D and others that might have been added along the alternative solution path for $G_1(X)$ must be reinstated. The kind of context switching that is required as a result of backtracking is, thus, fairly complex and some thought is required in devising a method for realizing it efficiently.

The second new aspect that needs to be dealt with in a satisfactory implementation of AUGMENT is that of program clauses containing logic variables. To see how such clauses might be produced, and also to understand what is involved in handling such clauses properly, let us consider the goal $\exists x\,(p(x) \supset g(x))$; we assume that p and g are predicate symbols here. Following the strategy already outlined, the attempt to solve this goal leads to an attempt to solve the goal $g(X)$ from a program that now also includes the clause $p(X)$. Notice that the symbol X that appears in these formulas is a logic variable and that this variable actually appears in the new program clause. The nature of this variable in the clause is different from that of the variables that usually appear in program clauses. While this variable can be instantiated, such an instantiation must be performed in a consistent way across all copies of the clause and must also be tied to the instantiation of X in the goal $g(X)$. Thus, suppose that the program from which we are attempting to solve the given goal contains the clauses

$$\forall x\,((q(x) \wedge p(b)) \supset g(x)), \text{ and}$$

$(p(a) \supset q(b))$.

Using the first clause in trying to solve $g(X)$ produces the subgoals $q(X)$ and $p(b)$. The first subgoal can be successfully solved by using the second clause and the added clause $p(X)$. However, as a result of this solution to the first subgoal, the added clause must be changed to $p(a)$. This clause can, therefore, not be used to solve the second subgoal, and this ultimately leads to a failure in the attempt to solve the overall goal.

The problem with logic variables in program clauses occurs again in the system N-Prolog that is presented in the next section and is discussed in more detail there. An actual interpreter for the language $\langle \mathcal{D}_2, \mathcal{G}_2, \vdash_I \rangle$ that includes a treatment of several of the issues outlined here is described in [Nadathur, 1993]. The question of implementing this interpreter efficiently has also been considered and we refer the interested reader to [Nadathur *et al.*, 1993] for a detailed discussion of this aspect. For the present purposes, it suffices to note that a procedure whose structure is similar to the one for constructing SLD-refutations can be used for finding uniform proofs for the extended language and that a satisfactory implementation of this procedure can be provided along the lines of usual Prolog implementations.

We have focused here on using the criterion developed in the last subsection in describing abstract logic programming languages in the context of first-order logic. However, the framework that has been described is quite broad and can be utilized in the context of other logics as well. It can, for instance, be used in the context of a higher-order logic to yield a higher-order version of the language $\langle \mathcal{D}_2, \mathcal{G}_2, \vdash_I \rangle$. Such a language has, in fact, been described [Miller *et al.*, 1991] and has provided the basis for a higher-order extension to Prolog that is called λProlog [Nadathur and Miller, 1988]. A discussion of some aspects of this extension also appears in the chapter on higher-order logic programming in this volume of the handbook. More generally, the framework can be utilized with a different set of logical symbols or with a different search interpretation given to the logical symbols considered here. Interpreted in this sense, our criterion has been used in conjunction with linear logic [Harland and Pym, 1991; Hodas and Miller, 1994] and a calculus of dependent types [Pfenning, 1989] to describe logic programming languages that have interesting applications.

3   Extending the logic programming paradigm

In the previous section we presented an abstract framework which attempts to capture the essence of the logic programming paradigm. We have seen that the Horn clause logic underlying Prolog fits this framework but that a much richer class of program clauses can be used if intuitionistic logic is employed in providing the underlying declarative semantics. Abstracting and formalizing the logic programming paradigm thus provides a mechanism to propose new logic programming languages. However, it also allows us to better understand logic programming languages developed independently of the framework. We illustrate this in this section with the consideration of two such existing logic programming languages.

One category of languages that we present, *N-Prolog* and the related *QN-Prolog*, extends Horn clause logic by permitting implication in goals and in the antecedent of program clauses. We shall see that this language is based on an abstract logic programming language. The proof procedures for N-Prolog and QN-Prolog may also be understood as ones that attempt to construct uniform proofs, and we illustrate this aspect in our presentation.

The second language presents a different situation, a datapoint seemingly outside the framework we have presented. The programming language family, called *near-Horn Prolog* (*nH-Prolog*), permits disjunction in the consequent of program clauses. This leads to some strikingly different characteristics relative to other logic programming languages, such as the possibility of disjunctive answers. (With a suitable encoding of classical negation one may view the logic as coextensive with full first-order logic.) The proof mechanism of one variant of nH-Prolog fits the structure of uniform proofs, a startling fact given the power of representation of the underlying logic. We show by illustration the key reasons why the strong proof restrictions hold for this variant.

The study of the nH-Prolog language we undertake here accomplishes two points simultaneously. First, it supports the claim that the nH-Prolog language is a very attractive way to approach the extended logic domain with regard to the logic programming paradigm. Second, understanding the relationship between the variant of nH-Prolog considered here and the notion of uniform proof enhances our understanding of both entities.

We begin our consideration of existing languages with N-Prolog.

3.1   A language for hypothetical reasoning

The N-Prolog language, developed by Gabbay and Reyle [Gabbay and Reyle, 1984b; Gabbay, 1985] introduces the hypothetical implication. This mechanism allows exploration of the consequences of a hypothetical situation, where additions are temporarily made to the database, or program, when certain queries are addressed. The basic system is sound and complete for positive intuitionistic logic, and Gabbay has shown that it can be extended to a complete procedure for positive classical logic by adding one inference rule (a "restart" rule).

We first present the propositional form of N-Prolog. We follow closely Gabbay and Reyle [Gabbay and Reyle, 1984b]. If P is a program and Q is a query, then P ? Q expresses the problem of determining if query Q follows from program P. P ? $Q = 1$ denotes success in processing Q; P ? $Q = 0$ denotes finite failure. If we let $P + A$ denote $P \cup \{A\}$, where P is a program and A is a clause, then the key novel deductive step of N-Prolog is to define P ? $(A \supset B)$ as $(P + A)$? B. That is, the conditional

$A \supset B$ as query is interpreted as asking B in the context of P augmented by the hypothetical fact A. We now formalize propositional N-Prolog.

An *N-clause* is defined inductively as an atom or as

$$A_1 \wedge A_2 \wedge \ldots \wedge A_n \supset B$$

where the A_i are N-clauses and B is an atom. An *N-program* or *database* is a set of N-clauses. An *N-goal* is any conjunction of N-clauses. For example, any Horn clause is an N-clause, as are $(((a \supset b) \supset c) \supset d)$ and $((a \supset b) \wedge c) \supset d$. The expression

$$(a \supset (b \supset c)) \supset ((a \supset b) \supset (a \supset c)),$$

an axiom in one formulation of intuitionistic logic, is not an N-clause, but the expression

$$((a \wedge b \supset c) \wedge (a \supset b) \wedge a) \supset c$$

that is intuitionistically equivalent to it is an N-clause. In general, formulas of form $A \supset (B \supset C)$ need to be rewritten in the intuitionistically equivalent form $A \wedge B \supset C$ in order to qualify as N-clauses.

There are three rules for computation for propositional N-Prolog.

(1) The rule for atoms has two parts: if Q is an atom then $P \: ? \: Q$ succeeds iff

    (a) $Q \in P$ or

    (b) for some clause $A_1 \wedge \ldots \wedge A_k \supset Q$ in P we have that $P \: ? \: (A_1 \wedge \ldots \wedge A_k)$ succeeds.

(2) The rule for conjunctions states that $P \: ? \: (A_1 \wedge \ldots \wedge A_k)$ succeeds iff each $P \: ? \: A_i$ succeeds.

(3) The rule for implication states that $P \: ? \: (A \supset B)$ succeeds iff $(P + A) \: ? \: B$ succeeds, where $P + A$ is the result of adding each conjunct of A to P.

To illustrate a deduction in N-Prolog we show that

$$P \: ? \: ((a \wedge b \supset c) \wedge (a \supset b) \wedge a) \supset c$$

succeeds for $P = \emptyset$, the empty program.

Example 3.1.1. Example: Show $\emptyset \: ? \: ((a \wedge b \supset c) \wedge (a \supset b) \wedge a) \supset c = 1$.

    1. $\emptyset \: ? \: ((a \wedge b \supset c) \wedge (a \supset b) \wedge a) \supset c$

    2. $a \wedge b \supset c, a \supset b, a \: ? \: c$

    3. $a \wedge b \supset c, a \supset b, a \: ? \: a \wedge b$

    4. Case 1: $a \wedge b \supset c, a \supset b, a \: ? \: a$

        This case succeeds immediately.

    5. Case 2: $a \wedge b \supset c, a \supset b, a \: ? \: b$

    6. $a \wedge b \supset c, a \supset b, a \: ? \: a$

This case now succeeds.

N-Prolog with quantifiers, which we might also call *general level N-Prolog* or *first-order N-Prolog*, addresses the extension of N-Prolog to the first-order level. The major complication in moving to the general level that is not shared by Prolog is the sharing of variables between program and goal. The task P ? $(a(X) \supset b(X))$ succeeds if $(P + a(X))$? $b(X)$ succeeds, where variable X now is shared by program and goal. (We hereafter adopt the Prolog convention of capital letters for variables.)

To handle the sharing of variables, N-Prolog with quantifiers, hereafter *QN-Prolog*, uses two classes of variables, universal and existential. Here universal variables are denoted by U_i, for i an integer; existential variables use other letters of the alphabet, also possibly with subscripts. (Of course, a commercial system might permit arbitrary words in place of the subscript.) Atoms now are predicate letters with terms that may contain variables of the two different kinds. *QN-clauses*, *QN-goals* and *QN-programs* generalize from the propositional form in the obvious way except no universal variables are permitted in QN-goals. Recall that in Prolog variables in goals behave as existential variables, and as universal variables in the program, but now that universal and existential variables co-exist in programs, an explicit mechanism is necessary. Some explicit replacement of universal variables by existential variables is necessary, as illustrated below.

For a formal definition of QN-Prolog the reader should consult [Gabbay and Reyle, 1984b]. We will use an example to illustrate the use of the two classes of variables. First, we emphasize the key attributes regarding variables use:

(1)   Existential variables may be shared among program clauses and goals, reflecting the view that the existential quantifiers associated with the variables are exterior to the entire expression (i.e. $\exists \vec{X}(P$? $Q)$);

(2)   Only existential variables occur in goals.

We adapt Example E2 (Section 4) from [Gabbay and Reyle, 1984b] for our illustration. Although somewhat contrived so as to present an interesting non-Horn structure in a compact example, the example does suggest that real databases (programs) exist where hypothetical implication occurs and thus processing can benefit from the use of QN-Prolog.

Example 3.1.2 (Example E2 in [Gabbay and Reyle, 1984b]).
Assume that we are given the following database:

(d1)   A person is neurotic if he/she is greatly disturbed when criticized by one of his/her friends.

(d2)   Mary gets greatly disturbed when Sally criticizes her.

(d3)   Sally criticizes everyone.

(d4) A person is a bad friend if there is someone who would become neurotic if this someone were befriended by the person.

The query is "Is there someone who is a bad friend?"
The database and query are formalized as follows:

(d1) $[f(U_1, U_2) \wedge cr(U_1, U_2) \supset d(U_2)] \supset n(U_2)$
(d2) $cr(s, m) \supset d(m)$
(d3) $cr(s, U_1)$
(d4) $[f(U_1, U_2) \supset n(U_2)] \supset b(U_1)$
(query) $b(Y)$

The query uses an existential variable, and all database clauses use universal variables.

We now follow [Gabbay and Reyle, 1984b] in presenting one possible computation sequence for this database and query.

1. d1,d2,d3,d4 ? $b(Y)$
2. d1,d2,d3,d4 ? $f(Y, X) \supset n(X)$ using d4
3. d1,d2,d3,d4,$f(Y, X)$? $n(X)$ using rule for implication
4. d1,d2,d3,d4,$f(Y, X)$? $f(Z, X) \wedge cr(Z, X) \supset d(X)$
     using d1
5. d1,d2,d3,d4,$f(Y, X), f(Z, X), cr(Z, X)$? $d(X)$
     using rule for implication
6. d1,d2,d3,d4,$f(Y, m), f(Z, m), cr(Z, m)$? $cr(s, m)$
     using d2
7. d1,d2,d3,d4,$f(Y, m), f(Z, m), cr(Z, m)$? $cr(s, m)$
     using d3.

In connection with this computation, it is interesting to note that in step 2 and in step 4 the universal variables U_2 and U_1 that appear in clauses d4 and d1 respectively are not instantiated during unification with the previous goal and have therefore to be renamed to an existential variable in the new goal. Note also that additions are made to the program in the course of computation that contain existential variables in them. An instantiation is determined for one of these variables in step 6 and this actually has the effect of changing the program itself.

Observe that the answer variable is uninstantiated; the bad friend exists, by the computation success, but is unnamed. The neurotic friend is seen to be Mary by inspection of the computation.

The derivation given by Gabbay and Reyle uses clause d3 at Step 7. Perhaps a more interesting derivation makes use of the augmented database at Step 7 and shows that clause d3 is unneeded. The intuition behind this alternative is that d1 says that for some instance of U_2 one can establish $n(U_2)$ by satisfying (an appropriate instance of) an implication, and d2 provides an appropriate implication for such an instance.

We now state the soundness and completeness result for QN-Prolog given in Gabbay [Gabbay, 1985].

Proposition 3.1.3. *P ? Q succeeds in QN-Prolog if and only if*

$$\vdash \exists \vec{X}[(\forall \vec{U})P \supset Q]$$

holds in intuitionistic logic for program (database) P and query Q where $\vec{X}$ denotes all the existential variables in P and Q and $\vec{U}$ denotes all the universal variables in P.

The above proposition brings out the connection between QN-Prolog and the discussion in the previous section. QN-Prolog is readily seen to be based on an abstract logic programming language contained in the language $\langle \mathcal{D}_2, \mathcal{G}_2, \vdash_I \rangle$ that is described in Subsection 2.3. This language is in fact created from the Horn clause language by permitting formulas of the form $D \supset A$ to appear in goals and in the antecedents of program clauses where D is itself a conjunction of program clauses under this definition. To ensure the existence of uniform proofs, i.e. proofs in which the succedent is singleton and also atomic whenever an antecedent inference figure is used, the derivability relation that needs to be adopted is $\vdash_I$. To reinforce the understanding of QN-Prolog as an abstract logic programming language we present the uniform proof implicit in the previous example using the sequent calculus described in the previous section.

In the presentation of the proof we adopt several suggestions made in Subsection 2.3 to improve the abstract interpreter efficiency. We delay the instantiations by use of logic variables as suggested for the abstract interpreter and as executed in the description of QN-Prolog. When the proof is read from the bottom (conclusion) upward, existential variables replace the instances that the ∀-L inference figures would normally introduce. The use of these variables signifies that one, perhaps undetermined, instance of the clause has been created. Other instances may similarly be created from the explicitly quantified version of the clause that is present in the antecedent of the sequent.

Several nonstandard inference figures are used to aid the presentation. The inference figure CI (clause incorporation) contains a formula in the antecedent of the upper sequent whose universal closure (zero or more applications of ∀-L) results in a clause already present in $\mathcal{P}$ and not explicitly listed in the lower sequent. We have used EG (existential generalization) simply to identify existential variables with their appropriate instantiation — an artifact of our delayed instantiation during goal-oriented (backward) proof development. We use the inference figure BC (backchain), suggested in the previous section, to save a step and simplify our deduction. The inference figure BC replaces ⊃-L and eliminates an initial upper sequent. (Also logic variables may be instantiated in the remaining upper sequent.) For example, the lowest use of BC in the deduction replaces the inference figure occurrence

$$\frac{\mathcal{P} \; \longrightarrow \; f(Y,X) \supset n(X) \qquad\qquad \mathcal{P}, b(Y) \; \longrightarrow \; b(Y)}{\mathcal{P}, [f(V,X) \supset n(X)] \supset b(V) \; \longrightarrow \; b(Y)} \supset\text{-L}$$

where $\supset$-L here is augmented by the instantiation of the logic variable V by Y.

With the modified inference figures suggested by the abstract interpreter of the preceding section, we observe that the modified I-proof is almost identical to that given in the QN-Prolog presentation.

Example 3.1.4 (A uniform proof of the Gabbay-Reyle example). As already noted, $\mathcal{P}$ corresponds here to the (universal closure of the) program presented earlier.

$$
\cfrac{
\cfrac{
\cfrac{
\cfrac{
\cfrac{
\cfrac{
\cfrac{
\cfrac{
\cfrac{
\cfrac{\mathcal{P}, f(Y,m), f(Z,m), cr(Z,m), c(s,m) \; \longrightarrow \; cr(s,m)}{\mathcal{P}, f(Y,m), f(Z,m), cr(Z,m), c(s,W) \; \longrightarrow \; cr(s,m)}\text{ EG}}{\mathcal{P}, f(Y,m), f(Z,m), cr(Z,m) \; \longrightarrow \; cr(s,m)}\text{ CI}}{\mathcal{P}, f(Y,X), f(Z,X), cr(Z,X), cr(s,m) \supset d(m) \; \longrightarrow \; d(X)}\text{ BC}}{\mathcal{P}, f(Y,X), f(Z,X), cr(Z,X) \; \longrightarrow \; d(X)}\text{ CI}}{\mathcal{P}, f(Y,X), f(Z,X) \wedge cr(Z,X) \; \longrightarrow \; d(X)}\text{ }\wedge\text{-L}}{\mathcal{P}, f(Y,X) \; \longrightarrow \; f(Z,X) \wedge cr(Z,X) \supset d(X)}\text{ }\supset\text{-R}}{\mathcal{P}, f(Y,X), [f(Z,W) \wedge cr(Z,W) \supset d(W)] \supset n(W) \; \longrightarrow \; n(X)}\text{ BC}}{\mathcal{P}, f(Y,X) \; \longrightarrow \; n(X)}\text{ CI}}{\mathcal{P} \; \longrightarrow \; f(Y,X) \supset n(X)}\text{ }\supset\text{-R}}{\mathcal{P}, [f(V,X) \supset n(X)] \supset b(V) \; \longrightarrow \; b(Y)}\text{ BC}}{\mathcal{P} \; \longrightarrow \; b(Y)}\text{ CI}}{\mathcal{P} \; \longrightarrow \; \exists Y b(Y)}\text{ }\exists\text{-R}
$$

The deductive power of N-Prolog can be extended to a proof procedure for classical logic by the introduction of a new rule of inference called a restart rule. Gabbay [Gabbay, 1985] calls the resulting system *NR-Prolog*. The propositional form of the restart rule states that at any point where the current goal is atomic, this atom can be replaced by the original query, and if this original query occurrence succeeds then the replaced goal is deemed to succeed. The original query might succeed at this point but not at the original occurrence because now the program has been enlarged by use of the rule for implications. One should note that any ancestor goal can replace a current goal because the ancestor goal could be regarded as the original query. (Use of clauses augmenting the program but introduced before the ancestor goal is not a problem, as we note below.)

The natural example to illustrate the use of the restart rule is Pierce's law. This formula is not valid intuitionistically, thus not provable in N-Prolog, as the reader can verify. We show that Pierce's law succeeds in NR-Prolog.

Example 3.1.5 (Pierce's law).

1. ? $((a \supset b) \supset a) \supset a$
2. $(a \supset b) \supset a ? a$ rule for implication
3. $(a \supset b) \supset a ? a \supset b$ using the only clause
4. $(a \supset b) \supset a, a ? b$ rule for implication
5. $(a \supset b) \supset a, a ? (a \supset b) \supset a) \supset a$ restart
6. $(a \supset b) \supset a, a, (a \supset b) \supset a ? a$ rule for implication
7. success

As can be seen above, the restart subdeduction succeeds. Thus b succeeds from $\{(a \supset b) \supset a, a\}$. Thus the original query succeeds.

In the above example ancestor goal a could have been the restart goal. Although $(a \supset b) \supset a$ was added to the program before a became a goal, it is re-derived in the restart, which can always reproduce the path to a. Thus, any ancestor goal restart is always permissible in NR-Prolog.

The restart rule at the first-order level is a simple generalization of the propositional case. The restart rule for *QNR-Prolog*, the extension of QN-Prolog by addition of this rule, is precisely as for the propositional case except that the reintroduced original goal must have all its (existential) variables replaced by new existential variables. See [Gabbay, 1985] for details.

The power of the restart rule is seen by comparing the following soundness and completeness theorem with the earlier theorem for QN-Prolog:

Proposition 3.1.6. *P ? Q succeeds in QNR-Prolog if*

$$\vdash \exists \vec{X}[(\forall \vec{U} P \supset Q]$$

holds in classical logic for program (database) P and query Q, where $\vec{X}$ denotes all the existential variables in P and Q and $\vec{U}$ denotes all the universal variables in P.

3.2 Near-Horn Prolog

We now shift our attention from an extension of Prolog (SLD-resolution) by hypothetical implication to an extension by disjunctive consequent. We wish to handle clauses with an indefinite conclusion, such as "jump_in_lake $\supset$ sink $\vee$ swim". This extension has received considerable attention recently, identified as a subarea (called disjunctive logic programming) with a first book devoted to the subarea (see [Lobo *et al.*, 1992]). Our focus is on proof procedures so we restrict ourselves to presenting (one version of) the Near-Horn Prolog (nH-Prolog) procedure mentioned earlier. This version of nH-Prolog was developed by Reed and Loveland [Reed, 1988; Reed, 1991; Loveland and Reed, 1991] based on earlier versions devised by Loveland [Loveland, 1987; Loveland, 1991].

The astute reader may recognize that the introduction of non-Horn clauses such as above returns us to the full descriptive power of first-order logic since every clause in a conjunctive normal form (cnf) presentation of a formula can be written as an implication of atoms. Namely, negative literals of the cnf clause appear (positively) in the antecedent of the implication and positive literals of the cnf clause appear in the consequent. Since SLD-resolution is a restriction of SL-resolution (or ME), the appropriate procedure family seems at hand. Unfortunately, these procedures have properties not compatible with the character of logic programming. A severe problem with the use of ME-based procedures is the need to access any literal of the input clause in executing the extension operation. With the clauses in positive implication format this means accessing antecedent atoms as well as consequent atoms. This requires a notion of contrapositive implications, which reverses the direction of implication. This can strongly disrupt the user's sense of computation sequence, which is key to severely limiting the branching that occurs in Prolog execution. Moreover, the ability to catch errors in the formulation of the program is strongly dependent on the procedural reading capability of the programmer, and the disruption caused by the introduction of unintuitive implications is high. This seems a fatal flaw to the notion of "program" in comparison to "axiom clause set" that separates logic programming from automated theorem proving. There certainly is reason to look to preserve implication direction as SLD-resolution does.

There are several important properties enjoyed by SLD-resolution, and its implementation as Prolog, that one would seek to preserve in extending to a new domain. Prolog (SLD-resolution) is goal oriented, allows a declarative and procedural reading capability, has a linear input format, uses a positive implication format, and needs no contrapositive occurrences of the implications. Moreover, the process is intuitionistically sound, which insures a certain constructive nature to the inference structure. The attractiveness of nH-Prolog is that it shares these properties with Prolog, except that the linearity and the procedural reading properties are local only. (A certain type of contrapositive is used, but not one that changes the direction of implication.) The degree of locality depends on the number of uses of non-Horn clauses in the computation. Low use of non-Horn clauses yields more traditional computation sequences. This is a major reason why near-Horn Prolog is so-named; the intended domain is clause sets with few non-Horn clauses.

Like SLD-resolution, nH-Prolog is intuitionistically sound, although the process of preparation of clauses uses transformations that are classically but not intuitionistically provable. We will consider a version of nH-Prolog that meets the uniform proof criteria, somewhat unexpectedly, given that the problem domain is all of first-order logic. (However, the above-mentioned clause preparation accounts for some of the apparent gap in these two statements. For example, the formula $\neg\neg A \supset A$, not intuitionistically provable, simply transforms to query A and program A.)

The nH-Prolog procedure (in all variants) can be regarded as deduction by case analysis. A deduction is divided into *blocks*, where each block is essentially a Prolog deduction of one case. Information on deferred cases is retained in a "deferred head" list within each deduction line. The case-analysis approach is effective when the number of non-Horn clauses is low, but is not as effective as, say, ME-type procedures when many non-Horn clauses are present, such as in some logic puzzles and mathematical theorems.

We present a variant known as *Inheritance near-Horn Prolog*, or *InH-Prolog*, because it is relatively simple to describe, has an underlying complete first-order proof procedure, yet also seems to be the preferred version for implementation when building a compiler for the language. See [Loveland and Reed, 1991] for a full discussion of related issues. See [Reed and Loveland, 1992] for one comparison of this variant with N-Prolog and a simplified problem reduction format of Plaisted. After presenting the procedure we give two example deductions; these illustrate the procedure and also the role of disjunction in a database.

We consider the language format. The general clause form is

$$A_1; \ldots; A_n \; :\text{-} \; B_1, \ldots, B_m$$

where the A_i, B_j are atoms. The semicolons denote "or", and, as usual, the commas denote "and". Thus, the semantics for the above clause is the implication

$$B_1 \wedge B_2 \ldots \wedge B_m \supset A_1 \vee \ldots \vee A_n.$$

A definite Horn clause is given by $n = 1$. A (possibly disjunctive) fact is given by $m = 0$. The $n = 0$ case is not permitted as such, but is transformed into a special-case Horn clause by use of the special atom FALSE, which is given the semantics of "false" by its role in the InH-Prolog procedure. (As we shall see later, this atom corresponds to the logical symbol $\perp$ introduced in Subsection 2.2.) Thus query clause ?- B_1, ... , B_m is written FALSE :- B_1, ... ,B_m and we use a fixed query ?- FALSE.

The reason for the introduction of special atom FALSE involves the manner of handling negative clauses. Negative clauses may appear in the program itself, unlike Horn clause programs. A traditional query form, e.g. ?- $q(X)$, is usable but then every negative program clause would have form $q(X)$:- B_1, ... , B_m instead of FALSE :- B_1, ... , B_m. This makes the program dependent on the query, a very awkward trait. Answer retrieval is accomplished from the query clause FALSE :- Q, where Q is the user's query. Although formally a program clause, this (single) clause would be outside the compiled program and instead interpreted since it changes with each query. See [Loveland and Reed, 1991] and [Smith and Loveland, 1988] for further discussion.

Some terminology is needed before presenting the InH-Prolog procedure. The head of a clause now possibly has multiple atoms, called *head atoms*, sometimes just *heads* when context permits. (The term *body atom*, for atoms in the clause body, is available but rarely used.) Goal clauses, used in recording the deduction, are notated :- G_1, ..., G_n except for the initial goal clause, the query, which is notated ?- G, in our case ?- FALSE.

The summary we give applies to all the nH-Prolog variants except where noted.

An InH-Prolog deduction may be regarded as blocks of Prolog deductions where each block differs only slightly from standard Prolog. The basic Prolog reduction inference step is the primary inference step of the InH-Prolog block, with the adjustment that if the called program clause is non-Horn then the head atoms not called are put aside for use in another block. We now amplify the form of the deduction.

For the presentation of an InH-Prolog deduction we use a line format that displays the current goal clause, the active head list and the deferred head list. (The various head lists are defined below.) The format is:

goal_clause # active_head-list [deferred_head_list]

We first state the inference rules of InH-Prolog for a block.

Reduction — if G_s is the selected goal atom of the preceding goal clause G (in usual implementations this will always be the leftmost goal atom) and $H_1;\ldots;H_n$:- $G_1,\ldots,G_m$ is a program clause, where G_s and H_i are unifiable, for some i, $1 \le i \le n$, then $(G_1, \ldots, G_m)\theta$ replaces $G_s\theta$ in $G\theta$, where θ is the most general unifier of G_s and H. The $H_i\theta$, $j \ne i$, are added to the *deferred head* list, with no variable renaming. Both the active and deferred head list pass to the next line; changes from line to line include only possible instantiation of variables shared with the goal clause and additions to the deferred head list as just described. The deferred head list is placed between brackets.

Cancellation — if G_s is the selected goal in goal clause G and G_s unifies with an active head A (defined below), then the next goal clause is $(G - \{G_s\})\theta$, where θ is the unifier of G_s and A.

Variables in the head list atoms can be instantiated during reduction through shared variables with goal clause atoms or during cancellation.

We now consider block structure, which is reflected in the initialization of the block. Blocks serve as subdeductions, a single case consideration in the analysis-by-cases characterization of the InH-procedure.

Block initiation — the first line of a block has the query ?- FALSE as goal clause. For *restart* blocks (blocks other than the first, or *start*, block) lists of *active* head atoms and deferred head atoms are declared that accompany each line of the block. If a block terminates successfully by deriving the empty clause as for Prolog, but with a nonempty deferred head list, then a successor restart block is created. A *distinguished* active head is defined for the new block, chosen by a user supplied selection function from the deferred head list of the final line of the preceding block. (For a standard implementation it will be the leftmost deferred head.) The deferred head list is the deferred head list of the final line of the preceding block, minus the now distinguished active head. For other nH-Prologs this defines the active and deferred head lists of the new block but InH-Prolog has also as active heads the active heads of the block in which the new distinguished active head was deferred. If one represents the block structure in tree form with a child block for each deferred head in a block, then the active heads in the new child block include the parent block deferred head as distinguished active head and the active heads of the parent block as the other active heads. No deferred head list exists, as the heads are immediately recorded in the children blocks. (The possibility that multiple heads from a clause can share variables complicates the tree format by requiring that binding information be passed between blocks. In the sequential format we are outlining, acquiring heads from the previous block handles shared bindings. However, special recording mechanisms are needed in InH-Prolog to identify the correct active heads in the preceding block.)

In the start block where no active head list exists, the separator symbol # is omitted until deferred heads are introduced.

The deduction terminates successfully when no new block can be formed, which occurs when the deferred head list is empty.

We distinguish the newest active head primarily because of the key cancellation requirement discussed in the next paragraph, but also because nH-Prolog deductions must have one restart block per deferred head, and the distinguished active head is the appropriate head atom to identify with the block. The active heads serve as conditional facts in the case-analysis view of the nH-Prologs.

The InH-Prolog procedure has added requirements that relate to search. A non-obvious property whose absence would make the procedure impractical is the cancellation requirement. This requirement states that a restart block is to be accepted in a deduction only if a cancellation has occurred using the distinguished active head. (Cancellation with other active heads may occur also, of course, but do not satisfy the requirement.) This demand keeps blocks relevant, and prunes away many false search branches. The underlying proof procedure is a complete proof procedure with this feature. We return to the importance of this later.

Another important search feature is *progressive search*. Although too complex to treat fully here we outline the feature. Recall that a restart block in InH-Prolog always begins with the initial query FALSE. (This is not true of the Unit nH-Prolog variant, originally called Progressive nH-Prolog [Loveland, 1987; Loveland, 1991] because it first incorporated this important search feature. However, this feature is useful for all variants.) If the program clauses were processed exactly as its "parent" block, then it would duplicate the computation with no progress made, unless the new distinguished active head can invoke a cancellation. Progressive search starts the search of the restart block where the "parent" block finished (roughly), so that a new search space is swept. More precisely, the initial portion of the restart block deduction duplicates the initial portion of the block where the current distinguished active head was deferred, the initial portion ending at that point of deferral. (The path to this point can be copied with no search time accrued.) In effect we insert a FAIL at this point and let normal Prolog backtracking advance the search through the remainder of the search space. If this search fails then the search continues "from the top", as a regular search pattern would begin the block. The search halts in failure when the initial path to the deferred head point is again reached. For a more precise description see [Loveland, 1991]. An interpreter for Unit nH-Prolog has proven the worth of this search strategy.

We present two examples of InH-Prolog deductions. The first has very short blocks but has multiple non-Horn clauses and an indefinite answer. The second example has less trivial blocks and yields a definite answer.

An answer is the disjunction of the different instantiations of the query clause which begin InH-Prolog blocks. Not every block begins with a query clause use; negative clauses also have head atom FALSE and may begin blocks. However, negative clauses are from the program so represent known information. Only uses of the query clause yield new information and warrant inclusion in the answer to a query. Nor does each use of a query clause yield a different instantiation; identical instantiations of answer literals are merged.

The deduction below shows a successful computation without any indication of the search needed to find it, as is true of any displayed deduction. It is natural to wonder how much search occurs before the query "men_req(X, Cond)" calls the correct clause in the successive restart blocks. (Following Prolog, strings beginning with capital letters are variables.) At the completion of the deduction we show that the cancellation requirement kills the attempt to repeat the start block and thus forces the system to backtrack immediately upon block failure to move to the next (and correct) clause to match the query.

Example 3.2.1 (The manpower requirement example).

Program:
    men_req(8,normal) :- cond(normal).
    men_req(20,wind_storm) :- cond(wind_storm).
    men_req(30,snow_removal) :- cond(snow_removal).
    cond(snow_removal); cond(wind_storm) :- cond(abnormal).
    cond(normal) ; cond(abnormal).

Query:

```
?- men_req(X,Cond).
```

Query clause:
```
FALSE :- men_req(X,Cond).
```

Deduction:
```
?- FALSE
:- men_req(X,Cond)
:- cond(normal)              % X=8, Cond=normal
:-                           # [cond(abnormal)]
restart
?- FALSE                     # cond(abnormal)
:- men_req(X1,Cond1)         # cond(abnormal)
:- cond(wind_storm)          # cond(abnormal)
                             % X=20, Cond1=wind_storm
:- cond(abnormal)            # cond(abnormal) [cond(snow_removal)]
:-                           # cond(abnormal) [cond(snow_removal)]
                             % cancellation with distinguished head
restart
?- FALSE                     # cond(snow_removal),cond(abnormal)
                             % The new distinguished head is placed
                             % leftmost in the active head list
:- men_req(X2,Cond2)         # cond(snow_removal),cond(abnormal)
:- cond(snow_removal)        # cond(snow_removal),cond(abnormal)
                             % X=30, Cond2=snow_removal
:-                           # cond(snow_removal),cond(abnormal)
                             % cancellation with distinguished head
```

The query answer is the disjunction of the various instantiations of the user query for successful blocks. Here the answer is:

men_req(8,normal) OR men_req(20,wind_storm) OR
             men_req(30,snow-removal)

We now show that the cancellation requirement aids the search process in the manner discussed before the deduction. A restart block with standard search rules would recompute the computation of the start block. However, if the following restart block were to follow the start block, and not be eliminated, then an infinite loop would be entered. (This restart block essentially repeats the start block.)

```
restart
?- FALSE                     # cond(abnormal)
:- men_req(X1,Cond1)         # cond(abnormal)
:- cond(normal)              # cond(abnormal)
```

:-   # cond(abnormal) [cond(abnormal)]

Because the distinguished active head "cond(abnormal)" is not used in cancellation this block would not be retained, normal backtracking would occur and the block of the deduction would be obtained. The progressive search feature discussed previously would also keep this block from being computed directly after the start block; the cancellation requirement allows a more standard search order to be used if desired. Also this illustrates the cancellation requirement mechanism; this discard feature is used many times other than repressing near-duplicate blocks.

The second example yields a definite answer. This is a commuting problem with an alternate behavior depending on the status of the office parking lot. If the problem were formulated to return a plan, then an indefinite answer would be returned [Loveland and Reed, 1991]. This example illustrates what we believe is a common structure for disjunctive logic programs. The non-Horn clause records the expected case ("park in office lot") and the error case ("lot is full"). Recovery possibilities are confirmed by the completion of the computation.

Example 3.2.2 (The commute example).

Program:
    car(al).
    drives(X,office_bldg) :- car(X).
    gets_to(X,office_bldg) :- parks(X,office_bldg).
    goes_to_mtg(X) :- gets_to(X,office_bldg).
    parks(X,commercial) :- car(X),lot_full(office_bldg).
    finds(X,office_bldg) :- drives(X,office_bldg), parks(X,commercial).
    gets_to(X,office_bldg) :- finds(X,office_bldg).
    parks(X,office_bldg); lot_full(office_bldg) :- drives(X,office_bldg).

Query:
    ?- goes_to_mtg(X).

Query clause:
    FALSE :- goes_to_mtg(X)

Deduction:
    ?- FALSE
    :- goes_to_mtg(X)
    :- gets_to(X,office_bldg)
    :- parks(X,office_bldg)
    :- drives(X,office_bldg)   # [lot_full(office_bldg)]
    :- car(X)   # [lot_full(office_bldg)]

```
 :-                                    #  [lot_full(office_bldg)]
                                       %  X=al
restart
   ?- FALSE
   :- goes_to_mtg(X1)                  #  lot_full(office_bldg)
   :- gets_to(X1,office_bldg)          #  lot_full(office_bldg)
   :- finds(X1,office_bldg)            #  lot_full(office_bldg)
   :- drives(X1,office_bldg), parks(X1,commercial)
                                       #  lot_full(office_bldg)
   :- car(X1), parks(X1,commercial)    #  lot_full(office_bldg)
   :- parks(al,commercial)             #  lot_full(office_bldg)
                                       %  X1=al
   :- car(al), lot_full(office_bldg)   #  lot_full(office_bldg)
   :- lot_full(office_bldg)            #  lot_full(office_bldg)
                                       %  cancellation
 :-                                    #  lot_full(office_bldg)
```

Query answer:
   goes_to_mtg(al)

Observe that the query answer above is the merge of the disjunction of two identical atoms, each corresponding to a block.

Unit nH-Prolog differs from InH-Prolog primarily by the use of only one active head atom, the distinguished active head, and by a possibly different restart block initial goal clause. The use of only one active head means a "constant time" inner loop speed (when a no-occurs-check unification is used, as for Prolog) rather than an inner-loop speed that varies with the length of the active list to be checked. (Pre-processing by a compiler usually makes the possibly longer active head list of InH-Prolog also process in near-constant time. This is not always possible, such as when multiple entries to the active head list share the same predicate letter.) The different restart initial goals can allow a shorter deduction to be written (and yield a shorter search time) but represent another branch point in the search and may in fact lengthen search time. (The latter is much less costly than first considerations indicate.) The search time tradeoff here is hard to quantify. Evidence at present suggests that InH-Prolog is superior when compilation is possible. For interpreters, Unit nH-Prolog seems to have the edge on speed, but is somewhat more complex to code.

We now consider how to represent the underlying inference system of InH-Prolog in a uniform proof format. One way is to rewrite non-Horn clauses in a classically equivalent form so that only rules acceptable to the uniform proof concept are used. We illustrate this approach by example, writing clauses as traditional implications (not Prolog notation), using ⊃ for implies and interpreting the atom FALSE as an alternative notation for $\perp$. Given the non-Horn clause $A \supset (B \vee C)$, we may rewrite this in the classically equivalent forms $(A \wedge (B \supset \text{FALSE})) \supset C$ and $(A \wedge (C \supset \text{FALSE})) \supset B$ with both clauses needed to replace $A \supset (B \vee C)$. With use of clauses of this form, InH-Prolog derivations can indeed be described as uniform proofs.

We choose a different approach for our major illustration, one that does not require us to rewrite the non-Horn clauses. We obtain the effect of case analysis and block initiation used by InH-Prolog by use of a derived rule meeting the uniform proof conditions. We justify the derived *restart* inference figure

$$\frac{\mathcal{P}, A \longrightarrow \text{FALSE} \qquad \mathcal{P}, B \longrightarrow B}{\mathcal{P}, A \vee B \longrightarrow B} \; \text{restart}$$

by the following derivation:

$$\frac{\dfrac{\mathcal{P}, A \longrightarrow \text{FALSE}}{\mathcal{P}, A \longrightarrow B} \bot\text{-R} \qquad \mathcal{P}, B \longrightarrow B}{\mathcal{P}, A \vee B \longrightarrow B} \; \vee\text{-L.}$$

There is a symmetric rule for $\mathcal{P}, A \vee B \longrightarrow A$ and this obviously generalizes for different size disjunctive clauses. The similarity in effect between the restart rule and the rewriting of the non-Horn clauses suggested earlier is obvious.

We give a uniform proof for the manpower requirement example. To shorten the proof tree we will combine the CI (Clause Incorporation) and BC (backchain) into one inference figure. Single symbol abbreviations are used for predicate and constant names and $\mathcal{P}$ denotes the formulas constituting the program for the example. We again use d1,d2,d3,d4 ? $f(Y, X) \supset n(X)$ "existential" variables in the CI inference figure to signify the creation of one instance of a clause when the proof is read from the bottom upward.

$$
\cfrac{
  \cfrac{
    \cfrac{
      \cfrac{
        \cfrac{
          \cfrac{\mathcal{P}, c(a), c(s) \longrightarrow c(s)}
                {\mathcal{P}, c(a), c(s), c(s) \supset m(30, s) \longrightarrow m(X_2, Y_2)} \text{BC}
        }
        {\mathcal{P}, m(X_2, Y_2) \supset \text{FALSE} \longrightarrow \text{FALSE}} \text{CI, BC}
      }
      {\mathcal{P}, c(a), c(s) \longrightarrow \text{FALSE}} \text{CI}
    \qquad \mathcal{P}, c(a), c(w) \longrightarrow c(w)}
    {\mathcal{P}, c(a) \longrightarrow c(a) \qquad \mathcal{P}, c(a), c(s) \vee c(w) \longrightarrow c(w)} \text{restart}
  }
  {\ldots}{\ldots}
$$

$$
\cfrac{
  \mathcal{P}, c(a) \longrightarrow c(a) \qquad
  \cfrac{
    \cfrac{\mathcal{P}, c(a), c(s) \vee c(w) \longrightarrow c(w)}
          {\mathcal{P}, c(a), c(a) \supset c(s) \vee c(w) \longrightarrow c(w)} \;\supset\text{-L}
  }{}
}{}
$$

$$
\cfrac{
  \cfrac{
    \cfrac{\mathcal{P}, c(a), c(a) \supset c(s) \vee c(w) \longrightarrow c(w)}
          {\mathcal{P}, c(a), c(w) \supset m(20, w) \longrightarrow m(X_1, Y_1)} \text{CI, BC}
  }{\mathcal{P}, c(a), m(X_1, Y_1) \supset \text{FALSE} \longrightarrow \text{FALSE}} \text{CI, BC}
}{\mathcal{P}, c(a) \longrightarrow \text{FALSE}} \text{CI}
\qquad \mathcal{P}, c(n) \longrightarrow c(n)
$$

$$
\cfrac{
  \cfrac{
    \cfrac{
      \cfrac{\mathcal{P}, c(a) \longrightarrow \text{FALSE} \qquad \mathcal{P}, c(n) \longrightarrow c(n)}
            {\mathcal{P}, c(n) \vee c(a) \longrightarrow c(n)} \text{restart}
    }{\mathcal{P}, c(n) \supset m(8, n) \longrightarrow m(X, Y)} \text{CI, BC}
  }{\mathcal{P}, m(X, Y) \supset \text{FALSE} \longrightarrow \text{FALSE}} \text{CI, BC}
}{\mathcal{P} \longrightarrow \text{FALSE}} \text{CI}
$$

We conclude this section with another example, one where the capability of the InH-Prolog procedure might seem to extend beyond the ability to represent the computation by a uniform proof. Indeed, the ability to model the computation by a uniform proof depends on the variant of InH-Prolog used, because the role of the query clause is significant in the associated uniform proof.

We are given the program consisting of the single clause $p(a); p(b)$, and ask the query

> ?- $p(X)$.

The sequent $p(a) \lor p(b) \longrightarrow \exists X p(X)$ has no uniform proof, so it is instructive to see the uniform proof for this InH-Prolog computation. By convention, the query is replaced by query clause FALSE :- $p(X)$ and query ?- FALSE. This transformation is justifiable in classical logic; in particular, the sequent $(\forall X(p(X) \supset \text{FALSE})) \supset \text{FALSE} \longrightarrow \exists X p(X)$ has a C-proof. The InH-Prolog computation of query ?- FALSE given program $p(a) \lor p(b), p(X) \supset \text{FALSE}$ succeeds, giving answer $p(a) \lor p(b)$. Using the various conventions described earlier and denoting the set $\{\forall X(p(X) \supset \text{FALSE}), p(a) \lor p(b)\}$ by $\mathcal{P}$, the associated uniform proof is given below.

$$
\cfrac{
  \cfrac{
    \cfrac{
      \cfrac{\dfrac{\mathcal{P}, p(a) \longrightarrow p(a)}{\mathcal{P}, p(a) \longrightarrow p(Z)}\text{ EG} \quad \mathcal{P}, p(a), \text{FALSE} \longrightarrow \text{FALSE}}{\mathcal{P}, p(a), p(Z) \supset \text{FALSE} \longrightarrow \text{FALSE}}\supset\text{-L}
    }{\mathcal{P}, p(a) \longrightarrow \text{FALSE}}\text{ CI} \quad
    \cfrac{\dfrac{\mathcal{P}, p(b) \longrightarrow p(b)}{\mathcal{P}, p(b) \longrightarrow p(Y)}\text{ EG}}{}\text{ restart}
  }{\mathcal{P}, p(a) \lor p(b) \longrightarrow p(Y)}
}{
  \cfrac{\mathcal{P} \longrightarrow p(Y) \quad \mathcal{P}, \text{FALSE} \longrightarrow \text{FALSE}}{\cfrac{\mathcal{P}, p(Y) \supset \text{FALSE} \longrightarrow \text{FALSE}}{\mathcal{P} \longrightarrow \text{FALSE}}\text{ CI}}\supset\text{-L}
}
$$

4 Conclusion

The material presented in this paper may be read in two ways. The first way is to consider the procedures as primary, starting with the historical introduction of procedures. This leads to the SLD-resolution procedure, which is the inference foundation for Prolog and anchors the traditional view of logic programming. Two extensions of the traditional notion of logic programming also appear. Included is an abstraction of the concept of logic programming that may be regarded as a derivative attempt to encode the essence of these procedures. An alternative view is to take the abstraction as primary and as setting the standard for acceptable logic programming languages. If this viewpoint is adopted, the abstraction provides guidance in constructing goal-directed proof procedures for logic programming — such procedures will essentially be ones that search for uniform proofs in the relevant context. Horn clause logic and the associated SLD-resolution procedure are illustrations of this viewpoint. However, richer exploitations of the general framework are also possible and this issue is discussed at length. The two procedures that conclude the paper serve as additional novel illustrations of the notion of searching for a uniform proof. N-Prolog is an excellent example of an extension of SLD-resolution that fits the uniform proof structure. The second example, near-Horn Prolog, also fits the uniform proof structure when we specify carefully the version (InH-Prolog) and the input format (use of query clause). That InH-Prolog is in fact a proof procedure for full (classical) first-order logic makes the fit within a uniform proof structure particularly interesting. However, recall that conversion of a given valid formula into the positive implication refutation logic format used by InH-Prolog may utilize several equivalences valid only classically.

Although the second way of reading the paper most likely is not the viewpoint the reader first adopts, it is a viewpoint to seriously consider. If the reader agrees with the paradigm captured by the structure of uniform proof, then he/she has a framework to judge not just the procedures presented here but future procedures that seek to extend our capabilities within the logic programming arena.

Acknowledgements

We wish to thank Robert Kowalski for suggestions that lead to an improved paper.

Loveland's work on this paper was partially supported by NSF Grants CCR-89-00383 and CCR-91-16203 and Nadathur's work was similarly supported by NSF Grants CCR-89-05825 and CCR-92-08465.

References

[Aït-Kaci, 1990] H. Aït-Kaci. *Warren's Abstract Machine: a Tutorial Reconstruction.* MIT Press, Cambridge, MA, 1990.

[Andrews, 1976] P. Andrews. Refutations by Matings. *IEEE Transactions on Computers*, C-25:801–807, 1976.

[Astrachan and Loveland, 1991] O. L. Astrachan and D. W. Loveland. METEORs: High performance theorem provers for Model Elimination. In R.S. Boyer, editor, *Automated Reasoning: Essays in Honor of Woody Bledsoe.* Kluwer Academic Publishers, Dordrecht, 1991.

[Astrachan and Stickel, 1992] O. L. Astrachan and M. E. Stickel. Caching and lemmaizing in Model Elimination theorem provers. In W. Bibel and R. Kowalski, editors, *Proceedings of the Eleventh Conference on Automated Deduction*, Lecture Notes in Artificial Intelligence 607, pages 224–238. Springer-Verlag, Berlin, June 1992.

[Bibel, 1982] W. Bibel. *Automated Theorem Proving.* Vieweg Verlag, Braunschweig, 1982.

[Bose *et al.*, 1991] S. Bose, E. M. Clarke, D. E. Long and S. Michaylov. PARTHENON: a parallel theorem prover for non-Horn clauses. *Journal of Automated Reasoning*, pages 153–181, 1991.

[Bowen, 1982] K. A. Bowen. Programming with full first-order logic. In J. E. Hayes, D. Michie and Y.-H. Pao, editors, *Machine Intelligence 10*, pages 421–440. Halsted Press, 1982.

[Chang and Lee, 1973] C. Chang and R. C. Lee. *Symbolic Logic and Mechanical Theorem Proving*. Academic Press, New York, 1973.

[Fitting, 1969] M. Fitting. *Intuitionistic Logic, Model Theory and Forcing*. North-Holland Publishing Company, 1969.

[Fitting, 1985] M. Fitting. A Kripke–Kleene semantics for logic programming. *Journal of Logic Programming*, 2(4):295–312, 1985.

[Fitting, 1990] M. Fitting. *First-order Logic and Automated Theorem Proving*. Springer-Verlag, 1990.

[Gabbay, 1985] D. M. Gabbay. N-Prolog: an extension of Prolog with hypothetical implication, Part 2. *Journal of Logic Programming*, 4:251–283, 1985.

[Gabbay and Reyle, 1984a] D. Gabbay and U. Reyle. N-Prolog: An extension to Prolog with hypothetical implications I. *Journal of Logic Programming*, 1(4):319–355, 1984.

[Gabbay and Reyle, 1984b] D. M. Gabbay and U. Reyle. N-Prolog: an extension of Prolog with hypothetical implication, Part 1. *Journal of Logic Programming*, 4:319–355, 1984.

[Gallier and Raatz, 1987] J. Gallier and S. Raatz. Hornlog: A graph-based interpreter for general Horn clauses. *Journal of Logic Programming*, 4(2):119–156, 1987.

[Gentzen, 1969] G. Gentzen. Investigations into logical deduction. In M. E. Szabo, editor, *The Collected Papers of Gerhard Gentzen*, pages 68–131. North Holland, Amsterdam, 1969.

[Green, 1969] C. Green. Theorem-proving by resolution as a basis for questions-answering systems. In B. Meltzer and D. Michie, editors, *Machine Intelligence 4*, pages 183–205. Edinburgh University Press, Edinburgh, 1969.

[Green and Raphael, 1968] C. Green and B. Raphael. The use of theorem-proving techniques in systems. In *Proceedings of the 23rd National Conference of the Association of Computing Machinery*, pages 169–181, Princeton, 1968. Brandon Systems Press.

[Harland and Pym, 1991] J. Harland and D. Pym. The uniform proof-theoretic foundation of linear logic programming (extended abstract). In V. Saraswat and K. Ueda, editors, *Proceedings of the 1991 International Logic Programming Symposium*, pages 304–318. MIT Press, 1991.

[Harrop, 1960] R. Harrop. Concerning formulas of the types $A \rightarrow B \vee$

C, $A \rightarrow (Ex)B(x)$ in intuitionistic formal systems. *Journal of Symbolic Logic*, 25:27–32, 1960.

[Hill, 1974] R. Hill. LUSH-resolution and its completeness. DCL Memo No. 78, School of Artificial Intelligence, University of Edinburgh, Edinburgh, Scotland, August 1974.

[Hodas and Miller, 1994] J. Hodas and D. Miller. Logic programming in a fragment of intuitionistic linear logic. *Information and Computation*, 110(2):327–365, May 1994.

[Kowalski, 1970] R. Kowalski. Search strategies for theorem proving. In B. Meltzer and D. Michie, editors, *Machine Intelligence 6*, pages 181–201. Edinburgh University Press, Edinburgh, 1970.

[Kowalski, 1979] R. Kowalski. *Logic for Problem Solving*. North-Holland, 1979.

[Kowalski and Kuehner, 1971] R. Kowalski and D. Kuehner. Linear resolution with selection function. *Artificial Intelligence*, pages 227–260, 1971.

[Letz *et al.*, 1991] R. Letz, J. Schumann, S. Bayerl, and W. Bibel. SETHEO: a high-performance theorem prover. *Journal of Automated Reasoning*, pages 183–212, 1991.

[Lloyd and Topor, 1984] J. Lloyd and R. Topor. Making Prolog more expressive. *Journal of Logic Programming*, 1(3):225–240, 1984.

[Lobo *et al.*, 1992] J. Lobo, J. Minker, and A. Rajasekar. *Foundations of Disjunction Logic Programming*. MIT Press, Cambridge, MA, 1992.

[Loveland, 1968] D. W. Loveland. Mechanical theorem proving by model elimination. *Journal of the Association for Computing Machines*, pages 236–251, 1968.

[Loveland, 1969] D. W. Loveland. A simplified format for the model elimination procedure. *Journal of the Association for Computing Machines*, pages 349–363, 1969.

[Loveland, 1970] D. W. Loveland. A linear format for resolution. In *Symposium on Automatic Demonstration*, Lecture Notes in Mathematics 125, pages 147–162. Springer-Verlag, Berlin, 1970.

[Loveland, 1978] D. W. Loveland. *Automated Theorem Proving: a Logical Basis*. North-Holland, Amsterdam, 1978.

[Loveland, 1987] D. W. Loveland. Near-Horn Prolog. In *Proceedings of the Fourth International Conference and Symposium on Logic Programming*, pages 456–469. MIT Press, Cambridge, MA, 1987.

[Loveland, 1991] D. W. Loveland. Near-Horn Prolog and beyond. *Journal of Automated Reasoning*, pages 1–26, 1991.

[Loveland and Reed, 1991] D. W. Loveland and D. W. Reed. A near-Horn Prolog for compilation. In J. Lassez and G. Plotkin, editors, *Computational Logic: Essays in Honor of Alan Robinson*, pages 542–564. MIT

Press, Cambridge, MA, 1991.

[Luckham, 1970] D. Luckham. Refinement theorems in resolution theory. In *Symposium on Automatic Demonstration*, Lecture Notes in Mathematics 125, pages 163–190. Springer-Verlag, Berlin, 1970.

[McCarty, 1988a] L. T. McCarty. Clausal intuitionistic logic I. Fixed point semantics. *Journal of Logic Programming*, 5(1):1–31, 1988.

[McCarty, 1988b] L. T. McCarty. Clausal intuitionistic logic II. Tableau proof procedures. *Journal of Logic Programming*, 5(2):93–132, 1988.

[Miller, 1989a] D. Miller. Lexical scoping as universal quantification. In G. Levi and M. Martelli, editors, *Sixth International Logic Programming Conference*, pages 268–283, Lisbon, Portugal, June 1989. MIT Press, Cambridge, MA.

[Miller, 1989b] D. Miller. A logical analysis of modules in logic programming. *Journal of Logic Programming*, 6:79–108, 1989.

[Miller, 1992] D. Miller. Unification under a mixed prefix. *Journal of Symbolic Computation*, 14:321–358, 1992.

[Miller et al., 1991] D. Miller, G. Nadathur, F. Pfenning and A. Scedrov. Uniform proofs as a foundation for logic programming. *Annals of Pure and Applied Logic*, 51:125–157, 1991.

[Nadathur, 1993] G. Nadathur. A proof procedure for the logic of hereditary Harrop formulas. *Journal of Automated Reasoning*, 11(1):115–145, August 1993.

[Nadathur and Miller, 1988] G. Nadathur and D. Miller. An overview of λProlog. In K. A. Bowen and R. A. Kowalski, editors, *Fifth International Logic Programming Conference*, pages 810–827, Seattle, Washington, August 1988. MIT Press.

[Nadathur et al., 1993] G. Nadathur, B. Jayaraman and K. Kwon. Scoping constructs in logic programming: Implementation problems and their solution. Technical Report CS-1993-17, Department of Computer Science, Duke University, July 1993.

[Paulson, 1987] L. R. Paulson. The representation of logics in higher-order logic. Technical Report Number 113, University of Cambridge, Computer Laboratory, August 1987.

[Pfenning, 1989] F. Pfenning. Elf: A language for logic definition and verified metaprogramming. In *Proceedings of the Fourth Annual Symposium on Logic in Computer Science*, pages 313–322. IEEE Computer Society Press, June 1989.

[Pohl, 1971] I. Pohl. Bi-directional search. In B. Meltzer and D. Michie, editors, *Machine Intelligence 6*, pages 127–140. Edinburgh University Press, Edinburgh, 1971.

[Prawitz, 1965] D. Prawitz. *Natural Deduction: A Proof-Theoretical Study*. Almqvist & Wiksell, 1965.

[Reed, 1988] D. W. Reed. Near-Horn Prolog: A first-order extension to Prolog. Master's thesis, Duke University, May 1988.

[Reed, 1991] D. W. Reed. *A Case-analysis Approach to Disjunctive Logic Programming*. PhD thesis, Duke University, December 1991.

[Reed and Loveland, 1992] D. W. Reed and D. W. Loveland. A comparison of three Prolog extensions. *Journal of Logic Programming*, 12:25–50, 1992.

[Robinson, 1965] J. A. Robinson. A machine-oriented logic based on the resolution principle. *Journal of the Association for Computing Machines*, 23–41, 1965.

[Schumann and Letz, 1990] J. Schumann and R. Letz. PARTHEO: a high performance parallel theorem prover. In M. Stickel, editor, *Proceedings of the Tenth International Conference on Automated Deduction*, Lecture Notes in Artificial Intelligence 449, pages 40–56, Berlin, June 1990. Springer-Verlag.

[Smith and Loveland, 1988] B. T. Smith and D. W. Loveland. A simple near-Horn Prolog interpreter. In *Proceedings of the Fifth International Conference and Symposium on Logic Programming*, Seattle, 1988.

[Stickel, 1984] M. E. Stickel. A Prolog technology theorem prover. *New Generation Computing*, 371–383, 1984.

[Stickel, 1988] M. E. Stickel. A Prolog Technology Theorem Prover: implementation by an extended Prolog compiler. *Journal of Automated Reasoning*, 353–380, 1988.

[Troelstra, 1973] A. Troelstra. *Metamathematical Investigation of Intuitionistic Arithmetic and Analysis*. Number 344 in Lecture Notes in Mathematics. Springer-Verlag, 1973.

[Warren, 1983] D. H. D. Warren. An abstract Prolog instruction set. Technical Note 309, SRI International, October 1983.

[Wos *et al.*, 1964] L. Wos, D. Carson and G. Robinson. The unit preference strategy in theorem proving. In *AFIPS Conference Proceedings 26*, pages 615–621, Washington, DC, 1964. Spartan Books.

[Wos *et al.*, 1965] L. Wos, G. Robinson, and D. Carson. Efficiency and completeness of the set of support strategy in theorem proving. *Journal of the Association for Computing Machines*, 536–541, 1965.

[Wos *et al.*, 1991] L. Wos, R. Overbeek, and E. Lusk. Subsumption, a sometimes undervalued procedure. In J. Lassez and G. Plotkin, editors, *Computational Logic: Essays in Honor of Alan Robinson*, pages 3–40. MIT Press, Cambridge, MA, 1991.

The Role of Abduction in Logic Programming

A. C. Kakas, R. A. Kowalski and F. Toni

Contents

1 Introduction

This paper extends and updates our earlier survey and analysis of work on the extension of logic programming to perform abductive reasoning [Kakas et al., 1993]. The purpose of the paper is to provide a critical overview of some of the main research results, in order to develop a common framework for evaluating these results, to identify the main unresolved problems, and to indicate directions for future work. The emphasis is not on technical details but on relationships and common features of different approaches. Some of the main issues we will consider are the contributions that abduction can make to the problems of reasoning with incomplete or negative information, the evolution of knowledge, and the semantics of logic programming and its extensions. We also discuss recent work on the argumentation-theoretic interpretation of abduction, which was introduced in the earlier version of this paper.

The philosopher Peirce first introduced the notion of abduction. In [Peirce, 1931–58] he identified three distinguished forms of reasoning.

Deduction, an analytic process based on the application of general rules to particular cases, with the inference of a result.

Induction, synthetic reasoning which infers the rule from the case and the result.

Abduction, another form of synthetic inference, but of the case from a rule and a result.

Peirce further characterised abduction as the "probational adoption of a hypothesis" as explanation for observed facts (results), according to known laws. "It is however a weak kind of inference, because we cannot say that we believe in the truth of the explanation, but only that it may be true"[Peirce, 1931–58].

Abduction is widely used in common-sense reasoning, for instance in diagnosis, to reason from effect to cause [Charniak and McDermott, 1985;

Pople, 1973]. We consider here an example drawn from [Pearl, 1987].

Example 1.0.1.

Consider the following theory T:

$$grass\text{-}is\text{-}wet \leftarrow rained\text{-}last\text{-}night$$
$$grass\text{-}is\text{-}wet \leftarrow sprinkler\text{-}was\text{-}on$$
$$shoes\text{-}are\text{-}wet \leftarrow grass\text{-}is\text{-}wet.$$

If we observe that our shoes are wet, and we want to know why this is so, $\{rained\text{-}last\text{-}night\}$ is a possible explanation, i.e. a set of hypotheses that together with the explicit knowledge in T implies the given observation. $\{sprinkler\text{-}was\text{-}on\}$ is another alternative explanation.

Abduction consists in computing such explanations for observations. It is a form of non-monotonic reasoning, because explanations which are consistent with one state of a knowledge base may become inconsistent with new information. In the example above the explanation *rained-last-night* may turn out to be false, and the alternative explanation *sprinkler-was-on* may be the true cause for the given observation. The existence of **multiple explanations** is a general characteristic of abductive reasoning, and the selection of "preferred" explanations is an important problem.

1.1 Abduction in logic

Given a set of sentences T (a theory presentation), and a sentence G (observation), to a first approximation, the abductive task can be characterised as the problem of finding a set of sentences Δ (abductive explanation for G) such that:

(1) $T \cup \Delta \models G$,

(2) $T \cup \Delta$ is consistent.

This characterisation of abduction is independent of the language in which T, G and Δ are formulated. The logical implication sign $\models$ in (1) can alternatively be replaced by a deduction operator $\vdash$. The consistency requirement in (2) is not explicit in Peirce's more informal characterisation of abduction, but it is a natural further requirement.

In fact, these two conditions (1) and (2) alone are too weak to capture Peirce's notion. In particular, additional restrictions on Δ are needed to distinguish abductive explanations from inductive generalisations [Console and Saitta, 1992]. Moreover, we also need to restrict Δ so that it conveys some reason why the observations hold, e.g. we do not want to explain one effect in terms of another effect, but only in terms of some cause. For both of these reasons, explanations are often restricted to belong to a special pre-specified, domain-specific class of sentences called **abducible**. In this paper we will assume that the class of abducibles is always given.

Additional criteria have also been proposed to restrict the number of candidate explanations:

- Once we restrict the hypotheses to belong to a specified set of sentences, we can further restrict, without loss of generality, the hypotheses to atoms (that "name" these sentences) which are predicates explicitly indicated as abducible, as shown by Poole [Poole, 1988].

- In Section 1.2 we will discuss the use of integrity constraints to reduce the number of possible explanations.

- Additional information can help to discriminate between different explanations, by rendering some of them more appropriate or plausible than others. For example Sattar and Goebel [Sattar and Goebel, 1989] use "crucial literals" to discriminate between two mutually incompatible explanations. When the crucial literals are tested, one of the explanations is rejected. More generally Evans and Kakas [Evans and Kakas, 1992] use the notion of corroboration to select explanations. An explanation fails to be corroborated if some of its logical consequences are not observed. A related technique is presented by Sergot in [Sergot, 1983], where information is obtained from the user during the process of query evaluation.

- Moreover various (domain specific) criteria of preference can be specified. They impose a (partial) order on the sets of hypotheses which leads to the discrimination of explanations [Brewka, 1989; Charniak and McDermott, 1985; Gabbay, 1991; Hobbs *et al.*, 1990; Poole, 1985; Poole, 1992; Stickel, 1989].

Cox and Pietrzykowski [Cox and Pietrzykowski, 1992] identify other desirable properties of abductive explanations. For instance, an explanation should be **basic**, i.e. should not be explainable in terms of other explanations. For instance, in Example 1.0.1 the explanation

$$\{grass\text{-}is\text{-}wet\}$$

for the observation

$$shoes\text{-}are\text{-}wet$$

is not basic, whereas the alternative explanations

$$\{rained\text{-}last\text{-}night\}$$
$$\{sprinkler\text{-}was\text{-}on\}$$

are.

An explanation should also be **minimal**, i.e. not subsumed by another one. For example, in Example 1.0.1 the explanation

$$\{rained\text{-}last\text{-}night,\ sprinkler\text{-}was\text{-}on\}$$

for the observation

$$shoes\text{-}are\text{-}wet$$

is not minimal, while the explanations

$$\{rained\text{-}last\text{-}night\}$$
$$\{sprinkler\text{-}was\text{-}on\}$$

are.

So far we have presented a semantic characterisation of abduction and discussed some heuristics to deal with the multiple explanation problem, but we have not described any proof procedures for computing abduction. Various authors have suggested the use of top-down, goal-oriented computation, based on the use of deduction to drive the generation of abductive hypotheses. Cox and Pietrzykowski [Cox and Pietrzykowski, 1992] construct hypotheses from the "dead ends" of linear resolution proofs. Finger and Genesereth [Finger and Genesereth, 1985] generate "deductive solutions to design problems" using the "residue" left behind in resolution proofs. Poole, Goebel and Aleliunas [Poole *et al.*, 1987] also use linear resolution to generate hypotheses.

In contrast, the ATMS [de Kleer, 1986] computes abductive explanations bottom-up. The ATMS can be regarded as a form of hyper-resolution, augmented with subsumption, for propositional logic programs [Reiter and De Kleer, 1987]. Lamma and Mello [Lamma and Mello, 1992] have developed an extension of the ATMS for the non-propositional case. Resolution-based techniques for computing abduction have also been developed by Demolombe and Fariñas del Cerro [Demolombe and Fariñas del Cerro, 1991] and Gaifman and Shapiro [Gaifman and Shapiro, 1989].

Abduction can also be applied to logic programming (LP). A **(general) logic program** is a set of Horn clauses extended by negation as failure [Clark, 1978], i.e. **clauses** of the form:

$$A \leftarrow L_1, \ldots, L_n$$

where each L_i is either an atom A_i or its negation $\sim A_i$,[1] A is an atom and each variable occurring in the clause is implicitly universally quantified. A is called the head and $L_1, \ldots, L_n$ is called the body of the clause. A logic program where each literal L_i in the body of every clause is atomic is said to be **definite**.

Abduction can be computed in LP by extending SLD and SLDNF [Chen and Warren, 1989; Eshghi and Kowalski, 1988; Eshghi and Kowalski, 1989;

---

[1] In the sequel we will represent negation as failure as $\sim$.

Kakas and Mancarella, 1990a; Kakas and Mancarella, 1990d; Denecker and De Schreye, 1992b; Teusink, 1993]. Instead of failing in a proof when a selected subgoal fails to unify with the head of any rule, the subgoal can be viewed as a hypothesis. This is similar to viewing abducibles as "askable" conditions which are treated as qualifications to answers to queries [Sergot, 1983]. In the same way that it is useful to distinguish a subset of all predicates as "askable", it is useful to distinguish certain predicates as abducible. In fact, it is generally convenient to choose, as abducible predicates, ones which are not conclusions of any clause. As we shall remark at the beginning of Section 5, this restriction can be imposed without loss of generality, and has the added advantage of ensuring that all explanations will be basic.

Abductive explanations computed in LP are guaranteed to be minimal, unless the program itself encodes non-minimal explanations. For example, in the propositional logic program

$$p \; \leftarrow \; q$$
$$p \; \leftarrow \; q, r$$

both the minimal explanation $\{q\}$ and the non-minimal explanation $\{q, r\}$ are computed for the observation p.

The abductive task for the logic-based approach has been proved to be highly intractable: it is NP-hard even if T is a set of acyclic [Apt and Bezem, 1990] propositional definite clauses [Selman and Levesque, 1990; Eiter and Gottlob, 1993], and is even harder if T is a set of any propositional clauses [Eiter and Gottlob, 1993]. These complexity results hold even if explanations are not required to be minimal. However, the abductive task is tractable for certain more restricted classes of logic programs (see for example [Eshghi, 1993]).

There are other formalisations of abduction. We mention them for completeness, but in the sequel we will concentrate on the logic-based view previously described.

- Allemand, Tanner, Bylander and Josephson [Allemand et al., 1991] and Reggia [Reggia, 1983] present a mathematical characterisation, where abduction is defined over sets of observations and hypotheses, in terms of coverings and parsimony.

- Levesque [Levesque, 1989] gives an account of abduction at the "knowledge level". He characterises abduction in terms of a (modal) logic of beliefs, and shows how the logic-based approach to abduction can be understood in terms of a particular kind of belief.

In the previous discussion we have briefly described both **semantics** and **proof procedures** for abduction. The relationship between semantics and proof procedures can be understood as a special case of the relationship between program specifications and programs. A program specification characterises what is the intended result expected from the execution of the program. In the same way semantics can be viewed as an abstract, possibly non-constructive definition of what is to be computed by the proof procedure. From this point of view, semantics is not so much concerned with explicating meaning in terms of truth and falsity, as it is with providing an abstract specification which "declaratively" expresses what we want to compute. This specification view of semantics is effectively the one adopted in most recent work on the semantics of LP, which restricts interpretations to Herbrand interpretations. The restriction to Herbrand interpretations means that interpretations are purely syntactic objects, which have no bearing on the correspondence between language and "reality". A purely syntactic view of semantics, based upon the notion of knowledge assimilation described in Section 2 below, is developed in [Kowalski, 1994].

One important alternative way to specify the semantics of a language, which will be used in the sequel, is through the **translation** of sentences expressed in one language into sentences of another language whose semantics is already well understood. For example if we have a sentence in a typed logic language of the form "there exists an object of type t such that the property p holds" we can translate this into a sentence of the form $\exists x \, (p(x) \wedge t(x))$, where t is a new predicate to represent the type t, whose semantics is then given by the familiar semantics of first-order logic. Similarly the typed logic sentence "for all objects of type t the property p holds" becomes the sentence $\forall x (p(x) \leftarrow t(x))$. Hence instead of developing a new semantics for the typed logic language, we apply the translation and use the existing semantics of first-order logic.

1.2   Integrity constraints

Abduction as presented so far can be restricted by the use of integrity constraints. Integrity constraints are useful to avoid unintended updates to a database or knowledge base. They can also be used to represent desired properties of a program [Lever, 1991].

The concept of integrity constraints first arose in the field of databases and to a lesser extent in the field of AI knowledge representation. The basic idea is that only certain knowledge base states are considered acceptable, and an integrity constraint is meant to enforce these legal states. When abduction is used to perform updates (see Section 2), we can use integrity constraints to reject abductive explanations.

Given a set of integrity constraints, I, of first-order closed formulae, the second condition (2) of the semantic definition of abduction (see Section 1.1) can be replaced by:

(2') $T \cup \Delta$ satisfies I.

As previously mentioned, we also restrict Δ to consist of atoms drawn from predicates explicitly indicated as abducible. Until the discussion in Section 5.7, we further restrict Δ to consist of **variable-free atomic sentences**.

In the sequel an **abductive framework** will be given as a triple $\langle T, A, I \rangle$, where T is a theory, A is the set of abducible predicates, i.e. $\Delta \subseteq A$ [2], and I is a set of integrity constraints.

There are several ways to define what it means for a knowledge base KB ($T \cup \Delta$ in our case) to satisfy an integrity constraint ϕ (in our framework $\phi \in I$). The **consistency view** requires that:

$$KB \text{ satisfies } \phi \text{ iff } KB \cup \phi \text{ is consistent.}$$

Alternatively the **theoremhood view** requires that:

$$KB \text{ satisfies } \phi \text{ iff } KB \models \phi.$$

These definitions have been proposed in the case where the theory is a logic program P by Kowalski and Sadri [Sadri and Kowalski, 1987] and Lloyd and Topor [Lloyd and Topor, 1985] respectively, where KB is the Clark completion [Clark, 1978] of P.

Another view of integrity constraints [Kakas, 1991; Kakas and Mancarella, 1990; Kowalski, 1990; Reiter, 1988; Reiter, 1990] regards these as **epistemic** or **metalevel** statements about the content of the database. In this case the integrity constraints are understood as statements at a different level from those in the knowledge base. They specify what must be true about the knowledge base rather than what is true about the world modelled by the knowledge base. When later we consider abduction in LP (see Sections 4,5), integrity satisfaction will be understood in a sense which is stronger than consistency, weaker than theoremhood, and arguably similar to the epistemic or metalevel view.

For each such semantics, we have a specification of the integrity checking problem. Although the different views of integrity satisfaction are conceptually very different, the integrity checking procedures based upon these views are not very different in practice (e.g. [Decker, 1986; Sadri and Kowalski, 1987; Lloyd and Topor, 1985]). They are mainly concerned with avoiding the inefficiency which arises if all the integrity constraints are retested after each update. A common idea of all these procedures is to render integrity checking more efficient by exploiting the assumption that the database before the update satisfies the integrity constraints, and therefore if integrity constraints are violated after the update, this violation should depend upon the update itself. In [Sadri and Kowalski, 1987]

---

[2]Here and in the rest of this paper we will use the same symbol A to indicate both the set of abducible predicates and the set of all their variable-free instances.

this assumption is exploited by reasoning forward from the updates. This idea is exploited for the purpose of checking the satisfaction of abductive hypotheses in [Eshghi and Kowalski, 1989; Kakas and Mancarella, 1990c; Kakas and Mancarella, 1990d]. Although this procedure was originally formulated for the consistency view of constraint satisfaction, it has proved equally appropriate for the semantics of integrity constraints in abductive logic programming.

1.3 Applications

In this section we briefly describe some of the applications of abduction in AI. In general, abduction is appropriate for reasoning with incomplete information. The generation of abducibles to solve a top-level goal can be viewed as the addition of new information to make incomplete information more complete.

Abduction can be used to generate causal explanations for **fault diagnosis** (see for example [Console *et al.*, 1989; Preist and Eshghi, 1992]). In medical diagnosis, for example, the candidate hypotheses are the possible causes (diseases), and the observations are the symptoms to be explained [Poole, 1988a; Reggia, 1983]. Abduction can also be used for model-based diagnosis [Eshghi, 1990; Reiter, 1987]. In this case the theory describes the "normal" behaviour of the system, and the task is to find a set of hypotheses of the form "some component A is not normal" that explains why the behaviour of the system is not normal.

Abduction can be used to perform **high level vision** [Cox and Pietrzykowski, 1992]. The hypotheses are the objects to be recognised, and the observations are partial descriptions of objects.

Abduction can be used in **natural language understanding** to interpret ambiguous sentences [Charniak and McDermott, 1985; Gabbay and Kempson, 1991; Hobbs, 1990; Stickel, 1988]. The abductive explanations correspond to the various possible interpretations of such sentences.

In **planning** problems, plans can be viewed as explanations of the given goal state to be reached [Eshghi, 1988; Shanahan, 1989].

These applications of abduction can all be understood as generating hypotheses which are causes for observations which are effects. An application that does not necessarily have a direct causal interpretation is **knowledge assimilation** [Kakas and Mancarella, 1990d; Kowalski, 1979; Kunifuji *et al.*, 1986; Miyaki *et al.*, 1984], described in greater detail below. The assimilation of a new datum can be performed by adding to the theory new hypotheses that are explanations for the datum. Knowledge assimilation can also be viewed as the general context within which abduction takes place. **Database view updates** [Bry, 1990; Kakas and Mancarella, 1990a; Console *et al.*, 1994] are an important special case of knowledge assimilation. Update requests are interpreted as observations to be explained. The explanations of the observations are transactions that satisfy the update request.

Another important application which can be understood in terms of a "non-causal" use of abduction is **default reasoning**. Default reasoning concerns the use of general rules to derive information in the absence of contradictions. In the application of abduction to default reasoning, conclusions are viewed as observations to be explained by means of assumptions which hold by default unless a contradiction can be shown [Eshghi and Kowalski, 1988; Poole, 1988]. As Poole [Poole, 1988] argues, the use of abduction avoids the need to develop a non-classical, non-monotonic logic for default reasoning. In Section 3 we will further discuss the use of abduction for default reasoning in greater detail. Because negation as failure in LP is a form of default reasoning, its interpretation by means of abduction will be discussed in section 4.

Some authors (e.g. Pearl [Pearl, 1988]) advocate the use of probability theory as an alternative approach to common sense reasoning in general, and to many of the applications listed above in particular. However, Poole [Poole, 1993] shows how abduction can be used to simulate (discrete) Bayesian networks in probability theory. He proposes the language of probabilistic Horn abduction: in this language an abductive framework is a triple $\langle T, A, I \rangle$, where T is a set of Horn clauses, A is a set of abducibles without definitions in T (without loss of generality, see Section 5), and I is a set of integrity constraints in the form of denials of abducibles only. In addition, for each integrity constraint, a probability value is assigned to each abducible, so that the sum of all the values of all the abducibles in each integrity constraint is 1. If the abductive framework satisfies certain assumptions, e.g. T is acyclic [Apt and Bezem, 1990], the bodies of all the clauses defining each non-abducible atom are mutually exclusive and these clauses are "covering", and abducibles in A are "probabilistically independent", then such a probabilistic Horn abduction theory can be mapped onto a (discrete) Bayesian network and vice versa.

2   Knowledge assimilation

Abduction takes place in the context of assimilating new knowledge (information, belief or data) into a theory (or knowledge base). There are four possible deductive relationships between the current knowledge base (KB), the new information, and the new KB which arises as a result [Kowalski, 1979; Kowalski, 1994].

1. The new information is already deducible from the current KB. The new KB, as a result, is identical with the current one.
2. The current KB = $KB_1 \cup KB_2$ can be decomposed into two parts. One part KB_1 together with the new information can be used to deduce the other part KB_2. The new KB is KB_1 together with the new information.

3. The new information violates the integrity of the current KB. Integrity can be restored by modifying or rejecting one or more of the assumptions which lead to the contradiction.

4. The new information is independent from the current KB. The new KB is obtained by adding the new information to the current KB.

In case (4) the KB can, alternatively, be augmented by an explanation for the new datum [Kakas and Mancarella, 1990d; Kowalski, 1979; Kunifuji *et al.*, 1986]. In [Kunifuji *et al.*, 1986] the authors have developed a system for knowledge assimilation (KA) based on this use of abduction. They have identified the basic issues associated with such a system and proposed solutions for some of these.

Various motivations can be given for the addition of an abductive explanation instead of the new datum in case (4) of the process of KA. For example, in natural language understanding or in diagnosis, the assimilation of information naturally demands an explanation. In other cases the addition of an explanation as a way of assimilating new data is forced by the particular way in which the knowledge is represented in the theory. This is the case, for instance, for the formulation of temporal reasoning in the Event Calculus [Kowalski and Sergot, 1986; Kowalski, 1992], as illustrated by the following example.

Example 2.0.1. The simplified version of the event calculus we consider contains an axiom that expresses the persistence of a property P from the time T_1 that it is initiated by an event E to a later time T_2:

$$
\begin{aligned}
holds\_at(P, T_2) \quad \leftarrow \quad & happens(E, T_1), \\
& T_1 < T_2, \\
& initiates(E, P), \\
& persists(T_1, P, T_2).
\end{aligned}
$$

New information that a property holds at a particular time point can be assimilated by adding an explanation in terms of the happening of some event that initiates this property at an earlier point of time together with an appropriate assumption that the property persists from one time to the other [Eshghi, 1988; Kakas and Mancarella, 1989; Shanahan, 1989; Van Belleghem *et al.*, 1994]. This has the additional effect that the new KB will imply that the property holds until it is terminated in the future by the happening of some event [Shanahan, 1989]. The fact that a property P cannot persist from a time T_1 to a later time T_2 if an event E happens at a time T between T_1 and T_2 such that E terminates P is expressed by the following integrity constraint:

$$\neg[persists(T_1, P, T_2) \wedge happens(E, T) \wedge terminates(E, P) \wedge T_1 < T < T_2].$$

Assimilating new information by adding explanations that satisfy the integrity constraints has the further effect of resolving conflicts between the current KB and the new information [Kakas and Mancarella, 1989; Shanahan, 1989]. For example, suppose that KB contains the facts [3]

$$happens(takes\_book(mary), t_0)$$
$$initiates(takes\_book(X), has\_book(X))$$
$$terminates(gives\_book(X, Y), has\_book(X))$$
$$initiates(gives\_book(X, Y), has\_book(Y))$$

Then, given $t_0 < t_1 < t_2$, the persistence axiom predicts $holds\_at(has\_book$ $(mary), t_1)$ by assuming $persists(t_0, has\_book(mary), t_1)$, and $holds\_at$ $(has\_book(mary), t_2)$ by assuming $persists(t_0, has\_book(mary), t_2)$. Both these assumptions are consistent with the integrity constraint. Suppose now that the new information $holds\_at(has\_book(john), t_2)$ is added to KB. This conflicts with the prediction $holds\_at(has\_book(mary), t_2)$. However, the new information can be assimilated by adding to KB the hypotheses $happens(gives\_book(mary, john), t_1)$ and $persists(t_1, has\_book(john), t_2)$ and by retracting the hypothesis $persists(t_0, has\_book(mary), t_2)$. Therefore, the earlier prediction $holds\_at(has\_book(mary), t_2)$ can no longer be derived from the new KB.

Note that in this example the hypothesis $happens(gives\_book(mary,$ $john), t_1)$ can be added to KB since it does not violate the further integrity constraint

$$\neg[happens(E, T) \wedge precondition(E, T, P) \wedge \sim holds\_at(P, T)]$$

expressing that an event E cannot happen at a time T if the preconditions P of E do not hold at time T. In this example, we may assume that KB also contains the fact

$$precondition(gives\_book(X, Y), has\_book(X)).$$

Once a hypothesis has been generated as an explanation for an external datum, it itself needs to be assimilated into the KB. In the simplest situation, the explanation is just added to the KB, i.e. only case (4) applies without further abduction. Case (1) doesn't apply, if abductive explanations are required to be basic. However case (2) may apply, and can be particularly useful for discriminating between alternative explanations for

---

[3]Note that here KB contains a definition for the abducible predicate $happens$. In Section 5 we will see that new predicates and clauses can be added to KB so that abducible predicates have no definitions in the transformed KB.

the new information. For instance we may prefer a set of hypotheses which entails information already in the KB, i.e. hypotheses that render the KB as "compact" as possible.

Example 2.0.2. Suppose the current KB contains

$$p \leftarrow q$$
$$p$$
$$r \leftarrow q$$
$$r \leftarrow s$$

and r is the new datum to be assimilated. The explanation $\{q\}$ is preferable to the explanation $\{s\}$, because q implies both r and p, but s only implies r. Namely, the explanation $\{q\}$ is more relevant.

Notice however that the use of case (2) to remove redundant information can cause problems later. If we need to retract previously inserted information, entailed information which is no longer explicitly in the KB might be lost.

It is interesting to note that case (3) can be used to check the integrity of abductive hypotheses generated in case (4).

Any violation of integrity detected in case (3) can be remedied in several ways [Kowalski, 1979]. The new input can be retracted as in conventional databases. Alternatively the new input can be upheld and some other assumptions can be withdrawn. This is the case with **view updates**. The task of translating the update request on the view predicates to an equivalent update on the extensional part (as in case (4) of KA) is achieved by finding an abductive explanation for the update in terms of variable-free instances of extensional predicates [Kakas and Mancarella, 1990a]. Any violation of integrity is dealt with by changing the extensional part of the database.

Example 2.0.3. Suppose the current KB consists of the clauses

$$sibling(X, Y) \leftarrow parent(Z, X), parent(Z, Y)$$
$$parent(X, Y) \leftarrow father(X, Y)$$
$$parent(X, Y) \leftarrow mother(X, Y)$$
$$father(john, mary)$$
$$mother(jane, mary)$$

together with the integrity constraints

$$X = Y \leftarrow father(X, Z), father(Y, Z)$$
$$X = Y \leftarrow mother(X, Z), mother(Y, Z)$$

$$X \neq Y \leftarrow mother(X, Z), father(Y, W)$$

where *sibling* and *parent* are view predicates, *father* and *mother* are extensional, and $=, \neq$ are "built-in" predicates such that

$X = X$ and

$s \neq t$ for all distinct variable-free terms s and t.

Suppose the view update

insert *sibling*(*mary*, *bob*)

is given. This can be translated into either of the two minimal updates

insert *father*(*john*, *bob*)

insert *mother*(*jane*, *bob*)

on the extensional part of the KB. Both of these updates satisfy the integrity constraints. However, only the first update satisfies the integrity constraints if we are given the further update

insert *mother*(*sue*, *bob*).

The general problem of belief revision has been studied formally in [Gärdenfors, 1988; Nebel, 1989; Nebel, 1991; Doyle, 1991]. Gärdenfors proposes a set of axioms for rational belief revision containing such constraints on the new theory as "no change should occur to the theory when trying to delete a fact that is not already present" and "the result of revision should not depend on the syntactic form of the new data". These axioms ensure that there is always a unique way of performing belief revision. However Doyle [Doyle, 1991] argues that, for applications in AI, this uniqueness property is too strong. He proposes instead the notion of "economic rationality", in which the revised sets of beliefs are optimal, but not necessarily unique, with respect to a set of preference criteria on the possible beliefs states. This notion has been used to study the evolution of databases by means of updates [Kakas, 1991a]. It should be noted that the use of abduction to perform belief revision in the view update case also allows results which are not unique, as illustrated in Example 2.0.3. Aravindan and Dung [Aravindan and Dung, 1994] have given an abductive characterisation of rational belief revision and have applied this result to formulate belief revision postulates for the view update problem.

A logic-based theory of the assimilation of new information has also been developed in the Relevance Theory of Sperber and Wilson [Sperber and Wilson, 1986] with special attention to natural language understanding. Gabbay, Kempson and Pitts [Gabbay *et al.*, 1994] have investigated how abductive reasoning and relevance theory can be integrated to choose between different abductive interpretations of a natural language discourse.

KA and belief revision are also related to truth maintenance systems. We will discuss truth maintenance and its relationship with abduction in Section 8.

3 Default reasoning viewed as abduction

Default reasoning concerns the application of general rules to draw conclusions provided the application of the rules does not result in contradictions. Given, for example, the general rules "birds fly" and "penguins are birds that do not fly" and the only fact about Tweety that Tweety is a bird, we can derive the default conclusion that Tweety flies. However, if we are now given the extra information that Tweety is a penguin, we can also conclude that Tweety does not fly. In ordinary, common sense reasoning, the rule that penguins do not fly has priority over the rule that birds fly, and consequently this new conclusion that Tweety does not fly causes the original conclusion to be withdrawn.

One of the most important formalisations of default reasoning is the default logic of Reiter [Reiter, 1980]. Reiter separates beliefs into two kinds, ordinary sentences used to express "facts" and default rules of inference used to express general rules. A **default rule** is an inference rule of the form

$$\frac{\alpha(X) : M\beta_1(X), \ldots, M\beta_n(X)}{\gamma(X)}$$

which expresses, for all variable-free instances t of X,[4] that $\gamma(t)$ can be derived if $\alpha(t)$ holds and each of $\beta_i(t)$ is consistent, where $\alpha(X)$, $\beta_i(X)$, $\gamma(X)$ are first-order formulae. Default rules provide a way of extending an underlying incomplete theory. Different applications of the defaults can yield different extensions.

As already mentioned in Section 1, Poole, Goebel and Aleliunas [Poole *et al.*, 1987] and Poole [Poole, 1988] propose an alternative formalisation of default reasoning in terms of abduction. Like Reiter, Poole also distinguishes two kinds of beliefs:

- beliefs that belong to a consistent set of first order sentences $\mathcal{F}$ representing "facts", and
- beliefs that belong to a set of first order formulae D representing defaults.

---

[4]We use the notation X to indicate a tuple of variables $X_1, \ldots, X_n$ and t to represent a tuple of terms $t_1, \ldots, t_n$.

Perhaps the most important difference between Poole's and Reiter's formalisations is that Poole uses sentences (and formulae) of classical first order logic to express defaults, while Reiter uses rules of inference. Given a Theorist framework $\langle \mathcal{F}, D \rangle$, default reasoning can be thought of as theory formation. A new theory is formed by extending the existing theory $\mathcal{F}$ with a set Δ of sentences which are variable-free instances of formulae in D. The new theory $\mathcal{F} \cup \Delta$ should be consistent. This process of theory formation is a form of abduction, where variable-free instances of defaults in D are the candidate abducibles. Poole [Poole, 1988] shows that the semantics of the theory formation framework $\langle \mathcal{F}, D \rangle$ is equivalent to that of an abductive framework $\langle \mathcal{F}', A, \emptyset \rangle$ (see Section 1.2) where the default formulae are all atomic. The set of abducibles A consists of a new predicate

$$p_w(x)$$

for each default formula

$$w(x)$$

in D with free variables x. The new predicate is said to "name" the default. The set $\mathcal{F}'$ is the set $\mathcal{F}$ augmented with a sentence

$$\forall X \, [p_w(X) \rightarrow w(X)]$$

for each default in D.

The theory formation framework and its correspondence with the abductive framework can be illustrated by the flying-birds example.

Example 3.0.1. In this case, the framework $\langle \mathcal{F}, D \rangle$ is [5]

$$
\begin{aligned}
\mathcal{F} \; = \{ \; & penguin(X) \rightarrow bird(X), \\
& penguin(X) \rightarrow \neg fly(X), \\
& penguin(tweety), \\
& bird(john) \} \\
D \; = \{ \; & bird(X) \rightarrow fly(X) \, \}.
\end{aligned}
\tag{3.1}
$$

The priority of the rule that penguins do not fly over the rule that birds fly is obtained by regarding the first rule as a fact and the second rule as a default. The atom $fly(john)$ is a default conclusion which holds in $\mathcal{F} \cup \Delta$ with

---

[5]Here, we use the conventional notation of first-order logic, rather than LP form. We use $\rightarrow$ for the usual implication symbol for first-order logic in contrast with $\leftarrow$ for LP. However, as in LP notation, variables occurring in formulae of $\mathcal{F}$ are assumed to be universally quantified. Formulae of D, on the other hand, should be understood as schemata standing for the set of all their variable-free instances.

$$\Delta = \{\, bird(john) \;\rightarrow\; fly(john) \,\}.$$

We obtain the same conclusion by naming the default (3.1) by means of a predicate $birds\text{-}fly(X)$, adding to $\mathcal{F}$ the new "fact"

$$birds\text{-}fly(X) \;\rightarrow\; [bird(X) \;\rightarrow\; fly(X)] \tag{3.2}$$

and extending the resulting augmented set of facts $\mathcal{F}'$ with the set of hypotheses

$$\Delta' = \{\, birds\text{-}fly(john) \,\}.$$

On the other hand, the conclusion $fly(tweety)$ cannot be derived, because the extension

$$\Delta = \{\, bird(tweety) \;\rightarrow\; fly(tweety) \,\}$$

is inconsistent with $\mathcal{F}$, and similarly the extension

$$\Delta' = \{\, birds\text{-}fly(tweety) \,\}$$

is inconsistent with $\mathcal{F}'$.

Poole shows that normal defaults without prerequisites in Reiter's default logic

$$\frac{:\,\mathrm{M}\beta(X)}{\beta(X)}$$

can be simulated by Theorist (abduction) simply by making the predicates $\beta(X)$ abducible. He shows that the default logic extensions in this case are equivalent to maximal sets of variable-free instances of the default formulae $\beta(X)$ that can consistently be added to the set of facts.

Maximality of abductive hypotheses is a natural requirement for default reasoning, because we want to apply defaults whenever possible. However, maximality is not appropriate for other uses of abductive reasoning. In particular, in diagnosis we are generally interested in explanations which are minimal. Later, in Section 5.1 we will distinguish between default and non-default abducibles in the context of abductive logic programming.

In the attempt to use abduction to simulate more general default rules, however, Poole needs to use integrity constraints. The new theory $\mathcal{F} \cup \Delta$ should be consistent with these constraints. Default rules of the form:

$$\frac{\alpha(X) :\, \mathrm{M}\beta_1(X), \ldots, \mathrm{M}\beta_n(X)}{\gamma(X)}$$

are translated into "facts", which are implications

$$\alpha(X) \wedge \mathrm{M}\beta_1(X) \wedge \ldots \wedge \mathrm{M}\beta_n(X) \;\rightarrow\; \gamma(X)$$

where M_{β_i} is a new predicate, and $M_{\beta_i}(X)$ is a default formula (abducible), for all $i = 1, \ldots, n$. Integrity constraints

$$\neg \beta_i(X) \rightarrow \neg M_{\beta_i}(X)$$

are needed to link the new predicates M_{β_i} appropriately with the predicates β_i, for all $i = 1, \ldots, n$. A further integrity constraint

$$\neg \gamma(X) \rightarrow \neg M_{\beta_i}(X),$$

for any $i = 1, \ldots, n$, is needed to prevent the application of the contrapositive

$$\neg \gamma(X) \wedge M_{\beta_1}(X) \wedge \ldots \wedge M_{\beta_n}(X) \rightarrow \neg \alpha(X)$$

of the implication, in the attempt to make the implication behave like an inference rule. This use of integrity constraints is different from their intended use in abductive frameworks as presented in Section 1.2.

Poole's attempted simulation of Reiter's general default rules is not exact. He presents a number of examples where the two formulations differ and argues that Reiter's default logic gives counterintuitive results. In fact, many of these examples can be dealt with correctly in certain extensions of default logic, such as cumulative default logic [Makinson, 1989], and it is possible to dispute some of the other examples. But, more importantly, there are still other examples where the Theorist approach arguably gives the wrong result. The most important of these is the now notorious Yale shooting problem of [Hanks and McDermott, 1986; Hanks and McDermott, 1987]. This can be reduced to the propositional logic program

 alive-after-load-wait-shoot ← alive-after-load-wait,
           ∼ abnormal-alive-shoot

 loaded-after-load-wait ← loaded-after-load,
          ∼ abnormal-loaded-wait
 abnormal-alive-shoot ← loaded-after-load-wait
 alive-after-load-wait
 loaded-after-load.

As argued in [Morris, 1988], these clauses can be simplified further: First, the facts *alive-after-load-wait* and *loaded-after-load* can be eliminated by resolving them against the corresponding conditions of the first two clauses, giving

 alive-after-load-wait-shoot ← ∼ abnormal-alive-shoot
 loaded-after-load-wait ← ∼ abnormal-loaded-wait
 abnormal-alive-shoot ← loaded-after-load-wait.

Then the atom *loaded-after-load-wait* can be resolved away from the second and third clauses leaving the two clauses

 alive-after-load-wait-shoot ← ∼ abnormal-alive-shoot

abnormal-alive-shoot ← ∼ *abnormal-loaded-wait.*

The resulting clauses have the form

$$p \leftarrow \sim q$$

$$q \leftarrow \sim r.$$

Hanks and McDermott showed, in effect, that the default theory, whose facts consist of

$$\neg q \rightarrow p$$

$$\neg r \rightarrow q$$

and whose defaults are the normal defaults

$$\frac{: M \neg q}{\neg q} \qquad \frac{: M \neg r}{\neg r}$$

has two extensions: one in which $\neg r$, and therefore q holds; and one in which $\neg q$, and therefore p holds. The second extension is intuitively incorrect under the intended interpretation. Hanks and Mc Dermott showed that many other approaches to default reasoning give similarly incorrect results. However, Morris [Morris, 1988] showed that the default theory which has no facts but contains the two non-normal defaults

$$\frac{: M \neg q}{p} \qquad \frac{: M \neg r}{q}$$

yields only one extension, containing q, which is the correct result. In contrast, all natural representations of the problem in Theorist give incorrect results.

As Eshghi and Kowalski [Eshghi and Kowalski, 1988], Evans [Evans, 1989] and Apt and Bezem [Apt and Bezem, 1990] observe, the Yale shooting problem has the form of a logic program, and interpreting negation in the problem as negation as failure yields only the correct result. This is the case for both the semantics and the proof theory of LP. Moreover, [Eshghi and Kowalski, 1988] and [Kakas and Mancarella, 1989] show how to retain the correct result when negation as failure is interpreted as a form of abduction.

On the other hand, the Theorist framework does overcome the problem that some default theories do not have extensions and hence cannot be given any meaning within Reiter's default logic. In the next section we will see that this problem also occurs in LP, but that it can also be overcome by an abductive treatment of negation as failure. We will also see that the resulting abductive interpretation of negation as failure allows us to regard LP as a hybrid which treats defaults as abducibles in Theorist but treats clauses as inference rules in default logic.

The inference rule interpretation of logic programs, makes LP extended with abduction especially suitable for default reasoning. Integrity constraints can be used, not for preventing application of contrapositives, but for representing negative information and exceptions to defaults.

Example 3.0.2. The default (3.1) in the flying-birds Example 3.0.1 can be represented by the logic program

$$fly(X) \leftarrow bird(X), birds\text{-}fly(X),$$

with the abducible predicate $birds\text{-}fly(X)$. Note that this clause is equivalent to the "fact" (3.2) obtained by renaming the default (3.1) in Theorist. The exception can be represented by an integrity constraint:

$$\neg fly(X) \leftarrow penguin(X).$$

The resulting logic program, extended by means of abduction and integrity constraints, gives similar results to the Theorist formulation of Example 3.0.1.

In Sections 4, 5 and 6 we will see other ways of performing default reasoning in LP. In Section 4 we will introduce negation as failure as a form of abductive reasoning. In Section 5 we will discuss abductive logic programming with default and non-default abducibles and domain-specific integrity constraints. In Section 6 we will consider an extended LP framework that contains clauses with negative conclusions and avoids the use of explicit integrity constraints in many cases. In Section 7 we will present an abstract argumentation-based framework for default reasoning which unifies the treatment of abduction, default logic, LP and several other approaches to default reasoning.

4   Negation as failure as abduction

We noted in the previous section that default reasoning can be performed by means of abduction in LP by explicitly introducing abducibles into rules. Default reasoning can also be performed with the use of negation as failure (NAF) [Clark, 1978] in general logic programs. NAF provides a natural and powerful mechanism for performing non-monotonic and default reasoning. As we have already mentioned, it provides a simple solution to the Yale shooting problem. The abductive interpretation of NAF that we will present below provides further evidence for the suitability of abduction for default reasoning.

To see how NAF can be used for default reasoning, we return to the flying-birds example.

Example 4.0.1. The NAF formulation differs from the logic program with abduction presented in the last section (Example 3.0.2) by employing a negative condition

$$\sim abnormal\text{-}bird(X)$$

instead of a positive abducible condition

$$birds\text{-}fly(X)$$

and by employing a positive conclusion

$$abnormal\text{-}bird(X)$$

in an ordinary program clause, instead of a negative conclusion

$$\neg\, fly(X)$$

in an integrity constraint. The two predicates *abnormal-bird* and *birds-fly* are opposite to one another. Thus in the NAF formulation the default is expressed by the clause

$$fly(X) \;\leftarrow\; bird(X),\, \sim abnormal\text{-}bird(X)$$

and the exception by the clause

$$abnormal\text{-}bird(X) \;\leftarrow\; penguin(X).$$

In this example, both the abductive formulation with an integrity constraint and the NAF formulation give the same result. We will see later in Section 5.5 that there exists a systematic transformation which replaces positive abducibles by NAF and integrity constraints by ordinary clauses. This example can be regarded as an instance of that transformation.

4.1   Logic programs as abductive frameworks

The similarity between abduction and NAF can be used to give an abductive interpretation of NAF. This interpretation was presented in [Eshghi and Kowalski, 1988] and [Eshghi and Kowalski, 1989], where negative literals are interpreted as abductive hypotheses that can be assumed to hold provided that, together with the program, they satisfy a canonical set of integrity constraints. A general logic program P is thereby transformed into an abductive framework $\langle P^*, A^*, I^* \rangle$ (see Section 1) in the following way.

- A new predicate symbol p^* (the opposite of p) is introduced for each p in P, and A^* is the set of all these predicates.

- P^* is P where each negative literal $\sim p(t)$ has been replaced by $p^*(t)$.
- I^* is a set of all integrity constraints of the form:[6]

$$\forall X \neg [p(X) \wedge p^*(X)] \text{ and}$$
$$\forall X [p(X) \vee p^*(X)].$$

The semantics of the abductive framework $\langle P^*, A^*, I^* \rangle$, in terms of **extensions** [7] $P^* \cup \Delta$ of P^*, where $\Delta \subseteq A^*$, gives a semantics for the original program P. A conclusion Q holds with respect to P if and only if the query Q^*, obtained by replacing each negative literal $\sim p(t)$ in Q by $p^*(t)$, has an abductive explanation in the framework $\langle P^*, A^*, I^* \rangle$. This transformation of P into $\langle P^*, A^*, I^* \rangle$ is an example of the method, described at the end of Section 1.1, of giving a semantics to a language by translating it into another language whose semantics is already known.

The integrity constraints in I^* play a crucial role in capturing the meaning of NAF. The denials express that the newly introduced symbols p^* are the negations of the corresponding p. They prevent an assumption $p^*(t)$ if $p(t)$ holds. On the other hand the disjunctive integrity constraints force a hypothesis $p^*(t)$ whenever $p(t)$ does not hold.

Hence we define the meaning of the integrity constraints I^* as follows: An extension $P^* \cup \Delta$ (which is a Horn theory) of P^* **satisfies** I^* if and only if for every variable-free atom p,

$$P^* \cup \Delta \not\models p \wedge p^*, \text{ and}$$
$$P^* \cup \Delta \models p \text{ or } P^* \cup \Delta \models p^*.$$

Eshghi and Kowalski [Eshghi and Kowalski, 1989] show that there is a one to one correspondence between stable models [Gelfond and Lifschitz, 1988] of P and abductive extensions of P^*. We recall the definition of stable model:

Let P be a general logic program, and assume that all the clauses in P are variable-free.[8] For any set M of variable-free atoms, let P_M be the Horn program obtained by deleting from P:

---

[6]In the original paper the disjunctive integrity constraints were written in the form

$$\text{Demo}(P^* \cup \Delta, p(t)) \vee \text{Demo}(P^* \cup \Delta, p^*(t)),$$

where t is any variable-free term. This formulation makes explicit a particular (meta-level) interpretation of the disjunctive integrity constraint. The simpler form

$$\forall X [p(X) \vee p^*(X)]$$

is neutral with respect to the interpretation of integrity constraints and allows the meta-level interpretation as a special case.

[7]This use of the term "extension" is different from other uses. For example, in default logic an extension is formally defined to be the deductive closure of a theory "extended" by means of the conclusions of default rules. In this paper we also use the term "extension" informally (as in Example 3.0.1) to refer to Δ alone.

[8]If P is not variable-free, then it is replaced by the set of all its variable-free instances.

i) each rule that contains a negative literal $\sim A$, with $A \in M$,

ii) all negative literals in the remaining rules.

If the minimal (Herbrand) model of P_M coincides with M, then M is a **stable model** for P.

The correspondence between the stable model semantics of a program P and abductive extensions of P^* is given by:

- For any stable model M of P, the extension $P^* \cup \Delta$ satisfies I^*, where $\Delta = \{p^* \mid p \text{ is a variable-free atom}, p \notin M\}$.

- For any Δ such that $P^* \cup \Delta$ satisfies I^*, there is a stable model M of P, where $M = \{p \mid p \text{ is a variable-free atom}, p^* \notin \Delta\}$.

Notice that the disjunctive integrity constraints in the abductive framework correspond to a totality requirement that every atom must be either true or false in the stable model semantics. Several authors have argued that this totality requirement is too strong, because it prevents us from giving a semantics to some programs, for example $p \leftarrow \sim p$. We would like to be able to assign a semantics to every program in order to have modularity, as otherwise one part of the program can affect the meaning of another unrelated part. We will see below that the disjunctive integrity constraint also causes problems for the implementation of the abductive framework for NAF.

Notice that the semantics of NAF in terms of abductive extensions is syntactic rather than model-theoretic. It is a semantics in the sense that it is a non-constructive specification. Similarly, the stable model semantics, as is clear from its correspondence with abductive extensions, is a semantics in the sense that it is a non-constructive specification of what should be computed. The computation itself is performed by means of a proof procedure.

4.2 An abductive proof procedure for LP

In addition to having a clear and simple semantics for abduction, it is also important to have an effective method for computing abductive explanations. Any such method will be very useful in practice in view of the many diverse applications of abductive reasoning, including default reasoning. The Theorist framework of [Poole, 1988; Poole *et al.*, 1987] provides such an implementation of abduction by means of a resolution based proof procedure.

In their study of NAF through abduction Eshghi and Kowalski [Eshghi and Kowalski, 1989] have defined an abductive proof procedure for NAF in logic programming. We will describe this procedure in some detail as it also serves as the basis for computing abductive explanations more generally within logic programming with other abducibles and integrity constraints (see Section 5). In this section we will refer to the version of the abductive proof procedure presented in [Dung, 1991].[9]

The abductive proof procedure interleaves two types of computation. The first type, referred to as the **abductive phase**, is standard SLD-resolution, which generates (negative) hypotheses and adds them to the set of abducibles being generated, while the second type, referred to as the **consistency phase**,[10] incrementally checks that the hypotheses satisfy the integrity constraints I^* for NAF. Integrity checking of a hypothesis $p^*(t)$ reasons forward one step using a denial integrity constraint to derive the new denial $\neg p(t)$, which is then interpreted as the goal $\leftarrow p(t)$. Thereafter it reasons backward in SLD-fashion in all possible ways. Integrity checking succeeds if all the branches of the resulting search space fail finitely, in other words, if the contrary of $p^*(t)$, namely $p(t)$, finitely fails to hold. Whenever the potential failure of a branch of the consistency phase search space is due to the failure of a selected abducible, say $q^*(s)$, a new abductive phase of SLD-resolution is triggered for the goal $\leftarrow q(s)$, to ensure that the disjunctive integrity constraint $q^*(s) \vee q(s)$ is not violated by the failure of both $q^*(s)$ and $q(s)$. This attempt to show $q(s)$ can require in turn the addition of further abductive assumptions to the set of hypotheses which is being generated.

To illustrate the procedure consider the following logic program, which is a minor elaboration of the propositional form of the Yale shooting problem discussed in Section 3.

Example 4.2.1.

$$
\begin{aligned}
s &\leftarrow \sim p \\
p &\leftarrow \sim q \\
q &\leftarrow \sim r.
\end{aligned}
$$

The query $\leftarrow s$ succeeds with answer $\Delta = \{p^*, r^*\}$. The computation is shown in Figure 1. Parts of the search space enclosed by a double box show the incremental integrity checking of the latest abducible added to the explanation Δ. For example, the outer double box shows the integrity check for the abducible p^*. For this we start from $\leftarrow p \equiv \neg p$ (resulting from the resolution of p^* with the integrity constraint $\neg (p \wedge p^*) \equiv \neg p \vee \neg p^*$) and resolve backwards in SLD-fashion to show that all branches end in failure, depicted here by a black box. During this consistency phase for p^* a new abductive phase (shown in the single box) is generated when q^* is selected since the disjunctive integrity constraint $q^* \vee q$ implies that failure of q^* is allowed only provided that q is provable. The SLD proof of q requires the

---

[9]As noticed by Dung [Dung, 1991], the procedure presented in [Eshghi and Kowalski, 1989] contains a mistake, which is not present, however, in the earlier unpublished version of the paper.

[10]We use the term "consistency phase" for historical reasons. However, in view of the precise definition of integrity constraint satisfaction, some other term might be more appropriate.

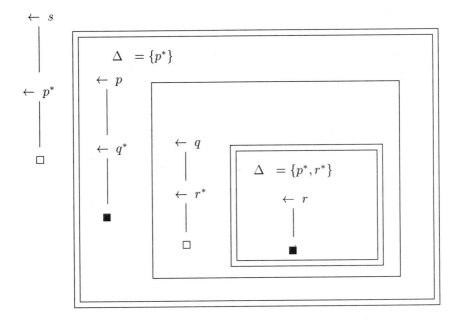

Fig. 1. Computation for Example 4.2.1

addition of r^* to Δ, which in turn generates a new consistency phase for r^* shown in the inner double box. The goal $\leftarrow r$ fails trivially because there are no rules for r and so r^* and the enlarged explanation $\Delta = \{p^*, r^*\}$ satisfy the integrity constraints. Tracing the computation backwards, we see that q holds, therefore q^* fails and, therefore p^* satisfies the integrity constraints and the original query $\leftarrow s$ succeeds.

In general, an abductive phase succeeds if and only if one of its branches ends in a white box (indicating that no subgoals remain to be solved). It fails finitely if and only if all branches end in a black box (indicating that some subgoal cannot be solved). A consistency phase fails if and only if one of its branches ends in a white box (indicating that integrity has been violated). It succeeds finitely if and only if all branches end in a black box (indicating that integrity has not been violated).

It is instructive to compare the computation space of the abductive proof procedure with that of SLDNF. It is easy to see that these are closely related. In particular, in both cases negative atoms need to be variable-free before they are selected. On the other hand, the two proof procedures have some important differences. A successful derivation of the abductive proof procedure will produce, together with the usual answer obtained from SLDNF, additional information, namely the abductive explanation Δ.

260 A. C. Kakas, R. A. Kowalski and F. Toni

This additional information can be useful in different ways, in particular to avoid recomputation of negative subgoals. More importantly, as the next example will show, this information will allow the procedure to handle non-stratified programs and queries for which SLDNF is incomplete. In this way the abductive proof procedure generalises SLDNF. Furthermore, the abductive explanation Δ produced by the procedure can be recorded and used in any subsequent revision of the beliefs held by the program, in a similar fashion to truth maintenance systems [Kakas and Mancarella, 1990d]. In fact, this abductive treatment of NAF allows us to identify a close connection between logic programming and truth maintenance systems in general (see Section 8). Another important difference is the distinction that the abductive proof procedure for NAF makes between the abductive and consistency phases. This allows a natural extension of the procedure to a more general framework where we have other hypotheses and integrity constraints in addition to those for NAF [Kakas and Mancarella, 1990a; Kakas and Mancarella, 1990b; Kakas and Mancarella, 1990c] (see Section 5.2).

To see how the abductive proof procedure extends SLDNF, consider the following program.

Example 4.2.2.

$$
\begin{aligned}
s &\leftarrow q \\
s &\leftarrow p \\
p &\leftarrow \sim q \\
q &\leftarrow \sim p.
\end{aligned}
$$

The last two clauses in this program give rise to a **two-step loop via NAF**, in the sense that p (and, similarly, q) "depends" negatively on itself through two applications of NAF. This causes the SLDNF proof procedure, executing the query $\leftarrow s$, to go into an infinite loop. Therefore, the query has no SLDNF refutation. However, in the corresponding abductive framework the query has two answers, $\Delta = \{p^*\}$ and $\Delta = \{q^*\}$, corresponding to the two stable models of the program. The computation for the first answer is shown in Figure 2. The outer abductive phase generates the hypothesis p^* and triggers the consistency phase for p^* shown in the double box. In general, whenever a hypothesis is tested for integrity, we can add the hypothesis to Δ either at the beginning or at the end of the consistency phase. When this addition is done at the beginning (as originally defined in [Eshghi and Kowalski, 1989]) this extra information can be used in any subordinate abductive phase. In this example, the hypothesis p^* is used in the subordinate abductive proof of q to justify the failure of q^* and consequently to render p^* acceptable. In other words, the acceptability of p^* as a hypothesis is proved under the assumption of p^*. The same abductive proof procedure, but where each new hypothesis is added to Δ only at

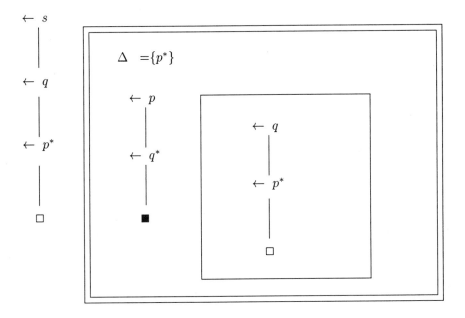

Fig. 2. Computation for Example 4.2.2

the successful completion of its consistency phase, provides a sound proof procedure for the well-founded semantics [Van Gelder *et al.*, 1988].

Example 4.2.3. Consider the query $\leftarrow p$ with respect to the abductive framework corresponding to the following program:

$$
\begin{aligned}
r &\leftarrow \sim r \\
r &\leftarrow q \\
p &\leftarrow \sim q \\
q &\leftarrow \sim p.
\end{aligned}
$$

Note that the first clause of this program give rise to a **one-step loop via NAF**, in the sense that r "depends" negatively on itself through one application of NAF. The abductive proof procedure succeeds with the explanation $\{q^*\}$, but the only set of hypotheses which satisfies the integrity constraints is $\{p^*\}$.

So, as Eshghi and Kowalski [Eshghi and Kowalski, 1989] show by means of this example, the abductive proof procedure is not always sound with respect to the above abductive semantics of NAF. In fact, following the result in [Dung, 1991], it can be proved that the proof procedure is sound for the class of order-consistent logic programs defined by Sato [Sato, 1990].

Intuitively, this is the class of programs which do not contain clauses giving rise to odd-step loops via NAF.

For the overall class of general logic programs, moreover, it is possible to argue that it is the semantics and not the proof procedure that is at fault. Indeed, Saccà and Zaniolo [Saccà and Zaniolo, 1990], Przymusinski [Przymusinski, 1990] and others have argued that the totality requirement of stable models is too strong. They relax this requirement and consider partial or three-valued stable models instead. In the context of the abductive semantics of NAF this is an argument against the disjunctive integrity constraints.

An abductive semantics of NAF without disjunctive integrity constraints has been proposed by Dung [Dung, 1991] (see Section 4.3 below). The abductive proof procedure is sound with respect to this improved semantics.

An alternative abductive semantics of NAF without disjunctive integrity constraints has been proposed by Brewka [Brewka, 1993], following ideas presented in [Konolige, 1992]. He suggests that the set which includes both accepted and refuted NAF hypotheses be maximised. For each such set of hypotheses, the logic program admits a "model" which is the union of the sets of accepted hypotheses together with the "complement" of the refuted hypotheses. For Example 4.2.3 the only "model" is $\{p^*, q, r\}$. Therefore, the abductive proof procedure is still unsound with respect to this semantics. Moreover, this semantics has other undesirable consequences. For example, the program

$$p \leftarrow\, \sim p, \sim q$$

admits both $\{\sim q\}$ and $\{\sim p\}$ as "models", while the only intuitively correct "model" is $\{\sim q\}$.

An alternative three-valued semantics for NAF has been proposed by Giordano, Martelli and Sapino [Giordano et al., 1993]. According to their semantics, given the program

$$p \leftarrow p$$

p and p^* are both undefined. In contrast, p^* holds in the semantics of [Dung, 1991], as well as in the stable model [Gelfond and Lifschitz, 1988] and well-founded semantics [Van Gelder et al., 1988]. Giordano, Martelli and Sapino [Giordano et al., 1993] modify the abductive proof procedure so that the modification is sound and complete with respect to their semantics.

Satoh and Iwayama [Satoh and Iwayama, 1992], on the other hand, show how to extend the abductive proof procedure of [Eshghi and Kowalski, 1989] to deal correctly with the stable model semantics. Their extension modifies the integrity checking method of [Sadri and Kowalski, 1987] and deals more generally with arbitrary integrity constraints expressed in the form of denials.

Casamayor and Decker [Casamayor and Decker, 1992] also develop an abductive proof procedure for NAF. Their proposal combines features of the Eshghi–Kowalski procedure with ancestor resolution.

Finally, we note that, to show that $\sim p$ holds for programs such as $p \leftarrow p$, it is possible to define a non-effective extension of the proof procedure that allows infinite failure in the consistency phases.

4.3   An argumentation-theoretic interpretation

Dung [Dung, 1991] replaces the disjunctive integrity constraints by a weaker requirement similar to the requirement that that the set of negative hypotheses Δ be a maximally consistent set. Unfortunately, simply replacing the disjunctive integrity constraints by maximality does not work, as shown in the following example.

Example 4.3.1.   With this change the program

$$p \leftarrow \sim q$$

has two maximally consistent extensions $\Delta_1 = \{p^*\}$ and $\Delta_2 = \{q^*\}$. However, only the second extension is computed both by SLDNF and by the abductive proof procedure. Moreover, for the same reason as in the case of the propositional Yale shooting problem discussed before, only the second extension is intuitively correct.

To avoid such problems Dung's notion of maximality is more subtle. He associates with every logic program P an abductive framework $\langle P^*, A^*, I^* \rangle$ where I^* contains only denials

$$\forall X \neg [p(X) \wedge p^*(X)]$$

as integrity constraints. Then, given sets Δ, E of (negative) hypotheses, i.e. $\Delta \subseteq A^*$ and $E \subseteq A^*$, E can be said to **attack** Δ (relative to $\langle P^*, A^*, I^* \rangle$) if $P^* \cup E \vdash p$ for some $p^* \in \Delta$. [11] Dung calls an extension $P^* \cup \Delta$ of P^* **preferred** if

- $P^* \cup \Delta$ is consistent with I^* and
- Δ is maximal with respect to the property that for every attack E against Δ, Δ attacks E (i.e. Δ "counterattacks" E or "defends" itself against E).

Thus a preferred extension can be thought of as a maximally consistent set of hypotheses that contains its own defence against all attacks. In [Dung, 1991] a consistent set of hypotheses Δ (not necessarily maximal) satisfying the property of containing its own defence against all attacks is said to be

---

[11] Alternatively, instead of the symbol $\vdash$ we could use the symbol $\models$, here and elsewhere in the paper where we define the notion of "attack".

admissible (to P^*). In fact, Dung's definition is not formulated explicitly in terms of the notions of attack and defence, but is equivalent to the one just presented.

Preferred extensions solve the problem with disjunctive integrity constraints in Example 4.2.3 and with maximal consistency semantics in Example 4.3.1. In Example 4.2.3 the preferred extension semantics sanctions the derivation of p by means of an abductive derivation with generated hypotheses $\{q^*\}$. In fact, Dung proves that the abductive proof procedure is sound with respect to the preferred extension semantics. In Example 4.3.1 the definition of preferred extension excludes the maximally consistent extension $\{p^*\}$, because there is no defence against the attack q^*.

The preferred extension semantics provides a unifying framework for various approaches to the semantics of negation in LP. Kakas and Mancarella [Kakas and Mancarella, 1993] show that it is equivalent to Saccà and Zaniolo's partial stable model semantics [Saccà and Zaniolo, 1990]. Like the partial stable model semantics, it includes the stable model semantics as a special case.

Dung [Dung, 1991] also defines the notion of **complete** extension. An extension $P^* \cup \Delta$ is complete if

- $P^* \cup \Delta$ is consistent with I^* and
- $\Delta = \{p^* \mid \text{for each attack } E \text{ against } \{p^*\}, \Delta \text{ attacks } E\}$
  (i.e. Δ is admissible and it contains all hypotheses it can defend against all attacks).

Stationary expansions [Przymusinski, 1991] are equivalent to complete extensions, as shown in [Brogi et al., 1992]. Moreover, Dung shows that the **well-founded model** [Van Gelder et al., 1988] is the smallest complete extension that can be constructed bottom-up from the empty set of negative hypotheses, by adding incrementally all admissible hypotheses. Thus the well-founded semantics is minimalist and sceptical, whereas the preferred extension semantics is maximalist and credulous. The relationship between these two semantics is further investigated in [Dung et al., 1992], where the well-founded model and preferred extensions are shown to correspond to the least fixed point and greatest fixed point, respectively, of the same operator.

Kakas and Mancarella [Kakas and Mancarella, 1991; Kakas and Mancarella, 1991a] propose an improvement of the preferred extension semantics. Their proposal can be illustrated by the following example.

Example 4.3.2. Consider the program

$$
\begin{aligned}
p &\leftarrow \; \sim q \\
q &\leftarrow \; \sim q.
\end{aligned}
$$

Similarly to Example 4.2.3, the last clause gives rise to a one-step loop via NAF, since q "depends" negatively on itself through one application of NAF. In the abductive framework corresponding to this program consider the set of hypotheses $\Delta = \{p^*\}$. The only attack against Δ is $E = \{q^*\}$, and the only attack against E is E itself. Thus Δ is not an admissible extension of the program according to the preferred extension semantics, because Δ cannot defend itself against E. The empty set is the only preferred extension. However, intuitively Δ should be "admissible" because the only attack E against Δ attacks itself, and therefore should not be regarded as an "admissible" attack against Δ.

To deal with this kind of example, Kakas and Mancarella [Kakas and Mancarella, 1991; Kakas and Mancarella, 1991a] modify Dung's semantics, increasing the number of ways in which an attack E can be defeated. Whereas Dung only allows Δ to defeat an attack E, they also allow E to defeat itself. They call a set of hypotheses Δ **weakly stable** if

- for every attack E against Δ, $E \cup \Delta$ attacks $E - \Delta$.

Moreover, they call an extension $P^* \cup \Delta$ of P^* a **stable theory** if Δ is maximally weakly stable. Note that here the condition "$P^* \cup \Delta$ is consistent with I^*" of the definition of preferred extensions and admissible sets of hypotheses is subsumed by the new condition. This is a consequence of another difference between [Kakas and Mancarella, 1991; Kakas and Mancarella, 1991a] and [Dung, 1991], namely that for each attack E against Δ the counter-attack is required to be against $E - \Delta$ rather than against E. In other words, the defence of Δ must be a genuine attack that does not at the same time also attack Δ. Therefore, if Δ is inconsistent, it contains as a subset an attack E, which can not be counterattacked because $E - \Delta$ is empty. In [Kakas and Mancarella, 1991a], Kakas and Mancarella show how these notions can also be used to extend the sceptical well-founded model semantics. In Example 4.3.2 above this extension of the well-founded model will contain the negation of p.

Like the original definition of admissible sets of hypotheses and preferred extension, the definition of weakly stable sets of hypotheses and stable theories was not originally formulated in terms of attack, but is equivalent to the one presented here.

Kakas and Mancarella [Kakas and Mancarella, 1991a] argue that the notion of defeating an attack needs to be liberalised further. They illustrate their argument with the following example.

Example 4.3.3. Consider the program P

$$
\begin{aligned}
s &\leftarrow \sim p \\
p &\leftarrow \sim q \\
q &\leftarrow \sim r \\
r &\leftarrow \sim p.
\end{aligned}
$$

The last three clauses give rise to a three-step loop via NAF, since p (and, similarly, q and r) "depends" negatively on itself through three applications of NAF. In the corresponding abductive framework, the only attack against the hypothesis s^* is $E = \{p^*\}$. But although $P^* \cup \{s^*\} \cup E$ does not attack E, E is not a valid attack because it is not stable (or admissible) according to the definition above.

To generalise the reasoning in this example so that it gives an intuitively correct semantics to any program with clauses giving rise to an odd-step loop via NAF, we need to liberalise further the conditions for defeating E. Kakas and Mancarella suggest a recursive definition in which a set of hypotheses is deemed acceptable if no attack against it is acceptable. More precisely, given an initial set of hypotheses Δ_0, a set of hypotheses Δ is **acceptable** to Δ_0 iff

for every attack E against $\Delta - \Delta_0$, E is not acceptable to $\Delta \cup \Delta_0$.

The semantics of a program P can be identified with any Δ which is maximally acceptable to the empty set of hypotheses $\emptyset$. As before with weak stability and stable theories, the consideration of attacks only against $\Delta - \Delta_0$ ensures that attacks and counterattacks are genuine, i.e. they attack the new part of Δ that does not contain Δ_0.

Notice that, as a special case, we obtain a basis for the definition:

Δ is acceptable to Δ_0 if $\Delta \subseteq \Delta_0$.

Therefore, if Δ is acceptable to $\emptyset$ then Δ is consistent.

Notice, too, that applying the recursive definition twice, and starting with the base case, we obtain an approximation to the recursive definition

Δ is acceptable to Δ_0 if for every attack E against $\Delta - \Delta_0$,
$E \cup \Delta \cup \Delta_0$ attacks $E - (\Delta \cup \Delta_0)$.

Thus, the stable theories are those which are maximally acceptable to $\emptyset$, where acceptability is defined by this approximation to the recursive definition.

A related argumentation-theoretic interpretation for the semantics of NAF in LP has also been developed by Geffner [Geffner, 1991]. This interpretation is equivalent to the well-founded semantics [Dung, 1993]. Based upon Geffner's notion of argumentation, Torres [Torres, 1993] has proposed an argumentation-theoretic semantics for NAF that is equivalent to Kakas and Mancarella's stable theory semantics [Kakas and Mancarella, 1991; Kakas and Mancarella, 1991a], but is formulated in terms of the following notion of attack: E attacks Δ (relative to P^*) if $P^* \cup E \cup \Delta \vdash p$ for some $p^* \in \Delta$.

Alferes and Pereira [Alferes and Pereira, 1994] apply the argumentation-theoretic interpretation introduced in [Kakas et al., 1993] to expand the well-founded model of normal and extended logic programs (see Section 5).

In the case of normal logic programming, their semantics gives the same result as the acceptability semantics in Example 4.3.3.

Simari and Loui [Simari and Loui, 1992] define an argumentation-theoretic framework for default reasoning in general. They combine a notion of acceptability with Poole's notion of "most specific" explanation [Poole, 1985], to deal with hierarchies of defaults.

In Section 7 we will present an abstract argumentation-theoretic framework which is based upon the framework for LP but unifies many other approaches to default reasoning.

4.4 An argumentation-theoretic interpretation of the abductive proof procedure

As mentioned above, the incorrectness (with respect to the stable model semantics) of the abductive proof procedure can be remedied by adopting the preferred extension, stable theory or acceptability semantics. This reinterpretation of the original abductive proof procedure in terms of an improved semantics, and the extension of the proof procedure to capture further improvements in the semantics, is an interesting example of the interaction that can arise between a program (proof procedure in this case) and its specification (semantics).

To illustrate the argumentation-theoretic interpretation of the proof procedure, consider again Figure 1 of Example 4.2.1. The consistency phase for p^*, shown in the outermost double box, can be understood as searching for any attack against $\{p^*\}$. The only attack, namely $\{q^*\}$, is counterattacked (thereby defending $\{p^*\}$) by assuming the additional hypothesis r^*, as this implies q. Hence the set $\Delta = \{p^*, r^*\}$ is admissible, i.e. it can defend itself against any attack, since all attacks against $\{p^*\}$ are counterattacked by $\{r^*\}$ and there are no attacks against $\{r^*\}$.

In general, the proof procedure constructs an admissible set of negative hypotheses in two steps. First, it constructs a set of hypotheses which is sufficient to solve the original goal. Then, it augments this set with the hypotheses necessary to defend the first set against attack.

The argumentation-theoretic interpretation suggests how to extend the proof procedure to capture more fully the stable theory semantics and more generally the semantics given by the recursive definition for acceptability. The extension, presented in [Toni and Kakas, 1995], involves temporarily remembering a (selected) attack E and using E itself together with the subset of Δ generated so far, to counterattack E, in the subordinate abductive phase.

For Example 4.3.2 of Section 4.3, as shown in Figure 3, to defend against the attack q^* on p^*, we need to temporarily remember q^* and use it in the subordinate abductive phase to prove q and therefore to attack q^* itself.

In the original abductive proof procedure of [Eshghi and Kowalski,

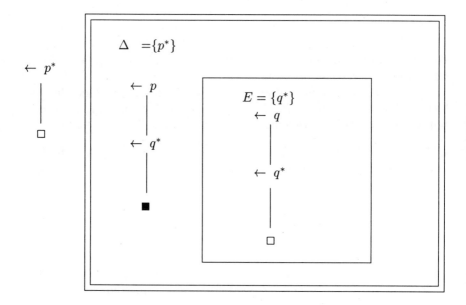

Fig. 3. Computation for Example 4.3.2 with respect to the revisited proof procedure

1989], hypotheses in defences are always added to Δ. However, in the proof procedure for the acceptability semantics defences D can not always be added to Δ, because even though D might be acceptable to Δ, $\Delta \cup D$ might not be acceptable to $\emptyset$. This situation arises for the three-step loop program of Example 4.3.3, where $D = \{q^*\}$ is used to defend $\Delta = \{s^*\}$ against the attack $E = \{p^*\}$, but $\Delta \cup D$ is not acceptable to $\emptyset$.

To cater for this characteristic of the acceptability semantics, the extended proof procedure non-deterministically considers two cases. For each hypothesis in a defence D against an attack E against Δ, the hypothesis either can be added to Δ or can be remembered temporarily to counterattack any attack E' against D, together with Δ and E. In general, a sequence of consecutive attacks and defences E, D, E', D', ... can be generated before an acceptable abductive explanation Δ is found, and the same non-deterministic consideration of cases is applied to D' and all successive defences in the sequence.

The definitions of admissible, stable and acceptable sets Δ of hypotheses all require that every attack against Δ be counterattacked. Although every superset of an attack is also an attack, the abductive proof procedure in [Eshghi and Kowalski, 1989] only considers those "minimal" attacks generated by SLD, [12] without examining superset attacks. This is possible because all supersets of an attack can be counterattacked in exactly the same way as the attack itself, which is generated by SLD. For this reason, the proof procedure of [Eshghi and Kowalski, 1989] is sound for the admissibility semantics. Unfortunately, supersets of attacks need to be considered to guarantee soundness of the proof procedure for the acceptability semantics. In [Toni and Kakas, 1995], however, Toni and Kakas prove that only certain supersets of "minimally generated" attacks need to be considered.

The additional features required for the proof procedure to capture more fully the acceptability semantics render the proof procedure considerably more complex and less efficient than proof procedures for simpler semantics. However, this extra complexity is due to the treatment of any odd-step loops via NAF and such programs seem to occur very rarely in practice. Therefore, in most cases it is sufficient to consider the approximation of the proof procedure which computes the preferred extension and stable theory semantics. This approximation improves upon the Eshghi-Kowalski proof procedure, since in the case of finite failure it terminates earlier, avoiding unnecessary computation.

5   Abductive logic programming

Abductive logic programming (ALP), as understood in the remainder of this paper, is the extension of LP to support abduction in general, and not only the use of abduction for NAF. This extension was introduced earlier in Section 1, as the special case of an abductive framework $\langle T, A, I \rangle$, where T is a logic program. In this paper we will assume, without loss of generality, that abducible predicates do not have definitions in T, i.e. do not appear in the heads of clauses in the program T.[13] This assumption has the advantage that all explanations are thereby guaranteed to be basic.

Semantics and proof procedures for ALP have been proposed by Eshghi and Kowalski [Eshghi and Kowalski, 1988], Kakas and Mancarella [Kakas and Mancarella, 1990] and Chen and Warren [Chen and Warren, 1989]. Chen and Warren extend the perfect model semantics of Przymusinski [Przymusinski, 1989] to include abducibles and integrity constraints over

---

[12]As illustrated in Section 1, these attacks are genuinely minimal unless the logic program encodes non-minimal explanations.

[13]In the case in which abducibile predicates have definitions in T, auxiliary predicates can be introduced in such a way that the resulting program has no definitions for the abducible predicates. This can be done by means of a transformation similar to the one used to separate extensional and intensional predicates in deductive databases [Minker, 1982]. For example, for each abducible predicate $a(X)$ in T we can introduce a new predicate $\delta_a(X)$ and add the clause

$$a(X) \leftarrow \delta_a(X).$$

The predicate $a(X)$ is no longer abducible, whereas $\delta_a(X)$ is now abducible.

abducibles. Here we shall concentrate on the proposal of Kakas and Mancarella, which extends the stable model semantics.

5.1 Generalised stable model semantics

Kakas and Mancarella [Kakas and Mancarella, 1990] develop a semantics for ALP by generalising the stable model semantics for LP. Let $\langle P, A, I \rangle$ be an abductive framework, where P is a general logic program, and let Δ be a subset of A. $M(\Delta)$ is a **generalised stable model** of $\langle P, A, I \rangle$ iff

- $M(\Delta)$ is a stable model of $P \cup \Delta$, and
- $M(\Delta) \models I$.

Here the semantics of the integrity constraints I is defined by the second condition in the definition above. Consequently, an abductive extension $P \cup \Delta$ of the program P **satisfies** I if and only if there exists a stable model $M(\Delta)$ of $P \cup \Delta$ such that I is true in $M(\Delta)$.

Note that in a similar manner, it is possible to generalise other model-theoretic semantics for logic programs, by considering only those models of $P \cup \Delta$ (of the appropriate kind, e.g. partial stable models, well-founded models etc.) in which the integrity constraints are all true.

Generalised stable models are defined independently from any query. However, given a query Q, we can define an abductive explanation for Q in $\langle P, A, I \rangle$ to be any subset Δ of A such that

- $M(\Delta)$ is a generalised stable model of $\langle P, A, I \rangle$, and
- $M(\Delta) \models Q$.

Example 5.1.1.   Consider the program P

$$p \leftarrow a$$
$$q \leftarrow b$$

with $A = \{a, b\}$ and integrity constraint I

$$p \leftarrow q.$$

The interpretations $M(\Delta_1) = \{a, p\}$ and $M(\Delta_2) = \{a, b, p, q\}$ are generalised stable models of $\langle P, A, I \rangle$. Consequently, both $\Delta_1 = \{a\}$ and $\Delta_2 = \{a, b\}$ are abductive explanations of p. On the other hand, the interpretation $\{b, q\}$, corresponding to the set of abducibles $\{b\}$, is not a generalised stable model of $\langle P, A, I \rangle$, because it is not a model of I as it does not contain p. Moreover, the interpretation $\{b, q, p\}$, although it is a model of $P \cup I$ and therefore satisfies I according to the consistency view of constraint satisfaction, is not a generalised stable model of $\langle P, A, I \rangle$, because it is not a stable model of P. This shows that the notion of integrity satisfaction for ALP is stronger than the consistency view. It is also possible to show that it is weaker than the theoremhood view and to argue that it is similar to the metalevel or epistemic view.

An alternative, and perhaps more fundamental way of understanding the generalised stable model semantics is by using abduction both for hypothetical reasoning and for NAF. The negative literals in $\langle P, A, I \rangle$ can be viewed as further abducibles according to the transformation described in Section 4. The set of abducible predicates then becomes $A \cup A^*$, where A^* is the set of negative abducibles introduced by the transformation. This results in a new abductive framework $\langle P^*, A \cup A^*, I \cup I^* \rangle$, where I^* is the set of special integrity constraints introduced by the transformation of Section 4.[14] The semantics of the abductive framework $\langle P^*, A \cup A^*, I \cup I^* \rangle$ can then be given by the sets Δ^* of hypotheses drawn from $A \cup A^*$ which satisfy the integrity constraints $I \cup I^*$.

Example 5.1.2.   Consider P

$$
\begin{aligned}
p &\leftarrow a, \sim q \\
q &\leftarrow b
\end{aligned}
$$

with $A = \{a, b\}$ and $I = \emptyset$. If Q is $\leftarrow p$ then $\Delta^* = \{a, q^*, b^*\}$ is an explanation for $Q^* = Q$ in $\langle P^*, A \cup A^*, I^* \rangle$. Note that b^* is in Δ^* because I^* contains the disjunctive integrity constraint $b \vee b^*$.

Kakas and Mancarella show a one to one correspondence between the generalised stable models of $\langle P, A, I \rangle$ and the sets of hypotheses Δ^* that satisfy the transformed framework $\langle P^*, A \cup A^*, I \cup I^* \rangle$. Moreover they show that for any abductive explanation Δ^* for a query Q in $\langle P^*, A \cup A^*, I \cup I^* \rangle$, $\Delta = \Delta^* \cap A$ is an abductive explanation for Q in $\langle P, A, I \rangle$.

Example 5.1.3.   Consider the framework $\langle P, A, I \rangle$ and the query Q of Example 5.1.2. We have already seen that $\Delta^* = \{a, q^*, b^*\}$ is an explanation for Q^* in $\langle P^*, A \cup A^*, I^* \rangle$. Accordingly the subset $\Delta = \{a\}$ is an explanation for Q in $\langle P, A, I \rangle$.

Note that the generalised stable model semantics as defined above requires that for each abducible a, either a or a^* holds. This can be relaxed by dropping the disjunctive integrity constraints $a \vee a^*$ and defining the set of abducible hypotheses A to include both a and a^*. Such a relaxation would be in the spirit of replacing stable model semantics by admissible or preferred extensions in the case of ordinary LP.

Generalised stable models combine the use of abduction for default reasoning (in the form of NAF) with the use of abduction for other forms of

---

[14]Note that the transformation described in Section 4 also needs to be applied to the set I of integrity constraints. For notational convenience, however, we continue to use the symbol I to represent the result of applying the transformation to I (otherwise we would need to use the symbol I^*, conflicting with the use of the symbol I^* for the special integrity constraints introduced in Section 4).

hypothetical reasoning. In the generalised stable model semantics, abduction for default reasoning is expressed solely by NAF. However, in the event calculus persistence axiom presented in Section 2 the predicate *persists* is a positive abducible that has a default nature. Therefore, instances of *persists* should be abduced unless some integrity constraint is violated. Indeed, in standard formulations of the persistence axiom the positive atom $persists(T_1, P, T_2)$ is replaced by a negative literal $\sim clipped(T_1, P, T_2)$ [Shanahan, 1989; Denecker and De Schreye, 1993]. In contrast, the abduction of *happens* is used for non-default hypothetical reasoning. The distinction between default reasoning and non-default abduction is also made in Konolige's proposal [Konolige, 1990], which combines abduction for non-default hypothetical reasoning with default logic [Reiter, 1980] for default reasoning. This proposal is similar, therefore, to the way in which generalised stable models combine abduction with NAF. Poole [Poole, 1989], on the other hand, proposes an abductive framework where abducibles can be specified either as default, like *persists*, or non-default, like *happens*. In [Toni and Kowalski, 1995], Toni and Kowalski show how both default and non-default abducibles can be reduced to NAF. This reduction is discussed in Section 5.5 below.

The knowledge representation problem in ALP is complicated by the need to decide whether information should be represented as part of the program, as an integrity constraint, or as an observation to be explained, as illustrated by the following example taken from [Baral and Gelfond, 1994].

Example 5.1.4.

$$fly(X) \leftarrow bird(X), \sim abnormal\_bird(X)$$
$$abnormal\_bird(X) \leftarrow penguin(X)$$
$$has\_beak(X) \leftarrow bird(X).$$

Suppose that *bird* is abducible and consider the three cases in which

$$fly(tweety)$$

is either added to the program, added to the integrity constraints, or considered as the observation to be explained. In the first case, the abducible *bird(tweety)* and, as a consequence, the atom *has_beak(tweety)* belong to some, but not all, generalised stable models. Instead, in the second case every generalised stable model contains *bird(tweety)* and *has_beak(tweety)*. In the last case, the observation is assimilated by adding the explanation {*bird(tweety)*} to the program, and therefore *has_beak(tweety)* is derived in the resulting generalised stable model. Thus, the last two alternatives have similar effects. Denecker and DeSchreye [Denecker and De Schreye, 1993] argue that the second alternative is especially appropriate for knowledge representation in the temporal reasoning domain.

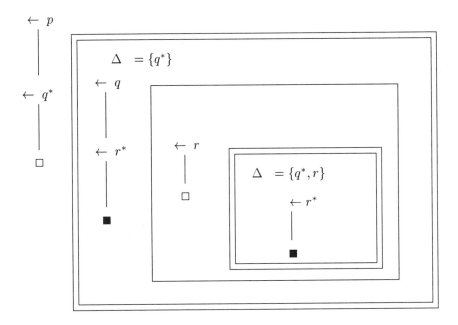

Fig. 4. Extended proof procedure for Example 5.2.1

5.2 An abductive proof procedure for ALP

In [Kakas and Mancarella, 1990a; Kakas and Mancarella, 1990b; Kakas and Mancarella, 1990c], a proof procedure is given to compute abductive explanations in ALP. This extends the abductive proof procedure for NAF [Eshghi and Kowalski, 1989] described in Section 4.2, retaining the basic structure which interleaves an abductive phase that generates and collects abductive hypotheses with a consistency phase that incrementally checks these hypotheses for integrity. We will illustrate these extended proof procedures by means of examples.

Example 5.2.1. Consider again Example 4.2.1. The abductive proof procedure for NAF fails on the query $\leftarrow p$. Ignoring, for the moment, the construction of the set Δ, the computation is that shown inside the outer double box of Figure 1 with the abductive and consistency phases interchanged, i.e. the type of each box changed from a double box to a single box and vice versa. Suppose now that we have the same program and query but in an ALP setting where the predicate r is abducible. The query will then succeed with the explanation $\Delta = \{q^*, r\}$ as shown in Figure 4. As before the computation arrives at a point where r needs to be proved. Whereas this failed before, this succeeds now by abducing r. Hence by adding the hypothesis r to the explanation we can ensure that

q^* is acceptable.

An important feature of the abductive proof procedures is that they avoid performing a full general-purpose integrity check (such as the forward reasoning procedure of [Kowalski and Sadri, 1988]). In the case of a negative hypothesis, q^* for example, a general-purpose forward reasoning integrity check would have to use rules in the program such as $p \leftarrow q^*$ to derive p. The optimised integrity check in the abductive proof procedure avoids this inference and only reasons forward one step with the integrity constraint $\neg (q \wedge q^*)$, deriving the resolvent $\leftarrow q$, and then reasoning backward from the resolvent.

Similarly, the integrity check for a positive hypothesis, r for example, avoids reasoning forward with any rules which might have r in the body. Indeed, in a case, such as Example 5.2.1 above, where there are no domain specific integrity constraints, the integrity check for a positive abducible, such as r, simply consists in checking that its complement, in our example r^*, does not belong to Δ.

To ensure that this optimised form of integrity check is correct, the proof procedure is extended to record those positive abducibles it needs to assume absent to show the integrity of other abducibles in Δ. So whenever a positive abducible, which is not in Δ, is selected in a branch of a consistency phase, the procedure fails on that branch and at the same time records that this abducible needs to be absent. This extension is illustrated by the following example.

Example 5.2.2.   Consider the program

$$
\begin{aligned}
p &\leftarrow \ \sim q, r \\
q &\leftarrow \ r
\end{aligned}
$$

where r is abducible and the query is $\leftarrow p$ (see Figure 5). The acceptability of q^* requires the absence of the abducible r. The simplest way to ensure this is by adding r^* to Δ. This, then, prevents the abduction of r and the computation fails. Notice that the proof procedure does not reason forward from r to test its integrity. This test has been performed backwards in the earlier consistency phase for q^*, and the addition of r^* to Δ ensures that it is not necessary to repeat it.

The way in which the absence of abducibles is recorded depends on how the negation of abducibles is interpreted. Under the stable and generalised stable model semantics, as we have assumed in Example 5.2.2 above, the required failure of a positive abducible is recorded by adding its complement to Δ. However, in general it is not always appropriate to assume that the absence of an abducible implies its negation. On the contrary, it may be appropriate to treat abducibles as open rather than closed (see Section 6.1), and correspondingly to treat the negation of abducible predicates as open.

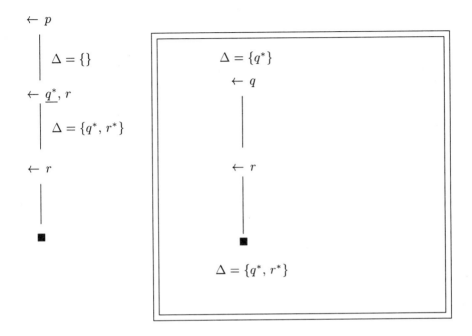

Fig. 5. Extended proof procedure for Example 5.2.2

As we shall argue later, this might be done by treating such a negation as a form of explicit negation, which is also abducible. In this case recording the absence of a positive abducible by adding its complement to Δ is too strong, and we will use a separate (purely computational) data structure to hold this information.

Integrity checking can also be optimised when there are domain specific integrity constraints, provided the constraints can be formulated as denials [15] containing at least one literal whose predicate is abducible. In this case the abductive proof procedure needs only a minor extension [Kakas and Mancarella, 1990b; Kakas and Mancarella, 1990c]: when a new hypothesis is added to Δ, the proof procedure resolves the hypothesis against any integrity constraint containing that hypothesis, and then reasons backward from the resolvent. To illustrate this extension consider the following example.

---

[15]Notice that any integrity constraint can be transformed into a denial (possibly with the introduction of new auxiliary predicates). For example:

$$p \leftarrow q \equiv \neg[q \wedge \neg p],$$
$$p \vee q \equiv \neg[\neg p \wedge \neg q].$$

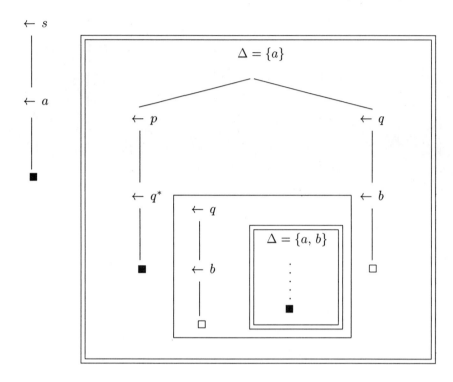

Fig. 6. Extended computation for Example 5.2.3

Example 5.2.3. Let the abductive framework be:

$$P: \quad s \leftarrow a \qquad\qquad I: \quad \neg[a \wedge p]$$
$$p \leftarrow\, \sim q \qquad\qquad\qquad \neg[a \wedge q]$$
$$q \leftarrow b$$

where a, b are abducible and the query is $\leftarrow s$ (see Figure 6).

Assume that the integrity check for a is performed Prolog-style, by re-solving first with the first integrity constraint and then with the second. The first integrity constraint requires the additional hypothesis b as shown in the innermost single box. The integrity check for b is trivial, as b appears only in the integrity constraint $\neg[b \wedge b^*]$ in I^*, and the goal $\leftarrow b^*$ trivially fails, given $\Delta = \{a, b\}$ (innermost double box). But $\Delta = \{a, b\}$ violates the integrity constraints, as can be seen by reasoning forward from b to q and then resolving with the second integrity constraint $\neg[a \wedge q]$. However, the proof procedure does not perform this forward reasoning and does not detect this violation of integrity at this stage. Nevertheless the proof procedure is sound because the violation is found later by backward reasoning when a is resolved with the second integrity constraint.

In summary, the overall effect of additional integrity constraints is to increase the size of the search space during the consistency phase, with no significant change to the basic structure of the backward reasoning procedure.

Even if the absence of abducibles is not identified with the presence of their complement, the abductive proof procedure [Kakas and Mancarella, 1990a; Kakas and Mancarella, 1990b; Kakas and Mancarella, 1990c] described above suffers from the same soundness problem shown in Section 4 for the abductive proof procedure for NAF. This problem can be solved similarly, by replacing stable models with any of the non-total semantics for NAF mentioned in Section 4 (partial stable models, preferred extensions, stable theories or acceptability semantics). Replacing the stable models semantics by any of these semantics requires that the notion of integrity satisfaction be revised appropriately. This is an interesting problem for future work.

The soundness problem can also be addressed by providing an argumentation-theoretic semantics for ALP which treats integrity constraints and NAF uniformly via an appropriately extended notion of attack. In Section 5.3 we will see that this alternative approach arises naturally from an argumentation-theoretic re-interpretation of the abductive proof procedure for ALP.

The proof procedure can be also modified to provide a sound computational mechanism for the generalised stable model semantics. This approach has been followed by Satoh and Iwayama [Satoh and Iwayama, 1991], as we illustrate in Section 5.4.

5.3 An argumentation-theoretic interpretation of the abductive proof procedure for ALP

Similarly to the LP case, the abductive proof procedure for ALP can be reinterpreted in argumentation-theoretic terms. For the ALP procedure, attacks can be provided as follows:

- via NAF:
  Relative to $\langle P^*, A \cup A^*, I \cup I^* \rangle$, E **attacks** Δ **via NAF** if
  E attacks Δ as in Section 4.3, i.e. $P^* \cup E \vdash p$ for some $p^* \in \Delta$,
  or
  a^* is in E, for some abducible a in Δ;
- via integrity constraints:
  Relative to $\langle P^*, A \cup A^*, I \cup I^* \rangle$, E **attacks** Δ **via an integrity constraint** $\neg(L_1 \wedge \ldots \wedge L_n)$ in I if $P^* \cup E \vdash L_1, \ldots, L_{i-1}, L_{i+1}, \ldots, L_n$, for some L_i in Δ. [16]

---

[16] Recall that the abductive proof procedure for ALP employs the restriction that each integrity constraint contains at least one literal with an abducible predicate.

To illustrate the argumentation-theoretic interpretation of the proof procedure for ALP, consider again Figure 6 of Example 5.2.3. The consistency phase for a, shown in the outer double box, can be understood as searching for attacks against $\{a\}$. There are two such attacks, $\{q^*\}$ and $\{b\}$, shown by the two branches in the figure. $\{q^*\}$ attacks $\{a\}$ via the integrity constraint $\neg(a \wedge p)$ in I, since q^* implies p. Analogously, $\{b\}$ attacks $\{a\}$ via the integrity constraint $\neg(a \wedge q)$ in I, since b implies q. The first attack $\{q^*\}$ is counterattacked by $\{b\}$, via NAF (as in Section 4.3), since this implies q. This is shown in the single box. The hypothesis b is added to Δ since the attack $\{b^*\}$ against $\{b\}$, via NAF, is trivially counterattacked by $\{b\}$, via NAF, as sketched in the inner double box. However, $\{b\}$ attacks $\{a\}$, as shown by the right branch in the outer double box. Therefore, Δ attacks itself, and this causes failure of the proof procedure.

The analysis of the proof procedure in terms of attacks and counterattacks suggests the following argumentation-theoretic semantics for ALP. A set of hypotheses Δ is **KM-admissible** if

- for every attack E against Δ,
  Δ attacks $(E - \Delta)$ via NAF alone.

In Section 6.5 we will see that the notion of KM-admissible set of hypotheses is similar to the notion of admissibility proposed by Dung [Dung, 1993b] for extended logic programming, in that only attacks via NAF are allowed to counterattack.

The argumentation-theoretic interpretation of ALP suggests several ways in which the semantics and proof procedure for ALP can be modified. Firstly, the notion of attack itself can be modified, e.g. following Torres' equivalent formulation of the stable theory semantics [Torres, 1993] (see Section 4.3). Secondly, the notion of admissibility can be changed to allow counterattacks via integrity constraints, as well as via NAF. Finally, as in the case of standard LP, the notion of admissibility can be replaced by other semantic notions such as weak stability and acceptability (see Section 4.3). The proof procedure for ALP can be modified appropriately to reflect each of these modifications. Such modifications of the semantics and the corresponding modifications of the proof procedure require further investigation.

Using the definition of well-founded semantics given in Section 4.3 (non-default) abducibles are always undefined, and consequently fulfill no function, in the well-founded semantics of ALP, as illustrated by the following example.

Example 5.3.1.   Consider the propositional abductive framework $\langle P, A, I \rangle$ where P is

$$p \leftarrow a$$

$A = \{a\}$, and $I = \emptyset$. The well-founded model of $\langle P, A, I \rangle$ is $\emptyset$.

In [Pereira *et al.*, 1991], Pereira, Aparicio and Alferes define an alternative, generalised well-founded semantics for ALP where first programs are extended by a set of abducibles as in the case of generalised stable models, and then the well-founded semantics (rather than stable model semantics) is applied to the extended programs. As a result, the well-founded models of an abductive framework are not unique. In the example above, $\emptyset$, $\{p^*, a^*\}$ and $\{p, a\}$ are the generalised well-founded models of $\langle P, A, I \rangle$. Note that in this application of the well-founded semantics, if an abducible is not in a set of hypotheses Δ then its negation does not necessarily belong to Δ. Thus the negation of an abducible is not interpreted as NAF. Moreover, since abducible predicates can be undefined some of the non-abducible predicates can also be undefined.

5.4 Computation of abduction through TMS

Satoh and Iwayama [Satoh and Iwayama, 1991] present a method for computing generalised stable models for logic programs with integrity constraints represented as denials. The method is a bottom-up computation based upon the TMS procedure of [Doyle, 1979]. Although the computation is not goal-directed, goals (or queries) can be represented as denials and be treated as integrity constraints.

Compared with other bottom-up procedures for computing generalised stable model semantics, which first generate stable models and then test the integrity constraints, the method of Satoh and Iwayama dynamically uses the integrity constraints during the process of generating the stable models, in order to prune the search space more efficiently.

Example 5.4.1. Consider the program P

$$
\begin{aligned}
p &\leftarrow q \\
r &\leftarrow \sim q \\
q &\leftarrow \sim r
\end{aligned}
$$

and the set of integrity constraints $I = \{\neg p\}$. P has two stable models $M_1 = \{p, q\}$ and $M_2 = \{r\}$, but only M_2 satisfies I. The proof procedure of [Satoh and Iwayama, 1991] deterministically computes only the intended model M_2, without first computing and then rejecting M_1.

In Section 8 we will see more generally that truth maintenance systems can be regarded as a form of ALP.

5.5 Simulation of abduction

Satoh and Iwayama [Satoh and Iwayama, 1991] also show that an abductive logic program can be transformed into a logic program without abducibles but where the integrity constraints remain. For each abducible predicate

p in A, a new predicate p' is introduced, which intuitively represents the complement of p, and a new pair of clauses [17]

$$p(X) \leftarrow \sim p'(X)$$
$$p'(X) \leftarrow \sim p(X)$$

is added to the program. In effect abductive assumptions of the form $p(t)$ are thereby transformed into NAF assumptions of the form $\sim p'(t)$. Satoh and Iwayama apply the generalised stable model semantics to the transformed program. However, the transformational semantics, which is effectively employed by Satoh and Iwayama, has the advantage that any semantics can be used for the resulting transformed program.

Example 5.5.1. Consider the abductive framework $\langle P, A, I \rangle$ of example 5.1.1. The transformation generates a new theory P' with the additional clauses

$$a \leftarrow \sim a'$$
$$a' \leftarrow \sim a$$
$$b \leftarrow \sim b'$$
$$b' \leftarrow \sim b.$$

P' has two generalised stable models that satisfy the integrity constraints, namely $M'_1 = M(\Delta_1) \cup \{b'\} = \{a, p, b'\}$, and $M'_2 = M(\Delta_2) = \{a, b, p, q\}$ where $M(\Delta_1)$ and $M(\Delta_2)$ are the generalised stable models seen in Example 5.1.1.

An alternative way of viewing abduction, which emphasises the defeasibility of abducibles, is **retractability** [Goebel *et al.*, 1986]. Instead of regarding abducibles as atoms to be consistently added to a theory, they can be considered as assertions in the theory to be retracted in the presence of contradictions until consistency (or integrity) is restored (c.f. Section 6.2).

One approach to this understanding of abduction is presented in [Kowalski and Sadri, 1988]. Here, Kowalski and Sadri present a transformation from a general logic program P with integrity constraints I, together with some indication of how to restore consistency, to a new general logic program P' without integrity constraints. Restoration of consistency is indicated by nominating one atom as retractable in each integrity constraint.[18] Integrity constraints are represented as denials, and the atom to be retracted must occur positively in the integrity constraint. The (informally specified) semantics is that whenever an integrity constraint of the form

$$\neg [p \wedge q]$$

---

[17]Satoh and Iwayama use the notation p^* instead of p' and explicitly consider only propositional programs.

[18]Many different atoms can be retractable in the same integrity constraint. Alternative ways of nominating retractable atoms correspond to alternative ways of restoring consistency in P.

has been violated, where the atom p has been nominated as retractable, then consistency should be restored by retracting the instance of the clause of the form

$$p \leftarrow r$$

which has been used to derive the inconsistency.

The transformation of [Kowalski and Sadri, 1988] replaces a program P with integrity constraints I by a program P' without integrity constraints which is always consistent with I; and if P is inconsistent with I, then P' represents one possible way to restore consistency (relative to the choice of the retractable atom).

Given an integrity constraint of the form

$$\neg [p \wedge q]$$

where p is retractable, the transformation replaces the integrity constraints and every clause of the form

$$p \leftarrow r$$

by

$$p \leftarrow r, \sim q$$

where the condition $\sim q$ may need to be transformed further, if necessary, into general logic program form, and where the transformation needs to be repeated for every integrity constraint. Kowalski and Sadri show that if P is a stratified program with appropriately stratified integrity constraints I, so that the transformed program P' is stratified, then P' computes the same consistent answers as P with I.

Notice that retracting abducible hypotheses is a special case where the abducibility of a predicate a is represented by an assertion

$$a(X).$$

The following example illustrates the behaviour of the transformation when applied to ALP.

Example 5.5.2. Consider the simplified version of the event calculus presented in example 2.0.1. If the integrity constraint

$$\neg [persists(T_1, P, T_2) \wedge happens(E, T) \wedge terminates(E, P) \wedge T_1 < T < T_2]$$

is violated, then it is natural to restore integrity by retracting the instance of $persists(T_1, P, T_2)$ that has led to the violation. Thus, $persists(T_1, P, T_2)$ is the retractible in this integrity constraint. By applying the transformation sketched above, the integrity constraint and the use of abduction can be replaced by the clauses obtained by further transforming

$$persists(T_1,\, P,\, T_2) \leftarrow\sim (happens(E,\, T), terminates(E,\, P), T_1 < T < T_2)$$

into general LP form.

One problem with the retractability semantics is that the equivalence of the original program with the transformed program was proved only in the case where the resulting transformed program is locally stratified. Moreover the proof of equivalence was based on a tedious comparison of search spaces for the two programs. This problem was addressed in a subsequent paper [Kowalski and Sadri, 1990] in which integrity constraints are re-expressed as extended clauses and the retractable atoms become explicitly negated conclusions. This use of extended clauses in place of integrity constraints with retractibles is discussed later in Section 6.3.

The transformation of [Kowalski and Sadri, 1988], applied to ALP, treats all abducibles as default abducibles. In particular, abducibles which do not occur as retractibles in integrity constraints are simply asserted in the transformed program P'. Therefore, this transformation can only be used to eliminate default abducibles together with their integrity constraints. A more complete transformation [Toni and Kowalski, 1995] can be obtained by combining the use of retractibles to eliminate integrity constraints with the transformation of [Satoh and Iwayama, 1991] for reducing non-default abducibles to NAF. The new transformation is defined for abductive frameworks where every integrity constraint has a retractible which is either an abducible or the NAF of an abducible.

As an example, consider the propositional abductive logic program $\langle P,\, A,\, I \rangle$ where P contains the clause

$$p \leftarrow a$$

a is in A, and I contains the integrity constraint

$$\neg[a \wedge q]$$

where a is retractible. If a is a default abducible, the transformation generates the logic program P'

$$p \leftarrow\sim a'$$
$$a' \leftarrow q$$
$$a \leftarrow\sim a'$$

where, as before, a' stands for the complement of a. The first clause in P' is obtained by replacing the positive condition a in the clause in P by the NAF literal $\sim a'$. The second clause replaces the integrity constraint in I. Note that this replaces "a should be retracted" if the integrity constraint $\neg[a \wedge q]$ is violated by "the complement a' of a should be asserted". Finally, the last clause in P' expresses the nature of a as a default abducible. Namely, a holds by default, unless some integrity constraint is violated. In this example, a holds if q does not hold.

If a is a non-default abducible, then the logic program P' obtained by transforming the same abductive program $\langle P, A, I \rangle$ also contains the fourth clause

$$a' \leftarrow\sim a$$

that, together with the third clause, expresses that neither a nor a' need hold, even if no integrity constraint is violated. Note that the last two clauses in P' are those used by Satoh and Iwayama [Satoh and Iwayama, 1991] to simulate non-default abduction by means of NAF.

Toni and Kowalski [Toni and Kowalski, 1995] prove that the transformation is correct and complete in the sense that there is a one-to-one correspondence between attacks in the framework $\langle P, A, I \rangle$ and in the framework corresponding to the transformed program P'. Thus, for any semantics that can be defined argumentation-theoretically there is a one-to-one correspondence between the semantics for an abductive logic program and the semantics of the transformed program. As a consequence, any proof procedure for LP which is correct for one of these semantics provides a correct proof procedure for ALP for the analogous semantics (and, less interestingly, vice versa).

In addition to the transformations from ALP to general LP, discussed above, transformations between ALP and disjunctive logic programming (DLP) have also been investigated. Inoue et al. [Inoue *et al.*, 1992a],[19] in particular, translate ALP clauses of the form

$$p \leftarrow q, a$$

where a is abducible, into DLP clauses

$$(p \wedge a) \vee a' \leftarrow q$$

where a' is a new atom that stands for the complement of a, as expressed by the integrity constraint

$$\neg (a \wedge a'). \tag{5.1}$$

A model generation theorem-prover (such as SATCHMO or MGTP [Fujita and Hasegawa, 1991]) can then be applied to compute all the minimal models that satisfy the integrity constraints (5.1). This transformation is related to a similar transformation [Inoue *et al.*, 1992] for eliminating NAF. Elsewhere [Sakama and Inoue, 1994], Sakama and Inoue demonstrate a

---

[19] A description of this work can also be found in [Hasegawa and Fujita, 1992].

one-to-one correspondence between generalised stable models for ALP and possible models [Sakama and Inoue, 1993] for DLP. Consider, for example, the abductive logic program $\langle P, A, I \rangle$ where P is

$$p \leftarrow a$$

$A = \{a\}$ and I is empty. $M_1 = \emptyset$ and $M_2 = \{a, p\}$ are the generalised stable models of $\langle P, A, I \rangle$. The program can be transformed into a disjunctive logic program P_D

$$p \leftarrow a$$
$$a \vee \epsilon.$$

P_D has possible models $M_1' = \{\epsilon\}$, $M_2' = \{a, p\}$ and $M_3' = \{\epsilon, a, p\}$, such that $M_1' - \{\epsilon\} = M_1$ and $M_2' - \{\epsilon\} = M_3' - \{\epsilon\} = M_2$.

Conversely, [Sakama and Inoue, 1994] shows how to transform DLP programs into ALP. For example, consider the disjunctive logic program P_D

$$a \vee b \leftarrow c$$
$$c$$

whose possible models are $M_1 = \{c, a\}$, $M_2 = \{c, b\}$ and $M_3 = \{c, a, b\}$. It can be transformed into an abductive logic program $\langle P, A, I \rangle$ where P consists of

$$a \leftarrow c, a'$$
$$b \leftarrow c, b'$$
$$c$$

a' and b' are new atoms, $A = \{a', b'\}$, and I consists of

$$\neg [c \wedge \sim a \wedge \sim b].$$

$\langle P, A, I \rangle$ has generalised stable models $M_1' = \{c, a, a'\}$, $M_2' = \{c, b, b'\}$ and $M_3' = \{c, a, a', b, b'\}$, such that, if HB is the Herbrand base of P_D, $M_i' \cap HB = M_i$, for each $i = 1, 2, 3$.

Whereas the transformation of [Sakama and Inoue, 1994] deals with inclusive disjunction, Dung [Dung, 1992] presents a simpler transformation that deals with exclusive disjunction, but works only for the case of acyclic programs. For example, the clause

$$p \vee q$$

can be replaced by the two clauses

$$p \leftarrow \sim q$$
$$q \leftarrow \sim p.$$

With this transformation, for acyclic programs, the Eshghi–Kowalski procedure presented in Section 4.2 is sound. For the more general case, Dung [Dung, 1992a] represents disjunction explicitly and extends the Eshghi-Kowalski procedure by using resolution-based techniques similar to those employed in [Finger and Genesereth, 1985].

5.6 Abduction through deduction from the completion

In the approaches presented so far, hypotheses are generated by backward reasoning with the clauses of logic programs used as inference rules. An alternative approach is presented by Console, Duprè and Torasso [Console *et al.*, 1991]. Here clauses of programs are interpreted as if-halves of if-and-only-if definitions that are obtained from the completion of the program [Clark, 1978] restricted to non-abducible predicates. Abductive hypotheses are generated deductively by replacing atoms by their definitions, starting from the observation to be explained.

Given a propositional logic program P with abducible predicates A without definitions in P, let P_C denote the completion of the non-abducible predicates in P. An **explanation formula** for an observation O is the most specific formula F such that

$$P_C \cup \{O\} \models F,$$

where F is formulated in terms of abducible predicates only, and F is **more specific** than F' iff $\models F \rightarrow F'$ and $\not\models F' \rightarrow F$.

Based on this specification, a proof procedure that generates explanation formulas is defined. This proof procedure replaces atoms by their definitions in P_C, starting from a given observation O. Termination and soundness of the proof procedure are ensured for hierarchical programs. The explanation formula resulting from the computation characterises all the different abductive explanations for O, as exemplified in the following example.

Example 5.6.1. Consider the following program P:

$$
\begin{array}{rcl}
wobbly\text{-}wheel & \leftarrow & broken\text{-}spokes \\
wobbly\text{-}wheel & \leftarrow & flat\text{-}tyre \\
flat\text{-}tyre & \leftarrow & punctured\text{-}tube \\
flat\text{-}tyre & \leftarrow & leaky\text{-}valve,
\end{array}
$$

where the predicates without definitions are considered to be abducible. The completion P_C is:

$$wobbly\text{-}wheel \leftrightarrow broken\text{-}spokes \lor flat\text{-}tyre$$
$$flat\text{-}tyre \leftrightarrow punctured\text{-}tube \lor leaky\text{-}valve.$$

If O is *wobbly-wheel* then the most specific explanation F is

$$broken\text{-}spokes \lor punctured\text{-}tube \lor leaky\text{-}valve,$$

corresponding to the abductive explanations

$$\Delta_1 = \{broken\text{-}spokes\},$$
$$\Delta_2 = \{punctured\text{-}tube\},$$
$$\Delta_3 = \{leaky\text{-}valve\}.$$

Console, Duprè and Torasso extend this approach to deal with propositional abductive logic programs with integrity constraints I in the form of denials of abducibles and of clauses expressing taxonomic relationships among abducibles. An explanation formula for an observation O is now defined to be the most specific formula F, formulated in terms of abducible predicates only, such that

$$P_C \cup I \cup \{O\} \models F.$$

The proof procedure is extended by using the denial and taxonomic integrity constraints to simplify F.

In the more general case of non-propositional abductive logic programs, the Clark equality theory CET [Clark, 1978], is used; the notion that F is more specific than F' requires that $F \rightarrow F'$ be a logical consequence of CET and that $F' \rightarrow F$ not be a consequence of CET. The explanation formula is unique up to equivalence with respect to CET. The proof procedure is extended to take into account the equality theory CET.

Denecker and De Schreye [Denecker and De Schreye, 1992a] compare the search space obtained by reasoning backward using the if-half of the if-and-only-if form of a definite program with that obtained by reasoning forward using the only-if half. They show an equivalence between the search space for SLD-resolution extended with abduction and the search space for model generation with SATCHMO [Manthey and Bry, 1988] augmented with term rewriting to simulate unification.

5.7   Abduction and constraint logic programming

ALP has many similarities with constraint logic programming (CLP). Recognition of these similarities has motivated a number of recent proposals to unify the two frameworks.

Both frameworks distinguish two kinds of predicates. The first kind is defined by ordinary LP clauses, and is eliminated during query evaluation. The second kind is "constrained" either by integrity constraints in the case of ALP or by means of a built-in semantic domain in the case of CLP. In both cases, an answer to a query is a "satisfiable" formula involving only the second kind of predicate.

Certain predicates, such as inequality, can be treated either as abducible or as constraint predicates. Treated as abducible, they are constrained by explicitly formulated integrity constraints such as

$$X < Z, Z < Y \to X < Y$$
$$\neg[X < Y \wedge Y < X].$$

Treated as constraint predicates, they are tested for satisfiability by using specialised algorithms which respect the semantics of the underlying domain. Constraints can also be simplified, replacing, for example,

$$2 < t \wedge 3 < t$$

by

$$3 < t.$$

Such simplification is less common in abductive frameworks.

A number of proposals have been made recently to unify the treatment of abducibles and constraints. Several of these, [Eshghi, 1988; Shanahan, 1989; Maim, 1992; Kakas and Michael, 1993] in particular, have investigated the implementation of specialised constraint satisfaction and simplification algorithms of CLP (specifically for inequality) by means of general-purpose integrity checking methods applied to domain-specific integrity constraints as in the case of ALP.

Kowalski [Kowalski, 1992a] proposes a general framework which attempts to unify ALP and CLP using if-and-only-if definitions for ordinary LP predicates and using integrity constraints for abducible and constraint predicates. Abduction is performed by means of deduction in the style of [Console *et al.*, 1991] (see Section 5.6). This framework has been developed further by Fung [Fung, 1993] and has been applied to job-shop scheduling by Toni [Toni, 1994]. A related proposal, to include user-defined constraint handling rules within a CLP framework, has been made by Frühwirth [Frühwirth, 1992].

Bürchert [Büchert, 1994] and Bürchert and Nutt [Büchert and Nutt, 1991], on the other hand, define a framework for general clausal resolution and show how abduction without integrity constraints can be treated as a special case of constrained resolution.

Another approach, which integrates both frameworks while preserving their identity, has been developed by Kakas and Michael [Kakas and Michael, 1995]. In this approach, the central notions of the two frameworks are combined, so that abduction and constraint handling cooperate to solve a common goal. Typically, the goal is reduced first by abduction to abducible hypotheses whose integrity checking reduces this further to a set of constraints to be satisfied in CLP.

Constructive abduction is the generation of non-ground abductive explanations, such as $\Delta = \{\exists X\, a(X)\}$. The integrity checking of such abducible hypotheses involves the introduction of equality assumptions, which can naturally be understood in CLP terms. A procedure for performing constructive abduction within a framework that treats equality as an abducible predicate and the Clark equality theory as a set of integrity constraint was first proposed by Eshghi [Eshghi, 1988]. Building upon this proposal, Kakas and Mancarella [Kakas and Mancarella, 1993a] extend the abductive proof procedure for LP in [Eshghi and Kowalski, 1989] (see Section 4.2) to combine constructive negation with constructive abduction in a uniform way, by reducing the former to the latter using the abductive interpretation of NAF.

The problem of constructive abduction has also been studied within the completion semantics. Denecker and De Schreye [1992b] define a proof procedure for constructive abduction, SLDNFA, which they show is sound and complete. Teusink [1993] extends Drabent's [1995] procedure, SLDNA, for constructive negation to perform constructive abduction and uses three-valued semantics to show soundness and completeness. In both proposals, [Denecker and De Schreye, 1992b] and [Teusink, 1993], integrity constraints are dealt with by means of a transformation, rather than explicitly.

6   Extended logic programming

Extended logic programming (ELP) extends general LP by allowing, in addition to NAF, a second, explicit form of negation. Explicit negation can be used, when the definition of a predicate is incomplete, to explicitly define negative instances of the predicate, instead of having them inferred implicitly using NAF.

Clauses with explicit negation in their conclusions can also serve a similar function to integrity constraints with retractibles. For example, the integrity constraint

$$\neg[persists(T_1, P, T_2) \wedge happens(E, T) \wedge terminates(E, P) \wedge T_1 < T < T_2]$$

with $persists(T_1, P, T_2)$ retractible can be reformulated as a clause with explicit negation in the conclusion

$\neg persists(T_1,\ P,\ T_2) \leftarrow happens(E,\ T), terminates(E,\ P), T_1 < T < T_2.$

6.1 Answer set semantics

In general logic programs, negative information is inferred by means of NAF. This is appropriate when the closed world assumption [Reiter, 1978], that the program gives a complete definition of the positive instances of a predicate, can safely be applied. It is not appropriate when the definition of a predicate is incomplete and therefore "open", as in the case of abducible predicates.

For open predicates it is possible to extend logic programs to allow **explicit negation** in the conclusions of clauses. In this section we will discuss the extension proposed by Gelfond and Lifschitz [Gelfond and Lifschitz, 1990]. This extension is based on the stable model semantics, and can be understood, therefore, in terms of abduction, as we have already seen.

Gelfond and Lifschitz define the notion of **extended logic programs**, consisting of clauses of the form:

$$L_0 \leftarrow L_1, \ldots, L_m, \sim L_{m+1}, \ldots, \sim L_n,$$

where $n \geq m \geq 0$ and each L_i is either an atom (A) or the explicit negation of an atom $(\neg A)$. This negation denoted by "$\neg$" is called "classical negation" in [Gelfond and Lifschitz, 1990]. However, as we will see below, because the contrapositives of extended clauses do not hold, the term "classical negation" can be regarded as inappropriate. For this reason we use the term "explicit negation" instead.

A similar notion has been investigated by Pearce and Wagner [Pearce and Wagner, 1991], who develop an extension of definite programs by means of Nelson's strong negation. They also suggest the possibility of combining strong negation with NAF. Akama [Akama, 1992] argues that the semantics of this combination of strong negation with NAF is equivalent to the answer set semantics for extended logic programs developed by Gelfond and Lifschitz.

The semantics of an extended program is given by its answer sets, which are like stable models but consist of both positive and (explicit) negative literals. Perhaps the easiest way to understand the semantics is to transform the extended program P into a general logic program P' without explicit negation, and to apply the stable model semantics to the resulting general logic program. The transformation consists in replacing every occurrence of explicit negation $\neg p(t)$ by a new (positive) atom $p'(t)$. The stable models of P' which do not contain a contradiction of the form $p(t)$ and $p'(t)$ correspond to the **consistent answer sets** of P. The corresponding answer sets of P contain explicit negative literals $\neg p(t)$ wherever the stable models contain $p'(t)$. In [Gelfond and Lifschitz, 1990] the answer sets are defined directly on the extended program by modifying the definition of the stable model semantics. The consistent answer sets of P also correspond to the generalised stable models (see Section 5.1) of P' with a set of integrity constraints $\forall X \neg [p(X) \wedge p'(X)]$, for every predicate p.

In the general case a stable model of P' might contain a contradiction of the form $p(t)$ and $p'(t)$. In this case the corresponding **inconsistent answer set** is defined to be the set of all the variable-free (positive and explicit negative) literals. It is in this sense that explicit negation can be said to be "classical". The same effect can be obtained by explicitly augmenting P' by the clauses

$$q(X) \leftarrow p(X), p'(X)$$

for all predicate symbols q and p in P'. Then the **answer sets** of P simply correspond to the stable models of the augmented set of clauses. If these clauses are not added, then the resulting treatment of explicit negation gives rise to a **paraconsistent** logic, i.e. one in which contradictions are tolerated.

Notice that, although Gelfond and Lifschitz define the answer set semantics directly without transforming the program and then applying the stable model semantics, the transformation can also be used with any other semantics for the resulting transformed program. Thus Przymusinski [Przymusinski, 1990] for example applies the well-founded semantics to extended logic programs. Similarly any other semantics can also be applied. As we have seen before, this is one of the main advantages of transformational semantics in general.

An important problem for the practical use of extended programs is how to distinguish whether a negative condition is to be interpreted as explicit negation or as NAF. This problem will be addressed in Sections 6.4 and 9.

6.2   Restoring consistency of answer sets

The answer sets of an extended program are not always consistent.

Example 6.2.1.   The extended logic program:

$$\neg fly(X) \leftarrow\sim bird(X)$$
$$fly(X) \leftarrow bat(X)$$
$$bat(tom)$$

has no consistent answer set.

As mentioned in Section 6.1, this problem can be dealt with by employing a paraconsistent semantics. Alternatively, in some cases it is possible to restore consistency by removing some of the NAF assumptions implicit in the answer set. In the example above we can restore consistency by rejecting the NAF assumption $\sim bird(tom)$ even though $bird(tom)$ does not hold. We then get the consistent set $\{bat(tom), fly(tom)\}$. This problem has been studied in [Dung and Ruamviboonsuk, 1991] and [Pereira *et al.*, 1991a]. Both of these studies are primarily concerned with the related problem of inconsistency of the well-founded semantics when applied to extended logic programs [Przymusinski, 1990].

To deal with the problem of inconsistency in extended logic programs, Dung and Ruamviboonsuk [Dung and Ruamviboonsuk, 1991] apply the preferred extension semantics to a new abductive framework derived from an extended logic program. An extended logic program P is first transformed into an ordinary general logic program P' by renaming explicitly negated literals $\neg p(t)$ by positive literals $p'(t)$. The resulting program is then further transformed into an abductive framework by renaming NAF literals $\sim q(t)$ by positive literals $q^*(t)$ and adding the integrity constraints

$$\forall X \neg [q(X) \wedge q^*(X)]$$

as described in Section 4.3. Thus if p' expresses the explicit negation of p the set A^* will contain p'^* as well as p^*. Moreover Dung includes in I^* additional integrity constraints of the form

$$\forall X \neg [p(X) \wedge p'(X)]$$

to prevent contradictions.

Extended preferred extensions are then defined by modifying the definition of preferred extensions in Section 4 for the resulting abductive framework with this new set I^* of integrity constraints. The new integrity constraints in I^* have the effect of removing a NAF hypothesis when it leads to a contradiction. Clearly, any other semantics for logic programs with integrity constraints could also be applied to this framework.

Pereira, Aparicio and Alferes [Pereira *et al.*, 1991a] employ a similar approach within the context of Przymuszynski's extended stable models [Przymusinski, 1990]. It consists in identifying explicitly all the possible sets of NAF hypotheses which lead to an inconsistency and then restoring consistency by removing at least one hypothesis from each such set. This method can be viewed as a form of belief revision, where if inconsistency can be attributed to an abducible hypothesis or a retractable atom (see Section 5.5), then we can reject the hypothesis to restore consistency. In fact Pereira, Aparicio and Alferes have also used this method to study counterfactual reasoning [Pereira *et al.*, 1991c]. Alferes and Pereira [Alferes and Pereira, 1993] have shown that this method of restoring consistency can also be viewed in terms of inconsistency avoidance.

This method [Pereira *et al.*, 1991a] is not able to restore consistency in all cases, as illustrated by the following example.

Example 6.2.2.
given the extended logic program

$$p \leftarrow q$$
$$q \leftarrow p$$
$$r \leftarrow \sim p$$
$$\neg r \leftarrow \sim p$$

the method of [Pereira *et al.*, 1991a] is unable to restore consistency by withdrawing the hypothesis p^*.

In [Pereira *et al.*, 1992] and [Pereira *et al.*, 1993], Pereira and Alferes present two different modifications of the method of [Pereira *et al.*, 1991a] to deal with this problem. For the program in Example 6.2.2, the method in [Pereira *et al.*, 1992] restores consistency by letting p undefined, while the method in [Pereira *et al.*, 1993] restores consistency by assigning p to truth. This second method is more suitable for diagnosis applications.

Both methods, [Dung and Ruamviboonsuk, 1991] and [Pereira *et al.*, 1991a; Pereira *et al.*, 1992; Pereira *et al.*, 1993], can deal only with inconsistencies that can be attributed to NAF hypotheses, as shown by the following example.

Example 6.2.3.   It is not possible to restore consistency by removing NAF hypotheses given the program:

$$p$$
$$\neg p.$$

However, Inoue [Inoue, 1994; Inoue, 1991] suggests a general method for restoring consistency, which is applicable to this case. This method (see also Section 6.3) is based on [Geffner, 1990] and [Poole, 1988] and consists in isolating inconsistencies by finding maximally consistent subprograms. In this approach a knowledge system is represented by a pair (P, H), where:

1. P and H are both extended logic programs,
2. P represents a set of facts,
3. H represents a set of assumptions.

The semantics is given using abduction as in [Poole, 1988] (see Section 3) by means of theory extensions $P \cup \Delta$ of P, with $\Delta \subseteq H$ maximal with respect to set inclusion, such that $P \cup \Delta$ has a consistent answer set.

In this approach, whenever the answer set of an extended logic program P is inconsistent, it is possible to restore consistency by regarding it as a knowledge system of the form

$$(\emptyset, P).$$

For Example 6.2.3 this will give two alternative semantics, $\{p\}$ or $\{\neg p\}$.

A similar approach to restoring consistency follows also from the work in [Kakas, 1992; Kakas *et al.*, 1994] (see Section 7), where argumentation-based semantics can be used to select acceptable (and hence consistent) subsets of an inconsistent extended logic program.

6.3 Rules and exceptions in LP

Another way of restoring consistency of answer sets is presented in [Kowalski and Sadri, 1990], where sentences with explicitly negated conclusions are given priority over sentences with positive conclusions. In this approach, extended clauses with negative conclusions are similar to integrity constraints with retractibles.

Example 6.3.1. Consider the program

$$fly(X) \leftarrow bird(X)$$
$$walk(X) \leftarrow ostrich(X)$$
$$bird(X) \leftarrow ostrich(X)$$
$$ostrich(john)$$

and the integrity constraint

$$\neg [fly(X) \wedge walk(X)],$$

with $fly(X)$ retractable. The integrity constraint is violated, because both $walk(john)$ and $fly(john)$ hold. Following the approach presented in Section 5.5, integrity can be restored by retracting the instance

$$fly(john) \leftarrow bird(john)$$

of the first clause in the program. Alternatively, the integrity constraint can be formulated as a clause with an explicit negative conclusion

$$\neg fly(X) \leftarrow walk(X).$$

In the new formulation it is natural to interpret clauses with negative conclusions as exceptions, and clauses with positive conclusions as default rules. In this example, the extended clause

$$\neg fly(X) \leftarrow walk(X)$$

can be interpreted as an exception to the "general" rule

$$fly(X) \leftarrow bird(X).$$

To capture the intention that exceptions should override general rules, Kowalski and Sadri [Kowalski and Sadri, 1990] modify the answer set semantics, so that instances of clauses with positive conclusions are retracted if they are contradicted by explicit negative information.

Kowalski and Sadri [Kowalski and Sadri, 1990] also present a transformation, which preserves the new semantics, and is arguably a more elegant form of the transformation presented in [Kowalski and Sadri, 1988] (see Section 5.5). In the case of the flying-birds example described above the new transformation gives the clause

$$fly(X) \leftarrow bird(X), \sim \neg fly(X).$$

This can be further transformed by "macroprocessing" the call to $\neg fly(X)$, giving the result of the original transformation in [Kowalski and Sadri, 1988]

$$fly(X) \leftarrow bird(X), \sim walk(X).$$

In general, the new transformation introduces a new condition

$$\sim \neg p(t)$$

into every clause with a positive conclusion $p(t)$. The condition is vacuous if there are no exceptions with $\neg p$ in the conclusion. The answer set semantics of the new program is equivalent to the modified answer set semantics of the original program, and both are consistent. Moreover, the transformed program can be further transformed into a general logic program by renaming explicit negations $\neg p$ by new positive predicates p'. Because of this renaming, positive and negative predicates can be handled symmetrically, and therefore, in effect, clauses with positive conclusions can represent exceptions to rules with (renamed) negative conclusions. Thus, for example, a negative rule such as

$$\neg fly(X) \leftarrow walk(X)$$

with a positive exception

$$fly(X) \leftarrow super\_ostrich(X)$$

can be transformed into a clause

$$\neg fly(X) \leftarrow walk(X), \sim fly(X)$$

and all occurrences of the negative literal $\neg fly(X)$ can be renamed by a new positive literal $fly'(X)$. This is not entirely adequate for a proper treatment of exceptions to exceptions. However, this approach can be extended, as we shall see in Section 6.6.

More direct approaches to the problem of treating positive and negative predicates symmetrically in default reasoning are presented in [Inoue, 1994; Inoue, 1991], following the methods of [Geffner, 1990] and [Poole, 1988] (see Section 6.2 for a discussion), and in [Kakas, 1992; Kakas *et al.*, 1994], based on an argumentation-theoretic framework (see Sections 6.4 and 7).

6.4 (Extended) Logic Programming without Negation as Failure

Kakas, Mancarella and Dung [Kakas *et al.*, 1994] show that the Kowalski–Sadri transformation presented in Section 6.3 can be applied in the reverse direction, to replace clauses with NAF by clauses with explicit negation together with a priority ordering between extended clauses. Thus, for example,

$$fly(X) \leftarrow bird(X), \sim walk(X)$$

can be transformed "back" to

$$fly(X) \leftarrow bird(X)$$
$$\neg fly(X) \leftarrow walk(X)$$

together with an ordering that indicates that the second clause has priority over the first. In general, the extended clauses

$$r : \ p \leftarrow q_1, \ldots, q_n$$
$$r_1 : \ \neg p \leftarrow s_1$$
$$\vdots$$
$$r_k : \ \neg p \leftarrow s_k$$

generated by transforming the clause

$$p \leftarrow q_1 \ldots q_n, \sim s_1, \ldots, \sim s_k$$

are ordered so that $r_j > r$ for $1 \leq j \leq k$. In [Kakas *et al.*, 1994], the resulting prioritised clauses are formulated in an ELP framework (with explicit negation) without NAF but with an ordering relation on the clauses of the given program.

This new framework for ELP is proposed in [Kakas *et al.*, 1994] as an example of a general theory of the acceptability semantics (see Section 4.3) developed within the argumentation-theoretic framework introduced in [Kakas *et al.*, 1993] (see Section 7). Its semantics is based upon an appropriate notion of attack between subtheories consisting of partially ordered extended clauses in a theory T. Informally, for any subsets E and Δ of T such that $E \cup \Delta$ have a contradictory consequence, E attacks Δ if and only if either E does not contain a clause which is lower than some clause in Δ or if E does contain such a clause, it also contains some clause which is higher than a clause in Δ. Thus, the priority ordering is used to break the symmetry between the incompatible sets E and Δ. Hence in the example above, if we have a bird that walks, then the subtheory which, in addition to these two facts, consists of the second clause

$$\neg fly(X) \leftarrow walk(X)$$

attacks the subtheory consisting of the clause

$$fly(X) \leftarrow bird(X)$$

and the same two facts, but not vice versa; so, the first subtheory is acceptable whereas the second one is not.

Kakas, Mancarella and Dung show that, with this notion of attack in the new framework with explicit negation but without NAF, it is possible to capture exactly the semantics of NAF in LP. This shows that, if LP is extended with explicit negation, then NAF can be simulated by introducing a priority ordering between clauses. Moreover, the new framework of ELP is more general than conventional ELP as it allows any ordering relation on the clauses of extended logic programs.

In the extended logic program which results from the transformation described above, if $\neg p$ holds then $\sim p$ holds in the corresponding general logic program, for any atom p. We can argue, therefore, that the transformed extended logic program satisfies the **coherence principle**, proposed by Pereira and Alferes [Pereira and Alferes, 1992], namely that whenever $\neg p$ holds then $\sim p$ must also hold. They consider the satisfaction of this principle to be a desirable property of any semantics for ELP, as illustrated by the following example, taken from [Alferes *et al.*, 1993].

Example 6.4.1. Given the extended logic program

$$\neg drivers\_strike$$
$$take\_bus \leftarrow \sim drivers\_strike$$

one should derive the conclusion *take_bus*.

The coherence principle automatically holds for the answer set semantics. Pereira and Alferes [Pereira and Alferes, 1992] and Alferes, Dung and Pereira [Alferes *et al.*, 1993] have defined new semantics for ELP that incorporates the coherence principle. These semantics are adaptations of

Przymusinski's extended stable model semantics [Przymusinski, 1990] and Dung's preferred extension semantics [Dung, 1991], respectively, to ELP. Alferes, Damasio and Pereira [Alferes *et al.*, 1994] provide a sound and complete proof procedure for the semantics in [Pereira and Alferes, 1992]. The proof procedure is implemented in Prolog by means of an appropriate transformation from ELP to general LP.

6.5 An argumentation-theoretic approach to ELP

The Dung and Ruamviboonsuk semantics for ELP [Dung and Ruamviboonsuk, 1991] in effect reduces ELP to ALP by renaming the explicit negation $\neg p$ of a predicate p to a new predicate p' and employing integrity constraints

$$\forall X \neg [p(X) \wedge p'(X)]$$

for all predicates p in the program. This reduction automatically provides us with an argumentation-theoretic interpretation of ELP, where attacks via these integrity constraints become **attacks via explicit negation**. Such notions of attack via explicit negation have been defined by Dung [Dung, 1993b] and Kakas, Mancarella and Dung [Kakas *et al.*, 1994]. Dung's notion can be formulated as follows: a set of NAF literals E [20] attacks another such set Δ via explicit negation (relative to a program P') [21] if

- $P' \cup E \cup \Delta \vdash p, p'$, for some atom p, and
  $P' \cup E \not\vdash p, p'$, and $P' \cup \Delta \not\vdash p, p'$, for all atoms p.

Kakas, Mancarella and Dung's notion can be formulated as follows: E attacks a non-empty set Δ via explicit negation (relative to a program P') if

- $P' \cup E \vdash l$ and $P' \cup \Delta \vdash \bar{l}$, for some literal l,

where $\bar{p} = p'$ and $\overline{p'} = p$.

Augmenting the notion of attack via NAF by either of these new notions of attack via explicit negation, we can define admissibility, weak stability and acceptability semantics similarly to the definitions in Section 4.3. However, the resulting semantics might give unwanted results, as illustrated by the following example given in [Dung, 1993b].

Example 6.5.1. Given the extended logic program

$$fly(X) \leftarrow bird(X), \sim ab\_bird(X)$$
$$\neg fly(X) \leftarrow penguin(X), \sim ab\_penguin(X)$$

---

[20]Note that, for simplicity, here we use NAF literals directly as hypotheses, without renaming them as positive atoms.

[21]P' stands for the extended logic program P where all explicitly negated literals of the form $\neg p(t)$ are rewritten as atoms $p'(t)$.

$$bird(X) \leftarrow penguin(X)$$
$$penguin(tweety)$$
$$ab\_bird(X) \leftarrow penguin(X), \sim ab\_penguin(X)$$

$\{ab\_penguin^*(tweety)\}$ attacks $\{ab\_bird^*(tweety)\}$ via NAF. However, $\{ab\_bird^*(tweety)\}$ attacks $\{ab\_penguin^*(tweety)\}$ via explicit negation (and vice versa). Therefore, $\{ab\_bird^*(tweety)\}$ counterattacks all attacks against it, and is admissible. As a consequence, $fly(tweety)$ holds in the extension given by $\{ab\_bird^*(tweety)\}$. However, intuitively $fly(tweety)$ should hold in no extension.

To cope with this problem, Dung [Dung, 1993b] suggests the following semantics, while keeping the definition of attack unchanged. A set of hypotheses is **D-admissible** if

- Δ does not attack itself, either via explicit negation or via NAF, and
- for every attack E against Δ, either via explicit negation or via NAF, Δ attacks E via NAF.

Note that, if ELP is seen as a special instance of ALP, then D-admissibility is very similar to KM-admissibility, presented in Section 5.3 for ALP, in that the two notions share the feature that counterattacks can only be provided by means of attacks via NAF.

It can be argued, however, that the problem in this example lies not so much with the semantics but with the representation itself. The last clause

$$ab\_bird(X) \leftarrow penguin(X), \sim ab\_penguin(X)$$

can be understood as attempting to assign a higher priority to the second clause of the program over the first. This can be done, without this last clause, explicitly in the ELP framework with priorities of [Kakas *et al.*, 1994] (Section 6.4) or in the rules and exceptions approach [Kowalski and Sadri, 1990] (Section 6.3).

An argumentation-theoretic interpretation for ELP has also been proposed by Bondarenko, Toni and Kowalski [Bondarenko *et al.*, 1993]. Their proposal, which requires that $P' \cup \Delta$ be consistent with the integrity constraints

$$\forall X \neg [p(X) \wedge p'(X)]$$

for each predicate p, instead of using a separate notion of attack via explicit negation, has certain undesirable consequences, as shown in [Alferes and Pereira, 1994]. For example, the program

$$p \leftarrow \sim p, \sim q$$

admits both $\{\sim q\}$ and $\{\sim p\}$ as admissible extensions, while the only intuitively correct extension is $\{\sim q\}$.

Alferes and Pereira [1994] use argumentation-theoretic notions to extend the well-founded semantics for ELP in [Pereira and Alferes, 1992]. Kakas, Mancarella and Dung [Kakas *et al.*, 1994] also define a well-founded semantics for ELP based upon argumentation-theoretic notions.

6.6 A methodology for default reasoning with explicit negation

Compared with other authors, who primarily focus on extending or modifying the semantics of LP to deal with default reasoning, Pereira, Aparicio and Alferes [Pereira *et al.*, 1991] develop a methodology for performing default reasoning with extended logic programs. Defaults of the form "normally if q then p" are represented by an extended clause

$$p \leftarrow q, \sim \neg nameqp, \sim \neg p \qquad (6.1)$$

where the condition *nameqp* can be understood as a name given to the default. The condition $\sim \neg p$ deals with exceptions to the conclusion of the rule, whilst the condition $\sim \neg nameqp$ deals with exceptions to the rule itself. An exception to the rule would be represented by an extended clause of the form

$$\neg nameqp \leftarrow r$$

where the condition r represents the conditions under which the exception holds. In the flying-birds example, the second clause of

$$fly(X) \leftarrow bird(X), \sim \neg birds\_fly, \sim \neg fly(X) \qquad (6.2)$$
$$\neg birds\_fly(X) \leftarrow penguin(X) \qquad (6.3)$$

expresses that the default named *birds_fly* does not apply for penguins.

The possibility of expressing both exceptions to rules as well as exceptions to predicates is useful for representing hierarchies of exceptions. Suppose we want to change (6.3) to the default rule "penguins usually don't fly". This can be done by replacing (6.3) by

$$\neg fly(X) \leftarrow penguin(X), \sim \neg penguins\_don't\_fly(X), \sim fly(X) \quad (6.4)$$

where *penguins_don't_fly* is the name assigned to the new rule. To give preference to the more specific default represented by (6.4) over the more general default (6.2), we add the additional clause

$$\neg birds\_fly(X) \leftarrow penguin(X), \sim \neg penguins\_don't\_fly(X).$$

Then to express that superpenguins fly, we can add the rule:

$$\neg penguins\_don't\_fly(X) \leftarrow superpenguin(X).$$

Pereira, Aparicio and Alferes [Pereira *et al.*, 1991] use the well-founded semantics extended with explicit negation to give a semantics for this methodology for default reasoning. However it is worth noting that any other semantics of extended logic programs could also be used. For example Inoue
[Inoue, 1994; Inoue, 1991] uses an extension of the answer set semantics
(see Section 6.2), but for a slightly different transformation.

6.7   ELP with abduction

Inoue [Inoue, 1991] (see also Section 6.3) and Pereira, Aparicio and Alferes
[Pereira *et al.*, 1991] investigate extended logic programs with abducibles
but without integrity constraints. They transform such programs into extended logic programs without abduction by adding a new pair of clauses

$$p(X) \leftarrow \sim \neg p(X)$$
$$\neg p(X) \leftarrow \sim p(X)$$

for each abducible predicate p. Notice that the transformation is identical to that of Satoh and Iwayama [Satoh and Iwayama, 1991] presented in
Section 5.5, except for the use of explicit negation instead of new predicates. Inoue [Inoue, 1991] and Pereira, Aparicio and Alferes [Pereira *et al.*,
1991] assign different semantics to the resulting program. Whereas Inoue
applies the answer set semantics, Pereira, Aparicio and Alferes apply the
extended stable model semantics of [Przymusinski, 1990]. Pereira, Aparicio
and Alferes [Pereira *et al.*, 1991b] have also developed proof procedures for
this semantics.

As mentioned above, Pereira, Aparicio and Alferes [Pereira *et al.*, 1991]
understand the transformed programs in terms of (three-valued) extended
stable models. This has the advantage that it gives a semantics to every
logic program and it does not force abducibles to be either believed or
disbelieved. But the advantage of the transformational approach, as we
have already remarked, is that the semantics of the transformed program
is independent of the transformation. Any semantics can be used for the
transformed program (including even a transformational one, e.g. replacing
explicitly negated atoms $\neg p(t)$ by a new atom $p'(t)$).

7   An abstract argumentation-based framework for default reasoning

Following the argumentation-theoretic interpretation of NAF introduced
in [Kakas *et al.*, 1993], Kakas [Kakas, 1992] generalised the interpretation
and showed how other logics for default reasoning can be based upon a
similar semantics. In particular, he showed how default logic can be understood in such terms and proposed a default reasoning framework based

on the argumentation-theoretic acceptability semantics (see Section 4.3) as an alternative to default logic.

Dung [Dung, 1993a] proposed an abstraction of the argumentation-theoretic interpretation of NAF introduced in [Kakas *et al.*, 1993], where arguments and the notion of one argument attacking another are treated as primitive concepts which can be superimposed upon any monotonic logic and can even be introduced into non-linguistic contexts. Stable, admissible, preferred, and well-founded semantics can all be defined in terms of sets of arguments that are able to attack or defend themselves against attack by other arguments. Dung shows that many problems from such different areas as AI, game theory and economics can be formulated and studied within this argumentation-theoretic framework.

Bondarenko, Toni and Kowalski [Bondarenko *et al.*, 1993] modified Dung's notion of an abstract argumentation-theoretic framework by defining an argument to be a monotonic derivation from a set of abductive assumptions. This new framework, like that of [Kakas, 1992], can be understood as a natural abstraction and extension of the Theorist framework in two respects. First, the underlying logic can be any monotonic logic and not just classical first-order logic. Second, the semantics of the non-monotonic extension can be formulated in terms of any argumentation-theoretic notion, and not just in terms of maximal consistency.

To give an idea of this framework, we show here how a simplified version of the framework can be used to define an abstract notion of stable semantics which includes as special cases stable models for logic programs, extensions for default logic [Reiter, 1980], autoepistemic logic [Moore, 1985] and non-monotonic logic II [McDermott, 1982]. We follow the approach of Bondarenko, Dung, Kowalski and Toni [Bondarenko *et al.*, 1997] (see also [Kakas, 1992]).

Let T be a set of sentences in any monotonic logic, $\vdash$ the provability operator for that logic and A a set of candidate abducible sentences. For any $\alpha \in A$, let $\overline{\alpha}$ be some sentence that represents the "contrary" of α. Then, a set of assumptions E is said to attack a set of assumptions Δ iff

- $T \cup E \vdash \overline{\alpha}$ for some $\alpha \in \Delta$.

Note that the notion of a sentence $\overline{\alpha}$ being the contrary of an assumption α can be regarded as a special case of the more general notion that α is retractible in an integrity constraint

$$\neg[\alpha \wedge \beta] \text{ (here } \beta \text{ is "a contrary" of } \alpha).$$

This more general notion is useful for capturing the semantics of ALP.

To cater for the semantics of LP, T is a general logic program, $\vdash$ is modus ponens and A is the set of all negative literals. The contrary of $\sim p$ is p.

For default logic, default rules are rewritten as sentences of the form

$$\gamma(x) \leftarrow \alpha(x) \wedge M\beta_1(x) \wedge \ldots \wedge M\beta_n(X)$$

(similarly to Poole's simulation of default logic, Section 3), where the underlying language is first-order logic augmented with a new symbol "M" which creates a sentence from a sentence not containing M, and with a new implication symbol $\leftarrow$ in addition to the usual implication symbol for first-order logic. The theory T is $\mathcal{F} \cup D$, where $\mathcal{F}$ is the set of "facts" and D is the set of defaults written as sentences. $\vdash$ is ordinary provability for classical logic augmented with modus ponens for the new implication symbol. (This is different from Poole's simulation, which treats $\leftarrow$ as ordinary implication.) The set A is the set of all sentences of the form $M\alpha$. The contrary of $M\alpha$ is $\neg\alpha$.

For autoepistemic logic, the theory T is any set of sentences written in modal logic. However, $\vdash$ is provability in classical (non-modal) logic. The set A is the set of all sentences of the form $\neg L\phi$ or $L\phi$. The contrary of $\neg L\phi$ is ϕ, whereas the contrary of $L\phi$ is $\neg L\phi$.

For non-monotonic logic II, T is any set of sentences of modal logic, as in the case of autoepistemic logic, but $\vdash$ is provability in modal logic (including the inference rule of necessitation, which derives $L\phi$ from ϕ). The set A is the set of all sentences of the form $\neg L\phi$. The contrary of $\neg L\phi$ is ϕ.

Given any theory T in any monotonic logic, candidate assumptions A and notion of the "contrary" of an assumption, a set of assumptions Δ is **stable** iff

- Δ does not attack itself and
- Δ attacks all $\{\alpha\}$ such that $\alpha \in A - \Delta$.

This notion of stability includes as special cases stable models in LP and extensions in default logic, autoepistemic logic and non-monotonic logic II.

Based upon this abductive interpretation of default logic, Satoh [Satoh, 1994] proposes a sound and complete proof procedure for default logic, by extending the proof procedure for ALP of [Satoh and Iwayama, 1992a].

At a similar level of abstraction, Kakas, Mancarella and Dung [Kakas *et al.*, 1994] also propose a general argumentation-theoretic framework based primarily on the acceptability semantics. As with LP, other semantics such as preferred extension and stable theory semantics can be obtained as approximations of the acceptability semantics. A sceptical form of semantics, analogous to the well-founded semantics for LP, is also given in [Kakas *et al.*, 1994], based on a strong form of acceptability.

Kakas, Mancarella and Dung define a notion of attack between conflicting sets of sentences, but these can be any subtheories of a given theory, rather than being subtheories drawn from a pre-assigned set of assumption sentences as in [Bondarenko *et al.*, 1993; Bondarenko *et al.*, 1997]. Also as in the special case of LP (see Section 4.3) this notion of attack together with the acceptability semantics ensures that defences are genuine counterattacks, i.e. that they do not at the same time attack the theory that we are trying to construct.

Because this framework does not separate the theory into facts and candidate assumptions, the attacking relation would be symmetric. To avoid this, a priority relation can be given on the sentences of the theory. As an example of this approach, Kakas, Mancarella and Dung propose a framework for ELP where programs are accompanied by a priority ordering on their clauses and show how in this framework NAF can be removed from the object-level language (see also Section 6.4). More generally, this approach provides a framework for default reasoning with priorities on sentences of a theory, viewed as default rules. It also provides a framework for restoring consistency in a theory T by using the acceptable subsets of T (see Sections 6.2 and 6.3).

Brewka and Konolige [Brewka and Konolige, 1993] also propose an abductive framework which unifies and provides new semantics for LP, autoepistemic logic and default logic, but does not use argumentation-theoretic notions. This semantics generalises the semantics for LP given in [Brewka, 1993].

8 Abduction and truth maintenance

In this section we will consider the relationship between truth maintenance (TM) and abduction. TM systems have historically been presented from a procedural point of view. However, we will be concerned primarily with the semantics of TM systems and the relationship to the semantics of abductive logic programming.

A TM system is part of an overall reasoning system which consists of two components: a domain dependent problem solver which performs inferences and a domain independent TM system which records these inferences. Inferences are communicated to the TM system by means of **justifications**, which in the simplest case can be written in the form

$$p \leftarrow p_1, \dots, p_n$$

expressing that the proposition p can be derived from the propositions $p_1, \dots, p_n$. Justifications include **premises**, in the case $n = 0$, representing propositions which hold in all contexts. Propositions can depend upon **assumptions** which vary from context to context.

TM systems can also record **nogoods**, which can be written in the form

$$\neg (p_1, \dots, p_n),$$

meaning that the propositions $p_1, \ldots, p_n$ are incompatible and therefore cannot hold together.

Given a set of justifications and nogoods, the task of a TM system is to determine which propositions can be derived on the basis of the justifications, without violating the nogoods.

For any such TM system there is a straightforward correspondence with abductive logic programs:

- justifications correspond to propositional Horn clause programs,
- nogoods correspond to propositional integrity constraints,
- assumptions correspond to abducible hypotheses, and
- contexts correspond to acceptable sets of hypotheses.

The semantics of a TM system can accordingly be understood in terms of the semantics of the corresponding propositional logic program with abducibles and integrity constraints.

The two most popular systems are the justification-based TM system (JTMS) of Doyle [Doyle, 1979] and the assumption-based TM system (ATMS) of deKleer [de Kleer, 1986].

8.1 Justification-based truth maintenance

A justification in a JTMS can be written in the form

$$p \leftarrow p_1, \ldots, p_n, \sim p_{n+1}, \ldots, \sim p_m,$$

expressing that p can be derived (i.e. is IN in the current set of beliefs) if $p_1, \ldots, p_n$ can be derived (are IN) and $p_{n+1}, \ldots, p_m$ cannot be derived (are OUT).

For each proposition occurring in a set of justifications, the JTMS determines an IN or OUT label, taking care to avoid circular arguments and thus ensuring that each proposition which is labelled IN has well-founded support. The JTMS incrementally revises beliefs when a justification is added or deleted.

The JTMS uses nogoods to record contradictions discovered by the problem solver and to perform **dependency-directed backtracking** to change assumptions in order to restore consistency. In the JTMS changing an assumption is done by changing an OUT label to IN.

Suppose, for example, that we are given the justifications

$$p \leftarrow \sim q$$
$$q \leftarrow \sim r$$

corresponding to the propositional form of the Yale shooting problem. As Morris [Morris, 1988] observes, these correctly determine that q is labelled IN and that r and p are labelled OUT. If the JTMS is subsequently informed that p is true, then dependency-directed backtracking will install a justification for r, changing its label from OUT to IN. Notice that this is similar to the behaviour of the extended abductive proof procedure described in Example 5.2.1, Section 5.2.

Several authors have observed that the JTMS can be given a semantics corresponding to the semantics of logic programs, by interpreting justifications as propositional logic program clauses, and interpreting $\sim p_i$ as NAF of p_i. The papers [Elkan, 1990; Giordano and Martelli, 1990; Kakas and Mancarella, 1990b; Pimentel and Cuadrado, 1989], in particular, show that a well-founded labelling for a JTMS corresponds to a stable model of the corresponding logic program. Several authors [Elkan, 1990; Fujiwara and Honiden, 1989; Kakas and Mancarella, 1990b; Reinfrank and Dessler, 1989], exploiting the interpretation of stable models as autoepistemic expansions [Gelfond and Lifschitz, 1988], have shown a correspondence between well-founded labellings and stable expansions of the set of justifications viewed as autoepistemic theories.

The JTMS can also be understood in terms of abduction using the abductive approach to the semantics of NAF, as shown in [Dung, 1991a; Giordano and Martelli, 1990; Kakas and Mancarella, 1990b]. This has the advantage that the nogoods of the JTMS can be interpreted as integrity constraints of the abductive framework. The correspondence between abduction and the JTMS is reinforced by [Satoh and Iwayama, 1991], which gives a proof procedure to compute generalised stable models using the JTMS (see Section 5.4).

8.2 Assumption-based truth maintenance

Justifications in ATMS have the more restricted Horn clause form

$$p \leftarrow p_1, \ldots, p_n.$$

However, whereas the JTMS maintains only one implicit context of assumptions at a time, the ATMS explicitly records with every proposition the different sets of assumptions which provide the foundations for its belief. In ATMS, assumptions are propositions that have been pre-specified as assumable. Each record of assumptions that supports a proposition p can also be expressed in Horn clause form

$$p \leftarrow a_1, \ldots, a_n$$

and can be computed from the justifications, as we illustrate in the following example.

Example 8.2.1. Suppose that the ATMS contains justifications

$$p \leftarrow a, b$$
$$p \leftarrow b, c, d$$
$$q \leftarrow a, c$$
$$q \leftarrow d, e$$

and the single nogood

$$\neg (a, b, e)$$

where a, b, c, d, e are assumptions. Given the new justification

$$r \leftarrow p, q$$

the ATMS computes explicit records of r's dependence on the assumptions:

$$r \leftarrow a, b, c$$
$$r \leftarrow b, c, d, e.$$

The dependence

$$r \leftarrow a, b, d, e.$$

is not recorded because its assumptions violate the nogood. The dependence

$$r \leftarrow a, b, c, d$$

is not recorded because it is subsumed by the dependence

$$r \leftarrow a, b, c.$$

Reiter and deKleer [Reiter and De Kleer, 1987] show that, given a set of justifications, nogoods, and candidate assumptions, the ATMS can be understood as computing minimal and consistent abductive explanations in the propositional case (where assumptions are interpreted as abductive hypotheses). This abductive interpretation of ATMS has been developed further by Inoue [Inoue, 1990], who gives an abductive proof procedure for the ATMS.

Given an abductive logic program P and goal G, the explicit construction in ALP of a set of hypotheses Δ, which together with P implies G and together with P satisfies any integrity constraints I, is similar to the record

$$G \leftarrow \Delta$$

computed by the ATMS. There are, however, some obvious differences. Whereas ATMS deals only with propositional justifications, relying on a separate problem solver to instantiate variables, ALP deals with general clauses, combining the functionalities of both a problem solver and a TM system.

The extension of the ATMS to the non-propositional case requires a new notion of minimality of sets of assumptions. Minimality as subset inclusion is not sufficient, but needs to be replaced by a notion of minimal consequence from sets of not necessarily variable-free assumptions [Lamma and Mello, 1992].

Ignoring the propositional nature of a TM system, ALP can be regarded as a hybrid of JTMS and ATMS, combining the non-monotonic negative assumptions of JTMS and the positive assumptions of ATMS, and allowing both positive and negative conditions in both justifications and nogoods [Kakas and Mancarella, 1990b]. Other non-monotonic extensions of ATMS have been developed in [Junker, 1989; Rodi and Pimentel, 1991].

It should be noted that one difference between ATMS and ALP is the requirement in ATMS that only minimal sets of assumptions be recorded. This minimality of assumptions is essential for the computational efficiency of the ATMS. However, it is not essential for ALP, but can be imposed as an additional requirement when it is needed.

9   Conclusions and future work

In this paper we have surveyed a number of proposals for extending LP to perform abductive reasoning. We have seen that such extensions are closely linked with other extensions including NAF, integrity constraints, explicit negation, default reasoning, belief revision and argumentation.

Perhaps the most important link, from the perspective of LP, is that between default abduction and NAF. On the one hand, we have seen that default abduction generalises NAF, to include not only negative but also positive hypotheses, and to include general integrity constraints. On the other hand, we have seen that logic programs with abduction and integrity constraints can be transformed into logic programs with NAF without integrity constraints. We have also seen that, in the context of ELP with explicit negation, NAF can be replaced by a priority ordering between clauses. The link between abduction and NAF includes both their semantics and their implementations.

The use of default abduction for NAF is a special case of abduction in general. The distinction between default and non-default abduction has been clarified. Semantics, proof procedures and transformations that respect this distinction have all been defined. However, more work is needed to study the integration of these two kinds of abduction in a common framework. The argumentation-based approach seems to offer a promising framework for such an integration.

We have seen the importance of clarifying the semantics of abduction and of defining a semantics that helps to unify the different forms of abduction, NAF, and default reasoning within a common framework. We have seen, in particular, that a proof procedure which is incorrect under one semantics (e.g. [Eshghi and Kowalski, 1989]) can be correct under another improved semantics (e.g. [Dung, 1991]). We have also introduced an argumentation-theoretic interpretation for the semantics of abduction applied to NAF, and we have seen that this interpretation can help to understand the relationships between different semantics.

The argumentation-theoretic interpretation of NAF has been abstracted and shown to unify and simplify the semantics of such different formalisms for default reasoning as default logic, autoepistemic logic and non-monotonic logic. In each case the standard semantics of these formalisms has been shown to be a special instance of a single abstract notion that a set of assumptions is a (stable) semantics if it does not attack itself but does attack all other assumptions it does not contain. The stable model semantics, generalised stable model semantics and answer set semantics are other special cases. We have seen that stable model semantics and its extensions have deficiencies which are avoided with admissibility, preferred extension, complete scenaria, weak stability, stable theory and acceptability semantics. Because these more refined semantics for LP can be defined abstractly for any argumentation-based framework, they automatically and uniformly provide improvements for the semantics of other formalisms for default reasoning.

Despite the many advances in the application of abduction to LP and to non-monotonic reasoning more generally, there is still much scope for further development. Important problems in semantics still need to be resolved. These include the problem of clarifying the role of integrity constraints in providing attacks and counterattacks in ALP.

The further development, clarification and simplification of the abstract argumentation-theoretic framework and its applications both to existing formalisms and to new formalisms for non-monotonic reasoning is another important direction for future research. Of special importance is the problem of relating circumscription and the if-and-only-if completion semantics to the argumentation-theoretic approach. An important step in this direction may be the "common sense" axiomatisation of NAF [Van Gelder and Schlipf, 1993] by Van Gelder and Schlipf, which augments the if-and-only-if completion with axioms of induction. The inclusion of induction axioms relates this approach to circumscription, whereas the rewriting of negative literals by new positive literals relates it to the abductive interpretation of NAF.

The development of systems that combine ALP and CLP is another important area that is still in its infancy. Among the results that might be expected from this development are more powerful systems that combine constructive abduction and constructive negation, and systems in which user-defined constraint handling rules might be formulated and executed efficiently as integrity constraints.

It is an important feature of the abductive interpretation of NAF that it possesses elegant and powerful proof procedures, which significantly extend SLDNF and which can be extended in turn to accommodate other abducibles and other integrity constraints. Different semantics for NAF require different proof procedures. It remains to be seen whether the inefficiency of proof procedures for the acceptability semantics, in particular, can somehow be avoided in practice.

We have seen that abductive proof procedures for LP can be extended to ALP. We have also seen that ALP can be reduced to LP by transformations. The comparative efficiency of the two different approaches to the implementation of ALP needs to be investigated further.

We have argued that the implementation of abduction needs to be considered within a broader framework of implementing knowledge assimilation (KA). We have seen that abduction can be used to assist the process of KA and that abductive hypotheses themselves need to be assimilated. Moreover, the general process of checking for integrity in KA might be used to check the acceptability of abductive hypotheses.

It seems that an efficient implementation of KA can be based upon combining two processes: backward reasoning both to generate abductive hypotheses and to test whether the input is redundant and forward reasoning both to test input for consistency and to test whether existing information is redundant. Notice that the abductive proof procedure for ALP already has this feature of interleaving backward and forward reasoning. Such implementations of KA need to be integrated with improvements of the abductive proof procedure considered in isolation.

We have seen that the process of belief revision also needs to be considered within a KA context. In particular, it could be useful to investigate relationships between the belief revision frameworks of [Doyle, 1991; Gärdenfors, 1988; Nebel, 1989; Nebel, 1991] and various integrity constraint checking and restoration procedures.

The extension of LP to include integrity constraints is useful both for abductive LP and for deductive databases. We have seen, however, that for many applications the use of integrity constraints with retractibles can be replaced by clauses with explicitly negated conclusions with priorities. Moreover, the use of explicit negation with priorities seems to have several advantages, including the ability both to represent and derive negative information, as well as to obtain the effect of NAF.

The relationship between integrity constraints with retractibles and explicit negation with priorities needs to be investigated further: To what extent does this relationship, which holds for abduction and default reasoning, hold for other uses of integrity constraints, such as those employed in deductive databases; and what are the implications of this relationship on the semantics and implementation of integrity constraints?

We have remarked upon the close links between the semantics of LP with abduction and the semantics of truth maintenance systems. The practical consequences of these links, both for building applications and for efficient implementations, need further investigation. What is the significance, for example, of the fact that conventional TMSs and ATMSs correspond only to the propositional case of logic programs?

We have seen the rapid development of the abduction-based argumentation-theoretic approach to non-monotonic reasoning. But argumentation has wider applications in areas such as law and practical reasoning more generally. It would be useful to see to what extent the theory of argumentation might be extended to encompass such applications. It would be especially gratifying, in particular, if such an extended argumentation theory might be used, not only to understand how one argument can defeat another, but also to indicate how conflicting arguments might be reconciled.

Acknowledgements

This research was supported by Fujitsu Research Laboratories and by the Esprit Basic Research Action Compulog II. The authors are grateful to Katsumi Inoue and Ken Satoh for helpful comments on an earlier draft, and to José Júlio Alferes, Phan Minh Dung, Paolo Mancarella and Luis Moniz Pereira for many helpful discussions.

References

[Akama, 1992] S. Akama. Answer set semantics and constructive logic with strong negation. Technical Report, 1992.

[Alferes et al., 1993] J. J. Alferes, P. M. Dung and L. M. Pereira. Scenario semantics of extended logic programs. *Proc 2nd International Workshop on Logic Programming and Nonmonotonic Reasoning*, Lisbon. L. M. Pereira and A. Nerode, eds. pp. 334–348, MIT Press, Cambridge, MA, 1993.

[Alferes and Pereira, 1994] J. J. Alferes and L. M. Pereira. An argumentation-theoretic semantics based on non-refutable falsity. *Proc. 4th Int. Workshop on Non-monotonic Extensions of Logic Programming*, Santa Margherita Ligure, Italy. J. Dix, L. M. Pereira and T. Przymusinski eds. 1994.

[Alferes and Pereira, 1993] J. J. Alferes and L. M. Pereira. Contradiction in logic programs: when avoidance equal removal, Parts I and II. *Proc. 4th Int. Workshop on Extensions of Logic Programming*, R. Dyckhoff ed. pp. 7–26. Lecture Notes in AI 798, Springer-Verlag, Berlin, 1993.

[Alferes et al., 1994] J. J. Alferes, C. V. Damasio and L. M. Pereira. Top-down query evaluation for well-founded semantics with explicit negation.

Proc. European Conference on Artificial Intelligence, ECAI '94, John Wiley, Amsterdam, 1994.

[Allemand *et al.*, 1991] D. Allemand, M. Tanner, T. Bylander and J. Josephson. The computational complexity of abduction. *Artificial Intelligence*, **49**, 25–60, 1991.

[Apt and Bezem, 1990] K. R. Apt and M. Bezem. Acyclic programs. *Proc. 7th International Conference on Logic Programming*, Jerusalem. pp. 579–597. MIT Press, Cambridge, MA, 1990.

[Aravindan and Dung, 1994] C. Aravindan and P. M. Dung. Belief dynamics, abduction and databases. *Proc. 4th European Workshop on Logics in AI*. Lecture Notes in AI, Springer Verlag, Berlin 1994.

[Baral and Gelfond, 1994] C. Baral and M. Gelfond. Logic programming and knowledge representation. *Journal of Logic Programming*, **19–20**, 73–148, 1994.

[Barbuti *et al.*, 1990] R. Barbuti, P. Mancarella, D. Pedreschi and F. Turini. A transformational approach to negation in logic programming. *Journal of Logic Programming*, **8**, 201–228, 1990.

[Bondarenko *et al.*, 1993] A. Bondarenko, F. Toni and R. A. Kowalski. An assumption-based framework for non-monotonic reasoning, *Proc. 2nd International Workshop on Logic Programming and Nonmonotonic Reasoning* Lisbon. L. M. Pereira and A. Nerode eds. 171–189. MIT Press, Cambridge, MA, 1993.

[Bondarenko *et al.*, 1997] A. Bondarenko, P. M. Dung, R. A. Kowalski and F. Toni. An abstract, argumentation-theoretic framework for default reasoning. To appear in *Artificial Intelligence*, 1997.

[Brewka, 1989] G. Brewka. Preferred subtheories: an extended logical framework for default reasoning. *Proc. 11th International Joint Conference on Artificial Intelligence*, Detroit, MI, 1043–1048, 1989.

[Brewka, 1993] G. Brewka. An abductive framework for generalised logic programs. *Proc. 2nd International Workshop on Logic Programming and Nonmonotonic Reasoning* Lisbon. L. M. Pereira and A. Nerode eds. 349–364. MIT Press, Cambridge, MA, 1993.

[Brewka and Konolige, 1993] G. Brewka and K. Konolige. An abductive framework for general logic programs and other non-monotonic systems. *Proc. 13th International Joint Conference on Artificial Intelligence*, Chambery, France, 9–15, 1993.

[Brogi *et al.*, 1992] A. Brogi, E. Lamma, P. Mello, and P. Mancarella. Normal logic programs as open positive programs. *Proc. ICSLP '92*, 1992.

[Bry, 1990] F. Bry. Intensional updates: abduction via deduction. *Proc. 7th International Conference on Logic Programming*, Jerusalem, 561–575, MIT Press, Cambridge, MA, 1990.

[Büchert, 1994] H.-J. Bürchert. A resolution principle for constrained logics. *Artificial Intelligence*, **66**, 235–271, 1994.

[Büchert and Nutt, 1991] H.-J. Bürchert and W. Nutt. On abduction and answer generation through constraint resolution. Technical Report, DFKI, Kaiserslautern, 1991.

[Casamayor and Decker, 1992] J. Casamayor and H. Decker. Some proof procedures for computational first-order theories, with an abductive flavour to them. *Proc. 1st Compulog-Net Workshop on Logic Programming in Artificial Intelligence*, Imperial College, London, 1992.

[Chan, 1988] D. Chan. Constructive negation based on the completed database. *Proc. 5th International Conference and Symposium on Logic Programming*, Washington, Seattle, 111–125, 1988.

[Charniak and McDermott, 1985] E. Charniak and D. McDermott. *Introduction to artificial intelligence*. Addison-Wesley, Menlo Park, CA, 1985.

[Chen and Warren, 1989] W. Chen and D. S. Warren. Abductive logic programming. Technical Report, Dept. of Comp. Science, State Univ. of New York at Stony Brook, 1989.

[Clark, 1978] K. L. Clark. Negation as failure. *Logic and Data Bases*, H. Gallaire and J. Minker, eds. pp. 293–322, Plenum Press, NY, 1978.

[Console and Saitta, 1992] L. Console and L. Saitta. Abduction, induction and inverse resolution. *Proc. 1st Compulog-Net Workshop on Logic Programming in Artificial Intelligence*, Imperial College, London, 1992.

[Console *et al.*, 1989] L. Console, D. Theseider Dupré and P. Torasso. A Theory for diagnosis for incomplete causal models. *Proc. 11th International Joint Conference on Artificial Intelligence*, Detroit, Mi, 1311–1317, 1989.

[Console *et al.*, 1991] L. Console, D. Theseider Dupré and P. Torasso. On the relationship between abduction and deduction. *Journal of Logic and Computation*, **2(5)**, 661–690, 1991.

[Console *et al.*, 1994] L. Console, M. L. Sapino and D. Theseider Dupré. The role of abduction in database view updating. *Journal of Intelligent Information Systems*, **4**, 261–280, 1995.

[Cox and Pietrzykowski, 1992] P. T. Cox and T. Pietrzykowski. Causes for events: their computation and applications. CADE '86, 608–621, 1992.

[de Kleer, 1986] J. de Kleer. An assumption-based TMS. *Artificial Intelligence*, **32**, 1986.

[Decker, 1986] H. Decker. Integrity enforcement on deductive databases. *Proc. EDS '86*, Charleston, SC, 271–285, 1986.

[Demolombe and Fariñas del Cerro, 1991] R. Demolombe and L. Fariñas del Cerro. An inference rule for hypotheses generation. *Proc. 12th International Joint Conference on Artificial Intelligence*, Sidney, 152–157, 1991.

[Denecker and De Schreye, 1992] M. Denecker and D. De Schreye. Temporal reasoning with abductive event calculus. *Proc. 1st Compulog-Net Workshop on Logic Programming in Artificial Intelligence*, Imperial College, London, 1992.

[Denecker and De Schreye, 1992a] M. Denecker and D. De Schreye. On the duality of abduction and model generation. *Proc. International Conference on Fifth Generation Computer Systems*, Tokyo, 650–657, 1992.

[Denecker and De Schreye, 1992b] M. Denecker and D. De Schreye. SLD-NFA: an abductive procedure for normal abductive programs. *Proc. International Conference and Symposium on Logic Programming*, 686–700, 1992.

[Denecker and De Schreye, 1993] M. Denecker and D. De Schreye. Representing incomplete knowledge in abductive logic programming. *Proc. ILSP'93*, Vancouver, 1993.

[Doyle, 1979] J. Doyle. A truth maintenance system. *Artificial Intelligence*, **12**, 231–272, 1979.

[Doyle, 1991] J. Doyle. Rational belief revision. *Proc. 2nd International Conference on Principles of Knowledge Representation and Reasoning*, Cambridge, MA, 163–174, 1991.

[Drabent, 1995] W. Drabent. What is failure? An approach to constructive negation. *Acta Informatica*, **32**, 27–60, 1995.

[Dung, 1991] P. M. Dung. Negation as hypothesis: an abductive foundation for logic programming. *Proc. 8th International Conference on Logic Programming*, Paris, 3–17, MIT Press, Cambridge, MA, 1991.

[Dung, 1991a] P. M. Dung. An abductive foundation for non-monotonic truth maintenance. *Proc. 1st World Conference on Fundamentals of Artificial Intelligence*, Paris. M. de Glas ed. 1991.

[Dung, 1992] P. M. Dung. Acyclic disjunctive logic programs with abductive procedure as proof procedure. *Proc. International Conference on Fifth Generation Computer Systems*, Tokyo, 555–561, 1992.

[Dung, 1992a] P. M. Dung. An abductive procedure for disjunctive logic programming. Technical Report, Dept. of Computing, Asian Institute of Technology, 1992.

[Dung, 1993] P. M. Dung. Personal communication, 1993.

[Dung, 1993a] P. M. Dung. On the acceptability of arguments and its fundamental role in nonmonotonic reasoning and logic programming. *Artificial Intelligence*, **77**, 321–357, 1994. (Extended Abstract in *Proc. International Joint Conference on Artificial Intelligence*, 852–859, 1993.)

[Dung, 1993b] P. M. Dung. An argumentation semantics for logic programming with explicit negation. *Proc. 10th International Conference on Logic Programming*, Budapest, Hungary, MIT Press, Cambridge, MA, 1993.

[Dung and Ruamviboonsuk, 1991] P. M. Dung and P. Ruamviboonsuk. Well-founded reasoning with classical negation. *Proc. 1st International Workshop on Logic Programming and Nonmonotonic Reasoning*, Washington, DC. A. Nerode, V. Marek and V. Subrahmahian, eds. 120–135, 1991.

[Dung et al., 1992] P. M. Dung, A. C. Kakas and P. Mancarella. Negation as failure revisited. Technical Report, 1992.

[Eiter and Gottlob, 1993] T. Eiter and G. Gottlob. The complexity of logic-based abduction. *Proc. 10th Symposium on Theoretical Aspects of Computing (STACS-93)*. P. Enjalbert, A. Finkel and K. W. Wagner, eds. pp. 70–79. Vol. 665 of Lecture Notes on Computer Science, Springer Verlag, Berlin, 1993. (Extended paper to appear in *Journal of the ACM*)

[Elkan, 1990] C. Elkan. A rational reconstruction of non-monotonic truth maintenance systems. *Artificial Intelligence*, **43**, 219–234, 1990.

[Eshghi, 1988] K. Eshghi. Abductive planning with event calculus. *Proc. 5th International Conference and Symposium on Logic Programming*, Washington, Seattle, 562–579, 1988.

[Eshghi, 1990] K. Eshghi. Diagnoses as stable models. *Proc. 1st International Workshop on Principles of Diagnosis*, Menlo Park, CA, 1990.

[Eshghi, 1993] K. Eshghi. A tractable set of abduction problems. *Proc. 13th International Joint Conference on Artificial Intelligence*, Chambry, France, 3–8, 1993.

[Eshghi and Kowalski, 1988] K. Eshghi and R. A. Kowalski. Abduction through deduction. Technical Report, Department of Computing, Imperial College, London, 1988.

[Eshghi and Kowalski, 1989] K. Eshghi and R. A. Kowalski. Abduction compared with negation by failure. *Proc. 6th International Conference on Logic Programming*, Lisbon, 234–255, MIT Press, Cambridge, MA, 1989.

[Evans, 1989] C. A. Evans. Negation as failure as an approach to the Hanks and McDermott problem. *Proc. 2nd International Symposium on Artificial intelligence*, Monterrey, Mexico, 1989.

[Evans and Kakas, 1992] C. A. Evans and A. C. Kakas. Hypothetico-deductive reasoning. *Proc. International Conference on Fifth Generation Computer Systems*, Tokyo, 546–554, 1992.

[Finger and Genesereth, 1985] J. J. Finger and M. R. Genesereth. RESIDUE: a deductive approach to design synthesis. Technical Report, no. CS-85-1035, Stanford University, 1985.

[Frühwirth, 1992] T. Frühwirth. Constraint simplification rules. Technical Report ECRC-92-18, 1992.

[Fujiwara and Honiden, 1989] Y. Fujiwara and S. Honiden. Relating the TMS to Autoepistemic Logic. *Proc. 11th International Joint Conference on Artificial Intelligence*, Detroit, MI, 1199–1205, 1989.

[Fujita and Hasegawa, 1991] M. Fujita and R. Hasegawa. A model generation theorem prover in KL1 using a ramified-stack algorithm. *Proc. 8th International Conference on Logic Programming*, Paris, 535–548, MIT Press, Cambridge, MA, 1991.

[Fung, 1993] T. H. Fung. *Theorem proving approach with constraint handling and its applications on databases*. MSc Thesis, Imperial College, London, 1993.

[Gabbay, 1991] D. M. Gabbay. Abduction in labelled deductive systems. A conceptual abstract. *Proc. of the European Conference on Symbolic and Quantitative Approaches for uncertainty '91*, R. Kruse and P. Siegel, eds. pp. 3–12. Vol. 548 of Lecture Notes on Computer Science, Springer Verlag, Berlin, 1991.

[Gabbay and Kempson, 1991] D. M. Gabbay and R. M. Kempson. Labelled abduction and relevance reasoning. *Workshop on Non-Standard Queries and Non-Standard Answers*, Toulouse, France, 1991.

[Gabbay *et al.*, 1994] D. M. Gabbay, R. M. Kempson and J. Pitts. Labelled abduction and relevance reasoning. *Non-standard queries and answers*, R. Demolombe and T. Imielinski, eds. pp. 155–185. Oxford University Press, 1994.

[Gaifman and Shapiro, 1989] H. Gaifman and E. Shapiro. Proof theory and semantics of logic programming. *Proc. LICS'89*, pp. 50–62. IEEE Computer Society Press, 1989.

[Gärdenfors, 1988] P. Gärdenfors. *Knowledge in Flux: Modeling the Dynamics of Epistemic States*. MIT Press, Cambridge, MA, 1988.

[Geffner, 1990] H. Geffner. Casual theories for non-monotonic reasoning. *Proc. AAAI '90*, 1990.

[Geffner, 1991] H. Geffner. Beyond negation as failure. *Proc. 2nd International Conference on Principles of Knowledge Representation and Reasoning*, Cambridge, MA, 218–229, 1991.

[Gelfond and Lifschitz, 1988] M. Gelfond and V. Lifschitz. The Stable model semantics for logic programs. *Proc. 5th International Conference and Symposium on Logic Programming*, Washington, Seattle, 1070–1080, 1988.

[Gelfond and Lifschitz, 1990] M. Gelfond and V. Lifschitz. Logic programs with classical negation. *Proc. 7th International Conference on Logic Programming*, Jerusalem, 579–597, MIT Press, Cambridge, MA, 1990.

[Giordano and Martelli, 1990] L. Giordano and A. Martelli. Generalized stable model semantics, truth maintenance and conflict resolution. *Proc. 7th International Confernece on Logic Programming*, Jerusalem, MIT Press, Cambridge, MA, 427–411, 1990.

[Giordano *et al.*, 1993] L. Giordano, A. Martelli and M. L. Sapino. A semantics for Eshghi and Kowalski's abductive procedure. *Proc. 10th International Conference on Logic Programming*, Budapest, 586–600, MIT Press, Cambridge, MA, 1993.

[Goebel et al., 1986] R. Goebel, K. Furukawa and D. Poole. Using definite clauses and integrity constraints as the basis for a theory formation approach to diagnostic reasoning. *Proc. 3rd International Conference on Logic Programming*, London, 1986, MIT Press, Cambridge, MA, .pp. 211–222. Vol 225 of Lecture Notes in Computer Science, Springer Verlag, Berlin, 1986.

[Hanks and McDermott, 1986] S. Hanks and D. McDermott. Default reasoning, non-monotonic logics, and the frame problem. *Proc. 8th AAAI '86*, Philadelphia, 328–333,1986.

[Hanks and McDermott, 1987] S. Hanks and D. McDermott. Non-monotonic logics and temporal projection. *Artificial Intelligence*, **33**, 1987.

[Hasegawa and Fujita, 1992] R. Hasegawa and M. Fujita. Parallel theorem provers and their applications. *Proc. International Conference on Fifth Generation Computer Systems*, Tokyo, 132–154, 1992.

[Hobbs, 1990] J. R. Hobbs. An integrated abductive framework for discourse interpretation. *Proc. AAAI Symposium on Automated Abduction*, Stanford, 10–12, 1990.

[Hobbs et al., 1990] J. R. Hobbs, M. Stickel, D. Appelt and P. Martin. Interpretation as abduction. Technical Report, 499, Artificial Intelligence Center, Computing and Engineering Sciences Division, Menlo Park, CA, 1990.

[Inoue, 1990] K. Inoue. An abductive procedure for the CMS/ATMS. *Proc. European Conference on Artificial Intelligence, ECAI '90*, International Workshop on Truth Maintenance, Stockholm, Springer Verlag Lecture notes in Computer Science, 1990.

[Inoue, 1991] K. Inoue. Extended logic programs with default assumptions. *Proc. 8th International Conference on Logic Programming*, Paris, 490–504, MIT Press, Cambridge, MA, 1991.

[Inoue, 1994] K. Inoue. Hypothetical reasoning in logic programs. *Journal of Logic Programming*, **18**, 191–227, 1994.

[Inoue et al., 1992] K. Inoue, M. Koshimura and R. Hasegawa. Embedding negation as failure into a model generation theorem prover. *Proc. 11th International Conference on Automated Deduction*, CADE '92, Saratoga Springs, NY, 1992.

[Inoue et al., 1992a] K. Inoue, Y. Ohta, R. Hasegawa and M. Nakashima. Hypothetical reasoning systems on the MGTP. Technical Report, ICOT, Tokyo (in Japanese), 1992.

[Junker, 1989] U. Junker. A correct non-monotonic ATMS. *Proc. 11th International Joint Conference on Artificial Intelligence*, Detroit, MI,

1049–1054, 1989.

[Kakas, 1991] A. C. Kakas. Deductive databases as theories of belief. Technical Report, Logic Programming Group, Imperial College, London, 1991.

[Kakas, 1991a] A. C. Kakas. On the evolution of databases. Technical Report, Logic Programming Group, Imperial College, London, 1991.

[Kakas, 1992] A. C. Kakas. Default reasoning via negation as failure. *Proc. ECAI-92 workshop on "Foundations of Knowledge Representation and Reasoning"*, G. Lakemeyer and B. Nebel, eds. Vol 810 of Lecture Notes in AI, Springer Verlag, Berlin, 1992.

[Kakas and Mancarella, 1989] A. C. Kakas and P. Mancarella. Anomalous models and abduction. *Proc. 2nd International Symposium on Artificial intelligence*, Monterrey, Mexico, 1989.

[Kakas and Mancarella, 1990] A. C. Kakas and P. Mancarella. Generalized Stable Models: a Semantics for Abduction. *Porc. 9th European Conference on artificial Intelligence, ECAI '90*, Stockholm, 385–391, 1990.

[Kakas and Mancarella, 1990a] A. C. Kakas and P. Mancarella. Database updates through abduction. *Proc. 16th International Conference on Very Large Databases, VLDB'90*, Brisbane, Australia, 1990.

[Kakas and Mancarella, 1990b] A. C. Kakas and P. Mancarella. On the relation of truth maintenance and abduction. *Proc. of the 1st Pacific Rim International Conference on Artificial Intelligence, PRICAI'90*, Nagoya, Japan, 1990.

[Kakas and Mancarella, 1990c] A. C. Kakas and P. Mancarella. Abductive LP. *Proc. NACLP '90,*, Workshop on Non-Monotonic Reasoning and Logic Programming, Austin, Texas, 1990.

[Kakas and Mancarella, 1990d] A. C. Kakas and P. Mancarella. Knowledge assimilation and abduction. *Proc. European Conference on Artificial Intelligence, ECAI '90*, International Workshop on Truth Maintenance, Stockholm, Springer Verlag Lecture notes in Computer Science, 1990.

[Kakas and Mancarella, 1991] A. C. Kakas and P. Mancarella. Negation as stable hypotheses. *Proc. 1st International Workshop on Logic Programming and Nonmonotonic Reasoning*, Washington, DC. A. Nerode, V. Marek and V. Subrahmanian eds., 1991.

[Kakas and Mancarella, 1991a] A. C. Kakas and P. Mancarella. Stable theories for logic programs. *Porc. ISLP '91*, San Diego, 1991.

[Kakas and Mancarella, 1993a] A. C. Kakas and P. Mancarella. Constructive abduction in logic programming. Technical Report, Dipartimento di Informatica, Università di Pisa, 1993.

[Kakas and Mancarella, 1993] A. C. Kakas and P. Mancarella. Preferred extensions are partial stable models. *Journal of Logic Programming*, **14**, 341–348, 1993.

[Kakas and Michael, 1993] A. C. Kakas and A. Michael. Scheduling through abduction. *Proc. ICLP'93 Post Conference workshop on Abductive Reasoning*, 1993.

[Kakas and Michael, 1995] A. C. Kakas and A. Michael. Integrating abductive and constraint logic programming. *Proc. 12th International Logic Programming Conference*, MIT Press, Cambridge, MA, 399–413, 1995.

[Kakas et al., 1993] A. C. Kakas, R. A. Kowalski and F. Toni. Abductive logic programming. *Journal of Logic and Computation*, **2**, 719–770, 1993.

[Kakas et al., 1994] A. C. Kakas, P. Mancarella and P. M. Dung. The acceptability semantics for logic programs. *Proc. 11th International Conference on Logic Programming*, Santa Margherita Ligure, Italy, 504–519, MIT Press, Cambridge, MA, 1994.

[Konolige, 1990] K. Konolige. A general theory of abduction. *Spring Symposium on Automated Abduction, Stanford University*, pp. 62–66, 1990.

[Konolige, 1992] K. Konolige. Using defualt and causal reasoning in diagnosis. *Proc. 3rd International Conference on Principles of Knowledge Representation and Reasoning*, Cambridge, 1992.

[Kowalski, 1979] R. A. Kowalski. *Logic for problem solving*. Elsevier, New York, 1979.

[Kowalski, 1987] R. A. Kowalski. Belief revision without constraints. *Computational Intelligence*, **3**, 1987.

[Kowalski, 1990] R. A. Kowalski. Problems and promises of computational logic. *Proc. Symposium on Computational Logic*, J. Lloyd ed. Springer Verlag Lecture Notes in Computer Science, 1990.

[Kowalski, 1992] R. A. Kowalski. Database updates in the event calculus. *Journal of Logic Programming*, **12**, 121–146, 1992.

[Kowalski, 1992a] R. A. Kowalski. A dual form of logic programming. Lecture Notes, Workshop in Honour of Jack Minker, University of Maryland, November 1992.

[Kowalski, 1994] R. A. Kowalski. Logic without model theory. *What is a Logical System?*, D. Gabbay, ed. Oxford University Press, 1994.

[Kowalski and Sadri, 1988] R. A. Kowalski and F. Sadri. Knowledge representation without integrity constraints. Technical Report, Department of Computing, Imperial College, London, 1988.

[Kowalski and Sadri, 1990] R. A. Kowalski and F. Sadri. Logic programs with exceptions. *Proc. 7th International Conference on Logic Programming*, Jerusalem, 598–613, MIT Press, Cambridge, MA, 1990.

[Kowalski and Sergot, 1986] R. A. Kowalski and M. Sergot. A logic-based calculus of events. *New Generation Computing*, **4**, 67–95, 1986.

[Kunifuji et al., 1986] S. Kunifuji, K. Tsurumaki and K. Furukawa. Consideration of a hypothesis-based reasoning system. *Journal of Japanese Society for Artificial Intelligence*, **1**, 228–237, 1986.

[Lamma and Mello, 1992] E. Lamma and P. Mello. An assumption-based truth maintenance system dealing with non ground justifications. *Proc. 1st Compulog-Net Workshop on Logic Programming in Artificial Intelligence*, Imperial College, London, 1992.

[Lever, 1991] J. M. Lever. *Combining induction with resolution in logic programming*. PhD Thesis, Department of Computing, Imperial College, London, 1991.

[Levesque, 1989] H. J.Levesque. A knowledge-level account of abduction. *Proc. 11th International Joint Conference on Artificial Intelligence*, Detroit, MI, 1061–1067, 1989.

[Lloyd and Topor, 1985] J. W. Lloyd and R. W. Topor. A basis for deductive database system. *Journal of Logic Programming*, **2**, 93–109, 1985.

[McDermott, 1982] D. McDermott. Nonmonotonic logic II: nonmonotonic modal theories. *JACM*, **29**, 1982.

[Maim, 1992] E. Maim. Abduction and constraint logic programming. *Proc. European Conference on Artificial Intelligence, ECAI '92*, Vienna, Austria, 1992.

[Makinson, 1989] D. Makinson. General theory of cumulative inference. *Proc. 2nd International Workshop on Monmonotonic reasoning*, Vol. 346 of Lecture Notes in Computer Science, Springer Verlag, Berlin, 1989.

[Manthey and Bry, 1988] R. Manthey and F. Bry. SATCHMO: a theorem prover implemented in Prolog. *Proc. 9th International Conference on Automated Deduction*, CADE '88, Argonne, IL, 415–434, 1988.

[Marek and Truszczynski, 1989] W. Marek and M. Truszczynski. Stable semantics for logic programs and default theories. *Proc. NACLP '89*, 243–256, 1989.

[Minker, 1982] J. Minker. On indefinite databases and the closed world assumption. *Proc. 6th International Conference on Automated Deduction*, CADE'82, New York. pp. 292–308. Vol 138 of Lecture Notes in Computer Science, Springer-Verlag, Berlin, 1982.

[Miyaki *et al.*, 1984] T. Miyaki, S. Kunifuji, H. Kitakami, K. Furukawa, A. Takeuchi and H. Yokota. A knowledge assimilation method for logic databases. *International Symposium on Logic Programming*, Atlantic City, NJ, pp. 118–125, 1984.

[Moore, 1985] R. Moore. Semantical considerations on non-monotonic logic. *Artificial Intelligence*, **25**, 1985.

[Morris, 1988] P. H. Morris. The anomalous extension problem in default reasoning. *Artificial Intelligence*, **35**, 383–399, 1988.

[Nebel, 1989] B. Nebel. A knowledge level analysis of belief revision. *Proc. 1st International Conference on Principles of Knowledge Representation and Reasoning*, Toronto, 301–311, 1989.

[Nebel, 1991] B. Nebel. Belief revision and default reasoning: syntax-based approaches. *Proc. 2nd International Conference on Principles of Knowledge Representation and Reasoning*, Cambridge, MA, 417–428, 1991.

[Pearce and Wagner, 1991] D. Pearce and G. Wagner. Logic programming with strong negation. *Proc. Workshop on Extensions of Logic Programming*, Lecture Notes in Computer Science, Springer Verlag, 1991.

[Pearl, 1987] J. Pearl. Embracing causality in formal reasoning. *Proc. AAAI '87,*, Washington, Seattle, 360–373, 1987.

[Pearl, 1988] J. Pearl. *Probabilistic reasoning in intelligent systems: Networks of plausible inference.* Morgan Kaufmann, San Mateo, CA, 1988.

[Peirce, 1931–58] C. S. Peirce. *Collected papers of Charles Sanders Peirce.* Vol.2, 1931–1958, C. Hartshorn and P. Weiss, eds. Harvard University Press, 1933.

[Pereira and Alferes, 1992] L. M. Pereira and J. J. Alferes. Well-founded semantics for logic programs with explicit negation. *Proc. 92 European Conference on Artificial Intelligence, ECAI 'Vienna,Austria*, 102–106, 1992.

[Pereira *et al.*, 1991] L. M. Pereira, J. N. Aparicio and J. J. Alferes. Nonmonotonic reasoning with well-founded semantics. *Proc. 8th International Conference on Logic Programming*, Paris, 1991. MIT Press, Cambridge, MA, 1991.

[Pereira *et al.*, 1991a] L. M. Pereira, J. N. Aparicio and J. J. Alferes. Contradiction removal within well-founded semantics. *Proc. 1st International Workshop on Logic Programming and Nonmonotonic Reasoning*, Washington, DC. A. Nerode, V. Marek and V. Subrahmanian eds., 1991.

[Pereira *et al.*, 1991b] L. M. Pereira, J. N. Aparicio and J. J. Alferes. Derivation procedures for extended stable models. *Proc. 12th International Joint Conference on Artificial Intelligence*, Sidney, 863–868, 1991.

[Pereira *et al.*, 1991c] L. M. Pereira, J. N. Aparicio and J. J. Alferes. Counterfactual reasoning based on revising assumptions. *Proc. ISLP '91*, San Diego, 1991.

[Pereira *et al.*, 1992] L. M. Pereira, J. J. Alferes and J. N. Aparicio. Contradiction removal semantics with explicit negation *Proc. Applied Logic Conference*, Amsterdam, 1992.

[Pereira *et al.*, 1993] L. M. Pereira, C. V. Damasio and J. J. Alferes. Diagnosis and debugging as contradiction removal. *Proc. 2nd International Workshop on Logic Programming and Nonmonotonic Reasoning* Lisbon. L. M. Pereira and A. Nerode eds. 316–330. MIT Press, Cambridge, MA, 1993.

[Pimentel and Cuadrado, 1989] S. G. Pimentel and J. L. Cuadrado. A truth maintenance system based on stable models. *Proc. NACLP '89*, 1989.

[Poole, 1985] D. Poole. On the comparison of theories: preferring the most specific explanation. *Proc. 9th International Joint Conference on Artificial Intelligence*, Los Angeles, CA, 144–147, 1985.

[Poole, 1987] D. Poole. Variables in hypotheses. *Proc. 10th International Joint Conference on Artificial Intelligence*, Milan, 905–908, 1987.

[Poole, 1988] D. Poole. A logical framework for default reasoning. *Artificial Intelligence*, **36**, 27–47, 1988.

[Poole, 1988a] D. Poole. Representing knowledge for logic-based diagnosis. *Proc. International Conference on Fifth Generation Computer Systems*, Tokyo, 1282–1290, 1988.

[Poole, 1989] D. Poole. Explanation and prediction: an architecture for default and abductive reasoning. *Computational Intelligence Journal*, **5**, 97–110, 1989.

[Poole, 1992] D. Poole. Logic programming, abduction and probability. *Proc. International Conference on Fifth Generation Computer Systems*, Tokyo, 530–538, 1992.

[Poole, 1993] D. Poole. Probabilistic Horn abduction and Bayesian networks. *Artificial Intelligence*, **64**, 81–129, 1993.

[Poole *et al.*, 1987] D. Poole, R. G. Goebel and T. Aleliunas. Theorist: a logical reasoning system for default and diagnosis. *The Knowledge Fronteer: Essays in the Representation of Knowledge*, N. Cercone and G. McCalla eds. pp. 331–352. Lecture Notes in Computer Science, Springer Verlag, 1987.

[Pople, 1973] H. E. Pople Jr. On the mechanization of abductive logic. *Proc. 3rd International Joint Conference on Artificial Intelligence*, 147–152, 1973.

[Preist and Eshghi, 1992] C. Preist and K. Eshghi. Consistency-based and abductive diagnoses as generalised stable models. *Proc. International Conference on Fifth Generation Computer Systems*, Tokyo, 514–521, 1992.

[Przymusinski, 1989] T. C. Przymusinski. On the declarative and procedural semantics of logic programs. *Journal of Automated Reasoning*, **5**, 167–205, 1989.

[Przymusinski, 1990] T. C. Przymusinski. Extended stable semantics for normal and disjunctive programs. *Proc. 7th International Conference on Logic Programming*, Jerusalem, 459–477, MIT Press, Cambridge, MA, 1990.

[Przymusinski, 1991] T. C. Przymusinski. Semantics of disjunctive logic programs and deductive databases. *Proc. DOOD '91*, 1991.

[Reggia, 1983] J. Reggia. Diagnostic experts systems based on a set-covering model. *International Journal of Man–Machine Studies*, **19**, 437–460, 1983.

[Reinfrank and Dessler, 1989] M. Reinfrank and O. Dessler. On the relation between truth maintenance and non-monotonic logics. *Proc. 11th International Joint Conference on Artificial Intelligence*, Detroit, MI, 1206–1212, 1989.

[Reiter, 1978] R. Reiter. On closed world data bases. *Logic and Databases*, H. Gallaire and J. Minker eds. pp. 55–76. Plenum, New York, 1978.

[Reiter, 1980] R. Reiter. A Logic for default reasoning. *Artificial Intelligence*, **13**, 81–132, 1980.

[Reiter, 1987] R. Reiter. A theory of diagnosis from first principle. *Artificial Intelligence*, **32**, 1987.

[Reiter, 1988] R. Reiter. On integrity constraints. *Proc. 2nd Conference on Theoretical Aspects of Reasoning about Knowledge*, Pacific Grove, CA, M. Y. Vardi ed. 1988.

[Reiter, 1990] R. Reiter. On asking what a database knows. *Proc. Symposium on Computational Logic*, J. Lloyd ed. Lecture Notes in Computer Science, Springer Verlag, 1990.

[Reiter and De Kleer, 1987] R. Reiter and J. de Kleer. Foundations of assumption-based truth maintenance systems: preliminary report. *Proc. AAAI '87*, Washington, Seattle, 183–188, 1987.

[Rodi and Pimentel, 1991] W. L. Rodi and S. G. Pimentel. A non-monotonic ATMS using stable bases. *Proc. 2nd International Conference on Principles of Knowledge Representation and Reasoning*, Cambridge, MA, 1991,

[Saccà and Zaniolo, 1990] D. Saccà and C. Zaniolo. Stable models and non determinism for logic programs with negation *Proc. ACM SIGMOD-SIGACT Symposium on Principles of Database Systems* pp. 205–217, 1990.

[Sadri and Kowalski, 1987] F. Sadri and R. A. Kowalski. An application of general purpose theorem-proving to database integrity. *Foundations of Deductive Databases and Logic Programming*, Minker ed. pp. 313–362. Morgan Kaufmann Publishers, Palo Alto, CA, 1987.

[Sakama and Inoue, 1993] C. Sakama and K. Inoue. Negation in disjunctive logic programs. *Proc. 10th International Conference on Logic Programming*, Budapest, 703–719, MIT Press, Cambridge, MA, 1993.

[Sakama and Inoue, 1994] C. Sakama and K. Inoue. On the equivalence between disjunctive and abductive logic programs. *Proc. 11th International Conference on Logic Programming*, Santa Margherita Ligure, Italy, 489–503, MIT Press, Cambridge, MA, 1994.

[Sato, 1990] T. Sato. Completed logic programs and their consistency. *Journal of Logic Programming*, **9**, 33–44, 1990.

[Satoh, 1994] K. Satoh. A top-down proof procedure for default logic by using abduction. *Proc. European Conference on Artificial Intelli-*

gence,ECAI '94, Amsterdam, 1994.

[Satoh and Iwayama, 1991] K. Satoh and N. Iwayama. Computing abduction using the TMS. *Proc. 8th International Conference on Logic Programming*, Paris, 505–518, MIT Press, Cambridge, MA, 1991.

[Satoh and Iwayama, 1992] K. Satoh and N. Iwayama. A correct top-down proof procedure for general logic programs with integrity constraints. *Proc. 3rd International Workshop on Extensions of Logic Programming*, pp. 19–34. 1992.

[Satoh and Iwayama, 1992a] K. Satoh and N. Iwayama. A query evaluation method for abductive logic programming. *Proc. International Conference and Symposium on Logic Programming*, 671–685, 1992.

[Sattar and Goebel, 1989] A. Sattar and R. Goebel. Using crucial literals to select better theories. Technical Report, Dept. of Computer Science, University of Alberta, Canada, 1989.

[Selman and Levesque, 1990] B. Selman and H. J. Levesque. Abductive and default reasoning: a computational core. *Proc. AAAI 90*, 343–348, 1990.

[Sergot, 1983] M. Sergot. A query-the-user facility for logic programming. *Integrated Interactive Computer Systems*. P. Degano and E. Sandewell eds. pp. 27–41. North Holland Press, 1983.

[Shanahan, 1989] M. Shanahan. Prediction is deduction but explanation is abduction. *Proc. 11th International Joint Conference on Artificial Intelligence*, Detroit, MI, 1055–1060, 1989.

[Simari and Loui, 1992] G. R. Simari and R. P. Loui. A mathematical treatment of defeasible reasoning and its implementation. *Artificial Intelligence*, **53**, 125–157, 1992.

[Sperber and Wilson, 1986] D. Sperber and D. Wilson. *Relevance: communication and cognition*. Blackwell, Oxford, UK, 1986.

[Stickel, 1988] M. E. Stickel. A prolog-like inference system for computing minimum-cost abductive explanations in natural-language interpretation. *Proc. International Computer Science Conference (Artificial Intelligence: Theory and Applications)*, Hong Kong, J.-L. Lassez and Shiu-Kai Chin eds. pp. 343–350, 1988.

[Stickel, 1989] M. E. Stickel. Rationale and methods for abductive reasoning in natural language interpretation. *Proc. International Scientific Symposium on Natural Language and Logic*, Hamburg, Germany. pp. 233–252. Lecture Notes in Artificial Intelligence, Springer Verlag, 1989.

[Teusink, 1993] F. Teusink. Using SLDFA-resolution with abductive logic programs. *ILPS '93* post-conference workshop "Logic Programming with Incomplete Information", 1993.

[Toni and Kakas, 1995] F. Toni and A. C. Kakas. Computing the acceptability semantics. *Proc. International Workshop on Logic Program-*

ming and Nonmonotonic Reasoning, V. W. Marek, A. Nerode and M. Truszczynski, eds. LNAI 928, Springer Verlag, 401–415, 1995.

[Toni and Kowalski, 1995] F. Toni and R. A. Kowalski. Reduction of abductive logic programs to normal logic programs. *Proc. 12th International Logic Programming Conference*, MIT Press,Cambridge, MA, 367–381, 1995.

[Toni, 1994] F. Toni. A theorem-proving approach to job-shop scheduling. Technical Report, Imperial College, London, 1994.

[Torres, 1993] A. Torres. Negation as failure to support. *Proc. 2nd International Workshop on Logic Programming and Nonmonotonic Reasoning* Lisbon. L. M. Pereira and A. Nerode eds. 223–243. MIT Press, Cambridge, MA, 1993.

[Van Belleghem *et al.*, 1994] K. Van Belleghem, M. Denecker and D. De Schreye. Representing continuos change in the abductive event calculus. *Proc. 11th International Conference on Logic Programming*, Santa Margherita Ligure, Italy, 225–239, MIT Press, Cambridge, MA, 1994.

[Van Gelder and Schlipf, 1993] A. Van Gelder and J. S. Schlipf. Commonsense axiomatizations for logic programs. *Journal of Logic Programming*, **17**, 161–195, 1993.

[Van Gelder *et al.*, 1988] A. Van Gelder, K. A. Ross and J. S. Schlipf. Unfounded sets and the well-founded semantics for general logic programs. *Proc. ACM SIGMOD-SIGACT, Symposium on Principles of Database Systems*, 1988.

[Wallace, 1987] M. Wallace. Negation by constraints: a sound and efficient implementation of negation in deductive databases. *Proc. 4th Symposium on Logic Programming*, San Francisco, 1987.

Semantics for Disjunctive and Normal Disjunctive Logic Programs

Jorge Lobo, Jack Minker and Arcot Rajasekar

Contents

1 Introduction

During the past 20 years, logic programming has grown from a new discipline to a mature field. Logic programming is a direct outgrowth of work that started in automated theorem proving. The first programs based on logic were developed by Colmerauer and his students [Colmerauer *et al.*, 1973] at the University of Marseilles in 1972 where the logic programming language PROLOG was developed. Kowalski [1974] published the first paper that formally described logic as a programming language in 1974. Alain Colmerauer and Robert Kowalski are considered the founders of the field of logic programming. van Emden and Kowalski [van Emden and Kowalski, 1976] laid down the theoretical foundation for logic programming. In the past decade the field has witnessed rapid progress with the publication of several theoretical results which have provided a strong foundation for logic programming and extended the scope of logic as a programming language. The objective of this article is to outline theoretical results that have been developed in the field of logic programming with particular emphasis to disjunctive logic programming. Disjunctive logic programming is an extension of logic programming and is useful in representing and reasoning with indefinite information.

A disjunctive logic program consists of a finite set of implicitly quantified universal clauses of the form:

$$A_1, \ldots, A_m \leftarrow B_1, \ldots, B_n \qquad m > 0 \text{ and } n \geq 0 \qquad (1)$$

where the A_i's and the B_j's are atoms. The atoms in the left of the implication sign form a disjunction and is called the *head* of the formula and those on the right form a conjunction and is called the *body* of the formula. The formula is read as "A_1 or A_2 or ... or A_m if B_1 and B_2 and ... and B_n." There are several forms of the formula that one usually distinguishes. If the body of the formula is empty, and the head is not, the formula is referred to as a *fact*. If both are not empty the formula is referred to as a *procedure*. A procedure or a fact is also referred to as a *logic program clause*. If both head and body of a formula are empty, then the formula is referred to as the *halt* statement. Finally, a *query* is a formula where the head of the formula is empty and the body is not empty. A finite set of such logic program clauses is said to constitute a *disjunctive* logic program. If the head of a logic program clause consists of a single atom, then it is called a *Horn or definite logic program clause*. A finite set of such definite logic program clauses is said to constitute a *Horn or definite* logic program. A definite logic program is a special case of disjunctive logic program. We shall also consider clauses of the form (1), where the B_i may be literals. By a *literal* we mean either an atom or the negation of an atom. A clause of the form (1) which contains literals in the body is referred to as a *normal* (when the head is an atom) or *general disjunctive* logic program clause. Similarly we also deal with queries which can have literals and we refer to them as *general queries*.

This article is divided into several sections. In the section *Positive consequences in logic programs*, we describe the theory developed to characterize logical consequences from definite and disjunctive logic programs whose forms are as in (1). In the section *Negation in logic programs*, we describe the theories developed to handle general queries in definite and disjunctive logic programs. In the section *Normal or general disjunctive logic programs* we discuss several topics: *stratified logic programs, well-founded and generalized well-founded logic programs* and *generalized disjunctive well-founded logic programs*. In the subsection *Stratified logic programs*, the theory for general logic programs with no recursion through negative literals in the body of a logic program clause is described. Such logic programs are called stratified logic programs. In the subsection *Well-founded and generalized well-founded logic programs*, we describe extensions to the theory that handle normal logic programs that are not stratifiable. In the subsection *Generalized disjunctive well-founded logic programs*, we extend the results to normal disjunctive logic programs. This permits the full gamut of possible logic programs to be discussed from a theoretical view. We do not treat theories in which the left hand side of a logic program clause may contain negated atoms.

2   Positive consequences in logic programs

A question that arises with any programming language is that of the semantics of the program. What does a program written in that language mean, and what programs can be written in the language? In logic programming the fact that one is dealing with a set of logical statements permits one to use concepts from classical logic to define a semantics for a logic program. It is convenient and sufficient to focus on the Herbrand domain of a logic program to capture the semantics of a logic program. By the *Herbrand domain* of a logic program P, denoted as U_P, we mean the set of all terms formed from the set of all constants in the logic program and recursively the set of all functions whose arguments are terms. If there are no constants in the logic program, then an arbitrary constant is added to the domain. Given the Herbrand domain, one can then consider the *Herbrand base*, denoted as B_P, which is the set of all ground predicates that can be constructed from the Herbrand domain. It is sufficient to define a semantics for the logic program over this domain [Lloyd, 1987]. We use *Herbrand interpretations*, which are subsets of the Herbrand base, to specify the semantics of logic programs. A *Herbrand model* (or model) of a logic program is an interpretation that satisfies all clauses in the logic program.

Example 2.0.1. Consider the following definite logic program:

$$P = \{path(X,Y) \leftarrow edge(X,Y)$$
$$path(X,Y) \leftarrow edge(X,Z), path(Z,Y)$$
$$edge(a,b) \leftarrow$$
$$edge(b,c) \leftarrow\}$$

Then, $U_P = \{a,b,c\}$
$$B_P = \{edge(a,a),\ edge(a,b),\ edge(a,c),$$
$edge(b,b),\ edge(b,a),\ edge(b,c),$
$edge(c,c),\ edge(c,a),\ edge(c,b),$
$path(a,a),\ path(a,b),\ path(a,c),$
$path(b,b),\ path(b,a),\ path(b,c),$
$path(c,c),\ path(c,a),\ path(c,b)\}$

$$I_1 = \{edge(b,b),\ path(a,b),\ path(c,b)\}$$
$$I_2 = \{edge(c,a),\ edge(b,a),\ path(b,b)\}$$

are two Herbrand interpretations of P.

$$M_1 = \{edge(a,b),\ edge(b,c),\ path(a,b),\ path(b,c),\ path(a,c)\}$$
$$M_2 = \{edge(a,b),\ edge(b,c),\ edge(c,c)$$
$$path(a,b),\ path(b,c),\ path(a,c)$$
$$path(b,a),\ path(a,a)\}$$

are two Herbrand models of P.

2.1 Definite logic programming

In their 1976 paper, van Emden and Kowalski [1976] defined different semantics for a definite logic program. These are referred to as model theoretic, proof theoretic (or procedural), and fixpoint (or denotational) semantics. Since we are dealing with logic, a natural semantics is to state that the meaning of a definite logic program is given by a Herbrand model of the theory. Hence, the meaning of the logic program is the set of atoms that are in the model. However, this definition is too broad as there may be atoms in the Herbrand model that one would not want to conclude to be true. For example, in the logic program given in Example 2.0.1, M_2 is a Herbrand model and includes atoms $edge(c,c)$, $path(b,a)$, $path(a,a)$. It is clear that the logic program does not state that any of these atoms are true. van Emden and Kowalski showed that for definite logic programs, the intersection of all Herbrand models of a logic program is a Herbrand model of the logic program. This property is called the Herbrand model intersection property. The intersection of all Herbrand models is the least Herbrand model as it is contained within all models. The least model captures all the ground atomic logical consequences of the logic program and represents the least amount of information that can be specified as true. The least Herbrand model of a logic program P is denoted as M_P.

Example 2.1.1. Consider the definite logic program P given in Example 2.0.1. The least Herbrand model of P is given by

$$M_P = \{edge(a,b),\ edge(b,c),\ path(a,b),\ path(b,c),\ path(a,c)\}$$

We can see that these are the only ground atoms which are logical consequences of P.

A second semantics that can be associated with a logic program is a procedural semantics. Gödel showed that one obtains the same results with proof theory as one does from model theory. Van Emden and Kowalski [1976] showed that if one uses a proof procedure called *linear resolution with selection function for definite logic programs (SLD-resolution)*, the ground atoms that are derivable using SLD from the logic program, forming the *SLD-success set, (SLD(P))* of the logic program, are exactly the same as the atoms in the least Herbrand model, M_P. SLD-resolution is a reduction type of processing and derives a sequence of queries, starting from the query. When a halt statement is derived, the SLD-resolution succeeds and the query is considered to be derivable using SLD-resolution. If no halt statement is obtained, the query is said to have failed.

Definition 2.1.2 ([van Emden and Kowalski, 1976]
(SLD-derivation)). Let P be a definite logic program, G be a query $= \leftarrow A_1, \ldots, A_m, \ldots A_n$. An SLD-derivation from P with top-query G consists of a (finite or infinite) sequence of queries $G_0 = G$, $G_1, \ldots$, such that for all $i \geq 0$, G_{i+1} is obtained from G_i as follows:

1. A_m is an atom in G_i and is called the selected atom
2. $A \leftarrow B_1, \ldots, B_q$ is a program clause in P (which is standarized apart with respect to G_i)
3. $A_m\theta = A\theta$ where θ is a substitution (most general)
4. G_{i+1} is the query $\leftarrow (A_1, \ldots, A_{m-1}, B_1, \ldots, B_q, A_{m+1}, \ldots, A_k)\theta$

In the example given below, we show an SLD-derivation of the halt statement.

Example 2.1.3. Consider the definite logic program P given in Example 2.0.1. Let $\leftarrow path(a, c)$ be the query to be solved.
Then we have the following SLD-derivation:

4. $\leftarrow path(a, c)$
5. $\leftarrow edge(a, Z)$, $path(Z, c)$ from the clause $path(X, Y) \leftarrow edge(X, Z), path(Z, Y)$
6. $\leftarrow path(b, c)$ from the clause $edge(a, b) \leftarrow$
7. $\leftarrow edge(b, c)$ from the clause $path(X, Y) \leftarrow edge(X, Y)$
8. $\leftarrow$ from the clause $edge(b, c) \leftarrow$

The query succeeds and is an element of the set SLD(P)

A third semantics is obtained by defining a mapping, T, from Herbrand interpretations to Herbrand interpretations. As in denotational semantics, if the domain over which the mapping, T, is defined is a complete lattice and the mapping is *continuous*, then the mapping, T, has a least fixpoint $(lfp(T))$, which is taken to be the meaning of the logic program. By a *fixpoint* of a mapping T, we mean an element I in the domain of T that satisfies the formula $T(I) = I$. The $lfp(T)$ is computed by iteratively applying the operator T starting with the bottom element of the lattice until a fixpoint is reached. The set of Herbrand interpretations forms a complete lattice over the partial ordering $\subseteq$. The bottom element of the lattice is the null set $\emptyset$. The following mapping, defined by van Emden and Kowalski [1976] is a continuous mapping.

Definition 2.1.4. [van Emden and Kowalski, 1976] Let P be a definite logic program, and let I be a Herbrand interpretation. Then

$$T_P(I) = \{A \in HB_P \mid A \leftarrow B_1, \ldots, B_n \text{ is a ground instance of a clause in } P,$$

and

$$B_1, \ldots, B_n \text{ are in } I\}$$

Example 2.1.5. Consider the definite logic program P given in Example 2.0.1. The least fixpoint of T_P is computed as follows:

$$T_P(\emptyset) = \{edge(a,b), edge(b,c)\}$$
$$T_P(\{edge(a,b), edge(b,c)\})$$
$$\quad = \{path(a,b), path(b,c), edge(a,b), edge(b,c)\}$$
$$T_P(\{path(a,b), path(b,c), edge(a,b), edge(b,c)\})$$
$$\quad = \{path(a,b), path(b,c), path(a,c), edge(a,b), edge(b,c)\}$$

The least fixpoint contains all the ground atoms which are logical consequences of P

The major result is that the model theoretic, the procedural and fixpoint semantics all capture the same meaning to a logic program: the set of ground atoms that are logical consequences of the logic program.

Theorem 2.1.6 ([van Emden and Kowalski, 1976]
(Horn Characterization—Positive)). *Let P be a definite logic program and $A \in HB_P$. Then the following are equivalent:*
  (a) A is in M_P
  (b) A is in least fixpoint of T_P
  (c) A is in $SLD(P)$
  (d) A is a logical consequence of P.

2.2 Disjunctive logic programming

In a disjunctive logic program, a minimal Herbrand model may not exist uniquely. Consider the disjunctive logic program

$$path(a,b), unconnected(b,a) \leftarrow \tag{3}$$

This clause is equivalent to

$$path(a,b) \vee unconnected(b,a) \tag{4}$$

and has two minimal Herbrand models, $\{path(a,b)\}$, and $\{unconnected(b,$

$a)\}$. Neither model contains the other. Furthermore, the intersection of the two minimal Herbrand models is not a model of the logic program. Hence, disjunctive logic programs do not have the Herbrand model intersection property of definite logic programs.

Although there is no unique minimal Herbrand model in a disjunctive logic program, there is a set of minimal Herbrand models. In 1982, Minker [1982] developed a suitable model theoretic semantics for disjunctive logic programs in terms of the minimal models. He showed that a ground clause is a logical consequence of a disjunctive logic program P if and only if it is true in every minimal Herbrand model of P. This semantics extends the unique minimal model theory of definite logic programs to disjunctive logic programs.

Example 2.2.1. Consider the following disjunctive logic program:

$P = \{(1) \; path(X, Y), unconnected(X, Y) \leftarrow point(X), point(Y) \; ;$

$(2) \; point(a) \; ;$

$(3) \; point(b)\}.$

The minimal Herbrand models of P are given by

$M_P^1 = \{path(a, a), path(a, b), path(b, a), path(b, b), point(a), point(b)\}$

$M_P^2 = \{unconnected(a, a), path(a, b), path(b, a), path(b, b), point(a),$
$point(b)\}$

$M_P^3 = \{path(a, a), unconnected(a, b), path(b, a), path(b, b), point(a),$
$point(b)\}$

$M_P^4 = \{path(a, a), path(a, b), unconnected(b, a), path(b, b), point(a),$
$point(b)\}$

$M_P^5 = \{path(a, a), path(a, b), path(b, a), unconnected(b, b), point(a),$
$point(b)\}$

$M_P^6 = \{unconnected(a, a), unconnected(a, b), path(b, a), path(b, b),$
$point(a), point(b)\}$

$M_P^7 = \{unconnected(a, a), path(a, b), unconnected(b, a), path(b, b),$
$point(a), point(b)\}$

$M_P^8 = \{unconnected(a, a), path(a, b), path(b, a), unconnected(b, b),$
$point(a), point(b)\}$

$M_P^9 = \{path(a, a), unconnected(a, b), unconnected(b, a), path(b, b),$
$point(a), point(b)\}$

$M_P^{10} = \{path(a, a), unconnected(a, b), path(b, a), unconnected(b, b),$
$point(a), point(b)\}$

$M_P^{11} = \{path(a, a), path(a, b), unconnected(b, a), unconnected(b, b),$
$point(a), point(b)\}$

$M_P^{12} = \{unconnected(a, a), unconnected(a, b), unconnected(b, a),$
$path(b, b), point(a), point(b)\}$

$M_P^{13} = \{unconnected(a, a), unconnected(a, b), path(b, a),$
$unconnected(b, b), point(a), point(b)\}$

$$M_P^{14} = \{unconnected(a,a), path(a,b), unconnected(b,a),$$
$$unconnected(b,b), point(a), point(b)\}$$
$$M_P^{15} = \{path(a,a), unconnected(a,b), unconnected(b,a),$$
$$unconnected(b,b), point(a), point(b)\}$$
$$M_P^{16} = \{unconnected(a,a), unconnected(a,b), unconnected(b,a),$$
$$unconnected(b,b), point(a), point(b)\}$$

We can see that every ground clause which is a logical consequence of P is true in every minimal Herbrand model of P

There is a corresponding result with respect to disjunctive logic programs that is similar to the Herbrand model intersection property. In contrast to definite logic programs, the ground logical consequences cannot necessarily be characterized by a set of ground atoms. To capture the logical consequences in a unique structure, the structure has to be defined over disjunctive clauses, rather than a structure dealing with atoms such as Herbrand base and interpretations. Minker and Rajasekar therefore defined the *disjunctive Herbrand base (DHB_P)* to consist of the set of all positive ground disjunctive clauses that can be constructed using the Herbrand base of a program. The DHB_P is used to define concepts similar to Herbrand interpretations and models of definite logic programs. Subsets of the DHB are referred to as *states*. A state is similar to a Herbrand interpretation. A structure corresponding to Herbrand models of definite programs is defined as follows.

Definition 2.2.2 ([Lobo *et al.*, 1989]). Consider a disjunctive logic program P. A *model-state* is defined to be a state of P such that

1. every minimal model of P is a model of the set of clauses in the model-state,
2. every minimal model of the model-state is a model of P.

The intersection of all model-states is a model-state and it is the least model-state. Lobo, Minker and Rajasekar [Lobo *et al.*, 1989] showed that the least model-state captures all the ground clausal logical consequences of the logic program and represents the least amount of information that can be specified as true. The least model-state of a disjunctive logic program P is denoted as MS_P.

Example 2.2.3. Consider the disjunctive logic program P given in Example 2.2.1. The least model-state of P is given by

$$MS_P = \{path(a,a) \vee unconnected(a,a), path(a,b) \vee unconnected(a,b),$$
$$path(b,a) \vee unconnected(b,a), path(b,b) \vee unconnected(b,b),$$
$$point(a), point(b)\}$$

We can see that every clause in MS_P is true in every minimal Herbrand model of P enumerated in Example 2.2.1.

To obtain the proof theoretic semantics of a disjunctive logic program, the inference system, *linear resolution with selection function for indefinite programs (SLI-resolution)*, developed by Minker and Zanon [1979] is used. SLI-resolution is defined using trees as the basic representation. Each node in the tree is a literal and there are two types of literals: marked literals or A-literals and unmarked literals or B-literals. A non-terminal node is always an A-literal whereas a terminal literal can be either an A- or a B-literal. These tree structures are called t-clauses. A t-clause can also be viewed as a pre-order representation of a resolution tree. It is a well-parenthesized expression such that every open parenthesis is followed by a marked literal. A t-clause is a special representation of a clause and embeds the information about the ancestry of each literal during a derivation. A literal is marked if it has been selected in an SLI-derivation. During derivation, an unmarked literal in the query t-clause is selected and marked. This literal can be either positive or negative. The selected literal is unified with a complementary literal in the program clause. The resolvent is attached as a subtree to the literal in the query clause. The t-clause is then made admissible and minimal by performing factoring, ancestry-resolution and truncation. The notions of factoring, ancestry-resolution and truncation are similar to that in SL-resolution [Kowalski and Kuehner, 1971]. Program and query clauses are represented in the form $(\varepsilon^* L_1 \ldots L_n)$, where ε is a special symbol, $*$ is a marking and the L_is are literals.

Example 2.2.4.

$$(\varepsilon^* \, path(X,Y) \, unconnected(X,Y) \, \neg point(X) \, \neg point(Y))$$

is a t-clause representation of

$$path(X,Y), unconnected(X,Y) \leftarrow point(X), point(Y)$$

We next give a formal definition for an SLI-derivation. First, we define two sets of literals which are used during resolution.

$\gamma_L = \{M :$ where M is a B-literal, and M is one node off the path from the root of $L\}$

$\delta_L = \{N :$ where N is an A-literal, and N is on the path between the root and $L\}$

A *t*-clause is said to satisfy the admissibility condition (AC) if for every occurrence of every B-literal L in it the following conditions hold:

(i) No two literals from γ_L and L have atoms which unify.

(ii) No two literals from δ_L and L have atoms which unify.

A *t*-clause is said to satisfy the minimality condition (MC) if there is no A-literal which is a terminal node.

γ_L and δ_L are used while performing factoring and ancestry-resolution respectively. AC and MC make sure that truncation, factoring and ancestry-resolution are performed as soon as possible. Now we have the framework for describing an SLI-resolution. We modify the definition given in [Minker and Zanon, 1979] and provide a definition similar to that of SLD-resolution.

Definition 2.2.5 ([Minker and Rajasekar, 1987]). Consider a t-clause C_0. Then C_n is a *tranfac-derivation* (truncation, ancestry and factoring) of C_0 when there is a sequence of t-clauses $C_0, C_1, \ldots, C_n$ such that for all i, $0 \le i \le n$, C_{i+1} is obtained from C_i by either t-factoring, t-ancestry, or t-truncation.

C_{i+1} is obtained from C_i by *t-factoring* iff

1. C_i is $(\alpha_1 \ L \ \alpha_2 \ M \ \alpha_3)$ or C_i is $(\alpha_1 \ M \ \alpha_2 \ L \ \alpha_3)$;
2. L and M have the same sign and unify with mgu θ ;
3. L is in γ_M (i.e., L is in an higher level of the tree);
4. C_{i+1} is $(\alpha_1\theta \ L\theta \ \alpha_2\theta \ \alpha_3\theta)$ or C_{i+1} is $(\alpha_1\theta \ \alpha_2\theta \ L\theta \ \alpha_3\theta)$

C_{i+1} is obtained from C_i by *t-ancestry* iff

1. C_i is $(\alpha_1 \ (L^* \ \alpha_2 \ (\alpha_3 \ M \ \alpha_4) \ \alpha_5) \ \alpha_6)$;
2. L and M are complementary and unify with mgu θ ;
3. L is in δ_M;
4. C_{i+1} is $(\alpha_1\theta \ (L\theta^* \ \alpha_2\theta \ (\alpha_3\theta \ \alpha_4\theta) \ \alpha_5\theta) \ \alpha_6\theta)$;

C_{i+1} is obtained from C_i by *t-truncation* iff

> either C_i is $(\alpha \ (L^*) \ \beta)$ and C_{i+1} is $(\alpha \ \beta)$.
> or C_i is (ε^*) and C_{i+1} is $\Box$.

Definition 2.2.6 ([Minker and Rajasekar, 1987]). Consider a t-clause C_i to be $(\varepsilon^* \ \alpha_1 \ L \ \beta_1)$ and a program-clause B_{i+1} to be $(\varepsilon^* \ \alpha_2 \ M \ \beta_2)$ which is standardized apart with respect to C_i. Let L to be an arbitrary literal in C_i selected for expansion. Then C_{i+1} is *derived* from C_i and B_j if the following conditions hold:

(a) L and M are complementary and unify with mgu $\theta'_{i+1} = \theta$;
(b) C'_{i+1} is $(\varepsilon^* \ \alpha_1\theta \ (L\theta^* \ \alpha_2\theta \ \beta_2\theta)\beta_1\theta)$
(c) C_{i+1} is a tranfac-derivation of C'_{i+1}
(d) C_{i+1} satisfies the admissibility and minimality conditions.

Definition 2.2.7 ([Minker and Rajasekar, 1987]). An *SLI-derivation* of a t-clause E from a disjunctive program P with top t-clause C is a sequence of t-clauses $(C_1, \ldots, C_n)$ such that:

- C_1 is a tranfac-derivation of C, and C_n is E;
- For all i, $1 \le i \le n$ C_{i+1} is derived from C_i and a program clause B_{i+1} in $P \cup \{C\}$

An SLI-derivation succeeds when it derives a null clause □. The example given next illustrates the SLI-derivation procedure.

Example 2.2.8. Consider the program P given in Example 2.2.1 augemented with the clauses

$$\{s(X,Y) \leftarrow path(X,Y),$$
$$s(X,Y) \leftarrow unconnected(X,Y)\}$$

Let $\leftarrow s(a,a)$ be the query to be solved. The t-clause representation of the augmented program is as follows:

(1) $\qquad (\varepsilon^* \; s(X,Y) \; \neg path(X,Y))$
(2) $\qquad (\varepsilon^* \; s(X,Y) \; \neg unconnected(X,Y))$
(3) $\qquad (\varepsilon^* \; path(X,Y) \; unconnected(X,Y) \; \neg point(X) \; \neg point(Y))$
(4) $\qquad (\varepsilon^* \; \neg point(a))$
(5) $\qquad (\varepsilon^* \; \neg point(b))$

and the query clause is translated into

(6) $\qquad (\varepsilon^* \; \neg s(a,a))$

We show that there is an SLI-refutation.

(6) $\qquad (\varepsilon^* \; \neg s(a,a))$ $\qquad\qquad\qquad$ query clause
(7) $\qquad (\varepsilon^* \; \overline{(\neg s(a,a)}^* \; \neg path(a,a))$ $\qquad\qquad$ t-derivation (6,1)
(8) $\qquad (\varepsilon^* \; (\neg s(a,a))^* \; \overline{(\neg path(a,a)}^* \; unconnected(a,a) \; \neg point(a)$
$\qquad\quad \neg point(a))))$ $\qquad\qquad\qquad\qquad\qquad$ t-derivation (7,3)
(9) $\qquad (\varepsilon^* \; (\neg s(a,a))^* \; (\neg path(a,a)^* \; unconnected(a,a) \; (\neg point(a)^*)$
$\qquad\quad \neg point(a))))$ $\qquad\qquad\qquad\qquad\qquad$ t-derivation (8,4)
(10) $\qquad (\varepsilon^* \; (\neg s(a,a))^* \; (\neg path(a,a)^* \; unconnected(a,a) \; \neg point(a))))$
$\qquad\qquad\qquad\qquad\qquad\qquad\qquad\qquad$ t-truncation (9)
(11) $\qquad (\varepsilon^* \; (\neg s(a,a))^* \; (\neg path(a,a)^* \; unconnected(a,a) \; (\neg point(a)^*))))$
$\qquad\qquad\qquad\qquad\qquad\qquad\qquad\qquad$ t-derivation (10,4)
(12) $\qquad (\varepsilon^* \; (\neg s(a,a))^* \; (\neg path(a,a)^* \; \underline{unconnected(a,a))))$
$\qquad\qquad\qquad\qquad\qquad\qquad\qquad\qquad$ t-truncation (11)
(13) $\qquad (\varepsilon^* \; (\neg s(a,a))^* \; (\neg path(a,a)^* \; (unconnected(a,a)^* \; \overline{s(a,a))))))$
$\qquad\qquad\qquad\qquad\qquad\qquad\qquad\qquad$ t-derivation (12,2)
(14) $\qquad (\varepsilon^* \; (\neg s(a,a))^* \; (\neg path(a,a)^* \; (unconnected(a,a)^* \; s(a,a)^*))))$
$\qquad\qquad\qquad\qquad\qquad\qquad\qquad\qquad$ t-ancestry (13)
(15) $\qquad \square$ $\qquad\qquad\qquad\qquad\qquad\qquad\qquad$ t-truncations (14) $\qquad \square$

As the proof theoretic semantics one should take the set of all positive ground clauses (that is, disjunctive clauses made of ground atoms from the Herbrand base) that one can derive from the logic program using SLI resolution. We call this set the *SLI-success set, (SLI(P)), of P.* The proof theoretic and the model theoretic semantics yield the same results.

Theorem 2.2.9 ([Minker and Zanon, 1979]). *Consider a disjunctive logic program P and a ground positive disjunctive clause C. Then,*

   $C \in SLI(P)$ *if and only if C is a logical consequence of P*

To obtain the fixpoint semantics of a disjunctive logic program, Minker and Rajasekar [1987a] modified the van Emden–Kowalski fixpoint operator T_P. When working with disjunctive logic programs, it is not possible to map Herbrand interpretations to Herbrand interpretations. The natural mapping with a disjunctive theory is to map a set of positive ground disjuncts to positive ground disjuncts. Minker and Rajasekar used the disjunctive Herbrand base, DHB_P, and its subsets to define a lattice for the mapping. Subsets of the DHB_P under the partial order $\subseteq$ form a lattice. Minker and Rajasekar defined their fixpoint operator to be:

Definition 2.2.10 ([Minker and Rajasekar, 1987a]). Let P be a disjunctive logic program, and let S be a state. Then

   $T_P(S) = \{C \in DHB(P) \mid C' \leftarrow B_1, \ldots, B_n$ is a ground instance of a clause in P,

   $B_1 \vee C_1, \ldots, B_n \vee C_n$ are in S, and C is the smallest factor of the clause $C' \vee C_1 \vee \ldots \vee C_n$, where the $C_i, 1 \leq i \leq n$ are positive clauses.$\}$

The smallest factor of a ground clause is another claus C' such that C' has only distinct ground atoms and is a subset of C. Minker and Rajasekar [1987a] showed that the operator T_P is continuous and the least fixpoint of T_P captures all the minimal ground clauses which are SLI-derivable from a disjunctive logic program P. By a minimal ground clause which is SLI-derivable we mean that no sub-clause of it is in the set $SLI(P)$.

Example 2.2.11. Consider the disjunctive logic program P given in Example 2.2.1. The least fixpoint of T_P is computed as follows:

   $T_P(\emptyset) = \{point(a), point(b)\}$
   $T_P(\{point(a), point(b)\})$
   $= \{path(a, a) \vee unconnected(a, a), path(a, b) \vee unconnected(a, b),$
   $path(b, a) \vee unconnected(b, a), path(b, b) \vee unconnected(b, b), point(a),$
   $point(b)\}$

This is the least fixpoint and contains all the minimal ground clauses which are derivable from P.

The major result in disjunctive logic programming is that the model semantics based on Herbrand models and model-states, the proof semantics and the fixpoint semantics yield the same semantics and capture the set of minimal positive clauses that are logical consequences of the logic program. Moreover, each of these semantics reduce to corresponding semantics for definite logic programs discussed in the previous section when

Semantics	Definite		Disjunctive	
	Theory	Reference	Theory	Reference
Positive Consequences				
Fixpoint Semantics	$T_P \uparrow \omega$	van Emden and Kowalski [1976]	$T_P^I \uparrow \omega$	Minker and Rajasekar [1987a]
Model Theory	Least Model	van Emden and Kowalski [1976]	Minimal Model Model-State	[Minker, 1982] Lobo *et al.* [1989]
Procedure	SLD	van Emden and Kowalski [1976]	SLI	Minker and Zanon [1979]

Table 1. Semantics for positive consequences for logic programs

applied to definite logic programs. Compare the following theorem with Theorem 2.1.6.

Theorem 2.2.12 ([Minker and Rajasekar, 1987a; Lobo *et al.*, 1989] Disjunction Characterization—Positive). *Let P be a disjunctive logic program and $C \in DHB_P$. Then the following are equivalent:*

(a) *C is true in every minimal Herbrand model of P*

(a') *C' is in MS_P, where C' is a sub clause of C*

(b) *C' is in the least fixpoint of T_P, where C' is a sub clause of C*

(c) *C is in $SLI(P)$*

(d) *C is a logical consequence of P.*

Table 1 summarizes the results discussed in this section.

3 Negation in logic programs

Given a definite or a disjunctive logic program, the only answers that may be derived are positive. It is not possible to answer a general query. One would have to permit negative information to be stored with the logic program. However, adding negative data could overwhelm a system as there is an unlimited amount of negative information that may apply. We describe several ways in which one may conclude negative information from definite or disjunctive theories without having to add negative data to the logic program. The theories of negation described below lead to nonmonotonic logics, important for commonsense reasoning. By a nonmonotonic logic is meant one in which the addition of a new truth to a theory may cause previous truths to become false. A logic program without negation is monotonic.

3.1 Negation in definite logic programs

Reiter [1978] and independently Clark [1978] were the first to address negation in definite logic programs and deductive databases. Their results appeared in a book edited by Gallaire and Minker [1978] entitled *Logic and*

Data Bases. To answer negated queries, Reiter defined the *closed world assumption (CWA)*. According to the CWA, one can assume a negated atom to be true if one cannot prove the atom from the logic program. Reiter showed that the union of the theory and the negated atoms proved by the CWA is consistent. Clark viewed negation of an atom as a lack of sufficient condition for provability of the atom. Clark argued that the logic program clauses in a definite logic program should be viewed as definitions of the atoms in the Herbrand base of the program. Hence they are necessary and sufficient to provide a proof for the atoms. That is, what one should do is consider the logic clauses as definitions to imply *if-and-only-if* conditions instead of only *if* conditions. To do so, one effectively reverses the *if* condition in the logic program clauses of a definite logic program P to be an *only-if* condition and then takes the union of this set of clauses with the original logic program clauses. The union of these two sets, augmented by Clark's equality theory (CET) [Clark, 1978] is referred to as the *Clark completion* of the program, and written comp(P). Clark shows that by using what is called the *negation as finite failure (NAF) rule* on the *if* definitions, one can conclude the negation of a ground atom if it fails finitely to prove the atom. He augmented SLD-resolution with this rule, and called it SLDNF-resolution, and showed that it is sound and complete with respect to the the the semantics defined by $comp(P)$.

Shepherdson [1984; 1985; 1987] showed a relationship between answers found using the CWA and the comp(P) theories of negation. He provides conditions under which they are the same and under which they may differ.

3.2   Negation in disjunctive logic progrtams

In his discussion of the CWA in 1978, Reiter [1978] showed that the CWA applied to disjunctive theories leads to inconsistencies. Consider the theory $\{p(a) \vee p(b)\}$. Since it is possible to prove neither $p(a)$ nor $p(b)$ by the CWA, one may assume $\neg p(a)$ and $\neg p(b)$. But the union is now inconsistent. That is, $\{p(a) \vee p(b), \neg p(a), \neg p(b)\}$ is inconsistent.

To overcome this problem, Minker [1982] defined the *generalized closed world assumption (GCWA)*. There are two ways to characterize the GCWA: model theoretic and proof theoretic.

Definition 3.2.1 ([Minker, 1982]). Let P be a disjunctive logic program. The set of negative literals that can be assumed using the GCWA is given by:
Model-theoretic definition:
$GCWA(P) = \{A \in HB_P \mid A$ not in any minimal Herbrand model of $P\}$
Proof-theoretic definition:
$GCWA(P) = \{A \in HB_P \mid \forall K, K$ is a positive (possibly empty) ground clause, $P \vdash A \vee K$ implies $P \vdash K\}$

Minker showed that these two definitions are equivalent.

Example 3.2.2. Consider the following definite logic program:

$P = \{$ (1) $path(X, Y), unconnected(X, Y) \leftarrow point(X), point(Y)$;
(2) $path(X, X) \leftarrow point(X)$
(3) $point(a)$;
(4) $point(b)\}$.

The minimal Herbrand models of P are given by

$$M_P^1 = \{path(a, a), path(a, b), path(b, a), path(b, b), point(a), point(b)\}$$
$$M_P^2 = \{path(a, a), unconnected(a, b), path(b, a), path(b, b), point(a),$$
$$point(b)\}$$
$$M_P^3 = \{path(a, a), path(a, b), unconnected(b, a), path(b, b), point(a),$$
$$point(b)\}$$
$$M_P^4 = \{path(a, a), unconnected(a, b), unconnected(b, a), path(b, b),$$
$$point(a), point(b)\}$$
$$GCWA(P) = HB_P - \bigcup_{i=1,2,3,4} M_P^i =$$
$$\{ unconnected(a, a)\ unconnected(b, b)\}$$

Answering negative queries with the GCWA is computationally difficult as shown by Chomicki and Subrahmanian [1989].

Lobo, Rajasekar and Minker [Lobo *et al.*, 1988] show that one can define a completion for a disjunctive logic program in a manner similar to the Clark completion [Clark, 1978] of definite logic programs. They refer to the completed theory for disjunctive logic programs as dcomp(P). They showed that a rule of negation called *negation as finite failure in disjunctive logic programs* can be defined, similar to the NAF-rule [Clark, 1978] of definite logic programs, and used to augment SLI-resolution to answer negative ground queries in disjunctive logic programs. They showed that this procedure, called SLINF-resolution, is sound and complete with respect to the completion of the disjunctive logic program. Rajasekar, Lobo and Minker [Rajasekar *et al.*, 1987] also show that a theory of negation similar to the closed world assumption called the *weak generalized closed world assumption (WGCWA)*, can be defined. They [Rajasekar *et al.*, 1987] showed that WGCWA is no more difficult to compute than negation in the CWA theory [Reiter, 1978] associated with definite logic programs. Hence, the WGCWA is computationally less complex than the GCWA [Minker, 1982]. In the WGCWA, we may assume the negation of an atom $p(a)$ if there is no positive ground clause that can be derived from the logic program that contains $p(a)$.

Definition 3.2.3 ([Rajasekar *et al.*, 1987]). Let P be a disjunctive logic program. The set of negative literals that can be assumed using the WGCWA is given by:

Semantics	Horn		Disjunctive	
	Theory	Reference	Theory	Reference
Negation				
Theory of	CWA	[Reiter, 1978]	GCWA	Minker [1982]
				Minker and
				Rajasekar [1987a]
negation			WGCWA	Ross and Topor [1987]
				Rajasekar *et al.* [1987]
Rule of	NAF	[Clark, 1978]	SN-rule	Minker and
				Rajasekar [1987]
negation			NAFFD-rule	[Rajasekar *et al.*, 1987]
Procedure	SLDNF	[Clark, 1978]	SLINF	Minker and
				Rajasekar [1987; 1987a]

Table 2. Semantics for Negative Consequences for Logic Programs

Proof-theoretic Definition:

$WGCWA(P) = \{A \in HB_P \mid \not\exists K, K$ is a positive (possibly empty) ground clause, P derives $A \vee K\}$.

We can consider the concept of *derivability* from a program P as equivalent to membership in the least fixpoint of T_P.

Example 3.2.4. Consider the disjunctive logic program P given in Example 3.2.2. The derivable consequences of P (as given by the least fixpoint of T_P)

$$= \{ \quad path(a,a) \vee unconnected(a,a), path(a,b) \vee unconnected(a,b),$$
$$path(b,a) \vee unconnected(b,a), path(b,b) \vee unconnected(b,b),$$
$$path(a,a), path(b,b), point(a), point(b)\}$$

$WGCWA(P) = \{\}$ since every ground atom in HB_P is in some clause which is derivable from P.

The WGCWA was discovered independently by Ross and Topor [1987] who call it the *disjunctive database rule (DDR)*. Rajasekar, Lobo and Minker [Rajasekar *et al.*, 1987] show that the GCWA implies the WGCWA. Both the GCWA and the WGCWA compute answers to negated atoms when they are ground formulae. When applied to Horn programs both the WGCWA and the GCWA reduce to the CWA.

Table 2 summarizes the results in negation for definite and disjunctive logic programs.

4   Normal or general disjunctive logic programs

Definite logic programs or disjunctive logic programs do not allow negated atoms in the right hand side of a logic program clause. This restricts the expressiveness that one may achieve in writing logic programs with negation in the body of a rule. As noted earlier, logic programs with negated atoms in the body of a logic program clause are referred to as normal (for program clauses with atomic heads) or normal disjunctive logic programs. One can, of course, write an equivalent formula for a disjunctive logic program which does not contain negated atoms, by moving the negated atom to the head of the logic program clause to achieve a disjunction of atoms in the head of the clause. This, however, has a different connotation than that intended by a negated atom in the body of a clause. It is intended in this case that the negated atom be considered solved by a default rule, such as the CWA or negation as finite failure.

As noted by Apt, Blair and Walker [Apt *et al.*, 1987], and also by Van Gelder [1987], by Naqvi [1986] and by Chandra and Harel [1985], problems arise with the intended meaning of a normal logic program in some instances. For example, the logic program $\{P = p(a) \leftarrow \neg q(a), q(a) \leftarrow p(a)\}$ raises questions as to its meaning. We describe alternative ways to handle normal definite logic programs and the corresponding approach with normal disjunctive logic programs.

4.1 Stratified definite logic programs

In a stratified logic program one allows normal logic programs which do not permit recursion through negation. For example, the program P given at the end of the previous section would not be permitted since there is recursion through negation. That is, we have two rules which need recursive application to solve and the application is through the negative literal $\neg q(a)$. When one excludes these constructs, one can place logic program clauses of the program into different strata, such that if a negative literal $\neg A$ occurs in the body of a program clause in some stratum S, then A occurs positively in the head of a program clause only in a stratum below S and if a positive literal A occurs in the body of a program clause in some stratum S, then A occurs positively in the head of a program clause in the same stratum or in a stratum below S. Stratified logic programs are a simple generalization of a class of logic programs introduced in the context of deductive databases by Chandra and Harel [1985].

Apt, Blair and Walker [1987] showed that if one has a stratified normal logic program, then one can find a fixpoint for the first stratum and then use this fixpoint as the starting point, find the fixpoint of the next stratum and continue until a fixpoint is obtained for the last stratum. This fixpoint is taken as the meaning of the logic program. They show that the fixpoint is a model and furthermore, is a minimal and supported model of the logic program.

Example 4.1.1. Consider the following normal program given by:

$$P = \{ \quad path(X,Y) \leftarrow \neg unconnected(X,Y),$$
$$unconnected(X,Y) \leftarrow point(X),\, point(Y)\; \neg edge(X,Y),$$
$$edge(X,Y) \leftarrow edge(X,Y),\, edge(Y,Z),$$
$$edge(a,b),\;\; edge(b,c),$$
$$edge(a,a),\;\; edge(b,b),\;\; edge(c,c),$$
$$point(a),\;\; point(b),\;\; point(c)\}$$

Then, the program can be stratified as follows:

$$P_1 = \{ \quad point(a),\;\; point(b),\;\; point(c),$$
$$edge(a,b),\; edge(b,c),$$
$$edge(X,Y) \leftarrow edge(X,Y),\, edge(Y,Z)\}$$
$$P_2 = \{ \quad unconnected(X,Y) \leftarrow \neg edge(X,Y)\}$$
$$P_3 = \{ \quad path(X,Y) \leftarrow \neg unconnected(X,Y)\}$$

Note that the atoms in the negative literals appearing in the body of a clause in stratum P_i appear only in the heads of clauses in stratum P_j with $j < i$. That is, the atoms appearing in these literals are *defined* in a stratum below them. Hence, there can be no recursion through these literals. In the case of positive literals appearing in the body of a clause in stratum P_i it can be seen that the atoms forming these literals are in the heads of clauses in stratum P_j with $j \le i$. again, this implies that these atoms are defined in the same stratum or in strata below. Recursion through these literals are allowed. The intended model is calculated iteratively as follows:

$$\begin{aligned}
M_{P_1} &= \text{least fixpoint of } T_{P_1}(\emptyset)\\
&= \{point(a),\; point(b),\; point(c),\\
&\quad edge(a,a),\; edge(b,b),\; edge(c,c),\\
&\quad edge(a,b),\; edge(b,c),\; edge(a,c)\}\\
M_{P_2} &= \text{least fixpoint of } T_{P_2}(M_{P_1})\\
&= \{unconnected(b,a),\; unconnected(c,b),\; unconnected(c,a)\} \bigcup M_{P_1}\\
M_{P_3} &= \text{least fixpoint of } T_{P_3}(M_{P_2})\\
&= \{path(a,a),\; path(b,b),\; path(c,c),\\
&\quad path(a,b),\; path(b,c),\; path(a,c)\} \bigcup M_{P_2}
\end{aligned}$$

$M_P = M_{P_3}$ is the intended meaning of the program using the Apt, Blair and Walker semantics.

The model semantics achieved by the theory developed by Apt, Blair and Walker [1987] is independent of the manner in which the logic program is stratified. Gelfond and Lifschitz [1988] show that M_P is also a *stable* model. Przymusinski [1988a] has defined the concept of a *perfect model* and has shown that every stratified logic program has exactly one perfect model. It is identical to the model obtained by Apt, Blair and Walker.

Theorem 4.1.2. *Let P be a stratified normal program. Then*

1. $T_P(M_P) = M_P$,
2. M_P is a *minimal Herbrand model of P*,
3. M_P is a *supported model of P*,
4. M_P is a *stable model of P*,
5. M_P is a *perfect model of P*.

In the procedural interpretation of normal disjunctive programs problems arise when a negated literal has to be evaluated and the literal contains a variable. In this case, the logic program is said to *flounder*. Chan [1988] has defined *constructive negation*, that will find correct answers even in the case of negated literals that contain variables. The underlying idea behind constructive negation is to answer queries using formulas involving only equality predicates. The following example illustrates the concept behind constructive negation.

Example 4.1.3. Consider the following normal program:

$$P = \{ \quad unconnected(X,Y) \leftarrow \neg path(X,Y),$$
$$path(X,Y) \leftarrow edge(X,Y)$$
$$path(X,Y) \leftarrow edge(X,Z), path(Z,Y)$$
$$edge(a,b) \leftarrow$$
$$edge(b,c) \leftarrow \}$$

and the query

$$\leftarrow unconnected(b,Y)$$

This query cannot be answered using the NAF rule [Clark, 1978] which requires that a negative literal be ground before it is selected in an SLDNF-derivation. Chan [1988] developed constructive negation which provides answers using inequality. An answer to the above query in his theory would be the inequality $\{Y \neq a\}$

4.2 Stratified disjunctive logic programs

Rajasekar and Minker [1988] apply the nonmonotonic fixpoint semantics developed by Apt, Blair and Walker to a closure operator $T^{\mathcal{C}}$ to develop a fixpoint theory for stratified disjunctive logic programs. The operator $T^{\mathcal{C}}$ is a modification of the operator T_P given in Definition 2.2.10 to handle negative literals in the body of the disjunctive program clauses. The operator uses the GCWA to handle negation. Given a set of positive ground clauses S, the canonical set, $can(S)$, is defined as a largest subset of S such that no clause in $can(S)$ is logically implied by another clause in $can(S)$.

Definition 4.2.1 ([Rajasekar and Minker, 1988]). For a disjunctive program P, a mapping $T_P^{\mathcal{C}} : 2^{DHB(P)} \rightarrow 2^{DHB(P)}$ is defined as follows:

Let S be the state of a program P, then

$$T_P^{\mathcal{C}}(S) = \{ \quad C \in DHB(P) : C' \leftarrow B_1, B_2, \ldots, B_n, \neg A_1, \neg A_2, \ldots,$$
$$\neg A_m \in HERB(P),$$
$$\forall i, 1 \leq i \leq n, s.t.\ B_i \text{ is an atom and } B_i \vee C_i \in S,$$
$$\forall i, 1 \leq i \leq m, s.t.\ A_i \text{ is an atom and no clause in } can(S)$$
$$\text{contains } A_i \text{ and}$$
$$C = s\text{-fac}(C' \vee C_1 \vee \ldots \vee C_n) \text{ where } \forall i, 1 \leq i \leq n, C_i$$
$$\text{can be empty}\}$$

Example 4.2.2. Consider the disjunctive program P given by:

$$P = \{ \quad path(X,Y) \leftarrow \neg unconnected(X,Y),$$
$$unconnected(X,Y), edge(X,Y) \leftarrow point(X), point(Y)$$
$$edge(X,Z) \leftarrow edge(X,Y), edge(Y,Z)$$
$$edge(a,b),\ edge(b,c),$$
$$edge(a,a),\ edge(b,b),\ edge(c,c),$$
$$point(a),\ point(b),\ point(c)\}.$$

P can be stratified as:

$$P_1 = \{ \quad point(a),\ point(b),\ point(c),$$
$$edge(a,b),\ edge(b,c),$$
$$(edge(a,a), edge(b,b), edge(c,c)$$
$$edge(X,Z) \leftarrow edge(X,Y), edge(Y,Z)\}$$
$$P_2 = \{ \quad unconnected(X,Y), edge(X,Y) \leftarrow point(X), point(Y)\}$$
$$P_3 = \{ \quad path(X,Y) \leftarrow \neg unconnected(X,Y)\}$$

Note that there is no recursion through negation. The explanation given in Example 4.1.1 also applies here. The intended meaning of P is computed as follows:

$$
\begin{aligned}
MS_{P_1} &= \text{least fixpoint of } T_{P_1}^{\mathcal{C}}(\emptyset) \\
&= \{point(a),\ point(b),\ point(c), \\
&\quad edge(a,a),\ edge(b,b),\ edge(c,c), \\
&\quad edge(a,b),\ edge(b,c),\ edge(a,c)\} \\
MS_{P_2} &= \text{least fixpoint of } T_{P_2}^{\mathcal{C}}(MS_{P_1}) \\
&= \{unconnected(a,b) \vee edge(a,b),\ unconnected(b,a) \vee edge(b,a), \\
&\quad unconnected(c,b) \vee edge(c,b),\ unconnected(b,c) \vee edge(b,c), \\
&\quad unconnected(a,c) \vee edge(a,c),\ unconnected(c,a) \vee edge(c,a), \\
&\quad unconnected(a,a) \vee edge(a,a),\ unconnected(b,b) \vee edge(b,b), \\
&\quad unconnected(c,c) \vee edge(c,c)\} \bigcup MS_{P_1} \\
MS_{P_3} &= \text{least fixpoint of } T_{P_3}^{\mathcal{C}}(MS_{P_2}) \\
&= \{path(a,a),\ path(b,b),\ path(c,c), \\
&\quad path(a,b),\ path(b,c),\ path(a,c)\} \bigcup MS_{P_2}
\end{aligned}
$$

Semantics	Horn		Disjunctive	
	Theory	Reference	Theory	Reference
Stratified Programs				
Fixpoint semantics	T_P	Apt *et al.* [1987]	$T_P^{\mathcal{C}}$	Rajasekar and Minker [1988]
			T_P^I	Ross and Topor [1987], Rajasekar and Minker [1988]
Model theory	Standard model	Apt *et al* [1987]	Standard state	Rajasekar and Minker [1988]
	Stable model	Gelfond and Lifschitz [1988]	Stable state	

Table 3. Stratification Semantics for Logic Programs

$MS_P = MS_{P_3}$ is the intended meaning of the program

Rajasekar and Minker [1988] show that the iterarted state MS_P reached by the stratified semantics is a logical fixpoint of $T_P^{\mathcal{C}}$. S is a logical fixpoint of T if $T(S) \to S$ and $S \to T(S)$. They also show that MS_P is a *stable* state and *supported* state. A stable state is similar in concept to the stable model of normal programs defined by Gelfond and Lifschitz [1988]. A supported state is defined similar to a supported Herbrand interpretation [Apt *et al.*, 1987]. In addition, Rajasekar and Minker [1988] develop an iterative definition for negation, called the *generalized closed world assumption for stratified logic programs (GCWAS)*, and show that the semantics captures this definition. A model-theoretic semantics is developed for stratified disjunctive logic programs which is shown to be the least state characterized by the fixpoint semantics that corresponds to a stable-state defined in a manner similar to the stable models of Gelfond and Lifschitz. A weaker semantics is also developed for stratification based on the WGCWA, called WGCWAS.

Theorem 4.2.3. *Let P be a stratified disjunctive program. Then*

1. $T_P^{\mathcal{C}}(MS_P) \Leftrightarrow MS_P$,

2. MS_P *is a supported state of P,*

3. MS_P *is a stable state of P.*

Lobo [1990] extends the concept of constructive negation, introduced by Chan for stratified logic programs, to apply to stratified disjunctive logic programs. The results include the theories of negation for disjunctive logic programs: the GCWAS and the WGCWAS.

Table 3 summarizes the results that have been obtained in stratified logic programs and stratified disjunctive logic programs.

4.3   Well-founded and generalized well-founded logic programs

There exist logic programs that are not stratifiable and yet we desire to compute answers to queries over these theories. An example of a logic program that is not stratifiable is given by the game tree program:

$$P = \{win(X) \leftarrow move(X,Y),\ \neg win(Y) \cup \{ \text{ clauses defining } move \ \} \ \}.$$

Van Gelder, Ross and Schlipf [Van Gelder *et al.*, 1988] define the concept of *well-founded semantics* to handle such logic programs. Przymusinski [1988b] presents the ideas of well-founded semantics in terms of two sets of atoms T and F. Atoms in T are assumed to be true and those in F are assumed to be false. If an atom is neither true nor false, it is assumed to be unknown. Thus, in the logic program,

$$P = \{p \leftarrow a,\ p \leftarrow b,\ a \leftarrow \neg b,\ b \leftarrow \neg a\}.$$

We can conclude that p, a, and b are all unknown. The atom p is considered *unknown* since it is defined using a and b both of which are *unknown*. Van Gelder, Ross and Schlipf [Van Gelder *et al.*, 1988] develop fixpoint and model theoretic semantics for such logic programs. Ross [1989b] and Przymusinski [1988b] develop procedural semantics. The three different semantics are equivalent.

If one analyzes the above logic program, another meaning to the logic program is also possible. In particular, the last two logic program clauses state that a is true if b is not true, and b is true if a is not true. Hence, if a is true then p must be true and if b is true p must be true. Thus, although we may not be able to conclude which of a or b are true, we can surely conclude that p must be true. Baral, Lobo and Minker [Baral *et al.*, 1989a] develop model theoretic, fixpoint and procedural semantics to capture the meaning of logic programs such as given above. They term this *generalized well-founded semantics (GWFS)*. The fixpoint definition is similar to the definitions of well-founded semantics of Przymusinski. Every atom proved to be true in the well-founded semantics is also true in the generalized well-founded semantics. However, some additional atoms may be proved true in the GWFS.

4.4   Generalized disjunctive well-founded semantics

Consider the following example:

Example 4.4.1. Let P be a disjunctive logic program:

$$P = \{\quad a \leftarrow \neg b,\ c,\ d,$$
$$b \leftarrow \neg a,$$
$$c \leftarrow \neg d,$$
$$d \leftarrow \neg c\}$$

$c \wedge d$ is false in all minimal models of this program. Therefore, it is reasonable to assume that a is false and b is true. But the GWFS discussed in the previous sub-section is not able to infer a to be false and b to be true for the above program. But, it is able to infer a to be false and b to be true for a simple variant of the above program, given to be:

$$P' = \{\quad a \leftarrow \neg b,\ e,$$
$$e \leftarrow c,\ d,$$
$$b \leftarrow \neg a,$$
$$c \leftarrow \neg d,$$
$$d \leftarrow \neg c\}.$$

Baral, Lobo and Minker [Baral *et al.*, 1989b] describe a semantics which solves the above problem in GWFS. The semantics is based on disjunctions and conjunctions of atoms instead of only sets of atoms. The disjuncts are assumed to be true and the conjuncts are assumed to be false. This allows the representation of indefinite information. That is, $\neg a \vee \neg b$ can be assumed to be true (by having $a \wedge b$ as false) without knowing if either $\neg a$ or $\neg b$ or both are true. The semantics is also general enough to extend the well-founded semantics to normal disjunctive programs. They also present a procedural semantics for the extended semantics and show how to restrict the procedure to compute the generalized well-founded semantics. Since the procedure handles not only atomic but also disjunctive information, factoring and bookkeeping for ancestry resolution are needed. In addition, the deduction of negative information is obtained using the GCWA which was proved to be more complex than the closed world assumption [Chomicki and Subrahmanian, 1989].

There have been other extensions of the well-founded theory to disjunctive logic programs. Ross [1989a] developed a *strong well-founded semantics* and Przymusinski [1990] developed what is called a *stationary semantics*. This work extends well-founded semantics to disjunctive logic programs.

Table 4 summarizes the results that have been obtained in well-founded semantics for definite and disjunctive logic programs.

5 Summary

We have described the foundational theory that exists for definite normal logic programs and the extensions that have been made to that theory and to disjunctive normal logic programs. The results are summarized in

Semantics	Horn		Disjunctive	
	Theory	Reference	Theory	Reference
	Well-Founded		Strong/ weak well-F/ stationary	
Normal Programs				
Fixpoint	I^∞	Van Gelder et al. [1988]		
Model	$M_{WF}(P)$	Van Gelder et al. [1988]	$M_{WF}^{S/W}(P)$ M_P	[Ross, 1989a] Przymusinski [1990]
Procedure	SLS	[Ross, 1989b]/ Przymusinski [1989]		
	General Well-Founded		General disjunctive well-founded	
Fixpoint	I^E	Baral et al. [1989a]	S^{ED}	Baral et al. [1989b]/ Baral et al [1989d]
Model	M_P^E	Baral [1989a]	MS_P^{ED}	Baral et al. [1989b]/ Baral et al. [1989d]
Procedure	SLIS	Baral et al. [1989d]	SLIS	[Baral et al., 1989c]/ [Baral et al., 1989d]

Table 4. Well founded semantics for logic programs

tables 1-4. The theory of definite and disjunctive logic programs applies equally to deductive databases where one typically assumes that the rules are function-free. A firm foundation now exists both for definite normal and disjunctive normal logic programs for deductive databases and logic programming.

Although we have developed model theoretic, proof theoretic and fixpoint semantics for disjunctive logic programs, efficient techniques will be required for computing answers to queries in disjunctive deductive databases and logic programs. Some preliminary work has been reported by Minker and Grant [1986b], Liu and Sunderraman [1990], and by Henschen and his students [Yahya and Henschen, 1985; Henschen and Park, 1986; Chi and Henschen, 1988]. However, a great deal of additional work is required regarding theoretical, implementational and applicative aspects of disjunctive logic programming. Questions regarding negation, efficient proof procedures and answer extraction are important areas which need to be looked into. Implementing a language based on disjunctive logic has open problems which need to be solved such as efficient data structure, subsumption algorithm, control strategies and extra logical features. Applications ranging from knowledge based systems, to common sense reasoning, to natural language processing seem to be appropriate domains for applying disjunctive logic programming. These areas and others need to be explored.

6   Addendum

Disjunctive logic programming has made significant progress since the paper was submitted in 1989.[1]

Semantics of disjunctive logic programming have been extended to include literals both in the head and in the body of disjunctive clauses and default negation in the body of clauses. In [Lobo *et al.*, 1992] the theoretical foundations of disjunctive logic programs including theories of negation, the semantics and the view update problem in disjunctive deductive databases are given. See [Minker, 1994] for work up to 1994; [Minker and Ruiz, 1996] for literature on disjunctive theories that contain literals in clauses and default negation in the body of clauses, and on theories that contain both literals and multiple default rules in the body of clauses.

Nonmonotonic reasoning and logic programming are closely related. Nonmonotonic theories such as circumscription, default reasoning and autoepistemic logic can be transformed to disjunctive logic programs. See Minker [1993; 1996] for references. Thus, disjunctive logic programs can serve as computational vehicles for nonmonotonic reasoning.

Complexity and properties of disjunctive logic programs have been studied extensively. Complexity results are known for most theories of extended disjunctive logic programs, see [Minker, 1996]. For references to work on properties of the consequence relations defined by the different semantics of disjunctive logic programs, see [Minker, 1996]. Based on properties of programs and their complexity, users may select the semantics of disjunctive logic programs of interest to them.

Disjunctive deductive databases are a subset of disjunctive logic programming. Such databases are function-free and hence on is dealing with finite theories. For theories and algorithms of disjunctive deductive databases, see [Fernández and Minker, 1995]. For work and references on the view update problem, see [Fernández, Grant and Minker, 1996]. For references to the role of disjunctive databases in knowledge bases, see [Minker, 1996].

Acknowledgements

We wish to express our appreciation to the National Science Foundation for their support of our work under grant number IRI-86-09170 and the Army Research Office under grant number DAAG-29-85-K-0-177.

References

[Apt *et al.*, 1987] K. R. Apt, H. A. Blair, and A. Walker. Towards a theory of declarative knowledge. In J. Minker, editor, *Foundations of Deduc-*

---

[1]This paper was written in 1989. the addendum specifies where references to work through 1996 may be found. Space did not permit citing all relevant work.

tive Databases and Logic Programming, pp. 89–148. Morgan Kaufmann, Washington, D.C., 1988.

[Baral et al., 1989a] C. Baral, J. Lobo, and J. Minker. Generalized well-founded semantics for logic programs. Technical report, Dept of Computer Science, University of Maryland, College Park Md 20742, 1989.

[Baral et al., 1989b] C. Baral, J. Lobo, and J. Minker. Generalized disjunctive well-founded semantics for logic programs : Declarative semantics. In Z. W. Ras, M. Zemankova and M. L. Emrich, editors, *Methodologies for Intelligent Systems*, **5**, pp. 465–473. North-Holland, 1990.

[Baral et al., 1989c] C. Baral, J. Lobo, and J. Minker. Generalized disjunctive well-founded semantics for logic programs : Procedural semantics. In Z. W. Ras, M. Zemankova and M. L. Emrich, editors, *Methodologies for Intelligent Systems*, **5**, pp. 456–464. North-Holland, 1990.

[Baral et al., 1989d] C. Baral, J. Lobo, and J. Minker. Generalized disjunctive well-founded semantics for logic programs. Technical report, Dept of Computer Science, University of Maryland, College Park Md 20742, 1989.

[Chan, 1988] D. Chan. Constructive negation based on the completed databases. In R.A. Kowalski and K.A. Bowen, editors, *Proc. 5th International Conference and Symposium on Logic Programming*, pp. 111–125, Seattle, Washington, August 15-19, 1988.

[Chandra and Harel, 1985] A. Chandra and D. Harel. Horn clause queries and generalizations. *Journal of Logic Programming*, 2(1):1–15, April 1985.

[Chi and Henschen, 1988] S. Chi and L. Henschen. Recursive query answering with non-Horn clauses. In E. Lusk and R. Overbeek, editors, *Proc. 9th International Conference on Automated Deduction*, pp. 294–312, Argonne, IL, May 23-26, 1988.

[Chomicki and Subrahmanian, 1989] J. Chomicki and V. S. Subrahmanian. Generalized closed world assumption is π_2^0 complete. *Information Processing Letters*, 34: 289–291, 1990.

[Clark, 1978] K. L. Clark. Negation as failure. In H. Gallaire and J. Minker, editors, *Logic and Data Bases*, pp. 293–322. Plenum Press, New York, 1978.

[Colmerauer et al., 1973] A. Colmerauer, H. Kanoui, R. Pasero, and P. Roussel. Un système de communication homme–machine en Français. Technical report, Groupe d'Intelligence Artificielle Université de Aix-Marseille II, Marseille, 1973.

[Fernández and Minker, 1995] J. A. Fernández and J. Minker. Bottom-up computation of perfect models for disjunctive theories. *Journal of Logic Programming*, 25: 33–51, 1995.

[Fernández, Grant and Minker, 1996] J. A. Fernández, J. Grant and J. Minker. Model theoretic approach to view updates in deductive databases. *Journal of Automated Reasoning*, 17:171–197, 1996.

[Gallaire and Minker, 1978] H. Gallaire and J. Minker, editors. *Logic and Databases*. Plenum Press, New York, April 1978.

[Gelfond and Lifschitz, 1988] M. Gelfond and V. Lifschitz. The stable model semantics for logic programming. In R. A. Kowalski and K. A. Bowen, editors, *Proc. 5th International Conference and Symposium on Logic Programming*, pp. 1070–1080, Seattle, Washington, August 15–19 1988.

[Henschen and Park, 1986] L. J. Henschen and H. Park. Compiling the GCWA in indefinite databases. In J. Minker, editor, *Foundations of Deductive Databases and Logic Programming*, pp. 395–438. Morgan Kaufmann, Washington, DC, 1988.

[Kowalski, 1974] R. A. Kowalski. Predicate logic as a programming language. *Proc. IFIP 4*, pp. 569–574, 1974.

[Kowalski and Kuehner, 1971] R. A. Kowalski and D. Kuehner. Linear resolution with selection function. *Artificial Intelligence*, **2**, 227–260, 1971.

[Liu and Sunderraman, 1990] K.C. Liu and R. Sunderraman. Indefinite and maybe information in relational databases. *ACM Transactions on Database Systems*, 15: 1–39, 1990.

[Lloyd, 1987] J.W. Lloyd. *Foundations of Logic Programming*. Springer–Verlag, second edition, 1987.

[Lobo, 1990] J. Lobo. On constructive negation for disjunctive logic programs. Submitted to NACLP 90.

[Lobo et al., 1988] J. Lobo, A. Rajasekar, and J. Minker. Weak completion theory for non-Horn programs. In R. A. Kowalski and K. A. Bowen, editors, *Proc. 5th International Conference and Symposium on Logic Programming*, pp. 828–842, Seattle, Washington, August 15–19 1988.

[Lobo et al., 1989] J. Lobo, J. Minker, and A. Rajasekar. Extending the semantics of logic programs to disjunctive logic programs. In G. Levi and M. Martelli, editors, *Proc. 6th International Conference on Logic Programming*, Lisbon, Portugal, June 19–23 1989.

[Lobo et al., 1992] J. Lobo, J. Minker and A. Rajasekar. *Foundations of Disjunctive Logic Programming*. The MIT Press, Cambridge, MA, 1992.

[Minker, 1982] J. Minker. On indefinite databases and the closed world assumption. In Vol. 138 of *Lecture Notes in Computer Science*, pp. 292–308. Springer-Verlag, Berlin, 1982.

[Minker, 1993] J. Minker. An overview of nonmonotonic reasoning and logic programming. *Journal of Logic Programming*, 17: 95–126, 1993.

[Minker, 1994] J. Minker. Overview of disjunctive logic programming. *Journal of Artificial Intelligence and Mathematics*, 12: 1–24, 1994.

[Minker, 1996] J. Minker. Logic and databases: a 20 year retrospective. In *Logic in Databases*, pp. 5–57, July 1996. Springer, Lecture Notes in Comp. Sci., 1154 Invited Keynote Address Int. Workshop LID'96 San Miniato, Italy Proceedings.

[Minker and Grant, 1986b] J. Minker and J. Grant. Answering queries in indefinite databases and the null value problem. In P. Kanellakis, editor, *Advances in Computing Research*, pp. 247–267, 1986.

[Minker and Rajasekar, 1987] J. Minker and A. Rajasekar. Procedural interpretation of non-Horn logic programs. In E. Lusk and R. Overbeek, editors, *Proc. 9th International Conference on Automated Deduction*, pp. 278–293, Argonne, IL, 23–26, May 1988.

[Minker and Rajasekar, 1987a] J. Minker and A. Rajasekar. A fixpoint semantics for disjunctive logic programs. *Journal of Logic Programming*, 9: 45–74, 1990.

[Minker and Ruiz, 1996] J. Minker and C. Ruiz. Mixing a default rule with stable negation. In *Proc. of the Fourth Int. Symp. on Art. Intell. and Mathematics*, pp. 122–125, 1996.

[Minker and Zanon, 1979] J. Minker and G. Zanon. An extension to linear resolution with selection function. *Information Processing Letters*, **14**, 191–194, 1982.

[Naqvi, 1986] S. A. Naqvi. A logic for negation in database systems. In J. Minker, editor, *Proc. Workshop on Foundations of Deductive Databases and Logic Programming*, pp. 378–387, Washington, DC, August 18–22, 1986.

[Przymusinski, 1990] T. C. Przymusinski. Stationary semantics for disjunctive logic programs. S. Debray and M. Hermenegildo, editors, *Proc of the North American Conference on Logic Programming*, Austin, TX, pp. 40–62, 1990.

[Przymusinski, 1988a] T. C. Przymusinski. Perfect model semantics. In R. A. Kowalski and K. A. Bowen, editors, *Proc. 5th International Conference and Symposium on Logic Programming*, pp. 1081–1096, Seattle, Washington, August 15–19 1988.

[Przymusinski, 1988b] T. C. Przymusinski. On constructive negation in logic programming. In E. Lusk and R. Overbeek, editors, *Proc. North American Conference of Logic Programming*, Cleveland, Ohio, October 16–20, 1989. Extended Abstract.

[Przymusinski, 1989] T. C. Przymusinski. Every logic program has a natural stratification and an iterated fixed point model. In *Proceedings 8th ACM SIGACT-SIGMOD-SIGART Symposium on Principle of Database Systems*, pp. 11–21, 1989.

[Rajasekar and Minker, 1988] A. Rajasekar and J. Minker. On stratified disjunctive programs. Technical Report CS-TR-2168 UMIACS-TR-88-99, Department of Computer Science, University of Maryland, College

Park, December 1988. In *Annals of Mathematics and Artificial Intelligence*, Vol. 1, 1990.

[Rajasekar *et al.*, 1987] A. Rajasekar, J. Lobo, and J. Minker. Weak generalized closed world assumption. *Journal of Automated Reasoning*, **5**, 293–307, 1989.

[Reiter, 1978] R. Reiter. On closed world data bases. In H. Gallaire and J. Minker, editors, *Logic and Data Bases*, pp. 55–76. Plenum Press, New York, 1978.

[Ross, 1989a] K. Ross. Well-founded semantics for disjunctive logic programs. In *Proc. 1st International Conference on Deductive and Object Oriented Databases*, Kyoto, Japan, December 4–6, 1989.

[Ross, 1989b] K. Ross. A procedural semantics for well founded negation in logic programs. In *Proc. 8th ACM SIGACT-SIGMOD-SIGART Symposium on Principle of Database Systems*, Philadelphia, PA, March, 29–31, 1989.

[Ross and Topor, 1987] K. A. Ross and R. W. Topor. Inferring negative information from disjunctive databases. *Journal of Automated Reasoning*, **4**, 397–424, 1988.

[Shepherdson, 1984] J. C. Shepherdson. Negation as finite failure: a comparison of Clark's completed database and Reiter's closed world assumption. *Journal of Logic Programming*, **1**, 51–79, 1984.

[Shepherdson, 1985] J. C. Shepherdson. Negation as failure: II. *Journal of Logic Programming*, **2**, 185–202, 1985.

[Shepherdson, 1987] J. C. Shepherdson. Negation in logic programming. In J. Minker, editor, *Foundations of Deductive Databases and Logic Programming*, pp. 19–88. Morgan Kaufman, Washington, DC, 1988.

[van Emden and Kowalski, 1976] M. H. van Emden and R. A. Kowalski. The semantics of predicate logic as a programming language. *Journal of the ACM*, **23**, 733–742, 1976.

[Van Gelder, 1987] A. Van Gelder. Negation as failure using tight derivations for general logic programs. In J. Minker, editor, *Foundations of Deductive Databases and Logic Programming*, pp. 1149–176. Morgan Kaufmann, Washington, DC, 1988.

[Van Gelder *et al.*, 1988] A. Van Gelder, K. Ross, and J. S. Schlipf. Unfounded sets and well-founded semantics for general logic programs. In *Proc. 7th Symposium on Principles of Database Systems*, pp. 221–230, 1988.

[Yahya and Henschen, 1985] A. Yahya and L. J. Henschen. Deduction in non-Horn databases. *Journal of Automated Reasoning*, **1**, 141–160, 1985.

Negation as Failure, Completion and Stratification

J. C. Shepherdson

Contents

1 Overview/introduction

1.1 Negation as failure, the closed world assumption and the Clark completion

The usual way of introducing negation into Horn clause logic programming is by 'negation as failure': if A is a ground atom

> *the goal $\neg A$ succeeds if A fails*
> *the goal $\neg A$ fails if A succeeds.*

This is obviously not classical negation, at least not relative to the given program P; the fact that A fails from P does not mean that you can prove $\neg A$ from P, e.g. if P is

$$a \leftarrow \neg b$$

then $? - b$ fails so, using negation as failure, $? - a$ succeeds, but a is not a logical consequence of P.

You could deal with classical negation by using a form of resolution which gave a complete proof procedure for full first order logic. To a logician this would be the natural thing to do. Two reasons are commonly given for why this is not done. The first is that it is believed by most, but not all, practitioners, that this would be infeasible because it would lead to a combinatorial explosion, whereas negation as failure does not, since it is not introducing any radically new methods of inference, just turning the old ones round. The second is that, in practical logic programming, negation as failure is often more useful than classical negation. This is the case when the program is a database, e.g. an airline timetable. You list all the flights there are. If there is no listed flight from Zurich to London at 12.31, then you conclude that there is no such flight. The implicit use of negation as failure here saves us the enormous labour of listing all the non-existent flights.

This implicit usage is made precise in the *closed world assumption*, one of the two commonest declarative semantics given for negation as failure. This was introduced by Reiter [1978] and formalises the idea that the database contains all the positive information about objects in the domain, that any positive ground literal which is not implied by the program is assumed to be false. Formally we define

$$CWA(P) = P \cup \{\neg A : A \text{ is a ground atom and } P \not\vdash A\},$$

and we also restrict consideration to term or Herbrand models whose domain of individuals consists of the ground terms.

Negation as failure (NF) is sound for the closed world assumption for both success and failure, i.e.

if ?−Q succeeds from P with answer θ using NF then $CWA(P) \vDash_H Qθ$,

if ? − Q fails from P using NF then $CWA(P) \vDash_H ¬Q$

where $T \vDash_H S$ means '*S is true in all Herbrand models of T* '.

The closed world assumption seems appropriate for programs representing the simpler kinds of database, but its more general use is limited by two facts:

1. *If P implies indefinite information about ground literals then $CWA(P)$ is inconsistent.*

   e.g. if P is the program above consisting of the single indefinite clause, $a \leftarrow ¬b$, then neither a nor b is a consequence of P so in forming $CWA(P)$ both $¬a$ and $¬b$ are added, and the original clause, which is equivalent to $a \lor b$, is inconsistent with these.

2. *Even if P consists of definite Horn clauses, NF may be incomplete for $CWA(P)$, i.e.*

   'if $CWA(P) \vDash_H Qθ$ then ?−Q succeeds from P with answer including θ using NF' fails to hold for some programs P.

   Indeed there may be no automatic proof procedure which is both sound and complete for $CWA(P)$, because there are P such that the set of negative ground literals which are consequences of $CWA(P)$ may be non-recursively enumerable.

A more widely applicable declarative semantics for NF was given by Clark [1978]. This is now usually called the (Clark) completion, $comp(P)$, of the original program P. It is based on 'the implied iff', the idea that when in a logic program you write

$$even(0) \leftarrow$$
$$even(s(s(x))) \leftarrow even(x),$$

what you usually intend is to give a comprehensive definition of the predicate *even*, that the clauses with even in their head are supposed to cover all the cases in which *even* holds, i.e.

$$even(y) \leftrightarrow (y = 0 \lor \exists x(y = s(s(x)) \land even(x))).$$

In the general case to form $comp(P)$ you treat each predicate symbol p like this, rewriting the clauses of P in which p appears in the head in the form of an iff definition of p. Since this introduces the equality predicate $=$ it is necessary to add axioms for that. These take the form of the usual equality axioms together with 'freeness axioms', which say that two terms are equal iff they are forced to be by the equality axioms; for example if

f and g are different unary function symbols one of the freeness axioms is $f(x) \neq g(y)$.

The basic result of [Clark, 1978] is that NF is sound for $comp(P)$ for both success and failure. Many logic programmers regard this as a justification for taking $comp(P)$ to be the declarative meaning of a logic program, indeed some of them take it so much for granted they do not feel the need to say that this is what they are doing. Quite apart from the lack of completeness which we discuss below, I think this is unsatisfactory. Although in everyday language we may often use 'if' when we mean 'iff', confusing them is responsible for many of the logical errors made by beginning students of mathematics. Since one of the merits of logic programming is supposed to be making a rapprochement between the declarative and procedural interpretation of a program, in the interests of Wysiwym— What you say is what you mean—logic programming, I think that if you mean 'iff' you should write 'iff'; if you want to derive consequences of $comp(P)$ you should write $comp(P)$, and if in order to carry out this derivation it is necessary to go via P then this should be done automatically. A practical reason for doing this would be that although in simple examples like the one given it is easy to understand the meaning of $comp(P)$ given P, this is no longer true when P contains 'recursive' clauses with the same predicate symbol occurring on both sides of the implication sign, or clauses displaying mutual recursion. Unfortunately writing $comp(P)$ instead of P would not solve all our problems because the fact that NF is usually incomplete for $comp(P)$ means that two programs with the same completion can behave differently with respect to NF. For example the program

$$a \leftarrow a$$
$$a \leftarrow \neg a$$

has completion

$$a \leftrightarrow a \vee \neg a$$

which is equivalent to the completion of

$$a \leftarrow$$

but the query $? - a$ succeeds with respect to the latter but not with respect to the former.

Despite these shortcomings of the closed world assumption and the completion, they dominate the current view of negation as failure to such an extent that a large part of this chapter will be taken up with their study. It must be admitted that the notion of the 'implied iff' is implicit in the use of negation as failure together with unification, and that the completion, although not as transparent as one would wish, is from the logical point of view one of the simplest declarative semantics which have been proposed for negation as failure.

1.2   Incompleteness of NF for *comp*(*P*)

We have noted above that although NF is not sound for *P* it is sound both for CWA(P) and *comp*(*P*). Although based on superficially similar considerations, CWA(P) and *comp*(*P*) can be very different; if *P* is $a \leftarrow \neg b$ then *comp*(*P*) is consistent but CWA(P) is not, if *P* is $p \leftarrow \neg p$ then CWA(P) is consistent but *comp*(*P*) is not, if *P* is $a \leftarrow \neg b, b \leftarrow a, a \leftarrow a$, then both CWA(P) and *comp*(*P*) are consistent but they are incompatible. We have seen above that there are many *P* for which NF is incomplete for CWA(P), in particular those *P* for which CWA(P) is inconsistent. The simple examples above show that NF is often incomplete for *comp*(*P*). This incompleteness is partially explained by the fact that the soundness result

> *if* ? − *Q succeeds from P with answer θ using NF then comp*(*P*) $\models$
> *Qθ,*
> *if* ? − *Q fails from P using NF then comp*(*P*) $\models \neg Q$

holds for weaker consequence relations than $\models$, for example for intuitionistic derivability $\vdash_I$, and for 3-valued consequence $\models_3$,(being true in all 3-valued models), as shown recently by Kunen [1987]. So we cannot have completeness for *comp*(*P*) using the classical 2-valued consequence relation unless these weaker consequence relations happen to coincide with the classical 2-valued one for the particular *comp*(*P*) in question. In fact we do not in general have completeness for either of the two weaker consequence relations or even for a kind of intersection of them, which allows only derivations which are sound for both intuitionistic 2-valued and classical 3-valued logic.

1.3   Floundering, an irremovable source of incompleteness

One reason for the incompleteness of NF is its inability to deal with non-ground negative literals. This is a price we have to pay for using a quantifier-free system. A query $? - p(x)$ is taken to mean $? - \exists p(x)$, and a query $? - \neg p(x)$ to mean $? - \exists \neg p(x)$. It is possible that both of these are true so it would be unsound to fail $? - \exists \neg p(x)$ just because $? - \exists p(x)$ succeeded. That is why NF is only allowed for ground negative literals. [Prolog is unsound because it allows NF on any goal]. This means that we cannot deal with queries of the form $? - \neg p(x)$, and in dealing with other queries we may *flounder*, or be unable to proceed because we reach a goal containing only non-ground negative literals.

It is time to be a little more precise about what we mean by NF. What is meant here is negation as finite failure formalised as the SLDNF-resolution of Lloyd [1987]. Program clauses are of the form

$$A \leftarrow L_1, \ldots, L_n$$

and queries are of the form

$$? - L_1, \ldots, L_n$$

where A is an atom and $L_1, \ldots, L_n$ are positive or negative literals. The negation of the query is written as a goal

$$\leftarrow L_1, \ldots, L_n$$

and when a positive literal L_i is selected from the current goal the computation tree proceeds in the same way as the SLD-resolution used for definite Horn clauses ; i.e. if L_i unifies with the head of a program clause

$$A \leftarrow M_1, \ldots, M_m$$

with mgu θ then there is a child goal

$$\leftarrow (L_1, \ldots, L_{i-1}, M_1, \ldots, M_m, L_{i+1}, \ldots, L_n)\theta.$$

When a ground negative literal $\neg B$ is selected you carry out a subsidiary computation on the goal $\leftarrow B$ before continuing with the main computation. If this results in a finitely failed tree then $\neg B$ succeeds and there is a child goal

$$\leftarrow L_1, \ldots, L_{i-1}, L_{i+1}, \ldots, L_n$$

resulting from its removal. If the goal $\leftarrow B$ succeeds then $\neg B$ fails so the main derivation fails at this point. If neither of these happens the main derivation has a *dead-end* here. This can arise because the derivation tree for $\leftarrow B$ has infinite branches but no successful ones, or if it, or some subsidiary derivation, flounders or has dead-ends.

The fact that we cannot deal with non-ground negative literals means that we can only hope to get completeness of SLDNF-resolution, for any semantics, for queries which do not flounder. In general the problem of deciding whether a query flounders is recursively unsolvable ([Börger, 1987]; a simpler proof is in [Apt, 1990]), so a strong overall condition on both the program and the query is often used which is sufficient to prevent this. A query is said to be *allowed* if every variable which occurs in it occurs in a positive literal of it; a program clause $A \leftarrow L_1, \ldots, L_n$ is allowed if every variable which occurs in it occurs in a positive literal of its body $L_1, \ldots, L_n$, and a program is *allowed* if all of its clauses are allowed. It is easy to show that if the program and the query are both allowed then the query cannot flounder, because the variables occurring in negative literals are eventually grounded by the positive literals containing them.

Allowedness is a very stringent condition which excludes many common Prolog constructs, such as the definition of equality ($equal(X, X)$), and both clauses in the standard definition of $member(X, L)$.

1.4 Cases where SLDNF-resolution is complete for $comp(P)$

If we accept the restriction described in the last section to programs and queries which are both allowed then there are some classes of programs for which SLDNF-resolution is complete for $comp(P)$. The simplest is the class of *definite* programs, whose clauses contain no negative literals. Here the use of NF is minimal; the only negative literals involved are those occurring in the query, and NF is only used once on each of these. There is no nested use of NF.

Another class is that of *hierarchical* programs introduced by Clark. These are free of recursion, that is to say the predicate symbols can be assigned to levels so that the predicate symbols occurring in the body of a clause are of lower levels than that occurring in the head. A much larger class has recently been given by Kunen [1989]. This is the class of programs which are *semi-strict* (or *call-consistent*, as it is more usually called now). Semi-strict means that no predicate symbol depends negatively on itself in the way that p does in the program $p \leftarrow \neg p$, or similarly via any number of intermediate clauses and predicate symbols, e.g. $p \leftarrow \neg q, q \leftarrow p$. Formally this is defined as follows:

We say $p \supseteq_{+1} q$ iff there is a program clause with p occurring in the head, and q occurring in a *positive* literal in the body. We say $\supseteq_{-1} q$ iff there is a clause with p occurring in the head, and q occurring in a *negative* literal in the body. Let $\geq_{+1}$ and $\geq_{-1}$ be the least pair of relations on the set of predicate symbols satisfying:

$$p \geq_{+1} p$$

and

$$p \supseteq_i q \,\&\, q \geq_j r \Rightarrow p \geq_{i,j} r.$$

Then the program is *semi-strict* if we never have $p \geq_{-1} p$.

For semi-strict programs the completeness requires also a condition involving the query, that the program is *strict with respect to the query*. This means that there is no predicate symbol p on which the query depends both positively and negatively, as does the query $? - a, b$ for the program

$$a \leftarrow p$$
$$b \leftarrow \neg p$$
$$p \leftarrow p.$$

Formally, if Q is a query, we say $Q \geq_i p$ iff either $a \geq_i p$ for some a occurring positively in Q, or $a \geq_{-i} p$ for some a occurring negatively in Q. The program is strict with respect to the query Q iff for no predicate symbol p do we have both $Q \geq_{+1} p$ and $Q \geq_{-1} p$.

The semi-strict programs include the *stratified* programs introduced by Apt *et al.* [1988]; these are like the hierarchical programs except that the condition that the level of every predicate symbol in the body be less than the level of the head is maintained for predicate symbols appearing negatively in the body, but for those appearing positively it is relaxed to 'less than or equal to'. The completeness result for stratified programs has been proved independently by Cavedon and Lloyd [1989].

Kunen's work clarifies the role of the hypotheses of strictness and allowedness. Allowedness gives completeness for the 3-valued semantics based on $comp(P)$, and strictness ensures that the 2-valued and 3-valued semantics coincide.

1.5   Semantics for negation via special classes of model

So far we have considered declarative semantics for logic programs of what we may call a purely logical kind. We have taken some set $S(P)$ of sentences e.g. $CWA(P)$ or $comp(P)$, determined by the program P, and taken this to be the declarative meaning of the program in the sense that when we ask a query $?Q$ we are asking whether Q (or, with the usual convention that free variables in queries are existentially quantified, $\exists Q$, the existential quantification of Q) is a logical consequence of $S(P)$. An ideal corresponding procedural semantics or automatic proof procedure would be sound and complete with respect to this declarative semantics, i.e. a query would succeed iff it was a consequence of $S(P)$, i.e. true in all models of $S(P)$. An alternative, model-theoretic approach, leaves the set of sentences P comprising the original program alone, but modifies the notion of consequence, by replacing 'true in all models of', by 'true in all models of a certain kind'. Some set $M(P)$ of one or more models of P, which are thought of as the only intended models, is singled out, and when we ask a query $?Q$ we are now considered to be asking whether Q is true in all models in $M(P)$.

The simplest semantics of this kind is the well known 'least fixpoint semantics' for a definite Horn clause program P, where $M(P)$ is taken to be the set consisting of the least fixpoint model of P. For example if P is the program

$$even(0) \leftarrow$$
$$even(s(s(x))) \leftarrow even(x),$$

the least fixpoint model is the Herbrand model with domain $\{0, s(0), s(s(0)) \ldots\}$ and $even(x)$ true for $x = 0, s(s(0)), \ldots$. This is the meaning one would attach to such a program if one regarded its clauses as being recursive definitions of the predicates in their heads. For definite

Horn clause programs, this least fixpoint semantics coincides with the semantics based on $CWA(P)$ because the least fixpoint model is a model, and the only model, of $CWA(P)$. It is also almost identical, for the usual positive queries, with the semantics based on considering all models of P. This is because the least fixpoint model is a generic model, and if Q is a conjunction of atoms then $\exists Q$ is true in the least fixpoint model of P iff it is true in all models of P. [However it is not true that an answer substitution which is correct for the least fixpoint model is correct in all models, e.g. in the example above the query $?even(y)$ has the correct answer $y = s(s(x))$ in the least fixpoint model, but not in all models.] For such positive queries $?Q$ the least fixpoint semantics also agrees with the semantics based on all models of $comp(P)$. This is because $comp(P) \models \exists Q$ iff $P \models \exists Q$. However this agreement no longer holds in general for queries containing negation. For example for the program P:

$$num(0) \leftarrow$$
$$num(x) \leftarrow num(s(x)),$$

the negative ground literal $\neg num(s(0))$ is true in the least fixpoint model of P but not in all models of $comp(P)$ or of P.

And when negative literals are allowed in the bodies of program clauses the least fixpoint model may no longer exist. A natural alternative then is to consider (as in Minker [1982]) a semantics based on the class of minimal Herbrand models of P. Apt *et al.* [1988] advocate a semantics based on the class of minimal Herbrand models of P which are also models of $comp(P)$, and Przymusinski [1988b] proposes an even more restricted class of *perfect* models.

We discuss these model-theoretic semantics in Section 2.8, but only briefly, because they are considered in more detail in Chapters 2.6 and 3.3 of this volume. They are not all directly related to negation as failure. For example negation as failure allows $?q$ to succeed from the program $P : q \leftarrow \neg p$, but q is not true in all minimal models of P. So negation as failure is not sound for the semantics based on all minimal models of P. It is sound for the semantics based on all minimal models of P which are also models of $comp(P)$, but since this in general a proper subset of the set of all models of $comp(P)$, negation as failure must be expected to be even more incomplete for this semantics than for the usual one based on *all* models of $comp(P)$.

1.6 Semantics for negation using non-classical logics

Gabbay [1986] (Section 2.10 below) shows how to obtain a semantics with respect to which a version of negation as failure is both sound and complete by using a modal logic with a provability operator $\square$. It is based on the idea that negation as failure treats $\neg A$ as $\neg provable(A)$. Gelfond [1987]

(Section 2.10 below) has related negation as failure to autoepistemic logic, replacing $\neg A$ by $\neg(A$ *is believed*$)$. Cerrito [1992; 1993] uses the linear logic of Girard [1987] to give (for the propositional case) a declarative semantics with respect to which negation as failure as used in Prolog is both sound and complete.

Three-valued logic affords some of the best fitting semantics for negation as failure. In Section 2.6 below we describe the work of Fitting [1985], Kunen [1987; 1989] and Stärk [1991; 1994; 1994] which shows that, in the very natural three-valued logic of Kleene [1952], SLDNF-resolution is sound with respect to $comp(P)$, and complete for a wide class of programs.

These are very successful attempts to discover the underlying logic of negation as failure. Their disadvantage is that the logics involved are more complicated and less familiar than classical logic so that they are not likely to help the naive programmer express his problem by means of a logic program, or to check the correctness of a program.

1.7 Constructive negation: an extension of negation as failure

Chan [1988] (Section 2.9 below) gives a way of dealing with the floundering problem of SLDNF-resolution by extending it so as to deal with non-ground negative literals. This is done by returning the negation of answers to query Q as answers to $\neg Q$. An answer substitution θ to a query Q with variables $x_1, \ldots, x_n$ can be written in equational form as

$$\exists (x_1 = x_1\theta \wedge \ldots \wedge x_n = x_n\theta)$$

where $\exists$ quantifies all variables except $x_1, \ldots, x_n$. When the SLDNF-tree for a query Q is finite, with answers $A_1, \ldots, A_k$ then

$$Q \leftrightarrow A_1 \vee \ldots \vee A_k$$

is a consequence of $comp(P)$ so if $comp(P)$ is the intended semantics it is legitimate to return

$$\neg(A_1 \vee \ldots \vee A_k)$$

as the answer to $\neg Q$. Chan's procedure of SLD-CNF resolution incorporates an algorithm for reducing the equality formulae (formulae with $=$ as the sole predicate symbol) returned in this way to a normal form which is not much more complicated than the equational form above of the usual type of answer given by a substitution. It is a promising way of getting a computational procedure which is more complete relative to the semantics based on $comp(P)$ than SLDNF-resolution. It is limited by the fact that an answer to $\neg Q$ can only be returned when Q has a finite derivation tree. This is true for all queries only when P is equivalent to a rather simple type of hierarchic program, although it may well be true for many programs and queries in practice.

1.8 Concluding remarks

Neither the closed world assumption nor the Clark completion provide a satisfactory declarative semantics for negation as failure since although it is sound for both of them it is not in general complete for either of them. And it is even more incomplete for the semantics based on minimal, perfect, well-founded or stable models of $comp(P)$. There are sound and complete semantics expressible in modal or linear logic but these seem too complicated to serve as a practical guide to the meaning of a program. I believe that this is inevitable; that the use of negation as failure is only justifiable in general by some very contorted logic, and that it is one of the impure features of present day logic programming which should only be used with great caution.

Those who are wedded to $comp(P)$ as the 'right', semantics for negation as failure must accept the incompleteness of negation as failure for this semantics, or confine themselves to programs and queries for which completeness has been proved for $comp(P)$, e.g. the allowed programs and queries which are definite, hierarchical or semi-strict (call-consistent) as described in Section 2.7. If they are prepared to think in terms of 3-valued logic then allowedness is enough. However, although $comp(P)$ is one of the simplest semantics proposed for negation as failure, it is often not easy to read off its meaning from P.

Comprehensive surveys of recent work can be found in the special issue (Vol 17, nos 2, 3, 4, November 1993) of the *Journal of Logic Programmng*, devoted to Non-monotonic Reasoning and Logic Programming and in [Apt, 1994].

I am grateful to K. R. Apt and K. Fine for reading earlier drafts very carefully and making several corrections and many improvements.

2 Main body

2.1 Negation in logic programming

Before taking up our main topic of negation as failure we mention briefly in this section some other kinds of negation used in logic programming.

The obvious treatment of negation—allowing the full use of classical negation in both program clauses and queries and using a theorem prover which is sound and complete for full first order logic—is generally believed to be infeasible because it leads to a combinatorial explosion. However there have been some attempts to do this, e.g. [Stickel, 1986; Naish, 1986; Poole and Goebel, 1986; Loveland, 1988; Sakai and Miyachi, 1986].

In some cases the use of negation can be avoided by renaming. If there are no occurrences in the program or query of $p(t_1, \ldots, t_n)$ for any terms

$t_1, \ldots, t_n$ then negative literals $\neg p(u_1, \ldots, u_n)$ can be made positive by introducing a new predicate $nonp(x_1, \ldots, x_n)$ for $\neg(x_1, \ldots, x_n)$. This was considered by Meltzer [1983]. A well known example of it is [Kowalski, 1979] where the statements

> *Every fungus is a mushroom or a toadstool.*
> *No boletus is a mushroom*

are made into Horn clauses by introducing the predicate *nonmushroom*:

> $toadstool(x) \leftarrow fungus(x),\ nonmushroom(x)$
> $nonmushroom(x) \leftarrow boletus(x).$

This trick obviously works, for the usual SLD-resolution, also when there are positive occurrences of $p(t_1, \ldots, t_n)$ provided none of these can be unified with any of the negative ones.

There is no problem in allowing *queries* containing negation if the program consists entirely of definite Horn clauses. The usual SLD-resolution is trivially still complete, because a query containing a negative literal cannot succeed, and it should not, because it is not a logical consequence of the program, since that has a model in which all predicates are true of everything.

There is also no problem in dealing with general Horn clause programs and queries, i.e. in allowing programs to contain negative Horn clauses as well as definite Horn clauses, and allowing goal clauses to be either negative or definite Horn clauses (so the queries, i.e. negations of goals, are conjunctions containing at most one negative literal). This depends on the well-known fact that if a set of Horn clauses is inconsistent then so is some subset containing just one negative clause. The query procedure is as follows:

First check the program for consistency by taking its positive part, i.e. the set of definite clauses in it, and querying this in turn with the negations of the negative program clauses (i.e. take each of these negative clauses as a goal). If any of these queries succeeds, i.e. if the empty clause can be derived from any of these goals, then the program is inconsistent. If the program is found to be consistent then proceed as follows:

If the query consists entirely of positive literals then discard any negative program clauses and test the query in the usual way with the positive part of the program. If the query contains a (single) negative literal then its negation can be written as a definite Horn clause G. If there are no negative program clauses then fail the query immediately because, as above, a negative query cannot be a consequence of a positive program. Otherwise add G to the positive part of the program and query it in turn with each of the negations of the negative program clauses (i.e. use each of these negative clauses as a goal). The only unusual feature is that answers to the query may no longer be of the familiar definite form, i.e. expressible by a single substitution. Instead every time G is used within one derivation of the empty clause, the value substitution is stored as one of the disjuncts of an indefinite answer substitution. For further details see [Sakai and Miyachi, 1983] or Gallier and Raatz [1987; 1989]. where the treatment is extended to include the equality relation.

2.2 Negation as failure; SLDNF-resolution

The basic principle of negation as failure is:
if A is a ground atom,

> *the goal $\neg A$ succeeds if A fails*
> *the goal $\neg A$ fails if A succeeds.*

This allows the usual SLD-resolution of Horn clause logic programming to be extended to the case where queries and the bodies of program clauses contain negative as well as positive literals. This is done, as described in Section 1.3 above, firstly by admitting only *computation rules* (rules for selecting a literal in the goal—sometimes called *selection rules*) which are safe in the sense of Lloyd [1987], i.e. which only select a negative literal if it is ground. When the ground negative literal $\neg A$ is selected the next step is to query A; if A succeeds then $\neg A$ fails, so the main derivation path fails at this point; if A fails on every evaluation path then $\neg A$ succeeds and the next goal is obtained by deleting $\neg A$ from the current goal. If A neither succeeds nor fails then the main derivation path ends here in an inconclusive *dead-end*. Since we are assuming that the program consists of a finite set of clauses, when all evaluation paths of A end in failure the whole derivation tree of A is finite by König's lemma, so this is usually described by saying that A *fails finitely* or has a *finitely failed tree*. Since only ground negative literals can be selected, if we reach a goal containing only non-ground negative literals we can proceed no further. Such a goal is called a *flounder* and the original derivation and query are said to *flounder*.

We will call this procedure SLDNF-*resolution*, following Lloyd [1987], which contains a very detailed recursive definition in terms of the depth of nesting of negation as failure calls. We find it more convenient to talk in terms of queries rather than goals. For us a *query* Q is a conjunction $L_1 \wedge \ldots \wedge L_n$ of literals, often written $? - L_1, \ldots, L_n$, and the corresponding goal is $\leftarrow L_1, \ldots, L_n$ i.e. the negation $\neg Q$ of the query. When Lloyd says '$P \cup \{\leftarrow Q\}$ has an SLDNF-refutation' we say 'Q *succeeds from* P *using* SLDNF-*resolution*', and when he says '$P \cup \{\leftarrow Q\}$ has a finitely failed SLDNF-tree' we say 'Q *fails from* P *using* SLDNF-*resolution*'.

Kunen [1989] gives a more succinct definition of these notions as follows. Let P be the program, R the set of all pairs (Q, θ) such that query Q succeeds with answer θ, and $\mathbf{F}$ the set of all queries which finitely fail. Then $\mathbf{R}, \mathbf{F}$ are defined by simultaneous recursion to be the least sets such that, denoting the identity substitution by 1,

1. $(\mathbf{true},1)\in \mathbf{R}$
2. If Q is $Q_1 \wedge A \wedge Q_2$ where A is a positive literal, if $A' \leftarrow Q'$ is a clause of P, if $\theta=\mathrm{mgu}(A,A')$ and $((Q_1 \wedge Q' \wedge Q_2)\sigma, \pi) \in \mathbf{R}$, then $(Q,(\sigma\pi)\mid Q) \in \mathbf{R}$.
3. If Q is $Q_1 \wedge \neg A \wedge Q_2$ where A is a positive *ground* literal, if $A \in \mathbf{F}$ and $(Q_1 \wedge Q_2, \sigma) \in \mathbf{R}$ then $(Q,\sigma) \in \mathbf{R}$.
4. Suppose Q is $Q_1 \wedge A \wedge Q_2$ where A is a positive literal. Suppose that for each clause $A' \leftarrow Q'$ of P, if A' is unifiable with A then $(Q_1 \wedge Q' \wedge Q_2)\mathrm{mgu}(A,A') \in \mathbf{F}$. Then $Q \in \mathbf{F}$.
5. If Q is $Q_1 \wedge \neg A \wedge Q_2$ where A is a positive *ground* literal and $(A,1) \in \mathbf{R}$ then $Q \in \mathbf{F}$. Here it is assumed that before computing an mgu the query clause and program clause are renamed to have distinct variables. Also $(\sigma\pi)\mid Q$ denotes the restriction of the substitution $\sigma\pi$ to the variables in Q.

One important difference between SLDNF-resolution and SLD-resolution is that, for the latter, any computation rule can be used, i.e. if a query succeeds with answer θ using one computation rule, then it does so using any other computation rule. This is no longer true for SLDNF-resolution; e.g. for the program

$$p \leftarrow p, q$$
$$r \leftarrow \neg p$$

the query $?-r$ succeeds if the 'last literal' rule is used but not if the Prolog 'first literal' rule is used. {The reason for this discrepancy is that whether a query fails using SLD-resolution may depend on the computation rule.} So it is hard to imagine a feasible way of implementing SLDNF-resolution, since to determine whether a query succeeds requires a search through all possible derivation trees, using all possible selections of literals. It is shown in Shepherdson [1985] that there are maximal computation rules R_m such that if a query succeeds with answer θ using any computation rule then it does so under R_m, and if it fails using any rule then it fails using R_m, but in Shepherdson [1991] a program is given for which there is no maximal recursive rule. What causes the difficulty is that in SLDNF-resolution once having chosen a ground negative literal $\neg A$ in a goal G you are committed to waiting possibly forever for the result of the query A before proceeding with the main derivation. What you need to do is to keep coming back and trying other choices of literal in G to see whether any of them fail, since when one of these exists it is not always possible to determine it in advance. This would be very complicated to implement. This is presumably why SLDNF-resolution insists that the evaluation of a negative call is pursued to completion before attending to siblings.

It is also important not to allow the use of negation as failure in the present form on non-ground negative literals. A query $?-p(x)$ is taken to mean $?-\exists x p(x)$, and a query $?-\neg p(x)$ to mean $?-\exists x \neg p(x)$. It is possible that both of these are true so it would be unsound to fail $? - \exists x \neg p(x)$ just because $? - \exists x p(x)$ succeeded. For example for the program

$$p(a)$$
$$q(b),$$

$? - p(x)$ should succeed because $? - p(a)$ succeeds, and $? - \neg p(x)$ should also succeed, because $? - \neg p(b)$ succeeds (using negation as failure legitimately on the ground negative literal $\neg p(b)$). Most Prolog implementations are unsound because they allow the use of negation as failure on non-ground negative literals, or even on more general goals. They are, of course also incomplete even for SLD-resolution because of their depth-first search, so it would appear to be very difficult to give a simple declarative semantics for negation as treated in Prolog.

This inability to handle non-ground negative literals means that if we reach a flounder, a goal containing only non-ground negative literals, we can, in SLDNF-resolution, proceed no further. This situation is a source of incompleteness in SLDNF-resolution. For the program $p(x) \leftarrow \neg r(x)$, the query $? - p(a)$ succeeds but $? - p(x)$ (meaning $? - \exists x p(x)$) does not. For the program

$$p(x) \leftarrow \neg q(x)$$
$$r(a)$$

the query $? - p(x), r(x)$ succeeds but the query $? - p(x)$ flounders. So the set of queries which succeed from a program P using SLDNF-resolution is not closed under either of the rules:

$$\frac{\phi(a)}{\exists x \phi(x)} \qquad \frac{A \wedge B}{A}$$

It is therefore impossible to find a declarative semantics for SLDNF-resolution which is sound and complete for all queries, i.e. a set $S(P)$ of sentences such that

$? - Q$ *succeeds from* P *using SLDNF-resolution iff* $S(P) \vdash \exists Q$.

Since the two rules of inference above are valid for intuitionistic and 3-valued logic, indeed for any logic which might conceivably be useful, it will not be possible to find such a semantics even if we weaken the classical derivability relation $\vdash$ to the intuitionistic or 3-valued or some other derivability relation. [For a further discussion of this point see [Fine, 1989], who distinguishes two souces of incompleteness. one arising from the classical and the other from the non-classical part of the logic.]

Börger [1987] ([Apt, 1990] has a simpler proof) has shown that the problem of deciding whether a query flounders is recursively undecidable. The usual way of dealing with the incompleteness due to floundering is to restrict attention to programs and queries satisfying some condition which prevents it. We discuss such conditions in Section 2.7. Since they are very restrictive we consider in Section 3.1 an alternative approach which extends SLDNF-*resolution* so that it can be applied, in some cases, to non-ground negative literals. For this extension, SLDNFS-resolution, it is possible to find a (rather complicated) semantics for which it is sound and complete for all programs and queries.

The practical logic programmer may not be disturbed by the incompleteness due to floundering because it may well be insignificant compared with the incompleteness forced by the limitations of time and space imposed by any implementation on a real machine. An interesting way of dealing with floundering has recently been proposed by Mancarella *et al.* [1988].

2.3   The closed world assumption, CWA(P)

The *closed world assumption* is one of the commonly accepted declarative semantics for negation in logic programming. It is particularly appropriate for database applications, being founded on the idea that the program (database) contains all the positive information about the objects in the domain. Reiter [1978] gave this a precise formulation by saying that any positive ground literal not implied by the program is taken to be false. He axiomatised this by adjoining the negations of these literals to the program P thus obtaining

$$CWA(P) = P \cup \{\neg A : A \text{ is a ground atom and } P \nvdash A\}.$$

He also restricted consideration to what in logic programming are usually called Herbrand models, i.e. models whose domain of individuals consists of the ground terms. This makes the closed world assumption (when it is consistent) categorical, i.e. if it has an Herbrand model that model must be unique, because a ground atom A must be true in it if it is a consequence of P and false if it is not a consequence of P.

{Actually in the usual logic programming situation, where P consists of clauses (or, more generally, universal sentences), and the query Q is an existential sentence, and neither P nor Q contains =, the restriction to Herbrand models is irrelevant, i.e.

$$CWA(P) \vDash_H Q \text{ iff } CWA(P) \vDash Q$$

where $T \vDash_H S$ means 'S is true in all Herbrand models of T'. This is because $CWA(P) \cup \neg Q$ consists of universal sentences not containing equality so, by the usual Herbrand–Skolem argument, if it has a model it has a Herbrand model. In particular if $CWA(P)$ is consistent it has a Herbrand model.}

If P is a definite Horn clause program then $CWA(P)$ is consistent, because the Herbrand interpretation in which a ground atom A is true iff $P \vdash A$, satisfies P (since if $B \leftarrow A_1, \ldots, A_r$ is a ground instance of a clause of P and $P \vdash A_1, \ldots, P \vdash A_r$ then $P \vdash B$); and it clearly satisfies the remaining axioms ($\neg A$ if $P \vdash A$) of $CWA(P)$. {This is of course the familiar least Herbrand model of P.}

The closed world assumption is a very strong presumption in favour of negative information and is often inconsistent. This is the case if the program implies indefinite information about ground atoms, e.g. if P is $p \leftarrow \neg q$, then neither p nor q is a consequence of P so both $\neg p$ and $\neg q$ belong to $CWA(P)$, and since $CWA(P)$ also contains P it is inconsistent. This condition is actually necessary and sufficient for the inconsistency of $CWA(P)$:

> $CWA(P)$ *is consistent iff for all ground atoms* $A_1, \ldots, A_r$,
> $P \vdash (A_1 \vee \ldots \vee A_r)$ *implies* $P \vdash A_i$ *for some* $i = 1, \ldots, r$.

The 'only if' part of this follows as in the example; the 'if' part follows from the compactness theorem, for if $CWA(P)$ is inconsistent so is some finite subset of it, so there exist $\neg A_1, \ldots, \neg A_r$ in $CWA(P)$ such that $P \cup \{\neg A_1, \ldots, \neg A_r\}$ is inconsistent, i.e. $P \vdash (A_1 \vee \ldots \vee A_r)$.

Indefinite information about non-ground literals need not imply the inconsistency of the closed world assumption, e.g. $CWA(P)$ is consistent for the program P:

$$p(x) \leftarrow \neg q(x)$$
$$p(a)$$
$$q(b).$$

However the consistency of the closed world assumption for certain extensions of P does imply that P is equivalent to a definite Horn clause program, and, by the remark above, conversely:

> *If* P *is a set of first order sentences, then* P *is equivalent to a set of definite Horn clauses iff* $CWA(P \cup S)$ *is consistent for each set* S *of ground atoms, possibly involving new constants.*

[For a proof see [Makowsky, 1986] or [Shepherdson, 1988b]; the result holds for first order logic with or without equality.]

This means that if you want to be able to apply the closed world assumption consistently to your program, and to any subsequent extension of it by positive facts, possibly involving new constants, then you are confined to definite Horn clause programs. This may be appropriate when the program is a simple kind of database but most logic programmers would consider it too restrictive and would therefore look for some other form of default reasoning for dealing with negation. Note that if the phrase 'possibly involving new constants' is omitted the result above fails, also that the consistency of the closed world assumption depends on the underlying language. The non-Horn program above satisfies the closed world assumption (i.e. $CWA(P)$ is consistent) if the Herbrand universe, i.e. the set of ground terms, is the usual one $\{a, b\}$ determined by the terms appearing in P, and it continues to do so if any more atoms from the corresponding Herbrand base $\{p(a), p(b), q(a), q(b)\}$ are added to the program. But if the Herbrand universe is enlarged to $\{a, b, c\}$ the closed world assumption becomes inconsistent. This ambiguity does not arise if the program is a definite Horn clause program, for the argument above shows that the closed world assumption for such a program is consistent whatever Herbrand universe is used.

Makowsky [1986] observed that the consistency of the closed world assumption is also equivalent to an important model-theoretic property:

> If P is a set of first order sentences then a term structure M is a model for $CWA(P)$ iff it is a generic model of P, i.e. for all ground atoms A, $M \vDash A$ iff $P \vDash A$.

{We use the words 'term structure' rather than 'Herbrand interpretation' here because in this more general setting where the sentences of P may not be all universal, the word 'Herbrand' would be more appropriately used for the language extended to include the Skolem functions needed to express these sentences in universal form.} This notion of a generic model is like that of a free algebraic structure; just as a free group is one in which an equation is true only if it is true in all groups, so a generic model of P is one in which a ground atom is true only if it is true in all models of P, i.e. is a consequence of P. So it is a unique most economical model of P in which a ground atom is true iff it has to be. If we identify a term model in the usual way with the subset of the base (set of ground atoms) which are true in it, then it is literally the smallest term model. It is easy to see that the genericity of a generic term model extends from ground atoms to existential quantifications of conjunctions of ground atoms:

> If M is a generic model of P, and Q is a conjunction of atoms, then $M \vDash \exists Q$ iff $P \vDash \exists Q$.

So a positive query is true in M iff it is a consequence of P, and one can behave almost as though one was dealing with a theory which had a unique model. This is one of the attractive features of definite Horn clause logic programming, which, as the results above show, does not extend much beyond it. But notice that if one is interested in answer substitutions then one cannot restrict consideration to a generic model, e.g. if P is:

$$p(0)$$
$$p(s(x))$$

then the identity substitution is a correct answer to the query $? - p(x)$ in the least Herbrand model, but is not a 'correct answer substitution', because $\forall x p(x)$ is not a consequence of P.

For negative queries not only is this genericity property lost, but as Apt *et al.* [1988] have pointed out, the set of queries which are true under the closed world assumption, i.e. true in the generic model, may not even be recursively enumerable, that is to say there may be no computable procedure for generating the set of queries which ought to succeed under the closed world assumption. To show this take a non-recursive recursively enumerable set W and a definite Horn clause program P with constant 0, unary function symbol s and unary predicate symbol p, such that

$$P \vdash p(s^n(0)) \text{ iff } n \in W.$$

[This is possible since every partial recursive function can be computed by a definite Horn clause program ([Andreka and Nemeti, 1978]). Now $\neg p(s^n(0))$ is true under the closed world assumption iff $n \notin W$. However, this situation does not arise under the conditions under which Reiter originally suggested the use of the closed world assumption, namely when there are no function symbols in the language. Then the Herbrand base is finite and so is the model determined by the closed world assumption, hence the set of true queries is recursive.

The relevance of the closed world assumption to this chapter is that negation as failure is sound for the closed world assumption for both success and failure, i.e.

if ? − *Q succeeds from P with answer θ using SLDNF-resolution
then CW A(P)* $\vDash_H$ *Qθ,*
if ? − *Q fails from P using SLDNF-resolution then CW A(P)* $\vDash_H$
¬Q.

For a proof see [Shepherdson, 1984]. However, SLDNF-resolution is usually incomplete for the closed world assumption. This is bound to be the case when the closed world assumption is inconsistent. Even for definite Horn clause programs, where the closed world assumption will be consistent, and even when there are no function symbols, SLDNF-resolution can be incomplete for the closed world assumption, e.g. for the program $p(a) \leftarrow p(a)$, and the query $? - \neg p(a)$, since this query ends in a dead-end.

{As noted above, the restriction to Herbrand models makes no difference in the first of the soundness statements above, i.e. it remains true when $\vDash_H$ is replaced by $\vdash$. This is not true of the second, where we are are dealing with the negation of a query. For example if P consists of the single clause $p(a) \leftarrow p(b)$ and Q is $p(x)$ then Q fails from P but $CW A(P) \vDash_H \neg Q$ is not true since there are non-Herbrand models of $CW A(P)$ containing elements c with $p(c)$ true.}

It is possible that one might want to apply the closed world assumption to some predicates but to protect from it other predicates where it was known that the information about them was incomplete. For reference to this notion of protected data see [Minker and Perlis, 1985; Jäger, 1988]

which study the model-theoretic aspects of this relativized closed world
assumption. For more details of the model-theory of the ordinary closed
world assumption see [Makowsky, 1986]. In Section 2.8 we discuss briefly
various model-theoretic semantics which can be regarded as weak forms of
the closed world assumption, e.g. the generalized closed world assumption
of [Minker, 1982], and the self-referential closed world assumption of [Fine,
1989]. However not all of these have an obvious relation to negation as
failure.

Summary: The closed world assumption is a natural and simple way of
dealing with negation for programs which represent simple databases, i.e.
definite Horn clause programs without function symbols. Its use outside
this range is limited: as soon as function symbols are introduced there may
not be any sound and complete computable proof procedure for it, and
if one goes beyond definite Horn clause programs it will be inconsistent,
either for the original program or for some extension of it by positive atoms.

We move on now to deal with the Clark completion of a program which
provides a more widely applicable semantics for negation as failure.

2.4   The Clark completion, $comp(P)$

The most widely accepted declarative semantics for negation as failure is
the 'completed database' introduced by Clark [1978]. This is now usually
called the completion or Clark completion of a program P and denoted by
$comp(P)$. We shall define this initially only when P is what Lloyd [1987]
calls a normal program, i.e. a set of clauses (not containing the predicate
$=$) of the form

$$A \leftarrow L_1, \ldots, L_m$$

where A is an atom and $L_1, \ldots, L_m$ are literals. [Later we shall consider
the extension of this definition to the case where the body of the clause
is an arbitrary first order formula.] To avoid tedious repetition we shall
assume, throughout this section, unless otherwise stated, that all programs
referred to are normal. Similarly goals and queries will be assumed to be
normal, i.e. of the forms $\leftarrow L_1, \ldots, L_m$, and $? - L_1, \ldots, L_m$, respectively.

To form $comp(P)$ you take each clause

$$p(t_1, \ldots, t_n) \leftarrow L_1, \ldots, L_m$$

of P in which the predicate symbol p appears in the head, rewrite it in
general form

$$p(x_1, \ldots, x_n) \leftarrow \exists y_1 \ldots \exists y_p (x_1 = t_1 \wedge \ldots \wedge x_n = t_n \wedge L_1 \wedge \ldots \wedge L_m.)$$

where $x_1, \ldots, x_n$ are new variables (i.e. not already occurring in any of
these clauses) and $y_1, \ldots, y_p$ the variables of the original clause. If the

general forms of all these clauses (we assume there are only finitely many) are:

$$p(x_1, \ldots, x_n) \leftarrow E_1$$
$$\ldots$$
$$p(x_1, \ldots, x_n) \leftarrow E_j$$

then the *completed definition* of p is

$$p(x_1, \ldots, x_n) \leftrightarrow E_1 \vee \ldots \vee E_j.$$

The empty disjunction is taken to be false, so if $j = 0$ i.e. there is no clause with p in its head, then the completed definition of p is

$$\neg p(x_1, \ldots, x_n).$$

The completion, $comp(P)$ of P is now defined to be the collection of completed definitions of each predicate symbol in P together with the equality and freeness axioms below, which we shall refer to as CET (Clark's equational theory).

equality axioms

$x = x$

$x = y \rightarrow y = x$

$x = y \wedge y = z \rightarrow x = z$

$x_1 = y_1 \wedge \ldots \wedge x_n = y_n \rightarrow (p(x_1, \ldots, x_n) \leftrightarrow p(y_1, \ldots y_n))$, for each predicate symbol p

$x_1 = y_1 \wedge \ldots \wedge x_n = y_n \rightarrow f(x_1, \ldots, x_n) = f(y_1, \ldots, y_n)$, for each function symbol f.

freeness axioms

$f(x_1, \ldots, x_n) \neq g(y_1, \ldots, y_m)$, for each pair of distinct function symbols f, g,

$f(x_1, \ldots, x_n) = f(y_1, \ldots, y_n) \rightarrow x_1 = y_1 \wedge \ldots \wedge x_n = y_n$, for each function symbol f,

$t(x) \neq x$, for each term $t(x)$ different from x in which x occurs.

The equality axioms are needed because the completed definitions of predicates contain the equality predicate. The freeness axioms are needed because in SLDNF-resolution terms such as $f(x_1, \ldots, x_n), g(y_1, \ldots, y_m)$ are not unifiable.

In stating these axioms constants are treated as 0-ary function symbols, and the axioms are stated for all the function and predicate symbols of the language. We assume that this language is given 'in advance of P' so to speak, rather than, as is often assumed in logic programming, being determined by the function and predicate symbols actually occurring in P. Note that, because it contains the freeness axioms, $comp(P)$, like $CWA(P)$, depends on the language as well as on P. For example if P is the program $p(a)$ and the language contains no function symbols and just one constant a, then $comp(P)$ consists of the equality axioms and $p(x) \leftrightarrow x = a$; but if the language has another constant b then $comp(P)$ contains the freeness axiom $a \neq b$. In the latter case $comp(P) \vdash \exists x \neg p(x)$, but not in the former case. For a precise statement of the way in which $comp(P)$ depends on the language of function symbols see Section 2.6. Note also that, like CWA(P), $comp(P)$ is an extension of P:

$$comp(P) \vdash P.$$

The basic result of [Clark, 1978] is that negation as failure is sound for $comp(P)$ for both success and failure:

> *if ? $- Q$ succeeds from P with answer θ using SLDNF-resolution*
> *then $comp(P) \vDash Q\theta$,*
> *if ? $- Q$ fails from P using SLDNF-resolution then $comp(P) \vDash$*
> $\neg Q$.

For a proof see [Lloyd, 1987, pp. 92, 93]. The key step in the proof is to show that $comp(P)$ implies that in an SLDNF-derivation tree a goal is equivalent to the conjunction of its child goals.

This soundness result can be strengthened by replacing the derivability relation $\vDash$ by $\vDash_3$ (truth in all 3-valued models, for a specific 3-valued logic—[Kunen, 1987, Section 2.7]) or by $\vdash_I$, the intuitionistic derivability relation ([Shepherdson, 1985]) or by a relation $\vdash_{3I}$, which admits only rules which are sound both for classical 3-valued and intuitionistic 2-valued logic ([Shepherdson, 1985]). This helps to explain why SLDNF-resolution is usually incomplete for $comp(P)$ with respect to the usual 2-valued derivability relation; in order to succeed a query must not only be true in all 2-valued models of $comp(P)$, it must be true in all 3-valued models, and must be derivable using only intuitionistically acceptable steps. For example, if P is the program $p \leftarrow \neg p$, then $comp(P)$ contains $p \leftrightarrow \neg p$ and is inconsistent in the 2-valued sense, so p is a 2-valued consequence of it, and if SLDNF-resolution were complete for $comp(P)$ then ? $- p$ should succeed. In fact it dead-ends. This can be explained by noting that there is a 3-valued model of $comp(P)$ in which p is not true but undefined. Similarly if P is the program

$$p \leftarrow q$$
$$p \leftarrow \neg q$$
$$q \leftarrow q,$$

whose completion contains $p \leftrightarrow (q \vee \neg q)$, the fact that ? $- p$ does not succeed using SLDNF- resolution can be explained by observing that p is not intuitionistically derivable from $comp(P)$, since the law of the excluded middle does not hold in intuitionistic logic.

Despite these kinds of incompleteness, and those due to floundering, pointed out in Section 1.3, $comp(P)$ is regarded by many logic programmers as the appropriate declarative semantics for the procedure of SLDNF-resolution applied to a program P, i.e. as the meaning they had in mind when they wrote down the program P. This is somewhat removed from the clarity aimed at in ideal logic programming, where the declarative meaning of a program should be apparent from the text of the program as written. Although in simple cases $comp(P)$ may be what most people have in mind when they write P, it is not always easy when writing P to foresee the effect of forming $comp(P)$, particularly when P contains clauses involving mutual recursion and negation. In fact we shall see later in this section that, using only clauses of the form $A \leftarrow \neg B$, where A and B are atoms, it is possible to construct a program P such that $comp(P)$ is essentially equivalent to any given formula of first order logic. However the same objection, that it is often not easy to read off the declarative meaning from the program as written, applies to the closed world assumption; indeed we saw that it could be impossible to decide whether $\neg A$ belonged to $CWA(P)$.

Whereas $CWA(P)$ depends only on the logical content of P, the completion, $comp(P)$, depends on the way P is written; the completion of $p \leftarrow \neg q$ contains $p \leftrightarrow \neg q$, and $\neg q$, which is equivalent to p and $\neg q$, but the completion of the logically equivalent program $q \leftarrow \neg p$ has these reversed.

The completion also differs from the closed world assumption in not implying a restriction to Herbrand models. At least that is the usual understanding. There are some people who impose this restriction on the completion, i.e. who regard a query $? - Q$ as a request to know whether $-Q$ is true in all Herbrand models of $comp(P)$. However, it should be noted that if this is done it may lead to non-computable semantics, i.e. [Shepherdson, 1988a]:

> *The set of negative ground literals $\neg A$ which are true in all Herbrand models of $comp(P)$, for a definite program P, may not be recursively enumerable.*

[Unlike the set of sentences which are true in all models of $comp(P)$, which is recursively enumerable by the Gödel completeness theorem. We saw above that the closed world assumption could give rise to non-computable semantics for a different reason, namely the non-recursive enumerability of the set of sentences $CWA(P)$.]

We have followed the usual convention here of using 'Herbrand model of $comp(P)$', to refer to a term model of $comp(P)$ over the language L used to express P, i.e. a model whose domain is the set of ground terms of L (the Herbrand universe of L), with functions given the free interpretation (e.g. the value of the function f applied to the term t is simply $f(t)$). This use of the term 'Herbrand' is rather misleading since it suggests that the Skolem–Herbrand theorem, that if a sentence has a model it has a

Herbrand model, should be applicable, and that restriction to Herbrand models should make no difference. The reason it does make a difference here is that for this theorem to apply the Herbrand universe must be large enough to contain Skolem functions enabling the sentence to be written in universal form. The appropriate Herbrand universe for $comp(P)$ would be one containing Skolem functions allowing the elimination of the existential quantifiers occurring on the right hand sides of the completed definitions of the predicate symbols of P. And even over that universe one could not restrict to free interpretations because $comp(P)$ contains the equality predicate. Nevertheless the 'Herbrand models' of $comp(P)$ are considered to be of particular interest, presumably because the Herbrand universe of the original language in which P is expressed is often the only domain of individuals the programmer wants to consider. There is a very neat fixpoint characterisation of these models which we now consider.

First we associate with the program P the operator T_P which maps a subset I of the Herbrand base (set of ground atoms) B_L into the subset $T_P(I)$ comprising all those ground atoms A for which there exists a ground instance

$$A \leftarrow L_1, \ldots, L_m$$

of a clause of P with all of $L_1, \ldots, L_m$ in I. $T_P(I)$ is the set of immediate consequences of I, i.e. those which can be obtained by applying a rule from P once only. [Note that T_P depends not only on the logical content of P but also on the way it is written e.g. adding the tautology $p \leftarrow p$ changes T_P.] Clearly

I is a model for P iff $T_P(I) \subseteq I$,

i.e. iff I is a pre-fixpoint of T_P. Following Apt *et al.* [1988] let us say an interpretation I is supported if for each ground atom A which is true in I there is a ground instance

$$A \leftarrow L_1, \ldots, L_m$$

of a clause of P such that $L_1, \ldots L_m$ are true in I. The terminology comes from the idea of negation as the default, that ground atoms are assumed false unless they can be supported in some way by the program. Clearly

I is supported iff $T_P(I) \supseteq I$,
I is a supported model of P iff it is a fixpoint of T_P, i.e.
$T_P(I) = I$.

The notion of being supported is equivalent to satisfying the 'only if' halves of the completed definitions of the predicate symbols in $comp(P)$, so it follows that:

I is a Herbrand model of $comp(P)$ iff it is a supported model of P.

I is a Herbrand model of comp(P) iff it is a fixpoint of T_P.

This fixpoint characterisation of Herbrand models of $comp(P)$ (due to Apt and van Emden [1982] for positive programs and to Apt *et al.* [1988] for normal programs) can be extended to arbitrary models by replacing the Herbrand base by the set of formal expressions $p(d_1, \ldots d_n)$ where p is a predicate symbol and $d_1, \ldots, d_n$ are elements of the domain; see [Lloyd, 1987, p. 81].

If P is composed of definite Horn clauses then T_P is continuous and has a least fixpoint $lfp(T_P)$ which is obtainable as $T_P \uparrow \omega$, the result of iterating T_P ω times starting from the empty set. This is the least Herbrand model of P and of $comp(P)$ (so $comp(P)$ is consistent). In general T_P is not continuous or even monotonic, so it may not have fixpoints, e.g. if P is $p \leftarrow \neg p$.

If P is a definite Horn clause program then $comp(P)$ adds no new positive information:

> If P is a definite Horn clause program and Q is a positive sentence, then $comp(P) \models Q$ implies $P \models Q$.

A positive sentence is one built up using only $\vee, \wedge, \forall, \exists$. This is an immediate consequence of the existence of the least fixpoint model in the case where Q is a ground atom, and the argument is easily extended to cover the case of a positive sentence [Shepherdson, 1988b].

The closed world assumption and the completion are superficially similar ways of extending a program. They are both examples of reasoning by default, assuming that if some positive piece of information cannot be proved in a certain way from P then it is not true. But for the closed world assumption the notion of proof involved is that of full first order logic, whereas for the completion it is 'using one of the program clauses whose head matches the given atom'. At first sight this is a narrower notion of proof, so that one would expect that more ground atoms should be false under the completion than under the closed world assumption, i.e. that $CWA(P)$ should be a consequence of $comp(P)$. But it is not so simple because $comp(P)$ adds, in the 'only if' halves of the completed definition of a predicate symbol p, new statements which can be used to prove things about predicates other than p. Also the closed world assumption involves a restriction to Herbrand models, which the completion, as usually defined does not. In fact when they are compatible it must be the closed world assumption which implies the completion, because the former is categorical. As the simple examples of Section 1.2 showed, either of the closed world assumption and the completion can be consistent and the other one not, or both can be separately consistent but incompatible. For conditions under which they are compatible, and the relation of $CWA(P) \cup comp(P)$ to $CWA(comp(P))$, see [Shepherdson, 1988b].

Although in defining $comp(P)$ above we assumed that P was a normal program, i.e. composed of clauses of the form

$$A \leftarrow L_1, \ldots, L_m,$$

where A is an atom and $L_1, \ldots, L_m$ are literals, the same definition could be applied when P is a set of sentences of the more general form

$$A \leftarrow W,$$

where W is a first order formula. This allows much more general statements to be made, but as Lloyd and Topor [1984] have observed, if one takes the view that the intended meaning of a program P is not P but $comp(P)$, then there is no gain in generality. Indeed they show how to transform such a program P into a normal program P' such that $comp(P')$ is essentially equivalent to $comp(P)$ (the precise sense of equivalence is explained later). It must be emphasised that the validity of this transformation depends crucially on the assumption that the meaning of the program is given by $comp(P)$. Their transformation makes $comp(P')$ equivalent to $comp(P)$; it does not make P' equivalent to P. If the intended meaning of the program was the program P actually written, then the appropriate way to obtain an equivalent normal program would be to introduce Skolem functions to get rid of the quantifiers. That would give a program P' essentially equiv-alent to P—but then $comp(P')$ would not be equivalent to $comp(P)$. So both methods of transformation change the relationship between P and $comp(P)$. Granted that the intended meaning is $comp(P)$, the transforma-tion of Lloyd and Topor is useful since it enables one to express $comp(P)$ using a P expressed in a form closer to natural language, and then convert P into a normal program P' on which one can use SLDNF-resolution to derive consequences of $comp(P')$, i.e. of $comp(P)$. One can also allow the *query* to be an arbitrary first order formula W, since if W has free variables $x_1, \ldots, x_n$, the effect of asking $? - W$ for the program P is the same as ask-ing $? - answer(x_1, \ldots, x_n)$ for the program P^* obtained by adding the clause $answer(x_1, \ldots, x_n) \leftarrow W$ to P. More precisely, $W\theta$ is a logical consequence of $comp(P)$ iff $answer(x_1, \ldots, x_n)\theta$ is a logical consequence of $comp(P^*)$, and $\neg W$ is a logical consequence of $comp(P)$ iff $\neg answer(x_1, \ldots, x_n)$ is a logical consequence of $comp(P^*)$. For a proof of this, and of the validity of the transformation of P into P' given below, see [Lloyd, 1987, Ch. 4].

The easiest way of effecting a transformation of a general program P into a normal program P' which sends $comp(P)$ into $comp(P')$ is to use the fact that every first order formula can be built up using $\neg, \vee,$ and $\exists$. Replacing

$$A \leftarrow W_1 \vee W_2$$

by

$$A \leftarrow W_1$$
$$A \leftarrow W_2$$

leaves the completion unaltered, as does replacing

$$A \leftarrow \exists x W$$

by

$$A \leftarrow W.$$

Replacing

$$A \leftarrow \neg W$$

by

$$A \leftarrow \neg p(x_1, \ldots, x_n)$$
$$p(x_1, \ldots, x_n) \leftarrow W$$

where $x_1, \ldots, x_n$ are the free variables of W, and p is a new predicate symbol, does change the completion, because it introduces a new predicate symbol, but the new completion, $comp(P')$, is a conservative extension of the old one, $comp(P)$, i.e. a formula not involving the new predicate symbols is a consequence of $comp(P')$ iff it is a consequence of $comp(P)$. {The reason for this is that if you leave out the new predicate symbols a model for $comp(P')$ is a model for $comp(P)$; conversely a model for $comp(P)$ can be extended to a model for $comp(P')$ by using the completed definition of p in $comp(P')$, i.e.

$$p(x_1, \ldots, x_n) \leftrightarrow W,$$

to define p.} If we now take each statement of the original general program P, rewrite its body in terms of $\neg, \vee,$ and $\exists$, and then, starting with the outermost connective of its body, successively apply these transformations we end up with a normal program P' such that $comp(P')$ is a conservative extension of $comp(P)$, so that in particular any query expressed in the original language is a consequence of $comp(P')$ iff it is a consequence of $comp(P)$.

The transformation just described is very uneconomical, and goes further than it needs. The clauses of the resulting normal program P' are of the very simple forms $A \leftarrow B, A \leftarrow \neg B$, where A and B are atoms. {In fact by replacing B by $\neg\neg B$, you can take them all in the latter form! This demonstrates that it is not always easy to predict the consequences of forming the completion of a program even if its individual clauses are very simple.} The body of a normal program clause is allowed to be a conjunction of literals, so there is no need for us to replace $A \wedge B$ by $\neg(\neg A \vee \neg B)$ and apply four transformation steps. The transformations given by Lloyd and Topor take account of this and are framed in terms of transforming if statements whose bodies are conjunctions, e.g. the rule for eliminating $\vee$ is to replace

$$A \leftarrow W_1 \wedge \ldots W_{i-1} \wedge (V \vee W) \wedge W_{i+1} \wedge \ldots W_m$$

by

$$A \leftarrow W_1 \wedge \ldots W_{i-1} \wedge V \wedge W_{i+1} \wedge \ldots W_m$$
$$A \leftarrow W_1 \wedge \ldots W_{i-1} \wedge V \wedge W_{i+1} \wedge \ldots W_m.$$

They are also as sparing as possible in the use of transformations to eliminate negation. The reason for this is that the whole point of the transformation of P into P' is to be able to use SLDNF-resolution on P' to find out whether queries are consequences of the completion $comp(P)$ of the original program P. And use of the new clause

$$A \leftarrow \neg p(x_1, \ldots, x_n)$$

resulting from our transformation of $A \leftarrow \neg W$, introduces, unless $n = 0$, a non-ground negative literal and is very likely to result in a flounder. Indeed if W has free variables which are not in A, it is bound to do so, since these variables can never be grounded. To avoid this as far as possible Lloyd and Topor replace (in a conjunct of the body as above)

$$
\begin{array}{lll}
\neg(V \wedge W) & \text{by} & \neg V \vee \neg W \\
(V \leftarrow W & \text{by} & V \vee \neg W \\
\neg(V \leftarrow W) & \text{by} & W \wedge \neg V \\
\neg(V \vee W) & \text{by} & \neg V \wedge \neg W \\
\neg\neg W & \text{by} & W \\
\exists x_1 \ldots \exists x_n W & \text{by} & W \\
\neg\forall x_1 \ldots \forall x_n W & \text{by} & \exists x_1 \ldots \exists x_n \neg W \\
\forall x_1 \ldots \forall x_n W & \text{by} & \neg\exists x_1 \ldots \exists x_n \neg W
\end{array}
$$

and, finally a conjunct $\neg\exists x_1 \ldots \exists_n W$ is dealt with as we dealt with negation above, i.e.

$$A \leftarrow W_1 \wedge \ldots \wedge W_{i-1} \wedge \neg\exists x_1 \ldots \exists x_n W \wedge W_{i+1} \wedge \ldots \wedge W_m$$

is replaced by

$$A \leftarrow W_1 \wedge \ldots \wedge W_{i-1} \wedge \neg p(y_1 \ldots y_k) \wedge W_{i+1} \wedge \ldots \wedge W_m$$

and

$$p(y_1, \ldots, y_k) \leftarrow \exists x_1 \ldots \exists x_n W$$

where $y_1, \ldots, y_k$ are the free variables in $\forall x_1 \ldots \forall x_n W$ and p is a new predicate symbol. This last transformation is the only one which introduces a new predicate symbol.

Although this method of transformation reduces the chance of floundering when using SLDNF-resolution on the transformed program it does not eliminate it, for the elimination of a universal quantifier $\forall x W(x)$ still leads to a clause with $\neg W(x)$ in its body. This may not give an inevitable flounder, e.g. if $W(x)$ is $p(x) \leftarrow q(x)$ this is further transformed to a clause with $q(x) \wedge \neg p(x)$ in its body, which will not flounder if x is grounded by $q(x)$. But if $W(x)$ is an atomic formula $p(x)$, or a formula starting with an existential quantifier it is bound to cause a flounder. In fact it is easily seen that the transformation of any formula containing an alternation of quantifiers leads to an inevitable flounder. This limits the use of such general programs in practice. It is not surprising that SLDNF-resolution, based as it is on SLD-resolution, which is complete only for the definite Horn clause fragment, should be incapable of dealing effectively with full first order logic. In fact this transformation method throws some light on the incompleteness of $comp(P)$ for normal programs. We have

> *Given any sentence ϕ of first order logic, you can construct a normal program P' such that $comp(P')$ is a conservative extension of ϕ, together with the equality and freeness axioms.*

To prove this take the general program P with statement

$$p \leftarrow (\neg \phi \wedge \neg p),$$

where p is a new 0-ary predicate symbol, together with

$$q(x_1, \ldots, x_n) \leftarrow q(x_1, \ldots, x_n)$$

for each n-ary predicate symbol in ϕ (this is to ensure that forming the completion does not add any statements about these predicates). Apart from the equality and freeness axioms $comp(P)$ is equivalent to

$$p \leftrightarrow (\neg \phi \wedge \neg p),$$

which is equivalent to $\neg p \wedge \phi$. Now transform this into a normal program P' such that $comp(P')$ is a conservative extension of $comp(P)$.

This means that if you regard $comp(P)$ as the correct declarative meaning of a normal program, so that when you ask a query you are asking whether it is a consequence of $comp(P)$, then you are dealing with the consequence relation of full first order logic and you need a complete proof procedure for that. It is only to be expected that SLDNF-resolution, which is SLD-resolution with a little trick for dealing with ground negative literals tacked on, should usually be very incomplete.

We have tacitly assumed in the above that the statements of the general program P do not contain the equality predicate $=$. It is possible to define *comp(P)* in the same way when they do, and it is possible to transform *P* into a normal program *P'* such that *comp(P')* is a conservative extension of *comp(P)*. To do this we deal with equations $t_1 = t_2$ as follows: use the equality and freeness axioms to reduce them successively either to false or to conjunctions of equations of the form $x = t$, where x is a variable, then replace all occurrences of x by t and discard the equation. However programs containing = are not usually considered in this way because the fact that forming the completion entails adding the freeness axioms means that = is severely constrained, and the meaning a statement involving it will have when the completion is made is not easy to predict. In fact for programs, normal or otherwise, involving =, the freeness axioms are inappropriate and a different treatment is called for; see [Jaffar *et al.*, 1984; Jaffar *et al.*, 1986a] for the case of SLD-resolution, [Shepherdson, 1992b] for SLDNF-resolution.

2.5   Definite Horn clause programs

For definite Horn clause programs there are some completeness results for negation as failure with respect to *comp(P)*. We start with definite queries, where negation as failure is not involved and SLDNF-resolution coincides with SLD-resolution (since the program is definite). Denote the existential quantification of *Q* by ∃*Q*.

   Let P be a definite Horn clause program and Q a definite query. Then using SLDNF-resolution with program P,

   1. *whatever computation rule is used Q succeeds with answer including θ iff comp(P) ⊨ Qθ,*
   2. *whatever computation rule is used Q succeeds iff comp(P) ⊨ ∃Q,*
   3. *if a fair computation rule is used Q fails iff comp(P) ⊨ ¬∃Q.*

   Here an 'answer including θ' means an answer θ' such that $\theta = \theta'\varphi$ for some substitution φ and all variables x in Q, and a *fair* computation rule is one where on each infinite evaluation path (some further instantiated version of) every literal in the goal is eventually chosen. The 'first (leftmost) literal' rule of Prolog is not fair and the conclusion of (3) does not hold, e.g. for the program $p \leftarrow p$ the query p, q does not fail with the Prolog rule although $\neg(p \wedge q)$ is a consequence of *comp(P)*. The Prolog rule could be made fair either by cycling the literals around, last to first, before choosing the first literal, or by putting the new literals introduced by unification at the right hand end. Both of these rules have the effect that all the original literals of a goal are chosen before any of their children. By considering the program $p \leftarrow p, q \leftarrow q$ and the query p, q it is easily seen that there is no fair rule of the kind defined in Lloyd [1987], where the selected literal depends only on the current goal, and permutation of literals is not allowed.

   (1), (2), (3) are easy consequences of the completeness of SLD-resolution for definite queries and the 'completeness of the negation as failure rule for definite programs and queries'; see [Lloyd, 1987, Chs 2, 3]. Let us see to what extent these results can be extended to normal queries , i.e. those of the form $A_1, \ldots, A_r, \neg B_1, \ldots, \neg B_s$ ([Apt, 1990, Section 6] contains a more thorough discussion of this). In this case the negation as failure rule is invoked only at the end of the computation, to declare a grounded $\neg B_j \theta$ a success or failure according to whether $B_j \theta$ fails or succeeds using SLD-resolution. The soundness of SLDNF-resolution with respect to $comp(P)$ implies that the 'only if' halves of (1),(2),(3), are true for all such queries, but the 'if' halves need additional conditions.

For normal queries Q containing negative literals,

1. above holds if the program P and query Q are allowed,
2. holds if the query Q is ground,
3. holds if Q is ground and contains no positive literals.

These results follow easily from the results above for definite queries. (1) depends on the fact that if the program and query are allowed then any computed answer to the query must be ground, because a variable in the query can only be removed by grounding. (2) is the same as (1) if Q is ground. (3) uses the fact that if $comp(P)$ implies a disjunction of ground atoms then it implies one of them, which follows from the existence of the least fixed point model. The following counter examples show that (1),(2),(3), do not hold if the conditions on Q are removed. The program $p(x) \leftarrow$ and allowed query $p(x), \neg q(x)$ violate (1). The allowed program $p(a) \leftarrow, p(f(a)) \leftarrow p(f(a))$ and allowed query $p(x), \neg p(f(x))$ violate (2) because $comp(P)$ implies $\neg p(f(f(a)))$ hence that either $x = a$ or $x = f(a)$ is a correct answer to the query, but it does not give a definite answer, and SLDNF-resolution can only give definite answers. (2) would, like (1), be true for all allowed programs and queries if the classical consequence relation $\models$ was replaced by the intuitionistic derivability relation $\vdash_I$, because $\exists Q$ is an intuitionistic consequence of $comp(P)$ iff some $Q\theta$ is. Finally the program $p \leftarrow p$ and query $p, \neg p$ violate (3).

For definite programs the relation between CWA(P) and $comp(P)$ is clear. According to CWA(P) all ground atoms not in the least fixed point model $T_P \uparrow \omega$ are deemed false, but $comp(P)$ implies the falsity only of the subset of these which fail under SLD-resolution. It can be shown ([Apt and van Emden, 1982]) that this latter set is the complement with respect to the Herbrand base B_P of the set $T_P \uparrow \omega$ obtained by starting with $T_P \downarrow 0 = B_P$ and defining $T \downarrow (\alpha + 1) = T_P(T_P \downarrow \alpha), T_P \downarrow \alpha = \cap_{\beta < \alpha} T_P \downarrow \beta$ for α a limit ordinal.

2.6 Three-valued logic

Three-valued logic seems particularly apt for dealing with programs, since they may either succeed or fail or go on forever giving no answer. And it seems particularly apt for discussing database knowledge where we know some things are true, some things are false, but about other things we do not know whether they are true or false. Kleene [1952] introduced such a logic to deal with partial recursive functions and predicates. The three truth values are **t**, true, **f**, false and **u**, undefined or unknown. A connective has the value **t** or **f** if it has that value in ordinary 2-valued logic for all possible replacements of **u**'s by **t** or **f**, otherwise it has the value **u**. For example $p \to q$ gets the truth value **t** if p is **f** or q is **t** but the value **u** if p, q are both **u**. (So $p \to p$ is not a tautology, since it has the value **u** if p has value **u**.) The universal quantifier is treated as an infinite conjunction so $\forall x \phi(x)$ is **t** if $\phi(a)$ is **t** for all a, **f** if $\phi(a)$ is **f** for some a, otherwise **u** (so it is the glb of truth values of the $\phi(a)$ in the partial ordering given by $\mathbf{t} \geq \mathbf{u}, \mathbf{f} \geq \mathbf{u}$). Similarly $\exists x \phi(x)$ is **t** if some $\phi(a)$ is **t**, **f** if all $\phi(a)$ are **f**, otherwise **u**.

This logic has been used in connection with logic programming by Mycroft [1983] and Lassez and Maher [1985]. Recent work of Fitting [1985] and Kunen [1987; 1989] provide an explanation of the incompleteness of negation as failure for 2-valued models of $comp(P)$. It turns out that negation as failure is also sound for $comp(P)$ in 3-valued logic, so it can only derive those consequences that are true not only in all 2-valued models but also in all 3-valued models.

Use of the third truth value avoids the usual difficulty with a non-Horn clause program P that the associated operator T_P which corresponds to one application of ground instances of the clauses regarded as rules, is no longer monotonic. To avoid asymmetric associations of T with true, let us call the corresponding operator for 3-valued logic Φ_P. This operates on pairs (T_0, F_0) of disjoint subsets of B_P, the Herbrand base of P, to produce a new pair $(T_1, F_1) = \Phi_P(T_0, F_0)$, the idea being that if the elements of T_0 are known to be true and the elements of F_0 are known to be false, then one application of the rules of P to ground instances shows that the elements of T_1 are true and the elements of F_1 are false.

Formally, for a ground atom A, we put A in T_1 iff some ground instance of a clause of P has head A and a body made true by (T_0, F_0), and we put A in F_1 iff all ground instances of clauses of P with head A have body made false by (T_0, F_0). In particular if A does not match the head of any clause of P it is put into F_1, which is in accordance with the default reasoning behind negation as failure.

A little care is needed in defining the notion of a 3-valued model and the notion of $comp(P)$. A 3-valued model of a set of sentences S is a non-empty domain together with interpretations of the various function symbols in the same way as in the 2-valued case. The equality relation '=' is interpreted as identity (hence is 2-valued), the sentences in S must all evaluate to t, and so must what Kunen calls CET or 'Clark's equational theory', i.e. the equality and freeness axioms listed above as part of $comp(P)$. If we were now to write the rest of $comp(P)$, the completed definitions of predicates, in the form

$$p(x_1, \ldots, x_n \leftrightarrow E_1 \vee \ldots E_j$$

using the Kleene truth table for $\leftrightarrow$ then we should be committing ourselves to 2-valued models, for $p \leftrightarrow p$ is not **t** but **u** when p is **u**. Kunen therefore replaces this $\leftrightarrow$ with Kleene's weak equivalence $\simeq$ which gives $p \simeq q$ the value **t** if p, q have the same truth value, **f** otherwise. (Note: Our notation here agrees with Fitting but not with Kunen who uses $\leftrightarrow$ instead of our $\simeq$ and $\equiv$ instead of our $\leftrightarrow$) This saves $comp(P)$ from the inconsistency it can have under 2-valued logic. For example if P is $p \leftarrow \neg p$ then the 2-valued $comp(P)$ is $p \leftrightarrow \neg p$, which is inconsistent; what Kunen uses is $p \simeq \neg p$ which has a model with p having the value **u**. Having done this, if we want $comp(P) \models_3 P$ to hold i.e. 3-valued models of $comp(P)$ also to be models of P then we must replace the $\rightarrow$ in the clauses of P by $\supset$ where $p \supset q$ is the 2-valued 'if p is true then q is true', which has the value **t** except when p is **t** and q is **f** or **u**, when it has the value **f**. (Actually this would still be true with the slightly stronger 2-valued connective which also requires 'and if q is **f** then p is **f**'.) $comp(P) \models_3 P$ does not hold if $\rightarrow$ is used in P because the program $p \leftarrow p$ has completion $p \simeq p$ which has a model where p is **u** which gives $p \leftarrow p$ the value **u** not **t**.

We may identify a pair (T, F) of disjoint subsets of the Herbrand base with the three valued structure which gives all elements of T the value **t**, all elements of F the value **f**, and all other elements of the Herbrand base the value **u**. The pairs (T, F) of disjoint subsets of B_p form a complete lattice with the natural ordering $\subseteq$.

We define $\Phi_P \uparrow \alpha$ as we defined $T_P \uparrow \alpha$, i.e. $\Phi_P \uparrow 0 = (\phi, , \phi), \Phi_P \uparrow (\alpha + I)\Phi_P(\Phi_P \uparrow \alpha), Phi_P \uparrow \alpha = \cup_{\beta < \alpha} \Phi_P \uparrow \beta$ for α a limit ordinal. We now have the analogue for Φ_P of the 2-valued properties of TP.

1. Φ_P *is monotonic.*
2. Φ_P *has a least fixed point given by* $\Phi_P \uparrow \alpha$ *for some ordinal* α.
3. *If* T, F *are disjoint then* (T, F) *is a 3-valued Herbrand model of* $comp(P)$ *iff it is a fixed point of* Φ_P.

In addition:

4. $comp(P)$ *is always consistent in 3-valued logic.*

For a proof see [Fitting, 1985]. The monotonicity is obvious and (2) is a well known consequence of that. (3) is also easily proved, as in the 2-valued case, and (4) follows from (2) and (3).

However, the operator Φ_P is not in general continuous and so the closure ordinal α, i.e. the α such that $\Phi_P \uparrow \alpha$ is the least fixed point, may be greater than ω. For example if P is :

$$p(f(x)) \leftarrow p(x)$$
$$q(a) \leftarrow p(x)$$

then it is easy to check that the closure ordinal is $\omega + 1$. Fitting shows that the closure ordinal can be as high as Church–Kleene ω_1, the first non recursive ordinal. Both Fitting and Kunen show also that a semantics based on this least fixed point as the sole model suffers from the same disadvantage as the closed world assumption, namely that the set of sentences, indeed even the set of ground atoms, that are true in this model may be non-recursively enumerable (as high as Π_1^1 complete in fact). The same is true of a semantics based on all 3-valued Herbrand models, for the programs in the examples constructed by Fitting and Kunen can be taken to have only one 3-valued Herbrand model.

Kunen proposes a very interesting and natural way of avoiding this non-computable semantics: Why should we consider only Herbrand models; why not consider all 3-valued models? In other words, ask whether the query Q is true in all 3-valued models of $comp(P)$. He shows that an equivalent way of obtaining the same semantics is by using the operator Φ_P but chopping it off at ω:

> A sentence ϕ has value $\mathbf{t}$ in all 3-valued models of $comp(P)$ iff it has value $\mathbf{t}$ in $\Phi_P \uparrow n$ for some finite n.

There are three peculiar features of this result. First, in determining the truth value of ϕ in $\Phi_P \uparrow n$, quantifiers are interpreted as ranging over the Herbrand universe, yet we get equivalence to truth in all 3-valued models. This may be partly explained by the fact that *the truth of this result depends on Φ_P and $comp(P)$ being formed using a language L_∞ with infinitely many function symbols*. (Where constants are treated as 0-ary functions. Actually Kunen uses a language with infinitely many function symbols of all arities, but the weaker condition above is sufficient.) For example if P is simply $p(a)$, then the usual language L_p associated with P has just one constant a, the Herbrand base is $\{p(a)\}$, and if Φ_P is evaluated wrt this, then $\forall x p(x)$ has value $\mathbf{t}$ in $\Phi_P \uparrow 1$. But $\forall x p(x)$ is not true in all 3-valued (or even all 2-valued) models of $comp(P)$, and it does not have value $\mathbf{t}$ in any $\Phi_P \uparrow n$ if Φ_P is evaluated wrt a language with infinitely many function symbols, because if b is a new constant (or the result $f(a, \ldots, a)$ of applying a new function symbol to a) then $p(b)$ has value $\mathbf{f}$ in $\Phi_P \uparrow 1$. Second, truth in some $\Phi_P \uparrow n$ is not the same as truth in $\Phi_P \uparrow \omega$, which is not usually a model of $comp(P)$. Third the result holds only for sentences built up from the Kleene connectives $\wedge, \vee, \neg, \rightarrow, \leftrightarrow, \forall, \exists$, which have the property that if they have the value $\mathbf{t}$ or $\mathbf{f}$ and one of their arguments changes from $\mathbf{u}$ to $\mathbf{t}$ or $\mathbf{f}$ then their value doesn't change. The weak equivalence $\simeq$ used in the sentences giving the completed definitions of the predicates in $comp(P)$ does not have this property, so the sentences of $comp(P)$—which obviously have value $\mathbf{t}$ in all 3-valued models of $comp(P)$—may not evaluate to $\mathbf{t}$ in any $\Phi_P \uparrow n$. For example if P is

$$p(0)$$
$$p(s(x)) \leftarrow p(x)$$

then the completed definition of p in $comp(P)$ is

$$p(y) \simeq [y = 0 \vee (\exists x)(y = s(x) \wedge p(x))].$$

This has value $\mathbf{f}$ in each $\Phi_P \uparrow n$ for finite n, because for $y = s^n(0)$ the left hand side is $\mathbf{u}$ but the right hand side is $\mathbf{t}$.

If Φ_P and $comp(P)$ are formed using a language L with only finitely many function symbols then [Shepherdson, 1988b] the corresponding result is

A sentence ϕ has value $\mathbf{t}$ in all 3-valued models of $comp(P) \cup \{DCA\}$ iff it has value $\mathbf{t}$ in $\Phi_P \uparrow n$ for some finite n.

Here DCA is the *domain closure* axiom for L

$$\forall x \bigvee_{f \in L} \exists y_1, \ldots, y_{r_f} (x = f(y_1, \ldots, y_{r_f}))$$

(where r_f is the arity of f), which states that every element is the value of a function in L (so it is satisfied in Herbrand models formed using L.).

It is worth noting here the way in which $comp(P)$ depends on the language L. As mentioned above this is due to $comp(P)$ containing the freeness axioms for L. Let us denote by $comp_L(P)$ the completion of P formed using the language L, by $G^k L$ the sentence expressing the fact that there are greater than or equal to k distinct elements which are not values of a function in L, and by G_L^∞ the set of sentences expressing the fact that there are infinitely many such elements. Let $L(P)$ denote the language of symbols occurring in the program. Then [Shepherdson, 1988a]:

Let $L_2 \supseteq L_1 \supseteq L(P)$. Then $comp_{L_2}(P)$ is a conservative extension of

1. *$comp_{L_1}(P)$ if L_1 has infinitely many function symbols,*
2. *$comp_{L_1}(P) \cup G_{L_1}^\infty$ if L_1 has finitely many function symbols and $L_2 - L_1$ contains a function symbol of positive arity or infinitely many constants,*
3. *$comp_{L_1}(P) \cup \{G_{L_1}^k\}$ if L_1 has finitely many function symbols and $L_2 - L_1$ contains no function symbol of positive arity but exactly k constants.*

These results are true in both 2- and 3-valued logic since only the equality predicate is involved, and this is always taken to be 2-valued.

Kunen shows that whether ϕ has value $\mathbf{t}$ in $\Phi_P \uparrow n$ is decidable, so when a language with infinitely many function symbols is used:

The set of Q such that $comp(P) \models_3 Q$ is recursively enumerable.

An alternative proof could be obtained by giving a complete and consistent deductive system for 3-valued logic, as Ebbinghaus [1969] has done for a very similar system of 3-valued logic. This alternative proof shows that the result holds for any language. For definite Horn clause programs 3-valued logic gives results which are in good agreement with those of 2-valued logic.

If P is a definite Horn clause program then

$$\Phi_P \uparrow \alpha = (T_P \uparrow \alpha, B_P - T_P \downarrow \alpha).$$

Since the closure ordinal of $T_P \uparrow$ for a definite Horn clause program P is ω, this shows that the closure ordinal of $\Pi_P \uparrow$ is the same as that of $T_P \downarrow$.

For definite programs and definite queries, where the 2-valued semantics of negation as failure in terms of $comp(P)$ is satisfactory, the 3-valued semantics agrees with it.

If P is a definite Horn clause program and Q is the existential closure of a conjunction of atoms then the following eight statements are equivalent: Q is true in all (2-valued, 3-valued) (models, Herbrand models) of (comp(P), P).

It is to be understood here that, as above, the clauses of P are written with $\rightarrow$ replaced by $\supset$. When this is done all 3-valued models of $comp(P)$ are models of P, so all the classes of models described are contained in the class of 3-valued models of P. Since they all contain the class of 2-valued Herbrand models of $comp(P)$, the result amounts to saying that if Q is true in all 2-valued Herbrand models of $comp(P)$ then it is true in all 3-valued models of P, which follows easily by considering the least fixed point model [Shepherdson, 1988b]. The result is true whatever language (containing $L(P)$) is used. But if 'existential' is replaced by 'universal' here then even the 2-valued parts of the result fail if the language used is $L(P)$. For example if P is $p(0)$, $p(s(x)) \leftarrow p(x)$ and Q is $\forall x p(x)$ then Q is true in all 2-valued Herbrand models of $comp(P)$, but not in all 2-valued models of $comp(P)$. However

> *If the language of symbols contains infinitely many constants, or a function symbol not in P, then the above equivalence result holds for all positive sentences.*

A positive sentence here means one built up from atomic sentences using only $\wedge, \vee, \forall, \exists$. The reason this holds is that new constants behave like variables; see [Shepherdson, 1988b] for details.

The relevance of 3-valued logic to negation as failure is given by Kunen's soundness and completeness results:

> *SLDNF-resolution is sound with respect to comp(P) in 3-valued logic, for normal programs P and normal queries Q, i.e.*
> *if Q succeeds with answer θ then $comp(P) \models_3 Q\theta$,*
> *if Q fails then $comp(P) \models_3 \neg \exists Q$.*

> *SLDNF-resolution is complete with respect to* $comp(P)$ *in 3-valued logic for normal allowed programs* P *and normal allowed queries* Q, *i.e.*
>
> *if* $comp(P) \vDash_3 Q\theta$ *then* Q *succeeds with answer including* θ,
> *if* $comp(P) \vDash_3 \neg\exists Q$ *then* Q *fails* .

Here a program is said to be *allowed* if every variable which occurs in a clause of it occurs in at least one positive literal in the body of that clause, a query is *allowed* if every variable in it occurs in at least one positive literal of it. It is easily verified that if the program and query are both allowed then the query cannot flounder, and this is what permits the completeness result. So for such programs and queries $comp(P)$ and 3-valued logic provide a perfectly satisfactory semantics. However, the allowedness condition is very stringent and excludes many common Prolog constructs, such as the definition of equality, $equal(x, x)$, and both clauses in the definition of $member(X, L)$. But Stärk [1994] has shown that the allowedness condition can be considerably weakened to one based on modes of predicates and data-flow analysis which is satisfied by most programs written in practice. The first result above is stated in [Kunen, 1987] (for a full proof see [Shepherdson, 1989]); the much deeper completeness result is proved in [Kunen, 1989]. Neither of them require the assumption used above that L contains infinitely many function symbols; they are valid for any L containing the function symbols of P (see [Shepherdson, 1988a; Shepherdson, 1989]).

Stärk [1991] gives a formal system for 3-valued logic, a fragment of Gentzen's sequent calculus LK, in which one can derive exactly the 3-valued consequence of $comp(P)$. Stärk [1994] shows that these 3-valued consequences of $comp(P)$ are the same as those in a certain 4-valued logic, and by representing a 4-valued relation by two 2-valued relations, they can be expressed as the classical 2-valued consequences of a set of formulae called *partial completion* of P. A similar theory has been introduced by Jäger [1993].

Other applications of many-valued logic to logic programming are to be found in the papers of Fitting [1986; 1987b; 1987a], Fitting and Ben-Jacob [1988] and Przymusinski [1991].

2.7 Cases where SLDNF-resolution is complete for $comp(P)$: hierarchical, stratified and call-consistent programs.

Clark [1978] proved completeness results for hierarchical programs. Apt *et al.* [1988] introduced the important notion of stratified program, showed that if P is stratified then $comp(P)$ is consistent, and conjectured a completeness result for stratified programs satisfying an additional strictness condition. This conjecture was proved by Cavedon and Lloyd [1989]. Sato

[1987] generalised the notion of stratifiability to *call-consistency* and showed that if P is call-consistent then $comp(P)$ is consistent. Finally Kunen [1987], using his completeness results above for 3-valued logic, proved completeness results for call-consistent programs which include all these results.

Informally a hierarchical program is one in which there are no recursive or mutually recursive definitions of predicates, a stratified one has no recursion through negation, and a call-consistent one has no predicate depending negatively on itself as p does in the program $p \leftarrow \neg p$ or similarly via intermediate clauses and predicate symbols, e.g. $p \leftarrow \neg q, q \leftarrow p$.

These notions can be defined formally in two ways. First in terms of the *dependency graph* of a program P. This is a directed graph whose nodes are the predicate symbols of P and which has an edge from p to q iff there is a clause in P with p in the head and q in the body. The edge is marked *positive* (resp. *negative*) if q occurs in a positive (resp. negative) literal in the body (an edge may be both positive and negative). Then a program is *hierarchical* iff its dependency graph contains no cycles, it is *stratified* iff its dependency graph contains no cycles containing a negative edge, it is *call-consistent* iff its dependency graph contains no cycle with an odd number of negative edges. Equivalent definitions can be given in terms of level mappings. A *level mapping* of a program is a mapping from its set of predicate symbols to the non-negative integers. A program P is hierarchical iff it has a level mapping such that in every clause of P the level of a predicate symbol in the body is strictly less than the level of the predicate symbol in the head. It is stratified iff the level of each predicate symbol in a positive literal in the body is less than or equal to the level of the predicate symbol in the head and each predicate symbol in a negative literal in the body is strictly less than the level of the predicate symbol in the head. Finally let us say a predicate symbol p *depends positively* (resp. *negatively*) on a predicate symbol q, written $p \geq_{+1} q$ (resp. $p \geq_{-1} q$) when there is a path (of length ≥ 0) in the dependency graph from p to q containing an even (resp. odd) number of negative edges. Then a program is call-consistent iff there is a level mapping such that $\mathrm{level}(p) \geq \mathrm{level}(q)$ if p depends positively or negatively on q, and $\mathrm{level}(p) > \mathrm{level}(q)$ if p depends both positively and negatively on q. Kunen gave an alternative definition of $p \geq_{+1} q$, $p \geq_{-1} q$ as follows. Define $p \supseteq_{+1} q$ (resp. $p \supseteq_{-1} q$) when there is a program clause with p in its head and q occurring in a positive (resp. negative) literal in its body. Let $\geq_{+1}, \geq_{-1}$ be the least pair of relations on the set of predicate symbols satisfying

$$p \geq_{+1} p$$
$$p \supseteq_i q \ \& \ q \geq_j r \Rightarrow p \geq_{i.j} r.$$

Kunen defined a program to be semi-strict iff there is no p such that $p \geq_{-1} p$. This is clearly seen to be equivalent to the first definition of call-consistent above.

Following Apt, Blair and Walker he defined a program to be strict iff there are no p, q such that $p \geq_{+1} q$ and $p \geq_{-1} q$. Finally if Q is a query, let us define $Q \geq_i p$ iff either $q \geq_i p$ for some q occurring positively in Q, or $q \geq_{-i} p$ for some q occurring negatively in Q. Then a program P is said to be *strict with respect* to Q iff for no predicate letter p do we have $Q \geq_{+1} p$ and $Q \geq_{-1} p$. [This condition excludes queries Q such as $p, \neg p$; here $\neg Q$ is a tautology so is a consequence of any $comp(P)$ but Q does not fail unless p succeeds or fails.]

Kunen [1987] proved:

> *If P is a call-consistent program which is strict wrt the query Q then*
> $comp(P) \vDash_2 \forall Q$ *implies* $comp(P) \vDash_3 \forall Q$,
> $comp(P) \vDash_2 \neg \exists Q$ *implies* $comp(P) \vDash_3 \neg \exists Q$.

[Actually the second part is not explicitly stated but follows by a similar argument]. Combining this with the 3-valued completeness results given in Section 2.6 above gives:

> *If P is an allowed, call-consistent normal program, Q is an allowed normal query, and P is strict with respect to Q, then SLDNF-resolution is complete with respect to $comp(P)$ in 2-valued logic for the query Q, i.e.*
> *if $comp(P) \vdash Q\theta$ then Q succeeds with answer θ*
> *if $comp(P) \vdash \neg \exists Q$ then Q fails.*

This does not include the result of Clark, that if call-consistent here is strengthened to hierarchical then the condition that P is strict with respect of Q is not needed. Kunen gives a version that includes this as follows. Let $\mathcal{P}$ be a subset of the predicate symbols of P which is *downward closed* i.e. if the predicate symbol in the head of a clause of P belongs to $\mathcal{P}$ then so do all predicate symbols in the body of the clause. Suppose that P restricted to $\mathcal{P}$ is hierarchical. Then the condition that P is strict with respect to Q can be weakened to: for no predicate letter p outside of $\mathcal{P}$ do we have $Q \geq_{+1} p$ and $Q \geq_{-1} p$.

These results extend to general programs (Section 2.4) where arbitrary first formulae are allowed in the bodies of program clauses, if the notions of allowed, call-consistent and strict are defined in the appropriate way; see [Cavedon, 1988] for details.

2.8 Semantics for negation in terms of special classes of models

We continue here the discussion begun in Section 1.5 of semantics based on the idea that the meaning of a program P is not a set of sentences (such as P, $comp(P)$ or, $CWA(P)$), but a set of $M(P)$ of models of P, and that when we ask a query $?Q$ we want to know whether Q is true in all models in $M(P)$. We have already discussed, in Section 1.5, the case where P is a definite Horn clause program and $M(P)$ is the singleton consisting of its least Herbrand model, and in Section 2.3 we have shown its close connection with the semantics based on $CWA(P)$. When P contains negation $CWA(P)$ may be inconsistent and P may not have a least Herbrand model. In attempting to find a weaker assumption which would be consistent for all consistent P, Minker [1982] was led to suggest replacing least Herbrand model by minimal Herbrand model, i.e. one not containing any proper submodel, where as usual we identify a Herbrand model with the subset of the Herbrand base B_p which is true in it. So he considers $M(P)$, the class of intended models of P, to be the class of minimal Herbrand models of P. He shows this semantics is closely related to the one based on his 'generalised closed world assumption', $GCWA(P)$, defined as follows:

$GCWA(P) = P \cup \{\neg A : A$ is a ground atom such that there is no disjunction B of ground atoms such that $P \vdash A \vee B$ but $P \nvdash B\}$.

Indeed the condition on A here is easily shown to be equivalent to:

A is a ground atom which is false in all minimal Herbrand models of P.

Since minimal models of P clearly satisfy $GCWA(P)$ this implies:

If a first order sentence Q is a consequence of $GCWA(P)$ then it is true in all minimal Herbrand models of P.

However, the converse is not generally true, for there may be models of $GCWA(P)$ which are not minimal Herbrand models of P. For example if P is $p(a) \leftarrow \neg p(b)$, i.e. $p(a) \vee p(b)$, there are two minimal Herbrand models of P, namely $\{p(a)\}$, $\{p(b)\}$, but $GCWA(P)$ is the same as P and has a non-minimal model $\{p(a), p(b)\}$. And the query $\exists x \neg p(x)$ is true in all minimal Herbrand models of P but is not a consequence of $GCWA(P)$. So $GCWA(P)$ is an incomplete attempt to characterise the minimal Herbrand models of P. The converse of the statement displayed above is true if Q is a positive query or, more generally the existential closure of a positive matrix (i.e. a formula built up from atoms using only $\wedge, \vee$). But $GCWA(P)$ is not really involved then, because if such a Q is true in all minimal Herbrand models of P it is actually a consequence of P alone. From the displayed statement above it follows that if such a Q is a consequence of $GCWA(P)$ then it is a already a consequence of P so addition of the generalised closed world assumption, like the closed world assumption, does not allow the derivation of any more positive information of this kind (in particular of ground atoms). This is usually thought to be a desirable feature, since closed world assumptions are usually intended as devices for uncovering implicit negative information, thus avoiding the need to state it explicitly, without adding unconsciously to the positive information of the program.

Minker's aim of providing a version of the closed world assumption which is consistent is achieved:

If P is consistent then so is GCWA(P)

This is true not only for normal programs P but for any program P consisting of universal sentences because it is easy to show that such P has a minimal Herbrand model.

$GCWA(P)$ is a generalisation of the $CWA(P)$ in the sense that it agrees with that when P is definite. The generalised closed world assumption is a kind of negation as failure in that $\neg A$ is assumed when A fails to be true in any minimal Herbrand model. However, negation as failure as defined here, i.e. as SLDNF-resolution, is not sound with respect to it. This is shown by the program $q \leftarrow \neg p$, where p fails but is not a consequence of $GCWA(P)$. Henschen and Park [1988] discuss computational proof procedures appropriate to the $GCWA(P)$ in the case of principal interest where P is a database, i.e. without function symbols (which Minker's original article restricted itself to). When function symbols are present there may be no sound and complete computational proof procedure for $GCWA(P)$. This follows from our example in Section 2.3 of a definite clause program for which the set of queries which are consequences of $CWA(P)$ is not recursively enumerable. The same is true for the set of queries true in all minimal Herbrand models of P, since for definite P this does coincide with the set of queries which are consequences of $GCWA(P)$ (i.e. of $CWA(P)$).

For further results on the $GCWA$ and other generalisation of the closed world assumption see Gelfond *et al.* [1986; 1989], Lifschitz [1988], Shepherdson [1988b], Brass and Lipeck [1989] and Yahya and Henschen [1985].

Apt *et al.* [1988] propose a semantics for negation which combines this approach with that of the Clark completion, i.e. applies both kinds of default reasoning. They suggest that the models of P which it is reasonable to study are those Herbrand models which are not only minimal but *supported*, i.e. a ground atom A is true only if there is a ground instance of a clause of P with head A and a body which is true. We saw in Section 2.4 that the supported models are the fixpoints of T_p, and the models of $comp(P)$. Apt, Blair and Walker say on p.100

> '... we are interested here in studying minimal and supported models ... this simply means we are looking for the minimal fixed points of the operator T_p.'

Since they go on to study the minimal fixed points of T_p it looks as though they intended the latter definition i.e. minimal supported models of P i.e. minimal models of $comp(P)$. But the first phrase suggests a stronger definition, i.e. models of $comp(P)$ which are also minimal models of P. To see the difference consider the program $p \leftarrow q, q \leftarrow \neg p, q \leftarrow q$. The only, and hence the minimal, model of $comp(P)$ is $\{p, q\}$; the only minimal model of P is $\{p\}$. There is no supported model of P (i.e. model of $comp(P)$) which is a minimal model of P. However, their main concern is with stratified programs, for which they establish the existence of a model satisfying the stronger first definition:

> If P is a stratified program then there is a minimal model of P which is also supported (i.e. a model of $comp(P)$, so $comp(P)$ is consistent).

There may be more than one model satisfying these conditions, e.g if P is the stratified program $p \leftarrow p, q \leftarrow \neg p$ there are two such models $\{p\}$ and $\{q\}$. They show that there is one such model M_p which is defined in a natural way and propose that it be taken as defining the semantics for the program P, i.e., that an ideal query evaluation procedure should make a query Q succeed if Q is true in M_p and fail if Q is false in M_p. They give two equivalent ways of defining M_p. A stratified program P can be partitioned

$$ P = P_1 \overset{\bullet}{\bigcup} \ldots \overset{\bullet}{\bigcup} P_n. $$

so that if a predicate occurs positively in the body of a clause in P_i, all clauses where it occurs in the head are in P_j with $j \leq i$, and if a predicate occurs negatively in the body of a clause in P_i, then all clauses where it occurs in the head are in P_j with $j < i$. (So P_i consists of the clauses defining ith level predicates.) Their first definition of M_p is to start with the empty set, iterate T'_{p_1} ω times then T'_{p_2} ω times, $\ldots$, T'_{p_n} ω times. (The operator T'_p here is defined by $T'_p(I) = T_p(I) \cup I$ and is more appropriate than T_p when that is nonmonotonic.) The other definition starts by defining $M(P_1)$ as the intersection of all Herbrand models of P_1, then $M(P_2)$ as the intersection of all Herbrand models of P_2 whose intersection with the Herbrand base of P_1 is $M(P_1)$, then $\ldots M(P_n)$ as the intersection of all Herbrand models of P_n whose intersection with the Herbrand base of P_{n-1} is $M(P_{n-1})$. Finally define $M_p = M(P_n)$. For the program above, this model is $\{q\}$, which does seem to be better in accordance with default reasoning than the other minimal model of $comp(P)$, namely $\{p\}$. There is no reason to suppose p is true, so p is taken to be false, hence q to be true. It seems natural to assign truth values to the predicates in the order in which they are defined, which is the essence of the above method. Moreover, a strong point in favour of the model M_p is that they show it does not depend on the actual way a stratifiable program is stratified, i.e., divided into levels.

Notice that like $comp(P)$, M_p depends not only on the logical content of P but on the way it is written, for $p \leftarrow \neg q$ and $q \leftarrow \neg p$ give different M_p.

Since SLDNF-resolution is sound for $comp(P)$ and M_p is a model of $comp(P)$, it is certainly sound for M_p but, since more sentences will be true in M_p than in all models of $comp(P)$, SLDNF-resolution will be even more incomplete for M_p than for $comp(P)$. For example, with the program above, where q is true in M_p but not in all models of $comp(P)$, there is no chance of proving q by SLDNF-resolution.

In general there may be no sound and complete computational proof procedure for the semantics based on M_p. This is shown by the example in 2.3 which shows this for $CWA(P)$, since for definite programs M_p is the least Herbrand model, so the semantics based on M_p coincides with that based on $CWA(P)$. However Apt, Blair and Walker do give an interpreter which is sound, and which is complete when there are no function symbols.

Przymusinski [1988b; 1988a] proposes an even more restricted class of models than the minimal, supported models, namely the class of *perfect* models. The argument for a semantics based on this class is that if one writes $p \vee q$, then one intends p, q to be treated equally; but, if one writes $p \leftarrow \neg q$ there is a presupposition that in the absence of contrary evidence q is false and hence p is true. He allows 'disjunctive databases,' i.e., clauses with more than one atom in the head, e.g.

$$C_1 \vee \ldots \vee C_p \leftarrow A_1 \wedge \ldots \wedge A_m \wedge \neg B_1 \wedge \ldots \wedge \neg B_n,$$

and his basic notion of priority is that the Cs here should have lower priority than the Bs and no higher priority than the As. To obtain greater generality, he defines this notion for ground atoms rather than predicates, i.e., if the above clause is a ground instance of a program clause he says that $C_i < B_j, C_i \leq A_k$. Taking the transitive closure of these relations establishes a relation on the ground atoms that is transitive (but may not be asymmetric and irreflexive if the program is not stratified).

His basic philosophy is

> ... if we have a model of DB and if another model N is obtained by possibly adding some ground atoms of M and removing some other ground atoms from M, then we should consider the new model N to be preferable to M only if the addition of a lower priority atom A to N is justified by the simultaneous removal from M of a higher priority atom B (i.e. such that $B > A$). This reflects the general principle that we are willing to minimize higher priority predicates, even at the cost of enlarging predicates of lower priority, in an attempt to minimize high priority predicates as much as possible. A model M will be considered perfect if there are no models preferable to it. More

formally:

[Definition 2.] Suppose that M and N are two different models of a disjunctive database DB. We say that N is preferable to M (briefly, $N < M$) if for every ground atom A in $N - M$ there is a ground atom B in $M - N$, such that $B > A$. We say that a model M of DB is perfect if there are no models preferable to M.

He extends the notion of stratifiability to disjunctive databases by requiring that in a clause

$$C_1 \vee \ldots \vee C_p \leftarrow A_1 \wedge \ldots \wedge A_m \wedge \neg B_1 \ldots \wedge \neg B_n$$

the predicates in $C_1, \ldots, C_p$ should all be of the same level i greater than that of the predicates in $B_1 \ldots B_n$ and greater than or equal to those of the predicates in $A_1 \ldots, A_m$. He then weakens this to *local stratifiability* by applying it to ground atoms and instances of program clauses instead of to predicates and program clauses. (The number of levels is then allowed to be infinite.) It is equivalent to the nonexistence of increasing sequences in the above relation $<$ between ground atoms.

He proves:

> *Every locally stratified disjunctive database has a perfect model. Moreover every stratified logic program P (i.e. where the head of each clause is a single atom) has exactly one perfect model, and it coincides with the model M_p of Apt, Blair, and Walker.*

He also shows that every perfect model is minimal and supported, if the program is positive disjunctive, then a model is perfect iff it is minimal, and a model is perfect if there are no minimal models preferable to it.

(Positive disjunctive means the clauses are of the form $C_1 \vee \ldots \vee C_p \leftarrow A_1 \wedge \ldots \wedge A_m$.) He also establishes a relation between perfect models and the concept of prioritized circumscription introduced by McCarthy [1984] and further developed by Lifschitz [1985]:

> Let $S_1, \ldots, S_r$ be any decomposition of the set S of all predicates of a database DB into disjoint sets. A model M of DB is called a model of prioritized circumscription of DB with respect to priorities $S_1 > S_2 > \ldots > S_r$, or—briefly—a model of $CIRC(DB, S_1 > S_2 > \ldots > S_r)$ if for every $i = 1, \ldots, r$ the extension in M of predicates from S_1 is minimal among all models M of DB in which the extension of predicates from $S_1, S_2, \ldots, S_{i-1}$ coincides with the extension of these predicates in M.

He shows

> Suppose that DB is a stratified disjunctive database and
> $\{S_1, S_1, \ldots S_r\}$ is a stratification of DB. A model of DB is
> perfect if and only if it is a model of prioritized circumscription
> $CIRC(DB, S_1 > S_2 > \ldots > S_r)$.

Przymusinska and Przymusinski [1988] extend the above results to a wider class of *weakly stratified program* and a corresponding wider class of *weakly perfect models*. The definitions are rather complicated but are based on the idea of removing 'irrelevant' predicate symbols in the dependency graph of a logic program and substituting components of this graph for its vertices in the definitions of stratification and perfect model.

Przymusinski [1988a] observed that the restriction to Herbrand models gives rise to what he calls the *universal query problem*. This is illustrated by the program P consisting of the single clause $p(a)$. Using the language defined by the program this has the sole Herbrand model $\{p(a)\}$ so that $\forall x p(x)$ is true in the least Herbrand model although it is not a consequence of P. So the semantics based on the least Herbrand model implies new positive information, and also prevents standard unification based procedures from being complete with respect to this semantics. One way of avoiding this problem is to consider Herbrand models not with respect to the language defined by the program but with respect to a language containing infinitely many function symbols of all arities, as in 2.6. This seems very cumbersome; given an interpretation for the symbols occurring in the program, to extend this to a model you would have to concoct meanings for all the infinitely many irrelevant constant and function symbols. A simpler way is to consider all models, or, as Przymusinski did, all models satisfying the equational axioms CET of Section 2.4 instead of just Herbrand models. He showed how to extend the notion of perfect model from Herbrand models to all such models, and proposed a semantics based on the class of *all* perfect models. He gave a 'procedural semantics' and showed it to be sound and complete (for non-floundering queries), for stratified programs with respect to this new perfect model semantics. It is an extension of the interpreter given by Apt, Blair and Walker. However, it is not a computational procedure. It differs from SLDNF-resolution by considering derivation trees to be failed not only when they are finitely failed, but also when all their branches either end in failure or are infinite. This cannot always be checked in a finite number of steps. Indeed there cannot be any computational procedure which is sound and complete for the perfect model semantics because for definite programs it coincides with the least Herbrand model semantics, and the example in Section 2.3 shows that the set of ground atoms false in this model may be non-recursively enumerable. Further results on stratified programs and perfect models are found in Apt and Pugin [1987], Apt and Blair [1988].

Van Gelder *et al.* [1988], building on an idea of Ross and Topor [1987] defined a semantics based on *well-founded models*. These are Herbrand models which are supported in a stronger sense than that defined above. It is explained roughly by the following example. Suppose that $p \leftarrow q$ and $q \leftarrow p$ are the only clauses in the program with p or q in the head. Then p needs q to support it and q needs p to support it so the set $\{p, q\}$ gets no external support and in a well-founded model all its members will be taken to be false. In order to deal with all programs they worked with partial interpretations and models. A *partial interpretation* I of a program P is a set of literals which is consistent, i.e. does not contain both p and $\neg p$ for any ground atom (element of the Herbrand base B_p) p. If p belongs to I then p is true in I, if $\neg p$ belongs to I then p is false in I, otherwise p is undefined in I. It is called a *total interpretation* if it contains either p or $\neg p$ for each ground atom p. A total interpretation I is a *total model* of P if every instantiated clause of P is satisfied in I. A *partial model* is a partial interpretation that can be extended to a total model. A subset A of the Herbrand base B_p is an *unfounded set of P with respect to the partial interpretation I* if each atom $p \in A$ satisfies the following condition: For each instantiated clause C of P whose head is p, at least one of the following holds:

1. Some literal in the body of C is false in I
2. Some positive literal in the body of C is in A.

The well-founded semantics uses conditions (1) and (2) to draw negative conclusions. Essentially it simultaneously infers all atoms in A to be false, on the grounds that there is no one atom in A that can be first established as true by the clauses of P, starting from 'knowing' I, so that if we choose to infer that all atoms in A are false there is no way we would later have to infer one as true. The usual notion of supported uses (1) only. The closed sets of Ross and Topor [1987] use (2) only. It is easily shown that the union of all unfounded sets with respect to I is an unfounded set, the greatest unfounded set of P with respect to I, denoted by $U_P(I)$. Now for each partial interpretation I an extended partial interpretation $W_P(P)$ is obtained by adding to I all those positive literals p such that there is an instantiated clause of P whose body is true in I (this part is like the familiar T_p operator) and all those negative literals $\neg p$ such that $p \in U_P(I)$. It is routine to show that U_P is monotonic and so has a least fixed point reached after iteration to some countable ordinal. This is denoted by $M_{wp}(P)$ and called the *well-founded partial model* of P. The *well-founded semantics* of P is based on $M_{wp}(P)$. In general $M_{wp}(P)$ will be a partial model, giving rise to a 3-valued semantics. Using the 3-valued logic of Section 2.6 $M_{wp}(P)$ is a 3-valued model of *comp(P)*, but in general it is not the same as the Fitting model defined in Section 2.6 as the least fixed point of p. Since the Fitting model is the least 3-valued model of *comp(P)* it is a subset of

$M_{wp}(P)$. For the program $p \leftarrow p$, in the Fitting model p is undefined, but in $M_{wp}(P)$ it is false (since the set $\{p\}$ is unfounded). However, for stratified programs this new approach agrees with the two previous ones:

> If P is locally stratified then its well-founded model is total and coincides with its unique perfect model, i.e. with the model M_p of Apt, Blair and Walker.

Przymusinski [1988b] extends this result to weakly stratified programs and weakly perfect models. He also shows how to extend SLS-resolution so that it is sound and complete for all logic programs (for non-floundering queries) with respect to the well-founded semantics. Ross [1989] gives a similar procedure. Przymusinski also shows that if the well-founded model is total the program is in a sense equivalent to a locally stratified program.

A closely related notion of *stable model* was introduced by Gelfond and Lifschitz [1988]. For a given logic program P they define a *stability transformation* S from total interpretations to total interpretations. Given a total interpretation I its transform $S(I)$ is defined in three stages as follows. Start with the set of all instantiations of clauses of P. Discard those whose bodies contain a negative literal which is false in I. From the bodies of those remaining discard all negative literals. This results in a set of definite clauses. Define $S(I)$ to be its least Herbrand model.

This transformation S is a 'shrinking' transformation, i.e. the set of positive literals true in $S(I)$ is a subset of those true in I. If I is a model of P the interpretation $S(I)$ may not be a model of P; it may shrink too much. However, the fixed points of S are always models of P. These are defined to be the *stable models* of P. A stable model is minimal (in terms of the set of positive literals) but not every minimal model is stable. Van Gelder *et al.* show that for total interpretations being a fixed point of S is the same as being a fixed point of their operator W_P. Since the well-founded model is the least fixed point of W_P it is a subset of every stable model of P. Furthermore

> If P has a well-founded total model then that model is the unique stable model.

The converse is not true.

Fine [1989] independently arrived, from a slightly different point of view, at a notion of *felicitous model*, which is equivalent to that of stable model. A felicitous model is one such that the falsehoods of the model serve to generate, via the program, exactly the truths of the model. His idea is that if you make a hypothesis as to which statements are false, and use the program to generate truths from this hypothesis then there are three possible outcomes: some statement is neither a posited falsehood nor a generated truth (a 'gap'); some statement is both a posited falsehood and a generated truth (a 'glut'); the posited falsehoods are the exact complements of the generated truths (no gap and no glut). A *happy hypothesis* is one which leads to no gaps and no glut, and a felicitous model is one where the hypothesis that the false statements are precisely those which are false in the model, is a happy hypothesis. Fine shows that the restriction to felicitous models can be viewed as a kind of self-referential closed world assumption.

To sum up. Plausible arguments have been given for each of the semantics discussed in this section. The minimal models of $comp(P)$ of Apt, Blair and Walker, the perfect models of Przymusinski, the well-founded models of van Gelder, Ross and Schlipf, and the stable models of Gelfond and Lifschitz are all models of $comp(P)$, so SLDNF-resolution is sound for them. So they all offer plausible semantics for negation as failure in general different from that based on $comp(P)$ because they are based on a subset of the models of $comp(P)$. The fact that for the important class of locally stratified programs they all coincide, giving a unique model Mp, which often appears to be 'the' natural model, adds support to their claim to be chosen as the intended semantics. However SLDNF-resolution will be even more incomplete for them than it is for the semantics based on $comp(P)$ and, as noted above there is, even for the class of definite programs, demonstrably no way of extending SLDNF-resolution to give a computable proof procedure which is both sound and complete for them.

2.9 Constructive negation; an extension of negation as failure

Chan [1988] gives a procedure, *constructive negation*, which extends negation as failure to deal with non-ground negative literals. This is done by returning the negation of answers to query Q as answers to $\neg Q$. If Q has variables $x_1, \ldots, x_n$ and succeeds with idempotent answer substitution θ for the program P we can write the answer in equational form as

$$Q \leftarrow \exists (x_1 = x_1\theta \wedge \ldots \wedge x_n = x_n\theta),$$

where $\exists$ quantifies the variables on the right hand side other than $x_1, \ldots, x_n$.

If there are a finite number of answers to the query Q then

$$Q \leftrightarrow A_1 \vee \ldots \vee A_k$$

is a consequence of $comp(P)$, so if $comp(P)$ is the intended semantics it is legitimate to return

$$\neg(A_1 \vee \ldots \vee A_k)$$

as the answer to $\neg Q$. For example if P is

$$\begin{aligned} p &\leftarrow \neg q(x) \\ q(a) &\leftarrow \end{aligned}$$

then $?q(x)$ has the answer $x = a$, so $?q(x)$ is given the answer $x \neq a$ and $?p$ the answer $\exists x (x \neq a)$.

If there are infinitely many answers to Q this procedure is not applicable, for example if P is

$$
\begin{aligned}
p(0) &\leftarrow \\
p(s(x)) &\leftarrow p(x)
\end{aligned}
$$

then $?p(x)$ has answers $x = 0, x = s(0), x = s^2(0), \ldots$ and there is no way of describing all these by a first order formula. And it will not work when there is an infinite branch in the derivation tree e.g. if P is

$$
\begin{aligned}
p(a) &\leftarrow \\
p(b) &\leftarrow p(b)
\end{aligned}
$$

then the only computed answer to $?p(x)$ is $x = a$, but the truth of $p(b)$ is not determined by $comp(P)$, so $p(x) \leftrightarrow x = a$ is not a consequence of $comp(P)$.

When the procedure does work it returns as answer to a query Q an equality formula E (i.e. a formula with $=$ as the only predicate symbol) such that

$$
Q \leftrightarrow E
$$

is a consequence of $comp(P)$. However if the formula E is built up in the way described above, then the alternations of existential quantification, disjunction and negation have the effect that E can be an arbitrarily complex first order equality formula. In order to make the answer E more intelligible Chan gives an algorithm for reducing the answer E at each stage to a fairly simple normal form N_E to which, assuming CET (Clark's equational theory, defined in Section 2.4 above), it is equivalent, i.e. such that

$$
CET \vdash \forall (E \leftrightarrow N_E).
$$

To allow this normal form N_E to be taken as simple as possible he assumes (as Kunen does in his 3-valued treatment given in Section 2.6 above) that the underlying language of constant and function symbols used is infinite. This language affects CET and since $comp(P)$ includes CET it affects $comp(P)$. Let us indicate this dependence on the language L by writing CET_L, $comp_L(P)$. In the first example above, if L is infinite (or indeed, if it contains any function symbol or any constant other than a) then the answer $\exists x (x \neq a)$ can be replaced by **true** because CET_L and hence $comp_L(P)$ imply the existence of an $x \neq a$ since CET_L implies that the different ground terms are unequal. This is the result given in this case by Chan's algorithm, which is incorporated into an extension of SLDNF-resolution called SLD-CNF resolution. If on the other hand, a is the only constant or function symbol in L then the answer $\exists x(x \neq a)$ cannot be simplified, because in some models of $comp_L(P)$ there will be elements other than a whereas in others there will not. Note the assumption that L is infinite excludes the usual Herbrand models based on the language defined by the program. In this example $\exists x(x \neq a)$ which has been replaced by **true** assuming L to be infinite is **false** in the usual Herbrand model whose domain is $\{a\}$. Chan's normal form for the equality formulae returned as answers is quite simple; you only need to add some universally quantified inequations to the equations $x_1 = x_1\theta \wedge \ldots \wedge x_n = x_n\theta$ which represent the familiar substitution type of answer. In fact further restrictions can be made; these are clearly stated in Przymusinski [1989a, theorem 8.1]. Assuming L is infinite, there is an algorithm for reducing any equality formula E to a *strictly normal equality formula* N_E such that

$$CET_L \vdash \forall(E \leftrightarrow N_E).$$

A *strictly normal equality formula* is a disjunction of *strictly simple equality formulae* each of which has the form

$$\exists y_1, \ldots, y_s(x_1 = t_1 \wedge \ldots \wedge x_m = t_m \wedge \forall(x_1' \neq s_1) \wedge \ldots \wedge \forall(x_m' \neq s_m))$$

where each t_i, s_i is either a non-variable term or one of the free variables of this formula distinct from x_i, x_i' respectively, where the $\forall$ in $\forall(x_i' \neq s_i)$ universally quantifies some (perhaps none) of the variables in s_i, where the $y_1, \ldots, y_s$ are distinct from $x_1, \ldots, x_m, x_1', \ldots, x_m'$, and each y_i occurs in at least one of the terms $t_1, \ldots, t_m$. Chan does not describe his normal form explicitly but from his examples and his reduction algorithm it would appear that he achieves the further restriction corresponding to the use of idempotent mgu, that the occurrence of x_i on the left hand side of $x_i = t_i$ is the only occurrence of x_i in the formula. But in order to achieve this he has to admit quantified inequations of the form $\forall(y_j \neq r_j)$ as well. For example, the formula

$$\exists y_1, y_2(x_1 = f(y_1, y_2) \wedge \forall z(x_1 \neq f(x_2, z)))$$

is in Przymusinski's normal form. The corresponding Chan normal form is

$$\exists y_1 y_2(x_1 = f(y_1, y_1) \wedge y_1 \neq x_2).$$

The reason why the assumption that L is infinite simplifies the normal forms for equality formulas is that CET_L is then a complete theory. Normal forms for the case of finite L have been given in Shepherdson [1988a]. The only difference is that closed formulae of the form $G_L^k, \neg G_L^k$ as defined in Section 2.6 may occur in the normal form. The formula G_L^k expresses the fact that there at least k distinct elements which are not values of a function in L. So if one is working with models for which the number of such elements is known, these can be replaced by **true** or **false** and the same normal forms as above are achievable, although the reduction algorithm will be more complicated than those of Chan and Przymusinski. One special case of interest is where one only wishes to consider models satisfying the domain closure axiom, DCA, of Section 2.6, which includes all the usual Herbrand models. Then all G_L^k would be replaced by **false**. Other normal forms for equality formulae have been given by Malcev [1971] and Maher [1988]. The normal forms of Chan and Przymusinski are probably the most intelligible and easily obtainable ones, but Maher's is also fairly simple—just a boolean combination of *basic formulae*. These are of the form

$$\exists y_1, \ldots, y_s (x_1 = t_1 \wedge \ldots \wedge x_m = t_m)$$

where $y_1, \ldots, y_s, x_1, \ldots, x_s$ are distinct variables and $x_1, \ldots, x_m$ do not occur in $t_1, \ldots, t_m$; so they are the answer formulae corresponding to the usual answer substitutions given by SLD- or SLDNF-resolution using idempotent mgu.

Chan's constructive negation is a procedure to translate a given query Q into an equality formula E which is equivalent to it with respect to the semantics $comp(P)$ i.e. such that

$$comp(P) \vdash \forall(Q \leftrightarrow E).$$

As we have seen above it does not always succeed. Clearly it can only succeed when Q is equality definable with respect to $comp(P)$ i.e. when there is such an equivalent equality formula. Let us say P is equality definable with respect to $comp(P)$ when all first order formulae Q are equality definable with respect to $comp(P)$. Przymusinski [1989a] considers equality definability with respect to different semantics. Since all perfect models of P are models of $comp(P)$, and all models of $comp(P)$ are models of P it is clear that:

> *If Q is equality definable with respect to P then it is equality definable with respect to $comp(P)$; if it is equality definable with respect to $comp(P)$ then it is equality definable with respect to the perfect model semantics.*

He shows that a program P is equality definable with respect to the perfect model semantics if it has no function symbols or more generally if it has the bounded term property defined by Van Gelder [Van Gelder, 1989]. The analogous result is not true for the semantics based on P or on $comp(P)$. Indeed Shepherdson [1988a] showed that P is equality definable with respect to $comp(P)$ iff there is a 2-level hierarchic program which is equivalent to P in the sense that its completion is a conservative extension of $comp(P)$. Przymusinski showed how to extend his SLS-resolution for stratified programs (cf. Section 2.8) to an 'SLSC-resolution' by augmenting it with constructive negation. With respect to the perfect model semantics the resulting procedure is always sound, and it is complete for equality definable programs, i.e. it is complete for all programs for which any procedure could be complete. However, like SLS-resolution, it is not a computable procedure.

Constructive negation is a significant attempt to deal with the problem of floundering and to produce answers when SLDNF-resolution flounders. Its limitations are that it can still only deal with a negative query $\neg A$ when the query A has a finite derivation tree. As noted above this is a fairly severe limitation.

2.10   Modal and autoepistemic logic

Gabbay [1989] presents a view of negation as failure as a modal provability notion.

> '... we use a variation of the modal logic of Solovay, originally introduced to study the properties of the Gödel provability predicate of Peano arithmetic, and show that $\neg A$ can be read essentially as 'A is not provable from the program'. To be more precise, $\neg A$ is understood as saying 'Either the program is inconsistent, or the program is consistent, in which case $\neg A$ means A is not provable from the program'.

In symbols
$$\neg A = \Box \, (\textbf{Program} \to \textbf{f}) \vee \sim \Box \, (\textbf{Program} \to A),$$
where $\neg$ is negation by failure, $\sim$ is classical negation, $\textbf{f}$ is falsity, and $\Box$ is the modality of Solovay. We provide a modal provability completion for a Prolog program with negation by failure and show that our new completion has none of the difficulties which plague the usual Clark completion.

We begin with an example. Consider the Prolog program $\neg A \to A$, where $\neg$ is negation by failure. This program loops. Its Clark completion is $\neg A \leftrightarrow A$, which is a contradiction, and does not satisfactorily give a logical content to the program.

We regard this program as saying:
$$(\underline{\text{Provable}} \; (\textbf{f}) \vee \sim \underline{\text{Provable}} \; (A) \,) \leftrightarrow A$$

In symbols, if x is the program and $\Box$ is the modality of provability, the program x says $(\Box(x \to \textbf{f}) \vee \sim \Box(x \to A)) \leftrightarrow A$ where $\sim$ is classical negation. In other words, the logical content of the program x is the fixed point solution (which can be proved to always exist) of the equation

$$x = [(\Box(x \to \textbf{f}) \vee \sim \Box(x \to A) \leftrightarrow A]$$

This solution turns out to be a consistent sentence of the modal logic of provability to be described later.

We now describe how to get the completion in the general case.

Let P be a Prolog program. Let $P1$ be its Clark completion. Let x be a new variable. Replace each $\neg A$ in the Clark completion $P1$ essentially by $(\Box(x \to f) \lor \sim \Box(x \to A))$. Thus $P1$ becomes $P2(x)$ containing $\Box, x$ and classical negation $\sim$. We claim that in the modal logic of provability, the modal completion of the program P is the X such that in the modal logic $\vdash X \leftrightarrow P2(x)$ holds. We have that a goal A succeeds from P iff (more or less) the modal completion of $P \vdash \Box A$. A more precise formulation will be given later. We denote the modal completion of P by $m(P)$.'

The modal completion is shown to exist and to be unique up to $\vdash$ equivalence. Defining $GA = A \land \Box A$, 'A is true and provable' (in a general provability logic A may be provable but not true), soundness and completeness results are proved:

> *for each atomic goal Q and substitution θ, $Q\theta$ succeeds under SLDNF-resolution iff $m(P) \vdash GQ\theta$ and $Q\theta$ fails from P iff $m(P) \vdash G\neg Q\theta$.*

The completeness result is based on a proof for the propositional case given by Terracini [1988a].

It should be noted that in this result 'succeeds' and 'finite' do not refer to SLDNF-resolution but to another version of negation as failure. This coincides with SLDNF-resolution when P is a propositional program, but when P contains individual variables '$Q\theta$ succeeds from P' means 'there exists η such that $Q\theta\eta$ is ground and succeeds from P^g under SLDNF-resolution'; similarly '$Q\theta$ fails from P' means 'η fails from P^g under SLDNF-resolution for all η for which $Q\theta\eta$ is ground'. Here P^g denotes the (possibly infinite) propositional program obtained by taking all ground instances of clauses of P. For example if P is $p \leftarrow \neg q(x)$ then P^g is $p \leftarrow \neg q(a)$ and the goal p is said to succeed, although in SLDNF-resolution from P it would flounder. This device enables the floundering problem to be dealt with and the predicate case reduced to the propositional case.

The modal logic of provability used is defined both semantically, in terms of Kripke type models consisting of finite trees, and also syntactically. Both of these definitions are rather complicated for predicate logic but the propositional form of the syntactic definition consists of the following schemas and rules:

1. $\vdash A$, if A is a substitution instance of a classical truth functional tautology.

2. The schemas:
   (a) $\vdash \Box(A \to B) \to (\Box A \to \Box B)$
   (b) $\vdash \Box(\Box(A \to B) \to (\Box A \to \Box B))$

3. The schemas
   (a) $\vdash \Box A \to \Box\Box A$
   (b) $\vdash \Box(\Box A \to \Box\Box A)$
4. The schemas
   (a) $\vdash \Box(\Box A \to A) \to \Box A$
   (b) $\vdash \Box[\Box(\Box A \to A) \to \Box A]$
5. For every atom q
   (a) $\vdash \Box(q \vee \Box f) \to \Box q$
   (b) $\vdash \Box(\sim q \vee \Box f) \to \Box \sim q$
   (c) $\vdash \Diamond\Diamond t$
6. $\dfrac{\vdash A, \vdash A \to B}{\vdash B}$

Here $\Diamond$ stands for $\neg\Box\neg A$. This is an extension of Solovay's modal logic of provability, which is itself obtained by extending the modal logic K_4 by Löb's axiom schemas 4(a). It is also described in [Terracini, 1988b]. The soundness and completeness results show that this is a very satisfactory semantics for negation as failure. Its main disadvantage is that the modal logic used is apparently rather complicated and, at present, not widely known. So it is doubtful whether this semantics would help writers of programs to understand their meaning and check their correctness. However, Gabbay argues convincingly that many of the day to day operations of logic programming have a modal meaning and that logic programmers should become more familiar with modal logic.

Gelfond [1987] and Przymusinska [1987] discussed negation as failure in terms of the *autoepistemic logic* of Moore [1985]. This is a propositional calculus augmented by a belief operator L where Lp is to be interpreted as 'p is believed'. Gelfond considers $\neg p$ in a logic program as intended to mean 'p is not believed'.

He defines the autoepistemic translation $I(F)$ of an *objective formula* F (i.e. a propositional formula not containing the belief operator L) to be the result of replacing each negative literal $\neg p$ in F by $\neg Lp$. The autoepistemic translation $I(P)$ of a logic program consists of the set of translations of all ground instances of clauses of P, i.e. the set of all clauses of the form

$$A \leftarrow B_1, \ldots, B_m, \neg LC_1, \ldots, \neg LC_n,$$

for all ground instances

$$A \leftarrow B_1, \ldots, B_m, \neg C_1, \ldots, \neg C_n \text{ of clauses from } P.$$

Let T be a set of autoepistemic formulae. Moore defined a *stable autoepistemic expansion* of T to be a set $E(T)$ of autoepistemic formulae which satisfies the fixed point condition

$$E(T) = C_n(T \cup \{Lf : f \text{ is in } E(T)\} \cup \{\neg Lf : f \text{ is not in } E(T)\})$$

where $C_n(S)$ denotes the set of autoepistemic logical consequences of S (formulae of the form Lg being treated as atoms). This intuitively represents a set of possible beliefs of an ideally rational agent who believes in all and only those facts which he can conclude from T and from his other beliefs. If this expansion is unique it can be viewed as the set of theorems which follow from T in the autoepistemic logic. The autoepistemic translation $I(P)$ of a logic program P does not always have such a unique expansion. The program $p \leftarrow \neg p$ has no consistent stable autoepistemic expansion because its translation is $p \leftarrow \neg p$ and it is easy to verify that both Lp and $\neg Lp$ must belong to such an expansion. On the other hand the program $p \leftarrow \neg q$, $q \leftarrow \neg p$ has two such expansions, one with $Cn(p)$ as its objective part, the other with $Cn(q)$ as its objective part. Gelfond and Przymusinska showed that for stratified propositional programs the autoepistemic and perfect model semantics coincide:

> *If P is a stratified propositional logic program then $I(P)$ has a unique stable autoepistemic expansion $E(I(P))$ and for every query Q, $PERF(P) \vDash Q$ iff $E(I(Q)) \vDash I(Q)$.*

Here $PERF(P)$ denotes the perfect model of P which, as noted in Section 2.8, coincides with the minimal supported model of Apt, Blair and Walker, with the well-founded total model and with the unique stable model.

Przymusinski [1989b; 1991] obtains results applicable to all logic programs by using a 3-valued autoepistemic logic. Let $M_{wp}(P)$ denote the 3-valued well-founded model defined in Section 2.8. He shows that if P is a logic program then $I(P)$ always has at least one stable autoepistemic expansion, and that the autoepistemic semantics coincides with the well-founded semantics:

> *For every ground atom A,*
> *A is true in $M_{wp}(P)$ iff A is believed in $I(P)$*
> *A is false in $M_{wp}(P)$ iff A is disbelieved in $I(P)$*
> *A is undefined in $M_{wp}(P)$ iff A is undefined in $I(P)$.*

Here A is believed (resp. disbelieved) in $I(P)$ if A is believed (resp. disbelieved) in all stable autoepistemic expansions of $I(P)$, otherwise we say A is undefined in $I(P)$.

For further details of autoepistemic logic see Konolige's chapter in Volume 3 of this Handbook.

2.11 Deductive calculi for negation as failure

The standard procedural descriptions of logic programming systems such as Prolog, SLD- and SLDNF-resolution are in terms of trees. This makes proving theorems about them rather awkward because the proofs somehow have to involve the tree structure. So it might be useful to have descriptions in the form of a deductive calculus of the familiar kind, based on axioms and rules of inference, so that proofs can be simply by induction on the length of the derivation. Mints [1986] gave such a calculus for pure Prolog, and Gabbay and Sergot [1986] implicitly suggested a similar calculus for negation as failure.

The definition of SLDNF-resolution given by Kunen [1989] which we reproduced in Section 1.3 can easily be put in the form of a Mints type calculus.

The meaning of the notation is as follows:

Y — A query, i.e. a sequence $L_1, \ldots, L_n, n \geq 0$ of literals.

$Y\theta$ — The result of applying the substitution θ to the goal Y.

$(Y; \theta)$ — The query Y succeeds with answer substitution θ.

(Y) — The query Y succeeds.

$\sim (Y)$ — The query Y fails finitely.

$\sim j(Y)$ — The goal $Y = A, X$ (where A is an atom) fails finitely if you consider only the branch starting with the attempt to unify A with the jth suitable program clause (i.e. whose head contains the same predicate as A does).

$i : A \leftarrow Z$ — The clause $A \leftarrow Z$ is (a variant of) the ith clause of the given program P which is suitable for (i.e. whose head contains the same predicate as) A.

The calculus operates on formulae of the forms

$$(Y; \theta), \ (Y), \ \sim j(Y), \ \sim (Y), \ i : A \leftarrow Z.$$

The axioms will be those formulae

$$i : A \leftarrow Z$$

such that $A \leftarrow Z$ is indeed the ith clause of P which is suitable for A, together with

$$(\textbf{true}; 1) \qquad\qquad (\text{START})$$

where 1 denotes the identity substitution. The rules of inference are:

Two rules allowing permutation of literals in a goal

$$\frac{(Q; \theta)}{(Q^\pi, \theta)} \qquad\qquad (\text{PERM})$$

$$\frac{\sim (Q)}{\sim (Q^\pi)} \qquad\qquad (\sim \text{PERM})$$

where Q^π denotes any permutation of the atoms of Q.

A rule corresponding to resolution

$$\frac{i : A' \leftarrow Z; (X\sigma, X\sigma; \pi)}{(A, X; (\sigma\pi) \mid (A, X))} \tag{RES}$$

where A is an atom and $\sigma = \text{mgu}\,(A, A')$. In all these rules $A' \leftarrow Z$ is as usual supposed to be a variant of the program clause which is standardised apart so as to have no variables in common with A, X.

A rule allowing you to pass from 'succeeds with answer θ' to 'succeeds',

$$\frac{(Q, \theta)}{(Q)} \tag{FIN}$$

Finally five rules for negation as failure,

$$\frac{\sim 1(Y); \sim 2(Y); \ldots; \sim k(Y)}{\sim (Y)} \tag{$\sim_1$}$$

where k is the number of suitable clauses for A, the first sub-goal of Y,

$$\frac{i : A' \leftarrow Z}{\sim i(A, Z)} \tag{$\sim_2$}$$

provided that A, A' are not unifiable,

$$\frac{i : A' \leftarrow Z; \sim (Z\sigma, X\sigma)}{\sim i(A, X)} \tag{$\sim_3$}$$

where $\sigma = \text{mgu}\,(A, A')$,

$$\frac{\sim (A); (Y; \theta)}{(\neg A, Y; \theta)} \tag{$\neg_1$}$$

if A is ground

$$\frac{(A)}{\sim (\neg A, X)}, \tag{$\neg_2$}$$

if A is ground.

If we take SLDNF-resolution to be defined in the familiar way in terms of trees, as in Lloyd [1987] then the statement that Kunen's definition given in Section 1.3 above is equivalent to it amounts to the statement:

A goal X succeeds under SLDNF-resolution from P iff (X) is derivable in this calculus; it succeeds with answer substitution θ iff $(X; \theta)$ is derivable in the calculus; it fails iff $\sim (X)$ is derivable in the calculus.

The proof is routine, by induction on the length of the derivation for the 'if' halves, and by induction on the number of nodes in the success

or failure tree for the 'only if' halves. For a survey of these calculi see
Shepherdson [1992a] which also gives the obvious extension of this calculus
to deal with the extended negation as failure rules described in Section 1.6
above:

> *if A fails then ¬A succeeds with answer θ*
> *if A succeeds with answer 1 then ¬A fails.*

References

[Andreka and Nemeti, 1978] H. Andreka and I. Nemeti. The generalised
completeness of Horn predicate logic as a programming langauge. *Acta
Cybernet*, 4:3–10, 1978.

[Apt, 1990] K. R. Apt. Introduction to logic programming. In J. van
Leeuwen, editor, *Handbook of Theoretical Computer Science*, Vol B,
Chapter 10. Elsevier Science, North Holland, Amsterdam, 1990.

[Apt and Bezem, 1991] K. R. Apt and M. Bezem. Acyclic programs. *New
Generation Computing*, 9:335–363, 1991.

[Apt and Blair, 1988] K. R. Apt and H. A. Blair. Arithmetic classification
of perfect models of stratified programs. Technical Report TR-88-09,
University of Texas at Austin, 1988.

[Apt, 1994] K. R. Apt and R. Bol. Logic programming and negation. *Journal of Logic Programming*, 1994.

[Apt and Pugin, 1987] K. R. Apt and J-M. Pugin. Management of stratified databases. Technical Report TR-87-41, University of Texas at
Austin, 1987.

[Apt and van Emden, 1982] K. R. Apt and M. H. van Emden. Contributions to the theory of logic programming. *Journal of the ACM*, 29:841–
863, 1982.

[Apt *et al.*, 1988] K. R. Apt, H. A. Blair, and A. Walker. Towards a theory
of declarative knowledge. In J. Minker, editor, *Foundations of Deductive
Databases and Logic Programming*, pp. 89–148. Morgan Kaufmann, Los
Altos, CA, 1988.

[Barbuti and Martelli, 1986] R. Barbuti and M. Martelli. Completeness of
SLDNF-resolution for structured programs. Preprint, 1986.

[Blair, 1982] H. A. Blair. The recursion theoretic complexity of the semantics of predicate logic as a programming language. *Information and
Control*, **54**, 24–47, 1982.

[Börger, 1987] E. Börger. Unsolvable decision problems for prolog programs. In E. Börger, editor, *Computer Theory and Logic*. Lecture Notes
in Computer Science, Springer-Verlag, 1987.

[Brass and Lipeck, 1989] S. Brass and U. W. Lipeck. Specifying closed
world assumptions for logic databases. In *Proc. Second Symposium on
Mathematical Fundamentals of Database Systems (MFDBS89)*, 1989.

[Cavedon, 1988] L. Cavedon. *On the Completeness of SLDNF-Resolution.* PhD thesis, Melbourne University, 1988.

[Cavedon, 1989] L. Cavedon. Continuity, consistency and completeness properties for logic programs (extended abstract). In *Proceedings of the Sixth International Conference on Logic Programming*, Lisbon, pp. 571–589, 1989.

[Cavedon and Lloyd, 1989] L. Cavedon and J. W. Lloyd. A completeness theorem for SLDNF-resolution. *Journal of Logic Programming*, 1989.

[Cerrito, 1992] S. Cerrito. A linear axiomatization of negation as failure. *Journal of Logic Programming*, **12**, 1–24, 1992.

[Cerrito, 1993] S. Cerrito. Negation and linear completion. In L. Farinas del Cerro and M. Pentonnen, editors, *Intensional Logic for Programming.* Oxford University Press, 1993.

[Chan, 1988] D. Chan. Constructive negation based on the completed database. Technical report, European Computer-Industry Research Centre, Munich, 1988.

[Clark, 1978] K. L Clark. Negation as failure. In H. Gallaire and J. Minker, editors, *Logic and Data Base*, pp. 293–322. Plenum, New York, 1978.

[Davis, 1983] M. Davis. The prehistory and early history of automated deduction. In J. Siekmann and G. Wrightson, editors, *Automation of Reasoning*, pp. 1–28. Springer, Berlin, 1983.

[Ebbinghaus, 1969] H. D. Ebbinghaus. Über eine prädikaten logik mit partiell definierten prädikaten and funktionen. *Arch. math. Logik*, **12**, 39–53, 1969.

[Fine, 1989] K. Fine. The justification of negation as failure. In J. E. Fenstad et al., editor, *Logic, Methodology and Philosophy of Science VIII.* Elsevier Science, Amsterdam, 1989.

[Fitting, 1985] M. Fitting. A Kripke-Kleene semantics for general logic programs. *Journal of Logic Programming*, *2*, 295–312, 1985.

[Fitting, 1986] M. Fitting. Partial models and logic programming. *Computer Science*, **48**, 229–255, 1986.

[Fitting, 1987a] M. Fitting. Logic programming on a topological bilattice. Technical report, H. Lehman College, (CUNY), Bronx, NY, 1987.

[Fitting, 1987b] M. Fitting. Pseudo-boolean valued prolog. Technical report, Research Report, H. Lehman College, (CUNY), Bronx, NY, 1987.

[Fitting, 1991] M. Fitting. Bilattices and the semantics of logic programming. *Journal of Logic Programming*, *11*, 91–116, 1991.

[Fitting and Ben-Jacob, 1988] M. Fitting and M. Ben-Jacob. Stratified and three-valued logic programming semantics. Technical report, Dept. of Computer Science, CUNY, 1988.

[Gabbay, 1986] D. M. Gabbay. Modal provability foundations for negation by failure, 1986. Preprint.

[Gabbay, 1989] D. M. Gabbay. Modal provability interpretation for negation by failure. In P. Schroeder-Heister, editor, *Extensions of Logic Programming*, pp. 179–222. LNCS 475, Springer-Verlag, Berlin, 1989.

[Gabbay and Sergot, 1986] D. M. Gabbay and M. J. Sergot. Negation as inconsistency. *Journal of Logic Programming*, **1**, 1–36, 1986.

[Gallier and Raatz, 1987] J. H. Gallier and S. Raatz. HORNLOG: A graph based interpreter for general Horn clauses. *Journal of Logic Programming*, **4**, 119–155, 1987.

[Gallier and Raatz, 1989] J. H. Gallier and S. Raatz. Extending SLD resolution methods to equational Horn clauses using E-unification. *Journal of Logic Programming*, **6**, 3–43, 1989.

[Gelfond, 1987] M. Gelfond. On stratified autoepistemic theories. In *Proceedings AAAI-87*, pp. 207–211. American Association for Artificial Intelligence, Morgan Kaufmann, Los Altos, CA, 1987.

[Gelfond and Lifschitz, 1988] M. Gelfond and V. Lifschitz. The stable model semantics for logic programming. In *5th International Conference on Logic Programming*, Seattle, 1988.

[Gelfond et al., 1986] M. Gelfond, H. Przymusinski, and T. Przymusinski. The extended closed world assumption and its relationship to parallel circumscription. In *Proceedings ACM SIGACT-SIGMOD Symposium on Principles of Database Systems*, Cambridge, MA, pp. 133–139, 1986.

[Gelfond et al., 1989] M. Gelfond, H. Przymusinski, and T. Przymusinski. On the relationship between circumscription and negation as failure. *Artificial Intelligence*, **39**, 265–316, 1989.

[Girard, 1987] J. Y. Girard. Linear logic. *Theoretical Computer Science*, **50**, 1987.

[Goguen and Burstall, 1984] J. A. Goguen and R. M. Burstall. Institutions: Abstract model theory for computer science. In E. Clark and D. Kozen, editors, *Proc. of Logic Programming Workshop*, pp. 221–256. Lecture Notes in Computer Science 164, Springer-Verlag, 1984.

[Haken, 1985] A. Haken. The intractability of resolution. *Theoretical Computer Science*, **39**, 297–308, 1985.

[Henschen and Park, 1988] L. J. Henschen and H-S. Park. Compiling the GCWA in indefinite databases. In J. Minker, editor, *Foundations of Deductive Databases and Logic Programming*, pp. 395–438. Morgan Kaufmann Publishers, Los Altos, CA, 1988.

[Hodges, 1985] W. Hodges. The logical basis of PROLOG, 1985. unpublished text of lecture, 10pp.

[Jaffar and Stuckey, 1986] J. Jaffar and P. J. Stuckey. Canonical logic programs. *Journal of Logic Programming*, **3**, 143–155, 1986.

[Jaffar et al., 1983] J. Jaffar, J. L. Lassez, and J. W. Lloyd. Completeness of the negation as failure rule. In *IJCAI-83, Karlsruhe*, pp. 500–506,

1983.

[Jaffar et al., 1984] J. Jaffar, J. L. Lassez, and M. J. Maher. A theory of complete logic programs with equality. *Journal of Logic Programming*, 1, 211–223, 1984.

[Jaffar et al., 1986a] J. Jaffar, J. L. Lassez, and M. J. Maher. Comments on general failure of logic programs. *Journal of Logic Programming*, **3**, 115–118, 1986.

[Jaffar et al., 1986b] J. Jaffar, J. L. Lassez, and M. J. Maher. Some issues and trends in the semantics of logic programs. In *Proceedings Third International Conference on Logic Programming*, pp. 223–241. Springer, 1986.

[Jäger, 1988] G. Jäger. Annotations on the consistency of the closed world assumption. Technical report, Computer Science Dept., Technische Hochschule, Zerich, 1988.

[Jäger, 1993] G. Jäger. Some proof-theoretic aspects of logic programming. In F. L. Bauer, W. Brauer, and H. Schwichtenberg, editors, *Logic and Algebra of Specification*, pp. 113–142. Springer-Verlag, 1993. Proceedings of the NATO Advanced Studies Institute on Logic and Algebra of Specification, Marktoherdorf, Germany, 1991.

[Kleene, 1952] S. C. Kleene. *Introduction to Metamathematics.* van Nostrand, New York, 1952.

[Kowalski, 1979] R. A. Kowalski. *Logic for Problem Solving.* North Holland, New York, 1979.

[Kunen, 1987] K. Kunen. Negation in logic programming. *Journal of Logic Programming*, **4**, 289–308, 1987.

[Kunen, 1989] K. Kunen. Signed data dependencies in logic programs. *Journal of Logic Programming*, **7**, 231–245, 1989.

[Lassez and Maher, 1985] J. L. Lassez and M. J. Maher. Optimal fixedpoints of logic programs. *Theoretical Computer Science*, 15–25, 1985.

[Lewis, 1978] H. Lewis. Renaming a set of clauses as a horn set. *Journal of the ACM*, **25**, 134–135, 1978.

[Lifschitz, 1985] V. Lifschitz. Computing circumscription. In *Proceedings IJCAI-85*, pp. 121–127, 1985.

[Lifschitz, 1988] V. Lifschitz. On the declarative semantics of logic programs with negation. In J. Minker, editor, *Foundations of Deductive Databases and Logic Programming*, pp. 177–192. Morgan Kaufmann, Los Altos, CA, 1988.

[Lloyd, 1987] J. W. Lloyd. *Foundations of Logic Programming.* Springer, Berlin., second edition, 1987.

[Lloyd and Topor, 1984] J. W. Lloyd and R. W. Topor. Making Prolog more expressive. *Journal of Logic Programming*, **1**, 225–240, 1984.

[Lloyd and Topor, 1985] J. W. Lloyd and R. W. Topor. A basis for deductive data base systems, II. *Journal of Logic Programming*, **3**, 55–68, 1985.

[Loveland, 1988] D. W. Loveland. Near-horn prolog. In J.-L. Lassez, editor, *Proc. ICLP'87*. MIT Press, Cambridge, MA, 1988.

[McCarthy, 1984] J. McCarthy. Applications of circumscription to formalizing common sense knowledge. In *AAAI Workshop on Non-Monotonic Reasoning*, pp. 295–323, 1984.

[Maher, 1988] M. J. Maher. Complete axiomatization of the algebras of finite, infinite and rational trees. In *Proc. of the Third Annual Symposium on Logic in Computer Science*, Edinburgh, pp. 345–357, 1988.

[Mahr and Makowsky, 1983] B. Mahr and J. A. Makowsky. Characterizing specification languages which admit initial semantics. In *Proc. 8th CAAP*, pp. 300–316. Lecture Notes in Computer Science 159, Springer-Verlag, 1983.

[Makowsky, 1986] J. A. Makowsky. Why Horn formulas matter in computer science: Initial structures and generic examples (extended abstract). Technical Report 329, Technion Haifa, 1986. Also in *Mathematical Foundations of Software Development, Proceedings of the International Joint Conference on Theory and Practice of Software Development* (TAPSOFT) (H. Ehrig *et al.*, Eds.), Lecture Notes in Computer Science 185, pp. 374–387, Springer, 1985. (Revised version May 15, 1986, 1-28, preprint.) The references in the text are to this most recent version.

[Malcev, 1971] A. Malcev. Axiomatizable classes of locally free algebras of various types. In *The Metamathematics of Algebraic Systems: Collected Papers*, chapter 23, pp. 262–281. North-Holland, Amsterdam, 1971.

[Mancarella *et al.*, 1988] P. Mancarella, S. Martini, and D. Pedreschi. Complete logic programs with domain closure axiom. *Journal of Logic Programming*, **5**, 263–276, 1988.

[Meltzer, 1983] B. Meltzer. Theorem-proving for computers: Some results on resolution and renaming. In J. Siekmann and G. Wrightson, editors, *Automation of Reasoning*, pp. 493–495. Springer, Berlin, 1983.

[Minker, 1982] J. Minker. On indefinite data bases and the closed world assumption. In *Proc. 6th Conference on Automated Deduction*, pp. 292–308. Lecture Notes in Computer Science 138, Springer-Verlag, 1982.

[Minker and Perlis, 1985] J. Minker and D. Perlis. Computing protected circumscription. *Journal of Logic Programming*, **2**, 1–24, 1985.

[Mints, 1986] G. Mints. Complete calculus for pure Prolog (Russian). *Proc. Acad. Sci. Estonian SSR*, *35*, 367–380, 1986.

[Moore, 1985] R. C. Moore. Semantic considerations on non-monotonic logic. *Artificial Intelligence*, **25**, 75–94, 1985.

[Mycroft, 1983] A. Mycroft. Logic programs and many-valued logic. In *Proc. 1st STACS Conf*, 1983.

[Naish, 1986] L. Naish. Negation and quantifiers in NU-Prolog. In *Proceedings Third International Conference on Logic Programming*, pp. 624–634. Springer, 1986.

[Naqvi, 1986] S. A. Naqvi. A logic for negation in database systems. In J. Minker, editor, *Proceedings of Workshop on Foundations of Deductive Databases and Logic Programming, Washington, DC*, 1986.

[Plaisted, 1984] D. A. Plaisted. Complete problems in the first-order predicate calculus. *Journal of Computer System Sciences*, **29**, 8–35, 1984.

[Poole and Goebel, 1986] D. L. Poole and R. Goebel. Gracefully adding negation and disjunction to Prolog. In *Proceedings Third International Conference on Logic Programming*, pp. 635–641. Springer, 1986.

[Przymusinska, 1987] H. Przymusinska. On the relationship between autoepistemic logic and circumscription for stratified deductive databases. In *Proceedings of the ACM SIGART International Symposium on Methodologies for Intelligent Systems*, Knoxville, TN, 1987.

[Przymusinska and Przymusinski, 1988] H. Przymusinska and T. Przymusinski. Weakly perfect model semantics for logic programs. In R. Kowalski and K. Bowen, editors, *Proceedings of the Fifth Logic Programming Symposium, Association for Logic Programming*, pp. 1106–1122. MIT Press, Cambridge, Mass, 1988.

[Przymusinski, 1988a] T. C. Przymusinski. On the declarative and procedural semantics of logic programs. *Journal of Automated Reasoning*, **4**, 1988. (Extended abstract appeared in: Przymusinski, T.C. [1988] Perfect model semantics. In R. Kowalski and K. Bowen, editors, *Proceedings of the Fifth Logic Programming Symposium*, pp. 1081–1096, Association for Logic Programming, MIT Press, Cambridge, MA.

[Przymusinski, 1988b] T. C. Przymusinski. On the semantics of stratified deductive databases. In J. Minker, editor, *Foundations of Deductive Database and Logic Programming*, pp. 193–216. Morgan Kaufmann, Los Altos, CA, 1988.

[Przymusinski, 1989a] T. C. Przymusinski. On constructive negation in logic pogramming. In *Proceedings of the North American Logic Programming Conference*, Cleveland, Ohio. MIT Press, Cambridge, MA, 1989. Addendum.

[Przymusinski, 1989b] T. C. Przymusinski. Three-valued non-monotonic formalisms and logic programming. In *Proceedings of the First International Conference on Principles of Knowledge Representation and Reasoning (KR'89)*, Toronto, 1989.

[Przymusinski, 1991] T. C. Przymusinski. Three-valued non-monotonic formalizations and semantics of logic programming. *Artificial Intelligence*, **49**, 309–343, 1991.

418   *J. C. Shepherdson*

[Reiter, 1978] R. Reiter. On closed world data bases. In H. Gallaire and J. Minker, editors, *Logic and Data Bases*, pp. 55–76. Plenum, New York, 1978.

[Ross, 1989] K. Ross. A procedural semantics for well founded negation in logic programs. In *Proceedings of the Eighth Symposium on Principles of Database Systems*. ACM SIGACT-SIGMOD, 1989.

[Ross and Topor, 1987] K. Ross and R. W. Topor. Inferring negative information from disjunctive databases. Technical Report 87/1, University of Melbourne, 1987.

[Sakai and Miyachi, 1983] K. Sakai and T. Miyachi. Incorporating naive negation into prolog. Technical Report TR-028, ICOT, 1983.

[Sakai and Miyachi, 1986] K. Sakai and T. Miyachi. Incorporating naive negation into PROLOG. In *Proceedings of a conference*, Clayton, Victoria, Australia, 3–8 Jan 1984, Vol. 1, pp. 1–12, 1986.

[Sato, 1987] T. Sato. On the consistency of first order logic programs. Technical Report 87-12, Electrotechnical Laboratory, Ibarki, Japan, 1987.

[Schmitt, 1986] P. H. Schmitt. Computational aspects of three valued logic. In *Proc. 8th Conference on Automated Deduction*, pp. 190–19. Lecture Notes in Computer Science, 230, Springer-Verlag, 1986.

[Shepherdson, 1984] J. C. Shepherdson. Negation as failure: A comparison of Clark's completed data base and Reiter's closed world assumption. *Journal of Logic Programming*, **1**, 51–81, 1984.

[Shepherdson, 1985] J. C. Shepherdson. Negations as failure II. *Journal of Logic Programming*, **3**, 185–202, 1985.

[Shepherdson, 1988a] J. C. Shepherdson. Language and equality theory in logic programming. Technical Report PM-88-08, Mathematics Dept., Univ. Bristol, 1988.

[Shepherdson, 1988b] J. C. Shepherdson. Negation in logic programming. In J. Minker, editor, *Foundations of Deductive Databases and Logic Programming*, pp. 19–88. Morgan Kaufann, Los Altos, CA, 1988.

[Shepherdson, 1989] J. C. Shepherdson. A sound and complete semantics for a version of negation as failure. *Theoretical Computer Science*, **65**, 343–371, 1989.

[Shepherdson, 1991] J. C. Shepherdson. Unsolvable problems for SLDNF-resolution. *Journal of Logic Programming*, **10**, 19–22, 1991.

[Shepherdson, 1992a] J. C. Shepherdson. Mints type deductive calculi for logic programming. *Annals of Pure and Applied Logic*, **56**, 7–17, 1992.

[Shepherdson, 1992b] J. C. Shepherdson. SLDNF-resolution with equality. *Journal of Automated Reasoning*, **8**, 297–306, 1992.

[Stärk, 1991] R. F. Stärk. A complete axiomatization of the three-valued completion of logic programs. *Journal of Logic and Computation*, **1**, 811–834, 1991.

[Stärk, 1994] R. F. Stärk. Input/output dependencies for normal logic programs. *Journal of Logic and Computation*, 4, 249–262, 1994.

[Stärk, 1994] R. F. Stärk. From logic programs to inductive definitions. Technical report, CIS, Universitaet Munich, 1994.

[Stickel, 1986] M. E. Stickel. A PROLOG technology theorem prover: Implementation by an extended PROLOG compiler. In *Proceedings Eighth International Conference on Automated Deduction*, Springer, pp. 573–587, 1986.

[Terracini, 1988a] L. Terracini. A complete bi-modal system for a class of models. *Atti dell'Academia delle Scienze di Torino*, **122**, 116–125, 1988.

[Terracini, 1988b] L. Terracini. Modal interpretation for negation by failure. *Atti dell'Academia delle Scienze di Torino*, **122**, 81–88, 1988.

[Van Gelder, 1988] A. Van Gelder. Negation as failure using tight derivations for general logic programs. In J. Minker, editor, *Foundations of Deductive Databases and Logic Programmming*, pp. 149–176. Morgan Kaufmann Publishers, Los Altos, CA, 1988. revised version in *Journal of Logic Programming*, **6**, 109-133, 1989.

[Van Gelder, 1989] A. Van Gelder. Negation as failure using tight derivations for general logic programs. *Journal of Logic Programming*, **6**, 109–133, 1989.

[Van Gelder et al., 1988] A. Van Gelder, K. Ross, and Schlipf. Unfounded sets and well-founded semantics for general logic programs. In *Proceedings of the Symposium on Principles of Database Systems, ACM SIGACT-SIGMOD*, 1988.

[Voda, 1986] P. J. Voda. Choices in, and limitations of, logic programming. In *Proc. 3rd International Conference on Logic Programming*, pp. 615–623. Springer, 1986.

[Yahya and Henschen, 1985] A. Yahya and L. Henschen. Deduction in non-horn databases. *Journal of Automated Reasoning*, **1**, 141–160, 1985.

Meta-Programming in Logic Programming
P. M. Hill and J. Gallagher

Contents

1 Introduction

A meta-program, regardless of the nature of the programming language, is a program whose data denotes another (object) program. The importance of meta-programming can be gauged from its large number of applications. These include compilers, interpreters, program analysers, and program transformers. Furthermore, if the object program is a logic or functional program formalizing some knowledge, then the meta-program may be regarded as a meta-reasoner for reasoning about this knowledge. In this chapter, the meta-program is assumed to be a logic program. The object program does not have to be a logic program although much of the work in this chapter assumes this.

We have identified three major topics for consideration. These are the theoretical foundations of meta-programming, the suitability of the alternative meta-programming techniques for different applications, and methods for improving the efficiency of meta-programs. As with logic programs generally, meta-programs have declarative and procedural semantics. The theoretical study of meta-programming shows that both aspects of the semantics depend crucially on the manner in which object programs are represented as data in a meta-program. The second theme of the paper is the problem of designing and choosing appropriate ways of specifying important meta-programming problems, including dynamic meta-programming and problems involving self-application. The third theme concerns efficient implementation of meta-programs. Meta-programming systems require representations with facilities that minimize the overhead of interpreting the object program. In addition, efficiency can be gained by transforming the meta-program, specializing it for the particular object program it is reasoning about. This chapter, which concentrates on these aspects of meta-programming, is not intended to be a survey of the field. A more complete survey of meta-programming for logic programming can be found in [Barklund, 1995].

Many issues in meta-programming have their roots in problems in logic which have been studied for several decades. This chapter emphasizes meta-programming solutions. It is not intended to give a full treatment of the underlying logical problems, though we try to indicate some connections to wider topics in meta-logic.

The meta-programs in this chapter are logic programs based on first order logic. An alternative approach, which we do not describe here, is to extend logic programming with features based on higher-order logic. Higher-order logic programming is an ongoing subject of research and is discussed by Miller and Nadathur [1995]. The higher-order logic programming language λProlog and its derivatives have been shown to be useful for many meta-programming applications, particularly when the object program is a functional program [Miller and Nadathur, 1987], [Hannan and

Miller, 1989], [Hannan & Miller, 1992].

To avoid confusion between a programming language such as Prolog and the language of an actual program, the programming language will be referred to as a programming *system* and the word *language* will be used to refer to the set of expressions defined by a specific alphabet together with rules of construction. Note that the programming system for the object program does not necessarily have to be the same as the programming system for the meta-program although this is often the case and most theoretical work on meta-programming in logic programming makes this assumption.

1.1 Theoretical foundations

The key to the semantics of a meta-program is the way the object program expressions are represented in the meta-program. However in logic programming there is no clear distinction between the data and the program, since the data is sometimes encoded as program clauses, and the question arises as to what kind of image of the object program can be included in the meta-program. Normally, a representation is given for each symbol of the object language. This is called a *naming relation*. Then rules of construction can be used to define the representation of the constructed terms and formulas. Each expression in the language of the object program should have at least one representation as an expression in the language of the meta-program.

It is straightforward to define a naming relation for the constants, functions, propositions, predicates and connectives in a language. For example, we can syntactically represent each object symbol s by its primed form s' or even by the same token s. However, although a meta-program symbol may be syntactically similar to the object symbol it represents, it may be in a different syntactic category. Thus a predicate is often represented as a function and a proposition as a constant. A connective in the object language may be represented as a connective, predicate, or function in the meta-program.

The main problem arises in the representation of the variables of the object language in the language of the meta-program. There are two options; either represent the object variables as ground terms or represent them as variables (or, more generally, non-ground terms). The first is called the *ground representation* and the second the *non-ground representation*. In logic, variables are normally represented as ground terms. Such a representation has been shown to have considerable potential for reasoning about an object theory. For example, the arithmetization of first order logic, illustrated by the Gödel numbering, has been used in first order logic to prove the well-known completeness and incompleteness theorems. As logic programming has the full power of a Turing machine, it is clearly possible to write declarative meta-programs that use the ground representation.

However, ease of programming and the efficiency of the implementation are key factors in the choice of technique used to solve a problem. So the support provided by a programming language for meta-programming often determines which representation should be used. Most logic programming systems have been based on Prolog and this has only provided explicit support for the representation of object variables as variables in the language of the meta-program. It was clear that there were several semantic problems with this approach and, as a consequence, for many years the majority of meta-programs in logic programming had no clear declarative semantics and their only defined semantics was procedural. The situation is now better understood and the problem has been addressed in two ways.

One solution is to clarify the semantics of the non-ground representation. This has been done by a number of researchers and the semantics is now better understood. The other solution is for the programmer to write meta-programs that use the ground representation. To save the user the work of constructing a ground representation, systems such as Reflective Prolog [Costantini and Lanzarone, 1989] and Gödel [Hill and Lloyd, 1994] that provide a built-in ground representation have been developed. There are advantages and disadvantages with each of these solutions. It is much more difficult to provide an efficient implementation when using the ground representation compared to the non-ground representation. However, the ground representation is far more expressive that the non-ground representation and can be used for many more meta-programming tasks. In Sections 2 and 3, we discuss the non-ground and ground representations, respectively, in more detail.

One other issue concerning the syntactic representation is how the theory of the object program is represented in the meta-program. The meta-program can either include the representation of the object program it is reasoning about as program statements, or represent the object program as a term in a goal that is executed in the meta-program. In the first case the components of the object program are fixed and the meta-program is specialized for just those object programs that can be constructed from these components. In the second case, the meta-program can reason about arbitrary object programs. These can be either fixed or constructed dynamically during the derivation procedure.

The syntactic representation of an object program as outlined above ignores the semantics of object expressions. As an example, consider an object program that implements the usual rules of arithmetic. In such a program, $1 < 2$ should be a true statement. Assuming a simple syntactic representation that represents this formula as a term, the truth of $1 < 2$ would be lost to the meta-program. Thus it is necessary to have relations in the meta-program that represent semantic properties of the object program so that, if, for example, the meta-program needed to reason about the truth of arithmetic inequalities in the object program, it would require a relation representing the truth of inequalities such as $1 < 2$. More generally, we take the concept of a *reflective principle* to cover the representation, in the meta-language, of 'truth of object formulas' and, also, the representation of the notions of validity, derivability, and related concepts such as inference rules and proofs.

In logic programming, a meta-program will normally require a variety of *reflective predicates* realising different reflective principles. For example, there may be a reflective predicate defining SLD-resolution for (the representation of) the object program. Other reflective predicates may define (using a representation of the object program) unification or a single derivation step. In fact, it is these more basic steps for which support is often required.

To make meta-programming a practical tool, many useful reflective predicates (based on a pre-defined representation) are often built into the programming system. However, a programming system cannot provide all possible reflective predicates even for a fixed representation. Thus a system that supports a representation with built-in reflective predicates must also provide a means by which a user can define additional reflective predicates appropriate for the particular application. The actual definition of the reflective predicates depends not only on the reflective principles it is intended to model but also on the representation. Later in this chapter, we discuss three reflective predicates in detail. One is *Solve*/2 which is defined for the non-ground representation and the others are *IDemo*/3 and *JDemo*/3 which are defined for the ground representation. Both Prolog and Gödel provide system predicates that are reflective. For example, in Prolog, the predicate `call/1` succeeds if its only argument represents the body of a goal and that goal succeeds with the object program. The Gödel system provides the predicate `Succeed` which has three arguments. `Succeed/3` is true if the third argument represents the answer that would be computed by the Gödel program represented in the first argument using the goal represented in the second argument.

1.2 Applications

We identify two important application requirements in this chapter. One is for meta-programs that can be applied to (representations of) themselves and the other is for meta-programs that need to reason about object programs that can change. We call the first, *self-applicable*, and the second, *dynamic* meta-programming.

There are many programming tools for which self-application is important. In particular; interpreters, compilers, program analysers, program transformers, program debuggers, and program specializers can be usefully applied to themselves. Self-applicable meta-programming is discussed in Section 4 and the use of self-applicable program specializers is discussed in Section 6.

For static meta-programming, where the object program is fixed, the meta-program can include the representation of the object program it is reasoning about in its program statements. However, frequently the purpose of the meta-program is to create an object program in a controlled way. For example, the object program may be a database that must change with time as new information arrives; the meta-program may be intended to perform hypothetical reasoning on the object program; or the object program may consist of a number of components and the meta-program is intended to reason with a combination of these components. This form of meta-programming in which the object program is changed or constructed by the meta-program we call *dynamic*. Section 5 explains the different forms of dynamic meta-programming in more detail.

Of course there are many applications which are both self-applicable and dynamic and for these we need a combination of the ideas discussed in these sections. One of these is a program that transforms other programs. As the usual motivation for transforming a program is to make its implementation more efficient, it is clearly desirable for the program transformer to be self-applicable. Moreover, the program transformer has to construct a new object program dynamically, possibly interpreting at different stages of the transformation (possibly temporary) versions of the object programs. We describe such an application in Section 6.

1.3 Efficiency improvements

Despite the fact that meta-programming is often intended to implement a more efficient computation of an object program, there can be a significant loss of efficiency even when the meta-program just simulates the reasoning of the object program. This is partly due to the extra syntax that is required in the representation and partly due to the fact that the compiler for the object program performs a number of optimizations which are not included in the meta-program's simulation. One way of addressing this problem is through program specialization. This approach is explained in Section 6. The main aim of specialization is to reduce the overhead associated with manipulating object language expressions. When dealing with a fixed object theory the overhead can largely be 'compiled away' by pre-computing, or 'partially evaluating' parts of the meta-program's computation.

A second reason for considering specialization is that it can establish a practical link between the ground and the non-ground representations. In certain circumstances a meta-program that uses a non-ground representation can be obtained by partially evaluating one that uses a ground representation.

$Cat(Tom)$
$Mouse(Jerry)$
$Chase(x, y) \leftarrow Cat(x) \wedge Mouse(y)$

Fig. 1. The Chase Program

$Member(x, [x|y])$
$Member(x, [z|y]) \leftarrow Member(x, y)$

$Member(x, Cons(x, y))$
$Member(x, Cons(z, y)) \leftarrow Member(x, y)$

Fig. 2. The Member Program

1.4 Preliminaries

The two principal representations, non-ground and ground, discussed in this chapter are supported by the programming systems, Prolog and Gödel, respectively. Since Prolog and Gödel have different syntax, we have, for uniformity, adopted a syntax similar to Gödel. Thus, for example, variables begin with a lower-case letter, non-variable symbols are either nonalphabetic or begin with an upper-case letter. The logical connectives are standard. Thus $\wedge$, $\neg$, $\leftarrow$, and $\exists$ denote conjunction, negation, left implication and existential quantification, respectively. The exception to the use of this syntax is where we quote from particular programming systems. In these cases, we adopt the appropriate notation.

Figures 1 and 2 contain two simple examples of logic programs (in this syntax) that will be used as object programs to illustrate the metaprogramming concepts in later sections. There are two syntactic forms for the definition of *Member* in Figure 2. One uses the standard list notation [...|...] and the other uses the constant *Nil* and function *Cons*/2 to construct a list. For illustrating the representations it is usually more informative to use the latter form although the former is simpler. The language of the program in Figure 1 is assumed to be defined using just the symbols *Cat*/1, *Mouse*/1, *Chase*/2, *Tom*, and *Jerry* occurring in the program. The language of the program in Figure 2 is assumed to include the non-logical symbols in the program in Figure 1, the predicate *Member*/2, the function *Cons*/2, the constant *Nil*, together with the natural numbers.

We summarize here the main logic programming concepts required for this chapter. Our terminology is based on that of [Lloyd, 1987] and the reader is referred to this book for more details. A *logic program* contains a set of program statements. A *program statement* which is a formula in first order logic is written as either

H

or

$$H \leftarrow B$$

where H is an atom and B is an arbitrary formula called the *body* of the statement. If B is a conjunction of literals (respectively, atoms), then the program statement is called a *normal* (respectively, *definite*) clause. A program is *normal* (respectively, *definite*) if all its statements are normal (respectively, definite). A *goal* for a program is written as

$$\leftarrow B$$

denoting the formula $\neg B$, where B is an arbitrary formula called the *body* of the goal. If B is a conjunction of literals (respectively, atoms), then the goal is *normal* (respectively, *definite*). As in Prolog and Gödel, an '_' is used to denote a unique variable existentially quantified at the front of the atom in which it occurs. It is assumed that all other free variables are universally quantified at the front of the statement or goal.

The usual procedural meaning given to a definite logic program is SLD-resolution. However, this is inadequate to deal with more general types of program statements. In logic programming, a (ground) negative literal $\neg A$ in the body of a normal clause or goal is usually implemented by 'negation as failure':

the goal $\neg A$ succeeds if A fails
the goal $\neg A$ fails if A succeeds.

Using the program as the theory, negation, as defined in classical logic, cannot provide a semantics for such a procedure. However, it has been shown that negation as failure is a satisfactory implementation of logical negation provided it is assumed that the theory of a program is not just the set of statements in the program, but is its *completion* [Clark, 1978]. A clear and detailed account of negation as failure and a definition of the completion of a normal program is given in [Shepherdson, 1994]. This definition can easily be extended to programs with arbitrary program statements. Moreover, it is shown in [Lloyd, 1987] that any program can be transformed to an equivalent normal program. Thus, in this chapter, we only consider object programs that are normal and, unless otherwise stated, that the semantics of a logic program is defined by its completion. The completion of a program P is denoted by comp(P).

In meta-programming, we are concerned, not only with the actual formulas in an object theory but also the language in which these formulas are written. This language which we call the *object language* may either be inferred from the symbols appearing in the object theory, or be explicitly declared. When the object theory is a Prolog program, then the language is inferred. However, when the object program is a Gödel program the language is declared. These declarations also declare the types of the symbols so that the semantics of the Gödel system is based on many-sorted logic.

The following notation is used in this chapter.

1. The symbols $\mathcal{L}$ and $\mathcal{M}$ denote languages. Usually $\mathcal{L}$ denotes an object language while $\mathcal{M}$ is the language of some meta-program.

2. The notation $E_{\mathcal{L}}$ means that E is an expression in a language $\mathcal{L}$. The subscript is omitted when the language is either obvious or irrelevant.

3. The representation of an expression E in another language $\mathcal{M}$ is written $\lceil E \rceil_{\mathcal{M}}$. The actual representation intended by this notation will depend on the context in which it is used. The subscript is omitted when the language is either obvious or irrelevant

4. If $\mathcal{L}$ is a language, then the set of representations of expressions of $\mathcal{L}$ in language $\mathcal{M}$ is written $\lceil \mathcal{L} \rceil_{\mathcal{M}}$.

We discuss a number of reflective predicates, but the key examples will realise adaptations of one or both of the following reflective principles. For all finite sets of sentences A and single sentences B of an object language $\mathcal{L}$,

$$A \vdash_{\mathcal{L}} B \text{ iff } Pr \vdash_{\mathcal{M}} Demo(\lceil A \rceil, \lceil B \rceil)$$

$$A \models_{\mathcal{L}} B \text{ iff } Pr \models_{\mathcal{M}} Demo(\lceil A \rceil, \lceil B \rceil)$$

where Pr denotes the theory of the meta-program with language $\mathcal{M}$ and $Demo/2$ denotes the reflective predicate. Such a program is often called a *meta-interpreter*.

A meta-program reasons about another (object) program. As this object program can itself be another meta-program, a *tower* of meta-programs can be constructed. Within such a tower, a meta-program can be assigned a *level*. The base level of the tower will be an object program, say P_0, which is not a meta-program. At the next level, a program P_1 will be a meta-program for reasoning about P_0. Similarly, if, for each $i \in \{1, \ldots, n\}$, P_{i-1} is an object program for P_i, then P_i is one level above the level of P_{i-1}. Normally, we are only concerned in any two consecutive levels and refer to the relative positions of an object program and its meta-program within such a tower as the *object level* and *meta-level*, respectively.

2 The non-ground representation

The non-ground representation requires the variables in the object program to be represented by non-ground terms in the meta-program. This section assumes, as in Prolog, that object variables are represented as variables in the meta-program. Before discussing the representation in more detail, we describe its historical background.

In the early work on logic programming it appears that there was an understanding that the Prolog system being developed should be self-applicable. That is, it should facilitate the interpretation of Prolog in

Prolog. The first implementation of a programming system based on the ideas of logic programming was Marseille Prolog [Colmerauer *et al.*, 1973]. This system was designed for natural language processing but it still provided a limited number of meta-programming features. However, the meta-programming predicates such as `clause`, `assert`, and `retract` that we are familiar with in Prolog (and now formally defined by the committee for the ISO standard for Prolog [ISO/IEC, 1995]) were introduced by D H D Warren and were first included as part of DEC-10 Prolog [Pereira *et al.*, 1978]. Moreover, the ability to use the meta-programming facilities of the Prolog system to interpret Prolog was first demonstrated in [Pereira *et al.*, 1978] with the following program.

```
execute(true).
execute((A,B)) :- execute(A), execute(B).
execute(A) :- clause(A,B), execute(B).
execute(A) :- A.
```

The program shows the ease by which Prolog programs can interpret themselves. It was stated that the last clause enabled the interpreter 'to cope with calls to ordinary Prolog predicates'. The main purpose for this clause was to enable the interpreter to cope with system predicates. The use of the variable A instead of a non-variable goal can be avoided by means of the `call` predicate which was also provided by DEC-10 Prolog. Thus the last clause in this interpreter could have been written as

```
execute(A) :- call(A).
```

Both the use of a variable for a goal and the provision of the `call` predicate corresponded to and was (probably) inspired by the *eval* function of Lisp.

Clark and McCabe [1979] illustrated how Prolog could be used for implementing expert systems. They made extensive use of the meta-programming facility that allows the use of a variable as a formula. Here the variable also occurred in the head of the clause or in an atom in the body of the clause to the left of the variable formula. The programmer had to ensure that the variable was adequately instantiated before the variable formula was called. For example in:

```
r(C) :- system(C), C.
```

either the call to r should have an atomic formula as its argument, or the predicate `system/1` would have to be defined so that it bound C to an atomic formula. The left to right computation rule of Prolog ensured that `system(C)` was called before C.

This meta-variable feature can be explained as a schema for a set of clauses, one for each relation used in the program. This explanation is credited to Roussel. Using just this meta-programming feature, Clark and McCabe showed how a proof tree could be constructed in solving a query to a specially adapted form of the expert system. A disadvantage of this approach was that the object program had to be explicitly modified by the programmer to support the production of the proof as a term.

Shapiro [1982] developed a Prolog interpreter for declarative debugging that followed the pattern of the `execute` program above. This was a program which was intended for debugging logic programs where the expected (correct) outcome of queries to a program is supplied by the programmer. The programmer can then ignore the actual trace of the execution. The meta-program was based on an interpreter similar to the above program from [Pereira *et al.*, 1978] but with the addition of an atom `system(A)` as a conjunct to the body of the last statement. `system/1` is intended to identify those predicates for which `clause/2` is undefined or explicit interpretation is not required.

A major problem with the use of meta-programs for interpreting other Prolog programs is the loss of efficiency caused by interpreting the object programs indirectly through a meta-program. Gallagher [1986] and Takeuchi and Furukawa [1986] showed that most of the overhead due to meta-programming in Prolog could be removed by partially evaluating the meta-program with respect to a specific object program. This important development and other research concerning program transformations encouraged further development of many kinds of meta-programming tools. For example, Sterling and Beer [1986; 1989] developed tools for transforming a knowledge base together with a collection of meta-programs for interpreting an arbitrary knowledge base into a program with the functionality of all the interpreters specialized for the given knowledge base.

It is clear that many of the meta-programming facilities of Prolog such as the predicates `var`, `nonvar`, `assert`, and `retract` do not have a declarative semantics. However, the predicates such as `clause` and `functor` are less problematical and can interpreted declaratively. In spite of this, the semantics of these predicates and a logical analysis of simple meta-programs that used them was not published until the first workshop on meta-programming in logic in 1988 [Abramson and Rogers, 1989]. Substantial work has been done since on the semantics of the Prolog style of meta-programming and some of this will be discussed later in this section. Since a proper theoretical account of any meta-program depends on the details of how the the object program is represented, in the next subsection we describe the simple non-ground representation upon which the Prolog meta-programming provision is based.

2.1 The representation

It can be seen from the above historical notes that the main motivation for a non-ground representation is its use in Prolog. Hence, the primary interest is in the case where variables are represented as variables and non-variable symbols are represented by constants and functions in the language of the meta-program.

Therefore, in this section, a non-ground representation is presented where variables are represented as variables and the naming relation for the non-logical symbols is summarized as follows.

Object symbol	Meta symbol
Constant	Constant
Function of arity n	Function of arity n
Proposition	Constant
Predicate of arity n	Function of arity n

Distinct symbols (including the variables) in the object language must be named by distinct symbols in the meta-language. For example, *Tom* and *Jerry* in the Chase program in Figure 1 could be named by constants, say *Tom′* and *Jerry′*. The predicates $Cat/1$, $Mouse/1$, and $Chase/2$ can be similarly represented by functions, say $Cat′/1$, $Mouse′/1$, and $Chase′/2$.

For a given naming relation, the representations $\lceil t \rceil$ and $\lceil A \rceil$ of a term t and atom A, are defined as follows.

- If t is a variable x, then $\lceil t \rceil$ is the variable x.
- If t is a constant C, then $\lceil t \rceil$ is the constant $C′$, where $C′$ is the name of C.
- If t is the term $F(t_1, \ldots, t_n)$, then $\lceil t \rceil$ is $F′(\lceil t_1 \rceil, \ldots, \lceil t_n \rceil)$, where $F′$ is the name of F.
- If A is the atom $P(t_1, \ldots, t_n)$, then $\lceil A \rceil$ is $P′(\lceil t_1 \rceil, \ldots, \lceil t_n \rceil)$, where $P′$ is the name of P.

For example, the atom *Cat(Tom)* is represented (using the above naming relation) by $Cat′(Tom′)$ and $Mouse(x)$ by $Mouse′(x)$. To represent non-atomic formulas, a representation of the logical connectives is required. The representation is as follows.

Object connective	Meta symbol
Binary connective	Function of arity 2
Unary connective	Function of arity 1

We assume the following representation for the connectives used in the examples here.

Object connective	Representation	
¬	Prefix function	$Not/1$
∧	Infix function	$And/2$
←	Infix function	$If/2$

Given a representation of the atomic formulas and the above representation of the connectives, the term $\lceil Q \rceil$ representing a formula Q is defined as follows.

- If Q is of the form $\neg R$, then $\lceil Q \rceil$ is *Not* $\lceil R \rceil$.
- If Q is of the form $R \wedge S$, then $\lceil Q \rceil$ is $\lceil R \rceil$ *And* $\lceil S \rceil$.
- If Q is of the form $R \leftarrow S$, then $\lceil Q \rceil$ is $\lceil R \rceil$ *If* $\lceil S \rceil$.

Continuing the above example using this naming relation, the formula

$Cat(Tom) \wedge Mouse(Jerry)$

is represented by the term

$Cat'(Tom')$ *And* $Mouse'(Jerry')$.

In this example, the name of an object symbol is distinct from the name of the symbol that represents it. However, there is no requirement that this should be the case. Thus, the names of the object symbol and the symbol that represents it can be the same. For example, with this representation, the atomic formula $Cat(Tom)$ is represented by the term $Cat(Tom)$. This is the trivial naming relation, used in Prolog. It does not in itself cause any amalgamation of the object language and meta-language; it is just a syntactic convenience for the programmer. We adopt this trivial naming relation together with the above representation of the connectives for the rest of this section.

A logic program is a set of normal clauses. It is clearly necessary that if the meta-program is to reason about the object program, there must be a way of identifying the clauses of a program. In Prolog, each clause in the program is represented as a fact (that is, a clause with the empty body). This has the advantage that the variables in the fact are automatically standardized apart each time the fact is used. We adopt this representation here. Thus it is assumed that there is a distinguished constant *True* and distinguished predicate *Clause*/2 in the meta-program defined so that each clause in the object program of the form

$h \leftarrow b.$

is represented in the meta-program as a fact

$Clause(\lceil h \rceil, \lceil b \rceil).$

and each fact

$h.$

is represented in the meta-program as a fact

$Clause(\lceil h \rceil, True).$

Thus, in Figure 1,

$Chase(x, y) \leftarrow Cat(x) \wedge Mouse(y).$

is represented by the fact

$Clause(Chase(x, y), Cat(x)$ *And* $Mouse(y)).$

The program in Figure 2 would be represented by the two facts.

Clause(*Member*(*x*, *Cons*(*x*, _)), *True*).
Clause(*Member*(*x*, *Cons*(_, *y*)), *Member*(*x*, *y*)).

An issue that has had much attention is whether the facts defining *Clause* accurately represent the object program. The problem is a consequence of the fact that, in Prolog, the language is not explicitly defined but assumed to be determined by the symbols used in the program and goal. Thus, the variables in the object program range over the terms in the language of the object program while the variables in the definition of *Clause* range, not only over the terms representing terms in the object program, but also over the terms representing the formulas of the object program. Thus, in Figure 1, the terms in the object language are just the two constants *Tom* and *Jerry*, while in a meta-program representing this program, the terms not only include *Tom* and *Jerry* but also *Cat(Tom)*, *Mouse(Jerry)*, *Cat(Cat(Tom))* and so on. Thus in the clause

Chase(*x*, *y*) ← *Cat*(*x*) ∧ *Mouse*(*y*).

in the object program, *x* and *y* are assumed to be universally quantified in a domain just containing *Tom* and *Jerry*, while in the fact

Clause(*Chase*(*x*, *y*), *Cat*(*x*) *And Mouse*(*y*)).

in the meta-program, *x* and *y* are assumed to be universally quantified in a domain that contains a representation of all terms and formulas of the object program.

There is a simple solution, that is, assume that the intended interpretation of the meta-program is typed. The types distinguish between the terms that represent terms in the object program and terms that represent the formulas. This approach has been developed by Hill and Lloyd [1989]. An alternative solution is to assume an untyped interpretation but restrict the object program so that its semantics is preserved in the meta-program. This approach has been explored by Martens and De Schreye [1992a], [1992b] using the concept of *language independence*. (Informally, a program is language independent when the perfect Herbrand models are not affected by the addition of new constants and functions.) In the next subsection, we examine how each of these approaches may be used to prove the correctness of the definition *Solve* with respect to the intended semantics.

2.2   Reflective predicates

By representing variables as variables, the non-ground representation provides implicit support for the reflection of the semantics of unification. For example, a meta-program may define a reflective predicate *Unify* by the fact

Unify(*u*, *u*)

so that the goal

$\leftarrow$ *Unify(*
      Member$(x,\, Cons(x,y)),$
      Member$(1,\, Cons(z,\, Cons(2,\, Cons(3, Nil))))$)

will succeed with

$x = 1, y = Cons(2,\, Cons(3, Nil)), z = 1.$

The ability to use the underlying unification mechanism for both the object program and its representation makes it easy to define reflective predicates whose semantics in the meta-program correspond to the semantics of the object program.

The meta-interpreter **V** in Figure 3 assumes that the object program is a normal logic program and defines the reflective predicate *Solve*/1. Given

Solve(*True*)
Solve((*a And b*)) $\leftarrow$
      Solve(*a*) $\wedge$
      Solve(*b*)
Solve(*Not a*) $\leftarrow$
      $\neg$*Solve*(*a*)
Solve(*a*) $\leftarrow$
      Clause(*a*,*b*) $\wedge$
      Solve(*b*)

Fig. 3. The Vanilla meta-interpreter **V**

a normal object program P, the program $\mathbf{V}_P$ consists of the program **V** together with a set of facts defining *Clause*/2 and representing P. For example, let P be the program in Figure 2, and $\leftarrow G$ the goal

$\leftarrow \neg Member(x,\, Cons(2,(Cons(3, Nil)))) \wedge$
    $Member(x,\, Cons(1,\, Cons(2,(Cons(3, Nil))))).$

Then both the goal $\leftarrow G$ and the goal $\leftarrow Solve(\lceil G \rceil)$

$\leftarrow$ *Solve*(
    $Not\ Member(x,\, Cons(2,(Cons(3, Nil))))\ And$
      $Member(x,\, Cons(1,\, Cons(2,(Cons(3, Nil)))))$)

have the computed answer

$x = 1.$

The predicate *Solve*/1 is intended to satisfy the following reflective principles which are adaptations of those given in Subsection 1.4:

$$P \vdash_{\mathcal{L}} Q \text{ iff } \mathbf{V}_P \vdash_{\mathcal{M}} Solve(\lceil Q \rceil)$$

$$\text{comp}(P) \models_{\mathcal{L}} Q \text{ iff comp}(\mathbf{V}_P) \models_{\mathcal{M}} Solve(\lceil Q \rceil)$$

Here Q is assumed to be a conjunction of ground literals although the reflective principles can easily be generalized for non-ground formulas. It has been shown that the relation *Solve*/1 has the intended semantics in program $\mathbf{V}_P$ if either the interpretation of $\mathbf{V}_P$ is typed or the object program represented by the definition of *Clause*/2 is language independent. Each of these conditions is described in turn.

We first consider using a typed interpretation of $\mathbf{V}_P$. There are (at least) two types in the interpretation, o and μ, where o is intended for object language terms and μ for object language formulas. The representation for the terms and formulas in the object language together with the intended types for their interpretation is as follows.

Object symbol	Meta symbol	Type
Constant	Constant	o
Function of arity n	Function of arity n	$o * \cdots * o \to o$
Proposition	Constant	μ
Predicate of arity n	Function of arity n	$o * \cdots * o \to \mu$
Binary connective	Function of arity 2	$\mu * \mu \to \mu$
Unary connective	Function of arity 1	$\mu \to \mu$

In addition, the predicates *Solve*/1 and *Clause*/2 have each of their arguments of type μ. The following result is proved in [Hill and Lloyd, 1989].

Theorem 2.2.1. *Let P be a normal program and $\leftarrow Q$ a normal goal. Let $\mathbf{V}_P$ be the program defined above. Then the following hold:*

1. *comp(P) is consistent iff comp($\mathbf{V}_P$) is consistent.*
2. *θ is a correct answer for comp(P)$\cup\{\leftarrow Q\}$ iff θ is a correct answer for comp($\mathbf{V}_P$)$\cup\{\leftarrow$ Solve(Q)$\}$.*
3. *$\neg Q$ is a logical consequence of comp(P) iff $\neg$ Solve(Q) is a logical consequence of comp($\mathbf{V}_P$).*

Theorem 2.2.2. *Let P be a normal program and $\leftarrow Q$ a normal goal. Let $\mathbf{V}_P$ be the program defined above. Then the following hold:*

1. *θ is a computed answer for $P\cup\{\leftarrow Q\}$ iff θ is a computed answer for $\mathbf{V}_P\cup\{\leftarrow$ Solve(Q)$\}$.*
2. *$P\cup\{\leftarrow Q\}$ has a finitely failed SLDNF-tree iff $\mathbf{V}_P\cup\{\leftarrow$ Solve(Q)$\}$ has a finitely failed SLDNF-tree.*

It is important to note here that, although the declarative semantics of $\mathbf{V}_P$ requires a model which is typed, the procedural semantics for the program P and for $\mathbf{V}_P$ is the same and that, apart from checking that the given goal is correctly typed, no run-time type checking is involved.

Martens and De Schreye have provided an alternative solution to the semantics of $\mathbf{V}_P$ that does not require the use of types. We now give a summary of the semantics that they have proposed. Their work requires the object programs to be stratified and satisfy the condition of language independence.

Definition 2.2.3. Let P be a program. A *language for P*[1] is any language $\mathcal{L}$ such that each clause in P is a well-formed expression in the language $\mathcal{L}$.

Let $\mathcal{L}_P$ be the language defined using just the symbols occurring in P. Then any language for P will be an extension of $\mathcal{L}_P$.

Definition 2.2.4. Let P be a stratified program. Then P is said to be *language independent* if the perfect Herbrand model of P is independent of the choice of language for P.

Language independence is an undecidable property. Thus it is important to find a subclass of the language independent programs that can be recognized syntactically. The following well-known concept of range restriction determines such a class.

Definition 2.2.5. A clause in a program P is *range restricted* if every variable in the clause appears in a positive literal in the body of the clause. A program is *range restricted* if all its clauses are range restricted.

It is shown in [Martens and De Schreye, 1992a] that the set of range restricted stratified programs is a proper subset of the language independent programs. It is also demonstrated that, if P is a definite program and G a definite goal, P is language independent if and only if all computed answers (using SLD-resolution) for $P \cup \{G\}$ are ground.

The correctness of the $\mathbf{V}_P$ program is stated in terms of the perfect model for the object program and the weakly perfect model for the meta-program. It is shown that if the object program P is stratified, then the program $\mathbf{V}_P$ has a weakly perfect model. Note that a stratified program always has a perfect model.[2]

We can now state the main result.

Theorem 2.2.6. *Let P be a stratified, language independent, normal program and $\mathbf{V}_P$ the meta-program, as defined above. Then, for every predicate p/n occurring in P the following hold.*

1. *If $t_1, \ldots, t_n$ are ground terms in the language defined by the symbols occurring in $\mathbf{V}_P$, then $Solve(p(t_1, \ldots, t_n))$ is true in the weakly perfect Herbrand model of $\mathbf{V}_P$ iff $p(t_1, \ldots, t_n)$ is true in the perfect Herbrand model of P.*

2. *If $t_1, \ldots, t_n$ are ground terms in the language defined by the symbols occurring in P, then $Solve(Not\ p(t_1, \ldots, t_n))$ is true in the weakly*

---

[1]Note that this definition of a language of a program just applies to the discussion of Martens and De Schreye's results and does not hold in the rest of this chapter.

[2]A definition of a weakly perfect model is in [Martens and De Schreye, 1992b]. A definition of a stratified program can be found in [Lloyd, 1987] as well as in [Martens and De Schreye, 1992b].

perfect Herbrand model of $\mathbf{V}_P$ *iff* $p(t_1, \ldots, t_n)$ *is not true in the perfect Herbrand model of P.*

The main issue distinguishing the typed and language independent approaches is the criterion that is used in determining the language of a program. Either the language of a program is inferred from the symbols it contains or the language can be defined explicitly by declaring the symbols. As the language of the program $\mathbf{V}_P$ must include a representation of all the symbols of the object program, it is clear that if we require the language of a program to be explicitly declared, the meta-program will need to distinguish between the terms that represent object terms and those that represent object formulas. This of course leads naturally to a typed interpretation. On the other hand, if the language of a program is fixed by the symbols actually appearing in that program, then we need to ensure the interpretation is unchanged when the program is extended with new symbols. This leads us to look at the concept of language independence which is the basis of the second approach.

The advantages of using a typed interpretation is that no extra conditions are placed on the object program. The usual procedural semantics for logic programming can be used for both typed and untyped programs. Thus the type information can be omitted from the program although it seems desirable that the intended types of the symbols be indicated at least as a comment to the program code. A possible disadvantage is that we must use many-sorted logic to explain the semantics of the meta-program instead of the better known unsorted logic. The alternative of coding the type information explicitly as part of the program is not desirable since this would create an unnecessary overhead and adversely affect the efficiency of the meta-interpreter.

The advantage of the language independence approach is that for definite language independent object programs, the semantics of the $\mathbf{V}$ program is based on that of unsorted first order logic. However, many common programs such as the program in Figure 2 are not language independent. Moreover, as soon as we allow negation in the bodies of clauses, any advantage is lost. Not only do we still require the language independence condition for the object program, but we can only compare the weakly perfect model of the meta-program with the perfect model of the object program.

We conclude this subsection by presenting in Figure 4 an extended form of the program $\mathbf{V}$ in Figure 3. This program, which is a typical example of what the non-ground interpretation can be used for is adapted from [Sterling and Shapiro, 1986]. The program $\mathbf{W}$ defines a predicate *PSolve*/2. The first argument of *PSolve*/2 corresponds to the single argument of *Solve* but the second argument must be bound to the program's proof of the first argument.

PSolve(*True, True*)
PSolve(*x And y, xproof And yproof*) ←
      PSolve(*x, xproof*) ∧
      PSolve(*y, yproof*)
PSolve(*Not x, True*) ←
      ¬*PSolve*(*x, _*)
PSolve(*x, x If yproof*) ←
      Clause(*x, y*) ∧
      PSolve(*y, yproof*)

Fig. 4. The Proof-Tree meta-interpreter **W**

Given a normal object program P, the program $\mathbf{W}_P$ consists of the program **W** together with a set of facts defining *Clause*/2 and representing P. If P is the program in Figure 2, then the goal

← *PSolve*(
      Not Member(*x, Cons*(2, (*Cons*(3, *Nil*)))) *And*
         Member(*x, Cons*(1, *Cons*(2, (*Cons*(3, *Nil*)))))),
      proof)

has the computed answer

$x = 1$
proof = *True And* (*Member*(1, *Cons*(1, *Cons*(2, *Cons*(3, *Nil*))))) *If True*).

2.3 Meta-programming in Prolog

The language Prolog has a number of built-in predicates that are useful for meta-programming. These can be divided into two categories: those with a declarative semantics and those whose semantics is purely procedural.

The first category includes functor/3, arg/3, and =../2. functor is true if the first argument is a term, the second is the name of the top-level function for this term and the third is its arity. arg is true if the first argument is a positive integer i, the second, of the form $f(t_1, \ldots, t_n)$ $(n \geq i)$, and the third, the ith argument t_i. For a Prolog meta-program containing the non-ground representation of the Chase program in Figure 1, the definition of the system predicates functor and arg would be:

```
functor(tom, tom, 0).
functor(jerry, jerry, 0).
functor(cat(_), cat, 1).
functor(mouse(_), mouse, 1).
functor(chase(_,_), chase, 2).

arg(1,cat(X),X).
arg(1,mouse(X),X).
```

```
arg(1,chase(X,Y),X).
arg(2,chase(X,Y),Y).
```

The predicate =.. is a binary infix predicate which is true when the left hand argument is a term of the form f or $f(t_1,\ldots,t_n)$ and the right hand argument is the list $[f,t_1,\ldots,t_n]$. This predicate is not really necessary and can be defined in terms of functor and arg.

```
Term =.. [Function| Args] :-
     functor(Term, Function, Arity),
     findargs(Arity, Args, Term).
```

```
findargs(0, [], _).
findargs(Argno, [Arg|Args], Term) :-
     arg(Argno, Term, Arg),
     Argno1 is Argno - 1,
     findargs(Argno1, Args, Term).
```

The second category includes meta-logical predicates such as var/1, nonvar/1, and atomic/1 and the dynamic predicates such as assert/1 and retract/1.

The predicate var/1 tests whether its argument is currently uninstantiated, while nonvar/1 is the opposite of var and tests whether its only argument is currently instantiated. atomic/1 succeeds if its argument is currently instantiated to a constant. These predicates are not declarative since computed answers are not correct answers. Consider the following Prolog goals.

```
?- var(X)
?- var(3)
```

The first goal succeeds with no binding, suggesting that var(X) is true for all instances of X, while the second goal fails.

The predicates assert/1 and retract/1 allow modification of the program being interpreted. On execution of assert(t), provided t is in the correct syntactical form for a clause, the current instance of t is added as a clause to the program. retract is the opposite of assert. On execution of retract(t), if there is a clause in the current program that unifies with t, then the first such clause will be removed from the program. Since these modify the program being executed and their effect is not undone on backtracking, it is clear that they do not have a declarative semantics.

3   The ground representation

In this section we review the work that has been done in meta-programming using the ground representation; that is, where any expression of the object program is represented by a ground expression in the meta-program. As in the previous section, we begin by outlining the historical background to the use of this representation.

Use of a ground representation in logic can be traced back to the work of Gödel, who gave a method (called a Gödel numbering) for representing expressions in a first order language as natural numbers [Gödel, 1931]. This was defined by giving each symbol of the logic a unique positive odd number, and then, using the sequence of symbols in a logical expression, a method for computing a unique number for that expression. It was not only possible to compute the representation of an expression, but also, given such a number, determine the unique expression that it represented. Using the properties of the natural numbers, this representation has been used in proving properties of the logic. Feferman [1962], who applied Gödel's ideas to meta-mathematics, introduced the concept of a reflective principle.

Weyhrauch [1980] designed a proof checker, called FOL, which has special support for expressing properties of a FOL structure (using a ground representation) in a FOL meta-theory. An important concept in FOL is the simulation structure. This is used in the meta-reasoning part of FOL for reflective axioms that define an intended interpretation of the representation of the object language in terms of other theories already defined in FOL (or in LISP). A FOL meta-theory has, as simulation structure, the object theory and the mappings between the language of the object theory and the language of the meta-theory. Weyhrauch generalized the reflection principle (as defined by Feferman) to be defined simply as a statement of a relation between a theory and its meta-theory. He gives, as an example, a statement of the correspondence between provability of a formula f in the object theory and a predicate $Pr/2$ in the metatheory. $Pr/2$ is intended to be true if the first argument represents the proof of f and the second argument represents f.

Bowen and Kowalski [1982] showed how the idea of using a representation similar to that used in FOL could be adapted for a logic programming system. The actual representation is not specified although a simple syntactic scheme is used in the paper whereby a symbol "$P(x, Bill)$" is used to denote a term of the meta-language which names $P(x, Bill)$. In addition, where a symbol, say A, is used to denote a term or formula of the object language, A' denotes the term in the meta-language representing A. In fact, the key point of this paper was not to give a detailed scheme for the representation of expressions in the object language, but to represent the provability relation $\vdash_{\mathcal{L}}$ for the object program with language $\mathcal{L}$ by means of a predicate $Demo/2$ in the meta-program with language $\mathcal{M}$. Thus, in the context of a set of sentences Pr of $\mathcal{M}$, $Demo$ represents $\vdash_{\mathcal{L}}$ if and only if, for all finite sets of sentences A and single sentences B of $\mathcal{L}$,

$$A \vdash_{\mathcal{L}} B \text{ iff } Pr \vdash_{\mathcal{M}} Demo(A', B').$$

It was not intended that $\neg Demo$ in Pr should represent unprovability since provability is semi-decidable.

The ideas of Bowen and Kowalski were demonstrated by Bowen and Weinberg [1985] using a logic programming system called MetaProlog, which extended Prolog with special meta-programming facilities. These consisted of three system predicates, demo/3, add_to/3, and drop_from/3. The first of these corresponded to the *Demo* predicate described by Bowen and Kowalski. The predicate demo/3 defines a relation between the representations of an object program P, a goal G, and a proof R. demo is intended to be true when G is a logical consequence of P and a proof of this is given by R. Predicates add_to/3, and drop_from/3 are relations between the representations of a program P, a clause C, and another program Q. add_to/3 and drop_from/3 are intended to be true when Q can be obtained from P by, respectively, adding or deleting the clause C. These predicates provided only the basic support for meta-programming and, to perform other meta-programming tasks, a meta-program has to use the non-declarative predicates in the underlying Prolog. Thus, although the theoretical work is based on a ground representation, meta-programming applications implemented in MetaProlog are often forced to use the non-ground representation.

Apart from the work of Bowen and Weinberg, meta-programming using the ground representation remained a mainly theoretical experiment for a number of years. Stimulation for furthering the research on this subject was brought about by the initiation in 1988 of a biennial series of workshops on meta-programming in logic. A paper [Hill and Lloyd, 1989] in the 1988 workshop built upon the ideas of Bowen and Kowalski and described a more general framework for defining and using the ground representation. In this representation, object clauses were represented as facts in the meta-program and did not allow for changing the object program. Subsequent work modified this approach so as to allow for more dynamic meta-programming [Hill and Lloyd, 1988]. Gödel is a programming system based on these ideas [Hill and Lloyd, 1994]. This system has considerable specialist support for meta-programming using a ground representation. Those aspects of Gödel, pertinent to the meta-programming facilities, are described in Subsection 3.3.

3.1 The representation

In Section 2, a simple scheme for representing a first order language based on that employed by Prolog was described. However, for most meta-programs such a representation is inadequate. Meta-programs often have to reason about the computational behaviour of the object program and, for this, only the ground representation is suitable. A program can be viewed from many angles; for example, the language, the order of statements, the modular structure. Meta-programs may need to reason about any of these.

In this subsection, we first consider the components that might constitute a program and how they may be represented.

In order to discuss the details of how components of an object program may be represented as terms in a meta-program, we need to understand the structure of the object program that is to be represented. Object programs are normally parsed at a number of structural levels, ranging from the individual characters to the modules (if the program is modular) that combine together to form the complete program. We assume here that an object program has some of the following structural levels.

1. Character
2. Symbol
3. Language element
4. Statement or declaration
5. Module
6. Program

For example, for a normal logic program (with a modular structure) these would correspond to the following.

1. Alphabetic and non-alphabetic character
2. Constant, function, proposition, predicate, connective, and variable
3. Term and formula
4. Clause
5. Set of predicate definitions
6. Logic program

Note that levels 1, 2, and 3 contribute to the language of a program, while levels 4, 5, and 6 are required for the program's theory. At each structural level a number of different kinds of tree structure (called here a *unit*) are defined. That is, a unit at a structural level other than the lowest will be a tree whose nodes are units defined at lower levels. At the lowest structural level, the units are the pre-defined characters allowed by the underlying programming system. Thus a subset of the trees whose nodes are units defined at or below a certain structural level will form the set of units at the next higher level. For example, in the program in Figure 2, M, (, and) are characters, *Member* and x, are symbols, and $Member(x, Cons(x, y))$ is a formula. Note that, as a tree may consist of just a single unit, some units may occur at more than one level. Thus the character x is also a variable as well as a term of the language. A representation will be defined for one or more of these structural levels of the object program. Moreover, it is usual for the representation to distinguish between these levels, so that, for example, a constant such as A may have three representations depending on whether it is being viewed as a character, constant, or term. Note that this provision of more than one representation for the different structural levels of a language is usual in logic. In particular, the arithmetization of

first order logic given by the Gödel numbering has a different number for
a constant when viewed as a symbol to that when it is viewed as a term.

The actual structural levels that may be represented depend on the
tasks the meta-program wishes to perform. In particular, if we wish to
define a reflective predicate that has an intended interpretation of SLD-
resolution, we need to define unification. For this, a representation of the
symbols is required. If we wish to be able to change the object program
using new symbols created dynamically, then a representation of the characters would be needed.

A representation is in fact a coding and, as is required for any cipher, a
representation should be invertible (injective) so that results at the meta-
level can be interpreted at the object-level[3]. Such an inverse mapping
we call here a *re-representation*. To ensure that not only the syntax and
structural level of the object element can be recovered but also the kind
of unit at that level (for example, if it is a language element in a logic
program, whether it is a term, atom, or formula) that is represented, the
representation has to include this information as part of the coding.

We give, as an example, a simple ground representation for a normal
program. This is used in the next subsection by the Instance-Demo program in Figure 5 and the SLD-Demo program in Figure 6. First we define the naming relation for each symbol in the language and then define
the representation for the terms and formulas (using just the connectives
$\wedge, \leftarrow, \neg$) that can be constructed from them. Individual characters are not
represented. For this representation, it is assumed that the language of
the meta-program includes three types: the type s for terms representing
object symbols; the type o for terms representing object terms; and the
type μ for terms representing object formulas. It is also assumed that the
language includes the type $List(a)$ for any type a together with the usual
list constructor *Cons* and constant *Nil*. The language must also include the
functions *Term*/2, *Atom*/2, *V*/1, *C*/1, *F*/1, *P*/1 *And*/2, *If*/2, and *Not*/1
whose intended types are as follows.

---

[3]There is, of course, an alternative explanation of why a representation must be
injective: it is the inverse of denotation. Since denotation must be functional (any term
has (at most) one denotation), the inverse of denotation must be injective.

Function	Type
Term	$s * List(o) \rightarrow o$
Atom	$s * List(o) \rightarrow \mu$
V	$Integer \rightarrow o$
C	$Integer \rightarrow s$
F	$Integer \rightarrow s$
P	$Integer \rightarrow s$
And	$\mu * \mu \rightarrow \mu$
If	$\mu * \mu \rightarrow \mu$
Not	$\mu \rightarrow \mu$

The representation of the variables, non-logical symbols, and connectives is as follows.

Object symbol	Representation		
Variable	Term	$V(n)$	$n \in Integer$
Constant	Term	$C(i)$	$i \in Integer$
Function	Term	$F(j)$	$j \in Integer$
Proposition/			
Predicate	Term	$P(k)$	$k \in Integer$
$\wedge$	Function	$And/2$	
$\leftarrow$	Function	$If/2$	
$\neg$	Function	$Not/1$	

To give the representation of the terms and formulas, suppose D is a constant represented by $C(i)$, G/n a function represented by $F(j)$, and Q/n a predicate represented by $P(k)$.

Object expression		Representation	
Constant	D	Term	$Term(C(i), [])$
Term	$G(t_1, \ldots, t_n)$	Term	$Term(F(j), [\lceil t_1 \rceil, \ldots, \lceil t_n \rceil])$
Atom	$Q(t_1, \ldots, t_n)$	Term	$Term(P(k), [\lceil t_1 \rceil, \ldots, \lceil t_n \rceil])$
Formula	$A \wedge B$	Term	$And(\lceil A \rceil, \lceil B \rceil)$
Formula	$\neg A$	Term	$Not(\lceil A \rceil)$
Formula	$A \leftarrow B$	Term	$If(\lceil A \rceil, \lceil B \rceil)$

As an example, consider the language of the program in Figure 2.

Object symbol	Representation
x	$V(0)$
y	$V(1)$
z	$V(2)$
Nil	$C(0)$
$i > 0$	$C(i)$
$i \leq 0$	$C(-i-1)$
Cons	$F(0)$
Member	$P(0)$

Thus the atom

$Member(x, [1, 2])$

is represented by the term

$Atom(\ P(0),$
$\qquad [\quad V(0),$
$\qquad\qquad Term($
$\qquad\qquad\quad F(0),$
$\qquad\qquad\quad [\quad Term(C(1), []),$
$\qquad\qquad\qquad\quad Term(F(0), [Term(C(2), []), Term(C(0), [])])\ ]\ )$
$\qquad\quad]\ ).$

The representation of a program clause which is a fact

H

is

$If([H], True)$

The representation of a program clause

$H \leftarrow B$

is

$If([H], [B])$

which is the same as the formula representation of $H \leftarrow B$.

The theory of a program is represented as a list of clauses. Using this representation, the Member program is represented by the following list:

$[\qquad If(Atom(P(0), [V(0), Term(F(0), [V(0), V(1)])]), True),$
$\qquad If(Atom(P(0), [V(0), Term(F(0), [V(1), V(2)])]),$
$\qquad\quad Atom(P(0), [V(0), V(2)]))\quad]$

This representation is defined for any normal programs and is used for many of the examples in this chapter. However, the main limitation with this representation is that there is no representation of the characters making up the object symbols. Thus this representation does not facilitate the generation of new object languages. In addition, it has been assumed that the object program has no module structure. By representing a module as a list of clauses and a program as a list of modules, a meta-program could reason about the structure of a modular program.

It can be seen that a representation such as the one described above that encodes structural information, is difficult to use and prone to user errors. An alternative representation is a string. A string, which is a finite sequence of characters, is usually indicated by enclosing the sequence in quotation marks. For example, "*ABC*" denotes the string *A,B,C*. With the string representation, the atom

$Member(x, [1, 2])$

is represented as

"$Member(x, [1, 2])$"

If a string concatenation function ++ is available, then unspecified components can be expressed using variables in the meta-program. For example

"$Member($" ++ x ++ "$, [1, 2])$"

defines a term that corresponds, using the previous representation to the (non-ground) term

$$Atom(\ P(0),$$
$$[\quad x,$$
$$Term($$
$$F(0),$$
$$[\quad Term(C(1), []),$$
$$Term(F(0), [Term(C(2), []), Term(C(0), [])]\ )\ ]\ )$$
$$]\ ).$$

As the string representation carries no structural information, this representation is computationally very inefficient. Thus, it is desirable for a representation such as a string as well as one that is more structurally descriptive to be available. The meta-programming system should then provide a means of converting from one representation to the other.

Most researchers on meta-programming define a specific representation suitable for their purposes without explaining why the particular representation was chosen. However, Van Harmelen [1992] has considered the many different ways in which a representation may be defined and how this may assist in reasoning about the object theory. We conclude this subsection with interesting examples of non-standard representations based on examples in his paper.

In the first example, the object theory encodes graphs as facts of the form $Edge(N_i, N_j)$ together with a rule defining the transitive closure.

$Connected(n_1, n_2) \leftarrow Edge(n_1, n_3) \wedge Connected(n_3, n_2)$

The representation assigns different terms to the object formulas, depending on their degree of instantiation.

Object formula	Representation
$Edge(N15, x)$	$GroundVar(Edge, N15, V(1))$
$Connected(N15, x)$	$GroundVar(Connected, N15, V(1))$
$Edge(x, N15)$	$VarGround(Edge, V(1), N15)$
$Connected(N15, x)$	$VarGround(Connected, V(1), N15)$
$Edge(x, y)$	$VarVar(Edge, V(1), V(2))$
$Connected(N15, N16)$	$GroundGround(Connected, N15, N16)$

With this representation, we can define the atoms that may be selected by means of a predicate *Selectable* in the meta-program.

$Selectable(GroundGround(\_, \_, \_))$
$Selectable(GroundVar(\_, \_, \_))$
$Selectable(VarGround(Edge, \_, \_))$

Moreover, with this representation, a meta-theory could be constructed containing the control assertion that the conjunction defining *Connected* should be executed from left to right if the first argument of *Connected* is given, but from right to left if the second argument is given.

The second example is taken from the field of knowledge-based systems and concerns the representation of the difference between implication when used to mean a causation and when used as a specialization. Such implications may require different inference procedures. The representation could be as follows.[4]

Object formula	Representation
$AcuteMenin \rightarrow Menin$	$TypeOf(AcuteMenin, Menin)$
$Meningococcus \rightarrow Menin$	$Causes(Meningococcus, Menin)$

The meta-program can then specify the inference steps that would be appropriate for each of these relations.

Although the idea of being able to define a representation tailored for a particular application is attractive, no programming system has been implemented that provides support for this.

3.2 Reflective predicates

With the ground representation, the reflective predicates have to be explicitly defined. For example, a predicate *GroundUnify*/2 that is intended to be true if some instance of its arguments represent identical terms in the object language, must be defined so that its completed definition corresponds to the Clark equality theory. Such a definition requires a full analysis of the terms representing object terms and atoms. This is computationally expensive compared with using *Unify*/2 to unify expressions in the non-ground representation (see Subsection 2.2).

---

[4] *Menin* and *AcuteMenin* are abbreviations of *Meningitis* and *Acute Meningitis*, respectively.

There are two basic styles of meta-interpreter that use the ground representation and have been discussed in the literature. The first style is derived from an idea proposed in [Kowalski, 1990] and has a similar form to the program **V** in Figure 3 but uses the ground rather than the nonground representation. In this subsection, we present, in Figure 5, an interpreter **I** based on this proposal. This style of meta-interpreter and similar meta-programs are being used in several programs although a complete version and a discussion of its semantics has not previously been published. In the second style the procedural semantics of the object program is intended to be a model of the meta-interpreter. For example, the meta-interpreter outlined in [Bowen and Kowalski, 1982] is intended to define SLD-resolution. An extension of this meta-interpreter for SLDNF-resolution in shown in [Hill and Lloyd, 1989] to be correct with respect to its intended interpretation. An outline of such a meta-interpreter **J** is given in Figure 6. The Gödel program SLD-Demo, also based on this style, is presented in the next subsection in Figure 9.

Both the programs **I** and **J** make use of the ground representation defined in the previous subsection. These programs require an additional type σ to be used for the bindings in a substitution. The function $Bind/2$ is used to construct such a binding. This has domain type $Integer * o$ and range type σ.

The meta-interpreter **I** in Figure 5 defines the predicate $IDemo/3$. This program is intended to satisfy the reflective principles

$$P \vdash_{\mathcal{L}} Q\theta \text{ iff } \mathbf{I} \vdash_{\mathcal{M}} IDemo(\lceil P \rceil, \lceil Q \rceil, \lceil Q\theta \rceil)$$

$$\text{comp}(P) \models_{\mathcal{L}} Q\theta \text{ iff } \text{comp}(\mathbf{I}) \models_{\mathcal{M}} IDemo(\lceil P \rceil, \lceil Q \rceil, \lceil Q\theta \rceil).$$

Here, Q is a conjunction of literals and θ a substitution that grounds Q. These reflective principles, which are adaptations of those given in Subsection 1.4, ensure that provability and logical consequence for the object program are defined in the meta-program.

The types of the predicates in Program **I** are as follows.

Predicate	Type
IDemo	$List(\mu) * \mu * \mu$
*IDemo*1	$List(\mu) * \mu$
InstanceOf	$\mu * \mu$
InstFormula	$\mu * \mu * List(\sigma) * List(\sigma)$
InstTerm	$o * o * List(\sigma) * List(\sigma)$
InstArgs	$List(o) * List(o) * List(\sigma) * List(\sigma)$

The above reflective principles intended for program **I** are similar to those intended for the meta-interpreter $\mathbf{V}_P$. Apart from the representation of the object variables, the main difference between these programs is that $\mathbf{V}_P$ includes the representation of the object program P. Thus, to make it

$IDemo(p, x, y) \leftarrow$
$\qquad InstanceOf(x, y) \wedge$
$\qquad IDemo1(p, y)$

$IDemo1(\_, True)$
$IDemo1(p, And(x, y)) \leftarrow$
$\qquad IDemo1(p, x) \wedge$
$\qquad IDemo1(p, y)$
$IDemo1(p, Not(x)) \leftarrow$
$\qquad \neg IDemo1(p, x)$
$IDemo1(p, Atom(q, xs)) \leftarrow$
$\qquad Member(z, p) \wedge InstanceOf(z, If(Atom(q, xs), b)) \wedge$
$\qquad IDemo1(p, b)$

$InstanceOf(x, y) \leftarrow InstFormula(x, y, [\,], \_)$

$InstFormula(Atom(q, xs), Atom(q, ys), s, s1) \leftarrow$
$\qquad InstArgs(xs, ys, s, s1)$
$InstFormula(And(x, y), And(z, w), s, s2) \leftarrow$
$\qquad InstFormula(x, z, s, s1) \wedge$
$\qquad InstFormula(y, w, s1, s2)$
$InstFormula(If(x, y), If(z, w), s, s2) \leftarrow$
$\qquad InstFormula(x, z, s, s1) \wedge$
$\qquad InstFormula(y, w, s1, s2)$
$InstFormula(Not(x), Not(z), s, s1) \leftarrow$
$\qquad InstFormula(x, z, s, s1)$
$InstFormula(True, True, s, s)$

$InstTerm(V(n), x, [\,], [Bind(n, x)])$
$InstTerm(V(n), x, [Bind(n, x)|s], [Bind(n, x)|s])$
$InstTerm(V(n), x, [Bind(m, y)|s], [Bind(m, y)|s1]) \leftarrow$
$\qquad n \neq m \wedge$
$\qquad InstTerm(V(n), x, s, s1)$
$InstTerm(Term(f, xs), Term(f, ys), s, s1) \leftarrow$
$\qquad InstArgs(xs, ys, s, s1)$

$InstArgs([\,], [\,], s, s)$
$InstArgs([x|xs], [y|ys], s, s2) \leftarrow$
$\qquad InstTerm(x, y, s, s1) \wedge$
$\qquad InstArgs(xs, ys, s1, s2)$

Fig. 5. The Instance-Demo program **I**

easier to compare the programs **V** and **I**, the first clause of **I** needs to be replaced by

$IDemo(p, x, y) \leftarrow$
$\qquad ObjectProgram(p) \wedge$
$\qquad InstanceOf(x, y) \wedge$
$\qquad IDemo1(p, y)$

and then define the program $\mathbf{I}_P$ to consist of this modified form of **I** together with a unit clause

$ObjectProgram(\lceil P \rceil)$

We expect that similar results to those of Theorems 2.2.1 and 2.2.2 will then apply to $\mathbf{I}_P$. Further research is needed to clarify the semantics of the program **I** in Figure 5 and the variation $\mathbf{I}_P$ described above.

The meta-interpreter **J** in Figure 6 defines the predicate $JDemo/3$. This program is intended to satisfy the reflective principle

$$P \vdash_{\mathcal{L}} Q\theta \text{ iff } \mathrm{comp}(\mathbf{I}) \models_{\mathcal{M}} JDemo(\lceil P \rceil, \lceil Q \rceil, \lceil Q\theta \rceil).$$

Here, Q denotes a conjunction of literals and θ a substitution that grounds Q. The types of the predicates in **J** are as follows.

Predicate	Type
$JDemo$	$List(\mu) * \mu * \mu$
$Derivation$	$List(\mu) * \mu * \mu * List(\sigma) * List(\sigma) * Integer$
$Resolve$	$\mu * \mu * \mu * List(\sigma) * List(\sigma) * \mu * Integer * Integer$
$MaxForm$	$\mu * Integer$
$SelectLit$	$\mu * \mu$
$Ground$	μ
$ReplaceConj$	$\mu * \mu * \mu * \mu$
$Rename$	$Integer * \mu * \mu * Integer$
$UnifyTerms$	$List(o) * List(o) * List(\sigma) * List(\sigma)$
$ApplyToForm$	$List(\sigma) * \mu * \mu$

It is intended that the first argument of $Derivation/6$ represents a normal program P, the second and third represent conjunctions of literals Q and R, the fourth and fifth represent substitutions θ and ϕ, and the sixth is an index n for renaming variables. $Derivation/6$ is true if there is an SLD-derivation of $P \cup \{\leftarrow Q\theta\}$ ending in the goal $\leftarrow R\phi$. The predicate $MaxForm/2$ finds the maximum of the variable indices (that is, n in $V(n)$) in the representation of a formula; $SelectLit/2$ selects a literal from the body of a clause; $Ground/1$ checks that a formula is ground; $Rename/4$ finds a variant of the formula in the second argument by adding the number in the first argument to the index of each of its variables and setting the last argument to the maximum of the new variable indices; $Resolve$ performs a single derivation step; $ReplaceConj/4$ removes an element from

$JDemo(p, x, y)$ ←
  $MaxForm(x, n)$ ∧
  $Derivation(p, x, True, [\,], s, n)$ ∧
  $ApplyToForm(s, x, y)$

$Derivation(\_, x, x, s, s, \_)$
$Derivation(p, x, z, s, t, n)$ ←
  $SelectLit(Atom(q, xs), x)$ ∧
  $Member(If(Atom(q, ys), ls), p)$ ∧
  $Resolve(x, Atom(q, xs), If(Atom(q, ys), ls), s, s1, z1, n, n1)$ ∧
  $Derivation(p, z1, z, s1, t, n1)$
$Derivation(p, x, z, s, s, \_)$ ←
  $SelectLit(Not(a), x)$ ∧
  $ApplyToForm(s, a, a1)$ ∧
  $Ground(a1)$ ∧
  $\neg Derivation(p, a1, True, [\,], , 0)$ ∧
  $ReplaceConj(x, Not(a), True, z)$

$Resolve(x, Atom(q, xs), If(Atom(q, ys), ls), s, t, z, m, n)$ ←
  $Rename(m, If(Atom(q, ys), ls), If(Atom(q, y1s), l1s), n)$ ∧
  $UnifyTerms(y1s, xs, s, t)$ ∧
  $ReplaceConj(x, Atom(q, xs), l1s, z)$

Fig. 6. The SLD-Demo program **J**

a conjunction and replaces it by another literal or conjunction of literals; *ApplyToForm*/3 applies a substitution to a formula; and *UnifyTerms*/4 finds an mgu for two lists of terms obtained by applying the substitution in the third argument to the lists of terms in the first and second arguments.

Programs **I** and **J** can be used with the Member program in Figure 2 as their object program. A goal for **I** or **J** that represents the object-level query

← $Member(x, [1, 2])$

is given in Figure 7 (where *Demo* denotes either *IDemo* or *JDemo*). Figure 7 also contains the computed answers for this goal using the programs in Figures 5 and 6.

The goal in Figure 7 has a ground term representing the object program. It has been observed that if a meta-interpreter such as **I** or **J** was used by a goal as above, but where the third argument representing the object program was only partly instantiated, then a program that satisfied the goal could be created dynamically. However, in practice, such a goal would normally flounder if SLDNF-resolution was used as the procedural semantics. Christiansen [1994] is investigating the use of constraint tech-

Goal

$\leftarrow$ *Demo*(
　　[　*If* (*Atom*(*P*(0), [*V*(0), *Term*(*F*(0), [*V*(0), *V*(1)])]), *True*),
　　　If (*Atom*(*P*(0), [*V*(0), *Term*(*F*(0), [*V*(1), *V*(2)])]),
　　　Atom(*P*(0), [*V*(0), *V*(2)]))　])
　　Atom(*P*(0), [
　　　V(0),
　　　Term(*F*(0),
　　　　[　*Term*(*C*(1), []),
　　　　　Term(*F*(0), [*Term*(*C*(2), []), *Term*(*C*(0), [])])])
　　]),
　　g,

Computed answers

g =　　*Atom*(*P*(0), [
　　　Term(*C*(1), []),
　　　Term(*F*(0),
　　　　[　*Term*(*C*(1), []),
　　　　　Term(*F*(0), [*Term*(*C*(2), []), *Term*(*C*(0), [])])])]),

g =　　*Atom*(*P*(0), [
　　　Term(*C*(2), []),
　　　Term(*F*(0),
　　　　[　*Term*(*C*(1), []),
　　　　　Term(*F*(0), [*Term*(*C*(2), []), *Term*(*C*(0), [])])])])

Fig. 7. Goal and computed answers for programs **I** and **J**

niques in the implementation of the meta-interpreter so as to avoid this problem. These techniques have the potential to implement various forms of reasoning including abduction and inductive logic programming.

The Instance-Demo program **I** relies on using the underlying procedures for unification and standardizing apart. Thus it would be difficult to adapt the program to define complex computation rules that involve non-trivial co-routining. However, the SLD-Demo program **J** can easily be modified to allow for arbitrary control strategies.

3.3　The language Gödel and meta-programming

The Gödel language [Hill and Lloyd, 1994] is a logic programming language that facilitates meta-programming using the ground representation.

The provision is mainly focussed on the case where the object program is another Gödel program, although there are also some basic facilities for representing and manipulating expressions in any structured language.

One of the first problems encountered when using the ground representation is how to obtain a representation of a given object program and goals for that program. It can be seen from the example in Figure 7, that a ground representation of even a simple formula can be quite a large expression. Hence constructing, changing, or even just querying such an expression can require a large amount of program code. The Gödel system provides considerable system support for the constructing and querying of terms representing object Gödel expressions. By employing an abstract data type approach so that the representation is not made explicit, Gödel allows a user to ignore the details of the representation. Such an abstract data type approach makes the design and maintenance of the meta-programming facilities easier. Abstract data types are facilitated in Gödel by its type and module systems. Thus, in order to describe the meta-programming facilities of Gödel, a brief account of these systems is given.

Each constant, function, predicate, and proposition in a Gödel program must be specified by a language declaration. The type of a variable is not declared but inferred from its context within a particular program statement. To illustrate the type system, we give the language declarations that would be required for the program in Figure 1:

```
BASE       Name.
CONSTANT   Tom, Jerry : Name.
PREDICATE  Chase      : Name * Name;
           Cat, Mouse : Name.
```

Note that the declaration beginning BASE indicates that Name is a base type. In the statement

```
Chase(x,y) <- Cat(x) & Mouse(y).
```

the variables x and y are inferred to be of type Name.

Polymorphic types can also be defined in Gödel. They are constructed from the base types, type variables called parameters, and type constructors. Each constructor has an arity ≥ 1 attached to it. As an example, we give the language declarations for the non-logical symbols used in the (second variant) of the program in Figure 2.

```
CONSTRUCTOR List/1.
CONSTANT    Nil    : List(a).
FUNCTION    Cons   : a * List(a) -> List(a)
PREDICATE   Member : a * List(a).
```

Here List is declared to be a type constructor of arity 1. The type List(a) is a polymorphic type that can be used generically. Gödel provides the usual syntax for lists so that [] denotes Nil and [x|y] denotes Cons(x,y). Thus, if 1 and 2 have type Integer, [1,2] is a term of type List(Integer).

The Gödel module system is based on traditional software engineering ideas. A program is a collection of modules. Each module has at most two parts, an export part and a local part. The part and name of the module is indicated by the first line of the module. The statements can occur only in the local part. Symbols that are declared or imported into the export part of the module are available for use in both parts of the module and other modules that import it. Symbols that are declared or imported into the local part (but not into the export part) of the module can only be used in the local part. There are a number of module conditions that prevent accidental interference between different modules and facilitate the definition of an abstract data type.

An example of an abstract data type is illustrated in the Gödel program in Figure 8 which consists of two modules, UseADT and ADT. In UseADT, the

```
MODULE UseADT.
IMPORT ADT.


EXPORT ADT.
BASE H,K.
CONSTANT C,D : H.
PREDICATE P : H * K * K;
          Q : H * H.

LOCAL ADT.
CONSTANT E : K.
FUNCTION F : H * K -> K.
P(u,F(u,E),E).
Q(C,D).
```

Fig. 8. Defining an abstract data type in Gödel

type K, which is imported from ADT, is an abstract data type. If the query

`<- Q(x,D) & P(x,y,z).`

was given to UseADT, then the displayed answer would be:

```
x = C,
y = <K>,
z = <K>
```

The system modules include general purpose modules such as Integers, Lists, and Strings as well as the modules that give explicit support for meta-programming. Integers provides the integers and the usual arithmetic operations on the integers. `Lists` provides the standard list notation explained earlier in this subsection as well as the usual list processing predicates such as `Member` and `Append`. The module `Strings` makes available the standard double quote notation for sequences of (ascii) characters. There is no type for an individual ascii character except as a string of length one.

Gödel provides an abstract data type `Unit` defined in the module `Units`. A `Unit` is intended to represent a term-like data structure. The module `Flocks` imports the module `Units` and provides an abstract data type `Flock` which is an ordered collection of terms of type `Unit`. Since `Flocks` and `Units` do not provide any reflective predicates, they cannot be regarded as complete meta-programming modules. However, `Flocks` are useful tools for the manipulation of any object language whose syntax can be viewed as a sequence of units. Thus `Flocks` can be used as the basis of a meta-program that can choose the object programming system and its semantics.

The four system modules for meta-programming are `Syntax`, `Programs`, `Scripts`, and `Theories`. The modules `Programs`, `Scripts`, and `Theories` support the ground representation of Gödel programs, scripts, and theories, respectively. A script is a special form of a program where the module structure is collapsed. Since program transformations frequently violate the module structure, `Scripts` is mainly intended for meta-programs that perform program transformations. A theory is assumed to be defined using an extension of the Gödel syntax to allow for arbitrary first order formulas as the axioms of the theory. The fourth meta-programming module `Syntax` is imported by `Programs`, `Scripts`, and `Theories` and facilitates the manipulation of expressions in the object language. We describe briefly here the modules `Syntax` and `Programs`. The modules `Scripts` and `Theories` are similar to `Programs` and details of all the meta-programming modules can be found in [Hill and Lloyd, 1994].

The module `Syntax` defines abstract data types including `Name`, `Type`, `Term`, `Formula`, `TypeSubst`, `TermSubst`, and `VarTyping` which are the types of the representations of, respectively, the name of a symbol, a type, a term, a formula, a type substitution, a term substitution, and a variable typing. (A *variable typing* is a set of bindings where each binding consists of a variable together with the type assigned to that variable.)

The module `Syntax` provides a large number of predicates that support these abstract data types. Many of these are concerned with the representation and can be used to identify and construct representations of object expressions. For example, `And` is a predicate with three arguments of type `Formula` and is true if the third argument is a representation of the conjunction of the formulas represented in the first two arguments. `Variable` has a single argument of type `Term` and is true if its argument is the representation of a variable.

The predicate `Derive` is an example of a reflective predicate in `Syntax`. `Derive` has the declaration

```
PREDICATE   Derive : Formula * Formula * Formula * Formula *
                     Formula * TermSubst * Formula.
```

Given an atom of the form $\mathtt{Derive}(f_1, f_2, f_3, f_4, f_5, f_6, f_7)$, then this is true if r_1 is the resultant derived from a resultant r with selected atom a and statement s using mgu t. Here, r_1 is the resultant represented by f_7, r is the resultant whose head is represented by f_1 and whose body is a conjunction of the formulas represented by f_2, f_3, and f_4; a is the atom represented by f_3; s (whose variables are standardized apart from the variables in r) is the statement represented by f_5.

The module Programs imports the module Syntax and defines the abstract data type Program. Program is the type of a term representing a Gödel program.

As in the module Syntax, many of the predicates in Programs are concerned with the representation. Some actually relate the object language syntax with the representation. For example, there is a predicate StringToProgramType/4 with declaration

```
PREDICATE   StringToProgramType : Program * String * String *
                                  List(Type).
```

that converts a type (represented as a string) to a list of representations of this type. There may be more than one type corresponding to the string due to overloading of the names of the symbols in the object program. There are other predicates for manipulating the elements of the abstract data type Program directly. Thus DeleteStatement, which has the declaration

```
PREDICATE   DeleteStatement : Program * String * Formula *
                              Program.
```

removes a statement from the module named in the second argument from the object program represented in the first.

Finally, there are several reflective predicates. For example, Succeed, which has the declaration

```
PREDICATE   Succeed : Program * Formula * TermSubst.
```

is true when its first argument is the representation of an object program, its second argument is the representation of the body of a goal in the language of this program, and its third argument is the representation of a computed answer for this goal and this program. The predicate Succeed is the Gödel equivalent of the *Demo* predicate.

The SLD-Demo program in Figure 9 defines a predicate SLDDemo/3 using some of the system predicates of Syntax and Programs although the only reflective system predicate used is Derive from Syntax. The predicate SLDDemo/3 is defined for definite programs and goals with the usual left to right selection rule. By changing the above definition of MyAnd/3, SLD-resolution can be defined with arbitrary selection rules. The program provides a starting point for a variety of extensions.

```
EXPORT SLDDemo.

IMPORT Programs.
PREDICATE SLDDemo : Program * Formula * Formula.


LOCAL SLDDemo.

SLDDemo(prog, query, query1) <-
      IsImpliedBy(query, query, res) &
      EmptyFormula(empty) &
      SLDDemo1(prog, res, res1) &
      IsImpliedBy(query1, empty, res1).

PREDICATE SLDDemo1 : Program * Formula * Formula.
DELAY SLDDemo1(p,r,_) UNTIL NONVAR(p) & NONVAR(r).
SLDDemo1(_, res, res).
SLDDemo1(prog, res, res1) <-
      EmptyFormula(empty) &
      IsImpliedBy(head, body, res) &
      MyAnd(atom, rest, body) &
      StatementMatchAtom(prog, _, atom, clause) &
      Derive(head, empty, atom, rest, clause, _, newres) &
      SLDDemo1(prog, newres, res1).

PREDICATE MyAnd : Formula * Formula * Formula.
MyAnd(atom, rest, body) <-
      And(atom, rest, body) &
      Atom(atom).
MyAnd(body, empty, body) <-
      EmptyFormula(empty) &
      Atom(body).
```

Fig. 9. An SLD-Demo program using the Gödel meta-programming modules

Although the predicates in the system modules Syntax and Programs can be used to construct the representation of a Gödel expression, this method would not be practical for a complete Gödel program. For this reason, there is a utility in the Gödel system that constructs the ground representation of an object program (of type Program) and writes this to a file. There is another utility that obtains the re-representation of a term of type Program and writes it to the appropriate files.

```
MODULE TestSLDDemo.

IMPORT SLDDemo, ProgramsIO.

PREDICATE Go: String * String * String.
Go(prog_string, goal_string, goal1_string) <-
    FindInput(prog_string ++ ".prm", In(stream)) &
    GetProgram(stream, prog) &
    MainModuleInProgram(prog, module) &
    StringToProgramFormula(prog,module,goal_string,[goal]) &
    SLDDemo(prog, goal, goal1) &
    ProgramFormulaToString(prog,module,goal1,goal1_string).
```

Fig. 10. Gödel program for testing the SLD-Demo program

To read from or write to a file containing a program representation, there is a system module **ProgramsIO** which provides the appropriate input and output system predicates. For example, to run the SLD-Demo program in Figure 9, we can use the module in Figure 10. This assumes that a file containing the ground representation of a program exists. Given a file **Chase.prm** containing a representation of a Gödel version of the program in Figure 1, a query of the form

```
<- Go("Chase", "Chase(Tom, x)",y).
```

has the answer

```
y = "Chase(Tom, Jerry)".
```

4   Self-applicability

There are a number of meta-programs that can be applied to (copies of) themselves. In this section we review the motivation for this form of meta-programming and discuss the various degrees of self-applicability that can be achieved by these programs.

The usefulness of self-applicability was demonstrated by Gödel in [1931] where the natural numbers represent the axioms of arithmetic and some fundamental theorems about logic are derived using the properties of arithmetic. Perlis and Subrahmanian [1994] give a description of many of the general issues surrounding self-reference in logic and artificial intelligence together with a comprehensive bibliography. The concept of self-applicability has been used to construct many well-known logical paradoxes, one of the most famous being the *liar paradox*:

This sentence is false.

Here, we are concerned with programming applications of self-applicability and how particular programming languages support such applications.

If the languages of the object program and meta-program are kept *separate*, we can prevent the problems of self-reference illustrated by the liar paradox above while being able to express the syntactic form of self-reference given in

This sentence has five words.

by replacing the words "This sentence" by a representation of the sentence. Provided a representation of the meta-program can be included as a term in a goal for the meta-program and object provability is defined in the meta-program, the meta-program is self-applicable although the object language and the language of meta-program are kept strictly separate.

Many goals for the meta-program that can also be expressed as goals for the object language can be solved more efficiently using the object program rather than using their representation in the meta-program. In order that the meta-program can use the object program directly, the language $\mathcal{M}$ of the meta-program needs to include the object language $\mathcal{L}$. Assuming $\mathcal{L} \subseteq \mathcal{M}$, Bowen and Kowalski [1982] defined the *amalgamation* of $\mathcal{L}$ and $\mathcal{M}$ to be the language $\mathcal{M}$ together with

- at least one ground term in $\mathcal{M}$ representing each term and formula of $\mathcal{L}$,

- a representation of the provability relation in $\mathcal{L}$ by means of a predicate in $\mathcal{M}$ (in the context of a set of sentences of $\mathcal{M}$), and

- linking rules for communicating goals and computed answers between the object language and its representation.

An amalgamation is said to be *strong* if the languages $\mathcal{L}$ and $\mathcal{M}$ are the same. Bowen and Kowalski [1982] showed that self-referential sentences were possible in this logic. They constructed a sentence J that asserts of itself that it is underivable. They show that neither J nor $\neg J$ is derivable in the logic so that J is clearly true. This establishes an incompleteness result for the amalgamated language. If $\mathcal{L}$ is a proper subset of $\mathcal{M}$, then the amalgamation is said to be *weak*. As we are not aware of any logic programming systems that allow the object language and language of the meta-program to be completely identified, only the weak form of amalgamation is discussed in this chapter.

4.1   Separated meta-programming

Normally, a self-applicable meta-program reasons about a copy of itself. This can be achieved with both the non-ground and ground representations, described in Sections 2 and 3. By using the meta-program as the object program for another meta-program, meta-meta-programs and higher towers of meta-programs can be constructed.

For example, the Instance-Demo program **I** given in Figure 5 can be applied to the representation of any normal logic program. Thus, as **I** is itself a normal program, **I** can be applied to a representation of itself. This is achieved by giving **I** a goal of the form:

$\leftarrow IDemo(\lceil\mathbf{I}\rceil, \lceil goal\rceil, g)$

where *goal* is the goal in Figure 7. We do not give the actual representation of **I** or $\lceil goal\rceil$ here, since these terms are large. This difficulty illustrates two of the problems of using towers of meta-programs. The terms used to represent the object program and goal are large and complex and also, because of the added structural information encoded in the terms, processing them is much less efficient than that using the original object code. This issue is discussed more fully in Section 6.

The Gödel system assumes that self-applicable meta-programs are separated. Utilities and certain IO predicates are provided for obtaining the representation and re-representation of a Gödel program. However, apart from these non-declarative facilities, there is no direct access to the object program from a meta-program. In contrast, in Prolog, the object program must be present in the meta-program in order to obtain its representation.

Self-application using separated meta-programming has many applications and is, we believe, the most useful form of self-applicability. In particular; interpreters, compilers, program analysers, program transformers, program debuggers, and program specializers can be usefully applied to themselves. In Section 3, we explained how the programming system Gödel provided support for meta-programming using the ground representation. This system has been designed so that self-applicable meta-programs can be developed. Towers of two or even three levels of program specializers have been achieved using the Gödel system although much work needs to be done to improve their efficiency [Gurr, 1993]. Section 6 explains how compilers and even compiler generators can be generated automatically from program specializers using self-application.

4.2 Amalgamated meta-programming

It is often desirable that not only should the object language be part of the meta-language but also, the object program be actually included in the meta-program. Hence we extend the above definition of weak amalgamation of languages to programs. We say that a meta-program is *amalgamated* if the languages of the meta-program and its object program are weakly amalgamated and the statements of the object program are included as part of the meta-program. With an amalgamated meta-program, a query for the meta-program that represents a query in the object language can be defined directly using the object program. For example, if P is a proposition in the object language represented by the constant P' in the language of the meta-program, then we could have a statement in the meta-program of the form:

$Demo(ThisProgram, P') \leftarrow P.$

In this example and in the examples below, *ThisProgram* is a constant in the meta-language that refers to the (ground) representation of an object program which is included in the meta-program.

A basic requirement for amalgamated meta-programming is that the semantics of the object program must be preserved. That is, the predicates defined in the object program must have the same definition in the amalgamated meta-program so that a goal written in the object language must be a logical consequence of the object program if and only if it is a logical consequence of the amalgamated meta-program.

In order to realize the advantages of amalgamated programming, there has to be a means by which the object program and its representation can communicate. Bowen and Kowalski define the following *linking rules* that should be satisfied by the reflective predicate *Demo*/2 in the amalgamated program for every formula B in the object program.

$$\frac{A \vdash B}{Pr \vdash Demo(\lceil A \rceil, \lceil B \rceil)} \qquad\qquad \frac{Pr \vdash Demo(\lceil A \rceil, \lceil B \rceil)}{A \vdash B}$$

These or similar rules are necessary for communication between the object program and its representation in the amalgamated meta-program.

To facilitate these linking rules, a means of computing the re-representation of the terms representing the terms of the object language must be provided. Also, a method for finding the representation of an object term is required. This *reflective requirement*, which concerns only the terms of the object language, may be realized by means of inference rules, functions, or relations. In each case, we consider how the predicate *Demo*/2 whose semantics is given by the above linking rules may be defined for the atomic formulas. The definition of *Demo*/2 for the non-atomic formulas is the same in every case. Thus, for formulas that are conjunctions of literals, the definition of *Demo*/2 would include the following clauses.

$Demo(p, a \wedge' b) \leftarrow Demo(p, a) \wedge Demo(p, b)$
$Demo(p, \neg'a) \leftarrow \neg Demo(p, a)$

where $\wedge'$ represents $\wedge$ and $\neg'$ represents $\neg$.

If the reflective requirement is realized by means of inference rules, then these must be built into the programming system. Thus the representation must also be fixed by the programming system. The inference rule that determines t from a term $\lceil t \rceil$ must first check that $\lceil t \rceil$ is ground and that it represents an object level term and secondly, if the object language is typed, that t is correctly typed in this language. The set of statements of the form

$Demo(\textit{ThisProgram}, P'(\lceil x_1 \rceil, \ldots, \lceil x_n \rceil)) \leftarrow P(x_1, \ldots, x_n)$

for each predicate P/n in the object language represented by a function P'/n in the language of the meta-program will provide a definition of

Demo/2 for the atomic formulas. Note that the x_i are universally quantified variables, quantified over the terms of the object language.

Note that, as the trivial naming relation is built into Prolog, the representation is trivially determined by means of an inference rule. However, there is no check that $\lceil t \rceil$ is ground before applying the inference rule. Reflective Prolog [Costantini and Lanzarone, 1989] (see below), is an example of a language with a non-trivial naming relation, but where the representation and re-representation are determined by inference rules.

If a re-representation was defined functionally, the meta-program would require a function such as *ReRepresent*/1. Thus, for each ground term t in the object language, the equality theory for the meta-program must satisfy

$$ReRepresent(\lceil t \rceil) = t$$

As this is part of a logic programming system where the equality theory is normally fixed by the unification procedure and constraint handling mechanisms, the evaluation method for this function would be built-in so that the representation would again be fixed by the programming system. Using this function, the definition of *Demo*/2 for the atomic formulas is given by a set of statements of the form

$Demo(ThisProgram, P'(y_1, \ldots, y_n)) \leftarrow$
$\qquad P(ReRepresent(y_1), \ldots, ReRepresent(y_n))$

for each predicate P/n in the object program.

For logic programming, the most flexible way in which a representation may be defined is as a relation, say *Represent*/2, where the first argument is an object term and the second its representation.

$Represent(t, \lceil t \rceil)$.

Then the definition of *Demo*/2, for each predicate P/n in the object language, would consist of a statement of the form

$Demo(ThisProgram, P'(y_1, \ldots, y_n)) \leftarrow$
$\qquad Represent(x_1, y_1) \wedge \ldots \wedge Represent(x_n, y_n) \wedge$
$\qquad P(x_1, \ldots, x_n)$

The predicate *Represent*/2 could be defined by the user and hence, as discussed in Subsection 3.1, can be chosen to suit a particular application. Thus, for the Member program in Figure 2, we would have the statement

$Demo(ThisProgram, Member'(y_1, \ldots, y_n)) \leftarrow$
$\qquad Represent(x_1, y_1) \wedge \ldots \wedge Represent(x_n, y_n) \wedge$
$\qquad Member(x_1, \ldots, x_n)$

For this example, the definition of *Represent*/2 would include the clauses

$Represent(Nil', Nil)$
$Represent(Cons'(x1, y1), Cons(x, y)) \leftarrow$
$\qquad Represent(x1, x) \wedge$
$\qquad Represent(y1, y)$

In Sections 2 and 3, we gave meta-programs that defined reflective predicates entirely at the meta-level. We have now shown that, if the meta-program is amalgamated, these reflective predicates can be defined using the object program directly. Usually, a combination of these two methods is preferred since the approach that executes a re-representation is usually more efficient, but the explicit representation of the procedural semantics provides greater flexibility. The level at which the explicit definition of the procedural semantics of the object programming system is replaced by a call to the object program using the re-representation determines the granularity of the interpreter. The greater the detail at which the procedure is defined explicitly, the greater the degree of granularity. Clearly efficiency will be decreased with increasing granularity.

Amalgamation not only facilitates greater computational efficiency for meta-programs but also provides an environment that allows interaction between the actual knowledge and the methods for reasoning about this knowledge. In particular, with an amalgamated language, not only can predicates at the meta-level be defined using object-level predicates, but also object-level predicates can use meta-level predicates in their definitions. A classic example of an application of this (taken from [Bowen and Kowalski, 1982]) is the coding of the legal rule that a person is innocent unless he or she is proven guilty.

$$Innocent(x) \leftarrow \neg Demo(ThisProgram, Guilty'(y)) \land$$
$$Represent(x, y).$$

An amalgamation can facilitate towers of meta-programming. For example, a meta-program can include the statement

$$Demo(ThisProgram, Demo'(ThisProgram, y)) \leftarrow$$
$$Represent(x, y) \land$$
$$Demo(ThisProgram, x).$$

where the predicate $Demo/2$ is represented by the function $Demo'/2$.

Note that at each meta-level, the definition of the predicate $Represent/2$ must be extended with the constants and functions of the previous meta-level. Suppose, for example, each meta-level uses an additional quote to represent the previous lower level. Then, just to represent the representation of the Member program in Figure 2, the following clauses would need to be added to the above definition of $Represent/2$.

$$Represent(Nil'', Nil')$$
$$Represent(Cons''(x1, y1), Cons'(x, y)) \leftarrow$$
$$Represent(x1, x) \land$$
$$Represent(y1, y)$$
$$Represent(Member''(x1, y1), Member'(x, y)) \leftarrow$$
$$Represent(x1, x) \land$$
$$Represent(y1, y)$$

At the next (third) meta-level, not only would the representation of Nil'', $Cons''/2$, and $Member''/2$ have to be defined by $Represent/2$ but also the representation of the function $Demo'/2$.

Each meta-level in a program could contain the representations of several programs at the previous level. The relationships between the different meta-levels in a program are sometimes called its *meta-level architecture*. The usual architectures in which each meta-level reasons about only one object program at the next lower level might be said to be "linear".

As the representation has to be explicitly defined using $Demo/2$ and $Represent/2$, there is always a top-most meta-level. This will contain symbols with no representation. Hence, without any 'higher-order' entensions, logic programming cannot be used for the strong form of amalgamation.

One of the problems of this amalgamation is that the representation needs to be made explicit. In the previous discussion, a representation of the symbols is given and then a representation of the terms and formulas is constructed in the standard way. However, it is often more convenient to hide the details of the representation from the programmer. Quine [1951] introduced the 'quasi-quotes' already used in this chapter to indicate a representation of some unspecified object expression. This (or similar syntax) can be used instead of an explicit representation. For example,

$\lceil Cons(x, Nil) \rceil$

would correspond (using the above representation) to the term

$Cons'(V(0), Nil')$

where $V(0)$ is the (ground) representation of x.

This syntax is not constructive. That is, there is no direct means of constructing larger expressions from their components. Note that, in the Gödel programming system, the use of abstract data types for meta-programming has a similar problem.

The main reason that terms representing object-level expressions have to be constructed dynamically is because the structure of components of these expressions may not be fully specified. The unspecified subexpressions are defined by variables that range not over the object terms but over the representations of arbitrary object expressions. Such variables are called *meta-variables*. Thus, instead of a programming system providing predicates for constructing terms representing object expressions, the syntax may distinguish between meta-variables and variables ranging over the object level terms. The partially specified object expression can then be enclosed in the quasi-quotes but those meta-variables that occur within their scope must be syntactically identifiable using some *escape* notation. For example, if the *escape* notation is an overline, $\overline{x}$ indicates that in the context of $\lceil \cdots \rceil$ x is a meta-variable. For example,

$\lceil Cons(\overline{x}, Nil) \rceil$

would correspond (using the above representation) to the term

$Cons'(x, Nil')$

where the x ranges over the terms in the language of the Member program. Moreover, $\lceil \overline{x} \rceil$ is equivalent to the meta-variable x[5]. With this notation, the clause in the definition of $Demo/2$ that defines the representation of $Member/2$ is as follows.

$Demo(\mathit{ThisProgram}, \lceil Member(\overline{x_1}, \ldots, \overline{x_n}) \rceil) \leftarrow$
$\qquad Member(x_1, \ldots, x_n).$

As explained in the previous subsection, Gödel is not intended for amalgamated meta-programming and provides no support for this. Prolog meta-programming facilities force the object program and a meta-program to be amalgamated but the actual switching between the object level and meta-level has to be programmed explicitly. In addition, most of the meta-programming facilities of Prolog are not declarative whereas the intention of using amalgamated meta-programs for representing knowledge is to provide a declarative representation of this knowledge.

A programming system called *Reflective Prolog* [Costantini and Lanzarone, 1989], [Costantini, 1990] is intended for amalgamated reasoning. In this language, the representation of the constants, functions, and predicates is defined by specially annotating the corresponding object symbols. There are three different kinds of variables: object variables, predicate meta-variables, and function meta-variables. The rules of substitution ensure that these may only be substituted by, respectively, an object term, a representation of a predicate, and a representation of a function. There are syntactic restrictions to keep the meta-levels distinct and prevent self-reference within a single atom. In addition to the object level and different meta-levels, a reflective Prolog program distinguishes between the meta-evaluation level and the base level. The meta-evaluation level is at the top of the meta-level architecture and includes a distinguished predicate Solve. The base level, containing an amalgamated theory, comprises the remaining meta-levels below it and cannot refer to any predicates in the meta-evaluation level. Procedurally, a definite Reflective Prolog program uses SLD-resolution whenever possible but automatically switches between the base level and meta-evaluation level in certain circumstances. The declarative semantics for such programs, called the *Least Reflective Herbrand Model*, is an adapted form of the well-known least Herbrand model.

A new system for amalgamated meta-programming called Alloy is described by Barklund [1995]. This system, which uses a syntax based on the

---

[5]This differs from Quine's notation where he uses x, y, z etc., to indicate the object variables (in his case, quantified over numbers) and Greek letters to indicate the meta-variables. Using this notation, $\lceil \mu \rceil = \mu$. The disadvantage of this notation is that only two levels are defined and these are assumed to be separated. There is no provision for more than two levels or for amalgamating the meta-levels.

quasi-quote and escape notation described above, is similar to and largely inspired by the ideas in Reflective Prolog. Alloy differs from Reflective Prolog in that it provides explicit support for the ground representation and for facilitating the definition of multiple meta-levels.

Towers of meta-programs and more general meta-level architectures have been shown to be useful in a number of areas. These include software engineering and legal reasoning. Software engineering defines methodologies for program development independent of any particular programming language or application. Tools for supporting these methodologies may distinguish three levels of reasoning. The object level is the application domain. Given the pre-conditions and post-conditions, the first meta-level defines what the program is intended to compute. Finally, the top-most meta-level defines a formalization of correct program development. More details concerning this application are given in [Dunin-Keplicz, 1994]. It is known that legal knowledge has a number of reasoning layers. For example, there may be a several primary legal rules that are intended for distinct situations. Then secondary rules specify when the primary rules are applicable, how to interpret them, or even how to construct new primary rules. In law, such techniques are often applied repeatedly, so that tertiary rules can be defined as meta-rules for the secondary rules and similarly for higher rules. It is shown in [Barklund and Hamfelt, 1994] that these layers can be put in a one-to one correspondence with the meta-levels of an amalgamated meta-program.

4.3 Ambivalent logic

The flexibility of the trivial naming relation with the non-ground representation in Prolog has encouraged a certain style of meta-programming to be adopted by Prolog programmers. However, first order logic does not provide many Prolog meta-programs with a declarative semantics. For example, a useful feature of Prolog allows an ambivalent syntax where terms and atoms are not distinguished except by their context in the clause, while substitution for variables is purely syntactic. Thus, expressions such as

```
demo(demo(X)) :- demo(X)
demo(X) :- X
```

are allowed. The first of these is easily explained as overloading the name demo as both a function and predicate symbol. The second of these can be understood as a schema for clauses of the form

$$demo(t) \leftarrow t$$

where the argument t is a ground term representing the ground formula t on the right of the arrow. However, the concept of a schema takes the semantics beyond that of first order logic.

There have been a number of proposals for extending first order logic with limited higher order features that may provide these aspects of Prolog with a semantics. Chen *et al.* [1993] have developed the logic Hilog. This is intended to give a logical basis for Prolog's ambivalent syntax. However, although Hilog does not distinguish between functions, predicates, terms, and atoms, it does not (as in Prolog) allow variables to range over arbitrary expressions in the language. Hilog is intended to provide a basis for a new logic programming system similar to Prolog but based on the logic of Hilog. Richards [1974] has defined an ambivalent logic that allows formulas to be treated as terms but not vice-versa. Another *ambivalent logic* is developed by Jiang [1994]. This employs features from both Richards' logic and Hilog. In Jiang's logic, there is no syntactic distinction between functions, predicates, terms, and formulas. Moreover, the semantics distinguishes between substitution (which is purely syntactic) and equality. The main purpose of this logic is to provide an expressive syntax for self-reference together with a suitable extension of first order logic for its semantics. However, it has also been used to show that the Vanilla program $\mathbf{V}_P$ in Section 2 (without the third clause that interprets negative formulas) has the intended semantics.

5   Dynamic meta-programming

We consider three forms of dynamic meta-programming: constructing a program using predefined components, updating a program, and transforming or synthesizing a program.

5.1   Constructing programs

The simplest and least dynamic means of creating a program is by combining program components called *modules* to form the complete program. There are several applications which require such a modular approach to programming. These include: the re-use of existing software; the development of programs incrementally; non-monotonic reasoning; and object-orientation with inheritance.

A number of operators that may be used to construct a complete program from a set of modules are defined in [Brogi *et al.*, 1990]. These form a sort of "command shell" for building new programs out of existing ones. In [Brogi *et al.*, 1992], it is shown how meta-programming techniques using the non-ground representation, can be used to define and implement these operators. We discuss here the use of meta-programming for two of the operators, union $\cup$ and intersection $\cap$. To explain these, we assume that there is a type *Module* for terms representing sets of clauses, a set of constants of type *Module* representing the sets of clauses that form the initial program components for constructing complete programs, and binary infix operators $\cap$ and $\cup$ with type *Module* $*$ *Module* $\rightarrow$ *Module*. Let P_1 and P_2 be two terms of type *Module*. Then:

$P_1 \cup P_2$ represents the module obtained by putting the clauses of modules

P_1 and P_2 together.

$P_1 \cap P_2$ represents the module consisting of all clauses defined in the following way:

If $\quad p(t_1, \ldots, t_n) \leftarrow B_1 \qquad$ is in the module represented by P_1,
$\quad\quad p(u_1, \ldots, u_n) \leftarrow B_2 \qquad$ is in the module represented by P_2,
and $\quad \theta$ is an mgu for $\{p(t_1, \ldots, t_n), p(u_1, \ldots, u_n)\}$,
then $p(t_1, \ldots, t_n)\theta \leftarrow B_1\theta, B_2\theta \quad$ is in the module represented by $P_1 \cap P_2$[6].

In the non-ground representation described in Section 2, the object program is represented in the meta-program by the definition of the predicate *Clause/2*. With this representation, a declarative meta-program cannot modify the (representation of) the object program. However, by adding an extra argument with type *Module* and replacing *Clause/2* by *OClause/3*, we can include in the representation of a clause the name of the module in which it occurs. Any expression formed from module names, and the operators $\cup$ and $\cap$ is called a *program term*. For example, given the facts:

OClause(P, *Cat*(*Tom*), *True*)
OClause(P, *Mouse*(*Jerry*), *True*)
OClause(Q, *Chase*(x, y), *Cat*(x) *And Mouse*(y))

for modules named P and Q, the program term $P \cup Q$ represents the Chase program in Figure 1. Moreover, with the set of facts:

OClause($P1$, *Cat*(*Tom*), *True*)
OClause($P1$, *Mouse*(*Jerry*), *True*)
OClause($P1$, *Chase*(x, y), *Cat*(x))
OClause($Q1$, *Cat*(*Tom*), *True*)
OClause($Q1$, *Mouse*(*Jerry*), *True*)
OClause($Q1$, *Chase*(x, y), *Mouse*(y))

for modules named $P1$ and $Q1$, the program term $P1 \cap Q1$ also represents the Chase program.

The operators $\cup$ and $\cap$ can be defined by extending program **V** in Figure 3 to give the Operator-Vanilla program **O** in Figure 11. As the operators have only been defined here in the case of definite programs, **O** does not have a clause for interpreting negative literals. Given a set of modules R, the program $\mathbf{O}_R$ consists of the program **O** together with the set of facts extending the definition of *OClause* and representing the modules in R.

The following result was proved in [Brogi *et al.*, 1992].

Theorem 5.1.1. *Let P and Q be object programs. Then, for any ground atom A in the object language,*

- $\mathbf{O}_{P,Q} \vdash OSolve(P \cup Q, A)$ *iff A is a logical consequence of $P \cup Q$*

---

[6]We assume that the statements are standardized apart so that they have no variables in common.

$OSolve(p, True)$
$OSolve(p, (b \; And \; c)) \leftarrow$
       $OSolve(p, b) \land$
       $OSolve(p, c)$
$OSolve(p, a) \leftarrow$
       $OClause(p, a, b) \land$
       $OSolve(p, b)$

$OClause(p \cup q, a, b) \leftarrow$
       $OClause(p, a, b)$
$OClause(p \cup q, a, b) \leftarrow$
       $OClause(q, a, b)$
$OClause(p \cap q, a, (b \; And \; c)) \leftarrow$
       $OClause(p, a, b) \land$
       $OClause(q, a, c)$

Fig. 11. The Operator-Vanilla interpreter **O**

- $\mathbf{O}_{P,Q} \vdash OSolve(P \cap Q, A)$ iff A is a logical consequence of $P \cap Q$

For example, given the program in Figure 11 together with the above clauses representing the Chase program, the goals

$\leftarrow OSolve(P \cup Q, Chase(x, y))$
$\leftarrow OSolve(P1 \cap Q1, Chase(x, y))$

would both succeed with computed answer

$x = Tom, \; y = Jerry.$

Composing programs with operators allows for programs to be only partly specified. The following result was proved in [Brogi *et al.*, 1990].

Theorem 5.1.2. *Let P be a (possibly non-ground) program term and G represent a goal for the program. Assume that the goal $\leftarrow OSolve(P, G)$ succeeds with computed answer θ. Then the goal represented by $G\theta$ can be proved in the program represented by any ground instance of $P\theta$.*

For example, given the program in Figure 11 together with the above clauses representing the Chase program, the goal

$\leftarrow OSolve(P \cup q, Chase(x, y))$

would succeed with computed answers

$q = Q, \; x = Tom, \; y = Jerry;$
$q = Q \cup v, \; x = Tom, \; y = Jerry;$
$\vdots$

5.2 Updating programs

A meta-program can modify an object program by inserting and removing statements. This form of meta-programming has many applications such as hypothetical reasoning, knowledge assimilation, and abduction. For example, in hypothetical reasoning, additional axioms are included as temporary hypotheses during a subcomputation. In knowledge assimilation, the program defining the current knowledge base has to be updated by the addition or deletion of clauses. These changes are usually constrained to satisfy certain integrity constraints as well as to cause minimal changes to the original knowledge base. Abductive reasoning is similar to the previous application except, in this case, only new facts may be added to the object program and no clauses may be deleted. Normally, there is an additional restriction that there is a predefined set of predicates called *abducibles* and the added facts must (partly) define an abducible predicate.

For these applications, it is necessary, if the meta-program is to be declarative, that the object program be represented as a term in the goal to the meta-program. Moreover, as first order logic does not allow quantifiers in terms, a ground representation must be used.

For knowledge assimilation, the changes to the object program are normally global and permanent. Thus, in the case of knowledge assimilation, it is particularly important that no unnecessary changes are made and the new knowledge base remains consistent. In [Kowalski, 1994], the problem of adding a statement S to the database D is discussed in detail. Four cases are described:

1. S is a logical consequence of D
2. $D = D_1 \cup D_2$ and D_2 is a logical consequence of $D_1 \cup \{S\}$.
3. S is inconsistent with D.
4. None of the relationships (1)–(3) holds.

It is assumed here that the knowledge base is a normal logic program whose semantics is taken to be its completion. In this case it is not appropriate to include the consistency checks (since all new facts will be inconsistent with the completion). Thus we only consider cases 1 and 2, and a third case when 1 and 2 do not hold. The program in Figure 12 defining the predicate *Assimilate*/3 (which is based on the program in [Kowalski, 1990]) shows how these requirements may be realized in logic programming using meta-programming techniques. To simplify the example, we have assumed that only facts may be added or removed. The program uses the representation given in Section 3, where the object program is represented by a list of terms representing the statements of the object program. The program also requires a definition of the reflective predicate *Demo* such as that of *IDemo* given in Figure 5 or *JDemo* given in Figure 6. The types of *Assimilate*/3 and *Remove*/2 are as follows.

$Assimilate(kb, s, kb) \leftarrow$
    $Demo(kb, s, \_)$
$Assimilate(kb, s, newkb) \leftarrow$
    $Remove(If(a, True), kb, kb1) \wedge$
    $Demo([If(s, True)|kb1], a, \_) \wedge$
    $Assimilate(kb1, s, newkb)$
$Assimilate(kb, s, [If(s, True)|kb]) \leftarrow$
    $\neg Demo(kb, s, \_) \wedge$
    $\neg(\exists a \exists kb1(Remove(If(a, True), kb, kb1) \wedge$
        $Demo([If(s, True)|kb1], a, \_)))$

$Remove(x, [x|xs], xs)$
$Remove(x, [\_|ys], zs) \leftarrow$
    $Remove(x, ys, zs)$

Fig. 12. Assimilating a ground fact into a database

Predicate	Type
Assimilate	$List(\mu) * \mu * List(\mu)$
Remove	$\mu * List(\mu) * List(\mu)$

$Remove/3$ is true if the first argument is an element of the list in the second argument and the third argument is obtained by removing this element.

It is natural to require certain integrity constraints to hold when facts are added to or removed from a knowledge base. These constraints are formulas that should be logical consequences of (the completion of) the updated knowledge base. A set of integrity constraints may be represented as a list of terms. Each term representing an integrity constraint from the set. The assimilation with integrity constraint checking is illustrated in Figure 13. This defines the predicate *AssimilateWithIC/4*.

Predicate	Type
AssimilateWithIC	$List(\mu) * List(\mu) * \mu * List(\mu)$

The first argument of *AssimilateWithIC/4* is the representation of the set of integrity constraints. If the knowledge base, consisting of the initial knowledge base (represented by the second argument) together with the fact which is to be assimilated (represented in the third argument), satisfies the integrity constraints (represented in the first argument), then the *Assimilate* predicate, defined in Figure 12, is called to update the knowledge base. The fourth argument of *AssimilateWithIC/4* contains the representation of the updated knowledge base.

As indicated in Section 3, the first logic programming system to provide declarative facilities for updating logic programs based on a ground repre-

$AssimilateWithIC([ic|ics], kb, s, newkb) \leftarrow$
$\quad Demo([If(s, True)|kb], ic, \_) \land$
$\quad AssimilateWithIC(ics, kb, s, newkb)$
$AssimilateWithIC([\,], kb, s, newkb) \leftarrow$
$\quad Assimilate(kb, s, newkb)$

Fig. 13. Checking integrity constraints

sentation was Meta-Prolog [Bowen and Weinberg, 1985]. However, it was built as an extension to Prolog so that it also inherited the non-declarative facilities of Prolog. The system Gödel, described in Subsection 3.3, provides considerable support for updating the theory of a program using its ground representation. For example, the system module Programs defines predicates InsertStatement/4 and DeleteStatement/4 for adding a statement to and removing a statement from a module in a program.

5.3 The three wise men problem

We illustrate the use of meta-programming for hypothetical reasoning by means of a well-known problem, *the three wise men*. This problem has been much studied by researchers in meta-reasoning and it is thought appropriate to show here how the standard techniques of meta-programming in logic programming can be used to solve this problem.

The three wise men puzzle is as follows. A king, wishing to find out which of his three wise men is the wisest, puts a hat on each of their heads and tells them that each hat is either black or white and at least one of the hats is white. The king does this in such a way that each wise man can see the hats of the other wise men, but not his own. In fact, each wise man has a white hat on. The king then successively asks each wise man if he knows the colour of his own hat. The first wise man answers "I don't know", as does the second. Then the third announces that his hat is white.

The reasoning of the third wise man is as follows. "Suppose my hat is black. Then the second wise man would see a black hat and a white hat, and would reason that, if his hat is black, the first wise man would see two black hats and hence would conclude that his hat is white since he knows that at least one of the hats is white. But the second wise man said he didn't know the colour of his hat. Hence my hat must be white."

The solution below, using pure logic programming, is intended to illustrate the use of meta-programming for hypothetical reasoning. In this solution, the king uses his knowledge to simulate the reasoning of the three wise men ($W1$, $W2$, $W3$). The king assumes that the third wise man uses his reasoning to simulate the reasoning of the second wise man and hence of the first. We use the ground representation given in Subsection 3.1 and assumed by the programs in Figures 5, 6, and 13. The constants and predicates used for the king's and wise men's knowledge bases together with their representation is as follows.

Object symbol	Representation
Black	$C(0)$
White	$C(1)$
*W*1	$C(11)$
*W*2	$C(12)$
*W*3	$C(13)$
Hat/2	$P(1)$
DontKnow/1	$P(2)$
Hear/2	$P(3)$
See/2	$P(4)$
DiffColor/2	$P(5)$
Same/2	$P(6)$

The predicate *Demo* is defined as either *IDemo* in Figure 5 or *JDemo* in Figure 6. *AssimilateWithIC* is defined in Figure 13. The knowledge of the king and his wise men consists of sets of normal clauses represented by a list of representations of these clauses in some order. There are two initial knowledge bases. One contains knowledge common to all the men.

Hat(*W*3, *White*) ← *Hat*(*W*2, *Black*) ∧ *Hat*(*W*1, *Black*)
Hat(*W*2, *White*) ← *Hat*(*W*1, *Black*) ∧ *Hat*(*W*3, *Black*)
Hat(*W*1, *White*) ← *Hat*(*W*3, *Black*) ∧ *Hat*(*W*2, *Black*)
Hear(*W*3, *W*2)
Hear(*W*3, *W*1)
Hear(*W*2, *W*1)
See(*x*, *y*) ← ¬*Same*(*x*, *y*)
DiffColor(*White*, *Black*)
DiffColor(*Black*, *White*)
Same(*x*, *x*)

This is represented by the single fact defining the predicate *CommonKb*/1.

CommonKb([
        If(*Atom*(*P*(1), [*C*(13), *C*(1)]),
          And(*Atom*(*P*(1), [*C*(12), *C*(0)]), *Atom*(*P*(1), [*C*(11), *C*(0)]))),
        If(*Atom*(*P*(1), [*C*(12), *C*(1)]),
          And(*Atom*(*P*(1), [*C*(11), *C*(0)]), *Atom*(*P*(1), [*C*(13), *C*(0)]))),
        If(*Atom*(*P*(1), [*C*(11), *C*(1)]),
          And(*Atom*(*P*(1), [*C*(13), *C*(0)]), *Atom*(*P*(1), [*C*(12), *C*(0)]))),
        If(*Atom*(*P*(3), [*C*(13), *C*(12)]), *True*),
        If(*Atom*(*P*(3), [*C*(13), *C*(11)]), *True*),
        If(*Atom*(*P*(3), [*C*(12), *C*(11)]), *True*),
        If(*Atom*(*P*(4), [*V*(1), *V*(2)]), *Not*(*Atom*(*P*(6), [*V*(1), *V*(2)]))),
        If(*Atom*(*P*(5), [*C*(1), *C*(0)]), *True*),

$$If(Atom(P(5), [C(0), C(1)]), True),$$
$$If(Atom(P(6), [V(1), V(1)]), True)$$
])

In addition to the above common knowledge base, the men will have certain commonly held constraints on what combination of knowledge is acceptable. As an example of such a constraint, we assume that all men know that a hat cannot be both black and white.

$$\neg(Hat(w, Black) \wedge Hat(w, White))$$

This can be represented in the fact defining the predicate *CommonIC*/1.

$CommonIC([$
   $Not(And($
    $Atom(P(1), [V(11), C(0)]),$
    $Atom(P(1), [V(11), C(1)]))))$
  ]).

The other knowledge base contains a list of facts describing the king's knowledge about the state of the world.

$Hat(W1, White)$
$Hat(W2, White)$
$Hat(W3, White)$
$DontKnow(W1)$
$DontKnow(W2)$

This is represented by the fact defining the predicate *KingKb*/1.

$KingKb([$
    $If(Atom(P(1), [C(11), C(1)]), True),$
    $If(Atom(P(1), [C(12), C(1)]), True),$
    $If(Atom(P(1), [C(13), C(1)]), True),$
    $If(Atom(P(2), [C(12)]), True),$
    $If(Atom(P(2), [C(11)]), True)$
  ])

The king and the wise men can use only their own knowledge when simulating other men's reasoning. The key to their reasoning is defined by the predicate *LocalKb*/3. Given the name of a wise man and a current knowledge base in the first and second arguments, respectively, then *LocalKb*/3 will be true if the third argument is bound to the part of the knowledge base of the wise man which is contained in the current knowledge base.

$$LocalKb(w, kb, localkb) \leftarrow LocalKb1(w, kb, kb, localkb)$$

The predicate *LocalKb*/3 calls *LocalKb1*/4. This predicate requires an extra copy of the initial knowledge base so that it can process all clauses represented by elements of the list and determine which should be included in the new knowledge base.

$LocalKb1(\_,\_,[],[])$
$LocalKb1(w,ikb,[k|kb],[k|lkb]) \leftarrow$
    $CommonKb(ckb) \wedge$
    $Member(k,ckb) \wedge$
    $LocalKb1(w,ikb,kb,lkb)$
$LocalKb1(w,ikb,[If(Atom(P(1),[w1,c]),True)|kb],$
        $[If(Atom(P(1),[w1,c]),True)|lkb]) \leftarrow$
    $Demo(ikb,Atom(P(4),[w,w1]),\_) \wedge$
    $LocalKb1(w,ikb,kb,lkb)$
$LocalKb1(w,ikb,[If(Atom(P(1),[w1,\_]),True)|kb],$
        $lkb) \leftarrow$
    $\neg Demo(ikb,Atom(P(4),[w,w1]),\_) \wedge$
    $LocalKb1(w,ikb,kb,ikb,lkb)$
$LocalKb1(w,ikb,[If(Atom(P(2),[w1]),True)|kb],$
        $[If(Atom(P(2),[w1]),True)|lkb]) \leftarrow$
    $Demo(ikb,Atom(P(3),[w,w1]),\_) \wedge$
    $LocalKb1(w,ikb,kb,lkb)$
$LocalKb1(w,ikb,[If(Atom(P(2),[w1]),True)|kb],$
        $lkbs) \leftarrow$
    $\neg Demo(ikb,Atom(P(3),[w,w1]),\_) \wedge$
    $LocalKb1(w,ikb,kbs,lkb)$

There are six statements defining *LocalKb1/4*. The first is the base case. The second ensures that common knowledge is included in the wise man's knowledge. The third (resp., fourth) deals with the case where the wise man can (resp., cannot) see a hat and the colour is known. The fifth (resp., sixth) deals with the case where the wise man can (resp., cannot) hear another man and that man says he doesn't know.

The predicate *Reason/3* simulates the reasoning of the men. Either the man in the first argument reasons that the colour of his hat is white because he believes the other two hats are black, or, if he has heard another wise man say "I do not know the colour of my hat", he hypothesises a colour for his own hat and by simulating the other man's reasoning, tries to obtain a contradiction. The predicate *AssimilateWithIC* checks that no integrity constraints are violated by the extra hypothesis.

$Reason(kb,w,c) \leftarrow$
    $Demo(kb,Atom(P(1),[w,V(1)]),Atom(P(1),[w,c]))$
$Reason(kb,w,c1) \leftarrow$
    $Demo(kb,Atom(P(2),[V(1)]),Atom(P(2),[w1])) \wedge$
    $LocalKb(w1,kb,newkb) \wedge$
    $Demo(kb,Atom(P(5),[V(1),V(2)]),Atom(P(5),[c1,c2])) \wedge$
    $CommonIC(ics) \wedge$
    $AssimilateWithIC(ics,newkb,Atom(P(1),[w,c2]),newkb1) \wedge$
    $Reason(newkb1,w1,\_)$

Finally, the predicate *King*/2 models the king's own reasoning. The king will deduce that the man in the first argument should be able to reason that the colour of his hat is the colour given in the second argument.

$King(w, c) \leftarrow$
$\qquad KingKb(kkb) \wedge$
$\qquad CommonKb(ckb) \wedge$
$\qquad Append(kkb, ckb, kb) \wedge$
$\qquad LocalKb(w, kb, lkb) \wedge$
$\qquad Reason(lkb, w, c)$

With the program consisting of these definitions together with the programs in Figures 5, 12, and 13 and the usual definitions of *Append*/3 and *Member*/2, the goal

$\leftarrow King(C(13), c)$

has just the computed answer

$c = C(1).$

Moreover, the goals

$\leftarrow King(C(11), c)$
$\leftarrow King(C(12), c)$

both fail[7].

Note that this program is not amalgamated, even in the weak sense, and only requires one level of meta-programming.

A number of alternative approaches to the solution of this problem have been made. Kim and Kowalski [1990] use full first order logic to give a representation and solution of the problem. This solution requires meta-level reasoning with a weak amalgamation. The solution in [Aiello *et al.*, 1988] also uses full first order logic but is designed for a more general framework of non-cooperative but loyal and perfect reasoners. Their solution has been machine-checked using a version of Weyhrauch's FOL system [Weyhrauch, 1982]. Nait Abdallah [1987] extends logic programming with a concept similar to a module called an *ion*. This solution is not expressed as a logic program and does not use meta-programming techniques. An alternative solution similar to the one given above using the Gödel system is in [Hill and Lloyd, 1994]. This was primarily designed to illustrate the meta-programming facilities in Gödel and differs in that its object program defining the wise men's knowledge is purely propositional and a query may only ask the third wise man the colour of his hat.

---

[7]The wise men program with these goals has been machine-checked using the Gödel system.

5.4   Transforming and specializing programs

A major application for meta-programming is in the transformation and specialization of programs. However, it appears that, although many transformation and specialization procedures and their proofs of correctness have been published, apart from the work of Gurr [1993], little work has been done to establish good declarative meta-programming styles for implementing such procedures.

When a program is specialized for a particular application or transformed to a more efficient program, although the new program may have little resemblance to the old program, it should preserve the semantics, at least with respect to the expected goals for the program. It is quite clear that the old object program has to be represented as a ground term in the goal to the meta-program. In addition, the computed answer of the meta-program should bind a variable in the goal to a ground term representing the transformed or specialized program.

It is difficult to discuss how program transformers and specializers can be implemented in logic programming without a concrete procedure in mind. Thus we consider the meta-programming requirements for a basic unfolding step and provide a skeleton logic program that realizes this step. To define an unfolding step, it is convenient to denote the body of a normal clause as a sequence of literals or conjunctions of literals. Thus, for example,

$$H \leftarrow L_1, \ldots, L_n$$

denotes the normal clause

$$H \leftarrow L_1 \wedge \cdots \wedge L_n.$$

The unfolding step for definite programs is defined as follows [Tamaki and Sato, 1984][8].

Definition 5.4.1. Let P be a normal program that includes the clause

$$C: \qquad A \leftarrow S, Q(\underline{t}), R.$$

Suppose, for $i = 1, \ldots, r$, the clauses

$$D_i: \qquad Q(\underline{t_i}) \leftarrow R_i$$

are variants (chosen to have no variables in common with C) of all the clauses in P whose heads unify with $Q(\underline{t})$. Let θ_i be the mgu of $Q(\underline{t})$ and $Q(\underline{t_i})$. Then the *result of unfolding C with respect to $Q(\underline{t})$* is the program P' obtained from P by replacing C by the r clauses

$$D_i': \qquad A\theta_i \leftarrow S\theta_i, R_i\theta_i, R\theta_i$$

obtained by resolving C with D_i wrt $Q(\underline{t})$.

This definition was first proved correct with respect to preservation of the success set by Tamaki and Sato [1984] for definite programs and later

---

[8]A tuple $t_1, \ldots, t_j$ is denoted here by $\underline{t}$.

$Unfold(p, If(h, b), Atom(q, xs), p1) \leftarrow$
$\quad SelectClause(If(h, b), p) \wedge$
$\quad SelectLit(Atom(q, xs), b) \wedge$
$\quad MaxForm(If(h, b), n) \wedge$
$\quad DeriveAll(p, If(h, b), Atom(q, xs), cs, n) \wedge$
$\quad Replace(p, If(h, b), cs, p1)$

$DeriveAll([], \_, \_, [], \_)$
$DeriveAll([pc|pcs], If(h, b), a, [c|cs], m) \leftarrow$
$\quad Resolve(b, a, pc, [], s, b1, m, n) \wedge$
$\quad ApplyToForm(s, If(h, b1), c) \wedge$
$\quad DeriveAll(pcs, If(h, b), a, cs, n)$
$DeriveAll([pc|pcs], If(h, b), a, cs, m) \leftarrow$
$\quad \neg Resolve(b, a, pc, [], \_, \_, m, \_) \wedge$
$\quad DeriveAll(pcs, If(h, b), a, cs, m)$

$Resolve(b, Atom(q, xs), If(Atom(q, ys), ls), s, t, r, m, n) \leftarrow$
$\quad Rename(m, If(Atom(q, ys), ls), If(Atom(q, y1s), l1s), n) \wedge$
$\quad UnifyTerms(y1s, xs, s, t) \wedge$
$\quad ReplaceConj(b, Atom(q, xs), l1s, r)$

Fig. 14. The unfolding program

by Seki [1989] and Gardner and Shepherdson [1991] for normal programs. Kanamori and Horiuchi [1987] showed that it preserves computed answers.

Figure 14 contains the top part of a program that performs an unfolding step, defined by the predicate *Unfold*/4. The ground representation given in Subsection 2.1 is assumed. The types of *Unfold*/4, *SelectClause*/2, *DeriveAll*/5, and *Replace*/4 are as follows.

Predicate	Type
Unfold	$List(\mu) * \mu * \mu * List(\mu)$
SelectClause	$\mu * List(\mu)$
DeriveAll	$List(\mu) * \mu * \mu * List(\mu) * Integer$
Replace	$List(\mu) * \mu * List(\mu) * List(\mu)$

The predicate *SelectClause*/2 selects a clause from a program; *DeriveAll*/5 attempts a derivation step for every clause in the program; and *Replace*/4 removes an element from a list and inserts a sublist of elements in its place. The remaining predicates are described in Subsection 3.2.

The unfold procedure requires certain basic steps: standardising apart the variables used in the program's clauses from the variables in the clause selected for unfolding, computing a unifier, and applying substitutions, and so on. Moreover at the heart of such a procedure is the need to construct a list of the representations of all clauses that satisfy certain conditions. This could also be be achieved by means of intensional sets (if these are provided) and then converting the set of clauses to a list. These basic steps are common to program transformers and specializers and many other similar meta-programs. Thus to simplify the writing of this kind of meta-programming application, predicates that perform these tasks should be provided by the meta-programming system.

Frequently, when transforming a program, the language has to be extended with new functions and predicates. The names of these symbols need to be generated by the meta-program. Thus, the meta-programming system needs to provide support for constructing new names for symbols and modifying the language of an object program. The representation given in Subsection 3.1 does not include a representation of the characters in the symbols of the object language and hence the representation is not adequate for program transformers that extend or change the object language.

The language of a Prolog program is determined by the functions and predicates used in the clauses and goal. Also, names of symbols can be converted to and from their corresponding lists of ascii codes by means of predicates such as name/2. Hence, new symbol names can be added to the representation of the object language. As the naming relation is trivial, this defines new symbol names for the object languages themselves. However, as Prolog does not support a ground representation, writing declarative meta-programs for transforming programs is extremely difficult.

The Gödel system not only includes predicates for adding and deleting statements, but also for changing the object language. For example, the system module `Programs` defines the predicate `ProgramConstantName/4` which will convert between a string of characters forming the name of a constant in an object language and its representation. The module `Strings` provides standard string processing predicates and functions. Thus, new names of symbols required for defining new object languages can be created and their representation obtained. Other predicates add and delete representations of names of symbols and their declarations to and from the representation of an object language. For example, the predicate `InsertProgramConstant/6` creates a representation of a new program from the representation $\lceil P \rceil$ of an existing program P by adding the representation of a constant to $\lceil P \rceil$. Moreover, the system module `Syntax` in Gödel provides many predicates for basic meta-programming tasks such as standardising apart, applying a substitution, and finding an mgu.

In Section 6, the use of meta-programming for program specialization is illustrated by partial evaluation. This technique uses partial information about the goal to create a specialized program. It is intended that the specialized program has the same semantics as the original program (when called with an appropriate goal) but improved efficiency.

6 Specialization of meta-programs

Meta-level computations involve an overhead for interpreting the representation of an object program. The more complex and expressive the representation, the greater the overhead is likely to be. The ground representation, in particular, is associated by many with inefficiency. It has been shown that the overhead can be "compiled away" for a meta-program that operates on a given object program. The method for doing this is based on a program transformation technique called program specialization which is a large topic in its own right and not limited to meta-programs in its application. However, the combination of meta-programming and program specialization appears a particularly fruitful one, and it is this aspect together with its applications that we discuss in this section.

6.1 Logic program specialization

Let P be a logic program and G a goal. The aim of specialization is to derive another program P' say, whose computations with G (and instances of G) give identical results to those given by P. For goals other than G and its instances, P' may give different results. The restriction of P to G is exploited to gain efficiency; in other words, P' should be more efficient than P, with respect to G.

The topic has been studied in a variety of programming languages, and is often called partial evaluation. A comprehensive treatment of partial evaluation, mainly for functional languages but with some sections on other languages, is given by Jones *et al.* [1993]. Partial evaluation was introduced into logic programming by Komorowski [1982] (who later called it partial deduction), and the basic principles and results were established by Lloyd and Shepherdson [1991]. A recent survey of techniques and results can be found in [Gallagher, 1993].

Our main interest in specialization is when P, the program to be specialized, is a meta-program. Suppose either P or the goal G with respect to which P is to be specialized contains the representation of an object program. In this case the aim of the specialization of P with respect to G is to compile away the representation of the object program.

In the following subsections we show the specialization of the Instance-Demo interpreter and the specialization of a resolution procedure applied to fixed object programs. The specialization of the Instance-Demo program (Figure 5) yields clauses syntactically isomorphic to the object language clauses, and therefore computations using the specialized *IDemo*/3 are almost identical to computations of the object program. The specialization of resolution yields a program containing low-level predicates manipulating terms, substitutions and so on. In fact specialization of a resolution interpreter is close to true compilation of the object program to a lower-level target language, and the low-level operations correspond to instructions in

$IDemo(p, x, y) \leftarrow InstanceOf(x, y) \wedge IDemo1(p, y)$

$IDemo1(\_, True).$
$IDemo1(p, And(x, y)) \leftarrow$
$\qquad IDemo1(p, x) \wedge$
$\qquad IDemo1(p, y)$
$IDemo1(p, Not(x)) \leftarrow$
$\qquad \neg IDemo1(p, x)$
$IDemo1(p, Atom(P(n), xs)) \leftarrow$
$\qquad Member(z, p) \wedge InstanceOf(z, If(Atom(P(n), xs), b)) \wedge$
$\qquad IDemo1(p, b)$

Fig. 15. The Instance-Demo interpreter **I**

$IDemo([$
$\quad If(Atom(P(0), [Var(0), Term(F(1), [Var(0), Var(1)])]), True),$
$\quad If(Atom(P(0), [Var(0), Term(F(1), [Var(1), Var(2)])]),$
$\qquad Atom(P(0), [Var(0), Var(2)]))],$
$\quad x, y) \leftarrow$
$\quad InstanceOf(x, y) \wedge$
$\quad IDemo1(y).$
$IDemo1(Atom(P(0), [x, Term(F(1), [x, z])])).$
$IDemo1(Atom(P(0), [x, Term(F(1), [y, z])])) \leftarrow$
$\quad IDemo1(Atom(P(0), [x, z])).$

Fig. 16. The specialized Instance-Demo interpreter

a target language such as Warren Abstract machine instructions.

6.1.1   Specialization of the Instance-Demo interpreter

The Instance-Demo program **I** in Figure 5 can be partially evaluated with respect to a given object program. Figure 15 shows again the top level procedures of this interpreter. When supplied with an object program P, **I** can be specialized by partial evaluation, with respect to the goal $\leftarrow IDemo(\lceil P \rceil, x, y)$. If the object program is the Member program (Figure 2) then the goal is as follows.

$\leftarrow IDemo([$
$\quad If(Atom(P(0), [Var(0), Term(F(1), [Var(0), Var(1)])]), True),$
$\quad If(Atom(P(0), [Var(0), Term(F(1), [Var(1), Var(2)])]),$
$\qquad Atom(P(0), [Var(0), Var(2)]))],$
$\quad x, y)$

A suitable partial evaluation of **I** with respect to this goal gives the result shown in Figure 16.

The example shows that substantial optimizations are obtainable by partial evaluation, since the overhead of handling the ground representation in the original program has been almost eliminated. In other words, computations with the specialized Instance-Demo program are almost identical to object-level computations with the object program. In the specialized program the clauses for *IDemo*1/2 are very similar to the clauses for *Member*/2 in the object program representation, except that the representations of variables have been replaced by meta-variables. This arises since the calls to $Member(z, p)$ and $InstanceOf(z, If(Atom(P(n), xs), b))$ have been completely unfolded, where p is the representation of the Member program. Secondly, the first argument of *IDemo*1/2 containing the object program has been completely eliminated from the specialized *IDemo*1/2 predicate by means of a well-known structure specialization applied by most logic program specialization systems [Gallagher and Bruynooghe, 1990]. Note that the Instance-Demo program (and hence also its partial evaluation) is typed and this ensures that the new meta-variables range over representations of object terms.

The close correspondence between the specialized Instance-Demo program and its original object program is somewhat surprising, and it is interesting to compare the natural interpretations of the original Instance-Demo program and the specialized program in Figure 16. In the original Instance-Demo program the intended domain of interpretation is the set of object language expressions, and the denotation of a term in the ground representation is the object term that it represents. On the other hand, in the specialized program the natural domain of interpretation is (an extension of) the domain of the Member program.

At first sight it is odd that partial evaluation has the effect of changing the intended interpretation of the Instance-Demo program as well as specializing its behaviour. This effect is not so surprising when one considers that the general Instance-Demo program handles arbitrary (uninterpreted) programs in the object language, whereas specialization with respect to a particular object program allows, indeed suggests, a particular interpretation of the object language. This induces a natural interpretation of the meta-language representations. More precisely, if the interpretation of a ground object term t is an object d in the domain of interpretation of the object language, then $\lceil t \rceil$ in the meta-language will also denote d. For terms $\lceil t \rceil$ where t is a non-ground object expression a reasonable interpretation of $\lceil t \rceil$ is the set of objects denoted by ground instances of t. Such an interpretation scheme can be applied to the specialized program in Figure 16. The interpretation of the specialized *IDemo*1 predicate in this case is that $IDemo1(Atom(P(0), [\lceil t_1 \rceil, \lceil t_2 \rceil]))$ is true iff some ground instance of $Member(t_1, t_2)$ is true.

Note that this interpretation gives non-standard, but quite reasonable interpretations for predicates such as *InstanceOf*/2, which are now interpreted as relations on the domain of the Member program rather than on the domain of object language expressions.

It is clear from the example above that a corresponding set of clauses for *IDemo*1/2 could be derived for any object program P. Suppose P is of form $[If(h_1, b_1), \ldots, If(h_n, b_n)]$, where $h_1, \ldots, h_n$ and $b_1, \ldots, b_n$ are the representations of the heads and bodies of the clauses respectively. The specialized Instance-Demo program contains a set of clauses $\{IDemo1(h'_1) \leftarrow IDemo1(b'_1), \ldots, IDemo1(h'_n) \leftarrow IDemo1(b'_n)\}$, where each h'_i and b'_i is obtained from h_i and b_i respectively by replacing the ground representation of variables by typed meta-variables.

Kowalski [1990] sketched the derivation of Solve-style interpreter containing non-ground clauses representing an object program, by unfolding a Demo interpreter. Kowalski's interpreter was similar to the Instance-Demo interpreter, but contained a set of ground unit clauses representing the object program instead of representing the program in an argument of *Demo*. The derivation was achieved by unfolding a call to a predicate performing substitution. The use of types (or corresponding sort predicates) in the Instance-Demo program is also essential to the process, a point missed by Kowalski, since otherwise the meta-variables may have unintended instances. Kowalski's argument, and the partial evaluation example above, suggest the conclusion that the typed non-ground representation of an object program is conceptually not far removed from a ground representation. The well-known limitations of the Solve-style interpreters are a consequence of the limitations of the Instance-Demo program.

However, as a technique for gaining efficiency in the ground representation, the partial evaluation of Instance-Demo is interesting. There is a superficial connection with the *ad hoc* implementation technique of "melting" ground representations by substituting meta-variables in place of ground representations of variables, in order to increase efficiency of meta-programming with the ground representation. This was used for example in the Logimix self-applicable partial evaluator for Prolog [Mogensen and Bondorf, 1993]).

6.1.2 Specialization of a resolution procedure

More complex and flexible interpreters than Instance-Demo (such as a resolution proof procedure) are more difficult to specialize effectively. Gurr [1993] achieved substantial efficiency improvements by partial evaluation of a resolution interpreter written for the ground representation in Gödel. This work and others [Kursawe, 1987], [Nilsson, 1993] aimed to show that specialization of logic program interpreters can produce results similar to standard techniques for compiling logic programs based on the Warren abstract machine. The connection between specialization and compilation will be further discussed in Section 6.2. Here we illustrate the idea using an example of the partial evaluation of resolution in Gurr's system.

$\leftarrow Resolve(g,$
$\qquad If(Atom(P(0),[V(0),V(0),Term(C(0),[]),$
$\qquad\qquad Term(F(0),[V(1),Term(F(0),[V(0),Term(C(0),[])])])])]),$
$\qquad\qquad Atom(P(1),[V(1)])),$
$\qquad s1,s2,g1,v1,v2)$

Fig. 17. Instantiated call to *Resolve*

Gurr partially evaluated a predicate *Resolve*/7 which we have already used in the SLD-Demo program in Figure 9. It is intended that the first argument of *Resolve*/7 represents a formula g; the second, a program clause c; the third, a substitution $s1$ to be applied to g; the fifth, the resolvent $g1$ of g and c (with substitution $s1$ applied to g); and the fourth, the resulting substitution $s2$. The remaining arguments $v1$ and $v2$ are indices for renaming variables during standardization apart. We do not show the code for *Resolve*/7 used by Gurr, which incorporates standardization apart, unification of the goal with the clause head, application of the substitution to the clause body, and composition of the unifier with the input substitution.

During partial evaluation of the resolution interpreter with a given object program, the aim is to generate a separate specialized call to *Resolve* for each clause in the object program. Consider the example used in [Gurr, 1993] where the object program contains a clause C:

$$P(x,x,A,F(y,F(x,A))) \leftarrow Q(y)$$

Figure 17 shows the call to *Resolve*/7 that is to be partially evaluated. The ground representation defined in Section 3 is used, where $P(0)$ represents P, $P(1)$ represents Q, $C(0)$ represents A, $F(0)$ represents F, and $V(0),V(1)$ represent x and y respectively. Figure 18 shows the result. A new predicate *Resolve$_C$*/6 has been created and the representation of the clause C (the second argument of *Resolve*) has been eliminated. The calls in the body to *UnifyTerms*, *GetConstant*, *GetFunction*, *UnifyVariable*, *UnifyConstant* and *UnifyValue* are the operations corresponding to the detailed matching of the parts of the head of the clause, and are the residual parts of the full resolution procedure written by Gurr. Note that the variable names from the clause have also completely disappeared since the standardization apart has effectively been carried out during partial evaluation. The body predicates are deliberately named after their analogous Warren abstract machine (WAM) instructions. This emphasizes the fact that partial evaluation with respect to a given object program achieves a similar result to compilation of the program.

We can compare specialization with the other main approach to improv-

$Resolve_C(Atom(P(0), [arg1, arg2, arg3, arg4]),$
        $subst\_in, subst\_out,$
        $Atom(P(1), [var]),$
        $v, v1) \leftarrow$
        $UnifyTerms(arg1, arg2, subst\_in, s1) \wedge$
        $GetConstant(arg3, Term(C(0), [\,]), s1, s2) \wedge$
        $GetFunction(arg4, Term(F(0), [t1, t2]), mode, s2, s3) \wedge$
        $UnifyVariable(mode, t1, var, v, v1) \wedge$
        $UnifyFunction(mode, t2, Term(F(0), [t21, t22], mode1, s3, s4) \wedge$
        $UnifyValue(mode1, arg1, t21, s4, s5) \wedge$
        $UnifyConstant(mode1, t22, Term(C(0), [\,]), s5, subst\_out)$

Fig. 18. Partial evaluation of *Resolve*

ing efficiency in meta-programs, namely "meta-programming facilities", such as those provided in Gödel or Reflective Prolog. Meta-programming facilities consist of essential meta-programming tools and commonly used procedures that are carefully coded, and provided to the programmer in libraries or as built-in procedures in the meta-language. Such facilities are specific to a given object language and a representation of it. This helps to avoid unnecessary inefficiency, but does not eliminate the overhead of using the representation. The advantage of such tools is that once written they are easily applicable. The disadvantage is that there will always be applications outside the scope of the given set of meta-programming facilities. For example, if one has to deal with object programs in a different language, or use a different representation, the built-in facilities may not be applicable.

Specialization has the advantage of being applicable to any object language and representation. Its disadvantage is that it has to be applied to each meta-program separately, though the Futamura projections discussed below alleviate this overhead.

Ideally, both approaches to efficiency improvement should be combined. A meta-programming system should provide some facilities for efficient handling of standard meta-programming problems, together with program specialization tools. The latter can gain further efficiency for the standard procedures, and also help to optimize meta-programs outside the scope of the standard facilities. This complementary approach to optimizing meta-programs suggests that built-in procedures should be written in such a way as to make them more "specializable" [Gurr, 1993], though what this means in practice is not yet completely understood.

6.2   Specialization and compilation

The specialization of meta-programs is analogous to compilation, and the relation between executing specialized and unspecialized meta-programs is analogous to the relation between running compiled and interpreted code. The comparison with compilation is actually quite extensive and is discussed further below. A functional notation is used though an equivalent, but more cumbersome, formulation in logic programming is possible.

Definition 6.2.1. A program specializer *written in* $\mathcal{M}$ *for* $\mathcal{L}$ is a function

$$PS_{\mathcal{M}} : \lceil \mathcal{L} \rceil_{\mathcal{M}} \to (\lceil \mathcal{L} \rceil_{\mathcal{M}} \to \lceil \mathcal{L} \rceil_{\mathcal{M}})$$

It is assumed that an object program $p_{\mathcal{L}}$ in $\mathcal{L}$ is a function with two arguments, and that the first argument is known but not the second. The specializer takes the representations of $p_{\mathcal{L}}$ with data $x_{\mathcal{L}}$ for the first argument of $p_{\mathcal{L}}$ and computes the representation of a specialized program $p_{\mathcal{L}}^x$.

The defining property of the specializer PS is the following:

$$PS_{\mathcal{M}}(\lceil p \rceil, \lceil x \rceil_{\mathcal{M}}) = \lceil p^x \rceil_{\mathcal{M}} \; \Rightarrow \; (\forall y) \, p(x, y) = p^x(y)$$

Definition 6.2.2. A language interpreter *written in* $\mathcal{M}$ *for* $\mathcal{L}$ is a function

$$I_{\mathcal{M}} : \lceil \mathcal{L} \rceil_{\mathcal{M}} \to (\lceil D \rceil_{\mathcal{M}} \to \lceil D \rceil_{\mathcal{M}})$$

(We assume that D is the language of input and output for programs in $\mathcal{L}$). That is, $I_{\mathcal{M}}$ takes the representations of a program $p_{\mathcal{L}}$ and some data x_D for $p_{\mathcal{L}}$ and computes the representation of the output, say y_D.

The analogy between compilation and interpreter specialization was first identified by Futamura [Futamura, 1971]. In the following we formulate the so-called Futamura projections in such a way as to emphasize meta-programming aspects.

Definition 6.2.3. First Futamura projection

Let $PS_{\mathcal{K}}$ be a program specializer written in $\mathcal{K}$ for $\mathcal{M}$. Let $I_{\mathcal{M}}$ be an interpreter for programs in $\mathcal{L}$. Then specialization of the interpreter with respect to a given program $p_{\mathcal{L}}$ is expressed by

$$PS_{\mathcal{K}}(\lceil I_{\mathcal{M}} \rceil_{\mathcal{K}}, \lceil \lceil p_{\mathcal{L}} \rceil_{\mathcal{M}} \rceil_{\mathcal{K}})$$

Note that the second argument is a "meta-meta" (or $meta^2$) object in the sense that it is the representation in $\mathcal{K}$ of an object already represented in $\mathcal{M}$.

The result of the first Futamura projection is the representation of a specialized program, say $\lceil I_{\mathcal{M}}^p \rceil_{\mathcal{K}}$. By Definition 6.2.1, $I_{\mathcal{M}}^p(x) = I_{\mathcal{M}}(p, x)$, so $I_{\mathcal{M}}^p$ preserves the functionality of p. $I_{\mathcal{M}}^p$ can be regarded as a "compiled" version of p since it maps input directly to output. This analogy becomes more concrete in practical program specialization systems, which effectively perform the parsing of the object program, leaving residual "execution" operations in the specialized program, as in real compilers.

Thus for instance, we could have $\mathcal{L}$ = Pascal, $\mathcal{M}$ = Scheme and $\mathcal{K}$ = Gödel, in which case I is an interpreter for Pascal written in Scheme, and PS is a specializer of Scheme programs, written in Gödel. The second argument in the first Futamura projection is a Gödel term encoding a Scheme representation of a Pascal program. The result is a Gödel representation of a Scheme program. Note that to run it as a Scheme program involves extracting the Scheme program from its Gödel representation. In summary, a Pascal program has been "compiled" into Scheme.

6.3　Self-applicable program specializers

We now consider the case where the program specializer is self-applicable. If $\mathcal{K} = \mathcal{M}$, then in principle the program $PS_{\mathcal{K}}$ can be applied to itself by constructing $\lceil PS_{\mathcal{K}} \rceil_{\mathcal{K}}$. The possibility of encoding a language in itself was established by Gödel numbering, as discussed in Section 4. It is then possible to "self-apply" PS, or more accurately, to apply PS to a representation of itself.

Definition 6.3.1. Second Futamura projection

The specialization of PS with respect to itself and an interpreter $I_{\mathcal{M}}$ is expressed by

$$PS_{\mathcal{K}}(\lceil PS_{\mathcal{K}} \rceil_{\mathcal{K}}, \lceil \lceil I_{\mathcal{M}} \rceil_{\mathcal{K}} \rceil_{\mathcal{K}})$$

Note that the second argument is $meta^2$. The result, namely $\lceil PS^{I_{\mathcal{M}}} \rceil_{\mathcal{K}}$, is the representation of a program which, when given a program $p_{\mathcal{L}}$, produces $\lceil I_{\mathcal{M}}^p \rceil_{\mathcal{K}}$. This is the representation of a compiled version of $p_{\mathcal{L}}$, as established by the first Futamura projection. Thus the second Futamura projection expresses the production of a compiler from an interpreter for $\mathcal{L}$.

Definition 6.3.2. Third Futamura projection

The specialization of PS with respect to itself and (a representation of) itself is expressed by

$$PS_{\mathcal{K}}(\lceil PS_{\mathcal{K}} \rceil_{\mathcal{K}}, \lceil \lceil PS_{\mathcal{K}} \rceil_{\mathcal{K}} \rceil_{\mathcal{K}})$$

Again, the second argument is $meta^2$, and is not the same as the first argument. The result $\lceil PS^{PS} \rceil_{\mathcal{K}}$ is a program which, when given $\lceil I_{\mathcal{M}} \rceil_{\mathcal{K}}$, produces $\lceil PS^{I_{\mathcal{M}}} \rceil_{\mathcal{K}}$. In other words, it returns the representation of a compiler of programs in $\mathcal{L}$, as established by the second Futamura projection. The third Futamura projection thus expresses the production of a compiler generator (that produces a compiler from a given interpreter).

The second and third projections provide a way of achieving the first projection in stages. This is useful where the same meta-program is to be executed with many different object programs. The "compiler" associated with that meta-program can be obtained using the second projection. If compilers for different meta-programs are to be produced, then the third projection is useful since it shows how to obtain a "compiler-generator" from a partial evaluator.

The effective implementation of the Futamura projections is the subject of current research. The effectiveness of the first Futamura projection is critical to the usefulness of the second and third, which are simply means to achieve the first projection (compilation) by stages. Interpreters, or indeed any meta-programs, do not appear to be any less complex than programs in general from the point of view of specialization. Therefore an effective specializer for the first projection should be also an effective general purpose specializer.

In order to perform the second and third projections the specializer should be effectively self-applicable. This requirement, added to the requirement of being a good general purpose specializer, has proved very difficult to meet. Program analysis methods based on abstract interpretation have been employed to complement partial evaluation and add to its effectiveness [Sestoft and Jones, 1988], [Mogensen and Bondorf, 1993], [Gurr, 1993]. Another approach to self-application is to use two or more versions of a specializer [Ruf and Weise, 1993], [Fujita and Furukawa, 1988]. A simple specializer can be applied to a complex one, or vice versa. In such a method, extra run-time computation in the compiled program or in the compiler produced by the projections is traded for less computation during the second and third Futamura projections respectively.

6.4 Applications of meta-program specialization

The uses of specialization with meta-programming are many, and we finish this section by indicating some areas of current research in which specialization of logic programs is relevant.

Implementing other languages and logics. First order logic, or fragments of it such as definite clauses or normal clauses, can be used as a meta-language for defining the semantics of other languages and logics. The Futamura projections then offer a general compilation mechanism to improve the computational efficiency of the semantics.

A proof system for a logic $\mathcal{L}$ can be constructed from a set of (abstract) syntax rules for defining expressions of $\mathcal{L}$, together with a set of inference rules of the form

$$\frac{\alpha_0, \ldots, \alpha_k}{\beta}$$

where $\alpha_0, \ldots, \alpha_k, \beta$ are expressions in $\mathcal{L}$, and β is inferred from $\alpha_0, \ldots,$ and α_k. Clearly these rules can be encoded as definite clauses, and the concept of theory, proof, theorem and so on can be defined by clauses. The procedural interpretation of clauses can then be used to search for theorems from given object theories. Such an approach may appear naive as a way to build efficient theorem proving systems but, when added to techniques of specialization, practical results are obtainable. The advantage of the method is its generality.

One experiment serves to illustrate this general framework. A theorem prover for first order clauses, based on the model elimination method, was written as a definite logic meta-program by de Waal and Gallagher [1994]. Here, the object language is full clausal logic, while definite clauses are the meta-language. The theorem prover was then specialized with respect to fixed object theories. The result for a given theory was a specialized theorem prover that can prove theorems only in the given theory, but much faster than the original prover. Theory-specific information, such as the uselessness of given object formulas or inference rules in a given proof, can also be obtained and exploited. This can be seen as an application of the first Futamura projection, where the theorem prover is an "interpreter" of clauses.

It appears that this experiment could be repeated for other theorem provers, since the method assumes only that the theorem prover can be written as a logic meta-program, an assumption that holds for any computable logic. This provides a general approach to using a uniform meta-language (logic programs) to implement other logics, and using specialization to get reasonable efficiency. In similar style, Jones *et al.* [1993] mention the possibility of using partial evaluation as a way of improving the efficiency of high-level functional meta-languages for programming language definition and implementation.

Expert systems and knowledge based systems.   A deductive data base or knowledge base can be viewed as a logic program. Expert systems can also be included under this heading. Procedures for querying, updating, checking integrity constraints, and similar tasks are thus meta-level procedures. The potential of using partial evaluation to optimize expert system query interpreters with respect to fixed bases of knowledge was identified by Levi and Sardu [1988] and by Sterling and Beer [1989].

Enhanced language interpreters.   In logic programming, interpreters for tracing computations, spying, timing and so on are sometimes written as "enhanced" versions of a standard or "vanilla" interpreter (see the Proof-Tree interpreter in Figure 4). That is, the standard interpreter is written as a meta-program (usually in the non-ground representation) augmented with operations that record or report the state of the computation at each step. The interpretation overhead is sometimes heavy, but partial evaluation offers a way to reduce this (for a given object program). Safra and Shapiro [1986] report extensive use of this technique for a concurrent logic programming system, where facilities such as deadlock detection were added to a standard interpreter. In their approach the second Futamura projection was constructed by hand since their partial evaluator was not self-applicable.

Optimizing non-standard procedural semantics. The dual reading of programs, declarative and procedural, represents one of the most distinctive features of logic programming. A program with clear declarative semantics can be regarded as a problem specification. Unfortunately, in order to achieve efficient computations, complex non-standard procedural semantics are often needed. Examples of these include coroutining, tabulation and forward checking. The use of such procedural readings is often precluded since they carry a lot of computational overhead. As a result programs are often made more efficient (with respect to standard procedural semantics) at the expense of declarative clarity.

Program specialization appears to offer a general approach to exploiting the dual reading more effectively. The overhead of complex procedural semantics can sometimes be drastically reduced if an interpreter for the semantics is available, written as a meta-program. In this case the Futamura projections can be applied to reduce the overhead. This method was advocated by Gallagher [1986] and illustrated on coroutining programs. Gurr [1993] also shows the compilation of a coroutining example. The work on "compiling control" [Bruynooghe *et al.*, 1989] is similar in its aims, but is not based explicitly on meta-programming.

The use of meta-programming combined with specialization as a program production technique is in its infancy. Applications such as those mentioned in this section indicate its generality and promise.

Acknowledgements

We are particularly indebted to John Lloyd and Frank Van Harmelen who have made many suggestions that have improved this chapter. We greatly appreciate their help. We also thank all those who, through discussion and by commenting on earlier drafts contributed to this work. These include Jonas Barklund, Tony Bowers, Henning Christiansen, Yuejun Jiang, Bob Kowalski, Bern Martens, Dale Miller, Alberto Pettorossi, Danny De Schreye, Sten-Åke Tärnlund, and Jiwei Wang.

Work on this chapter has been carried out while the first author was supported by a SERC grant GR/H/79862. In addition, the ESPRIT Basic Research Action 3012 (Compulog) and Project 6810 (Compulog 2) have provided opportunities to develop our ideas and understanding of this area by supporting many workshops and meetings and providing the funds to attend.

References

[Abramson and Rogers, 1989] H. Abramson and M. Rogers, eds. *Meta-Programming in Logic Programming*, MIT Press, 1989. Proceedings of the Meta88 Workshop.

[Aiello *et al.*, 1988] L. C. Aiello, D. Nardi and M. Schaerf. Reasoning about knowledge and ignorance, *in* 'Proceedings of the FGCS', pp. 618–627, 1988.

[Barklund, 1995] J. Barklund. Metaprogramming in logic, Technical Report UPMAIL 80, Department of Computer Science, University of Uppsala, Sweden. Also in *Encyclopedia of Computer Science and Technology*, Vol. 33, A. Kent and J. G. Williams (eds.), Marcel Dekker, 1995.

[Barklund and Hamfelt, 1994] H. Barklund and A. Hamfelt. Hierarchical representation of legal knowledge with meta-programming in logic, *Journal of Logic Programming* **18**(1), 55–80, 1994.

[Barklund *et al.*, 1995] J. Barklund, K. Boberg, P. Dell'Aqua and M. Veanes. Meta-programming with theory systems. In K. Apt and F. Turini, eds, *Meta-programming in Logic Programming*, MIT Press, 1995.

[Bowen and Kowalski, 1982] K. Bowen and R. A. Kowalski. Amalgamating language.and metalanguage in logic programming. In K. Clark & S.-A. Tärnlund, eds, *Logic Programming*, pp. 153–172. Academic Press, 1982.

[Bowen and Weinberg, 1985] K. Bowen and T. Weinberg. A meta-level extension of Prolog. In *Proceedings of 2nd IEEE Symposium on Logic Programming, Boston*, pp. 669–675. Computer Society Press, 1985.

[Brogi *et al.*, 1990] A. Brogi, P. Mancarella, D. Pedreschi and F. Turini. Composition operators for logic theories. In J. W. Lloyd, ed., *Computational Logic*, Springer-Verlag, pp. 117–134, 1990.

[Brogi *et al.*, 1992] A. Brogi, P. Mancarella, D. Pedreschi and F. Turini. Meta for modularising logic programming. In A. Pettorossi, ed., *Meta-Programming in Logic, Proceedings of the 3rd International Workshop, Meta-92*, Uppsala, Sweden, pp. 105–119. Springer-Verlag, 1992.

[Bruynooghe *et al.*, 1989] M. Bruynooghe, D. De Schreye and B. Krekels. Compiling control, *Journal of Logic Programming* **6**, 135–162, 1989.

[Chen *et al.*, 1993] W. Chen, M. Kifer and D. S. Warren. HiLog: A foundation for higher-order logic programming, *Journal of Logic Programming* **15**, 187–230, 1993.

[Christiansen, 1994] H. Christiansen. On proof predicates in logic programming, In A. Momigliano and M. Ornaghi, eds, *Proof-Theoretical Extensions of Logic Programming*, CMU, Pittsburgh, PA 15213–3890, USA, 1994. Proceedings of an ICLP-94 Post-Conference Workshop.

[Clark, 1978] K. L. Clark. Negation as failure. In H. Gallaire and J. Minker, eds, *Logic and Data Bases*, Plenum Press, pp. 293–322, 1978.

[Clark and McCabe, 1979] K. L. Clark and F. G. McCabe. The control facilities of IC-PROLOG, In D. Michie, ed., *Expert Systems in the Micro Electronic Age*, Edinburgh University Press, pp. 122–149, 1979.

[Colmerauer *et al.*, 1973] A. Colmerauer, H. Kanoui, R. Pasero and P. Roussel. Un système de communication homme–machine en Français, Technical report, Groupe d'Intelligence Artificielle, Université d'Aix Marseille II, Luminy, France, 1973.

[Costantini, 1990] S. Costantini. Semantics of a metalogic programming language. In M. Bruynooghe, ed., *Proceedings of the 2nd Workshop on Meta-programming in Logic*, Katholieke Universiteit, Leuven, Belgium, pp. 3–18, 1990.

[Costantini and Lanzarone, 1989] S. Costantini and G. Lanzarone. A metalogic programming language. In G. Levi and M. Martelli, eds, *6th International Conference on Logic Programming*, Lisbon, pp. 218–233. The MIT Press, Cambridge, MA, 1989.

[De Waal and Gallagher, 1994] D. De Waal and J. Gallagher. The applicability of logic program analysis and transformation to theorem proving. In *Proceedings of the 12th International Conference on Automated Deduction (CADE-12)*, Nancy, 1994.

[Dunin-Keplicz, 1994] B. Dunin-Keplicz. An architecture with multiple meta-levels for the development of correct programs. In F. Turini, ed., *Proceedings of the 4th International Workshop on Meta-Programming in Logic (Meta-94)*, 1994. to be published by Springer-Verlag.

[Feferman, 1962] S. Feferman. Transfinite recursive progressions of axiomatic theories, *The Journal of Symbolic Logic* **27**(3), 259–316, 1962.

[Fujita and Furukawa, 1988] H. Fujita and K. Furukawa. A self-applicable partial evaluator and its use in incremental compilation, *New Generation Computing* **6(2,3)**, 91–118, 1988.

[Futamura, 1971] Y. Futamura. Partial evaluation of computation process—an approach to a compiler–compiler, *Systems, Computers, Controls* **2**, 45–50, 1971.

[Gallagher, 1986] J. Gallagher. Transforming logic programs by specialising interpreters. In *Proceedings of the 7th European Conference on Artificial Intelligence (ECAI-86)*, Brighton, pp. 109–122, 1986.

[Gallagher, 1993] J. Gallagher. Specialisation of logic programs: A tutorial. In *ACM-SIGPLAN Symposium on Partial Evaluation and Semantics Based Program Manipulation*, Copenhagen, pp. 88–98, 1993.

[Gallagher and Bruynooghe, 1990] J. Gallagher and M. Bruynooghe. Some low-level source transformations for logic programs. In M. Bruynooghe, ed., *Proceedings of the 2nd Workshop on Meta Programming in Logic*, Katholieke Universiteit Leuven, Belgium, pp. 229–244, 1990.

[Gardner and Shepherdson, 1991] P. Gardner and J. Shepherdson. Unfold/fold transformations of logic programs. In J.-L. Lassez & G. Plotkin, eds, *Computational Logic: Essays in Honor of Alan Robinson*, MIT Press, pp. 565–583, 1991.

[Gödel, 1931] K. Gödel. Über formal unentscheidbare Sätze der Principia Mathematica und verwandter Systeme I. *Monatsh. Math. Phys.* **38**, 173–198, 1931. English translation in *From Frege to Gödel*, J. van Heijenoort, ed. pp. 592–617. Harvard University Press, 1967.

[Gurr, 1993] C. Gurr. A Self-applicable Partial Evaluator for the Logic Programming Language Gödel, PhD thesis, Dept. of Computer Science, University of Bristol, 1993.

[Hannan and Miller, 1989] J. Hannan and D. Miller. A meta-logic for functional programming. In H. Abramson & M. Rogers, eds, *Meta-Programming in Logic Programming*, MIT Press, chapter 24, pp. 453–476, 1989.

[Hannan & Miller, 1992] J. Hannan and D. Miller. From operational semantics to abstract machines, *Mathematical Structures in Computer Science* **2**(4), 415–459, 1992.

[Hill and Lloyd, 1988] P. Hill and J. Lloyd. Meta-programming for dynamic knowledge bases, Technical Report CS-88-18, Department of Computer Science, University of Bristol, 1988.

[Hill and Lloyd, 1989] P. Hill and J. Lloyd. Analysis of meta-programs. In H. Abramson and M. Rogers, eds, *Meta-Programming in Logic Programming*, MIT Press, pp. 23–52, 1989. Proceedings of the Meta88 Workshop, June 1988.

[Hill and Lloyd, 1994] P. Hill and J. Lloyd. *The Gödel Programming Language*, MIT Press, 1994.

[ISO/IEC, 1995] ISO/IEC 13211-1: 1995. Information Technology — Programming Languages — Part 1: General Core. International Standards Organisation, 1995.

[Jiang, 1994] Y. Jiang. Ambivalent logic as the semantic basis of meta-logic programming: I. In P. V. Hentenryck, ed., *Proceedings of the 11th International Conference on Logic Programming*, MIT Press, 1994 .

[Jones et al., 1993] N. Jones, C. Gomard and P. Sestoft. *Partial Evaluation and Automatic Software Generation*, Prentice Hall, 1993.

[Kanamori and Horiuchi, 1987] T. Kanamori and K. Horiuchi. Construction of logic programs based on generalised unfold/fold rules. In J.-L. Lassez, ed., *Proceedings of the Fourth International Conference on Logic Programming*, 1987.

[Kim and Kowalski, 1990] J. S. Kim and R. A. Kowalski. An application of amalgamated logic to multi-agent belief. In M. Bruynooghe, ed., *Proceedings of the 2nd Workshop on Meta Programming in Logic*, Katholieke Universiteit Leuven, Belgium, pp. 272–283, 1990.

[Komorowski, 1982] H. Komorowski. Partial evaluation as a means for inferencing data structures in an applicative language: A theory and implementation in the case of Prolog, In *9th ACM Symposium on Principles of Programming Languages*, Albuquerque, New Mexico, pp. 255–267, 1982.

[Kowalski, 1990] R. A. Kowalski. Problems and promises of computational logic. In J. W. Lloyd, ed., *Computational Logic*, Springer-Verlag, pp. 1–36, 1990.

[Kowalski, 1994] R. A. Kowalski. Logic without model theory. In D. M. Gabbay, ed., *What is a Logical system?*, Oxford University Press, 1994.

[Kursawe, 1987] P. Kursawe. How to invent a Prolog machine. *New Generation Computing* **5**, 97–114, 1987.

[Levi and Sardu, 1988] G. Levi and G Sardu. Partial evaluation of metaprograms in a 'multiple worlds' logic language. *New Generation Computing* **6**, 227–247, 1988.

[Lloyd, 1987] J. Lloyd. *Foundations of Logic Programming*, second edn, Springer-Verlag, 1987.

[Lloyd and Shepherdson, 1991] J. Lloyd and J. Shepherdson. Partial evaluation in logic programming. *The Journal of Logic Programming* **11**(3&4), 217–242, 1991.

[Martens and De Schreye, 1992a] B. Martens and D. De Schreye. Why untyped non-ground meta-programming is not (much of) a problem, Technical Report CW 159, Department of Computer Science, Katholieke Universiteit Leuven, 1992. An abridged version will published in the *Journal of Logic Programming*.

[Martens and De Schreye, 1992b] B. Martens and D. De Schreye. A perfect Herbrand semantics for untyped vanilla meta-programming. In K. Apt, ed., *Proceedings of the Joint International Conference on Logic Programming*, Washington, USA, pp. 511–525, 1992.

[Miller and Nadathur, 1987] D. Miller and G. Nadathur. A logic programming approach to manipulating formulas and programs. In S. Haridi, ed., *IEEE Symposium on Logic Programming*, San Francisco, pp. 379–388, 1987.

[Miller and Nadathur, 1995] D. Miller and G. Nadathur. Higher-order logic programming. In D. Gabbay, C. Hogger and J. Robinson, eds, *Handbook of Logic in Artificial Intelligence and Logic Programming*, Volume V: Deduction Methodologies, Oxford University Press, 1995.

[Mogensen and Bondorf, 1993] T. Mogensen and A. Bondorf. Logimix: A self-applicable Partial Evaluator for Prolog. In K.-K. Lau & T. Clement, eds, *Logic Program Synthesis and Transformation, Manchester 1992*, Springer-Verlag, 1993.

[Nait and Abdallah, 1987] M. Nait and Abdallah. Logic programming with ions, In T. Ottmann, ed., *Proceedings of the 14th International Colloquium on Automata, Languages, and Programming, LNCS 267*, pp. 11–20, 1987.

[Nilsson, 1993] U. Nilsson. Towards a methodology for the design of abstract machines for logic programming languages. *Journal of Logic Programming* **16**, 163–189, 1993.

[Pereira *et al.*, 1978] L. Pereira, F. Pereira and D. Warren. User's guide to DECsystem-10 Prolog, Technical report, Department of A.I., University of Edinburgh, 1978.

[Perlis and Subrahmanian, 1994] D. Perlis and V. S. Subrahmanian. Meta-languages, reflection principles, and self-reference. In D. Gabbay, C. Hogger & J. Robinson, eds, *Handbook of Logic in Artificial Intelligence and Logic Programming, Volume II: Deduction Methodologies*, Oxford University Press, 1994.

[Quine, 1951] W. Quine. *Mathematical Logic (Revised Edition)*, Harvard University Press, 1951.

[Richards, 1974] B. Richards. A point of self-reference. *Synthese*, 1974.

[Ruf and Weise, 1993] E. Ruf and D. Weise. On the specialization of online program specializers. *Journal of Functional Programming* **33**, 251–281, 1993.

[Safra and Shapiro, 1986] S. Safra and E. Shapiro. Meta interpreters for real. *in* In H.-J. Kugler, ed., *Information Processing 86*, North Holland, pp. 271–278, 1986.

[Seki, 1989] H. Seki. Unfold/Fold Transformation of Stratified Programs, In G. Levi & M. Martelli, eds, *6th International Conference on Logic Programming*, Lisbon, Portugal, The MIT Press, Cambridge, MA, 1989.

[Sestoft and Jones, 1988] P. Sestoft and N. Jones. The structure of a self-applicable partial evaluator. In H. Ganzinger and N. Jones, eds, *Programs as Data Objects*, North-Holland, 1988.

[Shapiro, 1982] E. Shapiro. *Algorithmic Program Debugging*, MIT Press, 1982. An ACM Distinguished Dissertation.

[Shepherdson, 1994] J. Shepherdson. Negation as failure: Completion and stratification, In D. Gabbay, C. Hogger & J. Robinson, eds, *Handbook of Logic in Artificial Intelligence and Logic Programming, Volume V: Logic Programming*, Oxford University Press, 1995.

[Sterling and Beer, 1986] L. Sterling and R. Beer. Incremental flavor-mixing of meta-interpreters for expert system construction. In *Proceedings of the 3rd Symposium on Logic Programming, Salt Lake City*, pp. 20–27, 1986.

[Sterling and Beer, 1989] L. Sterling and R. Beer. Metainterpreters for expert system construction. *Journal of Logic Programming* **6**, 163–178, 1989.

[Sterling and Shapiro, 1986] L. Sterling and E. Shapiro. *The Art of Prolog*, MIT Press, 1986.

[Takeuchi and Furukawa, 1986] A. Takeuchi and K. Furukawa. Partial evaluation of Prolog programs and its application to meta programming. In H.-J. Kugler, ed., *Information Processing 86*, Dublin, North Holland, pp. 415–420, 1986.

[Tamaki and Sato, 1984] H. Tamaki and T. Sato. Unfold/fold transformations of logic programs, In *Proceedings of the 2nd International Conference on Logic Programming*, Uppsala, Sweden, pp. 127–138, 1984 .

[Van Harmelen, 1992] F. Van Harmelen. Definable naming relations in metalevel systems, In A.Pettorossi, ed., *Meta-Programming in Logic, Proceedings of the 3rd International Workshop, META-92*, Springer-Verlag, 1992.

[Weyhrauch, 1980] R. Weyhrauch. Prolegomena to a theory of mechanised formal reasoning, *Artificial Intelligence* **13**, 133–170, 1980.

[Weyhrauch, 1982] R. Weyhrauch. An example of FOL using Metatheory. Formalizing reasoning systems and introducing derived inference rules. In *Proceedings of the 6th Conference on Automatic Deduction*, 1982.

Higher-Order Logic Programming
Gopalan Nadathur and Dale Miller

Contents

1   Introduction

Modern programming languages such as Lisp, Scheme and ML permit procedures to be encapsulated within data in such a way that they can subsequently be retrieved and used to guide computations. The languages that provide this kind of an ability are usually based on the functional programming paradigm, and the procedures that can be encapsulated in them correspond to functions. The objects that are encapsulated are, therefore, of higher-order type and so also are the functions that manipulate them. For this reason, these languages are said to allow for *higher-order programming*. This form of programming is popular among the users of these languages and its theory is well developed.

The success of this style of encapsulation in functional programming makes is natural to ask if similar ideas can be supported within the logic programming setting. Noting that procedures are implemented by predicates in logic programming, higher-order programming in this setting would correspond to mechanisms for encapsulating predicate expressions within terms and for later retrieving and invoking such stored predicates. At least some devices supporting such an ability have been seen to be useful in practice. Attempts have therefore been made to integrate such features into Prolog (see, for example, [Warren, 1982]), and many existing implementations of Prolog provide for some aspects of higher-order programming. These attempts, however, are unsatisfactory in two respects. First, they have relied on the use of *ad hoc* mechanisms that are at variance with the declarative foundations of logic programming. Second, they have largely imported the notion of higher-order programming as it is understood within functional programming and have not examined a notion that is intrinsic to logic programming.

In this chapter, we develop the idea of higher-order logic programming by utilizing a higher-order logic as the basis for computing. There are, of course, many choices for the higher-order logic that might be used in such a study. If the desire is only to emulate the higher-order features found in functional programming languages, it is possible to adopt a "minimalist" approach, i.e., to consider extending the logic of first-order Horn clauses—the logical basis of Prolog—in as small a way as possible to realize the additional functionality. The approach that we adopt here, however, is to enunciate a notion of higher-order logic programming by describing an analogue of Horn clauses within a rich higher-order logic, namely, Church's simple theory of types [Church, 1940]. Following this course has a number of pleasant outcomes. First, the extension to Horn clause logic that results from it supports, in a natural fashion, the usual higher-order programming capabilities that are present in functional programming languages. Second, the particular logic that is used provides the elegant mechanism of λ-terms as a means for constructing descriptions of predicates and this turns out to have benefits at a programming level. Third, the use of a higher-order logic blurs the distinction between predicates and functions— predicates correspond, after all, to their characteristic functions—and this makes it natural both to quantify over functions and to extend the mechanisms for constructing predicate expressions to the full class of functional expressions. As a consequence of the last aspect, our higher-order extension to Horn clauses contains within it a convenient means for representing and manipulating objects whose structures incorporate a notion of binding. The abilities that it provides in this respect are not present in *any* other programming paradigm, and, in general, our higher-order Horn clauses lead to a substantial enrichment of the notion of computation within logic programming.

The term "higher-order logic" is often a source of confusion and so it is relevant to explain the sense in which it is used here. There are at least three different readings for this term:

1. Philosophers of mathematics usually divide logic into first-order logic and second-order logic. The latter is a formal basis for all of mathematics and, as a consequence of Gödel's first incompleteness theorem, cannot be recursively axiomatized. Thus, higher-order logic in this sense is basically a model theoretic study [Shapiro, 1985].

2. To a proof theorist, all logics correspond to formal systems that are recursively presented and a higher-order logic is no different. The main distinction between a higher-order and a first-order logic is the presence in the former of predicate variables and comprehension, i.e., the ability to form abstractions over formula expressions. Cut-elimination proofs for higher-order logics differ qualitatively from those for first-order logic in that they need techniques such as Girard's "candidats de réductibilité," whereas proofs in first-order logics can generally be done by induction [Girard *et al.*, 1989]. Semantic arguments can be employed in this setting, but general models (including non-standard models) in the sense of Henkin [Henkin, 1950] must be considered.

3. To many working in automated deduction, higher-order logic refers to any computational logic that contains typed λ-terms and/or variables of some higher-order type, although not necessarily of predicate type. Occasionally, such a logic may incorporate the rules of λ-conversion, and then unification of expressions would have to be carried out relative to these rules.

Clearly, it is not sensible to base a programming language on a higher-order logic in the first sense and we use the term only in the second and third senses here. Note that these two senses are distinct. Thus, a logic can be a higher-order one in the second sense but not in the third: there have been proposals for adding forms of predicate quantification to computational logics that do not use λ-terms and in which the equality of expressions continues to be based on the identity relation. One such proposal appears in [Wadge, 1991]. Conversely, a logic that is higher-order in the third sense may well not permit a quantification over predicates and, thus, may not be higher-order in the second sense. An example of this kind is the specification logic that underlies the Isabelle proof system [Paulson, 1990].

Developing a theory of logic programming within higher-order logic has another fortunate outcome. The clearest and strongest presentations of the central results regarding higher-order Horn clauses require the use of the sequent calculus: resolution and model theory based methods that are traditionally used in the analysis of first-order logic programming are either not useful or not available in the higher-order context. It turns out that the sequent calculus is an apt tool for characterizing the intrinsic role of logical connectives within logic programming and a study such as the one undertaken here illuminates this fact. This observation is developed in a more complete fashion in [Miller *et al.*, 1991] and [Miller, 1994] and in the chapter by Loveland and Nadathur in this volume of the Handbook.

2 A motivation for higher-order features

We are concerned in this chapter with providing a principled basis for higher-order features in logic programming. Before addressing this concern, however, it is useful to understand the higher-order additions to this paradigm that are motivated by programming considerations. We explore this issue in this section by discussing possible enhancements to the logic of first-order Horn clauses that underlies usual logic programming languages.

Horn clauses are traditionally described as the universal closures of disjunctions of literals that contain at most one positive literal. They are subdivided into *positive* Horn clauses that contain exactly one positive literal and *negative* Horn clauses that contain no positive literals. This form of description has its origins in work on theorem-proving within classical first-order logic, a realm from which logic programming has evolved. Clausal logic has been useful within this context because its simple syntactic structure simplifies the presentation of proof procedures. Its use is dependent on two characteristics of classical first-order logic: the ability to convert arbitrary formulas to sets of clauses that are equivalent from the perspective of unsatisfiability, and the preservation of clausal form under logical operations like substitution and resolution. However, these properties do not hold in all logics that might be of interest. The conversion to clausal form is, for instance, not possible within the framework of intuitionistic logic. In a similar vein, substitution into a disjunction of literals may not produce another clause in a situation where predicates are permitted to be variables; as we shall see in Subsection 3.5, substitution for a predicate variable has the potential to change the top-level logical structure of the original formula. The latter observation is especially relevant in the present context: a satisfactory higher-order generalization of Horn clauses must surely allow for predicates to be variables and must therefore be preceded by a different view of Horn clauses themselves.

Fortunately there is a description of Horn clauses that is congenial to their programming application and that can also serve as the basis for a higher-order generalization. Let A be a syntactic variable for an atomic formula in first-order logic. Then we may identify the classes of (first-order) G- and D-formulas by the following rules:

$$G ::= A \mid G \wedge G \mid G \vee G \mid \exists x\, G$$
$$D ::= A \mid G \supset A \mid \forall x\, D$$

These formulas are related to Horn clauses in the following sense: within the framework of classical logic, the negation of a G-formula is equivalent to a set of negative Horn clauses and, similarly, a D-formula is equivalent to a set of positive Horn clauses. We refer to the D-formulas as *definite clauses*, an alternative name in the literature for positive Horn clauses, and to the G-formulas as *goal formulas* because they function as goals within the programming paradigm of interest. These names in fact motivate the symbol chosen to denote members of the respective classes of formulas.

The programming interpretation of these formulas is dependent on treating a collection of closed definite clauses as a program and a closed goal formula as a query to be evaluated; definite clauses and goal formulas are, for this reason, also called *program clauses* and *queries*, respectively. The syntactic structures of goal formulas and definite clauses are relevant to their being interpreted in this fashion. The matrix of a definite clause is a formula of the form A or $G \supset A$, and this is intended to correspond to (part of) the definition of a procedure whose name is the predicate head of A. Thus, an atomic goal formula that "matches" with A may be solved immediately or by solving the corresponding instance of G, depending on the case of the definite clause. The outermost existential quantifiers in a goal formula (which are usually left implicit) are interpreted as a request to find values for the quantified variables that produce a solvable instance of the goal formula. The connectives $\wedge$ and $\vee$ that may appear in goal formulas typically have search interpretations in the programming context. The first connective specifies an AND branch in a search, i.e. it is a request to solve both components of a conjoined goal. The goal formula $G_1 \vee G_2$ represents a request to solve either G_1 or G_2 independently, and $\vee$ is thus a primitive for specifying OR branches in a search. This primitive is not provided for in the traditional description of Horn clauses, but it is nevertheless present in most implementations of Horn clause logic. Finally, a search related interpretation can also be accorded to the existential quantifier. This quantifier can be construed as a primitive for specifying an infinite OR branch in a search, where each branch is parameterized by the choice of substitution for the quantified variable.[1]

We illustrate some of the points discussed above by considering a program that implements the "append" relation between three lists. The first question to be addressed in developing this program is that of the representation to be used for lists. A natural choice for this is one that uses the constant *nil* for empty lists and the binary function symbol *cons* to construct a list out of a "head" element and a "tail" that is a list. This representation makes use of the structure of first-order terms and is symptomatic of another facet of logic programming: the terms of the underlying logic provides the data structures of the resulting programming language. Now, using this representation of lists, a program for appending lists is given by the following definite clauses:

$$\forall L \, append(nil, L, L),$$
$$\forall X \, \forall L_1 \, \forall L_2 \, \forall L_3 (append(L_1, L_2, L_3) \supset$$
$$append(cons(X, L_1), L_2, cons(X, L_3))).$$

We assume that *append* in the definite clauses above is a predicate name, coincidental, in fact, with the name of the procedure defined by the clauses. The declarative intent of these formulas is apparent from their logical interpretation: the result of appending the empty list to any other list is the latter list and the result of appending a list with head X and tail L_1 to (another list) L_2 is a list with head X and tail L_3, provided L_3 is the result of appending L_1 and L_2. From a programming perspective, the two definite clauses have the following import: The first clause defines *append* as a procedure that succeeds immediately if its first argument can be matched with *nil*; the precise notion of matching here is, of course, first-order unification. The second clause pertains to the situation where the first argument is a non-empty list. To be precise, it stipulates that one way of solving an "append" goal whose arguments unify with the terms $cons(X, L_1)$, L_2 and $cons(X, L_3)$ is by solving another "append" goal whose arguments are the relevant instantiations of L_1, L_2 and L_3.

The definition of the *append* procedure might now be used to answer relevant questions about the relation of appending lists. For example, suppose that a, b, c and d are constant symbols. Then, a question that might be of interest is the one posed by the following goal formula:

$$\exists L \, append(cons(a, cons(b, nil)), cons(c, cons(d, nil)), L).$$

Consistent with the interpretation of goal formulas, this query corresponds to a request for a value for the variable L that makes

$$append(cons(a, cons(b, nil)), cons(c, cons(d, nil)), L)$$

a solvable goal formula. A solution for this goal formula may be sought by using the procedural interpretation of *append*, leading to the conclusion that the only possible answer to it is the value

$$cons(a, cons(b, cons(c, cons(d, nil))))$$

for L. A characteristic of this query is that the "solution path" and the final answer for it are both deterministic. This is not, however, a necessary facet of every goal formula. As a specific example, the query

$$\exists L_1 \exists L_2 \, append(L_1, L_2, cons(a, cons(b, cons(c, cons(d, nil)))))$$

may be seen to have five different answers, each of which is obtained by choosing differently between the two clauses for *append* in the course of a solution. This aspect of nondeterminism is a hallmark of logic programming and is in fact a manifestation of its ability to support the notion of search in a primitive way.

Our current objective is to expose possible extensions to the syntax of the first-order G- and D-formulas that permit higher-order notions to be realized within logic programming. One higher-order ability that is coveted in programming contexts is that of passing procedures as arguments to other procedures. The above discussion makes apparent that the mechanism used for parameter passing in logic programming is unification and that passing a value to a procedure in fact involves the binding of a variable. A further point to note is that there is a duality in logic programming between predicates and procedures; the same object plays one or the other of these roles, depending on whether the point-of-view is logical or that of programming. From these observations, it is clear that the ability to pass procedures as arguments must hinge on the possibility of quantifying over predicates.

Predicate quantification is, in fact, capable of providing at least the simplest of programming abilities available through higher-order programming. The standard illustration of the higher-order capabilities of a language is the possibility of defining a "mapping" function in it. Such "functions" can easily be defined within the paradigm being considered with the provision of predicate variables. For example, suppose that we wish to define a function that takes a function and a list as arguments and produces a new list by applying the given function to each element of the former list. Given the relational style of programming prevalent in logic programming, such a function corresponds to the predicate *mappred* that is defined by the following definite clauses:

$$\forall P \, mappred(P, nil, nil),$$
$$\forall P \, \forall L_1 \, \forall L_2 \, \forall X \, \forall Y \, ((P(X, Y) \wedge mappred(P, L_1, L_2)) \supset$$
$$mappred(P, cons(X, L_1), cons(Y, L_2))).$$

The representation that is used for lists here is identical to the one described in the context of the *append* program. The clauses above involve a quantification over P which is evidently a predicate variable. This variable can be instantiated with the name of an actual procedure (or predicate) and would lead to the invocation of that procedure (with appropriate arguments) in the course of evaluating a *mappred* query. To provide a particular example, let us assume that our program also contains a list of clauses defining the ages of various individuals, such as the following:

> $age(bob, 24)$,
> $age(sue, 23)$.

The procedure *mappred* can then be invoked with *age* and a list of individuals as arguments and may be expected to return a corresponding list of ages. For instance, the query

> $\exists L\, mappred(age, cons(bob, cons(sue, nil)), L)$

should produce as an answer the substitution $cons(24, cons(23, nil))$ for L. Tracing a successful solution path for this query reveals that, in the course of producing an answer, queries of the form $age(bob, Y_1)$ and $age(sue, Y_2)$ have to be solved with suitable instantiations for Y_1 and Y_2.

The above example involves an instantiation of a simple kind for predicate variables—the substitution of a name of a predicate. A question to consider is if it is useful to permit the instantiation of such variables with more complex predicate terms. One ability that seems worth while to support is that of creating new relations by changing the order of arguments of given relations or by projecting onto some of their arguments. There are several programming situations where it is necessary to have "views" of a given relation that are obtained in this fashion, and it would be useful to have a device that permits the generation of such views without extensive additions to the program. The operations of abstraction and application that are formalized by the λ-calculus provide for such a device. Consider, for example, a relation that is like the *age* relation above, except that it has its arguments reversed. Such a relation can be represented by the predicate term $\lambda X\, \lambda Y\, age(Y, X)$. As another example, the expression $\lambda X\, age(X, 24)$ creates from *age* a predicate that represents the set of individuals whose age is 24.

An argument can thus be made for enhancing the structure of terms in the language by including the operations of abstraction and application. The general rationale is that it is worth while to couple the ability to treat predicates as values with devices for creating new predicate valued terms. Now, there are mechanisms for combining predicate terms, namely the logical connectives and quantifiers, and the same argument may be advanced for including these as well. To provide a concrete example, let us assume that our program contains the following set of definite clauses that define the "parent" relation between individuals:

$parent(bob, john),$
$parent(john, mary),$
$parent(sue, dick),$
$parent(dick, kate).$

One may desire to create a grandparent relation based on these clauses. This relation is, in fact, implemented by the term

$\lambda X \, \lambda Y \, \exists Z \, (parent(X, Z) \wedge parent(Z, Y)).$

An existential quantifier and a conjunction are used in this term to "join" two relations in obtaining a new one. Relations of this sort can be used in meaningful ways in performing computations. For example, the query

$\exists L \, mappred(\lambda X \, \lambda Y \, \exists Z \, (parent(X, Z) \wedge parent(Z, Y)),$
$cons(bob, cons(sue, nil)), L)$

illustrates the use of the relation shown together with the *mappred* predicate in asking for the grandparents of the individuals in a given list.

Assuming that we do allow logical symbols to appear in terms, it is relevant to consider whether the occurrences of these symbols should be restricted in any way. The role that these symbols are intended to play eventually indicates the answer to this question. Predicate terms are to instantiate predicate variables that get invoked as queries after being supplied with appropriate arguments. The logical connectives and quantifiers that appear in terms therefore become primitives that direct the search in the course of a computation. This observation, when coupled with our desire to preserve the essential character of Horn clause programming while providing for higher-order features, leads to the conclusion that only those logical symbols should be permitted in terms that can appear in the top-level structure of goal formulas. This argues specifically for the inclusion of only conjunctions, disjunctions and existential quantifications. This restriction can, of course, be relaxed if we are dealing with a logic whose propositional and quantificational structure is richer than that of Horn clauses. One such logic is outlined in Section 9 and is studied in detail in [Miller *et al.*, 1991].

Our consideration of higher-order aspects began with the provision of predicate variables. In a vein similar to that for logical symbols, one may ask whether there are practical considerations limiting the occurrences of these variables. In answering this question, it is useful to consider the structure of definite clauses again. These formulas are either of the form $\forall \bar{x} \, A$ or $\forall \bar{x} \, (G \supset A)$. An intuitive justification can be provided for permitting predicate variables in at least two places in such formulas: in "argument" positions in A and as the "heads" of atoms in G. The possibility for predicate variables to appear in these two locations is, in fact, what supports the ability to pass procedures as arguments and to later invoke them as goals. Now, there are two other forms in which a predicate variable can appear in the formulas being considered, and these are as an argument of an atom in G and as the head of A. An examination of the definition of the *mappred* procedure shows that it is useful to permit predicate variables to appear within the arguments of atomic goal formulas. With regard to the other possibility, we recall that, from a programming perspective, a definite clause is to be viewed as the definition of a procedure whose name it given by the head of A. A consideration of this fact indicates that predicate variables are not usefully permitted in the head position in A.

We have been concerned up to this point with only predicate variables and procedures. There is, however, another higher-order facet that should be considered and this is the possibility of functions to be variables. There is a similarity between predicates and functions—predicates are, eventually, boolean valued functions—and so it seems reasonable to permit a quantification over the latter if it is permitted over the former. There is, of course, the question of whether permitting such quantifications results in any useful and different higher-order abilities. To answer this question, let us consider the "functional" counterpart of *mappred* that is defined by the following definite clauses:

$$\forall F \, mapfun(F, nil, nil),$$
$$\forall F \, \forall L_1 \, \forall L_2 \, \forall X \, (mapfun(F, L_1, L_2) \supset$$
$$mapfun(F, cons(X, L_1), cons(F(X), L_2))).$$

Reading these clauses declaratively, we see that *mapfun* relates a function and two lists just in case the second list is obtained by applying the function to each element of the first list. Notice that the notion of function application involved here is quite different from that of solving a goal. For example, if our terms were chosen to be those of some version of the λ-calculus, function evaluation would be based on β-conversion. Thus, the query

$$\exists L \, mapfun(\lambda X \, h(1, X), cons(1, cons(2, nil)), L)$$

would apply the term $\lambda X \, h(1, X)$ to each of 1 and 2, eventually producing the list $cons(h(1, 1), cons(h(1, 2), nil))$ as an instantiation for L. (We assume that the symbol h that appears in the query is a constant.) By placing suitable restrictions on the λ-terms that we use, we can make the operation of β-conversion a relatively weak one, and, in fact, strong enough only to encode the substitution operation. Such a choice of terms makes it conceivable to run queries like the one just considered in "reverse." In particular, a query such as

$$\exists F \, mapfun(F, cons(1, cons(2, nil)), cons(h(1, 1), cons(h(1, 2), nil)))$$

could be posed with the expectation of generating the term $\lambda X \, h(1, X)$ as a substitution for F. The ability to find such solutions is dependent critically on using a weak notion of functions and function evaluation and finding predicate substitutions through an apparently similar process of solving goals is *not* a feasible possibility. To see this, suppose that we are given the query

$$\exists P \, mappred(P, cons(bob, cons(sue, nil)), cons(24, cons(23, nil))).$$

It might appear that a suitable answer can be provided to this query and that this might, in fact, be the value *age* for P. A little thought, however, indicates that the query is an ill-posed one. There are too many predicate terms that hold of *bob* and 24 and of *sue* and 23—consider, for example, the myriad ways for stating the relation that holds of any two objects—and enumerating these does not seem to be a meaningful computational task.

The above discussion brings out the distinction between quantification over only predicates and quantification over both predicates and functions. This does not in itself, however, address the question of usefulness of permitting quantification over functions. This question is considered in detail in Sections 8 and 9 and so we provide only a glimpse of an answer to it at this point. For this purpose, we return to the two *mapfun* queries above. In both queries the new ability obtained from function variables and λ-terms is that of analyzing the process of substitution. In the first query, the computation involved is that of performing substitutions into a given structure, namely $h(1, X)$. The second query involves finding a structure from which two different structures can be obtained by substitutions; in particular, a structure which yields $h(1, 1)$ when 1 is substituted into it and $h(1, 2)$ when 2 is used instead. Now, there are several situations where this ability to analyze the structures of terms via the operation of substitution is important. Furthermore, in many of these contexts, objects that incorporate the notion of binding will have to be treated. The terms of a λ-calculus and the accompanying conversion rules are, as we shall see, appropriate tools for correctly formalizing the idea of substitution in the presence of bound variables. Using function variables and λ-terms can, therefore, provide for programming primitives that are useful in these contexts.

We have already argued, using the *mappred* example, for the provision of predicate variables in the arguments of (atomic) goal formulas. This argument can be strengthened in light of the fact that predicates are but functions of a special kind. When predicate variables appear as the heads of atomic goals, i.e., in "extensional" positions, they can be instantiated, thereby leading to the computation of new goals. However, as we have just observed, it is not meaningful to contemplate finding values for such variables. When predicate variables appear in the arguments of goals, i.e. in "intensional" positions, values can be found for them by structural analyses in much the same way as for other function variables. These two kinds of occurrences of predicate variables can thus be combined to advantage: an intensional occurrence of a predicate variable can be used to form a query whose solution is then sought via an extensional occurrence

of the same variable. We delay the consideration of specific uses of this
facility till Section 7.

3   A higher-order logic

A principled development of a logic programming language that incorporates the features outlined in the previous section must be based on a
higher-order logic. The logic that we use for this purpose is derived from
Church's formulation of the simple theory of types [Church, 1940] princi-
pally by the exclusion of the axioms concerning infinity, extensionality for
propositions, choice and description. Church's logic is particularly suited
to our purposes since it is obtained by superimposing logical notions over
the calculus of λ-conversion. Our omission of certain axioms is based on a
desire for a logic that generalizes first-order logic by providing a stronger
notion of variable and term, but that, at the same time, encompasses only
the most primitive logical notions that are relevant in this context; only
these notions appear to be of consequence from the perspective of computational applications. Our logic is closely related to that of [Andrews,
1971], the only real differences being the inclusion of η-conversion as a rule
of inference and the incorporation of a larger number of propositional connectives and quantifiers as primitives. In the subsections that follow, we
describe the language of this logic and clarify the intended meanings of
expressions by the presentation of a deductive calculus as well as a notion
of models. There are several similarities between this logic and first-order
logic, especially in terms of proof-theoretic properties. However, the richer
syntax of the higher-order logic make the interpretation and usefulness of
these properties in the two contexts different. We dwell on this aspect in
Subsection 3.5.

3.1   The language

The language underlying the formal system that we utilize in this chapter
is that of a typed λ-calculus. There are two major syntactic components
to this language: the types and the terms. The purpose of the types is to
categorize the terms based on a functional hierarchy. From a syntactic perspective, the types constitute the more primitive notion and the formation
rules for terms identify a type with each term.

The types that are employed are often referred to as *simple* types. They
are determined by a set S of *sorts* and a set C of *type constructors*. We
assume that S contains the sort o that is the type of propositions and at
least one other sort, and that each member of C has associated with it
a unique positive arity. The class of types is then the smallest collection
that includes (i) every sort, (ii) $(c\ \sigma_1\ \ldots\ \sigma_n)$, for every $c \in C$ of arity n
and $\sigma_1,\ldots,\sigma_n$ that are types, and (iii) $(\sigma \to \tau)$ for every σ and τ that
are types. Understood intuitively, the type $(\sigma \to \tau)$ corresponds to the

set of "function" terms whose domains and ranges are given by σ and τ respectively. In keeping with this intuition, we refer to the types obtained by virtue of (i) and (ii) as *atomic types* and to those obtained by virtue of (iii) as *function* types.

We will employ certain notational conventions with respect to types. To begin with, we will use the letters σ and τ, perhaps with subscripts, as metalanguage variables for types. Further, the use of parentheses will be minimized by assuming that $\to$ associates to the right. Using this convention, every type can be written in the form $(\sigma_1 \to \cdots \to \sigma_n \to \tau)$ where τ is an atomic type. We will refer to $\sigma_1, \ldots, \sigma_n$ as the *argument* types and to τ as the *target* type of the type when it is written in this form. This terminology is extended to atomic types by permitting the argument types to be an empty sequence.

The class of terms is obtained by the operations of *abstraction* and *application* from given sets of constants and variables. We assume that the constants and variables are each specified with a type and that these collections meet the following additional conditions: there is at least one constant and a denumerable number of variables of each type and the variables of each type are distinct from the constants and the variables of any other type. The *terms* or *formulas* are then specified together with an associated type in the following fashion:

(1) A variable or a constant of type σ is a term of type σ.

(2) If x is a variable of type σ and F is a term of type τ then $(\lambda x \, F)$ is a term of type $\sigma \to \tau$, and is referred to as an *abstraction* that *binds* x and whose *scope* is F.

(3) If F_1 is a term of type $\sigma \to \tau$ and F_2 is a term of type σ then $(F_1 \, F_2)$, referred to as the *application* of F_1 to F_2, is a term of type τ.

Once again, certain notational conventions will be employed in connection with terms. When talking about an arbitrary term, we will generally denote this by an uppercase letter that possibly has a subscript and a superscript. It will sometimes be necessary to display abstractions and we will usually depict the variable being abstracted by a lowercase letter that may be subscripted. When it is necessary to present specific (object-level) terms, we will explicitly indicate the symbols that are to be construed as constants and variables. In writing terms, we will omit parentheses by using the convention that abstraction is right associative and application is left associative. This usage will occur at both the object- and the meta-level. As a further shorthand, the abstraction symbol in a sequence of abstractions will sometimes be omitted: thus, the term $\lambda x_1 \ldots \lambda x_n \, T$ may be abbreviated by $\lambda x_1, \ldots, x_n \, T$. Finally, although each term is specified only in conjunction with a type, we will seldom mention the types of terms explicitly. These omissions will be justified on the basis that the types can either be inferred from the context or are inessential to the discussion at hand.

The rules of formation for terms serve to identify the well-formed subparts of any given term. Specifically, a term G is said to *occur* in, or to be a *subterm* or *subformula* of, a term F if (a) G is F, or (b) F is of the form $(\lambda x\, F_1)$ and G occurs in F_1, or (c) F is of the form $(F_1\, F_2)$ and G occurs in either F_1 or F_2. An occurrence of a variable x in F is either *bound* or *free* depending on whether it is or is not an occurrence in the scope of an abstraction that binds x. A variable x is a bound (free) variable of F if it has at least one bound (free) occurrence in F. F is a *closed* term just in case it has no free variables. We write $\mathcal{F}(F)$ to denote the set of free variables of F. This notation is generalized to sets of terms and sets of pairs of terms in the following way: $\mathcal{F}(\mathcal{D})$ is $\bigcup\{\mathcal{F}(F) \mid F \in \mathcal{D}\}$ if $\mathcal{D}$ is a set of terms and $\bigcup\{\mathcal{F}(F_1) \cup \mathcal{F}(F_2) \mid \langle F_1, F_2\rangle \in \mathcal{D}\}$ if $\mathcal{D}$ is a set of pairs of terms.

Example 3.1.1. Let $int \in S$ and $list \in C$ and assume that the arity of $list$ is 1. Then the following are legitimate types: int, $(list\, int)$ and $int \to (list\, int) \to (list\, int)$. The argument types of the last of these types are int and $(list\, int)$ and its target type is $(list\, int)$. Let $cons$ be a constant of type $int \to (list\, int) \to (list\, int)$, let 1 and 2 be constants of type int and let l be a variable of type $(list\, int)$. Then $\lambda l\,(cons\, 1\,(cons\, 2\, l))$ is a term. A cursory inspection reveals that the type of this term must be $(list\, int) \to (list\, int)$. The above term has one bound variable and no free variables, i.e., it is a closed term. However, it has as subterm the term $(cons\, 1\,(cons\, 2\, l))$ in which the variable l appears free.

The language presented thus far gives us a means for describing functions of a simple sort: abstraction constitutes a device for representing function formation and application provides a means for representing the evaluation of such functions. Our desire, however, is for a language that allows not only for the representation of functions, but also for the use of connectives and quantifiers in describing relations between such functions. Such a capability can be achieved in the present context by introducing a set of constants for representing these logical operations. To be precise, we henceforth assume that the set of constants is partitioned into the set of *parameters* or *nonlogical constants* and the set of *logical constants* with the latter comprising the following infinite list of symbols: $\top$ of type o, $\neg$ of type $o \to o$, $\wedge$, $\vee$ and $\supset$ of type $o \to o \to o$, and, for each σ, $\exists$ and $\forall$ of type $(\sigma \to o) \to o$. We recall that o is intended to be the type of propositions. The logical constants are to be interpreted in the following manner: $\top$ corresponds to the tautologous proposition, the *(propositional) connectives* $\neg$, $\vee$, $\wedge$, and $\supset$ correspond, respectively, to negation, disjunction, conjunction, and implication, and the family of constants $\exists$ and $\forall$ are, respectively, the existential and universal quantifiers. The correspondence between $\exists$ and $\forall$ and the quantifiers familiar from first-order logic may be understood from the following: the existential and universal quantification of x over P is written as $(\exists\,(\lambda x\,P))$ and $(\forall\,(\lambda x\,P))$ respectively. Under this representation, the dual aspects of binding and predication that accompany the usual notions of quantification are handled separately by abstractions and constants that are propositional functions of propositional functions. The constants that are used must, of course, be accorded a suitable interpretation for this representation to be a satisfactory one. For example, the meaning assigned to $\forall$ must be such that $(\forall\,(\lambda x\,P))$ holds just in case $(\lambda x\,P)$ corresponds to the set of all objects of the type of x.

Certain conventions and terminology are motivated by the intended interpretations of the type o and the logical constants. In order to permit a distinction between arbitrary terms and those of type o, we reserve the word "formula" exclusively for terms of type o. Terms of type $\sigma_1 \to \cdots \to \sigma_n \to o$ correspond to n-ary relations on terms and, for this reason, we will also refer to them as predicates of n-arguments. In writing formulas, we will adopt an infix notation for the symbols $\wedge$, $\vee$ and $\supset$; e.g., we will write $(\wedge\,F\,G)$ as $(F \wedge G)$. In a similar vein, the expressions $(\exists x\,F)$ and $(\forall x\,F)$ will be used as abbreviations for $(\exists\,(\lambda x\,F))$ and $(\forall\,(\lambda x\,F))$ Parallel to the convention for abstractions, we will sometimes write the expressions $\exists x_1 \ldots \exists x_n\,F$ and $\forall x_1 \ldots \forall x_n\,F$ as $\exists x_1, \ldots, x_n\,F$ and $\forall x_1, \ldots, x_n\,F$ respectively. In several cases it will only be important to specify that the "prefix" contains a sequence of some length. In such cases, we will use $\bar{x}$ an abbreviation for a sequence of variables and write $\lambda \bar{x}\,F$, $\exists \bar{x}\,F$ or $\forall \bar{x}\,F$, as the case might be.

Our language at this point has the ability to represent functions as well as logical relations between functions. However, the sense in which it can represent these notions is still informal and needs to be made precise. We do this in the next two subsections, first by describing a formal system that clarifies the meaning of abstraction and application and then by presenting a sequent calculus that bestows upon the various logical symbols their intended meanings.

3.2 Equality between terms

The intended interpretations of abstraction and application are formalized by the rules of λ-conversion. To define these rules, we need the operation of replacing all free occurrences of a variable x in the term T_1 by a term T_2 of the same type as x. This operation is denoted by $S_x^{T_2}T_1$ and is made explicit as follows:

(i) If T_1 is a variable or a constant, then $S_x^{T_2}T_1$ is T_2 if T_1 is x and T_1 otherwise.

(ii) If T_1 is of the form $(\lambda y\,C)$, then $S_x^{T_2}T_1$ is T_1 if y is x and $(\lambda y\,S_x^{T_2}C)$ otherwise.

(iii)   If T_1 is of the form $(C\ D)$, then $S_x^{T_2}T_1 = (S_x^{T_2}C\ S_x^{T_2}D)$.

In performing this operation of replacement, there is the danger that the free variables of T_2 become bound inadvertently. The term "T_2 is *substitutable for x in T_1*" describes the situations in which the operation is logically correct, i.e. those situations where x does not occur free in the scope of an abstraction in T_1 that binds a free variable of T_2. The rules of α-*conversion*, β-*conversion* and η-*conversion* are then, respectively, the following operations and their converses on terms:

(1)   Replacing a subterm $(\lambda x\, T)$ by $(\lambda y\, S_x^y T)$ provided y is substitutable for x in T and not free in T.

(2)   Replacing a subterm $((\lambda x\, T_1)\ T_2)$ by $S_x^{T_2}T_1$ provided T_2 is substitutable for x in T_1, and vice versa.

(3)   Replacing a subterm $(\lambda x\, (T\ x))$ by T provided x is not free in T, and vice versa.

The rules above, referred to collectively as the λ-conversion rules, may be used to define the following relations between terms:

Definition 3.2.1. T λ-*conv* (β-*conv*, $\equiv$) S just in case there is a sequence of applications of the λ-conversion (respectively α- and β-conversion, α-conversion) rules that transforms T into S.

The three relations thus defined are easily seen to be equivalence relations. They correspond, in fact, to notions of equality between terms based on the following informal interpretation of the λ-conversion rules: α-conversion asserts that the choice of name for the variable bound by an abstraction is unimportant, β-conversion relates an application to the result of evaluating the application, and η-conversion describes a notion of extensionality for function terms (the precise nature of which will become clear in Subsection 3.4). We use the strongest of these notions in our discussions below, i.e. we shall consider T and S equal just in case T λ-conv S.

It is useful to identify the equivalence classes of terms under the relations just defined with canonical members of each class. Towards this end, we say that a term is in β-*normal form* if it does not have a subterm of the form $((\lambda x\, A)\ B)$. If T is in β-normal form and S β-conv T, then T is said to be a β-normal form for S. For our typed language, it is known that a β-normal form exists for every term [Andrews, 1971]. By the celebrated Church–Rosser theorem for β-conversion [Barendregt, 1981], this form must be unique up to a renaming of bound variables. We may therefore use terms in β-normal form as representatives of the equivalence classes under the β-conv relation. We note that each such term has the structure

$$\lambda x_1 \ldots \lambda x_n\, (A\ T_1\ \ldots\ T_m)$$

where A is a constant or variable, and, for $1 \leq i \leq m$, T_i also has the same structure. We refer to the sequence $x_1, \ldots, x_n$ as the *binder*, to A as the *head* and to $T_1, \ldots, T_m$ as the *arguments* of such a term; in particular instances, the binder may be empty, and the term may also have no arguments. Such a term is said to be *rigid* if its head, i.e. A, is either a constant or a variable that appears in the binder, and *flexible* otherwise.

In identifying the canonical members of the equivalence classes of terms with respect to λ-conv, there are two different approaches that might be followed. Under one approach, we say that a term is in η-normal form if it has no subterm of the form $(\lambda x \, (A \, x))$ in which x is not free in A, and we say a term is in λ-normal form if it is in both β- and η-normal form. The other alternative is to say that a term is in λ-normal form if it can be written in the form $\lambda \bar{x} \, (A \, T_1 \, \ldots \, T_m)$ where A is a constant or variable of type $\sigma_1 \to \ldots \to \sigma_m \to \tau$ with τ being an atomic type and, further, each T_i can also be written in a similar form. (Note that the term must be in β-normal form for this to be possible.) In either case we say that T is a λ-normal form for S if S λ-conv T and T is in λ-normal form. Regardless of which definition is chosen, it is known that a λ-normal form exists for every term in our typed language and that this form is unique up to a renaming of bound variables (see [Barendregt, 1981] and also the discussion in [Nadathur, 1987]). We find it convenient to use the latter definition in this chapter and we will write $\lambda norm(T)$ to denote a λ-normal form for T under it. To obtain such a form for any given term, the following procedure may be used: First convert the term into β-normal form by repeatedly replacing every subterm of the form $((\lambda x \, A) \, B)$ by $S_x^B A$ preceded, perhaps, by some α-conversion steps. Now, if the resulting term is of the form $\lambda x_1, \ldots, x_m \, (A \, T_1 \, \ldots \, T_n)$ where A is of type $\sigma_1 \to \ldots \sigma_n \to \sigma_{n+1} \to \ldots \to \sigma_{n+r} \to \tau$, then replace it by the term

$$\lambda x_1, \ldots, x_m, y_1, \ldots, y_r \, (A \, T_1 \, \ldots \, T_n \, y_1 \, \ldots \, y_r)$$

where $y_i, \ldots, y_r$ are distinct variables of appropriate types that are not contained in $\{x_1, \ldots, x_m\}$. Finally repeat this operation of "fluffing-up" of the arguments on the terms $T_1, \ldots, T_n, y_1, \ldots, y_r$.

A λ-normal form of a term T as we have defined it here is unique only up to a renaming of bound variables (i.e., up to α-conversions). While this is sufficient for most purposes, we will occasionally need to talk of a unique normal form. In such cases, we use $\rho(F)$ to designate what we call the *principal normal form* of F. Determining this form essentially requires a naming convention for bound variables and a convention such as the one in [Andrews, 1971] suffices for our purposes.

The existence of a λ-normal form for each term is useful for two reasons. First, it provides a mechanism for determining whether two terms are equal by virtue of the λ-conversion rules. Second, it permits the properties of terms to be discussed by using a representative from each of the equivalence classes that has a convenient structure. Of particular interest to us is the structure of formulas in λ-normal form. For obvious reasons, we call a formula whose leftmost non-parenthesis symbol is either a variable or a parameter an *atomic formula*. Then one of the following is true of a formula in λ-normal form: (i) it is ⊤, (ii) it is an atomic formula, (iii) it is of the form ¬F, where F is a formula in λ-normal form, (iv) it is of the form $(F \vee G)$, $(F \wedge G)$, or $(F \supset G)$ where F and G are formulas in λ-normal form, or (v) it is of the form $(\exists x\, F)$ or $(\forall x\, F)$, where F is a formula in λ-normal form.

The β-conversion rule provides a convenient means for defining the operation of substitution on terms. A substitution is formally a (type preserving) mapping on variables that is the identity everywhere except at finitely many explicitly specified points. Thus, a substitution is represented by a set of the form $\{\langle x_i, T_i\rangle \mid 1 \leq i \leq n\}$, where, for $1 \leq i \leq n$, x_i is a distinct variable and T_i is a term that is of the same type as x_i but that is distinct from x_i. The application of a substitution to a term requires this mapping to be extended to the class of all terms and can be formalized as follows: if $\theta = \{\langle x_i, T_i\rangle \mid 1 \leq i \leq n\}$ and S is a term, then

$$\theta(G) = \rho(((\lambda x_1 \ldots \lambda x_n\, S)\, T_1\ \ldots\ T_n)).$$

It can be seen that this definition is independent of the order in which the pairs are taken from θ and that it formalizes the idea of replacing the free occurrences of $x_1, \ldots, x_n$ in S simultaneously by the terms $T_1, \ldots, T_n$. We often have to deal with substitutions that are given by singleton sets and we introduce a special notation for the application of such substitutions: if θ is $\{\langle x, T\rangle\}$, then $\theta(S)$ may also be written as $[T/x]S$.

Certain terminology pertaining to substitutions will be used later in the chapter. Given two terms T_1 and T_2, we say T_1 is an *instance* of T_2 if it results from applying a substitution to T_2. The *composition* of two substitutions θ_1 and θ_2, written as $\theta_1 \circ \theta_2$, is precisely the composition of θ_1 and θ_2 when these are viewed as mappings: $\theta_1 \circ \theta_2(G) = \theta_1(\theta_2(G))$. The *restriction* of a substitution θ to a set of variables $\mathcal{V}$, denoted by $\theta \uparrow \mathcal{V}$, is given as follows:

$$\theta \uparrow \mathcal{V} = \{\langle x, F\rangle \mid \langle x, F\rangle \in \theta \text{ and } x \in \mathcal{V}\}.$$

Two substitutions, θ_1 and θ_2, are said to be *equal* relative to a set of variables $\mathcal{V}$ if it is the case that $\theta_1 \uparrow \mathcal{V} = \theta_2 \uparrow \mathcal{V}$ and this relationship is denoted by $\theta_1 =_v \theta_2$. θ_1 is said to be *less general than* θ_2 relative to $\mathcal{V}$, a relationship denoted by $\theta_1 \preceq_v \theta_2$, if there is a substitution σ such that $\theta_1 =_v \sigma \circ \theta_2$. Finally, we will sometimes talk of the result of applying a substitution to a set of formulas and to a set of pairs of formulas. In the first case, we mean the set that results from applying the substitution to each formula in the set, and, in the latter case, we mean the set of pairs that results from the application of the substitution to each element in each pair.

3.3   The notion of derivation

The meanings of the logical symbols in our language may be clarified by providing an abstract characterization of proofs for formulas containing these symbols. One convenient way to do this is by using a sequent calculus. We digress briefly to summarize the central notions pertaining to such calculi. The basic unit of assertion within these calculi is a *sequent*. A sequent is a pair of finite (possibly empty) sets of formulas $\langle \Gamma, \Theta \rangle$ that is usually written as $\Gamma \longrightarrow \Theta$. The first element of this pair is referred to as the *antecedent* of the sequent and the second is called its *succedent*. A sequent corresponds intuitively to the assertion that in each situation in which all the formulas in its antecedent hold, there is at least one formula in its succedent that also holds. In the case that the succedent is empty, the sequent constitutes an assertion of contradictoriness of the formulas in its antecedent. A *proof* for a sequent is a finite tree constructed using a given set of *inference figures* and such that the root is labeled with the sequent in question and the leaves are labeled with designated *initial sequents*. Particular sequent systems are characterized by their choice of inference figures and initial sequents.

Our higher-order logic is defined within this framework by the inference figure schemata contained in Figure 1. Actual inference figures are obtained from these by instantiating Γ, Θ and Δ by sets of formulas, B, D, and P by formulas, x by a variable, T by a term and c by a parameter. There is, in addition, a proviso on the choice of parameter for c: it should not appear in any formula contained in the lower sequent in the same figure. Also, in the inference figure schemata λ, the sets Δ and Δ' and the sets Θ and Θ' differ only in that zero or more formulas in them are replaced by formulas that can be obtained from them by using the λ-conversion rules. The initial sequents of our sequent calculus are all the sequents of the form $\Gamma \longrightarrow \Theta$ where either $\top \in \Theta$ or for some atomic formulas $A \in \Delta$ and $A' \in \Theta$ it is the case that $A \equiv A'$.

Expressions of the form B, Δ and Θ, B that are used in the inference figure schemata in Figure 1 are to be treated as abbreviations for $\Delta \cup \{B\}$ and $\Theta \cup \{B\}$ respectively. Thus, a particular set of formulas may be viewed as being of the form Θ, B even though $B \in \Theta$. As a result of this view, a formula that appears in the antecedent or succedent of a sequent really has an arbitrary multiplicity. This interpretation allows us to eliminate the structural inference figures called contraction that typically appear in sequent calculi; these inference figures provide for the multiplicity of formulas in sequents in a situation where the antecedents and succedents are taken to be lists instead of sets. Our use of sets also allows us to drop another structural inference figure called exchange that is generally employed to ensure that the order of formulas is unimportant. A third kind of structural inference figure, commonly referred to as thinning or

$$\frac{B, D, \Delta \longrightarrow \Theta}{B \wedge D, \Delta \longrightarrow \Theta} \wedge\text{-L} \qquad \frac{\Delta \longrightarrow \Theta, B \qquad \Delta \longrightarrow \Theta, D}{\Delta \longrightarrow \Theta, B \wedge D} \wedge\text{-R}$$

$$\frac{B, \Delta \longrightarrow \Theta \qquad D, \Delta \longrightarrow \Theta}{B \vee D, \Delta \longrightarrow \Theta} \vee\text{-L}$$

$$\frac{\Delta \longrightarrow \Theta, B}{\Delta \longrightarrow \Theta, B \vee D} \vee\text{-R} \qquad \frac{\Delta \longrightarrow \Theta, D}{\Delta \longrightarrow \Theta, B \vee D} \vee\text{-R}$$

$$\frac{\Delta \longrightarrow \Theta, B}{\neg B, \Delta \longrightarrow \Theta} \neg\text{-L} \qquad \frac{B, \Delta \longrightarrow \Theta}{\Delta \longrightarrow \Theta, \neg B} \neg\text{-R}$$

$$\frac{\Delta \longrightarrow \Theta, B \qquad D, \Delta \longrightarrow \Gamma}{B \supset D, \Delta \longrightarrow \Theta \cup \Gamma} \supset\text{-L} \qquad \frac{B, \Delta \longrightarrow \Theta, D}{\Delta \longrightarrow \Theta, B \supset D} \supset\text{-R}$$

$$\frac{[T/x]P, \Delta \longrightarrow \Theta}{\forall x\, P, \Delta \longrightarrow \Theta} \forall\text{-L} \qquad \frac{\Delta \longrightarrow \Theta, [T/x]P}{\Delta \longrightarrow \Theta, \exists x\, P} \exists\text{-R}$$

$$\frac{[c/x]P, \Delta \longrightarrow \Theta}{\exists x\, P, \Delta \longrightarrow \Theta} \exists\text{-L} \qquad \frac{\Delta \longrightarrow \Theta, [c/x]P}{\Delta \longrightarrow \Theta, \forall x\, P} \forall\text{-R}$$

$$\frac{\Delta' \longrightarrow \Theta'}{\Delta \longrightarrow \Theta} \lambda$$

Fig. 1. Inference figure schemata

weakening, permits the addition of formulas to the antecedent or succedent. This ability is required in calculi where only one formula is permitted in the antecedent or succedent of an initial sequent. Given the definition of initial sequents in our calculus, we do not have a need for such inference figures.

Any proof that can be constructed using our calculus is referred to as a **C**-proof. A **C**-proof in which every sequent has at most one formula in its succedent is called an **I**-proof. We write $\Gamma \vdash_C B$ to signify that $\Gamma \longrightarrow B$ has a **C**-proof and $\Gamma \vdash_I B$ to signify that it has an **I**-proof. These relations correspond, respectively, to provability in higher-order classical and intuitionistic logic. Our primary interest in this chapter is in the classical notion, and unqualified uses of the words "derivation" or "proof" are to be read as **C**-proof. We note that this notion of derivability is identical to the notion of provability in the system $\mathcal{T}$ of [Andrews, 1971] augmented by the rule of η-conversion. The reader familiar with [Gentzen, 1969] may also compare the calculus LK and the one described here for **C**-proofs. One difference between these two is the absence of the inference figures of the form

$$\frac{\Gamma \longrightarrow \Theta, B \qquad B, \Delta \longrightarrow \Lambda}{\Gamma \cup \Delta \longrightarrow \Theta \cup \Lambda}$$

from our calculus. These inference figures are referred to as the *Cut* inference figures and they occupy a celebrated position within logic. Their omission from our calculus is justified by a rather deep result for the higher-order logic under consideration, the so-called *cut-elimination theorem*. This theorem asserts that the same set of sequents have proofs in the calculi with and without the Cut inference figures. A proof of this theorem for our logic can be modelled on the one in [Andrews, 1971] (see [Nadathur, 1987] for details). The only other significant difference between our calculus and the one in [Gentzen, 1969] is that our formulas have a richer syntax and the λ inference figures have been included to manipulate this syntax. This difference, as we shall observe presently, has a major impact on the process of searching for proofs.

3.4 A notion of models

An alternative approach to clarifying the meanings of the logical symbols in our language is to specify the role they play in determining the denotations of terms from abstract domains of objects. This may be done in a manner akin to that in [Henkin, 1950]. In particular, we assume that we are given a family of domains $\{D_\sigma\}_\sigma$, each domain being indexed by a type. The intention is that a term of type σ will, under a given interpretation for the parameters and an assignment for the variables, denote an object in the domain D_σ. There are certain properties that we expect our domains to satisfy at the outset. For each atomic type σ other than o, we assume that D_σ is some set of *individual objects* of that type. The domain D_o will correspond to a set of truth values. However, within our logic and unlike the logic dealt with in [Henkin, 1950], distinctions must be made between the denotations of formulas even when they have the same propositional content: as an example, it should be possible for $Q \vee P$ to denote a different object from $P \vee Q$, despite the fact that these formulas share a truth value under identical circumstances. For this reason, we take D_o to be a domain of *labeled* truth values. Formally, we assume that we are given a collection of labels, $\mathcal{L}$ and that D_o is a subset of $\mathcal{L} \times \{T, F\}$ that denotes a function from the labels $\mathcal{L}$ to the set $\{T, F\}$. For each function type, we assume that the domain corresponding to it is a collection of functions over the relevant domains. Thus, we expect $D_{\sigma \to \tau}$ to be a collection of functions from D_σ to D_τ.

We refer to a family of domains $\{D_\sigma\}_\sigma$ that satisfies the above constraints as a *frame*. We assume now that I is a mapping on the parameters that associates an object from D_σ with a parameter of type σ. The behavior of the logical symbols insofar as truth values are concerned is determined by their intended interpretation as we shall presently observe. However, their behavior with respect to labels is open to choice. For the purpose of fixing this in a given context we assume that we are given a predetermined label $\top_l$ and the following mappings:

$$\neg_l : \mathcal{L} \to \mathcal{L} \qquad \vee_l : \mathcal{L} \to \mathcal{L} \to \mathcal{L} \qquad \wedge_l : \mathcal{L} \to \mathcal{L} \to \mathcal{L}$$
$$\supset_l : \mathcal{L} \to \mathcal{L} \to \mathcal{L} \qquad \exists_l^\sigma : D_{\sigma \to o} \to \mathcal{L} \qquad \forall_l^\sigma : D_{\sigma \to o} \to \mathcal{L};$$

the last two are actually a family of mappings, parameterized by types. Let C be the set containing $\top_l$ and these various mappings. Then the tuple $\langle \mathcal{L}, \{D_\sigma\}_\sigma, I, C \rangle$ is said to be a *pre-structure* or *pre-interpretation* for our language.

A mapping ϕ on the variables is an *assignment* with respect to a pre-structure $\langle \mathcal{L}, \{D_\sigma\}_\sigma, I, C \rangle$ just in case ϕ maps each variable of type σ to D_σ. We wish to extend ϕ to a "valuation" function V_ϕ on all terms. The desired behavior of V_ϕ on a term H is given by induction over the structure of H:

(1) H is a variable of a constant. In this case

    (i)   if H is a variable then $V_\phi(H) = \phi(H)$,

    (ii) if H is a parameter then $V_\phi(H) = I(H)$,

    (iii) if H is $\top$ then $V_\phi(H) = \langle \top_l, T \rangle$

    (iv) if H is $\neg$ then $V_\phi(H)\langle l, p \rangle = \langle \neg_l(l), q \rangle$, where q is F if p is T and T otherwise,

    (v) if H is $\vee$ then $V_\phi(H)\langle l_1, p \rangle \langle l_2, q \rangle = \langle \vee_l(l_1)(l_2), r \rangle$, where r is T if either p or q is T and F otherwise,

    (vi) if H is $\wedge$ then $V_\phi(H)\langle l_1, p \rangle \langle l_2, q \rangle = \langle \wedge_l(l_1)(l_2), r \rangle$, where r is F if either p or q is F and T otherwise,

    (vii) if H is $\supset$ then $V_\phi(H)\langle l_1, p \rangle \langle l_2, q \rangle = \langle \supset_l(l_1)(l_2), r \rangle$, where r is T if either p is F or q is T and F otherwise,

    (viii) if H is $\exists$ of type $((\sigma \to o) \to o)$ then, for any $p \in D_{\sigma \to o}$, $V_\phi(H)(p) = \langle \exists_l^\sigma(p), q \rangle$, where q is T if there is some $t \in D_\sigma$ such that $p(t) = \langle l, T \rangle$ for some $l \in \mathcal{L}$ and q is F otherwise, and

    (ix) if H is $\forall$ of type $((\sigma \to o) \to o)$ then, for any $p \in D_{\sigma \to o}$, $V_\phi(H)(p) = \langle \forall_l^\sigma(p), q \rangle$, where q is T if for every $t \in D_\sigma$ there is some $l \in \mathcal{L}$ such that $p(t) = \langle l, T \rangle$ and q is F otherwise.

(2) H is $(H_1\ H_2)$. In this case, $V_\phi(H) = V_\phi(H_1)(V_\phi(H_2))$.

(3) H is $(\lambda x\ H_1)$. Let x be of type σ and, for any $t \in D_\sigma$, let $\phi(x := t)$ be the assignment that is identical to ϕ except that it maps x to t.

Then $V_\phi(H) = p$ where p is the function on D_σ such that $p(t) = V_{\phi(x:=t)}(H_1)$.

The definition of pre-structure is, however, not sufficiently restrictive to ensure that $V_\phi(H) \in D_\sigma$ for every term H of type σ. The solution to this problem is to deem that only certain pre-structures are acceptable for the purpose of determining meanings, and to identify these pre-structures and the meaning function simultaneously. Formally, we say a pre-structure $\langle \mathcal{L}, \{D_\sigma\}_\sigma, I, C \rangle$ is a *structure* or *interpretation* only if, for any assignment ϕ and any term H of type σ, $V_\phi(H) \in D_\sigma$ where V_ϕ is given by the conditions above. It follows, of course, that $V_\phi(H)$ is well defined relative to a structure. For a closed term H, $V_\phi(H)$ is independent of the assignment ϕ and may, therefore, be thought of as the denotation of H relative to the given structure.

The idea of a structure as defined here is similar to the notion of a *general model* in [Henkin, 1950], the chief difference being that we use a domain of labeled truth values for D_o. Note that our structures degenerate to general models in Henkin's sense in the case that the the the set of labels $\mathcal{L}$ is restricted to a two element set. It is of interest also to observe that the domains $D_{\sigma \to \tau}$ in our structures are collections of functions from D_σ to D_τ as opposed to functions in combination with a way of identifying them, and the semantics engendered is extensional in this sense. The axiom of extensionality is not a formula of our logic since its vocabulary does not include the equality symbol. However, it is easily seen that the effect of this axiom holds in our structures at a meta-level: two elements of the domain $D_{\sigma \to \tau}$ are equal just in case they produce the same value when given identical objects from D_σ. As a final observation, in the special case that the domains $D_{\sigma \to \tau}$ include all the functions from D_σ to D_τ we obtain a structure akin to the *standard* models of [Henkin, 1950].

Various logical notions pertaining to formulas in our language can be explained by recourse to the definition of V_ϕ. We say, for instance, that a formula H is satisfied by a structure and an assignment ϕ if $V_\phi(H) = \langle l, T \rangle$ relative to that structure. A *valid* formula is one that is satisfied by every structure and every assignment. Given a set of formulas Γ, and a formula A, we say that A is a logical consequence of Γ, written $\Gamma \models A$, just in case A is satisfied by every structure and assignment that also satisfies each member of Γ.

Given a finite set of formulas Θ, let $\vee\Theta$ denote the disjunction of the formulas in Θ if Θ is nonempty and the formula $\neg\top$ otherwise. The following theorem relates the model-theoretic semantics that is presented in this subsection for our higher-order logic to the proof-theoretic semantics presented in the previous subsection. The proof of this theorem and a fuller development of the ideas here may be found in [Nadathur, 1997].

Theorem 3.4.1. *Let* Γ, Θ *be finite sets of formulas. Then* $\Gamma \longrightarrow \Theta$ *has a* **C***-proof if and only if* $\Gamma \models (\vee\Theta)$.

3.5　Predicate variables and the subformula property

As noted in Subsection 3.3, the proof systems for first-order logic and our higher-order logic look similar: the only real differences are, in fact, in the presence of the λ-conversion rules and the richer syntax of formulas. The impact of these differences is, however, nontrivial. An important property of formulas in first-order logic is that performing substitutions into them preserves their logical structure — the resulting formula is in a certain precise sense a subformula of the original formula (see [Gentzen, 1969]). A similar observation can unfortunately not be made about formulas in our higher-order logic. As an example, consider the formula $F = ((p\ a) \supset (Y\ a))$; we assume that p and a are parameters of suitable type here and that Y is a variable. Now let θ be the substitution

$$\{\langle Y, \lambda z\,((p\ z) \wedge \forall x\,((z\ x) \supset (b\ x)))\rangle\},$$

where x, y and z are variables and b is a parameter. Then

$$\theta(F) \equiv (p\ a) \supset ((p\ a) \wedge \forall x\,((a\ x) \supset (b\ x))).$$

As can be seen from this example, applying a substitution to a formula in which a predicate variable appears free has the potential for dramatically altering the top-level logical structure of the formula.

The above observation has proof-theoretic consequences that should be mentioned. One consequence pertains to the usefulness of cut-elimination theorems. These theorems have been of interest in the context of logic because they provide an insight into the nature of deduction. Within first-order logic, for instance, this theorem leads to the subformula property: if a sequent has a proof, then it has one in which every formula in the proof is a subformula of some formula in the sequent being proved. Several useful structural properties of deduction in the first-order context can be observed based on this property. From the example presented above, it is clear that the subformula property does not hold under any reasonable interpretation for our higher-order logic even though it admits a cut-elimination theorem; predicate terms containing connectives and quantifiers may be generalized upon in the course of a derivation and thus intermediate sequents may have formulas whose structure cannot be predicted from the formulas in the final one. For this reason, the usefulness of cut-elimination as a device for teasing out the structural properties of derivations in higher-order logic has generally been doubted.

A related observation concerns the automation of deduction. The traditional method for constructing a proof of a formula in a logic that involves quantification consists, in a general sense, in substituting expressions for existentially quantified variables and then verifying that the resulting formula is a tautology. In a logic where the propositional structure remains invariant under substitutions, the search for a proof can be based on this structure and the substitution (or, more appropriately, unification) process may be reduced to a constraint on the search. However, the situation is different in a logic in which substitutions can change the propositional structure of formulas. In such logics, the construction of a proof often involves finding the "right" way in which to change the propositional structure as well. As might be imagined, this problem is a difficult one to solve in general, and no good method that is also complete has yet been described for determining these kinds of substitutions in our higher-order logic. The existing theorem-provers for this logic either sacrifice completeness [Bledsoe, 1979; Andrews *et al.*, 1984] or are quite intractable for this reason [Huet, 1973a; Andrews, 1989].

In the next section we describe a certain class of formulas from our higher-order logic. Our primary interest in these formulas is that they provide a logical basis for higher-order features in logic programming. There is an auxiliary interest, however, in these formulas in the light of the above observations. The special structure of these formulas enables us to obtain useful information about derivations concerning them from the cut-elimination theorem for higher-order logic. This information, in turn, enables the description of a proof procedure that is complete and that at the same time finds substitutions for predicate variables almost entirely through unification. Our study of these formulas thus also demonstrates the utility of the cut-elimination theorem even in the context of a higher-order logic.

4 Higher-order Horn clauses

In this section we describe a logical language that possesses all the enhancements to first-order Horn clauses that were discussed in Section 2. The first step in this direction is to identify a subcollection of the class of terms of the higher-order logic that was described in the previous section.

Definition 4.0.1. A *positive* term is a term of our higher-order language that does not contain occurrences of the symbols $\neg$, $\supset$ and $\forall$. The collection of positive terms that are in λ-normal form is called the *positive Herbrand universe* and is denoted by $\mathcal{H}^+$.

The structure of positive terms clearly satisfies the requirement that we wish to impose on the arguments of atomic formulas: these terms are constructed by the operations of application and abstraction and function (and predicate) variables may appear in them as also the logical symbols $\top$, $\vee$, $\wedge$ and $\exists$. As we shall see presently, $\mathcal{H}^+$ provides the domain of terms used for describing the results of computations. It thus plays the same role in our context as does the first-order Herbrand Universe in other discussions of logic programming.

A higher-order version of Horn clauses is now identified by the following definition.

Definition 4.0.2. A formula of the form $(p\ T_1\ \ldots\ T_n)$, where p is a parameter or a variable and, for $1 \le i \le n$, $T_i \in \mathcal{H}^+$ is said to be a *positive atomic formula*. Recall that such a formula is rigid just in case p is a parameter. Let A and A_r be symbols that denote positive and rigid positive atomic formulas respectively. Then the (higher-order) goal formulas and definite clauses are the G- and D-formulas given by the following inductive rules:

$$G ::= \top \mid A \mid G \wedge G \mid G \vee G \mid \exists x\, G$$
$$D ::= A_r \mid G \supset A_r \mid \forall x\, D$$

A finite collection of closed definite clauses is referred to as a *program* and a goal formula is also called a *query*.

There is an alternative characterization of the goal formulas just defined: they are, in fact, the terms in $\mathcal{H}^+$ of type o. The presentation above is chosen to exhibit the correspondence between the higher-order formulas and their first-order counterparts. The first-order formulas are contained in the corresponding higher-order formulas under an implicit encoding that essentially assigns types to the first-order terms and predicates. To be precise, let i be a sort other that o. The encoding then assigns the type i to variables and parameters, the type $i \to \cdots \to i \to i$, with $n+1$ occurrences of i, to each n-ary function symbol, and the type $i \to \cdots \to i \to o$, with n occurrences of i, to each n-ary predicate symbol. Looked at differently, our formulas contain within them a many-sorted version of first-order definite clauses and goal formulas. In the reverse direction, the above definition is but a precise description of the generalization outlined informally in Section 2. Of particular note are the restriction of arguments of atoms to positive terms, the requirement of a specific name for the "procedure" defined by a definite clause and the ability to quantify over predicates and functions. The various examples discussed in Section 2 can be rendered almost immediately into the current syntax, the main difference being the use of a curried notation.

Example 4.0.3. Let *list* be a unary type constructor, let *int* and i be sorts. Further, let *nil* and *nil'* be parameters of type $(list\ i)$ and $(list\ int)$ and let *cons* and *cons'* be parameters of type $i \to (list\ i) \to (list\ i)$ and $int \to (list\ int) \to (list\ int)$. The following formulas constitute a program under the assumption that *mappred* is a parameter of type

$$(i \to int \to o) \to (list\ i) \to (list\ int) \to o$$

and that P, L_1, L_2, X and Y are variables of the required types:

$\forall P\,(mappred\ P\ nil\ nil')$,
$\forall P, L_1, L_2, X, Y\,(((P\ X\ Y) \wedge (mappred\ P\ L_1\ L_2)) \supset$
$\qquad\qquad (mappred\ P\ (cons'\ X\ L_1)\ (cons\ Y\ L_2)))$.

Assuming that *age* is a parameter of type $i \to int \to o$, *bob* and *sue* are parameters of type i and L is a variable of type $(list\ int)$, the formula

$(mappred\ age\ (cons\ bob\ (cons\ sue\ nil))\ L)$

constitutes a query. If $mapfun$ is a parameter of type

$(int \to int) \to (list\ int) \to (list\ int) \to o$

and F, L_1, L_2 and X are variables of appropriate types, the following formulas, once again, constitute a program:

$\forall F\ (mapfun\ F\ nil\ nil),$
$\forall F, L_1, L_2, X\ ((mapfun\ F\ L_1\ L_2) \supset$
$\qquad\qquad\qquad (mapfun\ F\ (cons\ X\ L_1)\ (cons\ (F\ X)\ L_2))).$

If 1, 2, and h are parameters of type int, int, and $int \to int \to int$ respectively and L, X and F are variables of suitable types, the following are queries:

$(mapfun\ (\lambda X\ (h\ 1\ X))\ (cons\ 1\ (cons\ 2\ nil))\ L),$ and
$(mapfun\ F\ (cons\ 1\ (cons\ 2\ nil))\ (cons\ (h\ 1\ 1)\ (cons\ (h\ 1\ 2)\ nil))).$

Higher-order definite clauses and goal formulas are intended to provide for a programming paradigm in a manner analogous to their first-order counterparts. The notion of computation corresponds as before to solving a query from a given program. The desire to preserve the essential character of Horn clause logic programming dictates the mechanism for carrying out such a computation: an abstract interpreter for our language must perform a search whose structure is guided by the top-level logical symbol in the query being solved. There is, however, a potential problem in the description of such an interpreter caused by the possibility for predicate variables to appear in extensional positions in goal formulas. We recall from Section 3 that substitutions for such variables have the ability to alter the top-level logical structure of the original formula. In the specific context of interest, we see that goal formulas do not remain goal formulas under arbitrary instantiations. For example, consider the instantiation of the goal formula $\exists P\ (P\ a)$ with the term $\lambda x\ \neg(q\ x)$; we assume that P and x are variables here and that a and q are parameters. This instantiation produces the formula $\neg(q\ a)$ which is obviously not a goal formula. If such instantiations must be performed in the course of solving queries similar to the given one, an interpreter that proceeds by examining the top-level structure of only goal formulas cannot be described for our language. The computational mechanism for our language would, therefore, have to diverge even in principle from the one used in the first-order context.

Fortunately this problem has a solution that is adequate at least from a pragmatic perspective. The essential idea is to consider the domain of our computations to be limited to that of positive terms. In particular, instantiations with only positive terms will be used for definite clauses and goal formulas in the course of solving queries. Now, it is easily seen that "positive" instantiations of quantifiers in goal formulas and definite clauses yield formulas that are themselves goal formulas and definite clauses respectively. Problems such as those just discussed would, therefore, not arise in this context. We adopt this solution in our discussions below. Although this solution is adequate in a practical sense, we note that there is a question about its acceptability from a logical perspective; in particular, using it may be accompanied by a loss in logical completeness. We discuss this issue in the next section.

In presenting an abstract interpreter for our language, we find a notation for positive instances of a set of definite clauses useful. This notation is described below.

Definition 4.0.4. A (closed) *positive substitution* is a substitution whose range is a set of (closed) terms contained in $\mathcal{H}^+$. Let D be a closed definite clause. Then the collection of its closed positive instances, denoted by $[D]$, is

(i) $\{D\}$ if D is of the form A or $G \supset A$, and
(ii) $\bigcup\{[\varphi(D')] \mid \varphi$ is a closed positive substitution for $x\}$ if D is of the form $\forall x\, D'$.

This notation is extended to programs as follows: if $\mathcal{P}$ is a program,

$$[\mathcal{P}] = \bigcup\{[D] \mid D \in \mathcal{P}\}.$$

We now specify the abstract interpreter in terms of the desired search related interpretation for each logical symbol.

Definition 4.0.5. Let $\mathcal{P}$ be a program and let G be a closed goal formula. We use the notation $\mathcal{P} \vdash_O G$ to signify that our abstract interpreter succeeds on G when given $\mathcal{P}$; the subscript on $\vdash_O$ acknowledges the "operational" nature of the notion. Now, the success/failure behavior of the interpreter on closed goal formula is specified as follows:

(i) $\mathcal{P} \vdash_O \top$,
(ii) $\mathcal{P} \vdash_O A$ where A is an atomic formula if and only if $A \equiv A'$ for some $A' \in [\mathcal{P}]$ or for some $G \supset A' \in [\mathcal{P}]$ such that $A \equiv A'$ it is the case that $\mathcal{P} \vdash_O G$,
(iii) $\mathcal{P} \vdash_O G_1 \vee G_2$ if and only if $\mathcal{P} \vdash_O G_1$ or $\mathcal{P} \vdash_O G_2$,
(iv) $\mathcal{P} \vdash_O G_1 \wedge G_2$ if and only if $\mathcal{P} \vdash_O G_1$ and $\mathcal{P} \vdash_O G_2$, and
(v) $\mathcal{P} \vdash_O \exists x\, G$ if and only if $\mathcal{P} \vdash_O \varphi(G)$ for some φ that is a closed positive substitution for x.

The description of the abstract interpreter has two characteristics which require further explanation. First, it specifies the behavior of the interpreter only on closed goal formulas, whereas a query is, by our definition, an arbitrary goal formula. Second, while it defines what a computation should be, it leaves unspecified what the *result* of such a computation is.

The explanations of these two aspects are, in a certain sense, related. The typical scenario in logic programming is one where a goal formula with some free variables is to be solved relative to some program. The calculation that is intended in this situation is that of solving the existential closure of the goal formula from the program. If this calculation is successful, the result that is expected is a set of substitutions for the free variables in the given query that make it so. We observe that the behavior of our abstract interpreter accords well with this view of the outcome of a computation: the success of the interpreter on an existential query entails its success on a particular instance of the query and so it is reasonable to require a specific substitution to be returned as an "answer."

Example 4.0.6. Suppose that our language includes all the parameters and variables described in Example 4.0.3. Further, suppose that our program consists of the definite clauses defining *mappred* in that example and the following in which 24 and 23 are parameters of type *int*:

(*age bob* 24),
(*age sue* 23).

Then, the query

(*mappred age* (*cons bob* (*cons sue nil*)) *L*)

in which *L* is a free variable actually requires the goal formula

$\exists L$ (*mappred age* (*cons bob* (*cons sue nil*)) *L*).

to be solved. There is a solution to this goal formula that, in accordance with the description of the abstract interpreter, involves solving the following "subgoals" in sequence:

(*mappred age* (*cons bob* (*cons sue nil*)) (*cons'* 24 (*cons'* 23 *nil'*)))
(*age bob* 24) ∧ (*mappred age* (*cons sue nil*) (*cons'* 23 *nil'*))
(*age bob* 24)
(*mappred age* (*cons sue nil*) (*cons'* 23 *nil'*))
(*age sue* 23) ∧ (*mappred age nil nil'*)
(*age sue* 23)
(*mappred age nil nil'*).

The answer to the original query that is obtained from this solution is the substitution (*cons'* 24 (*cons'* 23 *nil'*)) for *L*.

As another example, assume that our program consists of the clauses for *mapfun* in Example 4.0.3 and that the query is now the goal formula

(*mapfun F* (*cons* 1 (*cons* 2 *nil*)) (*cons* (*h* 1 1) (*cons* (*h* 1 2) *nil*)))

in which *F* is a free variable. Once again we can construct the goal formula whose solution is implicitly called for by this query. Further, a successful solution path may be traced to show that an answer to the query is the value λx (*h* 1 *x*) for *F*.

We have, at this stage, presented a higher-order generalization to the Horn clauses of first-order logic and we have outlined, in an abstract fashion, a notion of computation in the context of our generalization that preserves the essential character of the notion in the first-order case. We have, through this discussion, provided a framework for higher-order logic programming. However, there are two respects in which the framework that we have presented is incomplete. First, we have not provided a justification based on logic for the idea of computation that we have described. We would like to manifest a connection with logic to be true to the spirit of logic programming in general and to benefit from possible declarative interpretations of programs in particular. Second, the abstract interpreter that has been described is not quite adequate as a basis for a practical programming language. As evidenced in Example 4.0.6, an unacceptable degree of clairvoyance is needed in determining if a given query has a successful solution—an answer to the query must be known at the outset. A viable evaluation procedure therefore needs to be described for supporting the programming paradigm outlined here. We undertake these two tasks in Sections 5 and 6 respectively.

5 The meaning of computations

We may attempt to explain the meaning of a computation as described in the previous section by saying that a query succeeds from a given program if and only if its existential closure is provable from, or a logical consequence of, the program. Accepting this characterization without further argument is, however, problematic. One concern is the treatment of quantifiers. From Definition 4.0.5 we see that only positive instances of definite clauses are used and success on existentially quantified goal formulas depends only on success on a closed positive instance of the goal. It is unclear that these restrictions carry over to the idea of provability as well. A related problem concerns the search semantics accorded to the logical connectives. We note, for instance, that success on a goal formula of the form $G_1 \vee G_2$ depends on success on either G_1 or G_2. This property does not hold of provability in general: a disjunctive formula may have a proof without either of the disjuncts being provable.

A specific illustration of the above problems is provided by the following derivation of the goal formula $\exists Y\,(p\,Y)$ from a program consisting solely of the definite clause $\forall X\,(X \supset (p\,a))$; we assume that p, a and b are parameters here and that X and Y are variables.

$$\dfrac{\dfrac{(p\ b)\ \longrightarrow\ (p\ b)}{\dfrac{(p\ b)\ \longrightarrow\ \exists Y\,(p\ Y)}{\ \longrightarrow\ \exists Y\,(p\ Y),\neg(p\ b)}\ \text{¬-R}}\quad \dfrac{(p\ a)\ \longrightarrow\ (p\ a)}{(p\ a)\ \longrightarrow\ \exists Y\,(p\ Y)}\ \text{∃-R}}{\dfrac{\neg(p\ b)\supset(p\ a)\ \longrightarrow\ \exists Y\,(p\ Y)}{\forall X\,(X\supset(p\ a))\ \longrightarrow\ \exists Y\,(p\ Y)}\ \text{∀-L}}\ \supset\text{-L}$$

The penultimate sequent in this derivation is

$$\neg(p\ b)\supset(p\ a)\ \longrightarrow\ \exists Y\,(p\ Y). \qquad\qquad (*)$$

The antecedent of this sequent is obtained by substituting a term that is not positive into a definite clause. This sequent obviously has a derivation. There is, however, no term T such that $\neg(p\ b)\supset(p\ a)\ \longrightarrow\ (p\ T)$ has a derivation. This is, of course, a cause for concern. If all derivations of

$$\forall X\,(X\supset(p\ a))\ \longrightarrow\ \exists Y\,(p\ Y)$$

involve the derivation of $(*)$, or of sequents similar to $(*)$, then the idea of proving $\exists Y\,(p\ Y)$ would diverge from the idea of solving it, at least in the context where the program consists of the formula $\forall X\,(X\supset(p\ a))$.

We show in this section that problems of the sort described in the previous paragraph do not arise, and that the notions of success and provability in the context of our definite clauses and goal formulas coincide. The method that we adopt for demonstrating this is the following. We first identify a **C'**-proof as a **C**-proof in which each occurrence of ∀-L and ∃-R constitutes a generalization upon a closed term from $\mathcal{H}^+$. In other words, in each appearance of figures of the forms

$$\dfrac{[T/x]P,\Delta\ \longrightarrow\ \Theta}{\forall x\,P,\Delta\ \longrightarrow\ \Theta}\qquad\qquad \dfrac{\Delta\ \longrightarrow\ \Theta,[T/x]P}{\Delta\ \longrightarrow\ \Theta,\exists x\,P}$$

it is the case that T is instantiated by a closed term from $\mathcal{H}^+$. We shall show then that if Γ consists only of closed definite clauses and Δ consists only of closed goal formulas, then the sequent $\Gamma\ \longrightarrow\ \Delta$ has a **C**-proof only if has a **C'**-proof. Now **C'**-proofs of sequents of the kind described have the following characteristic: every sequent in the derivation has an antecedent consisting solely of closed definite clauses and a succedent consisting solely of closed goal formulas. This structural property of the derivation can be exploited to show rather directly that the existence of a proof coincides with the possibility of success on a goal formula.

5.1   Restriction to positive terms

We desire to show that the use of only **C'**-proofs, i.e., the focus on positive terms, does not restrict the relation of provability as it pertains to definite clauses and goal formulas. We do this by describing a transformation from an arbitrary **C**-proof to a **C'**-proof. The following mapping on terms is useful for this purpose.

Definition 5.1.1. Let x and y be variables of type o and, for each σ, let z_σ be a variable of type $\sigma \to o$. Then the function *pos* on terms is defined as follows:

(i) If T is a constant or a variable

$$pos(T) = \begin{cases} \lambda x\, \mathsf{T} & \text{if } T \text{ is } \neg \\ \lambda x\, \lambda y\, \mathsf{T}, & \text{if } T \text{ is } \supset \\ \lambda z_\sigma\, \mathsf{T} & \text{if } T \text{ is } \forall \text{ of type } (\sigma \to o) \to o \\ T & \text{otherwise.} \end{cases}$$

(ii) $pos((T_1\, T_2)) = (pos(T_1)\, pos(T_2))$.
(iii) $pos(\lambda w\, T) = \lambda w\, pos(T)$.

Given a term T, the λ-normal form of $pos(T)$ is denoted by T^+.

The mapping defined above is a "positivization" operation on terms as made clear in the following lemma whose proof is obvious.

Lemma 5.1.2. *For any term T, $T^+ \in \mathcal{H}^+$. Further, $\mathcal{F}(T^+) \subseteq \mathcal{F}(T)$. In particular, if T is closed, then T^+ is a closed positive term. Finally, if $T \in \mathcal{H}^+$ then $T = T^+$.*

Another property of the mapping defined above is that it commutes with λ-conversion. This fact follows easily from the lemma below.

Lemma 5.1.3. *For any terms T_1 and T_2, if T_1 λ-converts to T_2 then $pos(T_1)$ also λ-converts to $pos(T_2)$.*

Proof. We use an induction on the length of the conversion sequence. The key is in showing the lemma for a sequence of length 1. It is easily seen that if T_2 is obtained from T_1 by a single application of the α- or η-conversion rule, then $pos(T_2)$ results from $pos(T_1)$ by a similar rule. Now, let A be substitutable for x in B. Then an induction on the structure of B confirms that $pos(S_x^A B) = S_x^{pos(A)} pos(B)$. Thus, if R_1 is $((\lambda x\, B)\, A)$ and R_2 is $S_x^A B$, it must be the case that $pos(R_1)$ β-converts to $pos(R_2)$. An induction on the structure of T_1 now verifies that if T_2 results from it by a single β-conversion step, then $pos(T_1)$ β-converts to $pos(T_2)$. ∎

We will need to consider a sequence of substitutions for variables in a formula in the discussions that follow. In these discussions it is notationally convenient to assume that substitution is a right associative operation. Thus $[R_2/x_2][R_1/x_1]T$ is to be considered as denoting the term obtained by first substituting R_1 for x_1 in T and then substituting R_2 for x_2 in the result.

Lemma 5.1.4. *If T is a term in $\mathcal{H}^+$ and $R_1, \ldots, R_n$ are arbitrary terms $(n \geq 0)$, then*

$$([R_n/x_n] \ldots [R_1/x_1]T)^+ = [(R_n)^+/x_n] \ldots [(R_1)^+/x_1]T.$$

In particular, this is true when T is an atomic goal formula or an atomic definite clause.

Proof. We note first that for any term $T \in \mathcal{H}^+$, $pos(T) = T$ and thus $T^+ = T$. Using Lemma 5.1.3, it is easily verified that

$$([R_n/x_n] \ldots [R_1/x_1]T)^+ = [(R_n)^+/x_n] \ldots [(R_1)^+/x_1]T^+.$$

The lemma follows from these observations. ∎

The transformation of a **C**-proof into a **C**′-proof for a sequent of the kind that we are interested in currently can be described as the result of a recursive process that works upwards from the root of the proof and uses the positivization operation on the terms generalized upon in the ∀-L and ∃-R rules. This recursive process is implicit in the proof of the following theorem.

Theorem 5.1.5. *Let Δ be a program and let Θ be a finite set of closed goal formulas. Then $\Delta \longrightarrow \Theta$ has a **C**-proof only if it also has a **C**′-proof.*

Proof. We note first that all the formulas in $\Delta \longrightarrow \Theta$ are closed. Hence, we may assume that the ∀-L and ∃-R inference figures that are used in the **C**-proof of this sequent generalize on closed terms (i.e., they are obtained by replacing T in the corresponding schemata by closed terms). The standard technique of replacing all occurrences of a free variable in a proof by a parameter may be used to ensure that this is actually the case.

Given a set of formulas Γ of the form

$$\{[R^1_{l_1}/z^1_{l_1}] \ldots [R^1_1/z^1_1]F_1, \ldots, [R^r_{l_r}/z^r_{l_r}] \ldots [R^r_1/z^r_1]F_r\},$$

where $r, l_1, \ldots, l_r \geq 0$, we shall use the notation Γ^+ to denote the set

$$\{[(R^1_{l_1})^+/z^1_{l_1}] \ldots [(R^1_1)^+/z^1_1]F_1, \ldots, [(R^r_{l_r})^+/z^r_{l_r}] \ldots [(R^r_1)^+/z^r_1]F_r\}.$$

Now let Δ be a set of the form

$$\{[T^1_{n_1}/x^1_{n_1}] \ldots [T^1_1/x^1_1]D_1, \ldots, [T^t_{n_t}/x^t_{n_t}] \ldots [T^t_1/x^t_1]D_t\},$$

i.e., a set of formulas, each member of which is obtained by performing a sequence of substitutions into a definite clause. Similarly, let Θ be a set of the form

$$\{[S^1_{m_1}/y^1_{m_1}] \ldots [S^1_1/y^1_1]G_1, \ldots, [S^s_{m_s}/y^s_{m_s}] \ldots [S^s_1/y^s_1]G_s\},$$

i.e., a set obtained by performing sequences of substitutions into goal formulas. We claim that if $\Delta \longrightarrow \Theta$ has a **C**-proof in which all the ∀-L and the ∃-R figures generalize on closed terms, then $\Delta^+ \longrightarrow \Theta^+$ must have a **C**′-proof. The theorem is an obvious consequence of this claim.

The claim is proved by an induction on the height of **C**-proofs for sequents of the given sort. If this height is 1, the given sequent must be an initial sequent. There are, then, two cases to consider. In the first case, for some i such that $1 \leq i \leq s$ we have that $[S^i_{m_i}/y^i_{m_i}] \ldots [S^i_1/y^i_1]G_i$ is ⊤. But then G_i must be an atomic formula. Using Lemma 5.1.4 we then see that

$[(S_{m_i}^i)^+/y_{m_i}^i]\ldots[(S_1^i)^+/y_1^i]G_i$ must also be $\top$. In the other case, for some i,j such that $1 \le i \le s$ and $1 \le j \le t$, we have that

$$[R_{n_j}^j/x_{n_j}^j]\ldots[R_1^j/x_1^j]D_j \equiv [S_{m_i}^i/y_{m_i}^i]\ldots[S_1^i/y_1^i]G_i$$

and, further, that these are atomic formulas. From the last observation, it follows that D_j and G_i are atomic formulas. Using Lemma 5.1.4 again, it follows that

$$[(R_{n_j}^j)^+/x_{n_j}^j]\ldots[(R_1^j)^+/x_1^j]D_j \equiv [(S_{m_i}^i)^+/y_{m_i}^i]\ldots[(S_1^i)^+/y_1^i]G_i.$$

Thus in either case it is clear that $\Delta^+ \longrightarrow \Theta^+$ is an initial sequent.

We now assume that the claim is true for derivations of sequents of the requisite sort that have height h, and we verify it for sequents with derivations of height $h+1$. We argue by considering the possible cases for the last inference figure in such a derivation. We observe that substituting into a definite clause cannot yield a formula that has $\wedge$, $\vee$, $\neg$ or $\exists$ as its top-level connective. Thus the last inference figure cannot be an $\wedge$-L, an $\vee$-L, a $\neg$-L or a $\exists$-L. Further, a simple induction on the heights of derivations shows that if a sequent consists solely of formulas in λ-normal form, then any **C**-proof for it that contains the inference figure λ can be transformed into a shorter **C**-proof in which λ does not appear. Since each formula in $\Delta \longrightarrow \Theta$ must be in λ-normal form, we may assume that the last inference figure in its **C**-proof is not a λ. Thus, the only figures that we need to consider are $\supset$-L, $\forall$-L, $\wedge$-R, $\vee$-R, $\neg$-R, $\supset$-R, $\exists$-R, and $\forall$-R.

Let us consider first the case for an $\wedge$-R, i.e., when the last inference figure is of the form

$$\frac{\Delta \longrightarrow \Theta', B \qquad \Delta \longrightarrow \Theta', D}{\Delta \longrightarrow \Theta', B \wedge D}$$

In this case $\Theta' \subseteq \Theta$ and for some i, $1 \le i \le s$,

$$[S_{m_i}^i/y_{m_i}^i]\ldots[S_1^i/y_1^i]G_i = B \wedge D.$$

Our analysis breaks up into two parts depending on the structure of G_i:

(1) If G_i is an atomic formula, we obtain from Lemma 5.1.4 that

$$[(S_{m_i}^i)^+/y_{m_i}^i]\ldots[(S_1^i)^+/y_1^i]G_i = (B \wedge D)^+ = B^+ \wedge D^+.$$

Now B and D can be written as $[B/y]y$ and $[D/y]y$, respectively. From the hypothesis it thus follows that

$$\Delta^+ \longrightarrow (\Theta')^+, B^+ \text{ and } \Delta^+ \longrightarrow (\Theta')^+, D^+$$

have **C**′-proofs. Using an $\wedge$-R inference figure in conjunction with these, we obtain a **C**′-proof for $\Delta^+ \longrightarrow \Theta^+$.

(2) If G_i is not an atomic formula then it must be of the form $G_i^1 \wedge G_i^2$. But then $B = [S_{m_i}^i/y_{m_i}^i]\ldots[S_1^i/y_1^i]G_i^1$ and $D = [S_{m_i}^i/y_{m_i}^i]\ldots[S_1^i/y_1^i]G_i^2$. It follows from the hypothesis that **C**′-proofs exist for

$$\Delta^+ \longrightarrow (\Theta')^+, [(S_{m_i}^i)^+/y_{m_i}^i]\ldots[(S_1^i)^+/y_1^i]G_i^1$$

and

$$\Delta^+ \longrightarrow (\Theta')^+, [(S^i_{m_i})^+/y^i_{m_i}]\dots[(S^i_1)^+/y^i_1]G^2_i.$$

A proof for $\Delta^+ \longrightarrow \Theta^+$ can be obtained from these by using an ∧-R inference figure.

An analogous argument can be provided when the last figure is ∨-R. For the case of ⊃ -L, we observe first that if the result of performing a sequence of substitutions into a definite clause D is a formula of the form $B \supset C$, then D must be of the form $G \supset A_r$ where G is a goal formula and A_r is a rigid positive atom. An analysis similar to that used for ∧-R now verifies the claim.

Consider now the case when the last inference figure is a ¬-R, i.e., of the form

$$\frac{B, \Delta \longrightarrow \Theta'}{\Delta \longrightarrow \Theta', \neg B}.$$

We see in this case that for some suitable i, $[S^i_{m_i}/y^i_{m_i}]\dots[S^i_1/y^i_1]G_i = \neg B$. But then G_i must be an atomic goal formula and by Lemma 5.1.4

$$[(S^i_{m_i})^+/y^i_{m_i}]\dots[(S^i_1)^+/y^i_1]G_i = (\neg B)^+ = \top.$$

Thus, $\Delta^+ \longrightarrow \Theta^+$ is an initial sequent and the claim follows trivially. Similar arguments can be supplied for ⊃ -R and ∀-R.

The only remaining cases are those when the last inference figure is a ∃-R or a ∀-L. In the former case the last inference figure must have the form

$$\frac{\Delta \longrightarrow \Theta', [T/w]P}{\Delta \longrightarrow \Theta', \exists w\, P}$$

where $\Theta' \subseteq \Theta$ and for some i, $1 \le i \le s$, $[S^i_{m_i}/y^i_{m_i}]\dots[S^i_1/y^i_1]G_i = \exists w\, P$. We assume, without loss of generality, that w is distinct from the variables $y^i_1, \dots, y^i_{m_i}$ as well as the variables that are free in $S^i_1, \dots, S^i_{m_i}$. There are once again two subcases based on the the structure of G_i:

(1) If G_i is an atomic formula, it follows from Lemma 5.1.4 that

$$[(S^i_{m_i})^+/y^i_{m_i}]\dots[(S^i_1)^+/y^i_1]G_i = (\exists w\, P)^+ = \exists w\, (P)^+.$$

Writing $[T/w]P$ as $[T/w][P/u]u$ and invoking the hypothesis, we see that a **C′**-proof must exist for $\Delta^+ \longrightarrow (\Theta')^+, [T^+/w]P^+$. Adding a ∃-R figure below this yields a derivation for $\Delta^+ \longrightarrow (\Theta')^+, \exists w\, (P)^+$, which is identical to $\Delta^+ \longrightarrow \Theta^+$. Further, this must be a **C′**-proof since T is a closed term by assumption and hence, by Lemma 5.1.2, T^+ must be a closed positive term.

(2) If G_i is a non-atomic formula, it must be of the form $\exists x\, G'_i$ where G'_i is a goal formula. But now $P = [S^i_{m_i}/y^i_{m_i}]\dots[S^i_1/y^i_1]G'_i$. Thus,

$$\Delta^+ \longrightarrow (\Theta')^+, [T^+/w][(S^i_{m_i})^+/y^i_{m_i}]\dots[(S^i_1)^+/y^i_1]G'_i$$

has a **C′**-proof by the hypothesis. By adding a ∃-R inference figure below this, we obtain a **C′**-proof for

$$\Delta^+ \longrightarrow (\Theta')^+, \exists w\, ([(S^i_{m_i})^+/y^i_{m_i}]\dots[(S^i_1)^+/y^i_1]G'_i).$$

Noting that

$$\exists w \left([(S_{m_i}^i)^+/y_{m_i}^i] \cdots [(S_1^i)^+/y_1^i] G_i' \right) \equiv [(S_{m_i}^i)^+/y_{m_i}^i] \cdots [(S_1^i)^+/y_1^i] \exists w\, G_i',$$

we see that the claim must be true.

The argument for ∀-L is similar to the one for the second subcase of ∃-R. ∎

As mentioned already, Theorem 5.1.5 implicitly describes a transformation on **C**-proofs. It is illuminating to consider the result of this transformation on the derivation presented at the beginning of this section. We invite the reader to verify that this derivation will be transformed into the following:

$$\cfrac{\longrightarrow \exists Y\,(p\,Y), \top \qquad \cfrac{\cfrac{(p\,a) \longrightarrow (p\,a)}{(p\,a) \longrightarrow \exists Y\,(p\,y)}\ \exists\text{-R}}{\top \supset (p\,a) \longrightarrow \exists Y\,(p\,Y)}\ \supset\text{-L}}{\forall X\,(X \supset (p\,a)) \longrightarrow \exists y\,(p\,Y)}\ \forall\text{-L}$$

Notice that there is no ambiguity about the answer substitution that should be extracted from this derivation for the existentially quantified variable Y.

5.2   Provability and operational semantics

We now show that the possibility of success on a goal formula given a program coincides with the existence of a proof for that formula from the program. Theorem 5.1.5 allows us to focus solely on **C′**-proofs in the course of establishing this fact, and we do this implicitly below.

The following lemma shows that any set of definite clauses is consistent.

Lemma 5.2.1. *There can be no derivation for a sequent of the form* $\Delta \longrightarrow$ *where* Δ *is a program.*

Proof. Suppose the claim is false. Then there is a least h and a program Δ such that $\Delta \longrightarrow$ has a derivation of height h. Clearly $h > 1$. Considering the cases for the last inference figure ($\supset$-L or ∀-L with the latter generalizing on a closed positive term), we see a sequent of the same sort must have a shorter proof. ∎

The lemma below states the equivalence of classical and intuitionistic provability in the context of Horn clauses. This observation is useful in later analysis.

Lemma 5.2.2. *Let* Δ *be a program and let* G *be a closed goal formula. Then* $\Delta \longrightarrow G$ *has a derivation only if it has one in which there is at most one formula in the succedent of each sequent.*

Proof. We make a stronger claim: a sequent of the form

$$\Delta \longrightarrow G_1,\ldots,G_n,$$

where Δ is a program and $G_1,\ldots,G_n$ are closed goal formulas, has a derivation only if for some i, $1 \le i \le n$, $\Delta \longrightarrow G_i$ has a derivation in which at most one formula appears in the succedent of each sequent.

The claim is proved by an induction on the heights of derivations. It is true when the height is 1 by virtue of the definition of an initial sequent. In the situation when the height is $h+1$, we consider the possible cases for the last inference figure in the derivation. The argument for $\wedge$-R and $\vee$-R are straightforward. For instance, in the former case the last inference figure in the derivation must be of the form

$$\frac{\Delta \longrightarrow \Theta,G_j^1 \qquad \Delta \longrightarrow \Theta,G_j^2}{\Delta \longrightarrow \Theta,G_j^1 \wedge G_j^2}$$

where for some j, $1 \le j \le n$, $G_j = G_j^1 \wedge G_j^2$ and $\Theta \subseteq \{G_1,\ldots,G_n\}$. Applying the inductive hypothesis to the upper sequents of this figure, it follows that there is a derivation of the requisite sort for $\Delta \longrightarrow G$ for some $G \in \Theta$ or for both $\Delta \longrightarrow G_j^1$ and $\Delta \longrightarrow G_j^2$. In the former case the claim follows directly, and in the latter case we use the two derivations together with an $\wedge$-R inference figure to construct a derivation of the required kind for $\Delta \longrightarrow G_j^1 \wedge G_j^2$.

Similar arguments can be provided for the cases when the last inference figure is $\exists$-R or $\forall$-L. The only additional observation needed in these cases is that the restriction to $\mathbf{C}'$-proofs ensures that the upper sequent in these cases has the form required for the hypothesis to apply.

We are left only with the case of $\supset$-L. In this case, the last inference figure has the form

$$\frac{\Delta' \longrightarrow \Gamma_2,G \qquad A,\Delta' \longrightarrow \Gamma_1}{G \supset A,\Delta' \longrightarrow \Gamma_1 \cup \Gamma_2}$$

where $\Delta = \{(G \supset A)\} \cup \Delta'$ and $\Theta = \Gamma_1 \cup \Gamma_2$. From Lemma 5.2.1 it follows that $\Gamma_1 \ne \emptyset$. By the hypothesis, we see that there is a derivation of the required kind for either $\Delta' \longrightarrow G_1$ for some $G_1 \in \Gamma_2$ or for $\Delta' \longrightarrow G$. In the former case, by adding $G \supset A$ to the antecedent of every sequent of the derivation, we obtain one for $\Delta \longrightarrow G_1$. In the latter case, another use of the inductive hypothesis tells us that there is a derivation of the desired kind for $A,\Delta' \longrightarrow G_2$ for some $G_2 \in \Gamma_1$. This derivation may be combined with the one for $\Delta' \longrightarrow G$ to obtain one for $\Delta \longrightarrow G_2$. ∎

The proof of the above lemma is dependent on only one fact: every sequent in the derivations being considered has a program as its antecedent and a set of closed goal formulas as its succedent. This observation (or one closely related to it) can be made rather directly in any situation where quantification over predicate variables appearing in extensional positions is not permitted. It holds, for instance, in the case when we are dealing with only first-order formulas. Showing that the observation also applies in the case of our higher-order formulas requires much work, as we have already seen.

Definition 5.2.3. The *length* of a derivation Ξ is defined by recursion on its height as follows:

(i)   It is 1 if Ξ consists of only an initial sequent.

(ii)   It is $l + 1$ if the last inference figure in Ξ has a single upper sequent whose derivation has length l.

(iii) It is $l_1 + l_2 + 1$ if the last inference figure in Ξ has two upper sequents whose derivations are of length l_1 and l_2 respectively.

The main result of this subsection requires the extraction of a successful computation from a proof of a closed goal formula from a program. The following lemma provides a means for achieving this end.

Lemma 5.2.4. *Let Δ be a program, let G be a closed goal formula and let $\Delta \longrightarrow G$ have a derivation of length l. Then one of the following is true:*

(i)   *G is $\top$.*

(ii)   *G is an atomic formula and either $G \equiv A$ for some A in $[\Delta]$ or for some $G' \supset A \in [\Delta]$ such that $G \equiv A$ it is the case that $\Delta \longrightarrow G'$ has a derivation of length less than l.*

(iii) *G is $G_1 \wedge G_2$ and there are derivations for $\Delta \longrightarrow G_1$ and $\Delta \longrightarrow G_2$ of length less than l.*

(iv)   *G is $G_1 \vee G_2$ and there is a derivation for either $\Delta \longrightarrow G_1$ or $\Delta \longrightarrow G_2$ of length less than l.*

(v)   *G is $\exists x\, G_1$ and for some closed positive term T it is the case that $\Delta \longrightarrow [T/x]G_1$ has a derivation of length less than l.*

Proof. We use an induction on the lengths of derivations. The lemma is obviously true in the case this length is 1: G is either $\top$ or G is atomic and $G \equiv A$ for some $A \in \Delta$. When the length is $l + 1$, we consider the cases for the last inference figure. The argument is simple for the cases of $\wedge$-R, $\vee$-R and $\exists$-R. For the case of $\supset$-L, i.e., when the last inference figure is of the form

$$\frac{\Delta' \longrightarrow G' \qquad A, \Delta' \longrightarrow G}{G' \supset A, \Delta' \longrightarrow G}$$

where $\Delta = \{G' \supset A\} \cup \Delta'$, the argument depends on the structure of G. If G is an atomic formula distinct from $\top$, the lemma follows from the hypothesis applied to $A, \Delta' \longrightarrow G$ except in the case when $G' \equiv A$. But in the latter case we see that $(G' \supset A) \in [\Delta]$ and a derivation for $\Delta \longrightarrow G'$ of length less than $l + 1$ can be obtained from the one for $\Delta' \longrightarrow G'$ by adding $(G' \supset A)$ to the antecedent of every sequent in that derivation. If G is $G_1 \wedge G_2$, we see first that there must be derivations for $A, \Delta' \longrightarrow G_1$ and $A, \Delta' \longrightarrow G_2$ of smaller length than that for $A, \Delta' \longrightarrow G$. But using the derivation for $\Delta' \longrightarrow G'$ in conjunction with these we obtain derivations for $G' \supset A, \Delta' \longrightarrow G_1$ and $G' \supset A, \Delta' \longrightarrow G_2$ whose lengths must be less than $l+1$. Analogous arguments may be provided for the other cases for the structure of G. Finally a similar (and in some sense simpler) argument can be provided for the case when the last inference figure is a $\forall$-L. ∎

The equivalence of provability and the operational semantics defined in the previous section is the content of the following theorem.

Theorem 5.2.5. *If Δ is a program and G is a closed goal formula, then $\Delta \vdash_C G$ if and only if $\Delta \vdash_O G$.*

Proof. Using Lemma 5.2.4 and an induction on the length of a derivation it follows easily that $\Delta \vdash_O G$ if $\Delta \vdash_C G$. In the converse direction we use an induction on the length of the successful computation. If this length is 1, $\Delta \longrightarrow G$ must be an initial sequent. Consider now the case where G is an atomic formula that is solved by finding a $G' \supset A \in [\Delta]$ such that $G \equiv A$ and then solving G'. By the hypothesis, $\Delta \longrightarrow G'$ has a derivation as also does $A \longrightarrow G$. Using an $\supset$-L in conjunction with these, we get a derivation for $G' \supset A, \Delta \longrightarrow G$. Appending a sequence of $\forall$-L inference figures below this, we get a derivation for $\Delta \longrightarrow G$. The argument for the remaining cases is simpler and is left to the reader. ∎

6 Towards a practical realization

A practical realization of the programming paradigm that we have described thus far depends on the existence of an efficient procedure for determining whether a query succeeds or fails relative to a given program. The abstract interpreter that is described in Section 4 provides the skeleton for such a procedure. However, this interpreter is deficient in an important practical respect: it requires a prior knowledge of suitable instantiations for the existential quantifiers in a goal formula. The technique that is generally used in the first-order context for dealing with this problem is that of delaying the instantiations of such quantifiers till a time when information is available for making an appropriate choice. This effect is achieved by replacing the quantified variables by placeholders whose values are determined at a later stage through the process of unification. Thus, a goal formula of the form $\exists x\, G(x)$ is transformed into one of the form $G(X)$ where X is a new "logic" variable that may be instantiated at a subsequent point in the computation. The attempt to solve an atomic goal formula A involves looking for a definite clause $\forall \bar{y}\, (G' \supset A')$ such that A unifies with the atomic formula that results from A' by replacing the universally quantified variables with logic variables. Finding such a clause results in an instantiation of the logic variables in A and the next task becomes that of solving a suitable instance of G'.

The approach outlined above is applicable to the context of higher-order Horn clauses as well. The main difference is that we now have to consider the unification of λ-terms in a situation where equality between these terms is based on the rules of λ-conversion. This unification problem has been studied by several researchers and in most extensive detail by [Huet, 1975]. In the first part of this section we expose those aspects of this problem and its solution that are pertinent to the construction of an actual interpreter for our language. We then introduce the notion of a $\mathcal{P}$-derivation as a generalization to the higher-order context of the SLD-derivations that are used relative to first-order Horn clauses [Apt and van Emden, 1982]. At one level, $\mathcal{P}$-derivations are syntactic objects for demonstrating success on a query and our discussions indicate their correctness from this perspective. At another level, they provide the basis for an actual interpreter for our programming paradigm: a symbol manipulating procedure that searches for $\mathcal{P}$-derivations would, in fact, be such an interpreter. Practicality requires that the ultimate procedure conduct such a search in a deterministic manner. Through our discussions here we expose those choices in search that play a critical role from the perspective of completeness and, in the final subsection, discuss ways in which these choices may be exercised by an actual interpreter.

6.1   The higher-order unification problem

Let us call a pair of terms of the same type a *disagreement pair*. A *disagreement set* is then a finite set, $\{\langle T_i, S_i \rangle \mid 1 \leq i \leq n\}$, of disagreement pairs, and a *unifier* for the set is a substitution θ such that, for $1 \leq i \leq n$, $\theta(T_i) = \theta(S_i)$. The *higher-order unification problem* can, in this context, be stated as the following: Given any disagreement set, to determine whether it has unifiers, and to explicitly provide a unifier if one exists.

The problem described above is a generalization of the well-known unification problem for first-order terms. The higher-order unification problem has certain properties that are different from those of the unification problem in the first-order case. For instance, the question of whether or not a unifier exists for an arbitrary disagreement set in the higher-order context is known to be undecidable [Goldfarb, 1981; Huet, 1973b; Lucchesi, 1972]. Similarly, it has been shown that most general unifiers do not always exist for unifiable higher-order disagreement pairs [Gould, 1976]. Despite these characteristics of the problem, a systematic search can be made for unifiers of a given disagreement set, and we discuss this aspect below.

Huet, in [Huet, 1975], describes a procedure for determining the existence of unifiers for a given disagreement set and, when unifiers do exist, for enumerating some of them. This procedure utilizes the fact that there are certain disagreement sets for which at least one unifier can easily be provided and, similarly, there are other disagreement sets for which it is easily manifest that no unifiers can exist. Given an arbitrary disagreement set, the procedure attempts to reduce it to a disagreement set of one of these two kinds. This reduction proceeds by an iterative use of two simplifying functions, called SIMPL and MATCH, on disagreement sets. The basis for the first of these functions is provided by the following lemma whose proof may be found in [Huet, 1975]. In this lemma, and in the rest of this section, we use the notation $\mathcal{U}(\mathcal{D})$ to denote the set of unifiers for a disagreement set $\mathcal{D}$.

Lemma 6.1.1. *Let* $T_1 = \lambda \bar{x} \, (H_1 \, A_1 \, \ldots \, A_r)$ *and* $T_2 = \lambda \bar{x} \, (H_2 \, B_1 \, \ldots \, B_s)$ *be two rigid terms of the same type that are in λ-normal form. Then* $\theta \in \mathcal{U}(\{\langle T_1, T_2 \rangle\})$ *if and only if*

(i) $H_1 = H_2$ *(and, therefore, $r = s$), and*
(ii) $\theta \in \mathcal{U}(\{\langle \lambda \bar{x} \, A_i, \lambda \bar{x} \, B_i \rangle \mid 1 \leq i \leq r\})$.

Given any term T and any substitution θ, it is apparent that $\theta(T) = \theta(\lambda norm(T))$. Thus the question of unifying two terms can be reduced to unifying their λ-normal forms. Let us say that T is rigid (flexible) just in case $\lambda norm(T)$ is rigid (flexible), and let us refer to the arguments of $\lambda norm(T)$ as the arguments of T. If T_1 and T_2 are two terms of the same type, their λ-normal forms must have binders of the same length. Furthermore, we may, by a sequence of α-conversions, arrange their binders to be identical. If T_1 and T_2 are both rigid, then Lemma 6.1.1 provides us a means for either determining that T_1 and T_2 have no unifiers or reducing the problem of finding unifiers for T_1 and T_2 to that of finding unifiers for the arguments of these terms. This is, in fact, the nature of the simplification effected on a given unification problem by the function SIMPL.

Definition 6.1.2. The function SIMPL on sets of disagreement pairs is defined as follows:

(1)   If $\mathcal{D} = \emptyset$ then $\text{SIMPL}(\mathcal{D}) = \emptyset$.
(2)   If $\mathcal{D} = \{\langle T_1, T_2 \rangle\}$, then the forms of T_1 and T_2 are considered.

   (a)   If T_1 is a flexible term then $\text{SIMPL}(\mathcal{D}) = \mathcal{D}$.
   (b)   If T_2 is a flexible term then $\text{SIMPL}(\mathcal{D}) = \{\langle T_2, T_1 \rangle\}$.
   (c)   Otherwise T_1 and T_2 are both rigid terms. Let $\lambda \bar{x} \, (C_1 \, A_1 \, \ldots \, A_r)$ and $\lambda \bar{x} \, (C_2 \, B_1 \, \ldots \, B_s)$ be λ-normal forms for T_1 and T_2. If $C_1 \neq C_2$ then $\text{SIMPL}(\mathcal{D}) = \mathbf{F}$; otherwise
        $$\text{SIMPL}(\mathcal{D}) = \text{SIMPL}(\{\langle \lambda \bar{x} \, A_i, \lambda \bar{x} \, B_i \rangle \mid 1 \leq i \leq r\}).$$

(3)   Otherwise $\mathcal{D}$ has at least two members. Let $\mathcal{D} = \{\langle T_1^i, T_2^i \rangle \mid 1 \leq i \leq n\}$.

(a)   If SIMPL($\{\langle T_1^i, T_2^i \rangle\}$) = **F** for some i then SIMPL($\mathcal{D}$) = **F**;

(b)   Otherwise SIMPL($\mathcal{D}$) = $\bigcup_{i=1}^{n}$ SIMPL($\{\langle T_1^i, T_2^i \rangle\}$).

Clearly, SIMPL transforms a given disagreement set into either the marker **F** or a disagreement set consisting solely of "flexible–flexible" or "flexible–rigid" terms. By an abuse of terminology, we shall regard **F** as a disagreement set that has no unifiers. The intention, then, is that SIMPL transforms the given set into a simplified set that has the same unifiers. The lemma below that follows from the discussions in [Huet, 1975] shows that SIMPL achieves this purpose in a finite number of steps.

Lemma 6.1.3. SIMPL *is a total computable function on sets of disagreement pairs. Further, if* $\mathcal{D}$ *is a set of disagreement pairs then* $\mathcal{U}(\mathcal{D}) = \mathcal{U}(\text{SIMPL}(\mathcal{D}))$.

The first phase in the process of finding unifiers for a given disagreement set $\mathcal{D}$ thus consists of evaluating SIMPL($\mathcal{D}$). If the result of this is **F**, $\mathcal{D}$ has no unifiers. On the other hand, if the result is a set that is either empty or has only flexible–flexible pairs, at least one unifier can be provided easily for the set, as we shall see in the proof of Theorem 6.2.7. Such a set is, therefore, referred to as a *solved set*. If the set has at least one flexible–rigid pair, then a substitution needs to be considered for the head of the flexible term towards making the heads of the two terms in the pair identical. There are essentially two kinds of "elementary" substitutions that may be employed for this purpose. The first of these is one that makes the head of the flexible term "imitate" that of the rigid term. In the context of first-order terms this is, in fact, the only kind of substitution that needs to be considered. However, if the head of the flexible formula is a function variable, there is another possibility: one of the arguments of the flexible term can be "projected" into the head position in the hope that the head of the resulting term becomes identical to the head of the rigid one or can be made so by a subsequent substitution. There are, thus, a set of substitutions, each of which may be investigated separately as a component of a complete unifier. The purpose of the function MATCH that is defined below is to produce these substitutions.

Definition 6.1.4. Let $\mathcal{V}$ be a set of variables, let T_1 be a flexible term, let T_2 be a rigid term of the same type as T_1, and let $\lambda \bar{x} (F\ A_1\ \ldots\ A_r)$, and $\lambda \bar{x} (C\ B_1\ \ldots\ B_s)$ be λ-normal forms of T_1 and T_2. Further, let the type of F be $\sigma_1 \to \cdots \to \sigma_r \to \tau$, where τ is atomic and, for $1 \leq i \leq r$, let w_i be a variable of type σ_i. The functions IMIT, PROJ, and MATCH are then defined as follows:

(i)   If C is a variable (appearing also in $\bar{x}$), then IMIT($T_1, T_2, \mathcal{V}$) = $\emptyset$; otherwise

$$\text{IMIT}(T_1, T_2, \mathcal{V}) = \{\{\langle F, \lambda w_1, \ldots, w_r \ (C \ (H_1 \ w_1 \ \ldots \ w_r) \ \ldots$$
$$(H_s \ w_1 \ \ldots \ w_r))\rangle\}\},$$

where $H_1, \ldots, H_s$ are variables of appropriate types not contained in $\mathcal{V} \cup \{w_1, \ldots, w_r\}$.

(ii) For $1 \le i \le r$, if σ_i is not of the form $\tau_1 \to \ldots \to \tau_t \to \tau$ then $\text{PROJ}_i(T_1, T_2, \mathcal{V}) = \emptyset$; otherwise,

$$\text{PROJ}_i(T_1, T_2, \mathcal{V}) = \{\{\langle f, \lambda w_1, \ldots, w_r \ (w_i \ (H_1 \ w_1 \ \ldots \ w_r) \ \ldots$$
$$(H_t \ w_1 \ \ldots \ w_r))\rangle\}\},$$

where $H_1, \ldots, H_t$ are variables of appropriate types not contained in $\mathcal{V} \cup \{w_1, \ldots, w_r\}$.

(iii) $\text{MATCH}(T_1, T_2, \mathcal{V}) = \text{IMIT}(T_1, T_2, \mathcal{V}) \cup (\bigcup_{1 \le i \le r} \text{PROJ}_i(T_1, T_2, \mathcal{V}))$.

The purpose of MATCH is to suggest a set of substitutions that may form "initial segments" of unifiers and, in this process, bring the search for a unifier closer to resolution. That MATCH achieves this effect is the content of the following lemma whose proof may be found in [Huet, 1975] or [Nadathur, 1987].

Lemma 6.1.5. *Let $\mathcal{V}$ be a set of variables, let T_1 be a flexible term and let T_2 be a rigid term of the same type as T_1. If there is a substitution $\theta \in \mathcal{U}(\{\langle T_1, T_2 \rangle\})$ then there is a substitution $\varphi \in \text{MATCH}(T_1, T_2, \mathcal{V})$ and a corresponding substitution θ' such that $\theta =_\mathcal{V} \theta' \circ \varphi$. Further, there is a mapping π from substitutions to natural numbers, i.e., a measure on substitutions, such that $\pi(\theta') < \pi(\theta)$.*

A unification procedure may now be described based on an iterative use of SIMPL and MATCH. The structure of this procedure is apparent from the above discussions and its correctness can be ascertained by using Lemmas 6.1.3 and 6.1.5. A procedure that searches for a $\mathcal{P}$-derivation, a notion that we describe next, actually embeds such a unification procedure within it.

6.2 $\mathcal{P}$-derivations

Let the symbols $\mathcal{G}$, $\mathcal{D}$, θ and $\mathcal{V}$, perhaps with subscripts, denote sets of formulas of type o, disagreement sets, substitutions and sets of variables, respectively. The following definition describes the notion of one tuple of the form $\langle \mathcal{G}, \mathcal{D}, \theta, \mathcal{V} \rangle$ being derivable from another similar tuple relative to a program $\mathcal{P}$.

Definition 6.2.1. Let $\mathcal{P}$ be a program. We say a tuple $\langle \mathcal{G}_2, \mathcal{D}_2, \theta_2, \mathcal{V}_2 \rangle$ is $\mathcal{P}$-derivable from another tuple $\langle \mathcal{G}_1, \mathcal{D}_1, \theta_1, \mathcal{V}_1 \rangle$ if $\mathcal{D}_1 \ne \mathbf{F}$ and, in addition, one of the following situations holds:

(1) *(Goal reduction step)* $\theta_2 = \emptyset$, $\mathcal{D}_2 = \mathcal{D}_1$, and there is a goal formula $G \in \mathcal{G}_1$ such that

(a) G is $\top$ and $\mathcal{G}_2 = \mathcal{G}_1 - \{G\}$ and $\mathcal{V}_2 = \mathcal{V}_1$, or

(b) G is $G_1 \wedge G_2$ and $\mathcal{G}_2 = (\mathcal{G}_1 - \{G\}) \cup \{G_1, G_2\}$ and $\mathcal{V}_2 = \mathcal{V}_1$, or

(c) G is $G_1 \vee G_2$ and, for $i = 1$ or $i = 2$, $\mathcal{G}_2 = (\mathcal{G}_1 - \{G\}) \cup \{G_i\}$ and $\mathcal{V}_2 = \mathcal{V}_1$, or

(d) $G \equiv \exists x \, P$ and for some variable $y \notin \mathcal{V}_1$ it is the case that $\mathcal{V}_2 = \mathcal{V}_1 \cup \{y\}$ and $\mathcal{G}_2 = (\mathcal{G}_1 - \{G\}) \cup \{[y/x]P\}$.

(2)   *(Backchaining step)* Let $G \in \mathcal{G}_1$ be a rigid positive atomic formula, and let $D \in \mathcal{P}$ be such that $D \equiv \forall \bar{x} \, (G' \supset A)$ for some sequence of variables $\bar{x}$ no member of which is in $\mathcal{V}_1$. Then $\theta_2 = \emptyset$, $\mathcal{V}_2 = \mathcal{V}_1 \cup \{\bar{x}\}$, $\mathcal{G}_2 = (\mathcal{G}_1 - \{G\}) \cup \{G'\}$, and $\mathcal{D}_2 = \text{SIMPL}(\mathcal{D}_1 \cup \{\langle G, A \rangle\})$. (Here, $\{\bar{x}\}$ denotes the set of variables occurring in the list $\bar{x}$.)

(3)   *(Unification step)* $\mathcal{D}_1$ is not a solved set and for some flexible-rigid pair $\langle T_1, T_2 \rangle \in \mathcal{D}_1$, either $\text{MATCH}(T_1, T_2, \mathcal{V}_1) = \emptyset$ and $\mathcal{D}_2 = \mathbf{F}$, or there is a $\varphi \in \text{MATCH}(T_1, T_2, \mathcal{V}_1)$ and it is the case that $\theta_2 = \varphi$, $\mathcal{G}_2 = \varphi(\mathcal{G}_1)$, $\mathcal{D}_2 = \text{SIMPL}(\varphi(\mathcal{D}_1))$, and, assuming φ is the substitution $\{\langle x, S \rangle\}$ for some variable x, $\mathcal{V}_2 = \mathcal{V}_1 \cup \mathcal{F}(S)$.

Let us call a finite set of goal formulas a *goal set*, and a disagreement set that is $\mathbf{F}$ or consists solely of pairs of positive terms a *positive disagreement set*. If $\mathcal{G}_1$ is a goal set and $\mathcal{D}_1$ is a positive disagreement set then it is clear, from Definitions 6.1.2, 6.1.4 and 6.2.1 and the fact that a positive term remains a positive term under a positive substitution, that $\mathcal{G}_2$ is a goal set and $\mathcal{D}_2$ a positive disagreement set for any tuple $\langle \mathcal{G}_2, \mathcal{D}_2, \theta_2, \mathcal{V}_2 \rangle$ that is $\mathcal{P}$-derivable from $\langle \mathcal{G}_1, \mathcal{D}_1, \theta_1, \mathcal{V}_1 \rangle$.

Definition 6.2.2. Let $\mathcal{G}$ be a goal set. Then we say that a sequence of the form $\langle \mathcal{G}_i, \mathcal{D}_i, \theta_i, \mathcal{V}_i \rangle_{1 \leq i \leq n}$ is a *$\mathcal{P}$-derivation sequence* for $\mathcal{G}$ just in case $\mathcal{G}_1 = \mathcal{G}$, $\mathcal{V}_1 = \mathcal{F}(\mathcal{G}_1)$, $\mathcal{D}_1 = \emptyset$, $\theta_1 = \emptyset$, and, for $1 \leq i < n$, $\langle \mathcal{G}_{i+1}, \mathcal{D}_{i+1}, \theta_{i+1}, \mathcal{V}_{i+1} \rangle$ is $\mathcal{P}$-derivable from $\langle \mathcal{G}_i, \mathcal{D}_i, \theta_i, \mathcal{V}_i \rangle$.

From our earlier observations it follows easily that, in a $\mathcal{P}$-derivation sequence for a goal set $\mathcal{G}$, each $\mathcal{G}_i$ is a goal set and each $\mathcal{D}_i$ is a positive disagreement set. We make implicit use of this fact in our discussions below. In particular, we intend unqualified uses of the symbols $\mathcal{G}$ and $\mathcal{D}$ to be read as syntactic variables for goal sets and positive disagreement sets, respectively.

Definition 6.2.3. A $\mathcal{P}$-derivation sequence $\langle \mathcal{G}_i, \mathcal{D}_i, \theta_i, \mathcal{V}_i \rangle_{1 \leq i \leq n}$ terminates, i.e., is not contained in a longer sequence, if

(a) $\mathcal{G}_n$ is either empty or is a goal set consisting solely of flexible atoms and $\mathcal{D}_n$ is either empty or consists solely of flexible–flexible pairs, or

(b) $\mathcal{D}_n = \mathbf{F}$.

In the former case we say that it is a *successfully terminated* sequence. If this sequence also happens to be a $\mathcal{P}$-derivation sequence for $\mathcal{G}$, then we call it a $\mathcal{P}$-*derivation of* $\mathcal{G}$ and we say that $\theta_n \circ \cdots \circ \theta_1$ is its *answer substitution*.[2] If $\mathcal{G} = \{G\}$ then we also say that the sequence is a $\mathcal{P}$-derivation of G.

Example 6.2.4. Let $\mathcal{P}$ be the set of definite clauses defining the predicate *mapfun* in Example 4.0.3. Further, let G be the goal formula

$$(mapfun\ F_1\ (cons\ 1\ (cons\ 2\ nil))\ (cons\ (h\ 1\ 1)\ (cons\ (h\ 1\ 2)\ nil)))$$

in which F_1 is a variable and all other symbols are parameters as in Example 4.0.3. Then the tuple $\langle \mathcal{G}_1, \mathcal{D}_1, \emptyset, \mathcal{V}_1 \rangle$ is $\mathcal{P}$-derivable from $\langle \{G\}, \emptyset, \emptyset, \{F_1\} \rangle$ by a backchaining step, if

$$\mathcal{V}_1 = \{F_1, F_2, L_1, L_2, X\},$$
$$\mathcal{G}_1 = \{(mapfun\ F_2\ L_1\ L_2)\}, \quad \text{and}$$
$$\mathcal{D}_1 = \{\langle F_1, F_2 \rangle, \langle X, 1 \rangle, \langle (F_1\ X), (h\ 1\ 1) \rangle,$$
$$\langle L_1, (cons\ 2\ nil) \rangle, \langle L_2, (cons\ (h\ 1\ 2)\ nil) \rangle\},$$

where F_2, L_1, L_2, and X are variables. Similarly, if

$$\mathcal{V}_2 = \mathcal{V}_1 \cup \{H_1, H_2\},$$
$$\mathcal{G}_2 = \{(mapfun\ F_2\ L_1\ L_2)\},$$
$$\theta_2 = \{\langle F_1, \lambda w\ (h\ (H_1\ w)\ (H_2\ w)) \rangle\}, \quad \text{and}$$
$$\mathcal{D}_2 = \{\langle L_1, (cons\ 2\ nil) \rangle, \langle L_2, (cons\ (h\ 1\ 2)\ nil) \rangle, \langle X, 1 \rangle,$$
$$\langle (H_1\ X), 1 \rangle, \langle (H_2\ X), 1 \rangle, \langle F_2, \lambda w\ (h\ (H_1\ w)\ (H_2\ w)) \rangle\},$$

then the tuple $\langle \mathcal{G}_2, \mathcal{D}_2, \theta_2, \mathcal{V}_2 \rangle$ is $\mathcal{P}$-derivable from $\langle \mathcal{G}_1, \mathcal{D}_1, \emptyset, \mathcal{V}_1 \rangle$ by a unification step. (H_1, H_2 and w are additional variables here.) It is, in fact, obtained by picking the flexible–rigid pair $\langle (F_1\ X), (h\ 1\ 1) \rangle$ from $\mathcal{D}_1$ and using the substitution provided by IMIT for this pair. If the substitution provided by PROJ_1 was picked instead, we would obtain the tuple $\langle \mathcal{G}_2, \mathbf{F}, \{\langle F_1, \lambda w\ w \rangle\}, \mathcal{V}_1 \rangle$.

There are several $\mathcal{P}$-derivations of G, and all of them have the same answer substitution: $\{\langle F_1, \lambda w\ (h\ 1\ w) \rangle\}$.

Example 6.2.5. Let $\mathcal{P}$ be the program containing only the definite clause $\forall X\ (X \supset (p\ a))$, where X is a variable of type o and p and a are parameters of type $i \to o$ and i, respectively. Then, the following sequence of tuples constitutes a $\mathcal{P}$-derivation of $\exists Y\ (p\ Y)$:

$$\langle \{\exists Y\ (p\ Y)\}, \emptyset, \emptyset, \emptyset \rangle, \quad \langle \{(p\ Y)\}, \emptyset, \emptyset, \{Y\} \rangle,$$
$$\langle \{X\}, \{\langle Y, a \rangle\}, \emptyset, \{Y, X\} \rangle, \quad \langle \{X\}, \emptyset, \{\langle Y, a \rangle\}, \{Y, X\} \rangle.$$

Notice that this is a successfully terminated sequence, even though the final goal set contains a flexible atom. We shall presently see that a goal set that contains only flexible atoms can be "solved" rather easily. In this particular case, for instance, the final goal set may be solved by applying the substitution $\{\langle X, \top \rangle\}$ to it.

---

[2]This is somewhat distinct from what might be construed as the result of a computation. The latter is obtained by taking the the final goal and disagreement sets into account and restricting the substitution to the free variables in the original goal set. We discuss this matter in Subsection 6.3.

A $\mathcal{P}$-derivation of a goal G is intended to show that G succeeds in the context of a program $\mathcal{P}$. The following lemma is useful in proving that $\mathcal{P}$-derivations are true to this intent. A proof of this lemma may be found in [Nadathur, 1987] or [Nadathur and Miller, 1990]. The property of the $\mathcal{P}$-derivability relation that it states should be plausible at an intuitive level, given Lemma 6.1.3 and the success/failure semantics for goals.

Lemma 6.2.6. *Let $\langle \mathcal{G}_2, \mathcal{D}_2, \theta_2, \mathcal{V}_2 \rangle$ be $\mathcal{P}$-derivable from $\langle \mathcal{G}_1, \mathcal{D}_1, \theta_1, \mathcal{V}_1 \rangle$, and let $\mathcal{D}_2 \neq \mathbf{F}$. Further let $\varphi \in \mathcal{U}(\mathcal{D}_2)$ be a positive substitution such that $\mathcal{P} \vdash_O G$ for every G that is a closed positive instance of a formula in $\varphi(\mathcal{G}_2)$. Then*

(i) $\varphi \circ \theta_2 \in \mathcal{U}(\mathcal{D}_1)$, and

(ii) $\mathcal{P} \vdash_O G'$ *for every G' that is a closed positive instance of a formula in* $\varphi \circ \theta_2(\mathcal{G}_1)$.

We now show the correctness of $\mathcal{P}$-derivations. An interesting aspect of the proof of the theorem below is that it describes the construction of a substitution that simultaneously solves a set of flexible atoms and unifies a set of flexible–flexible disagreement pairs.

Theorem 6.2.7. (Soundness of $\mathcal{P}$-derivations) *Let $\langle \mathcal{G}_i, \mathcal{D}_i, \theta_i, \mathcal{V}_i \rangle_{1 \leq i \leq n}$ be a $\mathcal{P}$-derivation of G, and let θ be its answer substitution. Then there is a positive substitution φ such that*

(i) $\varphi \in \mathcal{U}(\mathcal{D}_n)$, and

(ii) $\mathcal{P} \vdash_O G'$ *for every G' that is a closed positive instances of the goal formulas in $\varphi(\mathcal{G}_n)$.*

Further, if φ is a positive substitution satisfying (i) and (ii), then $\mathcal{P} \vdash_O G''$ for every G'' that is a closed positive instance of $\varphi \circ \theta(G)$.

Proof. The second part of the theorem follows easily from Lemma 6.2.6 and a backward induction on the index of a tuple in the given $\mathcal{P}$-derivation sequence. For the first part we exhibit a substitution—that is a simple modification of the one in Lemma 3.5 in [Huet, 1975]—and then show that it satisfies the requirements.

Let H_σ be a chosen variable for each atomic type σ. Then for each type τ we identify a term $\hat{E}_\tau$ in the following fashion:

(a) If τ is o, then $\hat{E}_\tau = \top$.

(b) If τ is an atomic type other than o, then $\hat{E}_\tau = H_\tau$.

(c) If τ is the function type $\tau_1 \to \cdots \to \tau_k \to \tau_0$ where τ_0 is an atomic type, then $\hat{E}_\tau = \lambda x_1 \ldots \lambda x_k \, \hat{E}_{\tau_0}$, where, for $1 \leq i \leq k$, x_i is a variable of type τ_i that is distinct from H_{τ_i}.

Now let $\varphi = \{ \langle Y, \hat{E}_\tau \rangle \mid Y \text{ is a variable of type } \tau \text{ and } Y \in \mathcal{F}(\mathcal{G}_n) \cup \mathcal{F}(\mathcal{D}_n) \}$.

Any goal formula in $\mathcal{G}_n$ is of the form $(P \, S_1 \, \ldots \, S_l)$ where P is a variable whose type is of the form $\sigma_1 \to \cdots \to \sigma_l \to o$. From this it is apparent that if $G \in \mathcal{G}_n$ then any ground instance of $\varphi(G)$ is identical to $\top$. Thus, it is clear that φ satisfies (ii). If $\mathcal{D}_n$ is empty then $\varphi \in \mathcal{U}(\mathcal{D}_n)$. Otherwise, let $\langle T_1, T_2 \rangle \in \mathcal{D}_n$. Since T_1 and T_2 are two flexible terms, it may be seen that $\varphi(T_1)$ and $\varphi(T_2)$ are of the form $\lambda y_1^1 \ldots \lambda y_{m_1}^1 \, \hat{E}_{\tau_1}$, and $\lambda y_1^2 \ldots \lambda y_{m_2}^2 \, \hat{E}_{\tau_2}$ respectively, where τ_i is a primitive type and $\hat{E}_{\tau_i} \notin \{y_1^i, \ldots, y_{m_i}^i\}$ for $i = 1, 2$. Since T_1 and T_2 have the same types and substitution is a type preserving mapping, it is clear that $\tau_1 = \tau_2$, $m_1 = m_2$ and, for $1 \le i \le m_1$, y_i^1 and y_i^2 are variables of the same type. But then $\varphi(T_1) = \varphi(T_2)$. ∎

We would like to show a converse to the above theorem that states that searching for a $\mathcal{P}$-derivation is adequate for determining whether a goal G succeeds or fails in the context of a program $\mathcal{P}$. The crux of such a theorem is showing that if the goals in the last tuple of a $\mathcal{P}$-derivation sequence succeed and the corresponding disagreement set has a unifier, then that sequence can be extended to a successfully terminated sequence. This is the content of the following lemma, a proof of which may be found in [Nadathur, 1987] and [Nadathur and Miller, 1990]. The lemma should, in any case, be intuitively acceptable, given the success/failure semantics for goals and Lemmas 6.1.3 and 6.1.5.

Lemma 6.2.8. *Let $\langle \mathcal{G}_1, \mathcal{D}_1, \theta_1, \mathcal{V}_1 \rangle$ be a tuple that is not a terminated $\mathcal{P}$-derivation sequence and for which $\mathcal{F}(\mathcal{G}_1) \cup \mathcal{F}(\mathcal{D}_1) \subseteq \mathcal{V}_1$. In addition, let there be a positive substitution $\varphi_1 \in \mathcal{U}(\mathcal{D}_1)$ such that, for each $G_1 \in \mathcal{G}_1$, $\varphi_1(G_1)$ is a closed goal formula and $\mathcal{P} \vdash_O \varphi_1(G_1)$. Then there is a tuple $\langle \mathcal{G}_2, \mathcal{D}_2, \theta_2, \mathcal{V}_2 \rangle$ that is $\mathcal{P}$-derivable from $\langle \mathcal{G}_1, \mathcal{D}_1, \theta_1, \mathcal{V}_1 \rangle$ and a positive substitution φ_2 such that*

(i) $\varphi_2 \in \mathcal{U}(\mathcal{D}_2)$,

(ii) $\varphi_1 =_{\mathcal{V}_1} \varphi_2 \circ \theta_2$,

(iii) *for each $G_2 \in \mathcal{G}_2$, $\varphi_2(G_2)$ is a closed goal formula that is such that $\mathcal{P} \vdash_O \varphi_2(G_2)$.*

Further, there is a mapping $\kappa_\mathcal{P}$ from goal sets and substitutions to ordinals, i.e., a measure on pairs of goal sets and substitutions, relative to $\mathcal{P}$ such that $\kappa_\mathcal{P}(\mathcal{G}_2, \varphi_2) < \kappa_\mathcal{P}(\mathcal{G}_1, \varphi_1)$. Finally, when there are several tuples that are $\mathcal{P}$-derivable from $\langle \mathcal{G}_1, \mathcal{D}_1, \theta_1, \mathcal{V}_1 \rangle$, such a tuple and substitution exist for every choice of (1) the kind of step, (2) the goal formula in a goal reduction or backchaining step, and (3) the flexible–rigid pair in a unification step.

In using this lemma to prove the completeness of $\mathcal{P}$-derivations, we need the following observation that is obtained by a routine inspection of Definition 6.2.2.

Lemma 6.2.9. *Let $\langle \mathcal{G}_2, \mathcal{D}_2, \theta_2, \mathcal{V}_2 \rangle$ be $\mathcal{P}$-derivable from $\langle \mathcal{G}_1, \mathcal{D}_1, \theta_1, \mathcal{V}_1 \rangle$ and let $\mathcal{D}_2 \ne \mathbf{F}$. Then $\mathcal{V}_1 \subseteq \mathcal{V}_2$. Further, if $\mathcal{F}(\mathcal{G}_1) \cup \mathcal{F}(\mathcal{D}_1) \subseteq \mathcal{V}_1$, then*

$$\mathcal{F}(\mathcal{G}_2) \cup \mathcal{F}(\mathcal{D}_2) \subseteq \mathcal{V}_2.$$

Theorem 6.2.10. (Completeness of $\mathcal{P}$-derivations) *Let φ be a closed positive substitution for the free variables of G such that $\mathcal{P} \vdash_O \varphi(G)$. Then there is a $\mathcal{P}$-derivation of G with an answer substitution θ such that $\varphi \preceq_{\mathcal{F}(G)} \theta$.*

Proof. From Lemmas 6.2.8 and 6.2.9 and the assumption of the theorem, it is evident that there is a $\mathcal{P}$-derivation sequence $\langle \mathcal{G}_i, \mathcal{D}_i, \theta_i, \mathcal{V}_i \rangle_{1 \leq i}$ for $\{G\}$ and a sequence of substitutions γ_i such that

(i) $\gamma_1 = \varphi$,

(ii) γ_{i+1} satisfies the equation $\gamma_i =_{\mathcal{V}_i} \gamma_{i+1} \circ \theta_{i+1}$,

(iii) $\gamma_i \in \mathcal{U}(\mathcal{D}_i)$, and

(iv) $\kappa_{\mathcal{P}}(\mathcal{G}_{i+1}, \gamma_{i+1}) < \kappa_{\mathcal{P}}(\mathcal{G}_i, \gamma_i)$.

From (iv) it follows that the sequence must be finite. From (iii) and Lemmas 6.1.3 and 6.1.5 it is evident, then, that it must be a successfully terminated sequence, i.e. a $\mathcal{P}$-derivation of G. Suppose that the length of the sequence is n. From (i), (ii), Lemma 6.2.9 and an induction on n, it can be seen that that $\varphi \preceq_{\mathcal{V}_1} \theta_n \circ \cdots \circ \theta_1$. But $\mathcal{F}(G) = \mathcal{V}_1$ and $\theta_n \circ \cdots \circ \theta_1$ is the answer substitution for the sequence. ∎

6.3 Designing an actual interpreter

An interpreter for a language based on our higher-order formulas may be described as a procedure which, given a program $\mathcal{P}$ and a query G, attempts to construct a $\mathcal{P}$-derivation of G. The search space for such a procedure is characterized by a set of states each of which consists of a goal set and a disagreement set. The initial state in the search corresponds to the pair $\langle \{G\}, \emptyset \rangle$. At each stage in the search, the procedure is confronted with a state that it must attempt to simplify. The process of simplification involves either trying to find a solution to the unification problem posed by the disagreement set, or reducing the goal set to an empty set or a set of flexible atomic goal formulas. Given a particular state, there are several ways in which an attempt might be made to bring the search closer to a resolution. However, Definition 6.2.1 indicates that the possible choices are finite, and Theorem 6.2.10 assures us that if these are tried exhaustively then a solution is bound to be found if one exists at all. Further, a solution path may be augmented by substitutions from which an answer can be extracted in a manner akin to the first-order case.

An exhaustive search, while being necessary for completeness, is clearly an inappropriate basis for an interpreter for a programming language, and a trade-off needs to be made between completeness and practicality. From Lemma 6.2.8 we understand that certain choices can be made by the interpreter without adverse effects. However, the following choices are critical:

(i) the disjunct to be added to the goal set in a goal reduction step involving a disjunctive goal formula,

(ii)   the definite clause to be used in a backchaining step, and

(iii) the substitution to be used in a unification step.

When such choices are encountered, the interpreter can, with an accompanying loss of completeness, explore them in a depth-first fashion with the possibility of backtracking. The best order in which to examine the options is a matter that is to be settled by experimentation. This issue has been explored in actual implementations of our language [Brisset and Ridoux, 1992; Miller and Nadathur, 1988; Elliott and Pfenning, 1991], and we comment briefly on the insights that have been gained from these implementations.

The description of the search space for the interpreter poses a natural first question: Should the unification problem be solved first or should a goal reduction step be attempted? A reasonable strategy in this context appears to be that of using a unification step whenever possible and attempting to reduce the goal set only after a solved disagreement set has been produced. There are two points that should be noted with regard to this strategy. First, an interpreter that always tries to solve an unsolved unification problem before looking at the goal set would function in a manner similar to standard Prolog interpreters which always solve the (straightforward) first-order unification problems first. Second, the attempt to solve a unification problem stops short of looking for unifiers for solved disagreement sets. The search for unifiers for such sets can be rather expensive [Huet, 1975], and may be avoided by carrying the solved disagreement sets forward as constraints on the remaining search. In fact, it appears preferable not to look for unifiers for these sets even after the goal set has been reduced to a "solved" set. When the search reaches such a stage, the answer substitution and the final solved disagreement and goal sets may be produced as a response to the original query. From Theorem 6.2.7 we see that composing any substitution that is a unifier for this disagreement set and that also "solves" the corresponding goal set with the answer substitution produces a complete solution to the query and the response of the interpreter may be understood in this sense. In reality, the presentation of the answer substitution and the mentioned sets can be limited to only those components that have a bearing on the substitutions for the free variables in the original query since it is these that constitute the result of the computation.

In attempting to solve the unification problem corresponding to a disagreement set, a flexible–rigid pair in the set may be picked arbitrarily. Invoking MATCH on such a pair produces a set of substitutions in general. One of these needs to be picked to progress the search further, and the others must be retained as alternatives to backtrack to in case of a failure. Certain biases may be incorporated in choosing from the substitutions provided by MATCH, depending on the kinds of solutions that are desired first. For example, consider the unification problem posed by the disagreement set $\{\langle(F\ 2), (cons\ 2\ (cons\ 2\ nil))\rangle\}$ where F is a variable of type $int \to (list\ int)$ and the other symbols are as in Example 4.0.3. There are four unifiers for this set:

$$\{\langle F, \lambda x\ (cons\ x\ (cons\ x\ nil))\rangle\}, \quad \{\langle F, \lambda x\ (cons\ 2\ (cons\ x\ nil))\rangle\},$$
$$\{\langle F, \lambda x\ (cons\ x\ (cons\ 2\ nil))\rangle\}, \text{ and } \{\langle F, \lambda x\ (cons\ 2\ (cons\ 2\ nil))\rangle\}.$$

If the substitutions provided by PROJ$_i$s are chosen first at each stage, then these unifiers will be produced in the order that they appear above, perhaps with the second and third interchanged. On the other hand, choosing the substitution provided by IMIT first results in these unifiers being produced in the reverse order. Now, the above unification problem may arise in a programming context out of the following kind of desire: We wish to unify the function variable F with the result of "abstracting" out all occurrences of a particular constant, which is 2 in this case, from a given data structure, which is an integer list here. If this is the desire, then it is clearly preferable to choose the PROJs substitutions before the substitution provided by IMIT. In a slightly more elaborate scheme, the user may be given a means for switching between these possibilities.

In attempting to solve a goal set, a nonflexible goal formula from the set may be picked arbitrarily. If the goal formula is either conjunctive or existential, then there is only one way in which it can be simplified. If the goal formula picked is $\{G_1 \vee G_2\}$ and the remaining goal set is $\mathcal{G}$, then, for the sake of completeness, the interpreter should try to solve $\{G_1\} \cup \mathcal{G}$ and $\{G_2\} \cup \mathcal{G}$ simultaneously. In practice, the interpreter may attempt to solve $\{G_1\} \cup \mathcal{G}$ first, returning to $\{G_2\} \cup \mathcal{G}$ only in case of failure. This approach, as the reader might notice, is in keeping with the one used in Prolog. In the case that the goal formula picked is atomic, a backchaining step must be used. In performing such a step, it is enough to consider only those definite clauses in the program of the form $\forall \bar{x}\ A$ or $\forall \bar{x}\ (G \supset A)$ where the head of A is identical to the head of the goal formula being solved, since all other cases will cause the disagreement set to be reduced to **F** by SIMPL. For completeness, it is necessary to use each of these definite clauses in a breadth-first fashion in attempting to solve the goal formula. Here again the scheme that is used by standard Prolog interpreters might be adopted: the first appropriate clause might be picked based on some predetermined ordering and others may be returned to only if this choice leads to failure.

The above discussion indicates how an interpreter can be constructed based on the notion of $\mathcal{P}$-derivations. An interpreter based on only these ideas would still be a fairly simplistic one. Several specific improvements (such as recognizing and handling special kinds of unification problems) and enhancements (such as those for dealing with polymorphism, a necessary practical addition) can be described to this interpreter. An examination of these aspects is beyond the scope of this chapter. For the interested reader, we mention that a further discussion of some of these aspects may be found in [Nadathur, 1987], that a detailed presentation of a particular interpreter appears in [Elliott and Pfenning, 1991], that a class of λ-terms with interesting unifiability properties is studied in [Miller, 1991] and that ideas relevant to compilation are explored in [Brisset and Ridoux, 1991; Kwon *et al.*, 1994; Nadathur *et al.*, 1995; Nadathur *et al.*, 1993].

7 Examples of higher-order programming

In this section, we present some programs in our higher-order language that use predicate variables and λ-terms of predicate type. We begin this discussion by describing a concrete syntax that will be used in the examples in this and later sections. We then present a set of simple programs that illustrate the idea of higher-order programming. In Subsection 7.3 we describe a higher-order logic programming approach to implementing goal-directed theorem proving based on the use of *tactics* and *tacticals*. We conclude this section with a brief comparison of the notion of higher-order programming in the logic programming and the functional programming settings.

7.1 A concrete syntax for programs

The syntax that we shall use is adapted from that of the language λProlog. In the typical programming situation, it is necessary to identify three kinds of objects: the sorts and type constructors, the constants and variables with their associated types and the definite clauses that define the various predicate symbols. We present the devices for making these identifications below and simultaneously describe the syntax for expressions that use the objects so identified.

We assume that the two sorts o and int corresponding to propositions and integers and the unary list type constructor list are available in our language at the outset. This collection can be enhanced by declarations of the form

```
kind    <Id>    type -> ... -> type.
```

in which <Id> represents a token that is formed out of a sequence of alphanumeric characters and that begins with a lowercase letter. Such a declaration identifies <Id> as a type constructor whose arity is one less than the number of occurrences of type in the declaration. A declaration of this kind may also be used to add new sorts, given that these are, in fact, nullary type constructors. As specific examples, if int and list were not primitive to the language, then they might be added to the available collections by the declarations

```
kind    int     type.
kind    list    type -> type.
```

The sorts and type constructors available in a given programming context can be used as expected in forming type expressions. Such expressions might also use the constructor for function types that is written in concrete syntax as ->. Thus, the type $int \to (list\ int) \to (list\ int)$ seen first in Example 3.1.1 would be written now as `int -> (list int) -> (list int)`.

The logical constants are rendered into concrete syntax as follows: ⊤ is represented by `true`, ∧ and ∨ are denoted by the comma and semicolon respectively, implication is rendered into `:-` after being written in reverse order (i.e., $G \supset A$ is denoted by `A :- G` where A and G are the respective translations of A and G), ¬ is not used, and ∀ and ∃ of type $(\tau \to o) \to o$ are represented by `pi` and `sigma` respectively. The last two constants are polymorphic in a sense that is explained below. To reduce the number of parentheses in expressions, we assume that conjunction and disjunction are right associative operators and that they have narrower scope than implication. Thus, the formula $(F \wedge (G \wedge H)) \supset A$ will be denoted by an expression of the form `A :- F,G,H`.

Nonlogical constants and variables are represented by tokens formed out of sequences of alphanumeric characters or sequences of "sign" characters. Symbols that consist solely of numeric characters are treated as nonlogical constants that have the type `int` associated with them. For other constants, a type association is achieved by a declaration of the form

```
type    <Id>    <Type>.
```

in which `<Id>` represents a constant and `<Type>` represents a type expression. As an example, if `i` has been defined to be a sort, then

```
type    f    (list i) -> i.
```

is a valid type declaration and results in `f` being identified as a constant of type `(list i) -> i`. The types of variables will be left implicit in our examples with the intention that they be inferred from the context.

It is sometimes convenient to identify a family of constants whose types are similar through *one* declaration. To accommodate this possibility, our concrete syntax allows for variables in type expressions. Such variables are denoted by capital letters. Thus, `A -> (list A) -> (list A)` is a valid type expression. A type declaration in which variables occur in the type is to be understood in the following fashion: It represents an infinite number of declarations each of which is obtained by substituting, in a uniform manner, closed types for the variables that occur in the type. For instance, the quantifier symbol `sigma` can be thought to be given by the type declaration

```
type    sigma    (A -> o) -> o.
```

This declaration represents, amongst others, the declarations

```
type    sigma    (int -> o) -> o.
```

```
type   sigma   ((int -> int) -> o) -> o.
```

The tokens `sigma` that appear in each of these (virtual) declarations are, of course, distinct and might be thought to be subscripted by the type chosen in each case for the variable `A`. As another example, consider the declarations

```
type   nil   (list A).
type   ::    A -> (list A) -> (list A).
```

The symbols `nil` and `::` that are identified by them serve as polymorphic counterparts of the constants *nil* and *cons* of Example 4.0.3: using "instances" of `nil` and `::` that are of type

```
(list int) and int -> (list int) -> (list int)
```

respectively, it is possible to construct representations of lists of objects of type `int`. These two symbols are treated as pre-defined ones of our language and we further assume that `::` is an infix and right-associative operator.

The symbol `\` is used as an infix and right-associative operator that denotes abstraction and juxtaposition with some intervening white-space serves as an infix and left-associative operator that represents application. Parentheses may be omitted in expressions by assuming that abstractions bind more tightly than applications. Thus, the expressions

```
x\x,  (x\x Y\Y)  and  x\y\z\(x z (y z))
```

denote, respectively, the terms

$$\lambda x\, x, \quad ((\lambda x\, x)\,(\lambda Y\, Y)) \quad \text{and} \quad \lambda x\, \lambda y\, \lambda z\, ((x\ z)\,(y\ z)).$$

Within formulas, tokens that are not explicitly bound by an abstraction are taken to be variables if they begin with an uppercase letter. A collection of definite clauses that constitute a program will be depicted as in Prolog by writing them in sequence, each clause being terminated by a period. Variables that are not given an explicit scope in any of these clauses are assumed to be universally quantified over the entire clause in which they appear. As an example, assuming that the declaration

```
type   append   (list A) -> (list A) -> (list A) -> o.
```

gives the type of the predicate parameter `append`, the following definite clauses define the append relation of Prolog:

```
append nil L L.
(append (X::L1) L2 (X::L3)) :- (append L1 L2 L3).
```

Notice that, in contrast to Prolog and in keeping with the higher-order nature of our language, our syntax for formulas and terms is a curried one. We depict a query by writing a formula of the appropriate kind preceded by the token `?-` and followed by a period. As observed in Section 4, the free variables in a query are implicitly existentially quantified over it and represent a means for extracting a result from a computation. Thus, the expression

```
?- (append (1::2::nil) (3::4::nil) L).
```

represents a query that asks for the result of appending the two lists 1::2::nil and 3::4::nil.

In conjunction with the append example, we see that variables may occur in the types corresponding to the constants and variables that appear in a "definite clause". Such a clause is, again, to be thought of as a schema that represents an infinite set of definite clauses, each member of this set being obtained by substituting closed types for the type variables that occur in the schema. Such a substitution is, of course, to be constrained by the fact that the resulting instance must constitute a well-formed definite clause. Thus, consider the first of the definite clause "schemata" defining append. Writing the types of nil, L and append as (list B), C and

```
        (list A) -> (list A) -> (list A) -> o,
```

respectively, we see that C must be instantiated by a type of the form (list D) and, further, that the same closed type must replace the variables A, B and D. Consistent with this viewpoint, the invocation of a clause such as this one must also be accompanied by a determination of the type instance to be used. In practice this choice can be delayed through unification at the level of types. This possibility is discussed in greater detail in [Nadathur and Pfenning, 1992] and we assume below that it is used in the process of solving queries.

A final comment concerns the inference of types for variables. Obvious requirements of this inference is that the overall term be judged to be well-formed and that every occurrence of a variable that is (implicitly or explicitly) bound by the same abstraction be accorded the same type. However, these requirements are, of themselves, not sufficiently constraining. For example, in the first definite clause for append, these requirements can be met by assigning the variable L the type (list int) or the type (list D) as indicated above. Conflicts of this kind are to be resolved by choosing a type for each variable that is most general in the sense that every other acceptable type is an instance of it. This additional condition can be sensibly imposed and it ensures that types can be inferred for variables in an unambiguous fashion [Damas and Milner, 1982].

7.2   Some simple higher-order programs

Five higher-order predicate constants are defined through the declarations in Figure 2. The intended meanings of these higher-order predicates are the following: A closed query of the form (mapred P L K) is to be solvable if P is a binary predicate, L and K are lists of equal length and corresponding elements of L and K are related by P; mapred is, thus, a polymorphic version of the predicate *mapred* of Example 4.0.3. A closed query of

```
type    mappred     (A -> B -> o) -> (list A) -> (list B) -> o.
type    forsome     (A -> o) -> (list A) -> o.
type    forevery    (A -> o) -> (list A) -> o.
type    trans       (A -> A -> o) -> A -> A -> o.
type    sublist     (A -> o) -> (list A) -> (list A) -> o.


(mappred P nil nil).
(mappred P (X::L) (Y::K)) :- (P X Y), (mappred P L K).


(forsome P (X::L)) :- (P X).
(forsome P (X::L)) :- (forsome P L).


(forevery P nil).
(forevery P (X::L)) :- (P X), (forevery P L).


(trans R X Y) :- (R X Y).
(trans R X Z) :- (R X Y), (trans R Y Z).


(sublist P (X::L) (X::K)) :- (P X), (sublist P L K).
(sublist P (X::L) K)      :- (sublist P L K).
(sublist P nil nil).
```

Fig. 2. Definition of some higher-order predicates

the form (forsome P L) is to be solvable if L is a list that contains at least one element that satisfies the predicate P. In contrast, a closed query of the form (forevery P L) is to be solvable only if *all* elements of L satisfy the predicate P. Assuming that R is a closed term denoting a binary predicate and X and Y are closed terms denoting two objects, the query (trans R X Y) is to be solvable just in case the objects given by X and Y are related by the transitive closure of the relation given by R; notice that the subterm (trans R) of this query is also a predicate. Finally, a closed query of the form (sublist P L K) is to be solvable if L is a sublist of K all of whose elements satisfy P.

Figure 3 contains some declarations defining a predicate called **age** that can be used in conjunction with these higher-order predicates. An interpreter for our language that is of the kind described in Section 6 will succeed on the query

?- mappred x\y\(age x y) (ned::bob::sue::nil) L.

relative to the clauses in Figures 2 and 3, and will have an answer substitution that binds L to the list (23::24::23::nil). This is, of course, the list of ages of the individuals ned, bob and sue, respectively. If the query

?- mappred x\y\(age y x) (23::24::nil) K.

```
kind   person   type.
type   bob      person.
type   sue      person.
type   ned      person.
type   age      person -> int -> o.

(age bob 24).
(age sue 23).
(age ned 23).
```

Fig. 3. A database of people and their ages

is invoked relative to the same set of definite clauses, two substitutions for K can be returned as answers: (sue::bob::nil) and (ned::bob::nil). Notice that within the form of higher-order programming being considered, non-determinism is supported naturally. Support is also provided in this context for the use of "partially determined" predicates, i.e., predicate expressions that contain variables whose values are to be determined in the course of computation. The query

```
?- (forevery x\(age x A) (ned::bob::sue::nil)).
```

illustrates this feature. Solving this query requires determining if the predicate x\(age x A) is true of ned, bob and sue. Notice that this predicate has a variable A appearing in it and a binding for A will be determined in the course of computation, causing the predicate to become further specified. The given query will fail relative to the clauses in Figures 2 and 3 because the three individuals in the list do not have a common age. However, the query

```
?- (forevery x\(age x A) (ned::sue::nil)).
```

will succeed and will result in A being bound to 23. The last two queries are to be contrasted with the query

```
?- (forevery x\(sigma Y\(age x Y)) (ned::bob::sue::nil)).
```

in which the predicate x\(sigma Y\(age x Y)) is completely determined. This query will succeed relative to the clauses in Figures 2 and 3 since all the individuals in the list (ned::bob::sue::nil) have an age defined for them.

An interpreter for our language that is based on the ideas in Section 6 solves a query by using a succession of goal reduction, backchaining and unification steps. None of these steps result in a flexible goal formula being selected. Flexible goal formulas remain in the goal set until substitutions performed on them in the course of computation make them rigid. This may never happen and the computation may terminate with such goal formulas being left in the goal set. Thus, consider the query

```
?- (P sue 23).
```

relative to the clauses in Figure 3. Our interpreter will succeed on this immediately because the only goal formula in its initial goal set is a flexible one. It is sensible to claim this to be a successful computation because there is at least one substitution — in particular, the substitution x\y\true for P — that makes this query a solvable one. It might be argued that there are meaningful answers for this query relative to the given program and that these should be provided by the interpreter. For example, it may appear that the binding of P to the term x\y\(age x y) (that is equal by virtue of η-conversion to age) should be returned as an answer to this query. However, many other similarly suitable terms can be offered as bindings for P; for example, consider the terms x\y\(age ned 23) and x\y\((age x 23), (age ned y)). There are, in fact, far too many "suitable" answer substitutions for this kind of a query for any reasonable interpreter to attempt to generate. It is for this reason that flexible goal formulas are never selected in the course of constructing a $\mathcal{P}$-derivation and that the ones that persist at the end are presented as such to the user along with the answer substitution and any remaining flexible–flexible pairs.

Despite these observations, flexible goal formulas can have a meaningful role to play in programs because the range of acceptable substitutions for predicate variables can be restricted by other clauses in the program. For example, while it is not sensible to ask for the substitutions for R that make the query

```
?- (R john mary).
```

a solvable one, a programmer can first describe a restricted collection of predicate terms and then ask if any of these predicates can be substituted for R to make the given query a satisfiable one. Thus, suppose that our program contains the definite clauses that are presented in Figure 4. Then, the query

```
?- (rel R), (R john mary).
```

is a meaningful one and is solvable only if the term

```
x\y\(sigma Z\((wife x Z), (mother Z y))).
```

is substituted for R. The second-order predicate rel specifies the collection of predicate terms that are relevant to consider as substitutions in this situation.

Our discussions pertaining to flexible queries have been based on a certain logical view of predicates and the structure of predicate terms. However, this is not the only tenable view. There is, in fact, an alternative viewpoint under which a query such as

```
?- (P sue 23).
```

can be considered meaningful and for which the only legitimate answer is

```
type    primrel    (person -> person -> o) -> o.
type    rel        (person -> person -> o) -> o.
type    mother     person -> person -> o.
type    wife       person -> person -> o.

(primrel mother).
(primrel wife).
(rel R) :- (primrel R).
(rel x\y\(sigma Z\((R x Z), (S Z y)))) :-
      (primrel R), (primrel S).
(mother jane mary).
(wife john jane).
```

Fig. 4. Restricting the range of predicate substitutions

the substitution of **age** for P. We refer the reader to [Chen *et al.*, 1993] for a presentation of a logic that justifies this viewpoint and for the description of a programming language that is based on this logic.

7.3   Implementing tactics and tacticals

To provide another illustration of higher-order programming, we consider the task of implementing the *tactics* and *tacticals* that are often used in the context of (interactive) theorem proving systems. As described in [Gordon *et al.*, 1979], a tactic is a primitive method for decomposing a goal into other goals whose achievement or satisfaction ensures the achievement or satisfaction of the original goal. A tactical is a high-level method for composing tactics into meaningful and large scale problem solvers. The functional programming language ML has often been used to implement tactics and tacticals. We show here that this task can also be carried out in a higher-order logic programming language. We use ideas from [Felty and Miller, 1988; Felty, 1993] in this presentation.

The task that is at hand requires us, first of all, to describe an encoding within terms for the notion of a goal in the relevant theorem proving context. We might use g as a sort for expressions that encode such goals; this sort, which corresponds to "object-level" goals, is to be distinguished from the sort o that corresponds to "meta-level" goals, i.e., the queries of our programming language. The terms that denote primitive object-level goals will, in general, be determined by the problem domain being considered. For example, if the desire is to find proofs for formulas in first-order logic, then the terms of type g will have to incorporate an encoding of such formulas. Alternatively, if it is sequents of first-order logic that have to be proved, then terms of type g should permit an encoding of sequents. Additional constructors over the type g might be included to support the encoding of compound goals. For instance, we will use below the constant truegoal of type g to denote the trivially satisfiable goal and the constant andgoal of type g -> g -> g to denote a goal formed out of the conjunction of two other goals. Other combinations such as the disjunction of two goals are also possible and can be encoded in a similar way.

A tactic in our view is a binary relation between a primitive goal and another goal, either compound or primitive. Thus tactics can be encoded by predicates of type g -> g -> o. Abstractly, if a tactic R holds of G1 and G2, i.e., if (R G1 G2) is solvable from a presentation of primitive tactics as a set of definite clauses, then satisfying the goal G2 in the object-language should suffice to satisfy goal G1.

An illustration of these ideas can be provided by considering the task of implementing a proof procedure for propositional Horn clauses. For simplicity of presentation, we restrict the propositional goal formulas that will be considered to be conjunctions of propositions. The objective will, of course, be to prove such formulas. Each primitive object-level goal therefore corresponds to showing some atomic proposition to be true, and such a goal might be encoded by a constant of type g whose name is identical to that of the proposition. Now, if p and q are two atomic propositions, then the goal of showing that their conjunction is true can be encoded in the object-level goal (andgoal p q). The primitive method for reducing such goals is that of backchaining on (propositional) definite clauses. Thus, the tactics of interest will have the form (R H G), where H represents the head of a clause and G is the goal corresponding to its body. The declarations in Figure 5 use these ideas to provide a tactic-style encoding of the four propositional clauses

```
p :- r,s.
q :- r.
s:- r,q.
r.
```

The tactics cl1tac, cl2tac, cl3tac and cl4tac correspond to each of these clauses respectively.

The declarations in Figure 6 serve to implement several general tacticals. Notice that tacticals are higher-order predicates in our context since they take tactics that are themselves predicates as arguments. The tacticals in Figure 6 are to be understood as follows. The orelse tactical is one that succeeds if either of the two tactics it is given can be used to successfully reduce the given goal. The try tactical forms the reflexive closure of a given tactic: if R is a tactic then (try R) is itself a tactic and, in fact, one that always succeeds, returning the original goal if it is unable to reduce it by means of R. This tactical uses an auxiliary tactic called idtac whose meaning is self-evident. The then tactical specifies the natural join of the two relations that are its arguments and is used to compose tactics: if R1 and

```
type    p    g.
type    q    g.
type    r    g.
type    s    g.

type    cl1tac    g -> g -> o.
type    cl2tac    g -> g -> o.
type    cl3tac    g -> g -> o.
type    cl4tac    g -> g -> o.

(cl1tac p (andgoal r s)).
(cl2tac q r).
(cl3tac s (andgoal r q)).
(cl4tac r truegoal).
```

Fig. 5. A tactic-style encoding of some propositional definite clauses

R2 are closed terms denoting tactics, and G1 and G2 are closed terms representing (object-level) goals, then the query (then R1 R2 G1 G2) succeeds just in case the application of R1 to G1 produces G3 and the application of R2 to G3 yields the goal G2. The maptac tactical is used in carrying out the application of the second tactic in this process since G2 may be not be a primitive object-level goal: maptac maps a given tactic over all the primitive goals in a compound goal. The then tactical plays a fundamental role in combining the results of step-by-step goal reduction. The repeat tactical is defined recursively using then, orelse, and idtac and it repeatedly applies the tactic it is given until this tactic is no longer applicable. Finally, the complete tactical succeeds if the tactic it is given completely solves the goal it is given. The completely solved goal can be written as truegoal and (andgoal truegoal truegoal) and in several other ways, and so the auxiliary predicate goalreduce is needed to reduce all of these to truegoal. Although the complete tactical is the only one that uses the predicate goalreduce, the other tacticals can be modified so that they also use it to simplify the structure of the goal they produce whenever this is possible.

Tacticals, as mentioned earlier, can be used to combine tactics to produce large scale problem solvers. As an illustration of this, consider the following definite clause

```
(depthfirst G) :-
 (complete (repeat (orelse cl1tac
                    (orelse cl2tac (orelse cl3tac cl4tac))))
            G truegoal).
```

in conjunction with the declarations in Figures 5 and 6. Assuming an

```
type then        (g -> g -> o) -> (g -> g -> o)
                                   -> g -> g -> o.
type orelse      (g -> g -> o) -> (g -> g -> o)
                                   -> g -> g -> o.
type maptac      (g -> g -> o) -> g -> g -> o.
type repeat      (g -> g -> o) -> g -> g -> o.
type try         (g -> g -> o) -> g -> g -> o.
type complete    (g -> g -> o) -> g -> g -> o.
type idtac       g -> g -> o.
type goalreduce  g -> g -> o.


(orelse R1 R2 G1 G2) :- (R1 G1 G2).
(orelse R1 R2 G1 G2) :- (R2 G1 G2).


(try R G1 G2) :- (orelse R idtac G1 G2).


(idtac G G).


(then R1 R2 G1 G2) :- (R1 G1 G3), (maptac R2 G3 G2).


(maptac R truegoal truegoal).
(maptac R (andgoal G1 G2) (andgoal G3 G4)) :-
     (maptac R G1 G3), (maptac R G2 G4).
(maptac R G1 G2) :- (R G1 G2).


(repeat R G1 G2) :- (orelse (then R (repeat R)) idtac G1 G2).


(complete R G1 truegoal) :-
     (R G1 G2), (goalreduce G2 truegoal).


(goalreduce (andgoal truegoal G1) G2) :- (goalreduce G1 G2).
(goalreduce (andgoal G1 truegoal) G2) :- (goalreduce G1 G2).
(goalreduce G G).
```

Fig. 6. Some simple tacticals

interpreter for our language of the kind described in Section 6, this clause defines a procedure that attempts to solve an object-level goal by a depth-first search using the given propositional Horn clauses. The query

```
?- (depthfirst p).
```

has a successful derivation and it follows from this that the proposition p is a logical consequence of the given Horn clauses.

7.4   A comparison with functional programming

The examples of higher-order programming considered in this section have
similarities to higher-order programming in the functional setting. In the
latter context, higher-order programming corresponds to the treatment,
perhaps in a limited fashion, of functions as values. For example, in a
language like ML [Milner *et al.*, 1990], function expressions can be constructed using the abstraction operation, bound to variables, and applied
to arguments. The semantics of such a language is usually extensional,
and so intensional operations on functions like that of testing whether two
function descriptions are identical are not supported by it. We have just
seen that our higher-order logic programming language supports the ability
to build predicate expressions, to bind these to variables, to apply them
to arguments and, finally, to invoke the resulting expressions as queries.
Thus, the higher-order capabilities present in functional programming languages are matched by ones available in our language. In the converse
direction, we note that there are some completely new higher-order capabilities present in our language. In particular, this language is based on
logic that has intensional characteristics and so can support computations
on the *descriptions* of predicates and functions. This aspect is not exploited
in the examples in this section but will be in those in the next.

In providing a more detailed comparison of the higher-order programming capabilities of our language that are based on an extensional view
with those of functional programming languages, it is useful to consider
the function `maplist`, the "canonical" higher-order function of functional
programming. This function is given by the following equations:

```
(maplist f nil) = nil
(maplist f (x::l)) = (f x)::(maplist f l)
```

There is a close correspondence between `maplist` and the predicate called
`mappred` that is defined in Subsection 7.2. In particular, let $\mathcal{P}$ be a program, let q be a binary predicate and let f be a functional program such
that (q t s) is provable from $\mathcal{P}$ if and only if (f t) evaluates to s; that
is, the predicate q represents the function f. Further, let $\mathcal{P}'$ be $\mathcal{P}$ extended
with the two clauses that define `mappred`. (We assume that no definite
clauses defining `mappred` appear in $\mathcal{P}$.) Then, for any functional programming language that is reasonably pure, we can show that (maplist f l)
evaluates to k if and only if (mappred q l k) is provable from $\mathcal{P}'$. Notice,
however, that `mappred` is "richer" than `mapfun` in that its first argument
can be a non-functional relation. In particular, if q denotes a non-functional
relation, then (mappred q) is an acceptable predicate and itself denotes a
non-functional relation. This aspect was illustrated earlier in this section
through the query

```
?- (mappred x\y\(age y x) (23::24::nil) K).
```

In a similar vein, it is possible for a predicate expression to be partially specified in the sense that it contains logic variables that get instantiated in the course of using the expression in a computation. An illustration of this possibility was provided by the query

```
?- (forevery x\(age x A) (ned::sue::nil)).
```

These additional characteristics of higher-order logic programming are, of course, completely natural and expected.

8 Using λ-terms as data structures

As noted in Section 2, the expressions that are permitted to appear as the arguments of atomic formulas in a logic programming language constitute the data structures of that language. The data structures of our higher-order language are, therefore, the terms of a λ-calculus. There are certain programming tasks that involve the manipulation of objects that embody a notion of binding; the implementation of theorem proving and program transformation systems that perform computations on quantified formulas and programs are examples of such tasks. Perspicuous and succinct representations of such objects can be provided by using λ-terms. The data structures of our language also incorporate a notion of equality based on λ-conversion and this provides useful support for logical operations that might have to be performed on the objects being represented. For example, following the discussion in Subsection 3.2, β-conversion can be used to realize the operation of substitution on these objects. In a similar sense, our language permits a quantification over function variables, leading thereby to the provision of higher-order unification as a primitive for taking apart λ-terms. The last feature is truly novel to our language and a natural outcome of considering the idea of higher-order programming in logic programming in its full generality: logic programming languages typically support intensional analyses of objects that can be represented in them, and the manipulation of λ-terms through higher-order unification corresponds to such examinations of functional expressions.

The various features of our language that are described above lead to several important applications for it in the realm of manipulating the syntactic objects of other languages such as formulas and programs. We refer to such applications as *meta-programming* ones and we provide illustrations of them in this section. The examples we present deal first with the manipulation of formulas and then with the manipulation of programs. Although our language has several features that are useful from this perspective, it is still lacking in certain respects as a language for meta-programming. We discussion this aspect in the last subsection below as a prelude to an extension of it that is considered in Section 9.

Before embarking on the main discussions of this section, it is useful to recapitulate the kinds of computations that can be performed on functional objects in our language. For this purpose, we consider the predicate `mapfun` that is defined by the following declarations.

```
type    mapfun    (A -> B) -> (list A) -> (list B) -> o.
```

```
(mapfun F nil nil).
(mapfun F (X::L) ((F X)::K))  :- (mapfun F L K).
```

This predicate is a polymorphic version of the predicate *mapfun* presented in Example 4.0.3 and it relates a term of functional type to two lists of equal length if the elements of the second list can be obtained by applying the functional term to the corresponding elements of the first list. The notion of function application that is relevant here is, of course, the one given by the λ-conversion rules. Thus, suppose that h is a nonlogical constant of type `int -> int -> int`. Then the answer to the query

```
?- (mapfun x\(h 1 x) (1::2::nil) L).
```

is one that entails the substitution of the term `((h 1 1)::(h 1 2)::nil)` for L. In computing this answer, an interpreter for our language would have to form the terms `((x\(h 1 x)) 1)` and `((x\(h 1 x)) 2)` that may subsequently be simplified using the λ-conversion rules. As another example, consider the query

```
?- (mapfun F (1::2::nil) ((h 1 1)::(h 1 2)::nil)).
```

Any $\mathcal{P}$-derivation for this query would have an associated answer substitution that contains the pair $\langle$F, x\(h 1 x)$\rangle$. A depth-first interpreter for our language that is of the kind described in Section 6 would have to consider unifying the terms (F 1) and (h 1 1). There are four incomparable unifiers for these two terms and these are the ones that require substituting the terms

```
    x\(h x x),  x\(h 1 x),  x\(h x 1),  and  x\(h 1 1)
```

respectively for F. Now, the terms (F 2) and (h 1 2) can be unified only under the second of these substitutions. Thus, if the interpreter selects a substitution for F distinct from the second one above, it will be forced to backtrack to reconsider this choice when it attempts to unify the latter two terms. As a final example, consider the query

```
?- (mapfun F (1::2::nil) (3::4::nil)).
```

This query does not succeed in the context of our language. The reason for this is that there is no λ-term of the kind used in our language that yields 3 when applied to 1 and 4 when applied to 2. Note that there are an infinite number of functions that map 1 to 3 and 2 to 4. However, none of these functions can be expressed by our terms.

As a final introductory remark, we observe that it is necessary to distinguish in the discussions below between the programs and formulas that are being manipulated and the ones in our language that carry out these

```
kind    term    type.
kind    form    type.

type    false   form.
type    truth   form.
type    and     form -> form -> form.
type    or      form -> form -> form.
type    imp     form -> form -> form.
type    all     (term -> form) -> form.
type    some    (term -> form) -> form.

type    a       term.
type    b       term.
type    c       term.
type    f       term -> term.
type    path    term -> term -> form.
type    adj     term -> term -> form.
type    prog    list form -> o.

prog ((adj a b) :: (adj b c) :: (adj c (f c)) ::
      (all x\(all y\(imp (adj x y) (path x y)))) ::
      (all x\(all y\(all z\(imp (and (adj x y) (path y z))
                                (path x z)))))) ::
      nil)
```

Fig. 7. A specification of an object-level logic and some definite clauses

manipulations. We do this by referring to the former as object-level ones and to the latter as ones of the meta-level.

8.1 Implementing an interpreter for Horn clauses

Formulas in a quantificational logic can be represented naturally within the terms of our language. The main concern in encoding these objects is that of capturing the nature of quantification. As noted in Subsection 3.1, the binding and predication aspects of a quantifier can be distinguished and the former can be handled by the operation of abstraction. Adopting this approach results in direct support for certain logical operations on formulas. For example, the equivalence of two formulas that differ only in the names used for their bound variables is mirrored directly in the equality of λ-terms by virtue of α-conversion. Similarly, the operation of instantiating a formula is realized easily through β-conversion. Thus, suppose the expression (all x\T) represents a universally quantified formula. Then the instantiation of this formula by a term represented by S is effected simply by writing the expression ((x\T) S); this term is equal, via β-conversion, to the term [S/x]T. The upshot of these observations is that a programmer using our language does not need to explicitly implement procedures for testing for alphabetic equivalence, for performing substitution or for carrying out other similar logical operations on formulas. The benefits of this are substantial since implementing such operations correctly is a non-trivial task.

We provide a specific illustration of the aspects discussed above by considering the problem of implementing an interpreter for the logic of first-order Horn clauses. The first problem to address here is the representation of object-level formulas and terms. We introduce the sorts **form** and **term** for this purpose; λ-terms of these two types will represent the objects in question. Object-level logical and nonlogical constants, functions, and predicates will be represented by relevant meta-level nonlogical constants. Thus, suppose we wish to represent the following list of first-order definite clauses:

$$adj(a, b),$$
$$adj(b, c),$$
$$adj(c, f(c)),$$
$$\forall x \forall y (adj(x, y) \supset path(x, y)) \text{ and}$$
$$\forall x \forall y \forall z (adj(x, y) \wedge path(y, z) \supset path(x, z)).$$

We might do this by using the declarations in Figure 7. In this program, a representation of a list of these clauses is eventually "stored" by using the (meta-level) predicate **prog**. Notice that universal and existential quantification at the object-level are encoded by using, respectively, the constants **all** and **some** of second-order type and that variable binding at the object-level is handled as expected by meta-level abstraction.

The clauses in Figure 8 implement an interpreter for the logic of first-order Horn clauses assuming the representation just described. Thus, given the clauses in Figures 7 and 8, the query

?- (prog Cs), (intep Cs (path a X)).

is solvable and produces three distinct answer substitutions, binding X to b, c and (f c), respectively. Notice that object-level quantifiers need to be instantiated at two places in an interpreter of the kind we desire: in dealing with an existentially quantified goal formula and in generating an instance of a universally quantified definite clause. Both kinds of instantiation are realized in the clauses in Figure 8 through (meta-level) β-conversion and the specific instantiation is delayed in both cases through the use of a logic variable.

In understanding the advantages of our language, it is useful to consider the task of implementing an interpreter for first-order Horn clause logic in a pure first-order logic programming language. This task is a much more involved one since object-level quantification will have to be represented in

```
type    interp       form -> form -> o.
type    backchain    form -> form -> form -> o.


(interp Cs (some B))   :- (interp Cs (B T)).
(interp Cs (and B C))  :- (interp Cs B), (interp Cs C).
(interp Cs (or B C))   :- (interp Cs B).
(interp Cs (or B C))   :- (interp Cs C).
(interp Cs A)          :- (backchain Cs Cs A).


(backchain Cs (and D1 D2) A)  :- (backchain Cs D1 A).
(backchain Cs (and D1 D2) A)  :- (backchain Cs D2 A).
(backchain Cs (all D) A)      :- (backchain Cs (D T) A).
(backchain Cs A A).
(backchain Cs (imp G A) A)    :- (interp Cs G).
```

Fig. 8. An interpreter for first-order Horn clauses

a different way and substitution will have to be explicitly encoded in such a language. These problems are "finessed" in the usual meta-interpreters written in Prolog (such as those in [Sterling and Shapiro, 1986]) by the use of non-logical features; in particular, by using the "predicate" clause.

8.2 Dealing with functional programs as data

Our second example of meta-programming deals with the problem of representing functional programs and manipulating these as data. Some version of the λ-calculus usually underlies a functional programming language and, towards dealing with the representation issue, we first show how untyped λ-terms might be encoded in simply typed λ-terms. Figure 9 contains some declarations that are relevant in this context. These declarations identify the sort tm that corresponds to the encodings of object-level λ-terms and the two constants abs and app that serve to encode object-level abstraction and application. As illustrations of the representation scheme, the untyped λ-terms $\lambda x\, x$, $\lambda x\, \lambda y\, (x\ y)$, and $\lambda x\, (x\ x)$ are denoted by the simply typed λ-terms (abs x\x), (abs x\(abs y\(app x y))), and (abs x\(app x x)), respectively. A notion of evaluation based on β-reduction usually accompanies the untyped λ-terms. Such an evaluation mechanism is not directly available under the encoding. However, it can be realized through a collection of definite clauses. The clauses defining the predicate eval in Figure 9 illustrate how this might be done. As a result of these clauses, this predicate relates two meta-level terms if the second encodes the result of evaluating the object-level term that is encoded by the first; the assumption in these clauses is that any "value" that is produced must be distinct from an (object-level) application. We note again

```
kind   tm   type.

type   abs   (tm -> tm) -> tm.
type   app   tm -> tm -> tm.
type   eval  tm -> tm -> o.

(eval (abs R) (abs R)).
(eval (app M N) V) :-
        (eval M (abs R)), (eval N U), (eval (R U) V).
```

Fig. 9. An encoding of untyped λ-terms and call-by-value evaluation

that application and β-conversion at the meta-level are used in the second clause for `eval` to realize the needed substitution at the object-level of an actual argument for a formal one of a functional expression.

The underlying λ-calculus is enhanced in the typical functional programming language by including a collection of predefined constants and functions. In encoding such constants a corresponding set of nonlogical constants might be used. For the purposes of the discussions below, we shall assume the collection presented in Figure 10 whose purpose is understood as follows:

(1)   The constants `fixpt` and `cond` encode the fixed-point and conditional operators of the object-language being considered; these operators play an essential role in realizing recursive schemes.

(2)   The constants `truth` and `false` represent the boolean values and `and` represents the binary operation of conjunction on booleans.

(3)   The constant `c` when applied to an integer yields the encoding of that integer; thus (`c 0`) encodes the integer 0. The constants `+`, `*`, `-`, `<` and `=` represent the obvious binary operators on integers. Finally, the constant `intp` encodes a function that recognizes integers: (`intp e`) encodes an expression that evaluates to true if `e` is an encoding of an integer and to false otherwise.

(4)   The constants `cons` and `nill` encode list constructors, `consp` and `null` encode recognizers for nonempty and empty lists, respectively, and the constants `car` and `cdr` represent the usual list destructors.

(5)   The constant `pair` represents the pair constructor, `pairp` represents the pair recognizer, and `first` and `second` represent the obvious destructors of pairs.

(6)   the constant `error` encodes the error value.

Each of the constants and functions whose encoding is described above has a predefined meaning that is used in the evaluation of expressions in the object-language. These meanings are usually clarified by a set of

```
type    cond    tm -> tm -> tm -> tm.
type    fixpt   (tm -> tm) -> tm.

type    truth   tm.
type    false   tm.
type    and     tm -> tm -> tm.

type    c       int -> tm.
type    +       tm -> tm -> tm.
type    -       tm -> tm -> tm.
type    *       tm -> tm -> tm.
type    <       tm -> tm -> tm.
type    =       tm -> tm -> tm.
type    intp    tm -> tm

type    nill    tm.
type    cons    tm -> tm -> tm.
type    null    tm -> tm.
type    consp   tm -> tm.
type    car     tm -> tm.
type    cdr     tm -> tm.

type    pair    tm -> tm -> tm.
type    pairp   tm -> tm.
type    first   tm -> tm.
type    second  tm -> tm.

type    error   tm.
```

Fig. 10. Encodings for some predefined constants and functions

equations that are satisfied by them. For instance, if $fixpt$ and $cond$ are the fixed-point and conditional operators of the functional programming language being encoded and $true$ and $false$ are the boolean values, then the meanings of these operators might be given by the following equations:

$$\forall x \,((fixpt \; x) = (x \; (fixpt \; x))),$$
$$\forall x \forall y \,((cond \; true \; x \; y) = x), \text{ and}$$
$$\forall x \forall y \,((cond \; false \; x \; y) = y).$$

The effect of such equations on evaluation can be captured in our encoding by augmenting the set of definite clauses for `eval` contained in Figure 9. For example, the definite clause

```
(eval (fixpt F) V) :- (eval (F (fixpt F)) V).
```

can be added to this collection to realize the effect of the first of the equations above. We do not describe a complete set of equations or an encoding of it here, but the interested reader can find extended discussions of this and other related issues in [Hannan and Miller, 1992] and [Hannan, 1993]. A point that should be noted about an encoding of the kind described here is that it reflects the effect of the object-language equations only in the evaluation relation and does not affect the equality relation of the metalanguage. In particular, the notions of equality and unification for our typed λ-terms, even those containing the new nonlogical constants, are still governed only by the λ-conversion rules.

The set of nonlogical constants that we have described above suffices for representing several recursive functional programs as λ-terms. For example, consider a tail-recursive version of the factorial function that might be defined in a functional programming language as follows:

$$fact\ n\ m\ =\ (cond\ (n = 0)\ m\ (fact\ (n - 1)\ (n * m))).$$

(The factorial of a non-negative integer n is to be obtained by evaluating the expression $(fact\ n\ 1)$.) The function $fact$ that is defined in this manner can be represented by the λ-term

```
(fixpt fact\(abs n\(abs m\
    (cond (= n (c 0)) m
          (app (app fact (- n (c 1))) (* n m)))))).
```

We assume below a representation of this kind for functional programs and we describe manipulations on these programs in terms of manipulations on their representation in our language.

As an example of manipulating programs, let us suppose that we wish to transform a recursive program that expects a single pair argument into a corresponding curried version. Thus, we would like to transform the program given by the term

```
(fixpt fact\(abs p\
  (cond (and (pairp p) (= (first p) (c 0)))
        (second p)
        (cond (pairp p)
              (app fact (pair (- (first p) (c 1))
                              (* (first p) (second p))))
              error)))))
```

into the factorial program presented earlier. Let the argument of the given function be p as in the case above. If the desired transformer is implemented in a language such as Lisp, ML, or Prolog then it would have to be a recursive program that descends through the structure of the term representing the functional program, making sure that the occurrences of the bound variable p in it are within expressions of the form (pairp p), (first p), or (second p) and, in this case, replacing these expressions respectively by a true condition, and the first and second arguments of the version of the program being constructed. Although this does not happen with the program term displayed above, it is possible for this descent to enter a context in which the variable p is bound locally, and care must be exercised to ensure that occurrences of p in this context are not confused with the argument of the function. It is somewhat unfortunate that the *names* of bound variables have to be considered explicitly in this process since the choice of these names has no relevance to the meanings of programs. However, this concern is unavoidable if our program transformer is to be implemented in one of the languages under consideration since a proper understanding of bound variables is simply not embedded in them.

The availability of λ-terms and of higher-order unification in our language permits a rather different kind of solution to the given problem. In fact, the following (atomic) definite clause provides a concise description of the desired relationship between terms representing the curried and uncurried versions of recursive programs:

```
(curry (fixpt q1\(abs x\(A (first x) (second x) (pairp x)
                        (r\s\(app q1 (pair r s)))))))
         (fixpt q2\(abs y\(abs z\(A y z truth (r\s\(app
                        (app q2 r) s))))))).
```

The first argument of the predicate curry in this clause constitutes a "template" for programs of the type we wish to transform: For a term representing a functional program to unify with this term, it must have one argument that corresponds to x, every occurrence of this argument in the body of the program must be within an expression of the form (first x), (second x) or (pairp x), and every recursive call in the program must involve the formation of a pair argument. (The expression r\s\(app q1 (pair r s)) represents a function of two arguments that applies q1 to the pair formed from its arguments.) The recognition of the representation of a functional program as being of this form results in the higher-order variable A being bound to the result of extracting the expressions (first x), (second x), (pairp x), and r\s\(app q1 (pair r s)) from the term corresponding to the body of this program. The desired transformation can be effected merely by replacing the extracted expressions with the two arguments of the curried version, truth and a recursive call, respectively. Such a replacement is achieved by means of application and β-conversion in the second argument of curry in the clause above.

To illustrate the computation described abstractly above, let us consider solving the query

```
?- (curry (fixpt fact\(abs p\
              (cond (and (pairp p) (= (first p) (c 0)))
                    (second p)
                    (cond (pairp p)
```

```
                            (app fact
                                 (pair (- (first p) (c 1))
                                       (* (first p) (second p))))
                            error)))))
                NewProg).
```

using the given clause for curry. The described interpreter for our language
would, first of all, instantiate the variable A with the term

```
u\v\p\q\(cond (and p (= u (c 0))) v
              (cond p (q (- u (c 1)) (* u v)) error).
```

(This instantiation for A is unique.) The variable NewProg will then be set
to a term that is equal via λ-conversion to

```
(fixpt q2 \(abs y\(abs z\(cond (and truth (= y (c 0))) z
     (cond truth (app (app q2 (- y (c1))) (* y z)) error)))))).
```

Although this is not identical to the term we wished to produce, it can be
reduced to that form by using simple identities pertaining to the boolean
constants and operations of the function programming language. A program transformer that uses these identities to simplify functional programs
can be written relatively easily.

As a more complex example of manipulating functional programs, we
consider the task of recognizing programs that are tail-recursive; such a
recognition step might be a prelude to transforming a given program into
one in iterative form. The curried version of the factorial program is an
example of a tail-recursive program as also is the program for summing two
non-negative integers that is represented by the following λ-term:

```
(fixpt sum\(abs n\(abs m\
            (cond (= n (c 0)) m
                  (app (app sum (- n (c 1))) (+ m (c 1))))))))).
```

Now, the tail-recursiveness of these programs can easily be recognized by
using higher-order unification in conjunction with their indicated representations. Both are, in fact, instances of the term

```
(fixpt f\(abs x\(abs y\
         (cond (C x y) (H x y)
               (app (app f (F1 x y)) (F2 x y)))))).
```

Further, the representations of only tail-recursive programs are instances
of the last term: Any closed term that unifies with the given "second-
order template" must be a representation of a recursive program of two
arguments whose body is a conditional and in which the only recursive
call appears in the second branch of the conditional and, that too, as the
head of the expression constituting that branch. Clearly any functional
program that has such a structure must be tail-recursive. Notice that all
the structural analysis that has to be performed in this recognition process

is handled completely within higher-order unification.

Templates of the kind described above have been used by Huet and Lang [Huet and Lang, 1978] to describe certain transformations on recursive programs. Templates are, however, of limited applicability when used alone since they can only recognize restricted kinds of patterns. For instance, the template that is shown above for recognizing tail-recursiveness will not identify tail-recursive programs that contain more than one recursive call or that have more than one conditional in their body. An example of such a program is the one for finding the greatest common denominator of two numbers that is represented by the following λ-term:

```
(fixpt gcd\(abs x\(abs y\
  (cond (= (c 1) x) (c 1)
        (cond (= x y) x
              (cond (< x y) (app (app gcd y) x)
                    (app (app gcd (- x y)) y)))))))
```

This program is tail-recursive but its representation is not an instance of the template presented above. Worse still, there is no second-order term all of whose closed instances represent tail-recursive programs and that also has the representations of the factorial, the sum and the greatest common denominator progams as its instances.

A recursive specification of a class of tail-recursive program terms that includes the representations of all of these programs can, however, be provided by using definite clauses in addition to second-order λ-terms and higher-order unification. This specification is based on the following observations:

(1) A program is obviously tail-recursive if it contains no recursive calls. The representation of such a program can be recognized by the template `(fixpt f\(abs x\(abs y\(H x y))))` in which H is a variable.

(2) A program that consists solely of a recursive call with possibly modified arguments is also tail-recursive. The second-order term

   `(fixpt f\(abs x\(abs y\(app (app f (H x y)) (G x y)))))`

   in which H and G are variables unifies with the representations of only such programs.

(3) Finally, a program is tail-recursive if its body consists of a conditional in which there is no recursive call in the test and whose left and right branches themselves satisfy the requirements of tail-recursiveness. Assuming that C, H1 and H2 are variables of appropriate type, the representations of only such programs unify with the λ-term

   `(fixpt f\(abs x\(abs y\(cond (C x y) (H1 f x y)`
   `(H2 f x y)))))`

   in a way such that the terms `(fixpt f\(abs x\(abs y\(H1 f x y))))` and `(fixpt f\(abs x\(abs y\(H2 f x y))))` represent tail-recursive

```
type    tailrec    tm -> o.

(tailrec (fixpt f\(abs x\(abs y\(H x y))))).
(tailrec (fixpt f\(abs x\(abs y\(app (app f (H x y))
                                     (G x y)))))).
(tailrec (fixpt f\(abs x\(abs y\(cond (C x y) (H1 f x y)
                                      (H2 f x y)))) :-
    (tailrec (fixpt f\(abs x\(abs y\(H1 f x y))))),
    (tailrec (fixpt f\(abs x\(abs y\(H2 f x y))))).
```

Fig. 11. A recognizer for binary tail-recursive functional programs

programs under the instantiations determined for H1 and H2.

These observations can be translated immediately into the definition of a one place predicate that recognizes tail-recursive functional programs of two arguments and this is done in Figure 11. It is easily verified that all three tail-recursive programs considered in this section are recognized to be so by tailrec. The definition of tailrec can be augmented so that it also transforms programs that it recognizes to be tail-recursive into iterative ones in an imperative language. We refer the reader to [Miller and Nadathur, 1987] for details.

8.3 A limitation of higher-order Horn clauses

Higher-order variables and an understanding of λ-conversion result in the presence of certain interesting meta-programming capabilities in our language. This language has a serious deficiency, however, with respect to this kind of programming that can be exposed by pushing our examples a bit further. We do this below.

We exhibited an encoding for a first-order logic in Subsection 8.1 and we presented an interpreter for the Horn clause fragment of this logic. A natural question to ask in this context is if we can define a (meta-level) predicate that recognizes the representations of first-order Horn clauses. It is an easy matter to write predicates that recognize first-order terms, atomic formulas, and quantifier-free Horn clauses. However, there is a problem when we attempt to deal with quantifiers. For example, when does a term of the form (all B) represent an object-level Horn clause? If we had chosen to represent formulas using only first-order terms, then universal quantification might have been represented by an expression of the form forall(x,B), and we could conclude that such an expression corresponds to a definite clause just in case B corresponds to one. Under the representation that we actually use, B is a higher-order term and so we cannot adopt this simple strategy of "dropping" the quantifier. We might try to mimic it by instantiating the quantifier. But with what should we perform the instantiation? The ideal solution is to use a new constant, say dummy, of type `term`; thus, (all B) would be recognized as a definite clause if (B dummy) is a definite clause. The problem is that our language does not provide a logical way to generate such a new constant. An alternative is to use just any constant. This strategy will work in the present situation, but there is some arbitrariness to it and, in any case, there are other contexts in which the newness of the constant is critical.

A predicate that recognizes tail-recursive functional programs of two arguments was presented in Subsection 8.2. It is natural to ask if it is possible to recognize tail-recursive programs that have other arities. One apparent answer to this question is that we mimic the clauses in Figure 11 for each arity. Thus, we might add the clauses

```
(tailrec (fixpt f\(abs x\(H x)))).
(tailrec (fixpt f\(abs x\(app (app f (h x)) (G x))))).
(tailrec (fixpt f\(abs x\(cond (C x) (H1 f x) (H2 f x))))) :-
      (tailrec (fixpt f\(abs x\(H1 f x)))),
      (tailrec (fixpt f\(abs x\(H2 f x)))).
```

to the earlier program to obtain one that also recognizes tail-recursive functional programs of arity 1. However, this is not really a solution to our problem. What we desire is a *finite* set of clauses that can be used to recognize tail-recursive programs of *arbitrary* arity. If we maintain our encoding of functional programs, a solution to this problem seems to require that we descend through the abstractions corresponding to the arguments of a program in the term representing the program discharging each of these abstractions with a new constant, and that we examine the structure that results from this for tail-recursiveness. Once again we notice that our language does not provide us with a principled mechanism for creating the new constants that are needed in implementing this approach.

The examples above indicate a problem in defining predicates in our language for recognizing terms of certain kinds. This problem becomes more severe when we consider defining relationships between terms. For example, suppose we wish to define a binary predicate called **prenex** that relates the representations of two first-order formulas only if the second is a prenex normal form of the first. One observation useful in defining this predicate is that a formula of the form $\forall x\, B$ has $\forall x\, C$ as a prenex normal form just in case B has C as a prenex normal form. In implementing this observation, it is necessary, once again, to consider dropping a quantifier. Using the technique of substitution with a dummy constant to simulate this, we might translate our observation into the definite clause

```
(prenex (all B) (all C)) :- (prenex (B dummy) (C dummy)).
```

Unfortunately this clause does not capture our observation satisfactorily and describes a relation on formulas that has little to do with prenex normal forms. Thus, consider the query

?- (prenex (all x\(p x x)) E).

We expect that the only answer to this query is the one that binds E to (all x\(p x x)), the prenex normal form of (all x\(p x x)). Using the clause for prenex above, the given goal would be reduced to

?- (prenex (p dummy dummy) (C dummy)).

with E being set to the term (all C). This goal should succeed only if (p dummy dummy) and (C dummy) are equal. However, as is apparent from the discussions in Section 6, there are four substitutions for C that unify these two terms and only one of these yields an acceptable solution to the original query.

The crux of the problem that is highlighted by the examples above is that a language based exclusively on higher-order Horn clauses does not provide a principled way to generate new constants and, consequently, to descend under abstractions in λ-terms. The ability to carry out such a descent, and, thereby, to perform a general recursion over objects containing bound variables that are represented by our λ-terms, can be supported by enhancing our language with certain new logical symbols. We consider such an enhancement in the next section.

9 Hereditary Harrop formulas

The deficiency of our language that was discussed in Subsection 8.3 arises from the fact that higher-order Horn clauses provide no abstraction or scoping capabilities at the level of predicate logic to match those present at the level of terms. It is possible to extend Horn clause logic by allowing occurrences of implications and universal quantifiers within goal formulas, thereby producing the logic of *hereditary Harrop formulas* [Miller *et al.*, 1991]. This enhancement to the logic leads to mechanisms for controlling the availability of the names and the clauses that appear in a program. It has been shown elsewhere that these additional capabilities can be used to realize notions such as modular programming, hypothetical reasoning, and abstract data types within logic programming [Miller, 1989b; Miller, 1990; Nadathur and Miller, 1988]. We show in this section that they can also be used to overcome the shortcoming of our present language from the perspective of meta-programming.

9.1 Universal quantifiers and implications in goals

Let Σ be a set of nonlogical constants and let $\mathcal{K}_\Sigma$ denote the set of λ-normal terms that do not contain occurrences of the logical constants $\supset$ and $\perp$ or of nonlogical constants that are not elements of Σ; notice that the only logical constants that *are* allowed to appear in terms in $\mathcal{K}_\Sigma$ are $\top$, $\wedge$, $\vee$, $\forall$, and $\exists$. Further, let A and A_r be syntactic variables for atomic formulas and rigid atomic formulas in $\mathcal{K}_\Sigma$, respectively. Then the *higher-order hereditary*

Harrop formulas and the corresponding goal formulas relative to Σ are the D- and G-formulas defined by the following mutually recursive syntax rules:

$$D ::= A_r \mid G \supset A_r \mid \forall x\, D \mid D \wedge D$$
$$G ::= \top \mid A \mid G \wedge G \mid G \vee G \mid \forall x\, G \mid \exists x\, G \mid D \supset G.$$

Quantification in these formulas, as in the context of higher-order Horn clauses, may be over function and predicate variables. When we use the formulas described here in programming, we shall think of a closed D-formula as a program clause relative to the signature Σ, a collection of such clauses as a program, and a G-formula as a query. There are considerations that determine exactly the definitions of the D- and G-formulas that are given here, and these are described in [Miller, 1990; Miller *et al.*, 1991].

An approach similar to that in Section 4 can be employed here as well in explaining what it means to solve a query relative to a program and what the result of a solution is to be. The main difference is that, in explaining how a closed goal formula is to be solved, we now have to deal with the additional possibilities for such formulas to contain universal quantifiers and implications. The attempt to solve a universally quantified goal formula can result in the addition of new nonlogical constants to an existing signature. It will therefore be necessary to consider generating instances of program clauses relative to different signatures. The following definition provides a method for doing this.

Definition 9.1.1. Let Σ be a set of nonlogical constants and let a closed positive Σ-*substitution* be one whose range is a set of closed terms contained in $\mathcal{K}_\Sigma$. Now, if D is a program clause, then the collection of its closed positive Σ-instances is denoted by $[D]_\Sigma$ and is given as follows:

(i)   if D is of the form A or $G \supset A$, then it is $\{D\}$,

(ii) if D is of the form $D' \wedge D''$ then it is $[D']_\Sigma \cup [D'']_\Sigma$, and

(iii) if D is of the form $\forall x\, D'$ then it is $\bigcup\{[\varphi(D')]_\Sigma \mid \varphi$ is a closed positive Σ-substitution for $x\}$.

This notation is extended to programs as follows: if $\mathcal{P}$ is a program,

$$[\mathcal{P}]_\Sigma = \bigcup\{[D]_\Sigma \mid D \in \mathcal{P}\}.$$

The attempt to solve an implicational goal formula will lead to an augmentation of an existing program. Thus, in describing an abstract interpreter for our new language, it is necessary to parameterize the solution of a goal formula by both a signature and a program. We do this in the following definition that modifies the definition of operational semantics contained in Definition 4.0.5 to suit our present language.

Definition 9.1.2. Let Σ be a set of nonlogical constants and let $\mathcal{P}$ and G be, respectively, a program and a goal formula relative to Σ. We then use the notation $\Sigma; \mathcal{P} \vdash_O G$ to signify that our abstract interpreter succeeds on G when given the signature Σ and the logic program $\mathcal{P}$. The success/failure behavior of the interpreter for hereditary Harrop formulas is itself specified as follows:

(i) $\Sigma; \mathcal{P} \vdash_O \top$,

(ii) $\Sigma; \mathcal{P} \vdash_O A$ where A is an atomic formula if and only if $A \equiv A'$ for some $A' \in [\mathcal{P}]_\Sigma$ or for some $(G \supset A') \in [\mathcal{P}]_\Sigma$ such that $A \equiv A'$ it is the case that $\Sigma; \mathcal{P} \vdash_O G$,

(iii) $\Sigma; \mathcal{P} \vdash_O G_1 \wedge G_2$ if and only if $\Sigma; \mathcal{P} \vdash_O G_1$ and $\Sigma; \mathcal{P} \vdash_O G_2$,

(iv) $\Sigma; \mathcal{P} \vdash_O G_1 \vee G_2$ if and only if $\Sigma; \mathcal{P} \vdash_O G_1$ or $\Sigma; \mathcal{P} \vdash_O G_2$,

(v) $\Sigma; \mathcal{P} \vdash_O \exists x\, G$ if and only if $\Sigma; \mathcal{P} \vdash_O [t/x]G$ for some term $t \in \mathcal{K}_\Sigma$ with the same type as x,

(vi) $\Sigma; \mathcal{P} \vdash_O D \supset G$ if and only if $\Sigma; \mathcal{P} \cup \{D\} \vdash_O G$, and

(vii) $\Sigma; \mathcal{P} \vdash_O \forall x\, G$ if and only if $\Sigma \cup \{c\}; \mathcal{P} \vdash_O [c/x]G$ where c is a nonlogical constant that is not already in Σ and that has the same type as x.

Let $\mathcal{P}$ be a program, let G be a closed goal formula and let Σ be any collection of nonlogical constants that includes those occurring in $\mathcal{P}$ and G. Using techniques similar to those in Section 5, it can then be shown that $\mathcal{P} \vdash_I G$ if and only if $\Sigma; \mathcal{P} \vdash_O G$; see [Miller *et al.*, 1991] for details. Thus $\vdash_O$ coincides with $\vdash_I$ in the context of interest. It is easy to see, however, that $\vdash_C$ is a stronger relation than $\vdash_O$. For example, the goal formulas $p \vee (p \supset q)$ and $(((r\ a) \wedge (r\ b)) \supset q) \supset \exists x((r\ x) \supset q)$ (in which p, q, r and a are parameters) are both provable in classical logic but they are not solvable in the above operational sense. (The signature remains unchanged in the attempt to solve both these goal formulas and hence can be elided.) The operational interpretation of hereditary Harrop formulas is based on a natural understanding of the notion of goal-directed search and we shall therefore think of the complementary logical interpretation of these formulas as being given by intuitionistic logic and not classical logic.

The main novelty from a programming perspective of a language based on hereditary Harrop formulas over one based on Horn clauses is the following: in the new language it is possible to restrict the scope of nonlogical constants and program clauses to selected parts of the search for a solution to a query. It is these scoping abilities that provide the basis for notions such as modular programming, hypothetical reasoning, and abstract data types in this language. As we shall see later in this section, these abilities also provide for logic-level abstractions that complement term-level abstractions.

A (deterministic) interpreter can be constructed for a language based on higher-order hereditary Harrop formulas in a fashion similar to that in the case of higher-order Horn clauses. There are, however, some differences in the two contexts that must be taken into account. First, the solution to a goal formula must be attempted in the context of a specific signature and program associated with that goal formula and not in

```
type   term   term -> o.
type   atom   form -> o.

(term a).
(term b).
(term c).
(term (f X)) :- (term X).

(atom (path X Y)) :- (term X), (term Y).
(atom (adj X Y)) :- (term X), (term Y).
```

Fig. 12. Recognizers for object-language terms and atomic formulas

a global context. Each goal formula must, therefore, carry a relevant signature and program. Second, the permitted substitutions for each logic variable that is introduced in the course of solving an existential query or instantiating a program clause are determined by the signature that is in existence at the time of introduction of the logic variable. It is therefore necessary to encode this signature in some fashion in the logic variable and to use it within the unification process to ensure that instantiations of the variable contain only the permitted nonlogical constants. Several different methods can be used to realize this requirement in practice, and some of these are described in [Miller, 1989a; Miller, 1992; Nadathur, 1993]).

9.2 Recursion over structures with binding

The ability to descend under abstractions in λ-terms is essential in describing a general recursion over representations of the kind described in Section 8 for objects containing bound variables. It is necessary to "discharge" the relevant abstractions in carrying out such a descent, and so the ability to generate new constants is crucial to this process. The possibility for universal quantifiers to appear in goal formulas with their associated semantics leads to such a capability being present in a language based on higher-order hereditary Harrop formulas. We show below that this suffices to overcome the problems outlined in Subsection 8.3 for a language based on higher-order Horn clauses.

We consider first the problem of recognizing the representations of first-order Horn clauses. Our solution to this problem assumes that the object-level logic has a fixed signature that is given by the type declarations in Figure 7. Using a knowledge of this signature, it is a simple matter to define predicates that recognize the representations of (object-level) terms and atomic formulas. The clauses for **term** and **atom** that appear in Figure 12 serve this purpose in the present context. These predicates are used in

```
type   defcl   form -> o.
type   goal    form -> o.

(defcl (all C))    :- (pi x\((term x) => (defcl (C x)))).
(defcl (imp G A))  :- (atom A), (goal G).
(defcl A)          :- (atom A).

(goal truth).
(goal (and B C))   :- (goal B), (goal C).
(goal (or B C))    :- (goal B), (goal C).
(goal (some C))    :- (pi x\((term x) => (goal (C x)))).
(goal A)           :- (atom A).
```

Fig. 13. Recognizing representations of first-order Horn clauses

Figure 13 in defining the predicate defcl and goal that are intended to be recognizers of encodings of object-language definite clauses and goal formulas respectively. We use the symbol => to represent implications in (meta-level) goal formulas in the program clauses that appear in this figure. Recall that the symbol pi represents the universal quantifier.

In understanding the definitions presented in Figure 13, it is useful to focus on the first clause for defcl that appears in it. This clause is not an acceptable one in the Horn clause setting because an implication and a universal quantifier are used in its "body". An attempt to solve the query

```
?- (defcl (all x\(all y\(all z\
          (imp (and (adj x y) (path y z)) (path x z)))))).
```

will result in this clause being used. This will, in turn, result in the variable C that appears in the clause being instantiated to the term

```
x\(all y\(all z\(imp (and (adj x y) (path y z))
                   (path x z)))).
```

The way in which this λ-term is to be processed can be described as follows. First, a new constant must be picked to play the role of a name for the bound variable x. This constant must be added to the signature of the object-level logic, in turn requiring that the definition of the predicate term be extended. Finally, the λ-term must be applied to the new constant and it must be checked if the resulting term represents a Horn clause. Thus, if the new constant that is picked is d, then an attempt must be made to solve the goal formula

```
(defcl (all y\(all z\(imp (and (adj d y) (path y z))
                     (path d z)))))
```

after the program has been augmented with the clause (term d). From the operational interpretation of implications and universal quantifiers de-

```
type    quantfree    form -> o.

(quantfree false).
(quantfree truth).
(quantfree A)           :- (atom A).
(quantfree (and B C)) :- ((quantfree B), (quantfree C)).
(quantfree (or  B C)) :- ((quantfree B), (quantfree C)).
(quantfree (imp B C)) :- ((quantfree B), (quantfree C)).
```

Fig. 14. Recognizing quantifier free formulas in a given object-language

scribed in Definition 9.1.2, it is easily seen that this is exactly the computation that is performed with the λ-term under consideration.

One of the virtues of our extended language is that it is relatively straightforward to verify formal properties of programs written in it. For example, consider the following property of the definition of defcl: If the query (defcl (all B)) has a solution and if T is an object-level term (that is, (term T) is solvable), then the query (defcl (B T)) has a solution, i.e., the property of being a Horn clause is maintained under first-order universal instantiation. This property can be seen to hold by the following argument: If the query (defcl (all B)) is solvable, then it must be the case that the query pi x\((term x) => (defcl (B x))) is also solvable. Since (term T) is provable and since universal instantiation and modus ponens holds for intuitionistic logic and since the operational semantics of our language coincides with intuitionistic provability, we can conclude that the query (defcl (B T)) has a solution. The reader will easily appreciate the fact that proofs of similar properties of programs written in other programming languages would be rather more involved than this.

Ideas similar to those above are used in Figures 16 and 15 in defining the predicate prenex. The declarations in these figures are assumed to build on those in Figure 7 and 12 that formalize the object-language and those in Figure 14 that define a predicate called quantfree that recognizes quantifier free formulas. The predicate merge that is defined in Figure 15 serves to raise the scopes of quantifiers over the binary connectives. This predicate is used in the definition of prenex in Figure 16. An interpreter for our language should succeed on the query

```
?- (prenex (or (all x\(and (adj x x) (and (all y\(path x y))
                                            (adj (f x) c))))
               (adj a b))
           Pnf).
```

relative to a program consisting of these various clauses and should produce the term

```
all x\(all y\(or (and (adj x x)
```

```
          (and (path x y) (adj (f x) c)))
     (adj a b)))
```

as the (unique) binding for Pnf when it does. The query

```
?- (prenex (and (all x\(adj x x)) (all z\(all y\(adj z y))))
          Pnf).
```

is also solvable, but could result in Pnf being bound to any one of the terms

```
all z\(all y\(and (adj z z) (adj z y))),
all x\(all z\(all y\(and (adj x x) (adj z y)))),
all z\(all x\(and (adj x x) (adj z x))),
all z\(all x\(all y\(and (adj x x) (adj z y)))), and
all z\(all y\(all x\(and (adj x x) (adj z y)))).
```

We now consider the task of defining a predicate that recognizes the representations of tail-recursive functions of arbitrary arity. We assume the same set of predefined constants and functions for our functional programming language here as we did in Subsection 8.2 and the encodings for these are given, once again, by the declarations in Figure 10. Now, our approach to recognizing the λ-terms of interest will, at an operational level, be the following: we shall descend through the abstractions in the representation of a program discharging each of them with a new constant and then check if the structure that results from this process satisfies the requirements of tail-recursiveness. The final test requires the constant that is introduced as the name of the function, i.e., the constant used to instantiate the top-level abstracted variable of M in the expression (fixpt M), to be distinguished from the other nonlogical constants. Thus, suppose that the expression that is produced by discharging all the abstractions is of the form (cond C M N). For the overall λ-term to be the representation of a tail-recursive program, it must, first of all, be the case that the constant introduced as the name of the function does not appear in the term C. Further, each of M and N should be a λ-term that contains an occurrence of the constant introduced as the name of the function at most as its head symbol or that represents a conditional that recursively satisfies the requirements being discussed.

The required distinction between constants and the processing described above are reflected in the clauses in Figure 17 that eventually define the desired predicate tailrec. Viewed operationally, the clauses for the predicates tailrec and trfn realize a descent through the abstractions representing the name and arguments of a function. Notice, however, that the program is augmented differently in each of these cases: headrec is asserted to hold of the constant that is added in descending through the abstraction representing the name of the function whereas term is asserted to hold of the new constants introduced for the arguments. Now, the predicates term and headrec that are also defined by the clauses in this figure recognize

```
type   merge  form -> form -> o.

(merge (and (all B) (all C)) (all D))    :-
    (pi x\((term x) => (merge (and (B x) (C x)) (D x)))).
(merge (and (all B) C) (all D))          :-
    (pi x\((term x) => (merge (and (B x) C) (D x)))).
(merge (and (some B) C) (some D))        :-
    (pi x\((term x) => (merge (and (B x) C) (D x)))).
(merge (and B (all C)) (all D))          :-
    (pi x\((term x) => (merge (and B (C x)) (D x)))).
(merge (and B (some C)) (some D))        :-
    (pi x\((term x) => (merge (and B (C x)) (D x)))).
(merge (or (some B) (some C)) (some D)) :-
    (pi x\((term x) => (merge (or (B x) (C x)) (D x)))).
(merge (or (all B) C) (all D))           :-
    (pi x\((term x) => (merge (or (B x) C) (D x)))).
(merge (or (some B) C) (some D))         :-
    (pi x\((term x) => (merge (or (B x) C) (D x)))).
(merge (or B (all C)) (all D))           :-
    (pi x\((term x) => (merge (or B (C x)) (D x)))).
(merge (or B (some C)) (some D))         :-
    (pi x\((term x) => (merge (or B (C x)) (D x)))).
(merge (imp (all B) (some C)) (some D)) :-
    (pi x\((term x) => (merge (imp (B x) (C x)) (D x)))).
(merge (imp (all B) C) (some D))         :-
    (pi x\((term x) => (merge (imp (B x) C) (D x)))).
(merge (imp (some B) C) (all D))         :-
    (pi x\((term x) => (merge (imp (B x) C) (D x)))).
(merge (imp B (all C)) (all D))          :-
    (pi x\((term x) => (merge (imp B (C x)) (D x)))).
(merge (imp B (some C)) (some D))        :-
    (pi x\((term x) => (merge (imp B (C x)) (D x)))).
(merge B B)                              :- (quantfree B).
```

Fig. 15. Raising the scopes of quantifiers

two different classes of λ-terms representing functional programs: (i) those that are constructed using the original set of nonlogical constants and the ones introduced for the arguments of programs and (ii) those in which the constant introduced as the name of the program also appears, but only as the head symbol. The predicate **term** is defined by reflecting the various type declarations in Figure 10 into the meta-language. This definition will, of course, get augmented to realize any extension that occurs to the first

```
type    prenex    form -> form -> o.

(prenex false false).
(prenex truth truth).
(prenex B B) :- (atom B).
(prenex (and B C) D)          :-
     (prenex B U), (prenex C V), (merge (and U V) D).
(prenex (or B C) D)           :-
     (prenex B U), (prenex C V), (merge (or U V) D).
(prenex (imp B C) D)          :-
     (prenex B U), (prenex C V), (merge (imp U V) D).
(prenex (all B) (all D))   :-
     (pi x\((term x) => (prenex (B x) (D x)))).
(prenex (some B) (some D)) :-
     (pi x\((term x) => (prenex (B x) (D x)))).
```

Fig. 16. Relating first-order formulas and their prenex normal forms

category of terms through the addition of new nonlogical constants. The conditions under which the predicate `headrec` should be true of a term can be expressed as follows: the term must either be identical to the constant introduced as the name of the function or it must be unifiable with the term (`app M N`) with `headrec` and `term` being true of the respective resulting instantiations of `M` and `N`. These conditions are obviously captured by the clause for `headrec` in Figure 17 and the one that is added in descending under the abstraction representing the name of the function. The final test for tail-recursiveness can be carried out easily using these predicates and this is, in fact, manifest in the definition of `trbody` in Figure 17.

Our last example in this section concerns the task of assigning types to expressions in our functional programming language. We shall, of course, be dealing with encodings of types and expressions of the object-language, and we need a representation for types to complement the one we already have for expressions. Figure 18 contains declarations that are useful for this purpose. The sort `ty` that is identified by these declarations is intended to be the meta-level type of terms that encode object-level types. We assume three primitive types at the object-level: those for booleans, natural numbers and lists of natural numbers. The nonlogical constants `boole`, `nat` and `natlist` serve to represent these. Further object-level types are constructed by using the function and pair type constructors and these are encoded by the binary constants `arrow` and `pairty`, respectively.

The program clauses in Figure 19 define the predicate `typeof` that relates the representation of an expression in our functional programming language to the representation of its type. These clauses are, for the most

```
type    term      tm -> o.
type    tailrec   tm -> o.
type    trfn      tm -> o.
type    trbody    tm -> o.
type    headrec   tm -> o.

(term (abs R))       :- (pi x\((term x) => (term (R x)))).
(term (app M N))     :- (term M), (term N).
(term (cond M N P)) :- (term M), (term N), (term P).
(term (fixpt R))     :- (pi x\((term x) => (term (R x)))).
(term truth).
(term false).
(term (and M N))     :- (term M), (term N).
(term (c X)).
(term (+ M N))       :- (term M), (term N).
(term (- M N))       :- (term M), (term N).
(term (* M N))       :- (term M), (term N).
(term (< M N))       :- (term M), (term N).
(term (= M N))       :- (term M), (term N).
(term (intp M))      :- (term M).
(term nill).
(term (cons M N))    :- (term M), (term N).
(term (null M))      :- (term M).
(term (consp M))     :- (term M).
(term (car M))       :- (term M).
(term (cdr M))       :- (term M).
(term (pair M N))    :- (term M), (term N).
(term (pairp M))     :- (term M).
(term (first M))     :- (term M).
(term (second M))    :- (term M).
(term error).

(tailrec (fixpt M))    :-
     (pi f\((headrec f) => (trfn (M f)))).
(trfn (abs R))            :- (pi x\((term x) => (trfn (R x)))).
(trfn R)                  :- (trbody R).
(trbody (cond M N P))  :- (term M), (trbody N), (trbody P).
(trbody M)                :- (term M); (headrec M).
(headrec (app M N))    :- (headrec M), (term N).
```

Fig. 17. Recognizing tail-recursive functional programs of arbitrary arity

```
kind   ty    type.

type   boole     ty.
type   nat       ty.
type   natlist   ty.
type   arrow     ty -> ty -> ty.
type   pairty    ty -> ty -> ty.
```

Fig. 18. Encoding types for functional programs

part, self explanatory. We draw the attention of the reader to the first two clauses in this collection that are the only ones that deal with abstractions in the representation of functional programs. Use is made in both cases of a combination of universal quantification and implication that is familiar by now in order to move the term-level abstraction into the meta-level. We observe, once again, that the manner of definition of the typing predicate in our language makes it easy to establish formal properties concerning it. For example, the following property can be shown to be true of typeof by using arguments similar to those used in the case of defcl: if the queries (typeof (abs M) (arrow A B)) and (typeof N A) have solutions, then the query (typeof (M N) B) also has a solution.

We refer the reader to [Felty, 1993; Pareschi and Miller, 1990; Hannan and Miller, 1992; Miller, 1991] for other, more extensive, illustrations of the value of a language based on higher-order hereditary Harrop formulas from the perspective of meta-programming. It is worth noting that all the example programs presented in this section as well as several others that are described in the literature fall within a sublanguage of this language called L_λ. This sublanguage, which is described in detail in [Miller, 1991], has the computationally pleasant property that higher-order unification is decidable in its context and admits of most general unifiers.

10   Conclusion

We have attempted to develop the notion of higher-order programming within logic programming in this chapter. A central concern in this endeavour has been to preserve the declarative style that is a hallmark of logic programming. Our approach has therefore been to identify an analogue of first-order Horn clauses in the context of a higher-order logic; this analogue must, of course, preserve the logical properties of the first-order formulas that are essential to their computational use while incorporating desirable higher-order features. This approach has led to the description of the so-called higher-order Horn clauses in the Simple Theory of Types, a higher-order logic that is based on a typed version of the lambda calculus. An actual use of these formulas in programming requires that a practically

```
type    typeof    tm -> ty -> o.

(typeof (abs M) (arrow A B))        :-
     (pi x\((typeof x A) => (typeof (M x) B))).
(typeof (fixpt M) A)                :-
     (pi x\((typeof x A) => (typeof (M x) A))).
(typeof (app M N) B)                :-
     (typeof M (arrow A B)), (typeof N A).
(typeof (cond C L R) A)             :-
     (typeof C boole), (typeof L A), (typeof R A).
(typeof truth  boole).
(typeof false  boole).
(typeof (and M N)  boole)           :-
     (typeof M boole), (typeof N boole).
(typeof (c X) nat).
(typeof (+ M N) nat)                :-
     (typeof M nat), (typeof N nat).
(typeof (- M N) nat)                :-
     (typeof M nat), (typeof N nat).
(typeof (* M N) nat)                :-
     (typeof M nat), (typeof N nat).
(typeof (< M N) boole)              :-
     (typeof M nat), (typeof N nat).
(typeof (= M N) boole)              :-
     (typeof M nat), (typeof N nat).
(typeof (intp M) boole)             :- (typeof M A).
(typeof nill  natlist).
(typeof (cons M N) natlist)         :-
     (typeof M nat), (typeof N natlist).
(typeof (null M) boole)             :- (typeof M natlist).
(typeof (consp M) boole)            :- (typeof M natlist).
(typeof (car M) nat)                :- (typeof M natlist).
(typeof (cdr M) natlist)            :- (typeof M natlist).
(typeof (pair M N) (pairty A B)) :-
     (typeof M A), (typeof N B).
(typeof (pairp M) boole)            :- (typeof M A).
(typeof (first M) A)                :- (typeof M (pair A B)).
(typeof (second M) B)               :- (typeof M (pair A B)).
(typeof error A).
```

Fig. 19. A predicate for typing functional programs

acceptable proof procedure exist for them. We have exhibited such a procedure by utilizing the logical properties of the formulas in conjunction with a procedure for unifying terms of the relevant typed λ-calculus. We have then examined the applications for a programming language that is based on these formulas. As initially desired, this language provides for the usual higher-order programming features within logic programming. This language also supports some unusual forms of higher-order programming: it permits λ-terms to be used in constructing the descriptions of syntactic objects such as programs and quantified formulas, and it allows computations to be performed on these descriptions by means of the λ-conversion rules and higher-order unification. These novel features have interesting uses in the realm of meta-programming and we have illustrated this fact in this chapter. A complete realization of these meta-programming capabilities, however, requires a language with a larger set of logical primitives than that obtained by using Horn clauses. These additional primitives are incorporated into the logic of hereditary Harrop formulas. We have described this logic here and have also outlined some of the several applications that a programming language based on this logic has in areas such as theorem proving, type inference, program transformation, and computational linguistics.

The discussions in this chapter reveal a considerable richness to the notion of higher-order logic programming. We note also that these discussions are not exhaustive. Work on this topic continues along several dimensions such as refinement, modification and extension of the language, implementation, and exploration of applications, especially in the realm of meta-programming.

Acknowledgements

We are grateful to Gilles Dowek for his comments on this chapter. Miller's work has been supported in part by the following grants: ARO DAAL03-89-0031, ONR N00014-93-1-1324, NSF CCR91-02753, and NSF CCR92-09224. Nadathur has similarly received support from the NSF grants CCR-89-05825 and CCR-92-08465.

References

[Andrews, 1971] Peter B. Andrews. Resolution in type theory. *Journal of Symbolic Logic*, 36:414–432, 1971.

[Andrews, 1989] Peter B. Andrews. On connections and higher-order logic. *Journal of Automated Reasoning*, 5(3):257–291, 1989.

[Andrews *et al.*, 1984] Peter B. Andrews, Eve Longini Cohen, Dale Miller, and Frank Pfenning. Automating higher order logic. In *Automated Theorem Proving: After 25 Years*, pages 169–192. American Mathematical Society, Providence, RI, 1984.

[Apt and van Emden, 1982] K. R. Apt and M. H. van Emden. Contributions to the theory of logic programming. *Journal of the ACM*, 29(3):841–862, 1982.

[Barendregt, 1981] H. P. Barendregt. *The Lambda Calculus: Its Syntax and Semantics*. North-Holland, 1981.

[Bledsoe, 1979] W. W. Bledsoe. A maximal method for set variables in automatic theorem-proving. In *Machine Intelligence 9*, pages 53–100. John Wiley, 1979.

[Brisset and Ridoux, 1991] Pascal Brisset and Olivier Ridoux. Naive reverse can be linear. In *Eighth International Logic Programming Conference*, Paris, France, June 1991. MIT Press.

[Brisset and Ridoux, 1992] Pascal Brisset and Olivier Ridoux. The architecture of an implementation of λProlog: Prolog/Mali. In Dale Miller, editor, *Proceedings of the 1992 λProlog Workshop*, 1992.

[Chen et al., 1993] Weidong Chen, Michael Kifer, and David S. Warren. HiLog: A foundation for higher-order logic programming. *Journal of Logic Programming*, 15(3):187–230, February 1993.

[Church, 1940] Alonzo Church. A formulation of the simple theory of types. *Journal of Symbolic Logic*, 5:56–68, 1940.

[Damas and Milner, 1982] Luis Damas and Robin Milner. Principal type schemes for functional programs. In *Proceedings of the Ninth ACM Symposium on Principles of Programming Languages*, pages 207–212. ACM Press, 1982.

[Elliott and Pfenning, 1991] Conal Elliott and Frank Pfenning. A semifunctional implementation of a higher-order logic programming language. In Peter Lee, editor, *Topics in Advanced Language Implementation*, pages 289–325. MIT Press, 1991.

[Felty, 1993] Amy Felty. Implementing tactics and tacticals in a higher-order logic programming language. *Journal of Automated Reasoning*, 11(1):43–81, August 1993.

[Felty and Miller, 1988] Amy Felty and Dale Miller. Specifying theorem provers in a higher-order logic programming language. In *Ninth International Conference on Automated Deduction*, pages 61–80, Argonne, IL, May 1988. Springer-Verlag.

[Gentzen, 1969] Gerhard Gentzen. Investigations into logical deduction. In M. E. Szabo, editor, *The Collected Papers of Gerhard Gentzen*, pages 68–131. North-Holland, 1969.

[Girard et al., 1989] Jean-Yves Girard, Paul Taylor, and Yves Lafont. *Proofs and Types*. Cambridge University Press, 1989.

[Goldfarb, 1981] Warren Goldfarb. The undecidability of the second-order unification problem. *Theoretical Computer Science*, 13:225–230, 1981.

[Gordon *et al.*, 1979] Michael J. Gordon, Arthur J. Milner, and Christopher P. Wadsworth. *Edinburgh LCF: A Mechanised Logic of Computation*, volume 78 of *Lecture Notes in Computer Science*. Springer-Verlag, 1979.

[Gould, 1976] W. E. Gould. A matching procedure for ω-order logic. Scientific Report No. 4, A F C R L, 1976.

[Hannan, 1993] John Hannan. Extended natural semantics. *Journal of Functional Programming*, 3(2):123–152, April 1993.

[Hannan and Miller, 1992] John Hannan and Dale Miller. From operational semantics to abstract machines. *Mathematical Structures in Computer Science*, 2(4):415–459, 1992.

[Henkin, 1950] Leon Henkin. Completeness in the theory of types. *Journal of Symbolic Logic*, 15:81–91, 1950.

[Huet, 1973a] Gérard Huet. A mechanization of type theory. In *Proceedings of the Third International Joint Conference on Artifical Intelligence*, pages 139–146, 1973.

[Huet, 1973b] Gérard Huet. The undecidability of unification in third order logic. *Information and Control*, 22:257–267, 1973.

[Huet, 1975] Gérard Huet. A unification algorithm for typed λ-calculus. *Theoretical Computer Science*, 1:27–57, 1975.

[Huet and Lang, 1978] Gérard Huet and Bernard Lang. Proving and applying program transformations expressed with second-order patterns. *Acta Informatica*, 11:31–55, 1978.

[Kwon *et al.*, 1994] Keehang Kwon, Gopalan Nadathur, and Debra Sue Wilson. Implementing polymorphic typing in a logic programming language. *Computer Languages*, 20(1):25–42, 1994.

[Lucchesi, 1972] C. L. Lucchesi. The undecidability of the unification problem for third order languages. Technical Report CSRR 2059, Department of Applied Analysis and Computer Science, University of Waterloo, 1972.

[Miller, 1989a] Dale Miller. Lexical scoping as universal quantification. In *Sixth International Logic Programming Conference*, pages 268–283, Lisbon, Portugal, June 1989. MIT Press.

[Miller, 1989b] Dale Miller. A logical analysis of modules in logic programming. *Journal of Logic Programming*, 6:79–108, 1989.

[Miller, 1990] Dale Miller. Abstractions in logic programming. In Peirgiorgio Odifreddi, editor, *Logic and Computer Science*, pages 329–359. Academic Press, 1990.

[Miller, 1991] Dale Miller. A logic programming language with lambda-abstraction, function variables, and simple unification. *Journal of Logic and Computation*, 1(4):497–536, 1991.

[Miller, 1992] Dale Miller. Unification under a mixed prefix. *Journal of Symbolic Computation*, pages 321–358, 1992.

[Miller, 1994] Dale Miller. A multiple-conclusion meta-logic. In S. Abramsky, editor, *Ninth Annual Symposium on Logic in Computer Science*, pages 272–281, Paris, July 1994.

[Miller and Nadathur, 1987] Dale Miller and Gopalan Nadathur. A logic programming approach to manipulating formulas and programs. In Seif Haridi, editor, *IEEE Symposium on Logic Programming*, pages 379–388, San Francisco, September 1987.

[Miller and Nadathur, 1988] Dale Miller and Gopalan Nadathur. λProlog Version 2.7. Distribution in C-Prolog and Quintus sources, July 1988.

[Miller et al., 1991] Dale Miller, Gopalan Nadathur, Frank Pfenning, and Andre Scedrov. Uniform proofs as a foundation for logic programming. *Annals of Pure and Applied Logic*, 51:125–157, 1991.

[Milner et al., 1990] Robin Milner, Mads Tofte, and Robert Harper. *The Definition of Standard ML*. MIT Press, 1990.

[Nadathur, 1987] Gopalan Nadathur. *A Higher-Order Logic as the Basis for Logic Programming*. PhD thesis, University of Pennsylvania, 1987.

[Nadathur, 1993] Gopalan Nadathur. A proof procedure for the logic of hereditary Harrop formulas. *Journal of Automated Reasoning*, 11(1):115–145, August 1993.

[Nadathur, 1997] Gopalan Nadathur. A notion of models for higher-order logic. Manuscript in preparation, 1997.

[Nadathur and Miller, 1988] Gopalan Nadathur and Dale Miller. An Overview of λProlog. In *Fifth International Logic Programming Conference*, pages 810–827, Seattle, Washington, August 1988. MIT Press.

[Nadathur and Miller, 1990] Gopalan Nadathur and Dale Miller. Higher-order Horn clauses. *Journal of the ACM*, 37(4):777–814, October 1990.

[Nadathur and Pfenning, 1992] Gopalan Nadathur and Frank Pfenning. The type system of a higher-order logic programming language. In Frank Pfenning, editor, *Types in Logic Programming*, pages 245–283. MIT Press, 1992.

[Nadathur et al., 1993] Gopalan Nadathur, Bharat Jayaraman, and Debra Sue Wilson. Implementation considerations for higher-order features in logic programming. Technical Report CS-1993-16, Department of Computer Science, Duke University, June 1993.

[Nadathur et al., 1995] Gopalan Nadathur, Bharat Jayaraman, and Keehang Kwon. Scoping constructs in logic programming: Implementation problems and their solution. *Journal of Logic Programming*, 25(2): 119–161, November 1995.

[Pareschi and Miller, 1990] Remo Pareschi and Dale Miller. Extending definite clause grammars with scoping constructs. In David H. D. Warren and Peter Szeredi, editors, *Seventh International Conference in Logic Programming*, pages 373–389. MIT Press, June 1990.

[Paulson, 1990] Lawrence C. Paulson. Isabelle: The next 700 theorem provers. In Peirgiorgio Odifreddi, editor, *Logic and Computer Science*, pages 361–386. Academic Press, 1990.

[Shapiro, 1985] Steward Shapiro. Second-order languages and mathematical practice. *Journal of Symbolic Logic*, 50(3):714–742, September 1985.

[Sterling and Shapiro, 1986] Leon Sterling and Ehud Shapiro. *The Art of Prolog: Advanced Programming Techniques*. MIT Press, 1986.

[Wadge, 1991] William W. Wadge. Higher-order Horn logic programming. In *1991 International Symposium on Logic Programming*, pages 289–303. MIT Press, October 1991.

[Warren, 1982] David H. D. Warren. Higher-order extensions to Prolog: Are they needed? In *Machine Intelligence 10*, pages 441–454. Halsted Press, 1982.

Constraint Logic Programming: A Survey

Joxan Jaffar and Michael J. Maher

Contents

1 Introduction

Constraint Logic Programming (CLP) began as a natural merger of two declarative paradigms: constraint solving and logic programming. This combination helps make CLP programs both expressive and flexible, and in some cases, more efficient than other kinds of programs. Though a relatively new field, CLP has progressed in several and quite different directions. In particular, the early fundamental concepts have been adapted to better serve in different areas of applications. In this survey of CLP, a primary goal is to give a systematic description of the major trends in terms of common fundamental concepts.

Consider first an example program in order to identify some crucial CLP concepts. The program below defines the relation $sumto(n, 1 + 2 + \cdots + n)$ for natural numbers n.

```
sumto(0, 0).
sumto(N, S) :- N >= 1, N <= S, sumto(N - 1, S - N).
```

The query `S <= 3, sumto(N, S)` gives rise to three answers ($N = 0, S = 0$), ($N = 1, S = 1$), and ($N = 2, S = 3$), and terminates. The computation sequence of states for the third answer, for example, is

$$S \leq 3, sumto(N, S).$$

$$S \leq 3, N = N_1, S = S_1, N_1 \geq 1, N_1 \leq S_1,$$
$$sumto(N_1 - 1, S_1 - N_1).$$

$$S \leq 3, N = N_1, S = S_1, N_1 \geq 1, N_1 \leq S_1,$$
$$N_1 - 1 = N_2, S_1 - N_1 = S_2, N_2 \geq 1, N_2 \leq S_2,$$
$$sumto(N_2 - 1, S_2 - N_2).$$

$$S \leq 3, N = N_1, S = S_1, N_1 \geq 1, N_1 \leq S_1,$$
$$N_1 - 1 = N_2, S_1 - N_1 = S_2, N_2 \geq 1, N_2 \leq S_2,$$
$$N_2 - 1 = 0, S_2 - N_2 = 0.$$

The constraints in the final state imply the answer $N = 2, S = 3$. Termination is reasoned as follows. Any infinite computation must use only the second program rule for state transitions. This means that its first three states must be as shown above, and its fourth state must be

$$S \leq 3, N = N_1, S = S_1, N_1 \geq 1, N_1 \leq S_1,$$
$$N_1 - 1 = N_2, S_1 - N_1 = S_2, N_2 \geq 1, N_2 \leq S_2,$$
$$N_2 - 1 = N_3, S_2 - N_2 = S_3, N_3 \geq 1, N_3 \leq S_3,$$
$$sumto(...)$$

We note now that this contains an unsatisfiable set of constraints, and in CLP, no further reductions are allowed.

This example shows the following key features in CLP:

- Constraints are used to specify the query as well as the answers.
- During execution, new variables and constraints are created.
- The collection of constraints in every state is tested as a whole for satisfiability before execution proceeds further.

In summary, constraints are: used for input/output, dynamically generated, and globally tested in order to control execution.

1.1 Constraint languages

Considerable work on constraint programming languages preceded logic programming and constraint logic programming. We now briefly survey some important works, with a view toward the following features. Are constraints used for input/output? Can new variables and/or constraints be dynamically generated? Are constraints used for control? What is the constraint solving algorithm, and to what extent is it complete? What follows is adapted from the survey in [Michaylov, 1992].

SKETCHPAD [Sutherland, 1963] was perhaps the earliest work that one could classify as a constraint language. It was, in fact, an interactive drawing system, allowing the user to build geometric objects from language primitives and certain constraints. The constraints are static, and were solved by local propagation and relaxation techniques. (See chapter 2 in [Leler, 1988] for an introduction to these and related techniques.)

Subsequent related work was THINGLAB [Borning, 1981] whose language took an object-oriented flavor. While local propagation and relaxation were also used to deal with the essentially static constraints, the system considered constraint solving in two different phases. When a graphical object is manipulated, a plan is generated for quickly re-solving the appropriate constraints for the changed part of the object. This plan was then repeatedly executed while the manipulation continued. Works following the THINGLAB tradition included the Filters project [Ege *et al.*, 1987] and Animus [Duisburg, 1986]. Another graphical system, this one focusing on geometrical layout, was JUNO [Nelson, 1985]. The constraints were constructed, as in THINGLAB, by text or graphical primitives, and the geometric object could be manipulated. A difference from the above mentioned works is that constraint solving was performed numerically using a Newton–Raphson solver.

Another collection of early works arose from MIT, motivated by applications in electrical circuit analysis and synthesis, and gave rise to languages for general problem solving. In the CONSTRAINTS language [Steele and Sussman, 1980], variables and constraints are static, and constraint solving was limited to using local propagation. An extension of this work [Steele, 1980] provided a more sophisticated environment for constraint programming, including explanation facilities. Some other related systems, EL/ARS [Stallman and Sussman, 1977] and SYN [de Kleer and Sussman, 1980], used the constraint solver MACSYMA [MathLab, 1983] to avoid the restrictions of local propagation. It was noted at this period [Steele, 1980] that there was a conceptual correspondence between the constraint techniques and logic programming.

The REF-ARF system [Fikes, 1970] was also designed for problem solving. One component, REF, was essentially a procedural language, but with nondeterminism because of constraints used in conditional statements. The constraints are static. They are, in fact, linear integer constraints, and all variables are bounded above and below. The constraint solver ARF used backtracking.

The Bertrand system [Leler, 1988] was designed as a meta-language for the building of constraint solvers. It is itself a constraint language, based on term rewriting. Constraints are dynamic here, and are used in control. All constructs of the language are based on augmented rewrite rules, and the programmer adds rules for the specific constraint solving algorithm to be implemented.

Post-CLP, there have been a number of works which are able to deal with dynamic constraints. The language 2LP [McAloon and Tretkoff, 1989] is described to be a CLP language with a C-like syntax for representing and solving combinatorial problems. Obtaining parallel execution is one of the main objectives of this work. The commercial language CHARME, also based on a procedural framework, arose from the work on CHIP (by essentially omitting the logic programming part of CHIP). ILOG-SOLVER, which is also commercial, is a library of constraint algorithms designed to work with C++ programs. Using a procedural language as a basis, [Freeman-Benson, 1991] introduced Constraint Imperative programming which has explicit constraints in the usual way, and also a new kind of constraints obtained by considering variable assignments such as $x = x + 1$ as time-stamped. Such assignments are treatable as constraints of the form $x_i = x_{i+1} + 1$. Finally, we mention Constraint Functional Programming [Darlington and Guo, 1992] whose goal is the amalgamation of the ideas of functional programming found in the HOPE language with constraints.

There is work on languages and systems which are not generally regarded as constraint languages, but are nevertheless related to CLP languages. The development of symbolic algebra systems such as MACSYMA [MathLab, 1983] concentrated on the solving of difficult algebraic problems. The programming language aspects are less developed. Languages for linear programming [Kuip, 1993] provide little more than a primitive documentation facility for the array of coefficients which is input into a linear programming module.

In parallel with the development of these constraint languages, much work was done on the modelling of combinatorial problems as Constraint Satisfaction Problems (CSPs) and the development of techniques for solving such problems. The work was generally independent of any host language. (A possible exception is ALICE [Lauriere, 1978] which provided a wide variety of primitives to implement different search techniques.) One important development was the definition and study of several notions of consistency. This work had a significant influence on the later development of the CLP language CHIP. We refer the reader to [Tsang, 1993] for an introduction to the basic techniques and results concerning CSPs. Finally, we mention the survey [Burg *et al.*, 1990] which deals not just with constraint programming languages, but with constraint-based programming techniques.

1.2 Logic Programming

Next, we consider conventional logic programming (LP), and argue by example that the power of CLP cannot be obtained by making simple changes to LP systems. The question at hand is whether predicates in a logic program can be meaningfully regarded as constraints. That is, is a predicate with the same declarative semantics as a constraint a sufficient implementation of the constraint as per CLP? Consider, for example, the logic program

```
add(0, N, N).
add(s(N), M, s(K)) :- add(N, M, K).
```

where natural numbers n are represented by $s(s(\cdots(0)\cdots))$ with n occurrences of s. Clearly, the meaning of the predicate $add(n, m, k)$ coincides with the relation $n + m = k$. However, the query add(N, M, K), add(N, M, s(K)), which is clearly unsatisfiable, runs forever in a conventional LP system. The important point here is that a global test for the satisfiability of the two *add* constraints is not done by the underlying LP machinery.

In this example, the problem is that the *add* predicate is not invoked with a representation of the *add* constraints collected so far, and neither does it return such a representation (after having dealt with one more constraint). More concretely, the second subgoal of the query above is not given a representation of the fact that $N + M = K$.

A partial solution to this problem is the use of a delay mechanism. Roughly, the idea is that invocation of the predicate is delayed until its arguments are sufficiently instantiated. For example, if invocation of add is systematically delayed until its first argument is instantiated, then add behaves as in CLP when the first argument is ground. Thus the query N = s(s(⋯ s(0)⋯)), add(N, M, K), add(N, M, s(K)) fails as desired. However, the original query add(N, M, K), add(N, M, s(K)) will be delayed forever.

A total solution could, in principle, be obtained by simply adding two extra arguments to the predicate. One would be used for the input representation, and one for the output. This would mean that each time a constraint is dealt with, a representation of the entire set of constraints accumulated must be manipulated and a new representation constructed. But this is tantamount to a meta-level implementation of CLP in LP. Furthermore, this approach raises new challenges to efficient implementation.

Since LP is an instance of CLP, in which constraints are equations over terms, its solver also requires a representation of accumulated constraints. It happens, however, that there is no need for an explicit representation, such as the extra arguments discussed above. This is because the accumulated constraints can be represented by a most general unifier, and this, of course, is globally available via a simple binding mechanism.

1.3 CLP languages

Viewing the subject rather broadly, constraint logic programming can be said to involve the incorporation of constraints and constraint "solving" methods in a logic-based language. This characterization suggests the possibility of many interesting languages, based on different constraints and different logics. However, to this point, work on CLP has almost exclusively been devoted to languages based on Horn clauses[1]. We now briefly describe these languages, concentrating on those that have received substantial development effort.

---

[1] We note, however, some work combining constraints and resolution in first-order automated theorem-proving [Stickel, 1984; Bürckert, 1990].

Prolog can be said to be a CLP language where the constraints are equations over the algebra of terms (also called the algebra of finite trees, or the Herbrand domain). The equations are implicit in the use of unification[2]. Almost every language we discuss incorporates Prolog-like terms in addition to other terms and constraints, so we will not discuss this aspect further. Prolog II [Colmerauer, 1982a] employs equations and disequations ($\neq$) over rational trees (an extension of the finite trees of Prolog to cyclic structures). It was the first logic language explicitly described as using constraints [Colmerauer, 1983].

CLP($\mathcal{R}$) [Jaffar *et al.*, 1992a] has linear arithmetic constraints and computes over the real numbers. Nonlinear constraints are ignored (delayed) until they become effectively linear. CHIP [Dincbas *et al.*, 1988a] and Prolog III [Colmerauer, 1988] compute over several domains. Both compute over Boolean domains: Prolog III over the well-known 2-valued Boolean algebra, and CHIP over a larger Boolean algebra that contains symbolic values. Both CHIP and Prolog III perform linear arithmetic over the rational numbers. Separately (domains cannot be mixed), CHIP also performs linear arithmetic over bounded subsets of the integers (known as "finite domains"). Prolog III also computes over a domain of strings. There are now several languages which compute over finite domains in the manner of CHIP, including `clp(FD)`[Diaz and Codognet, 1993], Echidna [Havens *et al.*, 1992], and Flang [Mantsivoda, 1993]. cc($\mathcal{FD}$) [van Hentenryck *et al.*, 1993] is essentially a second-generation CHIP system.

LOGIN [Aït-Kaci and Nasr, 1986] and LIFE [Aït-Kaci and Podelski, 1993a] compute over an order-sorted domain of feature trees. This domain provides a limited notion of object (in the object-oriented sense). The languages support a term syntax which is not first-order, although every term can be interpreted through first-order constraints. Unlike other CLP languages/domains, Prolog-like trees are essentially part of this domain, instead of being built on top of the domain. CIL [Mukai, 1987] computes over a domain similar to feature trees.

BNR-Prolog [Older and Benhamou, 1993] computes over three domains: the 2-valued Boolean algebra, finite domains, and arithmetic over the real numbers. In contrast to other CLP languages over arithmetic domains, it computes solutions numerically, instead of symbolically. Trilogy [Voda, 1988a; Voda, 1988b] computes over strings, integers, and real numbers. Although its syntax is closer to that of C, 2LP [McAloon and Tretkoff, 1989] can be considered to be a CLP language permitting only a subset of Horn clauses. It computes with linear constraints over integers and real numbers.

CAL [Aiba *et al.*, 1988] computes over two domains: the real num-

---

[2]The language Absys [Elcock, 1990], which was very similar to Prolog, used equations explicitly, making it more obviously a CLP language.

bers, where constraints are equations between polynomials, and a Boolean algebra with symbolic values, where equality between Boolean formulas expresses equivalence in the algebra. Instead of delaying non-linear constraints, CAL makes partial use of these constraints during computation. In the experimental system RISC-CLP(Real) [Hong, 1993] non-linear constraints are fully involved in the computation.

L_λ [Miller, 1991] and Elf [Pfenning, 1991] are derived from λ-Prolog [Miller and Nadathur, 1986] and compute over the values of closed typed lambda expressions. These languages are not based on Horn clauses (they include a universal quantifier) and were not originally described as CLP languages. However, it is argued in [Michaylov and Pfenning, 1993] that their operational behavior is best understood as the behavior of a CLP language. An earlier language, Le Fun [Aït-Kaci and Nasr, 1987], also computed over this domain, and can be viewed as a CLP language with a weak constraint solver.

1.4 Synopsis

The remainder of this paper is organized into three main parts. In part I, we provide a formal framework for CLP. Particular attention will be paid to operational semantics and operational models. As we have seen in examples, it is the operational interpretation of constraints, rather than the declarative interpretation, which distinguishes CLP from LP. In part II, algorithm and data structure considerations are discussed. A crucial property of any CLP implementation is that its constraint handling algorithms are incremental. In this light, we review several important solvers and their algorithms for the satisfiability, entailment, and delaying of constraints. We will also discuss the requirements of an inference engine for CLP. In part III, we consider CLP applications. In particular, we discuss two rather different programming paradigms, one suited for the modelling of complex problems, and one for the solution of combinatorial problems.

In this survey, we concentrate on the issues raised by the introduction of constraints to LP. Consequently, we will ignore, or pass over quickly, those issues inherent in LP. We assume the reader is somewhat familiar with LP and basic first-order logic. Appropriate background can be obtained from [Lloyd, 1987] for LP and [Shoenfield, 1967] for logic. For introductory papers on constraint logic programming and CLP languages we refer the reader to [Colmerauer, 1987; Colmerauer, 1990; Lassez, 1987; Frühwirth *et al.*, 1992]. For further reading on CLP, we suggest other surveys [Cohen, 1990; van Hentenryck, 1991; van Hentenryck, 1992], some collections of papers [Benhamou and Colmerauer, 1993; Kanellakis *et al.*, to appear; van Hentenryck, 1993], and some books [van Hentenryck, 1989a; Saraswat, 1989]. More generally, papers on CLP appear in various journals and conference proceedings devoted to computational logic, constraint processing, or symbolic computation.

1.5 Notation and terminology

This paper will (hopefully) keep to the following conventions. Upper case letters generally denote collections of objects, while lower case letters generally denote individual objects. u, v, w, x, y, z will denote variables, s, t will denote terms, p, q will denote predicate symbols, f, g will denote function symbols, a will denote a constant, a, b, h will denote atoms, A will denote a collection of atoms, θ, ψ will denote substitutions, c will denote a constraint, C, S will denote collections of constraints, r will denote a rule, P, Q will denote programs, G will denote a goal, $\mathcal{D}$ will denote a structure, D will denote its set of elements, and d will denote an element of D. These symbols may be subscripted or have an over-tilde. $\tilde{x}$ denotes a sequence of distinct variables $x_1, x_2, \ldots, x_n$ for an appropriate n. $\tilde{s}$ denotes a sequence of (not necessarily distinct) terms $s_1, s_2, \ldots, s_n$ for an appropriate n. $\tilde{s} = \tilde{t}$ abbreviates $s_1 = t_1 \wedge s_2 = t_2 \wedge \cdots \wedge s_n = t_n$. $\exists_{-\tilde{x}} \, \phi$ denotes the existential closure of the formula ϕ *except* for the variables $\tilde{x}$, which remain unquantified. $\tilde{\exists} \, \phi$ denotes the full existential closure of the formula ϕ.

A *signature* defines a set of function and predicate symbols and associates an arity with each symbol[3]. If Σ is a signature, a Σ-*structure* $\mathcal{D}$ consists of a set D and an assignment of functions and relations on D to the symbols of Σ which respects the arities of the symbols. A first-order Σ-formula is built from variables, function and predicate symbols of Σ, the logical connectives $\wedge, \vee, \neg, \leftarrow, \rightarrow, \leftrightarrow$ and quantifiers over variables $\exists, \forall$ in the usual way [Shoenfield, 1967]. A formula is closed if all variable occurrences in the formula are within the scope of a quantifier over the variable. A Σ-*theory* is a collection of closed Σ-formulas. A *model* of a Σ-theory T is a Σ-structure $\mathcal{D}$ such that all formulas of T evaluate to *true* under the interpretation provided by $\mathcal{D}$. A $\mathcal{D}$-*model* of a theory T is a model of T extending $\mathcal{D}$ (this requires that the signature of $\mathcal{D}$ be contained in the signature of T). We write $T, \mathcal{D} \models \phi$ to denote that the formula ϕ is valid in all $\mathcal{D}$-models of T.

In this paper, the set of function and predicate symbols defined in the constraint domain is denoted by Σ and the set of predicate symbols definable by a program is denoted by Π. A *primitive constraint* has the form $p(t_1, \ldots, t_n)$, where $t_1, \ldots, t_n$ are terms and $p \in \Sigma$ is a predicate symbol. Every *constraint* is a (first-order) formula built from primitive constraints. The class of constraints will vary, but we will generally consider only a subset of formulas to be constraints. An *atom* has the form $p(t_1, \ldots, t_n)$, where $t_1, \ldots, t_n$ are terms and $p \in \Pi$. A *CLP program* is a collection of *rules* of the form $a \leftarrow b_1, \ldots, b_n$ where a is an atom and the b_i's are atoms or constraints. a is called the *head* of the rule and $b_1, \ldots, b_n$ is called the *body*. Sometimes we represent the rule by $a \leftarrow c, B$, where c is the con-

---

[3]In a many-sorted language this would include associating a sort with each argument and the result of each symbol. However, we will not discuss such details in this survey.

junction of constraints in the body and B is the collection of atoms in the body, and sometimes we represent the rule by $a \leftarrow B$, where B is the collection of atoms and constraints in the body. In one subsection we will also consider programs with negated atoms in the body. A *goal* (or *query*) G is a conjunction of constraints and atoms. A *fact* is a rule $a \leftarrow c$ where c is a constraint. Finally, we will identify conjunction and multiset union.

To simplify the exposition, we assume that the rules are in a standard form, where all arguments in atoms are variables and each variable occurs in at most one atom. This involves no loss of generality since a rule such as $p(t_1, t_2) \leftarrow C, q(s_1, s_2)$ can be replaced by the equivalent rule $p(x_1, x_2) \leftarrow x_1 = t_1, x_2 = t_2, y_1 = s_1, y_2 = s_2, C, q(y_1, y_2)$. We also assume that all rules defining the same predicate have the same head and that no two rules have any other variables in common (this is simply a matter of renaming variables). However, in examples we relax these restrictions.

Programs will be presented in `teletype` font, and will generally follow the Edinburgh syntax. In particular, program variables begin with an upper case letter, $[Head|Tail]$ denotes a list with head $Head$ and tail $Tail$, and $[]$ denotes an empty list. In one variation from this standard we allow subscripts on program variables, to improve readability.

The semantics of CLP languages

Many languages based on definite clauses have quite similar semantics. The crucial insight of the CLP Scheme [Jaffar and Lassez, 1987; Jaffar and Lassez, 1986] and the earlier scheme of [Jaffar et al., 1984; Jaffar et al., 1986] was that a logic-based programming language, its operational semantics, its declarative semantics and the relationships between these semantics could all be parameterized by a choice of domain of computation and constraints. The resulting scheme defines the class of languages $CLP(\mathcal{X})$ obtained by instantiating the parameter $\mathcal{X}$.

We take the view that the parameter $\mathcal{X}$ stands for a 4-tuple $(\Sigma, \mathcal{D}, \mathcal{L}, \mathcal{T})$. Here Σ is a signature, $\mathcal{D}$ is a Σ-structure, $\mathcal{L}$ is a class of Σ-formulas, and $\mathcal{T}$ is a first-order Σ-theory. Intuitively, Σ determines the predefined predicate and function symbols and their arities, $\mathcal{D}$ is the structure over which computation is to be performed, $\mathcal{L}$ is the class of constraints which can be expressed, and $\mathcal{T}$ is an axiomatization of (some) properties of $\mathcal{D}$. In the following section, we define some important relationships between the elements of the 4-tuple, and give some examples of constraint domains.

We then give declarative and operational semantics for CLP programs, parameterized by $\mathcal{X}$. The declarative semantics are quite similar to the corresponding semantics of logic programs, and we cover them quickly. There are many variations of the resolution-based operational semantics, and we present the main ones. We also present the main soundness and completeness results that relate the two styles of semantics. Finally, we discuss some linguistic features that have been proposed as extensions to the basic CLP language.

2 Constraint domains

For any signature Σ, let $\mathcal{D}$ be a Σ-structure (the domain of computation) and $\mathcal{L}$ be a class of Σ-formulas (the *constraints*). We call the pair $(\mathcal{D}, \mathcal{L})$ a *constraint domain*. In a slight abuse of notation we will sometimes denote the constraint domain by $\mathcal{D}$. We will make several assumptions, none of which is strictly necessary, to simplify the exposition. We assume

- The terms and constraints in $\mathcal{L}$ come from a first-order language[4].
- The binary predicate symbol $=$ is contained in Σ and is interpreted as identity in $\mathcal{D}$[5].
- There are constraints in $\mathcal{L}$ which are, respectively, identically true and identically false in $\mathcal{D}$.
- The class of constraints $\mathcal{L}$ is closed under variable renaming, conjunction and existential quantification.

We will denote the smallest set of constraints which satisfies these assumptions and contains all primitive constraints – the constraints *generated* by the primitive constraints – by $\mathcal{L}_\Sigma$. In general, $\mathcal{L}$ may be strictly larger than $\mathcal{L}_\Sigma$ since, for example, universal quantifiers or disjunction are permitted in $\mathcal{L}$; it also may be smaller, as in Example 2.0.7 of Section 2 below. However, we will usually take $\mathcal{L} = \mathcal{L}_\Sigma$. On occasion we will consider an extension of Σ and $\mathcal{L}$, to Σ^* and $\mathcal{L}^*$ respectively, so that there is a constant in Σ^* for every element of D.

We now present some example constraint domains. In practice, these are not always fully implemented, but we leave discussion of that until later. Most general purpose CLP languages incorporate some arithmetic domain, including BNR-Prolog [Older and Benhamou, 1993], CAL [Aiba *et al.*, 1988], CHIP [Dincbas *et al.*, 1988a], CLP($\mathcal{R}$) [Jaffar *et al.*, 1992a], Prolog III [Colmerauer, 1988], RISC-CLP(Real) [Hong, 1993].

Example 2.0.1. Let Σ contain the constants 0 and 1, the binary function symbols $+$ and $*$, and the binary predicate symbols $=$, $<$ and $\leq$. Let D be the set of real numbers and let $\mathcal{D}$ interpret the symbols of Σ as usual (i.e. $+$ is interpreted as addition, etc). Let $\mathcal{L}$ be the constraints generated by the primitive constraints. Then $\Re = (\mathcal{D}, \mathcal{L})$ is the constraint domain of arithmetic over the real numbers. If we omit from Σ the symbol $*$ then the corresponding constraint domain $\Re_{Lin} = (\mathcal{D}', \mathcal{L}')$ is the constraint domain of linear arithmetic over the real numbers. If the domain is further

---

[4]Without this assumption, some of the results we cite are not applicable, since there can be no appropriate first-order theory $\mathcal{T}$. The remaining assumptions can be omitted, at the expense of a messier reformulation of definitions and results.

[5]This assumption is unnecessary when terms have a most general unifier in $\mathcal{D}$, as occurs in Prolog. Otherwise $=$ is needed to express parameter passing.

restricted to the rational numbers then we have a further constraint domain $\mathbf{Q}_{Lin}$. In constraints in $\Re_{Lin}$ and $\mathbf{Q}_{Lin}$ we will write terms such as 3 and $5x$ as abbreviations for $1+1+1$ and $x+x+x+x+x$ respectively[6]. Thus $\exists y\ 5x + y \leq 3 \wedge z \leq y - 1$ is a constraint in $\Re$, $\Re_{Lin}$ and $\mathbf{Q}_{Lin}$, whereas $x * x \leq y$ is a constraint only in $\Re$. If we extend $\mathcal{L}'$ to allow negated equations[7] (we will use the symbol $\neq$) then the resulting constraint domains $\Re^{\neq}_{Lin}$ and $\mathbf{Q}^{\neq}_{Lin}$ permit constraints such as $2x + y \leq 0 \wedge x \neq y$. Finally, if we restrict Σ to $\{0, 1, +, =\}$ we obtain the constraint domain $\Re_{LinEqn}$, where the only constraints are linear equations.

$\Re_{Lin}$ and $\mathbf{Q}_{Lin}$ (and $\Re^{\neq}_{Lin}$ and $\mathbf{Q}^{\neq}_{Lin}$) are essentially the same constraint domain: they have the same language of constraints and the two structures are elementarily equivalent [Shoenfield, 1967]. In particular, a constraint solver for one is also a constraint solver for the other.

Prolog and standard logic programming can be viewed as constraint logic programming over the constraint domain of finite trees.

Example 2.0.2. Let Σ contain a collection of constant and function symbols and the binary predicate symbol $=$. Let D be the set of finite trees where: each node of each tree is labelled by a constant or function symbol, the number of children of each node is the arity of the label of the node, and the children are ordered. Let $\mathcal{D}$ interpret the function symbols of Σ as tree constructors, where each $f \in \Sigma$ of arity n maps n trees to a tree whose root is labelled by f and whose subtrees are the arguments of the mapping. The primitive constraints are equations between terms, and let $\mathcal{L}$ be the constraints generated by these primitive constraints. Then $\mathcal{FT} = (\mathcal{D}, \mathcal{L})$ is the Herbrand constraint domain, as used in Prolog. Typical constraints are $x = g(y)$ and $\exists z\ x = f(z, z) \wedge y = g(z)$. (It is unnecessary to write a quantifier in Prolog programs because all variables that appear only in constraints are implicitly existentially quantified.)

It was pointed out in [Colmerauer, 1982b] that complete (i.e. always terminating) unification which omits the occurs check solves equations over the rational trees.

Example 2.0.3. We take Σ and $\mathcal{L}$ as in the previous example. D is the set of rational trees (see [Courcelle, 1983] for a definition) and the function symbols are interpreted as tree constructors, as before. Then $\mathcal{RT} = (\mathcal{D}, \mathcal{L})$ is the constraint domain of rational trees.

If we take the set of infinite trees instead of rational trees then we obtain a constraint domain that is essentially the same as $\mathcal{RT}$, in the same way that $\Re_{Lin}$ and $\mathbf{Q}_{Lin}$ are essentially the same: they have the same language

---

[6]Other syntactic sugar, such as the unary and binary minus symbol $-$, are allowed. Rational number coefficients can be used: all terms in the sugared constraint need only be multiplied by an appropriate number to reduce the coefficients to integers.

[7]Sometimes called *disequations*.

of constraints and the two structures are elementarily equivalent [Maher, 1988].

The next domain contains objects similar to the previous domains, but has a different signature and constraint language [Aït-Kaci *et al.*, 1992][8], which results in slightly different expressive power. It can be viewed as the restriction of domains over which LOGIN [Aït-Kaci and Nasr, 1986] and LIFE [Aït-Kaci and Podelski, 1993a] compute when all sorts are disjoint. The close relationship between the constraints and ψ-terms [Aït-Kaci, 1986] is emphasized by a syntactic sugaring of the constraints.

Example 2.0.4. Let $\Sigma = \{=\} \cup S \cup F$ where S is a set of unary predicate symbols (sorts) and F is a set of binary predicate symbols (features). Let D be the set of (finite or infinite) trees where: each node of each tree is labelled by a sort, each edge of each tree is labelled by a feature and no node has two outbound edges with the same label. Such trees are called *feature trees*. Let $\mathcal{D}$ interpret each sort s as the set of feature trees whose root is labelled by s, and interpret each feature f as the set of pairs (t_1, t_2) of feature trees such that t_2 is the subtree of t_1 that is reached by the edge labelled by f. (If t_1 has no edge labelled by f then there is no pair (t_1, t_2) in the set.) Thus features are essentially partial functions. The domain of feature trees is $\mathcal{FEAT} = (\mathcal{D}, \mathcal{L})$. A typical constraint is $wine(x) \wedge \exists y\ region(x, y) \wedge rutherglen(y) \wedge \exists y\ color(x, y) \wedge red(y)$, but there is also a sugared syntax which would represent this constraint as $x : wine[region \Rightarrow rutherglen, color \Rightarrow red]$.

The next constraint domain takes strings as the basic objects. It is used in Prolog III [Colmerauer, 1988].

Example 2.0.5. Let Σ contain the binary predicate symbol $=$, the binary function symbol $.$, a constant λ, and a number of other constants. D is the set of finite strings of the constants. The symbol $.$ is interpreted in $\mathcal{D}$ as string concatenation and λ is interpreted as the empty string. $\mathcal{L}$ is the set of constraints generated by equations between terms. Then $\mathcal{WE} = (\mathcal{D}, \mathcal{L})$ is the constraint domain of equations on strings, sometimes called the domain of word equations. An example constraint is $x.a = b.x$.

The constraint domain of Boolean values and functions is used in BNR-Prolog [Older and Benhamou, 1993], CAL [Aiba *et al.*, 1988], CHIP [Dincbas *et al.*, 1988a] and Prolog III [Colmerauer, 1988]. CAL and CHIP employ a more general constraint domain, which includes symbolic Boolean values.

Example 2.0.6. Let Σ contain the constants 0 and 1, the unary function symbol $\neg$, the binary function symbols $\wedge, \vee, \oplus, \Rightarrow$, and the binary predicate symbol $=$. Let D be the set $\{true, false\}$ and let $\mathcal{D}$ interpret the

---

[8]A variant of this domain, with a slightly different signature, is used in [Smolka and Treinen, 1992].

symbols of Σ as the usual Boolean functions (i.e. $\wedge$ is interpreted as conjunction, $\oplus$ is exclusive or, etc). Let $\mathcal{L}$ be the constraints generated by the primitive constraints. Then $\mathcal{BOOL} = (\mathcal{D}, \mathcal{L})$ is the (two-valued) Boolean constraint domain. An example constraint is $\neg(x \wedge y) = y$. In a slight abuse of notation, we allow a constraint $t = 1$ to be written simply as t so that, for example, $\neg(x \wedge y) \oplus y$ denotes the constraint $\neg(x \wedge y) \oplus y = 1$. For the more general constraint domain, let $\Sigma' = \Sigma \cup \{a_1, \ldots, a_i, \ldots\}$, where the a_i are constants. Let $\mathcal{L}'$ be the constraints generated by the Σ' primitive constraints and let $\mathcal{D}'$ be the free Boolean algebra generated by $\{a_1, \ldots, a_i, \ldots\}$. Then $\mathcal{BOOL}_\infty = (\mathcal{D}', \mathcal{L})$ is the Boolean constraint domain with infinitely many symbolic values[9]. A constraint $c(\tilde{x}, \tilde{a})$ is satisfiable in $\mathcal{BOOL}_\infty$ iff $\mathcal{D} \models \exists \tilde{x} \forall \tilde{y}\, c(\tilde{x}, \tilde{y})$.

The finite domains of CHIP are best viewed as having the integers as the underlying structure, with a limitation on the language of constraints.

Example 2.0.7. Let $D = \mathbf{Z}$ and $\Sigma = \{\{\in [m, n]\}_{m \leq n}, +, =, \neq, \leq\}$. For every pair of integers m and n, the interval constraint $x \in [m, n]$ denotes that $m \leq x \leq n$. The other symbols in Σ have their usual meaning. Let $\mathcal{L}$ be the constraints c generated by the primitive constraints, restricted so that every variable in c is subject to an interval constraint. Then $\mathcal{FD} = (\mathcal{D}, \mathcal{L})$ is the constraint domain referred to as finite domains. (The domain of a variable x is the finite set of values which satisfy all unary constraints involving x.) A typical constraint in $\mathcal{FD}$ is $x \in [1, 5] \wedge y \in [0, 7] \wedge x \neq 3 \wedge x + 2y \leq 5 \wedge x + y \leq 9$. The domain of x is $\{1, 2, 4, 5\}$.

There are several other constraint domains of interest that we cannot exemplify here for lack of space. They include pseudo-Boolean constraints (for example, [Bockmayr, 1993]), which are intermediate between Boolean and integer constraints, order-sorted feature algebras [Aït-Kaci and Poldeski, 1993b], domains consisting of regular sets of strings [Walinsky, 1989], domains of finite sets [Dovier and Rossi, 1993], domains of CLP(Fun(D)) which employ a function variable [Hickey, 1993], domains of functions expressed by λ-expressions [Miller and Nadathur, 1986; Aït-Kaci and Nasr, 1987; Miller, 1991; Pfenning, 1991; Michaylov and Pfenning, 1993], etc.

It is also possible to form a constraint domain directly from objects and operations in an application, instead of more general purpose domains such as those above. This possibility has only been pursued in a limited form, where a general purpose domain is extended by the *ad hoc* addition of primitive constraints. For example, in some uses of CHIP the finite domain

---

[9]Only finitely many constants are used in any one program, so it can be argued that a finite Boolean algebra is a more appropriate domain of computation. However, the two alternatives agree on satisfiability and constraint entailment (although not if an expanded language of constraints is permitted), and it is preferable to view the constraint domain as independent of the program. Currently, it is not clear whether the alternatives agree on other constraint operations.

is extended with a predicate symbol *element* [Dincbas *et al.*, 1988b]. The relation *element*(x, l, t) expresses that t is the x'th element in the list l. We discuss such extensions further in Section 9.2.

These constraint domains are expected to support (perhaps in a weakened form) the following tests and operations on constraints, which have a major importance in CLP languages. The first operation is the most important (it is almost obligatory), while the others might not be used in some CLP languages.

- The first is a test for *consistency* or *satisfiability*: $\mathcal{D} \models \tilde{\exists} c$.

- The second is the *implication* (or *entailment*) of one constraint by another: $\mathcal{D} \models c_0 \rightarrow c_1$. More generally, we may ask whether a disjunction of constraints is implied by a constraint: $\mathcal{D} \models c_0 \rightarrow \bigvee_{i=1}^{n} c_i$.

- The third is the *projection* of a constraint c_0 onto variables $\tilde{x}$ to obtain a constraint c_1 such that $\mathcal{D} \models c_1 \leftrightarrow \exists_{-\tilde{x}} c_0$. It is always possible to take c_1 to be $\exists_{-\tilde{x}} c_0$, but the aim is to compute the simplest c_1 with fewest quantifiers. In general it is not possible to eliminate all uses of the existential quantifier.

- The fourth is the detection that, given a constraint c, there is only one value that a variable x can take that is consistent with c. That is, $\mathcal{D} \models c(x, \tilde{z}) \wedge c(y, \tilde{w}) \rightarrow x = y$ or, equivalently, $\mathcal{D} \models \exists z \forall x, \tilde{y} \, c(x, \tilde{y}) \rightarrow x = z$. We say x is *determined* (or *grounded*) by c.

In Section 10 we will discuss problems and techniques which arise when implementing these operations in a CLP system. However, we point out here that some implementations of these operators – in particular, the test for satisfiability – are incomplete. In some cases it has been argued [Colmerauer, 1993b; Colmerauer, 1993a; Benhamou and Massat, 1993] that although an algorithm is incomplete with respect to the desired constraint domain, it is complete with respect to another (artificially constructed) constraint domain.

We now turn to some properties of constraint domains which will be used later. The first two – solution compactness and satisfaction completeness – were introduced as part of the CLP Scheme.

Definition 2.0.8. Let d range over elements of D and c, c_i range over constraints in $\mathcal{L}$, and let I be a possibly infinite index set. A constraint domain $(\mathcal{D}, \mathcal{L})$ is *solution compact* [Jaffar and Lassez, 1986; Jaffar and Lassez, 1987] if it satisfies the following conditions:

(SC_1) $\qquad\qquad \forall d \; \exists \{c_i\}_{i \in I} \; s.t. \; \mathcal{D} \models \forall x \; x = d \leftrightarrow \bigwedge_{i \in I} c_i(x)$

(SC_2) $\qquad\qquad \forall c \; \exists \{c_i\}_{i \in I} \; s.t. \; \mathcal{D} \models \forall \tilde{x} \; \neg c(\tilde{x}) \leftrightarrow \bigvee_{i \in I} c_i(\tilde{x})$

Roughly speaking, SC_1 is satisfied iff every element d of D can be defined by a (possibly infinite) conjunction of constraints, and SC_2 is satisfied iff the complement of each constraint c in $\mathcal{L}$ can be described by a (possibly infinite) disjunction of constraints.

The definition of SC_2 in [Jaffar and Lassez, 1986] is not quite equivalent to the definition in [Jaffar and Lassez, 1987] which we paraphrase above; see [Maher, 1992]. It turns out that SC_1 is not necessary for the results we present; we include it only for historical accuracy. There is no known natural constraint domain for which SC_2 does not hold. There are, however, some artificial constraint domains for which it fails.

Example 2.0.9. Let $\Re_{Lin}^+$ denote the constraint domain obtained from $\Re_{Lin}$ by adding the unary primitive constraint $x \neq \pi$. The negation of this constraint (i.e. $x = \pi$) cannot be represented as a disjunction of constraints in $\Re_{Lin}^+$. Thus $\Re_{Lin}^+$ is not solution compact.

The theory $\mathcal{T}$ in the parameter of the CLP scheme is intended to axiomatize some of the properties of $\mathcal{D}$. We place some conditions on $\mathcal{D}$ and $\mathcal{T}$ to ensure that $\mathcal{T}$ reflects $\mathcal{D}$ sufficiently. The first two conditions ensure that $\mathcal{D}$ and $\mathcal{T}$ agree on satisfiability of constraints, while the addition of the third condition guarantees that every unsatisfiability in $\mathcal{D}$ is also detected by $\mathcal{T}$. The theory $\mathcal{T}$ and these conditions mainly play a role in the completeness results of Section 6.

Definition 2.0.10. For a given signature Σ, let $(\mathcal{D}, \mathcal{L})$ be a constraint domain with signature Σ, and $\mathcal{T}$ be a Σ-theory. We say that $\mathcal{D}$ and $\mathcal{T}$ *correspond* on $\mathcal{L}$ if
- $\mathcal{D}$ is a model of $\mathcal{T}$, and
- for every constraint $c \in \mathcal{L}$, $\mathcal{D} \models \tilde{\exists}\, c$ iff $\mathcal{T} \models \tilde{\exists}\, c$.
We say $\mathcal{T}$ is *satisfaction complete* with respect to $\mathcal{L}$ if for every constraint $c \in \mathcal{L}$, either $\mathcal{T} \models \tilde{\exists}\, c$ or $\mathcal{T} \models \neg \tilde{\exists}\, c$.

Satisfaction completeness is a weakening of the notion of a complete theory [Shoenfield, 1967]. Thus, for example, the theory of the real closed fields [Tarski, 1951] corresponds and is satisfaction complete with respect to $\Re$ since the domain is a model of this theory and the theory is complete. Clark's axiomatization of unification [Clark, 1978] defines a satisfaction complete theory with respect to $\mathcal{FT}$ which is not complete when there are only finitely many function symbols [Maher, 1988].

The notion of independence of negative constraints plays a significant role in constraint logic programming[10]. In [Colmerauer, 1984], Colmerauer used independence of inequations to simplify the test for satisfiability of equations and inequations on the rational trees. (The independence of

---

[10]It is also closely related to the model-theoretic properties that led to an interest in Horn formulas [McKinsey, 1943; Horn, 1951].

inequations states: if a conjunction of positive and negative equational constraints is inconsistent then one of the negative constraints is inconsistent with the positive constraints.) Independence of negative constraints has been investigated in greater generality in [Lassez and McAloon, 1990]. The property has been shown to hold for several classes of constraints including equations on finite, rational and infinite trees [Lassez and Marriott, 1987; Lassez *et al.*, 1988; Maher, 1988], linear real arithmetic constraints (where only equations may be negated) [Lassez and McAloon, 1992], sort and feature constraints on feature trees [Aït-Kaci *et al.*, 1992], and infinite Boolean algebras with positive constraints [Helm *et al.*, 1991], among others [Lassez and McAloon, 1990]. We consider a restricted form of independence of negative constraints [Maher, 1993b].

Definition 2.0.11. A constraint domain $(\mathcal{D}, \mathcal{L})$ has the independence of negated constraints property if, for all constraints $c, c_1, \ldots, c_n \in \mathcal{L}$,

$$\mathcal{D} \models \bar{\exists} \, c \wedge \neg c_1 \wedge \cdots \wedge \neg c_n \text{ iff } \mathcal{D} \models \bar{\exists} \, c \wedge \neg c_i \text{ for } i = 1, \ldots, n.$$

The fact that $\mathcal{L}$ is assumed to be closed under conjunction and existential quantification is an important restriction in the above definition. For example, Colmerauer's work is not applicable in this setting since that dealt only with primitive constraints. Neither are many of the other results cited above, at least not in their full generality. However there are still several useful constraint domains known to have this property, including the algebras of finite, rational and infinite trees with equational constraints, when there are infinitely many function symbols [Lassez and Marriott, 1987; Maher, 1988], feature trees with infinitely many sorts and features [Aït-Kaci *et al.*, 1992], linear arithmetic equations over the rational or real numbers, and infinite Boolean algebras with positive constraints [Helm *et al.*, 1991].

Example 2.0.12. In the Herbrand constraint domain $\mathcal{FT}$ with only two function symbols, a constant a and a unary function f, it is easily seen that the following statements are true: $\mathcal{FT} \models \exists x, y, z \; x = f(y) \wedge \neg y = a \wedge \neg y = f(z)$; $\mathcal{FT} \models \exists x, y \; x = f(y) \wedge \neg y = a$; $\mathcal{FT} \models \exists x, y, z \; x = f(y) \wedge \neg y = f(z)$. This is an example of the independence of inequations for $\mathcal{FT}$. However, when we consider the full class of constraints of $\mathcal{FT}$ we have the following facts. The statement $\mathcal{FT} \models \exists x, y \; x = f(y) \wedge \neg y = a \wedge \neg \exists z \; y = f(z)$ is not true, since every finite tree y is either the constant a or has the form $f(z)$ for some finite tree z. On the other hand, both $\mathcal{FT} \models \exists x, y \; x = f(y) \wedge \neg y = a$ and $\mathcal{FT} \models \exists x, y \; x = f(y) \wedge \neg \exists z \; y = f(z)$ are true. Thus, for these function symbols – and it is easy to see how to extend this example to any finite set of function symbols – the independence of negated constraints does not hold.

As is clear from [Scott, 1982], constraint domains (and constraints) are closely related to the *information systems* (and their elements) used by

Scott to present his domain theory. Information systems codify notions of consistency and entailment among elements, which can be interpreted as satisfiability and implication of constraints on a single variable. Saraswat [Saraswat *et al.*, 1991; Saraswat, 1992] extended the notion of information system to *constraint systems*[11] (which allow many variables), and showed that some of the motivating properties of information systems continue to hold.

Constraint systems (we will not give a formal definition here) can be viewed as abstractions of constraint domains which eliminate consideration of a particular structure $\mathcal{D}$; the relation $\mathcal{D} \models c_1 \wedge \cdots \wedge c_n \to c$ among constraints $c, c_1, \ldots, c_n$ is abstracted to the relation $c_1, \ldots, c_n \vdash c$ (and the satisfiability relation $\mathcal{D} \models \tilde{\exists} c_1 \wedge \cdots \wedge c_n$ among constraints can be abstracted to a set Con of all consistent finite sets of constraints $\{c_1, \ldots, c_n\}$ [Scott, 1982; Saraswat, 1992]). Many of the essential semantic details of a constraint domain are still present in the corresponding constraint system, although properties such as solution compactness and independence of negated constraints cannot be expressed without more detail than a constraint system provides.

3   Logical semantics

There are two common logical semantics of CLP programs over a constraint domain $(\mathcal{D}, \mathcal{L})$. The first interprets a rule

$$p(\tilde{x}) \leftarrow b_1, \ldots, b_n$$

as the logic formula

$$\forall \tilde{x}, \tilde{y} \quad p(\tilde{x}) \vee \neg b_1 \vee \cdots \vee \neg b_n$$

where $\tilde{x} \cup \tilde{y}$ is the set of all free variables in the rule. The collection of all such formulas corresponding to rules of P gives a theory also denoted by P.

The second logical semantics associates a logic formula with each predicate in Π. If the set of all rules of P with p in the head is

$$
\begin{aligned}
p(\tilde{x}) &\leftarrow B_1 \\
p(\tilde{x}) &\leftarrow B_2 \\
&\cdots \\
p(\tilde{x}) &\leftarrow B_n
\end{aligned}
$$

then the formula associated with p is

---

[11]Although [Saraswat, 1992] does not treat consistency, only entailment.

$$\forall \tilde{x} \; p(\tilde{x}) \leftrightarrow \qquad \exists \tilde{y}_1 \; B_1$$
$$\lor \quad \exists \tilde{y}_2 \; B_2$$
$$\cdots$$
$$\lor \quad \exists \tilde{y}_n \; B_n$$

where $\tilde{y}_i$ is the set of variables in B_i except for variables in $\tilde{x}$. If p does not occur in the head of a rule of P then the formula is

$$\forall \tilde{x} \; \neg p(\tilde{x})$$

The collection of all such formulas is called the *Clark completion* of P, and is denoted by P^*.

A *valuation* v is a mapping from variables to D, and the natural extension which maps terms to D and formulas to closed $\mathcal{L}^*$-formulas. If X is a set of facts then $[X]_{\mathcal{D}} = \{v(a) \mid (a \leftarrow c) \in X, \mathcal{D} \models v(c)\}$. A $\mathcal{D}$-interpretation of a formula is an interpretation of the formula with the same domain as $\mathcal{D}$ and the same interpretation for the symbols in Σ as $\mathcal{D}$. It can be represented as a subset of $\mathcal{B}_{\mathcal{D}}$ where $\mathcal{B}_{\mathcal{D}} = \{p(\tilde{d}) \mid p \in \Pi, \tilde{d} \in D^k\}$. A $\mathcal{D}$-model of a closed formula is a $\mathcal{D}$-interpretation which is a model of the formula.

Let $\mathcal{T}$ denote a satisfaction complete theory for $(\mathcal{D}, \mathcal{L})$. The usual logical semantics are based on the $\mathcal{D}$-models of P and the models of $P^*, \mathcal{T}$. The least $\mathcal{D}$-model of a formula Q under the subset ordering is denoted by $lm(Q, \mathcal{D})$, and the greatest is denoted by $gm(Q, \mathcal{D})$. A *solution* to a query G is a valuation v such that $v(G) \subseteq lm(P, \mathcal{D})$.

4 Fixedpoint semantics

The fixedpoint semantics we present are based on one-step consequence functions $T_P^{\mathcal{D}}$ and $S_P^{\mathcal{D}}$, and the closure operator $[\![P]\!]$ generated by $T_P^{\mathcal{D}}$. The functions $T_P^{\mathcal{D}}$ and $[\![P]\!]$ map over $\mathcal{D}$-interpretations. The set of $\mathcal{D}$-interpretations forms a complete lattice under the subset ordering, and these functions are continuous on $\mathcal{B}_{\mathcal{D}}$.

$$T_P^{\mathcal{D}}(I) = \{p(\tilde{d}) \mid \quad p(\tilde{x}) \leftarrow c, b_1, \ldots, b_n \text{ is a rule of } P, a_i \in I, \; i = 1, \ldots, n,$$
$$v \text{ is a valuation on } \mathcal{D} \text{ such that}$$
$$\mathcal{D} \models v(c), \; v(\tilde{x}) = \tilde{d}, \text{ and } v(b_i) = a_i, \; i = 1, \ldots, n\}$$

$[\![P]\!]$ is the closure operator generated by $T_P^{\mathcal{D}}$. It represents a deductive closure based on the rules of P. Let Id be the identity function, and define $(f + g)(x) = f(x) \cup g(x)$. Then $[\![P]\!](I)$ is the least fixedpoint of $T_P^{\mathcal{D}} + Id$ greater than I, and the least fixedpoint of $T_{P \cup I}^{\mathcal{D}}$.

The function $S_P^{\mathcal{D}}$ is defined on sets of facts, which form a complete lattice under the subset ordering. We denote the closure operator generated from $S_P^{\mathcal{D}}$ by $\langle\!\langle P \rangle\!\rangle$. Both these functions are continuous.

$$S_P^{\mathcal{D}}(I) = \{p(\tilde{x}) \leftarrow c \mid \quad p(\tilde{x}) \leftarrow c', b_1, \ldots, b_n \text{ is a rule of } P,$$
$$a_i \leftarrow c_i \in I, \ i = 1, \ldots, n,$$
$$\text{the rule and facts renamed apart,}$$
$$\mathcal{D} \models c \leftrightarrow \exists_{-\tilde{x}} \, c' \wedge \bigwedge_{i=1}^{n} c_i \wedge a_i = b_i\}$$

We denote the least fixedpoint of a function f by $lfp(f)$ and the greatest fixedpoint by $gfp(f)$. These fixedpoints exist for the functions of interest, since they are monotonic functions on complete lattices. For a function f mapping $\mathcal{D}$-interpretations to $\mathcal{D}$-interpretations, we define the upward and downward iteration of f as follows.

$$
\begin{aligned}
f \uparrow 0 \quad &= \quad \emptyset \\
f \uparrow (\alpha + 1) \quad &= \quad f(f \uparrow \alpha) \\
f \uparrow \beta \quad &= \quad \bigcup_{\alpha < \beta} f \uparrow \alpha \quad \text{if } \beta \text{ is a limit ordinal}
\end{aligned}
$$

$$
\begin{aligned}
f \downarrow 0 \quad &= \quad \mathcal{B}_{\mathcal{D}} \\
f \downarrow (\alpha + 1) \quad &= \quad f(f \downarrow \alpha) \\
f \downarrow \beta \quad &= \quad \bigcap_{\alpha < \beta} f \downarrow \alpha \quad \text{if } \beta \text{ is a limit ordinal}
\end{aligned}
$$

We can take as semantics $lfp(S_P^{\mathcal{D}})$ or $lfp(T_P^{\mathcal{D}})$. The two functions involved are related in the following way: $[S_P^{\mathcal{D}}(I)]_{\mathcal{D}} = T_P^{\mathcal{D}}([I]_{\mathcal{D}})$. Consequently $[lfp(S_P^{\mathcal{D}})]_{\mathcal{D}} = lfp(T_P^{\mathcal{D}})$. $lfp(S_P^{\mathcal{D}})$ corresponds to the s-semantics [Falaschi *et al.*, 1989] for languages with constraints [Gabbrielli and Levi, 1991]. Fixedpoint semantics based on sets of clauses [Bossi *et al.*, 1992] also extend easily to CLP languages.

Based largely on the facts that the $\mathcal{D}$-models of P are the fixedpoints of $[\![P]\!]$ and the $\mathcal{D}$-models of P^* are the fixedpoints of $T_P^{\mathcal{D}}$, we have the following connections between the logical and fixedpoint semantics, just as in standard logic programming.

Proposition 4.0.1. *Let P, P_1, P_2 be CLP programs and Q a set of facts over a constraint domain $\mathcal{D}$ with corresponding theory $\mathcal{T}$. Then:*

- $T_P^{\mathcal{D}} \uparrow \omega = lfp(T_P^{\mathcal{D}}) = [lfp(S_P^{\mathcal{D}})]_{\mathcal{D}} = [\![P]\!](\emptyset)$
- $lm(P, \mathcal{D}) = [\{h \leftarrow c \mid P^*, \mathcal{D} \models (h \leftarrow c)\}]_{\mathcal{D}} = [\{h \leftarrow c \mid P^*, \mathcal{T} \models (h \leftarrow c)\}]_{\mathcal{D}}$
- $lm(P^*, \mathcal{D}) = lm(P, \mathcal{D}) = lfp(T_P^{\mathcal{D}})$
- $gm(P^*, \mathcal{D}) = gfp(T_P^{\mathcal{D}})$
- $[\![P]\!]([Q]_{\mathcal{D}}) = [\![P \cup Q]\!](\emptyset) = lm(P \cup Q, \mathcal{D})$
- $\langle\!\langle P \rangle\!\rangle(Q) = \langle\!\langle P \cup Q \rangle\!\rangle(\emptyset) = lfp(S_{P \cup Q}^{\mathcal{D}})$
- $\mathcal{D} \models P_1 \leftrightarrow P_2$ iff $[\![P_1]\!] = [\![P_2]\!]$

We will need the following terminology later. P is said to be $(\mathcal{D}, \mathcal{L})$-*canonical* iff $gfp(T_P^{\mathcal{D}}) = T_P^{\mathcal{D}} \downarrow \omega$. Canonical logic programs, but not constraint logic programs, were first studied in [Jaffar and Stuckey, 1986] which showed that every logic program is equivalent (wrt the success and finite failure sets) to a canonical logic program. The proof here was not constructive, but subsequently, [Wallace, 1989] provided an algorithm to generate the canonical logic program[12]. Like many other kinds of results in traditional logic programming, these results are likely to extend to CLP in a straightforward way.

5   Top-down execution

The phrase "top-down execution" covers a multitude of operational models. We will present a fairly general framework for operational semantics in which we can describe the operational semantics of some major CLP systems.

We will present the operational semantics as a transition system on *states*: tuples $\langle A, C, S \rangle$ where A is a multiset of atoms and constraints, and C and S are multisets of constraints. The constraints C and S are referred to as the *constraint store* and, in implementations, are acted upon by a constraint solver. Intuitively, A is a collection of as-yet-unseen atoms and constraints, C is the collection of constraints which are playing an *active* role (or are *awake*), and S is a collection of constraints playing a *passive* role (or are *asleep*). There is one other state, denoted by *fail*. To express more details of an operational semantics, it can be necessary to represent the collections of atoms and constraints more precisely. For example, to express the left-to-right Prolog execution order we might use a sequence of atoms rather than a multiset. However, we will not be concerned with such details here.

We will assume as given a *computation rule* which selects a transition type and an appropriate element of A (if necessary) for each state[13]. The transition system is also parameterized by a predicate *consistent* and a function *infer*, which we will discuss later. An initial goal G for execution is represented as a state by $\langle G, \emptyset, \emptyset \rangle$.

The transitions in the transition system are:

$$\langle A \cup a, C, S \rangle \rightarrow_r \langle A \cup B, C, S \cup (a = h) \rangle$$

if a is selected by the computation rule, a is an atom, $h \leftarrow B$ is a rule of P, renamed to new variables, and h and a have the same predicate symbol. The expression $a = h$ is an abbreviation for the conjunction of equations

---

[12]This proof was performed in the more general class of logic programs with negation.

[13]A computation rule is a convenient fiction that abstracts some of the behavior of a CLP system. To be realistic, a computation rule should also depend on factors other than the state (for example, the history of the computation). We ignore these possibilities for simplicity.

between corresponding arguments of a and h. We say a is *rewritten* in this transition.

$$\langle A \cup a, C, S \rangle \rightarrow_r fail$$

if a is selected by the computation rule, a is an atom and, for every rule $h \leftarrow B$ of P, h and a have different predicate symbols.

$$\langle A \cup c, C, S \rangle \rightarrow_c \langle A, C, S \cup c \rangle$$

if c is selected by the computation rule and c is a constraint.

$$\langle A, C, S \rangle \rightarrow_i \langle A, C', S' \rangle$$

if $(C', S') = infer(C, S)$.

$$\langle A, C, S \rangle \rightarrow_s \langle A, C, S \rangle$$

if $consistent(C)$.

$$\langle A, C, S \rangle \rightarrow_s fail$$

if $\neg consistent(C)$.

The $\rightarrow_r$ transitions arise from resolution, $\rightarrow_c$ transitions introduce constraints into the constraint solver, $\rightarrow_s$ transitions test whether the active constraints are consistent, and $\rightarrow_i$ transitions infer more active constraints (and perhaps modify the passive constraints) from the current collection of constraints. We write $\rightarrow$ to refer to a transition of arbitrary type.

The predicate $consistent(C)$ expresses a test for consistency of C. Usually it is defined by: $consistent(C)$ iff $\mathcal{D} \models \tilde{\exists}\, C$, that is, a complete consistency test. However, systems may employ a conservative but incomplete (or partial) test: if $\mathcal{D} \models \tilde{\exists}\, C$ then $consistent(C)$ holds, but sometimes $consistent(C)$ holds although $\mathcal{D} \models \neg\tilde{\exists}\, C$. One example of such a system is CAL [Aiba *et al.*, 1988] which computes over the domain of real numbers, but tests consistency over the domain of complex numbers.

The function $infer(C, S)$ computes from the current sets of constraints a new set of active constraints C' and passive constraints S'. Generally it can be understood as abstracting from S (or relaxing S) in the presence of C to obtain more active constraints. These are added to C to form C', and S is simplified to S'. We require that $\mathcal{D} \models (C \wedge S) \leftrightarrow (C' \wedge S')$, so that information is neither lost nor "guessed" by $infer$. The role that $infer$ plays varies widely from system to system. In Prolog, there are no passive constraints and we can define $infer(C, S) = (C \cup S, \emptyset)$. In CLP($\mathcal{R}$), non-linear constraints are passive, and $infer$ simply passes (the linearized version of) a constraint from S to C' when the constraint becomes linear in the context of C, and deletes the constraint from S. For example, if S

is $x * y = z \wedge z * y = 2$ and C is $x = 4 \wedge z \leq 0$ then $infer(C, S) = (C', S')$ where C' is $x = 4 \wedge z \leq 0 \wedge 4y = z$ and S' is $z * y = 2$.

In a language like CHIP, $infer$ performs less obvious inferences. For example, if S is $x = y + 1$ and C is $2 \leq x \leq 5 \wedge 0 \leq y \leq 3$ then $infer(C, S) = (C', S')$ where C' is $2 \leq x \leq 4 \wedge 1 \leq y \leq 3$ and $S' = S$. (Note that we could also formulate the finite domain constraint solving of CHIP as having no passive constraints, but having an incomplete test for consistency. However the formulation we give seems to reflect the systems more closely.) Similarly, in languages employing interval arithmetic over the real numbers (such as BNR-Prolog) intervals are active constraints and other constraints are passive. In this case, $infer$ repeatedly computes smaller intervals for each of the variables, based on the constraints in S, terminating when no smaller interval can be derived (modulo the precision of the arithmetic). Execution of language constructs such as the cardinality operator [van Hentenryck and Deville, 1991a], "constructive disjunction" [van Hentenryck et al., 1993] and special-purpose constructs (for example, in [Dincbas et al., 1988b; Aggoun and Beldiceanu, 1992]) can also be understood as $\rightarrow_i$ transitions, where these constructs are viewed as part of the language of constraints.

Generally, the active constraints are determined syntactically. As examples, in Prolog all equations are active, in $CLP(\mathcal{R})$ all linear constraints are active, on the finite domains of CHIP all unary constraints (i.e. constraints on just one variable, such as $x < 9$ or $x \neq 0$) are active, and in the interval arithmetic of BNR-Prolog only intervals are active.

The stronger the collection of active constraints, the earlier failure will be detected, and the less searching is necessary. With this in mind, we might wish $infer$ to be as strong as possible: for every active constraint c, if $infer(C, S) = (C', S')$ and $\mathcal{D} \models (C \wedge S) \rightarrow c$, then $\mathcal{D} \models C' \rightarrow c$. However, this is not always possible[14]. Even if it were possible, it is generally not preferred, since the computational cost of a powerful $infer$ function can be greater than the savings achieved by limiting search.

A *CLP system* is determined by the constraint domain and a detailed operational semantics. The latter involves a computation rule and definitions for *consistent* and *infer*. We now define some significant properties of CLP systems. We distinguish the class of systems in which passive constraints play no role and the global consistency test is complete. These systems correspond to the systems treated in [Jaffar and Lassez, 1986; Jaffar and Lassez, 1987].

Definition 5.0.1. Let $\rightarrow_{ris} = \rightarrow_r \rightarrow_i \rightarrow_s$ and $\rightarrow_{cis} = \rightarrow_c \rightarrow_i \rightarrow_s$. We say that

---

[14] For example, in $CLP(\mathcal{R})$, where linear constraints are active and non-linear constraints are passive, if S is $y = x * x$ then we can take c to be $y \geq 2kx - k^2$, for any k. There is no finite collection C' of active constraints which implies all these constraints and is not stronger than S.

a CLP system is *quick-checking* if its operational semantics can be described by $\rightarrow_{ris}$ and $\rightarrow_{cis}$. A CLP system is *progressive* if, for every state with a nonempty collection of atoms, every derivation from that state either fails, contains a $\rightarrow_r$ transition or contains a $\rightarrow_c$ transition. A CLP system is *ideal* if it is quick-checking, progressive, $infer$ is defined by $infer(C,S) = (C \cup S, \emptyset)$, and $consistent(C)$ holds iff $\mathcal{D} \models \tilde{\exists}\, C$.

In a quick-checking system, inference of new active constraints is performed and a test for consistency is made each time the collection of constraints in the constraint solver is changed. Thus, within the limits of *consistent* and *infer*, it finds inconsistency as soon as possible. A progressive system will never infinitely ignore the collection of atoms and constraints in the first part of a state during execution. All major implemented CLP systems are quick-checking and progressive, but most are not ideal.

A *derivation* is a sequence of transitions $\langle A_1, C_1, S_1 \rangle \rightarrow \cdots \rightarrow \langle A_i, C_i, S_i \rangle \rightarrow \cdots$. A state which cannot be rewritten further is called a *final state*. A derivation is *successful* if it is finite and the final state has the form $\langle \emptyset, C, S \rangle$. Let G be a goal with free variables $\tilde{x}$, which initiates a derivation and produces a final state $\langle \emptyset, C, S \rangle$. Then $\exists_{-\tilde{x}}\, C \wedge S$ is called the *answer constraint* of the derivation.

A derivation is *failed* if it is finite and the final state is *fail*. A derivation is *fair* if it is failed or, for every i and every $a \in A_i$, a is rewritten in a later transition. A computation rule is *fair* if it gives rise only to fair derivations. A goal G is *finitely failed* if, for any one fair computation rule, every derivation from G in an ideal CLP system is failed. It can be shown that if a goal is finitely failed then every fair derivation in an ideal CLP system is failed. A derivation *flounders* if it is finite and the final state has the form $\langle A, C, S \rangle$ where $A \neq \emptyset$.

The *computation tree* of a goal G for a program P in a CLP system is a tree with nodes labelled by states and edges labelled by $\rightarrow_r$, $\rightarrow_c$, $\rightarrow_i$ or $\rightarrow_s$ such that: the root is labelled by $\langle G, \emptyset, \emptyset \rangle$; for every node, all outgoing edges have the same label; if a node labelled by a state S has an outgoing edge labelled by $\rightarrow_c$, $\rightarrow_i$ or $\rightarrow_s$ then the node has exactly one child, and the state labelling that child can be obtained from S via a transition $\rightarrow_c$, $\rightarrow_i$ or $\rightarrow_s$ respectively; if a node labelled by a state S has an outgoing edge labelled by $\rightarrow_r$ then the node has a child for each rule in P, and the state labelling each child is the state obtained from S by the $\rightarrow_r$ transition for that rule; for each $\rightarrow_r$ and $\rightarrow_c$ edge, the corresponding transition uses the atom or constraint selected by the computation rule.

Every branch of a computation tree is a derivation, and, given a computation rule, every derivation following that rule is a branch of the corresponding computation tree. Different computation rules can give rise to computation trees of radically different sizes. Existing CLP languages use computation rules based on the Prolog left-to-right computation rule (which is not fair). We will discuss linguistic features intended to improve on this rule in Section 9.1.

The problem of finding answers to a query can be seen as the problem of searching a computation tree. Most CLP languages employ a depth-first search with chronological backtracking, as in Prolog (although there have been suggestions to use dependency-directed backtracking [De Backer and Beringer, 1991]). Since depth-first search is incomplete on infinite trees, not all answers are computed. The depth-first search can be incorporated in the semantics in the same way as is done for Prolog (see, for example, [Baudinet, 1988; Barbuti *et al.*, 1992]), but we will not go into details here. In Section 8 we will discuss a class of CLP languages which use a top-down execution similar to the one outlined above, but do not use backtracking.

Consider the transition

$$\langle A, C, S \rangle \to_g \langle A, C', \emptyset \rangle$$

where C' is a set of equations in $\mathcal{L}^*$ such that $\mathcal{D} \models C' \to (C \wedge S)$ and, for every variable x occurring in C or S, C' contains an equation $x = d$ for some constant d. Thus $\to_g$ grounds all variables in the constraint solver. We also have the transitions

$$\langle A, C, S \rangle \to_g fail$$

if no such C' exists (i.e. $C \wedge S$ is unsatisfiable in $\mathcal{D}$). A *ground derivation* is a derivation composed of $\to_r \to_g$ and $\to_c \to_g$.

We now define three sets that crystallize three aspects of the operational semantics. The success set $SS(P)$ collects the answer constraints to simple goals $p(\tilde{x})$. The finite failure set $FF(P)$ collects the set of simple goals which are finitely failed. The ground finite failure set $GFF(P)$ collects the set of grounded atoms, all of whose fair ground derivations are failed.

$SS(P) = \{p(\tilde{x}) \leftarrow c \mid \langle p(\tilde{x}), \emptyset, \emptyset \rangle \to^* \langle \emptyset, c', c'' \rangle, \ \mathcal{D} \models c \leftrightarrow \exists_{-\tilde{x}} c' \wedge c''\}$.
$FF(P) = \{p(\tilde{x}) \leftarrow c \mid \text{for every fair derivation, } \langle p(\tilde{x}), c, \emptyset \rangle \to^* fail\}$.
$GFF(P) = \{p(\tilde{d}) \mid \text{for every fair ground derivation, } \langle p(\tilde{d}), \emptyset, \emptyset \rangle \to^* fail\}$.

6 Soundness and completeness results

We now present the main relationships between the declarative semantics and the top-down operational semantics. To keep things simple, we consider only ideal CLP systems. However many of the results hold much more generally. The soundness results hold for any CLP system, because of restrictions we place on *consistent* and *infer*. Completeness results for successful derivations require only that the CLP system be progressive.

Theorem 6.0.1. *Consider a program P in the CLP language determined* *by a 4-tuple $(\Sigma, \mathcal{D}, \mathcal{L}, T)$ where $\mathcal{D}$ and T correspond on $\mathcal{L}$, and executing on an ideal CLP system. Then:*

1. $SS(P) = lfp(S_P^{\mathcal{D}})$ and $[SS(P)]_{\mathcal{D}} = lm(P, \mathcal{D})$.
2. If the goal G has a successful derivation with answer constraint c, then $P, T \models c \rightarrow G$.
3. Suppose T is satisfaction complete wrt $\mathcal{L}$. If G has a finite computation tree, with answer constraints $c_1, \ldots, c_n$, then $P^*, T \models G \leftrightarrow c_1 \vee \cdots \vee c_n$.
4. If $P, T \models c \rightarrow G$ then there are derivations for the goal G with answer constraints $c_1, \ldots, c_n$ such that $T \models c \rightarrow \bigvee_{i=1}^n c_i$. If, in addition, $(\mathcal{D}, \mathcal{L})$ has independence of negated constraints then the result holds for $n = 1$ (i.e. without disjunction).
5. Suppose T is satisfaction complete wrt $\mathcal{L}$. If $P^*, T \models G \leftrightarrow c_1 \vee \cdots \vee c_n$ then G has a computation tree with answer constraints $c_1', \ldots, c_m'$ (and possibly others) such that $T \models c_1 \vee \cdots \vee c_n \leftrightarrow c_1' \vee \cdots \vee c_m'$.
6. Suppose T is satisfaction complete wrt $\mathcal{L}$.
   The goal G is finitely failed for P iff $P^*, T \models \neg G$.
7. $gm(P^*, \mathcal{D}) = \mathcal{B}_{\mathcal{D}} - GFF(P)$.
8. Suppose $(\mathcal{D}, \mathcal{L})$ is solution compact. $T_P^{\mathcal{D}} \downarrow \omega = \mathcal{B}_{\mathcal{D}} - [FF(P)]_{\mathcal{D}}$.
9. Suppose $(\mathcal{D}, \mathcal{L})$ is solution compact.
   P is $(\mathcal{D}, \mathcal{L})$-canonical iff $[FF(P)]_{\mathcal{D}} = [\{h \leftarrow c \mid P^*, \mathcal{D} \models \neg(h \wedge c)\}]_{\mathcal{D}}$.

Most of these results are from [Jaffar and Lassez, 1986; Jaffar and Lassez, 1987], but there are also some from [Gabbrielli and Levi, 1991; Maher, 1987; Maher, 1993b]. Results 8 and 9 of the above theorem (which are equivalent) are the only results, of those listed above, which require solution compactness. In fact, the properties shown are equivalent to SC_2, the second condition of solution compactness [Maher, 1993b]; as mentioned earlier, SC_1 is not needed. In soundness results (2, 3 and half of 6), T can be replaced by $\mathcal{D}$. If we omit our assumption of a first-order language of constraints (see Section 2) then only results 1, 2, 3, 7, 8, 9 and the soundness half of 6 (replacing T by $\mathcal{D}$ where necessary) continue to hold.

The strong form of completeness of successful derivations (result 4) [Maher, 1987] provides an interesting departure from the conventional logic programming theory. It shows that in CLP it is necessary, in general, to consider and combine several successful derivations and their answers to establish that $c \rightarrow G$ holds, whereas only one successful derivation is necessary in standard logic programming. The other results in this theorem are more direct liftings of results in the logic programming theory.

The CLP Scheme provides a framework in which the lifting of results from LP to CLP is almost trivial. By replacing the Herbrand universe by an arbitrary constraint domain $\mathcal{D}$, unifiability by constraint satisfaction, Clark's equality theory by a corresponding satisfaction-complete theory, etc., most results (and even their proofs) lift from LP to CLP. The lifting is discussed in greater detail in [Maher, 1993b]. Furthermore, most operational aspects of LP (and Prolog) can be interpreted as logical operations, and consequently these operations (although not their implementations) also lift to CLP. One early example is matching, which is used in various LP systems (e.g. GHC, NU-Prolog) as a basis for affecting the computation rule; the corresponding operation in CLP is constraint entailment [Maher, 1987].

The philosophy of the CLP Scheme [Jaffar and Lassez, 1987] gives primacy to the structure $\mathcal{D}$ over which computation is performed, and less prominence to the theory $\mathcal{T}$. We have followed this approach. However, it is also possible to start with a satisfaction complete theory $\mathcal{T}$ (see, for example [Maher, 1987]) without reference to a structure. We can arbitrarily choose a model of $\mathcal{T}$ as the structure $\mathcal{D}$ and the same results apply. Another variation [Höhfeld and Smolka, 1988] considers a collection **D** of structures and defines *consistent*(C) to hold iff for some structure $\mathcal{D} \in \mathbf{D}$ we have $\mathcal{D} \models \bar{\exists}\, C$. Weaker forms of the soundness and completeness of successful derivations apply in this case.

7 Bottom-up execution

Bottom-up execution has its main use in database applications. The set-at-a-time processing limits the number of accesses to secondary storage in comparison to tuple-at-a-time processing (as in top-down execution), and the simple semantics gives great scope for query optimization.

Bottom-up execution is also formalized as a transition system. For every rule r of the form $h \leftarrow c, b_1, \ldots, b_n$ in P and every set A of facts there is a transition

$$A \rightsquigarrow A \cup \{h \leftarrow c' \mid a_i \leftarrow c_i, i = 1, \ldots, n \text{ are elements of}$$
$$A, \mathcal{D} \models c' \leftrightarrow c \wedge \bigwedge_{i=1}^n c_i \wedge b_i = a_i\}$$

In brief, then, we have $A \rightsquigarrow A \cup S_r^{\mathcal{D}}(A)$, for every set A and every rule r in P ($S_P^{\mathcal{D}}$ was defined in Section 4). An execution is a sequence of transitions. It is *fair* if each rule is applied infinitely often. The limit of ground instances of sets generated by fair executions is independent of the order in which transitions are applied, and is regarded as the result of the bottom-up execution. If Q is an initial set of facts and P is a program, and A is the result of a fair bottom-up execution then $A = SS(P \cup Q) = \langle\!\langle P \rangle\!\rangle(Q)$ and $[\![P]\!]([Q]_\mathcal{D}) = [A]_\mathcal{D}$.

An execution $Q = X_0 \rightsquigarrow X_1 \rightsquigarrow \cdots X_i \rightsquigarrow \cdots$ *terminates* if, for some m and every $i > m$, $X_i = X_m$. We say P is *finitary* if for every finite initial set of facts Q and every fair execution, there is a k such that $[X_i]_\mathcal{D} = [X_k]_\mathcal{D}$ for all $i \geq k$. However, execution can be non-terminating, even when the program is finitary and the initial set is finite.

Example 7.0.1. Consider the following program P on the constraint domain $\Re_{Lin}$:

```
p(X+1) ← p(X)
p(X) ← X ≥ 5
p(X) ← X ≤ 5
```

Straightforward bottom-up computation gives $\{p(x) \leftarrow x \geq 5, p(x) \leftarrow x \geq 6, p(x) \leftarrow x \geq 7, \ldots\} \cup \{p(x) \leftarrow x \leq 5, p(x) \leftarrow x \leq 6, p(x) \leftarrow x \leq 7, \ldots\}$, and does not terminate. We also have $lfp(T_P^{\mathcal{D}}) = T_P^{\mathcal{D}} \uparrow 1 = \{p(d) \mid d \in \Re\}$.

A necessary technique is to test whether a new fact is subsumed by the current set of facts, and accumulate only unsubsumed facts. A fact $p(\tilde{x}) \leftarrow c$ is *subsumed* by the facts $p(\tilde{x}) \leftarrow c_i, i = 1, \ldots, n$ (with respect to $(\mathcal{D}, \mathcal{L})$) if $\mathcal{D} \models c \rightarrow \bigvee_{i=1}^{n} c_i$. The transitions in the modified bottom-up execution model are

$$A \rightsquigarrow A \cup reduce(S_P^{\mathcal{D}}(A), A)$$

where $reduce(X, Y)$ eliminates from X all elements subsumed by Y. Under this execution model every finitary program terminates on every finite initial set Q.

Unfortunately, checking subsumption is computationally expensive, in general. If the constraint domain $(\mathcal{D}, \mathcal{L})$ does not satisfy the independence of negated constraints then the problem of showing that a new fact is not subsumed is at least NP-hard (see [Srivastava, 1993] for the proof in one constraint domain). In constraint domains with independence of negated constraints the problem is not as bad: the new fact only needs to be checked against one fact at a time [Maher, 1993b]. (Classical database optimizations are also more difficult without independence of negated constraints [Klug, 1988; Maher, 1993b].) A pragmatic approach to the problem of subsumption in $\Re_{Lin}$ is given in [Srivastava, 1993]. Some work avoids the problem of subsumption by allowing only ground facts in the database and intermediate computations.

Even with subsumption, there is still the problem that execution might not terminate (for example, if P is not finitary). The approach of [Kanellakis *et al.*, 1990] is to restrict the constraint domains $\mathcal{D}$ to those which only permit the computation of finitely representable relations from finitely representable relations. This requirement is slightly weaker than requiring that all programs are finitary, but it is not clear that there is a practical difference. Regrettably, very few constraint domains satisfy this condition, and those which do have limited expressive power.

The alternative is to take advantage of P and a specific query (or a class of queries). A transformation technique such as magic templates [Ramakrishnan, 1991] produces a program P^{mg} that is equivalent to P for the specific query. Other techniques [Kemp *et al.*, 1989; Mumick *et al.*, 1990; Srivastava and Ramakrishnan, 1992; Kemp and Stuckey, 1993] attempt to further limit execution by placing constraints at appropriate points in the program. Analyses can be used to check that execution of the resulting program terminates [Krishnamurthy *et al.*, 1988; Sagiv and Vardi, 1989; Brodsky and Sagiv, 1991], although most work has ignored the capability of using constraints in the answers.

Comparatively little work has been done on the nuts and bolts of implementing bottom-up execution for CLP programs, with all the work addressing the constraint domain $\Re_{Lin}$. [Kanellakis *et al.*, 1990] suggested the use of intervals, computed as the projection of a collection of constraints, as the basis for indexing on constrained variables. Several different data structures, originally developed for spatial databases or computational geometry, have been proposed as appropriate for indexing [Kanellakis *et al.*, 1990; Srivastava, 1993; Brodsky *et al.*, 1993]. A new data structure was presented in [Kanellakis *et al.*, 1993] which minimizes accesses to secondary storage. A sort-join algorithm for joins on constrained variables is given in [Brodsky *et al.*, 1993]. That paper also provides a query optimization methodology for conjunctive queries that can balance the cost of constraint manipulation against the cost of traditional database operations.

8 Concurrent constraint logic programming

Concurrent programming languages are languages which allow the description of collections of processes which may interact with each other. In concurrent constraint logic programming (CCLP) languages, communication and synchronization are performed by asserting and testing for constraints. The operational semantics of these languages are quite similar to the top-down execution described in Section 5. However, the different context in which they are used results in a lesser importance of the corresponding logical semantics.

For this discussion we will consider only the flat ask–tell CCLP languages, which were defined in [Saraswat, 1988; Saraswat, 1989] based on ideas from [Maher, 1987]. We further restrict our attention to languages with only committed-choice nondeterminism (sometimes called don't-care nondeterminism); more general languages will be discussed in Section 9. For more details of CCLP languages, see [Saraswat, to appear: 2; de Boer and Palamidessi, 1993].

Just as Prolog can be viewed as a kind of CLP language, obtained by a particular choice of constraint domain, so most concurrent logic languages can be viewed as concurrent CLP languages[15].

A program rule takes the form

$$h \leftarrow ask \; : \; tell \mid B$$

---

[15]Concurrent Prolog [Shapiro, 1983a] is not an ask–tell language, but [Saraswat, 1988] shows how it can be fitted inside the CCLP framework.

where h is an atom, B is a collection of atoms, and *ask* and *tell* are constraints. Many treatments of concurrent constraint languages employ a language based on a process algebra involving ask and tell primitives [Saraswat, 1989], but we use the syntax above to emphasize the similarities to other CLP languages.

For the sake of brevity, we present a simpler transition system to describe the operational semantics than the transition system in Section 5. However, implemented languages can make the same pragmatic compromises on testing consistency (and implication) as reflected in that transition system. The states in this transition system have the form $\langle A, C \rangle$ where A is a collection of atoms and C is a collection of constraints. Any state can be an initial state. The transitions in the transition system are:

$$\langle A \cup a, C \rangle \rightarrow_r \langle A \cup B, C \cup (a = h) \cup ask \cup tell \rangle$$

if $h \leftarrow ask : tell \mid B$ is a rule of P renamed to new variables $\tilde{x}$, h and a have the same predicate symbol, $\mathcal{D} \models C \rightarrow \exists \tilde{x} \; a = h \wedge ask$ and $\mathcal{D} \models \tilde{\exists} \; C \wedge a = h \wedge ask \wedge tell$. Roughly speaking, a transition can occur with such a rule provided the accumulated constraints imply the ask constraint and do not contradict the tell constraint. Some languages use only the ask constraint for synchronization. It is shown in [de Boer and Palamidessi, 1991] that such languages are strictly less expressive than ask–tell languages.

An operational semantics such as the above is not completely faithful to a real execution of the language, since it is possible for two atoms to be rewritten simultaneously in an execution environment with concurrency. The above semantics only allows rewritings to be interleaved. A 'true concurrency' semantics, based on graph-rewriting, is given in [Montanari and Rossi, 1993].

All ask–tell CCLP programs have the following *monotonicity* [Saraswat *et al.*, 1988] or *stability* [Gaifman *et al.*, 1991] property: If $\langle A, C \rangle \rightarrow_r \langle A', C' \rangle$ and $\mathcal{D} \models C'' \rightarrow C'$ then $\langle A, C'' \rangle \rightarrow_r \langle A', C'' \rangle$. This property provides for simple solutions to some problems in distributed computing related to reliability. When looked at in a more general framework [Gaifman *et al.*, 1991], stability seems to be one advantage of CCLP languages over other languages; most programs in conventional languages for concurrency are not stable. It is interesting to note that a notion of global failure (as represented in Section 5 by the state $fail$) destroys stability. Of course, there are also pragmatic reasons for wanting to avoid this notion in a concurrent language. A framework which permits non-monotonic CCLP languages is discussed in [de Boer *et al.*, 1993].

A program is *determinate* if every reachable state is determinate, where a state is determinate if every selected atom gives rise to at most one $\rightarrow_r$ transition. Consequently, for every initial state, every fair derivation rewrites the same atoms with the same rules, or every derivation fails. Thus non-failed derivations by determinate programs from an initial state differ from each other only in the order of rewriting (and the renaming of rules). Substantial parts of many programs are determinate[16]. The interest in determinate programs arises from an elegant semantics for such programs based upon closure operators [Saraswat *et al.*, 1991]. For every collection of atoms A, the semantics of A is given by the function $\mathcal{P}_A(C) = \exists_{-\tilde{x}} C'$ where $\langle A, C \rangle \to_r^* \langle A', C' \rangle$, $\tilde{x}$ is the free variables of $\langle A, C \rangle$, and $\langle A', C' \rangle$ is a final state. This semantics is extended in [Saraswat *et al.*, 1991] to a compositional and fully abstract semantics of arbitrary programs. A semantics based on traces is given in [de Boer and Palamidessi, 1990].

For determinate programs we also have a clean application of the classical logical semantics of a program [Maher, 1987]. If $\langle A, C \rangle \to_r^* \langle A', C' \rangle$ then $P^*, \mathcal{D} \models A \wedge C \leftrightarrow \exists_{-\tilde{x}} A' \wedge C'$ where $\tilde{x}$ is the free variables of $\langle A, C \rangle$. In cases where execution can be guaranteed not to suspend any atom indefinitely, the soundness and completeness results for success and failure hold (see Section 6).

9 Linguistic extensions

We discuss in this section some additional linguistic features for top-down CLP languages.

9.1 Shrinking the computation tree

The aim of $\to_i$ transitions is to extract as much information as is reasonable from the passive constraints, so that the branching of $\to_r$ transitions is reduced. There are several other techniques, used or proposed, for achieving this result.

In [Le Provost and Wallace, 1993] it is suggested that information can also be extracted from the atoms in a state. The constraint extracted would be an approximation of the answers to the atom. This operation can be expressed by an additional transition rule:

$$\langle A \cup a, C, S \rangle \to_x \langle A \cup a, C, S \cup c \rangle$$

where $extract(a, C) = c$. Here $extract$ is a function satisfying $P^*, \mathcal{D} \models (a \wedge C) \to c$. The evaluation of $extract$, performed at run-time, involves an abstract (or approximate) execution of $\langle a, C, \emptyset \rangle$. For example, if P defines p with the facts $p(1, 2)$ and $p(3, 4)$ then the constraint extracted by $extract(p(x, y), \emptyset)$ might be $y = x + 1$.

---

[16]For the programs we consider, determinate programs can be characterized syntactically by the following condition: for every pair of rules (renamed apart, except for identical heads) $h \leftarrow ask_1 \ : \ tell_1 \mid B_1$ and $h \leftarrow ask_2 \ : \ tell_2 \mid B_2$ in the program, we have $\mathcal{D} \models \neg(ask_1 \wedge ask_2 \wedge tell_1)$ or $\mathcal{D} \models \neg(ask_1 \wedge ask_2 \wedge tell_2)$. In languages where procedures can be hidden (as in many process algebra formulations) or there is a restriction on the initial states, the class of determinate programs is larger but is not as easily characterized.

A more widespread technique is to modify the order in which atoms are selected. Most CLP systems employ the Prolog left-to-right computation rule. This improves the "programmability" by providing a predictable flow of control. However, when an appropriate flow of control is data-dependent or very complex (for example, in combinatorial search problems) greater flexibility is required.

One solution to this problem is to incorporate a data-dependent computation rule in the language. The Andorra principle [Warren, 1987] involves selecting determinate atoms, if possible. (A determinate atom is an atom which only gives rise to one $\rightarrow_{ris}$ transition.) A second approach is to allow the programmer to annotate parts of the program (atoms, predicates, clauses, ...) to provide a more flexible computation rule that is, nonetheless, programmed. This approach was pioneered in Prolog II [Colmerauer, 1982a] and MU-Prolog [Naish, 1986]. The automatic annotation of programs [Naish, 1985] brings this approach closer to the first. A third approach is to introduce constructs from concurrent logic programming into the language. There are basically two varieties of this approach: guarded rules and guarded atoms. The former introduces a committed-choice aspect into the language, whereas the latter is a variant of the second approach. All these approaches originated for conventional logic programs, but the ideas lift to constraint logic programs, and there are now several proposals based on these ideas [Janson and Haridi, 1991; Smolka, 1991; Aït-Kaci and Poldeski, 1993c; van Hentenryck and Deville, 1991b; van Hentenryck *et al.*, 1993].

One potential problem with using guarded rules is that the completeness of the operational semantics with respect to the logical semantics of the program can be lost. This incompleteness was shown to be avoided in ALPS [Maher, 1987] (modulo infinitely delayed atoms), but that work was heavily reliant on determinacy. Smolka [Smolka, 1991] discusses a language of guarded rules which extends ALPS and a methodology for extending a predicate definition with new guarded rules such that completeness can be retained, even though execution would involve indeterminate committed-choice. The Andorra Kernel Language (AKL) [Janson and Haridi, 1991] also combines the Andorra principle with guarded rules. There the interest is in providing a language which subsumes the expressive power of CCLP languages and CLP languages.

Guarded atoms and, more generally, guarded goals take the form $c \rightarrow G$ where c is a constraint[17] and G is a goal. G is available for execution only when c is implied by the current active constraints. We call c the *guard constraint* and G the *delayed goal*. Although the underlying mechanisms are very similar, guarded atoms and guarded rules differ substantially as linguistic features, since guarded atoms can be combined conjunctively

---

[17]We also permit the meta-level constraint $ground(x)$.

whereas guards in guarded rules are combined disjunctively.

9.2   Complex constraints

Several language constructs that can be said simply to be complex constraints have been added to CLP languages. We can classify them as follows: those which implement Boolean combinations of (generally simple) constraints and those which describe an *ad hoc*, often application-specific, relation. Falling into the first category are some implementations of constraint disjunction [van Hentenryck *et al.*, 1993; De Backer and Beringer, 1993] (sometimes called 'constructive disjunction') and the cardinality operator [van Hentenryck and Deville, 1991a]. Into the second category fall the *element* constraint [Dincbas *et al.*, 1988b], and the *cumulative* constraint of [Aggoun and Beldiceanu, 1992], among others. These constraints are already accounted for in the operational semantics of Section 5, since they can be considered passive constraints in $\mathcal{L}$. However, it also can be useful to view them as additions to a better-known constraint domain (indeed, this is how they arose).

The cardinality operator can be used to express any Boolean combination of constraints. A use of this combinator has the form $\#(L, [c_1, \ldots, c_n], U)$, where the c_i are constraints and L and U are variables. This use expresses that the number of constraints c_i that are true lies between the value of L and the value of U (lower and upper bound respectively). By constraining $L \geq 1$ the combinator represents the disjunction of the constraints; by constraining $U = 0$ the combinator represents the conjunction of the negations of the constraints. The cardinality combinator is implemented by testing whether the constraints are entailed by or are inconsistent with the constraint store, and comparing the numbers of entailed and inconsistent constraints with the values of L and U. When L and U are not ground, the cardinality constraint can produce a constraint on these variables. (For example, after one constraint is found to be inconsistent U can be constrained by $U \leq n - 1$.)

In constraint languages without disjunction, an intended disjunction $c_1(\tilde{x}) \vee c_2(\tilde{x})$ must be represented by a pair of clauses

$$p(\tilde{x}) \leftarrow c_1(\tilde{x})$$
$$p(\tilde{x}) \leftarrow c_2(\tilde{x})$$

In a simple CLP language this representation forces a choice to be made (between the two disjuncts). Constructive disjunction refers to the direct use of a disjunctive constraint without immediately making a choice. Instead an active constraint is computed which is a safe approximation to the disjunction in the context of the current constraint store C. In the constraint domain $\mathcal{FD}$, [van Hentenryck *et al.*, 1993] suggests two possible approximations, one based on approximating each constraint $C \wedge c_i$ using the domain of each variable and the other (less accurately) approximating each constraint using the interval constraints for each variable. The disjunction of these approximations is easily approximated by an active constraint. For linear arithmetic [De Backer and Beringer, 1993] suggests the use of the convex hull of the regions defined by the two constraints as the approximation. Note that the constructive disjunction behavior could be obtained from the clauses for p using the methods of [Le Provost and Wallace, 1993].

In the second category, we mention two constructs used with the finite domain solver of CHIP. $element(X, L, T)$ expresses that T is the X'th element in the list L. Operationally, it allows constraints on either the index X or element T of the list to be reflected by constraints on the other. For example, if X is constrained so that $X \in \{1, 3, 5\}$ then $element(X, [1, 1, 2, 3, 5, 8], T)$ can constrain T so that $T \in \{1, 2, 5\}$ and, similarly, if T is constrained so that $T \in \{1, 3, 5\}$ then X is constrained so that $X \in \{1, 2, 4, 5\}$. Declaratively, the *cumulative* constraint of [Aggoun and Beldiceanu, 1992] expresses a collection of linear inequalities on its arguments. Several problems that can be expressed as integer programming problems can be expressed with *cumulative*. Operationally, it behaves somewhat differently from the way CHIP would usually treat the inequalities.

9.3   User-defined constraints

Complex constraints are generally "built in" to the language. There are proposals to extend CLP languages to allow the user to define new constraints, together with inference rules specifying how the new constraints react with the constraint store.

A basic approach is to use guarded clauses. The new constraint predicate is defined with guarded clauses, where the guards specify the cases in which the constraint is to be simplified, and the body is an equivalent conjunction of constraints. Using $ground(x)$ (or a similar construct) as a guard constraint, it is straightforward to implement local propagation (i.e. propagation of ground values). We give an example of this use in Section 11.1, and [Saraswat, 1987] has other examples. Some more general forms of propagation can also be expressed with guarded clauses.

The work [Frühwirth and Hanschke, 1993] can be seen as an extension of this method. The new constraints occur as predicates, and guarded rules (called constraint handling rules) are used to simplify the new constraints. However, the guarded rules may have two (or more) atoms in the head. Execution matches the head with a collection of constraint atoms in the goal and reduces to an equivalent conjunction of constraints. This method appears able to express more powerful solving methods than the guarded clauses. For example, transitivity of the user-defined constraint *leq* can be specified by the rule

```
leq(X, Y), leq(Y, Z) ==> true | leq(X, Z).
```

whereas it is not clear how to express this in a one-atom-per-head guarded clause. A drawback of having multiple atoms, however, is inefficiency. In particular, it is not clear whether constraint handling rules can produce incremental (in the sense defined in Section 10.1) constraint solvers except in simple cases.

A different approach [van Hentenryck *et al.*, 1991] proposes the introduction of 'indexical' terms which refer to aspects of the *state* of the constraint solver (thus providing a limited form of reflection)[18]. Constraints containing these terms are called indexical constraints, and from these indexical constraints user-defined constraints are built. Specifically, [van Hentenryck *et al.*, 1991] discusses a language over finite domains which can access the current domain and upper and lower bounds on the value of a variable using the indexical terms $dom(X)$, $max(X)$ and $min(X)$ respectively. Indexical constraints have an operational semantics: each constraint defines a method of propagation. For example, the constraint Y *in* $0..max(X)$ continually enforces the upper bound of Y to be less than or equal to the upper bound of X. This same behavior can be obtained in a finite domain solver with the constraint $Y \leq X$, but the advantage of indexical constraints is that there is greater control over propagation: with $Y \leq X$ we also propagate changes in the lower bound of Y to X, whereas we can avoid this with indexical constraints. A discussion of an implementation of indexical constraints is given in [Diaz and Codognet, 1993]. (One application of this work is a constraint solver for Boolean constraints [Codognet and Diaz, 1993]; we describe this application in Section 13.5.)

9.4 Negation

Treatments of negation in logic programming lift readily to constraint logic programming, with only minor adjustments necessary. Indeed many of the semantics for programs with negation are essentially propositional, being based upon the collection of ground instances of program rules. The perfect model [Przymusinski, 1988; Apt *et al.*, 1988; van Gelder, 1988], well-founded model [van Gelder *et al.*, 1988], stable model [Gelfond and Lifschitz, 1988] and Fitting fixedpoint semantics [Fitting, 1986], to name but a few, fall into this category. The grounding of variables in CLP rules by all elements of the domain (i.e. by all terms in $\mathcal{L}^*$) and the deletion of all grounded rules whose constraints evaluate to false produces the desired propositional rules (see, for example, [Maher, 1993a]).

Other declarative semantics, based on Clark's completion P^* of the

---

[18]This approach has been called a 'glass-box' approach.

program, also extend to CLP[19]. The counterpart of *comp(P)* [Clark, 1978; Lloyd, 1987] is $\mathcal{T}, P^*$, where $\mathcal{T}$ is satisfaction complete. Interestingly, it is necessary to consider the complete theory $\mathcal{T}$ of the domain if the equivalence of three-valued logical consequences of $\mathcal{T}, P^*$ and consequences of finite iterations of Fitting's Φ operator (as shown by Kunen [Kunen, 1987]), continues to hold for CLP programs [Stuckey, 1991].

SLDNF-resolution and its variants are also relatively untouched by the lifting to CLP programs, although, of course, they must use a consistency test instead of unification. The other main modification is that groundness must be replaced by the concept of a variable being determined by the current constraints (see Section 2). For example, a safe computation rule [Lloyd, 1987] may select a non-ground negated atom provided all the variables in the atom are determined by the current collection of constraints. Similarly, the definition of an allowed rule [Lloyd, 1987] for a CLP program requires that every variable either appear in a positive literal in the body or be determined by the constraints in the body. With these modifications, various soundness and completeness results for SLDNF-resolution and *comp(P)* extend easily to ideal CLP systems. An alternative implementation of negation, constructive negation [Chan, 1988], has been expanded and applied to CLP programs by Stuckey [Stuckey, 1991], who gave the first completeness result for this method.

9.5   Preferred solutions

Often it is desirable to express an ordering (or preference) on solutions to a goal. This can provide a basis for computing only the 'best' solutions to the query. One approach is to adapt the approach of mathematical programming (operations research) and employ an objective function [van Hentenryck, 1989a; Maher and Stuckey, 1989]. An optimization primitive is added to the language to compute the optimal value of the objective function[20].

CHIP and cc($\mathcal{FD}$) have such primitives, but they have a non-logical behavior. Two recent papers [Fages, 1993; Marriott and Stuckey, 1993b] discuss optimization primitives based upon the following logical characterization:

m is the minimum value of $f(\tilde{x})$ such that $G(\tilde{x})$ holds iff

$$\exists \tilde{x}\ (G(\tilde{x}) \wedge f(\tilde{x}) = m) \wedge \neg \exists \tilde{y}\ (G(\tilde{y}) \wedge f(\tilde{y}) < m)$$

Optimization primitives can be implemented by a branch and bound approach, pruning the computation tree of G based on the current minimum. A similar behavior can be obtained through constructive negation, using

---

[19]For example, the extension to allow arbitrary first-order formulas in the bodies of rules [Lloyd and Topor, 1984].

[20]We discuss only minimization; maximization is similar.

the above logical formulation [Fages, 1993; Marriott and Stuckey, 1993b], although a special-purpose implementation is more efficient. [Marriott and Stuckey, 1993b] gives a completeness result for such an implementation, based on Kunen's semantics for negation.

A second approach is to admit constraints which are not required to be satisfied by a solution, but express a preference for solutions which do satisfy them. Such constraints are sometimes called *soft* constraints. The most developed use of this approach is in hierarchical constraint logic programming (HCLP) [Borning *et al.*, 1989; Wilson and Borning, 1993]. In HCLP, soft constraints have different strengths and the constraints accumulated during a derivation form a constraint hierarchy based on these strengths. There are many possible ways to compare solutions using these constraint hierarchies [Borning *et al.*, 1989; Maher and Stuckey, 1989; Wilson and Borning, 1993], different methods being suitable for different problems. The hierarchy dictates that any number of weak constraints can be over-ruled by a stronger constraint. Thus, for example, default behavior can be expressed in a program by weak constraints, which will be over-ruled by stronger constraints when non-default behavior is required. The restriction to best solutions of a constraint hierarchy can be viewed as a form of circumscription [Satoh and Aiba, 1993].

Each of the above approaches has some programming advantages over the other, in certain applications, but both have problems as general-purpose methods. While the first approach works well when there is a natural choice of objective function suggested by the problem, in general there is no natural choice. The second approach provides a higher-level expression of preference but it cannot be so easily 'fine-tuned' and it can produce an exponential number of best answers if not used carefully. The approaches have the advantages and disadvantages of explicit (respectively, implicit) representations of preference. In the first approach, it can be difficult to reflect intended preferences. In the second approach it is easier to reflect intended preferences, but harder to detect inconsistency in these preferences. It is also possible to 'weight' soft constraints, which provides a combination of both approaches.

Implementation issues

The main innovation required to implement a CLP system is clearly in the manipulation of constraints. Thus the main focus in this part of the survey is on constraint solver operations, described in Section 10. Section 11 then considers the problem of extending the LP inference engine to deal with constraints. Here the discussion is not tied down to a particular constraint domain.

It is important to note that the algorithms and data structures in this part are presented in view of their use in top-down systems and, in particular, systems with backtracking. At the present, there is little experience in implementing bottom-up CLP systems, and so we do not discuss them here. However, some of the algorithms we discuss can be used, perhaps with modification, in bottom-up systems.

10 Algorithms for constraint solving

In view of the operational semantics presented in part I, there are several operations involving constraints to be implemented. These include: a satisfiability test, to implement *consistent* and *infer*; an entailment test, to implement guarded goals; and the projection of the constraint store onto a set of variables, to compute the answer constraint from a final state. The constraint solver must also be able to undo the effects of adding constraints when the inference engine backtracks. In this section we discuss the core efficiency issues in the implementation of these operations.

10.1 Incrementality

According to the folklore of CLP, algorithms for CLP implementations must be *incremental* in order to be practical. However, this prescription is not totally satisfactory, since the term incremental can be used in two different senses. On one hand, incrementality is used to refer to the *nature* of the algorithm. That is, an algorithm is incremental if it accumulates an internal state and a new input is processed in combination with the internal state. Such algorithms are sometimes called *on-line* algorithms. On the other hand, incrementality is sometimes used to refer to the *performance* of the algorithm. This section serves to clarify the latter notion of incrementality as a prelude to our discussion of algorithms in the following subsections. We do not, however, offer a formal definition of incrementality.

We begin by abstracting away the inference engine from the operational semantics, to leave simply the constraint solver and its operations. We consider the state of the constraint solver to consist of the constraint store C, a collection of constraints G that are to be entailed, and some backtrack points. In the initial state, denoted by $\emptyset$, there are no constraints nor backtrack points. The constraint solver reacts to a sequence of operations, and results in (a) a new state, and (b) a response.

Recall that the operations in CLP languages are:

- augment C with c to obtain a new store, determine whether the new store is satisfiable, and if so, determine which constraints in G are implied by the new store;
- add a new constraint to G;
- set a backtrack point (and associate with it the current state of the system);
- backtrack to the previous backtrack point (i.e. return the state of the system to that associated with the backtrack point);
- project C onto a fixed set of variables.

Only the first and last of these operations can produce a response from the constraint solver.

Consider the application of a sequence of operations $o_1, \ldots, o_k$ on a state Δ; denote the updated state by $\mathcal{F}(\Delta, o_1 \ldots o_k)$, and the sequence of responses to the operations by $\mathcal{G}(o_1 \ldots o_k)$. In what follows we shall be concerned with the average cost of computing $\mathcal{F}$ and $\mathcal{G}$. Using standard definitions, this cost is parameterized by the distribution of (sequences of) operations (see, for example, [Vitter and Flajolet, 1990]). We use average cost assuming the true distribution, the distribution that reflects what occurs in practice. Even though this distribution is almost always not known, we often have some hypotheses about it. For example, one can identify typical and often occurring operation sequences and hence can approximate the true distribution accordingly. The informal definitions below therefore are intended to be a guide, as opposed to a formal tool for cost analysis.

For an expression $exp(\tilde{o})$ denoting a function of $\tilde{o}$, define $AV[exp(\tilde{o})]$ to be the average value of $exp(\tilde{o})$, over all sequences of operations $\tilde{o}$. Note that the definition of average here is also dependent on the distribution of the $\tilde{o}$. For example, let $cost(\tilde{o})$ denote the cost of computing $\mathcal{F}(\emptyset, \tilde{o})$ by some algorithm, for *each* fixed sequence $\tilde{o}$. Then $AV[cost(\tilde{o})]$ denotes the average cost of computing $\mathcal{F}(\emptyset, \tilde{o})$ over *all* $\tilde{o}$.

Let Δ be shorthand for $\mathcal{F}(\emptyset, o_1 \ldots o_{k-1})$. Let A denote an algorithm which applies a sequence of operations on the initial state, giving the same response as does the constraint solver, but not necessarily computing the new state. That is, A is the batch (or off-line) version of our constraint solver. In what follows we discuss what it means for an algorithm to be incremental relative to some algorithm A. Intuitively A represents the best available batch algorithm for the operations.

At one extreme, we consider that an algorithm for $\mathcal{F}$ and $\mathcal{G}$ is 'non-incremental' relative to A if the average cost of applying an extra operation o_k to Δ is no better than the cost of the straightforward approach using A on $o_1 \ldots o_k$. We express this as

$$AV[cost(\Delta, o_k)] \geq AV[cost_A(o_1 \ldots o_k)].$$

At the other extreme, we consider that an algorithm for $\mathcal{F}$ and $\mathcal{G}$ is 'perfectly incremental', relative to A, if its cost is no worse than that of A. In other words, no cost is incurred for the incremental nature of the algorithm. We express this as

$$AV[cost(\emptyset, o_1 \ldots o_{k-1}) + cost(\Delta, o_k)] \leq AV[cost_A(o_1 \ldots o_k)].$$

In general, any algorithm lies somewhere in between these two extremes. For example, it will not be perfectly incremental as indicated by the cost formula above, but instead we have

$$AV\left[cost(\emptyset, o_1 \ldots o_{k-1}) + cost(\Delta, o_k)\right] = AV\left[cost_A(o_1 \ldots o_k)\right] + extra\_cost(o_1 \ldots o_k)$$

where the additional term $extra\_cost(o_1 \ldots o_k)$ denotes the extra cost incurred by the on-line algorithm over the best batch algorithm. Therefore, one possible "definition" of an incremental algorithm, good enough for use in a CLP system, is simply that its $extra\_cost$ factor is negligible.

In what follows, we shall tacitly bear in mind this expression to obtain a rough definition of incrementality[21]. Although we have defined incrementality for a collection of operations, we will review the operations individually, and discuss incrementality in isolation. This can sometimes be an oversimplification; for example, [Mannila and Ukkonen, 1986] has shown that the standard unification problem does not remain linear when backtracking is considered. In general, however, it is simply too complex, in a survey article, to do otherwise.

10.2 Satisfiability (non-incremental)

We consider first the basic problem of determining satisfiability of constraints independent of the requirement for incrementality. As we will see in the brief tour below of our sample domains, the dominant criterion used by system implementers is not the worst-case time complexity of the algorithm.

For the domain $\mathcal{FT}$, linear time algorithms are known [Paterson and Wegman, 1978], and for $\mathcal{RT}$, the best-known algorithms are almost linear time [Jaffar, 1984]. Even so, most Prolog systems implement an algorithm for the latter[22] because the *best*-case complexity of unification in $\mathcal{FT}$ is also linear, whereas it is often the case that unification in $\mathcal{RT}$ can be done without inspecting all parts of the terms being unified. Hence in practice Prolog systems are really implementations of CLP($\mathcal{RT}$) rather than CLP($\mathcal{FT}$). In fact, many Prolog systems choose to use straightforward algorithms which are slower, in the worst case, than these almost linear time algorithms. The reason for this choice (of algorithms which are quadratic time or slower in the worst case) is the belief that these algorithms are faster on average [Albert *et al.*, 1993].

For the arithmetic domain of $\Re_{LinEqn}$, the most straightforward algorithm is based on Gaussian elimination, and this has quadratic worst-case

---

[21]There are similar notions found in the (non-CLP) literature; see the bibliography [Ramalingam and Reps, 1993].

[22]This is often realized simply by omitting the 'occur-check' operation from a standard unification algorithm for $\mathcal{FT}$. Some Prolog systems perform such an omission naively, and thus obtain an incomplete algorithm which may not terminate in certain cases. These cases are considered pathological and hence are ignored. Other systems guarantee termination at slightly higher cost, but enjoy the new feature of cyclic data structures.

complexity. For the more general domain $\Re_{Lin}$, polynomial time algorithms are also known [Khachian, 1979], but these algorithms are not used in practical CLP systems. Instead, the Simplex algorithm (see eg. [Chvàtal, 1983]), despite its exponential time worst case complexity [Klee and Minty, 1972], is used as a basis for the algorithm. However, since the Simplex algorithm works over non-negative numbers and non-strict inequalities, it must be extended for use in CLP systems. While such an extension is straightforward in principle, implementations must be carefully engineered to avoid significant overhead. The main differences between the Simplex-based solvers in CLP systems is in the specific realization of this basic algorithm. For example, the $CLP(\mathcal{R})$ system uses a floating-point representation of numbers, whereas the solvers of CHIP and Prolog III use exact precision rational number arithmetic. As another example, in the $CLP(\mathcal{R})$ system a major design decision was to separately deal with equations and inequalities, enjoying a faster (Gaussian-elimination based) algorithm for equations, but enduring a cost for communication between the two kinds of algorithms [Jaffar *et al.*, 1992a]. Some elements of the CHIP solver are described in [van Hentenryck and Graf, 1991]. Disequality constraints can be handled using entailment of the corresponding equation (discussed in Section 10.4) since an independence of negative constraints holds [Lassez and McAloon, 1992].

For the domain of word equations $\mathcal{WE}$, an algorithm is known [Makanin, 1977] but no efficient algorithm is known. In fact, the general problem, though easily provable to be NP-hard, is not known to be in NP. The most efficient algorithm known still has the basic structure of the Makanin algorithm but uses a far better bound for termination [Koscielski and Pacholski, 1992]. Systems using word equations, Prolog III for example, thus resort to partial constraint solving using a standard delay technique on the lengths of word variables. Rajasekar's 'string logic programs' [Rajasekaar, 1993] also uses a partial solution of word equations. First, solutions are found for equations over the lengths of the word variables appearing in the constraint; only then is the word equation solved.

As with word equations, the satisfiability problem in finite domains such as $\mathcal{FD}$ is almost always NP-hard. Partial constraint solving is once again required, and here is a typical approach. Attach to each variable x a data structure representing $dom(x)$, its current possible values[23]. Clearly $dom(x)$ should be a superset of the projection space w.r.t. x. Define $min(x)$ and $max(x)$ to be the smallest and largest numbers in $dom(x)$ respectively. Now, assume that every constraint is written in so that each inequality is of the form $x < y$ or $x \leq y$, each disequality is of the form $x \neq y$, and each equation is of the form $x = n$, $x = y$, $x = y + z$, where x, y, z are variables

---

[23]The choice of such a data structure should depend on the size of the finite domains. For example, with small domains a characteristic vector is appropriate.

and n a number. Clearly every constraint in $\mathcal{FD}$ can be rewritten into a conjunction of these constraints.

The algorithm considers one constraint at a time and has two main phases. First, it performs an action which is determined by the form of the constraint: (a) for constraints $x \leq y$, ensure that $min(x) \leq max(y)$ by modifying $dom(x)$ and/or $dom(y)$ appropriately[24]; (b) for $x < y$, ensure that $min(x) < max(y)$; (c) for $x \neq y$, consider three subcases: if $dom(x) \cap dom(y) = \emptyset$ then the constraint reduces to *true*; otherwise, if $dom(x) = \{n\}$, then remove n from $dom(y)$ (and similarly for the case when $dom(y)$ is a singleton[25]); otherwise, nothing more need be done; (d) for $x = n$, simple make $dom(x) = \{n\}$; (e) for $x = y$, make $dom(x) = dom(y) = dom(x) \cap dom(y)$; (f) for $x = y + z$, ensure that $max(x) \geq min(y) + min(z)$ and $min(x) \leq max(y) + max(z)$. If at any time during steps (a) through (f) the domain of a variable becomes empty, then unsatisfiability has been detected. The second phase of this algorithm is that for each x such that $dom(x)$ is changed by some action in steps (a) through (f), all constraints (but the current one that gave rise to this action) that contain x are reconsidered for further action. Termination is, of course, assured simply because the domains are finite.

In the domain of Boolean algebra $\mathcal{BOOL}$, there are a variety of techniques for testing satisfiability. Since the problem is NP-complete, none of these can be expected to perform efficiently over all constraints. An early technique, pioneered by Davis and Putnam, is based upon variable elimination. The essential idea reduces a normal form representation into two smaller problems, each with one less variable. Binary decision diagrams [Bryant, 1986] provide an efficient representation. One of the two Boolean solvers of CHIP, for example, uses variable elimination and these diagrams. A related technique is based on enumeration and propagation. The constraints are expressed as a conjunction of simple constraints and then local propagation simplifies the conjunction after each enumeration step. See [Codognet and Diaz, 1993], for example. The method used in Prolog III [Benhamou, 1993] is a modification of SL-resolution whose main element is the elimination of redundant expressions. Another technique comes from operations research. Here the Boolean formula is restated in arithmetic form, with variables constrained to be 0 or 1. Then standard techniques for integer programming, for example cutting-planes, can be used. See [Chandru, 1991] for a further discussion of this technique. This technique has not been used in CLP systems. A more recent development is the adaptation of Buchberger's Groebner basis algorithm to Boolean algebras [Sakai *et al.*,

---

[24]In this case, simply remove from $dom(x)$ all elements bigger than $max(y)$, and remove from $dom(y)$ all elements smaller than $min(x)$. We omit the details of similar operations in the following discussion.

[25]If both are singletons, clearly the constraint reduces to either *true* or *false*.

to appear], which is used in CAL. Finally, there is the class of algorithms which perform Boolean unification; see the survey [Martin and Nipkow, 1989] for example. Here satisfiability testing is only part of the problem addressed, and hence we will discuss these algorithms in the next section.

The satisfiability problem for feature trees is essentially the same as the satisfiability problem for rational trees, provided that the number of features that may occur is bounded by a known constant [Aït-Kaci *et al.*, 1992]. (Generally this bounding constant can be determined at compile-time.) Two different sort constraints on the same variable clash in the same way that different function symbols on terms in $\mathcal{RT}$ clash. An equation between two feature tree variables (of the same sort) induces equations between all the subtrees determined by the features of the variables, in the same way as occurs in $\mathcal{RT}$. The main difference is that some sorts or features may be undetermined (roughly, unbound) in $\mathcal{FEAT}$.

10.3 Satisfiability (incremental)

As alluded to above, it is crucial that the algorithm that determines the satisfiability of a tentatively new constraint store be incremental. For example, a linear-time algorithm for a satisfiability problem is often as good as one can get. Consider a sequence of constraints $c_1, \ldots, c_k$ of approximately equal size N. A naive application of this linear-time algorithm to decide c_1, then $c_1 \wedge c_2, \wedge \cdots$, and finally $c_1 \wedge \cdots \wedge c_k$ could incur a cost proportional to Nk^2, on average. In contrast, a perfectly incremental algorithm as discussed in Section 10.1 has a cost of $O(Nk)$, on average.

In practice, most algorithms represent constraints in some kind of *solved form*, a format in which the satisfiability of the constraints is evident. Thus the satisfiability problem is essentially that of reducibility into solved form. For example, standard unification algorithms for $\mathcal{FT}$ represent constraints by (one variant of) its mgu, that is, in the form $x_1 = t_1(\tilde{y}), \ldots, x_n = t_n(\tilde{y})$ where each $t_i(\tilde{y})$ denotes a term structure containing variables from $\tilde{y}$, and no variable x_i appears in $\tilde{y}$. Similarly, linear equations in $\Re_{LinEqn}$ are often represented in parametric form $x_1 = le_1(\tilde{y}), \ldots, x_n = le_n(\tilde{y})$ where each $le_i(\tilde{y})$ denotes a linear expression containing variables from $\tilde{y}$, and no variable x_i appears in $\tilde{y}$. In both these examples, call the x_i *eliminable* variables, and the y_i *parametric* variables. For linear inequalities in $\Re_{Lin}$, the Simplex algorithm represents the constraints in an $n \times m$ matrix form $A\tilde{x} = B$ where A contains an $n \times n$ identity submatrix, defining the basis variables, and all numbers in the column vector B are nonnegative. For domains based on a unitary equality theory [Siekmann, 1989], the standard representation is the mgu, as in the case of $\mathcal{FT}$ (which corresponds to the most elementary equality theory). Word equations over $\mathcal{WE}$, however, are associated with an infinitary theory, and thus a unification algorithm for these equations [Jaffar, 1990] may not terminate. A solved form for word equations, or any closed form solution for that matter, is not known.

The first two kinds of solved form above are also examples of *solution forms*, that is, a format in which the set of all solutions of the constraints is evident. Here, any instance of the variables $\tilde{y}$ determines values for $\tilde{x}$ and thus gives one solution. The set of all such instances gives the set of all solutions. The Simplex format, however, is not in solution form: each choice of basis variables depicts just one particular solution.

An important property of solution forms (and sometimes of just solved forms) is that they define a convenient representation of the *projection* of the solution space with respect to any set of variables. More specifically, each variable can be equated with a substitution expression containing only parametric variables, that is, variables whose projections are the entire space. This property, in turn, aids incrementality as we now show via our sample domains.

In each of the following examples, let C be a (satisfiable) constraint in solved form and let c be the new constraint at hand. For $\mathcal{FT}$, the substitution expression for a variable x is simply x if x is not eliminable; otherwise it is the expression equated to x in the solved form C. This mapping is generalized to terms in the obvious way. Similarly we can define a mapping of linear expressions by replacing the eliminable variables therein with their substitution expressions, and then collecting like terms. For the domain $\Re_{Lin}$, in which case C is in Simplex form, the substitution expression for a variable x is simply x if x is not basic; otherwise it is the expression obtained by writing the (unique) equation in C containing x with x as the subject. Once again, this mapping can be generalized to any linear expression in an obvious way. In summary, a solution form defines a mapping θ which can be used to map any expression t into an equivalent form $t\theta$ which is free of eliminable variables.

The basic step of a satisfiability algorithm using a solution form is essentially this.

Algorithm 10.3.1. Given C, (a) Replace the newly considered constraint c by $c\theta$ where θ is the substitution defined by C. (b) Then write $c\theta$ into equations of the form $x = ...$, and this involves choosing the x and rearranging terms. Unsatisfiability is detected at this stage. (c) If the previous step succeeds, use the new equations to substitute out all occurrences of x in C. (d) Finally, simply add the new equations to C, to obtain a solution form for $C \wedge c$.

Note that the nonappearance of eliminable variables in substitution expressions is needed in (b) to ensure that the new equations themselves are in solved form, and in (c) to ensure that C, augmented with the new equations, remains in solution form.

The belief that this methodology leads to an incremental algorithm is based upon believing that the cost of dealing with c is more closely related to the size of c (which is small on average) than that of C (which is very large on average). This, in turn, is based upon believing that

- the substitution expressions for the eliminable variables in c, which largely determine the size of $c\theta$, often have a size that is independent of the size of C, and
- the number of occurrences of the new eliminable variable x in C, which largely determines the cost of substituting out x in C, is small in comparison to the size of C.

The domain $\mathcal{FT}$ provides a particularly good example of a solved form for which the basic algorithm 10.3.1 is incremental. Consider a standard implementation in which there is only one location for each variable, and all references to x are implemented by pointers. Given C in solved form, and given a new constraint c, there is really nothing to do to obtain $c\theta$ since the eliminable (or in this case, bound) variables in c are already pointers to their substitution expressions. Now if $c\theta$ is satisfiable and we obtain the new equations $x = ...$, then just one pointer setting of x to its substitution expression is required, and we are done. In other words, the cost of this pointer-based algorithm is focused on determining the satisfiability of $c\theta$ and extracting the new equations; in contrast, step (c) of global substitution using the new equations incurs no cost.

For $\Re_{LinEqn}$, the size of $c\theta$ can be large, even though the finally obtained equations may not be. For example, if C contain just $x_1 = u - v$, $x_2 = v - w$, $x_3 = w - u$, and c were $y = x_1 + x_2 + x_3$, then $c\theta$ is as big as C. Upon rearrangement, however, the finally obtained new equation is simply $y = 0$. Next, the substitution phase using the new equation also can enlarge the equations in C (even if temporarily), and rearrangement is needed in each equation substituted upon. In general, however, the above beliefs hold in practice, and the algorithm behaves incrementally.

We next consider the domain $\mathcal{RT}$ whose universally used solved form (due to [Colmerauer, 1982b]) is like that of $\mathcal{FT}$ with one important change: constraints are represented in the form $x_1 = t_1, \ldots, x_n = t_n$ where each t_i is an *arbitrary* term structure. Thus this solved form differs from that of $\mathcal{FT}$ in that the t_i can contain the variables x_j, and hence algorithm 1 is not directly applicable. It is easy to show that a constraint is satisfiable iff it has such a solved form, and further, the solved form is a fairly explicit representation of the set of all solutions (though not as explicit as the solution forms for $\mathcal{FT}$ or $\Re_{LinEqn}$). A straightforward satisfiability algorithm [Colmerauer, 1982b] is roughly as follows. Let x stand for a variable, and s and t stand for non-variable terms. Now, perform the following rewrite rules until none is applicable. (a) discard each $x = x$; (b) for any $x = y$, replace x by y throughout; (c) replace $t = x$ by $x = t$; (d) replace $f(s_1, \ldots, s_n) = f(t_1, \ldots, t_n)$, $n \geq 0$, by n equations $s_i = t_i$, $1 \leq i \leq n$; (e) replace $f(...) = g(...)$ by *false* (and thus the entire collection of constraints is unsatisfiable); (f) replace every pair of equations $x = t_1, x = t_2$, and say

t_1 is not bigger than t_2, by $x = t_1, t_1 = t_2$. Termination needs to be argued, but we will leave the details to [Colmerauer, 1982b].

We now discuss algorithms which do not fit exactly with Algorithm 1, but which employ a solved form. Consider first the Simplex algorithm for the domain $\Re_{Lin}$. The basic step of one pivoting operation within this algorithm is essentially the same as Algorithm 1. The arguments for incrementality for Algorithm 1 thus apply. The main difference from Algorithm 1 is that, in general, several pivoting operations are required to produce the final solved form. However, empirical evidence from CLP systems has shown that often the number of pivoting operations is small [Jaffar *et al.*, 1992a].

In the Boolean domain, Boolean unification algorithms [Martin and Nipkow, 1989] conform to the structure of Algorithm 1. One unification algorithm is essentially due to Boole, and we borrow the following presentation from [van Hentenryck, 1991]. Without loss of generality, assume the constraints are of the form $t(x_1, \ldots, x_n) = 0$ where the x_i are the variables in t. Assuming $n \geq 2$, rewrite $t = 0$ into the form

$$g(x_1, \ldots, x_{n-1}) \wedge x_n \oplus h(x_1, \ldots, x_{n-1}) = 0$$

so that the problem for $t = 0$ can be reduced to that of

$$\neg g(x_1, \ldots, x_{n-1}) \wedge h(x_1, \ldots, x_{n-1}) = 0$$

which contains one less variable. If this equation is satisfiable, then the 'assignment'

$$x_n = h(x_1, \ldots, x_{n-1}) \oplus \neg g(x_1, \ldots, x_{n-1}) \wedge y_n$$

where y_n is a new variable, describes all the possible solutions for x_n. This reduction clearly can be repeatedly applied until we are left with the straightforward problem of deciding the satisfiability of equations of the form $t \wedge x \oplus u = 0$ where t and u are ground. The unifier desired is given simply by collecting (and substituting out all assigned variables in) the assignments, such as that for x_n above.

The key efficiency problem here is, of course, that the variable elimination process gives rise to larger expressions, an increase which is exponential in the number of eliminated variables, in the worst case. So even though this algorithm satisfies the structure of Algorithm 1, it does not satisfy our assumption about the size of expressions obtained after substitution, and hence our general argument for incrementality does not apply here. Despite this, and the fact that Boole's work dates far back, this method is still used, for example, in CHIP [Büttner and Simonis, 1987].

Another unification algorithm is due to Löwenhein, and we adapt the presentation of [Martin and Nipkow, 1989] here. Let $f(x_1, \ldots, x_n) = 0$ be the equation considered. Let $\tilde{a}$ denote a solution. The unifier is then simply given by

$$x_i = y_i \vee f(\tilde{y}) \wedge (y_i \vee a_i), 1 \le i \le n$$

where the y_i are new variables. The basic efficiency problem is of course to determine $\tilde{a}$. The obtained unifiers are only slightly larger than f, in contrast to Boole's method. Thus Löwenhein's method provides a way of extending a constructive satisfiability test into a satisfiability test which has an incremental form. However, this method is not, to our knowledge, used in CLP languages.

Other algorithms for testing the satisfiability of Boolean constraints are considerably different from Algorithm 1. The Groebner basis algorithm produces a basis for the space of Boolean constraints implied by the constraint store. It is a solved form but not a solution form. The remaining algorithms mentioned in the previous subsection do not have a solved form. The algorithm used in Prolog III retains the set of literals implied to be true by the constraints, but the normal form does not guarantee solvability: that must be tested beforehand. Enumeration algorithms have the same behavior: they exhibit a solution, and may retain some further information, but they do not compute a solved form.

In the domain of feature trees $\mathcal{FEAT}$, equations occur only between variables. Thus Algorithm 1 does not address the whole problem. Existing algorithms [Aït-Kaci *et al.*, 1992; Smolka and Treinen, 1992] employ a solved form in which all implied equations between variables are explicit and there are no clashes of sort. Such solved forms are, in fact, solution forms. The implied equations are found by congruence closure, treating the features as (partial) functions, analogously to rule (d) in the algorithm for $\mathcal{RT}$.

In summary for this subsection, an important property for algorithms to decide satisfiability is that they have good average case behavior. More important, and even crucially so, is that the algorithm is incremental. Toward this goal, a common technique is to use a solved form representation for satisfiable constraints.

10.4 Entailment

Given satisfiable C, guard constraints G such that no constraint therein is entailed by C, and a new constraint c, the problem at hand is to determine the subset G_1 of G of constraints entailed by $C \wedge c$. We will also consider the problem of detecting groundness which is not, strictly speaking, an entailment problem. However, it is essentially the same as the problem of detecting groundness to a specific value, which is an entailment problem. In what follows the distinction is unimportant.

We next present a rule of thumb to determine whether an entailment algorithm is incremental in the sense discussed earlier. The important factor is not the number of constraints entailed after a change in the store, but instead, the number of constraints *not* entailed. That is, the algorithm must be able to ignore the latter constraints so that the costs incurred depend only on the number of entailed constraints, as opposed to the total number of guard constraints. As in the case of incremental satisfiability, the property of incremental entailment is a crucial one for the implementation of practical CLP systems.

We now briefly discuss modifications to some of the previously discussed algorithms for satisfiability, which provide for incremental entailment.

Consider the domain $\mathcal{FT}$ and suppose G contains only guard constraints of the form $x = t$ where t is some ground term[26]. Add to a standard implementation of a unification algorithm an index structure mapping variables x to just those guard constraints in G which involve x. (See [Carlsson, 1987] for a detailed description.) Now add to the process of constructing a solved form a check for groundness when variables are bound (and this is easily detectable). This gives rise to an incremental algorithm because the only guard constraints that are inspected are those $x = t$ for which x has just become ground, and not the entire collection G.

Just as with satisfiability, testing entailment is essentially the same over the domains $\mathcal{RT}$ and $\mathcal{FEAT}$. Four recent works have addressed this problem, all in the context of a CLP system, but with slightly differing constraint domains. We will discuss them all in terms of $\mathcal{RT}$. With some modifications, these works can also apply to $\mathcal{FT}$.

In [Smolka and Treinen, 1992; Aït-Kaci et al., 1992] a theoretical foundation is built. [Smolka and Treinen, 1992] then proposes a concrete algorithm, very roughly as follows: the to-be-entailed constraint c is added to the constraint store C. The satisfiability tester has the capability of detecting whether c is entailed by or inconsistent with C. If neither is detected then c', essentially a simplified form of c, is stored and the effect of adding c to C is undone. Every time a constraint is added to C that affects c' this entailment test is repeated (with c' instead of c).

The algorithm of [Podelski and van Roy, 1993] has some similarities to the previous algorithm, but avoids the necessity of undoing operations. Instead, operations that might affect C are delayed and/or performed on a special data-structure separate from C. Strong incrementality is claimed: if we replace average-case complexity by worst-case complexity, the algorithm satisfies our criterion for perfect incrementality.

[Ramachandran and van Hentenryck, 1993] goes beyond the problem of entailing equations to give an algorithm for entailment when both equa-

---

[26] As mentioned above, this discussion will essentially apply to guard constraints of the form *ground(x)*.

tions and disequations ($\neq$) are considered constraints. This algorithm has a rather different basis than those discussed above; it involves memorization of pairs of terms (entailments and disequations) and the use of a reduction of disequation entailment to several equation entailments.

For $\Re_{LinEqn}$, let G contain arbitrary equations e. Add to the algorithm which constructs the solved form a representation of each such equation e in which all eliminable variables are substituted out. Note, however, that even though these equations are stored with the other equations in the constraint store, they are considered as a distinct collection, and they play no direct role in the question of satisfiability of the current store. For example, a constraint store containing $x = z + 3, y = z + 2$ would cause the guard equation $y + z = 4$ to be represented as $z = 1$. It is easy to show that a guard equation e is entailed iff its representation reduces to the trivial form $0 = 0$, and similarly, the equation is refuted if its representation is of the form $0 = n$ where n is a nonzero number. (In our example, the guard equation is entailed or refuted just in case z becomes ground.) In order to have incrementality we must argue that the substitution operation is often applied only to very few of the guard constraints. This is tantamount to the second assumption made to argue the incrementality of Algorithm 1. Hence we believe our algorithm is incremental.

We move now to the domain $\Re_{Lin}$, but allow only equations in the guard constraints G. Here we can proceed as in the above discussion for $\Re_{LinEqn}$ to obtain an incremental algorithm, but we will have the further requirement that the constraint store contains all implicit equalities[27] explicitly represented as equations. It is then still easy to show that the entailment of a guard equation e need be checked only when the representation of e is trivial. The argument for incrementality given above for $\Re_{LinEqn}$ essentially holds here, provided that the cost of computing implicit equalities is sufficiently low.

There are two main works on the detection of implicit equalities in CLP systems over $\Re_{Lin}$. In [Studkey, 1989], the existence of implicit equalities is detected by the appearance of an equation of a special kind in the Simplex tableau at the end of the satisfiability checking process. Such an equation indicates some of the implicit equalities, but more pivoting (which, in turn, can give rise to more special equations) is generally required to find all of them. An important characteristic of this algorithm is that the extra cost incurred is proportional to the number of implicit equalities. This method is used in CLP($\mathcal{R}$) and Prolog III. CHIP uses a method based on [van Hentenryck and Graf, 1991]. In this method, a solved form which is more restrictive than the usual Simplex solved form is used. An equation in this

---

[27]These are equalities which are entailed by the store because of the presence of inequalities. For example, the constraint store $x + y \leq 3, x + y \geq 3$ entails the implicit equality $x + y = 3$.

form does not contribute to any implicit equality, and a whole tableau in this solved form implies that there are no implicit equalities. The basic idea is then to maintain the constraints in the solved form and when a new constraint is encountered, the search for implicit equalities can be first limited to variables in the new constraint. One added feature of this solved form is that it directly accommodates strict inequalities and disequations.

Next still consider the domain $\Re_{Lin}$, but now allow inequalities to be in G. Here it is not clear how to represent a guard inequality, say $x \geq 5$, in such a way that its entailment or refutation is detectable by some simple format in its representation. Using the Simplex tableau format as a solved form as discussed above, and using the same intuition as in the discussion of guard equations, we could substitute out x in $x \geq 5$ in case x is basic. However, it is not clear to which format(s) we should limit the resulting expression in order to avoid explicitly checking whether $x \geq 5$ is entailed[28]. Thus an incremental algorithm for checking the entailment of inequalities is yet to be found.

For $\mathcal{BOOL}$ there seems to be a similar problem in detecting the entailment of Boolean constraints. However, in the case of groundness entailment some of the algorithms we have previously discussed are potentially incremental. The Prolog III algorithm, in fact, is designed with the detection of groundness as a criterion. The algorithm represents explicitly all variables that are grounded by the constraints. The Groebner basis algorithm will also contain in its basis an explicit representation of grounded variables. Finally, for the unification algorithms, the issue is clearly the form of the unifier. If the unifier is in fully simplified form then every ground variable will be associated with a ground value.

In summary for this subsection, the problem of detecting entailment is not limited just to the cost of determining if a particular constraint is entailed. Incrementality is crucial, and this property can be defined roughly as limiting the cost to depend on the number of guard constraints affected by each change to the store. In particular, dealing (even briefly) with the entire collection of guard constraints each time the store changes is unacceptable.

Below, in Section 11.1, an issue related to entailment is taken up. Here we have focused on how to adapt the underlying satisfiability algorithm to be incremental for determining entailment. There we will consider the generic problem, independent of the constraint domain, of managing delayed goals which awake when certain constraints become entailed.

10.5 Projection

The problem at hand is to obtain a useful representation of the projection of constraints C w.r.t. a given set of variables. More formally, the problem

---

[28] And this can, of course, be done, perhaps even efficiently, but the crucial point is, once again, that we cannot afford to do this every time the store changes.

is: given *target* variables $\tilde{x}$ and constraints $C(\tilde{x}, \tilde{y})$ involving variables from $\tilde{x}$ and $\tilde{y}$, express $\exists \tilde{y}\, C(\tilde{x}, \tilde{y})$ in the most usable form. While we cannot define usability formally, it typically means both conciseness and readability. An important area of use is the output phase of a CLP system: the desired output from running a goal is the projection of the answer constraints with respect to the goal variables. Here it is often useful to have only the target variables output (though, depending on the domain, this is not always possible). For example, the output of $x = z + 1, y = z + 2$ w.r.t. to x and y should be $x = y - 1$ or some rearrangement of this, but it should not involve any other variable. Another area of use is in meta-programming where a description of the current store may be wanted for further manipulation. For example, projecting $\Re_{Lin}$ constraints onto a single variable x can show if x is bounded, and if so, this bound can be used in the program. Projection also provides the logical basis for eliminating variables from the accumulated set of constraints, once it is known that they will not be referred to again.

There are few general principles that guide the design of projection algorithms across the various constraint domains. The primary reason is, of course, that these algorithms have to be intimately related to the domain at hand. We therefore will simply resort to briefly mentioning existing approaches for some of our sample domains.

The projection problem is particularly simple for the domain $\mathcal{FT}$: the result of projection is $\tilde{x} = \tilde{x}\theta$ where θ is the substitution obtained from the solved form of C. Now, we have described above that this solved form is simply the mgu of C, that is, equations whose r.h.s. does not contain any variable on the l.h.s. For example, $x = f(y), y = f(z)$ would have the solved form $x = f(f(z)), y = f(z)$. However, the equations $x = f(y), y = f(z)$ are more efficiently stored internally as they are (and this is done in actual implementations). The solved form for x therefore is obtained only when needed (during unification for example) by fully dereferencing y in the term $f(y)$. A direct representation of the projection of C on a variable x, as required in a printout for example, can be exponential in the size of C. This happens, for example, if C is of the form $x = f(x_1, x_1)$, $x_1 = f(x_2, x_2), \ldots, x_n = f(a, a)$ because $x\theta$ would contain 2^{n+1} occurrences of the constant a. A solution would be to present the several equations equivalent to $x = x\theta$, such as the $n + 1$ equations in this example. This however is a less explicit representation of the projection; for example, it would not always be obvious if a variable were ground.

Projection in the domain $\mathcal{RT}$ can be done by simply presenting those equations whose l.h.s. is a target variable and, recursively, all equations whose l.h.s. appears in anything already presented. Such a straightforward presentation is in general not the most compact. For example, the equation $x = f(f(x, x), f(x, x))$ is best presented as $x = f(x, x)$. In general, the problem of finding the most compact representation is roughly equivalent to the problem of minimizing states in a finite state automaton [Colmerauer, 1982b].

```
let x₁, ..., xₙ be the target variables;
for (i = 1; i ≤ n; i = i + 1) {
    if (xᵢ is a parameter) continue;
    let e denote the equation xᵢ = r.h.s.(xᵢ) at hand;
    if (r.h.s.(xᵢ) contains a variable z of lower priority than xᵢ) {
        choose the z of lowest priority;
        rewrite the equation e into the form z = t;
        if (z is a target variable) mark the equation e as final;
        substitute t for z in the other equations ;
    } else mark the equation e as final;
}
return all final equations;
```

Fig. 1. *Projection algorithm for linear equations*

For $\Re_{LinEqn}$ the problem is only slightly more complicated. Recall that equations are maintained in parametric form, with eliminable and parametric variables. A relatively simple algorithm can be obtained by using a form of Gaussian elimination, and is informally described in Figure 1. It assumes there is some ordering on variables, and ensures that lower priority variables are represented in terms of higher priority variables. This ordering is arbitrary, except for the fact that the target variables should be of higher priority than other variables. We remark that a crucial point for efficiency is that the main loop in Figure 1 iterates n times, and this number (the number of target variables) is often far smaller than the total number of variables in the system. More details on this algorithm can be found in [Jaffar *et al.*, 1993].

For $\Re_{Lin}$, there is a relatively simple projection algorithm. Assume all inequalities are written in a standard form ... ≤ 0. Let C_x^+ (C_x^-) denote the subset of constraints C in which x has only positive (negative) coefficients. Let C_x^0 denote those inequalities in C not containing x at all. We can now describe an algorithm, due to Fourier [Fourier, 1824], which eliminates a variable x from a given C. If constraints c and c' have a positive and a negative coefficient of x, we can define $elim_x(c, c')$ to be a linear combination of c and c', which does not contain x[29]. A *Fourier step* eliminates x from a set of constraints C by computing $F_x(C) = \{elim_x(c, c') : c \in C_x^+, c' \in C_x^-\}$. It is easy to show that $\exists x C \leftrightarrow F_x(C)$. Clearly repeated applications of F

---

[29]Obtained, for example, by multiplying c by $1/m$ and c' by $(-1/m')$, where m and m' are the coefficients of x in c and c' respectively, and then adding the resulting equations together.

eliminating all non-target variables result in an equivalent set of constraints in which the only variables (if any) are target variables.

The main problem with this algorithm is that the worst-case size of $F_x(C)$ is $O(N^2)$, where N is the number of constraints in C. (It is in fact precisely $|C_x^0| + (|C_x^+| \times |C_x^-|) - (|C_x^+| + |C_x^-|)$.) In principle, the number of constraints needed to describe $\exists x\ C$ using inequalities over variables $var(C) - \{x\}$ is far larger than the number of inequalities in C. In practice, however, the Fourier step generates many *redundant* constraints[30]. See [Lassez *et al.*, 1989] for a discussion on such redundancy. Work by Černikov [Černikov, 1963] proposed tests on the generated constraints to detect and eliminate some redundant constraints. The output module of the CLP($\mathcal{R}$) system [Jaffar *et al.*, 1993] furthered these ideas, as did Imbert [Imbert, 1993b]. (Imbert [Imbert, 1993a] also considered the more general problem in which there are disequations.) All these redundancy elimination methods are *correct* in the following sense: if $\{\mathcal{C}_i\}_{i=1,2,...}$ is the sequence of constraints generated during the elimination of variables $x_1, \cdots, x_i$ from C, then $\mathcal{C}_i \leftrightarrow \exists x_1 \ldots x_i\ C$, for every i.

The survey [Chandru, 1993] contains further perspectives on the Fourier variable elimination technique. It also contains a discussion on how the essential technique of Fourier can be adapted to perform projection in other domains such as linear integer constraints and the Boolean domain.

We finish here by mentioning the non-Fourier algorithms of [Huynh *et al.*, 1990; Lassez and Lassez, 1991]. In some circumstances, especially when the matrix representing the constraints is dense, the algorithm of [Huynh *et al.*, 1990] can be far more efficient. It is, however, believed that typical CLP programs produce sparse matrices. The algorithm of [Lassez and Lassez, 1991] has the advantageous property that it can produce an approximation of the projection if the size of the projection is unmanageably large.

10.6 Backtracking

The issue here is to restore the state of the constraint solver to a previous state (or, at least, an equivalent state). The most common technique, following Prolog, is the trailing of constraints when they are modified by the constraint solver and the restoration of these constraints upon backtracking. In Prolog, constraints are equations between terms, represented internally as bindings of variables. Since variables are implemented as pointers to their bound values[31], backtracking can be facilitated by the simple mechanism of an untagged trail [Warren, 1983; Aït-Kaci, 1991]. This identifies the set of variables which have been bound since the last choice point. Upon backtracking, these variables are simply reset to become unbound.

---

[30] A constraint $c \in C$ is redundant in C if $C \leftrightarrow C - \{c\}$.

[31] Recall that this means that eliminable variables are not explicitly dereferenced on the r.h.s. of the equations in the solved form.

Thus in Prolog, the only information to be trailed is which variables have just become bound, and untrailing simply unbinds these variables.

For CLP in general, it is necessary to record *changes* to constraints. While in Prolog a variable's expression simply becomes more and more instantiated during (forward) execution, in CLP an expression may be completely changed from its original form. In $\Re_{LinEqn}$, for example, a variable x may have an original linear form and subsequently another. Assuming that a choice point is encountered just before the change in x, the original linear form needs to be trailed in case of backtracking. This kind of requirement in fact holds in all our sample domains with the exception of $\mathcal{FT}$ and $\mathcal{RT}$. Thus we have our first requirement on our trailing mechanism: the trail is a *value trail*, that is, each variable is trailed together with its associated expression. (Strictly speaking, we need to trail constraints rather than the expression with which a variable is associated. However, constraints are typically represented internally as an association between a variable and an expression.)

Now, the trailing of expressions is in general far more costly than the trailing of the variables alone. For this reason, it is often useful to avoid trailing when there is no choice point between the time a variable changes value from one expression to another. A standard technique facilitating this involves the use of *time stamps*: a variable is always time stamped with the time that it last changed value, and every choice point is also time stamped when created. Now just before a variable's value is to be changed, its time stamp n is compared with the time stamp m of the most recent choice point, and if $n > m$, clearly no trailing is needed[32].

Next consider the use of a *cross-reference* table for solved forms, such as those discussed for the arithmetic domains, which use parametric variables. This is an index structure which maps each parametric variable to a list of its occurrences in the solved form. Such a structure is particularly useful, and can even be crucial for efficiency, in the process of substituting out a parametric variable (step (c) in Algorithm 10.3.1). However, its use adds to the backtracking problem. A straightforward approach is to simply trail the entries in this table (according to time stamps). However, since these entries are in general quite large, and since the cross reference table is redundant from a semantic point of view, a useful approach is to *reconstruct* the table upon backtracking. The details of such reconstruction are straightforward but tedious, and hence are omitted here; see [Jaffar *et al.*, 1992a] for the case of the CLP($\mathcal{R}$) system. A final remark: this reconstruction approach has the added advantage of incurring cost only when backtracking actually takes place.

In summary, backtracking in CLP is substantially more complex than in Prolog. Some useful concepts to be added to the Prolog machinery are

---

[32] In Prolog, one can think of the stack position of a variable as the time stamp.

as follows: a value trail (and, in practice, a tagged trail as well because most systems will accommodate variables of different types, for example, the functor and arithmetic variables in CLP($\mathcal{R}$)); time stamps, to avoid repeated trailing for a variable during the lifetime of the same choice point; and finally, reconstruction of cross-references, rather than trailing.

11   Inference engine

This section deals with extensions to the basic inference engine for logic programming needed because of constraints. What follows contains two main sections. In the first, we consider the problem of an incremental algorithm to manage a collection of delayed goals and constraints. This problem, discussed independently of the particular constraint domain at hand, reduces to the problem of determining which of a given set of guard constraints (cf. Section 9) are affected as a result of change to the constraint store. The next section discusses extensions to the WAM, in both the design of the instruction set as well as in the main elements of the runtime structure. Finally, we give a brief discussion of work on parallel implementations.

11.1   Delaying/wakeup of goals and constraints

The problem at hand is to determine when a delayed goal is to be woken or when a passive constraint becomes active. The criterion for such an event is given by a guard constraint, that is, awaken the goal or activate the constraint when the guard constraint is entailed by the store[33]. In what follows, we use the term delayed constraint as synonymous with passive constraint, to emphasize the similarities with delayed goals.

The underlying implementation issue, as far as the constraint solver is concerned, is how to efficiently process just those guard constraints that are affected as a result of a new input constraint[34]. Specifically, to achieve incrementality, the cost of processing a change to the current collection of guard constraints should be related to the guard constraints affected by the change, and not to all the guard constraints. The following two items seem necessary to achieve this end.

First is a representation of what further constraints are needed so that a given guard constraint is entailed. For example, consider the delayed CLP($\mathcal{R}$) constraint $pow(x, y, z)$ (meaning $x = y^z$) which in general awaits the grounding of two of the three variables x, y, z. In constrast, the constraint $pow(1, y, z)$, only awaits the grounding of y (to a nonzero number)

---

[33] For guarded clauses, the problem is extended to determining which clause is to be chosen.

[34] However, significant changes to the inference engine are needed to handle delayed goals and guarded clauses. But these issues are the same as those faced by extending logic programming systems to implement delayed goals and/or guarded clauses (see, for example, [Tick, 1993]).

or z (to 1). In general, a delayed constraint is awoken by not one but a conjunction of several input constraints. When a subset of such input constraints has already been encountered, the runtime structure should relate the delayed constraint to (the disjunction of) just the remaining kinds of constraints which will awaken it.

Second, we require some index structure which allows immediate access to just the guard constraints affected as the result of a new input constraint. The main challenge is how to maintain such a structure in the presence of backtracking. For example, if changes to the structure were trailed using some adaptation of Prolog techniques [Warren, 1983], then a cost proportional to the number of entries can be incurred even though no guard constraints are affected.

The following material is a condensation of [Jaffar *et al.*, 1991].

11.1.1   Wakeup systems

For the purposes of this section, we will describe an instance of a constraint in the form $p(\$_1, \ldots, \$_n) \wedge C$ where p is the n-ary constraint symbol at hand, $\$_1, \ldots, \$_n$ are distinguished variables used as templates for the arguments of p, and C is a constraint (which determines the values of $\$_1, \ldots, \$_n$).

A *wakeup degree* represents a subset of the p constraints, and a *wakeup system* consists of a set of wakeup degrees, and further, these degrees are organized into an automaton where transitions between degrees are labelled by constraints called *wakeup conditions*[35]. Intuitively, a transition occurs when a wakeup condition becomes entailed by the store. There is a distinguished degree called *woken* which represents active p constraints. We proceed now with an example.

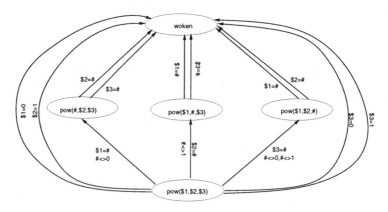

Fig. 2. Wakeup system for *pow/3*

---

[35] These are templates for the guard constraints.

Consider the CLP($\mathcal{R}$) constraint $pow(x, y, z)$ and see Figure 2. A wakeup degree may be specified by means of constraints containing $\$_1, \ldots, \$_3$ (for describing the three arguments) and some *meta-constants* $\#, \#_1, \#_2, \ldots$ (for describing unspecified values). Thus, for example, $\$_2 = \#$ specifies that the second argument is ground. Such a meta-language can also be used to specify the wakeup conditions. Thus, for example, the wakeup condition $\$_2 = \#, \# <> 0, \# <> 1$ attached to the bottom-most degree in figure 2 represents a transition of a constraint $pow(\$_1, \$_2, \$_3) \wedge C$, where C does not ground $\$_2$, into $pow(\$_1, \$_2, \$_3) \wedge C \wedge c$, where $C \wedge c$ does ground $\$_2$ into a number different from 0 and 1. The wakeup condition $\$_2 = 1$ which represents a transition to the degree *woken*, represents the fact that $pow(\$_1, 1, \$_3)$ is an active constraint (equivalent to $\$_1 = 1$). Similarly, $\$_3 = 1$ represents the transition to the active constraint $\$_1 = \$_2$. Note that there is no wakeup condition $\$_2 = 0$ because $pow(\$_1, 0, \$_3)$ (which is equivalent to $(\$_1 = 0 \wedge \$_3 \neq 0) \vee (\$_1 = 1 \wedge \$_3 = 0)$) is not active.

In general, there will be certain requirements on the structure of such an automaton to ensure that it does in fact define a mapping from p constraints into wakeup degrees, and that this mapping satisfies certain properties such as: it defines a partition, it maps only active constraints into *woken*, it is consistent with the wakeup conditions specifying the transitions, etc. A starting point will be a formalization of the meta-language used. These formal aspects are beyond the scope of this survey.

In summary, wakeup systems are an intuitive way to specify the organization of guard constraints. The wakeup degrees represent the various different cases of a delayed constraint which should be treated differently for efficiency reasons. Associated with each degree is a number of wakeup conditions which specify when an input constraint changes the degree of a delayed constraint. What is intended is that the wakeup conditions represent all the situations in which the constraint solver can efficiently update its knowledge about what further constraints are needed to wake the delayed constraint.

Before embarking on the runtime structure to implement delayed constraints such as *pow*, we amplify the abovementioned point about the similarities between delayed constraints and guarded clauses. Consider the guarded clause program:

```
pow(X,Y,Z) :-
    Y=1 | X=1.
pow(X,Y,Z) :-
    ground(X), X≠0, ground(Y), Y≠1 | Z=log(X)/log(Y).
pow(X,Y,Z) :-
    ground(X), X≠0, ground(Z) | Y=ᶻ√X.
pow(X,Y,Z) :-
    ground(Y), Y≠1, ground(Z) | X=Yᶻ.
pow(X,Y,Z) :-
    X=0 | Y=0, Z≠0.
pow(X,Y,Z) :-
    Z=0 | X=1.
pow(X,Y,Z) :-
    Z=1 | X=Y.
```

This program could be compiled into the wakeup system in Figure 2, where the three intermediate nodes reflect subexpressions in the guards that might be entailed without the entire guard being entailed. (More precisely, several *woken* nodes would be used, one for each clause body.) Thus wakeup systems express a central part of the implementation of (flat) guarded clauses. Since a guarded atom can be viewed as a one-clause guarded clause program for an anonymous predicate, wakeup systems are also applicable to implementing these constructs.

11.1.2 Runtime structure

Here we present an implementational framework in the context of a given wakeup system. There are three major operations with delayed goals or delayed constraints which correspond to the actions of delaying, awakening and backtracking:

1. adding a goal or delayed constraint to the current collection;
2. awakening a delayed goal or delayed constraint as the result of inputting a new (active) constraint, and
3. restoring the entire runtime structure to a previous state, that is, restoring the collection of delayed goals and delayed constraints to some earlier collection, and restoring all auxiliary structures accordingly.

In what follows, we concentrate on delayed constraints; as mentioned above, the constraint solver operations to handle delayed goals and guarded clauses are essentially the same.

The first of our two major structures is a stack containing the delayed constraints. Thus implementing operation 1 simply requires a push operation. Additionally, the stack contains constraints which are newer forms of constraints deeper in the stack. For example, if the constraint $pow(x, y, z)$ were in the stack, and if the input constraint $y = 3$ were encountered, then the new constraint $pow(x, 3, z)$ would be pushed, together with a pointer from the latter to the former. In general, the collection of delayed constraints contained in the system is described by the sub-collection of stacked constraints which have no inbound pointers.

Now consider operation 2. In order to implement this efficiently, it is necessary to have some access structure mapping an entailed constraint to just those delayed constraints affected. Since there are in general an infinite number of possible entailed constraints, a finite classification of them is required. A guard constraint, or simply guard for short, is an instance of a wakeup condition obtained by renaming the distinguished argument variables $\$_i$ into runtime variables. It is used as a template for describing the collection of entailed constraints (its instances) which affect the same sub-collection of delayed constraints. For example, suppose that the only delayed constraint is $pow(5, y, z)$ whose degree is $pow(\#, \$_2, \$_3)$ with wakeup conditions $\$_2 = \#$ and $\$_3 = \#$. Then only two guards need be considered: $y = \#$ and $z = \#$.

We now specify an index structure which maps a delayed constraint into a doubly linked list of occurrence nodes. Each node contains a pointer to a stack element containing a delayed constraint[36]. Corresponding to each occurrence node is a reverse pointer from the stack element to the occurrence node. Call the list associated with a delayed constraint $\mathcal{DW}$ a $\mathcal{DW}$-*list*, and call each node in the list a $\mathcal{DW}$-*occurrence node*.

Initially the access structure is empty. The following specifies what is done for the basic operations:

Delay Push the constraint C onto the stack, and for each wakeup condition associated with (the degree of) C, create the corresponding guard and $\mathcal{DW}$-list. All occurrence nodes here are pointed to C.

Process entailment Say $x = 5$ is now entailed. Find all guards which are implied by $x = 5$. If there are none, we are done. Otherwise, for each $\mathcal{DW}$-list L corresponding to each of these conditions, and for each constraint $C = p(...) \wedge C'$ pointed to in L, (a) delete all occurrence nodes pointing to C (using the reverse pointers), push the new delayed constraint $C'' = p(...) \wedge C' \wedge x = 5$ with a (downward) pointer to C, and finally, (c) construct the new $\mathcal{DW}$-lists corresponding to C'' as defined above for the delay operation.

Backtrack Restoring the stack during backtracking is easy because it only requires a series of pops. Restoring the list structure, however, is not as straightforward because no trailing/saving of the changes was performed. In more detail, the operation of backtracking is the following:

---

[36]The total number of occurrence nodes is generally larger than the number of delayed constraints.

(a) Pop the stack, and let C denote the constraint just popped. (b) Delete all occurrence nodes pointed to by C. If there is no pointer from C (and so it was a constraint that was newly delayed) to another constraint deeper in the stack, then nothing more need be done. (c) If there is a pointer from C to another constraint C' (and so C is the reduced form of C'), then perform the modifications to the access structure *as though* C' were being pushed onto the stack. These modifications, described above, involve computing the guards pertinent to C', inserting occurrence nodes, and setting up reverse pointers.

Note that the index structure obtained in backtracking may not be structurally the same as that of the previous state. What is important, however, is that it depicts the same *logical* structure as that of the previous state.

Figure 3 illustrates the entire runtime structure after the two constraints $pow(x, y, z)$ and $pow(y, x, y)$ are stored, in this order. Figure 4 illustrates the structure after a new input constraint makes $x = 5$ entailed.

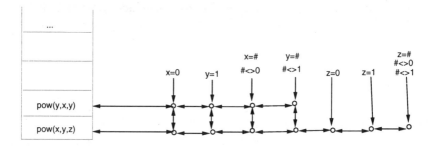

Fig. 3. The index structure

In summary, a stack is used to store delayed constraints and their reduced forms. An access structure maps a finite number of guards to lists of delayed constraints. The constraint solver is assumed to identify those conditions which are entailed. The cost of one primitive operation on delayed constraints (delaying a constraint, upgrading the degree of one delayed constraint, including awakening the constraint, and undoing the delay/upgrade of one constraint) is bounded by the (fixed) size of the underlying wakeup system. The total cost of an operation (delaying a new constraint, processing an entailed constraint, backtracking) on delayed constraints is proportional to the number of the delayed constraints affected by the operation.

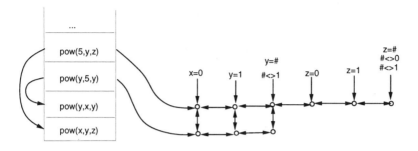

Fig. 4. The index structure after $x = 5$ is entailed

11.2 Abstract machine

This section discusses some major issues in the design of an abstract machine for the execution of CLP programs. The primary focus here will be on the design of the instruction set, with emphasis on the interaction between their use and information obtained from a potential program analyzer. Some elements of the runtime structure will also be mentioned.

In general, the essential features of the parts of an abstract machine dealing with constraints will differ greatly over CLP languages using different constraint domains. This is exemplified in the literature on CLP($\mathcal{R}$) [Jaffar *et al.*, 1992b], CHIP [Aggoun and Beldiceanu, 1993], and CLP($\mathcal{FD}$) [Diaz and Codognet, 1993]. The following presentation, though based on one work [Jaffar *et al.*, 1992b], contains material that is relevant to abstract machines for many CLP languages.

We begin by arguing that an abstract machine is the right approach in the first place. Abstract machines have been used for implementing programming languages for many reasons. Portability is one: only an implementation of the abstract machine needs to be made available on each platform. Another is simply convenience: it is easier to write a native code compiler if the task is first reduced to compiling for an abstract machine that is semantically closer to the source language. The best abstract machines sit at just the right point on the spectrum between the conceptual clarity of the high-level source language and the details of the target machine. In doing so they can often be used to express programs in exactly the right form for tackling the efficiency issues of a source language. For example, the Warren abstract machine [Warren, 1983; Aït-Kaci, 1991] revolutionized the execution of Prolog, since translating programs to the WAM exposed many opportunities for optimization that were not apparent at the source level. The benefit from designing an appropriate abstract machine for a given source language can be so great that even executing the abstract instruction code by interpretation can lead to surprisingly efficient implementations of a language. Many commercial Prolog systems compile to WAM-like code. Certainly more efficiency can be obtained from native code compilation, but the step that made Prolog usable was that of compiling to the WAM.

While the WAM made Prolog practical, global analysis shows the potential of making another major leap. For example, [Taylor, 1990] and [van Roy and Despain, 1990] used fairly efficient analyzers to generate high quality native code. Based on certain examples, they showed that the code quality was comparable to that obtained from a C compiler. In the case of CLP, the opportunities for obtaining valuable information from analysis are even greater than in Prolog. This is because the constraint solving step is in general far more involved than the unification step.

11.2.1 Instructions

Next we consider the design of an abstract machine instruction set, in addition to the basic instruction set of the WAM. While the examples presented will be for $CLP(\mathcal{R})$, the discussions are made for CLP systems in general. More details on this material can be obtained from the theses [Michaylov, 1992; Yap, 1994].

Our first requirement is a basic instruction for invoking the constraint solver. The format can be of the form

```
solve_xxx X₁ X₂ ... Xₙ
```

where xxx indicates the kind of constraint and the X_i denote the arguments. Typically these arguments are, as in the WAM, stack locations or registers. For example, in $CLP(\mathcal{R})$, there are instructions of the form `initpf` n and `addpf` n, X, where n is a number and X a (solver) variable. The former initializes a parametric form to contain just the number n. The latter adds an entry of the form $n * pf(X)$ to the parametric form being stored in an *accumulator*, where $pf(X)$ is the parametric form for X in the store. Thus the accumulator in general stores an expression exp of the form $n + n_1 * X_1 + \ldots + n_k * X_k$. Then, the instruction `solve_eq0` tests for the consistency of $exp = 0$ in conjunction with the store. If consistent, the solver adds the equation to the store; otherwise, backtracking occurs. There are similar instructions for inequalities.

There are important special kinds of constraints that justify making specialized versions of this basic instruction. While there are clearly many kinds of special cases, some specific to certain constraint domains, there are three cases which stand out:

1. the constraint is to be added to the store, but no satisfiability check is needed;
2. the constraint need not be added, but its satisfiability in conjunction

with the store needs to be checked;

3. the constraint needs to be added and satisfiability needs to be checked, but the constraint is never used later.

To exemplify the special case 1, consider adding the constraint $5 + X - Y = 0$ to the store. Suppose that $Y = Z + 3.14$ is already in the store, and that X is a new variable. A direct compilation results in the following. Note that the rightmost column depicts the current state of the accumulator.

```
initpf      5            accumulator : 5
addpf       1, X         accumulator : 5 + X
addpf       -1, Y        accumulator : 1.86 + X - Z
solve_eq0                solve : 1.86 + X - Z = 0
```

A better compilation can be obtained by using a specialized instruction solve_no_fail_eq X which adds the equation $X = exp$ to the store, where exp is the expression in the accumulator. The main difference here with solve_eq0 is that no satisfiability check is performed. For the above example, we now can have

```
initpf              -5        accumulator : -5
addpf               -1, Y     accumulator : -1.86 + Z
solve_no_fail_eq    X         add : X = -1.86 + Z
```

In summary for this special case, for CLP systems in general, we often encounter constraints which can be organized into a form such that its consistency with the store is obvious. This typically happens when a new variable appears in an equation, for example, and new variables are often created in CLP systems. Thus the instructions of the form solve_no_fail_xxx are justified.

Next consider the special case 2, and the following example CLP($\mathcal{R}$) program.

```
sum(0, 0).
sum(N, X) :-
    N >= 1,
    N1 = N - 1,
    X1 = X - N,
    sum(N1, X1).
```

Of concern to us here are constraints that, if added to the store, can be shown to become redundant as a result of future additions to the store. This notion of *future redundancy* was first described in [Jorgensen *et al.*, 1991]. Now if we execute the goal sum(N, X) using the second rule above, we obtain the subgoal

```
?- N >= 1, N1 = N - 1, X1 = X - N, sum(N1, X1).
```

Continuing the execution, we now have two choices: choosing the first rule we obtain the new constraint $N1 = 0$, and choosing the second rule we obtain the constraint $N1 \geq 1$ (among others). In each case the original constraint $N \geq 1$ is made redundant. The main point of this example is that the constraint $N \geq 1$ in the second rule should be implemented simply as a test, and not added to the constraint store. We hence define the new class of instructions solve_no_add_xxx.

This example shows that future redundant constraints do occur in CLP systems. However, one apparent difficulty with this special case is the problem of *detecting* its occurrence. We will mention relevant work on program analysis below. Meanwhile, we remark that experiments using CLP($\mathcal{R}$) have shown that this special case leads to the most substantial efficiency gains compared to the other two kinds of special cases discussed in this section [Michaylov, 1992; Yap, 1994].

Finally consider special case 3. Of concern here are constraints which are neither entailed by the store as in case 1 nor are eventually made redundant as in case 2, but which are required to be added to the store, and checked for consistency. What makes these constraints special is that after they have been added to the store (and the store is recomputed into its new internal form), their variables appear in those parts of the store that are never again referred to. Consider the sum program once again. The following sequence of constraints arises from executing the goal sum(7, X):

$$
\begin{array}{lrcl}
(1) & X1 & = & X - 7 \\
(2) & X1' & = & (X - 7) - 6 \\
(3) & X1'' & = & ((X - 7) - 6) - 5 \\
\ldots & & \ldots &
\end{array}
$$

Upon encountering the second equation $X1' = X1 - 6$ and simplifying into (2), note that the variable $X1$ will never be referred to in the future. Hence equation (1) can be deleted. Similarly, upon encountering the third equation $X1'' = X1' - 5$ and simplifying into (3), the variable $X1'$ will never be referred to in future and so (2) can be deleted. In short, only one equation involving X need be stored at any point in the computation. We hence add the class of instructions of the form add_and_delete X which informs the solver that after considering the constraint associated with X, it may delete all structures associated with X. In CLP($\mathcal{R}$), the corresponding instruction is addpf_and_delete n, X, the obvious variant of the previously described instruction addpf n, X. Compiling this sum example gives

```
(1)    init_pf             -7
       addpf               1, X
```

```
        solve_no_fail_eq      X1
(2)     init_pf               -6
        addpf_and_delete      1, X1
        solve_no_fail_eq      X1'
(3)     init_pf               -5
        addpf_and_delete      1, X1'
        solve_no_fail_eq      X1''
...       ...
```

Note that a different set of instructions is required for the first equation from that required for the remaining equations. Hence the first iteration needs to be unrolled to produce the most efficient code. The main challenge for this special case is, as in special case 2, the detection of the special constraints. We now address this issue.

11.2.2 Techniques for CLP program analysis

The kinds of program analysis required to utilize the specialized instructions include those techniques developed for Prolog, most prominently, detecting special cases of unification and deterministic predicates. Algorithms for such analysis have become familiar; see [Debray, 1989a; Debray, 1989b] for example. See [García and Hermenegildo, 1993], for example, for a description of how to extend the general techniques of abstract interpretation applicable in LP to CLP. Our considerations above, however, require rather specific kinds of analyses.

Detecting redundant variables and future redundant constraints can in fact be done without dataflow analysis. One simple method involves unfolding the predicate definition (and typically once is enough), and then, in the case of detecting redundant variables, simply inspecting where variables occur last in the unfolded definitions. For detecting a future redundant constraint, the essential step is determining whether the constraints in an unfolded predicate definition imply the constraint being analyzed.

An early work describing these kinds of optimizations is [Jorgensen *et al.*, 1991], and some further discussion can also be found in [Jaffar *et al.*, 1992b]. The latter first described the abstract machine CLAM for CLP($\mathcal{R}$), and the former first defined and examined the problem of our special case 2, that of detecting and exploiting the existence of future redundant constraints in CLP($\mathcal{R}$). More recently, [McDonald *et al.*, 1993] reported new algorithms for the problem of special case 3, that of detecting redundant variables in CLP($\mathcal{R}$). The work [Marriott and Stuckey, 1993a] describes, in a more general setting, a collection of techniques (entitled refinement, removal and reordering) for optimization in CLP systems. See also [Marriott *et al.*, 1994] for an overview of the status of CLP($\mathcal{R}$) optimization and [Michaylov, 1992; Yap, 1994] for detailed empirical results.

Despite the potential of optimization as reported in these works, the lack of (full) implementations leaves open the practicality of using these and other sophisticated optimization techniques for CLP systems in general.

11.2.3   Runtime structure

A CLP abstract machine requires the same basic runtime support as the WAM. Some data structures needed are a routine extension of those for the WAM – the usual register, stack, heap and trail organization. The main new structures pertain to the solver. Variables involved in constraints typically have a *solver identifier*, which is used to refer to that variable's location in the solver data structures.

The modifications to the basic WAM architecture typically would be:

- *Solver identifiers*
  It is often necessary to have a way to index from a variable to the constraints it is involved in. Since the WAM structure provides stack locations for the dynamically created variables, it remains just to have a tag and value structure to respectively (a) identify the variable as a solver variable, and (b) access the constraint(s) associated with this variable. Note that the basic unification algorithm, assuming functors are used in the constraint system, needs to be augmented to deal with this new type.

- *Tagged trail*
  As mentioned in Section 10.6, the trail in the WAM merely consists of a stack of addresses to be reset on backtracking. In CLP systems in general, the trail is also used to store changes to constraints. Hence a tagged value trail is required. The tags specify what operation is to be reversed, and the value component, if present, contains any old data to be restored.

- *Time-stamped data structures*
  Time stamps have been briefly discussed in Section 10.6. The basic idea here is that the data structure representing a constraint may go through several changes without there being a new choice point encountered during this activity. Clearly only one state of the structure need be trailed for each choice point.

- *Constraint accumulator*
  A constraint is typically built up using a basic instruction repeatedly, for example, the `addpf` instruction in CLP($\mathcal{R}$). During this process, the partially constructed constraint is represented in an accumulator. One of the `solve` instructions then passes the constraint to the solver. We can think of this linear form accumulator as a generalization of the accumulator in classical computer architectures, accumulating a partially constructed constraint instead of a number.

11.3   Parallel implementations

We briefly outline the main works involving CLP and parallelism. The opportunities for parallelism in CLP languages are those that arise, and have already been addressed, in the logic programming context (such as or-parallelism, and-parallelism, stream-parallelism), and those that arise because of the presence of a potentially computationally costly constraint solver.

The first work in this area [van Hentenryck, 1989b] was an experimental implementation of an or-parallel CLP language with domain $\mathcal{FD}$. That approach has been pursued with the development of the ElipSys system [Véron *et al.*, 1993], which is the most developed of the parallel implementations of CLP languages.

Atay [Atay, 1992; Atay *et al.*, 1993] presents the or-parallelization of 2LP, a language that computes with linear inequalities over reals and integers, but in which rules do not have local variables[37]. Another work deals with the or-parallel implementation of a CLP language over $\mathcal{FD}$ on massively parallel SIMD computers [Tong and Leung, 1993]. However the basis for the parallelism is not the nondeterministic choice of rules, as in conventional LP or-parallelism, but the nondeterministic choice of values for a variable.

Work on and-parallelism in logic programming depends heavily on notions of independence of atoms in a goal. [García *et al.*, 1993] addresses this notion in a CLP context, and identify notions of independence for constraint solvers which must hold if the advantages of and-parallelism in LP are to be fully realized in CLP languages. However, there has not, to our knowledge, been any attempt to produce an and-parallel implementation of a CLP language.

Two works address both stream-parallelism and parallelism in constraint solving. GDCC [Terasaki *et al.*, 1992] is a committed-choice language that can be crudely characterized as a committed-choice version of CAL. It uses constraints over domains of finite trees, Booleans, real numbers and integers. [Terasaki *et al.*, 1992] mainly discusses the parallelization of the Groebner basis algorithms, which are the core of the solvers for the real number and Boolean constraint domains, and a parallel branch-and-bound method that is used in the integer solver. Leung [Leung, 1993] addresses the incorporation of constraint solving in both a committed-choice language and a language based on the Andorra model of computation. He presents distributed solvers for finite domains, the Boolean domain and linear inequalities over the reals. The finite domain solver is based on [van Hentenryck, 1989a], the solver for the reals parallelizes the Simplex algorithm, and the Boolean solver parallelizes the unification algorithm of

---

[37]We say that a variable in a rule is *local* if it appears in the body of the rule, but not in the head.

[Büttner and Simonis, 1987].

Finally, [Burg *et al.*, 1992; Burg, 1992] reports the design and initial implementation of CLP($\mathcal{R}$) with an execution model in which the inference engine and constraint solver compute concurrently and asynchronously. One of the issues addressed is backtracking, which is difficult when the engine and solver are so loosely coupled.

11.3.1   Programming and Applications

In this final part, we discuss the practical use of CLP languages. The format here is essentially a selected list of successful applications across a variety of problem domains. Each application is given an overview, with emphasis on the particular programming paradigm and CLP features used.

It seems useful to classify CLP applications broadly into two classes. In one class, the essential CLP technique is to use constraints and rules to obtain a transparent representation of the (relationships underlying the) problem. Here the constraints also provide a powerful query language. The other class caters for the many problems which can be solved by enumeration algorithms, the combinatorial search problems. Here the LP aspect of CLP is useful for providing the enumeration facility while constraints serve to keep the search space manageable.

12   Modelling of complex problems

We consider here the use of CLP as a specification language: constraints allow the declarative interpretation of basic relationships, and rules combine these for complex relationships.

12.1   Analysis and synthesis of analog circuits

This presentation is adapted from [Heintze *et al.*, 1992], an early application of CLP($\mathcal{R}$). Briefly, the general methodology for representing properties of circuits is that constraints at a base level describe the relationship between variables corresponding to a subsystem, such as Ohm's law, and constraints at a higher level describe the interaction between these subsystems, such as Kirchhoff's law.

Consider the following program fragment defining the procedure circuit(N, V, I) which specifies that, across an electrical network N, the potential difference and current are V and I respectively. The network is specified in an obvious way by a term containing the functors resistor, series and parallel. In this program, the first rule states the required voltage–current relationship for a resistor, and the remaining rules combine such relationships in a network of resistors.

```
circuit(resistor(R), V, I) :- V = I * R.
circuit(series(N1, N2), V, I) :-
    I = I1,
    I = I2,
    V = V1 + V2,
    circuit(N1, V1, I1),
    circuit(N2, V2, I2).
circuit(parallel(N1, N2), V, I) :-
    V = V1, V = V2,
    I = I1 + I2,
    circuit(N1, V1, I1),
    circuit(N2, V2, I2).
```

For example, the query

```
?- circuit(series(series(resistor(R),resistor(R)),
       resistor(R)),V,5)
```

asks for the voltage value if a current value of 5 is flowing through a network containing just three identical resistors in series. (The answer is R = 0.0666667*V.) Additional rules can be added for other devices. For example, the piece-wise linear model of a diode described by the voltage–current relationship

$$I = \begin{cases} 10V + 1000 & \text{if } V < -100 \\ 0.001V & \text{if } -100 \le V \le 0.6 \\ 100V - 60 & \text{if } V > 0.6 \end{cases}$$

is captured by the rules:

```
circuit(diode, V, 10 * V + 1000) :- V < -100.
circuit(diode, V, 0.0001 * V) :- -100 <= V, V <= 0.6.
circuit(diode, V, 100 * V - 60) :- V > 0.6.
```

This basic idea can be extended to model AC networks. For example, suppose we wish to reason about an RLC network in steady-state. First, we dispense with complex numbers by representing $X + iY$ as a CLP($\mathcal{R}$) term c(X, Y), and use:

```
c_equal(c(Re, Im), c(Re, Im)).
c_add(c(Re1, Im1), c(Re2, Im2), c(Re1 + Re2, Im1 + Im2)).
c_mult(c(Re1, Im1), c(Re2, Im2), c(Re3, Im3)) :-
    Re3 = Re1 * Re2 - Im1 * Im2,
    Im3 = Re1 * Im2 + Re2 * Im1.
```

to implement the basic complex arithmetic operations of equality, addition and multiplication.

Now consider the following procedure circuit(N, V, I, W) which is like its namesake above except that the voltage and current values are now complex numbers, and the new parameter W, a real number, is the angular frequency. It is noteworthy that this significant extension of the previous program fragment for circuit has been obtained so easily.

```
circuit(resistor(R), V, I, W) :-
    c_mult(V, I, c(R, 0)).
circuit(inductor(L), V, I, W) :-
    c_mult(V, I, c(0, W * L)).
circuit(capacitor(C), V, I, W) :-
    c_mult(V, I, c(0, -1 / (W * C))).
circuit(series(N1, N2), V, I, W) :-
    c_equal(I, I1), c_equal(I, I2),
    c_add(V, V1, V2),
    circuit(N1, V1, I1, W),
    circuit(N2, V2, I2, W).
circuit(parallel(N1, N2), V, I, W) :-
    c_equal(V, V1), c_equal(V, V2),
    c_add(I, I1, I2),
    V = V1, V = V2,
    I = I1 + I2,
    circuit(N1, V1, I1, W),
    circuit(N2, V2, I2, W).
```

We close this example application by mentioning that the work in [Heintze *et al.*, 1992] not only contains further explanation of the above technique, but also addresses other problems such as the *synthesis* of networks and digital signal flow. Not only does the CLP approach provide a concise framework for modelling circuits (previously done in a more *ad hoc* manner), but it also provides additional functionality because relationships, as opposed to values, are reasoned about. Evidence that this approach can be practical was given; for example, the modelling can be executed at the rate of about 100 circuit components per second on an RS6000 workstation.

12.2 Options trading analysis

Options are contracts whose value is contingent upon the value of some underlying asset. The most common type of option are those on company shares. A *call option* gives the holder the right to buy a fixed number of shares at a fixed *exercise price* until a certain maturity/expiration date. Conversely, a *put option* gives the holder the right to sell at a fixed price. The option itself may be bought or sold. For example, consider a call option costing $800 which gives the right to purchase 100 shares at $50 per share within some period of time. This call option can be sold at the current market price, or exercised at a cost of $5000. Now if the price of the share is $60, then the option may be exercised to obtain a profit of $10 per share; taking the price of the option into account, the net gain is $200. After the specified period, the call option, if not exercised, becomes worthless. Figure 5 shows *payoff diagrams* which are a simple model of the relationship between the value of a call option and the share price. Sell options have similar diagrams. Note that c denotes the cost of the option and x the exercise price.

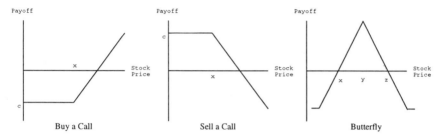

Fig. 5. Payoff diagrams

Options can be combined in arbitrary ways to form artificial financial instruments. This allows one to tailor risk and return in flexible ways. For example, the *butterfly* strategy in Figure 5 consists of buying two calls, one at a lower strike price x and one at a higher price z and selling two calls at the middle strike price y. This makes a profit if the share stays around the middle strike price and limits the loss if the movement is large.

The following presentation is due to Yap [Yap, 1994], based in his work using CLP($\mathcal{R}$). This material appeared in [Lassez *et al.*, 1987], and the subsequently implemented OTAS system is described in [Huynh and Lassez, 1988]. There are several main reasons why CLP, and CLP($\mathcal{R}$) in particular, are suitable for reasoning about option trading: there are complex trading strategies used which are usually formulated as rules; there is a combinatorial aspect to the problem as there are many ways of combining options; a combination of symbolic and numeric computation is involved; there are well developed mathematical valuation models and constraints on the relationships involved in option pricing, and finally, flexible 'what-if' type analysis is required.

A simple mathematical model of valuing options, and other financial instruments such as stocks and bonds, is with linear piecewise functions. Let the Heaviside function h and the ramp function r be defined as follows:

$$h(x, y) = \begin{cases} 0 & \text{if } x > y \\ 1 & \text{otherwise} \end{cases} \quad \text{and} \quad r(x, y) = \begin{cases} 0 & \text{if } x > y \\ y - x & \text{otherwise} \end{cases}$$

The payoff function for call and put options can now be described by the following matrix product which creates a linear piecewise function:

$$payoff = [h_1, h_2, r_1, r_2] \times \begin{bmatrix} h(b_1, s) \\ h(b_2, s) \\ r(b_1, s) \\ r(b_2, s) \end{bmatrix}$$

where s is the share price, b_i is either the strike price or 0, and h_i and r_i are multipliers of the Heaviside and ramp functions. In the following program, the variables S, X, R respectively denote the stock price, the exercise price and the interest rate.

```
h(X, Y, Z) :- Y < X, Z = 0.
h(X, Y, Z) :- Y >= X, Z = 1.
r(X, Y, Z) :- Y < X, Z = 0.
r(X, Y, Z) :- Y >= X, Z = Y - X.
value(Type, Buy_or_Sell, S, C, P, R, X, B, Payoff) :-
    sign(Buy_or_Sell, Sign),
    data(Type, S, C, P, R, X, B, B1, B2, H1, H2, R1, R2),
    h(B1, S, T1), h(B2, S, T2), r(B1, S, T3),
    r(B2, S, T4),
    Payoff = Sign*(H1*T1 + H2*T2 + R1*T3 + R2*T4).
```

The parameters for the piecewise functions can be expressed symbolically in the following tables, implemented simply as CLP facts.

```
sign(buy, -1).
sign(sell, 1).
data(stock, S, C, P, R, X, B, 0, 0, S*R, 0, -1, 0).
data(call, S, C, P, R, X, B, 0, X, C*R, 0, 0, -1).
data(put, S, C, P, R, X, B, 0, X, P*R-X, 0, 1, -1).
data(bond, S, C, P, R, X, B, 0, 0, B*R, 0, 0, 0).
```

This program forms the basis for evaluating option combinations. The following direct query evaluates the sale of a call option that expires *in-the-money*[38],

---

[38] That is, when the strike price is less than the share price.

```
?- Call = 5, X = 50, R = 1.05, S = 60,
   value(call, sell, S, Call, _, R, X, _, Payoff).
```

giving the answer, `Payoff = -4.75`. More general queries make use of the ability to reason with inequalities. We can ask for what share price does the value exceed 5,

```
?- Payoff > 5, C = 5, X = 50, R = 1.05, S = 60,
   value(call, sell, S, C, _, R, X, _, Payoff).
```

The answer constraints returned[39] illustrates the piecewise nature of the model,

```
Payoff = 5.25, S < 50;
Payoff = 55.25 - S, 50 <= S, S <= 50.25.
```

More complex combinations can be constructed by composing them out of the base financial instruments and linking them together with constraints. For example, the following is a combination of two calls and two puts,

```
?- R = 0.1,
Payoff = Payoff1 + Payoff2 + Payoff3 + Payoff4,
   P1 = 10, K1 = 20, value(put, sell, S, _, P1, R, K1,
   _, Payoff1),
   P2 = 18, K2 = 40, value(put, buy, S, _, P2, R, K2,
   _, Payoff2),
   C3 = 18, K3 = 60, value(call, buy, S, C3, _, R, K3,
   _, Payoff3),
   C4 = 18, K4 = 60, value(call, sell, S, C4, _, R, K4,
   _, Payoff4).
```

The answer obtained illustrates how combinations of options can be tailored to produce a custom linear piecewise payoff function.

```
Payoff = 5.7, S < 20;
Payoff = 25.7 - S, 20 <= S, S < 40;
Payoff = -14.3, 40 <= S, S < 60;
Payoff = S - 74.3, 60 <= S, S < 80;
Payoff = 5.7, 80 <= S.
```

The above is just a brief overview of the core ideas behind the work in [Lassez *et al.*, 1987]. Among the important aspects that are omitted are consideration of option pricing models, and details of implementing the de-

---

[39] We will use ';' to separate different sets of answer constraints in the output.

cision support system OTAS [Huynh and Lassez, 1988]. As in the circuit modelling application described above, the advantages of using CLP($\mathcal{R}$) here are that the program is concise and that the query language is expressive.

12.3   Temporal reasoning

It is natural and common to model time as an arithmetic domain, and indeed we do this in everyday life. Depending upon the application, a discrete representation (such as the integers) or a continuous representation (such as the reals) may be appropriate, and varying amounts of the arithmetic signature are needed (for example, we might use only the ordering, or use only a successor function). In this brief discussion we assume that time is linearly ordered, although this is not a universally accepted choice [Emerson, 1990].

Temporal logic [Emerson, 1990] is often used as a language for expressing time-related concepts. Temporal logic adds to standard first-order logic such constructs as *next* (meaning, roughly, 'in the next time instant'[40]), *always* (meaning 'in every future time instant'), and *sometime* (meaning 'in some future time instant'). The language Templog [Abadi and Manna, 1989] was designed based on a Horn-like subset of temporal logic in which the meaning of function symbols does not vary with time, but the meaning of predicate symbols does. It was shown in [Brzoska, 1991] that the operational behavior of Templog could be mimicked by a CLP language via the following natural translation: every predicate receives another argument, representing time. Then, at time t, *next* is represented by $t' = t + 1$, and the future (for *always* and *sometime*) is represented by $t' \geq t$. In later work [Brzoska, 1993], Brzoska has presented a more powerful temporal logic language which also can be viewed as, and implemented through, a CLP language.

Often we wish to manipulate the time parameter more directly than is possible in conventional temporal logic. For example, we may wish to express durations as well as times. We can do this if we include + in the signature of our domain modelling time. This is used in applications to scheduling, among others, as discussed in Section 13.

The use of simple constraint domains to model time has been explored extensively in the context of temporal databases. In this situation, an item of data might incorporate the time interval for which it is valid. Simple domains have been considered because of over-riding requirements for quick and terminating execution of queries, as discussed in Section 7. Furthermore, often the restriction is made that only one or two arguments in a tuple are time-valued, with the other arguments taking constant values.

---

[40]We assume that time is modelled by the integers.

[Baudinet *et al.*, 1993] surveys work in this area using an integer model of time.

13   Combinatorial search problems

CLP offers an easy realization of enumeration algorithms for the solving of combinatorial problems. Given decision variables $x_1, \ldots, x_n$, one uses a CLP program schema of the form

```
solve(X1, ... , Xn) :-
    constraints(X1, ... , Xn),
    enumerate(X1, ... , Xn).
```

to implement a 'constrain-and-generate' enumeration strategy (also called implicit enumeration), as opposed to naive enumerate-and-test strategy, to curtail the search space. We refer to the basic text [van Hentenryck, 1989a], chapter 2, for further introductory material to this CLP approach.

The above schema is used to represent the set of all solutions to the constraints. Often one desires an *optimal* solution according to some criterion, say the solution $a_1, \ldots, a_n$ to $x_1, \ldots, x_n$ that minimizes some given function $cost(x_1, \ldots, x_n)$. The simplest strategy to obtain this solution is simply to obtain and check each and every solution of `solve`. An easy improvement is obtained by augmenting the search with a *branch-and-bound* strategy. Briefly, the cost of the best solution encountered so far is stored and the continuing search is constrained to find only new solutions of better cost. More concretely, CLP systems typically provide predicates such as `minimize(solve(X1, ... , Xn, Cost), BestCost)` (and similarly `maximize(...)`) where `solve(X1, ... , Xn, Cost)` serves to obtain one solution as explained above, with cost `Cost`, and `BestCost` is a number representing the cost of the best solution found so far. (Initially, this number can be any sufficiently large number.) It is assumed here that the procedure `solve(X1, ... , Xn, Cost)` maintains a lower bound for a variable `Cost`, which is computed as the values of the decision variables are determined. The `minimize` procedure then essentially behaves as a repeated invocation of the goal `?- Cost < BestCost, solve(X1, ... , Xn, Cost)`. In general, the choice of a suitable cost function can be difficult. Finally, we refer the reader to the text [van Hentenryck, 1989a, Section 4.5.1] for a more detailed explanation of how branch-and-bound is used in CLP systems.

The constraint domain at hand is discrete and typically finite (since the enumeration must cover all candidate values for the sequence $x_1, \ldots, x_n$), and therefore constraint solving is almost always NP-hard. This in turn restricts implementations to the use of partial solvers, that is, not all constraints will be considered active. Recall that partial solvers are, however, required to be conservative in the sense that whenever unsatisfiability is reported, the tested constraints are indeed unsatisfiable.

In general, the primary efficiency issues are:

- How complete is the constraint solver? In general, there is tradeoff between the larger cost of a more complete solver and the smaller search space that such a solver can give rise to.
- What constraints to use to model the problem? A special case of this issue concerns the use of *redundant* constraints, that is, constraints that do not change the meaning of the constraint store. In general, redundant constraints will slow down a CLP system with a complete solver. With partial solvers, however, redundant constraints may be useful to the solver in case the equivalent information in the constraint store is not active.
- In which order do we choose the decision variables for enumeration? And should such order be dynamically determined?
- In which order do we enumerate the values for a given decision variable? And should such order be dynamically determined?

In this section, we will outline a number of CLP applications in specific combinatorial problem areas. In each subsection below, unless otherwise specified, we shall assume that the underlying constraint system is based on the integers.

13.1   Cutting stock

The following describes a two-dimensional cutting stock problem pertaining to furniture manufacturing, an early application of CHIP [Dincbas *et al.*, 1988b]. We are given a sawing machine which cuts a board of wood into a number of different sized shelves. The machine is able to cut in several configurations, each of which determines the number of each kind of shelf, and some amount of wood wasted. Let there be N different kinds of shelves, and M different configurations. Let $S_{i,j}$, $1 \leq i \leq M$, $1 \leq j \leq N$, denote the number of shelves j cut in configuration i. Let W_i, $1 \leq i \leq M$, denote the wastage in configuration i. Let R_i, $1 \leq i \leq N$ denote the number of shelves i required. The problem now can be stated as finding the configurations such that the required number of shelves are obtained and the wastage minimized.

In [Dincbas *et al.*, 1988b], there were 6 kinds of shelves, 72 configurations, and the number of boards to be cut was fixed at 4. Two solutions were then presented, which we now paraphrase.

Let X_i, $1 \leq i \leq 72$, denote the number of boards cut according to configuration i. Thus $X_1 + \cdots + X_{72} = 4$. The requirements on the number of shelves are expressed via the constraints $X_1 * S_{1,j} + \cdots + X_{72} * S_{72,j} \geq R_j$, for $1 \leq j \leq N$. The objective function, to be minimized, is $X_1 * W_1 + \cdots + X_{72} * W_{72}$. The straightforward program representation of all this is given below. The enumerate procedure has the range $\{0, 1, 2, 3, 4\}$. Note that solve is run repeatedly in the search for the solution of lowest Cost.

```
solve(X₁, ... , X₇₂, Cost) :-
    X₁ + ... + X₇₂ = 4,
    X₁ * S₁,₁ + ... + X₇₂ * S₇₂,₁ >= R₁,
    X₁ * S₁,₂ + ... + X₇₂ * S₇₂,₂ >= R₂,
    ...
    X₁ * S₁,₆ + ... + X₇₂ * S₇₂,₆ >= R₆,
    Cost = X₁ * W₁ + ... + X₇₂ * W₇₂,
    enumerate(X₁, ... , X₇₂).
```

The second solution uses the special CHIP constraint `element`, described above in Section 9.2. Recall that `element(X, List, E)` expresses that the X'th element of `List` is E. In this second approach to the problem, the variables X_i, $1 \le i \le 4$, denote the configurations chosen. Thus $1 \le X_i \le 72$. Let $T_{i,j}$, $1 \le i \le 4$, $1 \le j \le 6$, denote the number of shelves j in configuration i. Let $Cost_i$, $1 \le i \le 4$, denote the wastage in configuration i. Thus the required shelves are obtained by the constraints $T_{1,j} + \cdots + T_{4,j} \ge R_j$ where $1 \le j \le 6$, and the total cost is simply $Cost_1 + \cdots + Cost_4$.

In the program below, the constraints $X_1 \le X_2 \le X_3 \le X_4$ serve to eliminate consideration of symmetrical solutions. The following group of 24 `element` constraints serve to compute the $T_{i,j}$ variables in terms of the (given) $S_{i,j}$ values and the (computed) X_i values. The next group of 4 `element` constraints computes the $Cost_i$ variables in terms of the (given) W_i variables. The `enumerate` procedure has the range $\{1, 2, \ldots, 72\}$. Once again, `solve` is run repeatedly here in the search for the lowest `Cost`.

```
solve(X₁, ... , X₄, Cost) :-
    X₁ <= X₂, X₂ <= X₃, X₃ <= X₄,
    element(X₁, [S₁,ⱼ, ... , S₇₂,ⱼ], T₁,ⱼ),      % (1 ≤ j ≤ 6)
    element(X₂, [S₁,ⱼ, ... , S₇₂,ⱼ], T₂,ⱼ),
    element(X₃, [S₁,ⱼ, ... , S₇₂,ⱼ], T₃,ⱼ),
    element(X₄, [S₁,ⱼ, ... , S₇₂,ⱼ], T₄,ⱼ),
    element(X₁, [W₁, ... W₇₂], Cost₁),
    element(X₂, [W₁, ... W₇₂], Cost₂),
    element(X₃, [W₁, ... W₇₂], Cost₃),
    element(X₄, [W₁, ... W₇₂], Cost₄),
    T₁,ⱼ + T₂,ⱼ + T₃,ⱼ + T₄,ⱼ >= Rⱼ,             % (1 ≤ j ≤ 6)
    Cost = Cost₁ + Cost₂ + Cost₃ + Cost₄,
    enumerate(X₁, X₂, X₃, X₄).
```

The second program has advantages over the first. Apart from a smaller search space (approximately 10^7 in comparison with 10^{43}), it was able to avoid encountering symmetrical solutions. The timings given in [Dincbas *et al.*, 1988b] showed that the second program ran much faster. This comparison exemplifies the abovementioned fact that the way a problem is modelled can greatly affect efficiency.

13.2   DNA sequencing

We consider a simplified version of the problem of restriction site mapping (RSM). Briefly, a DNA sequence is a finite string over the letters $\{A, C, G, T\}$, and a restriction enzyme partitions a DNA sequence into certain fragments. The problem is then to reconstruct the original DNA sequence from the fragments and other information obtained through experiments. In what follows, we consider an abstraction of this problem which deals only with the lengths of fragments, instead of the fragments themselves.

Consider the use of two enzymes. Let the first enzyme partition the DNA sequence into $A_1, \ldots, A_N$ and the second into $B_1, \ldots, B_M$. Now, a simultaneous use of the two enzymes also produces a partition $D_1, \ldots, D_K$ corresponding to combining the previous two partitions. That is,

$$\forall i \exists j : A_1 \cdots A_i = D_1 \cdots D_j \text{ and}$$
$$\forall i \exists j : B_1 \cdots B_i = D_1 \cdots D_j, \text{ and conversely,}$$
$$\forall j \exists i : (D_1 \ldots D_j = A_1 \ldots A_i) \vee (D_1 \ldots D_j = B_1 \ldots B_i).$$

Let a_i denote the length of A_i; similarly for b_i and d_i. Let $\vec{a}_i$ denote the subsequence $(a_1, \ldots, a_i)$, $1 \leq i \leq N$. Similarly define $\vec{b}_i$ and $\vec{d}_i$. The problem at hand now can be stated as: given the *multisets* $\tilde{a} = \{a_1, \ldots, a_N\}$, $\tilde{b} = \{b_1, \ldots, b_M\}$ and $\tilde{d} = \{d_1, \ldots, d_K\}$, construct the *sequences* $\vec{a}_N = (a_1, \ldots, a_N)$, $\vec{b}_M = (b_1, \ldots, b_M)$ and $\vec{d}_K = (d_1, \ldots, d_K)$.

Our basic algorithm generates $d_1, d_2, \ldots$ in order and extends the partitions for $\vec{a}$ and $\vec{b}$ using the following invariant property which can be obtained from the problem definition above. Either

- d_k is aligned with a_i, that is, $d_1 + \cdots + d_k = a_1 + \cdots + a_i$, or
- d_k is aligned with b_j (but not with a_i[41],) that is, $d_1 + \cdots + d_k = b_1 + \cdots + b_j$.

In the program below, the main procedure `solve` takes as input three lists representing $\tilde{a}, \tilde{b}$ and $\tilde{d}$ in the first three arguments, and outputs in the remaining three arguments. Enumeration is done by choosing, at each recursive step of the `rsm` procedure, one of two cases mentioned above. Hence the two rules for `rsm`. Note that the three middle arguments of `rsm` maintain the length of the subsequences found so far, and in all calls, either `lenA = lenD < lenB` or `lenB = lenD < lenA` holds; the procedure `choose_initial` chooses the first fragment, and the first call to `rsm` is made with this invariant holding. Finally, the procedure `choose` deletes some element from the given list and returns the resultant list. Note that one more rule for `rsm` is needed in case the A and B fragments do align

---

[41]For simplicity we assume that we never have all three partitions aligned except at the beginning and at the end.

anywhere except at the extreme ends; we have omitted this possibility for simplicity.

```
solve(A, B, D, [AFrag|MapA], [BFrag|MapB],
[DFrag|MapD]) :-
    choose_initial(A, B, D, AFrag, BFrag, DFrag, A2, B2, D2),
    rsm(A2, B2, D2, AFrag, BFrag, DFrag, MapA, MapB, MapD).
rsm(A, B, D, LenA, LenB, LenD, MapA, MapB, MapD) :-
    empty(A), empty(B), empty(D),
    MapA = [], MapB = [], MapD = [].
rsm(A, B, D, LenA, LenB, LenD, [Ai|MapA], MapB,
[Dk|MapD]) :-
    LenA = LenD, LenA < LenB
    Dk <= LenB - LenA, Ai >= Dk,
    choose(Dk, D, D2),
    choose(Ai, A, A2),
    rsm(A2, B, D2, LenA + Ai, LenB, LenD + Dk,
    MapA, MapB, MapD).
rsm(A, B, D, LenA, LenB, LenD, MapA, [Bj|MapB],
[Dk|MapD]) :-
    LenB = LenD, LenB < LenA
    Dk <= LenA - LenB, Bj >= Dk,
    choose(Dk, D, D2),
    choose(Bj, B, B2),
    rsm(A, B2, D2, LenA, LenB + Bj, LenD + Dk,
    MapA, MapB, MapD).
```

This application of CLP is due to Yap [Yap, 1991; Yap, 1993] and it is important to note that the above program is a considerable simplification of Yap's program. A major omission is the consideration of errors in the fragment lengths (because these lengths are obtained from experimentation). A major point in Yap's approach is that it gives a robust and uniform treatment of the experimental errors inherent in the data as compared with many of the approaches in the literature. Furthermore, [Yap, 1993] shows how the simple two enzyme problem can be extended to a number of other problem variations. Because a map solution is just a set of answer constraints returned by the algorithm, it is easy to combine this with other maps, compare maps, verify maps, etc. This kind of flexibility is important as the computational problem of just computing a consistent map is intractable, and hence when dealing with any substantial amount of data, any algorithm would have to take into account data from many varieties of mapping experiments, as well as other information specific to the molecule in question.

13.3   Scheduling

In this class of problems, we are given a number of tasks, and for each task, a task duration. Each task also requires other resources to be performed, and there are constraints on precedences of task performance, and on resource usage. The problem is to schedule the tasks so that the resources are most efficiently used (for example, perform the tasks so that all are done as soon as possible).

Consider now a basic *job-shop* scheduling problem in which is given a number m of machines, j sequences of tasks, the task durations and the machine assigned to each task. The precedence constraints are that the tasks in each sequence (called a job) are performed in the sequence order. The resource constraints are that each machine performs at most one task at any given time.

In the program below, `precedences` sets up the precedence constraints for one job, and is called with two equally long lists. The first contains the task variables, whose values are the start times. The second list contains the durations of the tasks. Thus `precedences` is called once for each job. The procedure `resources` is called repeatedly, once for each pair of tasks T_1 and T_2 which must be performed without overlapping; their durations are given by D_1 and D_2.

```
precedences([T₁, T₂ | Tail], [D₁, D₂ | Tail2]) :-
    T₁ + D₁ <= T₂,
    precedences(Tail, Tail2).
precedences([], []).

resources(T₁, D₁, T₂, D₂) :- T₁ + D₁ <= T₂.
resources(T₁, D₁, T₂, D₂) :- T₂ + D₂ <= T₁.
```

A simple way to proceed is to fix an ordering of the tasks performed on each machine. This corresponds to choosing one of the two `resources` rules for each pair of tasks assigned to the same machine. This forms the basis of the `enumerate` procedure below. Once an ordering of tasks is fixed, it is a simple matter to determine the best start times for each task.

This can be done in the manner indicated in the `solve` procedure below. An important efficiency point is that by choosing a precedence between two tasks, the new constraints created by the use of `resources`, in conjunction with the precedence constraints, can reduce the number of possible choices for the remaining pairs. We assume that the procedure `define_cost` defines Cost in such a way that, in conjunction with other constraints, it provides a conservative lower bound of the real cost of the schedule determined so far. Its precise definition, omitted here, can be obtained in a similar way as in the second program of the cutting-stock example above.

```
solve(T₁, T₂, ... , Tₙ, Cost) :-
```

```
precedences( ... ), % one per job
...
precedences( ... ),
define_cost(T₁, T₂, ... , Tₙ, Cost),
enumerate(T₁, T₂, ... , Tₙ),
generate_start_times(T₁, T₂, ... , Tₙ).
enumerate(T₁, T₂, ... , Tₙ) :-
    resources( ... ), % one per pair of tasks assigned
    to same machine
    ...
    resources( ... ).
```

Finally, this `solve` procedure can be repeatedly run, within a branch-and-bound framework (with a special `minimize` predicate mechanism as explained above) to obtain the best solution over all possible orderings.

In this presentation of the program we have chosen to simply list all calls to `precedences` in the procedure `solve`, to focus on the important procedures in the program. A real program would use an auxiliary predicate to iterate over the jobs and generate the calls to `precedences`. Similarly, `enumerate` would iterate to generate calls to `resources`. Thus the program would be independent of the number of jobs or the pattern in which tasks are assigned to machines. Similar comments apply to other programs in this section.

There are variations and specializations of CLP approaches to this problem. Section 5.4.2 of [van Hentenryck, 1989a] and section 2 of [Dincbas *et al.*, 1990], on which this presentation is based, further discuss the problem and how particular features of CHIP can be useful. Another CHIP approach, but this time to a specific and practical scheduling problem, is reported in [Chamard *et al.*, 1992]. In [Aggoun and Beldiceanu, 1992], the focus is on a new feature of CHIP and how it can be used to obtain an optimal solution to a particular 10 jobs and 10 machine problem, which remained open until recently.

Real scheduling problems can involve more kinds of constraints than just those mentioned above. For example, one could require that there is at most a certain time elapsed between the completion of one task and the commencement of another. See [Wallace, 1993] for a more complete discussion of the CLP approach to the general scheduling problem.

13.4 Chemical hypothetical reasoning

This Prolog III application, described in some detail in [Jourdan *et al.*, 1990], uses both arithmetic and Boolean constraints. The problem at hand is that of elucidating chemical-reaction pathways, and we quote [Jourdan *et al.*, 1990]: given an *instantiation* of the (two-reagent) reaction schema $A + B \leadsto T + P_1 + \cdots + P_k$, determine the *pathway*, that is, the set of constituent reaction *steps*, as well as other molecules (or *species*) formed during the reaction.

The reaction step considered in [Jourdan *et al.*, 1990] contains at most two reactant molecules, and at most two product molecules, and so can be described in the form $R_1 + R_2 \longrightarrow P_1 + P_2$ where R_1, R_2, P_1, P_2 are (possibly empty) molecular formulas. The problem then is to determine, given an overall reaction, a collection of basic steps or pathway which explain the overall reaction. For example, given $C_7H_9N + CH_2O \rightsquigarrow C_{17}H_{18}N_2 + H_2O$, the following is a pathway which explains the reaction.

$$C_7H_9N + CH_2O \longrightarrow H_2O + C_8H_9N$$
$$C_8H_9N + C_8H_9N \longrightarrow C_{16}H_{18}N_2$$
$$C_8H_9N + C_{16}H_{18}N_2 \longrightarrow C_{17}H_{18}N_2 + C_7H_9N$$

Here C_8H_9N and $C_{16}H_{18}N_2$ are the previously unidentified species.

The program imposes constraints to express requirements for a chemical reaction and to exclude uninteresting reactions. In addition to the constraints on the number of molecules, there are two other constraints on reaction steps: for each chemical element, the number of reactant atoms equals the number of product atoms (i.e. the step is *chemically balanced*), and no molecular formula appears in both sides of a step.

There are also constraints on the pathway. Let the reaction schema under consideration be $A + B \rightsquigarrow T + P_1 + \cdots + P_k$. Then

- All pathway species must be formable from the two reagents A and B.
- Neither A nor B alone is sufficient to form the target product T. Here Boolean variables are used to express the dependency relation 'can be formed from'. For each pathway step $R_1, R_2 \longrightarrow P_1, P_2$ we state the Boolean constraint $a_1 \wedge a_2 \implies a_3 \wedge a_4$ where a_1, a_2, a_3, a_4 are Boolean variables associated with R_1, R_2, P_1, P_2 respectively. The constraint expresses that both P_1 and P_2 can be formed if both R_1 and R_2 can be formed. Let $\mathcal{B}$ denote the Boolean formulas thus constructed over all the steps in a pathway. Then expressing that species R does not, by itself, produce species P is tantamount to the satisfiability of the Boolean constraint $\mathcal{B} \wedge \neg(a_R \implies a_P)$, where a_R and a_P are the Boolean variables associated with R and P respectively. Since we have two original reagents, we will need two sets of Boolean variables and two sets of dependency constraints to avoid any interference between the two conditions.
- There is a notion of *pathway consistency* which is defined to be the satisfiability of a certain arithmetic formula constructed from the occurrences of species in the pathway. Essentially this formula is a conjunction of formulas $n_1 + n_2 = n_3 + n_4$, for each pathway step

$R_1 + R_2 \longrightarrow P_1 + P_2$, where $n_1, \ldots, n_4$ are the arithmetic variables of R_1, R_2, P_1, P_2 respectively.

- Finally, in the ultimate output of the program, no two pathways are identical, nor become identical under transformations such as permuting the reactants or products within a step, or switching the reactants and products in a step.

The program representation of a molecular formula is as a list of numbers, each of which specifies the number of atoms of a certain chemical element. We shall assume that there are only four chemical elements of interest in our presentation, and hence a molecular formula is a 4-tuple. A species is also represented by a 4-tuple (n, a, b, f) where n is an arithmetic variable (to be used in the formulation of the arithmetic formula mentioned above), a and b are Boolean variables (to be used in expressing the formation dependencies), and f is the species formula. A step $R_1 + R_2 \longrightarrow P_1 + P_2$ is represented by a 4-tuple (r_1, r_2, p_1, p_2) containing the identifiers of the representations of R_1, R_2, P_1 and P_2.

The listing below is a simplified and translated version of the Prolog III program in [Jourdan *et al.*, 1990]. In the main procedure `solve`, the first argument is a list of fixed size, say n, in which each element is a species template. The first three templates are given, and these represent the two initial reagents R_1, R_2 and final target T. Similarly, `Steps` is a list of fixed size, say m, in which each element is a step template. Thus n and m are parameters to the program. The undefined procedure `formula_of` obtains the species formula from a species, that is, it projects onto the last element of the given 4-tuple. Similarly, `arith_var_of`, `bool_var_a_of` and `bool_var_b_of` project onto the first, second and third arguments respectively.

The procedure `no_duplicates` asserts constraints which prevent duplicate species and steps, and it also prevents symmetrical solutions; we omit the details. Calls to the procedure `formation_dependencies` generate the formation dependencies. The procedure `both_reagents_needed` imposes two constraints, one for each reagent, that, in conjunction with the formation dependencies, assert that R_1 (respectively R_2) alone cannot produce T. Finally, `enumerate_species` is self-explanatory.

```
solve([R₁, R₂, T | Species], Steps) :-
    no_duplicates( ... ),
    balanced_step( ... ), % for each step in Steps
    pathway_step_consistency( ... ), % for each step in Steps
    formation_dependencies( ... ), % for each step in Steps
    both_reagents_needed(R₁, R₂, T),
    enumerate_species( ... ).
balanced_step(R₁, R₂, P₁, P₂) :-
    formula_of(R₁, (C₁, H₁, N₁, O₁)),
```

```
    formula_of(R₂, (C₂, H₂, N₂, O₂)),
    formula_of(P₁, (C₃, H₃, N₃, O₃)),
    formula_of(P₂, (C₄, H₄, N₄, O₄)),
    C₁ + C₂ = C₃ + C₄,
    H₁ + H₂ = H₃ + H₄,
    N₁ + N₂ = N₃ + N₄,
    O₁ + O₂ = O₃ + O₄.
pathway_step_consistency(R₁, R₂, P₁, P₂) :-
    arith_var_of(R₁, N₁), arith_var_of(R₁, N₂),
    arith_var_of(P₁, N₃), arith_var_of(P₁, N₄),
    N₁ + N₂ = N₃ + N₄.
formation_dependencies(R₁, R₂, P₁, P₂) :-
    bool_var_a_of(R₁, A₁), bool_var_b_of(R₁, B₁),
    bool_var_a_of(R₁, A₂), bool_var_b_of(R₂, B₂),
    bool_var_a_of(P₁, A₃), bool_var_b_of(P₁, B₃),
    bool_var_a_of(P₁, A₄), bool_var_b_of(P₂, B₄),
    A₁ ∧ A₂ ⟹ A₃ ∧ A₄,
    B₁ ∧ B₂ ⟹ B₃ ∧ B₄.
both_reagents_needed(R₁, R₂, T) :-
    bool_var_a_of(R₁, A₁), bool_var_b_of(R₂, B₁),
    bool_var_a_of(T, A₃), bool_var_b_of(T, B₃),
    ¬ (A₁ ⟹ A₃),
    ¬ (B₁ ⟹ B₃).
```

13.5 Propositional solver

As mentioned above in the discussion about the Boolean constraint domain, one approach to solving Boolean equations is to use clp(FD), representing the input formulas in a straightforward way using variables constrained to be 0 or 1. See section 3.3.2 of [Simonis and Dincbas, 1993] and [Codognet and Diaz, 1993] for example. What follows is from [Codognet and Diaz, 1993].

Assuming, without losing generality, that the input is a conjunction of equations of the form $Z = X \wedge Y$, $Z = X \vee Y$ or $X = \neg Y$, the basic algorithm is simply to represent each equation

$$Z = X \wedge Y \quad \text{by the } \mathcal{FD} \text{ constraints} \quad Z = X \times Y$$
$$Z \leq X \leq Z \times Y + 1 - Y$$
$$Z \leq Y \leq Z \times X + 1 - X$$
$$Z = X \vee Y \quad \text{by} \quad Z = X + Y - X \times Y$$
$$Z \times (1 - Y) \leq X \leq Z$$
$$Z \times (1 - X) \leq Y \leq Z$$
$$X = \neg Y \quad \text{by} \quad X = 1 - Y$$
$$Y = 1 - X$$

The following is a clp(FD) program fragment which realizes these representations. What is not shown is a procedure which takes the input equation and calls the **and**, **or** and **not** procedures appropriately, and an enumeration procedure (over the values 0 and 1) for all variables. In this program $val(X)$ delays execution of an $\mathcal{FD}$ constraint containing it until X is ground, at which time $val(X)$ denotes the value of X. The meanings of $min(X)$ and $max(X)$ are, respectively, the current lower and upper bounds on X maintained by the constraint solver, as discussed in Section 9.3. A constraint X *in* $s..t$ expresses that s and t are, respectively, lower and upper bounds for X.

```
and(X, Y, Z) :-
    Z in min(X)*min(Y) .. max(X)*max(Y),
    X in min(Z) .. max(Z)*max(Y) + 1 - min(Y),
    Y in min(Z) .. max(Z)*max(X) + 1 - min(X).
or(X, Y, Z) :-
    Z in min(X) + min(Y) - min(X)*min(Y) ..
    max(X) + max(Y) - max(X)*max(Y),
    X in min(Z)*(1 - max(Y)) .. max(Z),
    Y in min(Z)*(1 - max(X)) .. max(Z).
not(X, Y) :-
    X in 1 - val(Y),
    Y in 1 - val(X).
```

We conclude here by mentioning the authors' claim that this approach has great efficiency. In particular, it is several times faster than each of two Boolean solvers deployed in CHIP, and some special-purpose stand-alone solvers.

14 Further applications

The applications discussed in the previous two sections are but a sample of CLP applications. Here we briefly mention some others to indicate the breadth of problems that have been addressed using CLP languages and techniques.

We have exemplified the use of CLP to model analog circuits above. A considerable amount of work has also been done on digital circuits, in particular on verification [Simonis, 1989a; Simonis and Dincbas, 1987a; Simonis *et al.*, 1988; Simonis and Le Provost, 1989], diagnosis [Simonis and Dincbas, 1987b], synthesis [Simonis and Graf, 1990] and test-pattern generation [Simonis, 1989b]. Many of these works used the CHIP system. See also [Filkorn *et al.*, 1991] for a description of a large application. In civil engineering, [Lakmazaheri and Rasdorf, 1989] used CLP($\mathcal{R}$) for the analysis and partial synthesis of truss structures. As with electrical circuits, the constraints implement physical modelling and are used to verify truss and support components, as well as to generate spatial configurations. There is also work in mechanical engineering; [Sthanusubramonian, 1991] used CLP($\mathcal{R}$) to design gear boxes, and [Subramanian and Wang, 1993] combined techniques from qualitative physics and CLP($\mathcal{R}$) to design mechanical systems from behavior specifications. In general, engineering applications such as these use CLP to specify a hierarchical composition of complex systems and for rule-based reasoning.

Another important application area for CLP is finance. We mentioned the OTAS work above. Some further work is [Homiak, 1991] which also deals with option valuations, and [Berthier, 1989; Berthier, 1990; Broek and Daniels, 1991] which deal with financial planning. These financial applications have tended to take the form of expert systems involving sophisticated mathematical models.

There have been various proposals for including certainty measures and probabilities in logic programs to provide some built-in evidential reasoning that can be useful when writing expert systems. Original proposals [Shapiro, 1983b; van Emden, 1986] intended Prolog as the underlying language, but it is clear that CLP languages provide for more flexible execution of such expert systems.

Finally, we mention work on applying CLP languages to: music [Tobias, 1988], car sequencing [van Hentenryck, 1991], aircraft traffic control [Codognet *et al.*, 1992], building visual language parsers [Helm *et al.*, 1991], a warehousing problem [Bisdorff and Laurent, 1993], safety analysis [Corsini and Rauzy, 1993], frequency assignment for cellular telephones [Carlsson and Grindal, 1993], timetabling [Boizumault *et al.*, 1993], floor planning [Kanchanasut and Sumetphong, 1992], spacecraft attitude control [Skuppin and Buckle, 1992], interoperability of fiber optic communications equipment [Chadra *et al.*, 1992], interest rate risk management in banking [Gailly *et al.*, 1992], failure mode and effect analysis of complex systems [Gailly *et al.*, 1992], development of digitally controlled analog systems [Nerode and Kohn, 1993], testing of telecommunication protocols [Ladret, 1993], causal graph management [Rueher, 1993], factory scheduling [Evans, 1992], etc. The Applause Project [Li *et al.*, 1993] has developed applications that use the ElipSys system for manufacturing planning, tourist advice, molecular biology, and environment monitoring and control.

Acknowledgements

We would like to thank the following people for their comments on drafts of this paper and/or help in other ways: M. Bruynooghe, N. Heintze, P. van Hentenryck, A. Herold, J-L. Lassez, S. Michaylov, C. Palamidessi, K. Shuerman, P. Stuckey, M. Wallace, R. Yap. We also thank the anonymous referees for their careful reading and helpful comments.

References

[Abadi and Manna, 1989] M. Abadi and Z. Manna. Temporal Logic Programming, *Journal of Symbolic Computation*, **8**, 277–295, 1989.

[Aggoun and Beldiceanu, 1992] A. Aggoun and N. Beldiceanu. Extending CHIP to Solve Complex Scheduling and Packing Problems, In *Journées Francophones De Programmation Logique*, Lille, France, 1992.

[Aggoun and Beldiceanu, 1993] A. Aggoun and N. Beldiceanu. Overview of the CHIP Compiler System. In *Constraint Logic Programming: Selected Research*, F. Benhamou and A. Colmerauer, eds. pp. 421–435. MIT Press, 1993.

[Aiba *et al.*, 1988] A. Aiba, K. Sakai, Y. Sato, D. Hawley and R. Hasegawa. Constraint Logic Programming Language CAL, *Proc. International Conference on Fifth Generation Computer Systems 1988*, 263–276, 1988.

[Aït-Kaci, 1986] H. Aït-Kaci. An Algebraic Semantics Approach to the Effective Resolution of Type Equations, *Theoretical Computer Science*, **45**, 293–351, 1986.

[Aït-Kaci, 1991] H. Aït-Kaci. *Warren's Abstract Machine: A Tutorial Reconstruction*, MIT Press, 1991.

[Aït-Kaci and Nasr, 1986] H. Aït-Kaci and R. Nasr. LOGIN: A Logic Programming Language with Built-in Inheritance, *Journal of Logic Programming*, **3**, 185–215, 1986.

[Aït-Kaci and Nasr, 1987] H. Aït-Kaci, P. Lincoln and R. Nasr. Le Fun: Logic Equations and Functions, *Proc. Symposium on Logic Programming*, 17–23, 1987.

[Aït-Kaci and Podelski, 1993a] H. Aït-Kaci and A. Podelski. Towards a Meaning of LIFE, *Journal of Logic Programming*, **16**, 195–234, 1993.

[Aït-Kaci and Poldeski, 1993b] H. Aït-Kaci and A. Podelski. Entailment and Disentailment of Order-Sorted Feature Constraints, manuscript, 1993.

[Aït-Kaci and Poldeski, 1993c] H. Aït-Kaci and A. Podelski. A General Residuation Framework, manuscript, 1993.

[Aït-Kaci *et al.*, 1992] H. Aït-Kaci, A. Podelski and G. Smolka. A Feature-based Constraint System for Logic Programming with Entailment, *Theoretical Computer Science*, to appear. Also in: *Proc. International Conference on Fifth Generation Computer Systems 1992*, Vol. 2, 1992, 1012–1021.

[Albert *et al.*, 1993] L. Albert, R. Casas and F. Fages. Average-case Analysis of Unification Algorithms, *Theoretical Computer Science* 113, 3–34, 1993.

[Apt *et al.*, 1988] K. Apt, H. Blair and A. Walker. Towards a theory of declarative knowledge. In *Foundations of Deductive Databases and Logic Programming*, J. Minker, ed. pp. 89–148. Morgan Kaufmann, 1988.

[Atay, 1992] C. Atay. A Parallelization of the Constraint Logic Programming Language 2LP, Ph.D. thesis, City University of New York, 1992.

[Atay *et al.*, 1993] C. Atay, K. McAloon and C. Tretkoff. 2LP: A Highly Parallel Constraint Logic Programming Language, *Proc. 6th. SIAM Conf. on Parallel Processing for Scientific Computing*, 1993.

[Barbuti *et al.*, 1992] R. Barbuti, M. Codish, R. Giacobazzi and M.J. Maher. Oracle Semantics for Prolog, *Proc. 3rd Conference on Algebraic and Logic Programming*, LNCS 632, 100–115, 1992.

[Baudinet, 1988] M. Baudinet. Proving Termination Properties of Prolog: A Semantic Approach, *Proc. 3rd. Symp. Logic in Computer Science*, 334–347, 1988.

[Baudinet *et al.*, 1993] M. Baudinet, J. Chomicki and P. Wolper. Temporal deductive databases. In *Temporal Databases: Theory, Design and Implementation*, A. Tansel, J. Clifford, S. Gadia, S. Jajodia, A. Segev and R. Snodgrass, eds. Benjamin/Cummings, 1993.

[Benhamou, 1993] F. Benhamou. Boolean algorithms in PROLOG III. In *Constraint Logic Programming: Selected Research*, F. Benhamou and A. Colmerauer, eds. pp. 307–325. MIT Press, 1993.

[Benhamou and Colmerauer, 1993] F. Benhamou and A. Colmerauer, eds. *Constraint Logic Programming: Selected Research*, MIT Press, 1993.

[Benhamou and Massat, 1993] F. Benhamou and J-L. Massat. Boolean Pseudo-equations in Constraint Logic Programming, *Proc. 10th International Conference on Logic Programming*, 517–531, 1993.

[Berthier, 1989] F. Berthier. A Financial Model using Qualitative and Quantitative Knowledge, In F. Gardin, editor, *Proceedings of the International Symposium on Computational Intelligence 89*, Milano, 1–9, September 1989.

[Berthier, 1990] F. Berthier. Solving Financial Decision Problems with CHIP, In J.-L. Le Moigne and P. Bourgine, editors, *Proceeedings of the 2nd Conference on Economics and Artificial Intelligence— CECIOA 2*, Paris, 233–238, June 1990.

[Bisdorff and Laurent, 1993] R. Bisdorff and S. Laurent. Industrial Disposing Problem Solved in CHIP, *Proc. 10th International Conference on Logic Programming*, 831, 1993.

[Bockmayr, 1993] A. Bockmayr. Logic Programming with Pseudo-Boolean Constraints, in: *Constraint Logic Programming: Selected Research*, F. Benhamou and A. Colmerauer, eds. pp. 327–350. MIT Press, 1993.

[Boizumault *et al.*, 1993] P. Boizumault, Y. Delon and L. Peridy. Solving a real life exams problem using CHIP, *Proc. International Logic Programming Symposium,* 661, 1993.

[Borning, 1981] A. Borning. The Programming Language Aspects of ThingLab, a Constraint-oriented Simulation Laboratory, *ACM Transactions on Programming Languages and Systems,* 3(4), 252–387, October 1981.

[Borning *et al.*, 1989] A. Borning, M.J. Maher, A. Martindale and M. Wilson. Constraint Hierarchies and Logic Programming, *Proc. 6th International Conference on Logic Programming,* 149–164, 1989. Fuller version as Technical Report 88-11-10, Computer Science Department, University of Washington, 1988.

[Bossi *et al.*, 1992] A. Bossi, M. Gabbrielli, G. Levi and M.C. Meo. Contributions to the Semantics of Open Logic Programs, *Proc. Int. Conf. on Fifth Generation Computer Systems,* 570–580, 1992.

[Brodsky and Sagiv, 1991] A. Brodsky and Y. Sagiv. Inference of Inequality Constraints in Logic Programs, *Proc. ACM Symp. on Principles of Database Systems,* 1991.

[Brodsky *et al.*, 1993] A. Brodsky, J. Jaffar and M. Maher. Toward Practical Constraint Databases, *Proc. 19th International Conference on Very Large Data Bases,* 567–580, 1993.

[Broek and Daniels, 1991] J.M. Broek and H.A.M. Daniels. Application of CLP to Asset and Liability Management in Banks, *Computer Science in Economics and Management,* 4(2), 107–116, May 1991.

[Bryant, 1986] R. Bryant. Graph Based Algorithms for Boolean Function Manipulation, *IEEE Transactions on Computers* 35, 677–691, 1986.

[Brzoska, 1991] C. Brzoska. Temporal Logic Programming and its Relation to Constraint Logic Programming, *Proc. International Logic Programming Symposium,* 661–677, 1991.

[Brzoska, 1993] C. Brzoska. Temporal Logic Programming with Bounded Universal Modality Goals, *Proc. 10th International Conference on Logic Programming,* 239–256, 1993.

[Bürckert, 1990] H-J. Bürckert. A Resolution Principle for Clauses with Constraints. In *Proc. CADE-10,* M. Stickel, ed. pp. 178–192. LNCS 449, Springer-Verlag, 1990.

[Burg, 1992] J. Burg. Parallel Execution Models and Algorithms for Constraint Logic Programming over a Real-number Domain, Ph.D. thesis, Dept. of Computer Science, University of Central Florida, 1992.

[Burg *et al.*, 1990] J. Burg, C. Hughes, J. Moshell and S.D. Lang. Constraint-based Programming: A Survey, Technical Report IST-TR-90-16, Dept. of Computer Science, University of Central Florida, 1990.

[Burg et al., 1992] J. Burg, C. Hughes and S.D. Lang. Parallel Execution of CLP-ℜ Programs, Technical Report TR-CS-92-20, University of Central Florida, 1992.

[Büttner and Simonis, 1987] W. Büttner and H. Simonis. Embedding Boolean Expressions into Logic Programming, *Journal of Symbolic Computation*, 4, 191–205, 1987.

[Carlsson, 1987] M. Carlsson. Freeze, Indexing and other Implementation Issues in the WAM, *Proc. 4th International Conference on Logic Programming*, 40–58, 1987.

[Carlsson and Grindal, 1993] M. Carlsson and M. Grindal. Automatic Frequency Assignment for Cellular Telephones Using Constraint Satisfaction Techniques, *Proc. 10th International Conference on Logic Programming*, 647–665, 1993.

[Černikov, 1963] S.N. Černikov. Contraction of Finite Systems of Linear Inequalities (In Russian), *Doklady Akademiia Nauk SSSR*, 152, No. 5, 1075–1078, 1963. (English translation in *Soviet Mathematics Doklady*, 4, No. 5, 1520–1524, 1963.)

[Chadra et al., 1992] R. Chadra, O. Cockings and S. Narain. Interoperability Analysis by Symbolic Simulation, *Proc. JICSLP Workshop on Constraint Logic Programming*, 55–58, 1992.

[Chamard et al., 1992] A. Chamard, F. Decès and A. Fischler. Applying CHIP to a Complex Scheduling Problem, draft manuscript, Dassault Aviation, Department of Artificial Intelligence, 1992.

[Chan, 1988] D. Chan. Constructive Negation based on Completed Database, *Proc. 5th International Conference on Logic Programming*, 111–125, 1988.

[Chandru, 1993] V. Chandru. Variable Elimination in Linear Constraints, *The Computer Journal*, 36(5), 463–472, 1993.

[Chandru, 1991] V. Chandru and J.N. Hooker. Extended Horn Sets in Propositional Logic, *Journal of the ACM*, 38, 205–221, 1991.

[Chvàtal, 1983] V. Chvátal. *Linear Programming*, W.H. Freeman, New York, 1983.

[Clark, 1978] K.L. Clark. Negation as Failure. In *Logic and Databases*, H. Gallaire and J. Minker, eds. pp. 293–322. Plenum Press, New York, 1978.

[Codognet and Diaz, 1993] P. Codognet and D. Diaz. Boolean Constraint Solving using clp(FD), *Proc. International Logic Programming Symposium*, pp. 525–539, 1993.

[Codognet et al., 1992] P. Codognet, F. Fages, J. Jourdan, R. Lissajoux and T. Sola. On the Design of Meta(F) and its Applications in Air Traffic Control, *Proc. JICSLP Workshop on Constraint Logic Programming*, pp. 28–35, 1992.

[Cohen, 1990] J. Cohen. Constraint Logic Programming Languages, *CACM*, *33*, 52–68, July 1990.

[Colmerauer, 1982a] A. Colmerauer. Prolog-II Manuel de Référence et Modèle Théorique, Groupe Intelligence Artificielle, Université d'Aix-Marseille II, 1982.

[Colmerauer, 1982b] A. Colmerauer. Prolog and infinite trees. In *Logic Programming*, K. L. Clark and S.-A. Tarnlund, eds. pp. 231–251. Academic Press, New York, 1982.

[Colmerauer, 1983] A. Colmerauer. Prolog in 10 Figures, *Proc. 8th International Joint Conference on Artificial Intelligence*, pp. 487–499, 1983.

[Colmerauer, 1984] A. Colmerauer. Equations and Inequations on Finite and Infinite Trees, *Proc. 2nd. Int. Conf. on Fifth Generation Computer Systems*, Tokyo, pp. 85–99, 1984.

[Colmerauer, 1987] A. Colmerauer. Opening the Prolog III Universe, *BYTE Magazine*, August 1987.

[Colmerauer, 1988] A. Colmerauer. Prolog III Reference and Users Manual, Version 1.1, PrologIA, Marseilles, 1990.

[Colmerauer, 1990] A. Colmerauer. An Introduction to Prolog III, *CACM*, **33**, 69–90, July 1990.

[Colmerauer, 1993a] A. Colmerauer. Naive solving of non-linear constraints. In *Constraint Logic Programming: Selected Research*, F. Benhamou and A. Colmerauer, eds. pp. 89–112, MIT Press, 1993.

[Colmerauer, 1993b] A. Colmerauer. Invited talk at *Workshop on the Principles and Practice of Constraint Programming*, Newport, RI, April 1993.

[Corsini and Rauzy, 1993] M.-M. Corsini and A Rauzy. Safety Analysis by means of Fault Trees: an Application for Open Boolean Solvers, *Proc. 10th International Conference on Logic Programming*, p. 834, 1993.

[Courcelle, 1983] B. Courcelle. Fundamental properties of infinite trees. *Theoretical Computer Science*, **25**, 95–169, March 1983.

[Darlington and Guo, 1992] J. Darlington and Y.-K. Guo. A New Perspective on Integrating Functions and Logic Languages, *Proceedings of the 3rd International Conference on Fifth Generation Computer Systems*, Tokyo, 682–693, 1992.

[De Backer and Beringer, 1991] B. De Backer and H. Beringer. Intelligent Backtracking for CLP Languages, An Application to CLP($\mathcal{R}$), *Proc. International Logic Programming Symposium*, 405–419, 1991.

[De Backer and Beringer, 1993] B. De Backer and H. Beringer. A CLP Language Handling Disjunctions of Linear Constraints, *Proc. 10th International Conference on Logic Programming*, 550–563, 1993.

[de Boer and Palamidessi, 1990] F.S. de Boer and C. Palamidessi. A Fully Abstract Model for Concurrent Constraint Programming, *Proc. of TAPSOFT/CAAP*, LNCS 493, 296–319, 1991.

[de Boer and Palamidessi, 1991] F.S. de Boer and C. Palamidessi. Embedding as a Tool for Language Comparison, *Information and Computation* 108, 128–157, 1994.

[de Boer and Palamidessi, 1993] F.S. de Boer and C. Palamidessi. From Concurrent Logic Programming to Concurrent Constraint Programming, in: *Advances in Logic Programming Theory*, Oxford University Press. to appear.

[de Boer *et al.*, 1993] F. de Boer, J. Kok, C. Palamidessi and J. Rutten. Non-monotonic Concurrent Constraint Programming, *Proc. International Logic Programming Symposium,* 315–334, 1993.

[Debray, 1989a] S. K. Debray. Static Inference of Modes and Data Dependencies in Logic Programs, *ACM Transactions on Programming Languages and Systems* 11 (3), 418–450, 1989.

[Debray, 1989b] S. K. Debray and D.S. Warren. Functional Computations in Logic Programs, *ACM Transactions on Programming Languages and Systems* 11 (3), 451–481, 1989.

[de Kleer and Sussman, 1980] J. de Kleer and G.J. Sussman. Propagation of Constraints Applied to Circuit Synthesis, *Circuit Theory and Applications* 8, 127–144, 1980.

[Diaz and Codognet, 1993] D. Diaz and P. Codognet. A Minimal Extension of the WAM for clp(FD), *Proc. 10th International Conference on Logic Programming,* 774–790, 1993.

[Dincbas *et al.*, 1988a] M. Dincbas, P. Van Hentenryck, H. Simonis, and A. Aggoun. The Constraint Logic Programming Language CHIP, *Proceedings of the 2nd International Conference on Fifth Generation Computer Systems*, 249–264, 1988.

[Dincbas *et al.*, 1988b] M. Dincbas, H. Simonis and P. van Hentenryck. Solving a Cutting-stock Problem in CLP, *Proceedings 5th International Conference on Logic Programming*, MIT Press, 42–58, 1988.

[Dincbas *et al.*, 1990] M. Dincbas, H. Simonis and P. Van Hentenryck. Solving Large Combinatorial Problems in Logic Programming, *Journal of Logic Programming* 8 (1 and 2), 75–93, 1990.

[Dovier and Rossi, 1993] A. Dovier and G. Rossi. Embedding Extensional Finite Sets in CLP, *Proc. International Logic Programming Symposium*, 540–556, 1993.

[Duisburg, 1986] R. Duisburg. Constraint-based Animation: Temporal Constraints in the Animus System, Technical Report CR-86-37, Tektronix Laboratories, August 1986.

[Ege *et al.*, 1987] R. Ege, D. Maier and A. Borning. The Filter Browser:

Defining Interfaces Graphically, *Proc. of the European Conf. on Object-oriented Programming*, Paris, 155–165, 1987.

[Elcock, 1990] E. Elcock. Absys: The First Logic Programming Language—A Retrospective and Commentary, *Journal of Logic Programming*, 9, 1–17, 1990.

[Emerson, 1990] E. Emerson. Temporal and Modal Logic, in: *Handbook of Theoretical Computer Science*, Vol. B, Chapter 16, 995–1072, 1990.

[Evans, 1992] O. Evans. Factory Scheduling using Finite Domains, in: *Logic Programming in Action*, LNCS 636, Springer-Verlag, 45–53, 1992.

[Fages, 1993] F. Fages. On the Semantics of Optimization Predicates in CLP Languages, *Proc. 13th Conf. on Foundations of Software Technology and Theoretical Computer Science*, LNCS 761, 193–204, 1993.

[Falaschi et al., 1989] M. Falaschi, G. Levi, M. Martelli and C. Palamidessi. Declarative Modelling of the Operational Behavior of Logic Languages, *Theoretical Computer Science* 69, 289–318, 1989.

[Fikes, 1970] R.E. Fikes. REF-ARF: A system for solving problems stated as procedures, *Artificial Intelligence* 1, 27–120, 1970.

[Filkorn et al., 1991] T. Filkorn, R. Schmid, E. Tidén and P. Warkentin. Experiences from a Large Industrial Circuit Design Application, *Proc. International Logic Programming Symposium*, 581–595, 1991.

[Fitting, 1986] M. Fitting. A Kripke–Kleene Semantics for Logic Programs, *Journal of Logic Programming*, 4, 295-312, 1985.

[Fourier, 1824] J-B.J. Fourier. Reported in: Analyse des travaux de l'Académie Royale des Sciences, pendant l'année 1824, Partie mathematique, *Histoire de l'Académie Royale des Sciences de l'Institut de France*, Vol. 7, xlvii–lv, 1827. (Partial English translation in: D.A. Kohler. Translation of a Report by Fourier on his work on Linear Inequalities. *Opsearch*, Vol. 10, 38–42, 1973)

[Freeman-Benson, 1991] B.N. Freeman-Benson. Constraint Imperative Programming, PhD thesis, Department of Computer Science and Engineering, University of Washington, 1991.

[Frühwirth and Hanschke, 1993] T. Frühwirth and P. Hanschke. Terminological Reasoning with Constraint Handling Rules, *Proc. Workshop on Principles and Practice of Constraint Programming*, 82–91, 1993.

[Frühwirth et al., 1992] T. Frühwirth, A. Herold, V. Küchenhoff, T. Le Provost, P. Lim and M. Wallace. Constraint Logic Programming— An Informal Introduction, in: *Logic Programming in Action*, LNCS 636, Springer-Verlag, 3–35, 1992.

[Gabbrielli and Levi, 1991] M. Gabbrielli and G. Levi. Modeling Answer Constraints in Constraint Logic Programs, *Proc. 8th International Conference on Logic Programming*, 238–252, 1991.

[Gaifman et al., 1991] H. Gaifman, M.J. Maher and E. Shapiro. Replay,

Recovery, Replication and Snapshots of Nondeterministic Concurrent Programs, *Proc. 10th. ACM Symposium on Principles of Distributed Computation,* 1991.

[Gailly *et al.,* 1992] P.-J. Gailly, W. Krautter, C. Bisière and S. Bescos. The Prince project and its Applications, in: *Logic Programming in Action,* LNCS 636, Springer-Verlag, 54–63, 1992.

[García and Hermenegildo, 1993] M. García de la Banda and M. Hermenegildo. A Practical Approach to the Global Analysis of Constraint Logic Programs, *Proc. International Logic Programming Symposium,* 437–455, 1993.

[García *et al.,* 1993] M. García de la Banda, M. Hermenegildo and K. Marriott. Independence in Constraint Logic Programs, *Proc. International Logic Programming Symposium,* 130–146, 1993.

[Gelfond and Lifschitz, 1988] M. Gelfond and V. Lifschitz. The Stable Model Semantics for Logic Programming, *Proc. 5th International Conference on Logic Programming,* 1070–1080, 1988.

[Havens *et al.,* 1992] W. Havens, S. Sidebottom, G. Sidebottom, J. Jones and R. Ovans. Echidna: A Constraint Logic Programming Shell, *Proc. Pacific Rim International Conference on Artificial Intelligence,* 1992.

[Heintze *et al.,* 1992] N. Heintze, S. Michaylov and P.J. Stuckey. CLP($\mathcal{R}$) and Some Electrical Engineering Problems, *Journal of Automated Reasoning* 9, 231–260, 1992.

[Helm *et al.,* 1991] R. Helm, K. Marriott and M. Odersky. Building Visual Language Parsers, *Proc. Conf. on Human Factors in Computer Systems (CHI'91),* 105–112, 1991.

[Helm *et al.,* 1991] R. Helm, K. Marriott and M. Odersky. Constraint-based Query Optimization for Spatial Databases, *Proc. 10th ACM Symp. on Principles of Database Systems,* 181–191, 1991.

[Hickey, 1993] T. Hickey. Functional Constraints in CLP Languages, in: *Constraint Logic Programming: Selected Research,* F. Benhamou and A. Colmerauer, eds. pp. 355–381, MIT Press, 1993.

[Höhfeld and Smolka, 1988] M. Höhfeld and G. Smolka. Definite Relations over Constraint Languages, LILOG Report 53, IBM Deutschland, 1988.

[Homiak, 1991] D. Homiak. A CLP System for Solving Partial Differential Equations with Applications to Options Valuation, Masters Project, DePaul University, 1991.

[Hong, 1993] H. Hong. RISC-CLP(Real): logic programming with nonlinear constraints over the reals. In *Constraint Logic Programming: Selected Research,* F. Benhamou and A. Colmerauer, eds. pp. 133–159. MIT Press, 1993.

[Horn, 1951] A. Horn. On sentences which are true of direct unions of algebras. *Journal of Symbolic Logic*, **16**, 14–21, 1951.

[Huynh and Lassez, 1988] T. Huynh and C. Lassez. A CLP($\mathcal{R}$) Options Trading Analysis System, *Proceedings 5th International Conference on Logic Programming*, pp. 59–69, 1988.

[Huynh et al., 1990] T. Huynh, C. Lassez and J-L. Lassez. Practical issues on the projection of polyhedral sets. *Annals of Mathematics and Artificial Intelligence*, **6**, 295–315, 1992.

[Imbert, 1993a] J.-L. Imbert. Variable elimination for disequations in generalized linear constraint systems. *The Computer Journal*, **36**, 473–484, 1993.

[Imbert, 1993b] J.-L. Imbert. Fourier's Elimination: which to choose? *Proc. Workshop on Principles and Practice of Constraint Programming*, Newport, pp. 119–131, April 1993.

[Jaffar, 1984] J. Jaffar. Efficient unification over infinite terms. *New Generation Computing*, **2**, 207–219, 1984.

[Jaffar, 1990] J. Jaffar. Minimal and Complete Word Unification, *Journal of the ACM*, **37**, 47–85, 1990.

[Jaffar and Lassez, 1986] J. Jaffar and J.-L. Lassez. Constraint Logic Programming, Technical Report 86/73, Department of Computer Science, Monash University, 1986.

[Jaffar and Lassez, 1987] J. Jaffar and J.-L. Lassez. Constraint Logic Programming, *Proc. 14th ACM Symposium on Principles of Programming Languages*, Munich (January 1987), pp. 111–119.

[Jaffar and Stuckey, 1986] J. Jaffar and P. Stuckey. Canonical Logic Programs, *Journal of Logic Programming*, **3**, 143–155, 1986.

[Jaffar et al., 1984] J. Jaffar, J.-L. Lassez and M.J. Maher. A theory of complete logic programs with equality. *Journal of Logic Programming*, **1**, 211–223, 1984.

[Jaffar et al., 1986] J. Jaffar, J.-L. Lassez and M.J. Maher. A logic programming language scheme. In *Logic Programming: Relations, Functions and Equations*, D. DeGroot and G. Lindstrom, eds. pp. 441–467. Prentice-Hall, 1986.

[Jaffar et al., 1991] J. Jaffar, S. Michaylov and R.H.C. Yap. A Methodology for Managing Hard Constraints in CLP Systems, *Proc. ACM-SIGPLAN Conference on Programming Language Design and Implementation*, pp. 306–316, 1991.

[Jaffar et al., 1992a] J. Jaffar, S. Michaylov, P. Stuckey and R.H.C. Yap. The CLP($\mathcal{R}$) language and system. *ACM Transactions on Programming Languages*, **14**, 339–395, 1992.

[Jaffar et al., 1992b] J. Jaffar, S. Michaylov, P. Stuckey and R.H.C. Yap. An Abstract Machine for CLP($\mathcal{R}$), *Proceedings ACM-SIGPLAN*

Conference on Programming Language Design and Implementation, pp. 128–139, 1992.

[Jaffar *et al.*, 1993] J. Jaffar, M.J. Maher, P.J. Stuckey and R.H.C. Yap. Projecting CLP($\Re$) constraints. *New Generation Computing*, **11**, 449–469, 1993.

[Janson and Haridi, 1991] S. Janson and S. Haridi. Programming Paradigms of the Andorra Kernel Language, *Proc. International Logic Programming Symposium*, pp. 167–183, 1991.

[Jorgensen *et al.*, 1991] N. Jorgensen, K. Marriott and S. Michaylov. Some Global Compile-time Optimizations for CLP($\mathcal{R}$), *Proceedings 1991 International Logic Programming Symposium*, pp. 420–434, 1991.

[Jourdan *et al.*, 1990] J. Jourdan and R.E. Valdés-Pérez. Constraint Logic Programming Applied to Hypothetical Reasoning in Chemistry, *Proceedings North American Conference on Logic Programming*, pp. 154–172, 1990.

[Kanchanasut and Sumetphong, 1992] K. Kanchanasut and C. Sumetphong. Floor Planning Applications in CLP($\mathcal{R}$), *Proc. JICSLP Workshop on Constraint Logic Programming*, pp. 36–44, 1992.

[Kanellakis *et al.*, 1990] P. Kanellakis, G. Kuper and P. Revesz. Constraint query languages. *Journal of Computer and System Sciences*, to appear. Preliminary version appeared in *Proc. 9th ACM Symp. on Principles of Database Systems*, pp. 299–313, 1990.

[Kanellakis *et al.*, 1993] P. Kanellakis, S. Ramaswamy, D.E. Vengroff and J.S. Vitter. Indexing for Data Models with Constraints and Classes, *Proc. ACM Symp. on Principles of Database Systems*, 1993.

[Kanellakis *et al.*, to appear] P. Kanellakis, J-L. Lassez and V. Saraswat (Eds). *Principles and Practice of Constraint Programming*, MIT Press, to appear.

[Kemp *et al.*, 1989] D. Kemp, K. Ramarohanarao, I. Balbin and K. Meenakshi. Propagating Constraints in Recursive Deductive Databases, *Proc. North American Conference on Logic Programming*, pp. 981–998, 1989.

[Kemp and Stuckey, 1993] D. Kemp and P. Stuckey. Analysis based Constraint Query Optimization, *Proc. 10th International Conference on Logic Programming,* pp. 666–682, 1993.

[Khachian, 1979] L.G. Khachian. A polynomial algorithm in linear programming, *Soviet Math. Dokl.*, **20**, 191–194, 1979.

[Klee and Minty, 1972] V. Klee and G.J. Minty. How good is the Simplex algorithm? In *Inequalities-III*, O. Sisha, ed. pp. 159–175. Academic Press, New York, 1972

[Klug, 1988] A. Klug. On conjunctive queries containing inequalities. *Journal of the ACM*, **35**, 146–160, 1988.

[Koscielski and Pacholski, 1992] A. Koscielski and L. Pacholski. Complexity of Unification in Free Groups and Free Semigroups, *Proc. 31st Symp. on Foundations of Computer Science*, pp. 824–829, 1990.

[Krishnamurthy *et al.*, 1988] R. Krishnamurthy, R. Ramakrishnan and O. Shmueli. A Framework for Testing Safety and Effective Computability of Extended Datalog, *Proc. ACM Symp. on Management of Data*, pp. 154–163, 1988.

[Kuip, 1993] C.A.C. Kuip. Algebraic languages for mathematical programming. *European Journal of Operations Research*, **67**, 25–51, 1993.

[Kunen, 1987] K. Kunen. Negation in logic programming. *Journal of Logic Programming*, **4**, 289–308, 1987.

[Ladret, 1993] D. Ladret and M. Rueher. Contribution of Logic Programming to support Telecommunications Protocol Tests, *Proc. 10th International Conference on Logic Programming*, pp. 845–846, 1993.

[Lakmazaheri and Rasdorf, 1989] S. Lakmazaheri and W. Rasdorf. Constraint logic programming for the analysis and partial synthesis of Truss structures. *Artificial Intelligence for Engineering Design, Analysis, and Manufacturing*, **3**, 157–173, 1989.

[Lassez, 1987] C. Lassez. Constraint logic programming: a tutorial. *BYTE Magazine*, 171–176. August 1987,

[Lassez and Lassez, 1991] C. Lassez and J.-L. Lassez. Quantifier elimination for conjunctions of linear constraints via a convex hull algorithm. In *Symbolic and Numeric Computation for Artificial Intelligence*, B. Donald, D. Kapur and J.L. Mundy, eds. Academic Press, to appear. Also, IBM Research Report RC16779, T.J. Watson Research Center,

[Lassez and McAloon, 1990] J.-L. Lassez and K. McAloon. A Constraint Sequent Calculus, *Proc. of Symp. on Logic in Computer Science*, pp. 52–62, 1990.

[Lassez and McAloon, 1992] J.-L. Lassez and K. McAloon. A canonical form for generalized linear constraints. *Journal of Symbolic Computation*, **13**, 1–24, 1992.

[Lassez and Marriott, 1987] J.-L. Lassez and K.G. Marriott. Explicit representation of terms defined by counter examples. *Journal of Automated Reasoning*, **3**, 301–317, 1987.

[Lassez *et al.*, 1987] C. Lassez, K. McAloon and R.H.C. Yap. Constraint logic programming and options trading. *IEEE Expert*, **2**, Special Issue on Financial Software, August 1987, 42-50. 1991.

[Lassez *et al.*, 1988] J.-L. Lassez, M. Maher and K.G. Marriott. Unification revisited. In *Foundations of Deductive Databases and Logic Programming*, J. Minker, ed. pp. 587–625. Morgan Kaufmann, 1988.

[Lassez *et al.*, 1989] J.-L. Lassez, T. Huynh and K. McAloon. Simplifcation and Elimination of Redundant Linear Arithmetic Constraints, *Proc. North American Conference on Logic Programming*, Cleveland, pp. 35–51, 1989.

[Lauriere, 1978] J-L. Lauriere. A language and a program for stating and solving combinatorial problems. *Artificial Intelligence*, **10**, 29–127, 1978.

[Leler, 1988] W. Leler. *Constraint Programming Languages: Their Specification and Generation*, Addison-Wesley, 1988.

[Le Provost and Wallace, 1993] T. Le Provost and M. Wallace. Generalized constraint propagation over the CLP scheme. *Journal of Logic Programming*, **16**, 319–359, 1993.

[Leung, 1993] H.F. Leung. *Distributed Constraint Logic Programming*, Vol. 41, World-Scientific Series in Computer Science, World-Scientific, 1993.

[Li *et al.*, 1993] L.L. Li, M. Reeve, K. Schuerman, A. Véron. J. Bellone, C. Pradelles, Z. Palaskas, D. Stamatopoulos, D. Clark, S. Doursenot, C. Rawlings, J. Shirazi and G. Sardu, APPLAUSE: Applications Using the ElypSys Parallel CLP System, *Proc. 10th International Conference on Logic Programming*, pp. 847–848, 1993.

[Lloyd, 1987] J.W. Lloyd. *Foundations of Logic Programming*, Springer-Verlag, Second Edition, 1987.

[Lloyd and Topor, 1984] J.W. Lloyd and R.W. Topor. Making Prolog more expressive. *Journal of Logic Programming*, **1**, 93–109, 1984.

[McAloon and Tretkoff, 1989] K. McAloon and C. Tretkoff. 2LP: A Logic Programming and Linear Programming System, Brooklyn College Computer Science Technical Report No 1989-21, 1989.

[McDonald *et al.*, 1993] A. McDonald, P. Stuckey and R.H.C. Yap. Redundancy of Variables in CLP($\mathcal{R}$), *Proc. International Logic Programming Symposium*, pp. 75–93, 1993.

[McKinsey, 1943] J. McKinsey. The decision problem for some classes of sentences without quantifiers. *Journal of Symbolic Logic*, **8**, 61–76, 1943.

[Maher, 1987] M.J. Maher. Logic Semantics for a Class of Committed-Choice Programs, *Proc. 4th International Conference on Logic Programming*, pp. 858–876, 1987.

[Maher, 1988] M.J. Maher. Complete Axiomatizations of the Algebras of Finite, Rational and Infinite Trees, *Proc. 3rd. Symp. Logic in Computer Science*, pp. 348–357, 1988. Full version: IBM Research Report, T.J. Watson Research Center.

[Maher, 1992] M.J. Maher. A CLP View of Logic Programming, *Proc. Conf. on Algebraic and Logic Programming*, LNCS 632, pp. 364–383, 1992.

[Maher, 1993a] M.J. Maher. A transformation system for deductive database modules with perfect model semantics. *Theoretical Computer Science*, **110**, 377–403, 1993.

[Maher, 1993b] M.J. Maher. A Logic Programming View of CLP, *Proc. 10th International Conference on Logic Programming*, pp. 737–753, 1993. Full version: IBM Research Report, T.J. Watson Research Center.

[Maher and Stuckey, 1989] M.J. Maher and P.J. Stuckey. Expanding Query Power in CLP Languages, *Proc. North American Conference on Logic Programming*, pp. 20–36. 1989.

[Makanin, 1977] G.S. Makanin. The problem of solvability of equations in a free semigroup. *Math. USSR Sbornik*, **32**, 129–198, 1977. (English translation, AMS 1979).

[Mannila and Ukkonen, 1986] H. Mannila and E. Ukkonen. On the Complexity of Unification Sequences, *Proc. 3rd International Conference on Logic Programming*, pp. 122–133, 1986.

[Mantsivoda, 1993] A. Mantsivoda. Flang and its Implementation, *Proc. Symp. on Programming Language Implementation and Logic Programming*, LNCS 714, pp. 151–166, 1993.

[Marriott and Stuckey, 1993a] K.G. Marriott and P.J. Stuckey. The 3 R's of optimizing constraint logic programs: Refinement, removal and reordering, *Proc. 20th ACM Symp. Principles of Programming Languages*, pp. 334–344, 1993.

[Marriott and Stuckey, 1993b] K.G. Marriott and P.J. Stuckey. Semantics of CLP Programs with Optimization, Technical Report, University of Melbourne, 1993.

[Marriott *et al.*, 1994] K. Marriott, H. Søndergaard, P.J. Stuckey and R.H.C. Yap. Optimising Compilation for CLP(R), *Proc. Australian Computer Science Conf.*, pp. 551–560, 1994.

[Martin and Nipkow, 1989] U. Martin and T. Nipkow, Boolean unification—the story so far. *Journal of Symbolic Computation*, **7**, 275–293, 1989.

[MathLab, 1983] MathLab. *MACSYMA Reference Manual*, The MathLab Group, Laboratory for Computer Science, MIT, 1983.

[Michaylov, 1992] S. Michaylov. Design and Implementation of Practical Constraint Logic Programming Systems, Ph.D. Thesis, Carnegie Mellon University, Report CMU-CS-92-16, August 1992.

[Michaylov and Pfenning, 1993] S Michaylov and F. Pfenning. Higher-order Logic Programming as Constraint Logic Programming, *Proc. Workshop on Principles and Practice of Constraint Programming*, 1993.

[Miller, 1991] D. Miller. A Logic Programming Language with Lambda-abstraction, Function Variables, and Simple Unification. in *Extensions of Logic Programming: International Workshop*, Springer-Verlag LNCS 475, 253–281, 1991.

[Miller and Nadathur, 1986] D. Miller and G. Nadathur. Higher-order Logic Programming, *Proc. 3rd International Conference on Logic Programming*, pp. 448–462, 1986.

[Montanari and Rossi, 1993] U. Montanari and F. Rossi. Graph rewriting for a partial ordering semantics of concurrent constraint programming. *Theoretical Computer Science*, **109**, 225–256, 1993.

[Mukai, 1987] K. Mukai. Anadic Tuples in Prolog, Technical Report TR-239, ICOT, Tokyo, 1987.

[Mumick *et al.*, 1990] I.S. Mumick, S.J. Finkelstein, H. Pirahesh and R. Ramakrishnan. Magic Conditions, *Proc. 9th ACM Symp. on Principles of Database Systems*, pp. 314–330, 1990.

[Naish, 1985] L. Naish. Automating control for logic programs. *Journal of Logic Programming*, **2**, 167–183, 1985.

[Naish, 1986] L. Naish. *Negation and Control in PROLOG*, Lecture Notes in Computer Science 238, Springer-Verlag, 1986.

[Nelson, 1985] G. Nelson. JUNO, a constraint based graphics system. *Computer Graphics*, **19**, 235–243, 1985.

[Nerode and Kohn, 1993] A. Nerode and W. Kohn. Hybrid Systems and Constraint Logic Programming, *Proc. 10th International Conference on Logic Programming*, pp. 18–24, 1993.

[Older and Benhamou, 1993] W. Older and F. Benhamou. Programming in CLP(BNR), *Proc. Workshop on Principles and Practice of Constraint Programming*, pp. 239–249, 1993.

[Paterson and Wegman, 1978] M.S. Paterson and M.N. Wegman. Linear unification. *Journal of Computer and System Sciences*, **16**, 158–167, 1978.

[Pfenning, 1991] F. Pfenning. Logic programming in the LF logical framework. In *Logical Frameworks*, G. Huet and G. Plotkin, eds. pp. 149–181, Cambridge University Press, 1991.

[Podelski and van Roy, 1993] A. Podelski and P. van Roy. The Beauty and the Beast Algorithm: Testing Entailment and Disentailment Incrementally, draft manuscript, 1993.

[Przymusinski, 1988] T. Przymusinski. On the declarative semantics of deductive databases and logic programs. In *Foundations of Deductive Databases and Logic Programming*, J. Minker, ed. pp. 193-216. Morgan Kaufmann, 1988.

[Rajasekaar, 1993] A. Rajasekar. String Logic Programs, draft manuscript, Dept. of Computer Science, Univ. of Kentucky, 1993.

[Ramachandran and van Hentenryck, 1993] V. Ramachandran and P. van Hentenryck. Incremental Algorithms for Constraint Solving and Entailment over Rational Trees, *Proc. 13th Conf. on Foundations of Software Technology and Theoretical Computer Science*, LNCS 761, pp. 205–217, 1993.

[Ramakrishnan, 1991] R. Ramakrishnan. Magic templates: a spellbinding approach to logic programs. *Journal of Logic Programming*, **11**, 189–216, 1991.

[Ramalingam and Reps, 1993] G. Ramalingam and T. Reps. A Categorized Bibliography on Incremental Computation, *Proc. 17th ACM Symp. on Principles of Programming Languages*, pp. 502–510, 1993.

[Rueher, 1993] M. Rueher. A first exploration of PrologIII's capabilities. *Software–Practice and Experience*, **23**, 177–200, 1993.

[Sagiv and Vardi, 1989] Y. Sagiv and M. Vardi. Safety of Datalog Queries over Infinite Databases, *Proc. ACM Symp. on Principles of Database Systems*, pp. 160–171, 1989.

[Sakai *et al.*, to appear] K. Sakai, Y. Sato and S. Menju. Boolean Groebner Bases, to appear.

[Saraswat, 1987] V. Saraswat. CP as a General-purpose Constraint-language, *Proc. AAAI-87*, pp. 53–58, 1987.

[Saraswat, 1988] V. Saraswat. A Somewhat Logical Formulation of CLP Synchronization Primitives, *Proc. 5th International Conference Symposium on Logic Programming*, pp. 1298–1314, 1988.

[Saraswat, 1989] V. Saraswat. Concurrent Constraint Programming Languages, Ph.D. thesis, Carnegie-Mellon University, 1989. Revised version appears as *Concurrent Constraint Programming,* MIT Press, 1993.

[Saraswat, 1992] V. Saraswat. The Category of Constraint Systems is Cartesian-Closed, *Proc. Symp. on Logic in Computer Science*, pp. 341–345, 1992.

[Saraswat, to appear: 2] V. Saraswat. A Retrospective Look at Concurrent Logic Programming, in preparation.

[Saraswat *et al.*, 1988] V. Saraswat, D. Weinbaum, K. Kahn, and E. Shapiro. Detecting Stable Properties of Networks in Concurrent Logic Programming Languages, *Proc. 7th. ACM Symp. Principles of Distributed Computing*, pp. 210–222, 1988.

[Saraswat *et al.*, 1991] V. Saraswat, M. Rinard and P. Panangaden. Semantic Foundation of Concurrent Constraint Programming, *Proc. 18th ACM Symp. on Principles of Programming Languages*, pp. 333–352, 1991.

[Satoh and Aiba, 1993] K. Satoh and A. Aiba. Computing soft constraints by hierarchical constraint logic programming. *Journal of Informa-*

tion Processing, **7**, 1993,

[Scott, 1982] D. Scott. Domains for denotational semantics, *Proc. ICALP*, LNCS 140, 1982.

[Shapiro, 1983a] E. Shapiro. A Subset of Concurrent Prolog and its Interpreter, Technical Report CS83-06, Dept of Applied Mathematics, Weizmann Institute of Science, 1983.

[Shapiro, 1983b] E. Shapiro. Logic Programs with Uncertainties: A Tool for Implementing Expert Systems, *Proc. 8th. IJCAI*, pp. 529–532, 1983.

[Shoenfield, 1967] J.R. Shoenfield. *Mathematical Logic*, Addison-Wesley, 1967.

[Siekmann, 1989] J. Siekmann. Unification theory. *Journal of Symbolic Computation*, **7**, 207–274, 1989.

[Simonis, 1989a] H. Simonis. Formal verification of multipliers. In *Proceedings of the IFIP TC10/WG10.2/WG10.5 Workshop on Applied Formal Methods for Correct VLSI Design*, Leuven, Belgium, L.J.M. Claesen, ed. November 1989.

[Simonis, 1989b] H. Simonis. Test Generation using the Constraint Logic Programming language CHIP, *Proc. 6th International Conference on Logic Programming*, 1989.

[Simonis and Dincbas, 1987a] H. Simonis and M. Dincbas. Using an extended Prolog for digital circuit design, *IEEE International Workshop on AI Applications to CAD Systems for Electronics*, Munich, Germany, pp. 165–188, October 1987.

[Simonis and Dincbas, 1987b] H. Simonis and M. Dincbas. Using Logic Programming for Fault Diagnosis in Digital Circuits, *German Workshop on Artificial Intelligence (GWAI-87)*, Geseke, Germany, pp. 139–148, September 1987.

[Simonis and Dincbas, 1993] H. Simonis and M. Dincbas. Propositional calculus problems in CHIP. In *Constraint Logic Programming: Selected Research*, F. Benhamou and A. Colmerauer, eds. pp.269–285. MIT Press, 1993.

[Simonis and Graf, 1990] H. Simonis and T. Graf. Technology Mapping in CHIP, Technical Report TR-LP-44, ECRC, Munich, 1990.

[Simonis and Le Provost, 1989] H. Simonis and T. Le Provost. Circuit verification in chip: Benchmark results. *Proceedings of the IFIP TC10/WG10.2/WG10.5 Workshop on Applied Formal Methods for Correct VLSI Design*, Leuven, Belgium, pp. 125–129, November 1989.

[Simonis *et al.*, 1988] H. Simonis, H. N. Nguyen and M. Dincbas. Verification of digital circuits using CHIP, *Proceedings of the IFIP WG*

10.2 International Working Conference on the Fusion of Hardware Design and Verification, Glasgow, Scotland, July 1988.

[Skuppin and Buckle, 1992] R. Skuppin and T. Buckle. CLP and Spacecraft Attitude Control, *Proc. JICSLP Workshop on Constraint Logic Programming*, pp. 45–54, 1992.

[Smolka, 1991] G. Smolka. Residuation and guarded rules for constraint logic programming. In *Constraint Logic Programming: Selected Research*, F. Benhamou and A. Colmerauer, eds. pp. 405–419. MIT Press, 1993.

[Smolka and Treinen, 1992] G. Smolka and R. Treinen. Records for logic programming. Journal of Logic Programming, to appear. Also in: *Proceedings of the Joint International Conference and Symposium on Logic Programming*, pp. 240–254, 1992.

[Srivastava, 1993] D. Srivastava. Subsumption and indexing in constraint query languages with linear arithmetic constraints. *Annals of Mathematics and Artificial Intelligence*, **8**, 315–343, 1993.

[Srivastava and Ramakrishnan, 1992] D. Srivastava and R. Ramakrishnan. Pushing constraint selections. *Journal of Logic Programming*, **16**, 361–414, 1993.

[Stallman and Sussman, 1977] R.M. Stallman and G.J. Sussman. Forward reasoning and dependency directed backtracking in a system for computer aided circuit analysis. *Artificial Intelligence*, **9**, 135–196, 1977.

[Steele and Sussman, 1980] G. Steele and G.J. Sussman. CONSTRAINTS—a language for expressing almost hierarchical descriptions. *Artificial Intelligence*, **14**, 1–39, 1980.

[Steele, 1980] G.L. Steele. The Implementation and Definition of a Computer Programming Language Based on Constraints, Ph.D. Dissertation (MIT-AI TR 595), Dept. of Electrical Engineering and Computer Science, M.I.T. 1980.

[Sthanusubramonian, 1991] T. Sthanusubramonian. A Transformational Approach to Configuration Design, Master's thesis, Engineering Design Research Center, Carnegie Mellon University, 1991.

[Stickel, 1984] M. Stickel. Automated deduction by theory resolution. *Journal of Automated Reasoning*, **1**, 333-355, 1984.

[Studkey, 1989] P.J. Stuckey. Incremental linear constraint solving and detection of implicit equalities. *ORSA Journal of Computing*, **3**, 269–274, 1991.

[Stuckey, 1991] P. Stuckey. Constructive Negation for Constraint Logic Programming, *Proc. Logic in Computer Science Conference*, pp. 328–339, 1991. Full version in *Information and Computation*.

[Subramanian and Wang, 1993] D. Subramanian and C-S. Wang. Kinematic synthesis with configuration spaces, *Proc. Qualitative Reasoning 1993*, D. Weld, ed. pp. 228-239. 1993.

[Sutherland, 1963] I. Sutherland. A Man–Machine Graphical Communication System, PhD thesis, Massachusetts Institute of Technology, January 1963.

[Tarski, 1951] A. Tarski. *A Decision Method for Elementary Algebra and Geometry*, University of California Press, 1951.

[Taylor, 1990] A. Taylor. LIPS on a MIPS: Results from a Prolog Compiler for a RISC, *Proceedings 7th International Conference on Logic Programming*, pp. 174–185, 1990.

[Terasaki *et al.*, 1992] S. Terasaki, D.J. Hawley, H. Sawada, K. Satoh, S. Menju, T. Kawagishi, N. Iwayama and A. Aiba. Parallel Constraint Logic Programming Language GDCC and its Parallel Constraint Solvers, *Proc. International Conference on Fifth Generation Computer Systems 1992*, Volume I, pp. 330–346, 1992.

[Tick, 1993] E. Tick. The Deevolution of Concurrent Logic Programming Languages, draft manuscript, 1993.

[Tobias, 1988] J.C. Tobias, II. Knowledge Representation in the Harmony intelligent tutoring system, Master's thesis, Department of Computer Science, University of California at Los Angeles, 1988.

[Tong and Leung, 1993] B.M. Tong and H.F. Leung. Concurrent Constraint Logic Programming on Massively Parallel SIMD Computers, *Proc. International Logic Programming Symposium*, pp. 388–402, 1993.

[Tsang, 1993] E. Tsang. *Foundations of Constraint Satisfaction*, Academic Press, 1993.

[van Emden, 1986] M. van Emden. Quantitative deduction and its fixpoint theory. *Journal of Logic Programming*, 37–53, 1986.

[van Gelder, 1988] A. van Gelder. Negation as failure using tight derivations for general logic programs. In *Foundations of Deductive Databases and Logic Programming*, J. Minker, ed. pp. 149–176. Morgan Kaufmann, 1988.

[van Gelder *et al.*, 1988] A. van Gelder, K. Ross and J.S. Schlipf. Unfounded sets and well-founded semantics for general logic programs. Journal of the ACM, **38**, 620–650, 1991.

[van Hentenryck, 1989a] P. van Hentenryck. *Constraint Satisfaction in Logic Programming*, MIT Press, 1989.

[van Hentenryck, 1989b] P. van Hentenryck. Parallel Constraint Satisfaction in Logic Programming: Preliminary Results of CHIP within PEPSys, *Proc. 6th International Conference on Logic Programming*, pp. 165–180, 1989.

[van Hentenryck, 1991] P. van Hentenryck. Constraint logic programming. *The Knowledge Engineering Review*, **6**, 151–194, 1991.

[van Hentenryck, 1992] P. van Hentenryck. Constraint satisfaction using constraint logic programming. *Artificial Intelligence*, **58**, 113–159, 1992.

[van Hentenryck, 1993] P. van Hentenryck, ed. Special issue on constraint logic programming. *Journal of Logic Programming*, **16**, 1993.

[van Hentenryck and Deville, 1991a] P. van Hentenryck and Y. Deville. The Cardinality Operator: A New Logical Connective and its Application to Constraint Logic Programming, *Proc. International Conference on Logic Programming*, pp. 745–759, 1991.

[van Hentenryck and Deville, 1991b] P. van Hentenryck and Y. Deville. Operational Semantics of Constraint Logic Programming over Finite Domains, *Proc. Symp. on Programming Language Implementation and Logic Programming*, LNCS 528, pp. 395–406, 1991.

[van Hentenryck and Graf, 1991] P. van Hentenryck and T. Graf. Standard forms for rational linear arithmetics in constraint logic programming. *Annals of Mathematics and Artificial Intelligence*, **5**, 303–319, 1992.

[van Hentenryck *et al.*, 1991] P. van Hentenryck, V. Saraswat and Y. Deville. Constraint Processing in cc($\mathcal{FD}$), manuscript, 1991.

[van Hentenryck *et al.*, 1993] P. van Hentenryck, V. Saraswat and Y. Deville. Design, Implementations and Evaluation of the Constraint Language cc($\mathcal{FD}$), Technical Report CS-93-02, Brown University, 1993.

[van Roy and Despain, 1990] P. van Roy and A.M. Despain. The Benefits of Global Dataflow Analysis for an Optimizing Prolog Compiler, *Proceedings 1990 North American Conference on Logic Programming*, pp. 501–515, 1990.

[Véron *et al.*, 1993] A. Véron, K. Schuerman, M. Reeve and L.L. Li. Why and How in the ElipSys OR-parallel CLP system, *Proc. Conf. on Parallel Architectures and Languages Europe*, pp. 291–303, 1993.

[Vitter and Flajolet, 1990] J.S. Vitter and Ph. Flajolet. Average-case Analysis of Algorithms and Data Structures, *Handbook of Theoretical Computer Science*, Vol. A, pp. 431–524. Elsevier Science Publishers, Amsterdam, 1990.

[Voda, 1988a] P. Voda. The Constraint Language Trilogy: Semantics and Computations, Technical Report, Complete Logic Systems, 1988.

[Voda, 1988b] P. Voda. Types of Trilogy, *Proc. 5th International Conference on Logic Programming*, pp. 580–589, 1988.

[Walinsky, 1989] C. Walinsky. $CLP(\Sigma*)$: Constraint Logic Programming with Regular Sets, *Proc. 6th International Conference on Logic Programming*, pp. 181–196, 1989.

[Wallace, 1989] M. Wallace. A computable semantics for general logic programs. *Journal of Logic Programming*, **6**, 269–297, 1989.

[Wallace, 1993] M. Wallace. Applying constraints for scheduling. In *Constraint Programming*, B. Mayoh, E. Tyugu and J. Penjaam, eds. NATO Advanced Science Institute Series, Springer-Verlag, 1994.

[Warren, 1983] D.H.D. Warren. An Abstract PROLOG Instruction Set, Technical note 309, AI Center, SRI International, Menlo Park (October 1983).

[Warren, 1987] D.H.D. Warren. The Andorra Principle, presented at the Gigalips Workshop, 1987.

[Wilson and Borning, 1993] M. Wilson and A. Borning. Hierarchical constraint logic programming. *Journal of Logic Programming*, **16**, 277–318, 1993.

[Yap, 1991] R.H.C. Yap. Restriction Site Mapping in CLP($\mathcal{R}$), *Proceedings 8th International Conference on Logic Programming*, pp. 521–534. MIT Press, June 1991.

[Yap, 1993] R.H.C. Yap. A constraint logic programming framework for constructing DNA restriction maps. *Artificial Intelligence in Medicine*, **5**, 447–464, 1993.

[Yap, 1994] R.H.C. Yap. Contributions to CLP($\mathcal{R}$), Ph.D. thesis, Department of Computer Science, Monash University, January 1994 (expected).

Transformation of Logic Programs

Alberto Pettorossi and Maurizio Proietti

Contents

1   Introduction

Program transformation is a methodology for deriving correct and efficient programs from specifications.

In this chapter, we will look at the so called 'rules + strategies' approach, and we will report on the main techniques which have been introduced in the literature for that approach, in the case of logic programs. We will also present some examples of program transformation, and we hope that through those examples the reader may acquire some familiarity with the techniques we will describe.

The program transformation approach to the development of programs has been first advocated in the case of functional languages by Burstall and

Darlington [1977]. In that seminal paper the authors give a comprehensive account of some basic transformation techniques which they had already presented in [Darlington, 1972; Burstall and Darlington, 1975].

Similar techniques were also developed in the case of logic languages by Clark and Sickel [1977], and Hogger [1981], who investigated the use of predicate logic as a language for both program specification and program derivation.

In the transformation approach the task of writing a correct and efficient program is realized in two phases. The first phase consists in writing an initial, maybe inefficient, program whose correctness can easily be shown, and the second phase, possibly divided into various subphases, consists in transforming the initial program with the objective of deriving a new program which is more efficient.

The separation of the correctness concern from the efficiency concern is one of the major advantages of the transformation methodology. Indeed, using this methodology one may avoid some difficulties often encountered in other approaches. One such difficulty, which may occur when following the *stepwise refinement* approach, is the design of the invariant assertions, which may be quite intricate, especially when developing very efficient programs.

The experience gained during the past two decades or so shows that the methodology of program transformation is very valuable and attractive, in particular for the task of programming 'in the small', that is, for writing single modules of large software systems.

Program transformation has also the advantage of being adaptable to various programming paradigms, and although in this chapter we will focus our attention on the case of logic languages, in the relevant literature one can find similar results for the case of functional languages, and also for the case of imperative and concurrent languages.

The basic idea of the program transformation approach can be pictorially represented as in Fig. 1. From the initial program P_0, which can be viewed as the initial specification, we want to obtain a final program P_n with the same semantic value, that is, we want that $\mathbf{SEM}[P_0] = \mathbf{SEM}[P_n]$ for some given semantic function $\mathbf{SEM}$. The program P_n is often derived in various steps, that is, by constructing a sequence $P_0, \ldots, P_n$ of programs, called a *transformation sequence*, such that for $0 \leq i < n$, $\mathbf{SEM}[P_i] = \mathbf{SEM}[P_{i+1}]$, where P_{i+1} is obtained from P_i by applying a *transformation rule*.

In principle, one might obtain a program P_n such that $\mathbf{SEM}[P_0] = \mathbf{SEM}[P_n]$ by deriving intermediate programs whose semantic value is completely unrelated to $\mathbf{SEM}[P_0]$. This approach, however, has not been followed in practice, because it enlarges in an unconstrained way the search space to be explored when looking for those intermediate programs.

Sometimes, if the programs are nondeterministic, as it is the case of

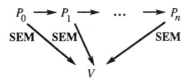

Fig. 1. The program transformation idea: from program P_0 we derive program P_n preserving the semantic value V.

most logic programs which produce a *set* of answers for any input query, we may allow transformation steps which are *partially correct*, but not *totally correct*, in the sense that for $0 \leq i < n$ and for every input query Q, $\mathbf{SEM}[P_i, Q] \subseteq \mathbf{SEM}[P_{i+1}, Q]$. (Here, and in what follows, the semantic function $\mathbf{SEM}$ is assumed to depend both on the program and the input query.)

As already mentioned, during the program transformation process one is interested in reducing the complexity of the derived program w.r.t. the initial program. This means that for the sequence $P_0, \ldots, P_n$ of programs there exists a cost function C which measures the computational complexity of the programs, such that $C(P_0) \geq C(P_n)$.

Notice that we may allow ourselves to derive a program, say P_i, for some $i > 0$, such that $C(P_0) < C(P_i)$, because subsequent transformations may lead us to a program whose cost is smaller than the one of P_0. Unfortunately, there is no general theory of program transformations which deals with this situation in a satisfactory way in all possible circumstances.

The efficiency improvement from program P_0 to program P_n is not ensured by an undisciplined use of the transformation rules. This is the reason why we need to introduce the so-called *transformation strategies*, that is, meta-rules which prescribe suitable sequences of applications of the transformation rules.

In logic programming there are many notions of efficiency which have been used. They are related either to the size of the proofs or to the machine model which is assumed for the execution of programs. In what follows we will briefly explain how the strategies which have been proposed in the literature may improve program efficiency, and we will refer to the original papers for more details on these issues.

So far we have indicated two major objectives of the program transformation approach, namely the preservation of the semantic value of the initial program and the reduction of the computational complexity of the derived program w.r.t. the initial one.

There is a third important objective which is often given less attention: the formalization of the program transformation process itself. The need for this formalization derives from the desire of making the program transformation approach a powerful programming methodology. In particular, via this formalization it is possible for the programmer to perform 'similar' transformations when starting from 'similar' initial programs, thus avoiding the difficulty of deciding which transformation rule should be applied at every step. It is also possible to make alternative program transformations by considering any program of a previously constructed sequence of programs and deriving from it a different sequence by applying different transformation rules.

The formalization of the program transformation process allows us to define various transformation strategies and, through them, to give suggestions to the programmer on how to transform the program at hand on the basis of the sequence of programs constructed so far.

However, it is not always simple to derive from a given program transformation sequence the strategies which can successfully be applied to similar initial programs. Research efforts are currently being made in this direction.

We often refer to the above three major objectives of the program transformation approach, that is, the preservation of semantics, the improvement of complexity, and the formalization of the transformation process itself, as the *transformation triangle*, with the following three vertices: (i) semantics, (ii) complexity, and (iii) methodology.

Finally, the program transformation methodology should be supported by an automatic (or semiautomatic) system, which both guides the programmer when applying the transformation rules, and also acquires in the form of transformation strategies, some knowledge about successful transformation sequences, while it is in operation.

Together with the 'rules + strategies' approach to program transformation, in the literature one also finds the so-called 'schemata' approach. We will not establish here the theoretical difference between these two approaches, and indeed that difference is mainly based on pragmatic issues. We will briefly illustrate the schemata approach in Section 5.3.

In Section 2 we will present a preliminary example of logic program transformation. It will allow the reader to have a better understanding of the various transformation techniques which we will introduce later. In Section 3 we will describe the transformation rules for logic programs, and in Section 4 we will study their correctness w.r.t. the various semantics which may be preserved. Section 5 is devoted to the introduction of the transformation strategies which are used for guiding the application of the rules. Then, in Section 6 we will consider the partial evaluation technique, and finally, in Section 7 we will briefly indicate some methodologies for program derivation which are related to program transformation.

2 A preliminary example

The 'rules + strategies' approach to program transformation as it was first introduced in [Burstall and Darlington, 1977] for recursive equation programs, is based on the use of two elementary transformation rules: the *unfolding rule* and the *folding rule*.

The unfolding rule consists in replacing an instance of the left hand side of a recursive equation by the corresponding instance of the right hand side. This rule corresponds to the 'replacement rule' used in [Kleene, 1971] for the computation of recursively defined functions. The application of the unfolding rule can also be viewed as a symbolic computation step.

The folding rule consists in replacing an instance of the right hand side of a recursive equation by the corresponding instance of the left hand side. Folding can be viewed as the inverse of unfolding, in the sense that, if we perform an unfolding step followed by a folding step, we get back the initial expression. Vice versa, unfolding can be viewed as the inverse of folding.

The reader who is not familiar with the transformation methodology, may wonder about the usefulness of performing a folding step, that is, of inverting a symbolic computation step, when one desires to improve program efficiency. However, as we will see in some examples below, the folding rule allows us to modify the recursive structure of the programs to be transformed and, by doing so, we will often be able to achieve substantial efficiency improvements.

Program derivation techniques following the 'rules + strategies' approach, have been presented in the context of logic programming in [Clark and Sickel, 1977; Hogger, 1981], where the basic derivation rules consist of the substitution of a formula by an equivalent formula.

Tamaki and Sato [1984] have adapted the unfolding and folding rules to the case of logic programs. Following the basic ideas relative to functional programs, they take an application of the unfolding rule to be equivalent to a computation step, that is, an application of SLD-resolution, and the folding rule to be the inverse of unfolding.

As already mentioned, during the transformation process we want to keep unchanged, at least in a weak sense, the semantic value of the programs which are derived, and in particular, we want the final program to be partially correct w.r.t. the initial program.

If from a program P_0 we derive by unfold/fold transformations a program P_1, then the least Herbrand model of P_1, as defined in [van Emden and Kowalski, 1976], is contained in the least Herbrand model of P_0 [Tamaki and Sato, 1984]. Thus, the unfold/fold transformations are partially correct w.r.t. the least Herbrand model semantics.

In general, unfold/fold transformations are not totally correct w.r.t. the least Herbrand model semantics, that is, the least Herbrand model of P_0 may be not contained in the one of P_1. In order to get total correctness one has to comply with some extra conditions [Tamaki and Sato, 1984].

The study of the various semantics which are preserved when using the unfold/fold transformation rules will be the objective of Section 4.

Let us now consider a preliminary example of program transformation where we will see in action some of the rules and strategies for transforming logic programs. In this example, together with the unfolding and folding rules, we will also see the use of two other transformation rules, called *definition rule* and *goal replacement rule*, and the use of a transformation strategy, called *tupling strategy*.

As already mentioned, the need for strategies which drive the application of the transformation rules and improve efficiency comes from the fact that folding is the inverse of unfolding, and thus we may construct a useless transformation sequence where the final program is equal to the initial program.

Let us consider the following logic program P_0 for testing whether or not a given list is a palindrome:

1. $pal([\,]) \leftarrow$
2. $pal([H]) \leftarrow$
3. $pal([H|T]) \leftarrow append(Y,[H],T), pal(Y)$
4. $append([\,],Y,Y) \leftarrow$
5. $append([H|X],Y,[H|Z]) \leftarrow append(X,Y,Z)$

We have that, given the lists X, Y, and Z, $append(X,Y,Z)$ holds in the least Herbrand model of P_0 iff Z is the concatenation of X and Y.

Both $pal(Y)$ and $append(Y,[H],T)$ visit the same list Y and we may avoid this double visit by applying the tupling strategy which suggests the introduction of the following clause for the new predicate *newp*:

6. $newp(L,T) \leftarrow append(Y,L,T), pal(Y)$

Actually, clause 6 has been obtained by a simultaneous application of the tupling strategy and the so-called *generalization strategy*, in the sense that in the body of clause 3 the argument $[H]$ has been generalized to the variable L. In Section 5, we will consider the tupling and the generalization strategies and we will indicate in what cases they may be useful for improving program efficiency.

By adding clause 6 to P_0 we get a new program P_1 which is equivalent to P_0 w.r.t. all predicates occurring in the initial program P_0, in the sense that each ground atom $q(\ldots)$, where q is a predicate occurring in P_0, belongs to the least Herbrand model of P_0 iff $q(\ldots)$ belongs to the least Herbrand model of P_1.

In order to avoid the double occurrence of the list Y in the body of clause 3, we now fold that clause using clause 6, that is, we replace '$append(Y,[H],T), pal(Y)$' which is an instance of the body of clause 6, by the corresponding instance '$newp([H],T)$' of the head of clause 6. Thus, we get:

3f. $pal([H|T]) \leftarrow newp([H],T)$

This folding step is the inverse of the step of unfolding clause 3f w.r.t. $newp([H],T)$.

Unfortunately, if we use the program made out of clauses 1, 2, 3f, 4, 5, and 6, we do not avoid the double visit of the input list, because *newp* is defined in terms of the two predicates *append* and *pal*. As we will show, a gain in efficiency is possible if we derive a definition of *newp* in terms of *newp* itself. This recursive definition of *newp* can be obtained as follows.

We first unfold clause 6 w.r.t. $pal(Y)$, that is, we derive the following three resolvents of clause 6 using clauses 1, 2, and 3, respectively:

7. $newp(L,T) \leftarrow append([\ ],L,T)$
8. $newp(L,T) \leftarrow append([H],L,T)$
9. $newp(L,T) \leftarrow append([H|Y],L,T), append(R,[H],Y), pal(R)$

We then unfold clauses 7, 8, and 9 w.r.t. the atoms $append([\ ],L,T)$, $append([H],L,T)$, and $append([H|Y],L,T)$, respectively, and we get

10. $newp(L,L) \leftarrow$
11. $newp(L,[H|L]) \leftarrow$
12. $newp(L,[H|U]) \leftarrow append(Y,L,U), append(R,[H],Y), pal(R)$

Now, in order to get a recursive definition of the predicate *newp* where no multiple visits of lists are performed, we would like to fold the entire body of clause 12 using clause 6, and in order to do so we need to have only one occurrence of the atom *append*. We can do so by applying the goal replacement rule (actually, the version formalized by rule R5.1 on page 713) which allows us to replace the goal '$append(Y,L,U)$, $append(R,[H],Y)$' by the equivalent goal '$append(R,[H|L],U)$'. Thus, we get the following clause:

13. $newp(L,[H|U]) \leftarrow append(R,[H|L],U), pal(R)$

We can fold clause 13 using clause 6, and we get:

13f. $newp(L,[H|U]) \leftarrow newp([H|L],U)$

Having derived a recursive definition of *newp*, the transformation process is completed. The final program we have obtained is as follows:

1. $pal([\ ]) \leftarrow$
2. $pal([H]) \leftarrow$
3f. $pal([H|T]) \leftarrow newp([H],T)$
4. $append([\ ],Y,Y) \leftarrow$
5. $append([H|X],Y,[H|Z]) \leftarrow append(X,Y,Z)$

10. $newp(L, L) \leftarrow$

11. $newp(L, [H|L]) \leftarrow$

13f. $newp(L, [H|U]) \leftarrow newp([H|L], U)$

In this final program no double visits of lists are performed, and the time complexity is improved from $O(n^2)$ to $O(n)$, where n is the size of the input list. The initial and final programs have the same least Herbrand model semantics w.r.t. the predicates *pal* and *append*.

Notice that if we are interested in the computation of the predicate *pal* only, in the final program we can discard clauses 4 and 5, which are unnecessary.

The crucial step in the above program transformation, which improves the program performance, is the introduction of clause 6 defining the new predicate *newp*. In the literature that step is referred to as a *eureka step* and the predicate *newp* is also called a *eureka predicate*.

It can easily be seen that eureka steps cannot, in general, be mechanically performed, because they require a certain degree of ingenuity. There are, however, many cases in which the synthesis of eureka predicates can be performed in an automatic way, and this is the reason why in practice the use of the program transformation methodology is very powerful.

In Section 5, we will consider the problem of inventing the eureka predicates and we will see that it can often be solved on the basis of syntactical properties of the program to be transformed by applying suitable transformation strategies.

3 Transformation rules for logic programs

In this section, we will present the most frequently used transformation rules for logic programs considered in the literature.

As already mentioned, the rules for transforming logic programs are directly derived from those used in the case of functional programs, but in adapting those rules, care has been taken, because logic programs compute *relations* rather than functions, and the *nondeterminism* inherent in relations does affect the various transformation techniques.

Moreover, for logic programs a rich variety of semantics can be defined and the choice of a particular semantics to be preserved affects the transformation rules to be used.

These facts motivate the large amount of research work which has been devoted to the extension of the transformation methodology to logic programs. Surveys of the work on logic program transformation have appeared in [Shepherdson, 1992; Pettorossi and Proietti, 1994].

3.1 Syntax of logic programs

Let us first briefly recall the syntax of logic programs and let us introduce the terminology which we will use. For other notions concerning logic programming not explicitly stated here we will refer to [Lloyd, 1987]. We assume that all our logic programs are written using symbols taken from a fixed language **L**. The Herbrand universe and the Herbrand base are constructed out of **L**, independently of the programs. This assumption which is sometimes made in the theory of logic programs (see, for instance, [Kunen, 1989]), in our case is motivated by the convenience of having a constant Herbrand universe while transforming programs.

An *atom* is a formula of the form: $p(t_1, \ldots, t_n)$ where p is an n-ary predicate symbol taken from **L**, and $t_1, \ldots, t_n$ are terms constructed out of variables, constants, and function symbols in **L**. A *literal* is either a *positive literal*, that is, an atom, or a *negative literal*, that is, a formula of the form: $\neg A$, where A is an atom.

A *goal* is a finite, possibly empty, *sequence* of literals not necessarily distinct. For clarity, a goal may also be written between round parentheses. In particular, if $L_1 \neq L_2$ the goals (L_1, L_2) and (L_2, L_1) are different, even though their semantics may be the same. Commas will be used to denote the associative concatenation of goals. Thus, $(L_1, \ldots, L_m), (L_{m+1}, \ldots, L_n)$ is equal to $(L_1, \ldots, L_m, L_{m+1}, \ldots, L_n)$.

A *clause* is a formula of the form: $H \leftarrow B$, where the *head* H is an atom and the *body* B is a (possibly empty) goal. The head and the body of a clause C are denoted by $hd(C)$ and $bd(C)$, respectively.

A *logic program* is a finite *sequence* (not a *set*) of clauses.

A *query* is a formula of the form: $\leftarrow G$, where G is a (possibly empty) goal. Notice that our notion of query corresponds to that of goal considered in [Lloyd, 1987].

Goals, clauses, logic programs, and queries are called *definite goals*, *definite clauses*, *definite logic programs*, and *definite queries*, respectively, if no negative literals occur in them. When we want to stress the fact that occurrences of negative literals are allowed, we will follow [Lloyd, 1987] and use the qualification *normal*. Thus, 'normal goal', 'normal clause', 'normal program', and 'normal query' are synonyms of 'goal', 'clause', 'program', and 'query', respectively. We will feel free to omit both qualifications 'definite' and 'normal' when they are irrelevant or understood from the context.

Given a term t, the set of variables occurring in t is denoted by $vars(t)$. A similar notation will also be adopted for the variables occurring in literals, goals, clauses, and queries.

A *substitution* is a finite mapping from variables to terms of the form: $\{X_1/t_1, \ldots, X_n/t_n\}$. The application of a substitution θ to a term t will be denoted by $t\theta$. Similar notation will be used for substitutions applied to literals, goals, clauses, and queries.

For other notions related to substitutions, such as *instance* and *most general unifier*, we refer to [Apt, 1990].

A *variable renaming* is a bijection from the set of variables of the language **L** onto itself. We assume that the variables occurring in a clause can be freely renamed, as usually done for bound variables in quantified formulas. This is required to avoid clashes of names, as, for instance, when performing resolution steps. Two clauses which differ only for a variable renaming are called *variants*.

For reasons of simplicity, we will identify any two computed answer substitutions obtained by resolution steps which differ only by the renaming of the clauses involved.

By a *predicate renaming* we mean a bijective mapping of the set of predicate symbols of $\mathbf{L}$ onto itself. Given a predicate renaming ρ and a program P, by $\rho(P)$ we denote the program obtained by replacing each predicate symbol p in P by $\rho(p)$. A similar notation will be adopted for the predicate renaming in queries.

Given a predicate p occurring in a logic program P, the *definition* of p in P is the subsequence of all clauses in P whose head predicate is p.

We will say that a predicate p *depends on* a predicate q in the program P iff either there exists in P a clause of the form: $p(\ldots) \leftarrow B$ such that q occurs in the goal B or there exists in P a predicate r such that p depends on r in P and r depends on q in P.

We say that a query (or a goal) Q depends on a clause of the form: $p(\ldots) \leftarrow B$ in a program P iff either p occurs in Q or there exists a predicate occurring in Q which depends on p. The *relevant part* $P_{rel}(Q)$ of program P for the query (or the goal) Q is the subsequence of clauses in P on which Q depends.

3.2 Semantics of logic programs

When deriving new programs from old ones, we need to take into account the semantics that is preserved. For the formal definition of the semantics of a logic program we explicitly consider the dependency on the input query, and thus we define a *semantics* of a set $\mathbf{P}$ of logic programs w.r.t. a set $\mathbf{Q}$ of queries to be a function $\mathbf{SEM} \colon \mathbf{P} \times \mathbf{Q} \to (\mathbf{D}, \leq)$, where $(\mathbf{D}, \leq)$ is a partially ordered set.

We will assume that every semantics $\mathbf{SEM}$ we consider is *preserved by predicate renaming*, that is, for every predicate renaming ρ, program P, and query Q, $\mathbf{SEM}[P, Q] = \mathbf{SEM}[\rho(P), \rho(Q)]$.

We will also assume that every semantics $\mathbf{SEM}$ is preserved by interchanging the order of two adjacent clauses with different head predicates. Thus, we may always assume that all clauses constituting the definition of a predicate are adjacent.

We say that two programs P_1 and P_2 in $\mathbf{P}$ are *equivalent* w.r.t. the semantics function $\mathbf{SEM}$ and the set $\mathbf{Q}$ of queries iff for every query Q in $\mathbf{Q}$ we have that $\mathbf{SEM}[P_1, Q] = \mathbf{SEM}[P_2, Q]$.

An example of semantics function can be provided by taking $\mathbf{P}$ to be the set of definite programs (denoted by $\mathbf{P}^+$), $\mathbf{Q}$ the set of definite queries (denoted by $\mathbf{Q}^+$), and $\mathbf{D}$ the powerset of the set of substitutions (denoted by $\mathcal{P}(\mathbf{Subst})$), ordered by set inclusion.

We now define the *least Herbrand model semantics* as the function **LHM**: $\mathbf{P}^+ \times \mathbf{Q}^+ \to (\mathcal{P}(\mathbf{Subst}), \leq)$ such that, for every $P \in \mathbf{P}^+$ and for every $\leftarrow G \in \mathbf{Q}^+$,

$$\mathbf{LHM}[P, \leftarrow G] = \{\theta \mid \text{every ground instance of } G\theta$$
$$\text{is a logical consequence of } P\}$$

where we identify the program P and the goal G with the logical formulas obtained by interpreting sequences of clauses (or atoms) as conjunctions and interpreting $\leftarrow$ as the implication connective. As usual, the empty sequence of atoms in the body of a clause is interpreted as *true*.

The least Herbrand model $\mathbf{M}(P)$ of a definite program P defined according to [van Emden and Kowalski, 1976] can be expressed in terms of the function **LHM** as follows:

$$\mathbf{M}(P) = \{A \mid A \text{ is a ground atom and } \mathbf{LHM}[P, \leftarrow A] = \mathbf{Subst}\}.$$

Thus, two programs P_1 and P_2 in $\mathbf{P}^+$ are equivalent w.r.t. **LHM** iff $\mathbf{M}(P_1) = \mathbf{M}(P_2)$.

In order to state various correctness results concerning our transformation rules w.r.t. different semantics functions (see Section 4), we need the following notion of *relevance* [Dix, 1995].

Definition 3.2.1 (Relevance). A semantics function **SEM**: $\mathbf{P} \times \mathbf{Q} \to (\mathbf{D}, \leq)$ is *relevant* iff for every program P in $\mathbf{P}$ and query Q in $\mathbf{Q}$, we have that $\mathbf{SEM}[P, Q] = \mathbf{SEM}[P_{rel}(Q), Q]$.

Thus, a semantics is relevant iff its value for a given program and a given query is determined only by the query and the clauses on which the query depends.

The least Herbrand model semantics and many other semantics we will consider are relevant but well-known semantics, such as the *Clark's completion* [Lloyd, 1987] and the *stable model semantics* [Gelfond and Lifschitz, 1988], are not.

3.3   Unfold/fold rules

As already mentioned, the program transformation process starting from a given initial program P_0 can be viewed as a sequence of programs $P_0, \ldots, P_k$, called a *transformation sequence* [Tamaki and Sato, 1984], such that program P_{j+1}, with $0 \leq j \leq k-1$, is obtained from program P_j by the application of a *transformation rule*, which may depend on $P_0, \ldots, P_j$. An application of a transformation rule is also called a *transformation step*.

Since most transformation rules can be viewed as the replacement of a given clause C by some new clauses $C_1, \ldots, C_n$, the transformation process can also be represented by means of trees of clauses [Pettorossi and Proietti,

1989], where the clauses $C_1, \ldots, C_n$ are viewed as the son-nodes of C. This tree-based representation will be useful for describing the transformation strategies (see Section 5).

The transformation rules we will present in this chapter are collectively called *unfold/fold rules* and they are a generalization of those introduced by [Tamaki and Sato, 1984]. Several special cases of these rules will be introduced in the subsequent sections, when discussing the correctness of the transformation rules w.r.t. different semantics of logic programs.

In the presentation of the rules we will refer to the transformation sequence $P_0, \ldots, P_k$ and we will assume that the variables of the clauses which are involved in each transformation rule are suitably renamed so that they do not have variables in common.

Rule R1. Unfolding. Let P_k be the program $E_1, \ldots, E_r, C, E_{r+1}, \ldots, E_s$ and C be the clause $H \leftarrow F, A, G$, where A is a *positive* literal and F and G are (possibly empty) goals. Suppose that

1. $D_1, \ldots, D_n$, with $n > 0$, is the subsequence of all clauses of a program P_j, for some j, with $0 \leq j \leq k$, such that A is unifiable with $hd(D_1), \ldots, hd(D_n)$, with most general unifiers $\theta_1, \ldots, \theta_n$, respectively, and
2. C_i is the clause $(H \leftarrow F, bd(D_i), G)\theta_i$, for $i = 1, \ldots, n$.

If we *unfold C w.r.t. A using P_j* we derive the clauses $C_1, \ldots, C_n$ and we get the new program $P_{k+1} = E_1, \ldots, E_r, C_1, \ldots, C_n, E_{r+1}, \ldots, E_s$.

The unfolding rule corresponds to the application of a resolution step to clause C with the selection of the positive literal A and the input clauses $D_1, \ldots, D_n$.

Example 3.3.1. Let P_k be the following program:

$p(X) \leftarrow q(t(X)), r(X), r(b)$
$q(a) \leftarrow$
$q(t(b)) \leftarrow$
$q(X) \leftarrow r(X)$

Then, by unfolding $p(X) \leftarrow q(t(X)), r(X), r(b)$ w.r.t. $q(t(X))$ using P_k itself we derive the following program P_{k+1}:

$p(b) \leftarrow r(b), r(b)$
$p(X) \leftarrow r(t(X)), r(X), r(b)$
$q(a) \leftarrow$
$q(t(b)) \leftarrow$
$q(X) \leftarrow r(X)$

Remark 3.3.2. There are two main differences between the unfolding rule in the case of logic programs and the unfolding rule in the case of functional programs.

The first difference is that, when we unfold a clause C w.r.t. an atom A in $bd(C)$ using a program P_j, it is not required that A be an instance of the head of a clause in P_j. We only require that A be unifiable with the head of at least one clause in P_j. This is related to the fact that a resolution step produces a *unifying* substitution, not a *matching* substitution, as it happens in a rewriting step for functional programs.

The second difference is that in the functional case it is usually assumed that the equations defining a program are mutually exclusive. Thus, by unfolding a given equation we may get at most one new equation. On the other hand, in the logic case there may be several clauses in a program P_j whose heads are unifiable with an atom A in the body of a clause C. As a result, by unfolding C w.r.t. A, we may derive more than one clause.

The unfolding rule is one of the basic transformation rules in all transformation systems for logic programs proposed in the literature. Our presentation of the rule follows [Tamaki and Sato, 1984] where, however, it is required that the program used for unfolding a clause is the one where this clause occurs, that is, with reference to our rule R1, P_j is required to be P_k.

Some derivation rules for logic programs similar to the unfolding rule have been considered in [Komorowski, 1982] and in [Clark and Sickel, 1977; Hogger, 1981], in the context of partial evaluation and program synthesis (see also Sections 6 and 7).

Gardner and Shepherdson [1991] have defined a transformation rule which can be considered as the unfolding of a clause w.r.t. a *negative* literal. Given the clause $C = H \leftarrow F, \neg A, G$ in a program P, where A is a ground atom, Gardner and Shepherdson's unfolding rule transforms P as follows:

1. either $\neg A$ is deleted from the body of C, if the query $\leftarrow A$ has a finitely failed SLDNF-tree in P,
2. or C is deleted from P, if the query $\leftarrow A$ has an SLDNF-refutation in P.

Gardner and Shepherdson's unfolding rule w.r.t. negative literals can be expressed in terms of the *goal replacement rule* (in case 1) and the *clause deletion rule* (in case 2). These rules will be introduced below.

Also Kanamori and Horiuchi [1987] and Sato [1992] allow unfolding steps w.r.t. negative literals. However, their notion of program goes beyond the definition of logic program which we consider here, and their transformation rules may more properly be regarded as rules for logic program synthesis starting from first-order logic specifications (see Section 7).

Rule R2. Folding. Let P_k be the program $E_1, \ldots, E_r, C_1, \ldots, C_n, E_{r+1}, \ldots, E_s$ and $D_1, \ldots, D_n$ be a subsequence of clauses in a program P_j, for some j, with $0 \leq j \leq k$. Suppose that there exist an atom A and two goals F and G such that for each i, with $1 \leq i \leq n$, there exists a substitution θ_i which satisfies the following conditions:

1. C_i is a variant of the clause $H \leftarrow F, bd(D_i)\theta_i, G$,
2. $A = hd(D_i)\theta_i$,
3. for every clause D of P_j not in the sequence $D_1, \ldots, D_n$, $hd(D)$ is not unifiable with A, and
4. for every variable X in the set $vars(D_i) - vars(hd(D_i))$, we have that
   - $X\theta_i$ is a variable which does not occur in (H, F, G) and
   - the variable $X\theta_i$ does not occur in the term $Y\theta_i$, for any variable Y occurring in $bd(D_i)$ and different from X.

If we *fold* $C_1, \ldots, C_n$ *using* $D_1, \ldots, D_n$ in P_j we derive the clause $C = H \leftarrow F, A, G$, and we get the new program $P_{k+1} = E_1, \ldots, E_r$, $C, E_{r+1}, \ldots, E_s$.

The folding rule is the inverse of the unfolding rule, in the sense that given a transformation sequence $P_0, \ldots, P_k, P_{k+1}$, where P_{k+1} is obtained from P_k by folding, there exists a transformation sequence $P_0, \ldots, P_k, P_{k+1}, P_k$, where P_k can be obtained from P_{k+1} by unfolding.

Notice that the possibility of inverting a folding step by performing an unfolding step, depends on the fact that for unfolding (as for folding) we can use clauses taken from any program of the transformation sequence constructed so far.

Example 3.3.3. Let us consider a transformation sequence P_0, P_1 where P_1 includes the clauses

$C_1. \ p(X) \leftarrow q(t(X), Y), r(X)$
$C_2. \ p(Z) \leftarrow s(Z), r(Z)$

and the definition of predicate a in P_0 consists of the clauses

$D_1. \ a(U) \leftarrow q(U, V)$
$D_2. \ a(t(W)) \leftarrow s(W)$

Clauses C_1, C_2 can be folded using D_1, D_2. Indeed, the conditions listed in the folding rule R2 are satisfied with $\theta_1 = \{U/t(X), V/Y\}$ and $\theta_2 = \{W/Z\}$. The derived clause is

$C. \ p(X) \leftarrow a(t(X)), r(X)$

Notice that by unfolding clause C using D_1 and D_2 we get again clauses C_1 and C_2.

The following example shows that condition 4 in rule R2 is necessary for ensuring that, after a folding step, we can perform an unfolding step which leads us back to the program we had before the folding step.

Example 3.3.4. Let C be $p(Z) \leftarrow q(Z)$ and D be $r \leftarrow q(X)$. Suppose that D is the only clause in P_j with head r. Clauses C and D satisfy conditions 1, 2, and 3 of the folding rule with $n = 1$ and $\theta_1 = \{X/Z\}$. However, they do not satisfy condition 4 because X does not occur in the head of D, and $X\theta_1$, which is Z, occurs in the head of C. By replacing the body of C by the head of D we get the clause $p(Z) \leftarrow r$. If we then unfold $p(Z) \leftarrow r$ using P_j we get $p(Z) \leftarrow q(X)$, which is *not* a variant of C.

Notice that, if a program P_k can be transformed into a program P_{k+1} by an unfolding step, it is not always possible to derive again P_k by means of a folding step applied to P_{k+1} (see the following example). Thus, we may say that folding is only a 'right-inverse' of unfolding.

Example 3.3.5. Let C be the clause $p(X) \leftarrow r(X)$ and D be the clause $r(t(X)) \leftarrow q(X)$. From program C, D, by unfolding C using the program C, D itself, we get the clause $C_1 = p(t(X)) \leftarrow q(X)$ and the program C_1, D. In order to get back C, D by folding, we would like to fold C_1 and derive (a variant of) C. There are only two ways of applying the folding rule to C_1. The first one is to use clause C_1 itself, thereby getting the clause $p(t(X)) \leftarrow p(t(X))$. The second one is to use clause D and if we do so we get the clause $p(t(X)) \leftarrow r(t(X))$. In neither case do we get a variant of C.

Our presentation of the folding rule is similar to the one in [Gergatsoulis and Katzouraki, 1994] where, however, during the application of the folding rule, the introduction of some equality atoms is also allowed. We will deal with the equality introduction in a separate rule.

Several folding rules which are special cases of rule R2 have been considered in the literature. These folding rules have various restrictions depending on: i) the choice of the program in the transformation sequence from where the clauses used for folding (i.e. $D_1, \ldots, D_n$) are taken, ii) the number of these clauses, and iii) whether or not these clauses are allowed to be recursive (i.e. predicates in the bodies of the clauses depend on predicates in the heads of those clauses).

We will present some of these special cases of the folding rule in subsequent sections. In particular, the rule originally introduced by Tamaki and Sato [1984] will be presented in Section 4.4.1 (see rule R2.2, page 726), when dealing with the preservation of the least Herbrand model semantics while transforming programs.

Rule R3. Definition introduction (or **Definition**, for short). We may get program P_{k+1} by adding to program P_k n clauses of the form: $p_i(\ldots) \leftarrow B_i$, for $i = 1, \ldots, n$, such that the predicate symbol p_i does not occur in $P_0, \ldots, P_k$.

The definition rule is said to be *non-recursive* iff every predicate symbols occurring in the bodies B_i's occurs in P_k as well.

Our presentation of the definition rule is similar to the one in [Maher, 1987] and it allows us to introduce one or more new predicate definitions each of which may consist of more than one clause.

Rule R4. Definition elimination. We may get program P_{k+1} by deleting from program P_k the clauses constituting the definitions of the predicates $q_1, \ldots, q_n$ such that, for $i = 1, \ldots, n$, q_i does not occur in P_0 and every predicate in P_k which depends on q_i is in the set $\{q_1, \ldots, q_n\}$.

The definition elimination rule can be viewed as an inverse of the definition introduction rule. It has been presented in [Maher, 1987], where it has been called *deletion*, and also in [Bossi and Cocco, 1993], where it has been called *restricting operation*.

The next rule we will introduce is the *goal replacement rule*, which allows us to replace a goal in the body of a clause by an *equivalent* goal. Equivalence between goals, as it is usually defined, depends on the semantics of the program P_k where the replacement takes place.

We now introduce a simple notion of goal equivalence which is parametric w.r.t. the semantics considered. A more complex notion will be given later.

Definition 3.3.6 (Goal equivalence). Two goals G_1 and G_2 are *equivalent* w.r.t. a semantics **SEM** and a program P iff $\mathbf{SEM}[P, \leftarrow G_1] = \mathbf{SEM}[P, \leftarrow G_2]$. (We will feel free to omit the references to **SEM** and/or P when they are understood from the context.)

Rule R5. Goal replacement. Let **SEM** be a semantics function, G_1 and G_2 two equivalent goals w.r.t. **SEM** and P_k, and $C = H \leftarrow L, G_1, R$ a clause in P_k. By *replacement* of goal G_1 by goal G_2 in C we derive the clause $D = H \leftarrow L, G_2, R$ and we get P_{k+1} from P_k by replacing C by D.

Example 3.3.7. Let **SEM** be the least Herbrand model semantics **LHM** defined in Section 3.2 and P_k be the following program:

$$C. \ p(X, Y) \leftarrow q(X, Y)$$
$$q(a, Y) \leftarrow$$
$$q(b, Y) \leftarrow q(b, Y)$$
$$r(X, X) \leftarrow$$

We have that $q(X, Y)$ is equivalent to $r(X, a)$ w.r.t. **LHM** and P_k. Thus, by replacement of $q(X, Y)$ in C we derive the clause

$$p(X, Y) \leftarrow r(X, a)$$

The above definition of goal equivalence does not take into account the clause where the goal replacement occurs. As a result, many substitutions of goals by new goals which produce from a program P_k a new program P_{k+1}, cannot be viewed as applications of our rule R5, even though P_k and P_{k+1} are equivalent programs.

Example 3.3.8. Let us consider the following clauses in a program P_k:

$C.\ sublist(N, X, Y) \leftarrow length(X, N), append(V, X, I), append(I, Z, Y)$
$A_1.\ append([\ ], L, L) \leftarrow$
$A_2.\ append([H|T], L, [H|U]) \leftarrow append(T, L, U)$

If we replace the goal '$append(V, X, I), append(I, Z, Y)$' in the body of C by the goal '$append(X, Z, J), append(V, J, Y)$' we get a program, say P_{k+1}, which is equivalent to P_k w.r.t. the least Herbrand model semantics **LHM**. However, the two goals '$append(V, X, I), append(I, Z, Y)$' and '$append(X, Z, J), append(V, J, Y)$' are not equivalent in the sense of Definition 3.3.6.

Indeed, the substitution $\theta = \{V/[\ ], X/[\ ], I/[\ ], Z/[\ ], Y/[\ ], J/[a]\}$ belongs to $\mathbf{LHM}[P_k, \leftarrow (append(V, X, I), append(I, Z, Y))]$ and does not belong to $\mathbf{LHM}[P_k, \leftarrow (append(X, Z, J), append(V, J, Y))]$.

In order to overcome the above mentioned limitation of the goal replacement rule R5, we now consider a weaker notion of goal equivalence which depends on a given set of variables. A similar notion was introduced, for definite programs and the computed answer substitution semantics, by Cook and Gallagher [1994]. We will then consider a version of the goal replacement rule based on this weaker notion of goal equivalence.

Definition 3.3.9 (Goal equivalence w.r.t. a set of variables). Let the program P_k be $C_1, \ldots, C_n$ and let **SEM** be a semantics function. Let us consider the following two clauses:

$D_1.\ newp_1(X_1, \ldots, X_m) \leftarrow G_1$
$D_2.\ newp_2(X_1, \ldots, X_m) \leftarrow G_2$

where $newp_1$ and $newp_2$ are distinct predicate symbols not occurring in P_k, $\{X_1, \ldots, X_m\}$ is a set of m variables, and G_1 and G_2 are two goals. Let V denote the set $\{X_1, \ldots, X_m\}$. We say that G_1 and G_2 are equivalent w.r.t. **SEM**, P_k and V, and we write $G_1 \equiv_v G_2$, iff

$$\mathbf{SEM}[(C_1, \ldots, C_n, D_1), \leftarrow newp_1(X_1, \ldots, X_m)]$$
$$= \mathbf{SEM}[(C_1, \ldots, C_n, D_2), \leftarrow newp_2(X_1, \ldots, X_m)].$$

If G_1 and G_2 are equivalent w.r.t. **SEM**, P_k, and V, we also say that the *replacement law* $G_1 \equiv_V G_2$ is *valid* w.r.t. **SEM** and P_k.

Since we have assumed that **SEM** is preserved by predicate renaming, we have that, for any set V of variables, $\equiv_V$ is an equivalence relation.

Rule R5.1   Clausal goal replacement. Let $C = H \leftarrow L, G_1, R$ be a clause in P_k. Suppose that goals G_1 and G_2 are equivalent w.r.t. **SEM**, P_k, and the set of variables $vars(H, L, R) \cap vars(G_1, G_2)$. By *clausal goal replacement* of G_1 by G_2 in C we derive the clause $D = H \leftarrow L, G_2, R$ and we get P_{k+1} by substituting D for C in P_k.

In Example 4.3.1 below we will see that rule R5.1 overcomes the above mentioned limitation of rule R5.

In the next section we will show that the clausal goal replacement rule R5.1 can be viewed as a derived rule, because its application can be mimicked by suitable applications of the transformation rules R1, R2, R3, R4, and R5 defined above. Thus, without loss of generality, we may consider rule R5 as the only goal replacement rule, when also rules R1, R2, R3, and R4 are available.

Various notions of goal equivalence and goal replacement have been introduced in the literature [Tamaki and Sato, 1984; Maher, 1987; Gardner and Shepherdson, 1991; Bossi *et al.*, 1992b; Bossi *et al.*, 1992a; Cook and Gallagher, 1994]. Each of these notions has been defined in terms of a particular semantics, while in our presentation we introduced a notion which has the advantage of being parametric w.r.t. the given semantics **SEM**.

We finally present a class of transformation rules which will collectively be called *clause replacement* rules and referred to as rule R6.

Rule R6. Clause replacement. From program P_k we get program P_{k+1} by applying one of the following four rules.

Rule R6.1 Clause rearrangement. We get P_{k+1} by replacing in P_k the sequence C, D of two clauses by D, C.

This clause rearrangement rule is implicitly used by many authors who consider a program as a set or a multiset of clauses.

Rule R6.2 Deletion of subsumed clauses. A clause C is *subsumed* by a clause D iff there exist a substitution θ and a (possibly empty) goal G such that $hd(C) = hd(D)\theta$ and $bd(C) = bd(D)\theta, G$. We may get program P_{k+1} by deleting from P_k a clause which is subsumed by another clause in P_k.

In particular, the rule for the deletion of subsumed clauses allows us to remove duplicate clauses.

Rule R6.3 Deletion of clauses with finitely failed body. Let C be a clause in program P_k of the form: $H \leftarrow A_1, \ldots, A_m, L, B_1, \ldots, B_n$ with $m, n \geq 0$. If literal L has a finitely failed SLDNF-tree in P_k, then we say that C has a *finitely failed body* in P_k and we get program P_{k+1} by deleting C from P_k.

The rules for the deletion of subsumed clauses and the deletion of clauses with finitely failed body are instances of the clause deletion rule introduced by Tamaki and Sato [1984] for definite programs. Other rules for deleting clauses from a given program, or adding clauses to a given program are studied in [Tamaki and Sato, 1984; Gardner and Shepherdson, 1991; Bossi and Cocco, 1993; Maher, 1993]. The correctness of those rules strictly depends on the semantics considered. For further details the reader may look at the original papers.

Rule R6.4 Generalization + equality introduction. Let us assume that the equality predicate '=' (written in infix notation) is defined by the clause $X = X \leftarrow$ in every program of the transformation sequence $P_0, \ldots, P_k$. Let us also consider a clause

C. $H \leftarrow A_1, \ldots, A_m$

in P_k, a substitution $\theta = \{X/t\}$, with X not occurring in t, and a clause

$GenC$. $GenH \leftarrow GenA_1, \ldots, GenA_m$

such that $C = GenC \, \theta$.

By *generalization + equality introduction* we derive the clause

D. $GenH \leftarrow X = t, GenA_1, \ldots, GenA_m$

and we get P_{k+1} by replacing C by D in P_k.

This transformation rule was formalized in [Proietti and Pettorossi, 1990].

4   Correctness of the transformation rules

In this section we will first present some correctness properties of the transformation rules which we introduced in the previous section. These properties are parametric w.r.t. the semantics function **SEM**. We will then give an overview of the main results presented in the literature concerning the correctness of the transformation rules w.r.t. various semantics for definite and normal programs.

We first introduce the notion of correctness of a transformation sequence w.r.t. a generic semantics function **SEM**.

Definition 4.0.1 (Correctness of a transformation sequence). Let **P** be a set of programs, **Q** a set of queries, and **SEM**: $\mathbf{P} \times \mathbf{Q} \rightarrow (\mathbf{D}, \leq)$ be a semantics function. A transformation sequence $P_0, \ldots, P_k$ of programs in **P** is *partially correct* (or *totally correct*) w.r.t. **SEM** iff for every query Q in **Q**, containing only predicate symbols which occur in P_0, we have that $\mathbf{SEM}[P_k, Q] \leq \mathbf{SEM}[P_0, Q]$ (or $\mathbf{SEM}[P_k, Q] = \mathbf{SEM}[P_0, Q]$).

A transformation rule is *partially correct* (or *totally correct*) w.r.t. **SEM** iff for every transformation sequence $P_0, \ldots, P_k$ which is partially correct (or totally correct) w.r.t. **SEM** and for any program P_{k+1} obtained from P_k by an application of that rule, we have that the extended transformation sequence $P_0, \ldots, P_k, P_{k+1}$ is partially correct (or totally correct) w.r.t. **SEM**.

A transformation step which allows us to derive P_{k+1} from a transformation sequence $P_0, \ldots, P_k$ is said to be *partially correct* (or *totally correct*) w.r.t. **SEM** iff for every query Q in **Q**, containing only predicate symbols which occur in P_k, we have that $\mathbf{SEM}[P_{k+1}, Q] \leq \mathbf{SEM}[P_k, Q]$ (or $\mathbf{SEM}[P_{k+1}, Q] = \mathbf{SEM}[P_k, Q]$).

Notice that, if a transformation sequence is constructed by performing a sequence of partially correct transformation steps, then it is partially correct. However, it may be the case that not all transformation steps realizing a partially correct transformation sequence are partially correct. Also, the application of a partially correct transformation rule may generate a transformation step which is not partially correct.

Similar remarks also hold for total correctness, instead of partial correctness.

Obviously, if $P_0, \ldots, P_k$ and $P_k, P_{k+1}, \ldots, P_n$ are partially correct (or totally correct) transformation sequences, also their 'concatenation' $P_0, \ldots, P_k, P_{k+1}, \ldots, P_n$ is partially correct (or totally correct). In what follows, by 'correctness' we will mean 'total correctness'.

The following lemma establishes a correctness result for the definition introduction and definition elimination rules assuming that **SEM** is relevant. In the subsequent sections we will give some more correctness results which hold with different assumptions on **SEM**.

Lemma 4.0.2 (Relevance). *The rules of definition introduction and definition elimination are totally correct w.r.t. any relevant semantics.*

4.1   Reversible transformations

We present here a simple method to prove that a transformation sequence constructed by applying partially correct rules is totally correct. This method is based on the notion of *reversible* transformation sequence.

Definition 4.1.1 (Reversible transformations). A transformation sequence $P_0, P_1, \ldots, P_{n-1}, P_n$ constructed by using a set **R** of rules is said to be *reversible* iff there exists a transformation sequence $P_n, Q_1, \ldots, Q_k, P_0$, with $k \geq 0$, which can be constructed by using rules in **R**.

A transformation step which allows us to derive P_{k+1} from P_k is said to be *reversible* iff P_k, P_{k+1} is a reversible transformation sequence. In particular, if P_k, P_{k+1} has been constructed by using a rule R_a and P_{k+1}, P_k can be constructed by using a rule R_b, then we say that a transformation step using R_a is *reversible* by an transformation step using R_b.

Notice that, in the above definition of reversible transformations the construction of the transformation sequence $P_n, Q_1, \ldots, Q_k, P_0$ is required to be independent of the construction of the transformation sequence $P_0, P_1, \ldots, P_{n-1}, P_n$. This independence condition is essential because, in general, we can derive a new program by using clauses occurring in a program which precedes the last one in the transformation sequence at hand. Thus, it may be the case that there exists a transformation sequence

$P_0, P_1, \ldots, P_{n-1}, P_n, R_1, \ldots, R_h, P_0$, for $h \geq 0$, but there is no transformation sequence $P_n, Q_1, \ldots, Q_k, P_0$. In this case the transformation sequence $P_0, P_1, \ldots, P_{n-1}, P_n$ is not reversible.

In particular, there are folding steps which are not reversible by unfolding steps, because the clauses to be used for unfolding are not available.

Example 4.1.2. Let us consider the following program:

$$P_0 : \qquad p \leftarrow q \qquad q \leftarrow q$$

By folding the first clause using itself, we get the program

$$P_1 : \qquad p \leftarrow p \qquad q \leftarrow q$$

This folding step is not reversible by any sequence of unfolding steps, because starting from program P_1, it is impossible to get program P_0 by applying the unfolding rule only.

The importance of the reversibility property is given by the following result, whose proof is straightforward.

Lemma 4.1.3 (Reversibility). *Let* **SEM** *be a semantics function and* **R** *a set of transformation rules.*

If a transformation step using a rule R_a *in* **R** *is reversible by a totally correct transformation step using a rule* R_b *in* **R**, *then the transformation step using* R_a *is totally correct.*

If the rules in **R** *are partially correct w.r.t.* **SEM**, *then any reversible transformation sequence using rules in* **R** *is totally correct w.r.t.* **SEM**.

Notice, however, that in general it is hard to check whether or not a transformation sequence is reversible.

We now consider instances of the folding rule and the goal replacement rule which always produce reversible transformation sequences.

Rule R2.1 In-situ folding. A folding step is called an *in-situ folding* iff, with reference to rule R2, we have that

- $P_k = P_j$ (that is, the clauses used for folding are taken from the last program, not from a previous program, in the transformation sequence at hand) and
- $\{C_1, \ldots, C_n\} \cap \{D_1, \ldots, D_n\} = \{\}$ (that is, no clause among $C_1, \ldots, C_n$ is used to fold $C_1, \ldots, C_n$).

Any in-situ folding step which derives a clause C from $C_1, \ldots, C_n$ in P_k using clauses $D_1, \ldots, D_n$ in P_k itself, is reversible by unfolding C using $D_1, \ldots, D_n$. Indeed, clauses $D_1, \ldots, D_n$ occur in P_{k+1} and by unfolding C using $D_1, \ldots, D_n$ we get $C_1, \ldots, C_n$. Thus, P_{k+1}, P_k is a transformation sequence which can be produced by an unfolding step.

A folding rule similar to in-situ folding has been considered by Maher [1990; 1993] in the more general context of logic programs *with constraints*.

Other instances of the in-situ folding rule have been proposed in [Maher, 1987; Gardner and Shepherdson, 1991].

We will see in Section 4.4 that the reversibility property of in-situ folding allows us to establish in a straightforward way some total correctness results for this rule. However, in-situ folding has limited power, in the sense that, as we will see in Section 5, most transformation strategies for improving program efficiency make use of folding steps which are not in-situ foldings.

Rule R5.2 Persistent goal replacement. Let C be a clause in P_k and goal G_1 be equivalent to goal G_2 w.r.t. a semantics **SEM** and program P_k. The goal replacement of G_1 by G_2 in C is said to be *persistent* iff G_1 and G_2 are equivalent w.r.t. **SEM** and the derived program P_{k+1}.

Any persistent goal replacement step which replaces G_1 by G_2 is reversible by a goal replacement step which performs the inverse replacement of G_2 by G_1. Thus, if the goal replacement rule is partially correct w.r.t. **SEM**, then any persistent goal replacement step is totally correct w.r.t. **SEM**.

In the following definition we introduce a variant of the goal replacement rule which is reversible if one considers relevant semantics.

Rule R5.3 Independent goal replacement. Let C be a clause in a program P and goal G_1 be equivalent to goal G_2 w.r.t. a semantics **SEM** and program P. The replacement of G_1 by G_2 in C is said to be *independent* iff C belongs to neither $P_{rel}(G_1)$ nor $P_{rel}(G_2)$ (that is, neither G_1 nor G_2 depends on C).

Lemma 4.1.4 (Reversibility of independent goal replacement). *Let* **SEM** *be a relevant semantics and goal G_1 be equivalent to goal G_2 w.r.t.* **SEM** *and program P. Any independent goal replacement of G_1 by G_2 in a clause of P is reversible by performing an independent goal replacement step.*

Proof. Let Q be the program obtained from P by replacing the goal G_1 by the goal G_2 in a clause C of P such that neither G_1 nor G_2 depends on C. We first show that this independent goal replacement step is persistent by proving that G_1 and G_2 are equivalent w.r.t. **SEM** and program Q, that is, $\mathbf{SEM}[Q, \leftarrow G_1] = \mathbf{SEM}[Q, \leftarrow G_2]$. Indeed, we have that

$\qquad \mathbf{SEM}[Q, \leftarrow G_1]$ (by relevance of **SEM**)

$\qquad = \mathbf{SEM}[Q_{rel}(G_1), \leftarrow G_1]$ (since $C \notin P_{rel}(G_1)$)

$\qquad = \mathbf{SEM}[P_{rel}(G_1), \leftarrow G_1]$ (by relevance of **SEM**)

$\qquad = \mathbf{SEM}[P, \leftarrow G_1]$ (since G_1 is equivalent to G_2 w.r.t. **SEM** and P)

$\qquad = \mathbf{SEM}[P, \leftarrow G_2]$ (by relevance of **SEM**)

$\qquad = \mathbf{SEM}[P_{rel}(G_2), \leftarrow G_2]$ (since $C \notin P_{rel}(G_2)$)

$= \mathbf{SEM}[Q_{rel}(G_2), \leftarrow G_2] \qquad$ (by relevance of $\mathbf{SEM}$)

$= \mathbf{SEM}[Q, \leftarrow G_2]$.

Since any independent goal replacement step is persistent, it is also reversible by performing the inverse independent goal replacement of G_2 by G_1 in the program Q. $\blacksquare$

4.2 A derived goal replacement rule

In this section we show that the clausal goal replacement rule can be derived from the following transformation rules: unfolding, in-situ folding, non-recursive definition introduction, definition elimination, and goal replacement, whenever the rules of non-recursive definition introduction and in-situ folding are totally correct w.r.t. the semantics $\mathbf{SEM}$. A different way of viewing the goal replacement rule as a sequence of transformation rules can be found in [Bossi *et al.*, 1992a].

Let P_k be the program $C_1, \ldots, C_n$ and let us consider clause C_i of the form $H \leftarrow L, G_1, R$. Suppose that the goal G_1 is equivalent to the goal G_2 w.r.t. $\mathbf{SEM}$, P_k, and $\{X_1, \ldots, X_m\} = vars(H, L, R) \cap vars(G_1, G_2)$.

By applying the clausal goal replacement rule R5.1 (page 713) we may replace G_1 by G_2 in C_i, thereby deriving the new clause D of the form $H \leftarrow L, G_2, R$ and the new program $P_{k+1} = C_1, \ldots, C_{i-1}, D, C_{i+1}, \ldots, C_n$.

The same program P_{k+1} can be derived by the sequence of the following five transformation steps.

Step 1. By the non-recursive definition rule we introduce the clauses

D_1. $newp_1(X_1, \ldots, X_m) \leftarrow G_1$
D_2. $newp_2(X_1, \ldots, X_m) \leftarrow G_2$

Then we get the program $C_1, \ldots, C_n, D_1, D_2$.

Step 2. Since $vars(H, L, R) \cap vars(G_1) \subseteq \{X_1, \ldots, X_m\}$, condition 4 of the folding rule is fulfilled. Also the other conditions 1, 2, and 3 are fulfilled. By in-situ folding of clause C_i using D_1 we derive the clause

F. $H \leftarrow L, newp_1(X_1, \ldots, X_m), R$

Thus, we get the new program

$$Q = C_1, \ldots, C_{i-1}, F, C_{i+1}, \ldots, C_n, D_1, D_2.$$

Step 3. The goals $newp_1(X_1, \ldots, X_m)$ and $newp_2(X_1, \ldots, X_m)$ are equivalent w.r.t. $\mathbf{SEM}$ and Q. Indeed, we have

$\mathbf{SEM}[(C_1, \ldots, C_{i-1}, C_i, C_{i+1}, \ldots, C_n, D_1), \leftarrow newp_1(X_1, \ldots, X_m)]$

(by the correctness of non-recursive definition introduction)

$= \mathbf{SEM}[(C_1, \ldots, C_{i-1}, C_i, C_{i+1}, \ldots, C_n, D_1, D_2), \leftarrow newp_1(X_1, \ldots, X_m)]$

(by the correctness of in-situ folding)

$= \mathbf{SEM}[(C_1, \ldots, C_{i-1}, F, C_{i+1}, \ldots, C_n, D_1, D_2), \leftarrow newp_1(X_1, \ldots, X_m)]$

and

$\mathbf{SEM}[(C_1, \ldots, C_{i-1}, C_i, C_{i+1}, \ldots, C_n, D_1), \leftarrow newp_1(X_1, \ldots, X_m)]$

(since G_1 and G_2 are equivalent w.r.t. $\mathbf{SEM}$, P_k, and $\{X_1, \ldots, X_m\}$)

$= \mathbf{SEM}[(C_1, \ldots, C_{i-1}, C_i, C_{i+1}, \ldots, C_n, D_2), \leftarrow newp_2(X_1, \ldots, X_m)]$

(by the correctness of non-recursive definition introduction)

$= \mathbf{SEM}[(C_1, \ldots, C_{i-1}, C_i, C_{i+1}, \ldots, C_n, D_1, D_2), \leftarrow newp_2(X_1, \ldots, X_m)]$

(by the correctness of in-situ folding)

$= \mathbf{SEM}[(C_1, \ldots, C_{i-1}, F, C_{i+1}, \ldots, C_n, D_1, D_2), \leftarrow newp_2(X_1, \ldots, X_m)].$

Thus, by applying the goal replacement rule R5, from clause F in program Q we derive the new clause

$M.\ H \leftarrow L, newp_2(X_1, \ldots, X_m), R$

and we get the new program $C_1, \ldots, C_{i-1}, M, C_{i+1}, \ldots, C_n, D_1, D_2$.

Step 4. By unfolding M w.r.t. $newp_2(X_1, \ldots, X_m)$ we get

$D.\ H \leftarrow L, G_2, R$

and the program $C_1, \ldots, C_{i-1}, D, C_{i+1}, \ldots, C_n, D_1, D_2$.

Step 5. Finally, by definition elimination we discard clauses D_1 and D_2, and we get exactly the program P_{k+1}, as desired.

We have also the converse result which we will show below, that is, if by goal replacement from program P_k we get program P_{k+1} and we assume that the non-recursive definition introduction rule and the independent goal replacement rule are totally correct w.r.t. $\mathbf{SEM}$, then we may apply the clausal goal replacement rule for deriving program P_{k+1} from program P_k.

Indeed, suppose that the goals G_1 and G_2 are equivalent w.r.t. $\mathbf{SEM}$ and $P_k = C_1, \ldots, C_n$. Also, consider the clauses

$D_1.\ newp_1(X_1, \ldots, X_m) \leftarrow G_1$
$D_2.\ newp_2(X_1, \ldots, X_m) \leftarrow G_2$

where $\{X_1, \ldots, X_m\}$ is any set of variables.

By the correctness of the non-recursive definition introduction rule we have that

$\mathbf{SEM}[(C_1, \ldots, C_n), \leftarrow G_1]$

$= \mathbf{SEM}[(C_1, \ldots, C_n, newp_1(X_1, \ldots, X_m) \leftarrow G_1), \leftarrow G_1]$ and

$\mathbf{SEM}[(C_1, \ldots, C_n), \leftarrow G_2]$

$= \mathbf{SEM}[(C_1, \ldots, C_n, newp_1(X_1, \ldots, X_m) \leftarrow G_1), \leftarrow G_2].$

Since the goals G_1 and G_2 are equivalent w.r.t. $\mathbf{SEM}$ and $(C_1, \ldots, C_n)$, that is, $\mathbf{SEM}[(C_1, \ldots, C_n), \leftarrow G_1] = \mathbf{SEM}[(C_1, \ldots, C_n), \leftarrow G_2]$, we have that

$\mathbf{SEM}[(C_1, \ldots, C_n,\ newp_1(X_1, \ldots, X_m) \leftarrow G_1),\ \leftarrow G_1]$

$= \mathbf{SEM}[(C_1, \ldots, C_n,\ newp_1(X_1, \ldots, X_m) \leftarrow G_1),\ \leftarrow G_2],$

that is, G_1 and G_2 are equivalent w.r.t. $\mathbf{SEM}$ and the program $(C_1, \ldots, C_n,$ $newp_1(X_1, \ldots, X_m) \leftarrow G_1)$.

As a consequence, we may apply the independent goal replacement rule and from program $(C_1, \ldots, C_n,\ newp_1(X_1, \ldots, X_m) \leftarrow G_1)$ we derive program $(C_1, \ldots, C_n,\ newp_1(X_1, \ldots, X_m) \leftarrow G_2)$.

Thus,

$\mathbf{SEM}[(C_1, \ldots, C_n, newp_1(X_1, \ldots, X_m) \leftarrow G_1), \leftarrow newp_1(X_1, \ldots, X_m)]$

(by the correctness of the independent goal replacement rule)

$= \mathbf{SEM}[(C_1, \ldots, C_n, newp_1(X_1, \ldots, X_m) \leftarrow G_2), \leftarrow newp_1(X_1, \ldots, X_m)]$

(since $\mathbf{SEM}$ is preserved by predicate renaming)

$= \mathbf{SEM}[(C_1, \ldots, C_n, newp_2(X_1, \ldots, X_m) \leftarrow G_2), \leftarrow newp_2(X_1, \ldots, X_m)].$

We conclude that: i) G_1 and G_2 are equivalent w.r.t. $\mathbf{SEM}$, P_k, and any set of variables (see Definition 3.3.9, page 713), and ii) the replacement of G_1 by G_2 in any clause of P_k may be viewed as an application of the clausal goal replacement rule.

To sum up the results presented in this section we have that, if the rules of non-recursive definition introduction, in-situ folding, and independent goal replacement are correct w.r.t. $\mathbf{SEM}$, then the goal replacement and clausal goal replacement are equivalent rules, in the sense that program Q can be derived from program P by using rules R1, R2, R3, R4, goal replacement (rule R5), and R6 iff Q can be derived from P by using rules R1, R2, R3, R4, clausal goal replacement (rule R5.1), and R6.

We will see that the non-recursive definition introduction, in-situ folding, and independent goal replacement rules are correct w.r.t. all semantics we will consider, and thus, when describing the correctness results w.r.t. those semantics, we can make no distinction between the goal replacement rule R5 and the clausal goal replacement rule R5.1.

4.3 The unfold/fold proof method

The validity of a replacement law is, in general, undecidable. However, if we use totally correct transformation rules only, then for any transformation sequence we need to prove a replacement law only once.

Indeed, if $G_1 \equiv_V G_2$ is valid w.r.t. a semantics $\mathbf{SEM}$ and a program P_k, then it is also valid w.r.t. $\mathbf{SEM}$ and Q for every program Q derived from P_k by using totally correct transformation rules.

In order to prove the validity of a replacement law, there are *ad hoc* proof methods depending on the specific semantics which is considered (see Section 7). As an alternative approach, one can use a simple method based on unfold/fold transformations which we call *unfold/fold proof method*.

This proof method was introduced by Kott for recursive equation programs [Kott, 1982] and its application to logic programs is described in [Boulanger and Bruynooghe, 1993; Proietti and Pettorossi, 1994a; Proietti and Pettorossi, 1994b].

The unfold/fold proof method can be described as follows. Given a program P, a semantics function **SEM**, and a replacement law $G_1 \equiv_V G_2$, with $V = \{X_1, \ldots, X_m\}$, we consider the clauses

$D_1.\ newp_1(X_1, \ldots, X_m) \leftarrow G_1$
$D_2.\ newp_2(X_1, \ldots, X_m) \leftarrow G_2$

and the programs $R_0 = C_1, \ldots, C_n, D_1$ and $S_0 = C_1, \ldots, C_n, D_2$.

We then construct two correct transformation sequences $R_0, \ldots, R_u$ and $S_0, \ldots, S_v$, such that R_u and S_v are equal modulo predicate renaming.

The validity of $G_1 \equiv_V G_2$ follows from the total correctness of the transformation sequences, and the assumption that **SEM** is preserved by predicate renaming.

Example 4.3.1. Consider again the program $P_k = C, A_1, A_2$ of the *Sublist* Example 3.3.8 (page 713). Suppose that we want to apply the clausal goal replacement rule to replace the goal $G_1 = (append(V, X, I), append(I, Z, Y))$ by the goal $G_2 = (append(X, Z, J), append(V, J, Y))$ in the body of the clause

$C.\ sublist(N, X, Y) \leftarrow length(X, N), append(V, X, I), append(I, Z, Y)$

We need to show the validity of the replacement law

$$append(V, X, I), append(I, Z, Y) \equiv_{\{X,Y\}} append(X, Z, J), append(V, J, Y)$$

where the equivalence w.r.t. the set $\{X, Y\}$ is justified by the fact that

$$vars(sublist(N, X, Y), length(X, N)) \cap vars(G_1, G_2) = \{X, Y\}.$$

As suggested by the unfold/fold proof method, we introduce the clauses

$D_1.\ newp_1(X, Y) \leftarrow append(V, X, I), append(I, Z, Y)$
$D_2.\ newp_2(X, Y) \leftarrow append(X, L, J), append(K, J, Y)$

We then consider the programs $R_0 = C, A_1, A_2, D_1$ and $S_0 = C, A_1, A_2, D_2$.

We now construct two transformation sequences starting from R_0 and S_0, respectively, as follows.

1. *Transformation sequence starting from R_0.*
   By unfolding clause D_1 in R_0 w.r.t. $append(V, X, I)$ we derive the following two clauses:

   $E_1.\ newp_1(X, Y) \leftarrow append(X, Z, Y)$

E_2. $newp_1(X,Y) \leftarrow append(T,X,U), append([H|U],Z,Y)$

and we get the program $R_1 = C, A_1, A_2, E_1, E_2$.
Then, by unfolding clause E_2 w.r.t. $append([H|U],Z,Y)$ we get

E_3. $newp_1(X,[H|V]) \leftarrow append(T,X,U), append(U,Z,V)$

and we get the program $R_2 = C, A_1, A_2, E_1, E_3$.
Finally, by folding clause E_3 using clause D_1 in R_0 we derive

E_4. $newp_1(X,[H|V]) \leftarrow newp_1(X,V)$

and we get the program $R_3 = C, A_1, A_2, E_1, E_4$.
2. *Transformation sequence starting from* S_0.
By unfolding clause D_2 in S_0 w.r.t. $append(K,J,Y)$ we derive two clauses

F_1. $newp_2(X,Y) \leftarrow append(X,L,Y)$
F_2. $newp_2(X,[H|U]) \leftarrow append(X,L,J), append(T,J,U)$

and we get the program $S_1 = C, A_1, A_2, F_1, F_2$.
By folding clause F_2 using clause D_2 in S_0 we get the clause

F_3. $newp_2(X;[H|U]) \leftarrow newp_2(X,U)$

and we derive the final program of this transformation sequence which is $S_2 = C, A_1, A_2, F_1, F_3$.

The derived programs R_3 and S_2 are equal up to predicate renaming (that is, for a renaming ρ which maps $newp_1$ to $newp_2$} we have $\rho(R_3) = S_2$) and the validity of the given replacement law is proved w.r.t. any semantics **SEM**, provided the transformation sequences R_0, R_1, R_2, R_3 and S_0, S_1, S_2 are correct w.r.t. **SEM**. We will show below that these transformation sequences are correct w.r.t. several semantics and, in particular, the least Herbrand model semantics **LHM**.

4.4   Correctness results for definite programs

Let us now consider definite programs and let us study the correctness properties of the transformation rules w.r.t. various semantics. We will first look at the correctness properties of the unfold/fold transformations w.r.t. both the least Herbrand model (Section 4.4.1) and the computed answer substitution semantics (Section 4.4.2). We will then take into account various semantics related to program termination, such as the finite failure semantics (Section 4.4.3) and the answer substitution semantics computed by the depth-first search strategy of Prolog (Section 4.4.4).

We will assume that the equivalence between goals, as well as the various instances of the goal replacement rule, refer to the semantics considered in each section.

4.4.1 Least Herbrand model

In this section we assume that the semantics function is **LHM** (page 707) and we present several partial correctness and total correctness results based on the work in [Tamaki and Sato, 1984; Tamaki and Sato, 1986; Maher, 1987; Gardner and Shepherdson, 1991; Gergatsoulis and Katzouraki, 1994].

The total correctness w.r.t. **LHM** of the unfolding steps is a straightforward consequence of the soundness and completeness of SLD-resolution w.r.t. the least Herbrand model semantics. As a consequence, by the reversibility lemma (page 717) any in-situ folding step is totally correct w.r.t. **LHM**.

In the general case, by applying the folding rule R2 to program P_k of a transformation sequence $P_0, \ldots, P_k$, we derive clauses which are true in the least Herbrand model of P_0. Thus, the folding rule is partially correct w.r.t. **LHM**. It is not totally correct, as is shown by the following example.

Example 4.4.1. Given the program

$$P_0: \qquad p \leftarrow q \qquad q \leftarrow$$

by folding the first clause using itself we get

$$P_1: \qquad p \leftarrow p \qquad q \leftarrow$$

We have that $\mathbf{LHM}[P_1, \leftarrow p] \neq \mathbf{LHM}[P_0, \leftarrow p]$, because p is true in the least Herbrand model of P_0 and it is false in the least Herbrand model of P_1.

The correctness of the definition introduction and elimination rules w.r.t. **LHM** follows from Lemma 4.0.2, since **LHM** is a relevant semantics.

Similarly to the case of the folding rule, also the goal replacement rule R5 is partially correct w.r.t. **LHM**. Indeed, by applying the goal replacement rule to program P_k of a transformation sequence $P_0, \ldots, P_k$, we derive clauses which are true in the least Herbrand model of P_0.

It is easy to see that, in general, the goal replacement rule is not totally correct. Indeed, the folding step considered in Example 4.4.1 may also be taken as an example of a goal replacement step which is not totally correct, because p is equivalent to q w.r.t. **LHM** and P_0.

However, there are some instances of the goal replacement rule which are totally correct. In particular, since **LHM** is a relevant semantics, by the partial correctness of the goal replacement rule, the reversibility lemma (page 717), and the reversibility of independent goal replacement lemma (page 718), the independent goal replacement rule is totally correct w.r.t. **LHM**.

Let us now consider the following two special cases of the goal replacement rule.

Rule R5.4 Goal rearrangement. By the *goal rearrangement* rule we replace a goal (G, H) in the body of a clause by the goal (H, G).

Rule R5.5 Deletion of duplicate goals. By the *deletion of duplicate goals* rule we replace a goal (G, G) in the body of a clause by the goal G.

Steps of goal rearrangement and deletion of duplicate goals are totally correct w.r.t. **LHM**. Indeed, they are persistent goal replacement steps, because they are based on the following equivalences w.r.t. **LHM**: $(G, H) \equiv_{vars(G,H)} (H, G)$ and $(G, G) \equiv_{vars(G)} G$, which hold w.r.t. any given program.

From these total correctness results it follows that, when dealing with the least Herbrand model semantics, we may assume that bodies of clauses are sets (not sequences) of atoms.

The total correctness of the clause replacement rules is also straightforward. Thus, since the rules for clause rearrangement (rule R6.1) and deletion of duplicate clauses (rule derived from rule R6.2) are totally correct w.r.t. **LHM**, we may assume that programs are sets (not sequences) of clauses.

However, we will see that some instances of the above rules are not correct when considering the computed answer substitution semantics (see Section 4.4.2, page 728) or the pure Prolog semantics (see Section 4.4.4, page 732).

As a summary of the results mentioned so far we have the following:

Theorem 4.4.2 (First correctness theorem w.r.t. LHM). *Let P_0, ..., P_n be a transformation sequence of definite programs constructed by using the following transformation rules: unfolding, in-situ folding, definition introduction, definition elimination, goal rearrangement, deletion of duplicate goals, independent goal replacement, and clause replacement. Then $P_0, \ldots, P_n$ is totally correct w.r.t. **LHM**.*

We have seen that the in-situ folding rule has the advantage of being a totally correct transformation rule, but it is a weak rule because it does not allow us to derive recursive definitions. In order to overcome this limitation we now present a different and more powerful version of the folding rule, called *single-folding*.

Let us first notice that by performing a folding step and introducing recursive clauses from non-recursive clauses, some infinite computations (due to a non-well-founded recursion) may replace finite computations, thereby affecting the semantics of the program and losing total correctness.

A simple example of this undesirable introduction of infinite computations is *self-folding*, where all clauses in a predicate definition can be folded using themselves. For instance, the definition $p \leftarrow q$ of a predicate p can be replaced by $p \leftarrow p$ (see Example 4.4.1, page 724).

This inconvenience can be avoided by ensuring that 'enough' unfolding steps have been performed before folding, so that 'going backward in the computation' (as folding does) does not prevail over 'going forward in the computation' (as unfolding does). This idea is the basis for various techniques in which total correctness is ensured by counting the number of unfolding and folding steps performed during the transformation sequence [Kott, 1978; Kanamori and Fujita, 1986; Bossi *et al.*, 1992a].

An alternative approach is based on the verification that some termination properties are preserved by the transformation process, thereby avoiding the introduction of infinite computations [Amtoft, 1992; Bossi and Etalle, 1994b; Bossi and Cocco, 1994; Cook and Gallagher, 1994].

The following definition introduces the version of the folding rule we have promised above. This version is a special case of rule R2 for $n = 1$.

Rule R2.2 Single-folding. Let C be a clause in program P_k and D be a clause in a program P_j, for some j, with $0 \leq j \leq k$. Suppose that there exist two goals F and G and a substitution θ such that:

1. C is a variant of $H \leftarrow F, bd(D)\theta, G$,

2. for every clause E of P_j different from D, $hd(E)$ is not unifiable with $hd(D)\theta$, and

3. for every variable X in the set $vars(D) - vars(hd(D))$, we have that
   - $X\theta$ is a variable which does not occur in (H, F, G) and
   - the variable $X\theta$ does not occur in the term $Y\theta$, for any variable Y occurring in $bd(D)$ and different from X.

By the *single-folding* rule, using clause D, from clause C we derive clause $H \leftarrow F, hd(D)\theta, G$.

This rule is called *T & S-folding* in [Pettorossi and Proietti, 1994].

We now present a correctness result analogous to the first correctness Theorem w.r.t. **LHM** for a transformation sequence including single-folding, rather than in-situ folding. We essentially follow [Tamaki and Sato, 1986], but we make some simplifying assumptions. By doing so, total correctness is ensured by easily verifiable conditions on the transformation sequence.

We assume that the set of the predicate symbols occurring in the transformation sequence $P_0, \ldots, P_n$ is partitioned into three sets, called *top predicates, intermediate predicates,* and *basic predicates,* respectively, with the following restrictions:

1. a predicate introduced by the definition rule is a *top predicate,*

2. an *intermediate predicate* does not depend in P_0 on any top predicate, and

3. a *basic predicate* does not depend in P_0 on any intermediate or top predicate.

Notice that this partition process is, in general, nondeterministic. In particular, we can choose the top predicates in P_0 in various ways. Notice also that dependencies of some intermediate predicates on top predicates may be introduced by folding steps (see the second correctness theorem below).

The approach we follow here is more general than the approach described in [Kawamura and Kanamori, 1990], where only two sets of predicates are considered (the so-called *new* predicates and *old* predicates).

Let us also introduce a new goal replacement rule, called *basic goal replacement*, which is a particular case of independent goal replacement.

Rule R5.6 Basic goal replacement. By the *basic goal replacement* rule we replace a goal G_1 in the body of a clause C by a goal G_2 such that any predicate occurring in G_1 or G_2 is a basic predicate and the head of C has a top or an intermediate predicate.

The following theorem establishes the correctness of transformation sequences which are constructed by applying a set of transformation rules including the single-folding rule and the basic goal replacement rule.

Theorem 4.4.3 (Second correctness theorem w.r.t. LHM). *Let $P_0, \ldots, P_n$ be a transformation sequence of definite programs constructed by using the following transformation rules: unfolding, single-folding, definition introduction, definition elimination, goal rearrangement, deletion of duplicate goals, basic goal replacement, and clause replacement. Suppose that no single-folding step is performed after a definition elimination step. Suppose also that when we apply the single-folding rule to a clause, say C, using a clause, say D, the following conditions hold:*
- *either D belongs to P_0 or D has been introduced by the definition rule,*
- *$hd(D)$ has a top predicate, and*
- *either $hd(C)$ has an intermediate predicate*
  or $hd(C)$ has a top predicate and C has been derived from a clause, say E, by first unfolding E w.r.t. an atom with an intermediate predicate and then performing zero or more transformation steps on a clause derived from the unfolding of E.

Then $P_0, \ldots, P_n$ is totally correct w.r.t. the semantics **LHM**.

The hypothesis that no single-folding step is performed after a definition elimination step is needed to prevent single-folding from being applied using a clause with a head predicate whose definition has been eliminated. This point is illustrated by the following example.

Example 4.4.4. Let us consider the transformation sequence

$P_0:$ $p \leftarrow q$ $p \leftarrow fail$ $q \leftarrow$
         (by definition introduction)
$P_1:$ $p \leftarrow q$ $p \leftarrow fail$ $q \leftarrow$ $newp \leftarrow q$

(by definition elimination)

P_2: $p \leftarrow q$ $p \leftarrow fail$ $q \leftarrow$

(by single-folding)

P_3: $p \leftarrow newp$ $p \leftarrow fail$ $q \leftarrow$

We may assume that *newp* is a top predicate and p is an intermediate predicate. However, the transformation sequence is not correct w.r.t. **LHM**, because the query $\leftarrow p$ succeeds in the initial program, while it fails in the final one.

The second correctness theorem w.r.t. **LHM** can be extended to other variants of the folding rule as described in [Gergatsoulis and Katzouraki, 1994].

4.4.2 Computed answer substitutions

We now consider a semantics function based on the notion of *computed answer substitutions* [Lloyd, 1987; Apt, 1990], which captures the procedural behaviour of definite programs more accurately than the least Herbrand model semantics.

The computed answer substitution semantics can be defined as a function

$$\textbf{CAS}: \textbf{P}^+ \times \textbf{Q}^+ \rightarrow (\mathcal{P}(\textbf{Subst}), \leq)$$

where $\textbf{P}^+$ is the set of definite programs, $\textbf{Q}^+$ is the set of definite queries, and $(\mathcal{P}(\textbf{Subst}), \leq)$ is the powerset of the set of substitutions ordered by set inclusion. We define the semantics **CAS** as follows:

$\textbf{CAS}[P, Q] = \{\theta \mid$ there exists an SLD-refutation of Q in P with computed answer substitution $\theta\}$.

CAS is a relevant semantics.

By the soundness and completeness of SLD-resolution w.r.t. **LHM**, we have that the equivalence of two programs w.r.t. **CAS** implies their equivalence w.r.t. **LHM**. However, the converse is not true. For instance, consider the following two programs:

P_1: $p(X) \leftarrow$
P_2: $p(X) \leftarrow$ $p(a) \leftarrow$

We have that $\textbf{LHM}[P_1, \leftarrow p(X)] = \textbf{LHM}[P_2, \leftarrow p(X)] = \textbf{Subst}$. However, we have that $\textbf{CAS}[P_1, \leftarrow p(X)] = \{\{\}\}$, whereas $\textbf{CAS}[P_2, \leftarrow p(X)] = \{\{\}, \{X/a\}\}$, where $\{\}$ is the identity substitution.

As a consequence, not all rules which are correct w.r.t. **LHM** are correct also w.r.t. **CAS**. In particular, the deletion of duplicate goals and the deletion of subsumed clauses do not preserve the **CAS** semantics, as is shown by the following examples.

Example 4.4.5. Let us consider the program

P_1: $p(X) \leftarrow q(X), q(X)$ $q(t(Y,a)) \leftarrow$ $q(t(a,Z)) \leftarrow$

By deleting an occurrence of $q(X)$ in the body of the first clause we get

P_2: $p(X) \leftarrow q(X)$ $q(t(Y,a)) \leftarrow$ $q(t(a,Z)) \leftarrow$

The substitution $\{X/t(a,a)\}$ belongs to $\mathbf{CAS}[P_1, \leftarrow p(X)]$ and not to $\mathbf{CAS}[P_2, \leftarrow p(X)]$.

Example 4.4.6. Let us consider the program

P: $p(X) \leftarrow$ $p(a) \leftarrow$

The clause $p(a) \leftarrow$ is subsumed by $p(X) \leftarrow$. However, if we delete $p(a) \leftarrow$ from the program P the $\mathbf{CAS}$ semantics is not preserved, because $\{X/a\}$ is no longer a computed answer substitution for the query $\leftarrow p(X)$.

There are particular cases, however, in which the deletion of duplicate goals and the deletion of subsumed clauses are correct w.r.t. $\mathbf{CAS}$. The following definitions introduce two such cases.

Rule R5.7 Deletion of duplicate ground goals. By the rule of *deletion of ground duplicate goals* we replace a *ground* goal (G, G) in the body of a clause by the goal G.

This rule is an instance of the persistent goal replacement rule (see rule R5.2, page 718).

Rule R5.8 Deletion of duplicate clauses. By the rule of *deletion of duplicate clauses* we replace all occurrences of a clause C in a program by a single occurrence of C.

Several researchers have addressed the problem of proving the correctness of the transformation rules w.r.t. $\mathbf{CAS}$ [Kawamura and Kanamori, 1990; Bossi *et al.*, 1992a; Bossi and Cocco, 1993]. We now present for the $\mathbf{CAS}$ semantics two theorems which correspond to the first and second correctness theorems w.r.t. the $\mathbf{LHM}$ semantics. As already mentioned, in these theorems the various instances of the goal replacement rule refer to the equivalence of goals w.r.t. $\mathbf{CAS}$.

Theorem 4.4.7 (First correctness theorem w.r.t. CAS). *Let $P_0, \ldots,$ P_n be a transformation sequence of definite programs constructed by using the following transformation rules: unfolding, in-situ folding, definition introduction, definition elimination, goal rearrangement, deletion of ground duplicate goals, independent goal replacement, clause rearrangement, deletion of duplicate clauses, deletion of clauses with finitely failed body, and generalization + equality introduction. Then $P_0, \ldots, P_n$ is totally correct w.r.t. $\mathbf{CAS}$.*

Theorem 4.4.8 (Second correctness theorem w.r.t. CAS). *Let $P_0,$ $\ldots, P_n$ be a transformation sequence of definite programs constructed by using the following transformation rules: unfolding, single-folding, definition introduction , definition elimination, goal rearrangement, deletion of* *ground duplicate goals, basic goal replacement, clause rearrangement, dele-tion of duplicate clauses, deletion of clauses with finitely failed body, and generalization + equality introduction. Suppose that no single-folding step is performed after a definition elimination step. Suppose also that when we apply the single-folding rule to a clause, say C, using a clause, say D, the following conditions hold:*

- *either D belongs to P_0 or D has been introduced by the definition rule,*
- *$hd(D)$ has a top predicate, and*
- *either $hd(C)$ has an intermediate predicate*
  or $hd(C)$ has a top predicate and C has been derived from a clause, say E, by first unfolding E w.r.t. an atom with an intermediate predicate and then performing zero or more transformation steps on a clause derived from the unfolding of E.

Then $P_0, \ldots, P_n$ is totally correct w.r.t. the semantics **CAS**.

4.4.3 Finite failure

In order to reason about the preservation of finite failure during program transformation we now consider the semantics function

$$\mathbf{FF} \colon \mathbf{P}^+ \times \mathbf{Q}^+ \to (\mathcal{P}(\mathbf{Subst}), \leq)$$

such that

$$\mathbf{FF}[P, Q] = \{\theta \mid \text{there exists a finitely failed SLD-tree for } Q\theta \text{ in } P\}.$$

The reader may verify that **FF** is a relevant semantics.

Work on the correctness of transformation rules w.r.t. **FF** has been presented in [Maher, 1987; Seki, 1991; Gardner and Shepherdson, 1991; Cook and Gallagher, 1994]. Similarly to the case of **LHM** and **CAS**, we have the following result, where the independent goal replacement rule is defined in terms of goal equivalence w.r.t. **FF**.

Theorem 4.4.9 (First correctness theorem w.r.t. FF). *Let $P_0, \ldots, P_n$ be a transformation sequence of definite programs constructed by using the following transformation rules: unfolding, in-situ folding, definition introduction, definition elimination, goal rearrangement, deletion of dupli-cate goals, independent goal replacement, and clause replacement. Then $P_0, \ldots, P_n$ is totally correct w.r.t.* **FF**.

However, the use of the rules listed in the second correctness theorems w.r.t. **LHM** and **CAS** (pages 727 and 729), may affect **FF**. In particular, if we allow folding steps which are not in-situ foldings, we may transform a finitely failing program into an infinitely failing program, as shown by the following example.

Example 4.4.10. Let us consider the transformation sequence, where p is a top predicate and q and r are intermediate predicates:

P_0: $p(X) \leftarrow q(X), r(X)$ $q(a) \leftarrow$ $r(b) \leftarrow r(b)$
                (by unfolding the first clause w.r.t. $r(X)$)
P_1: $p(b) \leftarrow q(b), r(b)$ $q(a) \leftarrow$ $r(b) \leftarrow r(b)$
                (by applying single-folding to the first clause)
P_2: $p(b) \leftarrow p(b)$ $q(a) \leftarrow$ $r(b) \leftarrow r(b)$

This transformation sequence satisfies the conditions stated in the second correctness theorem w.r.t. both **LHM** and **CAS**, but P_0 finitely fails for the query $\leftarrow p(b)$, while P_2 does not.

As we have shown in the above Example 4.4.10, if we allow folding steps which are not in-situ foldings, it may be the case that the derived transformation sequence is not correct w.r.t. **FF**.

The fact that such folding steps are not totally correct w.r.t. **FF** is related to the notion of fair SLD-derivation [Lloyd, 1987].

A possibly infinite SLD-derivation is *fair* iff it is either failed or for every occurrence of an atom A in the SLD-derivation, that occurrence of A or an instance (possibly via the identity substitution) of A which is derived from that occurrence, is selected for SLD-resolution within a finite number of steps.

Fairness of SLD-derivations is a sufficient condition for the completeness of SLD-resolution w.r.t. **FF**.

Let us consider a program P_1 and a query Q, and let us apply a folding step which replaces a goal B by an atom H, thereby obtaining a program, say P_2. We may view every SLD-derivation δ_2 of Q in the derived program P_2 as 'simulating' an SLD-derivation δ_1 of Q in P_1. Indeed, the simulated SLD-derivation δ_1 can be obtained by replacing in δ_2 the instances of H introduced by folding steps, with the corresponding instances of B.

By applying a folding step (which is not an in-situ folding) to a clause in P_1, we may derive a program P_2 such that a fair SLD-derivation for Q using P_2 simulates an unfair SLD-derivation for Q using P_1, as shown by the following example.

Example 4.4.11. Let us consider the program P_2 of Example 4.4.10 and the infinite sequence of queries

   $\leftarrow p(b)$ $\leftarrow p(b)$ $\leftarrow p(b)$ $\ldots$

which constitutes a fair SLD-derivation for the program P_2 and the query $\leftarrow p(b)$. The folding step which produces P_2 from P_1 replaces the goal $(q(b), r(b))$ by the goal $p(b)$. The above SLD-derivation can be viewed as a simulation of the following SLD-derivation for P_1:

   $\leftarrow p(b)$ $\leftarrow q(b), r(b)$ $\leftarrow q(b), r(b)$ $\ldots$

which is unfair, because it has been obtained by always selecting the atom $r(b)$ for performing an SLD-resolution step.

The Theorem 4.4.12 below is the analogue for the **FF** semantics of the second correctness theorems w.r.t. **LHM** and **CAS**. Its proof is based on the fact that an unfair SLD-derivation of a given program cannot be simulated by a fair SLD-derivation of a transformed program, if *all* atoms replaced in a folding step have previously been derived by unfolding. This condition is not fulfilled by the folding step shown in Example 4.4.10 because in the body of the clause $p(b) \leftarrow q(b), r(b)$ in P_1 the atom $q(b)$ has not been derived by unfolding.

Theorem 4.4.12 (Second correctness theorem w.r.t. FF). *Let P_0, ..., P_n be a transformation sequence of definite programs constructed by using the following transformation rules: unfolding, single-folding, definition introduction, definition elimination, goal rearrangement, deletion of duplicate goals, basic goal replacement, and clause replacement. Suppose that no single-folding step is performed after a definition elimination step. Suppose also that when we apply the single-folding rule to a clause, say C, using a clause, say D, the following conditions hold:*

- *either D belongs to P_0 or D has been introduced by the definition rule,*
- *$hd(D)$ has a top predicate, and*
- *either $hd(C)$ has an intermediate predicate*
  or $hd(C)$ has a top predicate and each atom of $bd(C)$ w.r.t. which the single-folding step is performed, has been derived in a previous transformation step by first unfolding a clause, say E, w.r.t. an atom with an intermediate predicate and then performing zero or more transformation steps on a clause derived from the unfolding of E.

*Then $P_0, \ldots, P_n$ is totally correct w.r.t. the semantics **FF**.*

4.4.4 Pure Prolog

In this section we consider the case where a definite program is evaluated using a Prolog evaluator. Its control strategy can be described as follows. The SLD-tree for a given program and a given query, is constructed by using the *left-to-right* rule for selecting the atom w.r.t. which SLD-resolution should be performed in a given goal. In this SLD-tree, the nodes which are sons of a given goal are ordered from left to right according to the order of the clauses used for performing the corresponding SLD-resolution step. Thus, in Prolog we have that the SLD-tree is an ordered tree, and it is visited in a depth-first manner. The use of the Prolog control strategy has two consequences: i) the answer substitutions are generated in a fixed order, possibly with repetitions, and ii) there may be some answer substitutions which cannot be obtained in a finite number of computation steps, because in the depth-first visit they are 'after' branches of infinite length. Therefore, by using Prolog control strategy SLD-resolution is not complete.

We will define a semantics function **Prolog** by taking into consideration the 'generation order' of the answer substitutions, their 'multiplicity', and their 'computability in finite time'. Thus, given a program P and a query Q, we consider the ordered SLD-tree T constructed as specified above.

The left-to-right ordering of brother nodes in T determines a left-to-right ordering of branches and leaves.

If T is finite then **Prolog**$[P, Q]$ is the sequence of the computed answer substitutions corresponding to the non-failed leaves of T in the left-to-right order.

If T is infinite we consider a (possibly infinite) sequence F of computed answer substitutions, each substitution being associated with a leaf of T. The sequence F is obtained by visiting from left to right the non-failed leaves which are at the end of branches to the left of the leftmost infinite branch. There are two cases: either F is infinite, in which case **Prolog**$[P, Q]$ is F or F is finite, in which case **Prolog**$[P, Q]$ is F followed by the symbol $\perp$, called the *undefined substitution*. All substitutions different from $\perp$ are said to be *defined*.

Thus, our semantics for Prolog is a function

$$\textbf{Prolog}: \textbf{P}^+ \times \textbf{Q}^+ \to (\textbf{SubstSeq}, \le)$$

where $\textbf{P}^+$ and $\textbf{Q}^+$ are the sets of definite programs and definite queries, respectively. $(\textbf{SubstSeq}, \le)$ is the set of finite or infinite sequences of defined substitutions, and finite sequences of defined substitutions followed by the undefined substitution $\perp$. Similar approaches to the semantics of Prolog can be found in [Jones and Mycroft, 1984; Debray and Mishra, 1988; Deville, 1990; Baudinet, 1992].

The sequence consisting of the substitutions $\theta_1, \theta_2, \ldots$ is denoted by $\langle \theta_1, \theta_2, \ldots \rangle$, and the concatenation of two sequences S_1 and S_2 in **SubstSeq** is denoted by $S_1 @ S_2$ and it is defined as the usual monoidal concatenation of finite or infinite sequences, with the extra property: $\langle \perp \rangle @ S = \langle \perp \rangle$, for any sequence S.

Example 4.4.13. Consider the following three programs:

P_1:	$p(a) \leftarrow$	$p(b) \leftarrow$	$p(a) \leftarrow$
P_2:	$p(a) \leftarrow$	$p(X) \leftarrow p(X)$	$p(b) \leftarrow$
P_3:	$p(a) \leftarrow$	$p(b) \leftarrow p(b)$	$p(a) \leftarrow$

We have that

$$\textbf{Prolog}[P_1, \leftarrow p(X)] = \langle \{X/a\}, \{X/b\}, \{X/a\} \rangle$$
$$\textbf{Prolog}[P_2, \leftarrow p(X)] = \langle \{X/a\}, \{X/a\}, \ldots \rangle$$
$$\textbf{Prolog}[P_3, \leftarrow p(X)] = \langle \{X/a\}, \perp \rangle.$$

The order $\le$ over **SubstSeq** expresses a 'less defined than or equal to' relation between sequences which can be introduced as follows.

For any two sequences of substitutions S_1 and S_2, the relation $S_1 \le S_2$ holds iff either $S_1 = S_2$ or $S_1 = S_3 @ \langle \perp \rangle$ and $S_2 = S_3 @ S_4$, for some S_3 and S_4 in **SubstSeq**. For instance, we have that: (i) for all substitutions η_1

and η_2 with $\eta_1 \neq \perp$ and $\eta_2 \neq \perp$, $\langle \eta_1, \perp \rangle \leq \langle \eta_1, \eta_2 \rangle$, and the sequences $\langle \eta_1 \rangle$ and $\langle \eta_1, \eta_2 \rangle$ are not comparable w.r.t. $\leq$, and (ii) for any (possibly empty) sequence S, $\langle \perp \rangle \leq S$.

Unfortunately, most transformation rules presented in the previous sections are not even partially correct w.r.t. **Prolog**. Indeed, it is easy to see that a clause rearrangement may affect the 'generation order' or the 'computability in finite time' of the answer substitutions, and the deletion of a duplicate clause may affect their multiplicity.

An unfolding step may affect the order of the computed answer substitutions as well as the termination of a program, as is shown by the following examples.

Example 4.4.14. By unfolding w.r.t. $r(Y)$ the first clause of the following program:

P_0: $p(X,Y) \leftarrow q(X), r(Y)$
        $q(a) \leftarrow$ $q(b) \leftarrow$ $r(a) \leftarrow$ $r(b) \leftarrow$

we get

P_1: $p(X,a) \leftarrow q(X)$ $p(X,b) \leftarrow q(X)$
        $q(a) \leftarrow$ $q(b) \leftarrow$ $r(a) \leftarrow$ $r(b) \leftarrow$

The order of the computed answer substitutions is not preserved by this unfolding step. Indeed, we have

$\quad$ **Prolog**$[P_0, \leftarrow p(X,Y)]$
$\quad\quad = \langle \{X/a, Y/a\}, \{X/a, Y/b\}, \{X/b, Y/a\}, \{X/b, Y/b\} \rangle$ and
$\quad$ **Prolog**$[P_1, \leftarrow p(X,Y)]$
$\quad\quad = \langle \{X/a, Y/a\}, \{X/b, Y/a\}, \{X/a, Y/b\}, \{X/b, Y/b\} \rangle$.

Example 4.4.15. By unfolding w.r.t. r the first clause of the following program:

P_0: $p \leftarrow q, r$ $q \leftarrow$ $q \leftarrow q$ $r \leftarrow fail$ $r \leftarrow$

we get

P_1: $p \leftarrow q, fail$ $p \leftarrow q$ $q \leftarrow$ $q \leftarrow q$ $r \leftarrow fail$ $r \leftarrow$

We have that **Prolog**$[P_0, \leftarrow p] \neq$ **Prolog**$[P_1, \leftarrow p]$, because

$\quad$ **Prolog**$[P_0, \leftarrow p] = \langle \{\}, \{\}, \ldots \rangle$ and **Prolog**$[P_1, \leftarrow p] = \langle \perp \rangle$.

Example 4.4.16. By unfolding w.r.t. $r(X)$ the first clause of the program

P_0: $p \leftarrow q(X), r(X)$ $q(a) \leftarrow q(a)$ $r(b) \leftarrow$

we get

P_1: $p \leftarrow q(b)$ $q(a) \leftarrow q(a)$ $r(b) \leftarrow$

We have that $\mathbf{Prolog}[P_0, \leftarrow p] \neq \mathbf{Prolog}[P_1, \leftarrow p]$, because

$$\mathbf{Prolog}[P_0, \leftarrow p] = \langle \bot \rangle \text{ and } \mathbf{Prolog}[P_1, \leftarrow p] = \langle \rangle.$$

We also have that the use of the folding rule does not necessarily preserve the **Prolog** semantics. In order to overcome this inconvenience, several researchers have proposed restricted versions of the unfolding and folding rules [Proietti and Pettorossi, 1991; Sahlin, 1993]. The following two instances of the unfolding rule can be shown to be totally correct w.r.t. **Prolog**.

Rule R1.1 Leftmost unfolding. The unfolding of a clause C w.r.t. the leftmost atom of its body is said to be a *leftmost unfolding* of C.

Rule R1.2 Single non-left-propagating unfolding. The unfolding of a clause $H \leftarrow F, A, G$ w.r.t. the atom A is said to be a *single non-left-propagating* unfolding iff i) there exists exactly one clause D such that A is unifiable with $hd(D)$ via a most general unifier θ, and ii) $H \leftarrow F$ is a variant of $(H \leftarrow F)\theta$.

This rule R1.2 is called *deterministic non-left-propagating unfolding* in [Pettorossi and Proietti, 1994]. If a folding step is both a single-folding and an in-situ folding, called here *single in-situ folding*, then it is reversible by an application of the single non-left-propagating unfolding rule. By the reversibility Lemma 4.1.3 (page 717), each single in-situ folding step is totally correct w.r.t. **Prolog**.

Since **Prolog** is relevant, the definition introduction and definition elimination rules are totally correct w.r.t. **Prolog**.

We also have that the goal replacement rule is partially correct, and by the reversibility lemma and the reversibility of independent goal replacement lemma (page 718) the independent goal replacement is totally correct w.r.t. **Prolog**.

Thus, we can state the following two results which are the analogues of the first and the second correctness theorems w.r.t. **LHM, CAS**, and **FF**. In the following Theorems 4.4.17 and 4.4.18 the instances of the goal replacement rule are defined in terms of the notion of goal equivalence w.r.t. **Prolog**.

Their proofs are based on the fact that an application of the leftmost unfolding rule can be viewed as 'a step forward in the computation' using the left-to-right computation rule.

Theorem 4.4.17 (First correctness theorem w.r.t. Prolog). *Let $P_0, \ldots, P_n$ be a transformation sequence of definite programs constructed by using the transformation rules: leftmost unfolding, single non-left-propagating unfolding, single in-situ folding, definition introduction, definition elimination, independent goal replacement, and generalization + equality introduction. Then $P_0, \ldots, P_n$ is totally correct w.r.t. Prolog.*

Theorem 4.4.18 (Second correctness theorem w.r.t. Prolog). *Let $P_0, \ldots, P_n$ be a transformation sequence of definite programs constructed by using the following transformation rules: leftmost unfolding, single non-left-propagating unfolding, single-folding, definition introduction, definition elimination, basic goal replacement, and generalization + equality introduction. Suppose that no single-folding step is performed after a definition elimination step. Suppose also that when we apply the single-folding rule to a clause, say C, using a clause, say D, the following conditions hold:*

- *either D belongs to P_0 or D has been introduced by the definition rule,*
- *$hd(D)$ has a top predicate, and*
- *either $hd(C)$ has an intermediate predicate*
  or $hd(C)$ has a top predicate and C has been derived from a clause, say E, by first performing a leftmost unfolding step w.r.t. an atom in $bd(E)$ with an intermediate predicate and then performing zero or more transformation steps on a clause derived from the unfolding of E.

Then $P_0, \ldots, P_n$ is totally correct w.r.t. the semantics **Prolog***.*

The following example shows that in the above Theorem 4.4.18 we cannot replace 'leftmost unfolding step' by 'single non-left-propagating unfolding step'.

Example 4.4.19. Let us consider the following initial program:

$$P_0: \qquad p \leftarrow q, r \qquad q \leftarrow fail \qquad r \leftarrow r, q$$

We assume that p is a top predicate and q, r, and $fail$ are intermediate predicates. By single non-left-propagating unfolding of $p \leftarrow q, r$ w.r.t. r, we get the program

$$P_1: \qquad p \leftarrow q, r, q \qquad q \leftarrow fail \qquad r \leftarrow r, q$$

If we now fold the first clause of P_1 using the first clause of P_0, we get

$$P_2: \qquad p \leftarrow p, q \qquad q \leftarrow fail \qquad r \leftarrow r, q$$

P_2 is not equivalent to P_0 w.r.t. **Prolog**, because

$$\mathbf{Prolog}[P_0, \leftarrow p] = \langle \rangle \quad \text{and} \quad \mathbf{Prolog}[P_2, \leftarrow p] = \langle \bot \rangle.$$

In this chapter we have considered only the case of pure Prolog, where the SLD-resolution steps have no side-effects. Properties which are preserved by unfold/fold rules when transforming Prolog programs with side-effects, including cuts, are described in [Deville, 1990; Sahlin, 1993; Prestwich, 1993b; Leuschel, 1994a].

4.5   Correctness results for normal programs

In this section we consider the case where the bodies of the clauses contain negative literals. There is a large number of papers dealing with transformation rules which preserve the various semantics proposed for logic programs with negation. In particular, some restricted forms of unfolding and folding have been shown to be correct w.r.t. various semantics, such as the computed answer substitution semantics and the finite failure semantics [Gardner and Shepherdson, 1991; Seki, 1991], the Clark's completion [Gardner and Shepherdson, 1991], the Fitting's and Kunen's three-valued extensions of Clark's completion [Fitting, 1985; Kunen, 1987; Bossi *et al.*, 1992b; Sato, 1992; Bossi and Etalle, 1994a], the perfect model semantics [Przymusinsky, 1987; Maher, 1993; Seki, 1991], the stable model semantics [Gelfond and Lifschitz, 1988; Maher, 1990; Seki, 1990], and the well-founded model semantics [Van Gelder *et al.*, 1989; Maher, 1990; Seki, 1990; Seki, 1993].

A uniform approach for proving the correctness of the unfold/fold transformation rules w.r.t. various non-monotonic semantics of logic programs (including stable model, well-founded model, and perfect model semantics) has been proposed by Aravindan and Dung [1995], who showed that the unfolding and some variants of folding transformations preserve the so-called *semantic kernel* of a normal logic program.

We will report here only on the results concerning the following three semantics [Lloyd, 1987]: i) computed answer substitutions, ii) finite failure, and iii) Clark's completion.

The computed answer substitution semantics for normal programs is a function

$$\textbf{CASNF: P} \times \textbf{Q} \rightarrow (\mathcal{P}(\textbf{Subst}), \leq)$$

where $\textbf{P}$ is the set of normal programs, $\textbf{Q}$ is the set of normal queries, and $(\mathcal{P}(\textbf{Subst}), \leq)$ is the powerset of the set of substitutions ordered by set inclusion. (The suffix '$\textbf{NF}$' stands for 'negation as failure'.) We define $\textbf{CASNF}$ as follows:

$$\textbf{CASNF}[P, Q] = \{\theta \mid \text{there exists an SLDNF-refutation of } Q \text{ in } P \\ \text{with computed answer substitution } \theta\}.$$

$\textbf{CASNF}$ is a relevant semantics.

For the correctness of a transformation sequence w.r.t. $\textbf{CASNF}$ there are results which are analogous to the ones for $\textbf{CAS}$. In particular, the statement of the first correctness theorem w.r.t. $\textbf{CAS}$ (page 729) is valid also for $\textbf{CASNF}$ if we replace 'definite programs' with 'normal programs' and $\textbf{CAS}$ with $\textbf{CASNF}$.

However, the first correctness theorem w.r.t. $\textbf{CAS}$ (and the new version for $\textbf{CASNF}$) does not ensure the correctness of transformation sequences which also include folding steps different from in-situ foldings.

If we want to perform transformation steps which are not applications of the in-situ folding rule, and still ensure their correctness, we may use Theorem 4.5.1 below, which combines the second correctness theorems w.r.t. $\textbf{CAS}$ and $\textbf{FF}$.

Following [Seki, 1991] in the hypotheses of Theorem 4.5.1 we assume that the programs are *stratified*.

We recall that a program is stratified iff for every program clause $p(\ldots) \leftarrow B$ and for every negative literal $\neg q(\ldots)$ in B, we have that q does not depend on p.

Theorem 4.5.1 (Second correctness theorem w.r.t. CASNF). *Let $P_0, \ldots, P_n$ be a transformation sequence of stratified normal programs constructed by using the following transformation rules: unfolding, single-folding, definition introduction, definition elimination, goal rearrangement, deletion of ground duplicate goals, basic goal replacement, clause rearrangement, deletion of duplicate clauses, deletion of clauses with finitely failed body, and generalization + equality introduction. Suppose that no single-folding step is performed after a definition elimination step. Suppose also that when we apply the single-folding rule to a clause, say C, using a clause, say D, the following conditions hold:*

- *either D belongs to P_0 or D has been introduced by the definition rule,*
- *$hd(D)$ has a top predicate, and*
- *either $hd(C)$ has an intermediate predicate*
  or $hd(C)$ has a top predicate and each atom of $bd(C)$ w.r.t. which the single-folding step is performed, has been derived in a previous transformation step by unfolding a clause, say E, w.r.t. an atom with an intermediate predicate and then performing zero or more transformation steps on a clause derived from the unfolding of E.

Then $P_0, \ldots, P_n$ is totally correct w.r.t. the semantics **CASNF**.

The finite failure semantics for normal programs, denoted **FF** as in the case of definite programs, has the same domain and codomain of **CASNF**. We define **FF** as follows:

$$\mathbf{FF}[P, Q] = \{\theta \mid \text{there exists a finitely failed SLDNF-tree for } Q\theta \text{ in } P\}.$$

For normal programs we may state some correctness results which are analogous to those stated in the case of definite programs. Indeed, the first and second correctness theorems w.r.t. **FF** (pages 730 and 732) continue to hold if we replace 'definite programs' with 'stratified normal programs' and we assume **FF** to be defined with reference to the set of normal programs and normal queries, instead of the set of definite programs and definite queries.

Now we consider the Clark's completion semantics.

Let **P** and **Q** be the sets of all normal programs and normal queries, respectively. For any program $P \in \mathbf{P}$, let $Comp(P)$ be the set of first order formulas, called the *completion* of P, and constructed as indicated in [Lloyd, 1987], except that $Comp(P)$ also contains a formula $\forall X \neg p(X)$ for every predicate p in the language **L** not occurring in P.

The Clark's completion semantics is defined by the function

$$\textbf{COMP: P} \times \textbf{Q} \rightarrow (\mathcal{P}(\textbf{Subst}), \leq)$$

such that

$$\textbf{COMP}[P, \leftarrow G] = \{\theta \mid Comp(P) \models \forall(G\theta)\}$$

where $\forall C$ denotes the universal closure of a conjunction C of literals, and similarly to the case of **LHM**, we identify any program P and any goal G with the corresponding logical formulas.

As already mentioned, **COMP** is not a relevant semantics. Thus, we cannot use the relevance lemma (page 716), and indeed, the definition introduction rule and the definition elimination rule are *not* totally correct w.r.t. **COMP**. To see this, let us consider the case where we add to a program P_1 whose completion is consistent, a new clause of form $newp(X) \leftarrow \neg newp(X)$. We get a new program, say P_2, whose completion contains the formula $newp(X) \leftrightarrow \neg newp(X)$ and it is inconsistent. Thus, $\textbf{COMP}[P_1, Q] \neq \textbf{COMP}[P_2, Q]$ for $Q = \leftarrow newp(X)$.

However, it can be shown that if the definition introductions are only non-recursive definition introductions then any step of non-recursive definition introduction or definition elimination is totally correct w.r.t. **COMP**.

The partial correctness w.r.t. **COMP** of the unfolding rule R1 and the folding rule R2 can easily be established, as illustrated by the following example.

Example 4.5.2. Let us consider the program

$$
\begin{array}{llll}
P_0: & p \leftarrow q, \neg r & q \leftarrow s, t & q \leftarrow s, u \\
& v \leftarrow t & v \leftarrow u & s \leftarrow \quad u \leftarrow
\end{array}
$$

whose completion is

$$
\begin{array}{ll}
Comp(P_0): & p \leftrightarrow q \wedge \neg r \quad q \leftrightarrow (s \wedge t) \vee (s \wedge u) \\
& v \leftrightarrow t \vee u \quad s \quad u \quad \neg r \quad \neg t
\end{array}
$$

By unfolding the first clause of P_0 w.r.t. q we get

$$
\begin{array}{llll}
P_1: & p \leftarrow s, t, \neg r & p \leftarrow s, u, \neg r & q \leftarrow s, t & q \leftarrow s, u \\
& v \leftarrow t & v \leftarrow u & s \leftarrow \quad u \leftarrow
\end{array}
$$

whose completion is

$$
\begin{array}{ll}
Comp(P_1): & p \leftrightarrow (s \wedge t \wedge \neg r) \vee (s \wedge u \wedge \neg r) \quad q \leftrightarrow (s \wedge t) \vee (s \wedge u) \\
& v \leftrightarrow t \vee u \quad s \quad u \quad \neg r \quad \neg t
\end{array}
$$

$Comp(P_1)$ can be obtained by replacing q in $p \leftrightarrow q \wedge \neg r$ of $Comp(P_0)$ by $(s \wedge t) \vee (s \wedge u)$ and then applying the distributive and associative laws. Since $q \leftrightarrow (s \wedge t) \vee (s \wedge u)$ holds in $Comp(P_0)$, we have that $Comp(P_1)$ is a logical consequence of $Comp(P_0)$.

From P_1 by folding the definition of p using the definition of v in P_1 itself, we get

$$P_2: \qquad p \leftarrow s, v, \neg r \qquad q \leftarrow s, t \qquad q \leftarrow s, u$$
$$\qquad v \leftarrow t \qquad v \leftarrow u \qquad s \leftarrow \qquad u \leftarrow$$

whose completion is

$$Comp(P_2): \qquad p \leftrightarrow s \wedge v \wedge \neg r \qquad q \leftrightarrow (s \wedge t) \vee (s \wedge u)$$
$$\qquad v \leftrightarrow t \vee u \qquad s \qquad u \qquad \neg r \qquad \neg t$$

$Comp(P_2)$ can be obtained from $Comp(P_1)$ by first using the associative, commutative, and distributive laws for replacing the formula $p \leftrightarrow (s \wedge t \wedge \neg r) \vee (s \wedge u \wedge \neg r)$ by $p \leftrightarrow (t \vee u) \wedge (s \wedge \neg r)$, and then substituting v for $t \vee u$. Since $v \leftrightarrow t \vee u$ holds in $Comp(P_1)$, we have that $Comp(P_2)$ is a logical consequence of $Comp(P_1)$.

In general, given a transformation sequence $P_0, \ldots, P_k$, if a program P_{k+1} can be obtained from a program P_k by an unfolding step using P_j, with $0 \leq j \leq k$, and both $Comp(P_j)$ and $Comp(P_k)$ are logical consequences of $Comp(P_0)$, then $Comp(P_{k+1})$ can be obtained from $Comp(P_k)$ by one or more replacements of a formula F by a formula G such that $F \leftrightarrow G$ is a logical consequence of $Comp(P_j)$. Thus, also $Comp(P_{k+1})$ is a logical consequence of $Comp(P_0)$.

A similar fact holds if P_{k+1} can be obtained from P_k by applying the folding rule, or the goal replacement rule, or the clause replacement rules. Thus, we have the following result.

Theorem 4.5.3 (Partial correctness w.r.t. COMP). *Let $P_0, \ldots, P_n$ be a transformation sequence of normal programs constructed by using the following rules: unfolding, folding, non-recursive definition introduction, definition elimination, goal replacement, and clause replacement. If no folding step is performed after a definition elimination step, then $P_0, \ldots, P_n$ is partially correct w.r.t. the semantics* **COMP**.

Unfortunately, the unfolding rule is not totally correct w.r.t. **COMP** as shown by the following example adapted from [Maher, 1987].

Example 4.5.4. Let us consider the program

$$P_0: \qquad p(X) \leftarrow q(X) \qquad p(X) \leftarrow \neg q(succ(X)) \qquad q(X) \leftarrow q(succ(X))$$

whose completion is (equivalent to)

$$Comp(P_0): \qquad \forall X (p(X) \leftrightarrow q(X) \vee \neg q(succ(X)))$$
$$\qquad \forall X (q(X) \leftrightarrow q(succ(X)))$$

together with the axioms of Clark's equality theory [Lloyd, 1987; Apt, 1990]. By unfolding the last clause of P_0 we get

$$P_1: \qquad p(X) \leftarrow q(X) \qquad p(X) \leftarrow \neg q(succ(X))$$

$$q(X) \leftarrow q(succ(succ(X)))$$

whose completion is (equivalent to)

$Comp(P_1)$: $\forall X\,(p(X) \leftrightarrow q(X) \vee \neg q(succ(X)))$
                 $\forall X\,(q(X) \leftrightarrow q(succ(succ(X))))$

together with the axioms of Clark's equality theory.

We have that $\forall X p(X)$ is a logical consequence of $Comp(P_0)$. On the other hand, $\forall X p(X)$ is not a logical consequence of $Comp(P_1)$. Indeed, let us consider the interpretation I whose domain is the set of integers, $p(x)$ holds iff $q(x)$ holds iff x is an even integer, and $succ$ is the successor function. I is a model of $Comp(P_1)$, whereas it is not a model of $\forall X p(X)$.

We may restrict the use of the unfolding rule so to make it totally correct w.r.t. **COMP**, as indicated in the following definition.

Rule R1.3 In-situ unfolding. The unfolding of a clause C in a program P_k w.r.t. an atom A using a program P_j is said to be an *in-situ unfolding* iff $P_j = P_k$, and $hd(C)$ is not unifiable with A.

If program P_{k+1} is derived from program P_k by performing an in-situ unfolding step, then the transformation sequence P_k, P_{k+1} is reversible by in-situ folding. Thus, by the reversibility lemma 4.1.3 (page 717) and the partial correctness theorem w.r.t. **COMP** (page 740), we have that every in-situ unfolding is totally correct w.r.t. **COMP**.

By similar arguments we can show the total correctness of any in-situ folding and independent goal replacement step, because, as the reader may verify, the independent goal replacement rule is reversible even though **COMP** is not a relevant semantics (and, thus, the reversibility of independent goal replacement lemma cannot be applied).

It is also straightforward to show the total correctness of any clause replacement step. Thus, we have the following result.

Theorem 4.5.5 (First correctness theorem w.r.t. COMP). *Let P_0, $\ldots, P_n$ be a transformation sequence of normal programs constructed by using the transformation rules: in-situ unfolding, in-situ folding, non-recursive definition introduction, definition elimination, independent goal replacement, and clause replacement. Then $P_0, \ldots, P_n$ is totally correct w.r.t.* **COMP**.

We end this section by showing, through the following example, that the hypotheses of the second correctness theorem w.r.t. **CASNF** are not sufficient to ensure the correctness of folding w.r.t. **COMP**.

Example 4.5.6. Let us consider the following transformation sequence:

P_0: $p \leftarrow q$ $q \leftarrow q$ $r \leftarrow p$ $r \leftarrow \neg q$
       (by in-situ unfolding of $p \leftarrow q$)
P_1: $p \leftarrow q$ $q \leftarrow q$ $r \leftarrow p$ $r \leftarrow \neg q$

(by single-folding of $p \leftarrow q$)

P_2: $p \leftarrow p$ $q \leftarrow q$ $r \leftarrow p$ $r \leftarrow \neg q$

where we assume that p and r are top predicates and q is an intermediate one.

By the second correctness theorem w.r.t. **CASNF** we have that P_0 and P_2 (and also P_1) are equivalent w.r.t. **CASNF**. Let us now consider the completions of P_0 and P_2, respectively:

$Comp(P_0)$: $p \leftrightarrow q$ $q \leftrightarrow q$ $r \leftrightarrow p \vee \neg q$
$Comp(P_2)$: $p \leftrightarrow p$ $q \leftrightarrow q$ $r \leftrightarrow p \vee \neg q$

We have that r is a logical consequence of $Comp(P_0)$. On the contrary, r is not a logical consequence of $Comp(P_2)$. Indeed, the interpretation where p is false, q is true, and r is false, is a model of $Comp(P_2)$, but not of r. Thus, P_0 and P_2 are not equivalent w.r.t. **COMP**.

It should be noted that in the above Example 4.5.6, P_0 is equivalent to P_2 w.r.t. other two-valued or three-valued semantics for normal programs such as the already mentioned Fitting's and Kunen's extensions of Clark's completion, perfect model, stable model, and well-founded model semantics.

For the case where unfolding and folding are not in-situ, the reader may find various correctness results w.r.t. the above mentioned semantics in [Seki, 1990; Seki, 1991; Sato, 1992; Seki, 1993; Aravindan and Dung, 1995; Bossi and Etalle, 1994a].

5   Strategies for transforming logic programs

The transformation process should be directed by some metarules, which we call *strategies*, because, as we have seen in Section 3, the transformation rules have inverses, and thus, they allow the final program of a transformation sequence to be equal to the initial program. Obviously, we are not interested in such useless transformations.

In this section we present an overview of some transformation strategies which have been proposed in the literature. They are used, in particular, for solving one of the crucial problems of the transformation methodology, that is, the use of the definition rule for the introduction of the so-called *eureka predicates*.

In [Feather, 1987; Partsch, 1990; Deville, 1990; Pettorossi and Proietti, 1994; Pettorossi and Proietti, 1996] one can find a treatment of the transformation strategies for both functional and logic programs.

For reasons of simplicity, when we describe the various transformation strategies we consider only the case of definite programs with the least Herbrand model semantics **LHM**.

We assume that the following rules are available: unfolding (rule R1, page 708), in-situ folding (rule R2.1, page 717), single-folding (rule R2.2, page 726), definition introduction (rule R3, page 711), definition elimination (rule R4, page 712), independent goal replacement (rule R5.3, page 718), goal rearrangement (rule R5.4, page 725), deletion of duplicate goals (rule R5.5, page 725), basic goal replacement (rule R5.6, page 727), and clause replacement (rule R6, page 714).

The correctness of those rules w.r.t. **LHM** is ensured by the first and the second correctness theorems w.r.t. **LHM** (pages 725 and 727).

In order to simplify our presentation, sometimes we will not mention the use of goal rearrangement and deletion of duplicate goals.

As already pointed out, from the correctness of the goal rearrangement, deletion of duplicate goals, clause rearrangement (rule R6.1, page 714), and deletion of duplicate clauses (rule derived from rule R6.2, page 714) it follows that the concatenation of sequences of literals and the concatenation of sequences of clauses are associative, commutative, and idempotent. Therefore, when dealing with goals or programs, we will feel free to use set-theoretic notations, such as $\{\dots\}$ and $\cup$, instead of sequence-theoretic notations.

Before giving the technical details concerning the transformation strategies we would like to present, we now informally explain the main ideas which justify their use.

Suppose that we are given an initial program and we want to apply the transformation rules to improve its efficiency. In order to do so, we usually need a preliminary analysis of the initial program by which we discover that the evaluation of a goal, say $A_1, \dots, A_n$, in the body of a program clause, say C, is inefficient, because it generates some redundant computations. For example, by analysing the initial program P_0 given in the palindrome example of Section 2 (page 702), we may discover that the evaluation of the body of the clause

3. $pal([H|T]) \leftarrow append(Y, [H], T), pal(Y)$

is inefficient because it determines multiple traversals of the list Y.

In order to improve the performance of P_0, we can apply the technique which consists in introducing a new predicate, say *newp*, by means of a clause, say N, with body $A_1, \dots, A_n$.

This initial transformation step can be formalized as an application of the so-called *tupling strategy* (page 746). Sometimes we also need a simultaneous application of the *generalization strategy* (page 747). Then we fold clause C w.r.t. the goal $A_1, \dots, A_n$ by using clause N, and we unfold clause N one or more times, thereby generating some new clauses.

This process can be viewed as a symbolic evaluation of a query which is an instance of $A_1, \dots, A_n$. This unfolding gives us the opportunity of improving our program, because, for instance, we may delete some clauses with finitely failed body, thereby avoiding failures at run-time, and we may delete duplicate atoms, thereby avoiding repeated computations.

Looking again at the palindrome example of Section 2, we see that by applying the tupling and generalization strategies, we have introduced the clause

6. $newp(L, T) \leftarrow append(Y, L, T), pal(Y)$

and we have used this clause 6 for folding clause 3. Then we have unfolded clause 6 w.r.t. the atoms $pal(\ldots)$ and $append(\ldots)$ and we have derived the clauses

10. $newp(L, L) \leftarrow$
11. $newp(L, [X|L]) \leftarrow$
13. $newp(L, [H|U]) \leftarrow append(R, [H|L], U), pal(R)$

These clauses for *newp*, together with clauses 1, 2, and 3f for *pal* and clauses 4 and 5 for *append*, avoid multiple traversals of the input list, but as the reader may verify, only when that list has at most three elements.

The efficiency improvements due to the unfoldings can be iterated at *each level of recursion*, and thus, they become computationally significant, only if we find a *recursive definition* of *newp*. In that case the multiple traversals of the input list will be avoided for lists of any length.

This recursive definition can often be obtained by performing a folding step using the clause initially introduced by tupling. In our palindrome example that clause is clause 6. By folding clause 13 using clause 6, we get

13f. $newp(L, [H|U]) \leftarrow newp([H|L], U)$

This recursive clause, together with clauses 10 and 11, indeed provides a recursive definition of *newp*, and it avoids multiple traversals of any input list.

In some unfortunate cases we may be unable to perform the desired folding steps for deriving the recursive definition of the predicates introduced by the initial applications of the tupling and generalization strategies. In those cases we may use some auxiliary strategies and we may introduce some extra eureka predicates which allow us to perform the required folding steps. Two of those auxiliary strategies are the *loop absorption strategy* and the already mentioned *generalization strategy*, both described in Section 5.1 below.

In [Darlington, 1981] the expression 'forced folding' is introduced to refer to the need for performing the folding steps for improving program efficiency. This *need for folding* plays an important role in the program transformation methodology, and it can be regarded as a meta-strategy. It is the need for folding that often suggests the appropriate strategy to apply at each step of the derivation.

The need for folding in program transformation is related to similar ideas in the field of automated theorem proving [Boyer and Moore, 1975] and program synthesis [Deville and Lau, 1994], where tactics for inductive proofs and inductive synthesis are driven by the need for applying suitable inductive hypotheses.

5.1 Basic strategies

We now describe some of the basic strategies which have been introduced in the literature for transforming logic programs. They are: tupling, loop absorption, and generalization. The basic ideas underlying these strategies come from the early days of program transformation and they were already present in [Burstall and Darlington, 1977].

The tupling strategy was formally defined in [Pettorossi, 1977] where it is used for tupling together different function calls which require common subcomputations or visit the same data structure.

The name 'loop absorption' was introduced in [Proietti and Pettorossi, 1990] for indicating a strategy which derives a new predicate definition when a goal is recurrently generated during program transformation. This strategy is present in various forms in a number of different transformation techniques, such as the above mentioned tupling, supercompilation [Turchin, 1986], compiling control [Bruynooghe *et al.*, 1989], as well as various techniques for partial evaluation (see Section 6).

Finally, the generalization strategy has its origin in the automated theorem proving context [Boyer and Moore, 1975], where it is used to generate a new generalized conjecture allowing the application of an inductive hypothesis.

The tupling, loop absorption, and generalization strategies are used in this chapter as building blocks to describe a number of more complex transformation techniques.

For a formal description of the strategies and their possible mechanization we now introduce the notion of *unfolding tree*. It represents the process of transforming a given clause by performing unfolding and basic goal replacement steps. This notion is also related to the one of *symbolic trace tree* of [Bruynooghe *et al.*, 1989], where, however, the basic goal replacement rule is not taken into account.

Definition 5.1.1 (Unfolding tree). Let P be a program and C a clause. An *unfolding tree* for $\langle P, C \rangle$ is a (finite or infinite) labelled tree such that

- the root is labelled by the clause C,
- if M is a node labelled by a clause D then
  either M has no sons,
  or M has $n(\geq 1)$ sons labelled by the clauses $D_1, \ldots, D_n$ obtained by unfolding D w.r.t. an atom of its body using P,
  or M has one son labelled by a clause obtained by basic goal replacement from D.

In an unfolding tree we also have the usual relations of 'descendant node' (or clause) and 'ancestor node' (or clause).

Given a program P and a clause C, the construction of an unfolding tree for $\langle P, C \rangle$ is nondeterministic. In particular, during the process of constructing an unfolding tree we need to decide whether or not a node should have son-nodes, and in case we decide that a node should have son-nodes constructed by unfolding, we need to choose the atom w.r.t. which that unfolding step should be performed. Those choices can be realized by using a function defined as follows.

Definition 5.1.2 (Unfolding selection rule). An *unfolding selection rule* (or *u-selection rule*, for short) is a function that, given an unfolding tree and one of its leaves, tells us whether or not we should unfold the clause in that leaf, and in the affirmative case it tells us the atom w.r.t. which that clause should be unfolded.

We now formally introduce the tupling, loop absorption, and generalization strategies.

S1. Tupling strategy. Let us consider a clause C of the form

$$H \leftarrow A_1, \ldots, A_m, B_1, \ldots, B_n$$

with $m \geq 1$ and $n \geq 0$. We introduce a new predicate *newp* defined by a clause T of the form

$$newp(X_1, \ldots, X_k) \leftarrow A_1, \ldots, A_m$$

where the arguments $X_1, \ldots, X_k$ are the elements of $vars(A_1, \ldots, A_m) \cap vars(H, B_1, \ldots, B_n)$. We then look for the recursive definition of the eureka predicate *newp* by performing some unfolding and basic goal replacement steps followed by suitable folding steps using clause T. We finally fold clause C w.r.t. the atoms $A_1, \ldots, A_m$ using clause T.

The tupling strategy is often applied when $A_1, \ldots, A_m$ share some variables. The program improvements which can be achieved by using this strategy are based on the fact that we need to evaluate only once the subgoals which are common to the computations determined by the tupled atoms $A_1, \ldots, A_m$. By tupling we can also avoid multiple visits of data structures and the construction of intermediate bindings.

S2. Loop absorption strategy. Suppose that a non-root clause C in an unfolding tree has the form

$$H \leftarrow A_1, \ldots, A_m, B_1, \ldots, B_n$$

with $m \geq 1$ and $n \geq 0$, and the body of a descendant D of C contains (as a subsequence of atoms) the instance $(A_1, \ldots, A_m)\theta$ of $A_1, \ldots, A_m$ via some substitution θ. Suppose also that the clauses in the path from C to D have been generated by applying no transformation rule, except for goal rearrangement and deletion of duplicate goals, to $B_1, \ldots, B_n$. We introduce a new predicate defined by the following clause A:

$$newp(X_1, \ldots, X_k) \leftarrow A_1, \ldots, A_m$$

where $\{X_1, \ldots, X_k\}$ is the minimum subset of $vars(A_1, \ldots, A_m)$ which is necessary to perform a single-folding step on C and a single-folding step on D, both using a clause whose body is $A_1, \ldots, A_m$. This minimum subset is determined by condition 3 for the applicability of the single-folding rule (page 726). We fold clause C using clause A and we then look for the recursive definition of the eureka predicate *newp*. This recursive definition can be found starting from clause A by first performing the unfolding steps and the basic goal replacement steps corresponding to the ones which lead from clause C to clause D, and then folding using clause A again.

S3. Generalization strategy. Let us consider a clause C of the form

$$H \leftarrow A_1, \ldots, A_m, B_1, \ldots, B_n$$

with $m \geq 1$ and $n \geq 0$. We introduce a new predicate *genp* defined by a clause G of the form

$$genp(X_1, \ldots, X_k) \leftarrow GenA_1, \ldots, GenA_m$$

where $(GenA_1, \ldots, GenA_m)\,\theta = (A_1, \ldots, A_m)$, for some substitution θ, and $\{X_1, \ldots, X_k\}$ is a superset of the variables which are necessary to fold C using a clause whose body is $GenA_1, \ldots, GenA_m$. We then fold C using G and we get

$$H \leftarrow genp(X_1, \ldots, X_k)\theta, B_1, \ldots, B_n$$

We finally look for the recursive definition of the eureka predicate *genp*.

A suitable form of the clause G introduced by generalization can often be obtained by matching clause C against one of its descendants, say D, in the unfolding tree generated during program transformation (see Example 5.2.2, page 753). In particular, we will consider the case where

1. D is the clause $K \leftarrow E_1, \ldots, E_m, F_1, \ldots, F_r$, and D has been obtained from C by applying no transformation rule, except for goal rearrangement and deletion of duplicate goals, to $B_1, \ldots, B_n$,
2. for $i = 1, \ldots, m$, E_i has the same predicate symbol of A_i,
3. $E_1, \ldots, E_m$ is not an instance of $A_1, \ldots, A_m$,
4. the goal $GenA_1, \ldots, GenA_m$ is the most specific generalization of $A_1, \ldots, A_m$ and $E_1, \ldots, E_m$, and
5. $\{X_1, \ldots, X_k\}$ is the minimum subset of $vars(GenA_1, \ldots, GenA_m)$ which is necessary to fold both C and D using a clause whose body is $GenA_1, \ldots, GenA_m$.

5.2 Techniques which use basic strategies

In this section we will present some techniques for improving program efficiency by using the tupling, loop absorption, and generalization strategies.

5.2.1 Compiling control

One of the advantages of logic programming over conventional imperative programming languages is that by writing a logic program one may easily separate the 'logic' part of an algorithm from the 'control' part [Kowalski, 1979]. By doing so, the correctness of an algorithm w.r.t. a given specification is often easier to prove. Obviously, we are then left with the problem of providing an efficient control.

Unfortunately, the naive Prolog strategy for controlling SLD-resolution (see Section 4.4.4) does not always give us the desired level of efficiency, because the search space generated by the nondeterministic evaluation of a program is explored without using any information about the program. Much work has been done in the direction of improving the control strategy of logic languages (see, for instance, [Bruynooghe and Pereira, 1984; Naish, 1985]).

We consider here a transformation technique, called *compiling control* [Bruynooghe *et al.*, 1989], which follows a different approach. Instead of enhancing the naive Prolog evaluator using a clever (and often more complex) control strategy, we transform the given program so that the derived program behaves using the naive evaluator as the given program behaves using an enhanced evaluator.

The main advantage of the compiling control approach is that we can use relatively simple evaluators which have small and efficient compilers.

The compiling control technique can also be used to 'compile' bottom-up and mixed evaluation strategies [De Schreye *et al.*, 1991; Sato and Tamaki, 1988] as well as lazy evaluation and coroutining [Narain, 1986]. Here we will only show the use of compiling control in the case where the control to be 'compiled' is a computation rule different from the left-to-right Prolog one. In this case, by applying the compiling control technique one can improve generate-and-test programs by simulating a computation rule which selects test predicates as soon as the relevant data are available.

A similar idea has also been investigated in the area of functional programming, within the so-called *filter promotion* strategy [Darlington, 1978; Bird, 1984]. Some other transformation techniques for improving generate-and-test logic programs, which are closely related to the compiling control technique and the filter promotion strategy, can be found in [Seki and Furukawa, 1987; Brough and Hogger, 1991; Träff and Prestwich, 1992].

The problem of 'compiling' a given computation rule C can be described as follows: given a program P_1 and a set Q of queries, we want to derive a new program P_2 which, for any query in Q, is equivalent to P_1 w.r.t. **LHM** and behaves using the left-to-right computation rule as P_1 does using the rule C [Bruynooghe *et al.*, 1989; De Schreye and Bruynooghe, 1989].

By 'equal behaviour' we mean that for a query in Q, the SLD-tree, say T_1, constructed by using P_1 and the computation rule C, is equal to the

SLD-tree, say T_2, constructed by using P_2 and the left-to-right computation rule, if

i) we look at T_1 and T_2 as directed trees with leaves labelled by 'success' or 'failure' and arcs labelled by most general unifiers (thus, we disregard the goals in the nodes),

ii) we replace zero or more non-branching paths of T_1 by single arcs, each of which is labelled by the composition of the most general unifiers labelling the corresponding path to be replaced, and

iii) we replace zero or more subtrees of T_1 whose roots have an outgoing arc only, and this arc is labelled by the identity substitution, as follows: every subtree is replaced by the subtree below the arc outgoing from its root.

We can formulate basic forms of compiling control in terms of the program transformation methodology as we now indicate. Given a program P_1, a set Q of queries, and a computation rule C, the program P_2 obtained by the compiling control technique can be derived by first constructing a suitable unfolding tree, say T, using the unfolding rule only, and then applying the loop absorption strategy. Some more complex forms of compiling control require the use of generalization strategies possibly more powerful than the strategy S3 (page 747).

Without loss of generality, we assume that every query in Q is of the form $\leftarrow q(\ldots)$ and in P_1 there exists only one clause, say R, whose head predicate is q. (Indeed, we can use the definition rule to comply with this condition.) The root clause of T is R and the nodes of T are generated by using a 'suitable' u-selection rule which simulates the evaluation of an 'abstract query' representing the whole set Q, by using the computation rule C. We will not give here the formal notions of 'simulation' and 'abstraction' which may be used to effectively construct the unfolding tree T from the given P_1, Q, and C. We refer to [Cousot and Cousot, 1977] for a formalization of the techniques of *abstract interpretation*, and to [De Schreye and Bruynooghe, 1989] for a method based on abstract interpretation for generating the tree T in a semi-automatic way.

We now give an example of application of the compiling control technique by using the tupling and the loop absorption strategies.

Example 5.2.1. [Common subsequences] Let sequences be represented as lists of items. We assume that for any given sequence X and Y, $subseq(X, Y)$ holds iff X is a subsequence of Y, in the sense that X can be obtained from Y by deleting some (possibly not contiguous) elements. Suppose that we want to verify whether or not a sequence X is a common subsequence of the two sequences Y and Z. The following program *Csub* does so by first verifying that X is a subsequence of Y, and then verifying that X is a subsequence of Z.

1. $csub(X, Y, Z) \leftarrow subseq(X, Y), subseq(X, Z)$
2. $subseq([\,], X) \leftarrow$
3. $subseq([A|X], [A|Y]) \leftarrow subseq(X, Y)$
4. $subseq([A|X], [B|Y]) \leftarrow subseq([A|X], Y)$

where for any sequence X, Y, and Z, $csub(X,Y,Z)$ holds iff X is a subsequence of Y and X is also a subsequence of Z.

Let Q be the set of queries $\{\leftarrow csub(X, s, t) \mid s$ and t are ground lists and X is an unbound variable$\}$ and the computation rule C be the following one:

> *if* the goal is '$subseq(w, x), subseq(y, z)$' and w is a proper subterm of y
> *then* C selects for resolution the atom $subseq(y, z)$
> *else* C selects for resolution the leftmost atom in the goal.

We may expect that the evaluation of a query in Q using the computation rule C, is more efficient than the evaluation of that query using the standard left-to-right Prolog computation rule, because the second occurrence of $subseq(\ldots)$ in a goal of the form '$subseq(\ldots), subseq(\ldots)$' is selected as soon as it gets suitably instantiated by the evaluation of the first occurrence. Thus, using the computation rule C, it may be the case that the evaluation of a goal of the form '$subseq(\ldots), subseq(\ldots)$' fails even if the first occurrence of $subseq(\ldots)$ has not been completely evaluated.

We now construct an unfolding tree T for $\langle Csub,$ clause $1\rangle$ by using the following u-selection rule U_C which simulates the computation rule C:

> *if* the body of the clause to be unfolded is '$subseq(w, x), subseq(y, z)$'
>   and w is a proper subterm of y
> *then* U_C selects for unfolding the atom $subseq(y, z)$
> *else* U_C selects for unfolding the leftmost atom in the body.

Clause 1 is the only clause whose head unifies with $csub(X, s, t)$.

A finite portion of T is depicted in Fig. 2, where a dashed arrow from clause M to clause N means that the body of M is an instance of the body of N.

Since the body of clause 10 is an instance of the body of clause 6, we apply the loop absorption strategy. We introduce the eureka predicate *newcsub* by the following clause:

11. $newcsub(A, X, Y, Z) \leftarrow subseq(X, Y), subseq([A|X], Z)$

and we fold clause 6, whereby obtaining

6f. $csub([A|X], [A|Y], Z) \leftarrow newcsub(A, X, Y, Z)$

We also have that the body of clause 7 is an instance of the body of clause 1. We fold clause 7 and we get

7f. $csub([A|X], [B|Y], Z) \leftarrow csub([A|X], Y, Z)$

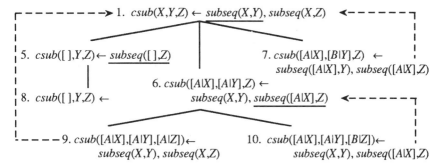

Fig. 2. An unfolding tree for $\langle Csub$, clause $1\rangle$ using the computation rule U_C. We have underlined the atoms selected for unfolding.

We now have to look for the recursive definition of the predicate *new-csub*. Starting from clause 11, we perform the unfolding step corresponding to the one which leads from clause 6 to clauses 9 and 10. We get the clauses

12. $newcsub(A, X, Y, [A|Z]) \leftarrow subseq(X, Y), subseq(X, Z)$
13. $newcsub(A, X, Y, [B|Z]) \leftarrow subseq(X, Y), subseq([A|X], Z)$

and by folding we get

12f. $newcsub(A, X, Y, [A|Z]) \leftarrow csub(X, Y, Z)$
13f. $newcsub(A, X, Y, [B|Z]) \leftarrow newcsub(A, X, Y, Z)$

The final program is made out of the following clauses:

8. $csub([\,], Y, Z) \leftarrow$
6f. $csub([A|X], [A|Y], Z) \leftarrow newcsub(A, X, Y, Z)$
7f. $csub([A|X], [B|Y], Z) \leftarrow csub([A|X], Y, Z)$
12f. $newcsub(A, X, Y, [A|Z]) \leftarrow csub(X, Y, Z)$
13f. $newcsub(A, X, Y, [B|Z]) \leftarrow newcsub(A, X, Y, Z)$

The correctness of the above transformation can easily be proved by applying the second correctness theorem w.r.t. **LHM** with the assumption that *newcsub* and *csub* are top predicates and *subseq* is an intermediate predicate. In particular, the single-folding step which generates clause 6f from clause 6 using clause 11, satisfies the conditions of that theorem, because: (i) clause 11 has been introduced by the definition rule, (ii) the head of clause 11 has a top predicate, and (iii) clause 6 has been derived from clause 1 by unfolding w.r.t. the intermediate atom $subseq(X, Y)$. Similar conditions ensure the correctness of the other single-folding steps.

Let us now compare the SLD-tree, say T_1, for *Csub*, a query of form $\leftarrow csub(X, s, t)$ in Q, and the computation rule C, with the SLD-tree, say T_2, for the final program, the query $\leftarrow csub(X, s, t)$, and the left-to-right computation rule.

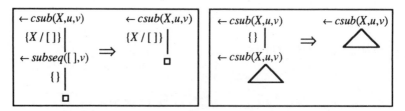

Fig. 3. Tree rewritings for the SLD-tree T_1.

As the reader may verify, the tree T_2 can be obtained from the tree T_1 by first replacing every query of the form '$\leftarrow subseq(x,b)$, $subseq(x,c)$' by the query '$\leftarrow csub(x,b,c)$' and every query of the form '$\leftarrow subseq(x,b)$, $subseq([a|x],c)$' by the query '$\leftarrow newcsub(a,x,b,c)$', and then by performing on the derived tree the rewritings shown in Fig. 3 for any unbound variable X and ground lists u and v.

5.2.2   Composing programs

A popular style of programming, which can be called *compositional*, consists in decomposing a given goal into easier subgoals, then writing program modules which solve these subgoals, and finally, composing the various program modules together. The compositional style of programming is often helpful for writing programs which can easily be understood and proved correct w.r.t. their specifications.

However, this programming style often produces inefficient programs, because the composition of the various subgoals does not take into account the interactions which may occur among the evaluations of these subgoals. For instance, let us consider a logic program with a clause of the form

$$p(X) \leftarrow q(X,Y), r(Y)$$

where in order to solve the goal $p(X)$ we are required to solve $q(X,Y)$ and $r(Y)$. The binding of the variable Y is not explicitly needed because it does not occur in the head of the clause. If the construction, the memorization, and the destruction of that binding are expensive, then our program is likely to be inefficient.

Similar problems occur when the compositional style of programming is applied for writing programs in other programming languages, different from logic. In imperative languages, for instance, one may construct several procedures which are then combined together by using various kinds of sequential or parallel composition operators. In functional languages, the small subtasks in which a given task is decomposed are solved by means of individual functions which are then combined together by using function application or tupling.

There are various papers in the literature which present techniques for improving the efficiency of the evaluation of programs written according to the compositional style of programming.

Similarly to the case discussed in Section 5.2.1, two approaches have been followed:

1. the improvement of the evaluator by using, for instance, garbage collection, memoing, and various forms of laziness and coroutining, and

2. the transformation of the given program into a semantically equivalent one which can be more efficiently evaluated by a non-improved, standard evaluator.

In the imperative and functional cases, various transformation methods have been proposed, such as: *finite differencing* [Paige and Koenig, 1982], *composition* or *deforestation* [Feather, 1982; Wadler, 1990], and *tupling* [Pettorossi, 1977]. (See also [Feather, 1987; Partsch, 1990; Pettorossi and Proietti, 1996] for surveys.)

For logic programs two main methods have been considered: *loop fusion* [Debray, 1988] and *unnecessary variable elimination* [Proietti and Pettorossi, 1995]. The aim of loop fusion is to transform a program which computes a predicate defined by the composition of two independent recursive predicates, into a program where the computations corresponding to these two predicates are performed by one predicate only. Using loop fusion one may avoid the multiple traversal of data structures and the construction of intermediate data structures.

The method presented in [Proietti and Pettorossi, 1995] may be used for deriving programs without unnecessary variables. A variable X of a clause C is said to be *unnecessary* if at least one of the following two conditions holds:

1. X occurs more than once in the body of C (in this case we say that X is a *shared* variable),

2. X does not occur in the head of C (in this case we say that X is an *existential* variable).

Since unnecessary variables often determine multiple traversals of data structures and construction of intermediate data structures, the results of unnecessary variable elimination are often similar to those of loop fusion.

In the following example we recast loop fusion and unnecessary variable elimination in terms of the basic strategies presented in Section 5.1.

Example 5.2.2. [Maximal number deletion] Suppose that we are given a list Xs of positive numbers. We want to delete from Xs every occurrence of its maximal number, say M. This can be done by first computing the value of M, and then visiting again Xs for deleting each occurrence of M. A program which realizes this algorithm is as follows:

1. $deletemax(Xs, Ys) \leftarrow maximal(Xs, M), delete(M, Xs, Ys)$
2. $maximal([\,], 0) \leftarrow$

3. $maximal([X|Xs], M) \leftarrow maximal(Xs, N), max(N, X, M)$
4. $delete(M, [\,], [\,]) \leftarrow$
5. $delete(M, [M|Xs], Ys) \leftarrow delete(M, Xs, Ys)$
6. $delete(M, [X|Xs], [X|Ys]) \leftarrow M \neq X, delete(M, Xs, Ys)$

where, for any positive number A, B, and M, $max(A, B, M)$ holds iff M is the maximum of A and B.

We would like to derive a program which traverses the list Xs once only. This could be done by applying the loop fusion method and obtaining a new program where the computations corresponding to $maximal$ and $delete$ are performed by one predicate only. A similar result can be achieved by eliminating the shared variables whose bindings are lists, and in particular, the variable Xs in clause 1.

To this aim we may apply the tupling strategy to the predicates $maximal$ and $delete$ which share the argument Xs. Since the atoms to be tupled together constitute the whole body of clause 1 defining the predicate $deletemax$, we do not need to introduce a new predicate, and we only need to look for the recursive definition of the predicate $deletemax$. After some unfolding steps, we get

7. $deletemax([\,], [\,]) \leftarrow$
8. $deletemax([M|Xs], Ys) \leftarrow maximal(Xs, N), max(N, M, M),$
$\qquad\qquad\qquad\qquad\qquad delete(M, Xs, Ys)$
9. $deletemax([X|Xs], [X|Ys]) \leftarrow maximal(Xs, N), max(N, X, M),$
$\qquad\qquad\qquad\qquad\qquad\qquad M \neq X, delete(M, Xs, Ys)$

As suggested by the tupling strategy, we may now look for a fold of the goal '$maximal(Xs, N)$, $delete(M, Xs, Ys)$' using clause 1. Unfortunately, no matching is possible because this goal is not an instance of '$maximal(Xs, M)$, $delete(M, Xs, Ys)$'. Thus, we apply the generalization strategy and we introduce the following clause:

10. $gen(Xs, P, Q, Ys) \leftarrow maximal(Xs, P), delete(Q, Xs, Ys)$

whose body is the most specific generalization of the following two goals: '$maximal(Xs, M)$, $delete(M, Xs, Ys)$', which is the body of clause 1, and '$maximal(Xs, N)$, $delete(M, Xs, Ys)$'. By folding clause 1 using clause 10, we get

1f. $deletemax(Xs, Ys) \leftarrow gen(Xs, M, M, Ys)$

We are now left with the problem of finding the recursive definition of the predicate gen introduced in clause 10. This is an easy task, because we can perform the unfolding steps corresponding to those leading from clause 1 to clauses 7, 8, and 9, and then we can use clause 10 for folding. After those steps we get the following program:

1f. $deletemax(Xs, Ys) \leftarrow gen(Xs, M, M, Ys)$

11. $gen([\ ], 0, Q, [\ ]) \leftarrow$
12. $gen([X|Xs], P, X, Ys) \leftarrow gen(Xs, N, X, Ys), max(N, X, P)$
13. $gen([X|Xs], P, Q, [X|Ys]) \leftarrow gen(Xs, N, Q, Ys), Q \neq X,$
$$max(N, X, P)$$

This program performs the desired list transformation in one visit. Indeed, let us consider a query of the form: $\leftarrow deletemax(l, Ys)$, where l is a ground list and Ys is an unbound variable. During the evaluation of that query, while visiting the input list l, the predicate $gen(l, P, Q, Ys)$ both computes the maximal number P and deletes all elements of l which are equal to P.

Notice also that no shared variable whose binding is a list occurs in the clauses defining *deletemax* and *gen*. Thus, we have been successful in eliminating the unnecessary variables at the expense of increasing nondeterminism (see clauses 12 and 13).

Now in order to avoid nondeterminism, we may continue our program derivation by looking for a program in which one avoids the evaluation of the goal $gen(Xs, N, Q, Ys)$ in clause 13, when the body of clause 12 fails after the evaluation of $gen(Xs, N, X, Ys)$.

This can be done by the application of the so called *clause fusion* [Debray and Warren, 1988; Deville, 1990]. This technique can be mimicked by applying our transformation rules as follows.

We first perform two generalization + equality introduction steps followed by a goal rearrangement step and we get

14. $gen([X|Xs], P, Q, Zs) \leftarrow gen(Xs, N, Q, Ys), max(N, X, P),$
$$Q = X, Zs = Ys$$
15. $gen([X|Xs], P, Q, Zs) \leftarrow gen(Xs, N, Q, Ys), max(N, X, P),$
$$Q \neq X, Zs = [X|Ys]$$

We then introduce the following definition:

16. $aux(Q, X, Zs, Ys) \leftarrow Q = X, Zs = Ys$
17. $aux(Q, X, Zs, Ys) \leftarrow Q \neq X, Zs = [X|Ys]$

and we fold clauses 14 and 15 by applying rule R2.1, thereby getting

18. $gen([X|Xs], P, Q, Zs) \leftarrow gen(Xs, N, Q, Ys), max(N, X, P),$
$$aux(Q, X, Zs, Ys)$$

We can then simplify clauses 16 and 17 by unfolding, and we obtain

19. $aux(X, X, Ys, Ys) \leftarrow$
20. $aux(Q, X, [X|Ys], Ys) \leftarrow Q \neq X$

Thus, the final program is made out of the clauses

1f. $deletemax(Xs, Ys) \leftarrow gen(Xs, M, M, Ys)$
11. $gen([\ ], 0, Q, [\ ]) \leftarrow$

18. $gen([X|Xs], P, Q, Zs) \leftarrow gen(Xs, N, Q, Ys), max(N, X, P),$
    $aux(Q, X, Zs, Ys)$

19. $aux(X, X, Ys, Ys) \leftarrow$

20. $aux(Q, X, [X|Ys], Ys) \leftarrow Q \neq X$

5.2.3   Changing data representations

The choice of appropriate data structures is usually very important for the design of efficient programs. In essence, this is the meaning of Wirth's motto 'algorithms + data structures = programs' [Wirth, 1976].

However, it is sometimes difficult to identify the data structures which allow very efficient algorithms before actually writing the programs. Moreover, complex data structures makes it harder to prove program correctness.

Program transformation has been proposed as a methodology for providing appropriate data structures in a *dynamic* way (see Chapter 8 of [Partsch, 1990]): first the programmer writes a preliminary version of the program implementing a given algorithm using simple data structures, and then he transforms their representations while preserving program semantics and improving efficiency.

An example of transformational change of data representations is the transformation of logic programs which use lists into equivalent programs which use *difference-lists*.

Difference-lists are data structures which are sometimes used for implementing algorithms that manipulate sequences of elements. The advantage of using difference-lists is that the concatenation of two sequences represented as difference-lists can often be performed in constant time, while the concatenation of standard lists takes linear time w.r.t. the length of the first list.

A difference-list can be thought of as a pair $\langle L, R \rangle$ of lists, denoted by $L \backslash R$, such that there exists a third list X for which the concatenation of X and R is L [Clark and Tärnlund, 1977]. In that case we say that the list X is *represented* by the difference-list $L \backslash R$. Obviously, a single list can be represented by many difference-lists.

Programs that use lists are often simpler to write and understand than the equivalent ones which make use of difference-lists. Several methods for transforming programs which use lists into programs which use difference-lists have been proposed in the literature [Hansson and Tärnlund, 1982; Brough and Hogger, 1987; Zhang and Grant, 1988; Marriot and Søndergaard, 1993; Proietti and Pettorossi, 1993].

The problem of deriving programs which manipulate difference-lists, instead of lists, can be formulated as follows.

Let $p(X, Y)$ be a predicate defined in a program P where Y is a list. We want to define the new predicate $diff\text{-}p(X, L \backslash R)$ which holds iff $p(X, Y)$ holds and Y is represented by the difference-list $L \backslash R$.

Let us assume that the concatenation of lists is defined in P by means of a predicate $append(X, Y, Z)$ which for any given list X, Y, and Z, holds iff the concatenation of X and Y is Z. Then, the desired transformation can often be achieved by applying the definition rule and introducing the following clause for the predicate *diff-p* [Zhang and Grant, 1988]:

D. $diff\text{-}p(X, L\backslash R) \leftarrow p(X, Y), append(Y, R, L)$

Then we have to look for a recursive definition of the predicate *diff-p*, which should depend neither on p nor on *append*.

This can be done, as clarified by the following example, by starting from clause D and performing some unfolding and goal replacement steps, based on the associativity property of *append*, followed by folding steps using D. We can then express p in terms of *diff-p* by observing that in the least Herbrand model of $P \cup \{D\}$, $diff\text{-}p(X, Y\backslash[\,])$ holds iff $p(X, Y)$ holds. Thus, in our transformed program the clauses for the predicate p can be replaced by the clause

E. $p(X, Y) \leftarrow diff\text{-}p(X, Y\backslash[\,])$

We leave it to the reader to check that this replacement of clauses can be performed by a sequence of in-situ folding, unfolding, and independent goal replacement steps, which are correct by the first correctness theorem w.r.t. **LHM** (page 725).

Example 5.2.3. [List reversal using difference-lists] Let us consider the following program for reversing a list:

1. $reverse([\,], [\,]) \leftarrow$
2. $reverse([H|T], R) \leftarrow reverse(T, V), append(V, [H], R)$
3. $append([\,], L, L) \leftarrow$
4. $append([H|T], L, [H|S]) \leftarrow append(T, L, S)$

Given a ground list l of length n and the query $\leftarrow reverse(l, R)$, where R is an unbound variable, this program requires $O(n^2)$ SLD-resolution steps. Indeed, for the evaluation of $\leftarrow reverse(l, R)$, clause 2 is invoked $n - 1$ times. Thus, $n - 1$ calls to *append* are generated, and the evaluation of each of those calls requires $O(n)$ SLD-resolution steps.

The above program can be improved by using a difference-list for representing the second argument of *reverse*. This is motivated by the fact that by clause 2 the list which appears as second argument of *reverse* is constructed by the predicate *append*, and as already mentioned, concatenation of difference-lists can be much more efficient than concatenation of lists.

We start off by applying the definition rule and introducing the clause

5. $diff\text{-}rev(X, L\backslash R) \leftarrow reverse(X, Y), append(Y, R, L)$

corresponding to clause D above.

The recursive definition of *diff-rev* can easily be derived as follows. We unfold clause 5 w.r.t. $reverse(X, Y)$ and we get

6. $diff\text{-}rev([\,], L \backslash R) \leftarrow append([\,], R, L)$
7. $diff\text{-}rev([H|T], L \backslash R) \leftarrow reverse(T, V), append(V, [H], Y),$
$\qquad\qquad\qquad\qquad\qquad\qquad append(Y, R, L)$

By unfolding, clause 6 is replaced by

8. $diff\text{-}rev([\,], R \backslash R) \leftarrow$

By using the unfold/fold proof method described in Section 4.3 we can prove the validity of the replacement law

F. $append(V, [H], Y), append(Y, R, L) \equiv_{\{V, H, R, L\}} append(V, [H|R], L)$

w.r.t. **LHM** and the current program made out of clauses 1, 2, 3, 4, 7, and 8.

Thus, we apply the goal replacement rule to clause 7 and we get

9. $diff\text{-}rev([H|T], L \backslash R) \leftarrow reverse(T, V), append(V, [H|R], L)$

We now fold clause 9 using clause 5 and we get

10. $diff\text{-}rev([H|T], L \backslash R) \leftarrow diff\text{-}rev(T, L \backslash [H|R])$

which, together with clause 8, provides the desired recursive definition of *diff-rev*.

The correctness of the transformation steps described above is ensured by the second correctness theorem w.r.t. **LHM** with the assumption that *diff-rev* is a top predicate, *reverse* is an intermediate predicate, and *append* is a basic predicate. Thus, in particular, the replacement performed to derive clause 9 is a basic goal replacement step, and the folding step which generates clause 10 from clause 9 using clause 5 is a single-folding step satisfying the conditions of that second correctness theorem, because: (i) clause 5 has been introduced by the definition rule, (ii) the heads of clauses 5 and 9 have top predicates, and (iii) clause 9 has been derived by first unfolding clause 5 w.r.t. the atom $reverse(X, Y)$ with intermediate predicate and then performing a basic goal replacement step.

Our final program that uses difference-lists is obtained by replacing the clauses defining *reverse* by the following clause (see clause *E* above):

11. $reverse(X, Y) \leftarrow diff\text{-}rev(X, Y \backslash [\,])$

The derived program is as follows:

11. $reverse(X, Y) \leftarrow diff\text{-}rev(X, Y \backslash [\,])$
8. $diff\text{-}rev([\,], R \backslash R) \leftarrow$
10. $diff\text{-}rev([H|T], L \backslash R) \leftarrow diff\text{-}rev(T, L \backslash [H|R])$

It takes $O(n)$ SLD-resolution steps for reversing a list of length n.

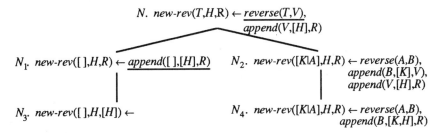

N. *new-rev(T,H,R) ← reverse(T,V),*
     append(V,[H],R)

N_1. *new-rev([ ],H,R) ← append([ ],[H],R)* N_2. *new-rev([K|A],H,R) ← reverse(A,B),*
                                                          append(B,[K],V),
                                                          append(V,[H],R)

N_3. *new-rev([ ],H,[H]) ←* N_4. *new-rev([K|A],H,R) ← reverse(A,B),*
                                        append(B,[K,H],R)

Fig. 4. An unfolding tree for the reverse program. We have underlined the atoms selected for unfolding.

A crucial step in the derivation of programs which use difference-lists is the introduction of the clause of the form

D. $diff\text{-}p(X, L \backslash R) ← p(X,Y), append(Y,R,L)$

which defines the eureka predicate *diff-p*. This eureka predicate can also be viewed as the invention of an *accumulator* variable, in the sense of the *accumulation strategy* [Bird, 1984]. Indeed, as indicated in Example 5.2.3, the argument R of $diff\text{-}rev(X, L \backslash R)$ can be viewed as an accumulator which at each SLD-resolution step stores the result of reversing the list visited so far.

In the following example we show that the invention of accumulator variables can be derived by using the basic strategies described in Section 5.1.

Example 5.2.4. [Inventing difference-lists by the generalization strategy] Let us consider again the initial program of Example 5.2.3 (page 757). We would like to derive a program for list reversal which does *not* use the *append* predicate. We can do so by applying the tupling strategy to clause 2 (because of the shared variable V) and introducing the eureka predicate *new-rev* by the following clause:

N. $new\text{-}rev(T, H, R) ← reverse(T, V), append(V, [H], R)$

As suggested by the tupling strategy, we then look for a recursive definition of *new-rev* by performing unfolding and goal replacement steps followed by folding steps using N. We have the additional requirement that the recursive definition of *new-rev* should not contain any call to *append*. This requirement can be fulfilled if the final folding steps are performed w.r.t. a conjunction of the atoms of the form '*reverse*(...), *append*(...)' and no other calls to *append* occur in the folded clauses.

The unfolding tree generated by some unfolding and goal replacement steps starting from clause N is depicted in Fig. 4.

Let us now consider clause N_4 in the unfolding tree of Fig. 4. If we were able to fold it using the root clause N, we would have obtained the required recursive definition of *new-rev*. Unfortunately, that folding step is not possible because the argument $[K, H]$ of the call of *append* in clause N_4 is not an instance of $[H]$ in clause N. Since N_4 is a descendant of N, we are in a situation where we can apply the generalization strategy. By doing so we introduce the new eureka predicate *gen-rev* defined by the following clause:

G. $gen\text{-}rev(U, X, Y, R) \leftarrow reverse(U, B), append(B, [X|Y], R)$

where the body of G is the most specific generalization of the body of N and the body of N_4.

The recursive definition of *gen-rev* can be found by performing the transformation steps which correspond to those leading from N to N_4 in the unfolding tree. We get the following clauses:

$gen\text{-}rev([\ ], X, Y, [X|Y]) \leftarrow$
$gen\text{-}rev([H|T], X, Y, R) \leftarrow gen\text{-}rev(T, H, [X|Y], R)$

We can then fold clause 2 using G and we get

2f. $reverse([H|T], R) \leftarrow gen\text{-}rev(T, H, [\ ], R)$

The final program is as follows:

1. $reverse([\ ], [\ ]) \leftarrow$
2f. $reverse([H|T], R) \leftarrow gen\text{-}rev(T, H, [\ ], R).$
$gen\text{-}rev([\ ], X, Y, [X|Y]) \leftarrow$
$gen\text{-}rev([H|T], X, Y, R) \leftarrow gen\text{-}rev(T, H, [X|Y], R)$

It has a computational behaviour similar to the program derived in Example 5.2.3 (page 757). In particular, the third argument of *gen-rev* is used as an accumulator.

5.3 Overview of other techniques

In this section we would like to give a brief account of some other techniques which have been presented in the literature for improving the efficiency of logic programs by using transformation methods.

5.3.1 Schema-based transformations

A common feature of the strategies we have described in Section 5.2 is that they are made out of sequences of transformation rules which are not specified in advance; on the contrary, they depend on the structure of the program at hand during the transformation process.

The schema-based approach to program transformation is complementary to the 'rules + strategies' approach and it consists in providing a catalogue of predefined transformations of *program schemata*.

A program schema (or simply, *schema*) S is an abstraction via a substitution θ, of a program P, where some terms, goals, and clauses are replaced by meta-variables, which once instantiated using θ, give us back the program P.

If a program schema S is an abstraction of a program P, then we say that P is an *instance* of S.

Two schemata S_1 and S_2 are *equivalent* w.r.t. a given semantics function **SEM** iff for all the values of the meta-variables the corresponding instances P_1 and P_2 are equivalent programs w.r.t. **SEM**.

The transformation of a schema S_1 into a schema S_2 is *correct* w.r.t. **SEM** iff S_1 and S_2 are equivalent w.r.t. **SEM**.

Usually, we are interested in a transformation from a schema S_1 to a schema S_2 if each instance of S_2 is more efficient than the corresponding instance of S_1.

Given an initial program P_1, the schema-based program transformation technique works as follows. We first choose a schema S_1 which is an abstraction via a substitution θ of P_1, then we choose a transformation from the schema S_1 to a schema S_2 in a given catalogue of correct schema transformations, and finally, we instantiate S_2 using θ to get the transformed program P_2.

The issue of proving the equivalence of program schemata has been addressed within various formalisms, such as flowchart programs, recursive schemata, etc. (see, for instance, [Paterson and Hewitt, 1970; Walker and Strong, 1972; Huet and Lang, 1978]). Some methodologies for developing logic programs using program schemata are proposed by several authors (see, for instance, [Deville and Burnay, 1989; Kirschenbaum *et al.*, 1989; Fuchs and Fromherz, 1992; Flener and Deville, 1993; Marakakis and Gallagher, 1994]) and some examples of logic program schema transformations can be found in [Brough and Hogger, 1987; Seki and Furukawa, 1987; Brough and Hogger, 1991]. The schema transformations presented in these papers are useful for *recursion removal* (see Section 5.3.2 below) and for reducing nondeterminism in generate-and-test programs (see Section 5.2.1, page 748).

An advantage of the schema-based approach over the strategy-based approach is that the application of a schema transformation requires little time, because it is simply the application of a substitution. However, the choice of a suitable schema transformation in the catalogue of the available transformations may be time consuming, because it requires the time for computing the matching substitution. On the other hand, one of the drawbacks of the schema-based approach is the space requirement for storing the catalogue itself. One more drawback is the fact that, when the program to be transformed is not an instance of any schema in the catalogue, then no action can be performed.

5.3.2   Recursion removal

Recursion is the main control structure for declarative (functional or logic) programs. Unfortunately, the extensive use of recursively defined procedures may lead to inefficiency w.r.t. time and space. In the case of imperative programs some program transformation techniques that remove recursion in favour of iteration have been studied, for instance, in [Paterson and Hewitt, 1970; Walker and Strong, 1972].

In logic programming languages, where no iterative constructs are available, recursion removal can be understood as a technique for deriving tail-recursive clauses from recursive clauses.

A definite clause is said to be *recursive* iff its head predicate also occurs in an atom of its body.

A recursive clause is said to be *tail-recursive* iff it is of the form

$$p(t) \leftarrow L, p(u)$$

where L is a definite goal. (For reasons of simplicity when dealing with recursion removal, we restrict ourselves to definite programs.)

A program is said to be tail-recursive iff all its recursive clauses are tail-recursive.

The elimination of recursion in favour of iteration can be achieved in two steps. First the given program is transformed into an equivalent, tail-recursive one, and then the derived tail-recursive program is executed in an efficient, iterative way by using an *ad hoc* compiler optimization, called *tail-recursion optimization* or *last-call optimization* (see [Bruynooghe, 1982] for a detailed description and the applicability conditions in the case of Prolog implementations).

Tail-recursion optimization makes sense only if we assume the left-to-right computation rule, so that, for instance, when the clause $p(t) \leftarrow L, p(u)$ is invoked, the recursive call $p(u)$ is the last call to be evaluated.

In principle, any recursive clause can be transformed into a tail-recursive one by simply rearranging the order of the atoms in the body. This transformation is correct w.r.t. **LHM** (see Section 4.4.1). However, goal rearrangements can increase the amount of nondeterminism, thus making useless the efficiency improvements due to tail-recursion optimization. Moreover, goal rearrangements do not preserve Prolog semantics (see Section 4.4.4), and tail-recursion optimization is usually applied to Prolog programs.

Many researchers have proposed more complex transformation strategies for obtaining tail-recursive programs without increasing the nondeterminism. We would like to mention the following three methods.

The first method consists in transforming *almost-tail-recursive* clauses into tail-recursive ones [Debray, 1985; Azibi, 1987; Debray, 1988] by using the unfold/fold rules. A clause is said to be almost-tail-recursive iff it is of the form

$$p(t) \leftarrow L, p(u), R$$

where L is a conjunction of atoms and R, called the *tail-computation*, is a conjunction of atoms whose predicates do not depend on p. Usually, the tail-computation contains calls to 'primitive predicates', such as the ones for computing concatenation of lists and arithmetic operations, like addition or multiplication of integers. The transformation techniques presented in [Debray, 1985; Azibi, 1987; Debray, 1988] use the generalization strategy and some replacement laws which are valid for the primitive predicates, such as the associativity of list concatenation, the associativity and the commutativity of addition, and the distributivity of multiplication over addition. Those techniques are closely related to the ones considered by [Arsac and Kodratoff, 1982] for functional programs.

The second method is based on schema transformations [Bloch, 1984; Brough and Hogger, 1987; Brough and Hogger, 1991], where some almost-tail recursive program schemata are shown to be equivalent to tail-recursive ones.

The third method consists in transforming a given program into a *binary program*, that is, a program whose clauses have only one atom in their bodies [Tarau and Boyer, 1990]. This transformation method is applicable to all programs and it is in the style of the continuation-based transformations for functional programs [Wand, 1980]. The transformation works by adding to each predicate an extra argument which encodes the next goal to be evaluated. This extra argument represents the so-called *continuation*.

For instance, the program

$$p \leftarrow$$
$$p \leftarrow p, q$$

is transformed into the program

$$p \leftarrow r(true)$$
$$r(G) \leftarrow G$$
$$r(G) \leftarrow r((q, G))$$

This transformation in itself does not improve efficiency. However, it allows us to use compilers based on a specialized version of the Warren Abstract Machine [Warren, 1983], and to perform further efficiency improving transformations [Demoen, 1993; Neumerkel, 1993].

5.3.3   Annotations and memoing

In the previous sections we have mainly considered transformations which do not make use of the extra-logical features of logic languages, like cuts, asserts, delay declarations, etc. In the literature, however, there are various papers which deal with transformation rules which preserve the operational semantics of full Prolog (see Section 4.4.4), and there are also some transformation strategies which work by inserting in a given Prolog program extra-logical predicates for improving efficiency by taking advantage of suitable properties of the evaluator. These strategies are related to some techniques which have been first introduced in the case of functional programs and are referred to as *program annotations* [Schwarz, 1982].

In the case of Prolog, a typical technique which produces annotated programs consists in adding a cut operator '!' in a point where the execution of the program can be performed in a deterministic way. For instance, the following Prolog program fragment:

$$p(X) \leftarrow C, BodyA$$
$$p(X) \leftarrow not(C), BodyB$$

can be transformed (if C has no side-effects) into

$$p(X) \leftarrow C, !, BodyA$$
$$p(X) \leftarrow BodyB$$

The derived code is more efficient than the initial one and behaves like an if-then-else statement.

Prolog program transformations based on the insertion of cuts are reported in [Sawamura and Takeshima, 1985; Debray and Warren, 1989; Deville, 1990].

Other techniques which introduce annotations for the evaluator are related to the automatic generation of *delay declarations* [Naish, 1985; Wiggins, 1992], which procrastinate calls to predicates until they are suitably instantiated.

A final form of annotation technique which has been used for improving program efficiency is the so-called *memoing* [Michie, 1968]. Results of previous computations are stored in a table together with the program itself, and when a query has to be evaluated, that table is looked up first. This technique has been implemented in logic programming by enhancing the SLDNF-resolution compiler through tabulations [Warren, 1992] or by using the 'assert' predicate for the run-time updating of programs [Sterling and Shapiro, 1994].

6   Partial evaluation and program specialization

Partial evaluation (also called *partial deduction* in the case of logic programming) is a program transformation technique which allows us to derive a new program from an old one when part of the input data is known at compile time. This technique which can be considered as an application of the *s-m-n* theorem [Rogers, 1967], has been extensively applied in the field of imperative and functional languages [Futamura, 1971; Ershov, 1977; Bjørner *et al.*, 1988; Jones *et al.*, 1993] and first used in logic programming by [Komorowski, 1982] (see also [Venken, 1984; Gallagher, 1986; Safra and Shapiro, 1986; Takeuchi, 1986; Takeuchi and Furukawa, 1986; Ershov *et al.*, 1988] for early papers on partial deduction, with special emphasis on the problem of partially evaluating meta-interpreters).

The resulting program may be more efficient than the initial program because, by using the partially known input, it is possible to perform at compile time some run-time computations.

Partial evaluation can be viewed as a particular case of *program specialization* [Scherlis, 1981], which is aimed at transforming a given program by exploiting the knowledge of the context where that program is used. This knowledge can be expressed as a precondition which is satisfied by the values of the input to the program.

Not much work has been done in the area of logic program specialization, apart from the particular case of partial deduction. However, some results are reported in [Bossi *et al.*, 1990] and in various papers by Gallagher and others [Gallagher *et al.*, 1988; Gallagher and Bruynooghe, 1991; de Waal and Gallagher, 1992]. In the latter papers the use of the abstract interpretation methodology plays a crucial role. Using this methodology one can represent and manipulate a possibly infinite set of input values which satisfies a given precondition, by considering, instead, an element of a finite abstract domain.

Abstract interpretations can be used before and after the application of program specialization, that is, during the so-called *preprocessing* phase and *postprocessing* phase. During the preprocessing phase, by using abstract interpretations we may collect information depending on the control flow, such as groundness of arguments and determinacy of predicates. This information can then be exploited for directing the specialization process. Examples of this preprocessing are the binding time analysis performed by the Logimix partial evaluator of [Mogensen and Bondorf, 1993] and the determinacy analysis performed by Mixtus [Sahlin, 1993].

During the postprocessing phase, abstract interpretations may be used for improving the program obtained by the specialization process, as indicated, for instance, in [Gallagher, 1993] where it is shown how one can get rid of the so-called *useless clauses*.

The idea of partial evaluation of logic programs can be presented as follows [Lloyd and Shepherdson, 1991]. Let us consider a normal program P and a query $\leftarrow A$, where A is an atom. We construct a finite portion of an SLDNF-tree for $P \cup \{\leftarrow A\}$ containing at least one non-root node. For this construction we use an *unfolding strategy* U which tells us the atoms which should be unfolded and when to terminate the construction of that tree. The notion of unfolding strategy is analogous to the one of u-selection rule (page 746), but it applies to goals, instead of clauses. The design of unfolding strategies which eventually terminate, thereby producing a *finite* SLDNF-tree, can be done within general frameworks like the ones described in [Bruynooghe *et al.*, 1992; Bol, 1993].

We then construct the set of clauses $\{A\theta_i \leftarrow G_i \mid i = 1, \ldots, n\}$, called *resultants*, obtained by collecting from each non-failed leaf of the SLDNF-tree the query $\leftarrow G_i$ and the corresponding computed answer substitution θ_i.

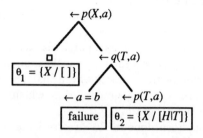

Fig. 5. An SLDNF-tree for $P \cup \{\leftarrow p(X,a)\}$ using U.

A *partial evaluation* of P w.r.t. the atom A is the program P_A obtained from P as follows. Let A be of the form $p(\ldots)$. We first replace the clauses of P which constitute the definition of the predicate symbol p by the set of resultants $\{A\theta_i \leftarrow G_i \mid i = 1,\ldots,n\}$, and then we throw away the definitions of the predicates, different from p, on which p does not depend after the replacement.

Example 6.0.1. Let us consider the following program P:

$$p([\,],Y) \leftarrow$$
$$p([H|T],Y) \leftarrow q(T,Y)$$
$$q(T,Y) \leftarrow Y = b$$
$$q(T,Y) \leftarrow p(T,Y)$$

and the atom $A = p(X,a)$. Let us use the unfolding strategy U which performs unfolding steps starting from the query $\leftarrow p(X,a)$ until each leaf of the SLDNF-tree is either a success or a failure or it is an atom with predicate p. We get the tree depicted in Fig. 5.

By collecting the goals and the substitutions corresponding to the leaves of that tree we have the following set of resultants:

$$p([\,],a) \leftarrow$$
$$p([H|T],a) \leftarrow p(T,a)$$

which constitute the partial evaluation P_A of P w.r.t. A. The clauses for q have been discarded because p does not depend on q in the above resultants.

If we use the program P_A, the evaluation of an instance of the query $\leftarrow p(X,a)$ is more efficient than the one using the initial program because the calls to the predicate q need not be evaluated and some failure branches are avoided.

The notion of partial evaluation of a program w.r.t. an atom can be extended to the notion of partial evaluation w.r.t. a set S of atoms by considering the union of the sets of resultants relative to the atoms in S.

We now introduce a *correctness* notion for partial evaluation which refers to the semantics **CASNF** and **FF** considered in Section 4. Analogous notions may be given with reference to other semantics.

Definition 6.0.2 (Correctness of partial evaluation). Let P be a program, Q be a query, and S be a set of atoms. A partial evaluation P_S of P w.r.t. S is *correct w.r.t.* Q iff we have that

- **CASNF**$[P, Q]$ = **CASNF**$[P_S, Q]$, and
- **FF**$[P, Q]$ = **FF**$[P_S, Q]$.

Theorem 6.0.5 below establishes a criterion for the correctness of partial evaluation. First we need the following definitions, where the notion of instance is relative to a substitution which may be the identity substitution.

Definition 6.0.3. Let R be a program or a query. Given a set S of atoms, we say that R is *S-closed* iff every atom in R with predicate symbol occurring in S is an instance of an atom in S.

Definition 6.0.4. Given a set S of atoms, we say that S is *independent* iff no two atoms in S have a common instance.

Theorem 6.0.5. [Lloyd and Shepherdson, 1991]. *Given a program P, a query Q, and a set S of atoms, let us consider a partial evaluation P_S of P w.r.t. S. If S is independent, and both P and Q are S-closed, then P_S is correct w.r.t. every instance of Q.*

In Example 6.0.1, the correctness w.r.t. every instance of the query $\leftarrow p(X, a)$ of the partial evaluation P_A of the program P follows from Theorem 6.0.5. Indeed, for the singleton $\{p(X, a)\}$ the independence property trivially holds, and the closedness property also holds because $p([\ ], a)$, $p([H|T], a)$, and $p(T, a)$ are all instances of $p(X, a)$.

The closedness and independence hypotheses cannot be dropped from Theorem 6.0.5, as it is shown by the following two examples.

Example 6.0.6. Suppose we want to partially evaluate the following program P:

$$p(a) \leftarrow p(b)$$
$$p(b) \leftarrow$$

w.r.t. the atom $p(a)$. We can derive the resultant $p(a) \leftarrow p(b)$. Let A be $\{p(a)\}$. Thus, a partial evaluation of P w.r.t. $p(a)$ is the program P_A:

$$p(a) \leftarrow p(b)$$

obtained by replacing the definition of p in P (that is, the whole program P) by the resultant $p(a) \leftarrow p(b)$. P_A is not $\{p(a)\}$-*closed* and we have that **CASNF**$[P_A, \leftarrow p(a)]$ = $\{\}$, whereas **CASNF**$[P, \leftarrow p(a)]$ = $\{\{\}\}$.

Example 6.0.7. Let us consider the following program P:

$$p \leftarrow q(X), \neg r(X)$$

$$q(X) \leftarrow$$

and the set S of atoms $\{p, q(X), q(a)\}$ which is not independent. A partial evaluation of P w.r.t. S is the following program P_S:

$$p \leftarrow q(X), \neg r(X)$$
$$q(X) \leftarrow$$
$$q(a) \leftarrow$$

The program P_S is *S-closed* and $\mathbf{CASNF}[P_S, \leftarrow p] = \{\{\}\}$, whereas $\mathbf{CASNF}[P, \leftarrow p] = \{\}$, because the unique SLDNF-derivation of $P \cup \{\leftarrow p\}$ flounders.

Lloyd and Shepherdson's theorem suggests the following methodology for performing correct partial evaluations. Given a program P and a query Q, we look for an independent set S of atoms and a partial evaluation P_S of P w.r.t. S such that both P_S and Q are S-closed.

Various strategies have been proposed in the literature for computing from a given program P and a given query Q, a suitable set S with the independence and closedness properties (see, for instance, [Benkerimi and Lloyd, 1990; Bruynooghe *et al.*, 1992; Gallagher, 1991; Martens *et al.*, 1992; Gallagher, 1993]). Some of them require generalization steps and the use of abstract interpretations.

Other techniques for partial evaluation and program specialization are based on the unfold/fold rules [Fujita, 1987; Bossi *et al.*, 1990; Sahlin, 1993; Bossi and Cocco, 1993; Prestwich, 1993a; Proietti and Pettorossi, 1993]. By using those techniques, given a program P and a query $\leftarrow G$, we introduce a new predicate *newp* defined by the clause

$D.\ newp(X_1, \ldots, X_n) \leftarrow G$

where $X_1, \ldots, X_n$ are the variables occurring in G.

Obviously, $newp(X_1, \ldots, X_n)$ and G are equivalent goals w.r.t. the semantics $\mathbf{CASNF}$ and the program $P \cup \{D\}$, and also w.r.t. $\mathbf{FF}$ and $P \cup \{D\}$. Moreover, we have that

$$\mathbf{CASNF}[P \cup \{D\}, \leftarrow newp(X_1, \ldots, X_n)] = \mathbf{CASNF}[P, \leftarrow G], \text{ and}$$
$$\mathbf{FF}[P \cup \{D\}, \leftarrow newp(X_1, \ldots, X_n)] = \mathbf{FF}[P, \leftarrow G].$$

Thus, we may look for a partial evaluation of the program $P \cup \{D\}$ w.r.t. $newp(X_1, \ldots, X_n)$, instead of a partial evaluation of P w.r.t. G.

The partial evaluation of $P \cup \{D\}$ w.r.t. $newp(\ldots)$ can be achieved by transforming $P \cup \{D\}$ into a program P_G such that

$$\mathbf{CASNF}[P \cup \{D\}, \leftarrow newp(X_1, \ldots, X_n)]$$
$$= \mathbf{CASNF}[P_G, \leftarrow newp(X_1, \ldots, X_n)], \text{ and}$$
$$\mathbf{FF}[P \cup \{D\}, \leftarrow newp(X_1, \ldots, X_n)]$$
$$= \mathbf{FF}[P_G, \leftarrow newp(X_1, \ldots, X_n)].$$

These two equalities hold if, for instance, we derive P_G from $P \cup \{D\}$ by using the definition, unfolding, and folding rules according to the restrictions of the second correctness theorems w.r.t. **CASNF** (page 738) and **FF** (page 732), respectively.

Let us now briefly compare the two approaches to partial evaluation we have mentioned above, that is, the one based on Lloyd and Shepherdson's theorem and the one based on the unfold/fold rules.

In the approach based on Lloyd and Shepherdson's theorem, the efficiency gains are obtained by constructing SLDNF-trees and extracting resultants. This process corresponds to the application of some unfolding steps, and since efficiency gains are obtained without using the folding rule, it may seem that this is an exception to the 'need for folding' meta-strategy described in Section 5. However, in order to guarantee the correctness of the partial evaluation of a given program P w.r.t. a set of atoms S, for each element of S we are required to find an SLDNF-tree whose leaves contain instances of atoms in S (see the closedness condition), and as the reader may easily verify, this requirement exactly corresponds to the 'need for folding'.

Conversely, the approach based on the unfold/fold rules does not require us to find the set S with the closedness and independence properties, but as we show in Example 6.0.8 below, we often need to introduce some auxiliary clauses by the definition rule and we also need to perform some final folding steps using those clauses.

Example 6.0.8 below also shows that in the partial evaluation approach based on the unfold/fold rules, the use of the renaming technique for structure specialization [Benkerimi and Lloyd, 1990; Gallagher and Bruynooghe, 1990; Gallagher, 1993; Benkerimi and Hill, 1993] which is often required in the first approach, is not needed. For other issues concerning the use of folding during partial evaluation the reader may refer to [Owen, 1989].

We now present an example of derivation of a partial evaluation of a program by applying the unfold/fold transformation rules and the loop absorption strategy.

Example 6.0.8. [String matching] [Sahlin, 1991; Gallagher, 1993]. Let us consider the following program *Match* for string matching:

1. $match(P, S) \leftarrow aux(P, S, P, S)$
2. $aux([\,], X, Y, Z) \leftarrow$
3. $aux([A|Ps], [A|Ss], P, S) \leftarrow aux(Ps, Ss, P, S)$
4. $aux([A|Ps], [B|Ss], P, [C|S]) \leftarrow \neg(A = B), aux(P, S, P, S)$

where the pattern P and the string S are represented as lists, and the relation $match(P, S)$ holds iff the pattern P occurs in the string S. For instance, the pattern [a,b] occurs in the string [c,a,b], but it does not occur in the string [a,c,b].

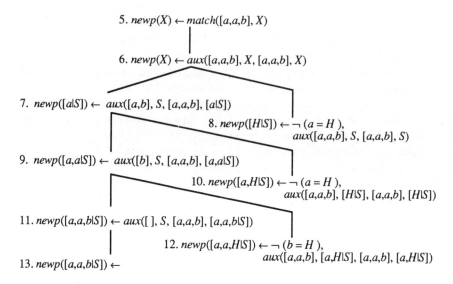

Fig. 6. An unfolding tree for $\langle Match, newp(X) \leftarrow match([a, a, b], X)\rangle$.

Let us now partially evaluate the given program *Match* w.r.t. the atom $match([a, a, b], X)$. In order to do so we first introduce the following definition:

5. $newp(X) \leftarrow match([a, a, b], X)$

whose body is the atom w.r.t. which the partial evaluation should be performed. As usual when applying the definition rule, the name of the head predicate is a new symbol, *newp* in our case. Then we construct the unfolding tree for $\langle Match$, clause $5\rangle$ using the u-selection rule which

i) unfolds a clause w.r.t. any atom of the form either $match(\ldots)$ or $aux(\ldots)$, and

ii) does not unfold a clause for which we can apply the loop absorption strategy, that is, a clause in whose body there is an instance of an atom which occurs in the body of a clause in an ancestor node.

We get the tree depicted in Fig. 6. In clause 8 of Fig. 6, the atom $aux([a, a, b], S, [a, a, b], S)$ is an instance of the body of clause 6 via the substitution $\{X/S\}$.

Analogously, in clause 10 the atom $aux([a, a, b], [H|S], [a, a, b], [H|S])$, and in clause 12 the atom $aux([a, a, b], [a, H|S], [a, a, b], [a, H|S])$ are instances of the body of clause 6.

Thus, we can apply the loop absorption strategy and we introduce the new definition:

14. $newq(S) \leftarrow aux([a, a, b], S, [a, a, b], S)$

We fold clause 6 (see Fig. 6) using clause 14 and we get:

6f. $newp(X) \leftarrow newq(X)$

Now the unfold/fold derivation continues by looking for the recursive definition of the predicate *newq*. This can be done by constructing the unfolding tree for $\langle Match, \text{clause } 14\rangle$. This tree is equal to the tree depicted in Fig. 6, except that clause 5 is deleted and the name *newp* is replaced by the name *newq*.

Thus, the leaves of the unfolding tree for $\langle Match, \text{clause } 14\rangle$ have the following clauses:

13q. $newq([a, a, b|S]) \leftarrow$
12q. $newq([a, a, H|S]) \leftarrow \neg(b = H), aux([a, a, b], [a, H|S], [a, a, b], [a, H|S])$
10q. $newq([a, H|S]) \leftarrow \neg(a = H), aux([a, a, b], [H|S], [a, a, b], [H|S])$
 8q. $newq([H|S]) \leftarrow \neg(a = H), aux([a, a, b], S, [a, a, b], S)$

By folding clauses 12q, 10q, and 8q, we get the following program:

6f. $newp(X) \leftarrow newq(X)$
13q. $newq([a, a, b|S]) \leftarrow$
12qf. $newq([a, a, H|S]) \leftarrow \neg(b = H), newq([a, H|S])$
10qf. $newq([a, H|S]) \leftarrow \neg(a = H), newq([H|S])$
 8qf. $newq([H|S]) \leftarrow \neg(a = H), newq(S)$

which is exactly the program produced by the Mixtus partial evaluator (see [Sahlin, 1991], page 124).

One of the most interesting motivations for developing the partial evaluation methodology is that it can be used for compiling programs and for deriving compilers from interpreters via the Futamura projections technique [Futamura, 1971]. For this last application it is necessary that the partial evaluator be self-applicable. This means that it should be able to partially evaluate itself. The interested reader may refer to [Jones et al., 1993] for a general overview, and to [Fujita and Furukawa, 1988; Fuller and Abramsky, 1988; Mogensen and Bondorf, 1993; Gurr, 1993; Leuschel, 1994a] for more details on the problem of self-applicability of partial evaluators in the logic languages Prolog and Gödel.

Partial evaluation has also been used in the area of deductive databases for deriving very efficient techniques for recursive query optimization and integrity checking. Some results in this direction can be found in [Sakama and Itoh, 1988; Bry, 1989; Leuschel, 1994b].

7 Related methodologies for program development

From what we have presented in the previous sections it is clear that the program transformation methodology for program development is very much related to various fields of artificial intelligence, theoretical computer science, and software engineering. Here we want to briefly indicate some of the techniques and methods which are used in those fields and are of relevance to the transformation methodology and its applications.

Let us begin by considering some *program analysis* techniques by which the programmer can investigate various program properties. Those properties may then be used for improving efficiency by applying transformation methods.

Program properties which are often useful for program transformation concern, for instance, the flow of computation, the use of data structures, the propagation of bindings, the sharing of information among arguments, the termination for a given class of queries, the groundness and/or freeness of arguments, and the functionality (or determinacy) of predicates.

Perfect knowledge about these properties is, in general, impossible to obtain, because of undecidability limitations. However, it is often the case that approximate reasoning can be carried out by using *abstract interpretation* techniques [Cousot and Cousot, 1977; Debray, 1992]. They make use of finite interpretation domains where information can be derived via a 'finite amount' of computation. The interpretation domains vary according to the property to be analysed and the degree of information one would like to obtain [Cortesi *et al.*, 1992].

A general framework, where program transformation strategies are supported by abstract interpretation techniques, is defined in [Boulanger and Bruynooghe, 1993]. Among the many transformation techniques which depend on program analysis techniques, we would like to mention: i) compiling control (see Section 5.2.1), where the information about the flow of computation is used for generating the unfolding tree, ii) the specialization method of [Gallagher and Bruynooghe, 1991], which is based on a technique for approximating the set of all possible calls generated during the evaluation of a given class of queries, iii) various techniques which insert cuts on the basis of determinacy information (see Section 5.3), and iv) various techniques implemented in the Spes system [Alexandre *et al.*, 1992; Bsaïes, 1992] in which *mode analysis* is used to mechanize several transformation strategies.

Very much related with these methodologies for the analysis of programs are the methodologies for the proof of properties of programs. They have been used for program verification, and in particular, for ensuring that a given set of clauses satisfies a given specification, or a given first order formula is true in a chosen semantic domain. These proofs may be used for guiding the application of suitable instances of the goal replacement rule.

Many proof techniques can be found in the literature, and in particular, in the field of theorem proving and automated deduction. For the ones which have been used for logic programs and may be adapted for program transformation we recall those in [Drabent and Małuszyński, 1988; Bossi and Cocco, 1989; Deransart, 1989].

The field of program transformation partially overlaps with the field of program synthesis (see [Deville and Lau, 1994] for a survey in the case of logic programs). Indeed, if we consider the given initial program as a program specification then the final program derived by transformation can be considered as an implementation of that specification. However, it is usually understood that program synthesis differs from program transformation because in program synthesis the specification is a somewhat implicit description of the program to be derived, and such implicit description often does not allow us to get the desired program by a sequence of simple manipulations, like those determined by standard transformation rules.

Moreover, it is often the case that the specification language differs from the executable language in which the final program should be written. This language barrier can be overcome by using transformation rules, but these techniques, we think, go beyond the area of traditional program transformation and belong to the field of logic program synthesis.

The transformational methods for developing logic programs are also closely related to methods for *logic program construction* [Sterling and Lakhotia, 1988; Deville, 1990; Sterling and Kirschenbaum, 1993], where complex programs are developed by enhancing and composing together simpler programs (see Section 5.2.2). However, the basic ideas and objectives of program construction are quite different from those of program transformation. In particular, the starting point for the above mentioned techniques for program construction is not a logic program, but a possibly incomplete and not fully formalized specification. Thus, the notion of semantics plays a minor role, in comparison with the techniques for program transformation. Moreover, the main objective of program construction is the improvement of the efficiency in software production, rather than the improvement of the efficiency of programs.

Finally, we would like to mention that the transformation and specialization techniques considered in this chapter have been partially extended to the case of concurrent logic programs [Ueda and Furukawa, 1988] and constraint logic programs [Hickey and Smith, 1991; Maher, 1993; Bensaou and Guessarian, 1994; Etalle and Gabbrielli, 1996].

Conclusions

We have looked at the theoretical foundations of the so-called 'rules + strategies' approach to logic program transformation. We have established a unified framework for presenting and comparing the various rules which have been proposed in the literature. That framework is parametric with respect to the semantics which is preserved during transformation.

We have presented various sets of transformation rules and the corresponding correctness results w.r.t. different semantics of definite logic programs, such as: the least Herbrand model, the computed answer substitutions, the finite failure, and the pure Prolog semantics.

We have also considered the case of normal programs, and using the proposed framework, we have presented the rules which preserve computed answer substitutions, finite failure, and Clark's completion semantics. We have briefly mentioned the results concerning the rules which preserve other semantics for normal programs.

We have also presented a unified framework in which it is possible to describe some of the most significant techniques for guiding the application of the transformation rules with the aim of improving program efficiency. We have singled out a few basic strategies, such as tupling, loop absorption, and generalization, and we have shown that various methods for compiling control, program composition, change of data representations, and partial evaluation, can be viewed as suitable applications of those strategies.

An area of further investigation is the characterization of the power of the transformation rules and strategies, both in the 'completeness' sense, that is, their capability of deriving all programs which are equivalent to the given initial program, and in the 'complexity' sense, that is, their capability of deriving programs which are more efficient than the initial program. No conclusive results are available in either direction.

A line of research that can be pursued in the future, is the integration of tools, like abstract interpretations, proofs of properties, and program synthesis, within the 'rules + strategies' approach to program transformation.

Unfortunately, the transformational methodology in the practice of logic programming has gained only moderate attention in the past. However, it is recognized that the automation of transformation techniques and their integrated use is of crucial importance for building advanced software development systems.

There is a growing interest in the mechanization of transformation strategies and the production of interactive tools for implementing program transformers. Moreover, some optimizing compilers already developed make use of various transformation techniques.

The importance of the transformation methodology will substantially increase if we extend its theory and applications also to the case of complex logic languages which manipulate constraints, and support both concurrency and object-orientation.

Acknowledgements

We thank M. Bruynooghe, J. P. Gallagher, M. Leuschel, M. Maher, and H. Seki for their helpful comments and advice on many issues concerning the transformation of logic programs. Our thanks go also to O. Aioni, P. Dell'Acqua, M. Gaspari and M. Kalsbeek for reading a preliminary version of this chapter.

References

[Alexandre *et al.*, 1992] F. Alexandre, K. Bsaïes, J. P. Finance, and A. Quéré. Spes: A system for logic program transformation. In *Proceedings of the International Conference on Logic Programming and Automated Reasoning, LPAR '92*, Lecture Notes in Computer Science 624, pages 445–447, 1992.

[Amtoft, 1992] T. Amtoft. Unfold/fold transformations preserving termination properties. In *Proc. PLILP '92*, Leuven, Belgium, Lecture Notes in Computer Science 631, pages 187–201. Springer-Verlag, 1992.

[Apt, 1990] K. R. Apt. Introduction to logic programming. In J. van Leeuwen, editor, *Handbook of Theoretical Computer Science*, pages 493–576. Elsevier, 1990.

[Aravindan and Dung, 1995] C. Aravindan and P. M. Dung. On the correctness of unfold/fold transformation of normal and extended logic programs. *Journal of Logic Programming*, 24(3):201–217, 1995.

[Arsac and Kodratoff, 1982] J. Arsac and Y. Kodratoff. Some techniques for recursion removal from recursive functions. *ACM Transactions on Programming Languages and Systems*, 4(2):295–322, 1982.

[Azibi, 1987] N. ·Azibi. *TREQUASI: Un système pour la transformation automatique de programmes Prolog récursifs en quasi-itératifs*. PhD thesis, Université de Paris-Sud, Centre d'Orsay, France, 1987.

[Baudinet, 1992] M. Baudinet. Proving termination properties of Prolog programs: A semantic approach. *Journal of Logic Programming*, 14:1–29, 1992.

[Benkerimi and Hill, 1993] K. Benkerimi and P. M. Hill. Supporting transformations for the partial evaluation of logic programs. *Journal of Logic and Computation*, 3(5):469–486, 1993.

[Benkerimi and Lloyd, 1990] K. Benkerimi and J. W. Lloyd. A partial evaluation procedure for logic programs. In S. Debray and M. Hermenegildo, editors, *Logic Programming: Proceedings of the 1990 North American Conference*, Austin, TX, USA, pages 343–358. The MIT Press, 1990.

[Bensaou and Guessarian, 1994] N. Bensaou and I. Guessarian. Transforming constraint logic programs. In *11th Symp. on Theoretical Aspects of Computer Science, STACS '94*, Lecture Notes in Computer Science 775, pages 33–46. Springer-Verlag, 1994.

[Bird, 1984] R. S. Bird. The promotion and accumulation strategies in transformational programming. *ACM Toplas*, 6(4):487–504, 1984.

[Bjørner *et al.*, 1988] D. Bjørner, A. P. Ershov, and N. D. Jones, editors. *Partial Evaluation and Mixed Computation*. North-Holland, 1988. IFIP TC2 Workshop on Partial and Mixed Computation, Gammel Avernæs, Denmark, 1987.

[Bloch, 1984] C. Bloch. Source-to-source transformations of logic programs. Master's thesis, Department of Applied Mathematics, Weizmann Institute of Science, Rehovot, Israel, 1984.

[Bol, 1993] R. Bol. Loop checking in partial deduction. *Journal of Logic Programming*, 16:25–46, 1993.

[Bossi and Cocco, 1989] A. Bossi and N. Cocco. Verifying correctness of logic programs. In *Proceedings TAPSOFT '89*, Lecture Notes in Computer Science 352, pages 96–110. Springer-Verlag, 1989.

[Bossi and Cocco, 1993] A. Bossi and N. Cocco. Basic transformation operations which preserve computed answer substitutions of logic programs. *Journal of Logic Programming*, 16(1&2):47–87, 1993.

[Bossi and Cocco, 1994] A. Bossi and N. Cocco. Preserving universal termination through unfold/fold. In *Proceedings ALP '94*, Lecture Notes in Computer Science 850, pages 269–286. Springer-Verlag, 1994.

[Bossi and Etalle, 1994a] A. Bossi and S. Etalle. More on unfold/fold transformations of normal programs: Preservation of Fitting's semantics. In L. Fribourg and F. Turini, editors, *Proceedings of LOPSTR'94 and META'94*, Pisa, Italy, Lecture Notes in Computer Science 883, pages 311–331, Springer-Verlag, 1994.

[Bossi and Etalle, 1994b] A. Bossi and S. Etalle. Transforming acyclic programs. *ACM Transactions on Programming Languages and Systems*, 16(4):1081–1096, July 1994.

[Bossi *et al.*, 1990] A. Bossi, N. Cocco, and S. Dulli. A method for specializing logic programs. *ACM Transactions on Programming Languages and Systems*, 12(2):253–302, April 1990.

[Bossi *et al.*, 1992a] A. Bossi, N. Cocco, and S. Etalle. On safe folding. In *Proceedings PLILP '92*, Leuven, Belgium, Lecture Notes in Computer Science 631, pages 172–186. Springer-Verlag, 1992.

[Bossi *et al.*, 1992b] A. Bossi, N. Cocco, and S. Etalle. Transforming normal programs by replacement. In A. Pettorossi, editor, *Proceedings 3rd International Workshop on Meta-Programming in Logic, Meta '92*, Uppsala, Sweden, Lecture Notes in Computer Science 649, pages 265–279. Springer-Verlag, 1992.

[Boulanger and Bruynooghe, 1993] D. Boulanger and M. Bruynooghe. Deriving unfold/fold transformations of logic programs using extended OLDT-based abstract interpretation. *Journal of Symbolic Computation*, 15:495–521, 1993.

[Boyer and Moore, 1975] R. S. Boyer and J. S. Moore. Proving theorems about Lisp functions. *Journal of the ACM*, 22(1):129–144, 1975.

[Brough and Hogger, 1987] D. R. Brough and C. J. Hogger. Compiling associativity into logic programs. *Journal of Logic Programming*, 4:345–359, 1987.

[Brough and Hogger, 1991] D. R. Brough and C. J. Hogger. Grammar-related transformations of logic programs. *New Generation Computing*, 9(1):115–134, 1991.

[Bruynooghe, 1982] M. Bruynooghe. The memory management of Prolog implementations. In K. L. Clark and S.-Å. Tärnlund, editors, *Logic Programming*, pages 83–98. Academic Press, 1982.

[Bruynooghe and Pereira, 1984] M. Bruynooghe and L. M. Pereira. Deduction revision by intelligent backtracking. In J. A. Campbell, editor, *Implementations of Prolog*, pages 253–266. Ellis Horwood, 1984.

[Bruynooghe et al., 1989] M. Bruynooghe, D. De Schreye, and B. Krekels. Compiling control. *Journal of Logic Programming*, 6:135–162, 1989.

[Bruynooghe et al., 1992] M. Bruynooghe, D. De Schreye, and B. Martens. A general criterion for avoiding infinite unfolding during partial deduction of logic programs. *New Generation Computing*, 11:47–79, 1992.

[Bry, 1989] F. Bry. Query evaluation in recursive data bases: Bottom-up and top-down reconciled. In *Proceedings 1st International Conference on Deductive and Object-Oriented Databases, Kyoto, Japan*, 1989.

[Bsaïes, 1992] K. Bsaïes. Static analysis for the synthesis of eureka properties for transforming logic programs. In *Proceedings 4th UK Conference on Logic Programming, ALPUK '92*, Workshops in Computing, pages 41–61. Springer-Verlag, 1992.

[Burstall and Darlington, 1975] R. M. Burstall and J. Darlington. Some transformations for developing recursive programs. In *Proceedings of the International Conference on Reliable Software, Los Angeles, CA,USA*, pages 465–472, 1975.

[Burstall and Darlington, 1977] R. M. Burstall and J. Darlington. A transformation system for developing recursive programs. *Journal of the ACM*, 24(1):44–67, January 1977.

[Clark and Sickel, 1977] K. L. Clark and S. Sickel. Predicate logic: A calculus for deriving programs. In *Proceedings 5th International Joint Conference on Artificial Intelligence, Cambridge, MA, USA*, pages 419–420, 1977.

[Clark and Tärnlund, 1977] K. L. Clark and S.-Å. Tärnlund. A first order theory of data and programs. In *Proceedings Information Processing '77*, pages 939–944. North-Holland, 1977.

[Cook and Gallagher, 1994] J. Cook and J. P. Gallagher. A transformation system for definite programs based on termination analysis. In L. Fribourg and F. Turini, editors, *Proceedings of LOPSTR'94 and META'94, Pisa, Italy*, Lecture Notes in Computer Science 883, pages 51–68, Springer-Verlag, 1994.

[Cortesi et al., 1992] A. Cortesi, G. Filé, and W. Winsborough. Comparison of abstract interpretations. In *Proceedings Nineteenth ICALP*,

Wien, Austria, Lecture Notes in Computer Science 623, pages 521–532. Springer-Verlag, 1992.

[Cousot and Cousot, 1977] P. Cousot and R. Cousot. Abstract interpretation: A unified lattice model for static analysis of programs by construction of approximation of fixpoints. In *Proceedings 4th ACM-SIGPLAN Symposium on Princples of Programming Languages (POPL '77)*, pages 238–252. ACM Press, 1977.

[Darlington, 1972] J. Darlington. *A Semantic Approach to Automatic Program Improvement*. PhD thesis, Department of Machine Intelligence, Edinburgh University, Edinburgh (Scotland) UK, 1972.

[Darlington, 1978] J. Darlington. A synthesis of several sorting algorithms. *Acta Informatica*, 11:1–30, 1978.

[Darlington, 1981] J. Darlington. An experimental program transformation system. *Artificial Intelligence*, 16:1–46, 1981.

[De Schreye and Bruynooghe, 1989] D. De Schreye and M. Bruynooghe. On the transformation of logic programs with instantiation based computation rules. *Journal of Symbolic Computation*, 7:125–154, 1989.

[De Schreye et al., 1991] D. De Schreye, B. Martens, G. Sablon, and M. Bruynooghe. Compiling bottom-up and mixed derivations into top-down executable logic programs. *Journal of Automated Reasoning*, 7:337–358, 1991.

[de Waal and Gallagher, 1992] D. A. de Waal and J. P. Gallagher. Specialization of a unification algorithm. In T. Clement and K.-K. Lau, editors, *Logic Program Synthesis and Transformation, Proceedings LOPSTR '91*, Manchester, UK, Workshops in Computing, pages 205–221. Springer-Verlag, 1992.

[Debray, 1985] S. K. Debray. Optimizing almost-tail-recursive Prolog programs. In *Proceedings IFIP International Conference on Functional Programming Languages and Computer Architecture*, Nancy, France, Lecture Notes in Computer Science 201, pages 204–219. Springer-Verlag, 1985.

[Debray, 1988] S. K. Debray. Unfold/fold transformations and loop optimization of logic programs. In *Proceedings SIGPLAN 88 Conference on Programming Language Design and Implementation*, Atlanta, GA, USA, SIGPLAN Notices, 23, (7), pages 297–307, 1988.

[Debray, 1992] S. K. Debray, editor. *Special Issue of the Journal of Logic Programming on Abstract Interpretation*, volume 12, Nos. 2&3. Elsevier, 1992.

[Debray and Mishra, 1988] S. K. Debray and P. Mishra. Denotational and operational semantics for Prolog. *Journal of Logic Programming*, 5:61–91, 1988.

[Debray and Warren, 1988] S. K. Debray and D. S. Warren. Automatic mode inference for logic programs. *Journal of Logic Programming*, 5:207–229, 1988.

[Debray and Warren, 1989] S. K. Debray and D. S. Warren. Functional computations in logic programs. *ACM TOPLAS*, 11(3):451–481, 1989.

[Demoen, 1993] B. Demoen. On the transformation of a Prolog program to a more efficient binary program. In K.-K. Lau and T. Clement, editors, *Logic Program Synthesis and Transformation, Proceedings LOPSTR '92*, Manchester, UK, Workshops in Computing, pages 242–252. Springer-Verlag, 1993.

[Deransart, 1989] P. Deransart. Proof methods of declarative properties of logic programs. In *Proceedings TAPSOFT '89*, Lecture Notes in Computer Science 352, pages 207–226. Springer-Verlag, 1989.

[Deville, 1990] Y. Deville. *Logic Programming: Systematic Program Development*. Addison-Wesley, 1990.

[Deville and Burnay, 1989] Y. Deville and J. Burnay. Generalization and program schemata. In *Proceedings NACLP '89*, pages 409–425. The MIT Press, 1989.

[Deville and Lau, 1994] Y. Deville and K.-K. Lau. Logic program synthesis. *Journal of Logic Programming*, 19, 20:321–350, 1994.

[Dix, 1995] J. Dix. A classification theory of semantics of normal logic programs: II weak properties. *Fundamenta Informaticae*, XII(3):257–288, 1995.

[Drabent and Małuszyński, 1988] W. Drabent and J. Małuszyński. Inductive assertion method for logic programs. *Theoretical Computer Science*, 1(1):133–155, 1988.

[Ershov, 1977] A. P. Ershov. On the partial computation principle. *Information Processing Letters*, 6(2):38–41, 1977.

[Ershov et al., 1988] A. P. Ershov, D. Bjørner, Y. Futamura, K. Furukawa, A. Haraldson, and W. Scherlis, editors. *Special Issue of New Generation Computing: Workshop on Partial Evaluation and Mixed Computation*, volume 6, Nos. 2&3. Ohmsha Ltd. and Springer-Verlag, 1988.

[Etalle and Gabbrielli, 1996] S. Etalle and M. Gabbrielli. Modular transformations of CLP programs. *Theoretical Computer Science*, 166:101–146, 1996.

[Feather, 1982] M. S. Feather. A system for assisting program transformation. *ACM Toplas*, 4(1):1–20, 1982.

[Feather, 1987] M. S. Feather. A survey and classification of some program transformation techniques. In L. G. L. T. Meertens, editor, *Proceedings IFIP TC2 Working Conference on Program Specification and Transformation*, Bad Tölz, Germany, pages 165–195. North-Holland, 1987.

[Fitting, 1985] M. Fitting. A Kripke–Kleene semantics for logic programs. *Journal of Logic Programming*, 2(4):295–312, 1985.

[Flener and Deville, 1993] P. Flener and Y. Deville. Logic program synthesis from incomplete specifications. *Journal of Symbolic Computation*, 15:775–805, 1993.

[Fuchs and Fromherz, 1992] N. E. Fuchs and M. P. J. Fromherz. Schema-based transformations of logic programs. In T. Clement and K.-K. Lau, editors, *Logic Program Synthesis and Transformation, Proceedings LOP-STR '91*, Manchester, UK, pages 111–125. Springer-Verlag, 1992.

[Fujita, 1987] H. Fujita. An algorithm for partial evaluation with constraints. Technical Memorandum TM-0367, ICOT, Tokyo, Japan, 1987.

[Fujita and Furukawa, 1988] H. Fujita and K. Furukawa. A self-applicable partial evaluator and its use in incremental compilation. *New Generation Computing*, 6(2&3):91–118, 1988.

[Fuller and Abramsky, 1988] D. A. Fuller and S. Abramsky. Mixed computation of Prolog programs. *New Generation Computing*, 6(2&3):119–141, 1988.

[Futamura, 1971] Y. Futamura. Partial evaluation of computation process—an approach to a compiler–compiler. *Systems, Computers, Controls*, 2(5):45–50, 1971.

[Gallagher, 1986] J. P. Gallagher. Transforming programs by specializing interpreters. In *Proceedings Seventh European Conference on Artificial Intelligence, ECAI '86*, pages 109–122, 1986.

[Gallagher, 1991] J. P. Gallagher. A system for specializing logic programs. Technical Report TR-91-32, University of Bristol, Bristol, U.K., 1991.

[Gallagher, 1993] J. P. Gallagher. Tutorial on specialization of logic programs. In *Proceedings of ACM SIGPLAN Symposium on Partial Evaluation and Semantics Based Program Manipulation, PEPM '93*, Copenhagen, Denmark, pages 88–98. ACM Press, 1993.

[Gallagher and Bruynooghe, 1990] J. P. Gallagher and M. Bruynooghe. Some low-level source transformations for logic programs. In M. Bruynooghe, editor, *Proceedings of the Second Workshop on Meta-Programming in Logic*, Leuven, Belgium, pages 229–246. Department of Computer Science, KU Leuven (Belgium), April 1990.

[Gallagher and Bruynooghe, 1991] J. P. Gallagher and M. Bruynooghe. The derivation of an algorithm for program specialisation. *New Generation Computing*, 6(2):305–333, 1991.

[Gallagher et al., 1988] J. P. Gallagher, M. Codish, and E. Shapiro. Specialization of Prolog and FCP programs using abstract interpretation. *New Generation Computing*, 6(2&3):159–186, 1988.

[Gardner and Shepherdson, 1991] P. A. Gardner and J. C. Shepherdson. Unfold/fold transformations of logic programs. In J.-L. Lassez and G. Plotkin, editors, *Computational Logic, Essays in Honor of Alan Robinson*, pages 565–583. The MIT Press, 1991.

[Gelfond and Lifschitz, 1988] M. Gelfond and V. Lifschitz. The stable model semantics for logic programming. In *Proceedings of the Fifth International Conference and Symposium on Logic Programming*, pages 1070–1080. The MIT Press, 1988.

[Gergatsoulis and Katzouraki, 1994] M. Gergatsoulis and M. Katzouraki. Unfold/fold transformations for definite clause programs. In *Proceedings Sixth International Symposium on Programming Language Implementation and Logic Programming (PLILP '94)*, Lecture Notes in Computer Science 844. Springer-Verlag, 1994.

[Gurr, 1993] C. A. Gurr. *A Self-Applicable Partial Evaluator for the Logic Programming Language Gödel*. PhD thesis, University of Bristol, Bristol, UK, 1993.

[Hansson and Tärnlund, 1982] Å. Hansson and S.-Å. Tärnlund. Program transformation by data structure mapping. In K. L. Clark and S.-Å. Tärnlund, editors, *Logic Programming*, pages 117–122. Academic Press, 1982.

[Hickey and Smith, 1991] T. J. Hickey and D. A. Smith. Towards the partial evaluation of CLP languages. In *Proceedings ACM Symposium on Partial Evaluation and Semantics Based Program Manipulation, PEPM '91*, New Haven, CT, USA, SIGPLAN Notices, 26, 9, pages 43–51. ACM Press, 1991.

[Hogger, 1981] C. J. Hogger. Derivation of logic programs. *Journal of the ACM*, 28(2):372–392, 1981.

[Huet and Lang, 1978] G. Huet and B. Lang. Proving and applying program transformations expressed with second-order patterns. *Acta Informatica*, 11:31–55, 1978.

[Jones and Mycroft, 1984] N. D. Jones and A. Mycroft. Stepwise development of operational and denotational semantics for Prolog. In *Proceedings 1984 International Symposium on Logic Programming*, Atlantic City, NJ, USA, pages 289–298, 1984.

[Jones et al., 1993] N. D. Jones, C. K. Gomard, and P. Sestoft. *Partial Evaluation and Automatic Program Generation*. Prentice Hall, 1993.

[Kanamori and Fujita, 1986] T. Kanamori and H. Fujita. Unfold/fold transformation of logic programs with counters. Technical Report 179, ICOT, Tokyo, Japan, 1986.

[Kanamori and Horiuchi, 1987] T. Kanamori and K. Horiuchi. Construction of logic programs based on generalized unfold/fold rules. In *Proceedings of the Fourth International Conference on Logic Programming*, pages 744–768. The MIT Press, 1987.

[Kawamura and Kanamori, 1990] T. Kawamura and T. Kanamori. Preservation of stronger equivalence in unfold/fold logic program transformation. *Theoretical Computer Science*, 75:139–156, 1990.

[Kirschenbaum *et al.*, 1989] M. Kirschenbaum, A. Lakhotia, and L. Sterling. Skeletons and techniques for Prolog programming. TR 89-170, Case Western Reserve University, 1989.

[Kleene, 1971] S. C. Kleene. *Introduction to Metamathematics*. North-Holland, 1971.

[Komorowski, 1982] H. J. Komorowski. Partial evaluation as a means for inferencing data structures in an applicative language: A theory and implementation in the case of Prolog. In *Ninth ACM Symposium on Principles of Programming Languages*, Albuquerque, New Mexico, USA, pages 255–267, 1982.

[Kott, 1978] L. Kott. About transformation system: A theoretical study. In *3ème Colloque International sur la Programmation*, pages 232–247, Paris (France), 1978. Dunod.

[Kott, 1982] L. Kott. The McCarthy's induction principle: 'oldy' but 'goody'. *Calcolo*, 19(1):59–69, 1982.

[Kowalski, 1979] R. A. Kowalski. Algorithm = Logic + Control. *Communications of the ACM*, 22(7):424–436, 1979.

[Kunen, 1987] K. Kunen. Negation in logic programming. *Journal of Logic Programming*, 4(4):289–308, 1987.

[Kunen, 1989] K. Kunen. Signed data dependencies in logic programs. *Journal of Logic Programming*, 7:231–246, 1989.

[Leuschel, 1994a] M. Leuschel. Partial evaluation of the real thing. In L. Fribourg and F. Turini, editors, *Proceedings of LOPSTR '94 and META '94*, Pisa, Italy, Lecture Notes in Computer Science 883, pages 122–137, Springer-Verlag, 1994.

[Leuschel, 1994b] M. Leuschel. Partial evaluation of the real thing and its application to integrity checking. Technical report, Computer Science Department, K.U. Leuven, Heverlee, Belgium, 1994.

[Lloyd, 1987] J. W. Lloyd. *Foundations of Logic Programming*. Springer-Verlag, Berlin, Second Edition, 1987.

[Lloyd and Shepherdson, 1991] J. W. Lloyd and J. C. Shepherdson. Partial evaluation in logic programming. *Journal of Logic Programming*, 11:217–242, 1991.

[Maher, 1987] M. J. Maher. Correctness of a logic program transformation system. IBM Research Report RC 13496, T. J. Watson Research Center, 1987.

[Maher, 1990] M. J. Maher. Reasoning about stable models (and other unstable semantics). IBM research report, T. J. Watson Research Center, 1990.

[Maher, 1993] M. J. Maher. A transformation system for deductive database modules with perfect model semantics. *Theoretical Computer Science*, 110:377–403, 1993.

[Marakakis and Gallagher, 1994] E. Marakakis and J. P. Gallagher. Schema-based top-down design of logic programs using abstract data types. In L. Fribourg and F. Turini, editors, *Proceedings of LOPSTR'94 and META'94*, Pisa, Italy, Lecture Notes in Computer Science 883, pages 138–153, Springer-Verlag, 1994.

[Marriot and Søndergaard, 1993] K. Marriot and H. Søndergaard. Difference-list transformation for Prolog. *New Generation Computing*, 11:125–177, 1993.

[Martens *et al.*, 1992] B. Martens, D. De Schreye, and M. Bruynooghe. Sound and complete partial deduction with unfolding based on well-founded measures. In *Proceedings of the International Conference on Fifth Generation Computer Systems*, pages 473–480. Ohmsha Ltd., IOS Press, 1992.

[Michie, 1968] D. Michie. Memo functions and machine learning. *Nature*, 218(5136):19–22, 1968.

[Mogensen and Bondorf, 1993] T. Mogensen and A. Bondorf. Logimix: A self-applicable partial evaluator for Prolog. In K.-K. Lau and T. Clement, editors, *Logic Program Synthesis and Transformation, Proceedings LOPSTR '92*, Manchester, UK, Workshops in Computing, pages 214–227. Springer-Verlag, 1993.

[Naish, 1985] L. Naish. *Negation and Control in Prolog*. Lecture Notes in Computer Science 238. Springer-Verlag, 1985.

[Narain, 1986] S. Narain. A technique for doing lazy evaluation in logic. *Journal of Logic Programming*, 3(3):259–276, 1986.

[Neumerkel, 1993] U. W. Neumerkel. *Specialization of Prolog Programs with Partially Static Goals and Binarization*. PhD thesis, Technical University Wien, Austria, 1993.

[Owen, 1989] S. Owen. Issues in the partial evaluation of meta-interpreters. In H. Abramson and M. H. Rogers, editors, *Meta-Programming in Logic Programming*, pages 319–339. The MIT Press, 1989.

[Paige and Koenig, 1982] R. Paige and S. Koenig. Finite differencing of computable expressions. *ACM Transactions on Programming Languages and Systems*, 4(3):402–454, 1982.

[Partsch, 1990] H. A. Partsch. *Specification and Transformation of Programs*. Springer-Verlag, 1990.

[Paterson and Hewitt, 1970] M. S. Paterson and C. E. Hewitt. Comparative schematology. In *Conference on Concurrent Systems and Parallel Computation Project MAC*, Woods Hole, Mass., USA, pages 119–127, 1970.

[Pettorossi, 1977] A. Pettorossi. Transformation of programs and use of tupling strategy. In *Proceedings Informatica 77*, Bled, Yugoslavia, pages 1–6, 1977.

[Pettorossi and Proietti, 1989] A. Pettorossi and M. Proietti. Decidability results and characterization of strategies for the development of logic programs. In G. Levi and M. Martelli, editors, *Proceedings of the Sixth International Conference on Logic Programming*, Lisbon, Portugal, pages 539–553. The MIT Press, 1989.

[Pettorossi and Proietti, 1994] A. Pettorossi and M. Proietti. Transformation of logic programs: Foundations and techniques. *Journal of Logic Programming*, 19,20:261–320, 1994.

[Pettorossi and Proietti, 1996] A. Pettorossi and M. Proietti. Rules and strategies for transforming functional and logic programs. *ACM Computing Surveys*, 28(2):360–414, 1996.

[Prestwich, 1993a] S. Prestwich. Online partial deduction of large programs. In *Proceedings ACM Sigplan Symposium on Partial Evaluation and Semantics-Based Program Manipulation, PEPM '93*, Copenhagen, Denmark, pages 111–118. ACM Press, 1993.

[Prestwich, 1993b] S. Prestwich. An unfold rule for full Prolog. In K.-K. Lau and T. Clement, editors, *Logic Program Synthesis and Transformation, Proceedings LOPSTR '92*, Manchester, UK, Workshops in Computing, pages 199–213. Springer-Verlag, 1993.

[Proietti and Pettorossi, 1990] M. Proietti and A. Pettorossi. Synthesis of eureka predicates for developing logic programs. In N. D. Jones, editor, *Third European Symposium on Programming, ESOP '90*, Lecture Notes in Computer Science 432, pages 306–325. Springer-Verlag, 1990.

[Proietti and Pettorossi, 1991] M. Proietti and A. Pettorossi. Semantics preserving transformation rules for Prolog. In *ACM Symposium on Partial Evaluation and Semantics Based Program Manipulation, PEPM '91*, Yale University, New Haven, CT, USA, pages 274–284. ACM Press, 1991.

[Proietti and Pettorossi, 1993] M. Proietti and A. Pettorossi. The loop absorption and the generalization strategies for the development of logic programs and partial deduction. *Journal of Logic Programming*, 16(1–2):123–161, 1993.

[Proietti and Pettorossi, 1994a] M. Proietti and A. Pettorossi. Synthesis of programs from unfold/fold proofs. In Y. Deville, editor, *Logic Program Synthesis and Transformation, Proceedings of LOPSTR '93*, Louvain-la-Neuve, Belgium, Workshops in Computing, pages 141–158. Springer-Verlag, 1994.

[Proietti and Pettorossi, 1994b] M. Proietti and A. Pettorossi. Total correctness of the goal replacement rule based on unfold/fold proofs. In M. Alpuente, R. Barbuti, and I. Ramos, editors, *Proceedings of the 1994 Joint Conference on Declarative Programming, GULP-PRODE '94*, pages 203–217. Universidad Politécnica de Valencia, Peñíscola, Spain, September 19–22, 1994.

[Proietti and Pettorossi, 1995] M. Proietti and A. Pettorossi. Unfolding-definition-folding, in this order, for avoiding unnecessary variables in logic programs. *Theoretical Computer Science*, 142(1):89–124, 1995.

[Przymusinsky, 1987] T. Przymusinsky. On the declarative semantics of stratified deductive databases and logic programs. In J. Minker, editor, *Foundations of Deductive Databases and Logic Programming*, pages 193–216. Morgan Kaufmann, 1987.

[Rogers, 1967] H. Rogers. *Theory of Recursive Functions and Effective Computability*. McGraw-Hill, 1967.

[Safra and Shapiro, 1986] S. Safra and E. Shapiro. Meta interpreters for real. In H. J. Kugler, editor, *Proceedings Information Processing 86*, pages 271–278. North-Holland, 1986.

[Sahlin, 1991] D. Sahlin. *An Automatic Partial Evaluator for Full Prolog*. PhD thesis, SICS, Sweden, 1991.

[Sahlin, 1993] D. Sahlin. Mixtus: An automatic partial evaluator for full Prolog. *New Generation Computing*, 12:7–51, 1993.

[Sakama and Itoh, 1988] C. Sakama and H. Itoh. Partial evaluation of queries in deductive databases. *New Generation Computing*, 6(2, 3):249–258, 1988.

[Sato, 1992] T. Sato. An equivalence preserving first order unfold/fold transformation system. *Theoretical Computer Science*, 105:57–84, 1992.

[Sato and Tamaki, 1988] T. Sato and H. Tamaki. Deterministic transformation and deterministic synthesis. In *Future Generation Computers*. North-Holland, 1988.

[Sawamura and Takeshima, 1985] H. Sawamura and T. Takeshima. Recursive unsolvability of determinacy, solvable cases of determinacy and their application to Prolog optimization. In *Proceedings of the International Symposium on Logic Programming*, Boston, USA, pages 200–207. IEEE Computer Society Press, 1985.

[Scherlis, 1981] W. L. Scherlis. Program improvement by internal specialization. In *Proc. 8th ACM Symposium on Principles of Programming Languagesi*, Williamsburgh, VA, pages 41–49. ACM Press, 1981.

[Schwarz, 1982] J. Schwarz. Using annotations to make recursive equations behave. *IEEE Transactions on Software Engineering SE*, 8(1):21–33, 1982.

[Seki, 1990] H. Seki. A comparative study of the well-founded and the stable model semantics: Transformation's viewpoint. In *Proceedings of the Workshop on Logic Programming and Non-monotonic Logic*, pages 115–123. Cornell University, USA, 1990.

[Seki, 1991] H. Seki. Unfold/fold transformation of stratified programs. *Theoretical Computer Science*, 86:107–139, 1991.

[Seki, 1993] H. Seki. Unfold/fold transformation of general logic programs for well-founded semantics. *Journal of Logic Programming*, 16(1&2):5–23, 1993.

[Seki and Furukawa, 1987] H. Seki and K. Furukawa. Notes on transformation techniques for generate and test logic programs. In *Proceedings of the International Symposium on Logic Programming*, San Francisco, CA, USA, pages 215–223. IEEE Press, 1987.

[Shepherdson, 1992] J. C. Shepherdson. Unfold/fold transformations of logic programs. *Mathematical Structures in Computer Science*, 2:143–157, 1992.

[Sterling and Kirschenbaum, 1993] L. Sterling and M. Kirschenbaum. Applying techniques to skeletons. In J.-M. Jacquet, editor, *Constructing Logic Programs*, chapter 6, pages 127–140. Wiley, 1993.

[Sterling and Lakhotia, 1988] L. Sterling and A. Lakhotia. Composing Prolog meta-interpreters. In R. A. Kowalski and K. A. Bowen, editors, *Proceedings Fifth International Conference on Logic Programming*, Seattle, WA, USA, pages 386–403. The MIT Press, 1988.

[Sterling and Shapiro, 1994] L. Sterling and E. Shapiro. *The Art of Prolog*. Second Edition, The MIT Press, 1994.

[Takeuchi, 1986] A. Takeuchi. Affinity between meta-interpreters and partial evaluation. In H. J. Kugler, editor, *Proceedings of Information Processing '86*, pages 279–282. North-Holland, 1986.

[Takeuchi and Furukawa, 1986] A. Takeuchi and K. Furukawa. Partial evaluation of Prolog programs and its application to meta-programming. In H. J. Kugler, editor, *Proceedings of Information Processing '86*, pages 279–282. North-Holland, 1986.

[Tamaki and Sato, 1984] H. Tamaki and T. Sato. Unfold/fold transformation of logic programs. In S.-Å. Tärlund, editor, *Proceedings Second International Conference on Logic Programming*, Uppsala, Sweden, pages 127–138. Uppsala University, 1984.

[Tamaki and Sato, 1986] H. Tamaki and T. Sato. A generalized correctness proof of the unfold/fold logic program transformation. Technical Report 86-4, Ibaraki University, Japan, 1986.

[Tarau and Boyer, 1990] P. Tarau and M. Boyer. Elementary logic programs. In P. Deransart and J. Małuszyński, editors, *Proceedings PLILP '90*, pages 159–173. Springer-Verlag, 1990.

[Träff and Prestwich, 1992] J. L. Träff and S. D. Prestwich. Meta-programming for reordering literals in deductive databases. In A. Pettorossi, editor, *Proceedings 3rd International Workshop on Meta-Programming in Logic, Meta '92*, Uppsala, Sweden, Lecture Notes in Computer Science 649, pages 280–293. Springer-Verlag, 1992.

[Turchin, 1986] V. F. Turchin. The concept of a supercompiler. *ACM TOPLAS*, 8(3):292–325, 1986.

[Ueda and Furukawa, 1988] K. Ueda and K. Furukawa. Transformation rules for GHC programs. In *Proceedings International Conference on Fifth Generation Computer Systems, ICOT*, Tokyo, Japan, pages 582–591, 1988.

[van Emden and Kowalski, 1976] M. H. van Emden and R. Kowalski. The semantics of predicate logic as a programming language. *Journal of the ACM*, 23(4):733–742, 1976.

[Van Gelder *et al.*, 1989] A. Van Gelder, K. Ross, and J. Schlipf. Unfounded sets and well-founded semantics for general logic programs. In *Proceedings of the ACM Sigact-Sigmod Symposium on Principles of Database Systems*, pages 221–230. ACM Press, 1989.

[Venken, 1984] R. Venken. A Prolog meta-interpretation for partial evaluation and its application to source-to-source transformation and query optimization. In T. O'Shea, editor, *Proceedings of ECAI '84*, pages 91–100. North-Holland, 1984.

[Wadler, 1990] P. L. Wadler. Deforestation: Transforming programs to eliminate trees. *Theoretical Computer Science*, 73:231–248, 1990.

[Walker and Strong, 1972] S. A. Walker and H. R. Strong. Characterization of flowchartable recursions. In *Proceedings 4th Annual ACM Symposium on Theory of Computing*, Denver, CO, USA, 1972.

[Wand, 1980] M. Wand. Continuation-based program transformation strategies. *Journal of the ACM*, 27(1):164–180, 1980.

[Warren, 1983] D. H. D. Warren. An abstract Prolog instruction set. Technical Report 309, SRI International, 1983.

[Warren, 1992] D. S. Warren. Memoing for logic programs. *Communications of the ACM*, 35(3):93–111, 1992.

[Wiggins, 1992] G. A. Wiggins. Negation and control in automatically generated logic programs. In A. Pettorossi, editor, *Proceedings 3rd International Workshop on Meta-Programming in Logic, Meta '92*, Uppsala, Sweden, Lecture Notes in Computer Science 649, pages 250–264. Springer-Verlag, 1992.

[Wirth, 1976] N. Wirth. *Algorithms + Data Structures = Programs*. Prentice-Hall, Inc., 1976.

[Zhang and Grant, 1988] J. Zhang and P. W. Grant. An automatic difference-list transformation algorithm for Prolog. In *Proceedings 1988 European Conference on Artificial Intelligence, ECAI '88*, pages 320–325. Pitman, 1988.

INDEX

References to footnotes are indicated by "*n*" after the page number

?-|- 4, 6
▷ ‖ → 4, 6, 44
?-⊢ 4, 6, 43
▷ |→ 5, 6
?- 5, 6, 11, 70
|- 5, 6, 37, 75
▷ ‖ 5, 6
→ 5, 6, 78
⊢ 6, 40, 75
⊨ 6, 7, 70
?-⊨ 6
∧ 8
. 25
≐ 28
⊥ 71, 192
⊓ 120
⊑ 120
↑ 120, 516
□ 166, 363, 406
⊤ 192
⊢*o* 193
? 213
≡ 387
↔ 387
≃ 387
◇ 408
[] 429
⌈⌉ 465
≼ 516
:: 551
\ 551
《 》 609
⟦ ⟧ 609

abducible hypotheses, retraction 281–2
abducibles, negation of 274–5
abducible sentences 237
abduction
   applications in AI 243–4
   argumentation-theoretic interpretation 236
   computation through TMS 279
   and constraint logic programming 287–8
   deduction from the completion 285–7
   default and non-default 308
   formalizations 240
   proof procedures 239

   semantics 308
   simulation 280–5
   use for various forms of reasoning 271–2
abductive framework 242
abductive logic programming [ALP] 269
   modification of semantics 278
abductive proof procedure 273–7
   abductive phase 258–60
   argumentation-theoretic interpretation 267–9, 277–9
   consistency phase 258, 258n, 260
   soundness 261–2
abductive reasoning 236–7
abductive task, intractability 240
abstract data type 455
   realization 208
abstract interpretation 111, 772
abstract interpreter 526–7
   for higher-order Horn clauses, deficiencies 537
abstract logic programming language 198
   examples 199–200, 205
abstract machine
   advantages 651–652
   design of instruction set 652–655
   runtime support 656
AC, *see* admissibility condition
acceptability semantics 296
accumulation strategy 759
admissibility condition [AC] 333
admissible chain 184
AKL, *see* Andorra Kernel Language
algebra 28; *see also* error...; functional...; initial...; relational...
allowed program 360–1, 391
Alloy 466
ALP, *see* abductive logic programming
α-conversion 514
ALPS 622
amalgamated language, incompleteness 460
amalgamated program 461
amalgamation 460
   advantages 464
ambivalent logic 467–8
analog circuits, analysis and synthesis 658–60